P9-DVD-594

# Two

Your decisions and actions are built around your **worldview**—how you think the world works, what you think your role in the world should be, and what you believe to be right and wrong behavior (ethics). How you act in the world reveals your worldview even though you may be unaware of many of its components.

There are many different worldviews based mostly on the cultures in which people are raised and educated. One of the most important goals of your education should be to understand and evaluate your worldview, modify it or adopt a new one if necessary, and see this as a lifelong process. To encourage you to articulate and evaluate your worldview, here are the environmental aspects of two opposing worldviews. These and other world-views are discussed in more detail in Chapter 27.

## Planetary Management Worldview

- We are the planet's most important species, and we are apart from and in charge of the rest of nature.

- There is always more, and it's all for us. Earth has an unlimited supply of resources to which we gain access through science and technology.

- All economic growth is good, more economic growth is better, and the potential for economic growth is unlimited.

- A healthy environment depends on a healthy economy.

- Our success depends on how well we can understand, control, and manage the planet for our benefit.

## An Earth Wisdom Worldview

- Nature exists for all of Earth's species, not just for us, and we are not apart from or in charge of the rest of nature. We need the earth, but the earth does not need us. The earth does not belong to us; we belong to the earth.

- There is not always more, and it's not all for us. Earth's resources are limited, should not be wasted, and should be used sustainably for us and all species.

- Some forms of economic growth are beneficial and some are harmful. Our goal should be to design economic and political systems that encourage Earth-sustaining growth and discourage or prohibit Earth-degrading growth.

- A healthy economy depends on a healthy environment. Our survival, life quality, and economies are totally de-pendent on the rest of nature (Earth capital).

- Our success as a species depends on learning to cooperate with one another and with the rest of nature instead of trying to dominate and manage Earth for our own use. Be-cause nature is so incredibly complex and always chang-ing, we will never have enough information and under-standing to manage the planet.

Two trees have been planted in a tropical rain forest for every tree used to make this book, courtesy of G. Tyler Miller, Jr., and Wadsworth Publishing Company. The author also sees that 50 trees are planted to compensate for the paper he uses and that several hectares of tropical rain forest are protected.

# Living in the Environment

*Principles, Connections, and Solutions*

EIGHTH EDITION

## G. TYLER MILLER, JR.

*Adjunct Professor of Human Ecology*
*St. Andrews' Presbyterian College*

**Wadsworth Publishing Company**
**Belmont, California**
**A Division of Wadsworth, Inc.**

: Jack Carey

umn Stanley

Ogus, Cynthia
Schutz

**Print Buyer:** Barbara Britton
**Art Editor:** Donna Kalal
**Permissions Editor:** Peggy Meehan
**Copy Editor:** Tom Briggs
**Photo Researcher:** Stephen Forsling
**Technical Illustrators:** Darwin and Vally Hennings, Tasa
  Graphic Arts, Inc., Susan Breitbard, and Teresa Roberts
**Box Logo Designs:** The Weller Institute
**Electronic Composition:** Edie Williams,
  Vargas/Williams/Design
**Disk Preparation:** Peter Penna, Penna Design & Production
**Color Separator:** H&S Graphics
**Printer:** Arcata Book Group/Hawkins
**Cover Design:** Andrew H. Ogus
**Part Opening Photographs:**
**Part 1:** © 1990 Tom Van Sant/The GeoSphere Project
**Part 2:** Brian Parker/Tom Stack & Associates
**Part 3:** United Nations
**Part 4:** H. Giardet/The Environmental Picture Library
**Part 5:** Gunter Ziesler/Bruce Coleman Ltd.
**Part 6:** Silvestris Fotoservice/NHPA
**Part 7:** Sam Kittner/SIPA Press
**Cover Photograph:** Oak Creek and Cathedral Rock, Arizona.
  © 1993 Larry Ulrich.

*This book is printed on acid-free recycled paper.*

I(T)P™

**International Thomson Publishing**
The trademark ITP is used under license.

Printed in the United States of America
1 2 3 4 5 6 7 8 9 10—98 97 96 95 94

**Library of Congress Cataloging in Publication Data**
Miller, G. Tyler (George Tyler)
    Living in the environment : principles, connections,
and solutions / G. Tyler Miller, Jr. — 8th ed.
        p.    cm. — (Wadsworth biology series)
    Includes bibliographical references and index.
    ISBN 0-534-19950-X (acid-free paper)
    1. Human ecology.  2. Environmental policy.  3. Environ-
mental sciences.  I. Title.  II. Series.
GF41.M54 1994
363.7—dc20                                    93-22763

# For Instructors and Students

**HOW I BECAME INVOLVED** In 1966 I heard a scientist give a lecture on the problems of overpopulation and environmental abuse. Afterward I went to him and said, "If even a fraction of what you have said is true, I will feel ethically obligated to give up my research on the corrosion of metals and devote the rest of my life to environmental issues. Frankly, I don't want to believe a word you have said, and I'm going into the literature to try to prove that your statements are either untrue or grossly distorted."

After six months of study I was convinced of the seriousness of these problems. Since then I have been studying, teaching, and writing about them. I have also attempted to live my life in an environmentally sound way—with varying degrees of success—by treading as lightly as possible on the earth (see pp. 694–695 for a summary of my own progress in attempting to work with nature). This book summarizes what I have learned in almost three decades of trying to understand environmental principles, problems, connections, and solutions.

**MY PHILOSOPHY OF EDUCATION** I agree with Norman Cousins that "the first aim of education should not be to prepare young people for careers, but to enable them to develop a respect for life." If we accomplish this, things we now dream and hope for become possible.

In our lifelong pursuit of knowledge, I believe we should do four things. First, we should question everything and everybody, as any good scientist does. Second, we should each develop a list of principles, concepts, and rules to guide us in making decisions and continually evaluate and modify this list as a result of experience. This is based on my belief that the purpose of our lifelong pursuit of education is to learn as little as we can—to learn how to sift through mountains of facts and ideas and find the few nuggets of wisdom that are useful and worth knowing. We need an *Earth Wisdom Revolution*, not an *information revolution*. This book is full of facts and numbers, but they are merely stepping-stones to laws, concepts, principles, connections, and solutions. And most statistics and facts are abstractions of human beings with the tears wiped off or living things whose lives we are threatening.

Third, I believe in interacting with what I read as a way to make learning more interesting and effective. I mark key sentences and paragraphs with a highlighter or pen. I put an asterisk in the margin next to something I think is important and double asterisks next to something that I think is especially important. I write comments in the margins, such as *Beautiful, Confusing, Bull, Wrong,* and so on. I fold down the top corner of pages with highlighted passages and the top and bottom corners of especially important pages. This way, I can flip through a book and quickly review the key passages. I urge you to interact in such ways with this book.

Finally, I believe that we have an ethical obligation to act on the always incomplete and usually controversial knowledge we have and not become "talking heads" or toe-dippers who refuse to jump into the dirty, difficult, uncertain, and challenging sea of life. In deciding how to walk more gently on the earth, I believe we should operate out of respect, compassion, and care for life, not out of immobilizing fear or guilt. Don't be overwhelmed by lists of what we can do, and don't feel guilty about all of the things you are not doing to help sustain the earth. No one can come close to doing all of these things, and you may disagree with many of the actions suggested by a diverse array of environmentalists. Choose the things you agree with and are willing to do and then try to expand your efforts.

**KEY FEATURES** This book is designed to be used in introductory courses on environmental science. Environmental science is a study of connections between parts of nature and between the problems we face, and it is the study of the possible solutions to these problems. Environmental science is an *interdisciplinary* study, combining ideas and information from natural sciences such as biology, chemistry, and geology and from social sciences such as economics, politics, and ethics to present a general idea of how nature works and how things are connected.

This book uses basic scientific laws, principles, and concepts to help us understand environmental and resource problems and the possible solutions to these problems. I have introduced only those concepts and principles needed to understand material in this book and have tried to present them simply but accurately. Key laws, principles, and concepts are summarized inside the back cover.

My aim is to provide a readable and accurate introduction to environmental science without the use of mathematics or complex scientific information. To help ensure that the material is accurate and up to date, I have consulted more than 10,000 research sources in the professional literature. This and previous editions have also been reviewed by more than 200 experts and teachers (see list on pp. x–xi).

The book is divided into seven major parts (see Brief Contents). Except for the foundation chapters in Parts I and II, the chapters can be covered in almost any order. In addition, most chapters and many sections within these chapters can be moved around or omitted to accommodate courses with different lengths and emphases.

After you review the Brief Contents, I urge you to read the list of laws, concepts, and principles given inside the back cover. In effect, it is a two-page summary of the key ideas in this book. Then I suggest that you turn to p. 701 and read the short Epilogue, which summarizes the major themes of this book.

I also relate the information in the book to the real world and to our individual lives. I use an array of boxes (each type with its own distinctive logo and background color) to spark interest, enhance visual impact, and eliminate long, tedious text passages. My goal is for you to flip randomly to almost any page and find a box or diagram that draws you into reading the text.

The 70 *Spotlight* boxes highlight and give further insights into environmental and resource problems. The 51 *Case Studies* give in-depth information about key issues and apply concepts. The 31 *Solutions* boxes summarize possible solutions to environmental problems or describe what individuals have done. In most cases, solutions are divided into two categories: prevention and control (reaction to problems). The 14 *Pro/Con* discussions outline both sides of controversial environmental and resource issues, while the 19 *Guest Essays* expose you to an individual environmental researcher's or activist's point of view. Finally, the 28 *Individuals Matter* boxes give examples of what we as individuals can do to help sustain the earth and thus ourselves and future generations. Earthcare is self-care.

As you look through the book, I think you'll find the 543 illustrations colorful and interesting, but they go beyond mere decoration—they are truly instructive. The 308 four-color diagrams (52 of them maps) and the 235 color photographs have been designed and selected to present complex ideas in understandable ways and to relate learning to the real world.

**MAJOR CHANGES IN THIS EDITION** *This new edition is a comprehensive revision.* Major changes include:

- Updating and revising material throughout the book. Because of rapid changes in data and information, an environmental science textbook needs to be updated every two years.

- Improving readability by reducing sentence and paragraph length, omitting unnecessary details,

examining chapter organization and flow, and writing in a more personal style.

- Adding brief Earth Stories at the beginning of each chapter to spark reader interest and provide useful information. Many describe what individuals have done to help us understand and sustain the earth.

- Adding factual recall questions (with answers) at the bottom of most pages.

- Emphasizing solutions to problems by adding 31 new boxes entitled Solutions and adding sections and subsections on solutions within most chapters.

- Adding 28 new Spotlights, 3 new Case Studies, 7 new Guest Essays, and 2 new Individuals Matter.

- Upgrading all diagrams to improve the color, add more detail, and give a more realistic 3-D effect.

- Adding 72 new color photos and 55 new diagrams and improving 17 existing diagrams.

- Adding 13 satellite photos of the earth.

- Adding 11 new maps and expanding a number of U.S. maps to include data on Canada, with the assistance of Daniel J. Boivin, Professor of Regional Planning, Université Laval, Quebec, Canada.

- Adding a new chapter on hazardous waste (Chapter 21).

- Completely rewriting and reorganizing Chapter 26, "Politics and Environment," and Chapter 27, "Worldviews, Ethics, and Sustainability."

- Increasing the scientific content by adding or expanding material on the nature of life (Section 4-1), types of organisms, the importance of insects, properties of air and water (including absolute and relative humidity), predator and prey characteristics, commensalism, the structure and composition of the atmosphere (Section 5-1), upwellings (Figure 5-8), weather extremes (tornadoes and tropical cyclones), kangaroo rat, coral reefs, mangrove swamps, thermal stratification and turnover of lakes, wetlands protection and restoration, population dynamics, density-dependent and density-independent checks on population growth, survivorship curves, origins of life and biodiversity (chemical and biological evolution), earth's resilience, mutations, adaptations, adaptive radiation, ecological succession, the evaluation of models of possible global warming and ozone depletion, soil formation (Figure 12-3), riparian zones, sustainable rangeland management, dose-response relationships, the importance of spiders, and lichens as air pollution indicators.

- Adding many new topics, including the giant panda (niche specialization), population stabilization in Japan, computer models and limits to growth, ecocities, land-use planning in Oregon, the neem tree, chemical prospecting in tropical forests, indigenous cultures and cultural extinction, alien species in Australia, the Everglades (problems and restoration), perennial crops, consequences of eating meat, salmon ranching and farming, reintroducing wolves to Yellowstone, recycled paper tradeoffs, wild game ranching, Earth Conservation Corps, ecotourism, biosphere reserves, the Energy Policy Act of 1992, the Mining Law of 1872, Earthship houses, dioxins, mussel invaders in the Great Lakes, jobs and the environment, environmental management, the Wise-Use movement, the 1992 Rio Earth Summit, ecofeminism, social ecology, environmental justice, green consumerism, and Earth education.

See pp. vii–ix for a more detailed summary of major changes for each chapter.

**WELCOME TO UNCERTAINTY, CONTROVERSY, AND CHALLENGE** There are no easy or simple answers to the environmental problems and challenges we face. We will never have scientific certainty or agreement about what we should do because science provides us with probabilities not certainties, and advances through continuous controversy. What is important is not what scientists disagree on (which represents the frontiers of knowledge still being developed and argued about) but what they generally agree on—the scientific consensus on concepts, problems, and possible solutions. Despite considerable research, we still know relatively little about how nature works at a time when we are altering nature at an accelerating pace. This uncertainty and the complexity and importance of these issues to present and future generations of humans and other species makes them highly controversial.

Intense controversy also arises because environmental science is a dynamic blend of natural and social sciences that sometimes questions the ways we view and act in the world around us. This interdisciplinary attempt to mirror reality asks us to evaluate our worldviews, values, and lifestyles and our economic and political systems. This can often be a threatening process.

Many environmental books and articles overwhelm us with the problems we face without suggesting ways we might deal with these problems. This book is loaded with solutions suggested by scientists and environmentalists with a wide range of viewpoints and expertise.

Don't take the numerous possible solutions given in this book as gospel. They are given to encourage you to think critically and to make up your own mind. My own views are constantly changing as I am exposed to new information and uncover new connections about how the earth and human societies work. Learning is always a work in progress. I don't believe there is any single "best" worldview, set of solutions, or political or economic philosophy for sustaining the earth. People with widely different worldviews, political persuasions, and

ideas can work together to help sustain the earth, and that is what counts.

An important lesson from nature is that a variety of life forms and arrangements (biodiversity) is the best way to respond to the environmental changes that always take place on Earth. By analogy, preserving and promoting cultural, political, and economic diversity is an important insurance policy in giving us the capacity to respond to changing conditions. We are all in this together, and we need to respect our differences and work together to find a rainbow of solutions to the problems and challenges we face.

Rosy optimism and gloom-and-doom pessimism are traps that usually lead to denial, indifference, and inaction. I have tried to avoid these two extremes and give a realistic—and yet hopeful—view of the future. My reading of history reveals that hope converted into action has been the driving force of our species. This book is filled with stories of individuals who have acted to help sustain the earth for us and all life and whose actions inspire us to do better.

I wish everything was more certain, but it isn't. Making difficult choices without ever having enough information is what being human is all about. It's an exciting time to be alive as we struggle to enter into a new relationship with the planet that is our only home.

**STUDY AIDS** Each chapter begins with a few general questions to give you an idea of how the chapter is organized and what you will be learning. When a new term is introduced and defined, it is printed in **boldface type.** There is also a glossary of all key terms at the end of the book.

Factual recall questions (with answers) appear at the bottom of most pages. You might cover the answer (on the right-hand page) with a piece of paper and then try to answer the question on the left-hand page. These questions are not necessarily related to the chapter in which they are found. Many give you previews of future topics and help reinforce learning.

Each chapter ends with a set of questions designed to encourage you to think critically and to apply what you have learned to your life. Some ask you to take sides on controversial issues and to back up your conclusions and beliefs. Individual and group projects, marked with an asterisk (*), also appear at the end of each chapter. Many additional projects are given in the Instructor's Manual and in *Green Lives, Green Campuses,* a supplement available with this book.

Readers who become especially interested in a particular topic can consult the list of Further Readings for each chapter, given in the back of the book. Appendix 1 contains a list of publications to help keep up to date on the book's material and a list of some key environmental organizations.

This book is also designed for future reference. I hope readers who value what they've learned from it will add the book to their personal library or give it to someone else who wants to learn about sustaining the earth.

## HELP ME IMPROVE THIS BOOK

Tell me how you think this book can be improved, and if you find any errors please let me know about them. Most errors can be corrected in subsequent printings of this edition, rather than waiting for a new edition. Send any errors you find and any suggestions for improvement to Jack Carey, Biology and Environmental Science Publisher, Wadsworth Publishing Company, 10 Davis Drive, Belmont, CA 94002. He will send them on to me.

## SUPPLEMENTS

The following supplements are available:

- Instructor's Manual (with test items), by Jane Heinze-Fry (Ph.D. in Science and Environmental Education). For each chapter, it lists goals and objectives; key terms; teaching suggestions; multiple-choice test questions with answers; projects, field trips, and experiments; term-paper and report topics; and audiovisual materials and computer software.

- *Green Lives, Green Campuses: An Activities Workbook*, by Jane Heinze-Fry, is designed to help students apply environmental concepts by investigating their lifestyles and by making an environmental audit of their campus.

- Laboratory Manual, by C. Lee Rockett (Bowling Green State University) and Kenneth J. Van Dellen (Macomb Community College).

- A set of 50 color acetates and 387 black-and-white transparency masters for making overhead transparencies or slides of line art is available to adopters.

- A special version of STELLA II software, a tool for developing critical thinking, is available, together with an accompanying workbook.

## ANNENBERG/CPB TELEVISION COURSE

This textbook is being offered as part of the Annenberg/CPB Project television series *Race to Save the Planet*, broadcast on PBS.

*Race to Save the Planet* is a 10-part public television series and a college-level telecourse examining the major environmental questions facing the world today, ranging from population growth to soil erosion, from the destruction of forests to climate changes induced by human activity. The series takes into account the wide spectrum of opinion about what constitutes an environmental problem, as well as the controversies about appropriate remedial measures. It analyzes problems and emphasizes the successful search for solutions. The course develops a number of key themes that cut across a broad range of environmental issues, including sustainability, the interconnection of the economy and the ecosystem, short-term versus long-term gains, and the trade-offs involved in balancing problems and solutions.

A study guide and a faculty guide, both available from Wadsworth Publishing Company, integrate the telecourse and my texts (*Living in the Environment* and *Environmental Science*). The television program was developed as part of the Annenberg/CPB Collection.

For further information about available television course licenses and duplication licenses, contact PBS Adult Learning Service, 1320 Braddock Place, Alexandria, VA 22314-1698 (1-800-ALS-AL5-8).

For information about purchasing videocassettes and print material, contact the Annenberg/CPB Collection, P.O. Box 2284, South Burlington, VT 05407-2284 (1-800-LEARNER).

## ACKNOWLEDGMENTS

I wish to thank the many students and teachers who responded so favorably to the seven editions of *Living in the Environment*, the four editions of *Environmental Science*, and the first edition of *Resource Conservation and Management*, and who offered many helpful suggestions for improvement and corrected errors. I am also deeply indebted to the reviewers who pointed out errors and suggested many important improvements in this book. Any errors and deficiencies left are mine.

The members of Wadsworth's talented and dedicated production team, listed on the copyright page, have also made vital contributions. Their labors of love are also gifts to helping sustain the earth. I especially appreciate the efforts of Vicki Friedberg, Andrew Ogus, Donna Kalal, and Edie Williams, who have worked so hard to make this book as good as it can be. My gratitude to two talented development editors, Mary Arbogast and Autumn Stanley, whose work in shaping this edition was superb. I also thank Autumn for writing 12 of the chapter-opening Earth Stories. My thanks also go to Wadsworth's hard-working sales staff, to Kristin Milotich for her cheerful efficiency, to Tom Briggs for superb copyediting, to Jane Heinze-Fry for her outstanding work on the Instructor's Manual and *Green Lives, Green Campuses*, to C. Lee Rockett and Kenneth J. Van Dellen for developing the Laboratory Manual to accompany this book, and to Kenneth J. Van Dellen as primary author of Chapter 7.

Special thanks go to Jack Carey, Biology and Environmental Science Publisher at Wadsworth, for his encouragement, help, twenty-five years of friendship, and superb reviewing system. It helps immensely to work with the best and most experienced editor in college textbook publishing.

I also wish to thank Peggy Sue O'Neal, my earthmate, spouse, and best friend, for her love and support of me and the earth. I dedicate this book to her and to the earth that sustains us all.

*G. Tyler Miller, Jr.*

# What's New in the Eighth Edition

## PART I

## HUMANS AND NATURE: AN OVERVIEW

### 1  Environmental Problems and Their Causes

1 color photo; 2 diagrams; opening Earth Story, "Living in an Exponential Age"; Spotlight, "The World's Most Overpopulated Country"; Guest Essay, "Simple Simon Environmental Analysis," by Anne H. Ehrlich and Paul R. Ehrlich

### 2  Brief History of Resource Use and Conservation

3 color photos; opening Earth Story, "Frontier Expansion and Biological Warfare"; update of major environmental events 1991–1993; Guest Essay, "Launching the Environmental Revolution," by Lester R. Brown

## PART II

## SCIENTIFIC PRINCIPLES AND CONCEPTS

### 3  Matter and Energy Resources: Types and Concepts

1 color photo; opening Earth Story, "Saving Energy, Saving Money, Saving Jobs"; expanded discussion of complex carbohydrates, proteins, and nucleic acids; Spotlight, "Keeping Track of Atoms and the Solar-Hydrogen Revolution"

### 4  Ecosystems and How They Work

9 color photos; 3 diagrams; 1 improved diagram; opening Earth Story, "Are Viruses Helping to Kill the Great Coral Reefs?"; Spotlight, "Have You Thanked Insects Today?"; Case Study, "The Vanishing Giant Panda"; discussions of the nature of life, absolute and relative humidity, condensation nuclei, and dew point; expanded treatment of five major kingdoms; predator and prey characteristics, and commensalism

### 5  Atmosphere, Climate, Weather, and Life

8 color photos; 4 diagrams; 3 improved diagrams; opening Earth Story, "Blowing in the Wind"; Spotlight, "The Kangaroo Rat: Water Miser and Keystone Species"; discussion of tornadoes and cyclones; expanded discussions of structure and composition of the atmosphere, and wetlands protection

### 6  Changes in Populations, Communities, and Ecosystems

3 color photos; 7 diagrams; 1 improved diagram; opening Earth Story, "From Rice Back to Rushes"; 2 Spotlights, "Earth: The Just Right, Resilient Planet" and "The Lesson of Evolution: Nature Always Bats Last"; Solutions, "Learning from Nature How to Live Sustainably"; discussions of density-dependent and density-independent checks on population growth, the origin of life and its diversity (chemical and biological evolution), and adaptive radiation; expanded discussions of population dynamics in nature, biological evolution and natural selection, and ecological succession

### 7  Geologic Processes: The Dynamic Earth

6 color photos; 3 diagrams; 2 improved diagrams; opening Earth Story, "Charles Darwin Reporting from Concepción, Chile"; new section (7-4), "Locating and Extracting Crustal Resources"; Spotlight, "Extracting Coal"; expanded discussion of environmental impacts of resource extraction

## PART III

## THE HUMAN POPULATION

### 8  Population Dynamics and Population Regulation

3 color photos; 4 diagrams; opening Earth Story, "Cops and Rubbers Day in Thailand"; Case Study, "The Graying of Japan"; Spotlight, "Using Computer Models to Evaluate Limits to Growth"; new

# Guest Authors, Guest Essayists, Reviewers

## GUEST AUTHORS AND GUEST ESSAYISTS

**Kenneth J. Van Dellen,** Professor of Geology and Environmental Science, Macomb Community College, is the primary author of Chapter 7. **Autumn Stanley,** writer and development editor, wrote 12 of the chapter-opening Earth Stories.

The following are authors of Guest Essays: **Lester R. Brown,** President, Worldwatch Institute; **Alberto Ruz Buenfil,** environmental activist, writer, and performer; **Robert D. Bullard,** Professor of Sociology, University of California, Riverside; **Vincent T. Covello,** Professor of Environmental Sciences, School of Public Health, and Director, Center for Risk Communication, Columbia University; **Herman E. Daly,** Senior Environmental Economist, World Bank; **Anne H. Ehrlich,** Senior Research Associate, Department of Biological Sciences, Stanford University; **Paul R. Ehrlich,** Bing Professor of Population Studies, Stanford University; **Lois Marie Gibbs,** Director, Citizens' Clearinghouse for Hazardous Wastes; **Garrett Hardin,** Professor Emeritus of Human Ecology, University of California, Santa Barbara; **Jim Hightower,** populist, author, and radio commentator; **Hugh Kaufman,** hazardous waste expert, Environmental Protection Agency; **Edward J. Kormondy,** Chancellor and Professor of Biology, University of Hawaii–Hilo/West Oahu College; **Amory B. Lovins,** energy policy consultant and Director of Research, Rocky Mountain Institute; **Jessica Tuchman Mathews,** Vice President, World Resources Institute; **Lester W. Milbrath,** Director of the Research Program in Environment and Society, State University of New York, Buffalo; **Peter Montague,** Senior Research Analyst, Greenpeace, and Director, Environmental Research Foundation; **Lynn Moorer,** environmental grass-roots leader; **Norman Myers,** consultant in environment and development; **David W. Orr,** Professor of Environmental Studies, Oberlin College; **David Pimentel,** Professor of Entomology, Cornell University; **Julian L. Simon,** Professor of Economics and Business Administration, University of Maryland.

## CUMULATIVE REVIEWERS

Barbara J. Abraham, Hampton College; Donald D. Adams, State University of New York at Plattsburgh; Larry G. Allen, California State University, Northridge; James R. Anderson, U.S. Geological Survey; Kenneth B. Armitage, University of Kansas; Gary J. Atchison, Iowa State University; Marvin W. Baker, Jr., University of Oklahoma; Virgil R. Baker, Arizona State University; Ian G. Barbour, Carleton College; Albert J. Beck, California State University, Chico; W. Behan, Northern Arizona University; Keith L. Bildstein, Winthrop College; Jeff Bland, University of Puget Sound; Roger G. Bland, Central Michigan University; Daniel J. Boivin, Université Laval; Georg Borgstrom, Michigan State University; Arthur C. Borror, University of New Hampshire; John H. Bounds, Sam Houston State University; Leon F. Bouvier, Population Reference Bureau;

Michael F. Brewer, Resources for the Future, Inc.; Mark M. Brinson, East Carolina University; Patrick E. Brunelle, Contra Costa College; Terrence J. Burgess, Saddleback College North; David Byman, Pennsylvania State University, Worthington-Scranton; Lynton K. Caldwell, Indiana University; Faith Thompson Campbell, Natural Resources Defense Council, Inc.; Ray Canterbery, Florida State University; Ted J. Case, University of San Diego; Ann Causey, Auburn University; Richard A. Cellarius, Evergreen State University; William U. Chandler, Worldwatch Institute; F. Christman, University of North Carolina, Chapel Hill; Preston Cloud, University of California, Santa Barbara; Bernard C. Cohen, University of Pittsburgh; Richard A. Cooley, University of California, Santa Cruz; Dennis J. Corrigan; George Cox, San Diego State University; John D. Cunningham, Keene State College; Herman E. Daly, The World Bank; Raymond F. Dasmann, University of California, Santa Cruz; Kingsley Davis, Hoover Institution; Edward E. DeMartini, University of California, Santa Barbara; Charles E. DePoe, Northeast Louisiana University; Thomas R. Detwyler, University of Wisconsin; Peter H. Diage, University of California, Riverside; Lon D. Drake, University of Iowa; T. Edmonson, University of Washington; Thomas Eisner, Cornell University; Michael Esler, Southern Illinois University; David E. Fairbrothers, Rutgers University; Paul P. Feeny, Cornell University; Nancy Field, Bellevue Community College; Allan Fitzsimmons, University of Kentucky; Andrew J. Friedland, Dartmouth College; Kenneth O. Fulgham, Humboldt State University; Lowell L. Getz, University of Illinois at Urbana-Champaign; Frederick F. Gilbert, Washington State University; Jay Glassman, Los Angeles Valley College; Harold Goetz, North Dakota State University; Jeffery J. Gordon, Bowling Green State University; Eville Gorham, University of Minnesota; Michael Gough, Resources for the Future; Ernest M. Gould, Jr., Harvard University; Peter Green, Golden West College; Katharine B. Gregg, West Virginia Wesleyan College; Paul K. Grogger, University of Colorado at Colorado Springs; L. Guernsey, Indiana State University; Ralph Guzman, University of California, Santa Cruz; Raymond Hames, University of Nebraska, Lincoln; Raymond E. Hampton, Central Michigan University; Ted L. Hanes, California State University, Fullerton; William S. Hardenbergh, Southern Illinois University at Carbondale; John P. Harley, Eastern Kentucky University; Neil A. Harriman, University of Wisconsin-Oshkosh; Grant A. Harris, Washington State University; Harry S. Hass, San Jose City College; Arthur N. Haupt, Population Reference Bureau; Denis A. Hayes, environmental consultant; Gene Heinze-Fry, Department of Utilities, State of Massachusetts; John G. Hewston, Humboldt State University; David L. Hicks, Whitworth College; Eric Hirst, Oak Ridge National Laboratory; S. Holling, University of British Columbia; Donald Holtgrieve, California State University, Hayward; Michael H. Horn, California State University, Fullerton; Mark A. Hornberger, Bloomsberg University; Marilyn Houck, Pennsylvania State University; Richard D. Houk, Winthrop College; Robert J. Huggett, College of William and Mary; Donald Huisingh, North Carolina State University; Marlene K. Hutt, IBM; David R. Inglis, University of Massachusetts; Robert Janiskee, University of South Carolina; Hugo H. John, University of Connecticut; Brian A. Johnson, University of Pennsylvania, Bloomsburg; David I. Johnson, Michigan State University; Agnes Kadar, Nassau Community College; Thomas L. Keefe, Eastern Kentucky University; Nathan Keyfitz, Harvard University; David Kidd, University of New Mexico; Edward J. Kormondy, University of Hawaii–Hilo/West Oahu College; John V. Krutilla, Resources for the Future, Inc.; Judith Kunofsky, Sierra Club; E. Kurtz; Theodore Kury, State University of New York, Buffalo; Steve Ladochy, University of Winnipeg; Mark B. Lapping, Kansas State University; Tom Leege, Idaho Department of Fish and Game; William S. Lindsay, Monterey Peninsula College; E. S. Lindstrom, Pennsylvania State University; M. Lippiman, New York University Medical Center; Valerie A. Liston, University of Minnesota; Dennis Livingston, Rensselaer Polytechnic Institute; James P. Lodge, air pollution consultant; Raymond C. Loehr, University of Texas at Austin; Ruth Logan, Santa Monica City College; Robert D. Loring, DePauw University; Paul F. Love, Angelo State University; Thomas Lovering, University of California, Santa Barbara; Amory B. Lovins, Rocky Mountain Institute; Hunter Lovins, Rocky Mountain Institute; Gene A. Lucas, Drake University; David Lynn; Timothy F. Lyon, Ball State University; Melvin G. Marcus, Arizona State University; Gordon E. Matzke, Oregon State University; Parker Mauldin, Rockefeller Foundation; Theodore R. McDowell, California State University; Vincent E. McKelvey, U.S. Geological Survey; John G. Merriam, Bowling Green State University; A. Steven Messenger, Northern Illinois University; John Meyers, Middlesex Community College; Raymond W. Miller, Utah State University; Arthur B. Millman, University of Massachusetts, Boston; Rolf Monteen, California Polytechnic State University; Ralph Morris, Brock University, St. Catherines, Ontario, Canada; William W. Murdoch, University of California, Santa Barbara; Norman Myers, environmetal consultant; Brian C. Myres, Cypress College; A. Neale, Illinois State University; Duane Nellis, Kansas State University; Jan Newhouse, University of Hawaii, Manoa; John E. Oliver, Indiana State University; Eric Pallant, Allegheny College; Charles F. Park, Stanford University; Richard J. Pedersen, U.S. Department of Agriculture, Forest Service; David Pelliam, Bureau of Land Management, U.S. Department of Interior; Rodney Peterson, Colorado State University; William S. Pierce, Case Western Reserve University; David Pimentel, Cornell University; Peter Pizor, Northwest Community College; Mark D. Plunkett, Bellevue Community College; Grace L. Powell, University of Akron; James H. Price, Oklahoma College; Marian E. Reeve, Merritt College; Carl H. Reidel, University of Vermont; Roger Revelle, California State University, San Diego; L. Reynolds, University of Central Arkansas; Ronald R. Rhein, Kutztown University of Pennsylvania; Charles Rhyne, Jackson State University; Robert A. Richardson, University of Wisconsin; Benjamin F. Richason III, St. Cloud State University; Ronald Robberecht, University of Idaho; William Van B. Robertson, School of Medicine, Stanford University; C. Lee Rockett, Bowling Green State University; Terry D. Roelofs, Humboldt State University; Richard G. Rose, West Valley College; Stephen T. Ross, University of Southern Mississippi; Robert E. Roth, The Ohio State University; Floyd Sanford, Coe College; David Satterthwaite, I.E.E.D., London; Stephen W. Sawyer, University of Maryland; Arnold Schecter, State University of New York, Syracuse; Frank Schiavo, San Jose State University, William H. Schlesinger, Ecological Society of America; Stephen H. Schneider, National Center for Atmospheric Research; Clarence A. Schoenfeld, University of Wisconsin, Madison; Henry A. Schroeder, Dartmouth Medical School; Lauren A. Schroeder, Youngstown State University; Norman B. Schwartz, University of Delaware; George Sessions, Sierra College; David J. Severn, Clement Associates; Paul Shepard, Pitzer College and Claremont Graduate School; Michael P. Shields, Southern Illinois University at Carbondale; Kenneth Shiovitz ; F. Siewert, Ball State University; E. K. Silbergold, Environmental Defense Fund; Joseph L. Simon, University of South Florida; William E. Sloey, University of Wisconsin–Oshkosh; Robert L. Smith, West Virginia University; Howard M. Smolkin, U.S. Environmental Protection Agency; Patricia M. Sparks, Glassboro State College; John E. Stanley, University of Virginia; Mel Stanley, California State Polytechnic University, Pomona; Norman R. Stewart, University of Wisconsin-Milwaukee; Frank E. Studnicka, University of Wisconsin–Platteville; William L. Thomas, California State University, Hayward; Tinco E. A. van Hylckama, Texas Tech University; Robert R. Van Kirk, Humboldt State University; Donald E. Van Meter, Ball State University; Gary Varner, Texas A&M University; John D. Vitek, Oklahoma State University; Lee B. Waian, Saddleback College; Warren C. Walker, Stephen F. Austin State University; Thomas D. Warner, South Dakota State University; Kenneth E. F. Watt, University of California, Davis; Alvin M. Weinberg, Institute of Energy Analysis, Oak Ridge Associated Universities; Brian Weiss; Anthony Weston, SUNY at Stony Brook; Raymond White, San Francisco City College; Douglas Wickum, University of Wisconsin–Stout; Charles G. Wilber, Colorado State University; Nancy Lee Wilkinson, San Francisco State University; John C. Williams, College of San Mateo; Ray Williams, Whittier College; Samuel J. Williamson, New York University; Ted L. Willrich, Oregon State University; James Winsor, Pennsylvania State University; Fred Witzig, University of Minnesota at Duluth; George M. Woodwell, Woods Hole Research Center; Robert Yoerg, Belmont Hills Hospital; Hideo Yonenaka, San Francisco State University; Malcolm J. Zwolinski, University of Arizona.

# Brief Contents

# Detailed Contents

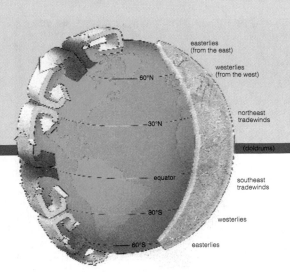

easterlies
(from the east)

westerlies
(from the west)

60°N

northeast
tradewinds

30°N

(doldrums)

equator

southeast
tradewinds

30°S

westerlies

60°S

easterlies

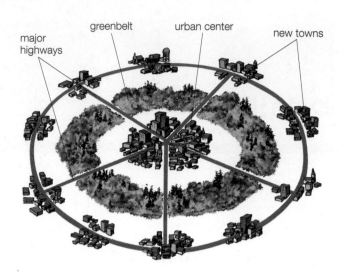

# Principles, Connections, Solutions:
# A Guide to Learning

With the emergence of the environment as one of today's most pressing and controversial concerns, the interdisciplinary field of environmental science is becoming increasingly important and interesting.

In this Eighth Edition of **Living in the Environment,** G. Tyler Miller, Jr., presents basic and easily understandable scientific principles to show how various parts of Earth's life support systems, environmental problems, and possible solutions are connected. The new subtitle for this edition, **"Principles, Connections, and Solutions,"** emphasizes this perspective.

This is a major revision of the world's most widely used environmental science textbook. The entirely new art program includes many illustrations and photographs that are more three-dimensional, colorful, detailed, and useful than ever before. The writing has never been better—it's clearer, more personal, livelier. And to ensure that information in the text is as current, accurate, and scientifically sound as possible, more scientific content has been added, well over 10,000 research sources in the professional literature have been consulted, and more than 200 experts have reviewed the material in this and earlier editions with a critical eye.

But in the end, it's the voice and experience of the author that sets this book apart. For 26 years, G. Tyler Miller, Jr., has devoted his full time to studying, teaching, and writing about the environment and its connections. He has challenged the two million students who have used his textbooks to question their assumptions, think problems through, and begin to lead more environmentally responsible lives.

The material that follows will enhance your ability to use and learn from this book.

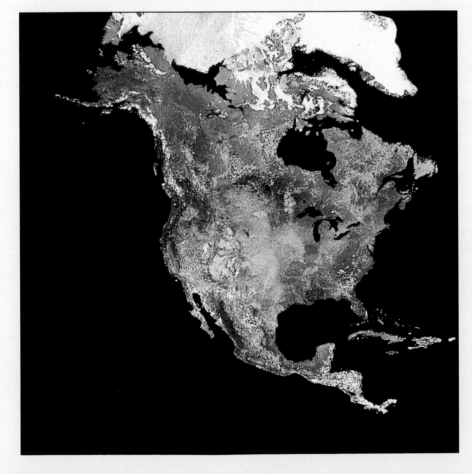

A view from space showing major biomes and surface features of most of North America. This is one of 13 spectacular new satellite photographs in this edition.

### How Farmers and a Monkey Saved a Forest

It's early morning in a tropical forest in the Central American country of Belize (Figure 9-3). Suddenly loud roars that trail off into wheezing moans—territorial wake-up calls of black howler monkeys (Figure

10-1)—rouse everyone in or near the wildlife sanctuary by the Belize River. These long-tailed primates live in small troops headed by a dominant male. Vegetarians, they travel slowly among the treetops, feeding on leaves, flowers, and fruits.

This species is the centerpiece of an experiment recruiting peasant farmers to preserve nearby tropical forests and wildlife. The project is the brainchild of

**Figure 10-1** Black howler monkey in a tropical forest in Belize. This is one of six howler monkey species in Latin America whose populations have declined as tropical forests in countries such as Guatemala and Mexico have been cleared. The black howler is one of the more than two-thirds of the world's 150 known species of primates threatened with extinction.

American Robert Horwich. Meeting in 1985 with the 300 people of Bermudian Landing, Robert suggested that the villagers establish a sanctuary that would benefit the local black howlers and themselves. He proposed that the farmers leave thin strips of forest along the edges of their fields to provide food for the howlers and let them travel through the sanctuary's patchwork of active garden plots and young and mature forest. Leaving strips of forest along the river, he noted, would also reduce soil erosion and river silting, yielding more fish for the villagers.

To date more than 100 farmers have done this, and the 47-square-kilometer (18-square-mile) sanctuary is now home for an estimated 1,100 black howlers. The idea has spread to seven other villages.

Now as many as 6,000 ecotourists visit the sanctuary each year to catch glimpses of its loudmouth monkeys and other wildlife. Villagers serve as tour guides, cook meals for the visitors, and lodge tourists overnight in their spare rooms. So long as ecotourism doesn't get so big that it destroys the howlers, this experiment can demonstrate the benefits of integrating ecology and economics by allowing local villagers to make money by helping sustain the forest and its wildlife.

Forests are home to 50–90% of Earth's species. They are also potentially renewable resources if used sustainably. However, forests—especially tropical forests and old-growth forests in the northwestern United States and southwestern Canada—are disappearing faster than any other biome as they are cleared for timber, paper pulp, fuelwood, cropland, livestock grazing, mining, reservoirs, and urbanization. They are also threatened by air pollution and by possible climate change that their destruction is helping to cause.

If these incredibly diverse and important forest biomes continue to vanish at the current rate, most will be gone within 30–50 years. Preventing further losses of these vital forms of Earth capital and helping to heal forests we have degraded are urgent priorities.

In this chapter we will answer the following questions:

- What are the major types of forests, and why are they such important ecosystems?
- How fast is tropical deforestation taking place, and why should we care about the problem?
- What are the causes of tropical deforestation and fuelwood shortages?
- What can be done to reduce tropical deforestation and fuelwood shortages?
- Why are the remaining old-growth forests in North America important, and what can be done to prevent their destruction?

### 10-1 Forests: Types and Importance

**TYPES OF FORESTS** Since agriculture began about 10,000 years ago, human activities have reduced Earth's forest cover by at least one-third to about 34% of the world's land area (p. 259 and Figures 5-11, 5-22, 5-24, and 5-26). Forests are disappearing almost everywhere, although losses in Europe and North America have been partially offset by new forest growth.

**Old-growth forests** are virgin (uncut) and old second-growth forests that have not been seriously disturbed for several hundred years. They contain massive trees hundreds or even thousands of years old. Examples include forests of Douglas fir, western hemlock, giant sequoia (Figure 4-9), and coastal redwoods (Figure 2-7) in the western United States; loblolly pine in the Southeast; and 60% of the world's tropical forests.

The understory zones and other vegetation in old-growth forests provide ecological niches for a variety of wildlife (Figure 4-37). These forests also have large numbers of standing dead trees (snags) and fallen logs (boles), which are habitats for a variety of plants, animals, and microorganisms. Their decay returns nutrients to the soil.

## NEW "EARTH STORIES"

Each chapter now opens with an "Earth Story" to introduce related material and spark interest. These stories, illustrated with exciting photographs, provide useful information. Many describe what individuals have already done to help sustain the earth, offering students inspiration and hope for the future.

## NEW SOLUTIONS BOXES

In addition to describing environmental problems, this new edition emphasizes more than ever before solutions to these problems. Each of 31 Solutions boxes, a new feature of this edition, highlights a particular environmental problem and offers possible ways to solve it. There are also sections and subsections of Solutions within most chapters.

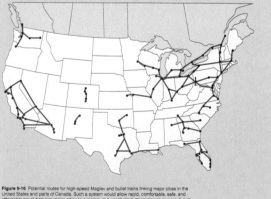

### High-Speed Regional Trains

**SOLUTIONS**

In western Europe and Japan a new generation of streamlined, comfortable, and low-polluting high-speed-rail (HSR) lines are being developed for medium-distance travel between cities within a region. These "bullet" or super-trains travel on new or upgraded existing tracks at speeds up to 320 kilometers (200 miles) per hour. They are ideal for trips of intermediate length—240–480 kilometers (150–300 miles). Journeys between major cities within a region on these trains are smoother and cheaper than an airplane.

In Japan such trains, which began operating in 1964, have carried over

3 billion passengers between Tokyo and Osaka without a single injury or fatality and depart and arrive on schedule 99% of the time. However, such systems are expensive to run and maintain, and must operate along heavily used transportation routes to be profitable.

A future alternative to the automobile and the airplane for medium-distance travel of 200–1,000 kilometers (120–620 miles) between cities is the *magnetic-levitation (Maglev) train*, which uses powerful superconducting electromagnets to suspend the train on a cushion of air a few centimeters above a guiding rail. Such trains zoom along without rail friction at speeds up to 500 kilometers (310 miles) per hour

and can carry 150–1,000 passengers, depending on the number of cars used. Germany and Japan have prototypes in operation.

Because these trains never touch the track they make little noise, require little maintenance, and can be elevated over existing median strips or other rights-of-way along highways, avoiding costly and disruptive land acquisitions. Maglev and bullet trains reduce energy consumption as well as greenhouse and other air emissions. A U.S. Maglev network could replace airplanes, buses, and private cars for most medium-distance travel between major American cities (Figure 9-16).

**Figure 9-16** Potential routes for high-speed Maglev and bullet trains linking major cities in the United States and parts of Canada. Such a system would allow rapid, comfortable, safe, and affordable travel between major cities in a region, and would slash dependence on cars, buses, and airplanes. (Data from High Speed Rail/Maglev Association)

Q: What is the largest source of CFC emissions in the United States?

### The Chipko Movement

In the late fifteenth century Jambeshwar, the son of a village leader in northern India, developed 29 principles for living and founded a Hindu sect, called the Bishnois, based on a religious duty to protect trees and wild animals. In 1730, when the Maharajah of Jodhpur in northern India ordered that the few remaining trees in the area be cut down, the Bishnois forbade it. Women rushed in and hugged the trees to protect them, but the Maharajah's minister ordered the work to proceed anyway. According to legend 363 Bishnois women died on that day.

In 1973 some women in the Himalayan village of Gopeshwar in northern India started the modern Chipko (an Indian word for "hug" or "cling to") movement to protect the remaining trees in a nearby forest from being cut down to make tennis rackets for export. It began when Chandi Prasad Bhatt, a village leader, urged villagers to run into the forest ahead of loggers and "hold fast," or "chipko," to protect the trees (Figure 10-25), thus reviving the tradition started several hundred years earlier by the Bishnois.

When the loggers came, local women, children, and men rushed into the forests, flung their arms around trees, and dared the loggers to let the axes fall on their backs. They were successful, and their action inspired women in other Himalayan villages to protect their forests. As a result, the commercial cutting of timber in the hills of the Indian state of Uttar Pradesh has been banned.

Since 1973 the Chipko movement, whose slogan is quoted at the

beginning of this chapter, has widened its efforts. Now the women—who still guard trees from loggers—also plant trees, prepare village forestry plans, and build walls to stop soil erosion.

The spreading actions of such Earth citizens should inspire us to help protect the earth. Sustaining the earth will come mostly from the bottom up by the actions of ordinary people, not from the top down.

**Figure 10-25** A member of the Chipko movement protecting a tree in northern India from being cut down for export. This is another example of a successful grass-roots group dedicated to sustaining the earth. Women are the driving force in this group.

In a like-spirited grass-roots movement, for two decades women and children in parts of India have gone into nearby forests, joined hands, and encircled trees to prevent commercial loggers from cutting them down (Individuals Matter, above).

*Forests precede civilizations, deserts follow them.*

FRANÇOIS-AUGUSTE-RENÉ DE CHATEAUBRIAND

A: Almost 40%

---

### Earth: The Just Right, Resilient Planet

Like Goldilocks tasting porridge at the house of the three bears, life as we know it is picky about temperature. Venus is much too hot, Mars is much too cold, and Earth is just right. Otherwise, you wouldn't be reading these words.

Life as we know it also depends on water. Again temperature is crucial. Earthly life needs average temperatures between the freezing and boiling points of water—between 0°C and 100°C (32°F and 212°F)—at Earth's typical atmospheric pressure.

Earth's orbit is the right distance from the sun to have these conditions. Much closer and it would be too hot—like Venus—for water vapor to condense to form rain; much farther away and it would be so cold—like Mars—that water would have existed only as ice. Earth also spins (Figure 5-5). Otherwise, the side facing the sun would be too hot, and the other side too cold, for water-based life to exist. So far, the temperature has been, like Baby Bear's porridge, just right.

Earth is also the right size. That is, it has enough gravitational mass to keep its iron-nickel core molten and its atmosphere around it. The slow transfer of this heat (geothermal energy) to the surface helps keep the planet at the right temperature for life. A much smaller Earth would not have enough gravitational mass to hold onto an atmosphere consisting of light molecules such as $N_2$, $O_2$, $CO_2$, and $H_2O$. And, thanks to the development of photosynthesizing bacteria over 2 billion years ago, an ozone sunscreen protects us from an overdose of ultraviolet light.

On a time scale of millions of years, Earth is also enormously resilient and adaptive. Earth's average temperatures have remained between the freezing and boiling points of water even though the sun's energy output has increased by about 30% over the 3.6 billion years since life arose. In short, Earth is just right for life as we know it to have arisen.

*chemical evolution of the earth.* This shows that Earth has the right physical and chemical conditions for life as we know it to exist (Spotlight, left).

A second conclusion from this body of evidence is that life on Earth developed in two phases:

*Phase 1: Chemical Evolution
(about 1 billion years)*

Part 1: Formation of Earth and its early crust and atmosphere

Part 2: Evolution of the nonliving biological molecules necessary for life—primarily the polymers DNA, RNA, proteins, and carbohydrates

Part 3: Evolution of systems of chemical reactions needed for linking these biopolymers in ways to produce the first living cells

*Phase 2: Biological Evolution
(about 3.6–3.8 billion years)*

Development of diverse species through genetic modification and natural selection of Earth's primitive cells and the organisms that followed

CHEMICAL EVOLUTION: SETTING THE STAGE FOR LIFE Billions of years ago, explosions of dying stars ripped through our galaxy and left behind a dense, swirling cloud of dust particles and hot gas extending trillions of kilometers across space in one of the spiral arms of our galaxy. As the cloud cooled, countless bits of matter gravitated toward one another. By 4.6 billion years ago the cloud had flattened into a slowly rotating disk. Our sun was born at the extremely dense, hot center of the disk. Extremely high temperatures in this core consisting of isotopes of hydrogen forced these nuclei together in nuclear fusion reactions (Figure 3-13) that would give off immense quantities of energy for the next 10 billion years.

Farther out from the center, the earth and other planets were forming as innumerable bits of matter were drawn together and coalesced. At some stage in its early life, Earth was a completely molten mass that did not cool for several hundred million years. As the cooling took place, the outermost portion of the molten sphere solidified to form a thin, hardened crust of rocks, devoid of atmosphere and oceans.

The planet's first atmosphere formed as molten rock frequently erupted through the thin crust, releasing gases from the molten interior or from below its crust. At first, water vapor released from the breakdown of rocks during volcanic eruptions evaporated in the intense heat blanketing the crust. Eventually, however, the crust cooled enough for this water vapor

sions of such items, that provide recognizable evidence of ancient organisms. The fossil record, however, is uneven. Some life forms left no fossils, some fossils have decomposed, and others are yet to be found.

Other sources of information include chemical analysis of ancient rocks and cores drilled out of buried ice, and analysis of the genetic makeup of fossil specimens. When this diverse evidence is pieced together, an important fact emerges: *The evolution of life has been linked, from the beginning, to the physical and*

\: 75%

---

## INDIVIDUALS MATTER BOXES

Thirty Individuals Matter boxes (5 new to this edition) demonstrate what individuals have already done or offer readers tips on how to adopt certain lifestyle changes to work with the earth. A new workbook, *Green Lives, Green Campuses,* is being offered as a supplement to this edition. It contains projects to help students evaluate the environmental impact of their lifestyles and guides them in making an environmental audit of their campus.

## INTEGRATING THEMES

Seven major themes—*Population, Energy and Energy Efficiency, Pollution Prevention and Waste Reduction, Biodiversity and Earth Capital, Economics and Environment, Solutions,* and *Individual Action and Earth Citizens*—are used to integrate the book (see inside front cover).

## SPOTLIGHTS

Seventy-two Spotlights (28 new to this edition) highlight and provide further insights into key environmental problems and concepts. This one, "Earth: The Just Right, Resilient Planet," demonstrates how Earth has the right physical and chemical conditions for life as we know it to exist.

## A PRINCIPLES-BASED APPROACH

The author has always used scientific principles as a foundation for helping students understand and think critically about environmental problems and their possible solutions—a trendsetting feature that has been expanded in this edition. The discussion here introduces a new section on the origin of life on Earth (chemical and biological evolution). Other new and expanded concepts include the nature of life, the five-kingdom classification of organisms, population dynamics, population density, ecological niche, primary and secondary ecological succession, half-lives of radioisotopes, the importance of insects, species interactions, climate and weather, coral reefs, mangroves, survivorship curves, mutations, adaptive radiations, and r- and K-strategists.

## PRO/CON BOXES

Fourteen Pro/Con boxes (4 new to this edition) present both sides of controversial environmental and resource issues to encourage critical thinking. Discussions of controversial issues are also found throughout much of the textual material. The Pro/Con box shown here presents arguments for and against the use of the automobile.

*New to This Edition:*
Factual recall questions with answers (shown here) at the bottom of each page.

## GUEST ESSAYS

Nineteen Guest Essays (7 new to this edition) provide various perspectives on the environment. The essays are written by both scholars and individuals actively engaged on the frontlines of environmental change. Shown here is the first page of one of the new Guest Essays in this edition (see pages 43 and 44 of the text for the complete essay).

---

### The Automobile

PRO/CON

The automobile is addictive. Its appeal is convenience and undreamed of mobility. To many people cars are also symbols of power, sex, excitement, and success.

Moreover, much of the world's economy is built on producing motor vehicles and supplying roads, services, and repairs for them. In the United States one of every six dollars spent and one of every six nonfarm jobs are connected to the automobile. Each day $200 million is spent building and rebuilding U.S. roads.

In spite of their benefits motor vehicles have many destructive effects on human lives and on air, water, land, and wildlife resources. Since 1885, when Karl Benz built the first automobile, almost 18 million people have been killed by motor vehicles, and the death toll increases by about 250,000 people per year—as many as were killed by the atomic bombs dropped on Hiroshima and Nagasaki. And each year about 10 million people are permanently disabled.

In the United States almost 15 million motor vehicle accidents kill around 40,000 people each year and injure almost 5 million people, at least 300,000 of them severely. More Americans have been killed by cars than were killed in all the country's wars. Each year the accidents cost

the United States more than $350 billion, about 8% of the GNP.

Motor vehicles are also the largest source of air pollution, laying a haze of smog over the world's cities (Figure 9-4). In the United States they produce at least 50% of the air pollution, even though emission standards are as strict as any in the world. Gains in fuel efficiency and emission reductions have been largely offset by the increase in cars and a doubling in the distance Americans traveled by car between 1970 and 1990.

Motor vehicles are the major cause of the world's oil addiction. Two-thirds of the oil used in the United States is devoted to transportation, with half the total consumed by motor vehicles. These vehicles generate 25% of U.S. carbon dioxide emissions, and leaky air conditioners in vehicles are the country's largest source of chlorofluorocarbon emissions, the primary culprits in the depletion of the ozone layer. Motor vehicles produce 14% of global $CO_2$ emissions and 28% of chlorofluorocarbon emissions. And leaks and spills of oil and gas routinely pollute surface water and groundwater.

By making long commutes and distant shopping possible, automobiles and highways have led to urban sprawl and reduced use of mass transit, bicycles, and walking. The typical American suburbanite

makes 13 trips per day to run errands. Ironically many people in the United States drive their cars to health clubs only to work out on treadmills or stationary bikes.

Worldwide at least a third of urban land is devoted to roads, parking lots, gasoline stations, and other automobile-related uses. In the United States more land is now devoted to cars than to housing. Half the land in an average American city is used for cars, prompting urban expert Lewis Mumford to suggest that the U.S. national flower should be the concrete cloverleaf.

In 1907 the average speed of horse-drawn vehicles through the borough of Manhattan was 18.5 kilometers (11.5 miles) per hour. Today cars and trucks with the potential power of 100–300 horses creep along Manhattan streets at 8 kilometers (5 miles) per hour. In Paris and Tokyo average auto speeds are even lower. If present trends continue, U.S. motorists will spend an average of two years of their lifetime in traffic jams. The U.S. economy loses at least $100 billion per year because of time lost in traffic delays. Building more roads is not the answer because, as economist Robert Samuelson put it, "Cars expand to fill available concrete." International experience indicates that it is more cost-effective to build rail systems within and between urban areas.

world's people, the United States has 35% of the world's cars and trucks (190 million vehicles). In LDCs most people travel by foot, bicycle, or motor scooter.

In the United States the car is now used for 86% of all trips (compared to about 45% in most western European countries), 98% of all urban transportation, and 86% of travel to work. Public transit is used for only 2.5% of all trips. Almost 75% of commuting cars carry only one person, and only 13% of commuters use car pools. Only about 5% of Americans use public transportation, and only 7% walk or use a bicycle to

get to and from work. Americans drive 3 billion kilometers (2 billion miles) each year—equal to more than 10 round trips to the sun and as far as the rest of the world combined. No wonder British author J. B. Priestley remarked, "In America, the cars have become the people."

By failing to make transportation strategy the basis of land-use planning, many of the world's cities have allowed the automobile to shape and dominate them. Now they are learning that the costs often outweigh the benefits (Pro/Con, above).

A: 100,000 (7,000 in the United States)

CHAPTER 9   243

---

### Launching the Environmental Revolution*

GUEST ESSAY

*Lester R. Brown*

*Lester R. Brown is president of the Worldwatch Institute, a private nonprofit research institute devoted to analysis of global environmental issues, which he founded in 1974. Under his leadership the institute publishes the annual State of the World Reports, considered by environmentalists and world leaders as the best source of information about key environmental issues; monographs on specific topics; World Watch magazine; and a series of Environmental Alert books. He is author of a dozen books, recipient of the MacArthur Foundation "Genius Award," and winner of the United Nations' 1989 environment prize. He has been described by the Washington Post as "one of the world's most influential thinkers."*

Our world of the mid-1990s faces potentially convulsive change. The question is, in what direction will it take us? Will the change come from strong worldwide initiatives that reverse the degradation of the planet and restore hope for the future, or will it come from continuing environmental deterioration that leads to economic decline and social instability?

Muddling through will not work. Either we will turn things around quickly or the self-reinforcing internal dynamic of the deterioration-and-decline scenario will take over. The policy decisions we make in the years immediately ahead will determine whether our children live in a world of development or decline.

There is no precedent for the rapid and substantial change we need to make. Building an environmentally sustainable future depends on restructuring the global economy, enacting major shifts in human reproductive behavior, and making dramatic changes in values and lifestyles. Doing all this quickly adds up to a revolution that is driven and defined by the need to restore and preserve the earth's environmental systems. If this *Environmental Revolution* succeeds, it will rank with the Agricultural and Industrial Revolutions as one of the great economic and social transformations in human history.

Like the Agricultural Revolution, it will dramatically alter population trends. While the former set the stage for enormous increases in human numbers, this revolution will succeed only if it stabilizes human population size, reestablishing a balance between people and natural systems on which they depend [Figure 2-4]. In contrast to the Industrial Revolution, which was based on a shift to fossil fuels, this new transformation will be based on a shift away from fossil fuels.

The two earlier revolutions were driven by technological advances—the first by the discovery of farming and the second by the invention of the steam engine, which

converted the energy in coal into mechanical power. The Environmental Revolution, while it will obviously need new technologies, will be driven primarily by the restructuring of the global economy so that it does not destroy its natural support systems.

The pace of the Environmental Revolution needs to be far faster than that of its predecessors. The Agricultural Revolution began some 10,000 years ago and the Industrial Revolution has been under way for about two centuries. But if the Environmental Revolution is to succeed, it must be compressed into a few decades.

Progress in the Agricultural Revolution was measured almost exclusively in the growth in food output that eventually enabled farmers to produce a surplus that could feed city dwellers. Similarly industrial progress was gauged by success in expanding the output of raw materials and manufactured goods. The Environmental Revolution will be judged by whether it can shift the world economy into an environmentally sustainable development path, one that leads to greater economic security, healthier lifestyles, and a worldwide improvement in the human condition.

Many still do not see the need for such an economic and social transformation. They see the earth's deteriorating physical condition as a peripheral matter that can be dealt with by minor policy adjustments. But 20 years of effort have failed to stem the tide of environmental degradation. There is now too much evidence on too many fronts to take these issues lightly.

Already the planet's degradation is damaging human health, slowing the growth in world food production, and reversing economic progress in dozens of countries. By the age of 10, thousands of children living in southern California's Los Angeles basin have respiratory systems that are permanently impaired by polluted air. Some 300,000 people in the former Soviet Union are being treated for radiation sickness caused by the Chernobyl nuclear power plant accident. The accelerated depletion of ozone in the stratosphere in the Northern Hemisphere will lead to an estimated additional 200,000 skin cancer fatalities over the next half century in the United States alone. Worldwide millions of lives are at stake. These examples, and countless others, show that our health is closely linked to that of the planet.

A scarcity of new cropland and fresh water plus the negative effects of soil erosion, air pollution, and hotter summers on crop yields are slowing the growth of the world grain harvest. Combined with continuing rapid population growth, this has reversed the steady rise in grain output per person that the world had become accustomed to. Between 1950 and 1984, the historical peak year, world grain production per person climbed by nearly 40%. Since then it has fallen roughly 1% per year, with the drop concentrated in poor countries. With food imports in these nations restricted by rising external debt, there are far more hungry people today than ever before.

(continued)

* Excerpt from an expanded version of these ideas in "Launching the Environmental Revolution," State of the World 1992 (New York: Norton, 1992).

A: About 25%

CHAPTER 2   43

### The Vanishing Giant Panda

The giant panda (Figure 4-36) is one of the world's most endangered animals. One reason is that it is so specialized, getting 99% of its food from bamboo. Worse, its digestive system absorbs only about 17% of the food it eats and its bamboo diet provides enough protein but very little energy. To survive, these animals must spend most of each day eating up to one-third of their body weight in bamboo.

Three million years ago giant pandas were widespread in China. But China's soaring population has pushed them into smaller and smaller areas in the remote, fog-shrouded western mountains. Today only about 800 giant pandas survive in the wild, in about 20 isolated "islands" of bamboo forest. These isolated populations of 10–50 animals are vulnerable to being wiped out and to inbreeding. One serious threat is illegal hunting. Although killing a giant panda in China brings an automatic death penalty, poachers still kill 40 or more pandas per year because their pelts bring $100,000 or more in Hong Kong and Japan.

Giant pandas are also biologically vulnerable to extinction. Only

about one cub per female survives every other year. Pandas are also quite finicky about picking mates, which becomes critical with their low numbers and isolated habitats.

Finally, bamboo dies off in cycles of 15–120 years, depending on the species. Then it takes several years for new bamboo sprouts to reach edible size. When bamboo was abundant this was no problem. The pandas simply moved to another area. Today, however, the few remaining pandas are confined to islands of forest dominated by a few bamboo species. When these plants die back, the pandas have no food source.

China has set aside 12 giant panda reserves, but the animals are threatened in 8 of them by poaching and by China's growing population. Fourteen new reserves have been proposed. Three of these would link existing reserves with migration corridors, to be planted with bamboo, and more corridors are planned. This would help end the animals' isolation, but it remains to be seen whether it will happen.

About 220 giant pandas are found in zoos and research centers in China (which has spent $25 million trying to save the species) and

**Figure 4-36** The giant panda, which is found in China, is a specialist species. It has a narrow food niche, surviving primarily on bamboo stalks and leaves.

elsewhere, but more captive pandas die than are born. Will this specialized species survive? Maybe in a few zoos, but within your lifetime it may disappear from the wild.

---

tors. When environments are changing rapidly, however, the adaptable generalist is usually better off than the specialist.

### 4-6 Interactions Between Species

**WAYS SPECIES INTERACT** When any two species in an ecosystem have some activities or requirements in common, they may interact to some degree. The principal types of species interactions are *interspecific competition, predation, parasitism, mutualism,* and *com-*

*mensalism*. Three of these interactions—parasitism, mutualism, and commensalism—are **symbiotic relationships** in which two or more kinds of organisms live together in an intimate association, with members of one or both species benefiting from the association. In mutualism and commensalism neither species is harmed by the interaction.

**COMPETITION BETWEEN SPECIES FOR LIMITED RESOURCES** As long as commonly used resources are abundant, different species can share them. This allows each species to come closer to occupying its **fundamental niche**: the full potential range of physical, chemical, and biological factors it could use if there were no competition from other species.

104

Q: How much of Earth's wetlands have been destroyed or polluted?

### CASE STUDIES

Forty-six Case Studies (3 new to this edition) offer in-depth information about key issues while applying environmental concepts. This one from Chapter 4 contains the latest information on the status of the giant panda. It applies the concept of ecological niche by showing how highly specialized feeding behavior coupled with habitat loss and hunting can make a species vulnerable to extinction.

*Key Terms*

Key terms are highlighted in **boldface** the first time they appear and are defined in the glossary at the end of the text. In addition, the index includes key terms and the page number where each term is first defined

*Factual Recall Question*

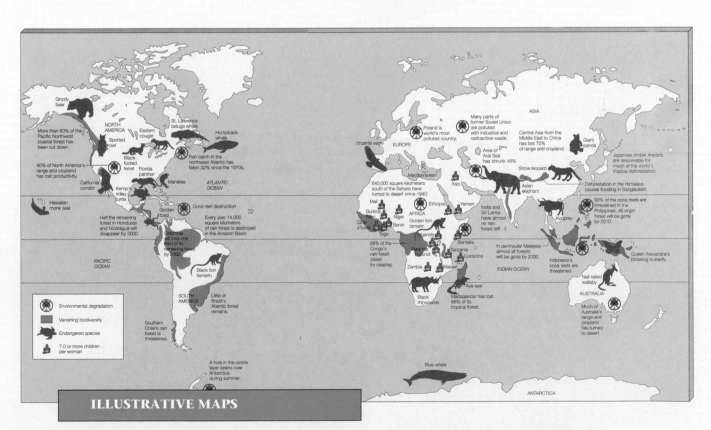

### ILLUSTRATIVE MAPS

Shown here is one of the 11 new maps created for this edition, bringing the total to 52 in all. This map shows serious environmental problems around the world. Other maps show the location of an area being discussed relative to the globe and to surrounding countries. Where data are available, U.S. maps have been expanded to include Canada.

The illustrations in each new edition of *Living in the Environment* keep getting better and better. In the new Eighth Edition each piece of existing art was redesigned to provide more realistic details, more vibrant color, and when possible, more three-dimensional effects. The result is a total of 308 full-color diagrams and 235 carefully selected photographs that simplify and demonstrate key concepts and ideas. Compare these examples from the Seventh and Eighth Editions.

### From the Eighth Edition

An illustration of how climate determines the types and amounts of natural vegetation you would expect to find in an undisturbed area.

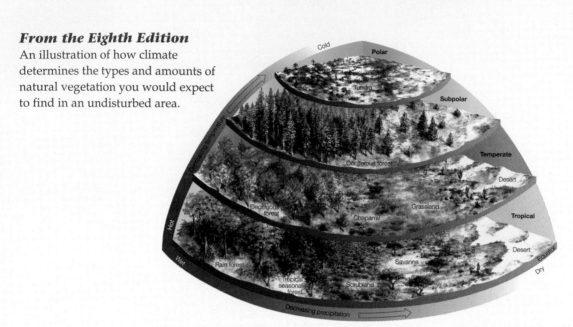

### From the Seventh Edition

## From the Eighth Edition

The three phases in the flow of water downhill from mountain head-water streams to wider, lower elevation streams to rivers, which empty into the ocean. Notice the improved detail and color in this new version.

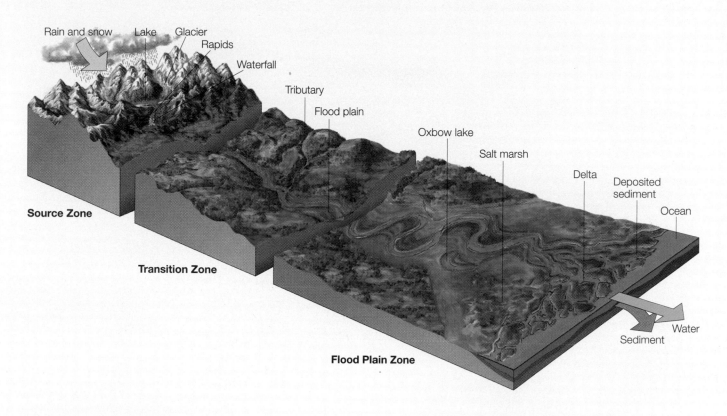

Rain and snow   Lake   Glacier

Rapids

Waterfall

Tributary

Flood plain

Oxbow lake

Salt marsh

Delta

Deposited sediment

Ocean

**Source Zone**

**Transition Zone**

**Flood Plain Zone**

Water

Sediment

## From the Seventh Edition

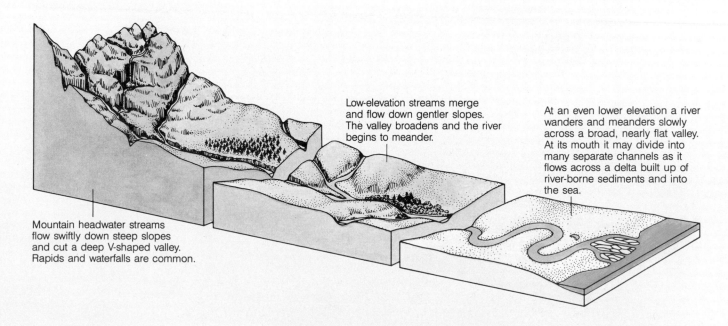

Low-elevation streams merge and flow down gentler slopes. The valley broadens and the river begins to meander.

At an even lower elevation a river wanders and meanders slowly across a broad, nearly flat valley. At its mouth it may divide into many separate channels as it flows across a delta built up of river-borne sediments and into the sea.

Mountain headwater streams flow swiftly down steep slopes and cut a deep V-shaped valley. Rapids and waterfalls are common.

# PART I
# Humans and Nature: An Overview

*The environmental crisis is an outward manifestation of a crisis of mind and spirit. There could be no greater misconception of its meaning than to believe it is concerned only with endangered wildlife, human-made ugliness, and pollution. These are part of it, but more importantly, the crisis is concerned with the kind of creatures we are and what we must become in order to survive.*

LYNTON K. CALDWELL

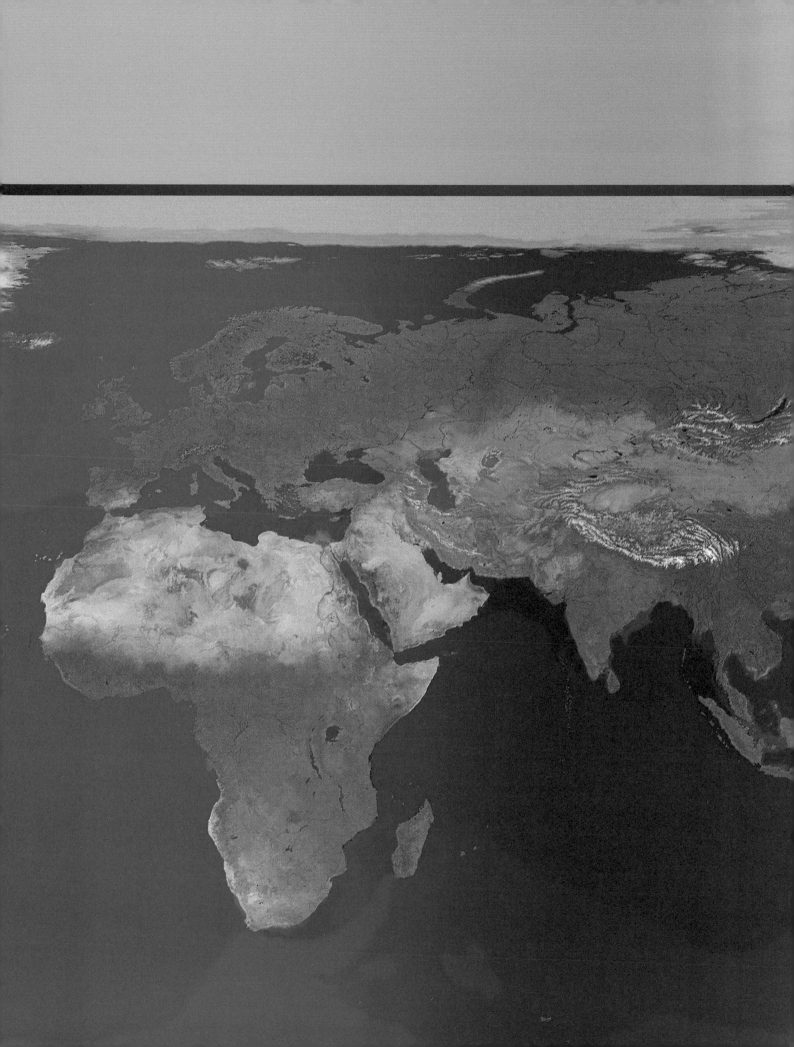

# 1 Environmental Problems and Their Causes

## Living in an Exponential Age

Once there were two kings who enjoyed playing chess, with the winner claiming a prize from the loser. After their match was over the winning king asked the loser to place one grain of wheat on the first square of the chessboard, two on the second, four on the third, and so on. The number of grains was to double each time until all 64 squares were filled.

The losing king, thinking he was getting off easy, agreed with delight. It was the biggest mistake he ever made. He bankrupted his kingdom and still could not produce the $2^{64}$ grains of wheat he had promised. In fact, it's probably more than all the wheat that has ever been harvested!

This is an example of **exponential growth**. As the loser learned, exponential growth is deceptive. It starts off slowly but after only a few doublings rises to enormous numbers, because each doubling is more than the total of all earlier growth.

Here is another example. Fold a piece of paper in half to double its thickness. If you could manage to do this 42 times, the stack would tower from Earth to the moon, 386,000 kilometers (240,000 miles) away. If you could double it 50 times, the folded paper would almost reach the sun, 149 million kilometers (93 million miles) away!

*Most environmental problems—population growth, excessive and wasteful resource use, wildlife extinction, and pollution—are growing exponentially.* For example,

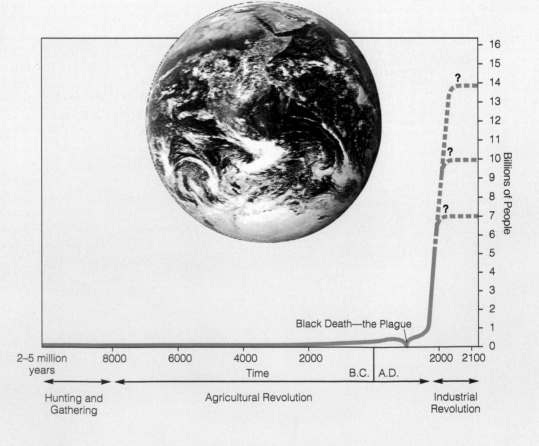

**Figure 1-1** The J-shaped curve of past exponential world population growth with projections to 2100. Notice that exponential growth starts off slowly but as time passes the curve becomes steeper and steeper. (Figure not to scale.) (Data from World Bank and United Nations; photo courtesy of NASA)

*We need to come together and choose a new direction. We need to transform our society into one in which people live in true harmony—harmony among nations, harmony among the races of humankind, and harmony with nature. . . . We will either reduce, reuse, recycle, and restore—or we will perish.*

REV. JESSE JACKSON

world population has more than doubled in only 43 years, from 2.5 billion in 1950 to 5.5 billion in 1993. Unless death rates rise sharply, it may reach 11 billion by 2045, and 14 billion by 2100 (Figure 1-1).

Exponential growth in population and resource use has drastically changed the face of the planet. Each year more forests, grasslands, and wetlands disappear, and the deserts grow larger. Vital topsoil washed or blown away from farmland and cleared forests clogs streams, lakes, and reservoirs with sediment. Underground water is pumped from wells faster than it can be replenished. Oceans are poisoned with our wastes. Every hour we drive as many as four wildlife species to extinction.

Burning fossil fuels and cutting down and burning forests raise the concentrations of carbon dioxide and other heat-trapping gases in the lower atmosphere. Within the next 40–50 years Earth's climate may become warm enough to disrupt agricultural productivity, alter water distribution, and drive countless species to extinction.

Extracting and burning fossil fuels pollute the air and water, and disrupt land. Other chemicals we add to the air drift into the upper atmosphere and deplete ozone gas, which now filters out much of the sun's harmful ultraviolet radiation. Toxic wastes from factories and homes poison the air, water, and soil. Agricultural pesticides contaminate some of our drinking water and food.

The bad news is the problems we face and their root causes, as outlined in this chapter. The good news is that it's not too late to replace our Earth-degrading actions with Earth-sustaining ones, as discussed throughout the rest of this book. The key is *Earth wisdom*—learning how Earth sustains itself—and integrating such lessons from nature into the ways we think and act. I hope you will join this *sustainability revolution*. There is no time to waste.

This chapter is an overview of environmental problems and will discuss:

- What is Earth capital? How are we depleting it?
- How fast is the human population increasing?
- What are Earth's main types of resources? How can they be depleted or degraded?
- What are the principal types of pollution? How can pollution be reduced?
- What are the root causes of the environmental problems we face?

## 1-1  Living Sustainably

**SOLAR CAPITAL AND EARTH CAPITAL**  Our existence, lifestyles, and economies depend totally on the sun and the earth. We can think of energy from the sun as **solar capital** and of the planet's air, water, fertile soil, forests, grasslands, wildlife, minerals, and natural purification and recycling processes as **Earth capital**.

The basic problem we face is that we are depleting and degrading Earth's natural capital at an accelerating rate (Figures 1-1 and 1-2). In a typical day we add 258,000 people to the world's population, clear 470 square kilometers (180 square miles) of tropical forests, create 170 square kilometers (66 square miles) of desert, erode 66 million metric tons (73 tons) of topsoil (Figure 1-3), eliminate 10–100 species, and add 71 million metric tons (78 million tons) of heat-trapping carbon dioxide and 1,600 metric tons (1,800 tons) of ozone-depleting chlorofluorocarbons to the atmosphere. To environmentalists, such behavior is unsustainable (Spotlight, p. 7).

A **sustainable society** is one that manages its economy and population size without doing irreparable environmental harm. It satisfies the needs of its people without depleting Earth capital and thus jeopardizing the prospects of future generations of humans or other species. This is done by regulating

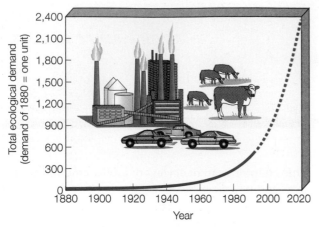

**Figure 1-2** J-shaped curve of exponential growth in the total demand on Earth's resources from agriculture, mining, and industry between 1890 and 1993. Projections to 2020 assume that resource use will continue to grow at the current rate of 5.5% per year. At that rate our total ecological demand on Earth's resources doubles every 13 years. If global economic output grew by only 3% a year, this would still double resource consumption every 23 years. (Data from United Nations, World Resources Institute, and Carrol Wilson, *Man's Impact on the Global Environment*, Cambridge, Mass.: MIT Press, 1970)

**Figure 1-3** Severe soil erosion on a hillside in Spain. Removal of forest cover often leads to this type of erosion. Wildlife habitat is lost, and streams can be polluted with eroded sediment.

population growth, by encouraging Earth-sustaining rather than Earth-degrading forms of economic development, and by minimizing poverty and human misery. It recognizes that without environmental security and economic and social justice, there can be no long-lasting economic and physical security. It also understands that with our current power to degrade our life

support systems, no country can be sustainable unless all countries work together to achieve these goals everywhere. We are all in this together.

## 1-2 Population Growth and the Wealth Gap

**LINEAR AND EXPONENTIAL GROWTH** Suppose you hop on a commuter train that accelerates by 1 kilometer (0.6 mile) per hour every second. After 5 seconds you would be traveling at 5 kilometers (3 miles) per hour; after 30 seconds your speed would be only 30 kilometers (19 miles) per hour. This is an example of **linear growth**, where a quantity increases by a constant amount per unit of time, as 1, 2, 3, 4, 5—or 1, 3, 5, 7, 9—and so on.

But suppose the train had a magic motor strong enough to increase its speed by 100% every second. After 5 seconds you would be moving at 64 kilometers per hour, and 1 second later you would be doing 128. After only 30 seconds you would be traveling 1 billion kilometers (620 million miles) per hour! This is an example, like the wheat on the chessboard, of the astounding power of *exponential growth*, where a quantity increases by a fixed percentage of the whole in a given time.

For a quantity such as resource use, population size, or money in a savings account, we may want to know how soon it will double. A quick way to calculate this **doubling time** in years is to use the **rule of 70**: 70/percentage growth rate = doubling time in years. For example, in 1993 the world's population grew by 1.7%. If that rate continues, Earth's population will double in 41 years (70/1.7 = 41 years)—more growth than has occurred in all of human history.

**THE J-SHAPED CURVE OF HUMAN POPULATION GROWTH** The increasing size of the human population provides an example of exponential growth, though not taking place at a uniform rate. For our first several million years our population grew only 0.002% per year, on average. This slow early growth creates the long horizontal part of the curve in Figure 1-1. Since then growth has speeded up. It reached an all-time high of 2.06% in 1970, before dropping to around 1.7% since 1985—which is still 850 times faster than in the first several million years of human existence (1.7%/0.002% = 850).

The relentless ticking of this population clock means that in 1993 the world's population of 5.5 billion people grew by 94 million (5.5 billion people x 0.017 = 94 million)—an average increase of 258,000 people per day, or 10,700 per hour.

Q: How many people are there in the world?

This means we are adding the equivalent of another Austria each month; an extra Canada every 14 weeks; almost another Mexico every year; and an extra United States every 2.5 years. As the population base grows, the number of people on Earth soars and the population growth curve rounds a bend and heads almost straight up, creating the J-shaped curve shown in Figure 1-1.

It took 2 million years to reach a billion people, 130 years to add the second billion, 30 years for the third, 15 years for the fourth, and only 12 years for the fifth. At present growth rates the sixth billion will be added during the 10-year period between 1987 and 1997, and the seventh only 9 years later in 2006. At the current rate of exponential growth, it takes about:

- 5 days to add people equal to the number of Americans killed in all U.S. wars

- 10 months to add 75 million people—the number killed by the bubonic plague (the Black Death) in the fourteenth century

- 1.7 years to add 165 million people—the number of people killed in all wars fought during the past 200 years

- 12 years to add 1.18 billion people—the population of China in 1993

This should give you some idea of what it means to go around the bend of the J curve of exponential growth.

**DIFFERENCES BETWEEN MORE AND LESS DEVELOPED COUNTRIES** Virtually all countries seek **economic growth:** increasing their capacity to provide goods and services for final use. Such growth is usually measured by an increase in a country's **gross national product (GNP):** the market value in current dollars of all goods and services produced by an economy for final use during a year. To show one person's slice of the economic pie, economists often calculate the **GNP per capita** (per person): the GNP divided by the total population.

Increases in GNP and GNP per capita have traditionally been used to indicate an increase in quality of life. However, they are actually poor indicators of life quality because they go up when we deplete Earth capital, produce waste and pollution, and affect human health. They give us misleading information about what we are doing and poor guidelines for evaluating what we should be doing to sustain the earth and our economic systems. Also, GNP per capita does not tell us how the wealth of a country is distributed among its people. For example, most less developed countries, such as moderately industrialized Mexico and Brazil, have small islands of affluence in a vast ocean of poverty.

## Don't Kill the Goose

SPOTLIGHT

Imagine you inherit $1 million. If you invest this capital at 10% interest, you will have a sustainable annual income of $100,000. That is, you can spend up to $100,000 per year without touching your capital.

But suppose you develop a taste for diamonds or a yacht—or all your relatives move in with you. Spend $200,000 per year and your million will be gone in 7 years. Even if you spend just $110,000 per year, you will be bankrupt in 18 years.

The lesson here is a very old one: Don't kill the goose that lays the golden eggs. Deplete your capital and you move from a sustainable to an unsustainable lifestyle. Get too greedy and you'll soon be needy.

The same lesson applies to Earth capital. With the help of solar energy, natural processes, developed over billions of years, renew the topsoil, water, air, forests, grasslands, and wildlife we and other species depend on, as long as we don't use these resources faster than they are renewed. Some of our wastes can also be diluted, decomposed, and recycled by natural processes as long as these processes are not overloaded.

Likewise, most of Earth's nonrenewable minerals can be recycled or reused if we don't contaminate them or mix them in landfills so that recycling and reuse are too costly. History also shows that we can often find substitutes as certain nonrenewable minerals become scarce.

Conserving energy and relying on virtually inexhaustible solar energy in the form of heat, wind, flowing water, and renewable wood and other forms of biomass are means to a sustainable lifestyle. The brief "fossil fuel age" we now live in is unsustainable because it depletes Earth's natural energy capital. By wasting less energy we could make these fuels last longer, reduce their massive environmental impact, and make an easier transition to a new, renewable-energy age.

The good news is that we can help sustain Earth for human beings and other species indefinitely by learning how to live off Earth income instead of Earth capital. Such **sustainable living** means taking no more potentially renewable resources from the natural world than can be replenished naturally and not overloading the capacity of the environment to cleanse and renew itself by natural processes.

The United Nations broadly classifies the world's countries as more or less developed. The **more developed countries (MDCs),** or *developed countries*, are highly industrialized, and most have high average GNPs per capita. They include the United States,

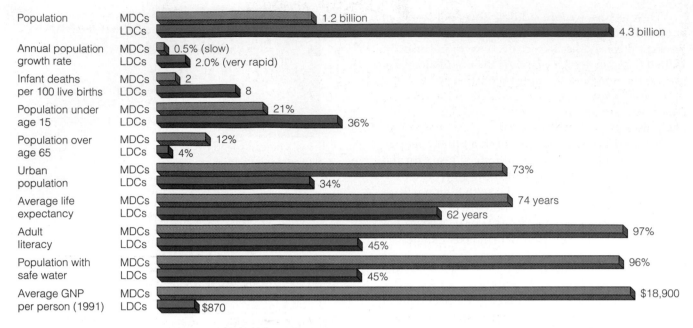

| | | |
|---|---|---|
| Population | MDCs | 1.2 billion |
| | LDCs | 4.3 billion |
| Annual population growth rate | MDCs | 0.5% (slow) |
| | LDCs | 2.0% (very rapid) |
| Infant deaths per 100 live births | MDCs | 2 |
| | LDCs | 8 |
| Population under age 15 | MDCs | 21% |
| | LDCs | 36% |
| Population over age 65 | MDCs | 12% |
| | LDCs | 4% |
| Urban population | MDCs | 73% |
| | LDCs | 34% |
| Average life expectancy | MDCs | 74 years |
| | LDCs | 62 years |
| Adult literacy | MDCs | 97% |
| | LDCs | 45% |
| Population with safe water | MDCs | 96% |
| | LDCs | 45% |
| Average GNP per person (1991) | MDCs | $18,900 |
| | LDCs | $870 |

**Figure 1-4** Some characteristics of more developed countries (MDCs) and less developed countries (LDCs) in 1993. (Data from United Nations and Population Reference Bureau)

Canada, Japan, the CIS,* Australia, New Zealand, and western European countries. These countries, with 1.2 billion people (22% of the world's population), command about 85% of the world's wealth and income, use 88% of its natural resources and 73% of its energy, and generate most of its pollution and wastes.

All other nations are classified as **less developed countries (LDCs)**, or *developing countries*, with low to moderate industrialization and GNPs per capita. Most lie in the Southern Hemisphere—in Africa, Asia, and Latin America. Their 4.3 billion people, or 78% of the world's population, have only about 15% of the wealth and income, and use only about 12% of the natural resources and 27% of the energy. The "less developed" label, invented by political scientists and economists in MDCs, is in some ways a misnomer because LDCs are highly developed culturally and in other ways.

Some analysts also distinguish between *poor* LDCs with low industrialization and GNPs per capita and *rapidly industrializing countries* (RICs) with moderate and rising industrialization and GNPs per capita. Examples of RICs include Thailand, Indonesia, and Malaysia in Southeast Asia, and Brazil, Mexico, and Chile in Latin America.

* The Commonwealth of Independent States (CIS) is a loose federation of 12 independent republics—Armenia, Azerbaijan, Belarus, Georgia, Kazakhstan, Kyrgyzstan, Moldova, Russia, Tajikstan, Turkmen-istan, Ukraine, and Uzbekistan—much of the former Soviet Union. As of this writing, Estonia, Latvia, and Lithuania had not joined the commonwealth. The composition of this alliance may change.

Figure 1-4 shows some general differences between MDCs and LDCs. Most of the projected increase in world population will take place in LDCs, where 1 million people are added every four days (Figure 1-5). By 2010 the combined populations of Asia and Africa are projected to be 5.3 billion—almost as many as now live on the entire planet.

**THE WEALTH GAP** The growing gap since 1960 between the rich and poor in GNP per capita has widened further since 1980 (Figure 1-6). The poor have received pitifully little of the wealth economists said would "trickle down" to them mostly as a result of economic growth and aid from MDCs. Between 1972 and 1992 the world's GNP rose $20 trillion, but only 15% went to LDCs. Each year LDCs pay MDCs four times more in debt interest than they receive in aid.

The rich have grown much richer, while the poor have stayed poor or grown even poorer. Today one in five people lives in luxury and the next three get by, while the fifth struggles to survive on less than $1 per day (Spotlight, p. 10).

Sooner or later there is a limit to exponentially growing resource use and the capacity of Earth's life support systems to absorb, dilute, and degrade the resulting waste and pollution. For example, if resource use grows exponentially at a rate of 5% per year, it will experience a 32-fold increase in 70 years; a 10% annual growth will yield a 1,024-fold increase. According to environmentalist David Brower, "It is cruel to pretend that the world's developing countries can reach the standard of living of the world's wealthy

Q: How many people are added to the world's population each day?

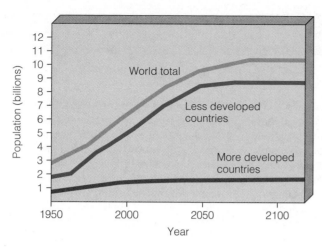

**Figure 1-5** Past and projected population size for MDCs, LDCs, and the world, 1950–2120. (Data from United Nations)

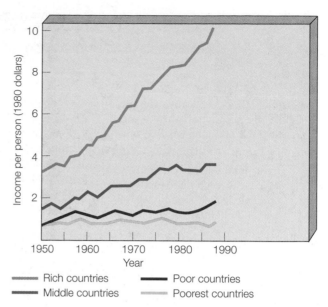

Rich countries     Poor countries
Middle countries     Poorest countries

**Figure 1-6** The wealth gap. Changes in the distribution of global income per person in four types of countries, 1950–1990. Instead of trickling down, most of the income from economic growth has flowed up, with the situation worsening since 1980. (Data from United Nations)

countries. . . . It is also clear that the wealthy countries can no longer maintain their standards of living. So we have to do something else. We can learn to live lightly on the earth."

<br>

## 1-3   Resources

**TYPES OF RESOURCES** A **resource** is anything we get from the living or nonliving environment to meet our needs and wants. *Material resources* are those whose quantities can be measured. Some, such as fresh air, fresh surface water, fertile soil, and wild edible plants, are directly available for use.

Most material resources, such as petroleum (oil), iron, groundwater (water occurring underground), and modern crops, aren't directly available, and their supplies are limited. They become resources only with some effort and technological ingenuity. Petroleum, for example, was a mysterious fluid until we learned how to find it, extract it, and refine it into gasoline, heating oil, and other products at affordable prices. On our short human time scale we classify material resources as perpetual, potentially renewable, and nonrenewable (Figure 1-9).

Solitude, beauty, knowledge, security, joy, and love are *nonmaterial*, or *intangible, resources*. Theoretically they are unlimited, but they can be threatened in a crowded and degraded environment.

**NONRENEWABLE MATERIAL RESOURCES**
**Nonrenewable**, or **exhaustible, resources** like copper, aluminum, coal, and oil exist in fixed quantities in the

earth's crust. We are extracting and using them much faster than the hundreds of millions of years it took to form them. Even if these resources are not physically exhausted, they can become **economically depleted**; that is, it costs too much to get what is left (typically when approximately 80% of the estimated supply has been extracted).

Some nonrenewable material resources can be recycled or reused to extend supplies. **Recycling** involves collecting and reprocessing a resource into new products. For example, aluminum cans can be collected, melted, and made into new beverage cans or other aluminum products. And glass bottles can be crushed and melted to make new bottles or other glass items. **Reuse** involves using a resource over and over in the same form. For example, glass bottles can be collected, washed, and refilled many times.

Other nonrenewable resources—such as coal, oil, and natural gas—can't be recycled or reused. Once burned, the useful energy in these fossil fuels is gone, leaving behind only waste heat and polluting exhaust gases. Most of the economic growth shown in Figure 1-6 has been fueled by nonrenewable oil, which is expected to be depleted within 40–80 years. Often we can find a substitute or a replacement for a scarce or expensive resource, but sometimes the replacements are inferior or too costly.

**PERPETUAL AND POTENTIALLY RENEWABLE MATERIAL RESOURCES** As long as the sun shines, there will be solar energy in the form of heat, wind,

## The Desperately Poor

Because of population growth and the wealth gap:

- One out of five persons is hungry or malnourished (Figure 1-7), lacks clean drinking water, and has decent housing (Figure 1-8) and adequate health care.

- One out of three persons lacks enough fuel to keep warm and to cook food.

- One out of four adults cannot read or write.

- More than half of humanity lacks sanitary toilets.

- One of every five people on Earth is desperately poor—unable to grow or buy enough food to stay healthy or work.

Life for the desperately poor is a harsh, daily struggle for survival. In urban slums and some rural villages, malnourished children and adults sit around wood or dung (dried manure) fires eating breakfasts of bread and coffee. The air is filled with the stench of refuse and open sewers.

Children and women carry heavy jars or cans of water, often for long distances, from muddy, contaminated streams, canals, or village water faucets. Some people sleep out on the street (Figure 1-8) or under makeshift canopies. Others sleep on dirt floors in crowded one-room shacks, made from straw, cardboard, rusting metal, or drainage pipes.

Parents—some with seven to nine children—are lucky to have an annual income of $300 (82¢ per day). Having many children makes good sense to most poor parents. Their children are a form of economic security, helping them grow food, tend livestock, work, or beg in the streets. And the two or three who live to adulthood will help their parents survive in old age (forties or fifties).

Each year 40 million of the desperately poor die from malnutrition (lack of protein and other nutrients needed for good health) or related diseases and from contaminated drinking water. This death toll of 110,000 people *per day* is equivalent

to 275 planes, each carrying 400 passengers, crashing every day. Half of those who die are children under age 5, with most dying from diarrhea or measles because they are weakened by malnutrition. While some put this death toll at about 20 million per year, even this lower estimate is appalling. *Those dying are unique human beings, not mere numbers or things.*

Because these deaths happen every day all over the world, but mostly in rural areas and urban slums in LDCs away from the scrutiny of TV cameras, they are not considered major news. Moreover, most people don't want to hear about them.

Most of these premature deaths could be prevented at little cost, typically only $5 per child per year. Such unnecessary deaths will continue, however, until we expand the concept of national and global security to include economic and environmental security for everyone, and greatly increase funding for these vital elements of our individual and collective security.

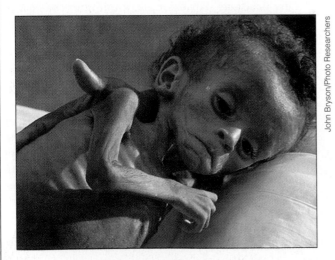

John Bryson/Photo Researchers

**Figure 1-7** One out of every three children under age 5, like this Brazilian child, suffers from malnutrition. Each day at least 40,000 children die—an average of 28 preventable deaths per minute.

United Nations

**Figure 1-8** One-fifth of the people in the world have inadequate housing, and at least 100 million have no housing. These homeless people in Calcutta, India, must sleep on the street.

Q: Where does everything that supports your life come from?

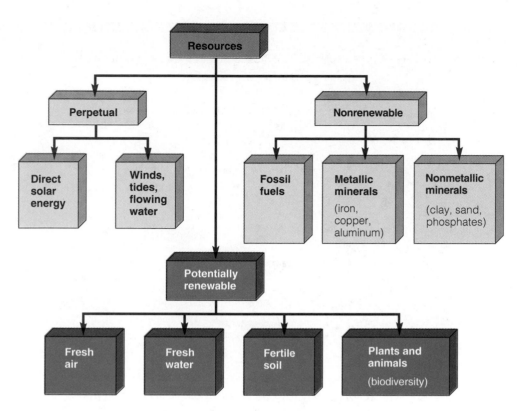

**Figure 1-9** Major types of material resources. This scheme isn't fixed; potentially renewable resources can become nonrenewable resources if used for a prolonged time at a faster rate than they are renewed by natural processes.

flowing water, and renewable wood that can be burned or broken down to provide energy. Solar energy is called a **perpetual resource** because it is expected to last at least 4 billion years while the sun completes its life cycle.

A **potentially renewable resource\*** theoretically can last as long as the sun is around because it can be renewed fairly rapidly through natural processes. Examples of such resources include forest trees, grassland grasses, wild animals, fresh lake and stream water, groundwater, fresh air, and fertile soil.

But even potentially renewable resources can be depleted. The highest rate at which a potentially renewable resource can be used without reducing its available supply is called its **sustainable yield**. If this natural replacement rate is exceeded, the available supply begins to shrink—a process known as **environmental degradation**.

Several types of environmental degradation can change potentially renewable resources into nonrenewable or unusable resources (Figure 1-10 and Spotlight on p. 14):

- *Covering productive land with water, concrete, asphalt, or buildings so that plant growth declines and wildlife habitats are lost.*

---

\* Most sources use the term *renewable resource*. I have added the word *potentially* to emphasize that these resources can be depleted if we use them faster than natural processes renew them.

- *Cultivating land without proper soil management, causing soil erosion and depletion of plant nutrients.* Topsoil is now eroding faster than it forms on about 33% of the world's cropland—a loss of about 23 billion metric tons (25 billion tons) of topsoil per year (Figure 1-3).

- *Irrigating cropland without good drainage, causing salinization or waterlogging.* Salt buildup has cut yields on one-fourth of all irrigated cropland, and waterlogging has reduced productivity on at least one-tenth.

- *Taking fresh water from underground sources (aquifers) and from streams and lakes faster than it is replaced by natural processes.* In the United States one-fourth of the groundwater withdrawn each year is not replenished.

- *Destroying wetlands and coral reefs.* Between 25% and 50% of the world's wetlands have been drained, built upon, or seriously polluted. Worldwide millions of hectares of wetlands are lost each year. The United States has lost 55% of its wetlands and loses another 150,000 hectares (371,000 acres) each year. Coral reefs are being destroyed or damaged in 93 of the 109 significant locations.

- *Cutting trees from large areas (deforestation) without adequate replanting* (Figure 1-3). Almost half of the world's tropical forests have been cleared. Each year about 170,000 square kilometers (66,000

A: The sun and the earth (Earth capital)

**Figure 1-10** A sampling of how some of Earth's natural systems, which support all life and all economies, are being assaulted at an accelerating rate as a result of the exponential growth of population and resource use. (Data from World Conservation Union, World Wildlife Fund, Conservation International, United Nations, Population Reference Bureau, U.S. Fish and Wildlife Service, and Daniel Boivin)

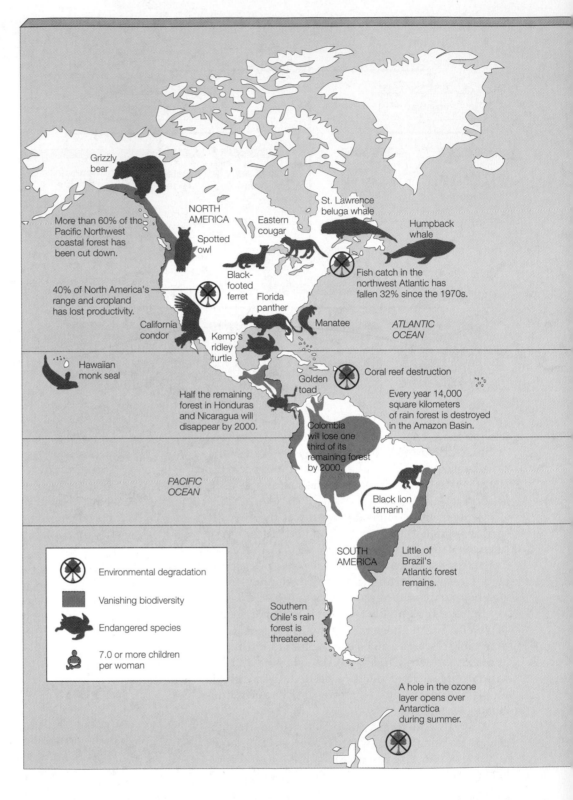

Grizzly bear

NORTH AMERICA

More than 60% of the Pacific Northwest coastal forest has been cut down.

Spotted owl

Eastern cougar

St. Lawrence beluga whale

Humpback whale

40% of North America's range and cropland has lost productivity.

Black-footed ferret

Florida panther

Fish catch in the northwest Atlantic has fallen 32% since the 1970s.

California condor

Kemp's ridley turtle

Manatee

ATLANTIC OCEAN

Hawaiian monk seal

Golden toad

Coral reef destruction

Half the remaining forest in Honduras and Nicaragua will disappear by 2000.

Every year 14,000 square kilometers of rain forest is destroyed in the Amazon Basin.

Colombia will lose one third of its remaining forest by 2000.

PACIFIC OCEAN

Black lion tamarin

SOUTH AMERICA

Little of Brazil's Atlantic forest remains.

Southern Chile's rain forest is threatened.

A hole in the ozone layer opens over Antarctica during summer.

Environmental degradation

Vanishing biodiversity

Endangered species

7.0 or more children per woman

square miles) of these forests are cut and an equivalent portion is degraded. Within 30–50 years there may be little of these forests left. In MDCs many of the remaining diverse, old-growth forests are being cleared and replaced with single-species tree farms, greatly reducing wildlife habitats and biodiversity.

- *Overgrazing of grassland by livestock, which converts productive grasslands into unproductive land or deserts (desertification). Each year almost 60,000 square kilometers (23,000 square miles) of new desert are formed. Almost two-thirds of U.S. rangeland is in fair to poor condition.*

Q: How long does it take to add 1 billion people at current growth rates?

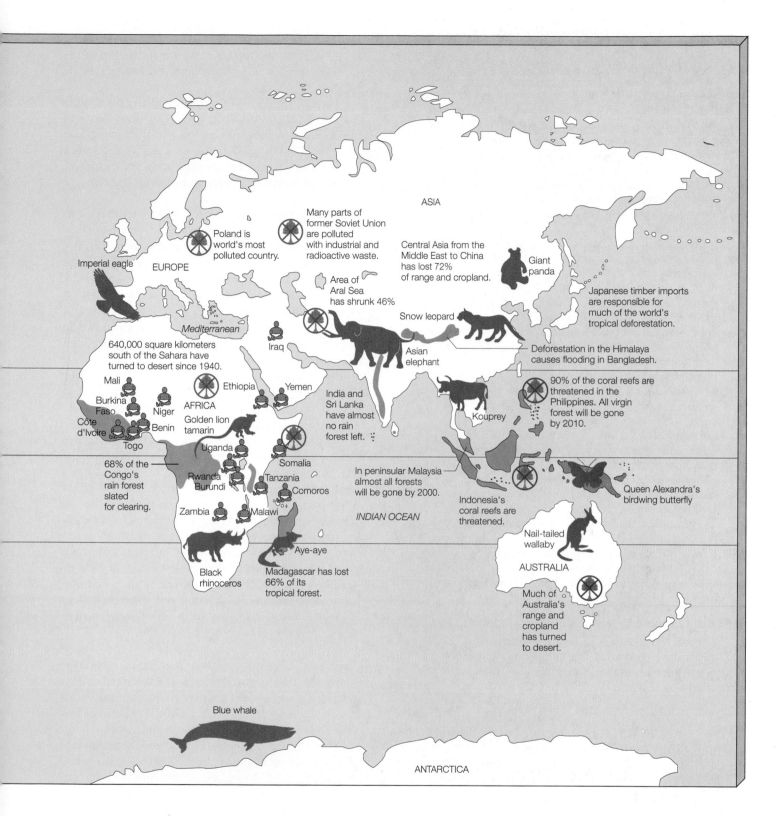

The following labels appear on the map:

ASIA

Poland is world's most polluted country.

Many parts of former Soviet Union are polluted with industrial and radioactive waste.

Central Asia from the Middle East to China has lost 72% of range and cropland.

Giant panda

Imperial eagle

EUROPE

Area of Aral Sea has shrunk 46%

Japanese timber imports are responsible for much of the world's tropical deforestation.

Snow leopard

Mediterranean

640,000 square kilometers south of the Sahara have turned to desert since 1940.

Iraq

Asian elephant

Deforestation in the Himalaya causes flooding in Bangladesh.

Mali

Ethiopia

Yemen

India and Sri Lanka have almost no rain forest left.

90% of the coral reefs are threatened in the Philippines. All virgin forest will be gone by 2010.

Burkina Faso

AFRICA

Niger

Kouprey

Côte d'Ivoire

Golden lion tamarin

Benin

Togo

Uganda

Somalia

Queen Alexandra's birdwing butterfly

68% of the Congo's rain forest slated for clearing.

Rwanda Burundi

Tanzania

Comoros

In peninsular Malaysia almost all forests will be gone by 2000.

Nail-tailed wallaby

Zambia

Malawi

Indonesia's coral reefs are threatened.

INDIAN OCEAN

AUSTRALIA

Black rhinoceros

Aye-aye

Madagascar has lost 66% of its tropical forest.

Much of Australia's range and cropland has turned to desert.

Blue whale

ANTARCTICA

- *Eliminating or decimating wild species through destruction of habitats, commercial hunting, pest control, and pollution.* Each year thousands of wildlife species become extinct, mostly because of human activities. If habitat destruction continues at present rates, as many as 1.5 million species could disappear over the next 25 years—a drastic loss of vital Earth capital.

- *Polluting renewable air, water, and soil so they are unusable.*

**RESOURCE SCARCITY** **Absolute resource scarcity** occurs when supplies of a resource cannot meet demand. **Relative resource scarcity** occurs when there is enough of a resource to meet the demand, but its distribution is unbalanced (Case Study, p. 15).

## The Tragedy of the Commons

One cause of environmental degradation is the overuse of **common-property resources**, which are owned by none and available to all. Most are potentially renewable. Examples include clean air, fish in the open ocean, migratory birds, Antarctica, gases of the lower atmosphere, and the ozone content of the upper atmosphere.

In 1968 biologist Garrett Hardin (Guest Essay, p. 226) called this the **tragedy of the commons**. It happens because each user reasons, "If I don't use this resource, someone else will. The little bit I use or pollute is not enough to matter." With few users, this logic works. However, the cumulative effect of many people trying to exploit a common-property resource is eventual exhaustion or destruction of the resource. Then no one can benefit from it. Therein lies the tragedy.

The obvious solution is to use common-property resources at rates below their sustainable yields or overload limits by reducing population, regulating access, or both. Unfortunately it is difficult to determine the sustainable yield of a forest, grassland, or animal population, partly because yields vary with weather, climate, and unpredictable biological factors. These uncertainties mean that *it is best to use a potentially renewable resource at a rate well below its estimated sustainable yield*. However, this is rarely done because it collides with the drive for short-term profit regardless of the future consequences.

Another guideline for managing the commons is **principle of multiple use**. According to this principle a national forest, for instance, should be used for several purposes, such as timbering, mining, grazing, recreation, wildlife preservation, and soil and water conservation. But resource managers find it hard to balance competing uses, and one use such as timber cutting may override the others.

## 1-4    Pollution

**WHAT IS POLLUTION?** Any addition to air, water, soil, or food that threatens the health, survival capability, or activities of humans or other living organisms is called **pollution**. Most pollutants are solid, liquid, or gaseous by-products or wastes produced when a resource is extracted, processed, made into products, and used. Pollution can also take the form of unwanted energy emissions, such as excessive heat, noise, or radiation.

A major problem is that people differ on acceptable levels of pollution, especially if they have to choose between pollution control and their jobs (Case Study, p. 17). As philosopher Georg Hegel pointed out, tragedy is not the conflict between right and wrong, but the conflict between right and right.

**SOURCES** Pollutants can enter the environment naturally (for example, from volcanic eruptions) or through human activities (for example, from burning coal). Most natural pollution is dispersed over a large area and diluted or broken down to harmless levels by natural processes. By contrast, most serious pollution from human activities occurs in or near urban and industrial areas, where pollutants are concentrated in small volumes of air, water, and soil. Industrialized agriculture is also a major source of pollution.

Some pollutants contaminate the areas where they are produced. Others are carried by winds or flowing water to other areas. Pollution does not respect state or national boundaries.

Some pollutants come from single, identifiable sources, such as the smokestack of a power plant, the drainpipe of a meat-packing plant, the chimney of a house, or the exhaust pipe of an automobile. These are called **point sources**. Other pollutants enter the air, water, or soil from dispersed, and often hard-to-identify, **nonpoint sources**. Examples are the runoff of fertilizers and pesticides from farmlands and suburban lawns and gardens into streams and lakes, and pesticides sprayed into the air or blown by the wind into the atmosphere. It is much easier and cheaper to identify and control pollution from point sources than from widely dispersed nonpoint sources.

**EFFECTS** Unwanted effects of pollutants are **(1)** disruption of life support systems, **(2)** damage to plant and animal species, **(3)** damage to human health, **(4)** damage to property, and **(5)** nuisance effects such as noise and unpleasant smells, tastes, and sights.

Three factors determine how severe the effects of a pollutant will be. One is its *chemical nature*—how active and harmful it is to living organisms. Another is its **concentration**—the amount per volume unit of air, water, soil, or body weight. One way to lower the concentration of a pollutant is to dilute it in a large volume of air or water. Until we started overwhelming the air and waterways with pollutants, dilution was the solution to pollution. Now it is only a partial solution.

A third factor is a pollutant's *persistence*—how long it stays in the air, water, soil, or body. **Degradable**, or **nonpersistent, pollutants** are broken down

**CASE STUDY**

Energy is needed to gain access to and use virtually all material resources, and oil is the main energy source for most MDCs and an increasing number of LDCs. When its price is adjusted for inflation, oil has been cheap since 1950 (Figure 1-11). Its low price has encouraged MDCs and LDCs to become heavily dependent on—indeed, addicted to—this important resource. Low prices have also encouraged waste of oil and discouraged the search for other sources of energy. Thus an oil shortage can cause economic shock waves.

Most MDCs first experienced a relative scarcity of oil between 1973 and 1979. Demand was high because of rapid oil-based economic growth during the 1960s. Also, the United States and many other MDCs were depending more on imported oil (Figure 1-12). A third factor was that between 1973 and 1979 the Organization of Petroleum Exporting Countries (OPEC)* controlled the supply, distribution, and price of oil. About 67% of the world's known and economically extractable oil deposits (proven reserves) are in the OPEC countries, compared with only 4% in the United States.

In 1973 OPEC produced 56% of the world's oil and supplied about 84% of all oil imported by other countries. In 1973 Arab members of OPEC reduced oil exports to the West and banned oil shipments to the United States because it had supported Israel in the 18-day Yom Kippur War with Egypt and Syria.

This embargo, lasting until March 1974, raised the average

price of crude oil (Figure 1-11). The result was double-digit inflation in the United States and many other countries, high interest rates, soaring international debt, and a global economic recession. Unhappy Americans waited for hours to buy gasoline and turned down thermostats in homes and offices. Nevertheless U.S. dependence on imported oil rose from 36% to 47% (67% of it from OPEC) between 1973 and 1977, mostly because the price of oil did not increase much between 1974 and 1977.

These relatively low prices sent a false message to consumers and set the stage for the second oil crisis of the 1970s, when Iran's 1979 Islamic revolution shut down most of that country's production. By 1981 the average world price of crude oil had risen to about $35 a barrel.

A combination of energy conservation (using energy more efficiently) and substitution of other energy sources for oil led to a drop in world consumption between 1979 and 1989. Because supply exceeded demand, the price of oil dropped

(continued)

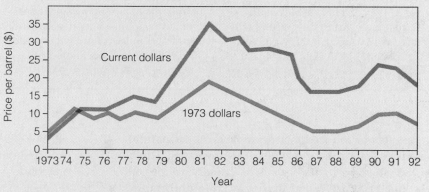

**Figure 1-11** Average world crude oil prices, 1973–1992. (Data from Department of Energy and Department of Commerce)

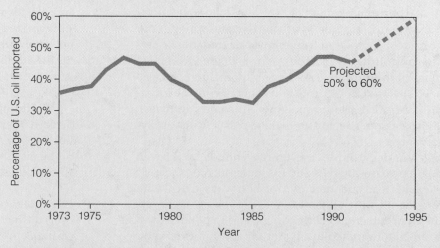

**Figure 1-12** Percentage of U.S. oil imported between 1973 and 1992 with projections to 1995. (Data from U.S. Department of Energy and Spears and Associates, Tulsa, Oklahoma)

* OPEC was formed in 1960 so that LDCs with much of the world's known and projected oil supplies could get a higher price for this resource and stretch remaining supplies by forcing the world to reduce oil use and waste. Today its 13 members are Algeria, Ecuador, Gabon, Indonesia, Iran, Iraq, Kuwait, Libya, Nigeria, Qatar, Saudi Arabia, the United Arab Emirates, and Venezuela.

from $35 to around $18 per barrel between 1981 and 1989, and fluctuated at around $18–$20 between 1989 and 1992. Adjusting for inflation, crude oil and gasoline in the United States cost about the same today as they did in 1974 (Figure 1-11).

When Iraq invaded Kuwait during the summer of 1990, the United States and other MDCs went to war, mostly to protect their access to oil in the Middle East, especially from Saudi Arabia, which has the world's largest oil reserves. As Christopher Flavin and Nicholas Lenssen put it, "Not only is the world addicted to cheap oil, but the largest liquor store is in a very dangerous neighborhood."

At the current rate of consumption, known world oil supplies will last for 42 years. Undiscovered oil that is thought to exist might last another 20–40 years. This means we

must start finding substitutes for oil now because history shows that it takes 50–60 years to phase in one or more replacements for a widely used energy resource.

Most resource analysts expect that some time before 2020 we will enter a period of increasing scarcity of and rising prices for oil, as we start approaching the end of the oil age. During this period OPEC countries are expected to supply at least 60% of all oil, dominate world oil markets, and raise oil prices sharply.

By 2010 the United States could depend on imports for 70% of its oil supply. This dependence and the likelihood for much higher oil prices could drain the United States (and other major oil-importing nations) of vast amounts of money, leading to severe inflation and widespread economic recession, and perhaps even to a major depression.

How can we deal with this addiction? The first step is to admit that we are "oilaholics." The next step is to begin recovery by changing our oil-wasting lifestyles to kick this Earth-degrading, and thus self-degrading, habit, and to begin shifting to greater dependence on perpetual and renewable energy resources.

Economic policies determine energy choices. By rewarding energy conservation and use of certain energy resources or by taxing the use of certain types of energy, the government can influence whether we move toward increased energy efficiency and use of perpetual and potentially renewable energy resources or continue our current wasteful use of nonrenewable ones. What have you done to reduce your own addiction to oil?

completely or reduced to acceptable levels by natural physical, chemical, and biological processes. Those broken down by living organisms (usually by specialized bacteria) are called **biodegradable pollutants**. Human sewage in a river, for example, is biodegraded fairly quickly by bacteria if it is not added faster than it can be broken down.

Unfortunately many of the substances we introduce into the environment take decades or longer to degrade. Examples of these **slowly degradable** or **persistent pollutants** include the insecticide DDT, most plastics, aluminum cans, and chlorofluorocarbons (CFCs)—used as coolants in refrigerators and air conditioners, as spray propellants (in some countries), and as foaming agents for making plastics such as Styrofoam.

**Nondegradable pollutants** cannot be broken down by natural processes. Examples include the toxic elements lead and mercury. The best ways to deal with nondegradable pollutants are to not release them into the environment, to recycle them, and to remove them from contaminated air, water, or soil (an expensive process).

We know little about the possible harmful effects of 80% of the 70,000 synthetic chemicals now in commercial use. Our knowledge about the effects of the

other 20% of these chemicals is limited, mostly because it is quite difficult, time consuming, and expensive to get this knowledge.

**DEALING WITH POLLUTION: PREVENTION AND CLEANUP** **Pollution prevention**, or **input pollution control**, reduces or eliminates the input of pollutants and wastes into the environment. This approach is summarized in biologist Barry Commoner's **law of pollution prevention**: If you don't put something into the environment, it isn't there. Pollution can be prevented, or at least reduced, by the three R's of resource use: *Reduce, Reuse, Recycle.*

**Pollution cleanup**, or **output pollution control**, deals with pollutants already in the environment. Relying mostly on pollution cleanup causes several problems. One is that, as long as population and consumption levels continue to grow, cleanup is only a temporary solution. For example, adding catalytic converters to cars has reduced air pollution. However, the increase in the number of cars has made this cleanup approach less effective.

Another problem is that cleanup often removes a pollutant from one part of the environment only to cause pollution in another part. We can collect garbage, but garbage must be burned (perhaps caus-

## Pollution and Jobs in Front Royal, Virginia

I spent my first 14 years in Front Royal, Virginia. It is a small town nestled in a valley where the Skyline Drive starts through Shenandoah National Park.

In 1938 the American Viscose Corporation built the world's largest rayon plant outside town. The plant provided 3,000 jobs for residents of Front Royal and nearby Warren County. I worked there during two college vacations.

When the wind blew in a certain direction, the air smelled like rotten eggs. Toxic hydrogen sulfide and carbon disulfide gas belched by the plant blackened silver overnight. It was foolish to paint your house white or a light color—within a few days the lead-based paint started turning black. However, no one paid much attention to those problems in the 1940s, because the plant supported the local economy, and people didn't start worrying about pollution until the 1970s.

In 1980 environmental officials charged the company, now Avtex Fibers, with severely polluting the South Fork of the Shenandoah River and groundwater near the plant with PCBs and other hazardous chemicals. The Shenandoah, a tributary of the Potomac, is a major water source for Washington, D.C. Avtex was forced to spend $750,000 to buy 23 properties with polluted wells.

In 1984 the Environmental Protection Agency (EPA) put the plant's chemical disposal area on its Superfund list of sites containing the country's highest levels of hazardous waste. Since then the EPA has sued Avtex and former plant owner FMC Corporation for a $9.1-million toxic-wastewater cleanup. State agencies have also sued Avtex for $9.3 million for numerous environmental and worker safety violations.

The EPA held a public meeting in September 1988 to discuss ways of cleaning up the plant and contaminated water supplies. The meeting turned into an emotional confrontation between local supporters and opponents of the cleanup effort. When one resident, barely holding back tears, urged that the plant be closed "for the sake of our children," a worker stood up and yelled, "What about our jobs? My children have to eat."

In November 1988 the state attorney general sued the company for $19.7 million in environmental damage caused by river and groundwater pollution. During 1989 Avtex topped the list in total emissions of toxic materials by U.S. industries.

Avtex laid off 500 of its 1,300 employees in the summer of 1989, citing environmental problems and lower profits because of increased competition. In February 1990 Avtex Fibers filed for bankruptcy and closed down its Front Royal plant and its corporate headquarters in Valley Forge, Pennsylvania. Its chairman and principal stockholder retired, and its remaining 800 employees lost their jobs.

Cleanup of the plant site and the contaminated Shenandoah River will cost millions of dollars and take at least a decade and possibly up to 30 years. Because the company filed for bankruptcy, federal and state officials may not recover much of the fines and cleanup money.

Suppose enforcement of government pollution control regulations meant that you would lose your job. If you could, would you choose unemployment and a cleaner environment or employment and a dirtier environment? Can you think of ways to avoid this dilemma?

---

ing air pollution and leaving a toxic ash that must be put somewhere); dumped into streams, lakes, and oceans (perhaps causing water pollution); buried (perhaps causing soil and groundwater pollution); or recycled or reused.

So far most efforts to improve environmental quality in the United States and other MDCs have used pollution cleanup based on *reacting* to problems that could have been prevented in the first place. The Commonwealth of Independent States (CIS, formerly part of the Soviet Union), many eastern European countries (especially Poland, the former East Germany, and the former Czechoslovakia), and most LDCs near the bottom of the economic ladder lag far behind in pollution control (Case Study, p. 18).

Both pollution prevention and pollution cleanup are needed, but environmentalists urge us to emphasize prevention because it works better and is cheaper than cleanup or repair. As Benjamin Franklin reminded us long ago, "An ounce of prevention is worth a pound of cure."

An increasing number of businesses have found that *pollution prevention pays*. It saves them money and at the same time helps the earth—a win-win strategy. So far, however, about 99% of environmental spending in the United States is devoted to pollution cleanup and only 1% to pollution prevention—a situation that environmentalists believe must be reversed over the next decade.

As you make decisions about what to buy and about how to solve environmental problems, ask yourself, "Is this a prevention (input) or a cleanup (output)

In 1985 the Polish Academy of Sciences described heavily industrialized Poland (Figure 1-13) as the most polluted country in the world. Air, water, and soil are so polluted that at least one-third of the people risk contracting environmentally induced cancers, respiratory illnesses, and a host of other diseases.

Coal supplies 80% of Poland's energy. Most of the country's industrial and power plants have no pollution control technology whatsoever or, at best, ineffective con-

trols. Satellite photographs show that the biggest clouds of smoke in Europe hang over southern Poland, partly because large coal-burning plants have shut down their pollution control equipment to save power and money.

Krakow, located in a river valley that traps pollution from its coal-burning steel mills, is one of the dirtiest and unhealthiest cities in the world (Figure 1-14). Air pollution in nearly every major city in Poland is reportedly 50 times legal limits. Sometimes motorists must turn on their lights during the day

to see. By 1990 an estimated 78% of the country's forests showed signs of air pollution damage, with roughly 32% suffering from moderate to severe damage.

About half of Poland's cities and 15% of its industrial facilities have no wastewater treatment systems. Even in Warsaw, the capital, only 5% of the sewage is treated. The rest is simply dumped into the Vistula River, which empties into the Baltic Sea.

Water present in 96% of the length of the country's monitored rivers is too polluted to drink, even after disinfection. Nearly 40% is unfit even for industrial use. The Polish Academy of Sciences projects that by the year 2000 the country will have no safe drinking water. Gdansk's sandy beaches have been closed for years, and many of the fish in the nearby bay contain excessive levels of mercury and have open sores.

A quarter of Poland's soil is believed to be too contaminated to grow food that is safe for livestock or people. In 1983 the government designated 27 "areas of ecological hazard" that make up about 11% of the country's land area and include 35% of its population. In 1988 the government declared five villages in the industrial region of Silesia unfit to live in because of toxic metals in the soil and water, and paid the villagers to relocate. Some 60% of the food grown around Krakow

**Figure 1-13** Where is Poland?

approach?" Our motto should be: *Pollution cleanup is better than doing nothing, but pollution prevention is the best way to walk more gently on the earth.*

## 1-5 The Crisis of Unsustainability: Problems and Causes

**KEY PROBLEMS** A number of interconnected environmental and resource problems make up the overall *crisis of unsustainability* we face. Four of these prob-

lems—global warming and the accompanying possible climate change, acid rain, depletion of stratospheric ozone, and urban air pollution—result from the chemicals we have put into the atmosphere (mostly from burning fossil fuels). A fifth problem is the continued poisoning of the soil and water by pesticides and numerous other toxic wastes as the result of not relying on pollution prevention. Another six problems—depletion of nonrenewable minerals (especially oil), depletion and contamination of groundwater, deforestation, soil erosion, conversion of productive cropland and grazing to desert (desertification), and species loss (biodiversity depletion)—result from

is considered unfit for human consumption because of contamination by toxic heavy metals.

Since the mid-1980s Polish citizens have organized to demand better environmental protection. Poland and all other eastern European countries now have one or more Green political parties, although many of these groups remain relatively weak.

Poland is struggling to move from a state-controlled economy to a free-market economy and to significantly reduce pollution. In 1990 Poland became the first country in eastern Europe to approve a comprehensive national environmental policy. It recommends the following major actions:

- Closing or redesigning the 80 worst industrial polluters and adding an additional 500 plants to this list based on further investigation

- Increasing coal washing to reduce air pollution emissions

- Setting stricter air pollution emission standards, including requiring all new cars sold in Poland to have catalytic converters by 1992 and to meet the emission standards of the European Community by 1995

- Improving drinking water supplies for urban areas by building 3,000 new wastewater treatment plants by 1995

The government has raised energy prices and increased the price of coal relative to oil and natural gas. This should decrease coal use and encourage improvements in energy efficiency.

Such efforts are hampered by Poland's $43-billion debt to Western MDCs—55% of its annual GNP — and by staggering cleanup costs. Cleaning up past damage and minimizing future damage will take 25–30 years and cost up to $260 billion—or more if the government fails to act.

With adequate aid and debt relief from MDCs, Poland could rapidly implement modern pollution control and energy efficiency technologies. Without such aid and without sustained action by its citizens and officials, Poland's already serious environmental problems will get worse. Other eastern European countries, and the CIS, face similar problems.

**Figure 1-14** The 700 smokestacks of the Nowa Huta steelworks belch out more than 455,000 metric tons (500,000 tons) of air pollutants a year, including 150 million metric tons (170 million tons) of toxic lead. These mills in Krakow, Poland, built in the 1930s, are the area's major employer. In 1989 mill officials agreed to reduce emissions of air pollutants from the mills by about one-third by 1992, but this goal was not reached.

exponentially growing depletion and degradation of Earth capital.

Population growth and poverty intensify these problems. World population will stabilize only when poverty is sharply reduced worldwide. And as long as LDCs are burdened by enormous foreign debts, they will feel driven to pay the interest on these debts by depleting and degrading their natural resources, mostly for export to MDCs.

Our problems are also worsened by political and economic systems that reward unsustainable economic growth, support the widening gap between the rich and the poor, hinder meeting the basic need for human justice and compassion, and fail to protect the rights of future generations of humans and other species. We cannot solve pollution problems by relying mostly on pollution cleanup and waste management instead of on pollution prevention and waste prevention.

**ROOT CAUSES** The first step in dealing with the crisis of unsustainability is to identify its underlying causes. They include:

- *Overpopulation.*
- *Overconsumption of resources by the affluent.*

**Figure 1-15** Simplified model of how three factors—population (P), affluence (A), and technology (T)—affect overall environmental degradation and pollution, or the environmental impact of population.

**People Overpopulation**

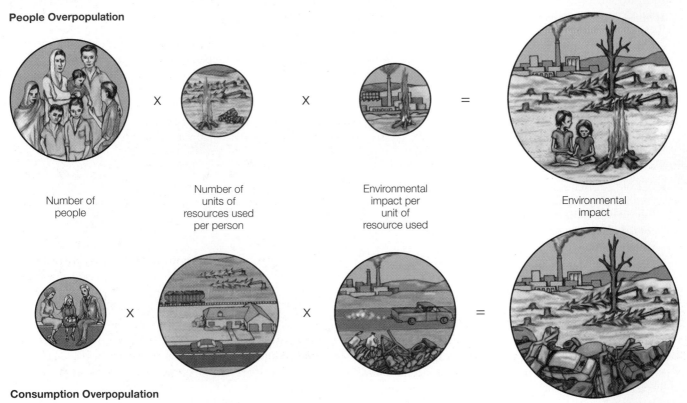

**Consumption Overpopulation**

**Figure 1-16** Two types of overpopulation based on the relative importance of the factors in the model shown in Figure 1-15. Circle size shows relative importance of each factor. People overpopulation is caused mostly by growing numbers of people. Consumption overpopulation is caused mostly by growing affluence (resource consumption).

- *Poverty or underconsumption of resources by the poor.* This is a result of our failure to achieve a more just distribution of global income (Figure 1-6) that meets everyone's basic needs.

- *Inefficiency.* This involves massive waste of energy, water, and other resources.

- *Addiction to fossil fuels.* This applies especially to oil and coal.

- *Oversimplification of Earth's life support systems.* The key factor here is excessive reduction of biodiversity.

- *Poor political and economic management.* This involves our failure to encourage Earth-sustaining forms of economic development and discourage Earth-degrading forms of economic and population growth.

- *Failure to have market prices represent the overall environmental cost of an economic good or service.* This promotes inefficiency and depletion of Earth capital for short-term profit by concealing the harmful effects of the products we buy.

- *Our urge to dominate and control nature.*

Q: How many children under age 5 die each day in LDCs of causes that could be prevented?

Environmentalists contend that the United States has the world's highest level of consumption overpopulation. With only 4.7% of the world's population it produces about 21% of all goods and services, uses about 25% of all processed mineral resources and nonrenewable energy and 33% of all paper and paperboard, and produces at least 25% of the pollution and trash, including 18% of the global emissions of greenhouse gases and 22% of ozone-destroying CFCs.

By contrast, India, with 16% of the world's population (3.4 times more people than the United States), produces 1% of all goods and services, uses about 3% of all mineral and nonrenewable energy resources, and produces about 3% of the pollution and trash, including about 4% of the global emissions of greenhouse gases and 0.7% of ozone-destroying CFCs. The average U.S. citizen consumes 50 times as much as the average citizen of India. If we take the average Indian's consumption as the norm, the environmental impact of 258 million Americans is equal to that of 12.9 billion Indians—more than twice the world's population.

According to biologist Paul Ehrlich, "A baby born in the United States will damage the planet 20 to 100 times more in a lifetime than a baby born into a poor family in an LDC. Each rich person in the United States does 1,000 times more damage than a poor person in an LDC." *This means that poor parents in an LDC would need 40–200 children to have the same environmental impact as 2 children in a typical family in the United States, and 2,000 children to equal the environmental impact of 2 children in a rich U.S. family.*

Germany, Japan, and most other MDCs with lifestyles comparable to those in the United States also suffer from consumption overpopulation. However, their environmental impact per person—except for Canada—is about half that per American mostly because they use energy more efficiently and pollute less.

**CONNECTIONS BETWEEN ROOT CAUSES AND PROBLEMS** Once we have identified the causes of our problems, the next step is to understand how they are connected to one another. The three-factor model in Figure 1-15 is a good starting point.

According to this model total environmental degradation and pollution—that is, the environmental impact of population—in a given area depend on three factors: **(1)** the number of people (population size, P), **(2)** the average number of units of resources each person uses (consumption per capita or affluence, A), and **(3)** the amount of environmental degradation and pollution produced for each unit of resource used (the environmental destructiveness of the technologies used to provide and use resources, T). This model, developed in the early 1970s by biologist Paul Ehrlich and physicist John Holdren, can be summarized in simplified form as Impact = Population x Affluence x Technology, or $I = P \times A \times T$.

**Environmental unsustainability**, or **overpopulation**, occurs when too many people deplete the resources that support life and economies, and introduce more wastes than the environment can handle. It happens when people exceed the **carrying capacity** of an area: the number of people an area can support given its resource base and the way those resources are used. The three factors in Figure 1-15 can interact to produce two types of environmental unsustainability or overpopulation (Figure 1-16).

**People overpopulation** exists where there are more people than the available supplies of food, water, and other important resources can support at a minimal level. Here, population size and the resulting degradation of potentially renewable resources as the poor struggle to stay alive tend to be the key factors determining total environmental impact. In the world's poorest LDCs people overpopulation causes premature death for 40 million people each year and absolute poverty for 1.2 billion.

**Consumption overpopulation** exists in MDCs, where only one-fifth of the world's people use resources at such a high rate that significant pollution, environmental degradation, and resource depletion occur. With this type of overpopulation high rates of resource use per person, and the resulting high levels of pollution and environmental degradation per person, are the key factors determining overall environmental impact (Spotlight, above).

We know from studying other species that when a population exceeds or *overshoots* the carrying capacity of its environment, it suffers a *dieback* that reduces its population to a sustainable size. How long will we be able to continue our exponential growth in population and resource use without suffering overshoot and dieback? No one knows, but warning signals from the earth (Figure 1-10) are forcing us to consider the question seriously.

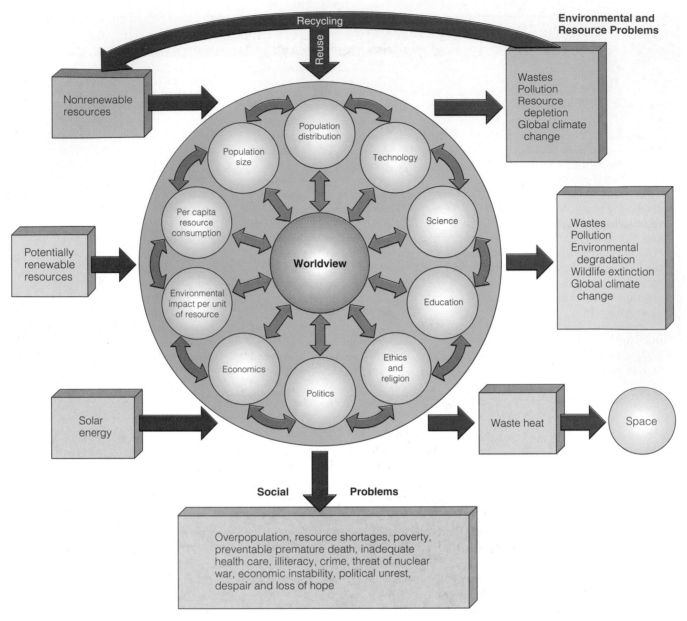

**Figure 1-17** Environmental, resource, and social problems are caused by a complex, poorly understood mix of interacting factors, as illustrated by this simplified model.

Many environmentalists believe that sustaining the earth will require that we cut our global environmental impact (I) in half over the next 50 years. However, if projected increases in population (doubling to 11 billion) and resource consumption (a modest 3% annual increase in economic growth per capita) over the next 50 years occur, our global environmental impact will increase eightfold. This massive increase in environmental impact could be offset by reducing the environmental destructiveness of the technologies used to produce the goods we consume to one-sixteenth of the current level (a 93% reduction) during the next five decades—an unlikely event. Such calculations show why many environmentalists believe that the only way we can prevent severe environmental overload is to mount a global program to simultaneously reduce each of the factors (P, A, and T) in the model shown in Figure 1-15 over the next 50 years—starting now.

The three-factor model in Figure 1-15 is useful in understanding the key factors leading to the crisis of unsustainability. However, the interconnected envi-

Q: What are proven reserves of a nonrenewable resource such as oil or copper?

ronmental, resource, and social problems we face are much more complex and involve a number of poorly understood interactions among a number of factors (Figure 1-17).

## 1-6 What Should Be Done?

**CONFLICTING WORLDVIEWS** There are conflicting views about how serious our environmental problems really are and what should be done about them (Guest Essays, pp. 24 and 26). These conflicts arise mostly out of differing **worldviews**: how individuals think the world works, what they think their role in the world should be, and what they believe is right and wrong behavior (ethics). People with widely differing worldviews can take the same data and arrive at quite different conclusions because they start with entirely different assumptions.

The environmental aspects of two opposing worldviews are summarized on the second page of the inside front cover spread. They are only two of many worldviews. However, their diametrically opposed beliefs can prod us into articulating our own worldview, evaluating proposed solutions to the problems we face, and deciding on actions we need to take to help sustain the earth and thus ourselves.

Once you change your worldview, it no longer makes sense to do things in the old ways. If enough people do this, then tremendous cultural change, once considered impossible, can take place rapidly.

**PLANETARY MANAGEMENT WORLDVIEW** Most people in today's industrial-consumer societies have a **planetary management worldview** summarized on the second page of the inside front cover spread. People with this and other human-centered worldviews see Earth as a place of unlimited resources. If we deplete a resource, they believe we will find substitutes. If resources become scarce or if substitutes can't be found, we can mine the moon, asteroids, or other planets. If we pollute an area, we can invent a technology to clean it up, dump it into space, or move into space ourselves. If we extinguish other species, we can use genetic engineering to create new and better ones.

According to this worldview we don't face a crisis of unsustainability. Continued economic growth and technological advances will produce a better world for everyone. Thus there is no need for us to make sacrifices now for future generations whose lives will be better. The environmental problems we face are mere-ly a minor detour along the highway of economic progress. We should and can control and manage the planet for our benefit.

**A SUSTAINABLE-EARTH WORLDVIEW** Growing numbers of people question the planetary management worldview. They know or at least suspect that our present political and economic systems are leading us to unsustainable use of Earth's natural capital and are searching for better worldviews. One of these alternatives is the **sustainable-Earth worldview*** summarized on the second page of the inside front cover spread.

People with this and most other life-centered worldviews believe that we do face a crisis of unsustainability. They believe that Earth's resources are finite and that ever-increasing population, production, and consumption will severely stress the natural processes that renew the air, water, and soil that support all life and economies. They compare our pursuit of unlimited economic growth and growth in the human population to being on a treadmill that moves faster and faster. They believe that, sooner or later, we will fall off the treadmill or cause it to break down because of our limited knowledge and managerial skills relative to the incredible complexity of Earth's life support systems.

According to biologist Gerald Durrell, "At the present rate of 'progress,' and unless something is done quickly, disaster stares us in the face. . . . We are bleeding our planet to death. We are led by saber-rattling politicians who are ignorant of biology . . . and surrounded by powerful commercial interests whose only interest in nature is often to rape it."

Instead of trying to dominate and manage Earth almost exclusively for our species, the key element in this life-centered approach is to cooperate with the rest of nature to help sustain all life and thus ourselves. We are to do this by learning as much as we can about how nature sustains itself and incorporating these Earth lessons into our lifestyles and economic, political, and ethical systems. Guidelines for doing this are summarized inside the back cover and discussed throughout this book. Various human-centered and life-centered worldviews are discussed in Chapter 27.

**WE CAN SUSTAIN THE EARTH** This chapter has presented you with an overview of the serious problems

---

* Others have used the terms *life-centered worldview, conserver worldview, holistic worldview,* and *deep ecology worldview* to describe this idea. I add the word *Earth* to emphasize that it's all of Earth's life support systems and life, not just human beings, that must be sustained.

*Julian L. Simon*

**GUEST ESSAY** *Julian L. Simon is professor of economics and business administration at the University of Maryland. He has effectively presented and defended the position that continued economic growth and technological advances will produce a less crowded, less polluted, and more resource-rich world. His many articles and books on this subject include* The Ultimate Resource, The Resourceful Earth, *and* Population Matters *(see Further Readings).*

This book, like most others discussing environmental and resource problems, begins with the proposition that there is an environmental and resource crisis. If this means that the situation of humanity is worse now than in the past, then the idea of a crisis—and all that follows from it—is dead wrong. In almost every respect important to humanity, the trends have been improving, not deteriorating.

Our world now supports 5.5 billion people. In the nineteenth century the earth could sustain only 1 billion. And 10,000 years ago, only 1 million people could keep themselves alive. People are living more healthily than ever before, too.

One would expect lovers of humanity—people who hate war and worry about famine in Africa—to jump with joy at this extraordinary triumph of the human mind and human organization over the raw forces of nature. Instead, they lament that there are so many human beings and wring their hands about the problems that more people inevitably bring.

The recent extraordinary decrease in the death rate—to my mind, the greatest miracle in history—accounts for the bumper crop of humanity. It took thousands of years to increase life expectancy at birth from the twenties to the thirties. Then, in just the last 200 years, life expectancy in the advanced countries jumped from the mid-thirties to the seventies. And, starting well after World War II, life expectancy at birth in the poor countries, even the very poorest, has leaped upward (averaging 62 in 1992) because of progress in agriculture, sanitation, and medicine. Average life expectancy at birth in

China, the world's most populous country, was 69 in 1992, an increase of 25 years since the 1950s. Is this not an astounding triumph?

In the short run another baby reduces income per person by causing output to be divided among more people. And as the British economist Thomas Malthus argued in 1798, more workers laboring with existing capital results in less output per worker. However, if resources are not fixed, then the Malthusian doctrine of diminishing resources, resurrected by today's doom-and-gloom analysts, does not apply. Given some time to adjust to shortages with known methods and new inventions, free people create additional resources.

It is amazing but true that a resource shortage resulting from population or income growth usually leaves us better off than if the shortage had never arisen. If firewood had not become scarce in seventeenth-century England, coal would not have been developed. If coal and whale oil shortages hadn't loomed, oil wells would not have been dug.

The prices of food, metals, and other raw materials have been declining by every measure since the beginning of the nineteenth century, and as far back as we know. That is, raw materials have been getting less scarce instead of more scarce throughout history, defying the commonsense notion that if one begins with an inventory of a resource and uses some up, there will be less left. This is despite, and indirectly because of, increasing population.

All statistical studies show that population growth doesn't lead to slower economic growth, though this also defies common sense. Nor is high population density a drag on economic development. Statistical comparison across nations reveals that higher population density is associated with faster instead of slower growth. Drive around on Hong Kong's smooth-flowing highways for an hour or two; you will then realize that a large concentration of human beings in a small area does not make comfortable existence impossible. It also allows for exciting economic expansion, if the system gives individuals the freedom to exercise their talents and pursue economic opportunities. The experience of densely populated Singapore makes it clear that Hong Kong is not unique.

we face and their root causes. They may seem overwhelming, and you may be tempted to think our situation is hopeless. This is not the case. *The most important message of this book is this: We can deal with the problems we face and begin to turn things around within the next 40–50 years if we begin now.* It will not be easy or painless, but it can—and must—be done.

The rest of this book presents a more detailed analysis of these problems along with proposed solutions. It also offers encouraging examples of things individuals and groups are doing to help sustain the earth, as well as a number of "Individuals Matter" boxes that suggest what you can do to help sustain the earth.

**Q:** What percentage of Earth's proven oil reserves are in OPEC nations?

In 1984 a blue-ribbon panel of scientists summarized their wisdom in *The Resourceful Earth*. Among the findings, besides those I have noted previously, were these:

- Many people are still hungry, but the food supply has been improving since at least World War II, as measured by grain prices, production per consumer, and the death rate from famines.

- Land availability won't increasingly constrain world agriculture in coming decades.

- In the United States the trend is toward higher-quality cropland, suffering less from erosion than in the past.

- The widely published report of increasingly rapid urbanization of U.S. farmland was based on faulty data.

- Trends in world forests are not worrisome, though in some places deforestation is troubling.

- There is no statistical evidence for rapid loss of plant and animal wildlife species in the next two decades. An increased rate of extinction cannot be ruled out if tropical deforestation continues unabated, but the linkage has not yet been demonstrated.

- Water does not pose a problem of physical scarcity or disappearance, although the world and U.S. situations do call for better institutional management through more rational systems of property rights.

- There is no compelling reason to believe that world oil prices will rise in coming decades. In fact, prices may fall well below current levels.

- Compared with coal, nuclear power is no more expensive and is probably much cheaper under most circumstances. It is also much cheaper than oil.

- Nuclear power gives every evidence of costing fewer lives per unit of energy produced than does coal or oil.

- Solar energy sources (including wind and wave power) are too dilute to compete economically for much of humankind's energy needs, though for specialized uses and certain climates they can make a valuable contribution.

- Threats of air and water pollution have been vastly overblown. Air and water in the United States have been getting cleaner, rather than dirtier.

We don't say that all is well everywhere, and we don't predict that all will be rosy in the future. Children are hungry and sick; people live out lives of physical or intellectual poverty and lack of opportunity; war or some other pollution may do us in. *The Resourceful Earth* does show that for most relevant matters we've examined, total global and U.S. trends are improving instead of deteriorating.

Also, we do not say that a better future happens automatically or without effort. It will happen because men and women—sometimes as individuals, sometimes as enterprises working for profit, sometimes as voluntary non-profit groups, and sometimes as governmental agencies—will address problems with muscle and mind, and will probably overcome, as has been usual through history.

We are confident that the nature of the physical world permits continued improvement in humankind's economic lot in the long run, indefinitely. Of course, there are always newly arising local problems, shortages, and pollution, resulting from climate or increased population and income and new technologies. Sometimes temporary large-scale problems arise. But the world's physical conditions and the resilience of a well-functioning economic and social system enable us to overcome such problems, and the solutions usually leave us better off than if the problem had never arisen. That is the great lesson to be learned from human history.

## Critical Thinking

1. Do you agree with the author's contention that there is no environmental, population, or resource crisis? Explain. How is it compatible with the data presented in Figure 1-10? After you've finished this course and this text, come back and answer this question again to see if your views have changed.

2. Do you feel you will be better off than your parents? What do you mean by better off? Do you think any children you might have will be better off than you? Explain.

The key to dealing with the problems we face is recognizing that *individuals matter*. Anthropologist Margaret Mead has summarized our potential for change: "Never doubt that a small group of thoughtful, committed citizens can change the world. Indeed it is the only thing that ever has." The choice is ours. We can continue to walk hard on the earth and thus ourselves, or we can learn to walk more gently on the earth.

*What's the use of a house if you don't have a decent planet to put it on?*

HENRY DAVID THOREAU

## Simple Simon Environmental Analysis

*Anne H. Ehrlich
and Paul R. Ehrlich*

**GUEST ESSAY**

*Anne H. Ehrlich is a senior research associate in Stanford's Department of Biological Sciences. Her many honors have included an honorary degree from Bethany College, the Global 500 Environmental Roll of Honor, and the Humanists' Award. The Ehrlichs have authored or coauthored more than 30 books and 600 articles dealing with population, the environment, ecology, and evolution. Paul R. Ehrlich is Bing Professor of population studies at Stanford University. His many honors include membership in the U.S. National Academy of Sciences, the Fellowship of the American Academy of Arts and Sciences, and the American Philosophical Society; the Crafoord Prize of the Swedish Academy of Sciences (given as the equivalent of the Nobel Prize); the American Association for the Advancement of Science/Scientific American Award for Science in the Service of Mankind; and a MacArthur Prize Fellowship.*

Today there are over 5.5 billion people in the human population, and population experts now project that it will reach a maximum size of 10–14 billion before it stops growing. It is not the number of people per se that causes concern, but the ways in which numbers, patterns of consumption, and choices of technology are now combining to destroy civilization's life support systems [Figures 1-15 and 1-16]. In 1992 a joint statement by the U.S. National Academy of Sciences and the British Royal Society on "Population Growth, Resource Consumption, and a Sustainable World" stated, among other warnings: "It is not prudent to rely on science and technology alone to solve problems created by rapid population growth, wasteful resource consumption, and harmful human practices."

Nevertheless, a few uninformed people claim that population growth is beneficial, the ozone hole is a hoax, global warming is too uncertain to justify action, the extinction of other organisms is no problem, and the degree of crowding possible in Hong Kong, Singapore, or the Netherlands can be accommodated over the entire planet. Julian Simon is the leading spokesperson for this view. He believes that a finite earth can hold an almost infinite number of people.

He also has maintained that resources are getting cheaper because they are infinite in supply. He believes, incorrectly, that resources are infinitely subdivisible (for example, petroleum, once it is divided into atoms, is no longer petroleum). But even if they were infinitely subdivisible, that would not make them infinite in quantity. Simon has simply resurrected a mathematical error known to the ancient Greeks (Zeno's paradox, which concluded that there is an infinite distance between any two points). He has even asserted that humanity could convert the entire universe (including itself and Simon, presumably) into copper!

Moving on from his clever "analysis," what are the facts?

- The connections between economic growth, population growth, and quality of life are much more subtle and complicated than Simon imagines. In many poor nations with rapidly growing populations, GNP *per person* has recently been shrinking, and quality of life is clearly declining.

- In *absolute numbers* more people are hungry today than ever—over a billion, according to the World Bank—although the *proportion* of hungry people has probably been reduced somewhat in recent decades. But can food production continue to increase at a faster rate than population growth? Agriculture is already running into problems such as a "cap" on rice yields and diminishing returns from green revolution technology. Moreover, per person food production has been falling in Africa for more than two decades.

- Land availability is very likely to constrain world agriculture, especially given that widespread degradation is occurring on a major portion of the world's farmland.

- In the United States production is now concentrated on the better-quality farmland for conservation rea-

## Critical Thinking

1. Is the world overpopulated? Explain. Is the United States suffering from consumption overpopulation? Explain.

2. Do you favor instituting policies designed to reduce population growth and stabilize **(a)** the size of the world's population as soon as possible and **(b)** the size of the U.S. population as soon as possible? Explain. What policies do you believe should be implemented?

3. Explain why you agree or disagree with the following propositions: **(a)** High levels of resource use by

the United States and other MDCs are beneficial. **(b)** MDCs stimulate the economic growth of LDCs by buying their raw materials. **(c)** High levels of resource use also stimulate economic growth in MDCs. **(d)** Economic growth provides money for more financial aid to LDCs and for reducing pollution, environmental degradation, and poverty.

4. Explain why you agree or disagree with the following proposition: The world will never run out of resources because technological innovations will produce substitutes or allow use of lower grades of scarce resources.

Q: What percentage of Earth's proven oil reserves are in the United States?

sons; but the amount of good land is not increasing, and even it is subject to degradation.

- The world (and the United States) is steadily losing prime farmland to urbanization. It is estimated that an area equivalent in size to Indiana, much of it farmland, will be built on in poor nations between 1980 and 2000.

- Trends in world forests are very worrisome—ask a biologist. Simon apparently doesn't know the difference between an old-growth virgin forest (with its critical biodiversity intact) and a tree farm. Sadly, in most temperate regions, only a tiny fraction of old-growth forests remains even though the total area of "forest" is approximately as large as a century ago. And the diversity-rich tropical forests are being cut down at unprecedented rates.

- Biologists have uncovered convincing evidence that major losses of biodiversity have already occurred through the widespread destruction of habitats on which other organisms are totally dependent.

- Yes, there is a lot of water on this planet, but it is often not available where or when needed, and much of it is polluted. Groundwater in many areas is being removed faster than it can be recharged. Since water is essential for high-yield agriculture, its scarcity in important agricultural regions is a serious concern. Some Earth scientists feel that water shortages will be the main factor limiting human population growth.

- The main problem now with oil is neither its supply nor its price, but the environmental costs of burning it and other fossil fuels, especially the injection of greenhouse gases into the atmosphere.

- Nuclear power is not cheap if the costs of development, waste disposal, decommissioning of worn-out plants, and insurance are properly factored in. The spread of nuclear weapons from use of nuclear power technology also adds enormous military defense costs.

- Nuclear power may cost fewer lives than coal if there are no major nuclear accidents; but the Chernobyl (which may eventually cost many more lives than the coal industry) and Three Mile Island accidents convinced the public that the risk was too high. Still, the possibility that a safe fission power technology could be developed should remain part of our thinking about future energy supplies.

- A solar energy economy in which electricity is generated (using some of it to make hydrogen as a versatile, portable fuel) is considered by most experts to be a feasible major energy option.

- Air pollution is not a minor matter. Besides causing serious direct threats to human health, agriculture, and forestry, it threatens to destroy the ozone shield, which is essential to the persistence of human and many other forms of life, and may lead to climate change severe enough to cause billions of premature deaths in the next century. Air and water pollution problems in the United States were abated by pollution control efforts in the 1970s, but in the 1980s they worsened again because the population and the economy continued to grow (producing more pollutants) with little improvement in pollution abatement.

You don't have to take our word for all this. The facts are readily available in numerous sources, and you can make your own assessment as to whether population growth, resource consumption, and environmental deterioration are real problems. But remember, while putting huge effort into solving nonexistent or trivial problems would be wasteful, failing to address or postponing actions on the truly serious problems we have outlined in this essay would be very costly indeed.

### Critical Thinking

1. How can Simon and the Ehrlichs take mostly the same data and come to such different conclusions?

2. Whom do you believe? Why?

5. Would you support a sharp increase in local, state, and federal taxes if you could be sure the money was used to help improve the environment?

6. Would you support greatly increasing the amount of land protected from development as wilderness, even if the land contained valuable minerals, oil, natural gas, timber, or other resources?

*7. What are the major resource and environmental problems in (a) the city, town, or rural area where you live and (b) the state where you live? Which of these problems affect you directly?

*8. Make a list of the resources you truly need. Then make another list of the resources that you use each day only because you want them. Then make a third list of resources you want and hope to use in the future.

---

* Critical Thinking topics preceded by an asterisk are either laboratory exercises or individual or class projects.

# 2 Brief History of Resource Use and Conservation

## Frontier Expansion and Biological Warfare

In 1500, before Europeans settled North America, some 60 to 125 million American bison grazed the grassy plains, prairies, and woodlands over much of the continent. A single herd might thunder past for several hours. Several Native American tribes depended heavily on the bison, not only for food but for clothing and shelter. They killed just the animals they needed to provide for themselves (Figure 2-1). By 1906, however, the once-vast range of the bison had shrunk to a tiny area, and the species had been driven nearly to extinction (Figure 2-2).

As settlers moved west after the Civil War, the sustainable balance between Native Americans and bison was upset. The Sioux, Apaches, Comanches, and other plains tribes traded bison skins to settlers for steel knives and firearms, and began killing more bison. The most relentless slaughter, however, was caused by the intruding white settlers.

As railroads pushed westward in the late 1860s, railroad companies hired professional bison hunters—like Buffalo Bill Cody—to supply construction crews with meat. Passengers also gunned down bison from train windows, purely for sport, leaving the carcasses to rot. Commercial hunters also shot millions of bison for their hides and their tongues (considered a delicacy), leaving the meat to rot. "Bone pickers" collected the bleached bones that whitened the prairies and shipped them east to be ground up as fertilizer. Farmers shot bison because they damaged crops, fences, telegraph poles, and sod houses, while ranchers killed them because they competed with cattle and sheep for grass. Finally, the U.S. Army killed bison as part of

**Figure 2-1** Plains Indians hunting American bison.

Buffalo Chase with Bows and Lances, 1832–33, George Catlin
National Museum of Amercan Art/Art Resouce

their campaign to subdue the plains tribes. At least 2.5 million bison perished each year between 1870 and 1875 in this form of biological warfare.

By 1892 only 85 bison were left. They were given refuge in Yellowstone National Park and protected by an 1893 law against the killing of wild animals in national parks.

In 1905, 16 people formed the American Bison Society to protect and rebuild the captive population. Soon thereafter the federal government established the National Bison Range near Missoula, Montana. Today there are an estimated 120,000 bison, about 80% of them on privately owned ranches.

About 10,000 bison are slaughtered each year for their meat (compared to 36 million cattle). Bison steak tastes sweeter than beef and has less fat and cholesterol than either beef or chicken. Some bison have been crossbred with cattle to produce hybrids, called beefalo. They grow faster and are easier to raise than cattle, with no need for expensive grain feed, and their meat is tasty. Some see bison and beefalo ranching as the wave of the future; others see it as a new threat to the American bison.

**Figure 2-2** The range of the North American bison shrank severely between 1500 and 1906.

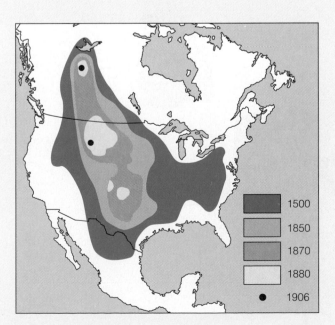

| | |
|---|---|
| | 1500 |
| | 1850 |
| | 1870 |
| | 1880 |
| ● | 1906 |

This chapter examines the major cultural shifts that have given our species ever-greater control over and more impact on Earth's life support systems. The chapter will focus on the following questions:

- What major impacts have hunter-gatherer societies, nonindustrialized, agricultural societies, and industrialized societies had on the environment?

- What are the major phases in the history of resource use, resource conservation, and environmental protection in the United States?

- How can we deal with the environmental and resource problems we face in the 1990s and beyond?

*p. 41*

*planned management of natural resources*

## 2-1 Cultural Change

Fossil evidence suggests that the current form of our species, *Homo sapiens sapiens*, has walked the earth for only about 40,000 years, an instant in the planet's estimated 4.6-billion-year existence. During the first 30,000 years we survived as mostly nomadic hunter-gatherers. Since then there have been two major cultural shifts, the *Agricultural Revolution*, which began 10,000–12,000 years ago, and the *Industrial Revolution*, which began about 275 years ago.

These cultural revolutions have given us much more energy (Figure 2-3) and new technologies with which to alter and control more of the planet to meet our basic needs and increasing wants. By expanding food supplies, lengthening average life spans, and raising average living standards, each shift increased the human population (Figure 2-4). The result has been skyrocketing resource use (Figure 1-2) and pollution and escalating environmental degradation (Figure 1-10).

Most environmentalists see an urgent need for a new cultural shift before we are overwhelmed by the exponential growth of people, pollution, and environmental degradation (Figure 1-15). This **Sustainable-Earth** or **Environmental Revolution** (Guest Essay,

p. 43) calls for us to halt population growth and to change our lifestyles, our political and economic systems, and the way we treat the earth so that we can help sustain it for ourselves and other species.

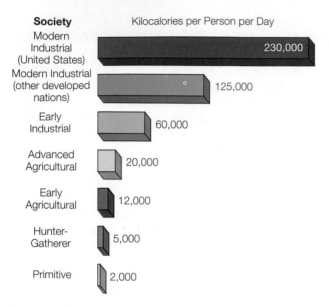

| Society | Kilocalories per Person per Day |
|---|---|
| Modern Industrial (United States) | 230,000 |
| Modern Industrial (other developed nations) | 125,000 |
| Early Industrial | 60,000 |
| Advanced Agricultural | 20,000 |
| Early Agricultural | 12,000 |
| Hunter-Gatherer | 5,000 |
| Primitive | 2,000 |

**Figure 2-3** Average direct and indirect daily energy use per person at various stages of human cultural development. A *calorie* is the amount of energy needed to raise the temperature of 1 gram of water 1°C (1.8°F). A *kilocalorie* is 1,000 calories. Food calories or calories expended during exercise are kilocalories (sometimes represented by Calories with a capital *C*).

During about three-fourths of our 40,000-year existence, we were **hunter-gatherers** who survived by gathering edible wild plants and by hunting and fishing (including shellfish) (Figure 2-5). Archaeological and anthropological evidence indicates that our hunter-gatherer ancestors lived in small bands of rarely more than 50 people who worked together to get enough food to survive. If food became scarce, they picked up their few possessions and moved on.

The earliest hunter-gatherers (and those still living this way today) survived only by having expert knowledge about their natural surroundings. They discovered that a variety of plants and animals could be eaten and used as medicines. They used stone-sharpened and -shaped sticks, other stones, and animal bones as primitive weapons for hunting and as tools for harvesting plants and for scraping hides for clothing and shelter. These dwellers in nature had three energy sources: **(1)** sunlight captured by plants (which also served as food for the animals they hunted), **(2)** fire, and **(3)** their own muscle power.

Usually the sexes shared work, food, and social power in these groups, although men gradually came to specialize in hunting, and women in gathering. Thus cooperation with one another and with nature was the guiding force of their existence.

Groups consciously tried to keep their population in balance with the food supply. Population control

**Figure 2-4** Expansion of Earth's carrying capacity for our species. Technological innovation has led to major cultural changes, and we have displaced and depleted species that compete with us for and provide us with resources. Dashed lines represent three alternative futures: **(1)** uninhibited human population growth, **(2)** population stabilization, and **(3)** growth followed by a crash and stabilization at a much lower level.

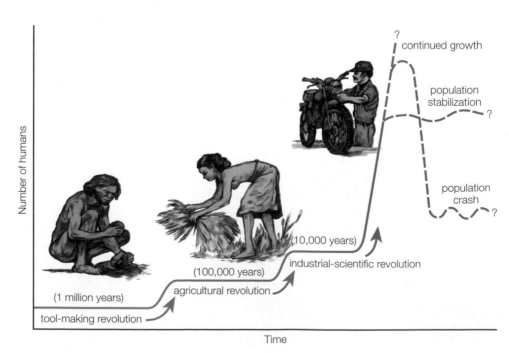

**Q:** How much of the oil used in the United States is imported?

practices varied with different cultures, but they included abstention from sexual intercourse, infanticide, herbal contraceptives, abortion, late marriage, and prolonged breast-feeding of infants (which provides some degree of birth control by inhibiting ovulation). Because of these measures, high infant mortality, and an average life expectancy of about 30 years, hunter-gatherer population grew very slowly (Figure 2-4).

Gradually the hunter-gatherers refined their tools and hunting practices. Some worked together to hunt herds of reindeer, woolly mammoths, European bison, and other big game. They used fire to flush game from thickets toward waiting hunters and to stampede herds into traps or over cliffs. Some learned that burning vegetation promoted the growth of food and forage plants.

Advanced hunter-gatherers had a greater impact on their environment than did early hunter-gatherers, especially in using fire to convert forests into grasslands. There is also evidence that they contributed to, and perhaps even caused, the extinction of some large game animals.

Because of their small numbers, nomadism, and dependence on their own muscle power to modify the environment, however, their environmental impact was fairly limited and localized. Both early and advanced hunter-gatherers were *dwellers in nature*, who trod lightly on the earth because they were not capable of doing more. They survived by being keenly aware of their intimate dependence on nature and by learning to work with nature and with one another.

## 2-3 Agricultural Societies

**THE AGRICULTURAL REVOLUTION** Some 10,000–12,000 years ago a cultural shift known as the **Agricultural Revolution** began in several regions of the world. This food-producing revolution involved a gradual move from a lifestyle based on nomadic hunting-and-gathering bands to one of settled agricultural communities, where people learned how to domesticate wild animals and cultivate wild plants. This shift may have resulted from climatic changes that forced humans either to adapt or to perish.

Plant cultivation may have begun in tropical forests. People discovered that they could grow various wild food plants from roots or tubers (fleshy underground stems). To prepare for planting they cleared small patches of forests by cutting down trees and other vegetation, and then burning the underbrush (Figure 2-6). The ashes fertilized the nutrient-poor soil. This was **slash-and-burn cultivation**.

These early growers also used **shifting cultivation** (Figure 2-6). After a garden had been used for several years, the soil would be depleted of nutrients or reinvaded by the forest. Then the growers moved and cleared a new plot. Each abandoned patch had to be left fallow (unplanted) for 10–30 years before the soil became fertile enough to grow crops again. By doing this early growers practiced sustainable cultivation.

These growers practiced **subsistence farming**, growing only enough food to feed their families. Their

**Figure 2-5** Most people who have lived on Earth have survived by hunting wild game and gathering wild plants. These !Kung tribesmen (left) in Africa are going hunting. The woman and child (right) are gathering wild plants in a tropical forest in the Amazon Basin of Brazil.

A: About 50%

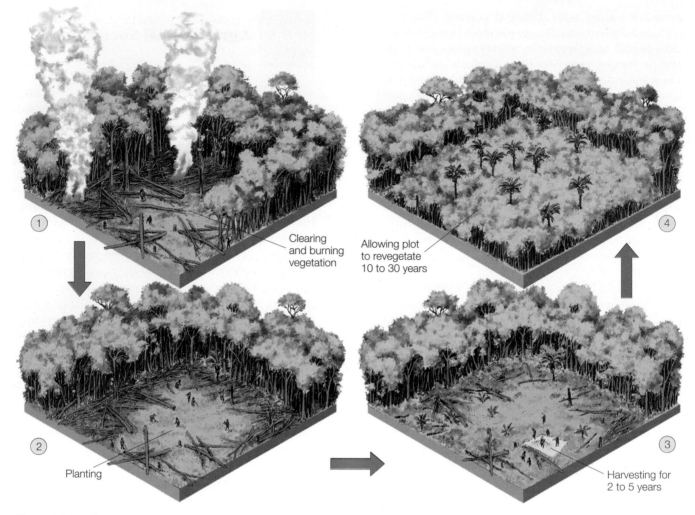

**Figure 2-6** The first crop-growing technique may have been a combination of slash-and-burn and shifting cultivation in tropical forests. This method is sustainable if only small plots of the forest are cleared, cultivated for no more than 5 years, and then allowed to lie fallow for 10–30 years to renew soil fertility.

dependence on human muscle power and crude stone or stick tools meant that they could cultivate only small plots; thus, they had relatively little impact on their environment.

About 7,000 years ago the invention of the metal plow, pulled by domesticated animals, allowed farmers to cultivate larger plots of land and to break up fertile grassland soils, which previously couldn't be cultivated because of their dense root systems. In some arid (dry) regions early farmers further increased crop output by diverting water from nearby streams into hand-dug ditches and canals to irrigate crops.

**EMERGENCE OF AGRICULTURE-BASED URBAN SOCIETIES** The gradual shift from hunting and gathering to farming had several significant effects:

- *Using domesticated animals to haul loads and perform other tasks increased the average energy use per person* (Figure 2-3).

- *Population increased, mostly because of a larger, more reliable food supply* (Figure 2-4).

- *People cleared increasingly larger fields and built irrigation systems to transfer water from one place to another.*

- *People began accumulating material goods.* Nomadic hunter-gatherers could not carry many possessions in their travels, but farmers living in one place could acquire as much as they could afford.

- *Farmers could grow more than enough food for their families.* They could use the surplus to barter with craftspeople who specialized in weaving, tool making, and pottery.

- *Urbanization—the formation of villages, towns, and cities—became practical.* Craftspeople and others with specialized occupations moved into permanent villages. Some villages grew into towns and cities, which served as centers for trade, government, and religion.

**Q:** Will the United States ever again be self-sufficient in oil?

- *Conflict between societies became more common as ownership of land and water rights became a valuable economic resource.* Armies and their leaders rose to power and conquered large areas of land. These rulers forced powerless people—slaves and landless peasants—to do the hard, disagreeable work of producing food and constructing things such as irrigation systems, temples, and walled fortresses.

- *Competition for land, water, and power led to male-dominated societies.* To survive, females had to give up the power they had shared in most hunter-gatherer societies to male warriors who could protect them and their children from aggressors.

- *The survival of wild plants and animals, once vital to humanity, no longer seemed to matter.* Wild animals competing with livestock for grass and feeding on crops became enemies to be killed or driven from their habitats. Wild plants invading crop-fields became weeds to be eliminated.

**ENVIRONMENTAL IMPACT** The growing populations of these emerging civilizations needed more food and more wood for fuel and buildings, so people cut down vast forests and plowed up large expanses of grassland. Such extensive land clearing degraded or destroyed the habitats of many wild plants and animals, causing or hastening their extinction.

Many of these cleared lands were poorly managed. Soil erosion, salt buildup in irrigated soils, and overgrazing of grasslands by huge herds of livestock helped turn fertile land into desert. Topsoil washed into streams, lakes, and irrigation canals, making them useless. The gradual degradation of the vital resource base of soil, water, forests, grazing land, and wildlife was a major factor in the downfall of many great civilizations (Guest Essay, p. 43).

The gradual spread of agriculture meant that most of the world's human population shifted from hunter-gatherers *in nature* to shepherds, farmers, and urban dwellers *against nature*. Their aim was to tame and control wild nature and to gain power and wealth by controlling other humans. Many analysts believe that this change is a major cause of today's environmental problems.

| 2-4 | **Industrial Societies: The Industrial Revolution** |

**EARLY INDUSTRIAL SOCIETIES** The next great cultural shift, the **Industrial Revolution**, began in England in the mid-1700s and spread to the United States in the 1800s. It multiplied energy consumption per capita and thus the power of humans to shape the earth to their will and to fuel economic growth (Figure 2-3). Production, trade, and distribution of goods all expanded.

The Industrial Revolution occurred when England had used up most of its forests. People began substituting coal for wood fuel. Coal fed the furnaces and foundries, which were often located near coal mines to minimize transportation costs. Thus the Industrial Revolution represented a shift from dependence on renewable wood and flowing water as energy sources to dependence on nonrenewable fossil fuels.

The availability of coal led to the invention of steam engines to pump water and perform other tasks, and eventually to an array of new machines powered by coal and later by oil and natural gas. The new machines in turn led to a switch from small-scale, localized production of handmade goods to large-scale production of machine-made goods in centralized factories in rapidly growing industrial cities.

Factory towns grew into cities as rural people came to the factories for work. There they worked long hours in noisy, dirty, and hazardous conditions. Other workers toiled in coal mines, which were also dangerous. In these industrial cities coal smoke belching from a profusion of chimneys was so heavy that many people died—mainly from lung ailments. Ash and soot covered everything, and some days the smoke was so thick that it blotted out the sun.

Fossil-fuel-powered farm machinery, commercial fertilizers, and new plant-breeding techniques increased the crop yields per acre, which meant that fewer farmers were needed. With a more reliable food supply, the human population began the sharp exponential upturn still going on today (Figures 1-1 and 2-4).

**ADVANCED INDUSTRIAL SOCIETIES** After World War I (1914–18) more efficient machines and mass-production techniques were developed, forming the basis of today's advanced industrial societies in the United States, Canada, Japan, and Western Europe. These societies are characterized by

- Higher production and consumption of goods, stimulated by mass advertising

- Greater dependence on nonrenewable resources such as fossil fuels, iron, and aluminum

- A shift from natural materials, which are environmentally harmless or are broken down and recycled by natural processes, to synthetics which break down slowly and often are toxic to humans and wildlife

- A jump in the amount of energy used per person for transportation, manufacturing, agriculture, lighting, and heating and cooling (Figure 2-3)

Advanced industrial societies benefit most people living in them. These benefits include

- Creation and mass production of many useful and economically affordable products

- A sharp increase in average agricultural productivity per person because of industrialized agriculture, in which a small number of farmers produce large amounts of food

- Higher average life expectancy because of better sanitation, hygiene, nutrition, and medical care

- A decrease in the rate of population growth in MDCs (Figure 1-4)

- Better health, birth control methods, education, average income, and old-age security

People in MDCs experience far more of these benefits than do people in LDCs.

**ENVIRONMENTAL IMPACT** These benefits to industrialized societies have been accompanied by the resource and environmental problems we face today. Industrialization feeds the idea that our role is to dominate and manage nature for our species.

## Resource Conservation and Environmental Protection in the United States

**2-5**

**AMERICA'S FIRST CONSERVATIONISTS** When Europeans first came to North America, in the fifteenth and sixteenth centuries, they found it populated with diverse groups of indigenous people—called Indians by the Europeans and now often referred to as Native Americans. For at least 10,000 years these peoples had practiced mostly hunting and gathering, and had survived by being immersed in and learning to work with nature.

Some Native Americans altered the land by burning forested areas to create habitats for elk, deer, and turkey which they then hunted. But most Native American cultures were based on a deep respect for the land and its animals, as summarized by a medicine woman of California's Wintu tribe:

*The white people never cared for the land or deer or bear. When the Indians kill meat, we eat it all up. When we dig roots, we make little holes. When we build houses we make little holes. . . . We don't chop down trees. We only use dead wood. But the white people plow up the ground, pull down the trees, kill everything. The tree says: "Don't. I am sore. Don't hurt me." But they chop it down and cut it up. The spirit of the land hates them. . . . The white people destroy all. They blast rocks and scatter them on the ground. The rock says: "Don't. You are hurting me." But the white people pay no attention. . . . How can the spirit of the Earth like the white man? . . . Everywhere the white man has touched the Earth it is sore.*

**FRONTIER EXPANSION AND RESOURCE USE (1607–1900)** When European colonists began settling North America in 1607, they found a vast continent with seemingly unlimited resources. Enormous flocks of geese, ducks, and passenger pigeons blotted out the sun. Forests seemed to stretch endlessly from the Atlantic coast to the Great Plains, and the forests beyond the Great Plains were even more dramatic (Figure 2-7).

Not surprisingly, these settlers had a **frontier worldview**. They saw a hostile wilderness to be conquered and cleared as fast as possible. This frontier attitude led to enormous resource waste because the settlers believed there would always be more.

In 1850 about 80% of the total land area of the territorial United States was government owned. Most of this land had been taken from indigenous Native Americans, who had lived on it sustainably for thousands of years.

After the Civil War the federal government turned its attention to expanding the frontier westward beyond the Missouri River. That meant displacing the Native American tribes who lived off the plains. This campaign involved waging war against these indigenous people and slaughtering bison—their major source of food—as described at the beginning of this chapter. By 1840 Native Americans had either been killed in battle or by disease (especially smallpox, sometimes deliberately transmitted through gifts of infected blankets) or been expelled from most of the eastern half of the United States.

The government signed dozens of treaties giving various nations and tribes large tracts of land—and routinely broke those treaties. By 1876 the remaining Native Americans had been pushed onto a few government-managed reservations. As a Sioux elder said in 1891: "They made us many promises, more than I can remember, but they never kept but one; they promised to take our land and they took it." In effect, everybody in the United States today—except Native Americans—lives on stolen land.

The elimination of North American bison and Native Americans from the plains opened these vast grazing lands for hundreds of thousands of cattle. In the early 1880s the invention of barbed wire allowed cattle barons and cattle companies (many of them British-owned) to fence off vast areas of public land. Although in 1885 Congress passed a law allowing prosecution of anyone who fenced in public land for

Q: Adjusting for inflation, how does the price of gasoline in the United States in 1993 compare with its price in 1950? In 1973?

private use, cattle companies often found ways around the law. This replacement of wild grazing animals with domesticated cattle left vast areas overgrazed and subject to erosion.

By 1900 more than half of the public land had been given away or sold at low cost to railroad, timber, and mining companies and to land speculators, states, schools, universities, and individual homesteaders. These low prices encouraged widespread abuse of the country's forest, grassland, wildlife, and mineral resources.

Between 1832 and 1870 some individuals had become alarmed at the scope of this depletion and degradation. These early conservationists—including George Catlin, Horace Greeley, Ralph Waldo Emerson, Frederick Law Olmsted, Charles W. Eliot, Henry David Thoreau, and George Perkins Marsh—proposed that part of the unspoiled wilderness owned by the government be protected as a legacy to future generations. However, their warnings were either ignored or vigorously opposed. Many people believed that the country's forests and wildlife would last forever and that people had the right to do as they pleased with private and public land.

**BEGINNINGS OF THE FEDERAL ROLE IN RESOURCE CONSERVATION (1870–1916)** In the late 1800s the first genuine American conservation movement emerged as more people realized how fast forests and wildlife were vanishing throughout the country. In 1872 the government set aside over 809,000 hectares (2 million acres) of forest, mostly in northwestern Wyoming, as Yellowstone National Park, and banned all hunting there. Though Congress acted mostly because it saw the land as essentially useless, this marked the beginning of the first wave of resource conservation in the United States.

In 1891 Congress passed the Forest Reserve Act, which set aside Yellowstone Timberland Reserve as the first federal forest reserve. The act also authorized the president to set aside more federal lands to ensure future timber supplies and to protect water resources. This was a turning point in establishing federal responsibility to protect public lands from unsustainable resource use. And in 1892 naturalist John Muir founded the Sierra Club, bringing private citizens together to lobby elected officials to protect public land from unsustainable development.

Between 1891 and 1897 Presidents Benjamin Harrison and Grover Cleveland banned timber cutting on large tracts of public land, located mostly in the West. Their actions were opposed by powerful and wealthy political foes, many of them westerners who had previously had unrestricted access to those public lands.

The Lacey Act of 1900 made it illegal to transport live or dead wild animals, or their parts, across state

**Figure 2-7** Sunlight filtering through a redwood grove in Muir Woods in northern California.

borders or to import foreign wildlife without a federal permit. Although this law reduced commercial hunting, it did not end the slaughter of wildlife.

More effective protection of forests and wildlife didn't come about until Theodore Roosevelt, an ardent conservationist, became president. His presidency (1901–1909) has been called the country's golden age of conservation.

Roosevelt first persuaded Congress to grant him executive powers to establish federal wildlife refuges. In 1903 he established the first federal refuge at Pelican Island off the east coast of Florida for preservation of the endangered brown pelican (Figure 2-8). Roosevelt also tripled the size of the forest reserves and transferred their administration from the Department of the Interior, known for lax enforcement, to the Department of Agriculture.

In 1905 Congress created the U.S. Forest Service to manage and protect the forest reserves. Roosevelt appointed Gifford Pinchot as its first chief. Pinchot pioneered scientific management of forest resources on public lands, using the principles of sustainable yield and multiple use. That same year the Audubon Society was founded to preserve the country's bird species.

**A:** It's about the same in both cases.

**Figure 2-8** The first national wildlife refuge was set up off the coast of Florida in 1903 to protect the brown pelican from extinction because of overhunting and loss of habitat. In the 1960s this species was again threatened with extinction when exposure to DDT and other persistent pesticides in the fish it eats caused reproductive losses. Now it is making a comeback.

In 1907 Congress, upset because Roosevelt had added vast tracts to the forest reserves, amended the Forest Reserve Act of 1891 to ban further executive withdrawals of public forests. This amendment also changed the name of the reserves to national forests, implying the possibility of some development. On the day before the change became law, Roosevelt defiantly reserved another 6.5 million hectares (16 million acres).

Early in this century the American conservation movement split over how the beautiful Hetch Hetchy Valley in what is now Yosemite National Park was to be used (Spotlight, p. 37). The *preservationist* school believed that wilderness areas should be left untouched. The *wise-use school* believed that wilderness and other public lands should be managed wisely to provide resources for the people.

In 1912 Congress created the U.S. National Park System. In 1916 it passed the National Park System Organic Act, dedicating national parks to preserving scenery, wildlife, and natural and historical objects for the use, viewing, health, and pleasure of people. In addition, the parks are to be maintained in a manner that leaves them unimpaired for future generations. The act also established the National Park Service within the Department of the Interior to manage the system.

During the Republican administrations of 1921–33 the government favored big business. Indeed, President Herbert Hoover (1929–33) proposed that the government return all remaining federal lands to the states or sell them to private interests for economic development. Luckily the Great Depression made the cost of owning such lands unattractive to state governments and private investors.

**EXPANDING FEDERAL ROLE IN RESOURCE MANAGEMENT (1933–60)** The second wave of national resource conservation began in the early 1930s, as President Franklin D. Roosevelt (1933–45) strove to prod the country out of the Great Depression, which lasted from 1929 to 1942. Cash-poor landowners eagerly sold large tracts of land at low prices to the government. Several government programs enacted during the Roosevelt administration had a lasting impact on U.S. environmental policy:

- The Civilian Conservation Corps (CCC) was created in 1933 to provide jobs for 2 million unemployed people. The CCC planted trees, developed parks and recreation areas, restored silted waterways, provided flood control, controlled soil erosion, and protected wildlife.

- The federal government built and operated many large dams in the arid western states, such as Hoover Dam on the Colorado River. These projects provided jobs, flood control, cheap irrigation water, and cheap electricity.

- The Taylor Grazing Act of 1934 was the first federal law to regulate grazing of domesticated livestock on public lands, especially in the West, which had been overgrazed by ranchers for many decades. This law required permits and fees for the use of federal grazing lands and placed limits on the number of animals that could be grazed. However, western congressional delegations managed to keep the Grazing Service and its successor, the Bureau of Land Management (BLM), poorly funded, understaffed, and without enforcement authority for another 40 years. This allowed many ranchers and mining and timber companies to continue abusing western public lands.

- The Migratory Bird Hunting Stamp Act of 1934 required waterfowl hunters to buy a federal duck hunting license. Since 1934 the sale of these permits has raised over $300 million for use in waterfowl research and the purchase of waterfowl refuge lands.

- The Soil Conservation Service was created in 1935 as part of the Department of Agriculture. Its mission was to correct the enormous erosion problems that had ruined many farms of the Great Plains states. This erosion, caused by the greatest drought in U.S. history and lack of soil conservation, contributed to the Great Depression by forcing many bankrupt farmers to migrate from the midwestern Dust Bowl to eastern and western cities in search of nonexistent jobs.

- In 1937 the Federal Aid in Wildlife Restoration Act (also known as the Pittman-Robertson Act) levied a federal tax on all sales of guns and ammunition.

Q: What percentage of U.S. environmental spending is devoted to preventing pollution?

SPOTLIGHT

In 1901 resource managers, led by Gifford Pinchot and San Francisco mayor James D. Phelan, proposed to dam the Tuolumne River running through Hetch Hetchy Valley to supply drinking water for San Francisco. Preservationists, led by John Muir, were opposed. After a bitter 12-year battle, the dam was built and the valley was flooded. Today the controversy continues, with preservationists pressing to have the dam removed.

Preservationists would keep large areas of public lands untouched so they can be enjoyed today and passed on unspoiled to future generations. After Muir's death in 1914, preservationists were led by forester Aldo Leopold, who said that the role of the human species should be to protect nature—not conquer it.

Another effective supporter of wilderness preservation was Robert Marshall of the U.S. Forest Service. In 1935 he and Leopold founded the Wilderness Society. More recent preservationist leaders include David Brower (former head of the Sierra Club and founder of Friends of the Earth, and Earth Island Institute), Ernest Swift, and Stewart L. Udall (a former secretary of the interior).

In contrast, wise-use resource managers see wilderness and other public lands as resources to be used to enhance economic growth and national strength and to provide the greatest benefit to the greatest number of people. In their view the government should protect these lands from harm by managing them efficiently and scientifically using the principles of sustainable yield and multiple use. Early wise-use resource managers included Theodore Roosevelt, Gifford Pinchot, John Wesley Powell, and Charles Van Hise.

Roosevelt and Pinchot thought conservation experts should form an elite corps of resource managers in the federal bureaucracy.

Shielded from political pressure, they could develop scientific management strategies. Pinchot angered Muir and other preservationists when he stated his "wise-use" principle:

*The first great fact about conservation is that it stands for development. There has been a fundamental misconception that conservation means nothing but the husbanding of resources for future generations. There could be no more serious mistake. . . . The first principle of conservation is the use of the natural resources now existing on this continent for the benefit of the people who live here now.*

Despite their basic differences both schools opposed delivering these public resources into the hands of a few for profit. Both groups have been disappointed. Since 1910 development rights to public lands have routinely been sold at below market prices to large corporate farms, ranches, mining companies, and timber companies. Taxpayers have subsidized this use of resources by absorbing the loss of potential revenue and paying for most of the resulting damage.

---

States have received more than $2.1 billion to buy land for wildlife conservation (mostly for game species), to support wildlife research, and to reintroduce wildlife in depleted areas. A similar law, the Federal Aid in Fish Restoration Act of 1950, helps state fisheries supply and conserve game fish through a tax on fishing equipment.

- The Bureau of Sport Fisheries in the Department of Commerce and the Bureau of Biological Survey in the Department of Agriculture were merged in 1940 to form the U.S. Fish and Wildlife Service. This new agency was placed in the Department of Interior and given the roles of managing the National Wildlife Refuge System and protecting wild species in danger of becoming extinct.

Between 1940 and 1960 there were few new developments in federal resource conservation policy because of preoccupation with World War II (1941–45) and economic recovery after the war. However, a few events during these years turned out to be forewarnings of later environmental problems. For example, in 1948 the United States suffered its first major air pollution disaster. When pollutants from a steel mill, a zinc smelter, and a sulfuric acid plant stagnated over the town of Donora, Pennsylvania, about 6,000 of the town's 14,000 inhabitants fell ill, and 20 died from breathing the polluted air. The incident caused some people to question belching smokestacks as an acceptable nuisance and a sign of economic progress.

Also, in 1948, William Voight warned about the dangers of rapid population growth and overpopulation in his book *The Road to Survival*. That same year, Fairfield Osborn wrote about the need to redouble efforts to protect and conserve the country's natural resources during the period of rapid economic growth after World War II. Unfortunately few people took either of these warnings seriously until the 1960s. And in 1949 *A Sand County Almanac*, a collection of essays by Aldo Leopold, was published, in which the author proposed a new land ethic and urged Americans to develop an ecological conscience to protect their

---

A: 1%; the other 99% is spent on pollution cleanup

**Figure 2-9** Foam on a creek in 1966 caused by nonbiodegradable additives in synthetic laundry detergents.

remaining wild lands and wildlife. This book is still widely used as a guide to Earth ethics and sustainable management of resources.

**RISE OF THE ENVIRONMENTAL MOVEMENT (1960–80)** The third wave of national resource conservation began during the short administration of John F. Kennedy (1961–63) and expanded under the administration of Lyndon B. Johnson (1963–68).

In 1962 biologist Rachel Carson published *Silent Spring*, which documented the pollution of air, water, and wildlife from pesticides such as DDT. This influential book helped broaden the concept of resource conservation to include preservation of the *quality* of the air, water, and soil—a concept that was under assault by a country experiencing rapid economic growth. Carson pointed out that "for the first time in the history of the world, every human being is now subjected to dangerous chemicals, from the moment of conception until death." Public response to Carson's book was unprecedented. Sadly she died in 1964 without knowing that her efforts were a driving force in the birth of what is now known as the environmental movement in the United States.

In 1964 Congress passed the Wilderness Act, largely because of tireless lobbying by Howard Zahniser, executive secretary of the Wilderness Society. The act authorized the government to protect undeveloped tracts of public land as part of the National Wilderness System unless Congress later decides they are needed for the national good. Land in this system is to be used only for nondestructive forms of recreation such as hiking and camping.

Between 1965 and 1970 the emerging science of ecology received widespread media coverage. At the same time, the popular writings of biologists such as Paul Ehrlich (Guest Essay, p. 26), Barry Commoner, and Garrett Hardin (Guest Essay, p. 226) awakened people to the interlocking relationships between population growth, resource use, and pollution (Figure 1-15). And during that same period, a number of events increased public awareness of pollution:

- In 1963 high concentrations of pollutants accumulated in the air above New York City, killing about 300 people and injuring thousands. Another 80 people died as a result of a similar event in New York City in 1966.

- In the mid-1960s foam from nonbiodegradable additives in laundry detergents and cleaners began appearing on streams (Figure 2-9).

- In 1969 the oil-polluted Cuyahoga River, running through Cleveland, Ohio, caught fire and burned for eight days. Two bridges were burned by the five-story-high flames.

- In 1969 oil leaking from an offshore well near Santa Barbara, California, coated beaches and wildlife.

- By the late 1960s Lake Erie had become severely polluted. Millions of fish died, including desirable species of commercial and game fish, and many beaches had to be closed.

- During the late 1960s and early 1970s the North American bald eagle (Figure 2-10), the grizzly bear, the whooping crane, the peregrine falcon, and other wildlife species were threatened with extinction from pollution and loss of habitat.

April 22, 1970, marked the first annual Earth Day in the United States. Some 20 million people in more than 2,000 communities took to the streets to demand better environmental quality. Elected officials got the message. Between 1969 and 1980 Congress passed numerous pieces of legislation to help protect the air, water, land, and wildlife (see Appendix 3 for a list of such legislation). These actions were instrumental in leading President Richard Nixon to establish the Environmental Protection Agency (EPA) in 1970. In 1972 the EPA banned most uses of the pesticide DDT in the United States, and Oregon passed the first beverage bottle recycling law. These accomplishments by government and by citizen-supported environmental groups were the fourth wave of national resource conservation.

A worldwide debate on the pros and cons of continuing population growth and destructive forms of industrialization and economic growth took place after Donella Meadows and her colleagues published *The Limits to Growth* in 1972. That same year representatives of 113 nations gathered at the UN Conference

Q: How much of the world's population is in the United States?

on the Human Environment in Stockholm, Sweden, to develop plans for international action to protect the global environment.

The 1973 OPEC oil embargo and the shutdown of Iranian oil production in 1979 led to oil shortages and sharp rises in the price of oil between 1973 and 1981 (Case Study, p. 15). This period of relative oil scarcity revealed the need to not waste energy resources, especially oil, and to develop solar and other renewable energy resources to replace oil.

In 1977 President Jimmy Carter created the Department of Energy to help the country deal with oil shortages. He, along with most conservationists, realized that the United States and other industrialized countries must develop a long-range energy strategy. During his term Carter also appointed a number of competent and experienced administrators to key posts in the EPA, the Department of the Interior, and the Department of Energy. He drew heavily on established environmental and conservation organizations for such appointees and for advice on environmental and resource policy. He also created the Superfund to clean up abandoned hazardous waste sites, such as the Love Canal suburb in Niagara Falls, New York.

Just before leaving office Carter used the Antiquities Act of 1906 to increase the amount of public land protected from development. He tripled the amount of land in the National Wilderness System, primarily by adding vast tracts in Alaska. This also doubled the area administered by the National Park Service.

Most efforts to make the United States face up to the upcoming end of the oil era have been undermined by the temporary oil glut since 1980 and by the low price of oil when adjusted for inflation (Figure 1-11). This continues to send a false message to many consumers and most elected officials that energy conservation and a need for oil substitutes are not high-priority items.

Several other noteworthy events occurred during this period. In 1974 chemists Sherwood Roland and Mario Molina suggested that chlorofluorocarbons (CFCs), used as refrigerants, as propellants in aerosols, and for making some plastics, were drifting upward to deplete ozone in the stratosphere, letting more deadly ultraviolet radiation from the sun reach the earth's surface. In 1978 the Love Canal housing development near Niagara Falls in New York was evacuated after discovery that it was built near a leaking toxic waste dump. And in 1979 the Three-Mile Island nuclear power plant in Pennsylvania experienced a partial meltdown.

**CONTINUING CONTROVERSY AND SOME RETRENCHMENT (1980–93)** The Federal Land Policy and Management Act of 1976 gave the Bureau of Land Management (BLM) its first real authority to manage

**Figure 2-10** Bald eagle with pink salmon at Kachemak Bay, Alaska. Some 250,000 American bald eagles soared over North America when this bird became the U.S. national symbol in 1782. During the late 1960s and early 1970s the bald eagle population in the lower 48 states declined because of loss of habitat, illegal hunting, and fragile eggs caused by uptake of pesticides in fish, their primary diet. Now this protected species is making a comeback.

the public lands under its control, 85% of which are in 12 western states. This angered a number of western interests, whose use of these lands was being restricted for the first time. Thus in the late 1970s a coalition of ranchers, miners, loggers, developers, farmers, politicians, and others launched a political campaign known as the *sagebrush rebellion*. Its primary goal was to remove most western lands from public ownership and turn them over to the states. Then they planned to persuade state legislatures to sell or lease the resource-rich lands at low prices to ranching, mining, timber, land development, and other private interests.

In 1981 Ronald Reagan, a self-declared sagebrush rebel and advocate of less federal control, became president. During his eight years in office Reagan mounted a massive attack on the conservation and environmental laws established over the previous 80 years by:

- Appointing people who opposed existing environmental, resource conservation, and land use legislation and policies to key positions in the Interior Department, BLM, and EPA—an action environmentalists likened to putting foxes in charge of the chicken house

- Barring established environmental and conservation organizations and leaders from giving advice on such appointments and on the administration's environmental and resource policies

- Making the enforcement of existing environmental and resource conservation laws difficult by encouraging drastic budget and staff cuts in enforcement agencies

- Greatly increasing energy and mineral development and timber cutting by private enterprise on public lands, allowing these resources to be sold at giveaway prices to private corporations

- Cutting federal funding for energy conservation research by 70% and for perpetual and renewable energy resources research by 85%, and eliminating tax incentives for residential solar energy and energy conservation

- Lowering automobile gas mileage standards and relaxing air and water quality standards

- Reducing funding for research and development on perpetual and renewable energy resources by 85%

Although Reagan was an immensely popular president, many people strongly opposed his environmental and resource policies. These policies were blunted by strong opposition in Congress, public outrage, and legal challenges by environmental and conservation organizations, whose memberships soared in this period.

The net effect of the Reagan years was to slow down the momentum of environmental protection and resource conservation built up in the 1970s. Instead of moving forward, environmental organizations spent much of their time and money struggling not to lose ground.

Upon his election in 1989, George Bush promised to be an environmental president. By 1992 when he left office Bush's environmental record was mixed, as he often failed to provide strong action and the national and global environmental leadership he had promised. Other significant environmental events in the 1980s and early 1990s included the following:

- 1986: A catastrophic explosion occurred at the Chernobyl nuclear power plant in the former Soviet Union and released large amounts of radioactivity into the atmosphere. This event mobilized global efforts to halt the spread of nuclear power as a way to produce electricity.

- 1986: After high levels of toxic dioxin were found in the town of Times Beach, Missouri, all residents were evacuated and the town bought by the EPA.

- 1987: After 13 years of argument and delay, 24 countries—including the United States—signed the Montreal Protocol and agreed to cut their emission of ozone-destroying CFCs in half by 1995.

- 1987: A Long Island, New York, garbage barge, the *Moro*, traveled 9,700 kilometers (6,000 miles) in an unsuccessful attempt to dump its load. This farcical journey became a symbol of the nation's mounting trash problems.

- 1988: NASA scientist James Hansen warned Congress that an enhanced greenhouse effect leading to rapid global warming over a few decades may be under way and could disrupt water and food supplies and raise sea levels.

- 1988: Several hundred local and regional grass-roots groups formed a national coalition called the "wise-use movement" to oppose further protection of wilderness, forests, and wildlife and to destroy the environmental movement in the United States by 1998. Many of these groups are financed mostly by developers and by timber, mining, oil, coal, and ranching interests.

- 1989: The oil tanker *Exxon Valdez* ran aground in Alaska's Prince William Sound and released 42 million liters (11 million gallons) of oil, the worst oil spill in U.S. waters in history.

- 1990: A UN report warned that emissions of carbon dioxide and other heat-trapping gases, caused mostly by burning of fossil fuels and deforestation, must be cut 60% by 2010 to prevent a harmful rise in average global atmospheric temperature by 2040.

- 1990: On April 22 the twentieth annual Earth Day took place. An estimated 200 million people in 141 nations participated—the largest global demonstration in history. The main goals of this event were to reach out to minorities and the poor throughout the world, to make people everywhere aware of the difference their actions could make in sustaining the earth (summarized in the slogan "Who Says You Can't Change the World"), and to get people involved in making every day Earth Day.

- 1991: The war in the Persian Gulf revealed U.S. oil addiction and dependence on imported oil, as well as illustrating the massive environmental damage caused by war.

- 1991: The United States and 38 other nations with a presence in Antarctica agreed to continue banning mining for minerals there for another 50 years and to limit tourism and marine pollution to protect native plant and animal wildlife.

- 1992: Representatives from 178 nations gathered at the Earth Summit in Rio de Janeiro, Brazil, to develop plans for international action to protect the global environment. Although important progress was made, President Bush was criticized for lack of leadership and vision, failure to sign a treaty to protect biodiversity, and watering down the treaty on global climate change.

Q: What percentage of the world's mineral resources and nonrenewable energy are used by the United States?

- 1993: Bill Clinton became president of the United States, promising to provide much needed national and global environmental leadership. Environmentalists were especially pleased that he chose Al Gore—considered to have a comprehensive understanding of environmental problems and possible solutions—as vice president and hope that Clinton's promise will be translated into action.

## 2-6 A New Environmental Revolution

Environmentalists warn that we must regain the lost momentum of the 1980s. Launching a new environmental revolution will require strong national and global leadership by the United States, the world's richest country as well as its largest polluter and user and waster of resources.

Dealing with global environmental and resource problems will involve much controversy and require us to make some trade-offs and significant changes in our worldviews, economic and political systems, and lifestyles. Specific actions most environmentalists believe are needed to help sustain the earth are presented throughout this book.

Our efforts will have to shift from pollution cleanup to pollution prevention (Guest Essay, below), waste disposal to waste prevention and reduction, species protection to habitat protection, and increased resource use to increased resource conservation. We will need to use our political and economic systems to reward Earth-sustaining economic activities and discourage those that harm the earth. We will have to allow parts of the world we have damaged to heal, help restore severely damaged areas, and protect remaining wild areas from destructive development. Governments will have to cooperate on an unprecedented scale to deal with a host of global and regional environmental problems (Guest Essay, p. 43).

The Agricultural Revolution took place over 10,000 years, and the Industrial Revolution over more than 200 years. Because of mushrooming population, resource consumption, pollution, and environmental degradation, we have only a few decades to bring about this new environmental revolution. Transforming our worldviews, lifestyles, and economic and social systems in such a short time is the greatest challenge our species has faced, but it can be done.

*We found our house—the planet—with drinkable water, with good soil to grow food, with clean air to breathe. We at least must leave it in as good a shape as we found it, if not better.*

REV. JESSE JACKSON

## A New Environmentalism for the 1990s and Beyond

GUEST ESSAY

### Peter Montague

*Peter Montague is senior research analyst for Greenpeace and director of the Environmental Research Foundation in Washington, D.C. The Foundation studies environmental problems and informs the public about environmental problems and the technologies and policies that might help solve them. He has served as project administrator of a hazardous-waste research program at Princeton University and has taught courses in environmental impact analysis at the University of New Mexico. He is the coauthor of two books on toxic heavy metals in the natural environment and is editor of Rachel, an informative and readable newsletter on environmental problems, focusing on hazardous waste.*

Environmentalism as we have known it for over 27 years is dead. The environmentalism of the 1970s advocated strict numerical controls on releases of *dangerous wastes* (any unwanted or uncontrolled materials that can harm living things or disrupt ecosystems) into the environment. Industry's ability to create new hazards, however, quickly outstripped government's ability to establish adequate controls and enforcement programs.

After so many years of effort by government and by concerned citizens (the environmental movement), the overwhelming majority of dangerous chemicals is still not regulated in any way. Even those few that are covered by regulations have not been adequately controlled.

In short, the *pollution management* approach to environmental protection has failed and stands discredited; *pollution prevention* is our only hope. An ounce of prevention really is worth a pound of cure.

Here, in list form, is the new environmentalism that is emerging:

(continued)

- *All waste disposal—landfilling, incineration, deep-well injection—is polluting because disposal means dispersal into the environment.* Once wastes are created they cannot be contained or controlled because of the scientific laws of matter and energy [Chapter 3]. The old environmentalism failed to recognize this important truth, and thus squandered enormous resources trying to achieve the impossible. We in the United States presently spend about $90 billion per year on pollution control. Yet, the global environment is increasingly threatened by a buildup of heat because of heat-trapping gases we emit into the atmosphere; at least half the surface of the planet is being subjected to damaging ultraviolet radiation from the sun as a result of ozone-depleting chemicals we have discharged into the atmosphere; and vast regions of the United States, Canada, and Europe are suffering from loss of forests, crop productivity, and fish as a result of acid rain (caused by releases of sulfur and nitrogen compounds, chiefly by power plants and automobiles) and other air pollutants. Soil and water are dangerously polluted at thousands of locales where municipal garbage and industrial wastes have been (and continue to be) dumped or incinerated; thousands of such sites remain to be discovered, according to U.S. government estimates.

- *The inevitable result of our reliance upon waste treatment and disposal systems has been an unrelenting buildup of exotic synthetic toxic materials in humans and other forms of life worldwide.* For example, breast milk of women in industrialized countries like the United States is so contaminated with pesticides and industrial hydrocarbons that, if human milk were bottled and sold commercially, it could be banned by the Food and Drug Administration (FDA) as unsafe for human consumption. If a whale today beaches itself on the shores of the United States and dies, its body must be treated as a "hazardous waste" because whales contain legally hazardous concentrations of PCBs (polychlorinated biphenyls).

- *The ability of humans and other life forms to adapt to changes in their chemical environment is strictly limited by the genetic code each form of life inherits.* Continued contamination occurring hundreds of times faster than we can adapt will drive humans to increasingly widespread sickness, to degradation of the species, and could ultimately lead to extinction.

- *Damage to humans (and to other life forms) is abundantly documented.* Birds, fish, and humans in industrialized countries like the United States are enduring steadily rising levels of cancer and other serious disorders attributable to pollution. An astonishing 88% of children under age 6 in the United States have enough toxic lead in their blood that they perform below par on standardized tests of physical, mental, and emotional development.

If we will but look, the handwriting is on the wall everywhere. To deal with these problems, industrial societies must abandon their reliance upon waste treatment and disposal and upon the regulatory system of numerical standards created by government to manage the damage that results from relying on waste disposal instead of waste prevention. We must—relatively quickly—move the industrialized and industrializing countries to new technical approaches accompanied by new industrial goals—namely, clean production or zero discharge systems.

The concept of "clean production" involves industrial systems that avoid or eliminate dangerous wastes and dangerous products, and minimize the use of raw materials, water, and energy. Goods manufactured in a clean production process must not damage natural ecosystems throughout their entire life cycle, including **(1)** raw materials selection, extraction, and processing; **(2)** product conceptualization, design, manufacture, and assembly; **(3)** materials transport during all phases; **(4)** industrial and household usage; and **(5)** reintroduction of the product into industrial systems or into the environment when it no longer serves a useful function.

Clean production does not include "end-of-pipe" pollution controls such as filters or scrubbers or chemical, physical, or biological treatment. Nor does it include measures that pretend to reduce the volume of waste by incineration or concentration, that mask the hazard by dilution, or that transfer pollutants from one environmental medium to another.

A new industrial pattern, and a new environmentalism, is thus emerging. It insists that the long-term well-being of humans and other species must be factored into our production and consumption plans. These new requirements are not optional; human survival depends upon our willingness to make, and pay for, the necessary changes.

### Critical Thinking

1. Do you agree with the author that the *pollution management* approach to environmental protection practiced during the past 25 years has failed and must be replaced with a *pollution prevention* approach? Explain.
2. List key economic, health, consumption, and lifestyle changes you might experience as a consequence of switching from pollution control to pollution prevention. What changes might the next generation face?

Q:  What percentage of the world's pollution is produced by the United States?

## Launching the Environmental Revolution*

**GUEST ESSAY**

*Lester R. Brown*

*Lester R. Brown is president of the World-watch Institute, a private nonprofit research institute devoted to analysis of global environmental issues, which he founded in 1974. Under his leadership the institute publishes the annual* State of the World Reports, *considered by environmentalists and world leaders as the best source of information about key environmental issues; monographs on specific topics;* World Watch *magazine; and a series of Environmental Alert books. He is author of a dozen books, recipient of the MacArthur Foundation "Genius Award," and winner of the United Nations' 1989 environment prize. He has been described by the* Washington Post *as "one of the world's most influential thinkers."*

Our world of the mid-1990s faces potentially convulsive change. The question is, In what direction will it take us? Will the change come from strong worldwide initiatives that reverse the degradation of the planet and restore hope for the future, or will it come from continuing environmental deterioration that leads to economic decline and social instability?

Muddling through will not work. Either we will turn things around quickly or the self-reinforcing internal dynamic of the deterioration-and-decline scenario will take over. The policy decisions we make in the years immediately ahead will determine whether our children live in a world of development or decline.

There is no precedent for the rapid and substantial change we need to make. Building an environmentally sustainable future depends on restructuring the global economy, enacting major shifts in human reproductive behavior, and making dramatic changes in values and lifestyles. Doing all this quickly adds up to a revolution that is driven and defined by the need to restore and preserve the earth's environmental systems. If this *Environmental Revolution* succeeds, it will rank with the Agricultural and Industrial Revolutions as one of the great economic and social transformations in human history.

Like the Agricultural Revolution, it will dramatically alter population trends. While the former set the stage for enormous increases in human numbers, this revolution will succeed only if it stabilizes human population size, reestablishing a balance between people and natural systems on which they depend [Figure 2-4]. In contrast to the Industrial Revolution, which was based on a shift to fossil fuels, this new transformation will be based on a shift away from fossil fuels.

The two earlier revolutions were driven by technological advances—the first by the discovery of farming and the second by the invention of the steam engine, which

* Excerpt from an expanded version of these ideas in "Launching the Environmental Revolution," *State of the World 1992* (New York: Norton, 1992).

converted the energy in coal into mechanical power. The Environmental Revolution, while it will obviously need new technologies, will be driven primarily by the restructuring of the global economy so that it does not destroy its natural support systems.

The pace of the Environmental Revolution needs to be far faster than that of its predecessors. The Agricultural Revolution began some 10,000 years ago and the Industrial Revolution has been under way for about two centuries. But if the Environmental Revolution is to succeed, it must be compressed into a few decades.

Progress in the Agricultural Revolution was measured almost exclusively in the growth in food output that eventually enabled farmers to produce a surplus that could feed city dwellers. Similarly industrial progress was gauged by success in expanding the output of raw materials and manufactured goods. The Environmental Revolution will be judged by whether it can shift the world economy into an environmentally sustainable development path, one that leads to greater economic security, healthier lifestyles, and a worldwide improvement in the human condition.

Many still do not see the need for such an economic and social transformation. They see the earth's deteriorating physical condition as a peripheral matter that can be dealt with by minor policy adjustments. But 20 years of effort have failed to stem the tide of environmental degradation. There is now too much evidence on too many fronts to take these issues lightly.

Already the planet's degradation is damaging human health, slowing the growth in world food production, and reversing economic progress in dozens of countries. By the age of 10, thousands of children living in southern California's Los Angeles basin have respiratory systems that are permanently impaired by polluted air. Some 300,000 people in the former Soviet Union are being treated for radiation sickness caused by the Chernobyl nuclear power plant accident. The accelerated depletion of ozone in the stratosphere in the Northern Hemisphere will lead to an estimated additional 200,000 skin cancer fatalities over the next half century in the United States alone. Worldwide millions of lives are at stake. These examples, and countless others, show that our health is closely linked to that of the planet.

A scarcity of new cropland and fresh water plus the negative effects of soil erosion, air pollution, and hotter summers on crop yields are slowing the growth of the world grain harvest. Combined with continuing rapid population growth, this has reversed the steady rise in grain output per person that the world had become accustomed to. Between 1950 and 1984, the historical peak year, world grain production per person climbed by nearly 40%. Since then it has fallen roughly 1% per year, with the drop concentrated in poor countries. With food imports in these nations restricted by rising external debt, there are far more hungry people today than ever before.

(continued)

On the economic front the signs are equally ominous: Soil erosion, deforestation, and overgrazing are adversely affecting productivity in the farming, forestry, and livestock sectors, slowing overall economic growth in agriculturally based economies. The World Bank reports that after three decades of broad-based economic gains, incomes fell during the 1980s in 40 LDCs. Collectively these nations contain more than 800 million people—almost three times the population of North America and nearly one-sixth that of the world. In Nigeria, the most populous country in the ill-fated group, average income fell a painful 29%, exceeding the fall in U.S. incomes during the depression decade of the 1930s.

Anyone who thinks these environmental, agricultural, and economic trends can easily be reversed need only look at population projections. Those of us born before the middle of this century have seen the world population more than double to 5.5 billion. We have witnessed the environmental effects of adding 3 billion people, especially in developing countries. We can see the loss of tree cover, the devastation of grasslands, the soil erosion, the crowding and poverty, the land hunger, and the air and water pollution associated with this addition of people. But what if 4.2 billion more people are added by 2050, over 90% of them in developing countries, as now projected by UN population experts?

The decline in living standards that was once predicted by some ecologists from the combination of continuing rapid population growth, spreading environmental degradation, and rising external debt has become a reality for one-sixth of humanity. Moreover, if a more comprehensive system of national economic accounting were used—one that incorporated losses of natural capital, such as topsoil and forests, the destruction of productive grasslands, the extinction of plant and animal species, and the health costs of air and water pollution, nuclear radiation,

and increased ultraviolet radiation—it might well show that most of humanity suffered a decline in living conditions in the 1980s.

Today we study archaeological sites of civilizations that were undermined by environmental deterioration. The wheatlands that made North Africa the granary of the Roman Empire are now largely desert. The early civilizations of the Tigris-Euphrates Basin declined as the waterlogging and salting of irrigation systems shrank their food supply. And the collapse of the Mayan civilization that flourished in the Guatemalan lowlands from the third century B.C. to the ninth century A.D. may have been triggered by deforestation and soil erosion.

No one knows for certain why centers of Mayan culture and art fell into neglect, nor whether the population of 1–3 million moved or died off, but recent progress in deciphering hieroglyphs in the area adds credence to the environmental decline hypothesis. One of those involved with the project, Linda Schele of the University of Texas, observes: "They were worries about war at the end. Ecological disasters, too. Deforestation. Starvation. I think the population rose to the limits their technology could bear. They were so close to the edge, if anything went wrong, it was all over."

Whether the Mayan economy had become environmentally unsustainable before it actually began to decline, we do not know. We do know that ours is.

## Critical Thinking

1. Do you agree with the author that we need to bring about an Environmental Revolution within a few decades? Explain.
2. Do you believe that this can be done by making minor adjustments in the global economy or that the global economy needs to be restructured to put less stress on Earth's natural systems?

# Critical Thinking

1. Would we be better off if agriculture had never been discovered and we were still hunter-gatherers? Explain.

2. List the most important benefits and drawbacks of an advanced industrial society such as the United States. Do the benefits outweigh the drawbacks? Explain. What are the alternatives?

3. Public forests, grasslands, wildlife reserves, and wilderness areas are owned by all citizens and managed for them by federal and state governments. In terms of the management policies for most of these lands, would you classify yourself as a preservationist, a wise-use resource manager, or somewhere between these two positions? Explain.

4. Many observers argue that the world's remaining hunter-gatherer societies should be given title to the land they and their ancestors have lived on for centuries and the right to be left alone by modern civilization. We have created protected reserves for endangered wild species, so why not create reserves for these endangered human cultures? What do you think?

5. Do you believe that a cultural change to a sustainable-Earth society over the next 50 years is desirable? Explain.

6. Do you believe that a cultural change to a sustainable-Earth society is possible over the next 50 years or so? What changes do you plan to make in your lifestyle to help bring about such a change?

# PART II
# Scientific Principles and Concepts

*Animal and vegetable life is too complicated a problem for human intelligence to solve, and we can never know how wide a circle of disturbance we produce in the harmonies of nature when we throw the smallest pebble into the ocean of organic life.*

GEORGE PERKINS MARSH

## Saving Energy, Saving Money, Saving Jobs

Osage, Iowa (population about 4,000), has become the energy efficiency capital of the United States. Its transformation began in 1974 when easy-going Wes Birdsall started going door to door preaching energy conservation to help his community deal with the energy crisis of 1973 (Case Study, p. 15). As general manager of Osage Municipal Gas and Electric Company, he wanted the townspeople to save energy and reduce their natural gas and electric bills. The utility would save money, too, by not having to buy more oil and generators.

Wes started his crusade by telling homeowners about the importance of insulating walls and ceilings and plugging leaky windows and doors. These repairs provided jobs for people selling and installing insulation, caulking, and energy-efficient windows.

Wes also advised people to replace their incandescent light bulbs with more efficient fluorescent bulbs and to turn down the temperature on water heaters and wrap them with insulation—an economic boon to local hardware and lighting stores. The utility company even gave away free water-heater blankets to anyone who asked. In addition, he urged people to save water and fuel by installing low-flow shower heads.

As people saw how much money they could save, Wes stepped up his campaign. He offered to give every building in town a free thermogram, an infrared scan that shows where heat escaped (Figure 3-1). When homeowners could see the energy (and money) hemorrhaging out of their buildings, they took action to plug these leaks—again helping the local economy. Teacher Ken Swenson and his family, who live in a large 865-square-meter (9,634-square-foot) house, can testify to the program's success. Their heating bill is only about $50 per year. A local knitting mill cut its utility bill nearly 40%.

**Figure 3-1** An infrared photo showing heat loss around the windows, doors, roofs, and foundations (red, white, and yellow colors) of houses and stores in Plymouth, Michigan. Wes Birdsall provided similar thermograms for houses in Osage, Iowa. The average U.S. house has heat leaks and air infiltration equivalent to leaving a window wide open during the heating season. Because of poor design, most U.S. houses and office buildings waste about half of the energy used to heat and cool them. Americans pay about $300 billion a year for this wasted heat—more than the entire annual military budget.

Wes then stepped up his campaign. He announced that no new houses could be hooked up to the company's natural gas line unless they met minimum energy-efficiency standards.

The results of this community-wide effort have been dramatic. Since 1974 the town has cut its natural gas consumption by 45%, no mean feat in a region where winter temperatures can plummet to –103°C (–80°F). In addition, the utility company saved enough money to prepay all its debt, accumulate a cash surplus, and cut inflation-adjusted electricity rates by a third (which attracted two new factories). Furthermore, each household saves more than $1,000 per year. This money is supporting jobs and circulating in the local economy rather than going out of town, and usually out of state, to buy energy. The town's lower fossil-fuel use also eases local air pollution and the threat of global warming. What is your local utility and community doing to improve energy efficiency and stimulate the local economy?

VANSCAN® Continuous Mobile Thermogram by Daedalus Enterprises, Inc.

This chapter looks at the world from a physical and chemical standpoint. Chapters 4–7 examine how key physical and chemical processes are integrated into the biological systems we call life. This chapter will answer the following questions:

- What is science? What is technology? What is environmental science?

- What are the basic forms of matter? What is matter made of? What makes matter useful to us as a resource?

- What are the major forms of energy? What energy resources do we rely on? What makes energy useful to us as a resource?

- What are physical and chemical changes? What scientific law governs changes of matter from one physical or chemical form to another?

- What are the three main types of nuclear changes that matter can undergo?

- What two scientific laws govern changes of energy from one form to another?

- How can we waste less energy? How much net useful energy is available from different energy resources?

- How are the scientific laws governing changes of matter and energy from one form to another related to resource use and environmental disruption?

## 3-1 Science, Technology, and Environmental Science

**WHAT IS SCIENCE?** Which of the following statements are true?

- Science emphasizes facts or data.

- Science establishes absolute truth about nature.

- Science has a method—a how-to scheme—for learning about nature.

- Science emphasizes logic over creativity, imagination, and intuition.

The answer is that they are all false or mostly false. Let's see why.

**Science** is an attempt to discover order in nature and then use that knowledge to make predictions or projections about what will happen in nature. In this search for order scientists try to answer two basic questions: **(1)** *What events happen in nature over and over with the same results?* and **(2)** *How or why do things happen this way?*

**WHAT DO SCIENTISTS DO?** Scientists collect **scientific data**, or facts, by making observations and taking measurements, but this is not the main purpose of science. As French scientist Henri Poincaré put it, "Science is built up of facts, but a collection of facts is no more science than a heap of stones is a house."

Scientists try to describe what is happening by organizing data into a generalization or scientific law. Thus scientific data are stepping stones to a **scientific law**, a description of the orderly behavior observed in nature—a summary of what we find happening in nature over and over in the same way. For example, after making thousands of measurements involving changes in matter, chemists concluded that in any physical change (such as converting liquid water to water vapor) or any chemical change (such as burning coal) no matter is created or destroyed. This summary of what we always observe in nature is called the *law of conservation of matter*, as discussed in more detail later in this chapter.

Scientists then try to explain how or why things happen the way a scientific law describes. For example, why does the law of conservation of matter work? To answer such questions, investigators develop a **scientific hypothesis**, an educated guess that explains a scientific law or certain scientific facts. More than 2,400 years ago Greek philosophers proposed that all matter is composed of tiny particles called atoms, but they had no experimental evidence to back up their *atomic hypothesis*.

If many experiments by different scientists support the hypothesis, it becomes a **scientific theory**—a well-tested and widely accepted scientific hypothesis. During the last two centuries scientists have done experiments that elevated the atomic hypothesis to the *atomic theory of matter*. This theory, in turn, explains the law of conservation of matter with the idea that in any physical or chemical change no atoms can be created or destroyed.

**ARE SCIENTIFIC THEORIES AND LAWS TRUE?** A favorite debating and advertising trick is to claim that something "has not been scientifically proved." But scientists can't establish absolute proof or truth. They are concerned only with how useful a theory or

a law is in describing, explaining, and predicting what happens in nature.

Science can disprove things, but it can never prove anything. Scientific laws and theories are based on statistical probabilities, not on certainties. Science gives us information in the following form: If we do so-and-so (say, add certain chemicals to the atmosphere at particular rates), there is a certain chance that we will cause various effects (such as change the climate or deplete ozone in the stratosphere). Scientific hypotheses and theories are also dynamic ideas that are constantly tested and challenged. Often they may be modified, or even discarded, because of new data or more useful explanations of current data.

Science advances by debate, argument, speculation, and controversy. Disputes among scientists are what the media usually report. Such disagreements make juicier stories, but what's really important is the *consensus* among scientists about various scientific ideas and issues. This substantial agreement—the real knowledge of science—rarely gets reported, giving the public a false idea of the nature of science and of scientific knowledge.

**SCIENTIFIC METHODS** The ways scientists gather data and formulate and test scientific hypotheses, laws, and theories are called **scientific methods**. A scientific method is a set of questions with no particular rules for answering them. The questions a scientist attempts to answer are these:

- What questions about nature should I try to answer?

- What relevant facts are already known, and what new data should I collect?

- How should I collect these data?

- How can I organize and analyze the data I have collected to develop a pattern of order or scientific law?

- How can I come up with a hypothesis to explain the law and use it to predict some new facts?

- Is this the simplest and only reasonable hypothesis?

- What new experiments should I run to test the hypothesis (and modify it if necessary) so it can become a scientific theory?

New discoveries happen in many ways. Some follow a data → law → hypothesis → theory sequence. Other times scientists simply follow a hunch or a bias and then do experiments to test it. Some discoveries occur when an experiment gives totally unexpected results and the scientist insists on finding out what happened. So, in reality, there are many methods of science rather than one scientific method.

Q: In terms of resource use and environmental impact, which is the most overpopulated country in the world?

Trying to discover order in nature requires logical reasoning, but it also requires imagination and intuition. As Albert Einstein once said, "Imagination is more important than knowledge, and there is no completely logical way to a new scientific idea." Intuition and creativity are as important in science as they are in poetry, art, music, and other great adventures of the human spirit that awaken us to the wonder, mystery, and beauty of the universe, the earth, and life.

**IS SCIENCE ALWAYS OBJECTIVE?** Science is often held up as being value-free and neutral, with scientists not allowing their personal beliefs and biases or outside pressures to influence their work. But scientists are ordinary human beings, with conscious and unconscious biases, values, opinions, and financial and other needs that can influence what questions they ask of nature, how they design experiments, and how they interpret the results. Open publishing of results and mutual criticism among scientists help correct for biases more than in other professions, but they do not remove them.

Doing most science today is so expensive that few scientists can finance their own research. This explains why about half the world's scientists work on military-related research and development and more than a third work directly or indirectly for large corporations. Much of this work is not published and thus is not open to evaluation and correction. If these scientists challenge or decline to publicly support the positions of organizations they depend on for a living, they may face unemployment or loss of research grants.

**WHAT IS TECHNOLOGY?** **Technology** is the creation of new products and processes that are supposed to improve our chances for survival, our comfort level, and our quality of life. In many cases technology develops from known scientific laws and theories. Scientists invented the laser, for example, by applying knowledge about the internal structure of atoms. Applied scientific knowledge about chemistry has given us nylon, pesticides, laundry detergents, pollution control devices, and countless other products.

Some technologies arose long before anyone understood the underlying scientific principles. For example, aspirin, extracted from the bark of a willow tree, relieved pain and fever long before anyone found out how it did so. Similarly, photography was invented by people who had no inkling of its chemistry. And farmers crossbred new strains of livestock and crops long before biologists understood the principles of genetics.

Science and technology differ in the way the information and ideas they produce are shared. Many of the results of scientific research are published and passed around freely to be tested, challenged, verified, or modified, a process that strengthens the validity of scientific knowledge and helps expose cheaters. In contrast, technological discoveries are often kept secret until the new process or product is patented.

**ENVIRONMENTAL SCIENCE: A HOLISTIC SCIENCE** For the past 250 years scientists have studied nature mostly by examining successively lower levels of organization of matter (Figure 3-2). This approach is called *reductionism*. It is based on the belief that if we can understand *subatomic particles, atoms, and molecules*, then we can work our way up the ladder of organizational levels of matter to understand *organisms* (distinct forms of life classified as species), *populations* (individuals of the same species living in a particular place or habitat), *communities* (populations of all species living in a particular habitat), *ecosystems* (a community of different species interacting with one another and their nonliving environment), the *ecosphere* (the collection of all of Earth's ecosystems), and eventually the *universe*.

The reductionist approach has taught us much about nature, but it provides an incomplete picture. Each higher level of organization of matter has properties that cannot be predicted or understood merely by understanding the lower levels that make up its structure. Even if you learn all there is to know about a particular tree, for example, you will know only a small part of how a forest works, and even less about the interactions between the forest and other living and nonliving parts of the environment.

The science of ecology has shown the need for combining reductionism with *holism* (sometimes spelled "wholism")—an attempt to describe all properties of a level of organization, not merely those based on the lower levels of organization that make up its underlying structure. This approach also attempts to understand and describe how the various levels of organization interact with one another and with their constantly changing environments. This challenging and incredibly complex task requires research and cooperation among disciplines. Unfortunately such research is rare, because most of the jobs and grants in scientific disciplines reward those who do specialized research in their disciplines.

**Environmental science** is the study of how we and other species interact with one another and with the nonliving environment of matter and energy. It is a holistic *physical and social science* that uses and integrates knowledge from physics, chemistry, biology (especially ecology), geology, geography, resource technology and engineering, resource conservation and management, demography (the study of population

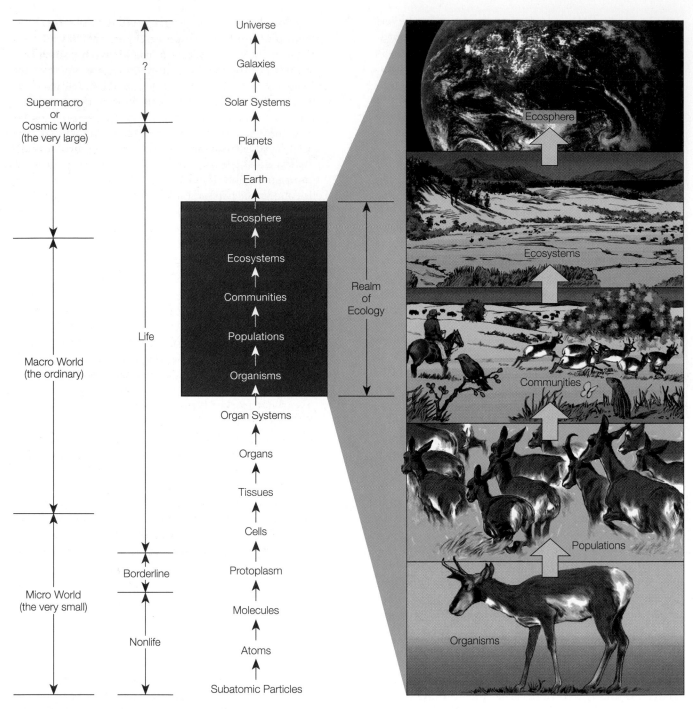

**Figure 3-2** Levels of organization of matter, according to size and function. This is one way scientists classify patterns of matter found in nature.

dynamics), economics, politics, and ethics. In other words, it is a study of how everything works and interacts—a study of connections in the common home of all living things.

### SCIENCE, TECHNOLOGY, AND THE FUTURE

Advances in science and technology have clearly improved the lives of many people. This progress, however, has also produced unforeseen effects, such as pol-

lution, that diminish the quality of our lives and threaten some of Earth's life support systems.

Our challenge as a society is to learn how to use scientific knowledge and technology to sustain the earth for humans and other species, and to improve the quality of life for all people—not to plunder the planet for short-term economic gain. This means that scientists and technologists need to consider the possible short- and long-range implications of their research, air these thoughts, and engage the public and decision makers in an ongoing debate about the ends that science should serve. To help achieve this goal, the education of all scientists and engineers should include courses on holistic and integrative thinking and on Earth ethics.

It's also important for nonscientists to have a basic knowledge of how nature works, because most decisions about how to use science and technology are made by nonscientists, usually with advice from scientists. Decision makers in business and government must have enough general knowledge of science and technology to ask tough questions of scientists and engineers, evaluate the answers, and make difficult decisions, usually with incomplete information.

<table>
<tr><td>3-2</td><td>

## Matter: Forms, Structure, and Quality
</td></tr>
</table>

**NATURE'S BUILDING BLOCKS: CHEMICAL AND PHYSICAL FORMS OF MATTER**   Matter is anything that has mass (the amount of material in an object) and takes up space. It includes the solids, liquids, and gases around you and within your body. Matter is found in three *chemical forms*: **elements** (the distinctive building blocks of matter that make up every material substance), **compounds** (two or more different elements held together in fixed proportions by attractive forces called *chemical bonds*), and **mixtures** (combinations of elements, compounds, or both).

All matter is built from the 109 known chemical elements. Ninety-two of them occur naturally, and the other 17 have been synthesized in laboratories. Each of these elements has a size, an internal structure, and other properties that make it unique, just as each of the 26 letters in the English alphabet is different from all the others. To simplify things, chemists represent each element by a one- or two-letter symbol, for example, hydrogen (H), carbon (C), oxygen (O), nitrogen (N), phosphorus (P), sulfur (S), chlorine (Cl), fluorine (F), bromine (Br), sodium (Na), calcium (Ca), and uranium (U).

If you had a super microscope to look at elements and compounds, you would discover that they are made up of three types of building blocks: **atoms** (the smallest unit of matter that is unique to a particular element), **ions** (electrically charged atoms), and **molecules** (combinations of atoms of the same or different elements held together by chemical bonds). Since ions and molecules are formed from atoms, atoms are the ultimate building blocks for all matter.

Some elements are found in nature as molecules. Examples are nitrogen and oxygen, which make up about 99% of the volume of the air we breathe. Two atoms of nitrogen (N) combine to form a nitrogen gas molecule with the shorthand formula $N_2$ (read as "N-two"). The subscript after the symbol of the element gives the number of atoms of that element in a molecule. Similarly most of the oxygen in the atmosphere exists as $O_2$ (read as "O-two") molecules. A small amount of oxygen, found mostly in the second layer of the atmosphere (stratosphere), exists as $O_3$ (read as "O-three") molecules; this type of oxygen is called *ozone*.

Elements can combine to form an almost limitless number of compounds, just as the letters of our alphabet have been combined to form almost a million English words. So far, chemists have identified more than 10 million compounds.

Matter is also found in three *physical states*: solid, liquid, and gas. Water, for example, exists as ice, liquid water, and water vapor depending on its temperature and pressure. The differences among the three physical states of a sample of matter are in the relative orderliness of its atoms, ions, or molecules, with solids having the most orderly arrangement and gases the least orderly.

**ATOMS AND IONS**   If you increased the magnification of your supermicroscope, you would find that each different type of atom is composed of a certain number of *subatomic particles*. The main building blocks of an atom are positively charged **protons** (represented by the symbol *p*), uncharged **neutrons** (*n*), and negatively charged **electrons** (*e*). Many other subatomic particles have been identified in recent years, but they need not concern us here.

Each atom consists of a relatively small center, or **nucleus**, containing protons and neutrons, and one or more electrons in rapid motion somewhere around the nucleus. We can describe electrons only in terms of the probability that they might be at various locations outside the nucleus.

The distinguishing feature of an atom of any given element is the number of protons in its nucleus, called its **atomic number**. The simplest element, hydrogen (H), has only 1 proton in its nucleus, so its atomic number is 1. Carbon (C), with 6 protons, has an atomic number of 6; uranium (U), a much larger atom, has 92 protons and an atomic number of 92.

Atoms normally have the same number of positively charged protons and negatively charged electrons and thus do not carry an electrical charge. For example, an uncharged atom of hydrogen has one positively charged proton in its nucleus and one negatively charged electron outside its nucleus. Similarly, each atom of uranium has 92 protons in its nucleus and 92 electrons outside.

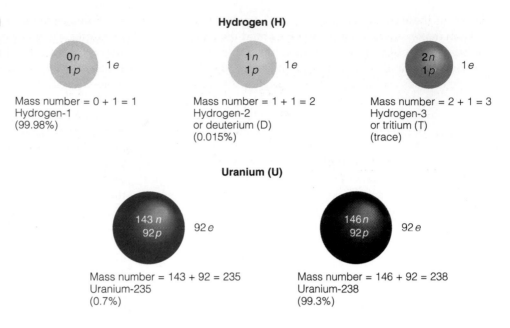

**Figure 3-3** Isotopes of hydrogen and uranium. All isotopes of hydrogen have an atomic number of 1 because each has one proton in its nucleus; similarly, all uranium isotopes have an atomic number of 92. However, each isotope of these elements has a different mass number because its nucleus contains a different number of neutrons. Figures in parentheses show the percent abundance by weight of each isotope in a natural sample of the element.

**Hydrogen (H)**

$0n$
$1p$  $1e$

Mass number = 0 + 1 = 1
Hydrogen-1
(99.98%)

$1n$
$1p$  $1e$

Mass number = 1 + 1 = 2
Hydrogen-2
or deuterium (D)
(0.015%)

$2n$
$1p$  $1e$

Mass number = 2 + 1 = 3
Hydrogen-3
or tritium (T)
(trace)

**Uranium (U)**

$143n$
$92p$  $92e$

Mass number = 143 + 92 = 235
Uranium-235
(0.7%)

$146n$
$92p$  $92e$

Mass number = 146 + 92 = 238
Uranium-238
(99.3%)

Protons and neutrons have essentially the same mass and are assigned a relative mass of 1. Each electron is assigned a relative mass of 0 because its mass is almost negligible compared with the mass of a proton or a neutron. This means that the approximate relative mass of an atom is determined by the number of neutrons plus the number of protons in its nucleus. This number is called its **mass number**. An atom of hydrogen with 1 proton and no neutrons has a mass number of 1, and an atom of uranium with 92 protons and 143 neutrons has a mass number of 235.

Although all atoms of an element have the same number of protons in their nuclei, they may have different numbers of uncharged neutrons in their nuclei and thus different mass numbers. These different forms of an element with the same atomic number but a different mass number are called **isotopes** of that element. Isotopes are identified by attaching their mass numbers to the name or symbol of the element. Hydrogen, for example, has three isotopes: hydrogen-1, or H-1; hydrogen-2, or H-2 (common name, deuterium); and hydrogen-3, or H-3 (common name, tritium). A natural sample of an element contains a mixture of its isotopes in a fixed proportion or percent abundance by weight (Figure 3-3).

Atoms of some elements can lose or gain one or more electrons to form *ions*: atoms or groups of atoms with one or more net positive (+) or negative (–) electrical charges. For example, an atom of sodium (Na) can lose one of its electrons and become a sodium ion with a positive charge of one ($Na^+$). An atom of chlorine (Cl) can gain an electron and become a chlorine ion with a negative charge of one ($Cl^-$). The number of positive or negative charges on an ion is shown as a superscript after the symbol for an atom or a group of atoms. Examples of other positive ions are calcium ions ($Ca^{2+}$) and ammonium ions ($NH_4^+$). Other common negative ions are nitrate ions ($NO_3^-$), sulfate ions ($SO_4^{2-}$), and phosphate ions ($PO_4^{3-}$).

**COMPOUNDS** Most matter exists as *compounds*—previously defined as combinations of different atoms or ions, of two or more different elements held together by chemical bonds. Chemists use a shorthand **chemical formula** to show the number of atoms (or ions) of each type found in the basic structural unit of a compound. The formula contains the symbols for each of the elements present and uses subscripts to show the number of atoms (or ions) of each element in the compound's basic structural unit.

Water, for example, is a *molecular compound*; each molecule consists of two hydrogen atoms chemically bonded to an oxygen atom, giving $H_2O$ (read as "H-two-O") molecules. Sodium chloride, or table salt, is an *ionic compound*, consisting of a network of oppositely charged ions ($Na^+$ and $Cl^-$) held together by the forces of attraction between opposite electric charges.

Table sugar, vitamins, plastics, aspirin, penicillin, and many other materials important to you and your lifestyle have one thing in common. They are *organic compounds*, containing atoms of the element carbon, usually combined with each other and with atoms of other elements such as hydrogen, oxygen, nitrogen, sulfur, phosphorus, chlorine, and fluorine.

Among the millions of known organic (carbon-based) compounds are:

Q: When did humans start shifting from hunting and gathering to agriculture?

- *Hydrocarbons*—compounds of carbon and hydrogen atoms. An example is methane ($CH_4$), the main component of natural gas.

- *Chlorinated hydrocarbons*—compounds of carbon, hydrogen, and chlorine atoms. Examples are DDT ($C_{14}H_9Cl_5$), an insecticide, and PCBs (such as $C_{12}H_5Cl_5$), oily compounds used as insulating materials in electric transformers.

- *Chlorofluorocarbons* (CFCs)—compounds of carbon, chlorine, and fluorine atoms. An example is Freon-12 ($CCl_2F_2$), used as a coolant in refrigerators and air conditioners, as an aerosol propellant, and as a foaming agent for making some plastics.

- *Simple carbohydrates* (simple sugars)—certain types of compounds of carbon, hydrogen, and oxygen atoms. An example is glucose ($C_6H_{12}O_6$), which most plants and animals break down in their cells to obtain energy.

Larger and more complex organic compounds, called *polymers*, consist of a number of basic structural or molecular units (*monomers*) linked together by chemical bonds. Some important types of organic polymers are:

- *Complex carbohydrates*—made up by linking together a number of simple-sugar molecules such as glucose. Examples are the complex starches in rice and potato plants.

- *Proteins*—produced in cells by linking together different numbers and sequences of about 20 different monomers, known as *amino acids*. Each amino acid contains carbon, hydrogen, oxygen, and nitrogen atoms, and a few also contain sulfur. Most animals, including humans, can make about 10 of these amino acids in their cells. Sufficient quantities of the other 10, known as *essential amino acids*, must be obtained from food intake to prevent protein deficiency diseases.

- *Nucleic acids*—made by linking together hundreds to thousands of four different types of monomers, called *nucleotides*, in different numbers and sequences. Nucleic acids contain carbon, hydrogen, oxygen, nitrogen, and phosphorus. Examples are various types of DNA and RNA in the cells of living organisms. A human cell contains 23 pairs of **chromosomes**, which together make up an individual's entire genetic endowment. Genetic information coded in the structure of DNA molecules found in your chromosomes is what makes you different from an oak leaf, an alligator, or a flea and from your mother and father. This information is contained in various sequences of nucleotides in parts of various cellular DNA molecules. These distinctive DNA segments are called **genes**. DNA molecules can replicate themselves and contain the instructions for assembling each new cell from a few kinds of "lifeless" molecules and for assembling the proteins each cell needs to survive and reproduce. RNA molecules help carry instructions provided by DNA molecules to parts of cells to produce proteins. DNA molecules can be viewed as a cell's administrators, proteins as its workforce, and RNA molecules as middle-level employees who carry and translate instructions from the administrator molecules needed to form the workforce molecules.

All other compounds are called *inorganic compounds*. Some of the inorganic compounds you will encounter in this book are sodium chloride (NaCl), water ($H_2O$), nitrous oxide ($N_2O$), nitric oxide (NO), carbon monoxide (CO), carbon dioxide ($CO_2$),* nitrogen dioxide ($NO_2$), sulfur dioxide ($SO_2$), ammonia ($NH_3$), sulfuric acid ($H_2SO_4$), and nitric acid ($HNO_3$).

**MATTER QUALITY** **Matter quality** is a measure of how useful a matter resource is, based on its availability and concentration. **High-quality matter** is organized and concentrated, and is usually found near the earth's surface. It has great potential for use as a matter resource. **Low-quality matter** is disorganized, dilute, or dispersed, and is often found deep underground or dispersed in the ocean or in the atmosphere. It usually has little potential for use as a matter resource (Figure 3-4).

An aluminum can is a more concentrated, higher-quality form of aluminum than aluminum ore with the same amount of aluminum. That's why it takes less energy, water, and money to recycle an aluminum can than to make a new can from aluminum ore.

**Entropy** is a measure of the disorder or randomness of a system. The greater the disorder of a sample of matter, the higher its entropy; the greater its order, the lower its entropy. Thus an aluminum can has a lower entropy (more order) than aluminum ore with the same amount of aluminum mixed with other materials. Similarly a piece of ice in which the water molecules are held in an ordered solid structure has a lower entropy (more order) than the highly dispersed water molecules in water vapor.

---

* Classifying compounds as organic or inorganic is somewhat arbitrary. All organic compounds contain one or more carbon atoms, but CO and $CO_2$ are classified as inorganic compounds.

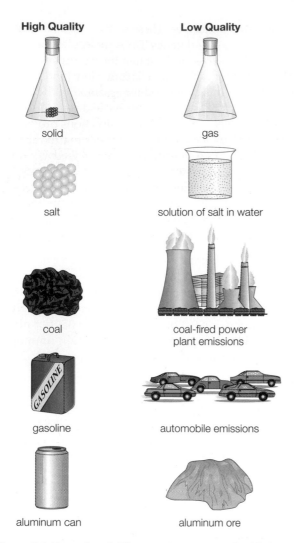

**High Quality**

solid

salt

coal

gasoline

aluminum can

**Low Quality**

gas

solution of salt in water

coal-fired power
plant emissions

automobile emissions

aluminum ore

**Figure 3-4** Examples of differences in matter quality. High-quality matter is fairly easy to get at and is concentrated. Low-quality matter is harder to get at and is more dispersed than high-quality matter.

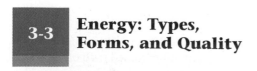

**3-3** | **Energy: Types, Forms, and Quality**

**TYPES** Like matter, energy affects every part of your life. You need it to keep your heart beating, to think, to breathe, to cook food, to travel by any method, and to warm or cool the buildings in which you live or work. Energy powers the factories, cars, bulldozers, airplanes, chain saws, giant power shovels, and electric motors and lights we use to improve our lives. Large amounts of energy are also used to extract metals from ores and to manufacture fertilizers, pesticides, plastics, CFCs, and other products.

**Energy** is the capacity to do work. You cannot pick up or touch energy, but you can use it to do work. You do work when you move matter, such as your arm or this book. Work or matter movement also is needed to boil liquid water and change it into steam or to burn natural gas to heat a house or cook food. Energy is also the heat that flows automatically from a hot object to a cold object. Touch a hot stove and you experience this energy flow in a painful way.

Energy comes in many forms: light; heat; electricity; chemical energy stored in the chemical bonds in coal, sugar, and other materials; moving matter such as water, wind (air masses), and joggers; and nuclear energy emitted from the nuclei of certain isotopes.

Scientists classify energy as either kinetic or potential. **Kinetic energy** is the energy that matter has because of its motion and mass. Wind (a moving mass of air), flowing streams, falling rocks, heat, electricity (flowing charged particles), and moving cars have kinetic energy.

**Heat** refers to the total kinetic energy of all the randomly moving atoms, ions, or molecules within a given substance, excluding the overall motion of the whole object. **Temperature** is a measure of the average speed of motion of the atoms, ions, or molecules in a sample of matter at a given moment. A substance can have a high heat content (much mass and many moving atoms, ions, or molecules) but a low temperature (low average molecular speed). For example, the total heat content of a lake is enormous, but its average temperature is low. On the other hand, a cup of hot coffee has a much lower heat content than a lake, but its temperature is much higher.

Radio waves, TV waves, microwaves, infrared radiation, visible light (the colors we see), ultraviolet radiation, X rays, gamma rays, and cosmic rays are forms of radiant energy traveling as waves and known as **electromagnetic radiation**. These forms of energy make up a wide band or spectrum of electromagnetic waves that differ in their wavelength (distance between two consecutive peaks or troughs) and energy content (Figure 3-5).

Cosmic rays, gamma rays, X rays, and ultraviolet radiation have enough energy to knock electrons from atoms and change them to positively charged ions. The resulting highly reactive electrons and ions can disrupt living cells, interfere with body processes, and cause many types of sickness, including various cancers. These potentially harmful forms of electromagnetic radiation are called **ionizing radiation**.

The other forms of electromagnetic radiation do not contain enough energy to form ions and are called **nonionizing radiation**. Some controversial evidence now suggests that long-term exposure to nonionizing radiation emitted by radios, TV sets, the video display terminals of computers, overhead electric power lines,

Q: Do scientists establish absolute proof or truth?

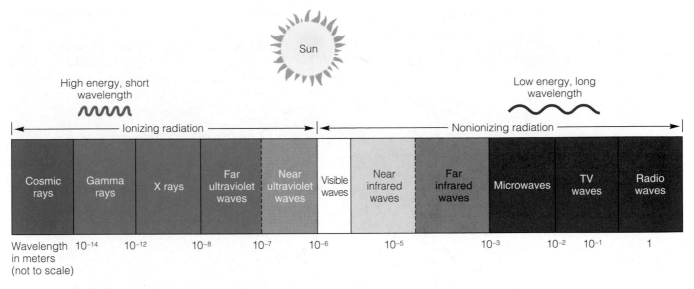

**Figure 3-5** The electromagnetic spectrum: the range of electromagnetic waves, which differ in wavelength (distance between successive peaks or troughs) and energy content.

electrically heated water beds, electric blankets, motors, and other electrical devices may also damage living cells.

**Potential energy** is stored energy that is potentially available for use. A rock held in your hand, an unlit stick of dynamite, still water behind a dam, and nuclear energy stored in the nuclei of atoms all have potential energy because of their position or the position of their parts. When you drop a rock held in your hand, its potential energy changes into kinetic energy. The chemical energy stored in molecules of gasoline and in the carbohydrates, proteins, and fats of food is also potential energy. When you burn gasoline in a car engine, the potential energy stored in the chemical bonds of its molecules changes into heat, light, and mechanical (kinetic) energy that propels the car.

An electric power plant burns some kind of fuel to make heat that is used to boil water into steam. The steam expands through turbines where its thermal energy (the energy of heat) is converted into kinetic energy. The turbines turn generators, and electromagnetic energy—electricity—comes out and is transmitted by wire to factories and buildings. When you flip a light switch you are at the end of the following energy chain: fuel → heat → steam → kinetic energy → electricity.

**ENERGY RESOURCES USED BY PEOPLE** *Some 99% of the energy used to heat Earth and all our buildings comes directly from the sun.* Without this direct input of solar energy Earth's average temperature would be –240°C (–400°F), and life as we know it would not have arisen. Solar energy also helps recycle the carbon, oxygen,

water, and other chemicals we and other organisms need to stay alive and healthy.

Broadly defined, **solar energy** includes both perpetual direct energy from the sun and several forms of energy produced indirectly by the sun's energy. These include wind, falling and flowing water (hydropower), and biomass (solar energy converted to chemical energy stored in the chemical bonds of organic compounds in trees and other plants). We use *wind turbines* and *hydroelectric power plants* to convert the indirect solar energy of wind and falling or flowing water into electricity.

*Passive* solar energy systems capture and store direct solar energy and use it to heat buildings and water without the use of mechanical devices. Examples are a well-insulated, fairly airtight house with large insulating windows that face the sun and the use of rock, concrete, or water to store and release heat slowly.

Direct solar energy can also be captured by *active* solar energy systems. For example, specially designed roof-mounted collectors concentrate direct solar energy; pumps then transfer this heat to water, to the interior of a building, or to insulated stone or water tanks that store and release heat slowly. *Solar cells* convert solar energy directly into electricity in one simple, nonpolluting step.

The 99% of energy that comes directly from the sun is not sold in the marketplace. The remaining 1%, the portion we generate to supplement the solar input, is *commercial energy* sold in the marketplace and *noncommercial energy* used by people who gather fuelwood, dung, and crop wastes for their own use. Most commercial energy comes from extracting and burn-

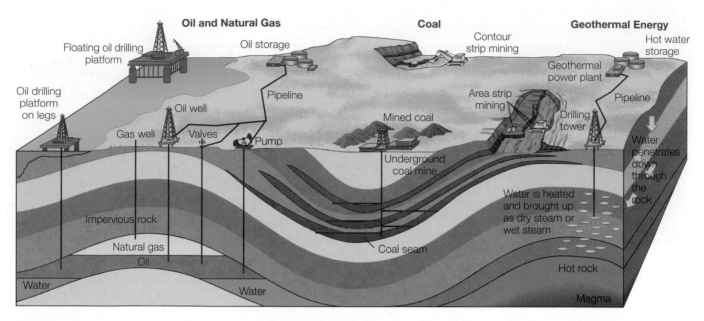

**Figure 3-6** Important energy resources from Earth's crust are geothermal energy, coal, oil, and natural gas. Uranium ore is also extracted from the crust and then processed to increase its concentration of uranium-235 (Figure 3-3), which can be used as a fuel in nuclear reactors to produce electricity.

ing mineral resources in the earth's crust (Figure 3-6), primarily fossil fuels. Most sources of noncommercial energy are potentially renewable biomass such as wood, but they may not be harvested sustainably.

MDCs and LDCs differ greatly in their sources of energy (Figure 3-7), the total amount used, and average energy use per person. The most important supplemental source of energy for LDCs is biomass—especially fuelwood—the main source of energy for heating and cooking for 70% of the people in LDCs. Much of this energy, which accounts for about 15% of the energy consumed by humans, is not sold in the marketplace. Within a few decades one-fourth of the world's population in MDCs may face an oil shortage, but one-third of the world's population in LDCs already faces a fuelwood shortage.

The United States is the world's largest user of energy: With only 4.7% of the population, it uses 25% of the commercial energy. By 1991 about 83% of the commercial energy used in the United States was provided by burning oil, coal, and natural gas (Figures 3-7 and 3-8). In contrast, India, with almost 16% of the world's people, uses only about 3% of the commercial energy. In 1993, 258 million Americans used more energy for air conditioning alone than 1.2 billion Chinese used for all purposes. The average American uses as much energy as 6 Mexicans, 153 Bangladeshis, or 500 Ethiopians.

The United States is also the world's largest waster of energy. Average per capita energy use in the United States is almost twice that of Japan and most western European MDCs (Figure 2-3).

**ENERGY QUALITY** Energy varies in its ability to do useful work. **Energy quality** is a measure of usefulness (Figure 3-9). **High-quality energy** is organized or concentrated and has great ability to perform useful work. That is, it has low entropy. Examples of these useful sources of energy are electricity, coal, gasoline, concentrated sunlight, nuclei of uranium-235, and heat concentrated in fairly small amounts of matter so that its temperature is high.

By contrast, **low-quality energy** is disorganized or dispersed and has little ability to do useful work. That is, it has high entropy. An example is heat dispersed in the moving molecules of a large amount of matter, such as the atmosphere or a large body of water, so that its temperature is relatively low. For instance, the total amount of heat stored in the Atlantic Ocean is greater than the amount of high-quality chemical energy stored in all the oil deposits of Saudi Arabia. However, the ocean's heat is so widely dispersed that it can't be used to move things or to heat things to high temperatures.

We use energy to accomplish certain tasks, each requiring a certain minimum energy quality (Figure 3-9). Electrical energy, which is very high-quality energy, is needed to run lights, electric motors, and electronic devices. We need high-quality mechanical energy to move a car, but we need only low-temperature air (less

**Q:** How much of the commercial energy used in the world comes from nonrenewable resources?

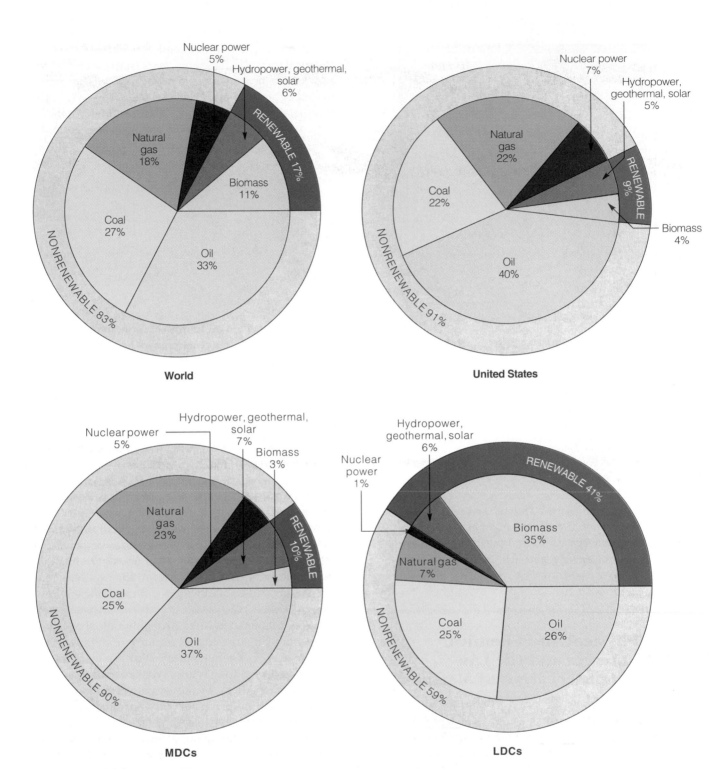

**Figure 3-7** Commercial energy use by source in 1991 for the world, the United States, MDCs, and LDCs. This amounts to only 1% of the energy used in the world. The other 99% of the energy used to heat Earth comes from the sun and is not sold in the marketplace. (Data from U.S. Department of Energy, British Petroleum, and Worldwatch Institute)

*Important*

**A:** 83% (78% from fossil fuels, 5% from nuclear power)

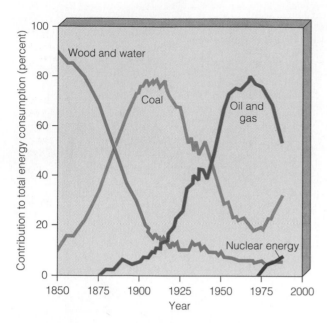

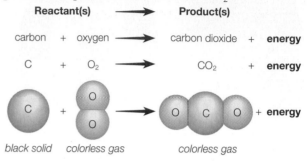

Energy is given off in this reaction, making coal a useful fuel. The reaction also shows how the burning of coal or any carbon-containing compounds, such as those in wood, natural gas, oil, and gasoline, adds carbon dioxide gas to the atmosphere.

**Figure 3-8** Shifts in the use of commercial energy resources in the United States since 1850. Shifts from wood to coal and then from coal to oil and natural gas have each taken about 50 years. Affordable oil is running out, and burning fossil fuels is the primary cause of air pollution and projected warming of the atmosphere. For these reasons most analysts believe we must make a new shift in energy resources over the next 50 years. (Data from U.S. Department of Energy)

in a chemical reaction. A chemical equation shows the chemical formulas for the *reactants* (starting chemicals) and the *products* (chemicals produced) with an arrow placed between them. For example, when coal burns completely, the solid carbon (C) it contains combines with oxygen gas ($O_2$) from the atmosphere to form the gaseous compound carbon dioxide ($CO_2$):

**THE LAW OF CONSERVATION OF MATTER: THERE IS NO AWAY** Earth loses some gaseous molecules to space, and it gains small amounts of matter from space, mostly in the form of occasional meteorites and cosmic dust. These losses and gains of matter are minute compared with Earth's total mass.

This means that *Earth has essentially all the matter it will ever have.* Fortunately over billions of years natural processes have evolved for continuously cycling key chemicals back and forth between the nonliving environment (soil, air, and water) and the living environment.

You, like most people, probably talk about consuming or using up material resources, but the truth is that we don't consume matter. We only use some of Earth's resources for a while. We take materials from the earth, carry them to another part of the globe, and process them into products. These products are used and then discarded, reused, or recycled.

We may change various elements and compounds from one physical or chemical form to another, but *in all physical and chemical changes we can't create or destroy any of the atoms involved. All we can do is rearrange them into different spatial patterns (physical changes) or different combinations (chemical changes).* This fact, based on many thousands of measurements of matter undergoing physical and chemical changes, is known as the **law of conservation of matter**. In describing chemical reactions chemists use a shorthand bookkeeping system to make sure no atoms are created or destroyed, as required by the law of conservation of matter (Spotlight, p. 60).

than 100°C) to heat homes and other buildings. It makes sense to match the quality of an energy source to the quality of energy needed to perform a particular task—this saves energy, and usually money (Guest Essay, p. 71).

## 3-4 Physical and Chemical Changes and the Law of Conservation of Matter

**PHYSICAL AND CHEMICAL CHANGES** A **physical change** is one that involves no change in chemical composition. For example, cutting a piece of aluminum foil into small pieces is a physical change—each cut piece is still aluminum. Changing a substance from one physical state to another is also a physical change. For example, when solid water, or ice, is melted or liquid water is boiled, none of the $H_2O$ molecules involved are altered; instead, the molecules are organized in different spatial patterns.

In a **chemical change**, or **chemical reaction**, there is a change in the chemical composition of the elements or compounds involved. Chemists use shorthand chemical equations to represent what happens

Q: How much of the commercial energy used in the United States comes from nonrenewable resources?

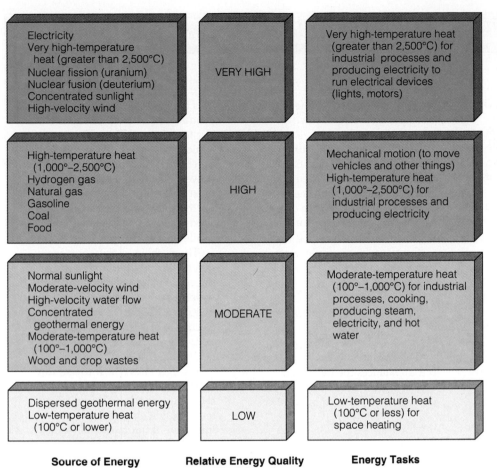

**Figure 3-9** Generalized ranking of the quality or usefulness of different sources of energy compared with the quality of energy needed to perform various energy tasks. *High-quality energy* is concentrated (low-entropy) and has great ability to perform useful work. *Low-quality energy* is dispersed (high-entropy) and has little ability to do useful work. To avoid unnecessary energy waste, it's best to match the quality of an energy source with the quality of energy needed to perform a task.

| Source of Energy | Relative Energy Quality (Usefulness) | Energy Tasks |
|---|---|---|
| Electricity<br>Very high-temperature heat (greater than 2,500°C)<br>Nuclear fission (uranium)<br>Nuclear fusion (deuterium)<br>Concentrated sunlight<br>High-velocity wind | VERY HIGH | Very high-temperature heat (greater than 2,500°C) for industrial processes and producing electricity to run electrical devices (lights, motors) |
| High-temperature heat (1,000°–2,500°C)<br>Hydrogen gas<br>Natural gas<br>Gasoline<br>Coal<br>Food | HIGH | Mechanical motion (to move vehicles and other things)<br>High-temperature heat (1,000°–2,500°C) for industrial processes and producing electricity |
| Normal sunlight<br>Moderate-velocity wind<br>High-velocity water flow<br>Concentrated geothermal energy<br>Moderate-temperature heat (100°–1,000°C)<br>Wood and crop wastes | MODERATE | Moderate-temperature heat (100°–1,000°C) for industrial processes, cooking, producing steam, electricity, and hot water |
| Dispersed geothermal energy<br>Low-temperature heat (100°C or lower) | LOW | Low-temperature heat (100°C or less) for space heating |

The law of conservation of matter means that there is no "away": *Everything we think we have thrown away is still here with us in one form or another.* We can collect dust and soot from the smokestacks of industrial plants, but these solid wastes must then be put somewhere. We can remove substances from polluted water at a sewage treatment plant, but the gooey sludge must either be burned (producing some air pollution), buried (possibly contaminating underground water supplies), or cleaned up and applied to the land as fertilizer (dangerous if the sludge contains nondegradable toxic metals, such as lead and mercury). Tall smokestacks can reduce some types of local air pollution but can increase air pollution in distant downwind areas. Banning DDT in the United States but still selling it abroad means that it can come back to us as DDT residues in imported coffee, fruit, and other foods.

We can make the environment cleaner and convert some potentially harmful chemicals into less harmful, or even harmless, physical or chemical forms. Nevertheless, the law of conservation of matter means that we will always be faced with the problem of what to do with some quantity of wastes. By placing much greater emphasis on pollution prevention and waste reduction, however, we can greatly reduce the amount of wastes we add to the environment (Guest Essay, p. 41).

 **3-5** **Nuclear Changes**

**NATURAL RADIOACTIVITY** In addition to physical and chemical changes, matter can undergo a third type of change, known as a **nuclear change**. This occurs when nuclei of certain isotopes spontaneously change or are forced to change into one or more different isotopes.  Three types of nuclear change are natural radioactive decay, nuclear fission, and nuclear fusion.

The law of conservation of matter does not apply to nuclear changes because they convert a small but measurable amount of the mass in a nucleus into energy. This type of change is governed by the **law of conservation of matter and energy**: *In any nuclear change the total amount of matter and energy involved remains the same.*

**A:** 91% (83% from fossil fuels, 8% from nuclear power)

A chemical equation must not violate the law of conservation of matter. This means that each side of the equation must have the same number of atoms of each element involved. If this is the case, the equation is said to be *balanced*. The equation illustrated earlier for the burning of carbon ($C + O_2 \rightarrow CO_2$) is balanced because there is one atom of carbon and two atoms of oxygen on each side of the equation.

If the number of atoms of one or more elements on each side of the equation differs, more than one of certain atoms or molecules must be involved so that no atoms are created or destroyed and the equation is balanced. The presence of more than one of a given atom or molecule is represented by placing whole numbers in front of the formula(s) in question. For example, when electricity is passed through water ($H_2O$), it can be broken down into hydrogen ($H_2$) and oxygen ($O_2$), as represented by the equation

$$H_2O \longrightarrow H_2 + O_2$$

2 hydrogens    2 hydrogens    2 oxygens
1 oxygen

**Unbalanced**

However, this equation is unbalanced because there is one atom of oxygen on the left and two on the right.

We can't change the subscripts of any of the formulas to balance this equation because then we would be changing the chemicals involved. Instead, we use different numbers of one or more of the molecules to balance the equation.

Suppose, for example, we use two water molecules:

$$2\,H_2O \longrightarrow H_2 + O_2$$

4 hydrogens    2 hydrogens    2 oxygens
2 oxygens

**Still Unbalanced**

This balances the oxygen atoms but unbalances the hydrogen atoms. We can correct this by producing two hydrogen molecules:

$$2\,H_2O \longrightarrow 2\,H_2 + O_2$$

4 hydrogens    4 hydrogens    2 oxygens
2 oxygens

**Balanced**

Now the equation is balanced, and the law of conservation of matter has not been violated.

The equation we just balanced may represent a chemical reaction that could dramatically change the world and your life. Hydrogen gas ($H_2$) is a clean-burning fuel that produces mostly water vapor when burned ($2\,H_2 + O_2 \rightarrow 2\,H_2O$). It could be used to replace oil and all other fossil fuels and nuclear power. This would also eliminate most of the world's air pollution. Furthermore, hydrogen would be produced from water, a widely available and cheap resource.

The problem is that there is not much $H_2$ around. It must be produced by passing energy through water. In other words, it takes energy to get this marvelous fuel. Using electricity or high temperatures to do this costs more than the hydrogen fuel is worth.

If we can learn how to use sunlight to decompose water, we will set in motion a *solar-hydrogen revolution* that will change the world as much as—if not more than—the Agricultural and Industrial Revolutions did. Scientists are hard at work trying to bring about this revolution. If they are successful, within your lifetime hydrogen may become the major fuel for powering vehicles, heating and cooling buildings, and providing electricity.

---

**Natural radioactive decay** is a nuclear change in which unstable isotopes spontaneously shoot out fast-moving particles, high-energy radiation, or both at a fixed rate. The unstable isotopes are called **radioactive isotopes**, or **radioisotopes**. This spontaneous process is called *radioactive decay*. It continues until the original isotope is changed into a new stable isotope, one that is not radioactive.

Radiation emitted by radioisotopes is damaging ionizing radiation. The most common form of ionizing energy released from radioisotopes is **gamma rays**, a form of high-energy electromagnetic radiation (Figure 3-5). High-speed particles emitted from the nuclei are a different form of ionizing radiation. The two most common types of ionizing particles emitted by radioactive isotopes are **alpha particles** (fast-moving, positively charged chunks of matter that consist of two protons and two neutrons) and **beta particles** (high-speed electrons). Figure 3-10 shows the relative penetrating power of alpha, beta, and gamma ionizing radiation. We are all exposed to small amounts of harmful ionizing radiation from both natural and human sources.

Each type of radioisotope decays spontaneously at a characteristic rate into a different isotope. This rate of decay can be expressed in terms of **half-life**—the time needed for *one-half* of the nuclei in a radioisotope to emit its radiation. Each radioisotope has a characteristic half-life, which may range from a few millionths of a second to several billion years (Table 3-1).

An isotope's half-life cannot be changed by temperature, pressure, chemical reactions, or any other factor. That is why radioactive dating is such a reliable method of determining the age of rocks, bones, and fossils.

Q: What percentage of the world's commercial energy is used by the United States?

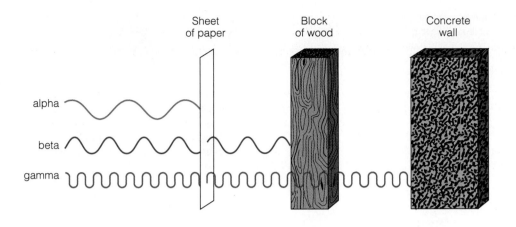

Sheet of paper

Block of wood

Concrete wall

alpha

beta

gamma

**Figure 3-10** The three principal types of ionizing radiation emitted by radioactive isotopes vary considerably in their penetrating power.

| Table 3-1 Half-Lives of Selected Radioisotopes | | |
|---|---|---|
| **Isotope** | **Half-Life** | **Radiation Emitted** |
| Potassium-42 | 12.4 hours | Alpha, beta |
| Iodine-131 | 8 days | Beta, gamma |
| Cobalt-60 | 5.27 years | Beta, gamma |
| Hydrogen-3 (tritium) | 12.5 years | Beta |
| Strontium-90 | 28 years | Beta |
| Carbon-14 | 5,370 years | Beta |
| Plutonium-239 | 24,000 years | Alpha, gamma |
| Uranium-235 | 710 million years | Alpha, gamma |
| Uranium-238 | 4.5 billion years | Alpha, gamma |

Half-life can also be used to estimate how long a sample of a radioisotope must be stored in a safe enclosure before it decays to what is considered a safe level. A general rule of thumb is that this takes about ten half-lives. Thus people would have to be protected from radioactive waste containing iodine-131 (which concentrates in the thyroid gland) for 80 days (10 x 8 days). Plutonium-239, which is produced in nuclear reactors and can cause lung cancer when inhaled in minute amounts, must be stored safely for 240,000 years (10 x 24,000 years)—six times longer than the latest version of our species has existed.

**NUCLEAR FISSION: SPLITTING NUCLEI** **Nuclear fission** is a nuclear change in which nuclei of certain isotopes with large mass numbers (such as uranium-235; Figure 3-3) are split apart into lighter nuclei when struck by neutrons; each fission releases two or three more neutrons and energy (Figure 3-11). Each of these neutrons, in turn, can cause an additional fission. For

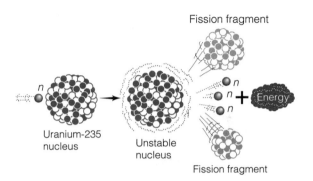

Fission fragment

$n$

Uranium-235 nucleus

Unstable nucleus

$n$
$n$
$n$
+ Energy

Fission fragment

**Figure 3-11** Fission of a uranium-235 nucleus by a neutron ($n$).

these multiple fissions to take place, there must be enough fissionable nuclei present to provide the **critical mass** needed for efficient capture of these neutrons.

Multiple fissions within a critical mass form a **chain reaction**, which releases an enormous amount of energy (Figure 3-12). Living cells can be damaged by the ionizing radiation released by the radioactive lighter nuclei and by high-speed neutrons produced by nuclear fission.

The fission process can be likened to filling the floor of a room with spring-loaded rat traps that throw two Ping-Pong balls into the air when they are sprung. If you open the door and throw a single Ping-Pong ball into the room and set off one trap, soon the room will be filled with a chain reaction of snapping traps and flying Ping-Pong balls—all caused by just one Ping-Pong ball (neutron).

In an atomic or nuclear fission bomb, an enormous amount of energy is released in a fraction of a second in an uncontrolled nuclear fission chain reaction. This reaction is initiated by an explosive charge, which suddenly pushes two masses of fissionable fuel together from all sides, causing the fuel to reach the critical mass needed for a chain reaction.

In the reactor of a nuclear electric power plant, the rate at which the nuclear fission chain reaction takes place is controlled, so that under normal operation

A: 25%

**Figure 3-12** A nuclear chain reaction initiated by one neutron triggering fission in a single uranium-235 nucleus. This shows only a few of the trillions of fissions caused when a single uranium-235 nucleus is split within a critical mass of uranium-235 nuclei. The elements krypton (Kr) and barium (Ba) shown here as fission fragments are only two of many possibilities.

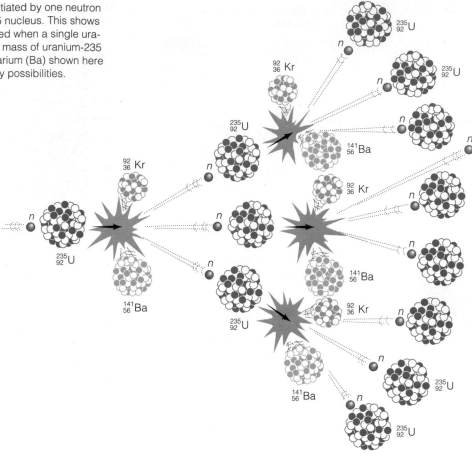

only one of each two or three neutrons released is used to split another nucleus. In conventional nuclear fission reactors nuclei of uranium-235 are split apart and release heat. The heat is used to produce high-pressure steam, which spins turbines, which in turn generate electricity.

**NUCLEAR FUSION: FORCING NUCLEI TO COMBINE** **Nuclear fusion** is a nuclear change in which two isotopes of light elements, such as hydrogen (Figure 3-3), are forced together at extremely high temperatures until they fuse to form a heavier nucleus, releasing energy in the process. Temperatures of at least 100 million°C are needed to force the positively charged nuclei (which strongly repel one another) to join together.

Nuclear fusion is much harder to initiate than nuclear fission, but once started, it releases far more energy per unit of fuel than does fission. Fusion of hydrogen nuclei to form helium nuclei is the source of energy in the sun and other stars.

After World War II the principle of *uncontrolled nuclear fusion* was used to develop extremely powerful hydrogen, or thermonuclear, weapons. These weapons

use the D-T fusion reaction, in which a hydrogen-2, or deuterium (D), nucleus and a hydrogen-3, or tritium (T), nucleus are fused to form a larger, helium-4 nucleus, a neutron, and energy (Figure 3-13).

Scientists have also tried to develop *controlled nuclear fusion*, in which the D-T reaction is used to produce heat that can be converted into electricity. Despite more than 40 years of research, however, this process is still at the laboratory stage. Even if it becomes technologically and economically feasible, it probably won't be a practical source of energy until 2050 or later.

## 3-6 The First and Second Laws of Energy

**FIRST LAW OF ENERGY: YOU CAN'T GET SOMETHING FOR NOTHING** After making millions of measurements, scientists have observed energy being

Q: How much of the commercial energy used in the United States is wasted?

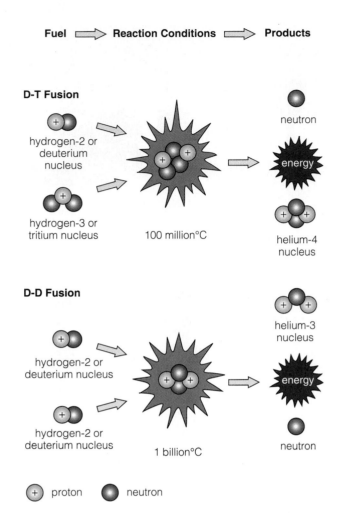

Fuel $\Longrightarrow$ Reaction Conditions $\Longrightarrow$ Products

**D-T Fusion**

hydrogen-2 or
deuterium
nucleus

hydrogen-3 or
tritium nucleus

100 million°C

neutron

energy

helium-4
nucleus

**D-D Fusion**

hydrogen-2 or
deuterium nucleus

hydrogen-2 or
deuterium nucleus

1 billion°C

helium-3
nucleus

energy

neutron

+ proton      neutron

**Figure 3-13** The deuterium-tritium (D-T) and deuterium-deuterium (D-D) nuclear fusion reactions, which take place at extremely high temperatures.

changed from one form to another in physical and chemical changes, but they have never been able to detect any energy being created or destroyed. This summary of what happens in nature is called the **law of conservation of energy**, also known as the **first law of energy** or **first law of thermodynamics**. This law does not apply to nuclear changes, however, where energy can be produced from small amounts of matter. This law means that when one form of energy is converted to another form in any physical or chemical change, energy input always equals energy output: *We can't get something for nothing in terms of energy quantity.*

**SECOND LAW OF ENERGY: YOU CAN'T BREAK EVEN** Because the first law of energy states that energy can be neither created nor destroyed, you might think that there will always be enough energy; yet, if you fill a car's tank with gasoline and drive around, or if you use a flashlight battery until it is dead, you have

lost something. If it isn't energy, what is it? The answer is energy quality (Figure 3-9).

Countless experiments have shown that in any conversion of energy from one form to another, there is always a decrease in energy quality (the amount of useful energy). These findings are expressed in the **second law of energy**, or the **second law of thermodynamics**: When energy is changed from one form to another, some of the useful energy is always degraded to lower-quality, more dispersed (higher-entropy), less useful energy. This degraded energy is usually in the form of heat, which flows into the environment and is dispersed by the random motion of air or water molecules. In other words *we can't break even in terms of energy quality because energy always goes from a more useful to a less useful form.* The more energy we use, the more low-grade energy (heat), or entropy, we add to the environment. No one has ever found a violation of this fundamental scientific law.

Consider three examples of the second energy law in action. First, when a car is driven, only about 10% of the high-quality chemical energy available in its gasoline fuel is converted into mechanical energy to propel the vehicle and into electrical energy to run its electrical systems. The remaining 90% is degraded heat that is released into the environment and eventually lost into space. Second, when electrical energy flows through filament wires in an incandescent light bulb, it is changed into about 5% useful light and 95% low-quality heat that flows into the environment. What we call a light bulb is really a heat bulb. A third example of the degradation of energy quality in living systems is illustrated in Figure 3-14.

The second energy law also means that *we can never recycle or reuse high-quality energy to perform useful work.* Once the concentrated energy in a piece of food, a liter of gasoline, a lump of coal, or a chunk of uranium is released, it is degraded to low-quality heat that becomes dispersed in the environment. We can heat air or water at a low temperature and upgrade it to high-quality energy, but the second energy law tells us that it will take more high-quality energy to do this than we get in return.

**LIFE AND THE SECOND ENERGY LAW** Life represents a creation and maintenance of ordered structures. Thus you might be tempted to think that life is not governed by the second law of thermodynamics.

However, to form and preserve the highly ordered arrangement of molecules and the organized network of chemical changes in your body, you must continually get and use high-quality matter and energy resources from your surroundings. As you use these resources, you add low-quality (high-entropy) heat and waste matter to your surroundings. For example,

A: 84% (43% of this energy is unnecessarily wasted)

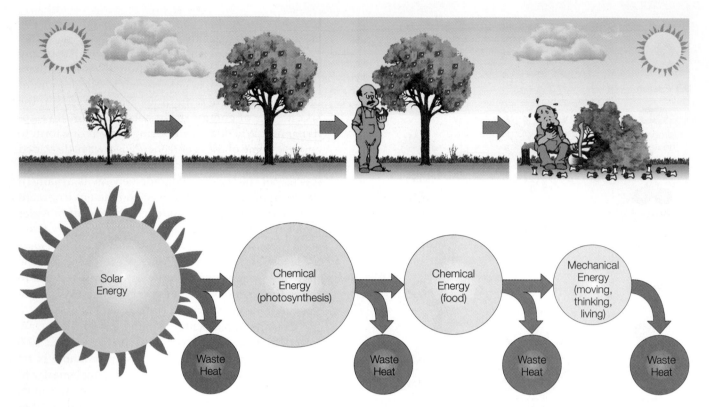

**Figure 3-14** The second energy law in action in living systems. When energy is changed from one form to another, some of the initial input of high-quality energy is degraded, usually to low-quality heat, which disperses in the environment.

your body continuously gives off heat equal to that of a 100-watt light bulb; this is the reason a closed room full of people gets warm. You also continuously give off molecules of carbon dioxide gas and water vapor, which become dispersed in the atmosphere.

Planting, growing, processing, and cooking food all require high-quality energy and matter resources that add low-quality (high-entropy) heat and waste materials to the environment. In addition, enormous amounts of low-quality heat and waste matter are added to the environment when concentrated deposits of minerals and fuels are extracted from the earth's crust, processed, and used to make roads, clothes, shelter, and other items or burned to heat or cool buildings or to transport you. *All forms of life are tiny pockets of order (low entropy) maintained by creating a sea of disorder (high entropy) in their environment.*

Because of the second energy law, the more energy we use (and waste), the more disorder (entropy) we create in the environment. The second law of energy tells us that we can't avoid this *entropy trap*, but we can reduce or minimize our production of entropy. This is the reason that reducing energy waste and switching from harmful nonrenewable energy resources to less harmful renewable and perpetual energy resources are the keys to a sustainable future for us and many other species.

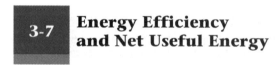 **Energy Efficiency and Net Useful Energy**

**INCREASING ENERGY EFFICIENCY** You may be surprised to learn that only 16% of all commercially produced energy that flows through the U.S. economy performs useful work or is used to make petrochemicals, which in turn are used to produce plastics, medicines, and many other products (Figure 3-15). This means that *84% of all commercial energy used in the United States is wasted.* About 41% of this energy is wasted automatically because of the degradation of energy quality imposed by the second energy law. However, about 43% is wasted unnecessarily mostly by using fuel-wasting motor vehicles, furnaces, and other devices and by living and working in leaky, poorly insulated buildings.

Much of this unnecessary energy waste can be eliminated by increasing the **energy efficiency** of the energy conversion devices we use (Guest Essay, p. 71). This is the percentage of total energy input that does useful work and is not converted to low-quality, essentially useless heat in an energy conversion system. The energy conversion devices we use vary considerably in their energy efficiencies (Figure 3-16).

Q: How much of the energy input of an incandescent light bulb is converted to light?

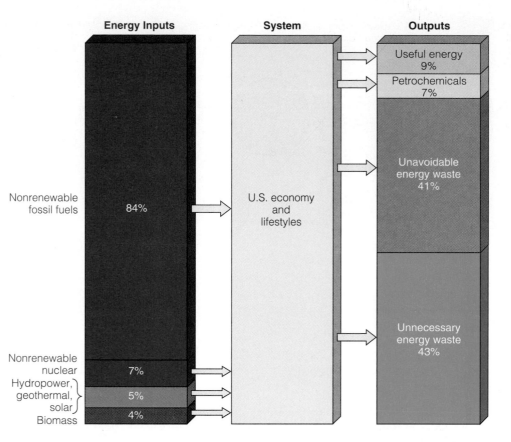

**Energy Inputs**

Nonrenewable fossil fuels — 84%

Nonrenewable nuclear — 7%

Hydropower, geothermal, solar — 5%

Biomass — 4%

**System**

U.S. economy and lifestyles

**Outputs**

Useful energy 9%

Petrochemicals 7%

Unavoidable energy waste 41%

Unnecessary energy waste 43%

**Figure 3-15** Flow of commercial energy through the U.S. economy. Note that only 16% of all commercial energy used in the United States ends up performing useful tasks or is converted to petrochemicals. The rest either is automatically and unavoidably wasted because of the second law of energy (41%) or is wasted unnecessarily (43%).

We can save energy and money by buying the most energy-efficient home heating systems, water heaters, cars, air conditioners, refrigerators, and other household appliances available. The energy-efficient models may cost more, but in the long run they usually save money by having a lower **life-cycle cost**: initial cost plus lifetime operating costs.

The net efficiency of the entire energy delivery process for a space heater, water heater, or car is determined by finding the efficiency of each step in the energy conversion process. For example, the sequence of energy-using and energy-wasting steps involved in using electricity produced from fossil or nuclear fuels is extraction → transportation → processing → transportation to power plant → electric generation → transmission → end use.

Figure 3-17 shows how net energy efficiency is determined for heating a well-insulated home **(1)** with electricity produced at a nuclear power plant, transported by wire to the home, and converted to heat (electric resistance heating), and **(2)** passively with an input of direct solar energy through windows facing the sun, with heat stored in rocks or water for slow release. This analysis shows that the process of converting the high-quality energy in nuclear fuel to high-quality heat at several thousand degrees, converting this heat to high-quality electricity, and then using the electricity to

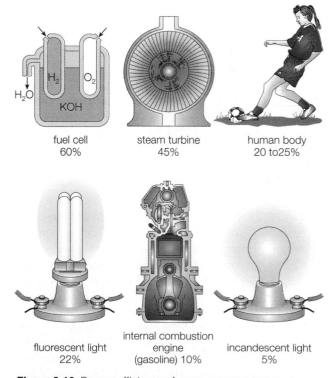

fuel cell 60%

steam turbine 45%

human body 20 to25%

fluorescent light 22%

internal combustion engine (gasoline) 10%

incandescent light 5%

**Figure 3-16** Energy efficiency of some common energy conversion devices.

A: 5% (the rest is heat, explaining why these light bulbs are really heat bulbs)

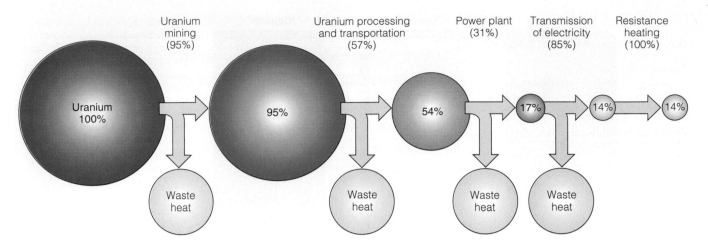

**Electricity from Nuclear Power Plant**

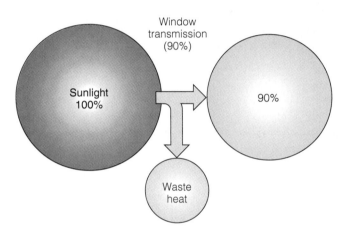

**Passive Solar**

**Figure 3-17** Comparison of net energy efficiency for two types of space heating. The cumulative net efficiency is obtained by multiplying the percentage shown inside the circle for each step by the energy efficiency for that step (shown in parentheses). Usually, the greater the number of steps in an energy conversion process, the lower its net energy efficiency. About 86% of the energy used to provide space heating by electricity produced at a nuclear power plant is wasted. By contrast, with passive solar heating, only about 10% of incoming solar energy is wasted.

provide low-quality heat for warming a house to only about 20°C (68°F), is extremely wasteful of high-quality energy. Burning coal, or any fossil fuel, at a power plant to supply electricity for space heating is also inefficient. By contrast, it is much less wasteful to use a passive or active solar heating system to obtain low-quality heat from the environment, store it in stone or water, and—if necessary—raise its temperature slightly to provide space heating or household hot water.

Using high-quality electrical energy to provide low-quality heating for living space or household water is like using a chain saw to cut butter or a sledgehammer to kill a fly. As a general rule, we should *match energy quality to energy tasks*: Don't use

high-quality energy to do a job that can be done with lower-quality energy (Figure 3-9).

Figure 3-18 lists the net energy efficiencies for a variety of space-heating systems. It shows that the most energy-efficient form of space heating is a superinsulated house. The most wasteful (least efficient) and most expensive way to heat a house is with electricity produced by a coal-burning power plant or a nuclear power plant. To prevent buildup of indoor air pollutants, any house should be equipped with an air-to-air heat exchanger. Use of such a device reduces slightly each of the net energy efficiencies shown in Figure 3-18.

Heat pumps are useful for space heating in warm climates (where they aren't needed much), but not in

**Q:** How much of the energy input of a screw-in fluorescent light bulb produces light?

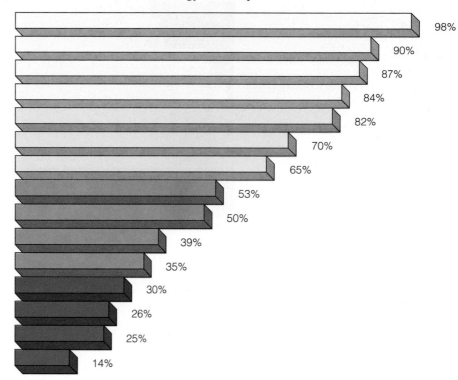

**Net Energy Efficiency**

| | |
|---|---|
| Superinsulated house (100% of heat)(R-43) | 98% |
| Passive solar (100% of heat) | 90% |
| Passive solar (50% of heat) plus high-efficiency natural gas furnace (50% of heat) | 87% |
| Natural gas with high-efficiency furnace | 84% |
| Electric resistance heating (electricity from hydroelectric power plant) | 82% |
| Natural gas with typical furnace | 70% |
| Passsive solar (50% of heat) plus high-efficiency wood stove (50% of heat ) | 65% |
| Oil furnace | 53% |
| Electric heat pump (electricity from coal-fired power plant) | 50% |
| High-efficiency wood stove | 39% |
| Active solar | 35% |
| Electric heat pump (electricity from nuclear plant) | 30% |
| Typical wood stove | 26% |
| Electric resistance heating (electricity from coal-fired power plant) | 25% |
| Electric resistance heating (electricity from nuclear plant) | 14% |

**Figure 3-18** Net energy efficiencies for various ways to heat an enclosed space such as a house. The most energy-efficient way to heat space is to build a *superinsulated house*. Such a house is so heavily insulated that even when winter temperatures fall to –40°C (–40°F), all of its space heating can usually be supplied by a combination of passive solar gain (about 59%), waste heat from appliances (33%), and body heat from occupants (8%).

cold climates because they then switch to wasteful, costly electric resistance heating. Also, most heat pumps in their air conditioning mode are much less efficient than many available stand-alone air conditioning units. Most heat pumps also require expensive repair every few years.

A similar analysis of net energy efficiency shows that the least efficient and most expensive way to heat water for washing and bathing is to use electricity produced by any type of power plant. The most efficient method is to use a tankless instant water heater fired by natural gas or liquefied petroleum gas (LPG). Such heaters are about the size of a bookcase loudspeaker and burn fuel only when the hot-water faucet is turned on. They heat the water instantly as it flows through a small burner chamber and provide hot water only when, and as long as, it is needed. Tankless heaters are widely used in many parts of Europe and are slowly beginning to appear in the United States. A well-insulated, conventional natural gas or LPG water heater is also fairly efficient, although all conventional natural gas and electric resistance heaters keep a large tank of water hot all day and night and can run out after a long shower or two.

In 1991 the average price of obtaining 250,000 kilocalories (1 million Btus) for heating space or water in the United States was $6.05 using natural gas, $7.56 using kerosene, $9.30 using oil, $9.74 using propane, and $24.15 using electricity. As these numbers suggest, if you like to throw away hard-earned dollars, use electricity to heat your house and bath water.

Perhaps the three least efficient energy-using devices in widespread use today are **(1)** incandescent light bulbs (which waste 95% of the energy input), **(2)** vehicles with internal combustion engines (which waste 90% of the energy in their fuel), and **(3)** nuclear power plants producing electricity for space or water heating (which waste 86% of the energy in their nuclear fuel; Figure 3-17). These devices were developed when energy was cheap and plentiful. To help sustain the earth and ourselves, we will have to replace them or greatly improve their energy efficiency (Guest Essay, p. 71).

**USING WASTE HEAT** We cannot recycle high-quality energy, but we can slow the rate at which waste heat flows into the environment when high-quality

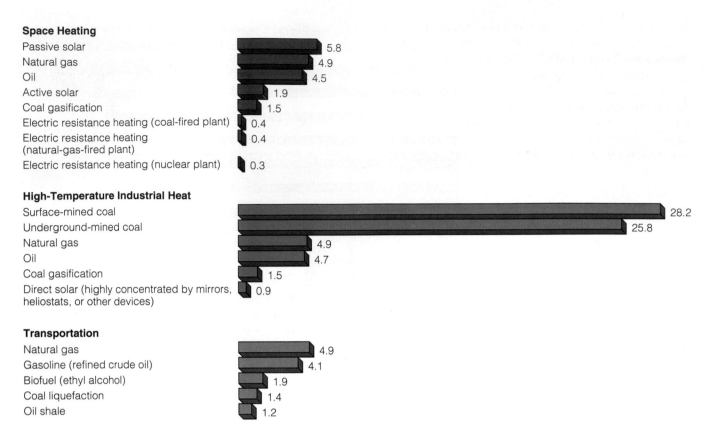

**Figure 3-19** Net useful energy ratios for various energy systems over their estimated lifetimes. (Data from Colorado Energy Research Institute, *Net Energy Analysis*, 1976; and Howard T. Odum and Elisabeth C. Odum, *Energy Basis for Man and Nature*, 3rd ed., New York: McGraw-Hill, 1981)

energy is degraded. The best way to do this is to heavily insulate a house and eliminate air leaks; then equip it with an air-to-air heat exchanger to prevent buildup of indoor air pollutants.

In some office buildings and stores waste heat from lights, computers, and other machines is collected and distributed to reduce heating bills during cold weather and is exhausted to reduce cooling bills during hot weather. Waste heat from industrial plants and electrical power plants can be distributed through insulated pipes and used to heat nearby buildings, greenhouses, and fish ponds, as is done in some parts of Europe.

Another way to use waste heat produced by industrial plants is **cogeneration**, the production of two useful forms of energy such as steam and electricity from the same fuel source. Waste heat from coal-fired and other industrial boilers can be used to produce steam that spins turbines and generates electricity at half the cost of buying it from a utility company. The electricity can be used by the plant or sold to the local power company for general use. Cogeneration is used in many industrial plants throughout Europe. If all large industrial boilers in the United States used cogeneration, there would be no need to build any electric power plants until 2020.

**NET USEFUL ENERGY: IT TAKES ENERGY TO GET ENERGY** The usable amount of high-quality energy from a given quantity of an energy resource is its **net useful energy**. It is the total useful energy available from the resource over its lifetime minus the amount of energy used (the first energy law), automatically wasted (the second energy law), and unnecessarily wasted in finding, processing, concentrating, and transporting it to users. For example, if 9 units of fossil fuel energy are needed to supply 10 units of nuclear, solar, or additional fossil fuel energy (perhaps from a deep well at sea), the net useful energy gain is only 1 unit of energy.

We can express this relationship as the ratio of useful energy produced to the useful energy used to produce it. In the example just given, the net energy ratio would be 10/9, or approximately 1.1. Thus the higher the ratio, or the equivalent real number, the greater the net useful energy yield. When the ratio is less than 1, there is a net energy loss over the lifetime of the system. Figure 3-19 lists estimated net useful

Q: How much of the energy in gasoline is used to move a motor vehicle powered by an internal combustion engine?

energy ratios for various systems of space heating, high-temperature heat for industrial processes, and gaseous and vehicle fuels.

Currently oil has a relatively high net useful energy ratio because much of it comes from large, accessible deposits such as those in Saudi Arabia and other parts of the Middle East. When those sources are depleted, however, the net useful energy ratio of oil will decline and prices will rise. Then more money and more high-quality fossil fuel will be needed to find, process, and deliver new oil from widely dispersed small deposits and deposits buried deep in the earth's crust or located in remote areas like Alaska, the Arctic, and the North Sea.

Conventional nuclear fission energy has a low net energy ratio because large amounts of energy are required to extract and process uranium ore, to convert it into a usable nuclear fuel, and to build and operate power plants. Energy is also needed to dismantle the plants after their 25–30 years of useful life and to store the resulting highly radioactive wastes for thousands of years.

## 3-8 Matter and Energy Laws and Environmental and Resource Problems

**THROWAWAY SOCIETIES** Because of the law of conservation of matter and the second law of energy, resource use by each of us automatically adds some waste heat and waste matter to the environment. Your individual use of matter and energy resources, and your additions of waste heat and matter to the environment, may seem small and insignificant. But you are only one of the 1.2 billion individuals in the MDCs using large quantities of matter and energy resources at a rapid rate. Meanwhile, the 4.3 billion people in the LDCs hope to be able to use more of these resources. And each year there are 94 million more consumers of Earth's energy and matter resources. Projected population growth alone will lead to a 70% jump in global energy use by 2025, even if per capita energy use stays at current levels. High rates of economic growth could triple energy use by 2025.

Most of today's advanced industrialized countries are largely *one-way societies*, or **throwaway societies**, sustaining continued economic growth by increasing the flow or *throughput* of planetary *sources* of materials and energy, through the economy, to planetary *sinks* (air, water, soil, organisms) where pollutants and wastes end up (Figure 3-20). The scientific laws of matter and energy tell us that if more and more people

continue to use and waste more and more energy and matter resources at an increasing rate, sooner or later the capacity of the local, regional, and global environments to dilute and degrade waste matter and absorb waste heat will be exceeded.

**MATTER-RECYCLING SOCIETIES** A stopgap solution to this problem is to convert from a throwaway society to a **matter-recycling society**. The goal of such a shift would be to allow economic growth to continue without depleting matter resources and without producing excessive pollution and environmental degradation. As we have learned, however, there is no free lunch when it comes to energy.

The two laws of energy tell us that *recycling matter resources always requires high-quality energy, which cannot be recycled*. In the long run a matter-recycling society based on continuing economic growth must have an inexhaustible supply of affordable high-quality energy. The environment must also have an infinite capacity to absorb and disperse waste heat and to dilute and degrade waste matter. Also, there is a physical limit to the number of times some materials, such as paper fiber, can be recycled before they become unusable. Thus *shifting from a throwaway society to a matter-recycling society is only a temporary solution to our problems*. Nevertheless, making such a shift is necessary to give us more time to convert to a sustainable-Earth society.

Suppose that affordable solar cells, nuclear fusion at room temperature, solar-produced hydrogen, or some other breakthrough were to guarantee an essentially infinite supply of affordable useful energy. Would that solve all our environmental and resource problems? No! The second energy law tells us that the faster we use energy to transform matter into products and to recycle those products, the faster low-quality heat and waste matter are dumped into the environment. Thus *the more we use energy to "conquer" Earth, the more stress we put on the environment*. Experts argue over how close we are to environmental overload, but the scientific laws of matter and energy indicate that limits do exist.

**SUSTAINABLE-EARTH SOCIETIES** The three scientific laws governing matter and energy changes indicate that the best long-term solution to our environmental problems is to shift from a society based on maximizing matter and energy flow (throughput) to a **sustainable-Earth society** (Figure 3-21).

Using these lessons from nature as guidelines, a sustainable-Earth society would:

- Reduce the throughput of matter and energy resources to prevent excessive depletion and degradation of planetary sources and overload of planetary sinks

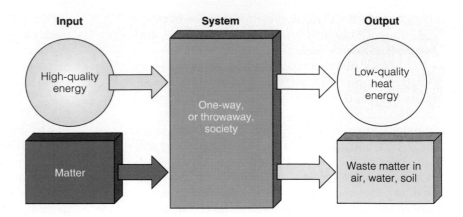

**Figure 3-20** The throwaway society of most industrialized countries is based on maximizing the rates of energy and matter flow, rapidly converting the world's high-quality matter and energy resources into waste, pollution, and low-quality heat.

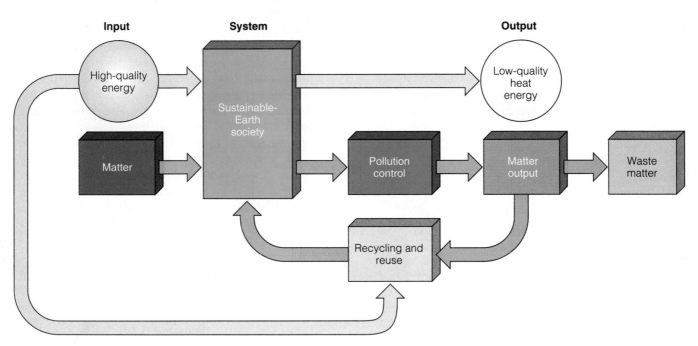

**Figure 3-21** A sustainable-Earth society, based on energy flow and matter recycling, reuses and recycles renewable matter resources, wastes less matter and energy, reduces unnecessary consumption, emphasizes pollution prevention and waste reduction, and controls population growth.

- Use energy more efficiently, and not use high-quality energy for tasks that require only moderate-quality energy (Figure 3-9)

- Shift from exhaustible and potentially polluting fossil and nuclear fuels to less harmful perpetual and renewable energy obtained from the sun and from Earth's natural cycles and flows

- Not waste potentially renewable resources, and use them no faster than the rate at which they are regenerated

- Not waste nonrenewable resources, and use them no faster than the rate at which a renewable resource, used sustainably, can be substituted for it

- Recycle and reuse at least 80% of the matter we now discard as trash

- Reduce use and waste of matter resources by making things that last longer and are easier to recycle, reuse, and repair

- Add wastes and pollutants to environmental sinks no faster than the rate at which they can be recycled, reused, absorbed, or rendered harmless to us and other species by natural processes

- Emphasize pollution prevention and waste reduction instead of pollution cleanup and waste management

- Bring human population growth to a halt to reduce stress on global life support systems

- Eliminate poverty, which degrades humans and the environment by forcing people to use resources unsustainably to stay alive

Q: What is the most inefficient and costly way to produce electricity for heating buildings or water?

*Amory B. Lovins*

**GUEST ESSAY** *Physicist and energy consultant Amory B. Lovins is one of the world's most recognized and articulate experts on energy strategy. In 1989 he received the Delphi Prize for environmental work; in 1990* The Wall Street Journal *named him as one of the 39 people most likely to change the course of business in the 1990s. He is research director at Rocky Mountain Institute, a nonprofit resource policy center that he and his wife, Hunter, founded in 1982 in Old Snowmass, Colorado. He has served as a consultant to 200 utilities, private industries, and international organizations, and to many national, state, and local governments. He is active in energy affairs in 31 countries and has published several hundred papers and a dozen books, including* Soft Energy Paths *and the nontechnical version of that work with L. Hunter Lovins,* Energy Unbound: Your Invitation to Energy Abundance *(see Further Readings).*

The answers you get depend on the questions you ask. But sometimes it seems so important to resolve a crisis that we forget to ask what problem we're trying to solve.

It is fashionable to suppose that we're running out of energy and that the solution is obviously to get lots more of it. But asking how to get more energy begs the question of how much we need. That depends not on how much we used in the past but on what we want to do in the future and how much energy it will take to do those things.

How much energy it takes to make steel, run a sewing machine, or keep ourselves comfortable in our house depends on how cleverly we use energy, and the more it costs, the smarter we seem to get. It is now cheaper, for example, to double the efficiency of most industrial electric motor drive systems than to fuel existing power plants to make electricity. *(Just this one saving can more than replace the entire U.S. nuclear power program.)* We know how to make lights five times as efficient as those presently in use and how to make household appliances that give us the same work as now, using one-fifth as much energy (saving money in the process).

Ten automakers have made good-sized, peppy, safe prototype cars averaging 29–59 kilometers per liter (62–138 miles per gallon). We know today how to make new buildings and many old ones so heat-tight (but still well ventilated) that they need essentially no energy to maintain comfort year-round, even in severe climates. (In fact, I live in one.)

These energy-saving measures are uniformly cheaper than going out and getting more energy. Detailed studies in more than a dozen countries have shown that supplying energy services in the cheapest way—by wringing more work from the energy we already have—would let us increase our standard of living while using several times less total energy (and electricity) than we do now. Those savings cost less than finding new domestic oil or operating existing power plants.

However, the old view of the energy problem included a worse mistake than forgetting to ask how much energy we needed: It sought more energy, in any form, from any source, at any price—as if all kinds of energy were alike. This is like saying, "All kinds of food are alike; we're running short of potatoes and turnips and cheese; but that's okay, we can substitute sirloin steak and oysters Rockefeller."

Some of us have to be more discriminating than that. Just as there are different kinds of food, so there are many different forms of energy, whose different prices and qualities suit them to different uses [Figure 3-9]. There is, after all, no demand for energy as such; nobody wants raw kilowatt-hours or barrels of sticky black goo. People instead want energy services: comfort, light, mobility, hot showers, cold beverages, and the ability to bake bread and make cement. We ought therefore to start at that end of the energy problem and ask, "What tasks do we want energy for, and what amount, type, and source of energy will do each task most cheaply?"

Electricity is a particularly high-quality, expensive form of energy. An average kilowatt-hour delivered in the United States in 1992 was priced at about 7¢, equivalent to buying the heat content of oil costing $116 per barrel—about six times the average world price in 1992. The average cost of electricity from nuclear plants (including fuel and operating expenses) beginning operation in 1988 was 13.5¢ per kilowatt-hour, equivalent on a heat basis to buying oil at about $216 per barrel.

Such costly energy might be worthwhile if it were used only for the premium tasks that require it, such as lights, motors, electronics, and smelters. But those special uses, only 8% of all delivered U.S. energy needs, are

(continued)

Because of the three basic scientific laws of matter and energy, we are all dependent on one another and on the rest of nature for our survival. Everything is connected to everything else, and we are all in it together. In the next chapter we will apply these laws to living systems and look at some biological principles that can teach us how to work with nature.

*The second law of thermodynamics holds, I think, the supreme position among laws of nature. . . . If your theory is found to be against the second law of thermodynamics, I can give you no hope.*

ARTHUR S. EDDINGTON

A: Nuclear power (only 14% efficient)

already met twice over by today's power stations. Two-fifths of our electricity is already spilling over into uneconomic, low-grade uses such as water heating, space heating, and air conditioning; yet no matter how efficiently we use electricity (even with heat pumps), we can never get our money's worth on these applications.

Thus, *supplying more electricity is irrelevant to the energy problem we have.* Even though electricity accounts for almost all of the federal energy research and development budget and for at least half of national energy investment, it is the wrong kind of energy to meet our needs economically. Arguing about what kind of new power station to build—coal, nuclear, solar—is like shopping for the best buy in antique Chippendale chairs to burn in your stove or brandy to put in your car's gas tank. *It is the wrong question.*

Indeed, *any kind of new power station is so uneconomical that if you have just built one, you will save the country money by writing it off and never operating it.* Why? Because its additional electricity can be used only for low-temperature heating and cooling (the premium "electricity-specific" uses being already filled up) and is the most expensive way of supplying those services. Saving electricity is much cheaper than making it.

The real question is, What is the cheapest way to do low-temperature heating and cooling? The answer is weather-stripping, insulation, heat exchangers, greenhouses, superwindows (which have as much insulating value as the outside wall of a typical house), window shades and overhangs, trees, and so on. These measures generally cost about half a penny per kilowatt-hour; the running costs alone for a new nuclear plant will be nearly 4¢ per kilowatt-hour, so it's cheaper not to run it. In fact, under the crazy U.S. tax laws, the extra saving from not having to pay the plant's future subsidies is probably so big that by shutting the plant down society can also recover the capital cost of having built it!

If we want more electricity, we should get it from the cheapest sources first. In approximate order of increasing price, these include:

- Converting to efficient lighting equipment. This would save the United States electricity equal to the output of 120 large power plants plus $30 billion a year in fuel and maintenance costs.

- Using more efficient motors to save half the energy used by motor systems. This would save electricity equal to the output of another 150 large power plants and repay the cost in about a year.

- Eliminating pure waste of electricity, such as lighting empty offices at headache level. Each kilowatt-hour saved can be resold without having to generate it anew.

- Displacing with good architecture, and with passive and some active solar techniques, the electricity now used for water heating and space heating and cooling. Some U.S. utilities now give low- or zero-interest weatherization loans, which you need not start repaying for ten years or until you sell your house—because it saves the utility millions of dollars to have available the electricity you don't use instead of building new power plants. Most utilities also offer rebates for buying efficient appliances.

- Making appliances, smelters, and the like cost-effectively efficient.

Just these five measures can quadruple U.S. electrical efficiency, making it possible to run today's economy, with no changes in lifestyles, using no power plants, whether old or new and whether fueled with oil, gas, coal, or uranium. We would need only the present hydroelectric capacity, readily available small-scale hydroelectric projects, and a modest amount of wind power. If we still wanted more electricity, the next cheapest sources would include:

- Industrial cogeneration, combined heat-and-power plants, low-temperature heat engines run by industrial waste heat or by solar ponds, filling empty turbine bays and upgrading equipment in existing big dams, modern wind machines or small-scale hydroelectric

## Critical Thinking

1. Do you think fraud is more or less likely in science than in other areas of knowledge? Explain.

2. To what extent are scientists responsible for the applications of knowledge they discover? Should scientists abandon research because of its possible harmful uses? Explain.

3. Explain why we don't really consume anything and why we can never really throw matter away.

4. A tree grows and increases its mass. Explain why this isn't a violation of the law of conservation of matter.

5. If there is no "away," why isn't the world filled with waste matter?

6. Use the second energy law to explain why a barrel of oil can be used only once as a fuel.

7. Explain why most energy analysts urge that the basis of any individual, corporate, or national energy plan should be improved energy efficiency. Is it an important part of your personal energy plan? Why or why not?

8. Explain why using electricity to heat a house and to supply household hot water by resistance heating is expensive and wasteful of energy. What energy tasks can be done best by electricity?

Q: What are the two most energy-efficient ways to heat interior space?

turbines in good sites, steam-injected natural gas turbines, and perhaps recent developments in solar cells with waste heat recovery.

It is only after we had clearly exhausted all these cheaper opportunities that we would even consider:

- Building a new central power station of any kind—the slowest and costliest known way to get more electricity (or to save oil).

To emphasize the importance of starting with energy end uses rather than energy sources, consider a sad little story from France, involving a "spaghetti chart" (or energy flowchart)—a device energy planners often use to show how energy flows from primary sources via conversion processes to final forms and uses. In the mid-1970s energy conservation planners in the French government started, wisely, on the right-hand side of the spaghetti chart. They found that their biggest need for energy was to heat buildings; and that even with good heat pumps, electricity would be the most costly way to do this. So they had a fight with their nationalized utility; they won, and electric heating was supposed to be discouraged or even phased out because it was so wasteful of money and fuel.

Meanwhile, down the street, the energy supply planners (who were far more numerous and influential in the French government) were starting on the left-hand side of the spaghetti chart. They said: "Look at all that nasty imported oil coming into our country! We must replace that oil. Oil is energy. . . . We need some other source of energy. Voilà! Reactors can give us energy; we'll build nuclear reactors all over the country." But they paid little attention to who would use that extra energy and no attention to relative prices.

Thus the two sides of the French energy establishment went on with their respective solutions to two different, indeed contradictory, French energy problems: *more energy of any kind* versus *the right kind to do each task*

*in the most inexpensive way.* It was only in 1979 that these conflicting perceptions collided. The supply side planners suddenly realized that the only thing they would be able to *sell* all that nuclear electricity for would be electric heating, which they had just agreed not to do.

Every industrial country is in this embarrassing position (especially if we include as "heating" air conditioning, which just means heating the outdoors instead of the indoors). Which end of the spaghetti chart we start on, or *what we think the energy problem is*, is not an academic abstraction: *It determines what we buy.* It is the fundamental source of disagreement about energy policy.

People starting on the left side of the spaghetti chart think the problem boils down to whether to build coal or nuclear power stations (or both). People starting on the right realize that *no* kind of new power station can be an economic way to meet the needs for using electricity to provide low- and high-temperature heat and for the vehicular liquid fuels that are 92% of our energy problem.

So if we want to provide our energy services at a price we can afford, let's get straight what question our technologies are supposed to answer. Before we argue about the meatballs, let's untangle the strands of spaghetti, see where they're supposed to lead, and find out what we really need the energy *for*!

## Critical Thinking

1. The author argues that building more nuclear, coal, or other electrical power plants to supply electricity for the United States is unnecessary and wasteful. Summarize the reasons for this conclusion, and give your reasons for agreeing or disagreeing with this viewpoint.

2. Do you agree or disagree that increasing the supply of energy, instead of concentrating on improving energy efficiency, is the wrong answer to U.S. energy problems? Explain.

9. **a.** Use the law of conservation of matter to explain why a matter-recycling society will sooner or later be necessary.
   **b.** Use the first and second laws of energy to explain why, in the long run, a sustainable-Earth society, not just a matter-recycling society, will be necessary.

*10. As a class project, determine the following information about your school.
   **a.** What energy sources are used for heating and cooling? How do these vary with the ages and types of buildings?
   **b.** How much money is spent on heating and cooling? How do these costs vary on a monthly basis

throughout the year? How do they vary with the ages and types of buildings?
   **c.** What is the rough energy efficiency of the devices used for heating, cooling, and lighting?
   **d.** What efforts have been made to improve the energy efficiency of heating, cooling, and lighting devices and to increase insulation and reduce air leaks during the past 10 years? How much money has been saved by such actions during this time? Use this information to draw up an energy-saving and money-saving plan for your school, and submit the results to appropriate officials.

A: Passive solar and natural gas

## Are Viruses Helping to Kill the Great Coral Reefs?

A previously unknown player in the arena of marine life has recently been exposed—viruses. Pioneer marine virologist Lita Proctor has shown that one drop of seawater may contain billions of these microscopic noncellular infectious agents.

These swarms of viruses may help control rapidly multiplying populations of marine bacteria, which would soon overwhelm ocean life if not kept in check. On the other hand, too many viruses could deplete vital marine bacteria. There are signs that the ocean's ancient balancing act between viruses and bacteria is being threatened, perhaps by the multitude of new viruses humans have been introducing into seawater through sewage and other waste disposal.

Other researchers are trying to find out what else ocean viruses may be killing besides bacteria. For example, oceanographer Curtis Suttle has found that in the laboratory marine viruses slow the population growth of photosynthetic marine algae by 80%.

If viruses attack algae in the ocean as ferociously as they do in the lab, they could cause a massive dieback in marine algae populations. Photosynthesizing algae in the oceans now remove about half the carbon dioxide we and other organisms put into the atmosphere. Reducing the uptake of this temperature-regulating gas in the atmosphere could accelerate projected global warming.

Marine viruses may also be harming coastal coral reefs found in tropical waters. They consist of coral animals—called polyps—covered with brightly colored algae (Figure 4-1, left). Recently many of these reefs have been losing their algae, and with them their brilliant colors (Figure 4-1, right). Scientists aren't sure why this coral bleaching is happening. But the work of Proctor and other researchers suggests that viruses could be involved in killing the colorful coral algae.

Other factors are probably involved as well. Some scientists suggest that warmer tropical water in some areas may be killing coral polyps or their algae. If so, increased coral bleaching may be an early warning sign of global warming. In some areas coral algae may be killed by oil spills, hurricanes, changes in water salinity, pesticide runoff, and excessive silt flowing into tropical coastal waters when soil erodes from cleared land. The thinning of the stratospheric

**Figure 4-1** A healthy coral reef in the Philippines covered by colorful algae (left) and a bleached coral reef in the Bahamas that has lost most of its algae (right). These diverse and productive ecosystems are being destroyed and damaged at an alarming rate.

Karl & Jill Wallin/FPG International

*If we love our children, we must love the earth with tender care and pass it on, diverse and beautiful, so that on a warm spring day 10,000 years hence they can feel peace in a sea of grass, can watch a bee visit a flower, can hear a sandpiper call in the sky, and can find joy in being alive.*

HUGH H. ILTIS

ozone layer, which shields living creatures from the sun's damaging ultraviolet radiation, may also contribute to coral bleaching.

Scientists are investigating other unexplained marine deaths. For example, unusual numbers of marine mammals are washing up on beaches, from striped dolphins in the Mediterranean to seals in the North Sea and Antarctica. Are viruses to blame? Again we don't know. However, antibodies to dog distemper and related viruses have shown up in the dead mammals.

Unraveling these and other biological mysteries requires us to answer some difficult questions: What organisms live in a coral reef, a field, or a pond? How do they get enough food and energy to stay alive? How do these organisms interact with one another? What changes might this coral reef, field, or pond undergo through time?

Ecology—created about 100 years ago by M.I.T. chemist Ellen Swallow—is the science that attempts to answer such questions. **Ecology**, from the Greek *oikos* (house, or place to live) and *logos* (study of), is the study of how organisms interact with one another and with their physical and chemical environment. The key word is *interact*. One way scientists pursue ecology is by examining various **ecosystems**: communities of species interacting with one another and with their nonliving environment of matter and energy.

Robert Wicklund

This chapter focuses on answering the following questions about ecosystems:

- What basic processes keep us and other organisms alive?
- What are the major living and nonliving parts of an ecosystem?
- What happens to energy in an ecosystem?
- What happens to matter in an ecosystem?
- What roles do different types of organisms play, and how do they interact in an ecosystem?

## 4-1  Life and Earth's Life Support Systems

**WHAT IS LIFE?**  The **cell** is the basic unit of life (Figure 3-2). Each cell is encased in an outer membrane or wall and contains genetic material (DNA) and other parts to perform its life functions. Organisms like bacteria consist of only one cell, but most of the organisms we are familiar with contain many cells. All forms of life:

- *Have a highly organized internal structure and organization.*

- *Have characteristic types of deoxyribonucleic acid, or DNA, molecules in each cell. DNA is the stuff genes— the basic units of heredity—are made of. These self-replicating molecules contain the instructions for making new cells from "lifeless" molecules and for assembling proteins and other molecules each cell needs to survive and reproduce.*

- *Can capture and transform matter and energy from their environment in order to survive, grow, and reproduce.*

- *Can maintain favorable internal conditions despite changes in their external environment if not overwhelmed.*

- *Arise through reproduction—the production of offspring by one or more parents—and in turn are capable of reproduction.*

**Figure 4-2** Our life support system: the general structure of the earth.

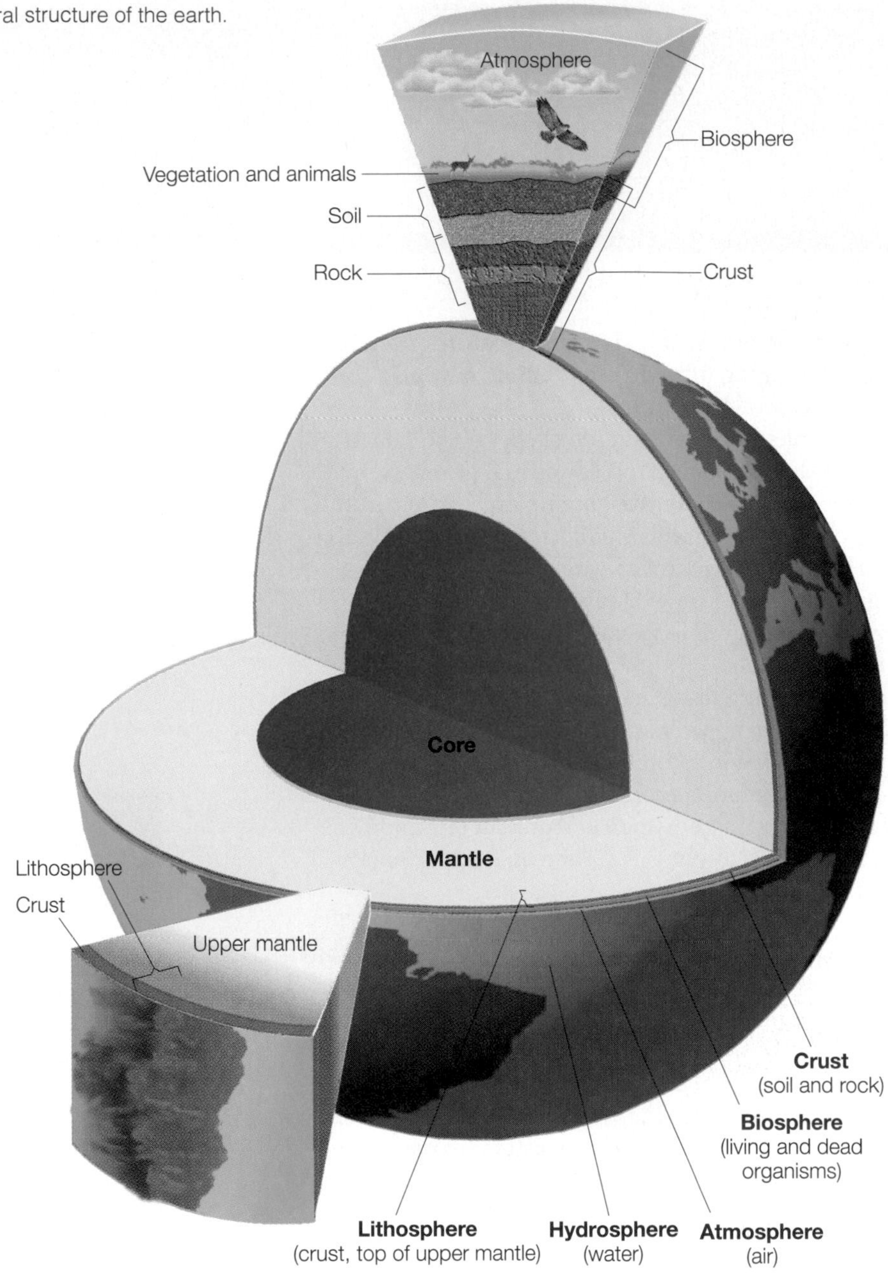

Atmosphere

Biosphere

Vegetation and animals

Soil

Rock

Crust

Lithosphere

Crust

Upper mantle

Core

Mantle

**Crust**
(soil and rock)

**Biosphere**
(living and dead
organisms)

**Lithosphere**
(crust, top of upper mantle)

**Hydrosphere**
(water)

**Atmosphere**
(air)

- *Can adapt to external change by **mutations**—random changes in their DNA molecules—and through combinations of existing genes during reproduction.* Most mutations are harmful, but some give rise to new genetic traits that allow the organisms to adapt to changing environmental conditions and have more offspring than those without such traits—a process called **natural selection**. Through successive generations these adaptive traits become more common. When such genetic changes in existing organisms form distinctly different new organisms, what biologists call **evolution** has occurred. Life forms that cannot adapt become fewer and may become extinct. These ongoing processes of extinction and evolution in response to environmental changes over billions of years have led to the diversity of life forms found on Earth today. This *biodiversity*—a vital part of Earth capital—sustains life and provides the genetic raw material for adaptation to future changes in environmental conditions.

**EARTH: A DYNAMIC PLANET** We can think of the earth as being made up of several layers or spheres (Figure 4-2):

- The **atmosphere**—a thin, gaseous envelope of air around the planet. Its inner layer, the **tropo-**

Q: What is the most energy-efficient fuel for powering a motor vehicle?

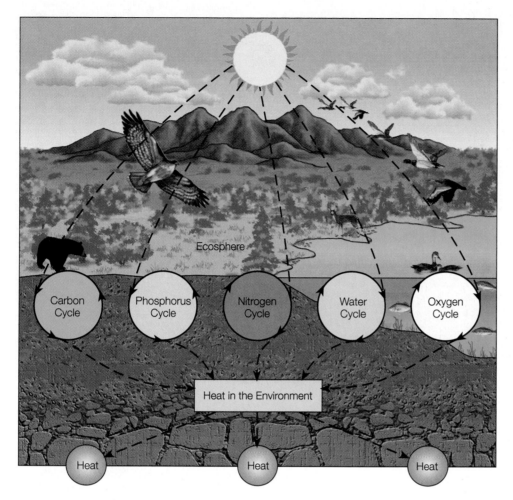

Ecosphere

Carbon Cycle

Phosphorus Cycle

Nitrogen Cycle

Water Cycle

Oxygen Cycle

Heat in the Environment

Heat

Heat

Heat

**Figure 4-3** Earth's life depends on the *one-way flow of energy* (dashed lines) from the sun through the ecosphere, the *cycling of critical elements* (solid lines around circles), and *gravity*, which keeps atmospheric gases from escaping into space and draws chemicals downward in the matter cycles. This simplified overview shows only a few of the many cycling elements.

**sphere**, extends only about 17 kilometers (11 miles) above sea level but contains most of the planet's air—mostly nitrogen (78%) and oxygen (21%). The next layer, stretching 17–48 kilometers (11–30 miles) above Earth's surface, is called the **stratosphere**. Its lower portion contains enough ozone ($O_3$) to filter out most of the sun's harmful ultraviolet radiation, thus allowing life on land to exist.

- The **hydrosphere**—liquid water (both surface and underground), frozen water (polar ice, icebergs, permafrost in soil), and water vapor in the atmosphere.

- The **lithosphere**—Earth's crust and upper mantle. It contains the fossil fuels and minerals we use and the soil chemicals (nutrients) needed to support plant life.

- The **ecosphere** or **biosphere**—the portion of Earth where living (biotic) organisms are found and interact with one another and with their nonliving (abiotic) environment. This zone of life includes most of the hydrosphere and parts of the lower atmosphere and upper lithosphere. It reaches from the deepest ocean floor 20 kilome-

ters (12 miles) upward to the tops of the highest mountains. If Earth were an apple, the ecosphere would be no thicker than the apple's skin, a haven for life between Earth's molten interior and the lifeless cold of space. *The goal of ecology is to learn how this thin global skin of air, water, soil, and organisms works and is sustained.*

**ENERGY FLOW, MATTER CYCLING, AND GRAVITY**
Life on Earth depends on three connected factors (Figure 4-3):

- The *one-way flow of high-quality (usable) energy* from the sun, through materials and living things on or near the earth's surface, then into the environment (mostly as heat dispersed into air or water molecules at a low temperature), and eventually into space as infrared radiation

- The *cycling of matter* required by living organisms through parts of the ecosphere

- *Gravity*, caused mostly by the attraction between the sun and the earth, which allows the planet to hold onto its atmosphere and causes the downward movement of chemicals in the matter cycles

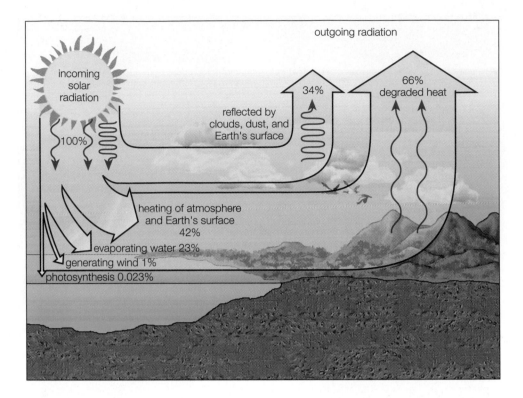

**Figure 4-4** The flow of energy to and from Earth. The ultimate source of energy in most ecosystems is sunlight.

- outgoing radiation
- incoming solar radiation
- 34% reflected by clouds, dust, and Earth's surface
- 66% degraded heat
- 100%
- heating of atmosphere and Earth's surface 42%
- evaporating water 23%
- generating wind 1%
- photosynthesis 0.023%

**THE SUN: SOURCE OF ENERGY FOR LIFE** The sun is a middle-aged star that lights and warms the planet. It also supplies the energy for *photosynthesis*, the process used by green plants and some bacteria to synthesize the compounds that keep them alive and feed most other organisms. Solar energy also powers the cycling of matter and drives the climate and weather systems that distribute heat and fresh water over Earth's surface. It is expected to provide Earth with energy for at least another 4 billion years.

The sun is a gigantic fireball of hydrogen (72%) and helium (28%) gases. Temperatures and pressures in its inner core are so high that hydrogen nuclei fuse to form helium nuclei (Figure 3-13), releasing enormous amounts of energy.

This nuclear fusion reactor radiates energy in all directions as electromagnetic radiation (Figure 3-5). At the speed of light this radiation makes the 150-million-kilometer (93-million-mile) trip between the sun and the earth in slightly more than 8 minutes. Earth, a tiny target in the vastness of space, receives only about one-billionth of this output, and much of that is either reflected away or absorbed by chemicals in the atmosphere. Most of the harmful, high-energy cosmic rays, gamma rays, X rays, and ultraviolet ionizing radiation never reach the planet's surface. Most of what reaches the troposphere is visible light and infrared radiation (heat) plus a small amount of ultraviolet radiation not absorbed by ozone in the stratosphere.

About 34% of the solar energy reaching the troposphere is reflected right back to space by clouds, chemicals, and dust and by the earth's surface of land and water (Figure 4-4). The ability of surfaces to reflect radiation, called **albedo**, depends on their color and texture. Clouds, ice, and snow have a high albedo, while forests have a low one. The albedo of the oceans, which cover three-quarters of the earth's surface, depends on the angle at which the sun's rays strike.

Most of the remaining 66% of solar energy warms the troposphere and land, evaporates water and cycles it through the ecosphere, and generates winds. A tiny fraction (0.023%), captured by green plants and bacteria, fuels photosynthesis to make the organic compounds that most life forms need to survive.

Most of this unreflected solar radiation is degraded into infrared radiation (which we experience as heat) as it interacts with the earth. How fast this heat flows through the atmosphere and back into space is affected by heat-trapping (greenhouse) gases, such as water vapor, carbon dioxide, methane, nitrous oxide, and ozone, in the troposphere. Without this atmospheric thermal "blanket," known as the *natural greenhouse effect*, Earth would be nearly as cold as Mars, and life as we know it could not exist.

**NUTRIENT CYCLES** Any chemical element or compound an organism must take in to live, grow, or reproduce is called a **nutrient**. Those needed in large amounts are called **macronutrients**. Carbon, oxygen, hydrogen, nitrogen, phosphorus, sulfur, calcium, magnesium, and potassium, and their compounds, are macronutrients that make up 97% of your body's mass

Q: On what three factors does life on Earth depend?

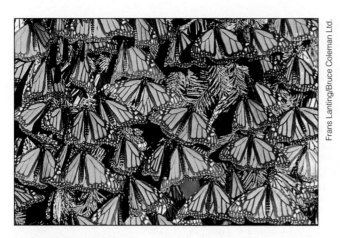

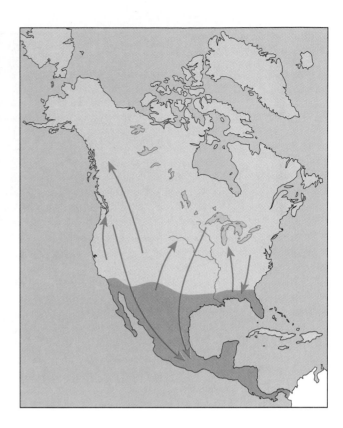

**Figure 4-5** A population of monarch butterflies wintering in Michoacán, Mexico (left). Monarchs winter in parts of Mexico and Central America (right). They head north during the spring and breed along the way. In the fall their offspring migrate south.

and more than 95% of the mass of all organisms. The 30-odd elements required by organisms in small, or trace, amounts are called **micronutrients**. Examples are iron, copper, zinc, chlorine, and iodine.

These nutrient elements and their compounds are continuously cycled from the nonliving environment (air, water, soil) to living organisms, and back to the nonliving environment in what are called **nutrient cycles**, or **biogeochemical cycles** (literally "life–earth–chemical" cycles). These cycles, driven directly or indirectly by incoming solar energy and gravity, include the carbon, oxygen, nitrogen, phosphorus, sulfur, and hydrologic (water) cycles (Figure 4-3).

Some nutrients, such as oxygen and carbon, cycle quickly and so are readily available for use by organisms. Others, like phosphorus, cycle slowly, explaining why the availability of phosphorus in soil often limits plant growth.

Earth's chemical cycles connect past, present, and future forms of life. Thus some of the carbon atoms in the skin of your right hand may once have been part of a leaf, a dinosaur's skin, or limestone rock. And some of the oxygen molecules you just inhaled may have been inhaled by your grandmother, Plato, or a hunter-gatherer who lived 25,000 years ago.

## 4-2    Ecosystem Components

**THE REALM OF ECOLOGY**  Ecology deals mainly with interactions among organisms, populations, communities, ecosystems, and the ecosphere (Figure 3-2).

An **organism** is any form of life. Organisms can be classified into **species**, groups of organisms that resemble one another in appearance, behavior, chemistry, and genetic structure. Most organisms reproduce sexually and are classified in the same species if they can breed with one another and produce fertile offspring under natural conditions.

We don't have the foggiest notion how many species exist on Earth. Estimates range from 5 million to 100 million, most of them insects, microscopic organisms, and tiny sea creatures. So far biologists have identified and named only about 1.4 million species. They know a fair amount about roughly one-third of these species and the detailed roles and interactions of only a few.

A **population** is a group of individuals of the same species occupying a given area at the same time (Figure 4-5). Examples are all sunfish in a pond, white oak trees in a forest, and people in a country. All members of the same population have certain structural, functional, and behavioral traits in common. In most natural populations individuals vary slightly in their genetic makeup so that they don't all look or behave exactly alike—something called *genetic diversity* (Figure 4-6).

The place where a population (or an individual organism) normally lives is known as its **habitat**. Populations of all the species occupying a particular place make up a **community** or **biological community**.

An *ecosystem*, recall, is a community of different species involved in a dynamic network of biological,

**Figure 4-6** Genetic diversity. Variation in shell color and banding patterns among populations of one species of snail found on Caribbean islands.

Alan Solem

chemical, and physical interactions that sustain it and allow it to respond to changing conditions. The size of an ecosystem—and thus a community—is arbitrary and is defined by the system we wish to study. All of Earth's ecosystems together make up the ecosphere.

Climate—long-term weather—is the main factor determining what type of life, especially what plants, will thrive in a given land area. Biologists have divided the terrestrial (land) portion of the ecosphere into **biomes**, large regions such as forests, deserts, and grasslands characterized by certain climatic conditions and inhabited by certain types of life, especially vegetation (Figure 4-7). Each biome consists of many ecosystems whose communities have adapted to small differences in climate, soil, and other environmental factors. Marine and freshwater portions of the ecosphere can be divided into aquatic life zones, containing numerous ecosystems. The major land biomes and aquatic life zones are discussed in more detail in Chapter 5.

**BIODIVERSITY** As environmental conditions have changed over billions of years, many species have become extinct and new ones have formed. The result of these changes is **biological diversity**, or **biodiversity**. It consists of the forms of life that can best survive the variety of conditions currently found on Earth and includes genetic diversity, species diversity, and ecological diversity.

As noted previously, *genetic diversity* is variability in the genetic makeup among individuals within a sin-

gle species (Figure 4-6). **Species diversity** is the variety of species on Earth and in different habitats of the planet. **Ecological diversity** is the variety of forests, deserts, grasslands, streams, lakes, oceans, and other biological communities that interact with one another and with their nonliving environments.

We are utterly dependent on this mostly unknown "biocapital." This rich variety of genes, species, and ecosystems gives us food, wood, fibers, energy, raw materials, industrial chemicals, and medicines, and pours hundreds of billions of dollars yearly into the world economy.

Earth's vast library of life forms and ecosystems also provides free recycling and purification services and natural pest control. Every species here today contains stored genetic information that represents thousands to millions of years of adaptation to Earth's changing environmental conditions and that is the raw material for future adaptations. Biodiversity is nature's "insurance policy" against disasters.

Some also include *human cultural diversity* as part of Earth's biodiversity. The variety of human cultures on the planet represents our "solutions" to survival and can help us adapt to changing conditions.

**TYPES OF ORGANISMS** Earth's diverse organisms are classified as eukaryotic or prokaryotic on the basis of their cell structure. All organisms except bacteria are **eukaryotic**: Their cells have a *nucleus* (genetic material surrounded by a membrane) and several other internal parts surrounded by membranes. Bacte-

Q: What five levels of the organization of matter are the focus of ecology?

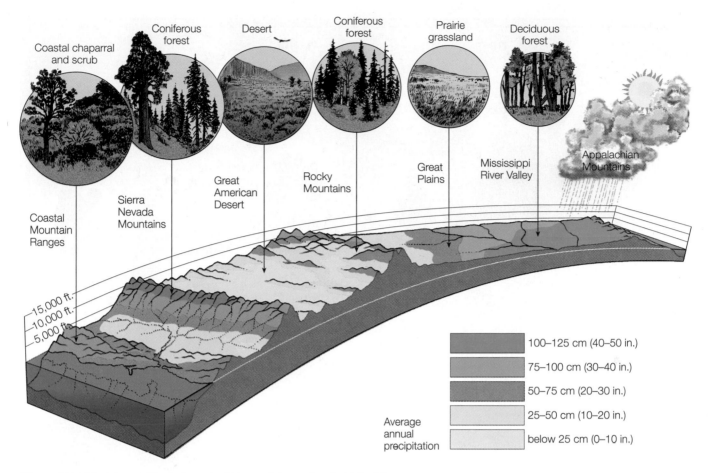

**Figure 4-7** Major biomes found along the 39th parallel crossing the United States. The differences mostly reflect changes in climate, mainly differences in average annual temperature and precipitation.

Average annual precipitation

| | |
|---|---|
| | 100–125 cm (40–50 in.) |
| | 75–100 cm (30–40 in.) |
| | 50–75 cm (20–30 in.) |
| | 25–50 cm (10–20 in.) |
| | below 25 cm (0–10 in.) |

rial cells are **prokaryotic**: They have no distinct nucleus or other internal parts enclosed by membranes. Although most of the organisms we see are eukaryotic, they could not exist without hordes of microscopic prokaryotic organisms (bacteria) toiling away unseen.

In this book Earth's organisms are classified into five kingdoms (Figure 4-8):

- **Monera (bacteria** and **cyanobacteria)** are single-celled, prokaryotic, microscopic organisms.

- **Protista (protists)** are mostly single-celled eukaryotic organisms such as diatoms, amoebas, golden brown and yellow-green algae, protozoans, and slime molds.

- **Fungi** are mostly many-celled (some microscopic), eukaryotic organisms such as mushrooms, molds, and yeasts.

- **Plantae (plants)** are mostly many-celled, eukaryotic organisms such as red, brown, and green algae, mosses, ferns, conifers (cone-bearing trees such as pine, juniper, redwood, and yew), and flowering

plants (cacti, grasses, beans, roses, bromeliads, and maple trees). They have developed impressive strategies for survival (Spotlight, p. 83).

- **Animalia (animals)** are many-celled, eukaryotic organisms. Most, called **invertebrates**, have no backbones (Figure 4-12). They include sponges, jellyfish, worms, arthropods (insects, shrimp, spiders), mollusks (snails, clams, octopuses), and echinoderms (sea stars, sea urchins). The **vertebrates**, animals with backbones (Figure 4-13), include fish (sharks, tuna), amphibians (frogs, salamanders), reptiles (turtles, crocodiles, snakes), birds (eagles, penguins, robins, ducks), and mammals (kangaroos, moles, bats, cats, rabbits, elephants, whales, seals, rhinos, humans). Insects and other arthropods such as spiders are vital to our existence (Spotlight, p. 84).

**LIVING COMPONENTS OF ECOSYSTEMS** The ecosphere and its ecosystems can be studied by being broken down into two parts: the living or **biotic**

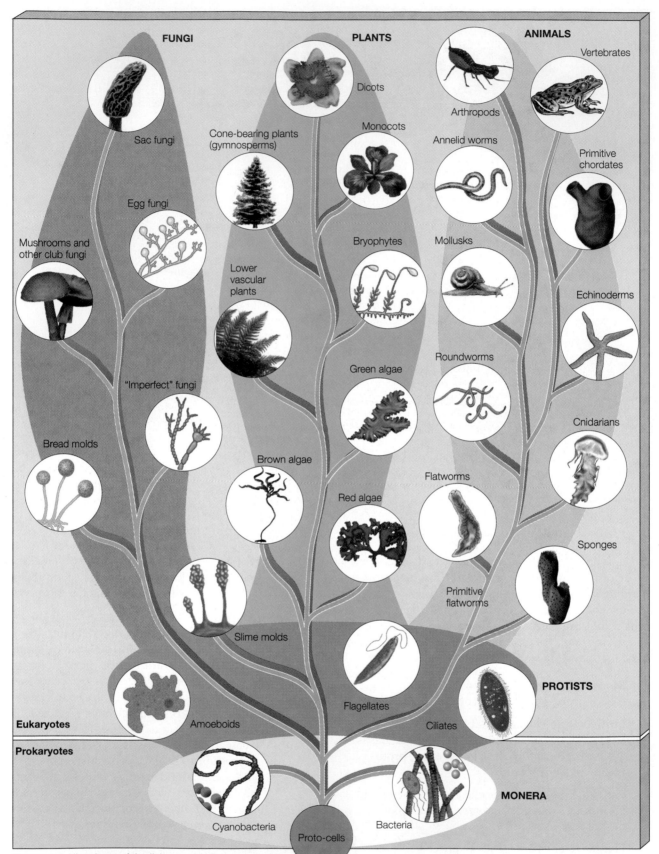

**Figure 4-8** Kingdoms of the living world. This is one of several ways that biologists classify Earth's diverse species into major groups. Most biologists believe that proto-cells gave rise to single-celled prokaryotes and that these in turn evolved into the more complex protists, fungi, plants, and animals that make up the planet's stunning biodiversity.

Q: What is the sun's source of energy?

## Some Survival Strategies of Plants

Over the eons plants have developed numerous survival techniques. Eucalyptus leaves turn their edges to the sun to minimize water loss. **Evergreens** like ferns, magnolias, pines, spruces, and sequoias (Figure 4-9) keep some leaves or needles all year. This allows them to carry out photosynthesis year-round in tropical climates or take maximum advantage of a short growing season in colder climates. The needles of certain conifers also contain "antifreeze" compounds that keep them from freezing.

Losing water—and heat—by evaporation through leaves is a disadvantage in a dry season and in winter. **Deciduous plants**, such as oak and maple trees, solve this problem and survive drought and cold by shedding their leaves.

**Succulent plants**, such as desert cacti (Figure 4-10), survive in dry climates by having no leaves, thus conserving scarce water. They store water and synthesize food in the fleshy tissue of their green stems and branches. Some also trap dew on their hairs.

Plants have different root systems to anchor them and to supply water and nutrients under different climatic conditions. Dandelions, carrots, and mesquite bushes have deep roots to obtain moisture from deep underground. Grasses and most cacti have fairly shallow roots with multiple branches that spread out to catch and quickly absorb water.

Some tropical forest species grow on tree branches rather than in soil. These **epiphytes**, or "air plants," have small seeds that are carried to tree limbs by birds and other animals or by the wind. They include mosses, ferns, lichens, and orchids (Figure 4-11).

Whit Bronaugh

**Figure 4-9** Giant sequoia trees are evergreen conifers found in just 75 groves along the western slopes of California's Sierra Nevada. Although coastal redwoods can grow taller, giant sequoias are Earth's most massive species. The 2,500- to 3,000-year-old General Sherman Tree, shown here, is about 84 meters (275 feet) high, and 11 meters (36 feet) in diameter. Notice how the people standing at its base are dwarfed. Its bark, which is more than 61 centimeters (2 feet) thick, helps protect it from fire, predators, and disease.

François Gohier/Ardea London

**Figure 4-10** These saguaro (pronounced sa-WA-ro) cacti in Arizona store water and produce food in their spongy stems and branches. They reduce water loss in the hot desert climate by having no leaves and by opening pores only at night. Their thorns discourage predators. These plants can reach heights of 15 meters (50 feet) and can swell to twice their normal size during the rainy season by absorbing water from a vast network of shallow roots. Their night-opening flowers are pollinated by nectar-eating bats.

Kenneth W. Fink/Ardea London

**Figure 4-11** This white orchid, an epiphyte from the tropical forests of Latin America, roots in the fork of a tree rather than the soil. It gets water from rain and humid air, and nutrients from bits of organic matter falling from the thick leaf canopy above. Epiphytes provide hiding and breeding sites for entire communities of frogs, birds, rodents, snakes, and insects—some of which live their entire lives in these aerial gardens. In this interaction between the epiphytes and their host tree, the epiphytes gain access to water and other nutrients and sunlight, and the tree is apparently unharmed.

**Figure 4-12** This cobalt blue sea star found on a barrier coral reef in Indonesia is an invertebrate.

**Figure 4-13** The peacock is a vertebrate. This courtship display can also scare off predators.

E. R. Degginger

Terry Domico/Earth Images

---

## Have You Thanked Insects Today?

**SPOTLIGHT**

Insects play important and largely unrecognized roles. A large fraction of Earth's plant species depend on insects for pollination and reproduction. Plants also owe their lives to the insects that help turn the soil around their roots and decompose dead tissue into nutrients the plants need. In turn, we and other land-dwelling animals depend on plants for food, either by eating them or by consuming plant-eating animals.

Indeed, if all insects were to disappear, we and most of Earth's amphibians, reptiles, birds, and other mammals would become extinct within a year because of the disappearance of most plant life. Earth would be covered with dead and rotting vegetation and animal carcasses being decomposed by unimaginable hordes of bacteria and fungi. The land would be largely devoid of animal life and covered by mats of wind-pollinated vegetation and clumps of small trees and bushes here and there.

This, however, is not a realistic scenario. Insects, which originated on land nearly 400 million years ago, are so diverse, abundant, and adaptable that they are virtually invincible. Some have asked whether insects will take over if the human race extinguishes itself. This is the wrong question. The roughly billion billion insects alive at any given time around the world have been in charge for millions of years. Insects can thrive without newcomers such as us, but we and most other land organisms would quickly perish without them.

---

components like plants and animals (Figure 4-8), and the nonliving or **abiotic** components like water, air, nutrients, and solar energy needed to sustain life. Figures 4-14 and 4-15 are greatly simplified diagrams showing a few of the components of ecosystems in a freshwater pond and in a field. Living organisms in ecosystems are usually classified as either *producers* or *consumers*, based on how they get food.

**Producers**—sometimes called **autotrophs** (self-feeders)—can make the organic nutrients they need from simple inorganic compounds in their environment. In most terrestrial ecosystems green plants are the producers. In aquatic ecosystems most of the producers are *phytoplankton*, floating and drifting bacteria and protists, mostly microscopic. Only producers make their own food. All other organisms are consumers living directly or indirectly on the food provided by producers.

Most producers use sunlight to make organic nutrients by **photosynthesis**. Although hundreds of chemical changes take place in sequence during photosynthesis, the overall net change can be summarized as follows:

carbon dioxide + water + **solar energy** $\longrightarrow$ glucose + oxygen

$6\,CO_2$ + $6\,H_2O$ + **solar energy** $\longrightarrow$ $C_6H_{12}O6$ + $6\,O_2$

In essence, radiant energy from the sun is converted into chemical energy stored in the chemical bonds that hold glucose and other organic carbohydrates together. Other nutrients, including nitrogen and phosphorus, come from compounds dissolved in water.

Although plants do most of the planet's photosynthesis today, bacteria "invented" this process. Photosynthetic bacteria still exist, including the highly successful cyanobacteria (once called blue-green algae).

Q: How do most producer organisms get the nutrients they need?

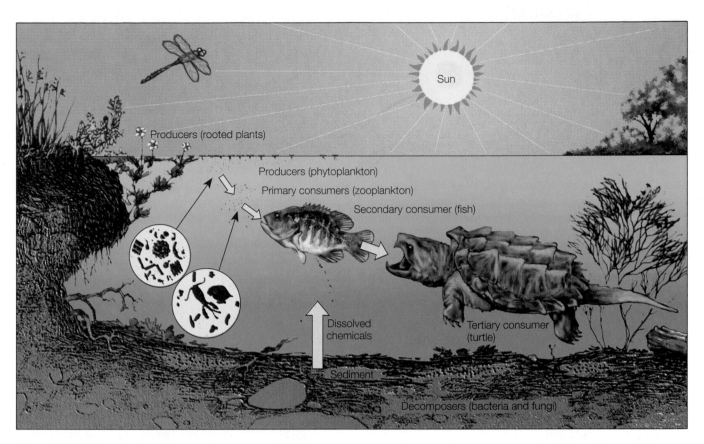

**Figure 4-14** Major components of a freshwater pond ecosystem.

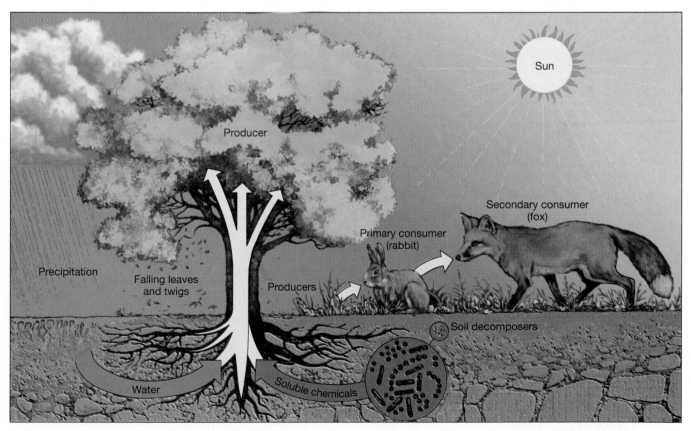

**Figure 4-15** Major components of an ecosystem in a field.

A: They produce them through photosynthesis.

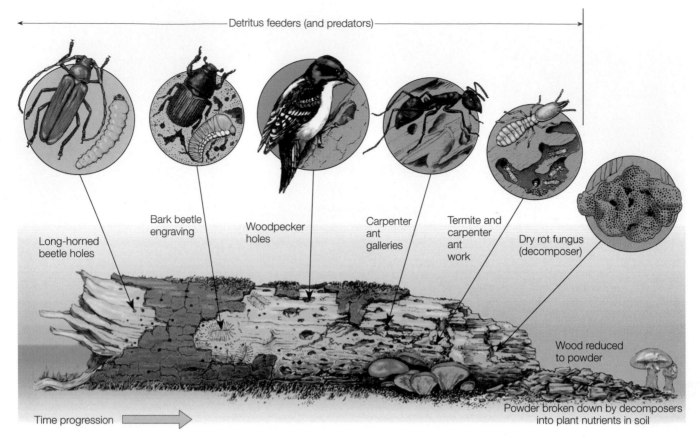

**Figure 4-16** Some detritivores, called *detritus feeders*, directly consume fragments of this log. Other detritivores, called *decomposers* (mostly fungi and bacteria), digest complex organic chemicals in fragments of the log into simpler inorganic nutrients. If these nutrients are not washed away or otherwise removed from the system, they can be used again by producers. The woodpecker shown in this diagram is not a detritivore. In its search for insects it pecks out fragments of organic matter that are consumed by detritivores.

A few producers, mostly specialized bacteria, can convert inorganic compounds from their environment into organic nutrients without sunlight—a process called **chemosynthesis**. In this case the source of energy is heat generated by the decay of radioactive elements deep in the earth's core and released at hotwater vents in the ocean's depths. In the pitch-dark around such vents specialized producer bacteria use the heat to convert dissolved hydrogen sulfide ($H_2S$) and carbon dioxide into organic nutrient molecules.

All other organisms in ecosystems are **consumers**, or **heterotrophs** (other-feeders), which get their organic nutrients by feeding on the tissues of producers or other consumers. There are several classes of consumers:

- **Herbivores** (plant-eaters) are called **primary consumers** because they feed directly on other producers.

- **Carnivores** (meat-eaters) feed on other consumers. Those called **secondary consumers** feed only on primary consumers. Most secondary consumers are animals, but a few such as the Venus flytrap trap and digest insects. **Tertiary (higher-level) consumers** feed only on other carnivores.

- **Omnivores** eat both plants and animals. Examples are pigs, rats, foxes, cockroaches, and humans.

- **Detritivores** (decomposers and detritus feeders) live off **detritus**, parts of dead organisms and cast-off fragments and wastes of living organisms (Figure 4-16).

- **Decomposers** digest the complex organic molecules in detritus into simpler inorganic compounds and absorb the soluble nutrients. These decomposers—mostly bacteria and fungi—(Figure 4-17) are an important source of food for worms and insects in the soil and water. **Detritus feeders**, such as crabs, carpenter ants, termites, and earthworms, extract nutrients from partly decomposed organic matter.

Producers and consumers use the chemical energy stored in glucose and other nutrients to drive

**Figure 4-17** Two types of decomposers are shelf fungi (left) and *Boletus luridus* mushrooms (right).

their life processes. This energy is released by the process of **aerobic respiration** (not the same as the breathing process called respiration), which uses oxygen to convert organic nutrients back into carbon dioxide and water. The net effect of the hundreds of changes in this complex process is

glucose + oxygen $\longrightarrow$ carbon dioxide + water + **energy**

$C_6H_{12}O_6$ + 6 $O_2$ $\longrightarrow$ 6 $CO_2$ + 6 $H_2O$ + **energy**

Thus, although the detailed steps differ, the net chemical change for aerobic respiration is the opposite of that for photosynthesis. Photosynthesis takes place during the day shift, when sunlight is available. Aerobic respiration can happen day or night.

The survival of any individual organism depends on the *flow of matter and energy* through its body. However, the community of organisms in an ecosystem survives primarily by a combination of *matter recycling* and *one-way energy flow* (Figure 4-18). Decomposers complete the cycle of matter by breaking detritus into inorganic nutrients usable by producers. Without decomposers the entire world would soon be knee-deep in plant litter, dead animal bodies, animal wastes, and garbage. In addition, the ecosphere needs only producers and decomposers to exist. We and all other consumers are unnecessary.

**NONLIVING PARTS OF ECOSYSTEMS** The nonliving, or abiotic, components of an ecosystem are physical and chemical factors that influence living organisms. Important physical factors affecting ecosystems are:

- Sunlight and shade
- Average temperature and temperature range
- Average precipitation and its timing
- Wind
- Latitude (distance from the equator)
- Altitude (distance above sea level)
- Nature of the soil (land ecosystems)
- Fire (land ecosystems)
- Water currents (aquatic ecosystems)
- Amount of suspended solid material (aquatic ecosystems)

The following are important chemical factors affecting ecosystems:

- Supply of water and air in the soil (land ecosystems)
- Supply of plant nutrients dissolved in soil moisture (land ecosystems) and in water (aquatic ecosystems)
- Level of toxic substances dissolved in soil moisture (land ecosystems) and in water (aquatic ecosystems)
- Salinity of water (aquatic ecosystems)
- Level of dissolved oxygen (aquatic ecosystems)

**TOLERANCE RANGES OF SPECIES** Each population in an ecosystem has a **range of tolerance** to variations in its physical and chemical environment (Figure

A: 5–20% (that is, a loss of 80–95%)

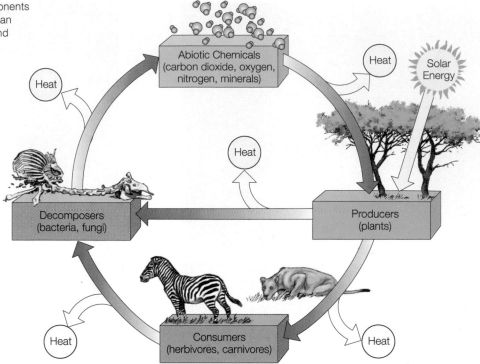

**Figure 4-18** The main structural components (energy, chemicals, and organisms) of an ecosystem are linked by energy flow and matter recycling.

4-19). For example, trout thrive in colder water than bass and perch, which in turn need colder water than catfish. Individuals within a population may have slightly different tolerance ranges for temperature, for example, because of small differences in their genetic makeup, health, and age. That is, it may take a little more heat to kill one brown trout than another. Thus, although a trout population may do best at one narrow band of temperatures (optimum level), a few individuals can survive both above and below that band. But, as Figure 4-19 shows, tolerance has its limits. Beyond them, no trout will survive.

These observations are summarized in the **law of tolerance**: *The existence, abundance, and distribution of a species in an ecosystem are determined by whether the levels of one or more physical or chemical factors fall within the range tolerated by the species.* A species may have a wide range of tolerance to some factors and a narrow range of tolerance to others. Most organisms are least tolerant during juvenile or reproductive stages of the life cycle. Highly tolerant species can live in a range of habitats with different conditions.

Some species can adjust their tolerance to physical factors such as temperature if change is gradual, just as you can tolerate a hotter bath by slowly adding hotter and hotter water. This adjustment to slowly changing new conditions, or **acclimation**, is a useful protective device. However, acclimation has limits. At each step the species comes closer to its absolute limit.

Suddenly, without warning, the next small change triggers a **threshold effect**, a harmful or even fatal reaction as the tolerance limit is exceeded—like adding that proverbial single straw that breaks the already heavily loaded camel's back.

The threshold effect explains why many environmental problems seem to arise suddenly. For example, spruce trees suddenly begin dying in droves, but the cause may be exposure to numerous air pollutants for decades. When whole forests die, as is happening in parts of Europe and North America, we're 10 or 20 years too late to do anything about it. The threshold effect also explains why we must prevent pollution to keep thresholds from being exceeded.

**LIMITING FACTORS IN ECOSYSTEMS** An ecological principle related to the law of tolerance is the **limiting factor principle**: *Too much or too little of any abiotic factor can limit or prevent growth of a population even if all other factors are at or near the optimum range of tolerance.* Such a factor is called a **limiting factor**.

Limiting factors in terrestrial ecosystems include temperature, water, light, and soil nutrients. For example, suppose a farmer plants corn in phosphorus-poor soil. Even if water, nitrogen, potassium, and other nutrients are at optimum levels, the corn will stop growing when it uses up the available phosphorus. Here, phosphorus determines how much corn will grow in the field. Growth can also be affected by too

Q: What are the three most productive types of ecosystems?

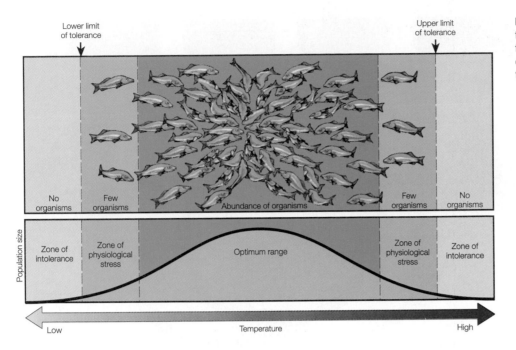

much of an abiotic factor. For example, plants can be killed by too much water or too much fertilizer.

In aquatic ecosystems **salinity** (the amounts of various salts dissolved in a given volume of water) is a limiting factor. It determines the species found in both marine (oceans) and freshwater ecosystems. Aquatic ecosystems can also be divided into surface, middle, and bottom layers or life zones. Important limiting factors for these layers are temperature, sunlight, **dissolved oxygen content** (the amount of oxygen gas dissolved in a given volume of water at a particular temperature and pressure), and availability of nutrients.

 ## 4-3 Energy Flow in Ecosystems

**FOOD CHAINS AND FOOD WEBS** *There is essentially no waste in functioning natural ecosystems.* All organisms, dead or alive, are potential sources of food for other organisms. A caterpillar eats a leaf; a robin eats the caterpillar; a hawk eats the robin. When plant, caterpillar, robin, and hawk all die, they in turn are consumed by decomposers.

The sequence of who eats or decomposes whom in an ecosystem is called a **food chain** (Figure 4-20). It determines how energy moves from one organism to another through the ecosystem. Ecologists assign every organism in an ecosystem to a *feeding level*, or **trophic level** (from the Greek *trophos*, "nourishment"),

depending on whether it is a producer or a consumer and on what it eats or decomposes. Producers belong to the first trophic level, primary consumers to the second trophic level, secondary consumers to the third trophic level, and so on. Detritivores process detritus from all trophic levels.

In the open ocean a typical food chain is phytoplankton → zooplankton → mackerel → tuna, with marine worms and bacteria decomposing all of these organisms when they die. Food chains rarely have more than four trophic levels or energy transfers.

Real ecosystems are more complex than this. Most consumers eat—and are eaten by—two or more types of organisms. Some animals feed at several trophic levels. Thus the organisms in most ecosystems form a complex network of feeding relationships called a **food web**. Figure 4-21 shows a simplified Antarctic food web. Trophic levels can be assigned in food webs just as in food chains.

**ECOLOGICAL PYRAMIDS** By counting the organisms at each trophic level, ecologists can graph this information to yield a **pyramid of numbers** for an ecosystem (Figure 4-22). Since the typical relationship is many producers to not so many primary consumers to just a few secondary consumers, the graph usually looks like a pyramid. For example, a million phytoplankton in a small pond may support 10,000 zooplankton, which in turn may support 100 perch, which might feed 1 person for a month or so. However, Figure 4-22 also shows there are exceptions to the pyramid shape.

A: Estuaries, swamps and marshes, and tropical rain forests

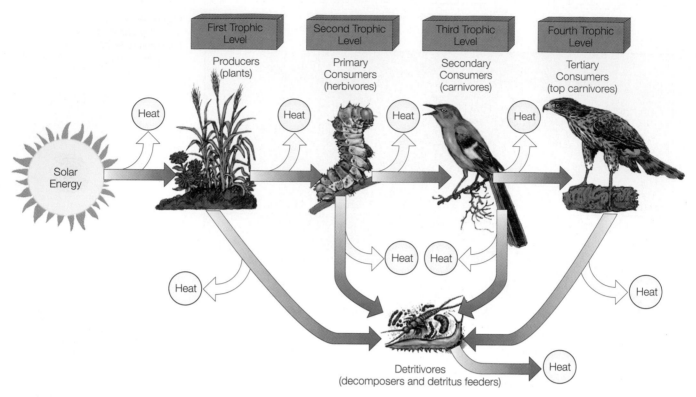

**Figure 4-20** A food chain. The arrows show how chemical energy in food flows through various trophic levels, with most of it degraded to heat in accordance with the second law of energy.

Each trophic level in a food chain or web contains a certain amount of **biomass**, the weight of all organic matter contained in its organisms. Ecologists estimate biomass by harvesting random patches or narrow strips in an ecosystem. The sample organisms are then sorted according to trophic levels, dried, and weighed. These data are used to plot a **pyramid of biomass** for the ecosystem (Figure 4-23). Here, too, the shape is not always pyramidal.

In a food chain or web, biomass (and thus chemical energy) is transferred from one trophic level to another, with some usable energy lost in each transfer. At each successive trophic level some of the available biomass is not eaten or is not digested or absorbed. Usable energy is also lost at each level, mostly as a result of the inevitable loss in energy quality imposed by the second law of energy.

The percentage of usable energy transferred from one trophic level to the next varies from 5% to 20% (that is, a loss of 80–95%), depending on the types of species and the ecosystem involved. The pyramid in Figure 4-24 illustrates this energy loss for a simple food chain, assuming a 90% energy loss with each transfer. This **pyramid of energy flow** shows that the more trophic levels or steps in a food chain or web, the greater the cumulative loss of usable energy. Figure 4-25 shows the actual pyramid and details of energy flow during one year for an aquatic ecosystem in Silver Springs, Florida.

The energy flow pyramid illustrates why Earth can support more people if they eat at lower trophic levels by consuming grains directly (for example, rice → human) rather than consuming grain-eaters (grain → steer → human). The large energy loss involved in going to each consecutive trophic level explains why food chains and webs rarely have more than four consecutive links. This is also why top carnivores like eagles, tigers, and white sharks are sparse in numbers and usually die off in large numbers when the ecosystems that support them are disrupted.

**PRODUCTIVITY OF PRODUCERS** The *rate* at which an ecosystem's producers capture and store chemical energy as biomass is the ecosystem's **gross primary productivity**. Figure 4-26 shows how this productivity varies in different parts of the earth. However, since the producers must use some of this biomass to stay alive, what we need to know is an ecosystem's **net primary productivity**.

| **net primary productivity** | = | rate at which producers produce chemical energy stored in biomass through photosynthesis | − | rate at which producers use chemical energy stored in biomass through aerobic respiration |
|---|---|---|---|---|

Q: How much of the world's net primary productivity on land is used by the world's 5.5 billion people?

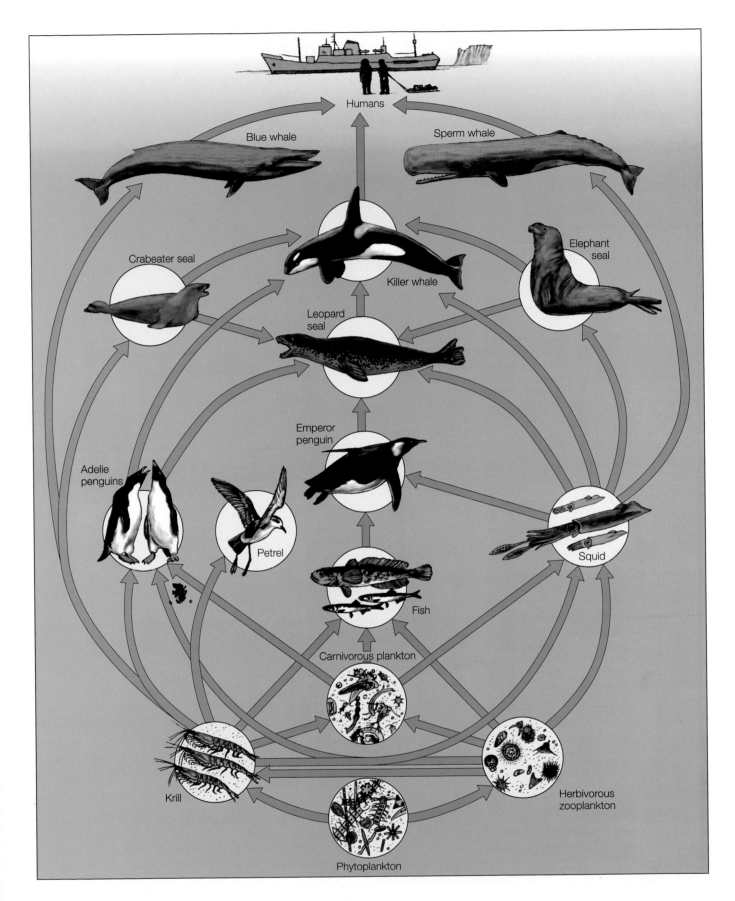

**Figure 4-21** Greatly simplified food web in the Antarctic. There are many more participants, including an array of decomposer organisms.

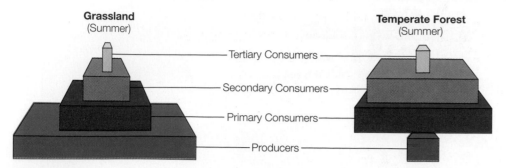

**Figure 4-22** Generalized graphs of numbers for two ecosystems. Numbers for grasslands and many other ecosystems taper off from the producer level to the higher trophic levels, forming a pyramid (left). For some ecosystems, however, the numbers take different shapes (right). For example, a redwood forest has a few large producers (the trees) that support a much larger number of small primary consumers (insects) that feed on the trees.

**Figure 4-23** Generalized graphs of biomass for two ecosystems. The size of each tier represents the dry weight per square meter of all organisms at that trophic level. For most land ecosystems the total biomass at each successive trophic level decreases. This yields a pyramid of biomass with a large base of producers, topped by a series of increasingly smaller trophic levels of consumers (left). In aquatic ecosystems the biomass of consumers can exceed that of producers (right). Here the producers are microscopic phytoplankton that grow and reproduce rapidly, not large plants that grow and reproduce slowly.

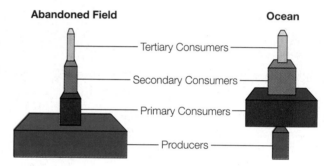

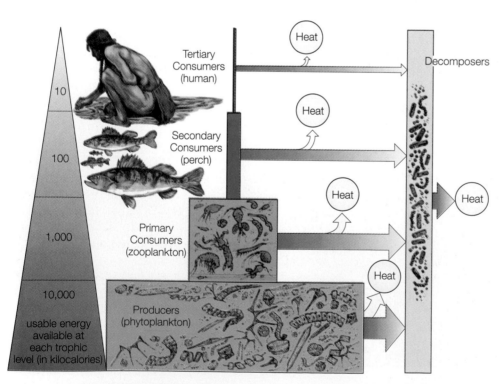

**Figure 4-24** Generalized pyramid of energy flow, showing the decrease in usable energy available at each succeeding trophic level in a food chain or web. This diagram shows a 90% loss in usable energy with each transfer from one trophic level to another. In nature such losses vary from 80% to 95%.

Q: What is the atmosphere's innermost layer called?

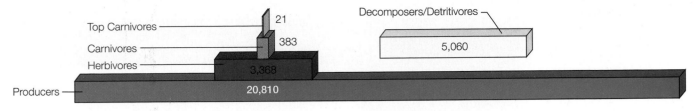

**Figure 4-25** Pyramid of energy flow (in kilocalories per square meter) for an aquatic ecosystem in Silver Springs, Florida, for one year. (Used by permission from Cecie Starr and Ralph Taggart, *Biology: The Unity and Diversity of Life*, 6th ed., Belmont, Calif.: Wadsworth, 1992)

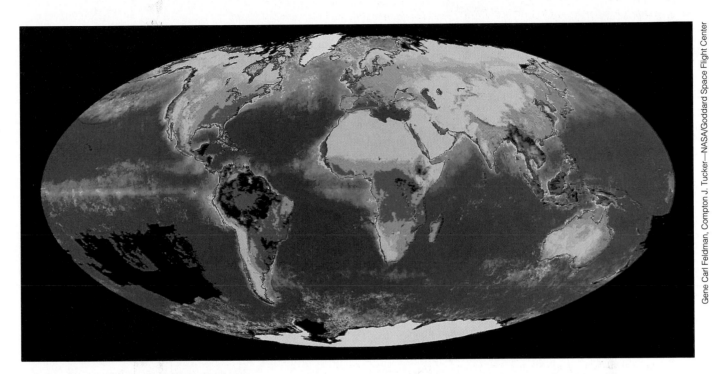

**Figure 4-26** Three years of satellite data on Earth's primary productivity. Rain forests and other highly productive areas appear as dark green, deserts as yellow. The concentration of phytoplankton, a primary indicator of ocean productivity, ranges from red (highest) to orange, yellow, green, and blue (lowest).

Net primary productivity, usually reported as the energy output of a specified area of producers over a given time (typically as kilocalories per square meter per year), is the basic food source or "income" for an ecosystem's consumers. It is the rate at which energy is stored in new biomass—cells, leaves, roots, stems—available for use by consumers. An estimated 59% of Earth's annual net primary productivity takes place on land, and the remaining 41% in oceans and other aquatic systems. Estuaries, swamps and marshes, and tropical rain forests are highly productive; open ocean, tundra (arctic grasslands), and desert are the least productive (Figure 4-27).

You might conclude that we should harvest plants in estuaries, swamps, and marshes to feed our hungry millions—or clear tropical forests and plant crops.

Wrong. The grasses in estuaries, swamps, and marshes cannot be eaten by people, but they are vital food sources (and spawning areas) for fish, shrimp, and other aquatic life that provide us and other consumers with protein. Thus we should protect, not harvest or destroy, these plants.

In tropical forests most nutrients are stored in vegetation rather than in the soil. When the trees are cleared, the nutrient-poor soils are rapidly depleted of their nutrients by frequent rains and by growing crops. Thus food crops can be grown only for a short time without massive applications of commercial fertilizers. Again, as with estuaries, swamps, and marshes, we should protect, not clear, these forests.

Humans now use or waste about 27% of the world's potential net primary productivity (40% for

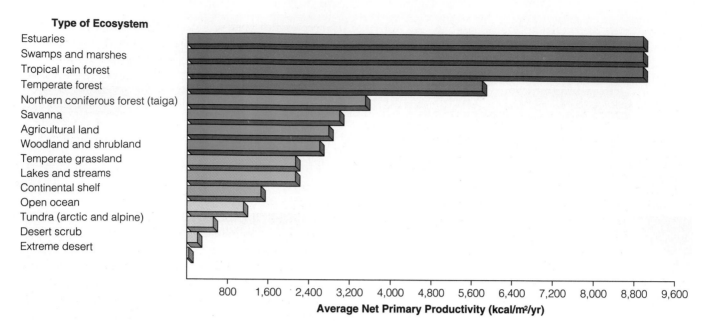

**Type of Ecosystem**

Estuaries
Swamps and marshes
Tropical rain forest
Temperate forest
Northern coniferous forest (taiga)
Savanna
Agricultural land
Woodland and shrubland
Temperate grassland
Lakes and streams
Continental shelf
Open ocean
Tundra (arctic and alpine)
Desert scrub
Extreme desert

800   1,600   2,400   3,200   4,000   4,800   5,600   6,400   7,200   8,000   8,800   9,600

**Average Net Primary Productivity (kcal/m²/yr)**

**Figure 4-27** Estimated average net primary productivity in major life zones and ecosystems. Values are given in kilocalories of energy produced per square meter per year.

**Figure 4-28** Simplified diagram of the global carbon cycle. The left portion shows the movement of carbon through marine ecosystems, and the right portion its movement through terrestrial ecosystems. (Used by permission from Cecie Starr and Ralph Taggart, *Biology: The Unity and Diversity of Life*, 6th ed., Belmont, Calif.: Wadsworth, 1992)

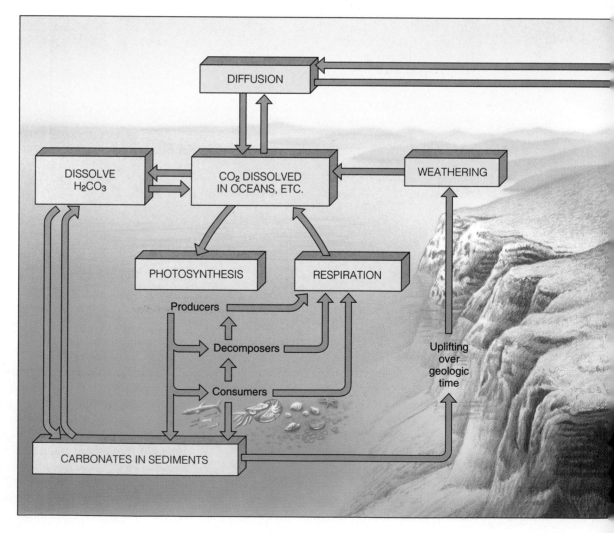

**Q:** What two gases make up 99% by volume of the air in the troposphere?

land systems). To do this our species has crowded out or eliminated other species. The resulting biodiversity impoverishment crisis is reducing Earth's carrying capacity for *all* species, including ourselves.

When earlier civilizations failed because they exceeded the carrying capacity of the land, people could expand into new areas. If we take over (or try to take over) 80% of the planet's primary land productivity as our population doubles over the next 40 years, most biologists believe we will exceed the carrying capacity in vast areas. There will be no place to expand to, and no place to hide from the consequences of such biological impoverishment.

## 4-4 Matter Cycling in Ecosystems

**CARBON CYCLE** Nutrients, the chemicals essential for life, move in the ecosphere and in mature ecosystems in biogeochemical cycles (Figure 4-3). In these cycles nutrients move from the environment, through organisms, and back to the environment. All are driven, directly or indirectly, by solar energy and by gravity.

Carbon is the basic building block of the carbohydrates, fats, proteins, nucleic acids such as DNA and RNA, and other organic compounds necessary for life. The **carbon cycle** is based on carbon dioxide gas, which makes up almost 0.036% by volume of the troposphere and is also dissolved in water.

Producers absorb $CO_2$ from the atmosphere (terrestrial producers) or water (aquatic producers) and use photosynthesis to convert it into complex carbohydrates. Then the cells in oxygen-consuming producers and consumers carry out aerobic respiration, which breaks down glucose and other complex organic compounds and converts the carbon back to $CO_2$ in the atmosphere or water for reuse by producers. This linkage between photosynthesis in producers and aerobic respiration in producers and consumers circulates carbon in the ecosphere and is a major part of the global carbon cycle (Figure 4-28). Oxygen and hydrogen, the other elements in carbohydrates, cycle almost in step with carbon.

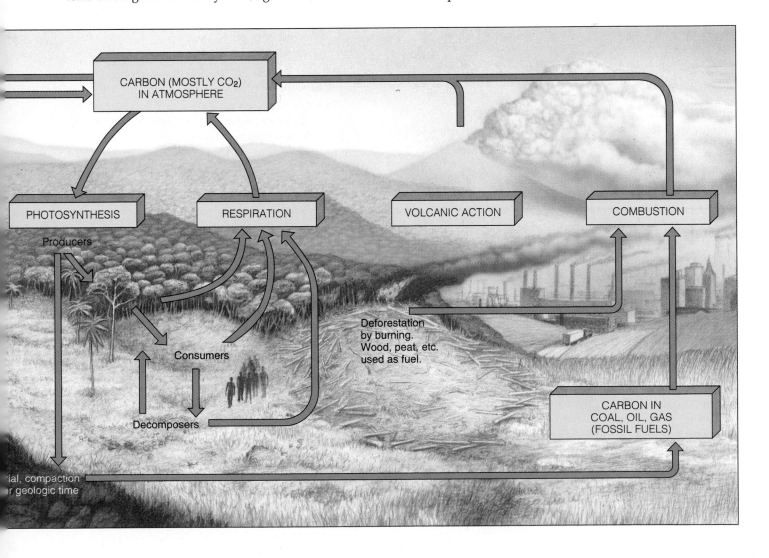

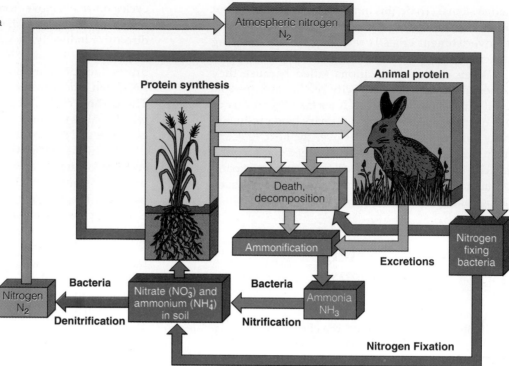

**Figure 4-29** Greatly simplified diagram of the nitrogen cycle in a terrestrial ecosystem. (Adapted from Carolina Biological Supply Company)

Carbon dioxide is the key component of nature's thermostat. If the carbon cycle removes too much $CO_2$ from the atmosphere, Earth will cool; if the cycle generates too much, Earth will get hotter. Thus even slight changes in the carbon cycle can affect climate and ultimately the types of life that can exist on the planet.

As Figure 4-28 shows, some carbon lies deep in the earth in fossil fuels—coal, petroleum, and natural gas—and is released to the atmosphere as carbon dioxide only when these fuels are extracted and burned. $CO_2$ also enters the atmosphere from aerobic respiration and from volcanic eruptions, which free carbon from rocks deep in the earth's crust.

The oceans also play a major role in regulating the level of carbon dioxide in the atmosphere. Carbon dioxide gas is readily soluble in water. Some of this dissolved $CO_2$ stays in the sea, and some is removed by photosynthesizing producers. As water warms, more dissolved $CO_2$ returns to the atmosphere.

In marine ecosystems some organisms take up dissolved $CO_2$ molecules, carbonate ions ($CO_3^{2-}$), or bicarbonate ions ($HCO_3^-$) from ocean water and form slightly soluble carbonate compounds such as calcium carbonate ($CaCO_3$) to build shells and the skeletons of marine organisms. When these organisms die, tiny particles of their shells and bone drift slowly to the ocean depths and are buried for eons (as long as 400 million years) in bottom sediments (Figure 4-28). In fact, most of the earth's carbon—10,000 times that in

the total mass of all life on Earth—is stored in the ocean floor sediments and on the continents. This carbon reenters the cycle very slowly when some of the sediments dissolve and form dissolved $CO_2$ gas that can enter the atmosphere. Geologic processes can also bring bottom sediments to the surface, exposing the carbonate rock to chemical attack by oxygen and conversion to $CO_2$ gas.

Especially since 1950, as world population and resource use have soared, we have disturbed the carbon cycle in two ways that add more carbon dioxide to the atmosphere than oceans and plants can remove:

- Forest and brush clearing, leaving less vegetation to absorb $CO_2$.

- Burning fossil fuels and wood, which produces $CO_2$ that flows into the atmosphere. Computer models of Earth's climate systems suggest that this $CO_2$, along with other heat-trapping gases we're adding to the atmosphere, could enhance the planet's natural greenhouse effect. This could alter climate patterns, disrupt global food production and wildlife habitats, and possibly raise the average sea level.

**NITROGEN CYCLE: BACTERIA IN ACTION** Organisms need nitrogen to make proteins, DNA, RNA, and other nitrogen-containing organic compounds. The nitrogen gas ($N_2$) that makes up 78% of the volume of

Q: What gas in the stratosphere keeps 99% of the sun's harmful ultraviolet radiation from reaching the earth's surface?

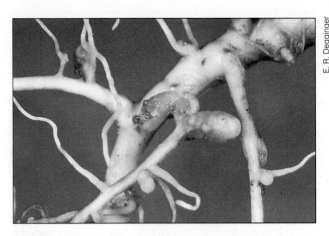

**Figure 4-30** Plants in the legume family have root nodules where *Rhizobium* bacteria "fix" nitrogen. That is, they change nitrogen gas ($N_2$) into ammonia ($NH_3$), which in soil water forms ammonium ions ($NH_4^+$) that are taken up by the roots of plants. This process benefits both species. The bacteria convert atmospheric nitrogen into a form usable by the plants, and the plants provide the bacteria with sugar.

the troposphere cannot be used directly as a nutrient by multicellular plants or animals. Fortunately bacteria convert nitrogen gas into water-soluble ionic compounds containing nitrate ions ($NO_3^-$) and ammonium ions ($NH_4^+$), which are taken up by plant roots as part of the **nitrogen cycle** (Figure 4-29).

The conversion of atmospheric nitrogen gas into other chemical forms useful to plants is called **nitrogen fixation**. It is done mostly by cyanobacteria in soil and water and by *Rhizobium* bacteria living in small nodules (swellings) on the roots of alfalfa, clover, peas, beans, and other legumes (Figure 4-30).

Plants convert inorganic nitrate ions and ammonium ions from soil water into DNA, proteins, and other, nitrogen-containing nutrients. Animals get their nitrogen by eating plants or plant-eating animals.

After nitrogen has served its purpose in living organisms, armies of specialized decomposer bacteria convert the nitrogen-rich organic compounds, wastes, cast-off particles, and dead bodies of organisms into simpler inorganic compounds such as ammonia gas ($NH_3$) and water-soluble salts containing ammonium ions ($NH_4^+$). Other specialized bacteria then convert these inorganic forms of nitrogen back into nitrite ($NO_2^-$) and nitrate ($NO_3^-$) ions in the soil and then into nitrogen gas, which is released to the atmosphere to begin the cycle again.

We intervene in the nitrogen cycle in the following ways:

- Emitting large quantities of nitric oxide (NO) into the atmosphere when any fuel is burned. (Most of this NO is produced when nitrogen and oxygen molecules in the air combine at high temperatures.) This nitric oxide combines with oxygen to form nitrogen dioxide ($NO_2$) gas, which can react with water vapor to form nitric acid ($HNO_3$). This acid is a component of acid deposition (commonly called acid rain), which can damage trees and kill fish.

- Emitting heat-trapping nitrous oxide ($N_2O$) gas into the atmosphere by the action of bacteria on livestock wastes and commercial inorganic fertilizers applied to the soil.

- Mining mineral deposits containing nitrate and ammonium ions for fertilizers.

- Depleting nitrate and ammonium ions from soil by harvesting nitrogen-rich crops.

- Adding excess nitrate and ammonium ions to aquatic ecosystems in agricultural runoff and discharge of municipal sewage. This excess of plant nutrients stimulates rapid growth of algae and other aquatic plants. The subsequent breakdown of dead algae by aerobic decomposers depletes the water of dissolved oxygen gas, killing great numbers of fish.

**PHOSPHORUS CYCLE** Phosphorus, mainly in the form of phosphate ions ($PO_4^{3-}$ and $HPO_4^{2-}$), is an essential nutrient of both plants and animals. It is a part of DNA molecules, which carry genetic information; other molecules, which store chemical energy for use by organisms in cellular respiration; certain fats in the membranes that encase plant and animal cells; and animal bones and teeth.

Phosphorus moves through water, Earth's crust, and living organisms in the **phosphorus cycle** (Figure 4-31). In this cycle phosphorus moves slowly from phosphate deposits on land and shallow ocean sediments to living organisms, and then back to the land and ocean. Bacteria are less important here than in the nitrogen cycle.

Phosphorus released by the slow breakdown, or weathering, of phosphate rock deposits is dissolved in soil water and taken up by plant roots. Wind can also carry phosphate particles long distances. Most soils contain little phosphorus because phosphate compounds are only slightly soluble in water and are found in few kinds of rocks. Thus phosphorus is the limiting factor for plant growth in many soils and aquatic ecosystems.

Animals get their phosphorus by eating producers or animals that have eaten producers. Animal wastes and the decay products of dead animals and producers return much of this phosphorus to the soil, to streams, and eventually to the ocean bottom as deposits of phosphate rock.

A: Ozone ($O_3$)

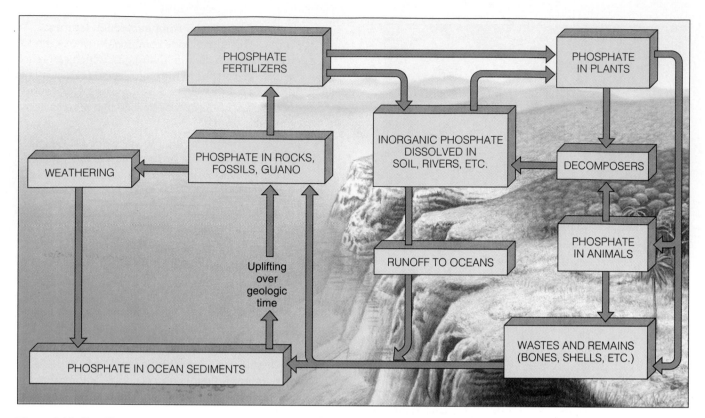

**Figure 4-31** Simplified diagram of the phosphorus cycle. (Used by permission from Cecie Starr and Ralph Taggart, *Biology: The Unity and Diversity of Life*, 6th ed., Belmont, Calif.: Wadsworth, 1992)

Some phosphate returns to the land as guano—the phosphate-rich manure of fish-eating birds such as pelicans and cormorants. This return is small, though, compared with the phosphate transferred from the land to the oceans each year by natural processes and human activities.

Over millions of years geologic processes may push up and expose the seafloor. Weathering then slowly releases phosphorus from the exposed rocks and allows the cycle to begin again.

We intervene in the phosphorus cycle chiefly in two ways:

- Mining large quantities of phosphate rock to produce commercial inorganic fertilizers and detergents.

- Adding excess phosphate ions to aquatic ecosystems in runoff of animal wastes from livestock feedlots, runoff of commercial phosphate fertilizers from cropland, and discharge of municipal sewage. As with nitrate and ammonium ions, too much of this nutrient causes explosive growth of cyanobacteria, algae, and aquatic plants, disrupting life in aquatic ecosystems.

**SULFUR CYCLE** Sulfur circulates through the ecosphere in the **sulfur cycle** (Figure 4-32). Much of the earth's sulfur is tied up underground in sulfide rocks (such as iron disulfide or pyrite) and minerals, including sulfate salts (such as hydrous calcium sulfate or gypsum) buried deep under ocean sediments.

However, sulfur also enters the atmosphere from several natural sources. Hydrogen sulfide ($H_2S$), a colorless, highly poisonous gas with a "rotten-egg" smell, comes from active volcanoes and from the breakdown of organic matter in swamps, bogs, and tidal flats caused by decomposers that don't use oxygen (anaerobic decomposers). Sulfur dioxide ($SO_2$), a colorless, suffocating gas, also comes from volcanoes. Particles of sulfate ($SO_4^{2-}$) salts, such as ammonium sulfate, enter the atmosphere from sea spray.

In the atmosphere sulfur dioxide reacts with oxygen to produce sulfur trioxide gas ($SO_3$), which in turn reacts with water vapor to produce tiny droplets of sulfuric acid ($H_2SO_4$). It also reacts with other chemicals in the atmosphere to produce tiny particles of sulfate salts. These droplets of sulfuric acid and particles of sulfate salts fall to Earth as components of acid

Q: What are the three major types of biomes?

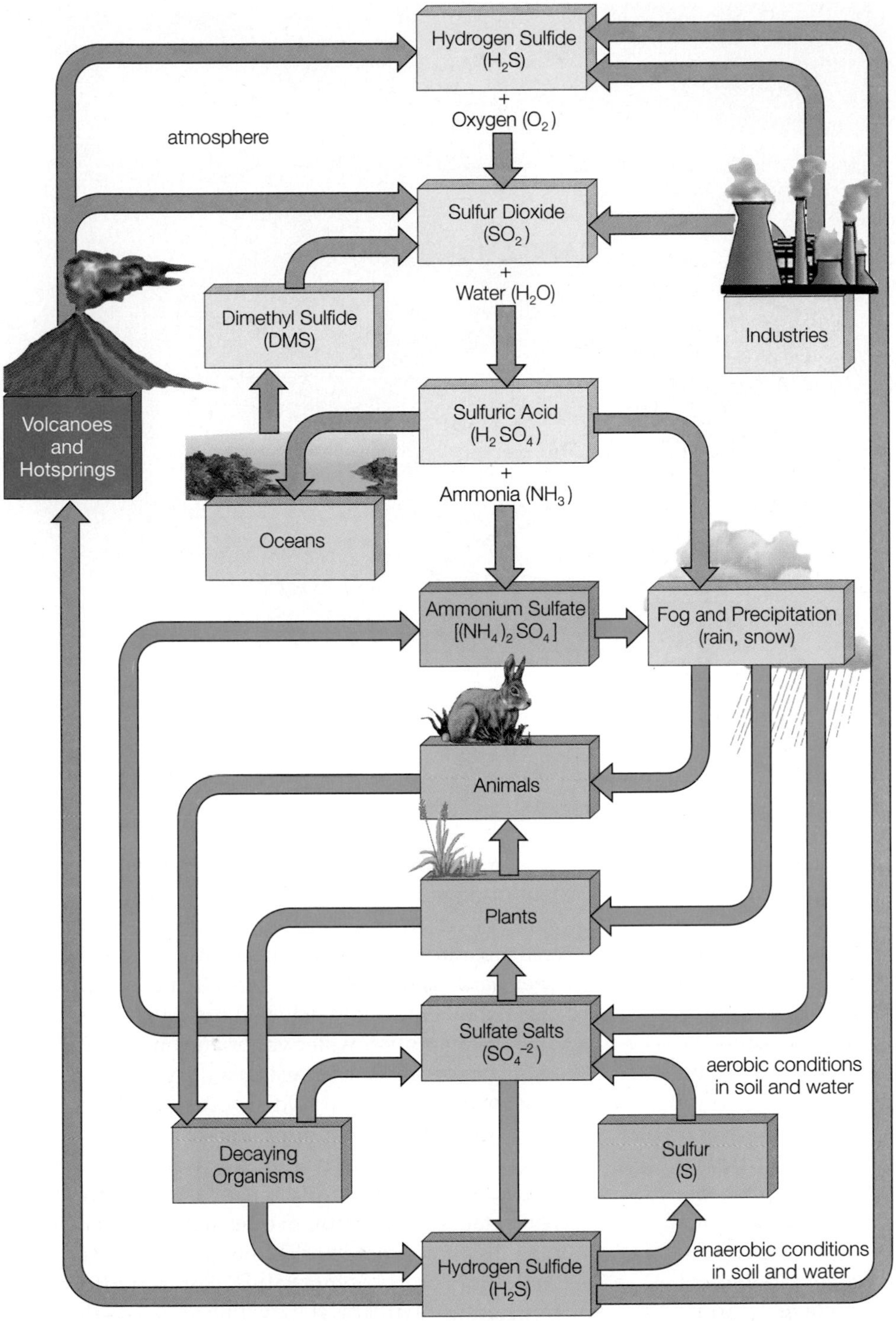

**Figure 4-32** Simplified diagram of the sulfur cycle.

deposition, which can harm trees and aquatic life. Droplets of sulfuric acid are also produced from dimethylsulfide (DMS) emitted into the atmosphere by many species of ocean plankton.

About a third of all sulfur, including 99% of the sulfur dioxide, that reaches the atmosphere comes from human activities. We intervene in the atmospheric phase of the sulfur cycle in two ways:

■ Burning sulfur-containing coal and oil to produce electric power, which produces about two-thirds of the human inputs of sulfur dioxide

■ Refining petroleum, smelting sulfur compounds of metallic minerals into free metals such as copper, lead, and zinc, and performing other industrial processes

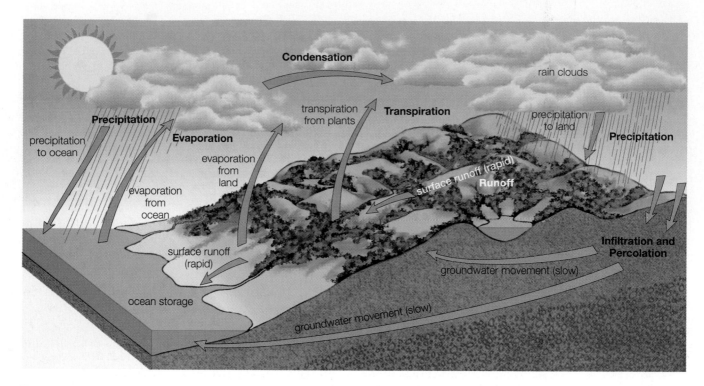

**Figure 4-33** Simplified diagram of the hydrologic cycle.

**HYDROLOGIC CYCLE** Without water the other nutrient cycles would not exist in their present forms, and the current forms of life on Earth—consisting mostly of water-containing cells and tissues—could not exist. The **hydrologic cycle** or **water cycle**, which collects, purifies, and distributes Earth's fixed supply of water, is shown in simplified form in Figure 4-33. The main processes in this water recycling and purifying cycle are *evaporation* (conversion of water into water vapor), *transpiration* (evaporation of water extracted by roots and transported upward from leaves or other parts of plants), *condensation* (conversion of water vapor into droplets of liquid water), *precipitation* (dew, rain, sleet, hail, snow), *infiltration* (movement of water into soil), *percolation* (downward flow of water through soil and permeable rock formations to groundwater storage areas), and *runoff* downslope back to the sea to begin the cycle again. At different phases of the cycle water is stored for varying amounts of time on the planet's surface (oceans, streams, reservoirs, glaciers) or in the ground.

The water cycle is powered by energy from the sun and by gravity. Incoming solar energy evaporates water from oceans, streams, lakes, soil, and vegetation into the atmosphere. About 84% of the moisture comes from the oceans, and the rest from land. The amount of mois-ture in the atmosphere at any one time is the equivalent of only about 25 millimeters (1 inch) of rainfall spread over Earth's entire surface. However, because this moisture is renewed, the average annual rainfall over Earth as a whole is 1 meter (40 inches), although actual rainfall varies widely in different places.

The amount of water vapor air can hold depends on its temperature, with warm air capable of holding more water vapor than cold air. **Absolute humidity** is the amount of water vapor found in a certain mass of air (usually expressed as grams of water per kilogram of air). **Relative humidity** is a measure (expressed in percentages) of the amount of water vapor in a certain mass of air compared with the maximum amount it could hold at that temperature. For example, a relative humidity of 60% at 27°C (80°F) means that each kilogram (or other mass unit) of air has 60% of the water vapor it could hold at that temperature.

Winds and air masses transport this water vapor over various parts of the earth's surface, often over long distances. Falling temperatures cause the water vapor to condense into tiny droplets that form clouds or fog. For precipitation to occur, air must contain **condensation nuclei**—tiny particles on which droplets of water vapor can collect. Volcanic ash, soil dust, smoke, sea salts, and particulate matter emitted by

Q: How much of Earth's tropical forests have been cleared or damaged?

factories, coal-burning power plants, and vehicles are sources of such particles. The temperature at which condensation occurs for a given amount of water vapor is called the **dew point**.

It takes millions of tiny water droplets adhering to a condensation nucleus to produce a drop of rain or a snowflake that will fall to the earth's surface. About 77% of this precipitation falls back into the sea, and the rest over land.

Some of the fresh water returning to the earth's surface as precipitation becomes locked in glaciers. Much of it collects in puddles and ditches, and runs off into nearby lakes and into streams, which carry water back to the oceans, completing the cycle.

Besides replenishing streams and lakes, surface water running off the land also causes soil erosion, which moves various nutrients through portions of other biogeochemical cycles. Water is the medium that carries rock debris from the mountains into valleys and eventually down to the ocean floor. It is the primary sculptor of Earth's landscape. Also, acidic rainwater reacts chemically with metallic minerals on Earth's surface, forming water-soluble metallic salts that are carried by rivers to the sea. This is one of the reasons the ocean is so salty.

Much of the water returning to the land seeps into or infiltrates surface soil layers. Some percolates downward into the ground, dissolving minerals from porous rocks on the way. There this mineral-laden water is stored as groundwater in the pores and cracks of rocks. This underground water, like surface water, flows downhill and seeps out into streams and lakes or comes out in springs. Eventually this water evaporates or reaches the sea to begin the cycle again. The average circulation rate of underground water in the hydrologic cycle is extremely slow (300–4,600 years) compared with that of water in lakes (13 years), in streams (13 days), and in the atmosphere (9 days). The turnover time for water in the ocean is about 37,000 years, and for ice in glaciers is about 16,000 years.

We intervene in the water cycle in two main ways:

- Withdrawing large quantities of fresh water from streams, lakes, and underground sources. In heavily populated or heavily irrigated areas withdrawals have led to groundwater depletion or intrusion of ocean salt water into underground water supplies.

- Clearing vegetation from land for agriculture, mining, roads, construction, and other activities. This reduces seepage that recharges groundwater supplies, increases the risk of flooding, and speeds surface runoff, producing more soil erosion and landslides.

## 4-5 Roles of Species in Ecosystems

**TYPES OF SPECIES IN ECOSYSTEMS** One way to look at an ecosystem's species is to divide them into four types:

- **Native species**, which normally live and thrive in a particular ecosystem.

- **Immigrant**, or **alien**, **species**, which migrate into an ecosystem or which are deliberately or accidentally introduced into an ecosystem by humans. Some of these species are beneficial, while others can take over and eliminate many native species.

- **Indicator species**, which serve as early warnings that a community or an ecosystem is being damaged. For example, the present decline of migratory, insect-eating songbirds in North America indicates that their summer habitats there and their winter habitats in the tropical forests of Latin America and the Caribbean are rapidly disappearing. Some indicator species, such as the brown pelican (Figure 2-8) and the North American bald eagle (Figure 2-10), and other birds of prey feed high in food chains and webs. This exposes them to high levels of fat-soluble toxic chemicals such as DDT and PCBs, which become more concentrated in the tissues of organisms at each successive trophic level. Some frogs, toads, salamanders, and other amphibians that live part of their lives in water and part on land are indicator species (Spotlight, p. 102).

- **Keystone species** affect many other organisms in an ecosystem.* For example, in tropical forests various species of bees, bats, ants, and hummingbirds play keystone roles in pollinating flowering plants, dispersing seed, or both. The loss of a keystone species can lead to population crashes and extinctions of other species that depend on it for certain services—a ripple or domino effect that spreads throughout an ecosystem. According to biologist E. O. Wilson, "The loss of a keystone species is like a drill accidentally striking a power line. It causes lights to go out all over." Sea otters,

---

* All species play some role in their ecosystem and thus are important. Some scientists consider all species equally important, but others consider certain species to be keystone or more important than others, at least in helping maintain the ecosystems they are a part of.

## The Mystery of Vanishing Amphibians

Amphibians first appeared about 350 million years ago. These cold-blooded creatures range in size from a frog that can sit on your thumb to a Japanese salamander about 1.5 meters (5 feet) long.

Fossil records suggest that frogs and toads, the oldest of today's amphibians, were living as long as 150 million years ago. Such endurance testifies to the adaptability of these organisms. Recently, however, hundreds of the world's estimated 5,100 amphibian species (including 2,700 species of frogs and toads) have been vanishing or dying back, even in protected wildlife reserves and parks (Figure 4-34).

Scientists have not identified any single reason for this decline. In some cases, such as Costa Rican golden toads, diebacks may be caused by prolonged drought. This causes breeding pools to dry up so that few if any tadpoles survive. Dehydration can also weaken amphibians, making them more susceptible to fatal viruses, bacteria, fungi, or protozoans.

In other cases the culprit may be pollution. Because amphibians live part of their lives in water and part on land, they are exposed to water, soil, and air pollutants. The soft, permeable skin that allows them to absorb oxygen from water also makes them extremely sensitive to water-borne pollutants. Their skin may also make them highly sensi-

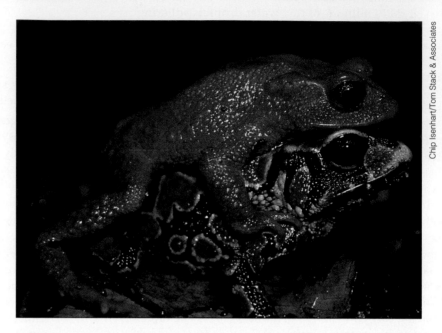

**Figure 4-34** A pair of golden toads mating. Populations of this species have dropped sharply in recent years, even in Costa Rica's protected Monteverde Cloud Forest Reserve. Prolonged drought may explain this population decline, but other factors may also be involved. The male's dazzling reddish-orange color helps it attract its mate.

tive to increases in ultraviolet radiation caused by depletion of ozone in the stratosphere. Their insect diet guarantees them abundant food, but in farming areas it also exposes them to pesticides.

In Asia, where frog legs are a delicacy, overhunting may play a part. In other areas migration or introduction of predators and competitors can threaten amphibian populations.

Scientists are concerned about the amphibians' decline for two reasons. First, it suggests that the

world's environmental health is deteriorating rapidly because amphibians are tough survivors. Second, amphibians, which outnumber birds and eat more insects than birds, play an important role in the world's ecosystems. In some habitats their extinction could also spell death for other species such as the reptiles, birds, and other amphibians that feed on them. As indicator species amphibians are sending us an important message.

---

for example, are keystone species that keep sea urchins from depleting kelp beds in offshore waters from Alaska to southern California. Remove the sea otter and there is not enough kelp left to support the diverse community of crustaceans, mollusks, fish, and marine mammals. Some keystone species, such as the alligator (Case Study, p. 103), wolf, leopard, lion, giant anteater, and giant armadillo, are top predators

that exert a stabilizing effect on their ecosystems by feeding on and regulating the populations of certain species.

**NICHE** The **ecological niche**, or simply **niche** (pronounced nitch), of a species is its total way of life or its role in an ecosystem. It includes all physical, chemical, and biological conditions a species needs to live and reproduce in an ecosystem.

## The American Alligator: A Keystone Species

The American alligator (Figure 4-35), America's largest reptile, has no natural predators except people. Hunters once killed large numbers of these animals for their exotic meat and for the supple belly skin used to make items such as shoes, belts, and pocketbooks. People also considered alligators to be useless, dangerous vermin and hunted them for sport or out of hatred. Between 1950 and 1960 hunters wiped out 90% of the alligators in Louisiana, and by the 1960s the alligator population in the Florida Everglades was also near extinction.

People who say "So what?" are overlooking the alligator's keystone role in subtropical, wetland ecosystems such as Florida's Everglades. Alligators dig deep depressions, or "gator holes," which collect fresh water during dry spells. These holes are refuges for aquatic life and supply fresh water and food for birds and other animals. Fertilized by alligator droppings, the holes become filled with lilies and other aquatic plants that provide shelter for nesting birds.

Large alligator nesting mounds also serve as nest sites for herons and egrets. As alligators move from gator holes to nesting mounds, they help keep areas of open water free of invading vegetation. Alligators also eat large numbers of predatory gar fish and thus help maintain populations of game fish such as bass and bream.

In 1967 the U.S. government placed the American alligator on the endangered species list. Averaging about 40 eggs per nest and protected from hunters, the alligator population had made a strong comeback in many areas by 1975—too strong, according to people who find alligators in their backyards and swimming pools.

The problem is that people are invading the alligator's natural habitats. And while the gator's diet consists mainly of snails, apples, sick fish, ducks, raccoons, and turtles, a pet or a person who falls into or swims in a canal, a pond, or some other area where a gator lives is subject to attack.

In 1977 the U.S. Fish and Wildlife Service reclassified the American alligator from endangered to threatened in Florida, Louisiana, and Texas, where 90% of the animals live. In 1987 this reclassification was extended to seven other states. As a threatened species, it is illegal to kill alligators,

**Figure 4-35** The American alligator is a keystone species in its marsh and swamp habitats in the southeastern United States. In 1967 it was classified as an endangered species. This protection allowed the species to recover enough for its status to be changed from endangered to threatened. Because of its thick skin, speed in the water, and powerful jaws, this species has no natural predators except humans.

but limited hunting by licensed professional game wardens is allowed in some areas to control the population. Florida, for example, with at least 1 million alligators, permits 7,000 kills per year. The comeback of the American alligator is an important success story in wildlife conservation.

---

Species can be broadly classified as specialists or generalists, according to their niches. **Specialist species** have narrow niches. They may be able to live in only one type of habitat, tolerate only a narrow range of climatic and other environmental conditions, or use only one or a few types of food. Examples of specialists are tiger salamanders, which can breed only in fishless ponds so their larvae won't be eaten; redcockaded woodpeckers, which carve nest-holes almost exclusively in longleaf pines at least 75 years old; and the giant panda (Case Study, p. 104).

In a tropical rain forest an incredibly diverse array of species survives by occupying specialized ecological niches in distinct layers of the forest's vegetation (Figure 4-37). The widespread clearing and degradation of such forests is dooming millions of such specialized species to extinction.

**Generalist species** have broad niches. They can live in many different places, eat a variety of foods, and tolerate a wide range of environmental conditions. Flies, cockroaches, mice, rats, white-tail deer, raccoons, and humans are all generalist species.

Is it better to be a generalist than a specialist? That depends. When environmental conditions are fairly constant, such as in a tropical rain forest, specialists have an advantage because they have fewer competi-

The giant panda (Figure 4-36) is one of the world's most endangered animals. One reason is that it is so specialized, getting 99% of its food from bamboo. Worse, its digestive system absorbs only about 17% of the food it eats and its bamboo diet provides enough protein but very little energy. To survive, these animals must spend most of each day eating up to one-third of their body weight in bamboo.

Three million years ago giant pandas were widespread in China. But China's soaring population has pushed them into smaller and smaller areas in the remote, fog-shrouded western mountains. Today only about 800 giant pandas survive in the wild, in about 20 isolated "islands" of bamboo forest. These isolated populations of 10–50 animals are vulnerable to being wiped out and to inbreeding. One serious threat is illegal hunting. Although killing a giant panda in China brings an automatic death penalty, poachers still kill 40 or more pandas per year because their pelts bring $100,000 or more in Hong Kong and Japan.

Giant pandas are also biologically vulnerable to extinction. Only about one cub per female survives every other year. Pandas are also quite finicky about picking mates, which becomes critical with their low numbers and isolated habitats.

Finally, bamboo dies off in cycles of 15–120 years, depending on the species. Then it takes several years for new bamboo sprouts to reach edible size. When bamboo was abundant this was no problem. The pandas simply moved to another area. Today, however, the few remaining pandas are confined to islands of forest dominated by a few bamboo species. When these plants die back, the pandas have no food source.

China has set aside 12 giant panda reserves, but the animals are threatened in 8 of them by poaching and by China's growing population. Fourteen new reserves have been proposed. Three of these would link existing reserves with migration corridors, to be planted with bamboo, and more corridors are planned. This would help end the animals' isolation, but it remains to be seen whether it will happen.

About 220 giant pandas are found in zoos and research centers in China (which has spent $25 million trying to save the species) and

**Figure 4-36** The giant panda, which is found in China, is a specialist species. It has a narrow food niche, surviving primarily on bamboo stalks and leaves.

elsewhere, but more captive pandas die than are born. Will this specialized species survive? Maybe in a few zoos, but within your lifetime it may disappear from the wild.

---

tors. When environments are changing rapidly, however, the adaptable generalist is usually better off than the specialist.

## 4-6 Interactions Between Species

**WAYS SPECIES INTERACT** When any two species in an ecosystem have some activities or requirements in common, they may interact to some degree. The principal types of species interactions are *interspecific competition, predation, parasitism, mutualism,* and *com-*

*mensalism.* Three of these interactions—parasitism, mutualism, and commensalism—are **symbiotic relationships** in which two or more kinds of organisms live together in an intimate association, with members of one or both species benefiting from the association. In mutualism and commensalism neither species is harmed by the interaction.

**COMPETITION BETWEEN SPECIES FOR LIMITED RESOURCES** As long as commonly used resources are abundant, different species can share them. This allows each species to come closer to occupying its **fundamental niche**: the full potential range of physical, chemical, and biological factors it could use if there were no competition from other species.

Q: How much of Earth's wetlands have been destroyed or polluted?

**Figure 4-37** Stratification of specialized plant and animal niches in various layers of a tropical rain forest. These specialized niches allow species to avoid or minimize competition for resources with other species and lead to the coexistence of a great diversity of species. Niche specialization is promoted by the adaptation of plants to the different levels of light available in the forest's layers and by hundreds of thousands of years of evolution in a fairly constant climate.

In most ecosystems each species faces competition from one or more other species for one or more of the same limited resources (such as food, sunlight, water, soil nutrients, or space) it needs. Because of such **interspecific competition**, parts of the fundamental niches of different species overlap significantly. When the fundamental niches of two competing species do overlap, one species may occupy more of its fundamental niche than the other species. This is done through two types of competitive interactions.

In **interference competition** one species may limit another's access to some resource, regardless of whether the resource is abundant or scarce. For example, one species of hummingbird may defend patches of spring wildflowers from which it gets nectar by chasing away individuals of other hummingbird species. Coral animals kill other nearby species of coral by poisoning and growing over them.

In pure **exploitation competition** two competing species have equal access to a specific resource but differ in how quickly or efficiently they exploit it. In this way one species gets more of the resource and thus hampers the growth, reproduction, or survival of the other species. When shared resources are abundant this type of interspecific competition does not occur.

Another process that reduces the degree of fundamental niche overlap is **resource partitioning**, the dividing up of scarce resources so that species with similar requirements use them at different times, in different ways, or in different places (Figure 4-38). In

**A:** 25–50% (55% in the United States, 91% in California)

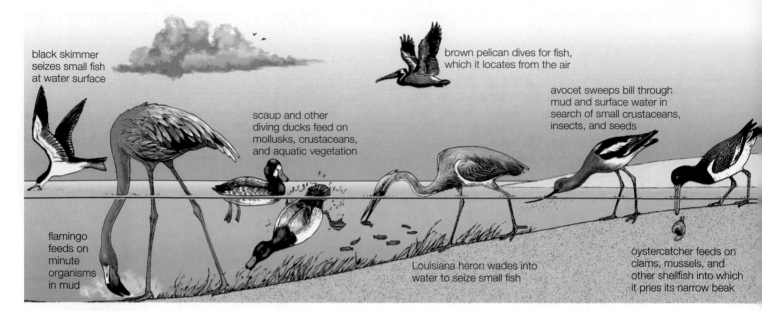

**Figure 4-38** Specialized feeding niches of various species of birds in a wetland. This resource partitioning allows them to reduce competition and share limited resources.

black skimmer seizes small fish at water surface

scaup and other diving ducks feed on mollusks, crustaceans, and aquatic vegetation

brown pelican dives for fish, which it locates from the air

avocet sweeps bill through mud and surface water in search of small crustaceans, insects, and seeds

flamingo feeds on minute organisms in mud

Louisiana heron wades into water to seize small fish

oystercatcher feeds on clams, mussels, and other shellfish into which it pries its narrow beak

effect, they "share the wealth," with each competing species occupying a **realized niche**, the portion of the fundamental niche that a species actually occupies. For example, hawks and owls feed on similar prey, but hawks hunt during the day and owls hunt at night. Where lions and leopards live in the same area, lions take mostly larger animals as prey and leopards take smaller ones. Some species of birds, such as warblers and tanagers, avoid competition by hunting for insects in different parts of the same coniferous trees.

Experiments have shown that no two species can occupy exactly the same fundamental niche indefinitely in a habitat where there is not enough of a particular resource to meet the needs of both species. This is called the **competitive exclusion principle**. As a result, one of the competing species must migrate to another area (if possible), shift its feeding habits or behavior, suffer a sharp population decline, or become extinct.

Competition can lead to diversity instead of extinction. When faced with competitive exclusion, species are often able to shift their niche to avoid competition.

**PREDATION** The most obvious form of species interaction in food chains and webs is **predation**. Members of a **predator** species feed on parts or all of an organism of a **prey** species, but do not live on or in the prey. Together the two kinds of organisms, such as lions and zebras, are said to have a **predator–prey relationship**. Predator–prey relationships can also include carni-

vore–prey, herbivore–plant, and parasite–host interactions. Examples of predators and their prey are shown in Figures 4-14, 4-15, 4-20, and 4-21.

Some predators hunt and kill live prey. Many shark species, for example, are key predators in the world's oceans (Case Study, p. 108). Other predators, called **scavengers**, feed on dead organisms that were either killed by other organisms or died naturally. Vultures, flies, crows, and some sharks are examples of scavengers.

Predators have a variety of methods that help them capture prey. Some carnivores, such as the cheetah, catch prey by being able to run fast, and others have keen eyesight (American bald eagle; Figure 2-10). Still others, such as wolves and African lions, cooperate in capturing their prey by hunting in packs. And humans have invented weapons and traps to capture prey.

Many predators stalk prey that is young, old, weak, sick, crippled, or in some way disabled. This natural weeding out of diseased and weak individuals also benefits the prey species by preventing the spread of disease and by leaving strong and healthy individuals for breeding.

Prey species have various protective mechanisms. Otherwise they would easily be captured and eaten. Some can run, swim, or fly fast; others have highly developed sight or a sense of smell that alerts them to the presence of a predator. Some have protective shells (turtles) or thick bark (giant sequoia; Figure 4-9); others have spines (porcupines) or thorns (cacti; Figure 4-10). Still others camouflage themselves by having certain shapes or colors (Figure 4-39) or the ability to

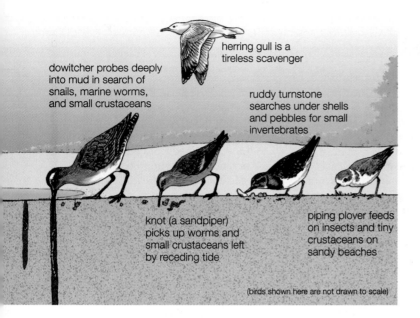

dowitcher probes deeply into mud in search of snails, marine worms, and small crustaceans

herring gull is a tireless scavenger

ruddy turnstone searches under shells and pebbles for small invertebrates

knot (a sandpiper) picks up worms and small crustaceans left by receding tide

piping plover feeds on insects and tiny crustaceans on sandy beaches

(birds shown here are not drawn to scale)

**Figure 4-39** Predator avoidance by camouflage. The African stoneplant avoids predators by closely resembling nearby stones. Can you find it?

change color (chameleon) so that they can hide by blending into their environment.

Some prey species give off chemicals that smell (skunks and skunk cabbages) or taste bad to their predators (buttercup) or irritate (bombardier beetles) or poison them (poison arrow frogs). The caterpillars of the monarch butterfly (Figure 4-5) eat milkweed, which contains chemicals that poison some of the milkweed's predators, but not monarch caterpillars. These poisons are incorporated into the caterpillar's body, and after its metamorphosis the adult monarch butterfly is foul-tasting and poisonous to some of its predators. The bright colors of the monarch butterfly (and other species such as the golden toad; Figure 4-34) warn predators that they are poisonous. Other butterfly species, such as the viceroy, are protected by looking like the monarch, a protective device known as *mimicry*. Some prey species attempt to scare off predators by puffing up or spreading their wings (the peacock; Figure 4-13), or by looking like a predator (Figure 4-40). Other prey gain some protection by living in large groups (schools of fish, herds of antelope).

**PARASITISM** Another type of predator–prey interaction is parasitism. A **parasite** is a predator that preys on another organism—its **host**—by living on or in the host for all or most of the host's life. The parasite is smaller than its host and draws nourishment from and gradually weakens the host, sometimes killing it. Tapeworms, disease-causing organisms (pathogens), and other parasites live inside their hosts. Lice, ticks,

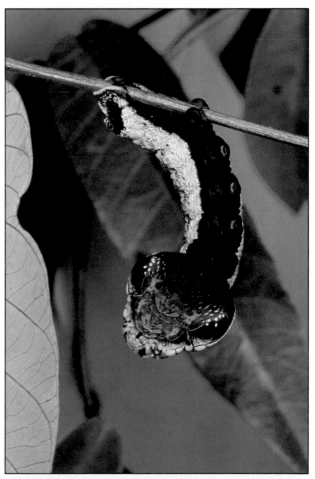

**Figure 4-40** Predator avoidance by behavior. When touched this snake caterpillar alters its body shape to look like the head of a snake. This puffed-up head "strikes" at whatever touches it.

**A:** About 4.6 billion years old

## Why We Need Sharks

Sharks lived in the oceans more than 400 million years ago, long before dinosaurs appeared. There are now about 350 species of sharks, whose size, behavior, and other characteristics differ widely. Sharks range in size from the dwarf dog shark—about the size of a large goldfish—to the whale shark—the world's largest fish at 18 meters (60 feet) long.

Various shark species are the key predators in the world's oceans, helping control the numbers of many other ocean predators. By feeding at the top of food webs, these shark species cull injured and sick animals from the ocean, thus keeping these species stronger and healthier.

Influenced by movies and popular novels, most people think of sharks as people-eating monsters. This is far from the truth. Every year a few species of shark—mostly great white, bull, bronze whaler, tiger, gray reef, blue (Figure 4-41), and oceanic whitetip—injure about 100 people worldwide and kill between 5 and 10. Most attacks are by great white sharks, which often feed on sea lions and other marine mammals, and sometimes mistake divers in black wet suits and swimmers on surfboards for their normal prey.

In a typical year about 10 or 12 shark attacks occur in U.S. waters (most of them off the Florida and southern California coasts), with only one or two of those attacks being fatal. If you are a typical ocean-goer, you are 150 times more likely to be killed by lightning and thousands of times more likely to be killed when you drive a car than to be killed by a shark.

For every shark that injures a person, we kill 1 million sharks—a total of more than 100 million sharks each year. The bodies of all the sharks humans kill each year would weigh more than seven aircraft carriers and, placed nose-to-tail, would encircle the earth five times.

Sharks are killed mostly for their fins (widely used in Asia as a soup ingredient at around $50 a bowl in some restaurants and as a pharmaceutical cure-all), livers, meat (especially mako and thresher), and jaws (especially great whites), or because we fear them. Some sharks (especially blue, mako, and oceanic whitetip) die when they are trapped in nets meant for swordfish, tuna, shrimp, and other commercially important species.

In the 1980s the U.S. commercial shark catch increased 15-fold and now has begun to threaten several species, including the thresher, mako, and hammerhead. In addi-

tion, shark fisheries in Nigeria, Nicaragua, Mexico, and the Arabian Sea have collapsed from overfishing. And great whites have almost vanished from South African waters, while Costa Rica has lost its hammerheads.

Sharks have several natural traits that make them vulnerable to overfishing. Unlike most other fish they have only a few offspring (between 2 and 10) once per year or once every two years. It takes most species 10 or 15 years (and in some cases 24 years) to reach sexual maturity and begin reproducing. They also have long gestation periods—as much as 24 months for some species.

About 89% of the U.S. commercial catch of sharks is discarded, mostly because of a wasteful practice called finning. When sharks are caught, most often only their fins are chopped off; the live, bleeding, and rudderless animals are then tossed overboard and eventually die because they cannot swim or feed properly.

Eating shark meat may be dangerous. In 1992 the Michigan Department of Agriculture advised consumers to eat shark meat no more than once a month after several samples sold by seafood distributors in Michigan and other states were found to contain unac-

mosquitoes, mistletoe plants, and lampreys (Figure 4-42) attach themselves to the outside of their hosts.

Some parasites move from one host to another, as fleas and ticks do. Others spend their adult lives attached to a single host. Examples are mistletoe, which feeds on oak tree branches, and tapeworms, which feed in the intestines of humans and other animals.

**MUTUALISM Mutualism** is a type of species interaction in which both participating species generally benefit. The honeybee and certain flowers have a mutual-

istic relationship. The honeybee feeds on a flower's nectar and in the process picks up pollen, pollinating female flowers when it feeds on them. Other examples are the mutualistic relationships between rhinos and oxpeckers (Figure 4-43) and between legume plants and *Rhizobium* bacteria that live in nodules on the plant's roots (Figure 4-30).

Another mutualistic relationship takes place between giant sequoias (Figure 4-9) and a fungus that infects their roots. The roots of these massive trees are usually only 1 or 2 meters (about 3–6 feet) deep and

Q: When did the first forms of life arise on Earth?

ceptably high levels of highly toxic methylmercury. Sharks—unlike most other fish—pick up high levels of methylmercury and other forms of mercury because they are top predators and eat a variety of fish that contain these toxins. Methylmercury can accumulate in the body and damage the nervous system, and is particularly harmful for fetuses and children.

Why should we care how many sharks are killed? Because they perform valuable services for us and other species. Sharks save human lives by helping us learn how to fight cancer, bacteria, and viruses because sharks seem to be free of almost all diseases, including cancer and eye cataracts, and are not affected by most toxic chemicals. Understanding why can help us improve human health.

Chemicals extracted from shark cartilage have killed cancerous tumors in laboratory animals and may someday be the basis of cancer-treating drugs. Another chemical extracted from shark cartilage is being used as an artificial skin for burn victims. Sharks' highly effective immune system allows wounds to heal quickly without becoming infected and is being studied for protection against AIDS. And shark corneas have been transplanted into human eyes.

**Figure 4-41** This blue shark and other types of sharks are key predators in the world's oceans. One of only a small number of shark species that occasionally attack swimmers, blue sharks prefer deep water and are a potential threat only to people swimming from boats in deep water.

Several steps are being taken to reduce the slaughter of sharks. In January 1993 the National Marine Fisheries Service imposed limits on the commercial and sport fishing catch for 39 of the most vulnerable species in U.S. waters. All sharks killed have to be brought ashore whole—a requirement designed to reduce finning. New laws in South Africa ban hunting of great whites within 320 kilometers (200 miles) of its coast. These steps are a good beginning, but they must be enacted and enforced on a global basis.

With more than 400 million years of evolution behind them, sharks have had a long time to get things right. We could undo most of this evolutionary wisdom in a few decades. Preventing this from happening begins with the recognition that sharks don't need us, but we and other species need them.

extend outward only about 15 meters (50 feet). How can such a shallow and relatively small root system take in enough water and nutrients to support its growth? The answer lies in the minute fungus that infects the roots of the sequoia and sends out billions of hairlike extensions into the soil around the tree's roots. The fungus gets nutrition and in turn helps the sequoia absorb much more water and many more nutrients than the tree's roots could absorb on their own.

Other important mutualistic relationships exist between animals and the vast armies of bacteria in their stomachs or intestines that break down (digest) their food. The bacteria gain a safe home with a steady food supply; the animal gains access to a large source of energy.

Research indicates that mutualism increases when resources become scarce. When there are not enough resources to go around, cooperative relationships between species for mutual benefit have survival value.

COMMENSALISM    In another type of species interaction, called **commensalism**, one species benefits

**Figure 4-42** Parasitism. Sea lampreys are parasites that use their suckerlike mouths to attach themselves to the sides of fish on which they prey. They then bore a hole in the fish with their teeth and feed on its blood.

**Figure 4-43** Mutualism. Oxpeckers feed on the ticks that infest the endangered black rhinoceros in Kenya. The rhino benefits by having parasites removed from its body, and oxpeckers benefit by having a dependable source of food. This and other species of rhinoceros face extinction because they are illegally killed for their horns and because their habitat is shrinking.

**Figure 4-44** Commensalism. This clownfish in the Coral Sea off Australia has a commensalistic relationship with deadly sea anemones, whose tentacles quickly paralyze most other fishes that touch them. The clownfish gains protection and food by feeding on scraps of food left over from fish killed by the sea anemones, which seem to be neither helped nor harmed by this relationship. All 26 species of clownfish are found only in association with various species of sea anemones.

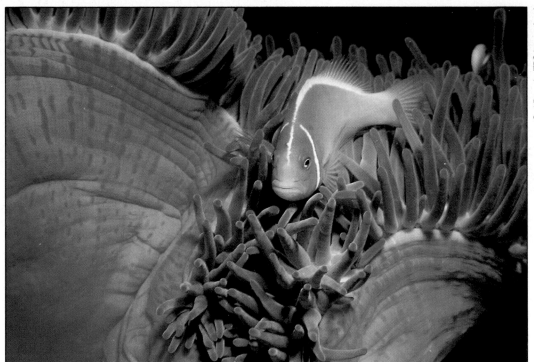

while the other is neither helped nor harmed to any great degree. An example is the relationship between various species of clownfish and sea anemones, marine animals with stinging tentacles that paralyze most fish that touch them (Figure 4-44). The clownfishes gain protection by living unharmed among the deadly tentacles and feed on the detritus left from the meals of the host anemone. The sea anemones seem to neither benefit nor suffer harm from this relationship.

On land there are commensalistic relationships between various trees and epiphytes or "air plants" that attach themselves to tree branches (Figure 4-11). The epiphytes benefit by obtaining water and nutrients from air or bark surfaces without penetrating or harming their hosts.

Q: How much of North America's original temperate deciduous forests has been cleared?

## INTERDEPENDENCE AND CONNECTEDNESS

The essential features of the living and nonliving parts of individual terrestrial and aquatic ecosystems, and of the ecosphere, are interdependence and connectedness. Without the services performed by diverse communities of species, we would be starving, gasping for breath, and drowning in our own wastes. We have also seen how some species survive by avoiding competition and by entering into nondestructive, often cooperative, relationships (mutualism and commensalism) with other species—examples that the human species could learn from. The next chapter shows how this interdependence is key to understanding Earth's major life zones and ecosystems.

*We sang the songs that carried in their melodies all the sounds of nature—the running waters, the sighing of winds, and the calls of the animals. Teach these to your children that they may come to love nature as we love it.*

GRAND COUNCIL FIRE OF AMERICAN INDIANS

## Critical Thinking

1. **a.** A bumper sticker asks, "Have you thanked a green plant today?" Give two reasons for appreciating a green plant.
   **b.** Trace the sources of the materials that make up the bumper sticker, and see whether the sticker itself is a sound application of the slogan.
   **c.** Explain how decomposers help keep you alive.

2. **a.** How would you set up a self-sustaining aquarium for tropical fish?
   **b.** Suppose you have a balanced aquarium sealed with a clear glass top. Can life continue in the aquarium indefinitely as long as the sun shines regularly on it?
   **c.** A friend cleans out your aquarium and removes all the soil and plants, leaving only the fish and water. What will happen?

3. Using the second law of energy, explain why there is such a sharp decrease in usable energy as energy flows through a food chain or web. Doesn't an energy loss at each step violate the first law of energy? Explain.

4. Using the second law of energy, explain why many poor people in LDCs exist mostly on a vegetarian diet.

5. Using the second law of energy, explain why, on a per weight basis, steak costs more than corn.

6. Why are there fewer lions than mice in an African ecosystem supporting both types of animals?

## Blowing in the Wind

Without wind most of the earth would be uninhabitable. The tropics would be unbearably hot and the rest of the planet would freeze. Winds also transport nutrients from one region to another. Dust rich in phosphates blows across the Atlantic from the Sahara Desert in Africa (Figure 5-1), replenishing rain-forest soils in Brazil. Iron-rich dust blowing from China's Gobi Desert falls into the Pacific Ocean between Hawaii and Alaska six or seven times a year and stimulates the growth of phytoplankton, the minute producers that support ocean food webs.

The bad news is that wind also transports harmful substances. Sulfur compounds and soot from oil-well fires in Kuwait have been detected over Wyoming, and deposits of DDT and PCBs have been found in Antarctica for decades. Cesium-137 blown from the Chernobyl nuclear power plant disaster in the Ukraine has made the lichen food of Lapland's reindeer radioactive. Reindeer meat, milk, and cheese, in turn, have become unfit to eat for the herders who depend on them.

There's mixed news as well. Clouds of particles from volcanic eruptions can ride the winds, encircle the globe, and change Earth's climate for a while. After

USGS/EROS Data Center

**Figure 5-1** Some of the dust shown here blowing from Africa's Sahara Desert can end up as soil nutrients in Amazonian rain forests.

Indonesia's Tambora blew up in 1815, for example, distant Europe experienced a "year without a summer" in 1816. This eruption, which injected 30–80 times as much ash into the atmosphere as the 1980 eruption of Mount St. Helens in Washington, reduced the amount of sunlight reaching the earth for several years.

On the other hand, volcanic ash, like blowing desert dust, adds valuable trace minerals to the soil where it settles. And emissions from the 1991 eruption of Mount Pinatubo in the Philippines—the largest of this century and the third largest in two centuries—may cool the earth for two to three years. This may temporarily offset and mask signs of possible global warming. In the short term this may be good news, but if it causes us to dismiss the possibility of long-term global warming, this is bad news.

The lesson is the same: *There is no away*, and wind—acting as part of the planet's circulatory system for heat, moisture, and plant nutrients—is one reason. Movement of soil particles from one place to another by wind and water is a natural process, but when we disturb the soil and leave it unprotected we hasten this process. As the Roman poet Virgil reminded us over 2,000 years ago: "Before we plow an unfamiliar patch/It is well to be informed about the winds."

Until recently wind has been a mostly invisible player, but now we have eyes for "seeing" the wind. Satellite pictures allow us to chart blowing dust clouds (Figure 5-1). Atmospheric chemists use laser probes from aircraft to identify substances in swirling wind plumes invisible to the human eye. Other sensors can detect trace gases caught in wind currents and record how their concentrations change over fractions of a second. It was these new technologies that showed the intimate connection between African desert and lush Amazonian rain forest. In coming years such technologies should help us learn more about the important roles of wind in the ecosphere.

In addition to its linking role, outlined here, wind is an important factor in climate through its influence on global air circulation patterns. Climate, in turn, is a key player in determining what kinds of life are found in different regions of the ecosphere, as we shall see in this chapter.

The discussion in this chapter answers several key questions:

- What layers are found in the atmosphere?
- What key factors determine variations in Earth's climate?
- What are the principal types of biomes?
- How does climate influence the type of biome found in a given area?
- What are the basic types of aquatic life zones, and what factors influence the kinds of life they contain?

## 5-1 Structure and Composition of the Atmosphere

**THE TROPOSPHERE: LIFE GIVER AND WEATHER BREEDER** We live at the bottom of a "sea" of air called the **atmosphere**. This thin envelope of life-sustaining gases surrounding the earth is divided into several layers characterized by abrupt changes in temperature due to differences in the absorption of incoming solar energy (Figure 5-2).

About 75% of the mass of Earth's air is found in the atmosphere's innermost layer, the **troposphere**, extending only about 17 kilometers (11 miles) above sea level at the equator and about 8 kilometers (5 miles) over the poles. If Earth were an apple, this lower layer containing the air we breathe would be no thicker than the apple's skin. This thin but nevertheless turbulent layer of rising and falling air currents and winds is the planet's weather breeder.

The composition of the atmosphere has varied considerably throughout Earth's long history. Today about 99% of the volume of clean, dry air in the troposphere consists of two gases: nitrogen (78%) and oxygen (21%). The remainder has slightly less than 1% argon (Ar), 0.036% carbon dioxide ($CO_2$), and trace amounts of neon (Ne), helium (He), methane ($CH_4$), krypton (Kr), hydrogen ($H_2$), Xenon (Xe), and chlorofluorocarbons (CFCs, put there by human activities).

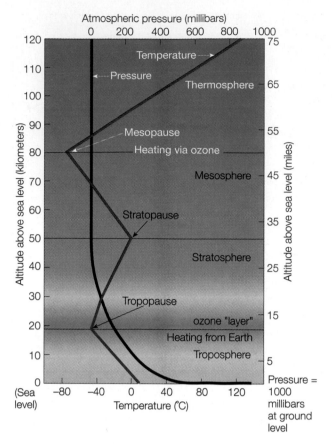

**Atmospheric pressure (millibars)**

**Figure 5-2** Earth's present atmosphere consists of several layers. Most ultraviolet radiation from the sun is absorbed by ozone ($O_3$) in the stratosphere, most of which is found in the so-called *ozone layer*, between 17 and 26 kilometers (11–16 miles) above sea level.

Air in the troposphere also holds water vapor in amounts varying from 0.01% by volume at the frigid poles to 5% in the humid tropics.

Temperature drops with altitude in the troposphere. At the top of this zone, however, there is a reversal and temperatures start to rise. The boundary where this occurs is called the *tropopause*; it limits mixing between the troposphere and upper layers.

### THE STRATOSPHERE: OUR GLOBAL SUNSCREEN

The tropopause marks the end of the troposphere and the beginning of the **stratosphere**, the atmosphere's second layer, which extends from about 17 to 48 kilometers (11–30 miles) above Earth's surface (Figure 5-2). It is a much more peaceful place than the troposphere. Although the stratosphere contains less matter than the troposphere, its composition is similar with two notable exceptions: Its volume of water vapor is

about 1,000 times less and its volume of ozone ($O_3$) about 1,000 times greater. Even so, if the ozone in the stratosphere were at sea-level pressures, it would amount to a thin skin of gas on Earth's surface no more than 0.005 centimeter (0.1 inch) thick. But in the stratosphere pressures are so low that these ozone molecules become dispersed in a layer at least 30 kilometers (20 miles) deep.

Stratospheric ozone is produced when some of its oxygen molecules interact with lightning and solar radiation. This thin gauze of ozone keeps about 99% of the harmful ultraviolet radiation (especially ultraviolet-B, or UV-B) given off by the sun from reaching Earth's surface. This filtering action protects us from increased sunburn, skin and eye cancer, cataracts, and damage to our immune system. This global sunscreen also prevents damage to some plants, aquatic organisms, and other land animals. Furthermore, it keeps much of the oxygen in the troposphere from being converted to toxic ozone. The trace amounts of ozone that do form in the troposphere as a component of urban smog damage plants, the respiratory systems of humans and other animals, and materials such as rubber.

Thus our good health and that of many other species depends on having enough "good" ozone in the stratosphere and as little as possible "bad" ozone in the troposphere. Unfortunately our activities are increasing the amount of bad ozone in the tropospheric air we must breathe and decreasing the amount of good ozone in the stratosphere.

Unlike in the troposphere, air in the stratosphere is calm, with little vertical mixing. Pilots like to fly in this layer because it has so little turbulence and such excellent visibility (due to the almost complete absence of clouds). Flying there also improves fuel efficiency because the thin air offers little resistance to the forward thrust of the plane. Again unlike in the troposphere, temperature rises with altitude in the stratosphere until there is another reversal at the *stratopause*, which marks the end of the stratosphere and the beginning of the atmosphere's next layer.

### MESOSPHERE AND THERMOSPHERE

Above the stratosphere the temperature begins falling with altitude in a layer called the **mesosphere** or middle layer (Figure 5-2). At the top of this layer there is another reversal of temperature called the *mesopause*. This marks the beginning of the **thermosphere,** where temperatures rise again. Temperatures are very high in this layer because its gaseous molecules are constantly bombarded by high-energy solar radiation and cosmic rays. This input of high-energy electromagnetic radiation also converts the gaseous molecules in this layer to ions.

Q: When did the first photosynthesizing cells arise on Earth?

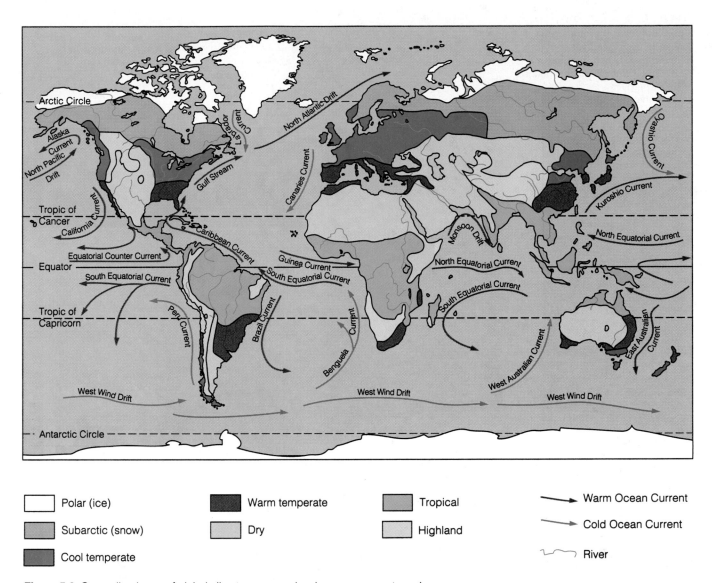

| | | | |
|---|---|---|---|
| ☐ Polar (ice) | ■ Warm temperate | ▨ Tropical | → Warm Ocean Current |
| ▨ Subarctic (snow) | ☐ Dry | ☐ Highland | → Cold Ocean Current |
| ■ Cool temperate | | | ∿ River |

**Figure 5-3** Generalized map of global climate zones and major ocean currents and drifts. Major variations in climate are dictated mainly by two variables: **(1)** the temperature, with its seasonal variations, and **(2)** the quantity and distribution of precipitation.

## Weather and Climate: A Brief Introduction

**WEATHER AND CLIMATE** Every moment at any spot on Earth the troposphere has a particular set of physical properties such as temperature, pressure, humidity, precipitation, sunshine, cloud cover, and wind direction and speed. These short-term properties of the troposphere at a given place and time are what we call **weather**.

**Climate** is the average weather of an area. It is the general pattern of atmospheric or weather conditions, seasonal variations, and weather extremes in a region averaged over a long period—at least 30 years. The two most important factors determining the climate of an area are temperature and precipitation (Figure 5-3).

**CLIMATE AND GLOBAL AIR CIRCULATION**
The temperature and precipitation patterns that lead to different climates are caused mostly by the way air circulates over the earth's surface. Several factors determine these patterns of global air circulation:

■ *Long-term variations in the amount of solar energy striking the earth.* These arise because of occasional changes in solar output, slight planetary shifts in which Earth's axis wobbles (22,000-year cycle) and tilts (44,000-year cycle) as it revolves around

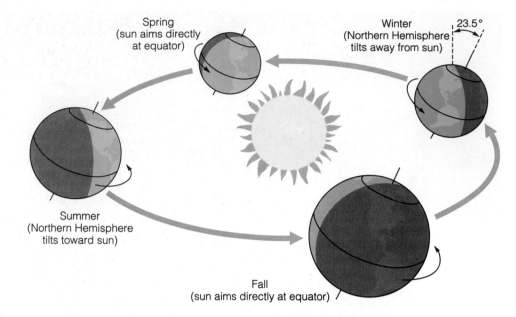

**Figure 5-4** Seasonal changes in climate (shown here for the Northern Hemisphere only) are caused by variations in the amount of solar energy reaching various areas of the earth. As Earth makes its annual revolution around the sun on an axis tilted about 23.5°, various regions are tipped toward or away from the sun, which causes changes in seasons.

Spring
(sun aims directly
at equator)

Winter
(Northern Hemisphere
tilts away from sun)

23.5°

Summer
(Northern Hemisphere
tilts toward sun)

Fall
(sun aims directly at equator)

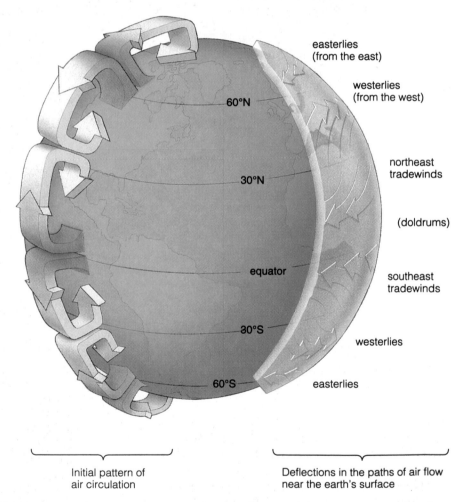

**Figure 5-5** Formation of prevailing surface winds, which disrupt the general flow of air from the equator to the poles and back to the equator. As Earth rotates, its surface turns faster beneath air masses at the equator and slower beneath those at the poles. This deflects air masses moving north and south to the west or east, creating six huge convection cells in which air swirls upward through a corkscrew pathway and down toward Earth's surface at different latitudes. The direction of air movement in these cells sets up belts of prevailing winds that distribute air and moisture over Earth's surface, affecting the general types of climate found in different areas and also driving the circulation of ocean currents. (Used by permission from Cecie Starr and Ralph Taggart, *Biology: The Unity and Diversity of Life*, 6th ed., Belmont, Calif.: Wadsworth, 1992)

easterlies
(from the east)

westerlies
(from the west)

60°N

northeast
tradewinds

30°N

(doldrums)

equator

southeast
tradewinds

30°S

westerlies

60°S

easterlies

Initial pattern of
air circulation

Deflections in the paths of air flow
near the earth's surface

the sun, and minute changes in the shape of its orbit around the sun (100,000-year cycle).

■ *Uneven heating of the earth's surface.* Air is heated much more at the equator where the sun's rays strike directly throughout the year than at the poles where sunlight strikes at a glancing angle, which spreads the incoming radiation over a much greater area and dilutes the heat input. These differences help explain why tropical regions near the equator are hot, polar regions are

Q: How many species are there on Earth?

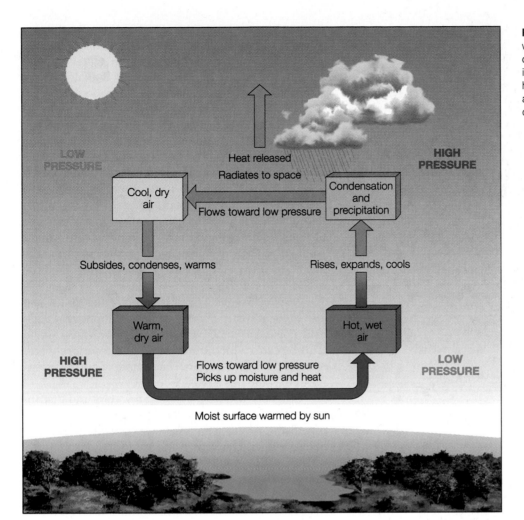

**Figure 5-6** Distribution of heat and water occurs because of vertical convection currents that stir up air in the troposphere and transport heat and water from one area to another in circular, convection cells.

cold, and temperate regions in between generally have intermediate temperatures.

- *The tilt of the earth's axis.* Earth's axis (an imaginary line connecting the North and South Poles) is tilted relative to its plane of revolution around the sun. Because of this tilt various regions are tipped toward or away from the sun as the earth makes its annual revolution (Figure 5-4). This creates opposite seasons in the Northern and Southern Hemispheres.

- *Rotation of the earth.* Earth's rotation on its axis prevents air currents from moving due north and south. Forces on the atmosphere created by this rotation deflect winds (moving air masses) to the right in the Northern Hemisphere and to the left in the Southern Hemisphere, in what is called the *Coriolis effect.* The result is six huge convection cells of swirling air masses—three north and three south of the equator (Figure 5-5).

- *Properties of air and water.* Hot and cold air have different properties. Cold air is denser (weighs more

per unit volume) than hot air and thus tends to sink through less dense, warmer air; hot air, being less dense, tends to rise. Hot air can also hold more water vapor than cold air. When heated by the sun, ocean water evaporates and removes heat from the oceans to the atmosphere. This moist, hot air expands, becomes less dense, and rises in fairly narrow vortexes that spiral upward creating an area of low pressure at the earth's surface. As this moisture-laden air rises it cools and releases moisture as condensation (because cold air can hold less water vapor than warm air). The heat released when water vapor condenses radiates into space. The resulting cooler, drier air becomes denser, sinks (subsides), and creates an area of high pressure. As this area flows across the earth's surface, it picks up heat and moisture and begins to rise again (Figure 5-6). The resulting small and giant convection cells circulate air, heat, and moisture both vertically and from place to place in the troposphere, leading to different climates and patterns of vegetation (Figure 5-7).

**A:** An estimated 5–100 million

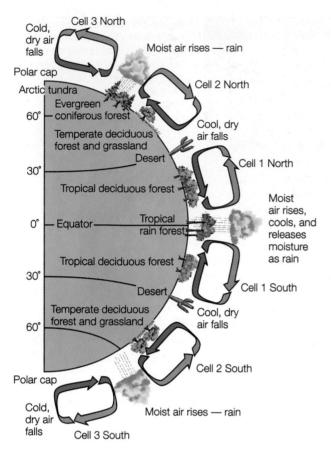

**Figure 5-7** Global air circulation and biomes. Heat and moisture are distributed over Earth's surface by vertical convection currents that form into six large convection cells (called Hadley cells) at different latitudes. The direction of air flow and the ascent and descent of air masses in these convection cells determine Earth's general climatic zones. The uneven distribution of heat and moisture over the planet's surface leads to the forests, grasslands, and deserts that make up Earth's biomes.

**CLIMATE AND OCEAN CURRENTS** Earth's rotation, the inclination of its axis, prevailing winds, uneven heating, and differences in water density cause warm and cold ocean currents that along with air masses above redistribute heat received from the sun (Figure 5-3). Generally cold currents flow from the polar areas toward the equator, and warm currents, driven by the wind and the earth's rotation, flow away from the equator. The deeper currents are driven partly by cooling (which makes water denser and causes it to sink) and partly by increased salinity (which has the same effect). In today's ocean, waters dense enough to fall to the bottom are found in only two regions, the northern North Atlantic and the frigid waters around Antarctica. The current created by sinking water in the northern North Atlantic has 20 times the volume flow of all the world's rivers.

Ocean currents, like air currents, redistribute heat and thus influence climate and vegetation, especially near coastal areas. For example, without the warm Gulf Stream, which transports 25 times more water than all the world's rivers, the climate of northwestern Europe would be subarctic.

Currents also help mix ocean waters and distribute nutrients and dissolved oxygen needed by aquatic organisms. Along some steep, western coasts of continents, almost-constant trade winds blow offshore, pushing surface water away from the shore. This outgoing surface water is replaced by an **upwelling** of cold, nutrient-rich bottom water (Figure 5-8). Some upwellings occur far from shore and others are found near shore. They bring plant nutrients from the deeper parts of the ocean to the surface and support large populations of phytoplankton, zooplankton, fish, and fish-eating seabirds.

**Figure 5-8** A *shore upwelling* shown here occurs when deep, cool, nutrient-rich waters are drawn up to replace surface water moved away from a steep coast by wind-driven currents. Such areas support large populations of phytoplankton, zooplankton, fish, and fish-eating birds. *Equatorial upwellings* occur in the open sea near the equator when northward and southward currents interact to push deep waters plus nutrients to the surface, thus greatly increasing primary productivity in such areas.

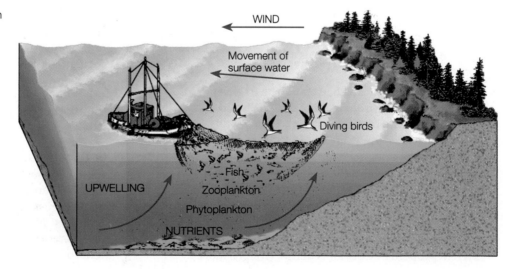

118

Every few years in the Pacific Ocean, however, normal coastal upwelling (Figure 5-9, left) is affected by periodic changes in climate patterns called the *El Niño–Southern Oscillation (ENSO)* (Figure 5-9, right). In an ENSO event the prevailing westerly winds weaken or stop blowing and surface water along the South and North American coasts becomes warmer. The upwelling of cold, nutrient-rich water is suppressed (Figure 5-9, right), which reduces primary productivity and causes a sharp decline in the populations of some fish species. A strong ENSO can trigger extreme weather changes over at least two-thirds of the globe, especially in the countries along the Pacific and Indian oceans. Some areas receive abnormally high rainfall; others suffer severe droughts.

**CLIMATE AND ATMOSPHERIC COMPOSITION: THE GREENHOUSE EFFECT AND THE OZONE LAYER** Small amounts of carbon dioxide and water vapor and trace amounts of ozone, methane, nitrous oxide, chlorofluorocarbons, and other gases in the troposphere play a key role in determining Earth's average temperatures and thus its climates.

These gases, known as **greenhouse gases**, act somewhat like the glass panes of a greenhouse or of a car parked in the sun with its windows rolled up: They allow light, infrared radiation, and some ultraviolet radiation from the sun to pass through the troposphere. Earth's surface absorbs much of this solar energy and degrades it to heat, which then rises into the troposphere (Figure 4-4). Some of this heat escapes into space, and some is absorbed by molecules of greenhouse gases, warming the air and radiating back toward the earth's surface. This trapping of heat in the troposphere is called the **greenhouse effect** (Figure 5-10). The basic theory behind the greenhouse effect is well established; for example, satellites equipped with infrared detectors have measured the effects of greenhouse gases on outgoing infrared radiation.

If there were no greenhouse gases, especially water vapor, Earth would be a cold and lifeless planet with an average surface temperature of –18°C (0°F) instead of its current 15°C (59°F). We and other species currently benefit from a comfortable level of greenhouse gases, with only minor and slow fluctuations, but global warming or cooling over decades instead of hundreds to thousands of years would be disastrous.

Ozone ($O_3$) is formed in the stratosphere as the sun's ultraviolet rays interact with regular oxygen molecules ($O_2$). As already mentioned, besides filtering out harmful ultraviolet radiation, ozone creates warm layers of air high in the stratosphere that prevent churning gases in the troposphere from entering the stratosphere (Figure 5-2). This thermal cap is

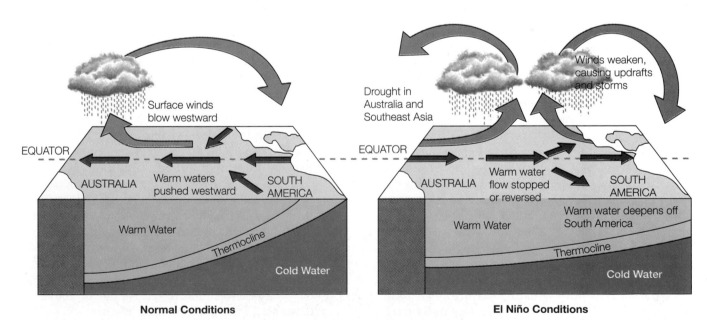

**Normal Conditions**          **El Niño Conditions**

**Figure 5-9** Surface winds blowing westward cause shore upwellings of cold, nutrient-rich bottom water in the tropical Pacific Ocean near the coast of Peru (left). The warm and cold waters are separated by a zone of gradual temperature change called a *thermocline*. Every few years a climate shift known as the *El Niño–Southern Oscillation (ENSO)* disrupts this pattern. Westward surface winds weaken, which depresses the coastal upwellings and warms the surface waters off South America (right). ENSOs typically occur every 3–4 years, although the interval has been as long as 7 years. Some ENSOs are minor, lasting only a few months. When an ENSO lasts 12–15 months, however, it severely disrupts populations of plankton, fish, and seabirds in upwelling areas.

**A:** About 1.4 million

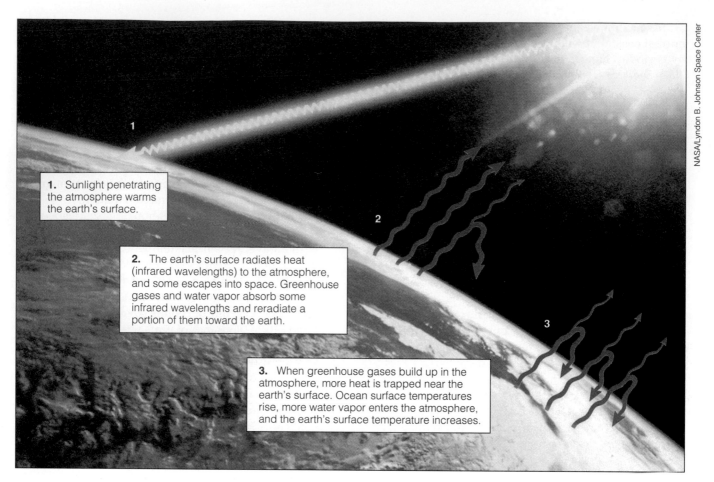

**1.** Sunlight penetrating the atmosphere warms the earth's surface.

**2.** The earth's surface radiates heat (infrared wavelengths) to the atmosphere, and some escapes into space. Greenhouse gases and water vapor absorb some infrared wavelengths and reradiate a portion of them toward the earth.

**3.** When greenhouse gases build up in the atmosphere, more heat is trapped near the earth's surface. Ocean surface temperatures rise, more water vapor enters the atmosphere, and the earth's surface temperature increases.

**Figure 5-10** The greenhouse effect. Without the atmospheric warming provided by this effect, Earth would be a cold and mostly lifeless planet. (Used by permission from Cecie Starr and Ralph Taggart, *Biology: The Unity and Diversity of Life*, 6th ed., Belmont, Calif.: Wadsworth, 1992)

important in determining the average temperature of the troposphere and thus Earth's current climates.

Any loss of ozone in the stratosphere or gain in greenhouse gases in the troposphere can change global climate, threatening our health and economies, and the survival of many other species. Yet we are steadily depleting ozone in the stratosphere and increasing the concentrations of greenhouse gases in the troposphere—ultimate global problems discussed in detail in Chapter 11.

**MICROCLIMATES** Mountains, valleys, and other topographical features of Earth's surface create local climatic conditions, or *microclimates*, that differ from the general climate of an area. For example, mountains interrupt the flow of prevailing surface winds and the movement of storms. When moist air blowing inland from an ocean reaches a mountain range, it cools as it is forced to rise and expand. This causes the air to lose most of its moisture in the form of rain and snow on the windward (wind-facing) slopes. As the drier air

mass flows down the leeward (away from the wind) slopes, it is compressed, becomes warmer, and thus can hold more moisture. This air draws moisture out of plants and soil it passes over rather than giving up moisture as precipitation. The lower precipitation and the resulting semiarid or arid conditions on the leeward side of high mountains is called the **rain shadow effect**. The Gobi Desert in Asia, for example, is in the rain shadow of the Himalayan mountain range, as the Mojave is of the Sierra Nevada in California.

People living near an ocean or lake enjoy cooler summers and warmer winters than those who live far away from water. This occurs because during the day land warms faster than water. As the air above the land warms, it expands and rises (Figure 5-6), pulling in a sea-to-land breeze as cooler, denser air above the water moves inland. At night this process is reversed, and there is a nighttime land-to-sea breeze because land cools faster than water.

Large clusters of plants also create microclimates because of their uptake and release of water, and their windbreak effect. Forests, for example, are warmer in

Q: What percentage of all species that have ever lived have become extinct?

winter and cooler in summer, and have lower wind speeds and a higher humidity, than nearby open land.

Cities too create distinct microclimates. Bricks, concrete, asphalt, and other building materials absorb and hold heat, and buildings break wind flows. Motor vehicles and the heating and cooling systems of buildings also release large quantities of heat and pollutants in an urban area. Thus cities tend to have more haze and smog, higher temperatures, and lower wind speeds than the surrounding countryside.

**WEATHER EXTREMES: TORNADOES AND TROPICAL CYCLONES** Two weather extremes are **(1)** violent storms called tornadoes, or twisters, which form over land, and **(2)** tropical cyclones, which form over warm ocean waters and sometimes pass over coastal land.

We don't know precisely what causes tornadoes, but we do know they occur only when a mass of cool, dry air overruns warm, humid air. This leads to thunderstorms and extremely turbulent conditions, and in some cases to the formation of a *tornado*, a funnel of spinning air on the underside of a cloud that can descend to the ground. Moving at speeds up to 480 kilometers (300 miles) per hour and roaring like a freight train, this spinning column of wind and debris can uproot trees, flatten entire neighborhoods, and fling cars and other large objects through the air. An average of 124 tornadoes hit the United States each year, most of them in Florida and in the Midwest—the world's most tornado-prone area.

*Tropical cyclones* are giant circular storm systems that develop over warm tropical waters, usually in the late summer or early fall. Tropical cyclones are called *hurricanes* in the Atlantic and *typhoons* in the Pacific. Their violent winds, which may blow at speeds of up to 320 kilometers (200 miles) per hour, bring torrential rains and towering waves. These storms can cover an area as much as 1,600 kilometers (1,000 miles) in diameter. If a hurricane reaches shore, as Andrew did in 1992 in Florida, it can be a killer. A hurricane's high winds and catastrophic flooding devastate a much larger area than a more localized and briefer tornado. Among the lower 48 states those areas at greatest risk from hurricanes lie on the east Atlantic and Gulf coasts.

**5-3**    **Biomes: Life on Land**

**CLIMATE AND VEGETATION** Why is one area of Earth's land surface a desert, another a grassland, and another a forest? Why are there different types of deserts, grasslands, and forests? What determines the types of life in these biomes when they are undisturbed by human activities?

The general answer to these questions is differences in climate—specifically differences in average temperature and average precipitation caused by global air circulation (Figure 5-7). Figure 5-11 shows the distribution of eleven **biomes**—regions with characteristic types of natural, undisturbed plant communities. By comparing this figure with Figure 5-3, you can see how the world's major biomes vary with climate. For plants, *precipitation is generally the limiting factor that determines whether a land area is desert, grassland, or forest* (Figure 5-12).

Average annual precipitation and temperature, along with soil type, are the most important factors determining the type of desert, grassland, or forest in a particular area. Acting together, these factors lead to tropical, temperate, and polar deserts, grasslands, and forests (Figures 5-13 and 4-7).

Climate and vegetation both vary with **latitude** (distance from the equator) and **altitude** (height above sea level). If you travel from the equator toward either pole, you will find colder and wetter climates (Figure 5-3) and zones of vegetation adapted to each (Figure 5-14). Similarly as elevation or height above sea level increases, the climate becomes colder and is often wetter. Thus, if you climb a tall mountain from its base to its summit, you will find changes in plant life similar to those you would find in traveling from equator to poles.

**DESERTS AND SEMIDESERTS** A *desert* is an area where the average precipitation is less than 25 centimeters (10 inches) per year and evaporation is rapid. Such areas have little vegetation or have widely spaced, mostly low vegetation. Deserts cover about 30% of Earth's land. They lie mainly between tropical and subtropical regions north and south of the equator (Figure 5-11) where dry air that has lost its moisture over the tropics falls back toward Earth (Figure 5-7). The atmosphere above deserts is a poor insulator because it contains little water vapor. This lack of moisture and the accompanying lack of vegetation allow the ground to radiate heat rapidly after the sun goes down, explaining why desert nights are often cold.

Low rainfall, combined with different average temperatures, create tropical, temperate, and cold deserts (Figure 5-13). *Tropical deserts*, such as the southern Sahara and the Namib in Africa (Figure 5-15), make up about one-fifth of the world's desert area. They are the driest places on Earth and typically have few plants and a hard, windblown surface strewn with rocks and some sand. In *temperate deserts* (Figure 4-10), such as the Mojave in southern California, daytime temperatures are hot in summer and cool in winter. In *cold deserts*, such as the Gobi in China, winters are cold and summers are warm or hot. In the typically semiarid zones between deserts and grasslands we find *semidesert*, dominated by thorn trees and shrubs adapted to a long dry season followed by brief, sometimes heavy, rains.

Desert plants and animals have evolved strategies to capture and conserve scarce water. Some of the plants are evergreens whose wax-coated leaves (cre-osote bush) cut down on evaporation. Some desert plants (mesquite) send down deep roots to tap into groundwater, while fleshy-stemmed, short (prickly pear) and tall (saguaro, Figure 4-10) cacti spread their shallow roots wide to collect scarce water for storage in their spongy tissues.

Most desert animals escape the heat by hiding in burrows or rocky crevices by day and being active during night or early morning hours. They also have

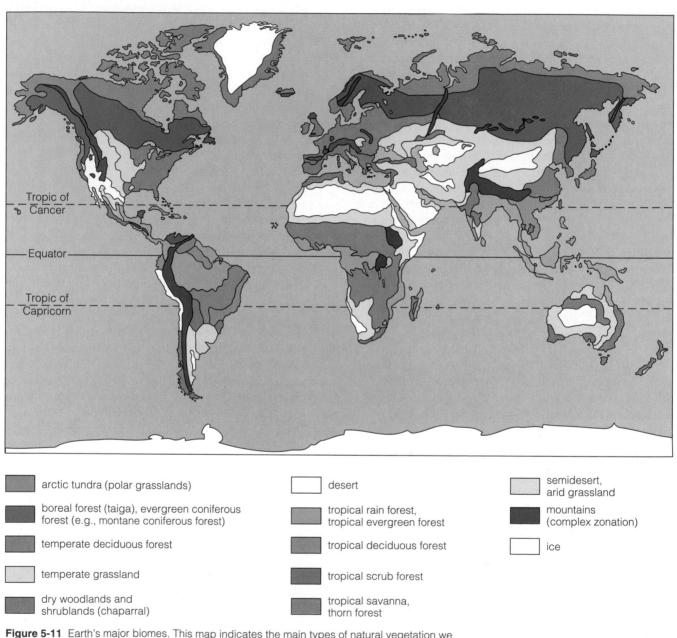

| | | |
|---|---|---|
| arctic tundra (polar grasslands) | desert | semidesert, arid grassland |
| boreal forest (taiga), evergreen coniferous forest (e.g., montane coniferous forest) | tropical rain forest, tropical evergreen forest | mountains (complex zonation) |
| temperate deciduous forest | tropical deciduous forest | ice |
| temperate grassland | tropical scrub forest | |
| dry woodlands and shrublands (chaparral) | tropical savanna, thorn forest | |

**Figure 5-11** Earth's major biomes. This map indicates the main types of natural vegetation we would expect to find in different undisturbed land areas, mostly because of differences in climate. Each biome contains many ecosystems whose communities have adapted to smaller differences in climate, soil, and other environmental factors within the biome. In reality, people have removed or altered much of this natural vegetation for farming, livestock grazing, cutting lumber and gathering fuelwood, mining, transferring water, and building villages and cities, thereby altering the biomes.

Q: What is the *first law of ecology*?

physical adaptations for conserving water (Spotlight, p. 125). Insects and reptiles have thick outer coverings to minimize water loss through evaporation. Some desert animals become dormant during periods of extreme heat or drought.

You might expect desert soils to be poor in plant nutrients, but some are nutrient-rich. In others it is only the lack of water that prevents the growth of plants found in wetter biomes. We have converted areas of such deserts into productive farmland by bringing water to them.

Because of the slow growth rate of plants, low species diversity, and shortages of water, deserts take a long time to recover from disruptions. For example, vegetation destroyed by livestock grazing and off-road vehicles may take decades to grow back. Vehicles can also cause the collapse of some underground burrows that are habitats for many desert animals.

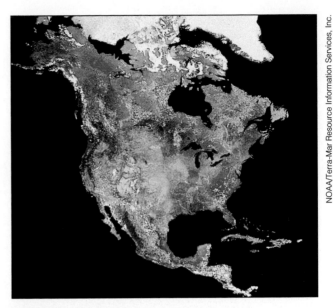

**Figure 5-12** View from space showing major biomes and surface features of most of North America.

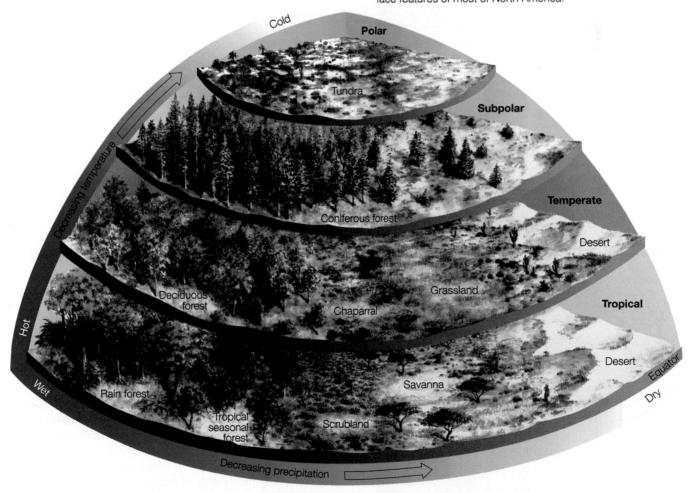

**Figure 5-13** Average precipitation and average temperature, acting together over a period of 30 or more years as limiting factors, determine the type of desert, grassland, or forest biome in a particular area. Although the actual situation is much more complex, this simplified diagram gives you a general idea of how climate determines the types and amounts of natural vegetation you would expect to find in an undisturbed area. (Adapted by permission of Macmillan Publishing Company, from Derek Elsom, *Earth*, New York: Macmillian, 1992. Copyright © 1992 by Marshall Editions Developments Limited.)

**A:** We can never do only one thing.

Latitude

Polar ice
and snow

Tundra (herbs,
lichens, mosses)

Coniferous forests

Deciduous forests

**Figure 5-14** Generalized effects of latitude and altitude on climate and biomes. Parallel changes in types of vegetation occur when we travel from equator to poles or from plain to mountaintop.

Gert Behrens/Ardea London

**Figure 5-15** Tropical desert. Only a few of the world's deserts are such vast expanses of sand and dunes, as shown in this photograph of the Namib of southwest Africa. Most are covered with rock or small stones, as well as some forms of scattered vegetation.

**GRASSLANDS** *Grasslands* occur where the average annual precipitation allows grass, and in some cases a few trees and shrubs, to grow, but is so erratic that drought and fire prevent large stands of trees from growing. Since grasses grow from the bottom, their stems can grow again after being devoured by herbivores. Grazing enhances primary productivity by stimulating growth of grasses, as long as the density of grazing animals is not too high. Grazing also helps keep out invading woody plants and preserves the mixtures of grasses and other vegetation preferred by most grassland herbivores.

The three main types of grasslands—tropical, temperate, and polar—result from combinations of low average precipitation with different average temperatures (Figure 5-13). *Tropical grasslands*—such as most savannas with scattered shrubs and stunted trees (Figure 5-17)—are found in areas with high average temperatures and low-to-moderate average precipitation. They occur in a wide belt on either side of the equator beyond the borders of tropical rain forests (Figure 5-11).

Tropical savannas have warm temperatures year-round, with two prolonged dry seasons and abundant rain the rest of the year. African tropical savannas contain enormous herds of *grazing* (grass- and herb-eating) and *browsing* (twig- and leaf-nibbling) hoofed animals, including wildebeest (Figure 5-17), gazelle, zebra, giraffe, and antelope. These and other large herbivores have specialized eating habits that minimize their competition for resources. For example, giraffes eat leaves and shoots from the tops of trees, while ele-

Q: What is the *second law of ecology*?

Altitude

Mountain
ice and snow

Tundra (herbs,
lichens, mosses)

Coniferous
forests

Deciduous
forests

Tropical forests

Tropical
forests

## Kangaroo Rat: Water Miser and Keystone Species

The kangaroo rat (Figure 5-16) is a remarkable mammal that has mastered the art of water conservation in its desert environment. As the desert's chief seed-eater, it is also a keystone species that helps support other desert species. By consuming seeds it helps keep desert shrubland from becoming grassland.

This rodent comes out of its burrow only at night when the air is cool and water evaporation has slowed. Its main source of food is dry seeds, which it quickly stuffs into its cheek pouches. After a night of foraging, it returns to its burrow and empties its cache of seeds.

In the cool burrow the seeds soak up water exhaled in the rodent's breath. The rat does not drink water; its water comes from recycled moisture in the seeds it eats and from water produced when the sugars in the seeds undergo aerobic respiration. Some of the water vapor in the rat's breath condenses on a cool inside surface of the nose and diffuses back to its body. Kangaroo rats have no sweat glands, so they don't lose water by perspiration. In addition, they save water by excreting hard, dry feces and thick, nearly solid urine from their superefficient kidneys.

B. & C. Calhoun/Bruce Coleman Ltd.

**Figure 5-16** This nocturnal kangaroo rat of the California desert is an expert in water conservation. It is also a keystone species because it consumes such vast quantities of seeds that desert shrubland is prevented from becoming grassland.

phants eat leaves and branches farther down. And Thompson's gazelles and wildebeests prefer short grass, while zebras graze on longer grass and stems.

During the dry season fires often sweep the savannas, and the great herds of grazing animals must migrate in search of food. The remains of these herbivores and their predators are picked over by hyenas, jackals, vultures, and other scavengers.

Another important savanna-dweller is the termite, which gathers wood detritus and other forms of cellulose, and carries it into huge nests or mounds. On top of this material it cultivates the fungi it feeds on. In turn this releases methane, a greenhouse gas.

Tropical savannas are efficient at converting carbon dioxide into carbohydrates through photosynthesis, equaling or even exceeding the net primary productivity of tropical rain forests. Much of the carbon removed from the atmosphere is locked up in the soil, in dead plant matter and in roots and underground stems. Thus deliberately burning savanna, plowing up its grasses, and converting it into cropland releases large quantities of carbon dioxide into the atmosphere. This may contribute as much to a projected enhanced greenhouse effect as (if not more than) the more publicized clearing and burning of tropical rain forests.

*Temperate grasslands* cover vast expanses of flat and gently rolling hills in the interiors of North and South America, Europe, and Asia (Figure 5-11). The winters are bitterly cold, but the hot, dry summers, as well as drought, occasional fires, and intense grazing, help prevent the growth of trees and bushes, except

**Figure 5-17** Serengeti tropical savanna in Tanzania, Africa, an example of one type of tropical grassland. Most savannas consist of grasslands punctuated by stands of deciduous shrubs and trees, which shed their leaves during the dry season and thus avoid excessive water loss. More large, hoofed, plant-eating mammals (ungulates), such as the herd of wildebeest shown here, live in this biome than anywhere else.

near rivers. Organic detritus breaks down slowly and thus accumulates to produce a fertile soil.

Types of temperate grasslands are the *tall-grass prairies* (Figure 5-18) and *short-grass prairies* (Figure 5-19) of the midwestern and western United States and Canada, the South American *pampas*, African *veld*, and the *steppes of* central Europe and Asia. Here winds blow almost continuously and evaporation is rapid, leading to recurring fires in the summer and fall. As long as the soil is not plowed, it is held in place by a thick network of grass roots; because of their fertile soils, however, many of the world's temperate grasslands have been cleared of their native grasses and used for growing crops (Figure 5-20). Overgrazing, mismanagement, and occasional prolonged droughts sometimes lead to severe wind erosion and loss of topsoil, which can convert these grasslands into desert or semidesert.

*Polar grasslands*, or *arctic tundra*, occur just south of the arctic polar ice cap (Figure 5-11). During most of the year these treeless plains are bitterly cold, swept by frigid winds and covered with ice and snow. Winters are long and dark, and the low average annual precipitation falls mostly as snow.

This biome is carpeted with a thick, spongy mat of low-growing plants (Figure 5-21). Most of the annual growth of these plants occurs during the summer when the sun shines almost around the clock.

Most of the tundra's permanent animal residents are small herbivores such as lemmings, hares, voles, and ground squirrels, which burrow underground to escape the cold. Their numbers are regulated by predators such as the lynx, arctic wolf, weasel, snowy owl, and arctic fox. Few species are present in large numbers. Most tundra animals do not hibernate be-

cause the summer is too short for them to build up adequate fat reserves.

One effect of the extreme cold is **permafrost**—a thick layer of ice beneath the soil surface that remains frozen year-round. The permafrost and the icy winter weather prevent the establishment of trees. In summer, water near the surface thaws, but the permafrost layer below stays frozen and keeps water melted at the surface from seeping into the ground. During this period the tundra is dotted with shallow lakes, bogs, marshes, and ponds. Hordes of mosquitoes, deerflies, blackflies, and other insects thrive in the shallow surface pools, and feed large colonies of migratory birds, especially waterfowl, which migrate from the south to nest and breed in the bogs and ponds. Caribou herds also arrive to feed on the summer vegetation, bringing along their predators, wolves.

Because of the cold, decomposition is slow; partially decomposed organic matter forms soggy peat bogs (the source of gardeners' peat moss), which contain about 95% of this biome's carbon. The low rate of decomposition, the shallow soil, and the slow growth rate of plants make the arctic tundra especially vulnerable to disruption. For example, vegetation destroyed by human activities can take decades to grow back.

Another type of tundra, called *alpine tundra*, occurs above the limit of tree growth but below the snow line on high mountains (Figure 5-14). The vegetation there is similar to that found in arctic tundra, but there is no permafrost layer. For a few weeks each summer the land blazes with color as wildflowers burst into bloom. The small plants that survive in this biome are grazed by elk and mountain goats, while golden eagles soar above looking for marmots and ground squirrels.

**Q:** What two countries have the world's largest populations?

Figure 5-18 A patch of tall-grass prairie in Mason County, Illinois, in early September. Grasses in this biome may be more than 2 meters (6.5 feet) high. Only about 1% of the original tall-grass prairie that once thrived in the midwestern United States and Canada remains. Because of their fertile soils, most have been cleared for corn, wheat, and soybeans, and for hog farming.

Figure 5-19 Bison grazing on a short-grass prairie to the east of the Rocky Mountains. Grasses in this biome are less than 0.6 meter (2 feet) high. Precipitation is too light and soils are too low in some plant nutrients to support taller grasses. These grasslands are widely used to graze unfenced cattle and sheep and, in some areas, to grow wheat and irrigated crops.

Figure 5-20 Replacement of a temperate grassland with a monoculture cropland near Blythe, California. When the tangled network of natural grasses is removed, the fertile topsoil is subject to severe wind erosion unless it is kept covered with some type of vegetation. If global warming accelerates as projected over the next 50 years, many of these grasslands may become too hot and dry for farming, thus threatening the world's food supply.

Figure 5-21 Polar grassland (arctic tundra) in Alaska in summer. During the long, dark, cold winter this land is covered with snow and ice. Its low-growing plants are adapted to the lack of sunlight and water, to freezing temperatures, and to constant high winds. Below the surface layer of soil is a thick layer of permafrost, which stays frozen year-round.

**Figure 5-22** Tropical rain forest in Monteverde Cloud Forest Reserve in Costa Rica. Although tropical rain forests cover only about 6% of Earth's land surface, they contain almost half of the world's growing wood and a third of its plant matter. They are also habitats for 50–80% of Earth's species. These biomes are being cut down and degraded at a rapid rate.

Brian Rogers/Biofotos

**FORESTS** Undisturbed areas with moderate-to-high average precipitation tend to be covered with *forest*, containing various species of trees and smaller forms of vegetation. *Tropical rain forests* are a type of evergreen broadleaf forest (Figure 5-22) found near the equator (Figure 5-11), where hot, moisture-laden air rises and dumps its moisture (Figure 5-7). They have a warm annual mean temperature that varies little daily or seasonally, high humidity, and heavy rainfall almost daily—ideal for trees. And the almost unchanging climate means that water and temperature are not limiting factors as in other biomes. Here soil nutrients are the main limiting factors.

There are several types of tropical rain forests depending on variations in altitude, temperature, and average rainfall. What they all have in common, however, is their astonishing biological diversity. A mature rain forest has more plant and animal species per unit of area than any other biome, although more mammal species live in the deserts, grasslands, and scrublands of South America than in its rain forests. These diverse life forms occupy specialized niches in distinct layers, based mostly on their need for sunlight (Figure 4-37).

For rain-forest plants, life is an endless struggle for sunlight. The tallest broadleaf evergreen trees emerge above the surrounding vegetation and capture direct sunlight. Beneath this *emergent layer* lies the *canopy*, where leaves and top branches of shorter trees overlap and allow only dim light to reach the *understory* of smaller trees. Vines, also called *lianas*, with their roots in the soil grow up tree trunks and loop through their branches until their leaves reach the canopy where sunlight is available. In the canopy they link tree crowns to one another, providing support for the giant trees in light storms. Rattan is a commercially valuable liana harvested from rain forests. Orchids (Figure 4-11) and other epiphytes attached to the trunks and limbs of canopy trees catch water and nutrients falling from above in their specially shaped leaves. Large epiphytes—some more than 2 meters (6 feet) in diameter—hold as much as 4 liters (1 gallon) of water and function as miniature ponds in the forest crown. A source of water for birds and monkeys, they also provide homes and moisture for spiders and insects, and places for frogs to lay eggs. Philodendrons have huge, dark green leaves to capture the sunlight in the dim understory. Many house and office plants come from the understory of tropical rain forests.

Even less light reaches the *shrub layer* near the ground, and only about 2% of the incoming sunlight reaches the dark *ground layer*, where there is relatively little vegetation. The popular image of the rain forest floor as a tangled, almost impenetrable jungle is accurate only along river banks, near clearings, or where a large tree has fallen and sunlight reaches the ground.

Much of the animal life, particularly insects, bats, and birds, lives in the sunny canopy layer, with its abundant shelter and food. Monkeys (Figure 5-23), apes (photo, p. 45), toads (Figure 4-34), geckos, sloths, snakes, chameleons, and other animals move up and down the trunks and vines to feed on insects, fruits, or leaves. Multitudes of tiny animals live on the ground, along with vast populations of termites and decom-

Q: At what rate is the world's population growing?

**Figure 5-23** Two of the astonishing diversity of species found in tropical forests. On the left is the world's largest flower, the flesh flower (*Rafflesia arnoldii*), growing in a tropical rain forest in Sumatra. The flower of this leafless plant can be as large as 1 meter (3.3 feet) in diameter and weigh up to 7 kilograms (15 pounds). The plant gives off a smell like rotting meat, presumably to attract flies and beetles that pollinate its flower. After blossoming for a few weeks the flower dissolves into a slimy black mass. On the right is a cotton top tamarin.

posers. Because of the warm, moist conditions, dropped leaves and dead animals break down fast; this rapid recycling of scarce soil nutrients is why there is little litter on the ground.

Because of the dense vegetation little wind blows in tropical rain forests, eliminating the possibility of wind pollination. Instead, many of the plants have evolved elaborate flowers (Figure 5-23) that attract particular insects, birds, or bats as pollinators.

Undisturbed tropical rain forests can sustain themselves indefinitely. Unfortunately, as we will see in Chapter 10, these storehouses of biodiversity are being cleared or degraded at an alarming rate. Within 50 years only scattered fragments might remain—causing a massive loss of Earth's vital biodiversity.

Moving a little farther from the equator, we find *tropical deciduous forests* (sometimes called tropical monsoon forests or tropical seasonal forests), usually located between tropical rain forests and tropical savannas (Figure 5-11). These forests are warm year-round. Most of their plentiful rainfall occurs during a wet (monsoon) season that is followed by a long dry season.

These forests are less complex than tropical rain forests. They contain a mixture of drought-tolerant evergreen trees and deciduous trees, which lose their leaves to help survive the dry season. Many tropical seasonal forests are being cleared for timber, grazing land, and agriculture, subjecting them to erosion, which can lead to desertification. Where the dry season is even longer, we find *tropical scrub forests* (Figure 5-11) containing mostly small deciduous trees and shrubs.

In scattered temperate areas with ample rainfall or moisture from ocean fogs, we find *temperate rain forests*. Along the west coast of North America from Canada to northern California these biomes are dominated by large conifers such as Sitka spruce, Douglas fir, and redwoods (Figure 2-7). Other temperate rain forests are dominated by broadleaf evergreens or contain a mixture of conifers and broadleaf evergreens. Because they contain stands of large, valuable trees, many of these ancient forests are being clear-cut for their lumber, further depleting Earth's biodiversity.

*Temperate deciduous forests* grow in areas with moderate average temperatures that change signifi-

A: 1.7% per year

**Figure 5-24** Temperate deciduous forest in Rhode Island during (clockwise from top left) winter, spring, summer, and fall.

Q: What continent has the world's highest population growth rate?

**Figure 5-25** Tree farm, or plantation, in North Carolina. Converting a diverse temperate deciduous forest to an even-aged stand of a single species (monoculture) increases the production of wood for timber or pulpwood but results in a loss of biodiversity. Such monocultures are more vulnerable to attacks by pests, disease, and air pollution than are the more diverse forests they replaced.

cantly during four distinct seasons (Figure 5-24). These areas have long summers, cold but not too severe winters, and abundant precipitation, often spread fairly evenly throughout the year.

This biome is dominated by a few species of broadleaf deciduous trees, such as oak, hickory, maple, poplar, sycamore, and beech. They survive the winter by dropping their leaves in the fall and becoming dormant. Each spring they sprout new leaves that change in the fall into a blazing array of reds and golds before dropping.

Mature temperate deciduous forests usually have a simpler structure than tropical rain forests, with more sunlight penetrating to the ground. At the top is a partly open canopy of leaves; below, an understory of shorter, shade-tolerant trees and shrubs; and on the forest floor a layer of ferns, mosses, and other low-growing plants. Compared with tropical rain forests, temperate deciduous forests contain relatively few tree species. However, the penetration of sunlight supports a richer diversity of plant life at ground level.

This layering of vegetation creates many niches for animal life. Hawks and owls nest in the canopy and keep down populations of mice and other small rodents, which would otherwise destroy much of the vegetation on the forest floor. Scarlet tanagers flit through the treetops, devouring beetles and caterpillars that harm oaks and other trees. Black bears nest and feed on the ground, and squirrels regularly commute between the canopy and the forest floor. Deer wander among the low-growing plants on the lighted forest floor.

Once, the temperate deciduous forests of the eastern United States were home for such large predators as bears, badgers, wolves, foxes, wildcats, and mountain lions. Today most of the predators have been killed or displaced, and the dominant mammal species is often the whitetail deer. Warblers, robins, and other bird species migrate to the forests during the summer to feed and breed, although many of these species are declining in numbers because of loss of their habitats.

All but about 0.1% of the original stands of temperate deciduous forests in North America have been cleared for farms, orchards, timber, and urban development. Some have been converted to intensely managed *tree farms* or *plantations*, where a single species is grown for timber, pulpwood, or Christmas trees (Figure 5-25).

*Evergreen coniferous forests*, also called *boreal forests* (meaning "northern forests") and *taigas* (meaning "swamp forests"), are found just south of the arctic tundra in northern regions across North America, Asia, and Europe with a subarctic climate (Figure 5-11). Winters are long, cold, and dry, and sunlight is available only 6–8 hours a day. Summers are short, with mild-to-warm temperatures, and the sun typically shines 19 hours a day.

These forests are dominated by a few species of coniferous evergreens such as spruce, fir, cedar, hemlock, and pine (Figure 5-26). The tiny, needle-shaped, wax-coated leaves of these trees can withstand the intense cold and drought of winter. Plant diversity is low in these forests because few species can survive the winters, when soil moisture is frozen. A few broadleaf deciduous species, such as aspen, birch, willow, and larch, are hardy enough to survive the short growing seasons in parts of these biomes.

The crowded needles of evergreen trees block out much of the light. Beneath the dense stands of trees, a carpet of fallen needles and leaf litter covers the nutrient-poor soil, making the soil acidic and preventing most other plants from growing on the dim forest floor.

During the frigid winters some mammals, such as beavers and squirrels, rely on food they stored up during the summer. Others, such as woodchucks and black bears, hibernate during the harsh months until spring. Moose, wolves, lynxes, and porcupines forage or prowl in search of prey throughout the winter.

During the brief summer the soil becomes water-logged, forming bogs, or muskegs, in low-lying areas of these forests. Warblers and other insect-eating birds arrive to feed on hordes of flies, mosquitoes, and caterpillars.

In settled areas of this biome in North America, farmers and ranchers have essentially eliminated large predators, such as timber wolves, which can prey on livestock. As a result, populations of moose, caribou, and mule deer have increased, devastating taiga vegetation. In the long run this reduces the ability of the land to support grazing livestock. Loggers have cut the trees from large areas of taiga in North America, and many of these remaining ancient forests may soon be cut. Much fur trapping has also taken place in this biome.

Most of the vast boreal forests that once covered Finland and Sweden have been cut, and some have been replaced with even-aged tree plantations. Within a decade the vast boreal forests of Siberia may also disappear as the Russian republics log them to earn hard currency. Boreal forests in Canada are also being cleared rapidly, mostly for export to Japan. The world's boreal forests are roughly two-thirds the size of the continental United States and extract three-quarters as much carbon dioxide from the atmosphere as do the tropical forests of the Amazon.

Boreal forests are especially vulnerable to acid deposition, ozone, and other forms of air pollution. Because they keep most of their needles, the trees are exposed to air pollution year-round, especially at high altitudes, where they can be almost continuously bathed in clouds and fog. Most life in nearby lakes and streams can be killed from runoff of water containing acids leached from the soil. Because trees grow slowly in the cold northern climate, these forests take a long time to recover from disruption.

## 5-4 Life in Water Environments

**WHY ARE THE OCEANS IMPORTANT?** A more accurate name for Earth would be Ocean, because oceans cover more than 70% of its surface (Figure 5-27). These oceans play key roles in the survival of virtually all life on Earth. Because solar heat is distributed through ocean currents (Figure 5-3) and because ocean water evaporates as part of the global hydrologic cycle (Figure 4-33), oceans play a major role in regulating Earth's climate. They also participate in other important biogeochemical cycles.

By serving as a gigantic reservoir for carbon dioxide (Figure 4-28), oceans help regulate the temperature of the troposphere. Oceans provide habitats for about 250,000 species of marine plants and animals, which are food for many organisms, including human beings. They also serve as a source of iron, sand, gravel, phosphates, magnesium, oil, natural gas, and many other valuable resources. Because of their size and currents, the oceans mix and dilute many human-pro-

**Figure 5-26** Evergreen coniferous forest (taiga or boreal forest) in Washington State. Many of the ancient forests along the coast from Canada to northern California have been clear-cut and replaced with tree plantations. There is intense pressure to clear-cut many of the remaining stands of these forests located in the national forests.

U.S. Forest Service

Q: Worldwide, what is the average number of children per woman?

duced wastes flowing or dumped into them to less harmful or even harmless levels, as long as they are not overloaded.

**OCEAN ZONES** Oceans have two major life zones: the coastal zone and the open sea (Figure 5-28). The **coastal zone** is the relatively warm, nutrient-rich, shallow water that extends from the high-tide mark on land to the gently sloping, relatively shallow edge of the *continental shelf*, the submerged part of the continents. Because of ample sunlight and nutrients deposited from land and stirred up by wind and ocean currents, this coastal zone has a very high net primary productivity per unit of area (Figure 4-27). Although it makes up less than 10% of the ocean's area, the coastal zone contains 90% of all marine species and is the site of most of the large commercial marine fisheries.

The sharp increase in water depth at the edge of the continental shelf separates the coastal zone from

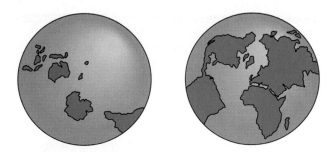

**Figure 5-27** The ocean planet. The oceans cover about 71% of Earth's surface. About 97% of Earth's water is in the interconnected oceans, which cover 90% of the planet's mostly ocean hemisphere (left) and 50% of its land-ocean hemisphere (right). The average depth of the world's oceans is 3.8 kilometers (2.4 miles).

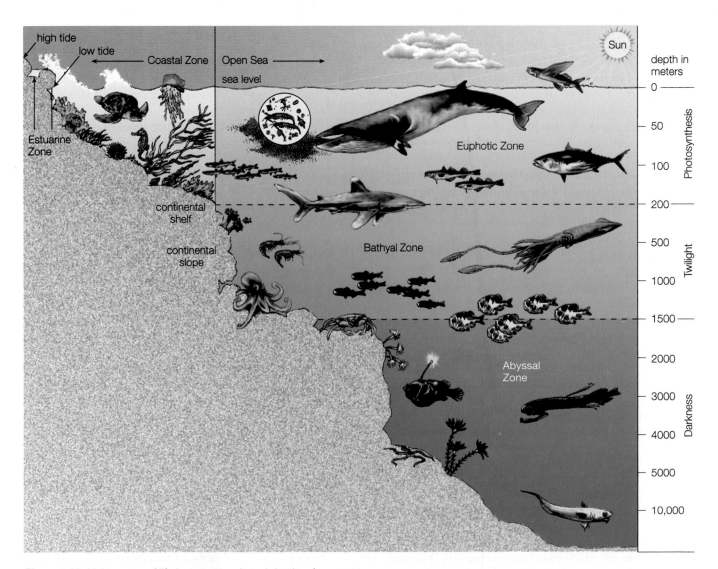

**Figure 5-28** Major zones of life in an ocean. Actual depths of zones may vary.

A: 3.3 (1.9 in MDCs, 3.8 in LDCs) in 1993

**Figure 5-29** Global distribution of coral reefs.

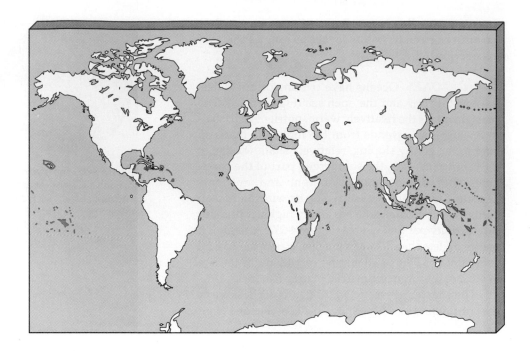

the **open sea**, which is divided into three vertical zones—euphotic, bathyal, and abyssal—based primarily on the penetration of sunlight (Figure 5-28). This vast volume contains only about 10% of all ocean species. The lighted upper (*euphotic*) zone is where photosynthesis takes place in the open sea. The coastal zone is all euphotic. The dimly lit *bathyal zone* and the dark *abyssal zone* are found only in the open sea.

The euphotic zone supports large populations of floating and drifting producers (mostly microscopic cyanobacteria and protists) called *phytoplankton*. They are fed upon by slightly larger, more mobile primary consumers called *zooplankton*, ranging in size from single-celled organisms to jellyfish. Feeding on them are a variety of consumers, from massive baleen whales to herrings, sardines, anchovies, and other small fish. These small fish are eaten by larger predators such as tuna, mackerel, and swordfish, and by marine mammals such as seals and orcas. Dead and decaying organisms fall to the ocean floor to feed microscopic decomposers and scavengers such as crabs and sea urchins. On parts of the dark, deep ocean floor near hydrothermal vents, scientists have discovered communities of organisms in which specialized microscopic bacteria use chemosynthesis to produce food for themselves and other organisms feeding on them.

Except at an occasional equatorial upwelling, average net primary productivity per unit of area in the open sea is quite low (Figure 4-27). This is because sunlight cannot penetrate the lower layers and because the surface layer normally has fairly low levels of nutrients for phytoplankton, which are the main photosynthetic producers of the open ocean.

**THE COASTAL ZONE: A CLOSER LOOK** The coastal zone includes several different ecosystems with the world's highest net primary productivities per unit of area (Figure 4-27). These include coral reefs, estuaries, and coastal wetlands.

The coastal zones of warm tropical and subtropical oceans often contain colorful **coral reefs** (Figures 4-1, left, and 5-29). They are formed by massive colonies containing billions of tiny coral animals, called polyps. These close relatives of jellyfish secrete a protective limestone crust around their soft bodies. When a coral polyp dies, this empty crust or outer skeleton remains as a framework for more growth. Thus the core of a reef is dead but covered by a thin skin of living coral. The resulting tangled maze of cracks, crevices, and caves formed by different types of coral provides shelter for a huge variety of marine plants and animals, including many colorful fish. Human activities are causing widespread destruction of and damage to these vital ecosystems, making them the most threatened ecosystems in the coastal zone (p. 74 and Case Study, p. 135).

An **estuary** is a partially enclosed coastal area at the mouth of a river where its fresh water, carrying fertile silt and runoff from the land, mixes with salty seawater (Figure 5-30). The constant water movement stirs up the nutrient-rich silt, making it available to producers. In an estuary temperature and salinity levels vary widely because of seasonal variations in stream flow and the daily rhythms of the tides.

A **wetland** is an area of land covered all or part of the year with salt water (called a **coastal wetland**) or fresh water (called an **inland wetland**, excluding lakes, ponds, and streams). About 5% of all wetlands in the

**Q:** What is the size of the U.S. population?

## The Importance of Coral Reefs

Coral reefs are among the world's oldest and most diverse and productive ecosystems—the marine equivalent of tropical rain forests. Coral reefs are a joint venture. Tiny, single-celled, photosynthesizing protists (dinoflagellates) living in or between the cells of coral animals synthesize organic food compounds for the polyps. In this mutualistic partnership the protists gain a protected habitat and some minerals from the polyps' body fluids and wastes. Algae and other producers, which give corals their bright colors, grow on the outside surfaces of coral animals and provide plentiful food for fish, starfish (Figure 4-12), and other marine animals. In fact, coral reefs support at least one-third of all marine fish species (Figure 4-1).

Coral reef ecosystems grow slowly and are easily disrupted. They thrive only in clear, clean, warm, and fairly shallow water of constant high salinity. They also need ample sunlight and enough wave action to provide dissolved oxygen and nutrients.

Coral reefs reduce the energy of incoming waves and help protect 15% of the world's coastlines from storms (Figure 5-29). By forming limestone shells, coral polyps take up carbon dioxide as part of the carbon cycle (Figure 4-28).

Despite their importance these ecosystems are being destroyed or damaged in 93 of their 109 significant locations. Natural threats include hurricanes, predation by crown-of-thorn starfish, and ocean warming from El Niño–Southern Oscillations (Figure 5-9). Normally reefs gradually recover from the ravages of nature, but human activities are upsetting this healing process.

The greatest human threats to these delicate ecosystems come from eroded soil produced by deforestation, construction, agriculture, and poor land management. The suspended soil sediment washes downriver to the sea where it smothers coral polyps or blocks their sunlight. The death of these polyps and their colorful algae coatings is one cause of coral reef bleaching (Figure 4-1, right). Other threats include viruses (p. 74), global warming, chemical pollution, nuclear weapons testing, anchor damage, dredging, overfishing, the dynamiting of fish, oil spills, mining coral (limestone) for use as building material, collecting coral for sale to local tourists and for export, and uncontrolled tourism.

Some 300 coral reefs in 65 countries are protected as reserves or parks, and another 600 have been recommended for protection. Also, some marine biologists are trying to replenish dead or dying reefs by scattering or gluing pieces of live coral onto the reef surface. These are important steps, but protecting and restoring reefs is difficult and expensive, and only half the countries with coral reefs have set aside reserves.

---

United States are coastal wetlands, which exend inland from estuaries. The other 95% are inland wetlands.

Estuaries and coastal wetlands are highly productive areas (Figure 4-27), supplying food and serving as spawning and nursery grounds for many marine fish and shellfish. Tens of millions of people in coastal LDCs depend on these ecosystems to get enough food to survive. They are also breeding grounds and habitats for waterfowl and other wildlife, including many endangered and threatened species.

Coastal wetlands dilute and filter out large amounts of nutrients and waterborne pollutants, helping protect the quality of waters used for swimming, fishing, and wildlife habitats. Just 0.4 hectare (1 acre) of tidal estuary provides $75,000 of free waste treatment and has an estimated value of $83,000 when production of fish for food and recreation is included. By comparison, 0.4 hectare (1 acre) of prime farmland in Kansas has a top value of $1,200 and an annual production value of $600.

In temperate areas coastal wetlands usually consist of a mix of *bays, lagoons, salt flats, mud flats,* and *salt marshes* (Figure 5-31), where grasses are the dominant vegetation. These highly productive ecosystems serve as nurseries and habitats for shrimp and many other aquatic animals.

In warm tropical climates where there is too much silt for coral reefs to grow, we find highly productive *mangrove swamps* (Figure 5-32). They are dominated by mangrove trees, any of about 55 species of trees and shrubs that can live partly submerged in the relatively salty environment of coastal swamps (Figure 5-33). Mangrove trees and shrubs get the oxygen they need in the oxygen-deficient silt bed of these swamps through roots, which protrude above the water at low tide and funnel oxygen down to the rest of their silt-covered roots. Mangrove swamps help protect the coastline from erosion, reduce damage from typhoons and hurricanes, trap sediment washed off the land, and provide breeding, nursery, and feeding grounds for some 2,000 species of wildlife.

Despite their ecological importance, mangroves have been under severe attack. Since 1970 Malaysia has lost half its mangrove area, much of it cut and converted to wood chips used in Japan. More than a quarter of Indonesia's mangroves have been cut and

**Figure 5-30** Space shuttle view of sediment plume at the mouth of Madagascar's Betsiboka River flowing into the estuary of the Mozambique Channel that separates the huge island from the African mainland. The massive amount of sediment results from topography, heavy rains, and clearing of forests for agriculture, making Madagascar the world's most eroded country.

**Figure 5-31** Salt marsh on Cape Cod on the coast of Massachusetts. These and other temperate coastal wetlands trap nutrients and sediment flowing in from rivers and nearby land, and thus have a high net primary productivity. They also filter out and degrade some of the pollutants deposited by rivers and land runoff.

drained to grow rice or rear shrimp. More than half of the mangroves in the Philippines have been converted into ponds used to raise prawns and milkfish.

Some coasts have steep *rocky shores* pounded by waves (Figure 5-34). Many organisms live in the numerous intertidal pools in the rocks. Other coasts have gently sloping *barrier beaches* at the water's edge. If not destroyed by human activities, one or more rows

of natural sand dunes on such beaches (with the sand held in place by the roots of grasses) serve as the first line of defense against the ravages of the sea (Figure 5-35). However, such beaches are prime sites for development, which usually destroys their protective dunes. When coastal developers remove the dunes or build behind the first set of dunes, minor hurricanes and sea storms can flood and even sweep away houses

Q: What is the average number of children per woman in the United States?

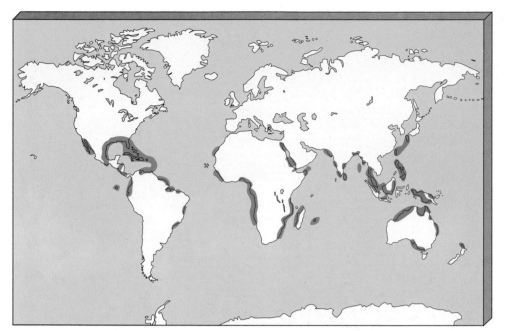

**Figure 5-32** Global distribution of mangroves. Since the mid-1960s some tropical coastal countries have lost half or more of their mangrove forests because of industrial logging for timber and fuelwood, conversion to ponds for raising fish and shellfish (aquaculture), conversion to rice fields and other agricultural land, and urban development. Mangroves are disappearing fastest in Asia, especially in the Philippines, Indonesia, and Java.

Alan Watson

**Figure 5-33** Mangrove swamp in Colombia.

and other buildings. Coastal dwellers mistakenly refer to these human-assisted disasters as natural disasters; federally supported insurance and disaster aid allows them to rebuild in these highly vulnerable areas and await the next disaster.

Along some coasts (such as most of North America's Atlantic and Gulf coasts) we find *barrier islands*: long, thin, low, offshore islands of sediment parallel to the shore. These islands protect the mainland, estuaries, lagoons, and coastal wetlands by dispersing the energy of approaching storm waves. Their low-lying

beaches are constantly shifting; gentle waves build them up and storms flatten and erode them. Longshore currents, which run parallel to the beaches, constantly take sand from one area and deposit it in another. Sooner or later many of the structures we build on low-lying barrier islands (Figure 5-36) and gently sloping barrier beaches are damaged or destroyed by flooding, severe beach erosion, and wind from major storms (including hurricanes).

Because of their immense value to us and other species, estuaries, coastal wetlands, barrier islands,

**Figure 5-34** Rocky shore beach in Acadia National Park, Maine. Organisms of most seashores must be able to withstand the tremendous force of incoming waves and the pull of the outgoing tide. Coasts like this one provide rocks to which organisms can attach themselves.

Richard Frear/National Park Service

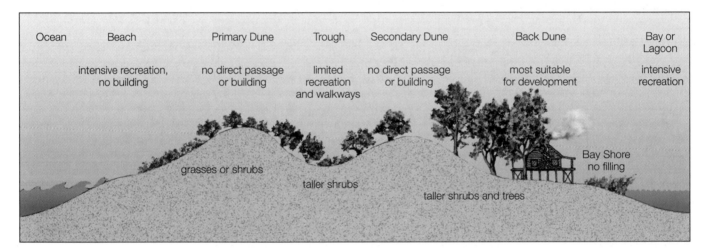

| Ocean | Beach | Primary Dune | Trough | Secondary Dune | Back Dune | Bay or Lagoon |
|---|---|---|---|---|---|---|
| | intensive recreation, no building | no direct passage or building | limited recreation and walkways | no direct passage or building | most suitable for development | intensive recreation |

grasses or shrubs

taller shrubs

taller shrubs and trees

Bay Shore no filling

**Figure 5-35** Primary and secondary dunes on a gently sloping beach play an important role in protecting the land from erosion by the sea. The roots of various grasses that colonize the dunes help hold the sand in place. Ideally construction and development should be allowed only behind the second strip of dunes, with walkways to the beach built over the dunes to keep them intact. Not only does this help preserve barrier beaches, but it helps protect structures from being damaged and washed away by wind, high tides, beach erosion, and flooding from storm surges. This type of protection is rare, however, because the short-term economic value of limited oceanfront land is considered to be much higher than its long-term ecological and economic values.

and natural sand dunes need to be protected and managed in ways that sustain their productivity (Case Study, p. 139).

**FRESHWATER LAKES** **Lakes** are large natural bodies of standing fresh water formed when precipitation, land runoff, or groundwater flowing from underground springs fills depressions in the earth. Causes of such depressions include glaciation (the Great Lakes of North America), crustal displacement accompanied by or resulting in earthquakes (Lake Nyasa in East Africa), and volcanic activity (Crater Lake in Oregon).

Lakes normally consist of four distinct zones (Figure 5-38), providing habitats and niches for different species. The *littoral zone* includes the shore and the shallow, nutrient-rich waters near the shore to the depth where rooted plants stop growing. It contains a variety of phytoplankton, rooted plants, and decomposers, as well as frogs, snails, snakes, and other consumers. The *limnetic zone*, like the euphotic zone of the

**Q:** How many people were added to the U.S. population in 1993?

In our desire to live near the coast, we are destroying or degrading the very resources that make coastal areas so enjoyable and valuable. Coastal zones are among our most densely populated and most intensely used—and polluted—ecosystems. Since 1900 the world may have lost half of its coastal wetlands. Asia has lost as much as 60% of its coastal wetlands area and Africa almost 30%. During the past 200 years nearly 55% of the area of estuaries and coastal wetlands in the United States has been destroyed or damaged, primarily by dredging and filling and by waste contamination. California alone has lost 91% of its original coastal wetlands, but Florida has lost the largest area of such wetlands in the United States.

These ecosystems are particularly vulnerable to toxic contamination because they trap pesticides, heavy metals, and other pollutants, concentrating them to very high levels. On any given day one-third of U.S. shellfish beds are closed to commercial or sport fishing because of contamination.

Fortunately about 45% of the area of estuaries and coastal wet-lands remains undeveloped. Each year, however, more of this land is developed or severely degraded, especially in the southeastern United States, where 83% of the remaining wetlands in the lower 48 states are found.

Beach erosion is a serious problem along most of the gently sloping beaches of barrier islands and mainland shores, with 30% of U.S. shoreline experiencing significant erosion. The main cause of this problem is that sea levels have been rising gradually for the past 12,000 years or so because the warmer climate since the last ice age has melted much of the ice and expanded the volume of seawater. Also, a shoreline is a dynamic system in which sediment from rivers and cliff erosion is continually being removed from one area by waves and currents and deposited in another. Thus beach erosion in one place and beach buildup in another is a natural process that we can do little to control.

Many states require that ocean-front structures be elevated and built of concrete. However, such structures can still be toppled by beach erosion and wind and wave damage as the average high-tide mark gradually moves inland. Engi-neers have tried several methods to halt or reduce beach erosion (Figure 5-37), but at best these are only temporary solutions because of the dynamic nature of shorelines.

The only permanent solution is to prevent development on remaining beach areas or to allow such development only behind protective dunes (Figure 5-35). Construction of seawalls, breakwaters, groins, and jetties should be banned or severely limited. Structures built too close to eroding beaches should be moved back from the water's edge, and any that are destroyed by storms or erosion should only be rebuilt farther inland. Eliminating federal flood insurance subsidies also would help protect beaches and would save taxpayers money by making individuals and corporations financially responsible for building in known high-risk areas. An urgent environmental priority should be to protect remaining unspoiled estuaries, coastal wetlands, mangroves, and beaches from destruction and degradation, and to manage those we have developed in sustainable ways.

(continued)

**Figure 5-36** Developed barrier island, Ocean City, Maryland—host to 8 million visitors a year. To keep up with shifting sands, officials spend millions of dollars to pump sand onto the beaches and to rebuild natural sand dunes; they may end up spending millions more to keep buildings from sinking. There is no effective protection against flooding and damage from severe storms, as residents on barrier islands in South Carolina learned when a devastating hurricane hit in 1989. Within a few hours a barrier island may be cut in two or destroyed by a hurricane. If global warming raises average sea levels as projected sometime in the next century, most of these valuable pieces of real estate will be underwater.

G. H. Demetrakas/O. C. Camera

A: 3.1 million (2 million more births than deaths and 1.1 million from legal and illegal immigration) CHAPTER 5

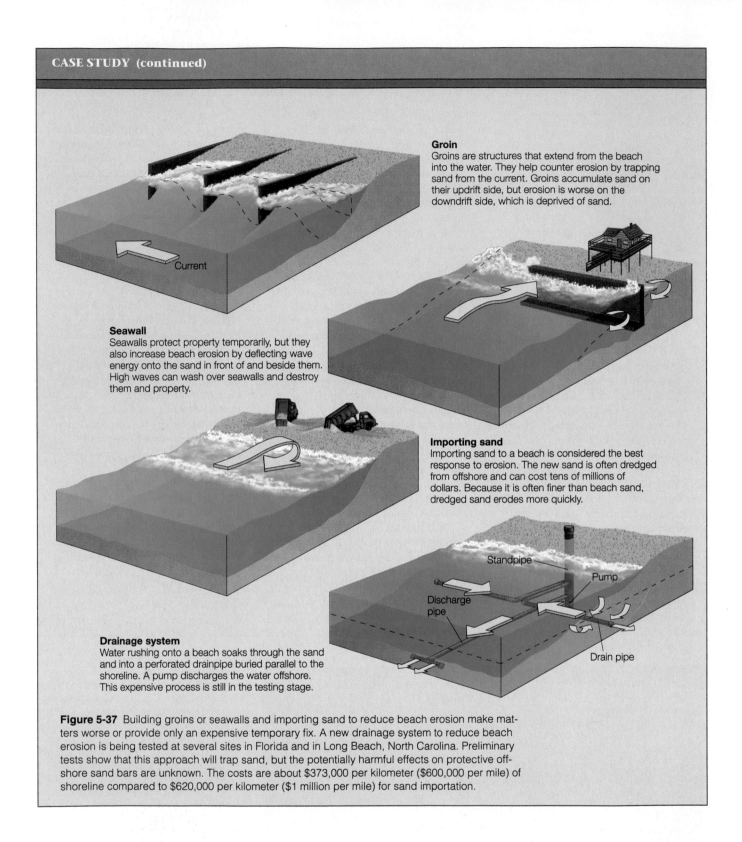

**Groin**
Groins are structures that extend from the beach into the water. They help counter erosion by trapping sand from the current. Groins accumulate sand on their updrift side, but erosion is worse on the downdrift side, which is deprived of sand.

Current

**Seawall**
Seawalls protect property temporarily, but they also increase beach erosion by deflecting wave energy onto the sand in front of and beside them. High waves can wash over seawalls and destroy them and property.

**Importing sand**
Importing sand to a beach is considered the best response to erosion. The new sand is often dredged from offshore and can cost tens of millions of dollars. Because it is often finer than beach sand, dredged sand erodes more quickly.

Standpipe

Pump

Discharge pipe

Drain pipe

**Drainage system**
Water rushing onto a beach soaks through the sand and into a perforated drainpipe buried parallel to the shoreline. A pump discharges the water offshore. This expensive process is still in the testing stage.

**Figure 5-37** Building groins or seawalls and importing sand to reduce beach erosion make matters worse or provide only an expensive temporary fix. A new drainage system to reduce beach erosion is being tested at several sites in Florida and in Long Beach, North Carolina. Preliminary tests show that this approach will trap sand, but the potentially harmful effects on protective offshore sand bars are unknown. The costs are about $373,000 per kilometer ($600,000 per mile) of shoreline compared to $620,000 per kilometer ($1 million per mile) for sand importation.

ocean (Figure 5-28), is the open-water surface layer that gets enough sunlight for photosynthesis. It contains varying amounts of phytoplankton, zooplankton, and fish, depending on the nutrients available. The *profundal zone* is the deep, open water where it is too dark for photosynthesis. It is inhabited by fish adapted to its cooler, darker water. The *benthic zone*, at the bottom of a lake, is inhabited mostly by decomposers (bacteria and fungi), detritus-feeding clams, and wormlike insect larvae.

A lake with a large or excessive supply of nutrients (mostly nitrates and phosphates) needed by pro-

**Q:** How many teenage women (ages 15–19) become pregnant each year in the United States?

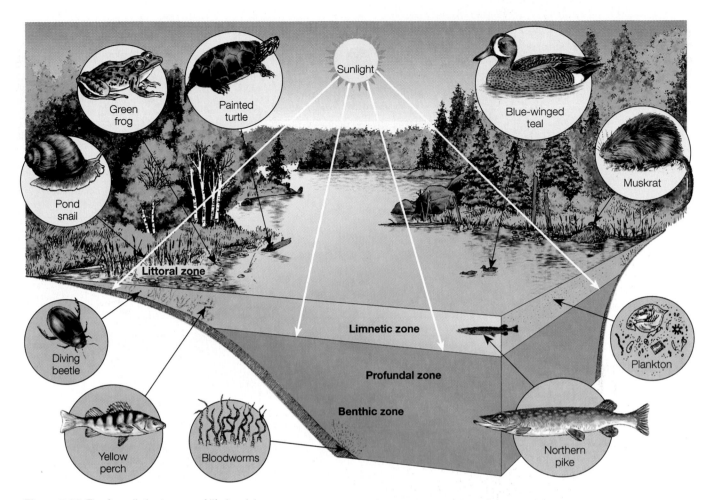

**Figure 5-38** The four distinct zones of life in a lake.

ducers is called a **eutrophic** (well-nourished) **lake** (Figure 5-39). Such lakes are typically shallow and have limited transparency. They have a high net primary productivity, with large populations of phytoplankton (especially cyanobacteria), many zooplankton, and diverse populations of fish, such as bass, sunfish, and yellow perch. In warm summer months the bottom layer of a eutrophic lake is often depleted of dissolved oxygen.

A lake with a small supply of nutrients is called an **oligotrophic** (poorly nourished) **lake** (Figure 5-39). This type of lake is often deep with steep banks. Because of its relatively low net primary productivity, such a lake usually has crystal-clear blue or green water. It has small populations of both phytoplankton and fish, such as smallmouth bass and lake trout. Many lakes fall somewhere between the two extremes of nutrient enrichment and are called **mesotrophic lakes**.

Most substances become denser as they go from gaseous to liquid to solid physical states. Luckily for us and for most freshwater organisms, water is an exception. It is densest as a liquid at 4°C (39°F). In other words, solid ice at 0°C (32°F) is less dense than

liquid water at 4°C (39°F), which is why ice floats on water. Otherwise, lakes and other bodies of standing fresh water in cold climates would freeze from the bottom up instead of from the surface down.

This unusual property of water causes *thermal stratification* of deep lakes in northern temperate areas with cold winters and warm summers (Figure 5-40). In summer such lakes become stratified into layers with different temperatures that hinder mixing. These lakes have an *epilimnion*, an upper layer of warm water with high levels of dissolved oxygen, and a *hypolimnion*, a lower layer of colder, denser water, usually with a lower concentration of dissolved oxygen. These layers are separated by a middle layer called a *thermocline*, where the water temperature changes rapidly with depth. The thermocline acts as a barrier to the transfer of nutrients and dissolved oxygen from the epilimnion to the hypolimnion.

In fall, when temperatures begin to drop, the surface layer sinks to the bottom when it cools to 4°C (39°F), and the thermocline disappears. This mixing, or *fall turnover*, brings nutrients from bottom sediments to the top and dissolved oxygen from the top to

**Figure 5-39** Eutrophic, or nutrient-rich, lake (top) and oligotrophic, or nutrient-poor, lake (bottom). Mesotrophic lakes fall between these two extremes of nutrient enrichment.

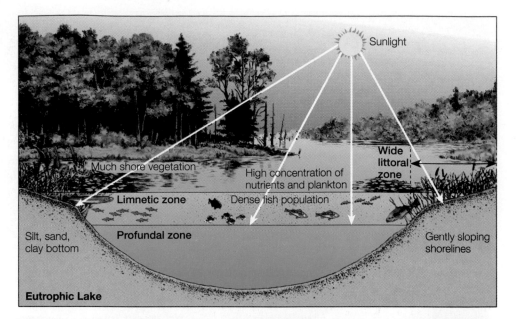

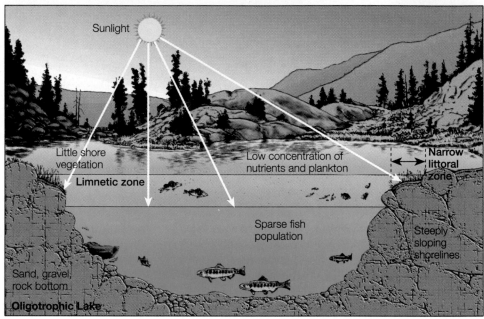

the bottom. And in spring, when the atmosphere warms, the lake's surface water warms to 4°C (39°F), reaches maximum density, and sinks through and below the cooler, less dense water. This brings the bottom water to the surface. During this *spring turnover* dissolved oxygen in the surface layer is moved downward and nutrients released by decomposition on the lake bottom are moved toward the surface.

**FRESHWATER STREAMS** Precipitation that doesn't sink into the ground or evaporate is **surface water**. This water becomes **runoff**, which flows into streams and eventually to the oceans to continue circulating in the hydrologic cycle (Figure 4-33). The entire land area that delivers water, sediment, and dissolved sub-

stances via small streams to a major stream (river), and ultimately to the sea, is called a **watershed**, or a **drainage basin**.

The downward flow of water from mountain highlands to the sea takes place in three phases in a *river system* (Figure 5-41). Because of different environmental conditions in each phase, a river system is a series of different ecosystems. First, narrow headwater or mountain highland streams with cold, clear water rush over waterfalls and rapids. As this turbulent water flows and tumbles downward, it dissolves large amounts of oxygen from the air. Here the plants are attached to rocks and the fish are cold-water fish, such as trout, which need lots of dissolved oxygen.

In the second phase the headwater streams merge

Q: What percentage of the world's population is under age 15?

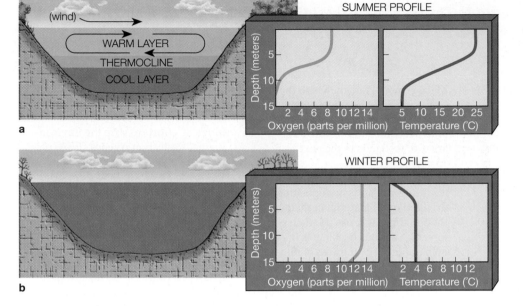

SUMMER PROFILE

Depth (meters)

Oxygen (parts per million)

Temperature (°C)

WINTER PROFILE

Depth (meters)

Oxygen (parts per million)

Temperature (°C)

**Figure 5-40  (a)** Thermal stratification and restriction on water mixing during summer for a lake in a temperate climate region. **(b)** There is little thermal stratification during the winter because once or twice a year such stratified lakes undergo a mixing or *turnover* in which temperature changes during various seasons cause changes in the densities of water in the top and bottom layers. (Used by permission from Cecie Starr and Ralph Taggart, *Biology: The Unity and Diversity of Life*, 6th ed., Belmont, Calif.: Wadsworth, 1992)

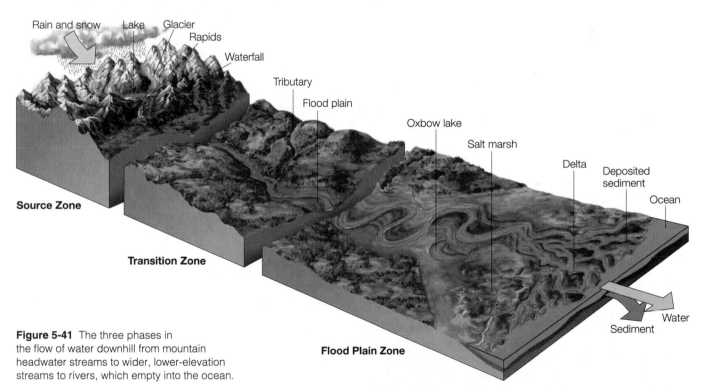

**Figure 5-41** The three phases in the flow of water downhill from mountain headwater streams to wider, lower-elevation streams to rivers, which empty into the ocean.

to form wider, deeper streams that flow down gentler slopes with fewer obstacles. The warmer water and other conditions in this phase support a variety of cold-water and warm-water fish species with slightly lower oxygen requirements.

In the third phase, these streams join into wider and deeper rivers that meander across broad, flat valleys. The main channels of these rivers support distinctive varieties of fish, whereas their backwaters support species similar to those in lakes. Meandering

streams are sometimes straightened, deepened, and widened to improve navigation and to help reduce flooding and bank erosion, but such *stream channelization* is controversial. At its mouth a river may divide into many channels as it flows across a delta and coastal wetlands and estuaries, where the river water mixes with ocean water and deposits of sediment (Figure 5-30).

As streams flow downhill they become powerful shapers of land. Over millions of years the friction of

Because some people see them as wastelands or health threats rather than ecological treasures, inland wetlands are being dredged, filled in, or paved over. Since 1780 about 55% of the original coastal and inland wetlands in the continental United States have been lost to development and agricultural use. Iowa, for example, has lost 99% of its inland wetlands, and Nebraska 91%. About 95% of remaining U.S. wetlands are inland, usually on or next to farmland. Each year some 1,200 square kilometers (470 square miles) of inland wetland are lost, about 80% to agriculture and the rest to mining, forestry, oil and gas extraction, highways, and urban development.

Other countries have suffered similar losses. For example, Canada, with 24% of the world's inland wetlands, has lost 14% of its original wetlands, mostly to agriculture. The United States has passed laws to help protect some of the 74% of U.S. wetlands that are privately owned—angering some of the owners who feel they should not be told how they can use their land.

The Tax Reform Act of 1985 eliminated the deduction for most wetland drainage expenses and removed the capital gains benefits for appreciation in land value created by destroying wetlands. The Farm Act of 1985 has a "swampbuster" provision that denies agricultural subsidies to farmers who drain wetlands and plant crops on them; however, it does not penalize farmers who merely drain wetlands. In addition, this law is hard to enforce, and even if fully enforced, it would apply to only about one-third of inland wetlands.

In 1990 Congress passed the North American Wetlands Conservation Act. It provides some $25 million per year for implementing the North American Waterfowl Management Plan, by which the Canadian and U.S. governments and conservation organizations plan to acquire and restore large areas of wetlands in the next 15 years.

A federal permit is now required for filling wetlands or depositing dredged or fill material in them, though this law too is poorly enforced. A serious problem is that only about 8% of the area of remaining inland wetlands is under federal protection, and federal, state, and local protection of wetlands is weak.

The stated goal of current federal policy is no net loss of the function and value of wetlands. Unfortunately this allows destruction of existing wetlands as long as an equal area of the same type of wetland is created or restored. Exceptions are also allowed. As a result, at least 14 hectares (34 acres) of U.S. wetlands are being destroyed every hour.

Some damaged wetlands can be partially restored, but we don't have enough knowledge to create new wetlands that even come close to duplicating the complexity of natural wetland ecosystems. Restoring and creating wetlands is also expensive. The result of destroying wetlands and replacing them with restored or created ones is a net loss of wetland ecological functions and values.

Uninformed observers wrongly identify temporary and seasonal wetlands as dry land and don't see why they shouldn't be used for agriculture or urban development. In reality, temporary and seasonal wetlands provide wildlife habitats, floodwater storage, and other important functions that permanent wetlands cannot.

In 1991 President George Bush bowed to pressure from developers and farmers and proposed that wetlands be redefined in a way that would make as much as one-third of the remaining wetlands (mostly temporary and seasonal wetlands) in the lower 48 states vulnerable to development. He also supported industry efforts to strip the Environmental Protection Agency (EPA) of its veto power (through the Clean Water Act) over wetland development permits. Permits then would be reviewed only by the Army Corps of Engineers, which is not charged by law with protecting water quality or aquatic ecosystems.

A panel of 40 scientists who evaluated this proposal for the Environmental Defense Fund concluded that this proposal would:

- Risk destroying a natural pollution control system that would cost $70 billion to replace

- Remove from protection at least one-third of all wetlands currently regulated under the Clean Water Act

- Threaten those wetlands most vital for flood control

- Jeopardize commercial fisheries in the Pacific Northwest and Gulf of Mexico

- Likely harm over 200 endangered and threatened species

Environmentalists have fought implementation of this regulation and urge Congress to insist that the definition of wetlands be based on science not politics.

According to a 1991 study by the National Academy of Sciences, the United States urgently needs a better system for protecting and reclaiming its wetlands. The immediate goal of such a program should be to prevent further losses by strengthening the protective laws, not weakening them. The goal over the next 15 years should be to restore the country's wetlands that have been damaged by development or pollution.

**144**

Q: How many legal immigrants are admitted to the United States each year?

**Figure 5-42** Prairie potholes in Minnesota. These depressions carved out by glaciers about 10,000 years ago hold water only a few weeks each spring. This type of inland wetland stores water for groundwater recharge and provides rest stops and feeding and breeding areas for migratory waterfowl. Stretching from Iowa and Minnesota to the high plains of Alberta, Canada, many of these wetlands have been converted into cropland.

moving water levels mountains and cuts deep canyons. The rock and soil the water removes is deposited as sediment in low-lying areas.

**INLAND WETLANDS** Lands covered with fresh water at least part of the year (excluding lakes, reservoirs, and streams) and located away from coastal areas are called **inland wetlands**. They include bogs, marshes, prairie potholes (Figure 5-42), swamps, mud flats, floodplains, bogs, fens, wet meadows, and the wet arctic tundra (Figure 5-21) in summer. Some of these wetlands are huge and others are small. Shallow marshes and swamps are among the world's most productive ecosystems per unit of area (Figure 4-27).

Some wetlands are covered with water year-round. Others, such as prairie potholes, floodplain wetlands, and bottom-land hardwood swamps, are *seasonal wetlands* that are underwater or soggy for only a short time each year. Some stay dry for years before filling again with water.

Inland wetlands provide habitats for a myriad of fish, waterfowl, and other wildlife, including many threatened and endangered species (43% of such species are in the United States). Floodplain wetlands near rivers help regulate stream flow by storing water during periods of heavy rainfall and releasing it slowly, which reduces riverbank erosion and flood damage. One study estimated that a swamp near Boston, Massachusetts, provides more than $17 million per year in flood protection. Inland wetlands—sometimes called nature's kidneys—also improve water quality by filtering, diluting, and degrading sediments and pollutants as water flows through. Seasonal wetlands can purify water more efficiently than can deep, stagnant swamps.

By storing water many seasonal and year-round wetlands allow increased infiltration, thus helping recharge groundwater supplies. Inland wetlands are used for recreation, especially waterfowl hunting, and for growing crops such as blueberries, cranberries, and rice. They also play significant roles in the global cycles of carbon, nitrogen, and sulfur. Despite the ecological importance of year-round and seasonal inland wetlands, however, they are under attack (Spotlight, p. 144).

The lesson to be learned from this chapter's overview of climate and Earth's land and water ecosystems is that everything is connected, as expressed in the quote at the beginning of this chapter. The challenge is to discover such connections, especially the strongest and most important ones, before we weaken or destroy them.

*Earth and water, if not too blatantly abused, can produce again and again for the benefit of all.*

STEWART L. UDALL

## Critical Thinking

1. List a limiting factor for each of the following ecosystems: **(a)** a desert, **(b)** the surface layer of the open sea, **(c)** the arctic tundra, **(d)** the floor of a tropical rain forest, and **(e)** the bottom of a deep lake.

2. Since the deep oceans are vast and located far away from human habitats, why not use them as the depository for our radioactive and other hazardous wastes? Give your reasons for agreeing or disagreeing with this proposal.

3. Why are coastal and inland wetlands and coral reefs such important ecosystems? Why have so many of these vital ecosystems been destroyed by human activities? What factors in your lifestyle contribute to the destruction and degradation of wetlands?

4. Why are there no coral reefs around the mouths of the Amazon and Congo rivers?

5. Suppose you buy coral for use in an aquarium, take samples of coral from a reef on a diving trip, damage a coral reef when you drop the anchor of the boat you are using, or discharge sewage from the boat. Explain how each of these actions can reduce Earth's biodiversity, possibly enhance global warming, and mean that sometime in the future you or your descendants might not have enough food or water.

6. Someone tries to sell you several brightly colored pieces of coral. Explain in biological terms why this is a ripoff.

\*7. What type of biome do you live in or near? What effects have human activities had on the characteristic vegetation and animal life normally found in this biome? How is your own lifestyle affecting this biome?

\*8. If possible, visit a nearby lake. Would you classify it as oligotrophic, mesotrophic, or eutrophic? What are the primary factors contributing to its nutrient enrichment? Which of these are related to human activities?

A: About 1 million

## From Rice Back to Rushes

Something there is that doesn't love a marsh. Our deepest fears are linked somehow with swamps, quicksand, and the "things" that lurch out of them. This ancient fear is reflected in our literature. In *Beowulf*, an Anglo-Saxon poem dating from the eighth century, the monster Grendel rises from the marsh. And Conan Doyle set the scene for his Sherlock Holmes tale about the hound of the Baskervilles on a misty moor where the unwary can sink out of sight in quagmires.

Driven by such fears and by ignorance about the ecological importance of wetlands, as well as by desire for land and hunger for profit, we have drained swamps and marshes relentlessly for centuries (Spotlight, p. 144). Now, belatedly, we begin to question that campaign against wild nature. For example, a hectare of Georgia salt marsh produces more biomass than a hectare of corn. Wetlands are highly efficient, too, at filtering pollutants from water flowing through them—nature's free sewage treatment plants. Can we turn back the clock to restore or rehabilitate vanished marshes?

Pat and Tom Leeson/Photo Researchers, Inc.

**Figure 6-1** Migration of snow geese in eastern Oregon along the Pacific Flyway.

California rancher Jim Callender decided to try. His motives were mixed; he wanted a place to hunt ducks as well as a restored wetland habitat. In 1982 he bought 20 hectares (50 acres) of Sacramento Valley ricefield that had been a marsh until the early 1970s. The previous owner had been thorough in his destruction—bulldozing, draining, leveling, uprooting the native plants, and spraying with chemicals to kill the snails and other food of the waterfowl.

Aided by a water bank program of the U.S. Fish and Wildlife Service, by the sale of his agricultural rights in the form of a conservation easement (also to Fish and Wildlife), and by guidance of biologists from the California Waterfowl Association (CWA), Jim and his friends set out to work in reverse. They hollowed out low areas, built up islands, replanted tules and bulrushes, brought back smartweed and other plants needed by birds, and planted fast-growing Peking willows. After six years of care, hand-planting, and annual seeding with a mixture of watergrass, smartweed, and rice, the marsh is once again a part of the Pacific Flyway used by migratory waterfowl (Figure 6-1). Many birds pass through, and some stay. Mallards and widgeons nest there, for example, as do wood ducks.

All kinds of hawks, shorebirds, and songbirds also live or forage in the marsh. The native insects and snails are back in force, and the local mammals have moved back in as well, including muskrat, deer, and beaver.

The tens of millions of migrating birds that once darkened the December sun in the Sacramento Valley and kept residents of Chico and Gridley awake with their cries may never come again. But Jim Callender and a few others have shown that at least part of the continent's wetlands heritage can be reclaimed, with canny planning and hard work. Such Earth healing is vital, but the real challenge is to protect remaining wetlands from having to be healed.

Organisms, populations, communities, and ecosystems are dynamic, always changing and adapting in response to changes in their environment. Understanding this adaptation process—and its limits—can help us sustain living systems rather than damage and destroy them. It can even help us restore an ecosystem we once destroyed.

This chapter focuses on answers to the following questions:

- How are living systems affected by environmental stress?
- How can populations of species change and adapt to environmental stress?
- How can communities and ecosystems change and adapt to small- and large-scale environmental stress?
- What impacts do human activities have on populations, communities, and ecosystems?
- What efforts are being made to restore ecosystems damaged by human activities?

## 6-1 Responses of Living Systems to Environmental Stress

**HOMEOSTASIS AND INFORMATION FEEDBACK**
To survive you must maintain your body temperature within a certain range (Figure 4-19) whether the temperature outside is steamy or freezing. This phenomenon is called **homeostasis**: the maintenance of favorable internal conditions despite fluctuations in external conditions.

Homeostatic systems have three essential elements: **(1)** a *receptor*, or *sensor*, to detect the environmental conditions; **(2)** a *comparator* to evaluate information from the receptor and make decisions; and **(3)** an *effector*, which executes commands from the comparator. These systems operate through **information feedback**, in which information fed back into a system causes it to change. This circuit of sensing, evaluating, and reacting to changes in environmental conditions is called a **feedback loop**.

Information feedback can be negative or positive. **Negative feedback**—also known as *corrective feedback*—is a flow of information into a system that counteracts the effects of change in external conditions to maintain a particular state. In effect, a *negative feedback loop* "says no" to a change in external conditions.

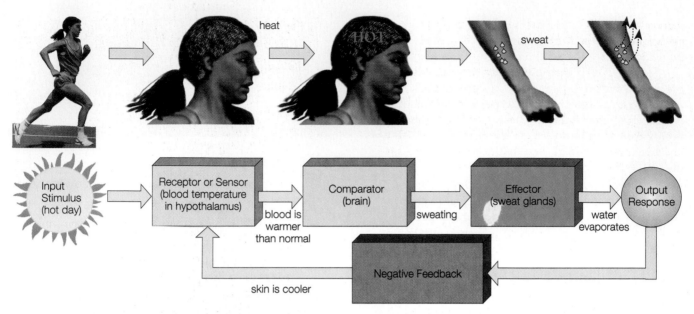

**Figure 6-2** Keeping cool on a hot day—a human temperature control system based on negative feedback of information to counteract a change in environmental conditions (arrows show flow of information). This is the major way organisms maintain homeostasis.

Negative feedback keeps your body temperature around 37°C (98°F), as shown in Figure 6-2. If you go outdoors on a hot day, *sensors* in your skin detect the high temperature and send that information as a nerve signal to your brain's hypothalamus (*comparator*). Your brain then sends a nerve impulse to sweat glands in your skin (*effectors*) to activate sweating, a cooling mechanism. Evaporation requires energy. Thus, as sweat evaporates, it removes heat from your skin. When your body has cooled down, this new information (*output response*) reaches your skin sensors, which feed it back to the brain. Then your brain sends a new message to your skin effectors to slow or stop the sweating process.

**Positive feedback**—also known as *amplifying feedback*—occurs when a change in the system in one direction provides information that causes the system to change further in the same direction. In effect, a *positive feedback loop* "says yes" to a change in external conditions. For example, if your body temperature exceeds 42°C (108°F), the negative-feedback-temperature-control system breaks down and switches to positive feedback. Your body can't get rid of heat fast enough and your metabolic rate (rate of the chemical reactions necessary for life) increases. This produces more body heat, which speeds up the chemical reactions even further, producing more body heat and so on—until you die.

Positive feedback is not always harmful. Mutualism (Figure 4-43) is a positive feedback relationship in which different species enter into a cooperative interaction that benefits both species—a *win-win* relationship. Competition is also a positive feedback system,

at least for the victor (predator), who gets more of scarce resources than the loser (prey). This *win-lose* system is limited, however, by negative feedback when the available resources (prey population) fall below the needs of the predator population.

Like humans all living systems contain a network of interconnected negative and positive feedback loops. Since the beginning of life on Earth, organisms not only have adapted to changing environmental conditions but have modified the environment in ways that have proven to be beneficial to life in general. This modified version of the *Gaia* (pronounced GUY-uh) *hypothesis*, proposed in the early 1970s by British chemist and inventor James Lovelock and American biologist Lynn Margulis, is now accepted by many scientists.

The Gaia hypothesis does not mean that the entire earth is alive. As Lovelock puts it, Gaia is like a tree: 99% of it, bark and wood, is dead, but the tree itself is kept alive and well by interactions between its living and dead parts and with its external environment. By analogy Earth consists mostly of dead matter covered by a thin film of life—the biosphere (Figure 4-2). The life that makes up only a tiny fraction of Earth's mass is sustained by sunlight and interactions with Earth's dead matter and other forms of life.

**TIME DELAYS** Systems regulated by information feedback show a **time delay**, or lapse between receiving a stimulus and taking corrective action. Time delays can protect a system from information overload or overshoot, and prevent hasty responses, but too long a delay can mean that corrective action comes too late. For example, a smoker exposed to cancer-causing

Q: How many illegal immigrants enter the United States each year?

(carcinogenic) chemicals in cigarette smoke may not get lung cancer for 20 or 30 years. By then, it's too late for a negative feedback (not to smoke) to be effective.

Environmental examples of the harmful effects of prolonged time delays are toxic dumps, depletion of the ozone layer, projected global warming and climate change from an enhanced greenhouse effect, destruction of forests from prolonged exposure to air pollutants, and reduction of the population of a species to the point where it is in danger of becoming extinct. Similarly, if the human population overshoots the carrying capacity of a particular area or of the entire planet, the result is a population crash or dieback of people through disease, famine, or possibly a war over scarce resources.

**SYNERGISTIC INTERACTIONS** In arithmetic 1 plus 1 always equals 2. But in nature 1 plus 1 may add up to more than 2, because of synergistic interactions. A **synergistic interaction** occurs when two or more processes interact so that the combined effect is greater than the sum of their separate effects (1 plus 1 equals 3 or even 10).

Our projections may seriously underestimate environmental problems if we ignore or don't understand synergy. For example, chlorofluorocarbons we put into the troposphere drift upward and destroy ozone in the stratosphere. The resulting increase in ultraviolet-B (UV-B) radiation reaching Earth damages phytoplankton in the ocean that use photosynthesis to remove carbon dioxide ($CO_2$) from the troposphere. If this damage reached significant levels, the capacity of the oceans to remove and store atmospheric $CO_2$ would be greatly reduced, and global warming would accelerate and intensify because of this synergistic interaction between ozone depletion and an enhanced greenhouse effect.

On the other hand, synergistic interactions can counteract or ease some environmental problems. For example, widespread tree planting in the tropics would remove considerable $CO_2$ from the atmosphere. If this planting took place on already damaged land (probably as tree plantations), it could lessen the need to cut older tropical forests for lumber, reduce soil erosion, and help heal the planting site. It would also preserve biodiversity, help regulate water flow, and reduce flooding.

We need much more research on environmental synergistic interactions. With such information we can anticipate, counteract, and even prevent some environmental problems.

**TYPES AND EFFECTS OF ENVIRONMENTAL STRESS**
The problem that all forms of life face is that environmental conditions change—sometimes gradually and sometimes suddenly—and put stresses on organisms, populations, communities, and ecosystems (Table 6-1).

## Table 6-1 Unfavorable Changes Affecting Ecosystems

**Natural Changes**

| | |
|---|---|
| Catastrophic | Drought |
| | Flood |
| | Fire |
| | Volcanic eruption |
| | Earthquake |
| | Hurricane |
| | Landslide |
| | Change in stream course |
| | Disease |
| Gradual | Changes in climate |
| | Immigration |
| | Adaptation and evolution |
| | Changes in plant and animal life (ecological succession) |

**Human-Caused Changes**

| | |
|---|---|
| Catastrophic | Deforestation |
| | Overgrazing |
| | Plowing |
| | Erosion |
| | Pesticides |
| | Fires |
| | Mining |
| | Toxic releases (can also be gradual) |
| | Urbanization (can also be gradual) |
| Gradual | Salt buildup in soil from irrigation (salinization) |
| | Waterlogging of soil from irrigation |
| | Compaction of soil from agricultural equipment |
| | Depletion of groundwater (aquifers) |
| | Water pollution (can also be catastrophic) |
| | Air pollution (can also be catastrophic) |
| | Loss and degradation of wildlife habitat (can also be catastrophic) |
| | Killing of predator and "pest" species |
| | Introduction of alien species |
| | Overhunting |
| | Overfishing |
| | Excessive tourism |

A: 200,000–500,000

## Table 6-2 Some Effects of Environmental Stress

**Organism Level**

Physiological and biochemical changes

Psychological disorders

Behavioral changes

Fewer or no offspring

Genetic defects in offspring (mutagenic effects)

Birth defects (teratogenic effects)

Cancers (carcinogenic effects)

Death

**Population Level**

Population increase or decrease

Change in age structure (old, young, and weak may die)

Survival of strains genetically resistant to stress

Loss of genetic diversity and adaptability

Extinction

**Community–Ecosystem Level**

Disruption of energy flow

  Decrease or increase in solar energy uptake and heat output

  Changes in trophic structure in food chains and webs

Disruption of chemical cycles

  Depletion of essential nutrients

  Excessive addition of nutrients

Simplification

  Reduction in species diversity

  Reduction or elimination of habitats and filled ecological niches

  Less complex food webs

  Possibility of lowered stability

  Possibility of ecosystem collapse

Table 6-2 summarizes the results of environmental stress on various living systems in which one or more environmental factors fall outside tolerable levels for various species (Figure 4-19).

Here are some signs of ill health in stressed ecosystems:

- Primary productivity often drops.

- Nutrient leakage increases.

- Sensitive (indicator) species decline in numbers or become extinct.

- Diseases and populations of insect pests increase.

- Species diversity drops although this may be off-set by invasions of insect pests, disease organisms, and other species.

- Contaminants are present.

## 6-2 Population Responses to Stress: Population Dynamics

**CHARACTERISTICS OF POPULATIONS** **Population size** is the number of individuals making up a population. That number determines the size of the population's gene pool and thus affects survival. Very small populations can easily become extinct—more individuals may die than are born because adults cannot find mates. Such populations are also more vulnerable to disease, predation, or catastrophes such as flooding or rapid climate change. Genetically close individuals in small populations may also breed, which can produce weak or malformed offspring and reduce the genetic diversity needed to adapt to changes in environmental conditions. By contrast, when populations become too large, many individuals may starve or become easier targets for predators.

**Population density** is the number of individuals of a population found in a certain space at a given time—the number of rabbits per hectare or the number of fathead minnows per liter of pond water, for example. However, **ecological population density**, the number of individuals of a population per unit of habitat area, is a better measure of the space suitable for a population to live in. Both types of density may vary with social characteristics, mating behavior, changes in seasons, or other factors.

Population density also affects a population's ability to survive. For some species individuals in dense populations may be more susceptible to disease. For other species, such as school fish and herd animals, high population density may offer some protection against predators.

**Population dispersion** refers to the general pattern in which the members of a population exist in their habitat. The most common pattern is *clumping*—for example, a herd of elephants or a stand of pines. One reason for clumping is that resources needed for survival and reproduction are rarely distributed uniform-

Q: What is the estimated value of women's unpaid work at home?

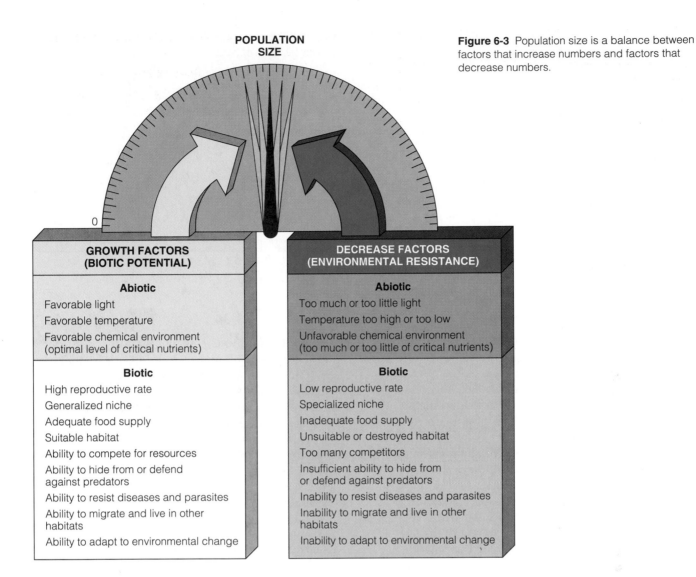

**POPULATION SIZE**

**Figure 6-3** Population size is a balance between factors that increase numbers and factors that decrease numbers.

| GROWTH FACTORS (BIOTIC POTENTIAL) | DECREASE FACTORS (ENVIRONMENTAL RESISTANCE) |
|---|---|
| **Abiotic** | **Abiotic** |
| Favorable light | Too much or too little light |
| Favorable temperature | Temperature too high or too low |
| Favorable chemical environment (optimal level of critical nutrients) | Unfavorable chemical environment (too much or too little of critical nutrients) |
| **Biotic** | **Biotic** |
| High reproductive rate | Low reproductive rate |
| Generalized niche | Specialized niche |
| Adequate food supply | Inadequate food supply |
| Suitable habitat | Unsuitable or destroyed habitat |
| Ability to compete for resources | Too many competitors |
| Ability to hide from or defend against predators | Insufficient ability to hide from or defend against predators |
| Ability to resist diseases and parasites | Inability to resist diseases and parasites |
| Ability to migrate and live in other habitats | Inability to migrate and live in other habitats |
| Ability to adapt to environmental change | Inability to adapt to environmental change |

ly. Also, some parts of a habitat offer more protection for prey or better hunting conditions for predators. Most mature plant communities are mosaics of clumps.

Individuals in some populations may be *randomly dispersed* over their habitat. An example is solitary insect-eating spiders living on a forest floor uniformly covered with similar leaf litter. Other species may be fairly *uniformly dispersed* over their habitat. This type of distribution is common among desert plants, such as the creosote bush, that compete intensely for the scarce annual rainfall. All three types of population dispersion may vary in response to mating habits or to seasonal changes. Population dispersion is also affected by the movement of individuals into or out of the population area.

**Age structure** is the proportion of individuals of each age in a population. Common age categories are prereproductive, reproductive, and postreproductive. A large percentage of individuals in the prereproduc-

tive and reproductive categories means a high potential for population growth.

Populations change in size, density, dispersion, and age distribution in response to changes in environmental conditions, such as the availability of food. These changes are called **population dynamics**.

**POPULATION SIZE** Four variables—births, deaths, immigration, and emigration—govern population size. A population gains individuals by birth and immigration and loses them by death and emigration:

$$\text{population change rate} = \left( \begin{array}{c} \text{births} \\ + \\ \text{immigration} \end{array} \right) - \left( \begin{array}{c} \text{deaths} \\ + \\ \text{emigration} \end{array} \right)$$

These variables in turn depend on changes in resource availability or other environmental changes (Figure 6-3).

Populations vary in their capacity for growth. The **biotic potential** of a population is the *maximum* rate

A: $4 trillion annually

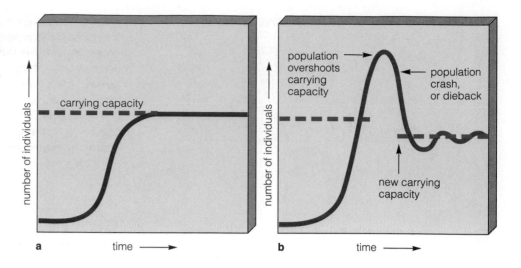

**Figure 6-4** **(a)** Idealized S-shaped curve of population growth. **(b)** Population curve when crash or dieback occurs. These idealized curves only approximate what goes on in nature.

($r_{max}$) at which it can increase when there are no limits on its growth. Animal species have different biotic potentials because of variations in **(1)** when reproduction starts and stops (reproductive span), **(2)** how often reproduction occurs, **(3)** how many live offspring are born each time (litter size), and **(4)** how many offspring survive to reproductive age.

No population can grow exponentially indefinitely. In the real world an exploding population reaches some size limit imposed by a shortage of one or more limiting factors, such as light, water, space, and nutrients. There are always limits to growth in nature.

**Environmental resistance** consists of all the factors acting jointly to limit the growth of a population. They determine the **carrying capacity (K)**, the number of individuals of a given species that can be sustained indefinitely in a given area. Carrying capacity is determined by many factors, including predation, competition between species, migration, and climate. The carrying capacity for a population can vary with seasonal or abnormal changes in the weather or supplies of food, water, nesting sites, or other crucial environmental resources.

Because of environmental resistance, any population growing exponentially starts out slowly, goes through a rapid growth phase, and then levels off once the carrying capacity of the area is reached. In most cases the size of such a population fluctuates slightly above and below the carrying capacity. A plot of this type of growth yields an *S-shaped curve* (Figure 6-4a). Sometimes, however, a population temporarily overshoots the carrying capacity (Figure 6-4b). This happens because of a *reproductive time lag*, the time required for the birth rate to fall and the death rate to rise in response to resource limits. Unless large numbers of individuals can move to an area with more

favorable conditions, the population will suffer a *dieback* or *crash*, falling back to a lower level that typically fluctuates around the area's carrying capacity. An area's carrying capacity can also be lowered because of resource destruction and degradation during the overshoot period.

Humans are not exempt from this phenomenon. Ireland, for example, experienced a population crash after a fungus infection destroyed the potato crop in 1845. About 1 million people died and 3 million people emigrated to other countries.

Technological, social, and other cultural changes have extended Earth's carrying capacity for the human species (Figure 2-4). We have increased food production, controlled many diseases, and used energy and matter resources at a rapid rate to make normally uninhabitable areas of Earth habitable. A crucial question is how long we will be able to keep doing this on a planet with finite size and resources.

**DENSITY-DEPENDENT AND DENSITY-INDEPENDENT CHECKS ON POPULATION GROWTH** Some limiting factors become more influential as a population's density increases. Examples of such *density-dependent population controls* are competition for resources, predation, parasitism, and disease. When prey populations become increasingly dense, for example, their members face greater competition for resources. They also have a greater risk of being killed by predators or being invaded by parasites or disease-causing organisms.

Infectious disease is a classic example of this type of population control. In dense populations disease spreads faster, increasing the death rate and leaving fewer individuals who can reproduce; in sparse popu-

Q: How many of the world's people live in urban areas?

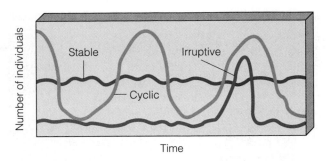

**Figure 6-5** General types of idealized population change curves found in nature.

lations disease spreads more slowly and has less effect on population growth.

In some species physiological and sociological control mechanisms limit reproduction as population density rises. For example, overcrowding in populations of mice and rats causes hormonal changes that can inhibit sexual maturity, lower sexual activity, and cut milk production in nursing females. Stress caused by crowding in these and several other species also reduces the number of offspring produced per litter through mechanisms such as spontaneous abortion. Crowding may also lead to population control in some species through cannibalism and killing of the young.

*Density-independent population controls* exert their effects on populations more or less regardless of population density. Examples include floods, hurricanes, severe drought, unseasonal temperature changes, fire, human destruction of habitat (such as clearing a forest of its trees), and changes in the chemical environment that increase the death rate and lower the reproduction rate.

## POPULATION DYNAMICS IN NATURE

The idealized S-shaped and crash or dieback curves of population growth shown in Figure 6-4 can be observed in laboratory experiments. In nature, however, we find three general types of population change curves: relatively stable, irruptive, and cyclic (Figure 6-5).

A species whose population size fluctuates slightly above and below its carrying capacity (as long as that capacity doesn't change significantly) has a relatively *stable* population size. Such stability is characteristic of many species in undisturbed tropical rain forest habitats (Figure 4-37), where there is little variation in average temperature and rainfall.

Some species, such as the raccoon, normally have a fairly stable population. However, the population may occasionally explode, or *irrupt*, to a high peak and then crash to a relatively stable lower level. The population explosion is due to some factor that temporarily increases carrying capacity for the population. Examples are better weather, more food, or fewer predators, including humans.

Some species undergo sharp increases in their numbers followed by seemingly periodic crashes. Predators are sometimes blamed, but the actual causes of such "boom-bust" cycles are poorly understood.

## REPRODUCTIVE STRATEGIES AND SURVIVAL

Each species has a characteristic mode of reproduction. At one extreme are species that produce hordes of offspring early in their life cycle. The offspring, usually small and short-lived, mature rapidly with little or no parental care. Typically many of them die before they can reproduce.

Species with this capacity for a high rate of population growth (r) (many offspring in a short time) are called **r-strategists**. Algae, bacteria, rodents, annual plants, many fish, and most insects are examples. Such species tend to be *opportunists*, reproducing rapidly when conditions are favorable or when a new habitat or niche becomes available—a cleared forest or a newly plowed field, for example. Unfavorable environmental conditions, however, can cause such populations to crash. Hence, most r-strategists go through "boom-bust" cycles.

At the other extreme are **K-strategists**, species that produce a few, often fairly large offspring and often look after them for a long time to ensure that most reach reproductive age. Living in fairly stable environments and tending to maintain their population size near their habitat's carrying capacity (K), they are called K-strategists. Their populations typically follow an S-shaped growth curve (Figure 6-4). Examples are sharks, most larger mammals—including humans, elephants, rhinoceroses, and whales—birds of prey, and large, long-lived plants, such as the saguaro cactus (Figure 4-10). The reproductive strategies of most species fall somewhere between these two extremes.

Species with different reproductive strategies tend to have different life expectancies, the length of time an individual of a certain age in a given species can expect to survive. This information is often presented as a **survivorship curve**, which shows the number of survivors in each age group for a particular species.

Three types of survivorship curves are common in nature (Figure 6-6). *Late-loss (type I)* curves are typical for K-strategists and *early-loss (type III)* curves for r-strategists. Species with *constant-loss (type II)* curves typically have intermediate reproductive strategies.

**Figure 6-6** Three generalized types of survivorship curves for populations of different species. For a type I population (elephant in East Africa) there is high survivorship until a certain age, then high mortality. A type II population (song thrush) shows a fairly constant death rate at all ages. For a type III population (sea star) survivorship is low early in life. Many animal and protist populations have survivorship curves that lie somewhere between those characteristic of type II and type III. Many plant species have curves closer to type III. (Adapted by permission from Cecie Starr and Ralph Taggart, *Biology: The Unity and Diversity of Life*, 6th ed., Belmont, Calif.: Wadsworth, 1992)

## 6-3    Population Responses to Stress: Adaptation and the Origins of Life

**ORIGINS OF LIFE AND ITS DIVERSITY** How did life originate on Earth? How did it evolve to its present system of diverse species living in an interlocking network of matter cycles, energy flow, and species interactions?

We don't know the full answers to these questions, but a widely accepted body of evidence suggests what might have happened. Some of this evidence comes from chemical experiments simulating possible atmospheric compositions and energy sources on the primitive Earth to see whether this could lead to the formation of the molecules necessary for life. Most of what we know of Earth's life history, however, comes from **fossils**—mineralized or petrified skeletons, bones, shells, body parts, leaves, and seeds, or impres-

154

## Earth: The Just Right, Resilient Planet

Like Goldilocks tasting porridge at the house of the three bears, life as we know it is picky about temperature. Venus is much too hot, Mars is much too cold, and Earth is just right. Otherwise, you wouldn't be reading these words.

Life as we know it also depends on water. Again temperature is crucial. Earthly life needs average temperatures between the freezing and boiling points of water—between 0°C and 100°C (32°F and 212°F)—at Earth's typical atmospheric pressure.

Earth's orbit is the right distance from the sun to have these conditions. Much closer and it would be too hot—like Venus—for water vapor to condense to form rain; much farther away and it would be so cold—like Mars—that water would have existed only as ice. Earth also spins (Figure 5-5). Otherwise, the side facing the sun would be too hot, and the other side too cold, for water-based life to exist. So far, the temperature has been, like Baby Bear's porridge, just right.

Earth is also the right size. That is, it has enough gravitational mass to keep its iron–nickel core molten and its atmosphere around it. The slow transfer of this heat (geothermal energy) to the surface helps keep the planet at the right temperature for life. A much smaller Earth would not have enough gravitational mass to hold onto an atmosphere consisting of light molecules such as $N_2$, $O_2$, $CO_2$, and $H_2O$. And, thanks to the development of photosynthesizing bacteria over 2 billion years ago, an ozone sunscreen protects us from an overdose of ultraviolet light.

On a time scale of millions of years, Earth is also enormously resilient and adaptive. Earth's average temperatures have remained between the freezing and boiling points of water even though the sun's energy output has increased by about 30% over the 3.6 billion years since life arose. In short, Earth is just right for life as we know it to have arisen.

*chemical evolution of the earth.* This shows that Earth has the right physical and chemical conditions for life as we know it to exist (Spotlight, left).

A second conclusion from this body of evidence is that life on Earth developed in two phases:

### Phase 1: Chemical Evolution (about 1 billion years)

Part 1: Formation of Earth and its early crust and atmosphere

Part 2: Evolution of the nonliving biological molecules necessary for life—primarily the polymers DNA, RNA, proteins, and carbohydrates

Part 3: Evolution of systems of chemical reactions needed for linking these biopolymers in ways to produce the first living cells

### Phase 2: Biological Evolution (about 3.6–3.8 billion years)

Development of diverse species through genetic modification and natural selection of Earth's primitive cells and the organisms that followed

**CHEMICAL EVOLUTION: SETTING THE STAGE FOR LIFE** Billions of years ago, explosions of dying stars ripped through our galaxy and left behind a dense, swirling cloud of dust particles and hot gas extending trillions of kilometers across space in one of the spiral arms of our galaxy. As the cloud cooled, countless bits of matter gravitated toward one another. By 4.6 billion years ago the cloud had flattened into a slowly rotating disk. Our sun was born at the extremely dense, hot center of the disk. Extremely high temperatures in this core consisting of isotopes of hydrogen forced these nuclei together in nuclear fusion reactions (Figure 3-13) that would give off immense quantities of energy for the next 10 billion years.

Farther out from the center, the earth and other planets were forming as innumerable bits of matter were drawn together and coalesced. At some stage in its early life, Earth was a completely molten mass that did not cool for several hundred million years. As the cooling took place, the outermost portion of the molten sphere solidified to form a thin, hardened crust of rocks, devoid of atmosphere and oceans.

The planet's first atmosphere formed as molten rock frequently erupted through the thin crust, releasing gases from the molten interior or from below its crust. At first, water vapor released from the breakdown of rocks during volcanic eruptions evaporated in the intense heat blanketing the crust. Eventually, however, the crust cooled enough for this water vapor

sions of such items, that provide recognizable evidence of ancient organisms. The fossil record, however, is uneven. Some life forms left no fossils, some fossils have decomposed, and others are yet to be found.

Other sources of information include chemical analysis of ancient rocks and cores drilled out of buried ice, and analysis of the genetic makeup of fossil specimens. When this diverse evidence is pieced together, an important fact emerges: *The evolution of life has been linked, from the beginning, to the physical and*

**Figure 6-7** Earth as it may have looked about 4 billion years ago. The moon, then presumably closer to the earth, looms on the horizon.

to condense and fall to the surface as rain, dissolving minerals from rocks and collecting in depressions to form the early oceans that covered most of the globe (Figure 6-7).

Studying the light given off by the sun and other stars indicates that hydrogen (H), helium (He), carbon (C), nitrogen (N), and oxygen (O) are the most abundant elements in the universe. Thus, C, H, N, and O—the four elements that are the major components of living organisms—were probably abundant on the prebiotic Earth. Basic chemistry predicts that three gases—methane ($CH_4$), ammonia ($NH_3$), and water vapor ($H_2O$)—are likely to have formed from these elements and comprised most of Earth's primitive atmosphere. Some scientists believe that carbon dioxide ($CO_2$) was abundant, along with smaller amounts of hydrogen cyanide (HCN), hydrogen sulfide ($H_2S$), and carbon monoxide (CO) as well. Whatever the composition of this primitive atmosphere, chemists agree that it had almost no free oxygen gas ($O_2$). This element is so chemically reactive that it would have combined into compounds. The only reason today's atmosphere has so much $O_2$ is that plants and some bacteria produce it in vast quantities through photosynthesis. But this is getting ahead of the story.

Energy was readily available to drive the synthesis of biological molecules from the chemicals found in Earth's primitive atmosphere—an idea first proposed in 1923 by Russian biochemist Alexander Oparin. There was no ozone layer, so the planet was exposed to intense ultraviolet (UV) light, cosmic rays, and other forms of solar radiation (Figure 3-5). Electrical discharges (lightning), radioactivity, heat from volcanoes, and even the shock waves from meteorite impacts may also have been important.

In 1953 American chemist Harold C. Urey and one of his graduate students, Stanley L. Miller, set out to test Oparin's hypothesis. Miller mixed hydrogen, methane, ammonia, and water in a sterilized reaction chamber, recirculated the mixture, and kept bombarding it with a spark discharge to simulate lightning and heat. Within one week several amino acids (the building-block molecules of proteins), some simple carbohydrates, and several small organic compounds necessary for life formed from the inorganic molecules.

Over the past 35 years other researchers have verified and expanded on this work. Many details are missing or hotly debated, but the basic hypothesis—that the molecules necessary for life can be produced by exposing various simple inorganic molecules

**Q:** Worldwide, how many people are homeless?

believed to have existed on the prebiotic Earth to energy—remains viable. Another possibility is that simple organic molecules necessary for life formed elsewhere in the universe, perhaps on dust particles in space, and reached Earth on meteorites.

During the 300 million years after the first rains began, organic compounds formed in the early atmosphere (or arriving from space) dissolved and accumulated in the shallow waters of the earth. Over such long periods untold numbers of complex organic molecules and assemblies of these molecules formed in this primitive organic soup.

Indirect evidence suggests that the first living cells, probably bacteria, emerged between 3.6 and 3.8 billion years ago. No one knows how these first bacterial cells arose from the slow-cooking organic soup. But after several hundred million years of different chemical combinations, conglomerates of proteins and other biopolymers may have combined to form membrane-bound *proto-cells*, small globules that could take up materials from their environment, grow, and divide, much like living cells.

Over time, it is believed, these proto-cells developed into simple prokaryotic cells having the properties we describe as life (Figure 4-8). These cells probably developed at least 10 meters (30 feet) below the ocean's surface, protected by water from the intense UV radiation that bathed the earth. With these first cells the stage was set for the drama of life to begin 3.6–3.8 billion years ago (Figures 4-8 and 6-8).

BIOLOGICAL EVOLUTION AND THE ATMOSPHERE: THE OXYGEN REVOLUTION These single-celled bacteria multiplied and underwent genetic changes (mutated) for about a billion years in Earth's warm, shallow seas. This led to a variety of new types of prokaryotic cells (bacteria) and the emergence of the first *eukaryotic cells* between 2.6 billion and 700 million years ago. Lynn Margulis and other biologists suggest that the first eukaryotic cell formed as a result of a symbiotic association among various prokaryotic cells—if correct, another example of how the thread of cooperation runs through all of life. Genetic changes in these eukaryotic cells spawned an amazing variety of protists and fungi and, beginning about 600 million years ago, plants and animals (Figures 4-8 and 6-8).

During this long, early period life could not have developed on land. There was no ozone layer to shield the DNA and other molecules of early life from bombardment by UV radiation.

Then, about 2.3–2.5 billion years ago, something happened in the ocean that would change Earth forever—the development of photosynthetic bacteria. These cells could remove carbon dioxide from the atmosphere and, powered by sunlight, combine it with water to make the carbohydrates they needed. In the process they emitted oxygen ($O_2$) into the atmosphere. Some of this oxygen reacted with methane in the atmosphere, eventually reducing this gas to trace levels. This *oxygen revolution* taking place over almost 2 billion years eventually led to our current atmosphere.

The transfer of oxygen from the ocean to the atmosphere may have been speeded up by geologic events during this period. Sediments from severe erosion of mountain ranges pushed up by lithospheric plates slamming into one another (Figure 7-6) may have buried vast amounts of organic matter on the ocean floor. This would prevent the organic matter from being decomposed by oxygen-consuming bacteria, leaving more oxygen in the ocean for escape into the atmosphere.

As oxygen proliferated, some was converted by incoming solar energy into ozone ($O_3$), which began forming a shield in the lower stratosphere that protected life forms from the sun's deadly UV radiation, allowing green plants to live closer to the surface of the ocean. As the production of oxygen snowballed, more UV light was filtered out, more life forms developed, and these produced still more oxygen. About 500 million years ago it was safe to go to the beach, so to speak, and the first plants began existing on land. Over the next several hundred million years this led to a variety of land plants and animals, mammals, and eventually the first humans (Figure 6-8).

Because of photosynthesis most of the carbon dioxide in the atmosphere was replaced with oxygen, resulting in today's oxygen–nitrogen atmosphere. Luckily cells developed that removed oxygen from the atmosphere for their aerobic respiration. Because of the resulting balance between photosynthesis and respiration in the carbon and oxygen cycles (Figure 4-28), we and other oxygen-consuming organisms have enough oxygen to survive but not so much that we would be poisoned or burned to death.

BIOLOGICAL EVOLUTION AND NATURAL SELECTION **Biological evolution**, or **evolution**, is a process by which species change their genetic composition over time in ways that make them better adapted to their environment and form new species. Evolution explains how life has changed over the past 3.6–3.8 billion years (Figure 6-8) and why it is so diverse today. According to this concept all species on Earth today are direct descendants of organisms that lived 3.6–3.8 billion years ago. Each species is a living genetic library of traits developed over an immense time span against nearly impossible odds that allow it to survive and reproduce today.

There is still controversy over the details and some of the mechanisms of evolution, but the general

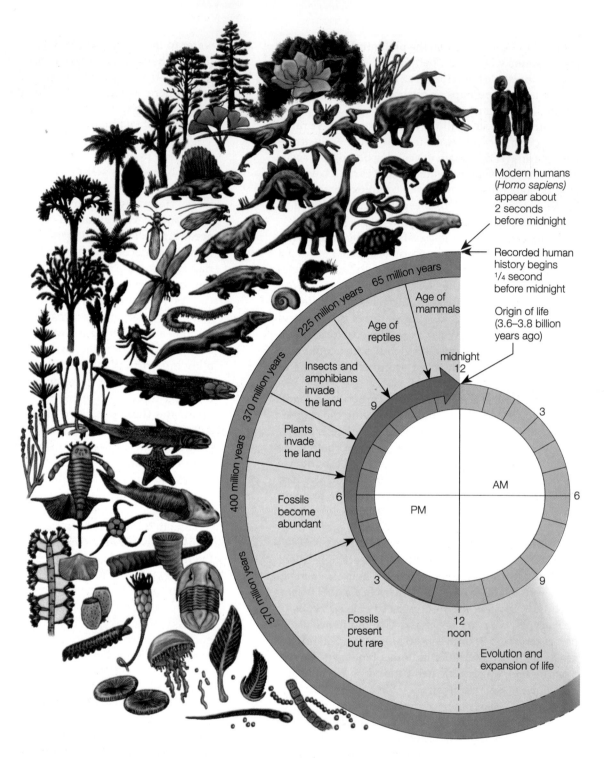

**Figure 6-8** Greatly simplified history of biological evolution of life on Earth, which was preceded by about 1 billion years of chemical evolution. The early span of biological evolution on Earth, between 3.8 billion and about 570 million years ago, was dominated by microorganisms (mostly bacteria and later protists). Plants and animals evolved only about 570 million years ago, and we arrived on the scene only a short time ago. If we compress Earth's roughly 3.8-billion-year history of life to a 24-hour time scale, our closest human ancestors (*Homo sapiens*) appeared about 2 seconds before midnight, and our species (*Homo sapiens sapiens*) appeared less than 1 second before midnight. Agriculture began only ¼ second before midnight, and the Industrial Revolution has been around for only seven thousandths of a second. Despite our brief time on Earth, humans may be hastening the extinction of more species in a shorter time than ever before in Earth's long history. (Adapted from George Gaylord Simpson and William S. Beck, *Life: An Introduction to Biology*, 2nd ed., New York: Harcourt Brace Jovanovich, 1965)

Q: How many motor vehicles are there in the world?

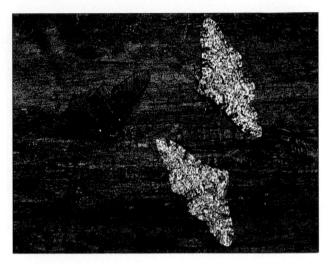

**Figure 6-9** Two color varieties of peppered moths found in England. In the mid-1800s, before the Industrial Revolution, the speckled, light-gray form of this moth was prevalent. These night-flying moths rested on light-gray, speckled lichens on tree trunks during the day. Their color camouflaged them from their bird predators. A dark-gray form also existed but was quite rare. However, during the Industrial Revolution, this dark form became the common one, especially near industrial cities, where soot and other pollutants from factory smokestacks began killing lichens and darkening tree trunks. In this new environment the dark form blended in with the blackened trees while the light form was highly visible to its bird predators. Through natural selection the dark form began to survive and reproduce faster than its light-colored kin. (Both varieties appear in each photo. Can you spot them?)

scientific consensus on it is called the **theory of evolution**. This idea is often attributed to Charles Darwin, the young Englishman whose five-year voyage as a naturalist on the HMS *Beagle* started him thinking about the origin of Earth's biological diversity. Darwin, however, did not come up with the concept of evolution, an idea widely discussed in his time and dating back to ancient Greece. What Darwin did was to propose a reasonable *mechanism* for evolutionary change. According to Darwin individuals don't evolve; *populations* do by means of *natural selection*—still considered the dominant mechanism for evolution. He published his findings in book form (*Origin of Species*) in 1859, but almost 70 years passed before advances in genetics led to widespread acceptance of his theory of natural selection.

Here is a capsule summary of the modern consensus on Darwin's original idea: A population of a particular species can change its genetic composition, or gene pool, in ways that enable it to better adapt to changes in environmental conditions. This can happen because not all individuals of a population have exactly the same genes.

One source of this genetic diversity in sexually reproducing species is **mutation**, or **gene mutation**, a random change in the kind, structure, sequence, or number of component parts of a cell's DNA that can yield changes in anatomy, physiology, or behavior in offspring. Such mutations in DNA molecules can be transmitted to offspring in several ways:

- When DNA is copied every time a cell divides

- During *sexual reproduction* when offspring are produced by the union of a male sperm and a female ovum (egg)

- During the *production of ova (eggs) or sperm cells*, known as *gametes*

- By *crossing over*, in which shifts of genetic material from one chromosome to another occur during the production of germ cells, which make sperm in males and ova in females

- By *exposure to an external agent* such as chemicals called mutagens and high-energy ionizing radiation (Figure 3-5) such as ultraviolet light, cosmic rays, X rays, and radioactivity (Figure 3-10)

Mutations lead to *genetic variation* among individuals in a population (Figure 4-6). Mutations may favor, hinder, or have little effect on the survival and reproduction of the population. Most mutations are harmful and many are quickly repaired by the cells, but harmful mutations passed on to offspring can cause fetal death or birth defects. Every so often, however, a mutation gives its bearer and most of its offspring better chances for survival and reproduction; these beneficial mutations are called **adaptations**.

Individuals with a genetic variation, such as coloration (Figure 6-9), that allows them to survive changes in environmental conditions have a *selective*

A: About 570 million (460 million cars, 110 million trucks)

**Figure 6-10** Coevolution. Many flowering plants have co-evolved with animals such as hummingbirds, which transfer pollen from one flower to another so the plant species can reproduce. Through coevolution the flowers of the plant shown here have a distinct color and depth that attract certain species of hummingbirds. In turn, species of hummingbirds have evolved beak lengths and responses to specific flower colors and shapes that enable them to feed on certain flower species. This helps reduce competition and niche overlap between various hummingbird species.

*advantage* over other members of the same population. Such individuals are more likely to reproduce and will leave behind more offspring with the same favorable adaptations, a phenomenon known as **differential reproduction**.

As long as environmental conditions don't change again in unfavorable ways, the offspring of these more successful or better-adapted individuals gradually increase in numbers and come to predominate. This leads to a shift in the **gene pool** or genetic composition of the population.

The process by which some genes and gene combinations in a population are reproduced more than others is called **natural selection**. Darwin called it "survival of the fittest." "Fittest" does not mean strongest, biggest, or most aggressive. It refers to one thing only: reproductive success. The fittest are individuals whose genetic traits equip them to survive and reproduce better than other individuals under existing environmental conditions.

Some species can adapt much faster than others. Genetically diverse r-strategists (weeds, mosquitoes, rats, bacteria) can quickly produce hordes of short-lived offspring. Thus they can adapt to a change in environmental conditions through natural selection in a short time. For example, when a chemical pesticide is used against an insect population, a few resistant individuals usually survive. They can rapidly breed new populations more genetically resistant to that chemical. Thus chemical pesticides in the long run

tend to increase, not decrease, the populations of species we consider pests.

By contrast, K-strategist species (elephants, tigers, sharks, humans) may have only low-to-moderate genetic diversity. They have long generation times and cannot produce large numbers of offspring rapidly. For such species, adaptation to an environmental stress by natural selection typically takes thousands or even millions of years. If they don't have that much time or have low genetic diversity, they become extinct.

It is important to note that *natural selection and the evolution of new life forms that follows does not lead inexorably toward "perfect" organisms.* Even if it did such organisms would soon cease to be perfect because the environment is constantly changing.

**COEVOLUTION** Physical and chemical changes in environmental conditions are the most familiar agents of evolutionary change. But some biologists have proposed that interactions between species (Section 4-6) can also result in natural selection and evolution. According to this hypothesis, when two species interact over a long period, changes in one species can lead to changes in the other. This process is **coevolution**.

For example, a carnivore may become more efficient at hunting. However, if certain individuals of its prey have traits that allow them to get away, they pass these adaptive traits on to their offspring. Then the predator may evolve ways to overcome this new trait, leading the prey to new adaptations, and so on.

Similarly plants may evolve defenses, such as camouflage, thorns, or poison, against efficient herbivores. This, in turn, can lead their herbivore consumers to evolve ways to counteract those defenses. Animals such as golden toads (Figure 4-34) may also evolve poisons that protect them from their predators. Through coevolution animals may also develop camouflage to hide them or to make them more effective predators.

Coevolution enhances or leads to mutualism (Figure 4-43), commensalism (Figure 4-44), and other symbiotic relationships between species. Many flowering plants depend on animals for pollination and seed dispersal, and these animals in turn depend on those same plants for nutrition. For example, hummingbirds have coevolved with plants whose flower colors attract them and whose flower shapes are adapted to their beak lengths (Figure 6-10). The birds get nectar that only they can reach, and the plant gets pollinated.

**SPECIATION AND EXTINCTION** Earth's 5–100 million species are believed to be the result of two processes over the past 3.6–3.8 billion years. One is **speciation**: the formation of two species from one as a

Q: What percentage of the world's cars are found in the United States?

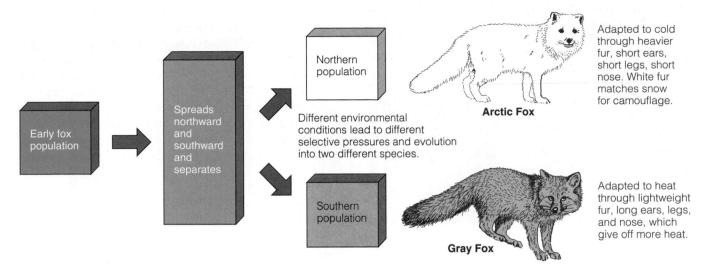

Northern population

Adapted to cold through heavier fur, short ears, short legs, short nose. White fur matches snow for camouflage.

**Arctic Fox**

Early fox population

Spreads northward and southward and separates

Different environmental conditions lead to different selective pressures and evolution into two different species.

Southern population

Adapted to heat through lightweight fur, long ears, legs, and nose, which give off more heat.

**Gray Fox**

**Figure 6-11** Geographic isolation leading to reproductive isolation and speciation.

result of divergent natural selection in response to changes in environmental conditions.

A common speciation mechanism is *geographic isolation*, the situation in which populations of a species become separated in areas with different environmental conditions for fairly long periods—typically for 1,000–100,000 generations—as when part of the group migrates in search of food and doesn't return (Figure 6-11). Populations may also become separated by a physical barrier or when a few individuals are carried to a new area by wind, water, or humans. Examples of physical barriers include those caused by earthquakes, movement of plates making up the lithosphere, and other geological events (Chapter 7). Even a new highway can become a barrier.

After long geographic separation, during which the two groups don't interbreed, they may begin to diverge in their genetic makeup because of different selection pressures. If this *reproduction isolation* continues long enough, members of the separated populations may become so different that they can't interbreed and produce fertile offspring. Then one species has become two (Figure 6-11).

In a few rapidly reproducing organisms (mostly r-strategists) speciation may take place in thousands or even hundreds of years. With most species (especially K-strategists), however, it takes from tens of thousands to millions of years. Given this time scale, it is difficult to observe and document the appearance of a new species.

The second key process affecting the various species on Earth is **extinction**: A species ceases to exist because it cannot genetically adapt and successfully reproduce under new environmental conditions. When the rules of the game change, a species may vanish entirely, or it may evolve into a new and better-adapted species.

Extinction is nothing new on Earth. Biologists estimate that 99% of all the species that have lived are now extinct. Some species inevitably disappear as local conditions change. This is *background extinction*. In contrast, a **mass extinction** is an abrupt rise in extinction rates above the background level. It is a catastrophic, widespread—often global— event in which not just one species but major groups of species are wiped out simultaneously. Fossil and geological evidence indicates that Earth's species have experienced five great mass extinctions—at roughly 26-million-year intervals—with smaller ones in between. The last mass extinction took place about 65 million years ago when the dinosaurs became extinct for disputed reasons after thriving for 140 million years.

A crisis for one species, however, is an opportunity for another. The fact that 5–100 million species exist today means that speciation, on average, has kept ahead of extinction. Evidence shows that Earth's mass extinctions have been followed by periods of recovery and **adaptive radiations** in which new species evolved to fill new or vacant ecological niches in changed environments. The disappearance of dinosaurs at the end of the Mesozoic Era about 65 million years ago, for example, was followed by an evolution explosion for mammals (Figure 6-12). This adaptive radiation marked the beginning of the Cenozoic Era (the past 65 million years).

Speciation minus extinction equals *biodiversity*, one of the planet's most important resources. Extinction is a natural process, but one of our goals should be to *not* reduce Earth's biodiversity by our actions (Spotlight, p. 163).

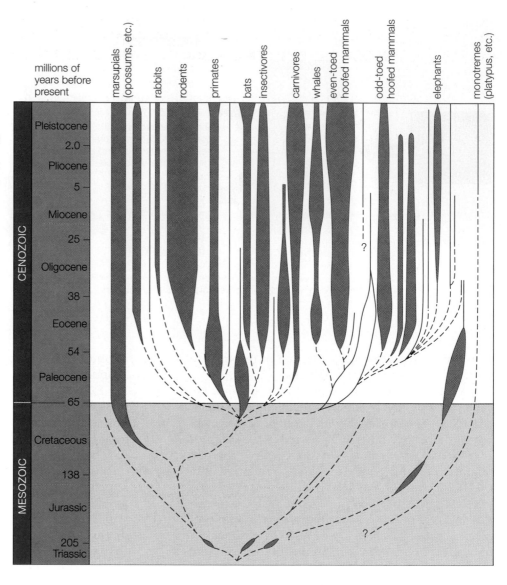

**Figure 6-12** Adaptive radiation of mammals in the first 10–12 million years of the Cenozoic Era, which began about 65 million years ago and which continues today. This speciation explosion is thought to have resulted when huge numbers of vacant and new environmental niches became available after the mass extinction of dinosaurs near the end of the Mesozoic Era. (Used by permission from Cecie Starr, *Biology: Concepts and Applications*, Belmont, Calif.: Wadsworth, 1991)

| 6-4 | **Community–Ecosystem Responses to Stress** |

**ECOLOGICAL SUCCESSION** One characteristic of most communities and ecosystems is that the types of species in a given area are usually changing. This gradual process of change in the composition and function of communities is called **ecological succession**, or **community development**.

Succession is a normal process in nature. It reflects the results of the continuing struggle between species with different adaptations for food, light, space, nutrients, and other survival resources. Ecological succession can result in a progression from immature, rapidly changing, unstable communities to more mature, self-sustaining communities when this process is not disrupted by large-scale natural events or human actions.

Ecologists recognize two types of ecological succession, primary and secondary, depending on the conditions at a particular site at the beginning of the process. **Primary succession** involves the development of biotic communities in a barren habitat with no or very little topsoil (Figure 6-13). Examples of such areas include the rock or mud exposed by a retreating glacier or a mudslide, newly cooled lava, a new sandbar deposited by a shift in ocean currents, and surface-mined areas from which all topsoil has been removed.

After such a large-scale disturbance life usually returns, first with a few hardy **pioneer species**—microbes, mosses, and lichens. They are usually r-strategists with the ability to establish large populations quickly in a new area—species Edward O. Wilson calls nature's sprinters.

Q: What percentage of the world's population owns cars?

So far humans may be the most adaptable animal species that ever existed. The main reason is that our adaptations are not restricted to genetic mutations leading to the slow process of biological evolution. Unlike other species we can adapt our behavior in a generation or less through cultural changes (Chapter 2). These cultural changes have allowed us to invade and dominate all types of habitats and to extract and use huge amounts of Earth's net primary productivity (Figure 4-27) and other resources.

This short 10,000-year "success" may have gone to our heads. It bolsters many people's belief that we are the planet's most important species, that Earth's riches are all for us, that we will never run out of resources because of our cleverness in exploiting nature, that we needn't follow nature's laws, and that technology will allow us to fix whatever problems we create.

Many environmentalists believe that such a worldview is a recipe for disaster. They warn that if we stress the tough and adaptable fabric of nature too far, it will "snap back" to put our fragile species in its place by a massive dieback—or perhaps even eliminate us as an evolutionary experiment that went wrong.

A major way we are altering nature is by causing the greatest mass extinction since dinosaurs vanished 65 million years ago. Indeed, we have become the "terminator" species behind this sixth great extinction spasm. Already our actions are leading to the premature loss of at least six species per hour. This hemorrhage of biodiversity and priceless genetic information results mostly from our destruction or degradation of major habitats containing most of the world's plant productivity (Figure 4-27) and biological wealth. As population and resource consumption increase over the next 30 years, we

may cause the extinction of up to a quarter of Earth's species, each the product of millions to billions of years of evolution.

Such catastrophic losses cannot be recouped by formation of new species. It took tens of millions of years after each of Earth's five great mass extinctions for evolution to allow life to recover to at least the level of biodiversity before each extinction. Genetic engineering cannot stop the holocaust because genetic engineers do not create new genes. They transfer genes or gene fragments from one organism to another and thus rely on natural biodiversity for their raw material.

According to biodiversity expert E. O. Wilson, "If this planet were under surveillance by biologists from another world, I think they would look at us and say, 'Here is a species in the mid-stages of self-destruction.'" The evolutionary lesson to be learned from nature is that no species can get too big for its britches, at least not for long.

Sometimes the species of this pioneer community make the area suitable for species with different niche requirements, a process called *facilitation*. More common is *inhibition*, in which the early species create conditions that hinder invasions and growth by other species. Then succession can proceed only when a fire, heavy grazing, bulldozing, or some other disturbance removes most of the pioneer species. In other cases later species are largely unaffected by the presence of earlier species, a phenomenon known as *tolerance*.

The more common type of succession is **secondary succession**, which begins in an area where the natural vegetation has been removed or destroyed but where the soil or bottom sediment has not been covered or removed. Examples of candidates for secondary succession include abandoned farmlands, burned or cut forests, heavily polluted streams, and land that has been dammed or flooded to produce a reservoir or pond. Because some soil or sediment is present, new vegetation can usually sprout within only a few weeks. In the central (Piedmont) region of North Carolina, for example, European settlers cleared

the mature forests of native oak and hickory, and replanted the land with crops. Later some of the land was abandoned. Figure 6-14 shows how such abandoned farmland, covered with a thick layer of soil, has undergone secondary succession until after about 150 years the area again supports a mature oak and hickory forest.

It is tempting to conclude that ecological succession is an orderly sequence, with each successional stage leading predictably to the next, more stable stage until an area is occupied by a *mature* or *climax community*, dominated by plant species Edward O. Wilson calls nature's long-distance runners. Research has shown, however, that this does not necessarily happen. The exact sequence of species and community types that appear during primary or secondary succession can be highly variable. We cannot predict the course of a given succession or view it as some preordained progress toward an ideally adapted climax community. Immature ecosystems and mature ecosystems have strikingly different characteristics, as summarized in Table 6-3.

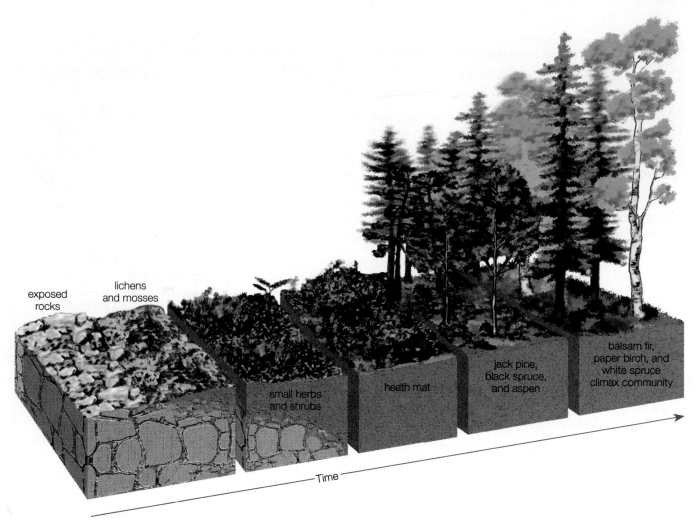

exposed rocks

lichens and mosses

small herbs and shrubs

heath mat

jack pine, black spruce, and aspen

balsam fir, paper birch, and white spruce climax community

Time

**Figure 6-13** Primary ecological succession of plant communities over several hundred years on bare rock exposed by a retreating glacier on Isle Royale in northern Lake Superior.

**DOES DIVERSITY LEAD TO STABILITY?** Organisms, populations, communities, and ecosystems have some ability to withstand or recover from externally imposed changes or stresses (Table 6-1)—provided those stresses are not too severe. In other words they have some degree of *stability*.

This stability, however, is maintained only by constant dynamic change. Although an organism's structure is fairly stable over its life span, it is continually gaining and losing matter and energy. Similarly in a mature tropical rain forest some trees will die and others will take their place. Some species may disappear, and the number of individual species in the forest may change. Unless it is cut, burned, or blown down, however, you will recognize it as a tropical rain forest 50 years from now.

It's useful to distinguish between three aspects of stability in living systems. **Inertia**, or **persistence**, is the ability of a living system to resist being disturbed or altered. **Constancy** is the ability of a living system, such as a population, to maintain a certain size or keep its numbers within certain limits. **Resilience** is the ability of a living system to bounce back after an outside disturbance that is not too drastic.

Communities and ecosystems are so complex and variable that ecologists have little understanding of how they maintain some degree of inertia and resilience while undergoing continual change in response to changes in environmental conditions. A major problem is the difficulty of conducting controlled experiments. Identifying and observing even a tiny fraction of the interacting variables in simple communities and ecosystems is virtually impossible. Greatly simplified ecosystems can be set up and observed under laboratory conditions, but extrapolating the results of such experiments to much more complex natural communities and ecosystems is difficult, if not impossible.

At one time ecologists believed that the higher the species diversity in an ecosystem, the greater its stability.

Q: What percentage of cars carrying people to and from work in the United States have only one passenger?

**Figure 6-14** Secondary ecological succession of plant communities on an abandoned farm field in North Carolina. After the farmland was abandoned it took about 150 years for the area once again to be covered with a mature oak and hickory forest.

| Table 6-3 Ecosystem Characteristics at Immature and Mature Stages of Ecological Succession | | |
|---|---|---|
| **Characteristic** | **Immature Ecosystem** | **Mature Ecosystem** |
| **Ecosystem Structure** | | |
| Plant size | Small | Large |
| Species diversity | Low | High |
| Trophic structure | Mostly producers, few decomposers | Mixture of producers, consumers, and decomposers |
| Ecological niches | Few, mostly generalized | Many, mostly specialized |
| Community organization (number of interconnecting links | Low | High |
| **Ecosystem Function** | | |
| Food chains and webs | Simple, mostly plant → herbivore with few decomposers | Complex, dominated by decomposers |
| Efficiency of nutrient recycling | Low | High |
| Efficiency of energy use | Low | High |

According to this hypothesis an ecosystem with a diversity of species has more ways to respond to most environmental stresses because it does not have "all its eggs in one basket." Research indicates, however, that there are numerous exceptions to this intuitively appealing idea.

There is, of course, some minimum threshold of species diversity below which ecosystems cannot function. For example, no ecosystem can function without some plants and decomposers (Figure 4-18). Beyond this it is difficult to know whether simple ecosystems are less stable than complex ones and to distinguish the threshold below which complex ecosystems fail.

Part of the problem is that ecologists disagree on how to define stability and diversity. Does an ecosystem need both high inertia and high resilience to be considered stable? Evidence indicates that some ecosystems have one of these properties but not the other. For example, California redwood forests (Figure 2-7) and tropical rain forests (Figures 4-37 and 5-22) have high species diversity and high inertia. This means they are hard to alter significantly or to destroy. However, once a large tract of either one is severely degraded, the ecosystem resilience is so low that the forest may never be restored. The soil nutrients and other conditions needed for recovery may no longer be present.

Grasslands, by contrast, are much less diverse than most forests, burn easily, and thus have low inertia. However, because most of their plant matter is underground, in the roots, these ecosystems have high resilience, which allows them to recover quickly. A grassland can be destroyed only if its roots are plowed up and something else is planted in its soil (Figure 5-20), or if it is severely overgrazed by livestock or other herbivores.

Another difficulty is that populations, communities, and ecosystems are rarely, if ever, at equilibrium. Instead, nature is in a continuing state of disturbance and fluctuation. Change and turmoil, more than constancy and balance, are the rule. When disturbed, natural systems may change and operate within new limits, rather than return to some "perfect" equilibrium state when the source of change is removed. Indeed, ecologists now recognize that disturbances of ecosystems are not abnormal but are integral parts of the way nature works.

## 6-5 Human Impact on Ecosystems: Learning from Nature

**SIMPLIFYING ECOSYSTEMS** In modifying natural ecosystems for our use, we usually simplify them: We plow grasslands, clear forests, and fill in wetlands.

Then we replace their thousands of interrelated plant and animal species with one crop (Figure 5-20) or with one kind of tree (Figure 5-25)—called **monocultures**—or with buildings, highways, and parking lots.

We spend a lot of time, energy, and money trying to protect monocultures from continual invasion by unwanted pioneer species, which we call *weeds* if they are plants (because weeds and annual crop plants typically occupy the same niches), *pests* if they are insects or other animals, and *pathogens* if they are fungi, viruses, or disease-causing bacteria. Weeds, pests, and pathogens can wipe out an entire monoculture crop unless it is protected by pesticides or by some form of biological control.

When fast-breeding insect species begin to undergo natural selection and develop genetic resistance to chemical pesticides, the salespeople urge farmers to

Q: What percentage of Americans use public transportation to get to and from work?

## Genetic Engineering: Savior or Monster?

"Genetic engineers" have learned how to splice genes and recombine sequences of existing DNA molecules in organisms to produce DNA with new genetic characteristics (recombinant DNA). In other words they use laboratory techniques to transfer traits from one species to another to make new genetic combinations (Figure 6-15) instead of waiting for new genetic combinations to evolve through natural selection.

This rapidly developing technology excites many scientists and investors. They see it as a way to increase crop and livestock yields and to produce, patent, and sell crop varieties with greater resistance to diseases, pests, frost, and drought, and with more protein than in existing varieties. They hope to create bacteria that can destroy oil spills, degrade toxic wastes, concentrate metals found in low-grade ores, and to serve as biological "factories" for new vaccines, drugs, and therapeutic hormones. Gene therapy, proponents argue, could eliminate certain genetic diseases and other genetic afflictions.

When the U.S. Supreme Court ruled in 1980 that genetically engineered organisms could be patented, investors began pouring billions of dollars into the fledgling biotech industry, with dreams of more billions in profits. The livestock industry, for example, hopes to develop specialized eating machines such as animals without legs (so theycouldn't waste energy by moving around) and chickens without feathers (to eliminate the need for plucking).

Already genetic engineering has produced a drug to reduce heart attack damage and agents to fight diabetes, hemophilia, and some forms of cancer. It has also been used to diagnose AIDS and cancer. Genetically altered bacteria have been used to manufacture more effective vaccines and human-growth hormones.

(continued)

---

use stronger doses or switch to a new pesticide. As a result natural selection in the pests increases to the point that these chemicals eventually become ineffective. This process illustrates biologist Garrett Hardin's **first law of ecology**: *We can never do merely one thing.* Any intrusion into nature has multiple effects, many (perhaps most) of them unpredictable because of our limited understanding of how nature works (Spotlight, p. 166).

Our actions should take into account the **second law of ecology**, or principle of connectedness: *Everything is connected to and intermingled with everything else; we are all in it together.* There is no independence in nature. No species is an island, and simplifying nature for our purposes can disrupt nature in ways that can decrease our ability to survive. The goal of ecology, however, is not the impossible one of trying to find out how everything is connected, but to discover the strongest and most important connections—still difficult enough.

Cultivation is not the only way people simplify ecosystems. Ranchers, who don't want bison or prairie dogs competing with sheep for grass, eradicate those species, as well as wolves, coyotes, eagles, and other predators that occasionally kill sheep. In addition, far too often, ranchers allow livestock to overgraze grasslands until erosion converts these ecosystems to simpler and less productive deserts. The cutting of vast areas of diverse tropical rain forests destroys part of Earth's biodiversity forever. And people tend to overfish and overhunt some species to extinction or near extinction, another way of simplifying ecosystems. Finally the burning of fossil fuels in industrial plants, homes, and vehicles creates air pollutants that return to Earth as acidic compounds in fog, rain, and solid particles that can disrupt and simplify forest and aquatic ecosystems.

Another problem with the simplified ecosystems and habitats we create is that they leak. Nutrients are quickly lost from monoculture crop fields, tree farms, cities, and suburbs, and must be replaced at great financial and environmental cost.

The price we pay for creating, maintaining, and protecting such stripped-down ecosystems is high: It includes time, money, increased use of matter and energy resources, reduced biodiversity, and loss of natural landscape. The challenge is to maintain a balance between simplified, human ecosystems and the neighboring, more complex (mature) natural ecosystems on which our simplified systems and other forms of life depend, and to slow down the rates at which we are altering nature for our purposes.

During the past 40,000 or so years the human species has used its intelligence to develop technologies and cultural mechanisms to gain increasing control over Earth's nonliving and living resources, and thus expand the planet's carrying capacity for humans (Figure 2-4). We have also learned to speed up genetic change in other species—first through crossbreeding

R. L. Brinster and R. E. Hammer/School of Veterinary Medicine, University of Pennsylvania

**Figure 6-15** An example of genetic engineering. The six-month-old mouse on the left is normal. The other mouse of the same age contains a human-growth hormone gene in the chromosomes of all its cells. In general, mice with the human-growth hormone gene grow two to three times as fast and reach a size twice that of mice without the gene.

In agriculture gene transfer has been used to develop strawberries that resist frost, and smaller cows that produce more milk. Toxin-producing genes have been transferred from bacteria to plants, increasing the plants' immunity to insect attack. Genetic technology has also produced salmon and carp that grow faster and bigger than conventional varieties.

Some people are worried that biotechnology may run amok. Most recognize that it is unrealistic to stop genetic engineering altogether,

but they argue that it should be kept under strict control. They believe that we don't understand how nature works well enough to have unregulated control over the genetic characteristics of humans and other species.

Critics also fear that unregulated biotechnology could lead to the development of "superorganisms." If such organisms were released deliberately or accidentally into the environment, they could have unpredictable, possibly harmful, effects. For example, bacteria genetically altered to clean up ocean oil spills by degrading the oil would wreak havoc if they were able to multiply rapidly and began degrading the world's remaining oil supplies.

Genetically engineered organisms might also mutate, change their form and behavior, and then migrate. Unlike defective cars and other products, they couldn't be recalled.

The risk of this or other biotech catastrophies is small. Nevertheless, critics fear that the potential profits from biotechnology are so enormous that, without strict controls, greed—not ecological wisdom and restraint—will prevail. They contend that rules proposed by the Environmental Protection Agency in 1988 for regulation of biotechnology are wholly inadequate.

Genetic scientists answer that it is highly unlikely that the release of genetically engineered species

would cause serious and widespread ecological problems. To have a serious effect, such organisms would have to be outstanding competitors and resistant to predation. In addition, they would have to be capable of becoming dominant in ecosystems and in the ecosphere. Critics point out that this has happened many times when we have accidentally or deliberately introduced alien organisms into biological communities. Proponents respond that genetically engineered bacteria meant to be released into any environment can be genetically modified so that they cannot live long there.

In 1989 a committee of prominent ecologists appointed by the Ecological Society of America warned that the ecological impacts of new combinations of genetic traits from different species would be difficult to predict. Thus their report called for a case-by-case review of any proposed environmental releases, as well as carefully regulated, small-scale field tests before any bioengineered organism is put into commercial use.

This controversy illustrates the difficulty of balancing the actual and potential benefits of a technology with its actual and potential risks of harm. What restrictions, if any, do you believe should be placed on genetic engineering research and use? How would you enforce any restrictions?

and recently through genetic engineering (Pro/Con, p. 167).

**SOME LESSONS FROM NATURE** It should be clear from the brief discussion of principles in this and the previous two chapters that living systems have six key features: *interdependence, diversity, resilience, adaptability, unpredictability,* and *limits.* We can also use the concepts developed in Chapters 3–6 to see how nature is perpetuated and sustained (Solutions, p. 169).

## 6-6 Healing Ecosystems

**REHABILITATING AND RESTORING ECOSYSTEMS** Another facet of sustainable living is to help heal wounds we have inflicted on nature. Luckily much of the environmental damage we cause is reversible. Forests can be replanted, topsoil can be

Q: How much of the U.S. working population lives within biking distance of work?

SOLUTIONS

Life on Earth is sustained despite finite resources and ever-changing environmental conditions because:

- Plants capture nonpolluting solar energy and convert it to chemical energy that keeps them, plant-eating animals, and decomposers alive.

- Organisms participate in biogeochemical cycles that provide them with nutrients and dispose of waste by recycling vital nutrients for reuse.

- Soil, water, air, plants, and animals are renewed through natural processes.

- Complex networks of positive and negative feedback loops give organisms and populations the information and control mechanisms they need to respond or adapt to changing conditions.

- Synergistic interactions amplify cooperative efforts.

- Natural populations adapt (change their genetic makeup) in response to changes in environmental conditions.

- Biodiversity varies but persists because a rainbow of species (species diversity), and a profusion of genetic variety within species (genetic diversity), and ecosystems (ecological diversity) have evolved over billions of years.

- Natural population size and growth rates for a species are controlled by interactions with other species and the nonliving environment.

- Organisms—except the human species—generally use only what they need to survive, stay healthy, and reproduce.

To live sustainably on Earth, we need to recognize three things: **(1)** We are a part of—not apart from—Earth's web of life; **(2)** our survival, lifestyles, and economies are totally dependent on the sun and the earth; and **(3)** everything is connected to everything. We are connected to all organisms through our evolutionary history carried in our DNA and through our interactions with air, water, soil, and other forms of life. The destiny of all species is a shared one.

We need not stop growing food or building cities, but we must recognize that such changes have far-reaching and unpredictable consequences (Guest Essay, p. 171). The key lesson is that we need Earth wisdom, care, restraint, humility, cooperation, and love as we alter the ecosphere to meet our needs and wants. Earth care is life care and self-care.

---

replenished, streams can be cleaned up, and wetlands can be restored (p. 146). Researchers are creating a new discipline of *rehabilitation and restoration ecology* devoted to renewing damaged areas and ecosystems.

When a degraded ecosystem is abandoned, in most cases it will eventually recover, at least partially, through ecological succession (Figure 6-14). But *natural restoration* usually takes a long time. For example, it typically takes more than a century for slash-and-burn clearing in a tropical forest (Figure 2-6) to be fully reforested. If the site is cleared by bulldozer, natural recovery will take at least 1,000 years. Large cleared areas of tropical rain forests, however, may become grasslands or deserts.

By studying how natural ecosystems recover, scientists are learning how to speed up our repair operations. *Rehabilitation* involves making degraded land useful for humans again on a sustainable basis, including stopping soil erosion and desert creep, and allowing the land once again to produce food or wood for fuel and timber.

*Active restoration* is more ambitious. Its goal is to take a degraded site and reestablish a community of organisms close to what would be found naturally. It is used mostly to partly reestablish unique or rare ecosystems in parts of the world where most ecosystems have been damaged. Often, it's not necessary to plant anything. All that's needed is to find the strongest types of natural growth, protect them, and remove all plant and animal species not native to the area so that natural ecological succession can take place.

Scientists and concerned citizens, with the aid of dedicated volunteers, have successfully restored or rehabilitated some damaged ecosystems. This isn't easy—it takes money and hard work (Spotlight, p. 170)—but the long-term costs of doing nothing are much higher.

**THE VALUES OF EARTH HEALING** Sometimes government agencies allow developers to destroy one ecosystem if they protect or restore a similar one of roughly the same size. Although preferable to wanton destruction of ecosystems, this tradeoff approach defeats the main purpose of ecosystem restoration, which is to repair previous damage, not to legitimize further destruction.

The dedicated scientists who are carrying out ecological rehabilitation and restoration projects to reforest, regreen, and rewater parts of the earth we have degraded, and the many volunteers who help them,

## Tall-Grass Prairie Restoration

**SPOTLIGHT**

An important restoration project has focused on restoring areas of tall-grass prairie that once blanketed the midwestern United States (Figure 5-18). Since 1936 scientists from the Aboretum of the University of Wisconsin–Madison have worked to restore the Curtis Prairie, a project conceived by Aldo Leopold in 1934. After over 50 years of painstaking work and research, tall grasses again wave over parts of the Curtis Prairie, much as they did before farmers plowed it up and planted crops.

Another pioneering example of prairie restoration is found at the Morton Arboretum near Chicago. Illinois has lost all but 0.01% of its original prairie. In 1962 Ray Schulenberg began reestablishing a patch of prairie by collecting seeds from remnants of prairie in the area, raising seedlings in a greenhouse, and then planting them on a plot of land at the arboretum. For two years workers removed nonnative weeds by hand. After the prairie grasses became established, they used controlled burning each spring to remove weeds and encourage the growth of perennial prairie plants. Today the site is covered with healthy prairie plants. It is used for educational purposes and as a refuge for endangered species of local plants and insects.

The largest prairie restoration project is being carried out at the Fermi National Accelerator Laboratory in Batavia, Illinois, by Schulenberg and Robert Betz, a biochemist at Northeastern Illinois University in Chicago. Schulenberg and Betz found remnants of virgin Illinois prairie in old cemeteries, on embankments, and on other patches of land. In 1972 they transplanted these by hand to a 4-hectare (10-acre) patch at the Fermi Laboratory site.

Each year since then volunteers have carefully prepared more land, sowed it with native prairie plants, weeded it by hand, reseeded the plots, removed exotic invaders, and used controlled burning to speed up ecological succession. Today more than 180 hectares (445 acres) of the plot have been restored with prairie plants. New native species are introduced each year, with the goal of eventually establishing the 150–200 species that once flourished on the entire 240-hectare (593-acre) site.

are important and inspiring examples of people caring for the earth. Expanding and supporting this emerging field designed to heal rather than hurt the earth must become a major priority.

Anyone can become involved in such Earth healing. For example, a group of volunteers can revitalize a creek or revegetate a small abandoned plot of land in a city. Partially repairing parts of Earth's damaged fabric will also help show that it is easier and cheaper not to hurt the earth in the first place.

*What has gone wrong, probably, is that we have failed to see ourselves as part of a large and indivisible whole. For too long we have based our lives on a primitive feeling that our "God-given" role was to have "dominion over the fish of the sea and over the fowl of the air and over every living thing that moveth upon the earth." We have failed to understand that the earth does not belong to us, but we to the earth.*

ROLF EDBERG

## Critical Thinking

1. Explain how 1 plus 1 does not always equal 2 in an organism or ecosystem.

2. Give two examples of time delays not discussed in this chapter. How can time delays be harmful? How can they be helpful?

3. Someone tells you not to worry about air pollution because through natural selection the human species will develop lungs that can detoxify pollutants. How would you reply?

4. Are human beings or insects such as flies and mosquitoes better able to adapt to environmental change? Defend your choice, and explain the primary way each of these species can adapt to environmental change.

5. How may a species bring about changes in local conditions so that the species becomes extinct in a given ecosystem? Could human beings do this to themselves? Explain.

6. Why is a simplified ecosystem such as a cornfield much more vulnerable to harm from insects, plant diseases, and fungi than a more complex, natural ecosystem such as a grassland? Why are natural ecosystems less vulnerable?

7. Do you believe that genetic engineering should be widely used? Explain. What restrictions, if any, would you place on its use? How would you enforce such restrictions, especially in secret biological warfare facilities?

*8. Visit a nearby land area or pond and look for signs of ecological succession. If possible, compare the types of species found on an abandoned farm field or lot with another nearby area that is at a more mature stage of ecological succession.

Q: What percentage of Americans walk or use a bicycle to get to and from work?

# We Propose and Nature Disposes

*Edward J. Kormondy*

**GUEST ESSAY** *Edward J. Kormondy is chancellor and professor of biology at the University of Hawaii–Hilo/West Oahu College. He has taught at the California State University at Los Angeles, the University of Southern Maine, the University of Michigan, Oberlin College, and Evergreen State College. Among his many research articles and books are* Concepts of Ecology *and* Readings in Ecology *(both published by Prentice-Hall). He has been a major force in biological education and for several years was director of the Commission on Undergraduate Education in the Biological Sciences.*

Energy flows—but downhill only in terms of its quality; chemical nutrients circulate—but some stagnate; populations stabilize—but some go wild; communities age—but some age faster. These dynamic and relentless processes are as characteristic of ecosystems as thermonuclear fusion reactions are characteristic of the sun.

Thinking we can escape the operation of these and other laws of nature is like thinking we can stop Earth from revolving or make rain fall up. Yet we have peopled Earth only for hundreds of millions to endure starvation and malnutrition; deliberately dumped wastes only to ensure contamination; purposefully simplified agricultural systems only to cause widespread crop losses from pest invasions. Such actions suggest that we believe energy and food automatically increase as people multiply, that things stay where they are put, that simplification of ecosystems aids in their productivity. Such actions indicate that we have ignored basic, inexorable, and unbreakable laws of ecosystems. We have proposed, but nature has disposed, often in unexpected ways counter to our intent.

We proposed more people, more mouths to be fed, more space to be occupied. Nature disposed by placing an upper limit on the rate at which plants can produce organic nutrients for themselves and for the people and other animals that feed on them. It also disposed by using and degrading energy quality at and between all trophic levels in the biosphere's intricate food webs, and by imposing an upper limit on the total space that is available and can be occupied by humans and other species.

Ultimately the only way there can be more and more people is for each person to have less and less food and fuel energy, and less and less physical space. Absolute limits to growth are imposed both by thermodynamics and by space. We may argue about what these limits are and when they will be reached, but there are limits and, if present trends continue, they will be reached. The more timely questions then become qualitative: What quality of life will we have within these limits? What kind of life do you want? What quality of life will future generations have?

We proposed exploitative use of resources and indiscriminate disposal of human and technological wastes.

Nature disposed and, like a boomerang, the consequences of our acts came back to hit us. On the one hand, finite oil, coal, and mineral resource supplies are significantly depleted—some nearing exhaustion. On the other hand, air, water, and land are contaminated, perhaps beyond restoring.

Nature's laws limit each resource; some limits are more confining than others, some more critical than others. Earth is finite, and its resources are therefore finite.

Yet another of nature's laws is that fundamental resources—elements and compounds—circulate, some fully and some partially. They don't stay where they are put. They move from the land to the water and the air, just as they move from the air and water to the land. Must not our proposals for using resources and discharging wastes be mindful of ultimate limits and Earth's chemical recycling processes? What about your own patterns of resource use and waste disposal?

We proposed simplification of our agricultural systems to ease the admittedly heavy burden of cultivation and harvest. Nature has disposed otherwise, however. Simple ecosystems such as a cornfield are youthful ones and, like our own youth, are volatile, unpredictable, and unstable. Young ecosystems do not conserve nutrients, and agricultural systems in such a stage must have their nutrients replaced artificially and expensively by adding commercial inorganic fertilizers. Young agricultural systems essentially lack resistance to pests and disease and have to be protected artificially and expensively by pesticides and other chemicals. These systems are also more subject to the whims of climate and often have to be expensively irrigated. Must not our proposals for managing agricultural systems be mindful of nature's managerial strategy of providing biological diversity to help sustain most complex ecosystems? What of your own manicured lawn?

The take-home lesson is a rather straightforward one: We cannot propose without recognizing how nature disposes of our attempts to manage Earth's resources for human use. We are shackled by basic ecological laws of energy flow, chemical recycling, population growth, and community aging processes. We have plenty of freedom within these laws, but like it or not we are bounded by them. You are bounded by them. What do you propose to do? And what might nature dispose in return?

## Critical Thinking

1. List the patterns of your life that are in harmony with the laws of energy flow and chemical cycling, and those that are not.

2. Set up a chart with examples of "we propose and nature disposes," but add a third column titled "we repropose," based on using ecological principles to work with nature.

## Charles Darwin Reporting from Concepción, Chile

The coastal city of Concepción, Chile, had been hit by earthquakes before—in 1570, 1730, and 1751. When another quake hit on February 20, 1835, its effects were reported to the world by Charles Darwin, who sailed into Talcahuano Bay on the HMS *Beagle* soon after the earth shook.

The whole coast, said Darwin, was "strewed over with timber and furniture as if a thousand ships had been wrecked. . . . The storehouse at Talcahuano had been burst open, and great bags of cotton, yerba, and other valuable merchandise were scattered on the shore." Not a building was left standing, either in Concepción itself or in the Port of Talcahuano; 70 other villages were destroyed, and a great wave (tsunami) nearly washed away what little was left of Talcahuano.

Quiriquina Island in the harbor was as plainly marked by the earthquake itself as the shore had been by the resulting tsunami. Cracks as big as a yard wide ran north and south through the ground. Enormous masses of rock had fallen from the cliffs onto the beach, and the survivors expected more to fall with the first rains.

"The effect of the vibration on the hard primary slate [forming] the foundation of the island," Darwin noted, "was still more curious; the superficial parts of some narrow ridges were as completely shivered as if

**Figure 7-1** San Andreas Fault (left) as it crosses part of the Carrizo Plain between San Francisco and Los Angeles. This fault, which extends almost the full length of California, is responsible for minor and major earthquakes. Cracks (right) in the earth caused by an earthquake in Santa Cruz, California.

*Civilization exists by geological consent, subject to change without notice.*

WILL DURANT

they had been blasted by gunpowder." He estimated that the island lost as much area in the few minutes of the quake as it would normally lose to sea and weather in a whole century. This effect must be confined near the surface, he thought, or "there would not exist a block of solid rock throughout Chile."

Darwin had been some miles away at Valdivia when the earthquake struck. What he felt, lying down in the woods to rest, was fairly mild: "The rocking of the ground was fairly sensible. . . . There was no difficulty in standing upright, but the motion made me almost giddy. . . . It lasted only two minutes, but felt much longer and affected me deeply. A bad earthquake at once destroys our oldest associations; the earth, the very emblem of solidity, has moved beneath our feet like a thin crust over a fluid—one second of time has created in the mind a strange idea of insecurity, which hours of reflection would not have produced." Indeed, once you have felt the earth move beneath your feet, you are never quite the same again (Figure 7-1).

We live on a dynamic planet. Energy from the sun and from Earth's interior and the cycling of water created continents, mountains, valleys, plains, and ocean basins—in a process that continues to change our landscape. **Geology** is the science devoted to the study of Earth's dynamic history. Geologists analyze and study rocks and Earth's interior and surface features and processes. It is from Earth's crust that mineral resources and soil come, as well as the elements that make up living organisms.

As Charles Darwin learned firsthand, Earth's dynamic processes also generate a variety of natural hazards: earthquakes, volcanic eruptions, floods, landslides, and subsidence (sinking or collapsing) of parts of its surface. We can best avoid or minimize harm from such hazards by not living in places where they pose a serious risk. However, many people continue to live in and move to such areas either because they have no other choice or because they believe the benefits outweigh the risks.

*Note:* **Kenneth J. Van Dellen**, professor of geology and environmental science, Macomb Community College, is the primary author of this chapter, with assistance from G. Tyler Miller, Jr.

In this chapter we will seek answers to the following questions:

- What are the principal structural and chemical components of Earth?
- What are the major processes occurring on and in the earth?
- How does the rock cycle recycle earth materials and concentrate resources?
- What natural hazards can affect us?
- What are the time scales of geologic processes?

## 7-1 Earth Structure and Composition

As the primitive earth cooled over eons, its interior separated into three major, concentric zones, which geologists identify as the core, the mantle, and the crust (Figure 7-2). What we know about the earth's deep interior comes mostly from indirect evidence of various kinds, such as density measurements, seismic (earthquake) wave studies, measurements of heat flow from the interior, analyses of lava, and research on meteorite composition.

**CORE** Earth's central zone, the **core**, begins a little less than half of the 6,300-kilometer (3,900-mile) distance from the surface to its center. The *inner core* is a solid ball about 1,200 kilometers (700 miles) in diameter, made mostly of iron with perhaps some nickel. Although its temperature may be 4,300°C (7,700°F) or more, the inner core is not liquid, because the extreme pressure there prevents melting. The *outer core*, which surrounds the inner core, is liquid, with a temperature of 3,700–4,300°C (6,700–7,700°F). It currently extends between depths of about 2,900 and 5,200 kilometers (1,800–3,200 miles), but its base is gradually rising because as the earth continues to cool more material solidifies into inner core. The outer and inner cores make up 31% of the mass and 16% of the volume of the earth.

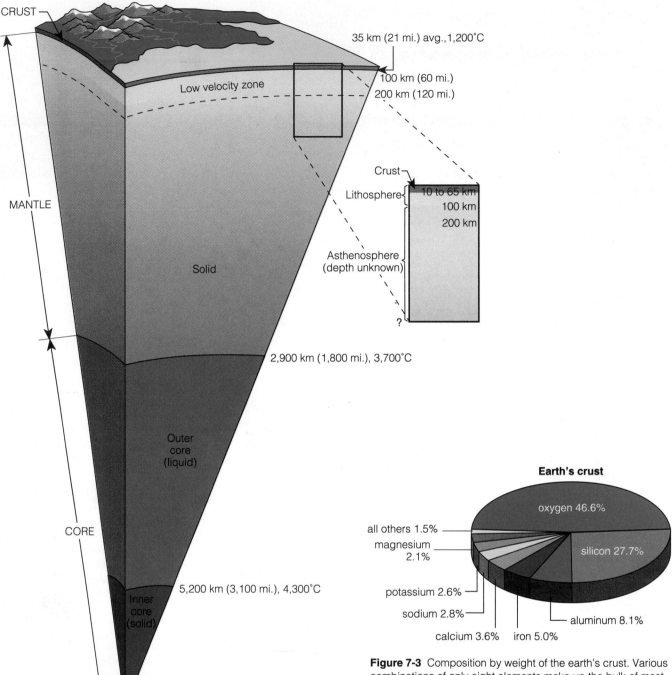

CRUST

35 km (21 mi.) avg.,1,200°C

100 km (60 mi.)
200 km (120 mi.)

Low velocity zone

MANTLE

Solid

Crust
Lithosphere
10 to 65 km
100 km
200 km

Asthenosphere
(depth unknown)

?

2,900 km (1,800 mi.), 3,700°C

Outer
core
(liquid)

CORE

5,200 km (3,100 mi.), 4,300°C

Inner
core
(solid)

6,400 km (3,900 mi.), 4,300°C?

**Figure 7-2** Earth's internal zones. (Surface features are not to scale.)

**Earth's crust**

oxygen 46.6%

all others 1.5%

magnesium
2.1%

silicon 27.7%

potassium 2.6%

sodium 2.8%

aluminum 8.1%

calcium 3.6%    iron 5.0%

**Figure 7-3** Composition by weight of the earth's crust. Various combinations of only eight elements make up the bulk of most minerals.

**MANTLE** Earth's core is surrounded by a thick, solid zone called the **mantle**, which begins at a depth of 10–65 kilometers (6–40 miles) (Figure 7-2). This zone makes up 82% of Earth's volume and 68% of its mass. Iron is a major constituent of the mantle, as of the core, but oxygen, silicon, and magnesium are also present in large proportions.

The outermost part of the mantle is rigid and strong, but apparently temperature and pressure conditions at a depth of 100–200 kilometers (60–120 miles) are such that rock partially melts; perhaps 1–10% is liquid. Because earthquake waves slow when they reach this zone, like a car hitting a deep puddle of water, it is also called the *low-velocity zone*. Below this zone the mantle is apparently completely solid again.

**CRUST** The **crust** (Figure 7-2) is the thinnest of Earth's zones and makes up only 2% of the planet's

Q: How many people have been killed by motor vehicles since the first automobile was built in 1885?

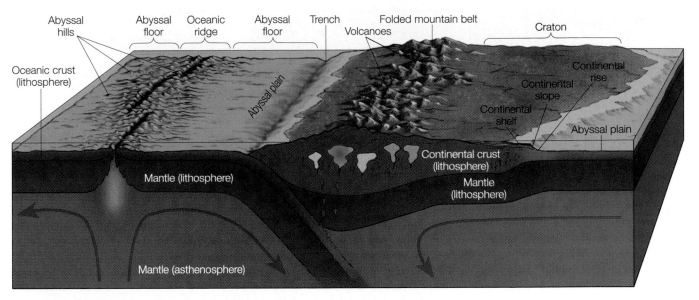

**Figure 7-4** Major features of the earth's crust and upper mantle. The lithosphere is the rigid, brittle outer zone, composed of the crust and outermost mantle. The asthenosphere is a zone in the mantle that can be deformed by heat and pressure like most forms of plastic.

volume and 1% of its mass. Its thickness varies from 10–65 kilometers (16–40 miles). Only eight elements make up 98.5% of the weight of the earth's crust (Figure 7-3).

The two categories of crust—oceanic crust and continental crust—differ in composition, density, and thickness (Figure 7-4). These differences give Earth two distinct elevations, with the continents rising above the ocean basins.

*Oceanic crust,* which covers about 71% of Earth's surface, is up to 10 kilometers (6 miles) thick. This relatively dense, low-lying crust provides a place for a large part of Earth's water to collect as oceans. Three prominent features of oceanic crust are the oceanic ridge system, the abyssal floor, and the trenches (Figure 7-4).

The *oceanic ridge system,* which extends into all oceans, winds around the surface somewhat like the seams of a baseball. With a total length of more than 80,000 kilometers (50,000 miles), it is 1,500–2,500 kilometers (930–1550 miles) wide and rises 2–3 kilometers (1–2 miles) above the abyssal floor.

The *abyssal floor* consists of deep-ocean basins, usually found on both sides of oceanic ridges. Part of it consists of numerous abyssal hills, found also on the oceanic ridge system, and part is flat abyssal plains, where abyssal hills have been buried by sediment. It is about 5 kilometers (3 miles) below sea level.

*Trenches,* the lowest areas of the earth's surface, are typically about 8 kilometers (5 miles) below sea level. The bottom of the deepest one, in the Pacific Ocean, is 11 kilometers (7 miles) below sea level.

*Continental crust* is higher and thicker than oceanic crust (Figure 7-4). It is as much as 65 kilometers (40 miles) thick under high mountain ranges and averages 35 kilometers (22 miles) thick. Continental crust has a lower density than oceanic crust, so that it "floats" much higher on the denser mantle.

Continents consist of folded mountain belts and cratons. In *folded mountain belts,* such as the Appalachians, Alps, Andes, and Himalaya, the rocks have been severely deformed and fractured, and intruded by molten rock material called **magma**. A *craton* is a nonmountainous part of a continent, where earlier mountains have been eroded away.

The *continental shelf* is the part of a craton flooded by the sea (Figure 7-4). Ecologically the edge of the ocean is the shoreline, but geologically it is the *continental slope,* the seaward edge of the continental shelf.

## 7-2 Internal and External Earth Processes

**INTERNAL PROCESSES: CONVECTION CELLS AND MANTLE PLUMES** Geologic changes originating from within the earth are called *internal processes.* Generally they build up the planet's surface. Heat from the earth's interior provides the energy for these processes, but gravity also plays a role.

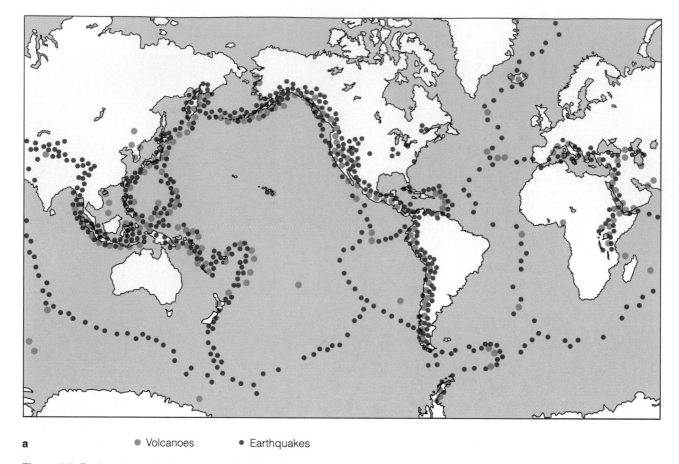

a          ● Volcanoes      ● Earthquakes

**Figure 7-5** Earthquakes and volcanoes are distributed mostly in bands along the planet's surface **(a)**. These bands correspond to lithospheric plate boundaries **(b)**. Divergent plate boundaries are marked by oceanic ridges and rift valleys. Convergent plate boundaries are marked by volcanic island chains or folded mountain belts and, usually, trenches. Transform faults, a third type of plate boundary, connect the other two types of plate boundaries. (A few examples on this map are marked with black arrows.)

Residual heat from the formation of the earth is still being given off as the inner core cools and the outer core both cools and solidifies. Continued decay of radioactive elements in the crust, especially the continental crust, adds to the flow of heat from within.

The deep heat causes much of the mantle to deform and flow slowly like heated plastic (in the same way that a red-hot iron horseshoe behaves plastically) from the top of the low-velocity zone to an undefined depth. Some researchers place the base of this plastic region, known as the **asthenosphere**, at a depth of as little as 200 kilometers (120 miles), limiting it to the low-velocity zone; others think it is deeper, perhaps extending all the way to the core—2,900 kilometers (1,800 miles) below the surface.

Indirect evidence suggests that at least two kinds of movement are occurring in the asthenosphere: convection cells and mantle plumes. Measurements of heat flow from the interior and observations of other phenomena indicate that the solid rock of the mantle moves in huge *convection cells*, following a pattern resembling convection in the atmosphere (Figure 5-7)

or in a pot of boiling soup. Another type of movement occurs at a *mantle plume*. There mantle rock flows slowly upward in a column like smoke from a chimney on a cold, calm morning. When it reaches the top of the plume, it moves out in a radial pattern. It is as if the material were flowing up an umbrella through the handle and then moving out in all directions from the tip of the umbrella to the rim. Both convection currents and mantle plumes move upward as the heated material is displaced by heavier, cooler material sinking under the influence of gravity.

**INTERNAL PROCESSES: PLATE TECTONICS** A map of Earth's earthquakes and volcanoes shows that most of these phenomena occur along certain lines or belts on the earth's surface (Figure 7-5a). The areas of the earth outlined by these major belts are called **plates** (Figure 7-5b). They are about 100 kilometers (60 miles) thick and are composed of the crust and the rigid, outermost part of the mantle above the asthenosphere, a combination called the **lithosphere**. These plates move constantly, carried by the slowly flowing astheno-

       Q: Worldwide, how many people are killed each year by motor vehicles?

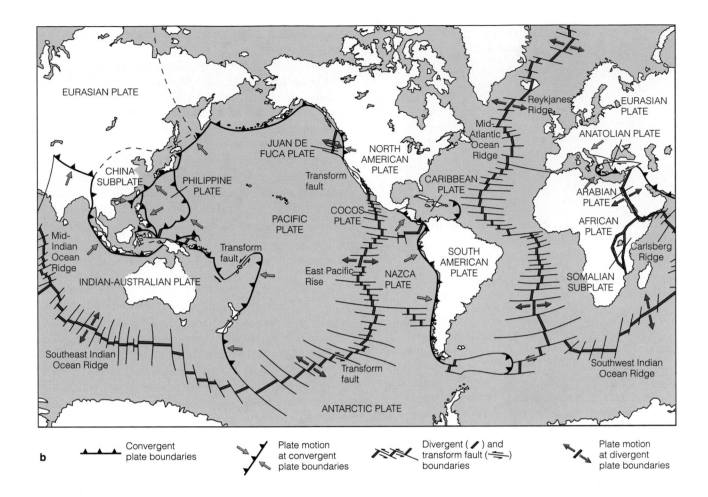

**b**

| | |
|---|---|
| ▲▲▲ | Convergent plate boundaries |
| | Plate motion at convergent plate boundaries |
| | Divergent ( ╱ ) and transform fault ( ⇌ ) boundaries |
| | Plate motion at divergent plate boundaries |

sphere like large pieces of ice floating on the surface of a lake during the spring breakup. Some plates move faster than others, but a typical speed is about the rate at which fingernails grow.

The theory explaining the movements of the plates and the processes that occur at their boundaries is called **plate tectonics**. The concept, which became widely accepted by geologists in the 1960s, was developed from an earlier idea called *continental drift*. Throughout Earth's history continents have split and joined as plates have drifted thousands of kilometers back and forth across the planet's surface. For example, geologic evidence indicates that about 225 million years ago the continents we now call Europe, Asia, North America, and South America were combined as one continent. This gigantic continental mass, named *Pangaea*, broke into pieces that gradually drifted apart as a result of movements of Earth's plates, and the continents eventually reached their present positions (Figure 7-32). In the process the Atlantic Ocean was formed.

Lithospheric plates have three types of boundaries: divergent, convergent, and transform fault (Figure 7-6). At a **divergent plate boundary** the plates move apart in opposite directions ( ← | → ). Because

many divergent plate boundaries are along the oceanic ridge system, geologists often refer to them as *oceanic spreading centers*. Divergent plate boundaries can also occur on continents when great blocks of Earth's crust are pushed up and moved apart, forming a rift valley between them into which water will flow if there is a link to the ocean. An example is the East African rift valleys. If divergence continues there, a new ocean will eventually develop.

As the plates move apart, the lowering of pressure causes very hot rock in the upper mantle to melt. This magma moves upward into the rift, some of it flowing out on the surface and some cooling underground. When it solidifies it adds to the separating plates, both underground and on the surface, and produces new lithosphere.

Volcanoes and lava flows along the East African rift valleys are associated with rifting, as is the volcanism along the oceanic spreading centers. Earthquakes also result from the separation of plates, but most have relatively little effect on people because they generally occur in the oceans (Figure 7-5a).

Where the tops of adjacent convection cells flow toward each other, the plates are pushed together ( → | ← ), producing a **convergent plate boundary** (Figure

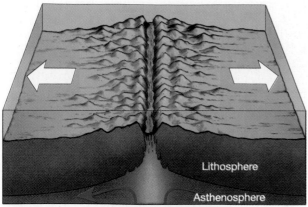

**Oceanic ridge at a divergent plate boundary**

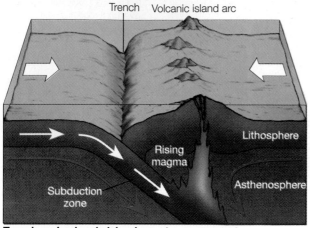

**Trench and volcanic island arc at a convergent plate boundary**

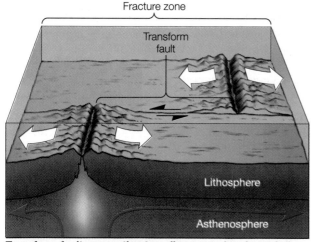

**Transform fault connecting two divergent plate boundaries**

**Figure 7-6** Types of boundaries between Earth's lithospheric plates. All three boundaries occur both in oceans and on continents.

7-6). These boundaries occur where folded mountains are developing. Some are found at a *volcanic island arc*, such as Japan, the Aleutian Islands, or the islands of the Caribbean. Others are at a continental margin, such as the Andes Mountains of South America or the

Cascade Range in the northwestern United States (Figure 7-5b).

At most convergent plate boundaries oceanic lithosphere is carried downward (subducted) under the island arc or the continent at a **subduction zone**. A trench ordinarily forms at the boundary between the two converging plates (Figure 7-4). As it descends some of the lithospheric material melts, producing volcanoes, and the rest is incorporated into the mantle. Stresses in the plate undergoing subduction cause earthquakes at convergent plate boundaries (Figure 7-5b). Only oceanic lithosphere is dense enough to subduct.

The third type of plate boundary, called a **transform fault**, occurs where plates move in opposite but parallel directions along a fracture (fault) in the lithosphere (Figure 7-6). Like the other types of plate boundaries, most transform faults are on the ocean floor. California's San Andreas Fault is one of the exceptions (Figures 7-1 and 7-7). Transform faults are the sites of earthquakes, most of which do not affect people. Transform faults on land do pose a risk, however, as the San Andreas Fault has demonstrated. Ordinarily volcanism does not occur at transform faults.

The movement of the lithospheric plates is important to us for several reasons. Plate motion produces mountains (including volcanoes), the oceanic ridge system, trenches, and other features of Earth's surface (Figure 7-4). Certain natural hazards are likely to be found at plate boundaries (Figure 7-5a). Plate movements and interactions also concentrate many of the minerals we extract and use.

The theory of plate tectonics also helps explain how certain patterns of biological evolution occurred. By reconstructing how continents have drifted around for millions of years, we can trace how life forms migrated from one area to another when continents that are now far apart were joined together (Figure 7-32).

Many details of plate tectonic theory are missing, and it is constantly being updated and revised. So far, however, this theory has greatly advanced our knowledge of how the earth's geological, chemical, and biological processes are interconnected and interact in ways that help sustain life on Earth in the face of continuous changes in environmental conditions.

**EXTERNAL PROCESSES: EROSION, WEATHERING, AND MASS WASTING** Geological changes based directly or indirectly on energy from the sun and on gravity, instead of on heat in the earth's interior, are called *external processes*. Whereas internal processes generally build up the earth's surface, external processes tend to lower it.

The sun causes water to evaporate from the earth, as part of the hydrologic cycle (Figure 4-33). Precipitation in the form of rain can run off in streams, infiltrate into the ground as groundwater, and collect in lakes

Q: How much of the air pollution in the United States is produced by motor vehicles?

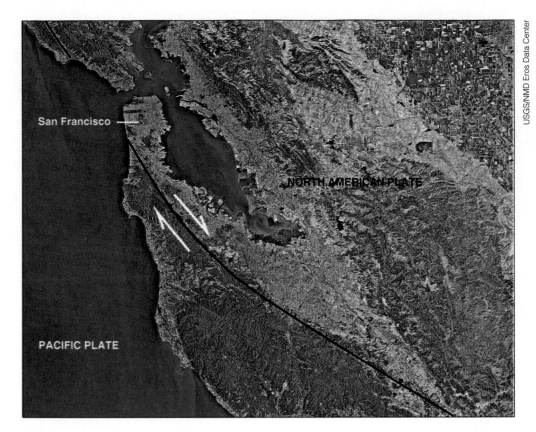

USGS/NMD Eros Data Center

**Figure 7-7** The San Andreas Fault in California is a transform fault on a continent. It connects an oceanic ridge segment in the Gulf of California with one off the coast of northern California and marks the boundary between the North American and the Pacific plates in that region. The relative movement is indicated by the arrows. When part of the fault locks, strain builds until the fault ruptures and movement occurs along the fault. The sudden release of strain produces an earthquake. The 1989 Loma Prieta earthquake near San Francisco, which killed 67 people, involved part of the San Andreas Fault. As long as the San Andreas Fault is active, Los Angeles will slowly move northward toward San Francisco.

and oceans. Snow can melt and do the same, or it may accumulate as snow fields that develop into glacier ice. Groundwater, streams, and glaciers remove loosened material, as well as material not yet separated, and deposit it in other places, a process called **erosion**. Waves and currents, generated by winds resulting from solar energy, do the same along the shores of lakes and oceans, and so does the wind itself (Figures 5-1 and 7-8). Streams are the most important agent of erosion, operating everywhere on Earth except in the polar regions. They produce ordinary valleys and canyons, and may form deltas where streams flow into lakes and oceans.

Gravity plays an important role in these processes. It is involved in the circulation of air in convection cells (Figures 5-6 and 5-7), which leads to precipitation, and in the downslope flow of water and the movement of glaciers. Gravity also causes sliding, flowing, and falling of rock and soil. In general, these processes have a leveling effect on the earth's surface.

Loosened material that can be eroded is usually produced by **weathering**. Weathering can occur as a result of mechanical processes, chemical processes, or both. In *mechanical weathering* a large rock mass is broken into smaller fragments of the original material, as though someone had used a hammer or a jackhammer. The most important agent of mechanical weathering is *frost wedging*, in which water collects in pores and

cracks of rock, expands upon freezing, and splits off pieces of the rock. Another important agent of mechanical weathering is fracturing in rocks from stress caused by the slow erosional removal of heavy overlying rock.

In *chemical weathering*, a mass of rock is decomposed by one or more chemical reactions, resulting in products that are chemically different from the original material. The products usually include both solid and dissolved components. Most chemical weathering involves reaction of rock material with oxygen, carbon dioxide, and moisture in the atmosphere and the ground (Figure 7-9).

Disintegration of rock by mechanical weathering accelerates chemical weathering by increasing the surface area that can be attacked by chemical weathering agents. This is similar to the way granulated sugar dissolves much faster than a large chunk of sugar. Chemical weathering is also aided by higher temperatures and precipitation, occurring most rapidly in tropical climates and next most rapidly in temperate climates.

Weathering is responsible for the development of soil. *Bed rock*, the solid rock mass of the earth, is sometimes exposed by weathering. Usually, however, bed rock lies under a blanket of unconsolidated material called *regolith*. If the regolith results from mechanical and chemical weathering, as most does, it is *residual regolith*; if it is deposited by wind, water, or ice, it is *transported regolith*.

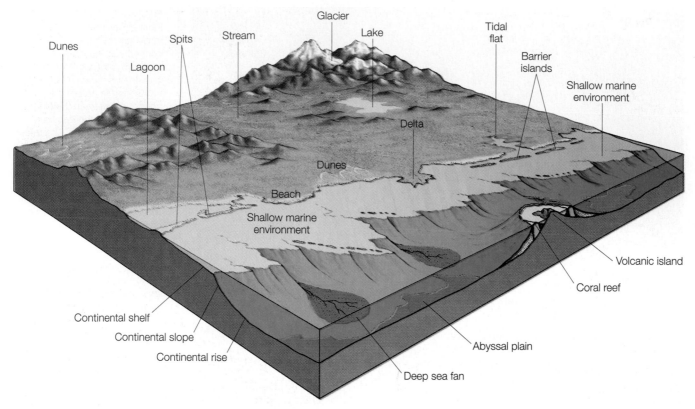

**Figure 7-8** Solar energy—through the hydrologic cycle and wind—and the force of gravity, along with the activities of organisms such as reef-building corals (Figure 4-1), have produced a variety of landforms and sedimentary environments.

Kenneth J. Van Dellen

**Figure 7-9** Chemical weathering of rock deposited by a glacier. Air and water weathered the surface of the granitelike rock, producing a shell of weathering products that surrounds it like the rind of an orange, except on the front where it has washed off. Weathering also happened in a fracture through the rock. The quartz grains of the parent rock are still present in the weathering rind, but some of the silicates have reacted with oxygen and carbonic acid to form clay, brown iron oxide, and soluble products. This is how soil is formed and how some trace elements are added to soil and groundwater. (The lens cap in the photo shows the relative size of the rock.)

Regolith or rock masses newly detached from underlying material may move downslope in various ways under the influence of gravity, without being carried in, on, or under a glacier, stream, or other agent of erosion. This transport of material is called **mass wasting**. The terms used to classify the types of mass wasting, such as *rockfall, rockslide, slump, creep, earthflow,* and *mudflow,* give clues to their characteristics. Mass wasting is most common on the sides of mountains above valleys and on the coasts of oceans and large lakes. Whenever streams, glaciers, or waves erode the landscape, producing cliffs or steep slopes, there is a potential for mass wasting. However, under the right conditions, it can occur even on quite gentle slopes.

Another agent of erosion is a **glacier** (Figure 7-8)—a flowing body of ice, formed in a region where snowfall exceeds melting. Under the influence of gravity, glaciers move slowly down a valley on a mountainside, as in the Alps, or over a wide area, as in Antarctica. Glaciers erode by abrasion and by their own unique process, called *plucking,* in which glacial ice freezes to rock and pulls fragments out when the glacier flows. Glaciers transport most of their eroded sediment within the ice, at or near the underside of the glacier.

Q: How much of the oil used in the United States is consumed by motor vehicles?

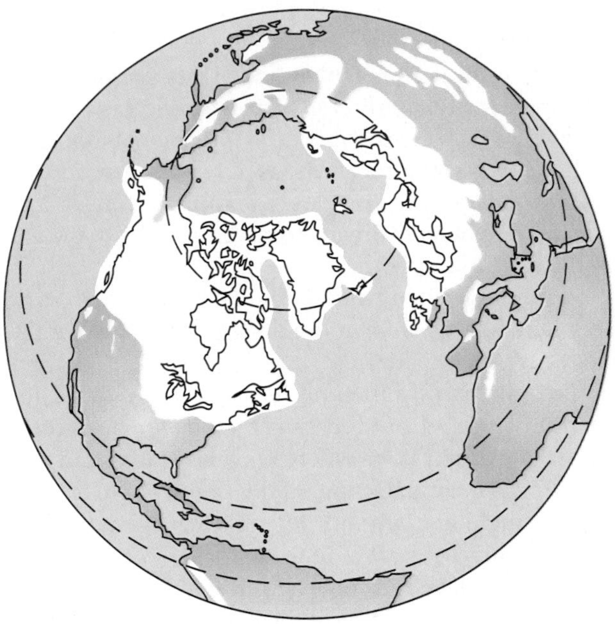

**Figure 7-11** A few minerals consist of a single element. One example is gold, shown here in the crevice of a rock in Colorado.

**Figure 7-12** Most rock-forming minerals consist of quartz, a form of silica (silicon dioxide, $SiO_2$).

**Figure 7-10** The region that was covered by ice at various times during the most recent glaciation, which ended about 10,000 years ago. During the past 2.0–2.5 million years, much of the Northern Hemisphere was covered several times with thick ice sheets. These glacial periods alternated with warmer interglacial periods. Moving ice sheets, up to 3 kilometers (2 miles) thick in the north and 1.6 kilometers (1 mile) thick in the Great Lakes area, modified much of the earth's surface by erosion and deposition as they advanced and melted back.

During the last ice age, which ended about 10,000 years ago, ice sheets called continental glaciers covered vast areas of North America, Europe, and Asia (Figure 7-10). In North America ice scoured and gouged rock from parts of Canada and New England, and dumped the sediment as *moraines* such as those that wrapped around Lakes Michigan, Huron, and Erie like multistrand necklaces. The Great Lakes, the largest mass of fresh water in the world, occupy glacially eroded stream valleys that filled with water as the glaciers melted back.

Human activities, particularly those that destroy the vegetation, accelerate erosion. Overgrazing, overcultivating, timbering, surface mining, construction, and off-road vehicles all can contribute to erosion. Soils and soil erosion are discussed in more detail in Chapter 12.

## 7-3  Mineral Resources and the Rock Cycle

**MINERALS AND ROCKS**  A **mineral** is an element or an inorganic compound that occurs naturally and is solid. It usually has a crystalline internal structure made up of an orderly, three-dimensional arrangement of atoms or ions. All of the earth's crust, except the rather small proportion composed of organic material, is made of minerals.

Some minerals consist of a single element, such as gold (Figure 7-11), silver, diamond (carbon), and sulfur. However, most of the over 2,000 identified minerals occur as inorganic compounds formed by various combinations of the eight elements that make up 98.5% by weight of the earth's crust (Figure 7-3). Examples are salt, mica, and quartz (Figure 7-12), all of which, along with many others, have economic importance. Other minerals are important mainly as rock formers.

**Rock** is any material that makes up a large, natural, continuous part of the earth's crust. Some kinds of rock, such as limestone (calcium carbonate, or $CaCO_3$) and quartzite (silicon dioxide, or $SiO_2$), contain only one mineral, but most rocks consist of two or more minerals. A few kinds of rocks are made of nonmineral material.

**THE ROCK CYCLE** Geologic processes constantly redistribute the chemical elements within and at the surface of the earth. Based on the way it forms, rock is placed in three broad classes: igneous, sedimentary, and metamorphic.

**Igneous rock** can form below the earth's surface as well as on it when magma wells up from the upper mantle or deep crust, cools, and hardens into rock. Igneous rock masses such as granite (Figure 7-13) that form underground are called *igneous intrusions*. These generally form beneath sites of volcanic activity, which are mostly at convergent and divergent plate boundaries (Figures 7-5 and 7-6). They appear at the earth's surface only after the rocks above them have eroded away. Because rock is a good heat insulator, igneous intrusions usually cool very slowly, allowing enough time for mineral grains or crystals to grow

Kenneth J. Van Dellen

**Figure 7-13** This granite consists of four types of mineral grains or crystals. The magma from which it formed cooled very slowly, so large crystals developed from the melt. (The staple in the photo shows the relative size of the crystals.) Because granite is hard, strong, and weather-resistant, and takes a fine polish, it is widely used in office buildings and monuments.

until they are large enough to be distinguished easily without magnification.

When magma reaches the earth's surface from volcanoes or through cracks, it is called **lava**. After cooling and hardening it is *extrusive igneous rock*, also called lava or lava rock. The rapid cooling produces either a fine-grained or glassy texture, because large crystals do not have time to form. Basalt, obsidian, and pumice are examples.

Although often covered by sedimentary rocks or soil, igneous rocks form the bulk of the earth's crust. They also are the main source of many nonfuel mineral resources. Granite and its relatives are used for monuments and as decorative stone in buildings, basalt as crushed stone where gravel is scarce, and volcanic rocks in landscaping. Many of the popular gemstones, such as diamond, tourmaline, garnet, ruby, and sapphire, are part of igneous rocks.

**Sedimentary rock** forms from sediment in several ways. Most such rocks are formed when preexisting rocks are weathered and eroded into small pieces, transported from their sources, and deposited in a body of surface water. As these deposited layers become buried and compacted, the resulting pressure causes their particles to bond together to form sedimentary rocks such as sandstone and shale. Some sedimentary rocks, such as dolomite and limestone, are formed from the compacted shells, skeletons, and other remains of dead organisms. Lignite and bituminous coal are sedimentary rocks derived from plant remains (Figure 7-14). Other sedimentary rocks, such as rock salt, gypsum, and several limestones, are precipitated from solution.

In most places sedimentary rocks are not more than 100 meters (330 feet) thick, but they cover nearly three-fourths of Earth's land surface. Besides making up much of the planet's scenic landscape, some sedimentary rocks are important resources. Limestone, for

**Figure 7-14** Stages in the formation of coal over millions of years. Peat is a soil material made of moist, partially decomposed organic matter. Lignite and bituminous coal are sedimentary rocks, and anthracite is a metamorphic rock.

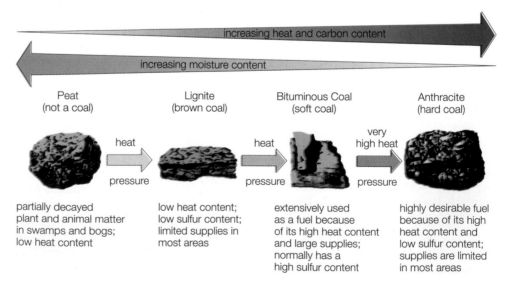

Q: Worldwide, how much of urban land is devoted to roads and parking?

example, is used as crushed stone, as building stone, as flux in blast furnaces for smelting iron ore, and with shale for making Portland cement.

**Metamorphic rock** is produced when a preexisting rock is subjected to high temperatures (which may cause it to melt partially), high pressures, chemically active fluids, or a combination of those agents. Anthracite (Figure 7-14), slate used for roofs and floors of buildings (Figure 7-15), and marble (formed from limestone and also used in buildings, sculptures, and monuments) are economically important metamorphic rocks. Talc, asbestos, graphite, titanium, and some gems are also found in metamorphic rocks.

Rocks are constantly being exposed to various physical and chemical conditions that over time can change them. The interaction of processes that change rocks from one type to another is called the **rock cycle** (Figure 7-16). Recycling material over millions of years, this slowest of Earth's cyclic processes is responsible for concentrating mineral resources on which humans depend.

## CLASSIFICATION OF MINERAL RESOURCES

A **mineral resource** is a concentration of naturally occurring solid, liquid, or gaseous material, in or on the earth's crust, in such form and amount that its extraction and conversion into useful materials are currently or potentially profitable. Internal and external Earth processes have produced numerous mineral resources, which are mostly essentially nonrenewable because of

**Figure 7-15** These rocks, near Negaunee, Michigan, were once layers of mud that included some layers of sand. They then became shale with sandstone beds. As a result of a mountain-building event about 1.75 billion years ago, they have been tilted to near vertical, and metamorphosed to slate (dark) with quartzite (light).

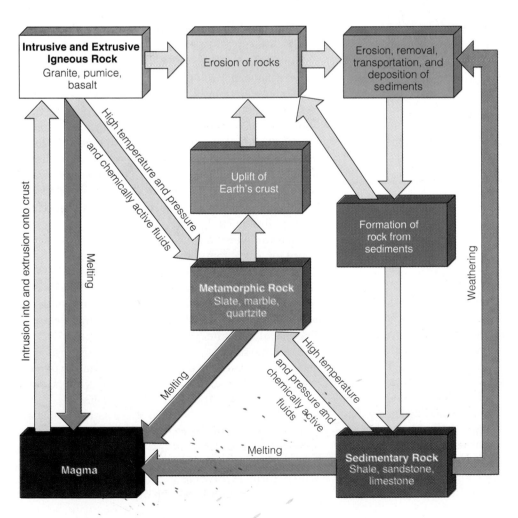

**Figure 7-16** The rock cycle, the slowest of Earth's cyclic processes. Earth's materials are recycled over millions of years by three processes: melting, erosion, and metamorphism. These processes produce igneous, sedimentary, and metamorphic rocks, respectively. Rock of any of the three classes can be converted to rock of either of the other two classes or can even be recycled within its own class.

A: At least 33% (50% in the United States)

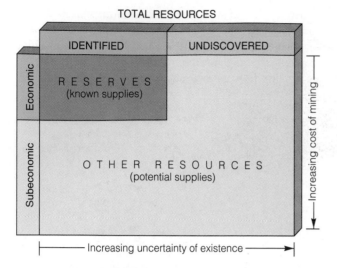

TOTAL RESOURCES

IDENTIFIED | UNDISCOVERED

Economic

R E S E R V E S
(known supplies)

Subeconomic

O T H E R   R E S O U R C E S
(potential supplies)

Increasing cost of mining

Increasing uncertainty of existence

**Figure 7-17** General classification of mineral resources by the U.S. Geological Survey. Note that this is not an area graph depicting abundance of reserves relative to other resources.

Kenneth J. Van Dellen

**Figure 7-18** This rock, known as Lake Superior Banded Iron Formation (or BIF), consists of alternating bands of shiny gray hematite, an iron oxide; and red jasper, a flintlike rock that is colored red by iron oxide. Most of our iron comes from rock similar to this that was deposited in many parts of the world between 1.8 and 3.2 billion years ago. This outcrop of rock is near Ishpeming, Michigan.

the slowness of the rock cycle. They include *energy resources* (coal, oil, natural gas, uranium, geothermal energy; Figure 3-6), *metallic mineral resources* (iron, copper, aluminum), and *nonmetallic mineral resources* (salt, gypsum, clay, sand, phosphates, water, soil; Figure 1-9).

The U.S. Geological Survey divides mineral resources into two broad categories, identified and undiscovered, based on degree of geologic understanding and certainty that the resource exists (Figure 7-17). **Identified resources** are deposits of a particular mineral resource that have a known location, quantity, and quality or that are estimated from direct geological evidence and measurements. **Reserves** are identified resources

that can be extracted economically at present prices with current mining technology. **Undiscovered resources** are potential supplies of a particular mineral resource that are believed to exist on the basis of geologic knowledge and theory, though specific locations, quality, and amounts are unknown. **Other resources** are identified and unidentified resources not classified as reserves.

Most published estimates of particular mineral resources refer only to reserves. Reserves can be increased when exploration finds previously undiscovered, economic-grade mineral resources. They can also be increased when identified subeconomic-grade mineral resources become economically viable because of new technology or higher prices.

**FORMATION AND CONCENTRATION OF MINERAL RESOURCES** Some metals seem more abundant than they really are in the earth's crust because slow-acting, infrequent, or localized processes have selectively concentrated them into ores. An **ore** is a metal-yielding material that can be economically extracted at a given time.

Copper, for example, makes up 0.0058% by weight of the earth's crust, but copper ore must contain at least 0.5% copper; thus the concentration of copper in ore is at least 86 times (0.5/0.0058) its average crustal abundance. Aluminum ore must have 3.7 times the average crustal abundance of that metal, and iron 5 times. However, the gold in gold ore must be concentrated 1,600 times its crustal average, and mercury an astonishing 100,000 times.

This limited and uneven concentration of nonrenewable metal resources raises serious questions about the wisdom of extracting concentrated deposits and scattering them all over the countryside in landfills, junkyards, or refuse dumps. Instead, we should think of discarded items made of these nonrenewable materials as potential resources to be recycled and reused to reduce energy use, extraction of virgin minerals, pollution, and waste.

Groundwater that circulates down to subduction zones of high temperature and pressure beneath developing mountains (Figure 7-6) can dissolve materials from rocks there and form mineral deposits elsewhere. Also, water containing dissolved minerals can be released in the late stages of the cooling of magma. These waters, called *hydrothermal solutions*, may be injected into fissures and pores, where they form veins and other types of ore deposits. Lead, zinc, copper, tin, gold, silver, mercury, tungsten, and molybdenum are some of the metals found in such deposits.

Sulfide ores of several of these same metals are produced by hydrothermal solutions at undersea hot springs, called *black smokers* because of the black specks of metal sulfides in the water. These vents, which form at divergent plate boundaries on the seafloor, also support marine organisms that produce

Q: What is the average government subsidy per car in the United States?

Earth's rocks and the fossils in them help us decipher some of the planet's history. The oldest known indication of life is found in 3.5- billion-year-old rocks that contain peculiar limestone structures called *stromatolites*, produced by and covered with a mat of fossilized marine cyanobacteria (Figure 7-19).

Chemical analysis of these ancient rocks shows that the cyanobacteria were photosynthetic. Because photosynthesis releases oxygen, dissolved oxygen gradually accumulated in the seawater. As the oxygen level increased, the gas eventually began to escape into the atmosphere, leading to the modern oxygen-rich troposphere and UV-filtering ozone in the stratosphere that together made possible the existence of life on land. One strand of evidence that the atmospheric oxygen content was changing is that red sediments, which are colored by strongly oxidized iron, appear in rocks as old as 2.5–2.8 billion years.

C. A. Henley/Biofotos

**Figure 7-19** Stromatolites in Shark Bay, Australia. These limestone structures are similar to those deposited as much as 3.5 billion years ago by photosynthetic cyanobacteria (formerly known as blue-green algae). A matlike cyanobacterial community covers the outer surface of living stromatolites. Tiny particles of calcium carbonate collect among the filamentous organisms when the tide is high and water covers the structures. Over time this slowly builds up thin layers of rock. About 2 billion years ago stromatolites probably were a common feature on Earth, but today they still exist only in a few places.

The rocks that form the major economically important deposits of iron ore were laid down because of the release of oxygen into the oceans by these ancient cyanobacteria. The oxygen combined with dissolved iron in these ancient oceans, changing it to a less soluble form that precipitated out of solution, settled to the bottom of the ocean, and became part of sediments. Over millions of years, these deposits formed thick deposits of Lake Superior Banded Iron Formation that are mined today from Minnesota and Michigan (Figure 7-18) to Australia. This is a striking example of how life, the atmosphere, and Earth's crust have interacted over billions of years.

organic nutrients by chemosynthesis. These deposits are mined in places where the seafloor has been shoved up above sea level, such as Cyprus (for which copper is named) and Japan.

Erosion of igneous, metamorphic, and sedimentary rocks leads to the concentration of several kinds of mineral resources. Seawater contains many soluble weathering products brought in from the land, but the only minerals we currently get from the sea are salt, bromine, and magnesium. These same materials are also obtained from natural *brine*—a concentrated solution of salts derived from seawater or desert lakes by evaporating some of the water.

Weathering in the tropics produces residual soils known as *laterite*. They are red from the iron oxide they contain and are usually rather hard. All of our aluminum and some iron, manganese, and nickel come from laterites.

Solid grains and fragments of economic-grade minerals that have been eroded from rocks are carried by streams and deposited at places along the stream channel or in beaches and offshore sands. This type of deposit, called a *placer* (pronounced PLASS-er), may concentrate titanium, gold, diamond, platinum, tin, niobium, tantalum, or uranium. The gold the forty-niners panned for in the California gold rush was in placers eroded from veins, the "mother lode," on the west slope of the Sierra Nevada.

Mineral resources have also been concentrated by consolidation of sediment into sedimentary rock or formation of sedimentary rock when changed conditions cause dissolved materials to precipitate out of solution. Examples include banded iron formations (the main source of iron ore; Figure 7-18), sandstone, and the sediments of former sand dunes, beaches, and stream deposits. Analyses of such deposits give us evidence about interactions among the earth's crust, atmosphere, and life during the planet's long history (Spotlight, above).

When water in marine lagoons or desert lakes evaporates partly or completely, with nearly constant replacement of lost water, various minerals, called *evaporites*, are deposited. Salt, gypsum (used in drywall and plaster of Paris), potassium minerals (potash used in commercial inorganic fertilizers), and soda ash and sodium sulfate (used in glass, insecticides, paper, and other products) are evaporites.

A: $1,600 per year

**Figure 7-20** This open-pit copper mine in Bingham, Utah, the largest humanmade hole in the world, is 4.0 kilometers (2.5 miles) in diameter and 0.8 kilometer (0.5 mile) deep. It produces 227,000 metric tons (250,000 tons) of copper a year, along with fairly large amounts of gold, silver, and molybdenum, and releases enormous amounts of toxic chemicals. The amount of material removed from this mine is seven times the amount moved to build the Panama Canal.

Organisms have also contributed to sedimentary mineral resources. Certain bacteria extract sulfur from gypsum and anhydrite (calcium sulfate minerals), producing rich deposits of pure sulfur that occur underground in places along the Gulf Coast of the United States. Phosphate rock deposits, which are formed in the phosphorous cycle (Figure 4-31), are phosphate bones and teeth of fish and other organisms or chemically precipitated phosphate, or sometimes both. Peat, lignite, and bituminous coal result from the transformation of accumulated plant remains (Figure 7-14). Petroleum and natural gas result indirectly from sedimentary processes involving the remains of organisms.

## 7-4 Locating and Extracting Crustal Resources

**FINDING AND MINING CRUSTAL RESOURCES**
Mining companies use several methods to find promising mineral deposits. Geological information about plate tectonics (Figure 7-5) and mineral formation suggests areas for closer study. Aerial photos and satellite images sometimes reveal rock formations associated with certain minerals. Other instruments on planes and satellites can detect mineral deposits by their effects on Earth's magnetic or gravitational fields.

After profitable deposits of minerals are located, deep deposits are extracted by **subsurface mining** and shallow deposits by **surface mining**. Subsurface mining disturbs less than one-tenth as much land as surface mining and usually produces less waste material. However, it leaves much of the resource in the ground and is more dangerous and expensive than surface mining. For example, roofs and walls of underground mines collapse, trapping and killing miners; explosions of dust and natural gas injure or kill them; and prolonged inhalation of mining dust causes lung diseases.

In surface mining, mechanized equipment strips away the **overburden** of soil and rock, and usually discards it, a waste material called **spoil**. Surface mining extracts about 90% by weight of mineral and rock resources and more than 60% by weight of the coal in the United States.

The type of surface mining used depends on the resource being sought and on the local topography. In **open-pit mining** machines dig holes and remove ores such as iron and copper (Figure 7-20). This method is also used for sand and gravel and for building stone

**Q:** What percentage of Earth's land area is covered by forests?

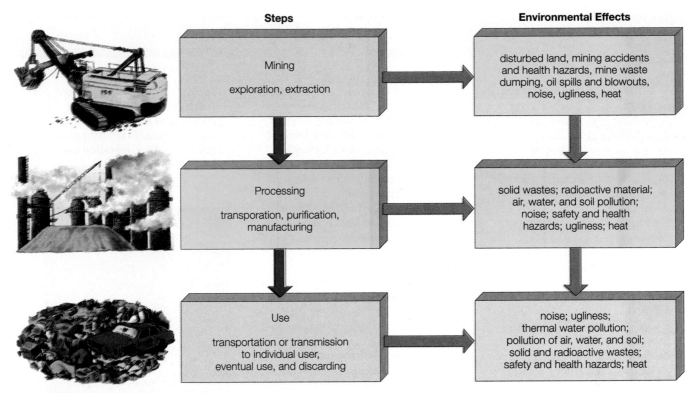

| Steps | Environmental Effects |
|---|---|
| **Mining**<br><br>exploration, extraction | disturbed land, mining accidents and health hazards, mine waste dumping, oil spills and blowouts, noise, ugliness, heat |
| **Processing**<br><br>transporation, purification, manufacturing | solid wastes; radioactive material; air, water, and soil pollution; noise; safety and health hazards; ugliness; heat |
| **Use**<br><br>transportation or transmission to individual user, eventual use, and discarding | noise; ugliness; thermal water pollution; pollution of air, water, and soil; solid and radioactive wastes; safety and health hazards; heat |

**Figure 7-21** Some harmful environmental effects of resource extraction, processing, and use. The energy used to carry out each step causes further pollution and environmental degradation. This harm could be minimized by requiring that the full costs of the pollution and environmental degradation caused by mining, processing, and manufacturing companies be included in the price of their products. Many of these "external" costs are now passed on to society as a whole in the form of poorer health, increased health and insurance costs, and increased taxes to deal with pollution and environmental degradation.

such as limestone, sandstone, slate, granite, and marble. Another form of surface mining is **dredging**, in which chain buckets and draglines scrape up underwater mineral deposits.

**Strip mining** is surface mining in which bulldozers, power shovels, or stripping wheels remove the overburden in strips. It is used mostly for removing coal (Spotlight, p. 188) and some phosphate rock.

**ENVIRONMENTAL IMPACTS** The mining, processing, and use of crustal resources requires enormous amounts of energy and often causes land disturbance, erosion, and air and water pollution (Figure 7-21).

After extraction from the ground many resources must be separated from other matter, a process that can pollute the air and water. Ore, for example, typically contains two parts: the ore mineral, which contains the desired metal, and the **gangue**, which is the waste mineral material. **Beneficiation**, or separation in a mill of the ore mineral from the gangue, produces waste called **tailings**.

Mining can affect the environment in several ways. Most noticeable are scarring and disruption of the land surface (Figures 7-20 and 7-22), and the ugli-

ness of spoil heaps and tailings. Underground fires in coal mines sometimes cannot be put out. Land above underground mines collapses or subsides, causing roads to buckle, houses to tilt, railroad tracks to bend, sewer lines to crack, gas mains to break, and groundwater systems to be disrupted. In addition, spoil heaps and tailings can be eroded by wind and water. The air can be contaminated with dust and toxic substances, and water pollution is a serious concern.

*Acid mine drainage* occurs when aerobic bacteria produce sulfuric acid from iron sulfide minerals in spoil from coal mines and some ore mines. Rainwater seeping through the mine or mine wastes may carry the acid to nearby streams, destroying aquatic life and contaminating surface water supplies (Figure 7-25). It may also infiltrate the ground and contaminate groundwater. Other harmful materials running off, or dissolved from underground mines or aboveground mining wastes, are radioactive uranium compounds and compounds of toxic metals such as lead, arsenic, or cadmium.

Most ore minerals do not consist of pure metal, so **smelting** is done to separate the metal from the other elements in the ore mineral. Without effective

Surface mining is used to extract almost two-thirds of the coal used in the United States. Most surface-mined coal is removed by area strip mining or contour strip mining, depending on the terrain.

*Area strip mining* is used where the terrain is fairly flat. An earthmover strips away the overburden, and then a power shovel digs a cut to remove a mineral deposit, such as coal. After the mineral is removed, the trench is filled with overburden, and a new cut is made parallel to the previous one. This process is repeated for the entire deposit. If the land is not restored, this type of mining leaves a wavy series of highly erodible hills of rubble called *spoil banks* (Figure 7-22).

*Contour strip mining* is used in hilly or mountainous terrain. A power shovel cuts a series of terraces into the side of a hill (Figure 7-23). An earthmover removes the overburden and a power shovel extracts the coal, with the overbur-

den from each new terrace dumped onto the one below. Unless the land is restored, a wall of dirt is left in front of a highly erodible bank of soil and rock called a *highwall*. Sometimes giant augers are used to drill horizontally into a hillside to extract underground coal.

In the United States contour strip mining for coal is used mostly in the mountainous Appalachian region. If the land is not restored (Figure 7-24), this type of surface mining has a devastating impact on the land.

*Subsurface mining* is used to remove coal too deep to be extracted by surface mining. Miners dig a deep vertical shaft, blast subsurface tunnels and rooms to get to the deposit, and haul the coal or ore to the surface. In the *room-and-pillar method* as much as half of the coal is left in place as pillars to prevent the mine from collapsing. In the *longwall method* a narrow tunnel is dug and then supported by movable metal pillars. After a cutting machine has removed the coal or ore from part of

the mineral seam, the roof supports are moved forward, allowing the earth behind the supports to collapse. No tunnels are left behind after the mining operation has been completed.

**Figure 7-22** Effects of area strip mining of coal near Mulla, Colorado. Restoration of newly strip-mined areas is now required in the United States, but many previously mined areas have not been restored.

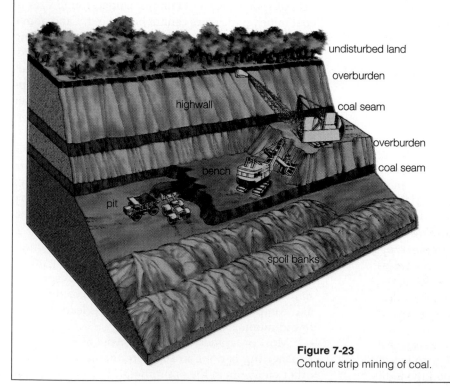

undisturbed land
overburden
coal seam
overburden
coal seam
highwall
bench
pit
spoil banks

**Figure 7-23**
Contour strip mining of coal.

**Figure 7-24** Grantsville, Maryland. With the land returned to its original contour and grass planted to hold the soil in place, it is hard to tell that this was once a site of surface coal mining. However, about three-fourths of the coal that can be surface mined in the United States is in the West, in arid and semi-arid regions, where the climate and the soil usually prevent full restoration.

Q: What percentage of Earth's land area is covered by tropical forests?

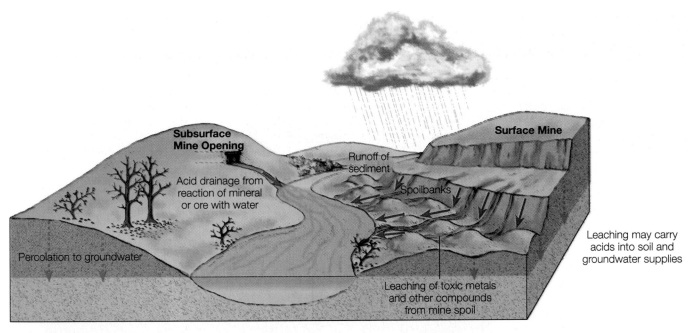

**Figure 7-25** Degradation and pollution of a stream and groundwater by runoff of acids—called acid mine drainage—and toxic chemicals from surface and subsurface mining operations. These substances can kill fish and other aquatic life. In the United States acid mine drainage has damaged over 26,000 kilometers (16,000 miles) of streams, mostly in Appalachia and in the West.

**Figure 7-26** Sulfur dioxide and other fumes from a nickel smelter that has operated for several decades at Sudbury, Ontario, Canada, have killed the forest once found on this land around the smelter.

pollution control equipment, smelters emit enormous quantities of air pollutants, which damage vegetation and soils in the surrounding area. Pollutants include sulfur dioxide, soot, and tiny particles of arsenic, cadmium, lead, and other toxic elements and compounds found in many ores. For example, decades of uncontrolled sulfur dioxide emissions from copper-smelting operations near Copperhill and Ducktown, Tennessee, killed all vegetation over a wide area around the smelter. Another dead zone has been created around

the Sudbury, Ontario, nickel smelter in Canada (Figure 7-26). New dead zones are forming in parts of eastern Europe, the Commonwealth of Independent States, and Chile. Smelters also cause water pollution and produce liquid and solid hazardous wastes that must be disposed of safely.

The burning of fossil fuels, the manufacture of items from mineral resources, and the use and discarding of many of these items produce solid waste (Chapter 19), hazardous waste (Chapter 21), air pollution (Chapter 22), and water pollution (Chapter 23).

## 7-5 Natural Hazards

Earth's internal and external processes cause **natural hazards**, events that destroy or damage wildlife habitats and kill or harm humans and damage property. Earthquakes and volcanoes are the result of internal Earth processes. Floods and mass wasting are the result of external Earth processes.

**EARTHQUAKES** Stress can cause solid rock to deform elastically until it suddenly fractures and is displaced along the fracture, producing a *fault* (Figures 7-1 and 7-7). The faulting or a later abrupt movement on an

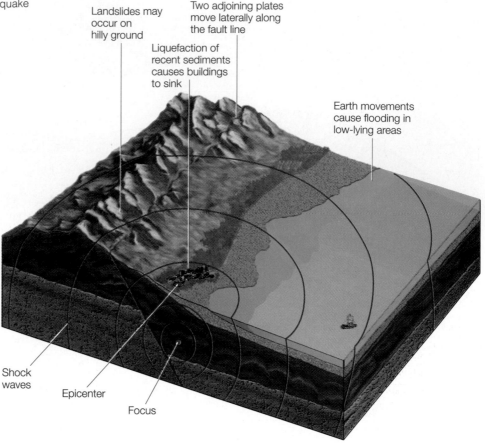

**Figure 7-27** Major features of an earthquake and its effects.

Landslides may occur on hilly ground

Liquefaction of recent sediments causes buildings to sink

Two adjoining plates move laterally along the fault line

Earth movements cause flooding in low-lying areas

Shock waves

Epicenter

Focus

existing fault causes an **earthquake**. Movements may occur repeatedly on an existing fault separated by irregular intervals of quiet that sometimes last many years.

Three kinds of human activities have caused or increased earthquake activity, also called seismic activity. The added load of water in Lake Mead behind Hoover Dam caused numerous tremors in the early years after the dam was completed, and this has happened elsewhere as well. Underground nuclear testing and deep-well disposal of liquid wastes have also caused minor earthquakes, most of which have not done much damage.

An earthquake has certain features and impacts (Figure 7-27). Earthquakes set up shock waves that radiate out from the center of movement like ripples in a pool of water. Reports of an earthquake commonly mention the focus and the epicenter. The *focus* is the point of initial movement, and the *epicenter* is the point on the surface directly above the focus. The epicenter may not be on the fault, either because the fault does not reach the surface or because the fault is not vertical and, therefore, surfaces some distance away from the epicenter. When the stressed parts of the earth suddenly fracture or shift, energy is released as shock waves that move outward from the earthquake's focus.

One way of measuring the severity of an earthquake is by its **magnitude** on the Richter scale. The magnitude is a measure of the amount of energy released in the earthquake, as indicated by the amplitude (size) of the vibrations when they reach the recording instrument. Using this scale seismologists rate earthquakes as *insignificant* (less than 4 on the Richter scale), *minor* (4–4.9), *damaging* (5–5.9), *destructive* (6–6.9), *major* (7–7.9), and *great* (over 8). The northern California earthquake of 1989 had a Richter magnitude of 7.1 and caused damage within a radius of 97 kilometers (60 miles) from its epicenter (Figure 7-28).

Each higher step on the Richter scale represents an amplitude that is 10 times greater than the step below, so a magnitude 5 earthquake is 10 times greater than a magnitude 4, and a magnitude 6 quake is 100 times greater than a magnitude 4. The amount of energy released is in the range of 30 times greater for each higher step on the scale. Earthquakes often have *aftershocks* that gradually decrease in frequency over a period of up to several months, and some have *foreshocks* from seconds to weeks before the main shock.

A map of earthquake epicenters shows that earthquakes are most common at all three types of lithospheric plate boundaries (Figure 7-5a), but they also

Q: How rapidly are the world's remaining tropical forests vanishing?

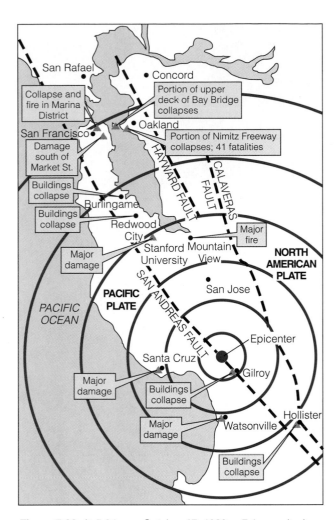

**Figure 7-28** At 5:04 P.M., October 17, 1989, a 7.1-magnitude earthquake occurred in northern California along the San Andreas Fault (Figure 7-7). It was the largest earthquake in northern California since 1906, when the great San Francisco quake and the resulting fires destroyed much of San Francisco. In the 1989 quake the most extensive damage was within a radius of 32 kilometers (20 miles) from the epicenter, but seismic waves caused major damage as far away as San Francisco and Oakland. Sixty-seven people were killed, and official damage estimates were as high as $10 billion. This was North America's costliest natural disaster until Hurricane Andrew devastated Florida in 1992.

## Earthquakes and Mass Wasting in the Peruvian Andes

**CASE STUDY** On May 31, 1970, a major disaster occurred on Nevado Huascaran, a 6,768-meter (22,190-foot) peak in the Cordillera Blanca region of the Peruvian Andes. It began with a 7.7-magnitude earthquake in the subduction zone near the Pacific coast, about 100 kilometers (60 miles) west of the mountain.

This earthquake turned out to be the deadliest ever recorded in the Western Hemisphere. It shook down the adobe homes of villagers and triggered thousands of small landslides.

The earthquake also dislodged a huge mass of overhanging rock and ice from the glacier near the top of the mountain. This material fell about 900 meters (3,000 feet), partially melted on impact, and picked up rock debris. Then the mixture of water, mud, rock, and ice swept down on the village of Yungay at speeds approaching 500 kilometers (310 miles) per hour.

At Yungay at least 20,000 people were killed, mostly from this debris avalanche, and throughout the region the death toll reached about 70,000. There were three main causes for this tremendous loss of life and property: the earthquake itself, the avalanche, and floods sent downstream when the avalanche reached the Rio Santa. This shows how one geologic event can trigger a chain of events.

This was not the first natural disaster in this area. In 1870 Yungay was wiped out by a debris avalanche, and several other villages were destroyed by another in 1941. Still another demolished several villages and killed at least 3,500 people in 1962.

---

occur at many intraplate sites away from plate boundaries. Shallow-focus earthquakes, those with a focal depth less than 70 kilometers (43 miles), occur in all earthquake zones and are generally more damaging than deeper ones. Intermediate- and deep-focus earthquakes, those with a focal depth between 70 kilometers (43 miles) and 700 kilometers (430 miles), occur only at convergent plate boundaries (Figure 7-5). Divergent plate boundaries at oceanic spreading centers, such as the Mid-Atlantic Ridge, present a rather low risk of damage from earthquakes because they are either far from land or not near densely populated areas.

*Intraplate seismicity* (as in Hawaii) may be related to the movement of magma at mantle plumes or to settling over a magma chamber. At other intraplate sites, such as the New Madrid fault zone in the region south of the southern tip of Illinois, earthquakes revealed the presence of old faults. The cause of many intraplate earthquakes that have occurred in the eastern United States is unknown.

The primary effects of earthquakes include shaking and sometimes permanent vertical or horizontal displacement of the ground. These may have serious effects on people and structures, such as buildings, bridges, freeway overpasses, dams, and pipelines. Secondary effects of earthquakes include various types of mass wasting (such as rockfalls and rockslides; Case Study, above), urban fires, and flooding due to

---

**Figure 7-29 (a)** Expected damage from earthquakes in Canada. Because Canada is not as heavily populated as the United States, overall earthquake damage is expected to be less severe. **(b)** Expected damage from earthquakes in the contiguous United States. Except for a few regions along the Atlantic and the Gulf Coast, virtually every part of the continental United States is subject to some risk from earthquakes, but several areas have a risk of moderate-to-major damage. Earthquakes occur along fault zones such as the San Andreas (Figure 7-7) or in intraplate areas such as the New Madrid zone south of the tip of Illinois. This latter zone is now considered by some to be the area of highest risk for a major earthquake in the lower 48 states. (Data from U.S. Geological Survey and *Energy, Mines, and Resources Canada*, 1976)

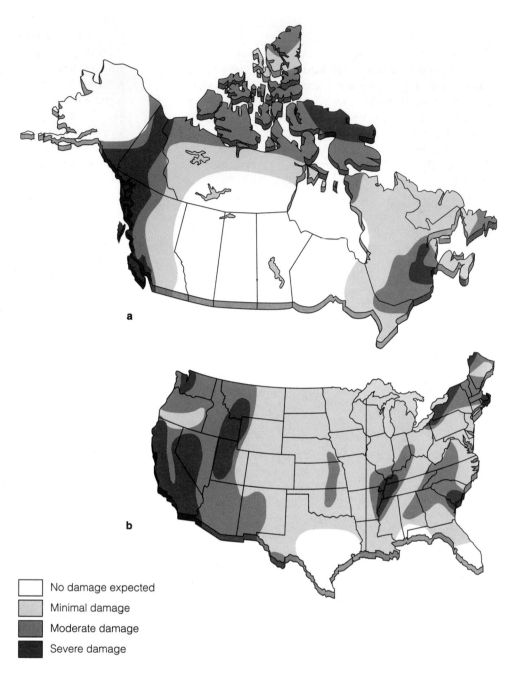

| | No damage expected |
| | Minimal damage |
| | Moderate damage |
| | Severe damage |

subsidence of land. Coastal areas can also be severely damaged by large, earthquake-generated water waves, called *tsunamis* (misnamed "tidal waves," although they have nothing to do with tides), that travel as fast as 950 kilometers (590 miles) per hour. Two of the worst earthquakes, in terms of lives lost, happened in China, with about 830,000 killed in 1556 and 500,000 in 1976.

Loss of life and property from earthquakes can be reduced. To do this we must locate active fault zones, make maps showing where ground conditions are more subject to shaking, establish building codes that regulate the placement and design of buildings in areas of high risk, and, hopefully, learn to predict when and where earthquakes will occur.

Because movement on a fault may be infrequent, it is sometimes difficult to determine whether a fault is active. Thus it is important to look at historical records of earthquakes and to do geologic field research that can indicate how recently a fault has moved. Maps indicating earthquake risk, based on such research,

Q: At current loss rates, when will most remaining tropical forests be gone?

have been developed and are being continually revised (Figure 7-29).

Actual prediction of earthquakes will have to be based primarily on *precursor phenomena*, events that precede an earthquake, as well as on the pattern and frequency of earthquakes in an area. Seismologists are collecting data on precursor phenomena on active faults in many places around the world, but the San Andreas (Figure 7-7) is the most heavily instrumented fault anywhere. Precursor phenomena include such characteristics of earth materials as slight tilting of rock and changes in electrical and magnetic properties, the amount of radon (a radioactive gas) dissolved in groundwater, the speed of seismic waves passing through the area from nearby quakes, and even the unusual behavior of animals that may be able to sense an imminent earthquake.

VOLCANOES An active **volcano** occurs where magma reaches the earth's surface through a central vent or a long crack (fissure). Such volcanic activity can release *ejecta* (debris ranging from large chunks of lava rock to ash that may be glowing hot), liquid lava, and gases (water vapor, carbon dioxide, sulfur dioxide, nitrogen, and others) into the environment.

Volcanic activity is concentrated, for the most part, in the same areas as seismic activity (Figure 7-5a). It usually occurs at divergent and convergent plate boundaries (Figure 7-5b), sometimes at intraplate sites, and perhaps at a few transform faults.

The volcanoes at convergent plate boundaries include Fujiyama (part of the volcanic island arc in Japan), Mount St. Helens in Washington (Case Study, p. 194), and Mount Pinatubo in the Philippines (which erupted in 1991). All have the steep, flaring cone shape characteristic of volcanoes at convergent plate boundaries. They usually erupt explosively and eject particulate matter and gases into the atmosphere that can reflect some incoming sunlight and cause short-term (1–4 years) global atmospheric cooling.

Volcanic eruptions at divergent boundaries, as in the islands of Iceland and the East African rift valleys, are ordinarily quieter. There lava typically just flows, or sprays into the air in a steady stream, from fissures, although steep cones occasionally occur.

Intraplate volcanism has an eruptive style related to the geologic location. Those in the ocean, as on Hawaii, erupt very quietly, like those at divergent boundaries, but from the summit or flanks of cones. This produces a broad, gently sloping cone, down which the lava flows in a stream. The main hazard from the Hawaiian volcanoes is lava flows, which can cover roads and villages and ignite brush, trees, and homes in the process.

Prediction of volcanic activity has improved considerably during this century, but every volcano has its own personality. As with earthquake maps, the eruptive history of a volcano or volcanic center gives some indication of where the risks are. Much experience has been gained at the Hawaii Volcano Observatory on Kilauea in predicting eruptions there, and research is currently being done at Mount St. Helens and in other places, such as Japan, which has 10% of the world's active volcanoes. Volcanologists are now studying precursor phenomena such as tilting or swelling of the cone, changes in magnetic and thermal properties of the volcano, changes in gas composition, and increased seismic activity.

Control of volcanic eruptions would seem impossible, but there has been some success with it. Experimental techniques include damming lava flows, mudflows, and debris flows, bombing lava flows, and spraying lava flows with water, all of which have worked in at least some cases.

We tend to think of volcanic activity in negative terms, but it also provides some benefits. One is outstanding scenery in the form of majestic mountains, some lakes (such as Crater Lake in Oregon, Figure 17-1), and other landforms. Geothermal phenomena, such as geysers and hot springs, have aesthetic value as well as economic value in the tourist and travel industry. Geothermal energy is also an important energy source in some areas (Figure 3-6) and may be more widely used in the future (Section 17-7). Perhaps the most important benefit of volcanism is the highly fertile soils produced by the weathering of lava.

STREAM FLOODS AND FLOOD CONTROL Natural flooding by streams, the most common type of flooding, is caused primarily by heavy rain or rapid melting of snow, which causes water in the stream to overflow the channel in which it normally flows and to cover the adjacent area. Geologically the flat valley floor next to a stream channel is called a **floodplain**. However, for legal purposes, the term is often applied to any low area with the potential for flooding, including certain coastal areas.

Valleys with floodplains are popular places for human habitation. In some cases the wide valley floor slopes gently down away from the channel, and the channel has a ridge, called a *natural levee*, on both sides. The levees are made of fine sand and coarse silt, deposited as sediment each time the stream overflows the channel. A flood here can easily inundate the entire floodplain because the stream is higher than most of the natural levee.

In other areas, where a stream has widened its valley by lateral erosion, the floodplain slopes toward the

**CASE STUDY**

Because volcanic eruptions may be infrequent even in areas of active volcanism, the public is likely to be rather unaware of, and unconcerned about, the risks. Public awareness in the United States was increased when, after 123 years of dormancy, Mount St. Helens in the Cascade Range erupted on May 18, 1980 (Figure 7-30). This eruption has been described as the worst volcanic disaster in U.S. history.

The blast had the explosive force of a 30-megaton bomb, 1,500 times as powerful as the one that demolished Hiroshima. Devastation occurred in three semicircular zones north of the volcano. In the direct blast zone (the "tree-removal zone"), extending about 13 kilometers (8 miles), everything was obliterated or carried away. Beyond the direct blast zone (in the "tree-down zone") to 30 kilometers (19 miles) out, the blast of dense, ash-laden air blew down the trees like matchsticks so their tops point away from the blast. In the "seared zone," 1–2 kilometers (0.6–1.2 miles) beyond the second zone, trees were left standing but were scorched brown.

The explosion also threw ash more than 7 kilometers (4 miles) up into the atmosphere, high enough to be injected into the global atmospheric circulation patterns. Most of the huge cloud of ash traveled eastward and, several hours after the explosion, darkened the sky enough to trigger automatic streetlights during the morning hours in Yakima and Spokane, Washington. Within two weeks the ash cloud had traveled around the globe and eventually circled the planet several times before the ash settled to the ground.

The heat of the eruption rapidly melted snow and glacial ice on the mountain. Mudflows, mixtures of volcanic debris and water, flowed down the stream valleys, clogging the Toutle, Cowlitz, and Columbia rivers. Such mudflows commonly flow down steep slopes at speeds of 30–70 kilometers (19–43 miles) per hour, so you can't outrun one and you may not be able to outdrive some, especially if you are in heavy traffic. The Mount St. Helens eruption did not produce a lava flow although it could have.

The Mount St. Helens eruption ejected a relatively small amount of ash and other materials compared with those of some other famous volcanoes. When Tambora in Indonesia erupted in 1815, for example, killing 50,000–90,000 people, it threw out so much ash (30–80 times more than Mount St. Helens) that sunlight was partially blocked out. The troposphere cooled so much that 1816 became known as "the year without a summer."

Although this most recent eruption of Mount St. Helens was not a major one, it still had serious consequences. About 60 people died, including a geologist who was gathering data. More than 200 cabins and homes were destroyed, and many more were damaged. Tens of thousands of hectares of forest were obliterated, along with campgrounds and bridges. An estimated 7,000 big-game animals (bear, deer, and elk) died, as did all birds and most small mammals in the blast area. Salmon hatcheries were damaged, and crops, including alfalfa, apples, potatoes, and wheat, were lost. Many people living in the area lost their jobs.

On the plus side, however, trace elements from the ash added to the soil may benefit agriculture in the long run. Also, volcano visitor centers and other tourism promotions brought new jobs and income.

In the years since 1980 some volcanic activity has continued, and the risk of further eruptions remains. There is also some risk of flooding if debris dams holding back drainage fail.

Mount St. Helens is the most studied volcano in history. These investigations should help save lives and increase our knowledge of this type of geologic event. By 1990 many biologists were surprised at how fast various forms of life had begun colonizing many of the most devastated areas—an instance of primary succession (Figure 6-13) in action.

---

stream. This type of stream usually lacks levees. In this case a low-discharge flood will affect only the part of the floodplain near the channel, and a larger one will affect areas farther away from the channel.

People have settled on floodplains since the beginnings of agriculture. The soil is fertile and water is available for irrigation. Communities have access to the water for transportation of people or goods. The beauty of the stream may be an attraction, and flood-plains are flat surfaces—ideal sites, in many ways, for buildings, highways, and railroads. People may decide that all of these benefits outweigh the risk of flooding, if they are even aware of the risk.

On marine coasts flooding is due most often to the wind-driven storm surges and rain-swollen streams associated with tropical cyclones (typhoons and hurricanes). Flooding can also occur on the shorelines of large inland lakes. For example, the low ground

Q: Worldwide, how many trees are planted for each 10 cut?

**Figure 7-30** Mount St. Helens, a composite volcano in Washington, near the Washington–Oregon border, before (top left), during (above), and after (bottom left) its major eruption in May of 1980. It is one in a chain of volcanoes less than 1 million years old that stretches 1,500 kilometers (930 miles) from Lassen Peak in northern California to Mount Garibaldi in British Columbia. A composite volcano typically has a steep conical shape. It develops adjacent to a subduction zone at a convergent plate boundary and erupts explosively. As a result of this eruption, much of the northern side of the mountain was blown away and the altitude of the summit was reduced by about 450 meters (1,475 feet).

around the west end of Lake Erie is occasionally flooded when strong east winds blow the water inland.

While earthquakes and volcanic eruptions are dramatic and severe, flooding is a more common type of natural disaster because areas susceptible to flooding are so numerous. Each year flooding kills thousands of people and causes tens of billions of dollars in property damage. In 1959, for example, floods in North China followed by famine and disease killed an estimated 2 million people. A 25-year analysis revealed that 39% of the deaths from natural hazards were caused by floods, followed by typhoons and hurricanes (36%), earthquakes (13%), gales and thunderstorms (5%), and volcanic eruptions (2%).

The main way humans increase the probability of flooding is by removing vegetation—through timbering operations, overgrazing by livestock, construction, forest fires, certain mining activities, and urbanization.

Vegetation retards surface runoff, increasing infiltration; when the vegetation is removed by human activities or natural occurrences, precipitation reaches streams more directly, often with a large load of sediment, which increases the chance of flooding.

The first step in designing a flood control strategy is to construct a *flood-frequency curve*, which illustrates the average recurrence interval between various levels of discharge (stream flow). This entails estimating how often, *on average*, a flood of a certain size occurs. This doesn't tell us when floods will occur, but it gives a general idea of how frequently they might occur based on past history.

Various ways have been developed to reduce the hazard of stream flooding, each with a mix of advantages and disadvantages. *Channelization* deepens, widens, or straightens a section of a stream. Sometimes the channel is lined with concrete to accommodate a higher discharge. This, in turn, increases the discharge downstream and may cause increased erosion upstream.

A *flood control dam* retains flood water, releasing it downstream over an extended time. The dam may also provide such secondary benefits as hydroelectric power, water for irrigation, and recreational facilities. However, the reservoir of the dam gradually fills with sediment until it is useless. Also, the weight of the water in the reservoir may put stress on the rocks, causing earthquakes. Tragically some flood control dams have failed for one reason or another, causing catastrophic, unpredicted flooding.

*Artificial levees* are sometimes built where there are no natural ones and sometimes on top of the natural ones. They may be permanent or temporary, in the form of sandbags placed when a flood is imminent. If the levee breaks or the flood spills over it, however, floodwater may be trapped between the levee and the valley wall long after the stream discharge has decreased.

From an environmental viewpoint *floodplain management* is the best approach. Using a flood-frequency curve, a plan is developed to prohibit certain types of buildings or activities in the high-risk zone, to elevate or otherwise flood-proof buildings that are allowed on the legally defined floodplain, and to construct a floodway that allows flood water to flow through the community with minimal damage. A good example of floodway use is in Scottsdale, Arizona, where the floodway forms a beautiful greenbelt, 11 kilometers (7 miles) long, through the city. It contains five parks, bike paths, tennis courts, golf courses, and other features.

The Federal Flood Disaster Protection Act passed by Congress in 1973 requires that, to be eligible for federal flood insurance, local governments must adopt such floodplain development regulations. It also denies federal funding to proposed construction projects in designated flood hazard areas.

Despite these efforts, in 1990 more than 16.8 million households and $758 billion worth of property were located on floodplains in the United States. On the average floods kill more than 200 people and cause over $4 billion in property losses per year in the United States, with California, Florida, Texas, and Louisiana being the four most flood-prone states.

The federal flood insurance program underwrites $185 billion in policies because private insurance companies are unwilling to fully insure people who live in flood-prone areas against damages. This federal program actually encourages many people to build on floodplains and low-lying coastal areas with a high risk of flooding. It would make more economic sense and save taxpayers money if the government would buy the 2% of the country's land that repeatedly floods, instead of continuing to make disaster payments.

**MASS WASTING** Frost action forces rock apart on the face of a cliff and causes a *rockfall*. Soil on a mountainside outside Los Angeles becomes saturated by an infrequent rain and, having lost its vegetative cover in a recent brushfire, becomes a *mudflow*. A large mass of rock is jarred loose by an earthquake and creates a *rockslide*. Frost wedging, burrowing animals, and grazing cattle cause the soil on a hillside to move slowly downhill in a process called *creep*. These are some common types of mass wasting.

Several factors affect whether mass wasting is likely to occur and, if it does, what kind it will be. One of the most important is how steeply the land slopes—sooner or later, some type of mass wasting is likely to occur on any steep slope. The earth material, soil or bed rock, in a region is also an important factor. In the case of bed rock, the strength of the rock, the presence of fractures, and the orientation of layering or other zones of weakness may all play a role.

Water frequently contributes to mass wasting. A small amount of water in the pores of earth material may actually improve the stability of regolith, as anyone who has built a sand castle knows, but the weight it adds contributes to instability. Saturation with water, however, forces soil particles apart, and can cause a mudflow of water-saturated regolith even on a moderate slope. Saturation and mudflows can also occur as a result of high precipitation during a storm or rapid melting of ice and snow.

The effect of vegetation on mass wasting varies. In some instances vegetation contributes to mass wasting by slowing the fall of rain on slopes, which helps water to infiltrate and saturate the soil. In others, it inhibits mass wasting by removing water from the ground and putting it into the air through transpiration, and by holding the soil together with its roots.

**Q:** What percentage of the earth's species live in tropical forests?

Mass wasting can also be triggered by volcanic eruptions and earthquakes (Case Study, p. 191).

Some human activities contribute to mass wasting, often in places where it causes loss of property and maybe injury and death. An example is the building of homes on terraces cut into hillsides, which oversteepens the slope and overloads the surface, greatly increasing the chances of mass wasting. Roadcuts through mountain ridges and along slopes and high walls from contour strip mining (Figure 7-23) are sometimes unstable as well. Mass wasting caused by clear-cutting of timber and building of logging roads is a serious problem in the Cascade Range in Oregon.

The first step in coping with mass wasting is to identify areas of risk. People proposing to build on a potentially unstable site should get professional help during the planning stage. It would be best to avoid construction on an unstable site, but if there are strong reasons for going ahead, there may be ways to reduce the risk in individual cases. Some factors that contribute to mass wasting, such as earthquakes, are unavoidable. It is possible, however, to install drainage systems to remove water from a slope, and certain types of vegetation can be planted to increase stability. Well-designed retention walls may also be effective in some cases.

**SUBSIDENCE** Subsidence is a vertical movement of large rock masses that is not slope-related. For example, collapse can occur in volcanic regions when magma underlying an area withdraws and the unsupported rock drops, producing a caldera, and in limestone regions when the roof of a cavern, formed by solution, collapses to make a sinkhole (Figure 7-31). Collapse can also occur in underground coal mines, as has happened in Wyoming and Pennsylvania, and in iron mines, as has happened in Michigan, resulting in loss of homes and lives.

Subsidence may involve only a sinking of the ground, without significant fracturing, as a result of thawing or very slow downward warping of the crust over a broad area. Subsidence that happens rapidly, such as in sinkhole formation, may be especially hazardous, but slow warping can also cause serious structural damage to buildings.

Pumping of groundwater or oil has caused subsidence. For example, groundwater withdrawal has caused parts of Houston, Texas, to subside as much as 3 meters (10 feet), and some areas of Mexico City have subsided as much as 8.5 meters (28 feet). In some places artificial recharge of groundwater by the injection of storm water or used water has helped restore the pressure and slow subsidence. Pumping of oil has caused subsidence in Long Beach, California.

Although humans contribute to some natural hazards, most would happen even if there were no people on Earth. However, we could greatly reduce the loss of life and property by not building houses on wave-cut cliffs next to the ocean, on floodplains along streams, or on other hazardous sites. We cannot expect natural processes to come to a halt for us.

**Figure 7-31** Subsidence in Winter Park, Florida, in May 1981. This large sinkhole developed rapidly one evening. By morning it was about 80 meters (260 feet) across and had swallowed a house, parts of two businesses, portions of pavement on two streets, a large part of a municipal swimming pool, and several cars. It caused $2 million in damage.

## 7-6 Geologic and Other Time Frames

Earth is constantly changing. Throughout Earth's history the atmosphere has changed (Section 6-3 and Spotlight, p. 185), the climate has changed, the geography has changed, the types and numbers of organisms have changed, and some kinds of geologic processes have slowed or accelerated (Figure 7-32). Some of these changes are so slow that we are unaware of them; others are much faster.

Weather changes in a matter of minutes or hours, and climate over decades to centuries. Populations can change their size and age distribution in response to changes in environmental conditions within hours to decades (Figure 6-5). As environmental conditions have changed, some of Earth's species have become extinct and new species have arisen (Figure 6-8). Speciation usually takes thousands to millions of years, depending mostly on the reproductive ability of each species.

A: At least 50% (some say 90%)

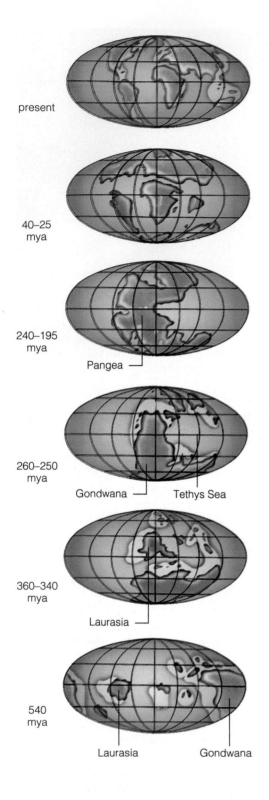

present

40–25
mya

240–195
mya

Pangea

260–250
mya

Gondwana — Tethys Sea

360–340
mya

Laurasia

540
mya

Laurasia          Gondwana

**Figure 7-32** Major geological and biological events in the evolution of the earth and its organisms, many of which take place over millions to billions of years. These changes make those over the last 40,000 years in which our species has existed seem like an eye-blink. The time spans of the different eras are not to scale. (Used by permission from Cecie Starr and Ralph Taggart, *Biology: The Unity and Diversity of Life*, 6th ed., Belmont, Calif.: Wadsworth, 1992)

| Era | Period | Epoch | Millions of Years Ago (mya) | |
|---|---|---|---|---|
| CENOZOIC | Quaternary | Recent | 0.01- | |
| | | Pleistocene | 1.65 | |
| | Tertiary | Pliocene | 5 | |
| | | Miocene | 25 | |
| | | Oligocene | 38 | |
| | | Eocene | 54 | |
| | | Paleocene | 65 | |
| MESOZOIC | Cretaceous | Late | 100 | |
| | | Early | 138 | |
| | Jurassic | | 205 | |
| | Triassic | | 240 | |
| PALEOZOIC | Permian | | 290 | |
| | Carboniferous | | 360 | |
| | Devonian | | 410 | |
| | Silurian | | 435 | |
| | Ordovician | | 505 | |
| | Cambrian | | 550 | |
| PROTEROZOIC | | | 2,500 | |
| ARCHEAN | | | | |

Q:  What percentage of tropical forest plants have been studied for their possible use as human resources?

## Range of Global Diversity
### (marine and terrestrial)

## Times of Major Geologic and Biological Events

1.65 mya to present. Major glaciations. Modern humans emerge and begin what may be greatest **mass extinction** of all time on land, starting with Ice Age hunters.

65–1.65 mya. Unprecedented mountain building as continents rupture, drift, collide. Major climatic shifts; vast grasslands emerge. Major **radiations** of flowering plants, insects, birds, mammals. Origin of earliest human forms.

65 mya. Asteroid impact? **Mass extinction** of all dinosaurs and many marine organisms.

135–65 mya. Pangea breakup continues, broad inland seas form. Major **radiations** of marine invertebrates, fishes, insects, dinosaurs. Origin of angiosperms (flowering plants).

181–135 mya. Pangea breakup begins. Rich marine communities. Major **radiations** of dinosaurs.

205 mya. Asteroid impact? Mass extinction of many organisms in seas, some on land; dinosaurs, mammals survive.

240–205 mya. Recovery, **radiations** of marine invertebrates, fishes, dinosaurs. Gymnosperms the dominant land plants. Origin of mammals.

240 mya. **Mass extinction.** Nearly all species in seas and on land perish.

280–240 mya. Pangea, worldwide ocean form; shallow seas squeezed out. Major **radiations** of reptiles, gymnosperms.

360–280 mya. Tethys Sea forms. Recurring glaciations. Major **radiations** of insects, amphibians. Spore-bearing plants dominate; gymnosperms present. Origin of reptiles.

370 mya. **Mass extinction** of many marine invertebrates, most fishes.

435–360 mya. Laurasia forms, Gondwana moves north. Vast swamplands, early vascular plants. **Radiations** of fishes continue. Origin of amphibians.

435 mya. Glaciations as Gondwana crosses South Pole. **Mass extinction** of many marine organisms.

500–435 mya. Gondwana moves south. Major **radiations** of marine invertebrates, early fishes.

550–500 mya. Land masses dispersed near equator. Simple marine communities. Origin of animals with hard parts.

700–550 mya. Supercontinent Laurentia breaks up; widespread glaciations.

2,500–570 mya. Oxygen present in atmosphere. Origin of aerobic metabolism. Origin of protistans, algae, fungi, animals.

3,800–2,500 mya. Origin of photosynthetic bacteria.

4,600–3,800 mya. Formation of earth's crust, early atmosphere, oceans. Chemical evolution leading to origin of life (anaerobic bacteria).

4,600 mya. Origin of earth.

A: 1%

Some geological changes in the earth's interior and crust have taken place on a time scale of millions to billions of years. Changes from mass wasting, erosion, volcanic eruption, and some subsidence can happen very rapidly. We and other species who inhabit Earth today are the beneficiaries of processes such as landscape development, biological change, and resource concentration, acting over eons.

In the finger snap of geologic time we have been on Earth (Figure 6-8), we have had a powerful impact on the environment, accelerating natural processes and introducing processes and changes that would not have occurred without us. We have the responsibility to be stewards of Earth, to tend it and care for it, and to help heal some of the wounds we have inflicted. Such Earth healing takes time. Large-scale air pollution such as acid deposition and water pollution from factories, farms, and lawns could be prevented, and the damaged ecosystems would be renewed in a matter of decades. Desertification could be reversed within a century. Tropical forests can grow back within 1,000 years. Soil cover in severely eroded areas can be renewed in 10,000 years—the same length of time it would take for the ozone layer and the global climate to return to the condition they were in before the Industrial Revolution. However, it will take many millions of years before a new burst of speciation will be able to expand into the empty niches we have created by our present mass extinction of Earth's wildlife over only a few decades.

*A civilization writes its record on the land.*

WALTER CLAY LOWDERMILK

# Critical Thinking

1. In what important ways would conditions on the earth's surface be different if the outer core were not liquid?

2. List some of the ways, positive and negative, that plate tectonics is important to you.

3. Discuss the ways, positive and negative, that external Earth processes (mass wasting, weathering, stream erosion, and so on) are important to you.

4. What would happen if plate tectonics stopped? What would happen if erosion and mass wasting stopped? If you were "in charge," would you eliminate either group of processes? Explain.

5. What crustal resources do you use every day? Make a table to show what materials are used and how they are used.

6. Discuss how both geologic processes and earlier organisms have produced environmental conditions that allow the present variety of life to exist.

*7. On a map of your state, do the following:
   a. Indicate where various types of crustal resources are extracted, distinguishing each type with a symbol or a colored spot.
   b. Mark where igneous, sedimentary, and metamorphic rocks occur. (You may have to combine two types in certain areas.)
   c. Show where various natural hazards exist. Describe what is being done to reduce the risk from those hazards.

*8. What mineral resources are extracted in your local area? What mining methods are used? Do local, state, or federal laws require restoration of the landscape after mining is completed? If so, how stringently are those laws enforced?

*9. Dissolve some copper sulfate in warm water to produce a concentrated solution, and let it cool slowly. Observe the size of the crystals that form. Then do the same thing but cool the solution quickly by placing it in an ice bath or refrigerator and noting the size of the crystals that form. This demonstrates the difference between the crystalline grains on intrusive (slow-cooling) and extrusive (rapid-cooling) igneous rock.

*10. Find out where earthquakes and volcanic eruptions have occurred during the past 30 years and locate them by sticking small flags on a map of the world or placing dots on Figure 7-5a. Compare their locations with the plate boundaries shown in Figure 7-5b.

PART III

# The Human Population

*We need the size of population in which human beings can fulfill their potentialities; in my opinion we are already overpopulated from that point of view; not just in places like India and China and Puerto Rico, but also in the United States and Western Europe.*

GEORGE WALD (Nobel Laureate, Biology)

## Cops and Rubbers Day in Thailand

In 1960 Thailand's (Figure 8-15) population was growing rapidly at a rate of 3.2% per year. The average Thai family had 6.4 children. Today its population is growing at a rate of 1.4%, and the average number of children per family is 2.4. And since 1960 the country's average per capita income has doubled.

There are several reasons for this impressive feat: the creativity of the government-supported family-planning program; the openness of the Thai people to new ideas; the willingness of the government to work with the private, nonprofit Population and Community Development Association (PCDA), and support of family planning by the country's Buddhist religious leaders (95% of Thais are Buddhist). Buddhist scripture teaches that "many children make you poor."

This remarkable transition was catalyzed by the charismatic leadership of Mechai Viravidaiya, a former government economist and public relations genius, who launched the PCDA. He established an imaginative, high-profile program to persuade Thais to have fewer children.

Anywhere there was a crowd PCDA workers handed out condoms—at festivals, movie theaters, even traffic jams. Demonstrations and ads were used to familiarize children and adults with condoms. Mechai told people to touch condoms and not be embarrassed by them. School children held condom-blowing championships (Figure 8-1, left).

He showed how a condom could be used as a tourniquet for deep cuts and snake bites and to carry coins or a beverage. Humorous songs were written about condom use and the reasons to have no more than two children. Mechai also persuaded traffic police to hand out condoms on New Year's Eve, now known as "Cops and Rubbers Day."

Distribution of condoms, now commonly called "mechais" in Thailand, was only part of the campaign. The PCDA had birth control carts giving out pills, spermicidal foam, and condoms at bus stations and public events. It paid the insurance of taxi drivers willing to dispense condoms and birth control pills in their cabs. On the Thai king's birthday the PCDA offers free vasectomies. Sterilization is now the most widely used form of birth control in the country.

Today 95% of the Thai people want only two children and 66% use birth control—almost the same percentage as in Europe. Thailand's population is still growing, but much more slowly than before. Their experience shows that creativity and dedication by individuals can cut population growth quickly.

All is not completely rosy. While Thailand has done well in slowing population growth, it has been less successful in improving public health, especially maternal health and control of AIDS and other sexually transmitted diseases. Its capital, Bangkok, is one of the world's most polluted and congested cities (Figure 8-1, right).

Thailand's family-planning success needs to be transplanted to other areas. Every time your heart beats, three more babies are born. We are now adding about 258,000 people each day, more than at any other time during our short span on Earth.

Both birth and death rates are coming down, but death rates have fallen more sharply than birth rates. If this trend continues, one of two things will proba-

Population and Community Development Association, Bangkok, Thailand

**Figure 8-1** Thai children blowing up condoms (left) and a crowded floating market in Bangkok (right).

*We shouldn't delude ourselves: The population explosion will come to an end before very long. The only remaining question is whether it will be halted through the humane method of birth control, or by nature wiping out our surplus.*

PAUL H. EHRLICH

bly happen during your lifetime: The number of people on Earth will at least double and perhaps triple, or the world will experience an unprecedented population crash, with hundreds of millions of people—perhaps billions—dying prematurely.

Marco Corsetti/FPG International

This chapter is devoted to answering the following questions:

- How is population size affected by rates of birth, death, fertility, and migration?
- How is population size affected by the percentage of males and females at each age level?
- How can we control population growth?
- What success have India and China had in controlling population growth?

 **8-1**

# Factors Affecting Human Population Size

**BIRTH RATES AND DEATH RATES** Populations grow or decline through the interplay of three factors: births, deaths, and migration. The **birth rate**, or **crude birth rate**, is the number of live births per 1,000 persons in a population in a given year. The **death rate**, or **crude death rate**, is the number of deaths per 1,000 persons in a population in a given year. Figure 8-2 shows the crude birth and death rates for various groups of countries in 1993.

When the birth rate of an area is greater than the death rate, its population grows (assuming no net migration into or out of the area). When the death rate equals the crude birth rate, population size remains stable, a condition known as **zero population growth (ZPG)**. When the death rate exceeds the birth rate, population size decreases.

The annual rate at which the size of a population changes is called the **annual rate of natural population change**. It is usually expressed as a percentage.

$$\text{annual rate of population change (\%)} = \frac{\text{birth rate} - \text{death rate}}{1,000 \text{ persons}} \times 100$$

$$= \frac{\text{birth rate} - \text{death rate}}{10}$$

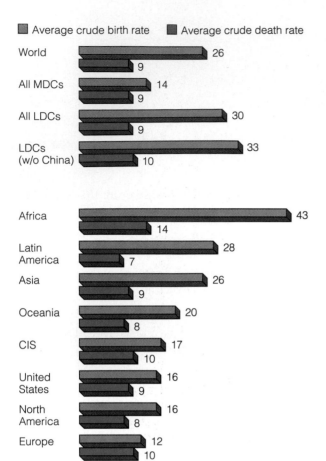

**Figure 8-2** Average crude birth and death rates for various groups of countries in 1993. (Data from Population Reference Bureau)

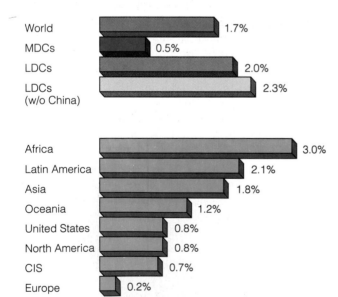

**Figure 8-3** Average annual rate of population change for various groups of countries in 1993. (Data from Population Reference Bureau)

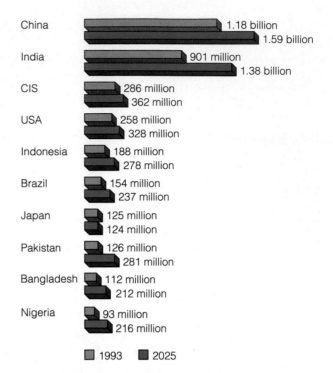

**Figure 8-4** The world's 10 most populous countries in 1993, with projections of their population size in 2025. (Data from World Bank and Population Reference Bureau)

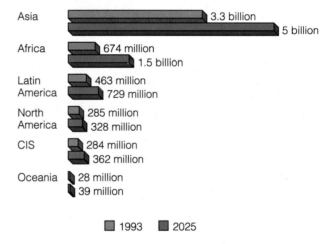

**Figure 8-5** Population projections by region, 1993–2025. (Data from United Nations and Population Reference Bureau)

The world's annual rate of population growth dropped 15% between 1965 and 1993, from 2% to 1.7%. This is good news, but the population base rose by almost three-fourths from 3.2 billion to 5.5 billion during the same period. Thus the world's population grew in 1993 by 94 million (5.5 billion x 1.7% = 94 million) compared to 70 million in 1965 (3.5 billion x 2.0% = 70 million) even though the growth rate was higher in 1965. This 15% drop in the growth rate is akin to learning that a truck heading straight at you has slowed

Q: What country is the largest importer of tropical lumber?

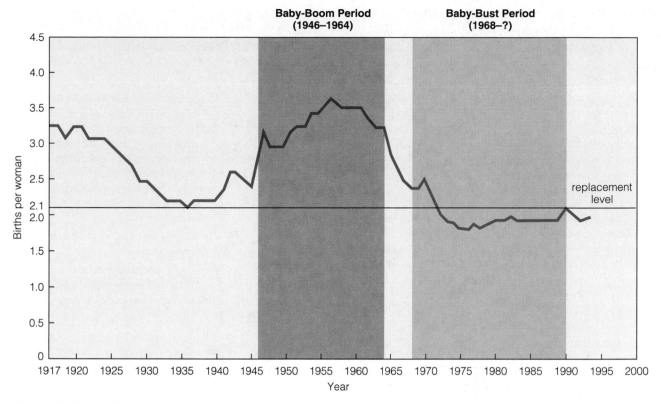

**Figure 8-6** Total fertility rate for the United States between 1917 and 1993. (Data from Population Reference Bureau and U.S. Census Bureau)

from 100 kilometers per hour to 85 kilometers per hour while its weight has increased by 72%.

Figure 8-3 gives the annual population change rates for major parts of the world in 1993. An annual population growth rate of 1–3% may seem small, but such exponential rates lead to enormous increases in population size over a 100-year period.

The impact of exponential population growth on population size is much greater in countries with a large existing population base. In terms of sheer numbers of people, China and India dwarf all other countries, making up 38% of the world's population (Figure 8-4). One person in five is Chinese, and 59% of the world's population is Asian. Figure 8-5 shows how the population in various regions is projected to grow between 1993 and 2025.

**FERTILITY RATES** Two types of fertility rates affect a country's population size and growth rate. **Replacement-level fertility** is the number of children a couple must bear to replace themselves. The actual average replacement-level fertility rate is slightly higher than two children per couple (2.1 in MDCs and as high as 2.5 in some LDCs), mostly because some female children die before reaching their reproductive years.

The most useful measure of fertility for projecting future population change is the **total fertility rate (TFR)**: an estimate of the average number of children that would be born alive to a woman during her lifetime if she passed through all her childbearing years (ages 15–44) conforming to age-specific fertility rates of a given year. In simpler terms TFR is an estimate of the average number of children a woman will have during her childbearing years.

In 1993 the average total fertility rate was 3.4 children per woman for the world as a whole, 1.9 in MDCs (down from 2.5 in 1950), and 3.8 in LDCs (down from 6.5 in 1950). If the world's total fertility rate remains at 3.4, its population will reach 694 billion by 2150—391 times the current population! Clearly, this is not possible, but it does illustrate the enormous power of exponential growth (p. 3). Population experts expect TFRs in MDCs to remain around 1.9 and those in LDCs to drop to around 2.3 by 2025—the basis of the projections in Figure 8-5. That is good news, but it will still lead to a projected world population of around 9 billion by 2025, with most of this growth taking place in LDCs.

Since 1972 the total fertility rate for the United States has been at or below the replacement level (Figure 8-6). This doesn't mean that the country's population has stabilized or is declining, however (Case Study, p. 206).

**A:** Japan (60%), followed by the United States and Great Britain

## Will U.S. Population Stabilize?

The population of the United States has grown from 4 million in 1790 to 258 million in 1993—a 64-fold increase—even while the country's total fertility rate has oscillated wildly (Figure 8-6). At the peak of the post–World War II baby boom (1946–64) in 1957, the TFR reached 3.7 children per woman. Since then it has generally declined, remaining at or below replacement level since 1972.

Various factors contributed to this decline:

- Widespread use of effective birth control methods.
- Availability of legal abortions.
- Social attitudes favoring smaller families.
- Greater social acceptance of childless couples.

- Increasing cost of raising a family. It will cost $86,000–$168,000 to raise a child born in 1992 to age 18.
- Rise in the average age at marriage between 1958 and 1991 from 20.1 to 24.1 for women and from 22.8 to 26.3 for men.
- More women working outside the home. In 1993 more than 70% of American women of childbearing age worked outside the home; their childbearing rate was one-third that of women not in the paid labor force.

The drop in the total fertility rate has led to a decline in the annual rate of population growth in the United States, but the country has not yet reached zero population growth (ZPG), nor is it even close. The main reasons for this are:

- The large number of women (58 million) born during the baby-boom period who are still moving through their childbearing years. Even though the total fertility rate has remained at or below replacement level for 21 years, there has been a large increase in the number of potential mothers.
- High levels of legal and illegal immigration.
- An increase in the number of unmarried women (including teenagers) having children.

In 1993 the U.S. population of 258 million grew by 1.2%—faster than that of any other industrialized country. This added 3.1 million people: 2.0 million more births than deaths, 900,000 legal immigrants, and at least 200,000 illegal immigrants.

**FACTORS AFFECTING BIRTH RATES AND FERTILITY RATES** The most significant factors affecting a country's average birth rate and total fertility rate are:

- *Average level of education and affluence.* Rates are usually lower in MDCs, where levels of both education and affluence are higher than in LDCs.

- *Importance of children as a part of the family labor force.* Rates tend to be lower in MDCs and higher in LDCs (especially in rural areas).

- *Urbanization.* People living in urban areas usually have better access to family planning services and tend to have fewer children than those living in rural areas, where children are needed to help grow food, collect firewood and water, and perform other survival tasks.

- *Cost of raising and educating children.* Rates tend to be lower in MDCs, where raising children is much more costly because children don't enter the labor force until their late teens or early twenties.

- *Educational and employment opportunities for women.* Rates tend to be low when women have access to education and paid employment outside the home.

- *Infant mortality rate.* In areas with low infant mortality rates, people tend to have fewer children because they don't need to replace children who have died.

- *Average marriage age* (or more precisely, the average age at which women give birth to their first child). People have fewer children when the average marriage age of women is 25 or older.

- *Availability of private and public pension systems.* Pensions eliminate the need for parents to have many children to support them in old age.

- *Availability of reliable methods of birth control.* Widespread availability tends to reduce birth and fertility rates (Figures 8-7 and 8-8). New methods of birth control are also being developed, but many may not be available in the United States (Spotlight, p. 209).

- *Religious beliefs, tradition, and cultural norms that influence the number of children couples want to have.* In many LDCs these factors tend to favor large families.

Figure 1-1 shows three projections of world population growth through the next century. But such projections are not predictions of what will necessarily

## Extremely Effective

Total abstinence — 100%

Abortion — 100%

Sterilization — 99.6%

Hormonal implant (Norplant) — 99%

## Highly Effective

IUD with slow-release hormones — 98%

IUD plus spermicide — 98%

Vaginal pouch ("female condom") — 97%

IUD — 95%

Condom (good brand) plus spermicide — 95%

Oral contraceptive — 94%

## Effective

Cervical cap — 89%

Condom (good brand) — 86%

Diaphragm plus spermicide — 84%

Rhythm method (Billings, Sympto-Thermal) — 84%

Vaginal sponge impregnated with spermicide — 83%

Spermicide (foam) — 82%

## Moderately Effective

Spermicide (creams, jellies, suppositories) — 75%

Rhythm method (daily temperature readings) — 74%

Withdrawal — 74%

Condom (cheap brand) — 70%

## Unreliable

Douche — 40%

Chance (no method) — 10%

**Figure 8-7** Typical effectiveness of birth control methods in the United States. Percentages are based on the number of undesired pregnancies per 100 couples using a specific method as their sole form of birth control for a year. For example, a 94% effectiveness rating for oral contraceptives means that for every 100 women using the pill regularly for one year, 6 will get pregnant. Effectiveness rates tend to be lower in LDCs because of human error and lack of education. (Data from Alan Guttmacher Institute)

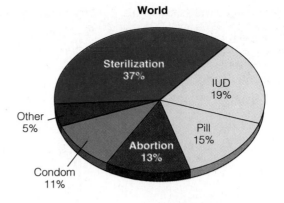

**World**

Sterilization 37%
IUD 19%
Pill 15%
Abortion 13%
Condom 11%
Other 5%

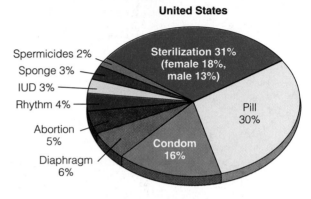

**United States**

Spermicides 2%
Sponge 3%
IUD 3%
Rhythm 4%
Abortion 5%
Diaphragm 6%
Sterilization 31% (female 18%, male 13%)
Pill 30%
Condom 16%

**Figure 8-8** Estimated percentage of couples of reproductive age in the world and the United States using various birth control methods in 1989 (including sterilization and induced abortion.) Worldwide there are 36–53 million induced abortions each year (26–31 million of them legal and 10–22 million illegal). Poorly performed abortions take the lives of 100,000–200,000 women each year. (Data from UN Population Division, Population Crisis Committee, U.S. National Center for Health Statistics, and National Academy of Sciences)

take place. Instead, they are possibilities based on present trends and certain assumptions about people's future reproductive behavior.

**FACTORS AFFECTING DEATH RATES** The rapid growth of the world's population over the past 100 years was not caused by a rise in crude birth rates. Rather, it was due largely to a decline in crude death rates, especially in the LDCs (Figure 8-9).

The principal interrelated reasons for this general drop in death rates are:

- *Better nutrition* because of higher levels of food production and better distribution

- *Fewer infant deaths and longer average life expectancy* because of improved personal hygiene, sanitation, and water supplies, which have curtailed the spread of infectious diseases

- *Improvements in medical and public health technology*, including antibiotics, immunization, and insecticides

A: 0.1%

**Figure 8-9** Changes in crude birth and death rates for MDCs and LDCs between 1775 and 1993, and projected rates (dashed lines) to 2000. (Data from Population Reference Bureau and United Nations)

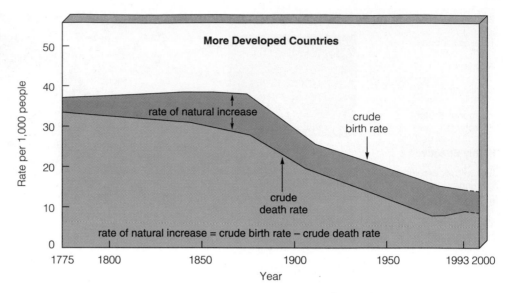

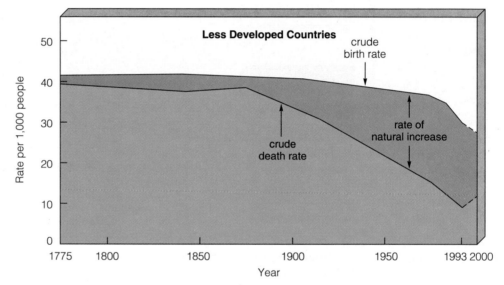

Two useful indicators of overall health in a country or region are **life expectancy**—the average number of years a newborn infant can be expected to live—and the **infant mortality rate**—the number of babies out of every 1,000 born each year that die before their first birthday (Figure 8-10).

The maximum *average* life expectancy for humans is projected at 85 years. It is encouraging that life expectancy has increased since 1965, and averaged 75 in MDCs and 62 in LDCs in 1993. But in the world's 41 poorest countries, mainly in Asia and Africa, average life expectancy is only 47 years.

Between 1900 and 1993 average life expectancy at birth rose sharply in the United States from 47 to 75 (79 for females and 72 for males); yet, in 1993, the average life expectancy at birth for people in 18 countries was higher than that for people in the United States. Japan has the highest life expectancy (79), followed by Sweden (78).

*Because it reflects the general level of nutrition and health care, infant mortality is probably the single most important measure of a society's quality of life.* A high infant mortality rate usually indicates insufficient food (undernutrition), poor nutrition (malnutrition), and a high incidence of infectious disease (usually from contaminated drinking water). Between 1965 and 1993 the world's infant mortality dropped 31% in MDCs and 35% in LDCs. This is an impressive achievement, but it still means that at least 12 million infants die each year of preventable causes.

Although the U.S. infant mortality rate of 9 per 1,000 in 1993 was low by world standards, 29 other countries had lower rates. Several factors keep it higher than it could be, including:

- Inadequate health care for poor women during pregnancy and for their babies after birth
- Drug addiction among pregnant women
- The high birth rate among teenage women (Case Study, p. 210)

Q: What percentage of the people in LDCs rely on biomass (mostly wood, crop residues, and dung) for heating and cooking?

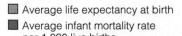

■ Average life expectancy at birth
■ Average infant mortality rate
　　per 1,000 live births

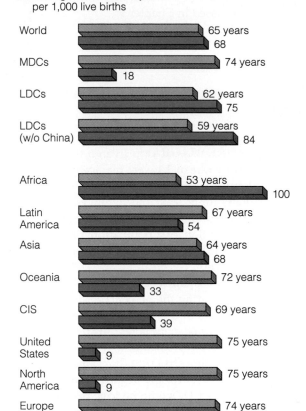

| | Life expectancy | Infant mortality |
|---|---|---|
| World | 65 years | 68 |
| MDCs | 74 years | 18 |
| LDCs | 62 years | 75 |
| LDCs (w/o China) | 59 years | 84 |
| Africa | 53 years | 100 |
| Latin America | 67 years | 54 |
| Asia | 64 years | 68 |
| Oceania | 72 years | 33 |
| CIS | 69 years | 39 |
| United States | 75 years | 9 |
| North America | 75 years | 9 |
| Europe | 74 years | 11 |

**Figure 8-10** Average life expectancy at birth and average infant mortality rate for various groups of countries in 1993. (Data from Population Reference Bureau)

International Development Research Center, Ottawa, Canada

**Figure 8-11** Camp of drought refugees in Burkina Faso, West Africa, depicts the plight of some of the estimated 10 million people driven from their homes worldwide by environmental degradation. Only a handful of countries accept immigrants.

## U.S. Birth Control Options: More or Less?

Researchers are working to develop new and better methods of birth control. Examples include biodegradable implants that don't require surgical removal, a two-year pregnancy vaccine, a contraceptive for men that reduces sperm count, morning-after contraceptives, chemicals for nonsurgical sterilization, and female and male sterilization procedures that can be reversed more easily.

The process of developing, testing, and evaluating the safety of a new contraceptive takes at least 15 years and $50 million or more. Despite the importance of population control, worldwide expenditures on reproductive research and contraceptive development have declined from a high of $250 million per year in the early 1970s to $200 million per year today—an average of only 4¢ per person.

Contraceptive research and development by private drug firms has virtually stopped in the United States, mostly because of the difficulty and expense of getting FDA approval for new contraceptives, fear of liability suits, and the high cost of liability insurance. Drug companies also make more money selling daily birth control pills than longer-range contraceptive pills, vaccines, or implants that prevent conception for one month to five years.

The United States is the only major industrialized country that is decreasing government emphasis on family planning and government-supported research on new forms of birth control. Since 1979 federal funding for fertility control research has dropped 25% (adjusted for inflation) because of budget cuts and political pressure from prolife groups. Most population experts fear that unless government and private funding of contraceptive research is at least doubled, few if any of the possible improved forms of birth control will be available in the United States.

**MIGRATION** The rate of population change for a specific geographic area is also affected by movement of people into (immigration) and out of (emigration) that area:

$$\text{population change rate} = \left(\begin{array}{c}\text{births} \\ + \\ \text{immigration}\end{array}\right) - \left(\begin{array}{c}\text{deaths} \\ + \\ \text{emigration}\end{array}\right)$$

Most countries control their rates of population growth to some extent by restricting immigration. Only a few countries accept large numbers of immigrants or refugees (Figure 8-11). This means that population

## Teenage Pregnancy in the United States

**CASE STUDY**

The United States has the highest teenage pregnancy rate of any industrialized country, about six times higher than the rate in Japan and most European countries, and 2 times higher than in Canada. Every year in the United States approximately 1 million teenage women—one in every nine ages 15–19—become pregnant. Some 83% of these pregnancies are not planned. About 590,000 of these young women give birth; the remaining 410,000 have abortions, accounting for almost 25% of abortions performed in the United States.

Teenage pregnancies cost state and federal governments (that is, taxpayers) at least $21 billion a year. Babies born to teenagers are more likely to have a low birth weight—the most important factor in infant deaths—thus increasing the country's infant mortality rate.

Why is the teenage pregnancy rate in the United States so high? UN studies show that American teenagers aren't more sexually active than those in other MDCs, but they are less likely to have learned what precautions to take to prevent pregnancy.

In Sweden, by contrast, which has a teenage pregnancy rate about one-fifth that of the United States, every child receives a thorough grounding in basic reproductive biology by age 7. By age 12 each child has been told about the various types of contraceptives.

A 1991 Gallup poll revealed that 87% of adult Americans favor sex education in the schools, including information about birth control and sexually transmitted diseases, and school clinics that dispense contraceptives with parental consent. Almost 60% of those favoring such programs believed they should start in kindergarten (14%) or by the fourth grade (43%).

Many analysts urge that effective sex education programs be developed in which American children are made aware of the values of abstinence and the various types of contraceptives by age 12 and that school-based health clinics be opened in all junior and senior high schools. These proposals are vigorously opposed by groups who fear that early sex education will lead to increased sexual activity. What do you think should be done about sex education and teenage pregnancy?

change for most countries is determined mainly by the difference between their birth rate and death rate.

Migration within countries, especially from rural to urban areas, plays an important role in the popula-

tion dynamics of cities, towns, and rural areas. This migration affects the population distribution within countries, as discussed in Chapter 9.

## 8-2 Population Age Structure

**AGE STRUCTURE DIAGRAMS** Even if the replacement-level fertility rate of 2.1 were magically achieved globally by tomorrow, the world's population would keep on growing for at least another 60 years! Why? The answer lies in an understanding of the **age structure**, or age distribution, of a population: the percentage of the population, or the number of people of each sex, at each age level.

Demographers construct a population age structure diagram by plotting the percentages or numbers of males and females in the total population in three age categories: *prereproductive* (ages 0–14), *reproductive* (ages 15–44), and *postreproductive* (ages 45–85+). Figure 8-12 shows the age structure diagrams for countries with rapid, slow, zero, and negative growth rates.

Kenya and most LDCs with rapidly growing populations, for example, have pyramid-shaped age structure diagrams. These countries have a high ratio of children under age 15 (the broad base of the pyramid) to adults over age 65 (the narrow top of the pyramid). In contrast, the diagrams for the United States and most other MDCs undergoing slow population growth have a narrower base. Such countries have a much smaller proportion of their population under age 15 and a larger proportion above age 65 than countries experiencing rapid population growth. MDCs that have achieved or nearly achieved zero population growth, such as Italy and Denmark, have roughly equal numbers of people at each age level, yielding a nearly rectangular diagram. And countries such as Hungary and Germany, which are experiencing a slow population decline (negative growth rates), have roughly equal numbers of people at most age levels but lower numbers under age 5, resulting in a narrower base.

**AGE STRUCTURE AND POPULATION GROWTH MOMENTUM** Any country with many people below age 15 has a powerful built-in momentum to increase its population size unless death rates rise sharply. The number of births rises even if women have only one or two children, because of the large number of women moving into their reproductive years.

Today half of the world's 2.6 billion women are in the reproductive ages of 15–49, and one of every three

Q: How many people cannot find or buy enough fuelwood to meet their basic needs?

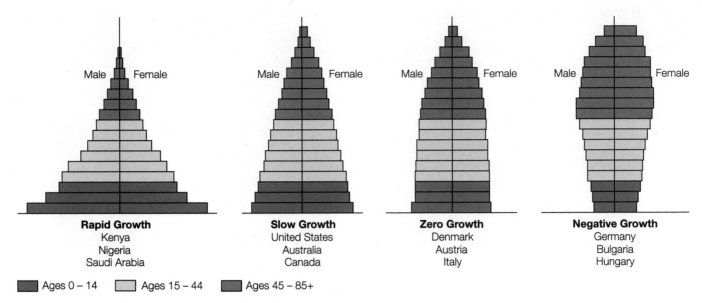

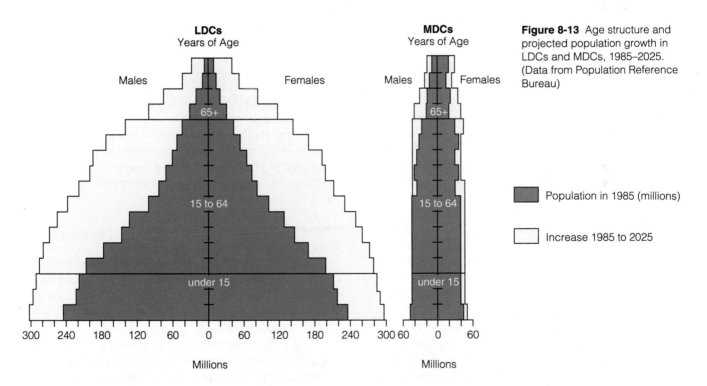

**Figure 8-12** Population age structure diagrams for countries with rapid, slow, zero, and negative population growth rates. Bottom portions represent prereproductive years (ages 0–14), middle portions represent reproductive years (ages 15–44), and top portions represent postreproductive years (ages 45–85+). (Data from Population Reference Bureau)

**Figure 8-13** Age structure and projected population growth in LDCs and MDCs, 1985–2025. (Data from Population Reference Bureau)

persons on this planet is under 15 years old and poised to move into their prime reproductive years. In LDCs the number is even higher—36% compared with 21% in MDCs. Figure 8-13 shows the powerful momentum for population growth in LDCs caused by these large numbers of young people. Even if each female in this group has only two children, world population will still grow for 60 years unless the death rate rises sharply. And women in LDCs now average 3.8 children, not even close to replacement level. This powerful force for continued population growth, mostly in LDCs, will be slowed only by an effective program to reduce birth rates or a catastrophic rise in death rates.

**MAKING PROJECTIONS FROM AGE STRUCTURE DIAGRAMS** A baby boom took place in the United States between 1946 and 1964 (Figure 8-6). This 80-million-person bulge, known as the *baby-boom generation*,

A: 1.5 billion—almost one of every three persons on Earth

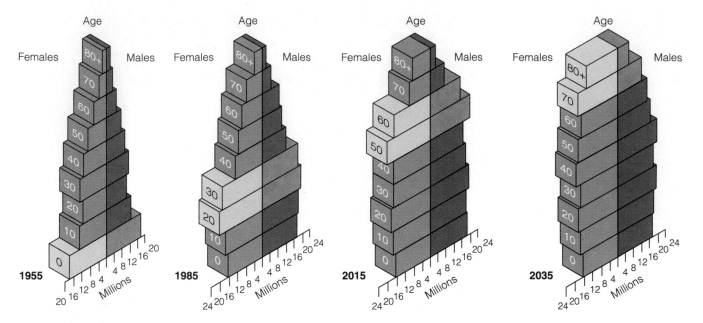

**Figure 8-14** Tracking the baby-boom generation in the United States. (Data from Population Reference Bureau and U.S. Census Bureau)

will move upward through the country's age structure during the 90-year period between 1946 and 2040 as baby boomers leave young adulthood behind, and enter middle, and then old age (Figure 8-14).

Today baby boomers make up nearly half of all adult Americans. They dominate the population's demand for goods and services, and companies not providing products and services for this aging population group can go bankrupt. In addition, baby boomers, making up about 60% of registered voters in 1993, play an increasingly important role in deciding who gets elected and what laws are passed.

During their working years baby boomers will create a large surplus of money in the Social Security trust fund. However, unless changes in funding procedures are made, the retired baby boomers will use up this surplus by 2048. Elderly baby boomers will also put severe strains on health care services.

The economic burden of helping support so many retired baby boomers will be on the *baby-bust generation*, the much smaller group of people born between 1970 and 1985, when total fertility rates fell sharply (Figure 8-6). Retired baby boomers may use their political clout to force members of the baby-bust generation to pay higher income, health care, and Social Security taxes.

In some respects the baby-bust generation should have an easier time than the baby-boom generation. Fewer people will be competing for education, jobs, and services, and labor shortages may drive up wages, at least for jobs requiring education or technical training beyond high school. On the other hand, the baby-bust group may find it hard to get job promotions as they reach middle age because most upper-level positions will be occupied by the much larger baby-boom group. And many baby boomers may delay retirement because of improved health and the need to build up adequate retirement funds.

From these few projections we see that any baby-boom bulge or baby-bust indentation in the age structure of a population creates social and economic changes that ripple through a society for decades.

**POPULATION DECLINE** Natural population decrease (more deaths than births) is already a reality in Hungary and Germany. Most other European countries are at or near zero population growth and could undergo population declines in the next century. Japan also faces this prospect sometime after 2025 (Case Study, p. 213).

If population decline is gradual, its negative effects can usually be managed. But rapid population decline, like rapid population growth, can lead to severe economic and social problems. For example, once a country reaches zero population growth and then experiences a rapid population decline, the proportion of the population made up of older people rises sharply. Older people consume a large share of medical, social security, and other costly public services. A country with a declining population can also face labor shortages unless it relies on greatly increased automation, immigration of foreign workers, or both.

Q: By 2000 how many people may not be able to get enough fuelwood?

## The Graying of Japan

**CASE STUDY**

In only seven years, between 1949 and 1956, Japan (Figure 8-15) cut its birth rate, total fertility rate, and population growth rate in half, mostly because of a liberal abortion law and access to family planning implemented by the post–World War II U.S. occupation forces and the Japanese government. Since 1956 these rates have declined further.

In 1949 Japan's total fertility rate was 4.5. In 1993 it was 1.5—one of the world's lowest—and is projected to fall to 1.35 in 1996. Average life expectancy at birth is 79 years—the highest in the world. Japan also has one of the world's lowest death rates for infants under one year of age. Japan's population of 124 million in 1993 is growing very slowly and is projected to be the same in 2025.

As Japan approaches zero population growth, it is beginning to face some of the problems of an aging population. Between 1993 and 2010 Japan's population age 65 or older is expected to increase 13% to 21%, and by 2045 to reach 27%.

Japan's universal health insurance and pension systems used about 41% of Japan's national income in 1993. This economic burden is projected to rise to 60% or higher in 2020, with at least two-thirds of the expenditures for pen-

sions and the virtually free health care provided to the elderly. Economists worry that the steep taxes needed to fund these services could discourage economic growth.

Since 1980 Japan has been feeling the effects of a declining work force. This is one reason it has invested heavily in automation and has encouraged women to work outside the home.

The population of Japan is 99% Japanese. Fearing a breakdown in its social cohesiveness, the government has been unwilling to increase

immigration to provide more workers. Despite this official policy the country is becoming increasingly dependent on illegal immigrants to keep its economic engines running. How Japan deals with these problems will provide ideas for the United States and other countries as they make the transition to zero population growth and, eventually, to population decline.

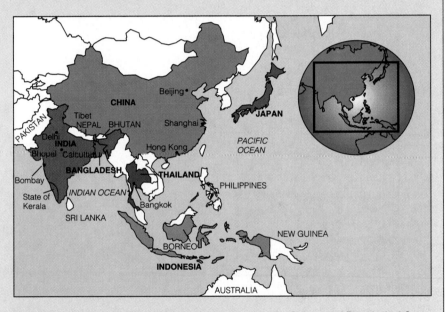

**Figure 8-15** Where are Japan, Thailand, Indonesia, India, China, and Bangladesh?

---

Fearing that declining populations will threaten their economic and national security, some European countries have offered economic incentives to encourage more births. Examples include giving couples who have children housing or other benefits and paying women while they are on maternity leave and guaranteeing their jobs if they decide to return to work after giving birth. In some cases such incentives slowed the rate of decline, but not enough to prevent eventual population decline. Massive immigration is also a solution to population decline and labor shortages, but so far Japan and most European countries have opposed this approach.

**8-3** | **Influencing Population Change**

CONTROLLING MIGRATION  A government can influence the size and rate of growth or decline of its population by encouraging a change in any of the three basic demographic variables: births, deaths, and migration. Only a few countries, chiefly Canada, Australia, and the United States (Case Study, p. 214), allow large annual increases in population from immigration, and some countries encourage emigration to reduce population pressures.

A: 3 billion

# Immigration and Population Growth in the United States

Between 1820 and 1993 the United States admitted almost twice as many immigrants and refugees as all other countries combined. However, the number of legal immigrants has varied during different periods because of changes in immigration laws and rates of economic growth (Figure 8-16).

Between 1820 and 1960 most legal immigrants came from Europe. Since then most have come from Asia and Latin America. Almost two-thirds of new U.S. immigrants live in just five states: California, New York, Texas, Florida, and Illinois.

Between 1960 and 1991 the number of legal immigrants per year rose from 265,000 to about 1 million (1.8 million in 1991)—twice as many legal immigrants as in all other countries combined. Each year 200,000–500,000 more people enter illegally, most from Mexico and other Latin American countries. This means that in 1993 legal and illegal immigrants increased the U.S. population by 1.2–1.5 million people, accounting for 37–43% of the country's population growth. These figures do not include refugees, who are admitted under other regulations. Soon immigration is expected to be the primary factor increasing the population of the United States (Figure 8-17). In 1992 the U.S. Census Bureau projected that between 1992 and 2050 the U.S. population would increase by 50% from 258 million to 383 million—mostly because of immigra-

tion and high fertility rates among women in many ethnic groups.

Some demographers and environmentalists call for an annual ceiling of no more than 450,000 people for all categories of legal immigration, including refugees. They argue that this will allow the country to reach zero population growth sooner and

reduce the enormous environmental impact of consumption overpopulation (Figure 1-16).

Some opponents of the country's open-door policy portray legal immigrants as either job stealers or welfare recipients, but recent studies indicate that this is not true. Many immigrants take low-paying,

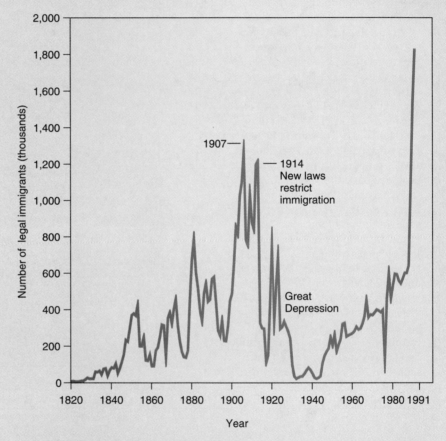

**Figure 8-16** Legal immigration to the United States, 1820–1993. The much higher rates since 1989 represent a combination of normal immigration levels of around 700,000 per year plus illegal immigrants living in the country for years who were granted legal status under the Immigration Reform and Control Act of 1986. (Data from U.S. Immigration and Naturalization Service)

**INFLUENCING BIRTHS** Because raising the death rate is not ethically acceptable, lowering the birth rate is the focus of most efforts to slow population growth. Today about 93% of the world's population and 91% of the people in LDCs live in countries with fertility reduction programs. Three general approaches to

decreasing birth rates are economic development, family planning, and socioeconomic changes.

The funding for and effectiveness of these programs vary widely from country to country. Few governments spend more than 1% of the national budget on them. There is also controversy over

Q: What percentage of the original old-growth forests in the United States have been cut?

often menial jobs that many Americans don't want. Also, immigrants draw very lightly on Social Security and Medicare, and they make virtually the same demands as other Americans do on other kinds of welfare spending. Moreover, a typical working immigrant adds about $3,000 a year to the Social Security trust fund. As workers and consumers, trained immigrants also contribute to economic growth. They create jobs, sometimes helping ailing businesses stay alive. But illegal immigrants can strain state and local budgets. For example, California's auditor general estimated in 1992 that illegal immigrants cost the state $3 billion per year.

In 1986 Congress passed a new law designed to help control illegal immigration, primarily from Mexico and other Latin American countries. The law prohibits the hiring of illegal immigrants and requires employers to check the documents of new employees. Employers who knowingly hire illegal immigrants can be fined, and repeat offenders sentenced to prison for up to six months. The bill also authorized funds to enforce the law, to increase border patrol staff by 50%, and to deport illegal immigrants.

Critics charge that illegal immigrants can get around the law with fake documents because employers are not responsible for verifying the authenticity of documents. Besides, despite more funds, the Immigration and Naturalization Service does not have enough money or staff to enforce the new law effectively or to patrol more than a small fraction of the 3,140-kilometer (1,950-mile) U.S.–Mexico border. And with nearly 60% of Mexico's labor force unemployed or underemployed, many Mexicans and other Latin American immigrants think being caught and sent back is a minor risk compared with remaining in poverty.

Some analysts favor changing immigration law to give preference to highly educated English speakers with valuable professional skills. Others argue that such a policy would amount to a brain drain of educated and talented people from LDCs that need these important human resources. It would also diminish the historical role of the United States as a place of opportunity for the world's poor and oppressed. Despite these arguments Congress voted in 1990 to increase the number of immigrants with special skills and talents admitted each year from 54,000 to 140,000.

What, if anything, do you think should be done about legal and illegal immigration into the United States?

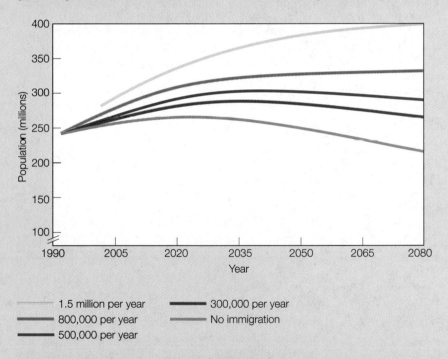

**Figure 8-17** Immigration to and projected population growth of the United States, 1990–2080. These projections assume that fertility levels will remain around 1.9 children per woman during this period. These projections may be too low because traditionally most immigrants have tended to have large families. (Data from U.S. Bureau of the Census and Population Reference Bureau)

whether population growth is good or bad (Pro/Con, p. 216).

**CONNECTIONS: COMPUTER MODELING AND LIMITS TO GROWTH** Individuals, businesses, and governments continually make plans based on what they think might or might not happen in the future. Mostly we use intuitive mental models to project alternative futures based on making assumptions about which existing trends are the most important and then extending (extrapolating) them into the future. If we use different assumptions we can get quite different

Because of differing concepts of carrying capacity and differing worldviews, experts disagree as to what level of population is too high.

To some the planet is already overpopulated (Figure 1-16). Others project that if everyone existed at a minimum survival level, the earth could support 20–48 billion people. This would require that everyone exist only on a diet of grain, that all arable land be cultivated, and that much of the earth's crust be mined to a depth of 1.6 kilometers (1 mile). Still others believe the planet could support 7–12 billion people at a decent standard of living by distributing land and food more equitably and by shifting from use of less abundant resources (such as lead, tin, uranium, oil, and natural gas) to use of more abundant resources (such as aluminum, glass, and solar energy).

Maximum sustainable population, however, is a slippery number that can move up or down with climate change, environmental degradation, and advances in technology. Let's assume for the moment that these optimistic estimates are technologically and environmentally feasible. Even so, many analysts doubt that our social and political structures can adapt to such a crowded and stressful world, and believe that the chances of mass destruction through warfare would increase sharply as countries competed for dwindling resources.

Others believe that asking how many people the world can support is the wrong question—like asking how many cigarettes one can smoke before getting lung cancer. Instead, they say, we should be asking what the *optimum sustainable population* of Earth might be. Such an optimum level would allow most, if not all, people to live with reasonable comfort and freedom without impairing the ability of the planet to sustain future generations.

Again, no one knows what this optimum population might be. Some consider it a meaningless question; some put it at 20 billion, others at 8 billion, and others at a level below today's population size.

Critics of the view that Earth is overpopulated point out that the world now supports 5.5 billion people whose average life span is longer than at any time in the past.

Things are getting better, not worse, for many of the world's people. They say that talk of a population crash is alarmist, that the world can support billions more people, and that people are the world's most valuable resource for solving problems. More people increase economic productivity by creating and applying new knowledge, and stimulate economic growth by becoming consumers. These analysts are confident that human ingenuity will permit continued improvement in humanity's lot into the indefinite future (Guest Essay, p. 24).

Some believe that if population declines in the MDCs, their economies will suffer and their power will decrease. To these analysts the primary cause of poverty is not population growth but the lack of free and productive economic systems in LDCs. And they argue that without more babies MDCs with declining populations will face a shortage of workers, taxpayers, scientists and engineers, consumers, and soldiers needed to maintain healthy economic growth, national security, and global power and influence. They also contend that the aging societies in MDCs will be

results. Put garbage in and you get garbage out. Since we can't know the future, this and all forms of modeling are exploratory projections of what *might* happen—not predictions or forecasts of what *will* happen.

The human mind can handle only a small number of variables and trends at one time. This problem is complicated even further because of the time delays and synergistic interactions found in complex social and ecological systems (Section 6-1), as well as the potential effects of totally unexpected events. Experience suggests that we can write a simple formula that often describes our attempts to make future plans and change the world using intuitive mental models or thinking: STS = LTP (short-term solution equals long-term problem).

Since 1970 *system dynamics computer modeling* has been used to mimic the behavior of complex systems and to make projections about how key variables can interact. Systems analysts develop mathematical equations that represent key variables and their interactions resulting from feedback loops, time delays, synergistic interactions, and other properties of complex systems. Then the equations are fed into a computer and used to project future dynamic behavior of the system and to test the potential effects of various policy decisions on the system. One of the nice things about such models is that we can play with them by asking, What if we do so and so? and running the model to project what the results might be (Spotlight, p. 219).

ECONOMIC DEVELOPMENT AND THE DEMOGRAPHIC TRANSITION Demographers examined the birth and death rates of western European countries that industrialized during the nineteenth century. From these data they developed a hypothesis of

Q: When did Earth's last ice age end?

less innovative and dynamic. These analysts urge the governments of the United States and other MDCs to prevent this by giving tax breaks and other economic incentives to couples who have more than two children.

Others opposed to population regulation feel that all people should be free to have as many children as they want. Some view population regulation as a violation of their deep religious beliefs, while others see it as an intrusion into their personal privacy and freedom. And minorities sometimes regard it as a form of genocide to keep their numbers and power from rising.

Proponents of population regulation point out that currently we are not providing adequate basic necessities for one out of five people on Earth (Spotlight, p. 10). They see people overpopulation in LDCs and consumption overpopulation in MDCs (Figure 1-16) as threats to Earth's life support systems. They believe that the world is already overpopulated and that we must slow world population growth (Guest Essay, p. 226). They contend that if we don't sharply lower birth rates, we are deciding by default to raise death rates. These analysts recognize that population growth is not the only cause of our environmental and resource problems. They believe, however, that adding several hundred million more people in MDCs and several billion more in LDCs will intensify many environmental and social problems by increasing resource use and waste, increasing environmental degradation and pollution, causing rapid climate change, and reducing biodiversity.

Despite promises about sharing the world's wealth, the gap between rich and poor has been getting wider since 1960 (Figure 1-6). Proponents of population regulation believe this is caused by a combination of population growth in LDCs and unwillingness of MDCs to share the world's resources more fairly.

Those favoring population regulation point out that technological innovation, not sheer numbers of people, is the key to military and economic power. Otherwise, England, Germany, Japan, and Taiwan, with fairly small populations, should have little global economic and military power, and China and India should rule the world. Also, as world military tensions ease, people are becoming aware that environmental security is now the key to both economic and national security.

Proponents of population regulation believe that the United States and other MDCs, rather than encouraging births, should establish an official goal of stabilizing their populations by 2025 and then begin a gradual population decline. This would help reduce their severe environmental impact on the ecosphere. It would also set a good example for LDCs to reduce their population growth more rapidly and adopt sustainable forms of economic development.

These analysts believe that people should have the freedom to produce as many children as they want only so long as this does not reduce the quality of other people's lives now and in the future by impairing the ability of Earth to sustain life. Limiting an individual's freedom to protect the freedom of all is the basis of most laws in modern societies. What do you think?

---

population change known as the **demographic transition**: As countries become industrialized, first their death rates and then their birth rates decline.

This transition takes place in four distinct phases (Figure 8-18). In the *preindustrial stage* harsh living conditions lead to a high birth rate (to compensate for high infant mortality) and a high death rate. Thus there is little population growth.

In the *transitional stage* industrialization begins, food production rises, and health care improves. Death rates drop, but birth rates remain high, so the population grows rapidly (typically 2.5–3% a year).

In the *industrial stage* industrialization is widespread. The birth rate drops and eventually approaches the death rate, primarily because couples in cities realize that children are expensive to raise and that having too many children hinders them from taking advantage of job opportunities in an expanding economy. Population growth continues, but at a slower and perhaps fluctuating rate, depending on economic conditions. Most MDCs are now in this third phase.

In the *postindustrial stage* the birth rate declines even further to equal the death rate, thus reaching zero population growth. Then the birth rate falls below the death rate, and total population size slowly decreases. Emphasis shifts from unsustainable to sustainable forms of economic development.

In most LDCs today death rates have fallen much more than birth rates (Figure 8-9). In other words, these LDCs, mostly in Southeast Asia, Africa, and Latin America, are still in the transitional phase, halfway up the economic ladder, with high population growth rates. Some economists believe that LDCs will make the demographic transition over the next few decades without increased family-planning efforts. But many population analysts fear that the

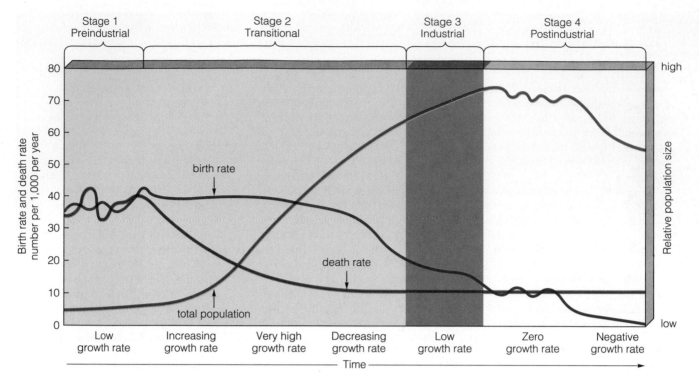

**Figure 8-18** Generalized model of the demographic transition.

rapid population growth in many LDCs will outstrip economic growth and overwhelm local life support systems—causing many of these countries to be caught in a *demographic trap*.

Furthermore, some of the conditions that allowed the MDCs to develop are not available to today's LDCs. Even with large and growing populations, many LDCs do not have enough skilled workers to produce the high-technology products needed to compete in today's economic environment. Most low-and middle-income LDCs also lack the capital and resources needed for rapid economic development. Also, the amount of money being given or loaned to LDCs—struggling under tremendous debt burdens—has been decreasing since 1980. Indeed, since the mid-1980s the LDCs have paid MDCs about $50 billion a year more (mostly in debt interest) than they have received from these countries.

**FAMILY PLANNING** Family-planning programs provide educational and clinical services that help couples choose how many children to have and when to have them. Such programs vary from culture to culture; but most provide information on birth spacing, birth control (Figures 8-7 and 8-8), breastfeeding (Spotlight, p. 222), and prenatal care as well as distribute contraceptives. In some cases, they also perform abortions and sterilizations, often without charge or at low rates.

Family-planning services were first introduced in LDCs in the 1940s and 1950s by private physicians and women's groups. Since then, the International Planned Parenthood Federation, the Planned Parenthood Federation of America, the United Nations Fund for Population Activities, the U.S. Agency for International Development, the Ford Foundation, the World Bank, and other organizations have helped countries carry out family planning by providing technical assistance, funding, or both.

Family planning has been an important factor in increasing the percentage of couples in LDCs using contraception from 10% in the 1960s to 51% today and in the drop in total fertility rate in LDCs from 6 in 1960 to 3.8 in 1993. Family planning also saves a government money by reducing the need for various social services. It also has health benefits. In LDCs, for example, about 1 million women per year die from pregnancy-related causes. Half of these deaths could be prevented by effective family-planning and health care programs. Family-planning programs also help control the spread of AIDS and other sexually transmitted diseases.

The effectiveness of family planning has varied depending on program design and funding. It has been a significant factor in reducing birth and fertility rates in populous countries such as China (Section 8-4), Indonesia (Case Study, p. 223), and Brazil. In Brazil—the world's eighth most populous country—

Q: What is the greenhouse effect?

In the early 1970s Jay Forrester, Donella Meadows, Dennis Meadows, Jørgen Randers, and their associates developed dynamic world computer models to evaluate the limits to growth of the human population and industrialization. The models looked at the dynamic interaction of five major variables: population, pollution, use of nonrenewable resources, industrial output per capita, and food output per capita.

In 1972 the projections of the model were published in *The Limits to Growth*. These projections indicated that if economic, resource use, and population trends in the early 1970s continued unchanged, the limits to physical growth on this planet would be reached within 100 years and result in economic and ecological collapse. The model was also used to demonstrate that certain policy changes could forestall such collapse.

The projections of this model challenged the basic assumptions of today's industrial societies—namely, that new advances in technology place no physical limits on industrial growth and population growth. *Limits to Growth* (with sales of 9 million copies in 29 languages) generated intense debate and research efforts.

Twenty years later, in 1992, the authors of the original study updated their work in *Beyond the Limits: Confronting Global Collapse, Envisioning a Sustainable Future*. Their updated computer modeling projects that the world has already overshot some of its limits and that, if current trends continue unchanged, we face global economic and environmental collapse sometime in the next century.

By feeding various policy decisions on population, resource use, pollution control, and industrial and food output per capita into their model, the researchers were able to project a range of outcomes, from collapse to economic and environmental sustainability, a few of which are discussed in this Spotlight. This dynamic computer model allows us to ask *what if* questions, such as the ones that follow.

**Question 1** *What if the world's population and industrial output continue to expand exponentially at 1990 rates with no major policy changes?* Figure 8-19 summarizes the results projected by the model in this business-as-usual scenario. This standard run projects that this would lead to overshoot and collapse of the system sometime within the next 100 years. In this case the collapse would be caused by depletion of nonrenewable resources and environmental overload. Another run of the model shows that doubling the projected supply of nonrenewable resources would delay overshoot and collapse by about 20 years. If

(continued)

**State of the World**

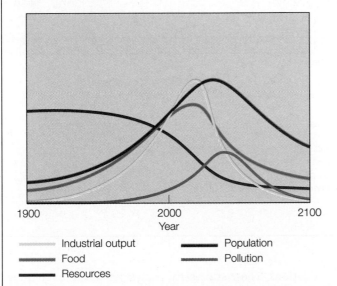

**Material Standard of Living**

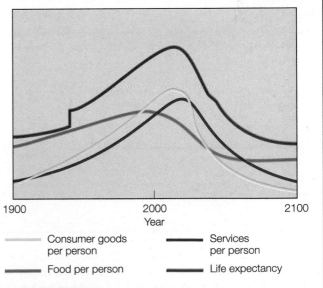

Legend (State of the World):
- Industrial output
- Food
- Resources
- Population
- Pollution

Legend (Material Standard of Living):
- Consumer goods per person
- Food per person
- Services per person
- Life expectancy

**Figure 8-19** Computer model scenario projecting what might happen if the world's population and economic growth continue growing exponentially at 1990 levels assuming no major policy changes or technological innovations. (Used by permission from Donella Meadows et al., *Beyond the Limits: Confronting Global Collapse, Envisioning a Sustainable Future*, Chelsea Green Publishing Co., Post Mills, Vt., 1992)

everyone had no more than two children beginning in 1995 and economic growth continued at 1990 levels, collapse could be delayed another 20 years. Even if no more children were born beginning in 1995, the system would still eventually collapse. In other words, according to this model the people already alive today are enough to drive the world to economic and social collapse if current per capita consumption and industrial output trends continue.

**Question 2** *What if we can use technology to double nonrenewable*

*resource supplies, pollution control effectiveness, crop and timber yields, soil erosion protection, and the efficiency of resource use within 20 years?* Figure 8-20 shows that this would allow population to grow to about 12.5 billion by 2100 and industrial output to continue rising until about 2050. After that industrial output per person would fall along with life expectancy because of the high cost of maintaining and improving technology and because of environmental overload.

**Question 3** *How can we avoid overshoot and collapse and make a fairly*

*smooth transition to a sustainable future?* Figure 8-21 shows one scenario of how this could be done by improving technology within 20 years as in Figure 8-20, making birth control available to everyone by 1995, and stabilizing per capita industrial output at 1990 levels.

The developers of this model stress that the model gives only projections, not predictions. Instead of viewing the projections as models of doom, they see them as challenges, opportunities, and possible guidelines for achieving economically and environmentally sustain-

**State of the World**

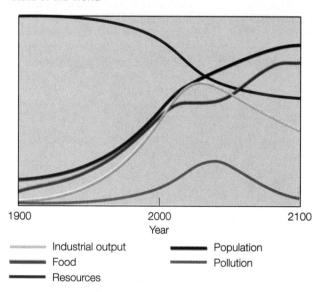

**Material Standard of Living**

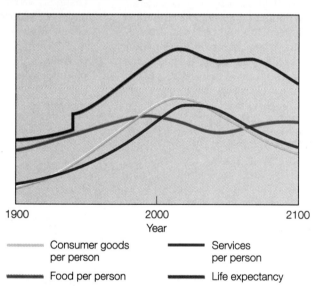

**Figure 8-20** Computer model scenario projecting what might happen if, beginning in 1995, we can use technology to double supplies of nonrenewable resources, crop and timber yields, soil erosion protection, and the efficiency of resource use within 20 years. (Used by permission from Donella Meadows et al., *Beyond the Limits: Confronting Global Collapse, Envisioning a Sustainable Future*, Chelsea Green Publishing Co., Post Mills, Vt., 1992)

for instance, the fertility rate fell from 6.8 in 1965 to 3.1 in 1993. However, because 35% of Brazilians are under age 15, the country's population is projected to rise from 151 million to 237 million between 1993 and 2025. Family planning has also played a major role in reducing population growth in Thailand (p. 202), Mexico, and several other LDCs with moderate-to-small populations. These successful programs based on committed leadership, local implementation, and wide availability of contraceptives show that population rates can be decreased significantly within two to three decades.

Family planning, however, has had moderate-to-poor results in more populous LDCs such as India,

Q: Is there doubt about the validity of the greenhouse effect?

able societies. According to their model this can be achieved by:

- Using nonrenewable material and energy resources at much lower rates

- Using potentially renewable resources no faster than they can regenerate themselves

- Dramatically reducing resource waste (and thus pollution and environmental degradation) by using all resources at maximum efficiency

- Halting the exponential growth of population and harmful industrial outputs by emphasizing sufficiency, equity (fairer resource and wealth distribution), and quality of life rather than quantity of people and goods

- Developing approaches to end poverty

They believe that making these changes requires an emphasis on love, generosity, cooperation, and compassion more than on competition, productivity, and technology.

**State of the World**

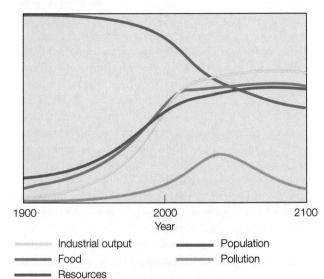

**Material Standard of Living**

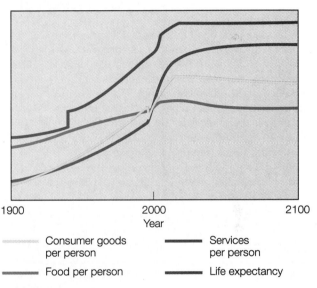

**Figure 8-21** Computer model scenario projecting how we might avoid overshoot and collapse, and make a fairly smooth transition to a sustainable future. This run assumes that, beginning in 1995, we can accomplish the same improvements in technology represented by the model in Figure 8-19 within 20 years. It also assumes that, beginning in 1995, 100% effective birth control is made available to everyone, that no couple has more than two children, and that industrial output per capita is stabilized at $350 (equivalent to the average standard of living in Europe in 1990). Another computer run shows that waiting until 2015 to implement these changes would lead to collapse and overshoot sometime around 2075, followed by a transition to sustainability by 2100. (Used by permission from Donella Meadows et al., *Beyond the Limits: Confronting Global Collapse, Envisioning a Sustainable Future*, Chelsea Green Publishing Co., Post Mills, Vt., 1992)

Egypt, Bangladesh, Pakistan, and Nigeria. Results have also been poor in 79 less populous LDCs—especially in Africa and Latin America—where population growth rates are usually very high.

The delivery of family-planning services in many LDCs is still woefully inadequate, particularly in rural areas. At least 300 million women in LDCs want to limit the number and determine the spacing of their children but lack access to such services. Extending family-planning services to these women and to those who will soon be entering their reproductive years could prevent an estimated 5.8 million births a year and more than 130,000 abortions a day. According to the Alan Guttmacher Institute, a nonprofit research group,

A: No. Without it, Earth would be too cold for life as we know it to exist.

CHAPTER 8    221

## Breastfeeding

Although it is not a reliable method of birth control, regular breastfeeding does prevent some women from ovulating, and thus delays their next possible pregnancy. Studies have shown that pregnancy is rare among nursing mothers who have not yet resumed their monthly menstrual cycles. Generally women who are feeding their infant only breast milk are 98% protected from pregnancy for six months after delivery. However, *any supplement to the breast milk can interfere with this natural contraceptive protection.* Breastfeeding also helps reduce infant mortality rates because mother's milk provides a baby with antibodies to help prevent disease, as well as usually being the most nutritious food available for infants in poor families.

Unfortunately breastfeeding is declining in many LDCs, mostly because large corporations have promoted the use of infant formulas instead of mother's milk—telling poor mothers that formula is more modern and is better for their baby. Buying infant formula when free breast milk is available is an unnecessary expense for a poor family struggling to survive. Moreover, poor people, lacking fuel, often prepare formula with unboiled, contaminated water and use unsterilized bottles. Thus using formula can lead to more infant illnesses and deaths.

widespread use of Ovral, a contraceptive also used as a morning-after pill, could prevent as many as 800,000 abortions and 2 million unwanted pregnancies per year.

Family planning could be provided in LDCs to all couples who want it for about $10 billion a year—less than four days' worth of world military spending. Currently only about $4.5 billion is being spent. If MDCs provided two-thirds of the $10 billion, each person in the MDCs would spend only $7.70 a year to help reduce world population by 2.7 billion by shrinking average family size from 3.8 to 2.1 children.

**ECONOMIC REWARDS AND PENALTIES** Some population experts argue that family planning, even coupled with economic development, cannot lower birth and fertility rates fast enough to avoid a sharp rise in death rates in many LDCs. The main reason for this is that most couples in LDCs want three or four

children—well above the 2.1 fertility rate needed to bring about population stabilization.

These experts call for increased emphasis on bringing about socioeconomic change to help regulate population size. The key is improving the quality of life, especially in rural areas of LDCs, so that people don't feel that they must have large families to assure that enough children survive to support elderly family members. They call for better basic health care and education, expanded women's rights, increased equity in land ownership, and fair prices for agricultural products.

About 20 countries offer small payments to individuals who agree to use contraceptives or to be sterilized. They also pay doctors and family-planning workers for each sterilization they perform and each IUD they insert. In India, for example, a person receives about $15 for being sterilized, the equivalent of about two weeks' pay for an agricultural worker. Such payments are most likely to attract people who already have all the children they want, however.

Some countries, such as China, penalize couples who have more than a certain number of children—usually one or two—by raising their taxes, charging other fees, or (as in Singapore, Hong Kong, Ghana, and Malaysia) not allowing income tax deductions for a couple's third child. Families who have more children than the prescribed limit may also lose health care benefits, food allotments, and job choice. Such economic penalties can be psychologically coercive for the poor. Programs that withhold food or increase the cost of raising children punish innocent children for the actions of their parents.

Experience has shown that economic rewards and penalties designed to reduce fertility work best if they:

- Nudge rather than push people to have fewer children

- Reinforce existing customs and trends toward smaller families

- Do not penalize people who produced large families before the programs were established

- Increase a poor family's income or land

Once population growth is out of control, a country may be forced to use coercive methods to prevent mass starvation and hardship. This is what China has had to do (Section 8-4).

A few countries have tried to use economic incentives to increase the birth rate. Since the 1930s, for example, France has had vigorous probirth policies. All parents get substantial subsidies and services to help with child rearing. Despite these efforts, however, France's total fertility rate has fallen from 2.7 children per woman in 1960 to 1.8 in 1993.

Q: Why is there concern over a potentially enhanced greenhouse effect?

**CHANGES IN WOMEN'S ROLES** Another socioeconomic method of regulating population, as well as promoting human rights, would be to improve the condition of women. Today women do almost all of the world's domestic work and child care, mostly without pay. They also do more than half the work associated with growing food, gathering fuelwood, and hauling water. Women also provide more health care with little or no pay than all the world's organized health services put together. As one Brazilian woman put it, "For poor women the only holiday is when you are asleep."

The worldwide economic value of women's domestic work is estimated at $4 trillion annually. This unpaid work is not included in the GNP of countries, so the central role of women in an economy is both unrecognized and unrewarded.

Despite their vital economic and social contributions, most women in LDCs don't have a legal right to own land or to borrow money to increase agricultural productivity. Although women work two-thirds of all hours worked in the world, they get only one-tenth of the world's income and own a mere 1% of the world's land. Many are abused or beaten by their husbands, who, in effect, own them as slaves. Furthermore, women make up about 60% of the more than 900 million adults who can neither read nor write. And women suffer the most malnutrition, because men and children are usually fed first where food supplies are limited.

Because of poor health care, complications in pregnancy and childbirth, and unsafe abortion, are the leading killers of women of reproductive age in LDCs. About 1 million women, 95% of them in LDCs, die annually from pregnancy-related causes—a figure that is expected to rise to at least 2 million by 2000. Most of these unnecessary deaths could be prevented by a *safe motherhood program*—including strengthened family-planning services and improved prenatal and delivery care.

Numerous studies have shown that better education is a strong factor leading women to have fewer children. Educated women are more likely than uneducated women to be employed outside the home. They also marry later and lose fewer infants to death.

Giving more women the opportunity to become educated and to work at meaningful, paid jobs outside the home will require some major social changes. Making these changes will be difficult because of the long-standing political and economic domination of society by men throughout the world. In addition, in many countries competition between men and women for already scarce jobs will become even more intense by 2000, when an additional billion people will be looking for work.

**CASE STUDY**

**Indonesia**

Indonesia (Figure 8-15) is the fifth most populous country, with a population of 188 million in 1993. It has one of the world's most successful family-planning programs. Between 1970 and 1993 its birth rate dropped from 44 to 26 per 1,000, the TFR fell from 5.5 to 3.0 children per woman, and the number of couples using contraceptives jumped from close to zero to 50%.

Despite such progress Indonesia still has a long way to go in reducing its population growth. Its population is still growing at a rate of 1.7% per year and, mostly because 37% of its population is under age 15, is projected to reach almost 278 million by 2025.

Indonesia, like most LDCs and MDCs, is faced with a rising pregnancy rate among unmarried teenagers. In 1987 the government began family-planning education for out-of-school teenagers. Sometime in the 1990s government officials expect to have a required population education course in grades 4–12, where students will learn about the economic and environmental implications of population growth.

However, sex education is not being included in the public school curriculum. In a country where 90% of the population is Muslim, the government is fearful that doing so would provoke political instability by alienating Muslim religious leaders.

## 8-4 Case Studies: Population Regulation in India and China

**INDIA** India (Figure 8-15) started the world's first national family-planning program in 1952, when its population was nearly 400 million. In 1993, after 41 years of population control efforts, India was the world's second most populous country, with a population of 900 million.

In 1952 India was adding 5 million people to its population each year. In 1993 it added 18 million—49,300 more mouths to feed each day. Future population growth is fueled by the 36% of India's population under age 15 and is projected to reach 1.4 billion by 2025, and possibly 1.9 billion before leveling off early in the twenty-second century.

India's people are among the poorest in the world. The average income per person is equivalent to less than $350 a year, and for at least one-third of the population it is less than $100 a year—27¢ a day. To add to the problem, nearly half of India's labor force is unemployed or can find only occasional work.

Currently India produces enough food to give its population an adequate survival diet, but widespread poverty means that many people don't have enough land to grow or enough money to buy the food they need. Almost one-third of the present population goes hungry. Life expectancy is only 58 years, and the infant mortality rate is 91 deaths per 1,000 live births.

Some analysts fear that India's already serious hunger and malnutrition problems will worsen as its population continues to grow rapidly. About 40% of India's cropland is degraded as a result of soil erosion, waterlogging, salinization, overgrazing, and deforestation; and roughly 80% of the country's land is subject to repeated droughts—often lasting two to five years.

Without its long-standing family-planning program, India's numbers would be growing even faster. However, the results of the program have been disappointing. Factors contributing to this failure have been poor planning, bureaucratic inefficiency, the low status of women (despite constitutional guarantees of equality), extreme poverty, and a lack of administrative and financial support.

The roots of the problem are deeper. About three out of every four people in India live in one of the 560,000 rural villages, where birth rates tend to be higher than in urban areas and where the illiteracy rate for women is typically 80–90%. For years the government has provided information about the advantages of small families; yet, Indian women still have an average of 3.9 children because most couples believe they need many children as a source of cheap labor and old-age survival insurance. Almost one-third of Indian children die before age 5, reinforcing that belief. And although 90% of Indian couples know of at least one method of birth control, only 49% actually use one. Finally, many social and cultural norms favor large families as well as a strong preference for male children, which means that some couples will keep having children until they produce one or more boys.

In 1976 Indira Gandhi's government started a program that offered financial incentives for sterilization. The program, which was supposed to be voluntary, failed almost immediately, however, because officials allegedly used coercion to meet sterilization quotas in a few rural areas. The resulting backlash played a role in Gandhi's election defeat in 1977.

In 1978 the government took a new approach, raising the legal minimum age for marriage from 18 to 21 for men and from 15 to 18 for women. The 1981 census, however, showed no drop in the population growth rate between 1971 and 1981. Since then the government has increased family-planning efforts and funding, with the goal of achieving 60% contraceptive use—compared to 49% in 1993—and replacement-level fertility by 2000.

The government is also considering job and housing incentives for couples who agree to meet family-planning goals. In addition, the government is pushing to raise the legal marriage age again, increase female literacy and employment opportunities for women, and decrease infant mortality, all of which could help reduce fertility levels. Whether these efforts will succeed remains to be seen.

**CHINA** Since 1970 China (Figure 8-15) has made impressive efforts to feed its people and bring its population growth under control. Between 1972 and 1985 China achieved a remarkable drop in its crude birth rate, from 32 to 18 per 1,000 people; and its total fertility rate dropped from 5.7 to 2.1 children per woman. Since 1985 China's infant mortality rate has been less than one-half the rate in India. Life expectancy in China is 71 years—12 years higher than in India. China's average per capita income of $370 is similar to that in India.

To achieve a sharp drop in fertility, China has established the most extensive, intrusive, and strict population control program in the world. Couples are strongly urged to postpone the age at which they marry and to have no more than one child (Figure 8-22). Married couples have ready access to free sterilization, contraceptives, and abortion. Paramedics and mobile units ensure access even in rural areas. Couples who pledge not to have more than one child are given extra food, larger pensions, better housing, free medical care, and salary bonuses; their child will be provided with free school tuition and with preferential treatment in employment when he or she enters the job market. Those who break the pledge lose all the benefits. All leaders are expected to set an example by limiting their own family size. The result is that 71% of married women in China are using contraception compared to only 43% in other LDCs.

These are drastic measures, but government officials realized in the 1960s that the only alternative to strict population control was mass starvation. Between 1958 and 1962 alone an estimated 30 million Chinese starved to death.

China is a dictatorship. Thus, unlike India, which is a democracy, China has been able to impose a unified policy from the top down. Moreover, Chinese society is fairly homogeneous and has a widespread common written language. India, by contrast, has over 1,600 languages and dialects and numerous religions, which

Q: What are the main greenhouse gases?

**Figure 8-22** Poster encouraging couples in China to have no more than one child. Couples who comply are given economic rewards, while those who do not suffer economic penalties.

makes it more difficult to educate people about family planning and to institute population regulation policies.

Despite these efforts China's population control program has faltered since 1985. Between 1985 and 1993 the birth rate rose from 17 to 20 per 1,000; the average total fertility rate increased from 2.1 to 2.2; and the annual population growth rate rose from 1% to 1.3%. The primary reasons for these increases were the large number of women moving into their childbearing years, some relaxation of the government's stringent policies, and a strong preference for male children. Since 1990 the number of homeless and hungry people in China has also been rising.

China's leaders have a goal of reaching zero population growth by 2000 with a population of l.2 billion, followed by a slow decline to a population of 0.6–1.0 billion by 2100. Achieving this goal will be very difficult, because 27% of the Chinese people are under age 15. As a result the United Nations projects that the population of China may be around 1.2 billion by 2000, 1.6 billion by 2025, and 1.7 billion before reaching zero population growth perhaps around 2100.

Most countries do not want to use the coercive elements of China's program. Coercion is not only incompatible with democratic values and notions of basic human rights but ineffective in the long run because sooner or later people resist being coerced. Other parts of this program, however, could be used in many LDCs. Especially useful is the practice of localizing the program, rather than asking the people to go to distant centers. Perhaps the best lesson that other countries can learn from China's experience is not to wait to curb population growth until the choice is between mass starvation and coercive measures that severely restrict human freedom.

## 8-5 Solutions: Cutting Global Population Growth

Lester Brown, (Guest Essay, p. 43) president of the Worldwatch Institute, urges the leaders of countries to adopt a goal of cutting world population growth in half during the 1990s by reducing the average global birth rate from 26 to 18 per 1,000 people.

The experience of countries such as China, Japan (Case Study, p. 213), and Thailand (p. 202) indicate that this is a realistic goal. Each of us plays an important role in controlling global population growth.

*Short of thermonuclear war itself, rampant population growth is the gravest issue the world faces over the decades immediately ahead.*

Robert S. McNamara

## Critical Thinking

1. Why are falling birth rates not necessarily a reliable indicator of future population growth trends?

2. Why is it rational for a poor couple in India to have six or seven children? What changes might induce such a couple to think of their behavior as irrational?

3. Project what your own life may be like at ages 25, 45, and 65 on the basis of the present population age structure of the country in which you live.

4. Do you believe there are physical limits to growth on Earth? Explain.

5. Do you believe that all U.S. high schools and colleges should have health clinics that make contraceptives

## Moral Implications of Cultural Carrying Capacity

*Garrett Hardin*

**GUEST ESSAY**

*As long-time professor of human ecology at the University of California at Santa Barbara, Garrett Hardin made important contributions to the joining of ethics and biology. He has raised hard ethical questions, sometimes taken unpopular stands, and forced people to think deeply about environmental problems and their possible solutions. He is best known for his 1968 essay "The Tragedy of the Commons," which has had a significant impact on the disciplines of economics and political science, and on the issue of management of potentially renewable resources. His many books include* Promethean Ethics *and* Filters Against Folly: How to Survive Despite Economists, Ecologists, and the Merely Eloquent *(see Further Readings).*

For many years Angel Island in San Francisco Bay was plagued with too many deer. A few animals transplanted there early in this century lacked predators and rapidly increased to nearly 300 deer—far beyond the carrying capacity of the island. Scrawny, underfed animals tugged at the heartstrings of Californians, who carried extra food for them from the mainland to the island.

Such charity worsened the plight of the deer. Excess animals trampled the soil, stripped the bark from small trees, and destroyed seedlings of all kinds. The net effect was to lower the carrying capacity, year by year, as the deer continued to multiply in a deteriorating habitat.

State game managers proposed that the excess deer be shot by skilled hunters. "How cruel!" some people protested. Then the managers proposed that coyotes be imported to the island. Though not big enough to kill adult deer, coyotes can kill defenseless young fawns, thus reducing the size of the herd. However, the Society for the Prevention of Cruelty to Animals was adamantly opposed to such human introduction of predators.

In the end, it was agreed that some deer would be exported to some other area suitable for deer life. A total of 203 animals were caught and trucked many miles away. From the fate of a sample of animals fitted with radio collars, it was estimated that 85% of the transported deer died within a year (most of them within two months) from various causes: predation by coyotes, bobcats, and domestic dogs; shooting by poachers and legal hunters; and being run over by automobiles.

The net cost (in 1982 dollars) for relocating each animal that survived for a year was $2,876. The state stopped financing the program, and no volunteers stepped forward to pay future bills.

Angel Island is a microcosm of the planet as a whole. Organisms reproduce exponentially, but the environment doesn't increase at all. The moral is a simple ecological commandment: *Thou shalt not transgress the carrying capacity.*

Now let's look at the human situation. A competent physicist has placed the human carrying capacity of the globe at 50 billion—about 10 times the present world population. Before you are tempted to urge women to have more babies, however, consider what Robert Malthus said nearly 200 years ago: "There should be no more people in a country than could enjoy daily a glass of wine and piece of beef for dinner."

A diet of grain or bread and water is symbolic of minimum living standards; wine and beef are symbolic of higher living standards that make greater demands on the environment. When land that could produce plants for direct human consumption is used to grow grapes for wine or corn for cattle, fewer calories get to the human population. Since carrying capacity is defined as the *maximum* number of animals (humans) an area can support, using part of the area to support such cultural luxuries as wine and beef reduces the carrying capacity. This reduced capacity is called the *cultural carrying capacity*. Cultural carrying capacity is always less than simple carrying capacity.

Energy is the common coin in which all competing demands on the environment can be measured. Energy saved by giving up a luxury can be used to produce more bread and support more people. We could increase the simple carrying capacity of the earth by giving up any (or all) of the following "luxuries": street lighting, vacations, private cars, air conditioning, and artistic performances of all sorts—drama, dance, music, and lectures. Since the heating of buildings is not as efficient as multiple layers of clothing, space heating could be forbidden as a luxury.

Is that all? By no means. To come closer to home, look at this book. Its production and distribution consumes a great deal of energy. In fact, the energy bill for higher education as a whole is very high (which is one reason tuition costs so much). By giving up all education beyond the eighth grade, we could free enough energy to sustain millions of additional human lives.

---

available to students and provide prenatal care for pregnant teenage women? Explain. Should such services be available at the junior high school level, when many teenagers first become sexually active? Explain.

6. **a.** Should the number of legal immigrants and refugees allowed into the United States each year be sharply reduced? Explain.

   **b.** Should illegal immigration into the United States be sharply decreased? Explain. If so, how would you go about achieving this?

7. Should families in the United States be given financial incentives and be persuaded to have more children to prevent population decline? Explain.

8. Debate the following resolution: The United States has a serious consumption overpopulation problem

Q: What are the four main sources of human emissions of greenhouse gases?

At this point a skeptic might well ask: "Does God give a prize for the maximum population?" From this brief analysis we can see that there are two choices. We can maximize the number of human beings living at the lowest possible level of comfort, or we can try to optimize the quality of life for a much smaller population.

What is the carrying capacity of the earth? is a scientific question. Scientifically it may be possible to support 50 billion people at a "bread" level. Is that what we want? The question What is the cultural carrying capacity? requires that we debate questions of value, about which opinions differ.

An even greater difficulty must be faced. So far, we have been treating the capacity question as a *global* question, as if there were a global sovereignty to enforce a solution on all people. However, there is no global sovereignty ("one world"), nor is there any prospect of one in the foreseeable future. We must make do with nearly 200 national sovereignties. That means, as concerns the capacity problem, that we must ask how nations are to coexist in a finite global environment if different sovereignties adopt different standards of living.

Consider a redwood forest [Figure 2-7], which produces no human food. Protected in a park, the trees do not even produce lumber for houses. Because people have to travel many kilometers to visit it, the forest is a net loss in the national energy budget. However, those who are fortunate enough to wander quietly through the cathedral-like aisles of soaring trees report that the forest does something precious for the human spirit.

Now comes an appeal from a distant land where millions are starving because their population has overshot the carrying capacity. We are asked to save lives by sending food. So long as we have surpluses, we may safely indulge in the pleasures of philanthropy. But the typical population in such poor countries increases by 2.3% a year—*or more*; that is, the country's population doubles every 30 years—*or less*. After we have run out of our surpluses, then what?

A spokesperson for the needy makes a proposal: "If you would only cut down your redwood forests, you could use the lumber to build houses and then grow potatoes on the land, shipping the food to us. Since we are all passengers together on Spaceship Earth, are you not duty bound to do so? Which is more precious, trees or humans?"

This last question may sound ethically compelling, but let's look at the consequences of assigning a preemptive and supreme value to human lives. At least 2 billion people in the world are poorer than the 34 million legally "poor" in America, and their numbers are increasing by about 40 million per year. Unless this increase is brought to a halt, sharing food and energy on the basis of need would require the sacrifice of one amenity after another in rich countries. The final result of sharing would be complete poverty everywhere on the face of the earth to maintain the earth's simple carrying capacity. Is that the best humanity can do?

To date there has been an overwhelmingly negative reaction to all proposals to make international philanthropy conditional upon the stopping of population growth by the poor, overpopulated recipient nations. Foreign aid is governed by two apparently inflexible assumptions:

- The right to produce children is a universal, irrevocable right of every nation, no matter how hard it presses against the carrying capacity of its territory.

- When lives are in danger, the moral obligation of rich countries to save human lives is absolute and undeniable.

Considered separately, each of these two well-meaning doctrines might be defended; together, they constitute a fatal recipe. If humanity gives maximum carrying capacity precedence over problems of cultural carrying capacity, the result will be universal poverty and environmental ruin. Or do you see an escape from this harsh dilemma?

## Critical Thinking

1. What population size do you believe would allow the world's people to have a good quality of life? What do you believe is the cultural carrying capacity of the United States? Should the United States have a national policy to establish this population size as soon as possible? Explain.

2. Do you support the two principles this essay lists as the basis of foreign aid to needy countries? If not, what changes would you make in the requirements for receiving such aid?

and should adopt an official policy to stabilize its population and reduce unnecessary resource waste and consumption as rapidly as possible.

9. What are some ways in which women are discriminated against in the United States? On your campus? In what ways, if any, do these forms of discrimination affect fertility?

10. Why has China been more successful than India in reducing its rate of population growth? Do you agree with China's present population control policies? Explain. What alternatives, if any, would you suggest?

*11. Survey members of your class to determine how many children they plan to have, and tally the results.

# 9 Population Distribution: Urban Living

## Is Your City Green? The Ecocity Concept in Davis, California

Today's cities aren't sustainable. They have become dependent on distant sources for their food, water, energy, and materials. Their very presence damages the nearby air, water, soil, and wildlife. Virtually every city can become more self-sufficient, however, by relying more on locally available resources and then using them more sustainably.

Such a sustainable and ecologically healthy city—called an *ecocity* or *green city*—creates far less pollution and waste than conventional cities. Emphasis is on pollution prevention, reuse, recycling, and efficient use of resources (Figure 3-21). Per capita solid waste is greatly reduced, and at least 80% of what is produced is recycled, composted, or reused. An ecocity takes advantage of locally available energy sources and requires that buildings, vehicles, and appliances meet high energy-efficiency standards.

Trees and plants adapted to the local climate and soils are planted throughout the ecocity to provide shade and beauty, to reduce pollution and noise, and to supply habitats for wildlife. Abandoned lots and polluted creeks are cleaned up and restored. Nearby forests, grasslands, wetlands, and farms are preserved instead of being devoured by urban sprawl. Much of the city's food comes from nearby organic farms, solar greenhouses, community gardens, and small gardens on rooftops and in yards and window boxes.

An ecocity is a people-oriented city—not a car-oriented city. Its residents are able to walk or bike to most places, including work, or take low-polluting mass transit. It is designed, retrofitted, and managed to provide a sense of community built around cooperative and vibrant neighborhoods.

The ecocity concept is not a futuristic dream. The citizens and elected officials of Davis, California—a city of about 40,000 people northeast of San Francisco—committed themselves in the early 1970s to making it an ecologically sustainable city.

**Figure 9-1** Solar home in Village Homes development in Davis, California.

Virginia Thigpen

City building codes encourage the use of solar energy for water and space heating. All new homes must meet high standards of energy efficiency. When an existing home changes hands, the buyer must bring it up to the energy conservation standards for new homes. In Davis's Village Homes development, America's first solar neighborhood, all houses are heated by solar energy (Figure 9-1). They face into a common open space reserved for people and bicycles; no cars have access to the interior area. The neighborhood also has orchards, vineyards, and a large community garden. Since 1975 the city has cut its use of energy for heating and cooling in half.

Davis has a solar power plant, which sells some of the electricity it produces to the regional utility company. Eventually the city plans to generate all of its electricity.

The city discourages the use of automobiles and encourages the use of bicycles by closing some streets to automobiles and by building bicycle paths and lanes. Any new housing tract must have a separate bicycle lane, and some city employees are given bikes. As a result, 28,000 bikes account for 40% of all in-city transportation, and less land is needed for parking spaces. This heavy dependence on the bicycle is aided by the city's warm climate and flat terrain.

Davis limits the type and rate of its growth, and maintains a mix of homes for people with low, medium, and high incomes. Development of the fertile farmland surrounding the city for residential or commercial use is restricted.

Davis and other cities—Arcosanti, Arizona; Cerro Gordo, Oregon; Osage, Iowa (p. 46); Horsen, Denmark; and Tapiola, Finland (Case Study, p. 253), for example—are blazing the trail by developing Earth-sustaining neighborhoods that involve people in making their city a better place to live.

The quality of urban life affects every person and every species on the planet. Today almost 45% of the world's population lives in urban areas, and by 2025 this figure is expected to increase to 61%. As the planet becomes more urbanized, reshaping existing cities and designing new ones to work with nature must become one of our top priorities.

This chapter will focus on answering the following questions:

- How is the world's population distributed between rural and urban areas?
- What factors determine how urban areas develop?
- What are the pros and cons of living in an urban area?
- How do transportation systems shape urban areas and growth?
- How can we manage land use in urban areas?
- How can cities be made more livable and sustainable?

## 9-1 Urbanization and Urban Growth

**THE FUTURE IS URBAN** Cities generate and concentrate wealth. They are the main centers for new jobs, education, innovation, culture, and trade. An **urban area** is often defined as a town or city with a population of more than 2,500 people, although some countries set the minimum at 10,000–50,000. A country's **degree of urbanization** is the percentage of its population living in an urban area. **Urban growth** is the rate of growth of urban populations, which grow in two ways: **(1)** by natural increase (more births than deaths) and **(2)** by immigration (mostly from rural areas).

At current rates the world's population will double in 41 years, the urban population in 22 years, and the urban population of LDCs in only 15 years. Several trends are important in understanding the problems and challenges of urbanization and urban growth on our rapidly urbanizing planet:

- The percentage of the population living in urban areas increased from 14% to 45% (73% in MDCs and 34% in LDCs) between 1900 and 1993 (Figure 9-2). It is projected that by 2025 61% of the world's people will be living in urban areas. During the 1990s about 83% of the world's population increase is expected to take place in urban areas—adding about 78 million people a year to these already overburdened areas.

- The number of large cities is mushrooming. Today 1 of every 10 persons lives in a city with a million or more inhabitants, and many of these live in *megacities* with 10 million or more people (Table 9-1). The United Nations projects that by 2000 there will be 26 megacities, more than two-thirds of them in LDCs.

- LDCs, with 34% urbanization, contain 1.5 billion people—more than the total population of Europe, North America, Latin America, and Japan combined. LDCs are projected to reach at least 57% urbanization by 2025 (Figure 9-2).

- In MDCs, with 73% urbanization, urban growth is slower than in LDCs, but MDCs should reach 84% urbanization by 2025 (Figure 9-2).

- Poverty is urbanizing as more poor people migrate from rural to urban areas.

- Despite being centers of commerce and industry, many cities suffer from extreme poverty and social and environmental decay.

**HYPER-URBANIZATION IN LDCs** The most extensive and rapid rural-to-urban migration is in LDCs (Figure 9-2). Yet these countries can't provide adequate food, services, shelter, and jobs for their present urban populations.

People are pulled to urban areas in search of jobs and a better life. They may also be pushed into urban areas by modern mechanized agriculture, which uses less farm labor and allows large landowners to buy out subsistence farmers who cannot afford to modernize. Without jobs or land these people are forced to move to cities.

For example, with 74% of its population living in urban areas, Brazil is more than twice as urbanized as most LDCs. Attracted by the prospect of jobs, many of the rural poor have migrated to Rio de Janeiro and São Paulo, which by 2000 is expected to be the world's second most populous city. As a safety valve for its

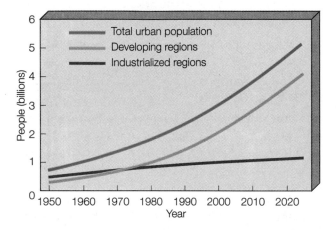

**Figure 9-2** Urban population growth in MDCs and LDCs, 1950–2025. (Data from United Nations and Population Reference Bureau)

| Table 9-1 The 10 Largest Megacity Urban Areas in the World, 1992 and 2000 | | | |
|---|---|---|---|
| **1992** | | **2000** | |
| Urban Area | Population (millions) | Urban Area | Projected Population (millions) |
| Tokyo–Yokohama | 25.8 | Mexico City | 25.6 |
| São Paulo | 19.2 | São Paulo | 22.1 |
| New York–N.E. New Jersey | 16.2 | Tokyo–Yokohama | 18.8 |
| Mexico City | 15.3 | Shanghai | 17.0 |
| Shanghai | 14.1 | New York–N.E. New Jersey | 16.8 |
| Bombay | 13.3 | Calcutta | 15.7 |
| Los Angeles | 11.9 | Bombay | 15.4 |
| Greater Buenos Aires | 11.8 | Beijing | 14.0 |
| Seoul | 11.6 | Los Angeles | 13.9 |
| Beijing | 11.4 | Jakarta | 13.7 |
| Data from United Nations | | | |

Q: What greenhouse gas is being emitted into the atmosphere in the largest quantity from human activities?

exploding population, the Brazilian government has encouraged migration of the landless poor to the vast Amazon Basin (Figure 9-3). This policy is supported by large landowners, who want to defuse pressures for more equitable land distribution in agricultural areas, and by wealthy ranchers, who receive government subsidies to establish cattle ranches by clearing tropical forests in the Amazon Basin.

Urban growth in LDCs is also fueled by government policies that distribute most income and social services to urban dwellers at the expense of rural dwellers. For example, in many LDCs where 70% of the population is rural, only about 20% of the national budget goes to the rural sector. The result is the urbanization of poverty as the city becomes a poverty trap, not an oasis of economic opportunity for these urban immigrants (Case Study, p. 232). Those fortunate enough to get a job must work long hours for low wages. These jobs may expose them to dust, hazardous chemicals, excessive noise, and dangerous machinery. As one observer put it, "The rich get the profits, the poor get the poisons."

Worldwide an estimated 150 million people are homeless (Figure 1-8). Worse still, the United Nations estimates that at least 1 billion people—18% of the world's population—live in the crowded slums of central cities and in the vast, mostly illegal squatter settlements or shantytowns that ring the outskirts of most cities in LDCs. Squatters, whose numbers are rising rapidly, are rarely included in urban population estimates such as those given in Table 9-1.

In squatter settlements—such as the one in Rio de Janeiro, Brazil, shown on p. 201—people generally live illegally on public or private land that no one else wants because it is too wet, too dry, too steep, too dangerous (subject to landslides, flooding, or fumes from industrial plants), or too polluted (city dumps). Most of the squatters live in shacks made from corrugated metal, plastic sheets, cardboard, discarded packing crates, or whatever building materials they can come up with. The inhabitants live in constant fear of having their settlements bulldozed or burned by city officials.

Many cities refuse to provide these settlements with adequate drinking water, sanitation facilities, electricity, food, health care, housing, schools, and jobs. Not only do cities lack the needed money, but officials fear that improving services will attract even more of the rural poor.

Despite joblessness, squalor, overcrowding, and rampant disease, most squatter and slum residents are better off than the rural poor they left behind. With better access to family-planning programs, they tend to have fewer children, who have better access to schools. Even so, nearly half of all school-age children in urban areas of LDCs drop out before they finish the fourth grade to work or care for younger children.

Many squatter settlements provide a sense of community and a vital survival safety net for the poor. Families can share child care, health care, and money or goods during hard times, and can organize to improve their conditions (Solutions, p. 234).

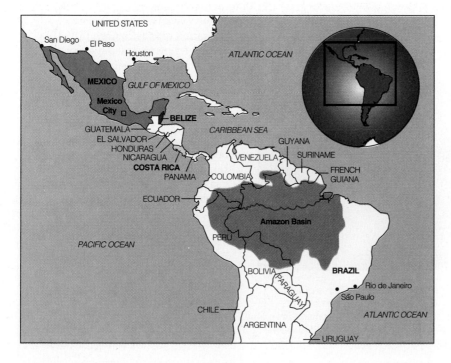

**Figure 9-3** Where are Brazil, Mexico, Belize, and Costa Rica?

**CASE STUDY**

In 1993 Mexico's (Figure 9-3) population of 90 million was growing at 2.3% a year. Between 1965 and 1993 Mexico's total fertility rate dropped from 6.7 to 3.8. However, because 39% of Mexicans are under age 15, the population should reach 143 million by 2025.

In 1993 the population of the capital, Mexico City, was 16.2 million—the world's most populous city. Every day an additional 1,000 poverty-stricken rural peasants pour into the city, hoping to find a better life.

The city suffers from severe air pollution, high unemployment (close to 50%), deafening noise, congestion, and a soaring crime rate. One-third of the city's people live in crowded slums (called barrios) or squatter settlements, without running water or electricity. And at least 8 million people—as many as live in New York City—live without sewer facilities, which means huge amounts of human waste are left in gutters and vacant lots every day. When the winds pick up dried excrement, a "fecal snow" often falls on parts of the city—leading to widespread salmonella and hepatitis infections—particularly among infants. About half of the city's garbage is left in the open to rot, attracting armies of rats and swarms of flies.

Some 3.5 million motor vehicles and 30,000 factories (making up half of the country's industry) spew pollutants into the atmosphere. Air pollution is intensified because the city lies in a basin surrounded by mountains, and frequent thermal inversions trap pollutants at ground level (Figure 9-4). Since 1982 the amount of contamination in the city's smog-choked air more than tripled.

Breathing the air is like smoking two packs of cigarettes a day, and birds have dropped dead flying through the smog. The air and water pollution cause an estimated 100,000 premature deaths a year. According to a World Health Organization study, 7 out of 10 babies born in Mexico City have unsafe levels of lead in their blood—threatening to stunt the intellectual development of an entire generation of children.

World Health Organization maximum allowable levels of ozone are exceeded 300–320 days per year—the world's worst ozone pollution. In March 1992 the city had record smog and ozone levels. On some days schools had to be closed, and the government ordered nearly 300 factories to curtail production by 70% and banned 40% of the cars from city streets. Street vendors who normally peddled chewing gum and stuffed animals at busy intersections sold surgical masks instead.

The air is so bad that residents are urged not to exercise outdoors. Some doctors have advised parents to take their children and leave the city—permanently. These problems, already at crisis levels, will become even worse if the city grows as projected to 25.6 million people by the end of this century.

The Mexican government is industrializing other parts of the country in an attempt to slow migration to Mexico City. In 1991 the government closed the city's huge state-run oil refinery and ordered many of the industrial plants in the basin to go elsewhere by 1994. Cars have also been banned from a 50-block central zone. Taxis built before 1965 have been taken off the streets, and trucks can only burn liquefied petroleum gas (LPG). The government began phasing in unleaded gasoline in 1991, but it will be years before millions of older lead-burning vehicles are eliminated. And as of 1993, all new cars in Mexico were required to have catalytic converters (output devices for reducing pollution emissions), but new cars represent only about 5% of the cars on the road each year. If you were in charge of Mexico City, what would you do?

United Nations

**Figure 9-4** The air in Mexico City ranks with the dirtiest in the world. This is due to a combination of topography, a large population, industrialization, large numbers of motor vehicles, and too little emphasis on reducing rural-to-urban migration and preventing and controlling pollution. Breathing the city's air has been compared to smoking two packs of cigarettes a day. This photo was taken on a bright, sunny morning.

Q: What country is the largest emitter of greenhouse gases?

**Figure 9-5** Computer composite of current major urban regions in the lower 48 states as revealed by night illumination detected by satellite sensors.

**THE UNITED STATES AND OTHER MDCs** In 1800 only 5% of Americans lived in cities. Since then three major internal population shifts have taken place in the United States:

- *Migration to large central cities.* Currently about 75% of Americans live in the nation's 350 *metropolitan areas*—cities and towns with at least 50,000 people (Figure 9-5). More than half of the country's population lives in large metropolitan areas with 1 million or more residents (Figure 9-6). The most urbanized state is California (93%) and the least urbanized is Vermont (32%). By 1995 some 83% of the U.S. population will probably live in urban areas.

- *Migration from large central cities to suburbs and smaller cities.* Since 1970 this type of migration has followed new jobs to such areas. Today about 41% of the country's urban dwellers live in central cities, and 59% in suburbs.

- *Migration from the North and East to the South and West.* Since 1980 about 80% of the U.S. population increase has occurred in the South and West, particularly near the coasts. This shift is expected to continue.

Since 1920 many of the worst urban environmental problems in the United States and other MDCs have been significantly reduced. Most people have better working and housing conditions. Air and water quality have improved. Better sanitation, public water supplies, and medical care have slashed rates of sickness and death from malnutrition and transmissible diseases such as measles, diphtheria, typhoid fever, pneumonia, and tuberculosis.

Many cities in MDCs now face deteriorating services, aging infrastructures (streets, schools, bridges, housing, sewers), budget crunches from lost tax revenues and rising costs, environmental degradation, and neighborhood collapse. Jobs, many businesses,

**Figure 9-6** Major urban regions in the United States and Canada by 2000. Nearly half (48%) of Americans live in *consolidated metropolitan areas* with 1 million or more people. (Data from U.S. Census Bureau and Statistics Canada)

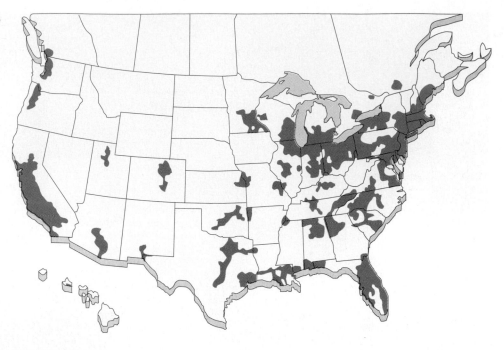

## Organizing for Survival and a Better Life

**SOLUTIONS**

A few squatter communities have organized to improve their living conditions. They have gradually turned flimsy shacks into solid buildings and worked together to lay out streets, build schools, and bring in water and electricity lines.

One example is Rio de Janeiro's Santa Marta slum, home for 11,500 of the city's 2 million squatters. Residents organized a day-care program and brought in water lines, electricity, health clinics, and drainage systems to prevent mud slides.

In Villa El Salvador outside Lima, Peru, a network of women's groups and neighborhood associations planted half a million trees, trained hundreds of door-to-door health workers, and built 300 community kitchens, 150 day-care centers, and 26 schools. Through their own efforts the 300,000 people now have homes with electricity, over half have running water and sewers, and trees and gardens flourish in what was once desert. In addition, illiteracy has fallen to 3%—one of the lowest rates in Latin America—and infant mortality is 40% below the national average.

Such success stories are rare, but they show what can be done. Governments can encourage the self-help process by giving squatters ownership of their occupied land. Then the squatters have more incentive to make improvements, because they know the land can't be taken from them.

and middle- and upper-class people have moved to the suburbs.

As a result, violence, drug traffic and abuse, crime, and decay have increased in parts of central cities. In these areas the poor, the elderly, the unemployed (typically 50% or higher in economically depressed inner-city areas), the homeless (an estimated 3.5 million in the United States), the handicapped, and others who cannot afford to leave are trapped in a downward spiral of poverty. Most available jobs pay only the minimum wage, offering little chance to escape the poverty trap.

### SPATIAL PATTERNS OF URBAN DEVELOPMENT

Three generalized models of urban structure are shown in Figure 9-7. A *concentric-circle city*—such as New York City—develops outward from its central business district (CBD) in a series of rings as the area grows in population and size. Typically industries and businesses in the CBD are ringed by housing zones that become more affluent toward the suburbs. In many LDCs, however, the affluent cluster in the central city and many of the poor live in squatter settlements that spring up on the outskirts.

A *sector city* grows in pie-shaped wedges, or ribbons. These growth sectors develop when commercial, industrial, and housing districts push outward from the CBD along major transportation routes. An example is the large urban area stretching from San Francisco to San Jose.

A *multiple-nuclei city* develops around a number of independent centers, or satellite cities, rather than a

Q: How much must global $CO_2$ emissions be cut by 2030 to slow projected global warming to an acceptable rate?

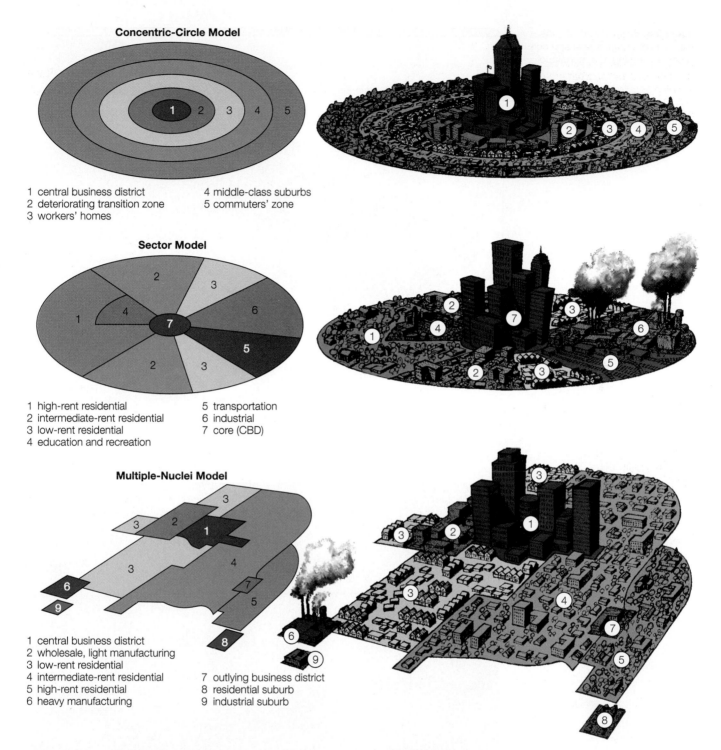

**Concentric-Circle Model**

1 central business district
2 deteriorating transition zone
3 workers' homes
4 middle-class suburbs
5 commuters' zone

**Sector Model**

1 high-rent residential
2 intermediate-rent residential
3 low-rent residential
4 education and recreation
5 transportation
6 industrial
7 core (CBD)

**Multiple-Nuclei Model**

1 central business district
2 wholesale, light manufacturing
3 low-rent residential
4 intermediate-rent residential
5 high-rent residential
6 heavy manufacturing
7 outlying business district
8 residential suburb
9 industrial suburb

**Figure 9-7** Three models of urban spatial structure. Although no city perfectly matches any of them, these simplified models can be used to identify general patterns of urban development. (Modified with permission from Harm J. deBlij, *Human Geography*, New York: John Wiley, 1977)

single center. Los Angeles comes fairly close to this pattern. Some cities develop in a combination of these patterns.

As they grow outward urban areas may merge with other urban areas to form *megalopolises*. For example, the remaining open space between Boston and Washington, D.C., is rapidly urbanizing and merging. This sprawling 800-kilometer-long (500-mile) urban area, sometimes called *Bowash*, has almost 60 million people—more than twice Canada's entire population (Figure 9-8). Megalopolises have developed all over the world; in the United States (Figure 9-6); in Europe

**Figure 9-8** Bowash and Chipitts—examples of urban sprawl and coalescence, leading to a megalopolis.

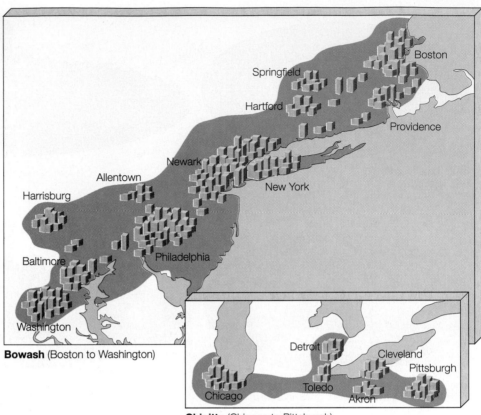

**Bowash** (Boston to Washington)

**Chipitts** (Chicago to Pittsburgh)

**Figure 9-9** Satellite photo of part of Paris, France, with the Seine River running through the city. This city is spreading out toward Amsterdam, Holland, to form a megalopolis.

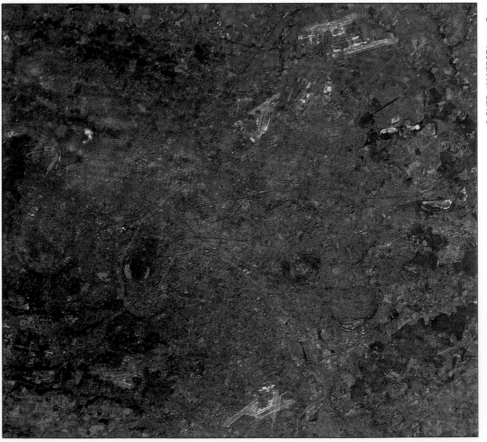

© CNES, 1992/SPOT Image Corp.

Q: How many trees would each person have to plant each year to absorb the $CO_2$ put into the atmosphere?

**Figure 9-10** Aigues-Mortes, France. For security reasons walls were built around the city between the fourteenth and sixteenth centuries. Today most of the population still lives within these walls.

**Figure 9-11** Sun City, Arizona—a prime example of urban sprawl made possible by the car culture. This retirement community of more than 60,000 people is nearly totally dependent on the outside for its resources. Its demands for water are beginning to exceed the available supply.

between Amsterdam and Paris (Figure 9-9); in Japan from a fusion of Tokyo, Nagoya, and Osaka (Tokama); and in the Brazilian Industrial Triangle made up of São Paulo, Rio de Janeiro, and Belo Horizonte.

If a city cannot spread outward it grows upward and downward, occupying a relatively small area with a high population density. Those are the only avenues of expansion for cities or urban areas such as Manhattan, Tokyo, and Hong Kong.

Most people living in such compact cities walk, ride bicycles, or use energy-efficient mass transit. Residents often live in multistory apartment buildings;

with few outside walls, heating and cooling costs are reduced. Many European cities are compact (Figure 9-10) and tend to be more energy-efficient than the dispersed cities of the United States, Canada, and Australia, where there is often ample land for outward expansion.

A combination of cheap gasoline, plentiful land, and a network of highways leads to dispersed, car-culture cities with a low population density—often called *urban sprawl* (Figure 9-11). Most people living in such a city rely on gas-guzzling cars for transportation and live in single-family houses, with unshared walls that

A: 1,000 (4,500 per American because of their larger input)

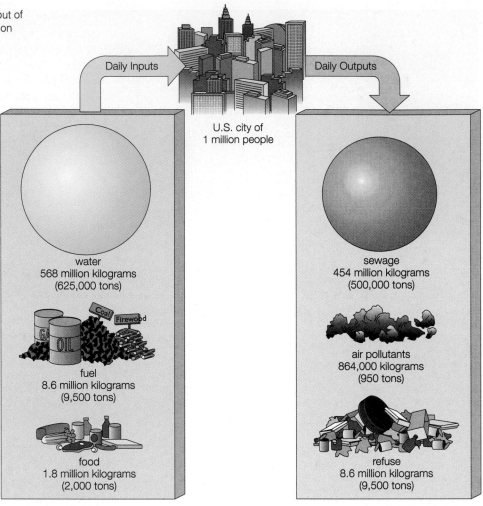

**Figure 9-12** Typical daily input and output of matter and energy for a U.S. city of I million people.

Daily Inputs

Daily Outputs

U.S. city of
1 million people

water
568 million kilograms
(625,000 tons)

fuel
8.6 million kilograms
(9,500 tons)

food
1.8 million kilograms
(2,000 tons)

sewage
454 million kilograms
(500,000 tons)

air pollutants
864,000 kilograms
(950 tons)

refuse
8.6 million kilograms
(9,500 tons)

lose and gain heat rapidly unless they are well insulated and airtight. Suburbanites living in a single-family home on a one-tenth-hectare (quarter-acre) lot use far more energy and other resources, and generate much more waste per person, than city dwellers living in smaller quarters closer to their work. Urban sprawl also eats up unspoiled natural habitats, paves over fertile farmland, and destroys the sense of community.

## 9-2 Urban Resource and Environmental Problems

**EFFECTS OF URBAN AREAS ON RESOURCES AND ENVIRONMENT** Cities as they are designed today are not self-sustaining. They survive only by importing food, water, energy, minerals, and other resources from nearby and distant farmlands, forests, mines,

and watersheds. They produce enormous quantities of wastes that can pollute air, water, and land within and outside their boundaries (Figure 9-12). In the words of Theodore Roszak:

> *The supercity . . . stretches out tentacles of influence that reach thousands of miles beyond its already sprawling parameters. It sucks every hinterland and wilderness into its technological metabolism. It forces rural populations off the land and replaces them with vast agroindustrial combines. Its investments and technicians bring the roar of the bulldozer and oil derrick into the most uncharted quarters. It runs its conduits of transport and communication, its lines of supply and distribution through the wildest landscapes. It flushes its wastes into every nearby river, lake, and ocean or trucks them away to other areas. The world becomes its garbage can.*

**VEGETATION** Urban areas generally have few trees, shrubs, or other natural vegetation that absorb air pollutants, give off oxygen, help cool the air as water evaporates from their leaves, muffle noise, provide

Q: What is the average amount of $CO_2$ each American adds to the atmosphere each year?

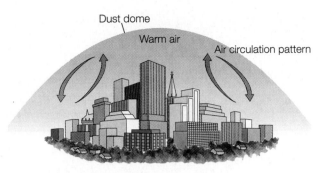

**Figure 9-13** An urban heat island causes patterns of air circulation that create a dust dome over the city. Winds elongate the dome toward downwind areas. A strong cold front can blow the dome away and lower urban pollution levels.

wildlife habitats, and give aesthetic pleasure. As one observer remarked, "Most cities are places where they cut down the trees and then name the streets after them."

This is a tragic loss. According to the American Forestry Association (AFA) one city tree provides over $57,000 worth of air conditioning, erosion and storm water control, wildlife shelter, and air pollution control over a 50-year lifetime. Just three trees properly placed or preserved around a house can cut air conditioning costs 10%–50%.

Cities also produce little of their own food. However, individuals can supplement their food supply by planting community gardens in unused lots and by using window-box and balcony planters and gardens or greenhouses built on the roofs of apartment buildings. Even abandoned cars can be filled with soil and used to grow food—"vegetable cars". Such urban gardens are common in many cities in eastern Europe and the Commonwealth of Independent States (CIS). In the Hague, Netherlands, and in an elementary school in Carborro, North Carolina, schoolchildren learn to compost cafeteria food waste and use the compost to grow vegetables on the school grounds or in communal gardens.

In addition to growing more of their own food, cities can encourage farmers' markets. This lowers food prices by allowing farmers to sell directly to customers and helps keep nearby farmland from being swallowed up by urban sprawl.

**URBAN MICROCLIMATE** Urbanization alters the local climate. Generally cities are warmer, rainier, foggier, and cloudier than suburbs and nearby rural areas.

The cars, factories, furnaces, lights, and people in cities generate enormous amounts of heat. Tall buildings and paved streets and parking areas in cities absorb heat and obstruct cooling winds. Rainfall runs off fast, so that little standing water is available to cool the air through evaporation. This combination of effects creates an **urban heat island** surrounded by cooler suburban and rural areas. The dome of heat also traps pollutants, especially tiny solid particles (suspended particulate matter), creating a **dust dome** above urban areas (Figure 9-13). Concentrations of suspended particulate matter over urban-industrial areas may be 10–1,000 times higher than over rural areas.

If wind speeds increase, the dust dome elongates downwind to form a **dust plume**, which can spread the city's pollutants for hundreds of kilometers. As cities grow and merge (Figure 9-8), individual heat islands also merge. This can affect the climate of a large area and keep polluted air from being adequately diluted and cleansed. Cities can save money and counteract the heat-island effect by enacting tree-planting programs, mandating lighter and more reflective paints and building materials, and establishing high energy-efficiency standards for vehicles, buildings, and appliances.

**WATER, RUNOFF, AND FLOODING** As cities grow and their water demands increase, expensive reservoirs and canals must be built and deeper wells drilled. This siphoning of water to urban areas deprives rural and wild areas of surface water, and sometimes depletes underground water faster than it is replenished.

Covering land with buildings, asphalt, and concrete means that precipitation runs off quickly and can overload sewers and storm drains, contributing to water pollution and flooding in cities and downstream areas. In car-dominated cities stormwater running off roads and parking lots is contaminated with oil, salt (for deicing roads), and toxic liquids; in suburbs large amounts of fertilizers and pesticides run off lawns and golf courses. Large, unbroken expanses of concrete or asphalt can also prevent rainwater and melting snow from entering the soil to renew groundwater.

Moreover, many cities are built on floodplains, areas subject to natural flooding. Floodplains are considered prime land for urbanization because they are flat, accessible, and near rivers.

Many of the world's largest cities are in coastal areas. If an enhanced greenhouse effect increases the average atmospheric temperature as projected, a rise in average sea level of even a meter or so could flood many of these cities sometime during the next century.

**SOLID WASTE AND POLLUTION** Urban residents are generally subjected to much higher concentrations of pollutants than people in rural areas. Litter and garbage are abundant in slums and squatter villages, where solid waste pickup services often don't exist. This invites disease-carrying rodents.

In 1988 the World Health Organization warned that nearly 1 billion city dwellers are being exposed to

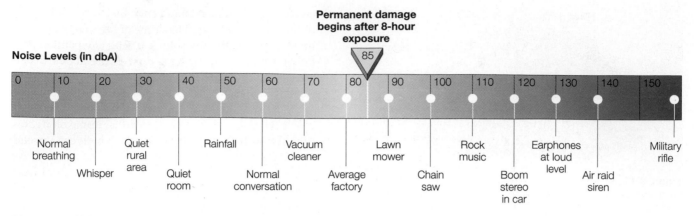

**Figure 9-14** Noise levels (in decibel-A or dbA sound pressure units) of common sounds.

health hazards from air pollutants, with 50–85% caused by motor vehicles. Smog is now a virtually unavoidable aspect of urban life in most of the world (Figure 9-4). Other major sources of air pollution, especially in LDCs, are smoky factories and the burning of wood, charcoal, and coal for cooking and heating. And many children suffer from lead poisoning after ingesting or inhaling particles of toxic lead present in paint, plaster, and caulking of older buildings.

Air pollution control since 1970 has helped keep levels of some air pollutants from rising in many urban areas in MDCs, but levels are beginning to rise in some cities because of more people, more cars, more factories, and other activities that burn fossil fuels. Air pollution control in most cities in LDCs is lax because of lenient pollution laws, lack of enforcement, corrupt officials, inadequate testing equipment, and a shortage of funds.

Water purification and wastewater treatment plants, and fairly strict pollution control laws, have reduced water pollution in most MDCs. In LDCs, however, few cities can afford to build and maintain such systems for their rapidly growing urban populations. For example, the 50-year-old sewer system in Cairo, Egypt, was built to serve 2 million; it is completely inadequate for Cairo's current population of 11 million people. Less than 16% of India's urban residents are served by even partial sewer systems and water treatment facilities.

About 200 million people in cities in LDCs do not have safe drinking water. Where the poor are forced to use contaminated water, diarrhea, dysentery, typhoid, and cholera are widespread and infant mortality is high. Inner-city dwellers are exposed to much higher than average amounts of lead in their drinking water because old plumbing often contains lead-based pipe or joint cementing compounds. Air pollution is discussed in more detail in Chapter 22, water pollution in Chapter 23, solid waste in Chapter 19, and hazardous waste in Chapter 21.

**NOISE POLLUTION** According to the Environmental Protection Agency, nearly half of all Americans, mostly urban residents, are regularly exposed to **noise pollution**—any unwanted, disturbing, or harmful sound that impairs or interferes with hearing, causes stress, hampers concentration and work efficiency, or causes accidents. Every day one of every nine Americans (28 million people) lives, works, or plays around noise of sufficient duration and intensity to cause some permanent hearing loss, and that number is rising rapidly. Noise is the most widespread occupational hazard.

The lives of 40 million more Americans, mostly urban dwellers, are significantly disrupted by noise pollution from cars, trucks, buses, jackhammers, construction equipment, motorcycles, power lawn mowers, vacuum cleaners, sirens, and unwanted loud music. Millions of people who listen to loud music using home and car stereos, portable stereos ("boom boxes") held close to the ear, and earphones are also damaging their hearing.

To determine harmful levels of noise, sound pressure is measured in decibels (db). Sounds also have pitch (frequency), and high-pitched sounds seem louder and more annoying than low-pitched sounds at the same intensity. Normally sound pressure measurement is weighted for high-pitched sounds, to which people are more sensitive, and measured in decibel-A (dbA) units (Figure 9-14). Sound pressure becomes damaging at about 75 dbA and painful at around 120 dbA; it can kill at 180 dbA. Sounds above 120 dbA can leave one with a high-pitched whine or ringing in the ears. Persistent ringing in the ears is called tinnitus, a distressing disorder for which there is no treatment.

You are being exposed to a sound level high enough to cause permanent hearing damage if you need to raise your voice to be heard above the racket, a noise causes your ears to ring, or nearby speech seems muffled. Prolonged exposure to lower noise levels and

Q: What is the role of ozone ($O_3$) gas in the stratosphere?

## Controlling Noise

Basically, there are five ways to control noise:

- Modify noisy activities and devices to produce less noise.
- Shield noisy devices or processes.
- Shield workers or other receivers from the noise.
- Move noisy operations or things away from people.
- Use antincise—a new technology that cancels out noise with noise.

Modern urban societies can reduce excessive noise by building and using quieter industrial machinery, jackhammers, airplane and vehicle motors, vacuum cleaners (which are deliberately made loud because people think quiet models are not picking up much dirt), and other noisy machines. Newer automobiles today are quieter than older ones. Commercial airliners are 50–70% quieter than those of the 1960s and 1970s, though they could be made much quieter.

Noisy factory operations can be totally or partially enclosed by walls. Houses and other buildings can be insulated to reduce sound transfer (and energy waste). Workers can wear protective devices to reduce the amount of noise entering their ears or can work in booths. New airports and flight patterns can be located to minimize people's exposure to noise. Governments can set noise control standards for equipment, and cities can enact and strictly enforce noise control laws.

The newest development is antinoise or noise-cancellation technology in which sound is created that will cancel out other sound. Sweden's Electrolux, for example, is planning a line of household appliances that will be hushed with antinoise. In Sheboygan, Wisconsin, a huge fan in a plastics plant is being quieted with noise cancellation. Antinoise mufflers that reduce engine noise in cars and trucks by at least 10% may soon be available. Fuel efficiency will also be improved because the engine exhaust will no longer have to be channeled through the series of confining chambers in conventional mufflers.

The control of noise pollution in the United States has lagged behind that in the CIS and many western European and Scandinavian countries. Noise is not effectively controlled in the United States because industries have resisted strict workplace noise standards. In 1981 the Reagan administration shut down the EPA's noise control program and dropped noise emission labeling on items such as power tools and lawnmowers. As of 1993 funding for the EPA's noise-pollution control program had not been reinstated. In most cities enforcement of noise control laws is lax.

Federal laws require U.S. employers to use engineering or other controls to adhere to certain noise standards (said to be too high by most hearing specialists), but *only to the extent feasible*. Compliance is limited and enforcement is lax because the law does not specify what is feasible.

By contrast, Europeans have developed quieter jackhammers, pile drivers, and air compressors costing little more than their noisy counterparts. Most European countries also require that small sheds and tents be used to muffle construction noise. Some countries quiet the clanging of garbage collection by using rubberized collection trucks. Subway cars in Montreal and Mexico City have rubberized wheels to reduce noise. In France cars must have separate highway and city horns, the latter much quieter than the former. What do you think should be done to reduce noise pollution?

---

occasional loud sounds may not damage your hearing but can greatly increase internal stress.

Because the db and dbA scales are logarithmic, a 10-fold increase in sound pressure occurs with each 10-decibel rise. Thus a rise from 30 dbA (quiet rural area) to 60 dbA (normal restaurant conversation) represents a 1,000-fold increase in sound pressure on the ear.

Studies have shown that by age 30 most Americans have been exposed to enough noise to lose 5 dbA of their hearing sensitivity and can't hear anything above 16,000 cycles per second (Hz). By age 65 most people have a 40-dbA reduction in hearing sensitivity and can't hear sounds above 8,000 cycles per second (Hz).

Increasing exposure to noise in urban areas throughout the world over the past 40 years has accelerated this normal pattern of hearing loss. For example, studies have shown that 60% of the incoming students at the University of Tennessee have significant high-frequency hearing loss. In effect, these and many other young people are entering their twenties with the hearing capability of people in their sixties.

Annoyance is usually the first response to excessive noise. When a person is exposed to a sudden noise or a persistent loud noise, adrenaline is released, the heart beats faster, blood pressure rises, and muscles tense. Harmful effects from prolonged exposure to excessive noise include permanent hearing loss, high blood pressure (hypertension), muscle tension, migraine headaches, higher cholesterol levels, gastric ulcers, irritability, insomnia, and psychological disorders including increased aggression. Noise can be reduced in several ways (Solutions, above).

---

A: It filters out high-energy ultraviolet radiation from the sun.

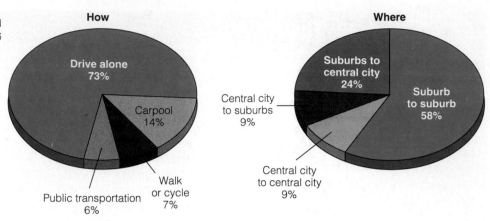

**Figure 9-15** How people in the United States get to work. Every day about 86 million Americans drive to and from work alone. In Denver, Houston, Phoenix, and Los Angeles, 90% of the people commute to work by car. (Data from U.S. Census Bureau)

**How**

Drive alone
73%

Carpool
14%

Walk
or cycle
7%

Public transportation
6%

**Where**

Suburbs to
central city
24%

Suburb
to suburb
58%

Central city
to suburbs
9%

Central city
to central city
9%

## LAND CONVERSION AND SOCIAL DISRUPTION

As urban areas expand, they swallow up rural land, especially flat or gently rolling cropland with well-drained, fertile soil. For example, each year about 526,000 hectares (1.3 million acres) of rural land—mostly cropland—are converted to urban developments, rights-of-way, highways, and airports in the United States. This is equivalent in area to building a 1-kilometer-wide (0.6-mile) highway between New York City and Los Angeles each year. Once prime agricultural land is paved over or built upon, it is lost for food production. As land values near urban areas rise, taxes on nearby farmland rise to the point where many farmers are forced to sell their land. They realize that they can make much more money growing houses and shopping centers than corn and cows.

The outward expansion of cities creates numerous problems for the once-rural counties, villages, and towns. Narrow country roads and town streets become congested with traffic. Town and county health, school, police, fire, water, sanitation, and other services are overwhelmed. Air pollution, crime, noise, congestion, and water pollution increase.

Suburbanized towns and counties must raise taxes to meet the demand for new public services. Some townspeople profit from the increased jobs and economic growth, and new migrants from central cities escape some of the crime, crowding, high costs, and other problems they faced. However, other long-time residents are forced out because of rising prices, higher property taxes, decreased environmental quality, and disruption of their way of life. Unless growth is carefully controlled, which is rare, residents eventually experience the central-city problems they were hoping to avoid.

## 9-3 Transportation and Urban Development

**TRANSPORTATION OPTIONS** The decision to build highways between cities, and freeways and beltways within urban areas, is probably the most far-reaching land-use, energy policy, and environmental decision a country, state, or city makes. These methods of moving people and goods by car and truck profoundly shape where we live and work, how we get from place to place (Figure 9-15), how urban areas grow (Figure 9-7), how much energy we waste, and how much pollution we produce.

People in urban areas move from one place to another primarily by three types of transportation:

- *Individual transit* by private automobile, taxi, motorcycle, motor scooter, bicycle, and walking
- *Mass transit* by bus and rail systems (subway, train, and trolley)
- *Paratransit* involving car pools, van pools, jitneys, or van taxis traveling along fixed routes, and dial-a-ride systems

**MOTOR VEHICLES** Worldwide there are about 550 million motor vehicles—440 million cars and 110 million trucks—more than a 10-fold increase since 1950. At this rate the global motor vehicle population will reach 740 million by 2000 and 1.2 billion by 2030.

Only 8% of the world's population own cars. About 89% of these cars are in MDCs, especially in the United States, Australia, Canada, and other large, affluent countries. Despite having only 4.7% of the

Q: Worldwide, how many people die each year from skin cancer?

## The Automobile

PRO/CON

The automobile is addictive. Its appeal is convenience and undreamed of mobility. To many people cars are also symbols of power, sex, excitement, and success.

Moreover, much of the world's economy is built on producing motor vehicles and supplying roads, services, and repairs for them. In the United States one of every six dollars spent and one of every six nonfarm jobs are connected to the automobile. Each day $200 million is spent building and rebuilding U.S. roads.

In spite of their benefits motor vehicles have many destructive effects on human lives and on air, water, land, and wildlife resources. Since 1885, when Karl Benz built the first automobile, almost 18 million people have been killed by motor vehicles, and the death toll increases by about 250,000 people per year—as many as were killed by the atomic bombs dropped on Hiroshima and Nagasaki. And each year about 10 million people are permanently disabled.

In the United States almost 15 million motor vehicle accidents kill around 40,000 people each year and injure almost 5 million people, at least 300,000 of them severely. More Americans have been killed by cars than were killed in all the country's wars. Each year the accidents cost the United States more than $350 billion, about 8% of the GNP.

Motor vehicles are also the largest source of air pollution, laying a haze of smog over the world's cities (Figure 9-4). In the United States they produce at least 50% of the air pollution, even though emission standards are as strict as any in the world. Gains in fuel efficiency and emission reductions have been largely offset by the increase in cars and a doubling in the distance Americans traveled by car between 1970 and 1990.

Motor vehicles are the major cause of the world's oil addiction. Two-thirds of the oil used in the United States is devoted to transportation, with half the total consumed by motor vehicles. These vehicles generate 25% of U.S. carbon dioxide emissions, and leaky air conditioners in vehicles are the country's largest source of chlorofluorocarbon emissions, the primary culprits in the depletion of the ozone layer. Motor vehicles produce 14% of global $CO_2$ emissions and 28% of chlorofluorocarbon emissions. And leaks and spills of oil and gas routinely pollute surface water and groundwater.

By making long commutes and distant shopping possible, automobiles and highways have led to urban sprawl and reduced use of mass transit, bicycles, and walking. The typical American suburbanite makes 13 trips per day to run errands. Ironically many people in the United States drive their cars to health clubs only to work out on treadmills or stationary bikes.

Worldwide at least a third of urban land is devoted to roads, parking lots, gasoline stations, and other automobile-related uses. In the United States more land is now devoted to cars than to housing. Half the land in an average American city is used for cars, prompting urban expert Lewis Mumford to suggest that the U.S. national flower should be the concrete cloverleaf.

In 1907 the average speed of horse-drawn vehicles through the borough of Manhattan was 18.5 kilometers (11.5 miles) per hour. Today cars and trucks with the potential power of 100–300 horses creep along Manhattan streets at 8 kilometers (5 miles) per hour. In Paris and Tokyo average auto speeds are even lower. If present trends continue, U.S. motorists will spend an average of two years of their lifetime in traffic jams. The U.S. economy loses at least $100 billion per year because of time lost in traffic delays. Building more roads is not the answer because, as economist Robert Samuelson put it, "Cars expand to fill available concrete." International experience indicates that it is more cost-effective to build rail systems within and between urban areas.

world's people, the United States has 35% of the world's cars and trucks (190 million vehicles). In LDCs most people travel by foot, bicycle, or motor scooter.

In the United States the car is now used for 86% of all trips (compared to about 45% in most western European countries), 98% of all urban transportation, and 86% of travel to work. Public transit is used for only 2.5% of all trips. Almost 75% of commuting cars carry only one person, and only 13% of commuters use car pools. Only about 5% of Americans use public transportation, and only 7% walk or use a bicycle to get to and from work. Americans drive 3 billion kilometers (2 billion miles) each year—equal to more than 10 round trips to the sun and as far as the rest of the world combined. No wonder British author J. B. Priestley remarked, "In America, the cars have become the people."

By failing to make transportation strategy the basis of land-use planning, many of the world's cities have allowed the automobile to shape and dominate them. Now they are learning that the costs often outweigh the benefits (Pro/Con, above).

**CYCLING AND WALKING** Worldwide there are almost twice as many bicycles as cars, and annual bicycle sales exceed automobile sales. A bicycle is an inexpensive form of transportation, burns no fossil fuels, produces no pollution, takes few resources to make, and is the most energy-efficient form of transportation (including walking).

In urban traffic cars and bicycles move at about the same average speed. Using separate bike paths or lanes running along roads, bicycle riders can make most trips shorter than 8 kilometers (5 miles) faster than a car. Separate bike and pedestrian paths or lanes that are smooth and wide enough, bike and pedestrian overpasses and underpasses at intersections, stoplights at intersections that allow cyclists and pedestrians to proceed before motor vehicles, low speed limits, and speed bumps, trees, or other barriers to slow down motor traffic greatly improve safety for cyclists and pedestrians.

Chinese cities often provide exclusive pedestrian/bicycle lanes and bridges for the country's 300 million cyclists (Figure 8-22). Many cities in the Netherlands, Germany, Sweden, Denmark, other western European countries, and Japan have taken back the streets for pedestrians, cyclists, and children's play by banning cars or slowing motor traffic in residential and shopping areas. Studies in the United States, the United Kingdom, and Germany have shown that creating automobile-free zones in city centers increases local business sales by 25% or more. Nevertheless in the United States bicycles and walking are used for less than 10% of urban trips compared with 40% in many European cities.

For longer trips secure bike parking spaces can be provided at mass transit stations, or buses and trains can be equipped to carry bicycles. Such bike-and-ride systems are widely used in Japan, Germany, the Netherlands (with more bicycle paths than any other country), and Denmark. Bike-and-ride commuting also is beginning to catch on in Atlanta, Boston, Milwaukee, San Francisco, Seattle, and Washington, D.C. And in Washington, D.C., one pizza chain has used bicycles for pizza delivery since 1985, cutting delivery time by 75% in the car-clogged city. So far, however, only a handful of U.S. cities—such as Davis, California; Seattle, Washington; Boulder, Colorado; and Palo Alto, California—actively encourage bicycling.

Bicycles won't replace cars in the U.S. urban sprawls, but between 1977 and 1992 the number of Americans bicycling to work (the "no-pollute commute") rose from 500,000 to 3.2 million. This is an encouraging trend, but it still represents only 2% of all commuters. By contrast, in the Netherlands bicycle travel makes up 30% of all urban trips, and in Japan 15% of all commuters ride bicycles to work or to commuter-rail stations.

**MASS TRANSIT** Although the U.S. population increased by 125 million between 1946 and 1993, the number of riders on all forms of mass transit dropped from 23.4 million to 8–9 million. In the United States mass transit accounts for only 7% of all passenger travel, compared with 15% in Germany and 47% in Japan.

While automobiles and highways multiplied and cities sprawled, the U.S. trolley system was dismantled. In 1917 all major U.S. cities had efficient trolley or streetcar systems run by electricity. Together with bus systems, they attracted 20 million riders in the 1920s and 24 million in 1945. As a high school student in Richmond, Virginia, in the 1940s, I could go almost anywhere in the city on a streetcar quickly, easily, and cheaply.

By 1950 privately owned streetcar systems in 100 major cities had been purchased by a holding company (National City Lines) formed by General Motors, Firestone Tire, Standard Oil, Phillips Petroleum, and Mack Truck (which also made buses), and dismantled to increase sales of buses and cars. The courts found the companies guilty of conspiracy to eliminate about 90% of the country's light-rail system, but the damage had already been done. The executives responsible were fined $1 each, and each company paid a fine of $5,000, less than the profit from replacing a single streetcar with a bus. General Motors alone had made $25 million in additional bus and car sales by the time the case was tried.

Another spur to the U.S. car culture was the huge government investment in 4.8 million kilometers (3 million miles) of roads and a 72,000-kilometer (45,000-mile) interstate highway system. Only 20% of the federal gasoline tax goes to mass transit; the rest, to highways. This encourages states and cities to invest in highways instead of in mass transit.

The federal tax code also discriminates against mass transit and those who cycle or walk to work. In the United States only 10% of commuting employees pay for parking, mainly because employers can deduct the expense of providing parking for workers from their taxes. This gives auto commuters a tax-free fringe benefit worth $200–$400 a month in major cities. On the other hand, employers can write off only $15 per month for employees who use public transit and nothing for those who walk or bike to work. Tax benefits for company cars are another subsidy. Higher government subsidies for big trucks also help discourage the hauling of freight by more energy-efficient railroads.

The key to breaking this cycle is to make drivers pay directly for most of the true costs of auto use. According to a World Resources Institute study federal, state, and local government auto subsidies in the United States amount to at least $300 billion per year (almost 5% of the country's GNP)—an average of $1,600 per vehicle. Taxpayers (drivers and nondrivers)

Q: How long do CFCs stay in the atmosphere?

foot this bill but generally are unaware that it is part of their car-use expenses. If drivers had to pay these hidden costs directly as a gasoline tax, they would be paying about $5 per gallon in taxes. They're paying this anyway but don't associate these hidden costs with their driving.

Besides drastically raising gasoline taxes while phasing out hidden automobile tax subsidies, government could also make direct costs of cars more visible by raising registration and license fees and by basing car sales and property taxes on fuel economy and emission levels. Making people pay directly for these and other costs of automobile use—estimated at about $1 a mile—would greatly increase the use of fuel-efficient cars, mass transit (funded by the increased tax revenue), and bicycles, and would make cities more compact, energy efficient, and livable.

**RAIL SYSTEMS** Rail systems, usually operated by electric engines, fall into four categories:

- *Rapid rail* (also called the underground, tube, metro, or subway), which operates on exclusive rights-of-way in tunnels or on elevated tracks
- *Suburban or regional trains*, which connect the central city with surrounding areas or provide transportation between major cities in a region (Solutions, p. 246)
- *Streetcars (or trams)*, which move on streets with other traffic
- *Light rail (or trolleys)*—more modern versions of streetcars, which can run either with other traffic or on exclusive rights-of-way

Rapid-rail and suburban train systems can transport large numbers of people at high speed, but they are efficient only where many people live along a narrow corridor and can easily reach properly spaced stations.

In recent years some U.S. cities have built successful rapid-rail systems. Since Atlanta's system opened in 1979, for example, it has steadily added riders and opened new stations. Pittsburgh has cleaner air and renewed business vitality, partly because of its new rapid-rail system, which opened in 1985.

One of the world's most successful rapid-rail systems is in Hong Kong. Fare revenues on this $4.2-billion system exceed operating costs by 50%, even though fares for most trips range from 25¢ to 65¢. Several factors contribute to its success. Hong Kong is compact and densely packed, making it ideal for a rapid-rail system running through a heavily populated corridor. Most residents live in high-rise apartment buildings, and half of the population can walk to a subway station in five minutes. Also, most people depend on public transportation because only 1 in 30 owns a car.

Over the past two decades 21 large cities in LDCs, including Cairo, Shanghai, and Mexico City, have built rapid-rail systems. These systems, which are often used as showcases of modernization, have improved transport service in dense city centers, but often at great cost. Critics believe that this money could have been better spent expanding and modernizing bus systems that could carry many more people at a much lower cost.

San Diego, Sacramento, San Jose, Los Angeles, Seattle, Buffalo, and Portland (Oregon) in the United States and Toronto, Edmonton, and Calgary in Canada have recently built light-rail systems. In Portland 43% of all people commuting downtown ride buses and a light-rail system, a shift to mass transit that has dramatically improved the city's air quality. In Toronto more than three-fourths of downtown commuters use public transportation to get to work.

A light-rail line costs about one-tenth as much to build per kilometer as a highway or a heavy-rail system. Although the start-up cost of a light-rail system is higher than for a comparable-load bus system, its operating costs are much lower. By linking trolley cars together, a light-rail system can carry up to 400 people with one driver, compared with 40–50 passengers on a bus. Trolleys are also cleaner and quieter than buses. Despite its advantages, rail carries only 0.4% of the passengers and 38% of the freight (down from 80% in 1925) between U.S. cities. In China, rail carries 56% of the passengers and 80% of the freight between cities.

**BUSES AND PARATRANSIT** Bus systems are more flexible than rail systems. They can be routed throughout sprawling cities and rerouted overnight if transportation patterns change. Bus systems also require less capital and have lower operating costs than heavy-rail systems.

However, because they must offer low fares to attract riders, bus systems often cost more money to operate than they bring in. To make up for losses, bus companies tend to cut service, reduce maintenance, and seek government subsidies. Furthermore, unless they operate in separate express lanes, buses get caught up in traffic congestion.

Diesel buses, especially in LDCs, emit large quantities of pollutants, although the cars needed to carry an equal number of passengers would create more air pollution. Not only does the technology exist to minimize such emissions, but buses can run on less-polluting fuels, such as natural gas (used in China and Brazil) and propane (used in parts of Europe).

Because buses are cost-effective only when full, they are sometimes supplemented by car pools, van pools, jitneys, and dial-a-ride systems. Dial-a-ride systems are on the rise in American cities. Passengers call for a van, minibus, or tax-subsidized taxi, which picks

**SOLUTIONS**

In western Europe and Japan a new generation of streamlined, comfortable, and low-polluting high-speed-rail (HSR) lines are being developed for medium-distance travel between cities within a region. These "bullet" or super-trains travel on new or upgraded existing tracks at speeds up to 320 kilometers (200 miles) per hour. They are ideal for trips of intermediate length—240–480 kilometers (150–300 miles). Journeys between major cities within a region on these trains are smoother and cheaper than an airplane.

In Japan such trains, which began operating in 1964, have carried over 3 billion passengers between Tokyo and Osaka without a single injury or fatality and depart and arrive on schedule 99% of the time. However, such systems are expensive to run and maintain, and must operate along heavily used transportation routes to be profitable.

A future alternative to the automobile and the airplane for medium-distance travel of 200–1,000 kilometers (120–620 miles) between cities is the *magnetic-levitation (Maglev) train*, which uses powerful superconducting electromagnets to suspend the train on a cushion of air a few centimeters above a guiding rail. Such trains zoom along without rail friction at speeds up to 500 kilometers (310 miles) per hour

and can carry 150–1,000 passengers, depending on the number of cars used. Germany and Japan have prototypes in operation.

Because these trains never touch the track they make little noise, require little maintenance, and can be elevated over existing median strips or other rights-of-way along highways, avoiding costly and disruptive land acquisitions. Maglev and bullet trains reduce energy consumption as well as greenhouse and other air emissions. A U.S. Maglev network could replace airplanes, buses, and private cars for most medium-distance travel between major American cities (Figure 9-16).

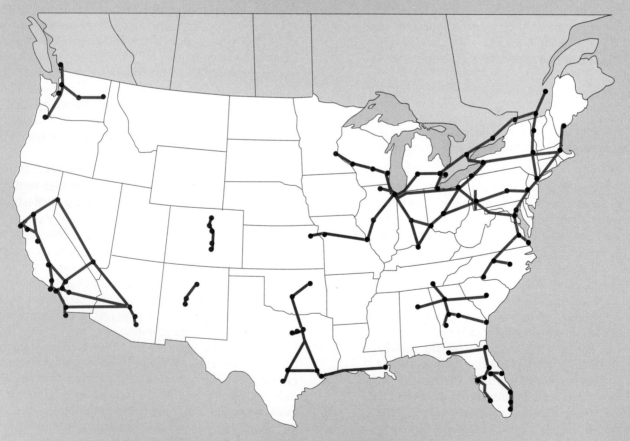

**Figure 9-16** Potential routes for high-speed Maglev and bullet trains linking major cities in the United States and parts of Canada. Such a system would allow rapid, comfortable, safe, and affordable travel between major cities in a region, and would slash dependence on cars, buses, and airplanes. (Data from High Speed Rail/Maglev Association)

Q: What is the largest source of CFC emissions in the United States?

them up at their doorstep, usually in 20–50 minutes. Two-way radios and computerized routing can increase the efficiency of these systems, but the rather expensive dial-a-ride systems are the least efficient mass transportation system in terms of energy costs per passenger kilometer.

In Mexico City, Caracas, and Cairo large fleets of jitneys—small vans or minibuses that travel regular routes but stop on demand—carry millions of passengers each day. Laws banning jitney service in the United States were repealed in 1979, despite objections by taxi and transit companies. Since then privately owned jitney service has flourished in San Diego, San Francisco, and Los Angeles, and may spread to other cities.

## 9-4 Urban Land-Use Planning and Control

**CONVENTIONAL LAND-USE PLANNING AND URBAN DECAY** Most urban areas and some rural areas use some form of **land-use planning** to decide the best present and future use of each parcel of land in the area. Land-use planning involves mapping out suitable locations for houses, industries, businesses, open space, parks, roads, water and sewer lines, reservoirs, hospitals, schools, waste treatment plants, and so on. Then zoning regulations or other devices are used to control how the land is used.

Because land is such a valuable economic resource, land-use planning is a complex and controversial process involving competing values and intense power struggles. Most land-use planning is based on the assumption that substantial future growth in population and economic development should be encouraged, regardless of the environmental and other consequences. Typically this leads to uncontrolled or poorly controlled urban growth and sprawl.

A major reason for allowing this usually destructive process is that 90% of the revenue that local governments use to provide schools, roads, police and fire protection, public water and sewer systems, welfare services, and other obligations comes from *property taxes*, taxes on all buildings and property proportional to their economic value. When an area is economically developed, property values and thus local tax revenues go up.

However, the costs of providing more services to accommodate population and economic growth often exceed the revenue from increased property values. Because local governments can rarely raise property taxes enough to meet expanding needs, they often try to raise more money by promoting further economic growth. Typically the long-term result is a treadmill of economic growth eventually leading to environmental decay. Then businesses and residents move away, decreasing the tax base, reducing tax income, and causing further environmental and social decay as governments are forced to cut the quantity and quality of services or to raise the tax rate (which drives more people away and worsens the situation).

**ECOLOGICAL LAND-USE PLANNING** Environmentalists challenge the "all-growth-is-good" dogma that is the basis of most land-use planning. They urge communities to use comprehensive, regional **ecological land-use planning**, in which all major variables are considered and integrated into a model designed to anticipate present and future needs and problems, and to propose solutions for an entire region (Solutions, p. 248, left). Emphasis is placed on blending economics and ecology to control the nature and speed of urban and suburban growth in ways that can minimize environmental degradation, pollution, and social decay.

Ecological land-use planning sounds good on paper, but it is not widely used for several reasons:

- There is intense pressure by economically and politically powerful people to develop urban land for short-term economic gain, with little regard for long-term ecological and economic losses.

- Local officials seeking election every few years usually focus on short-term rather than long-term problems and can often be influenced by economically powerful developers.

- Officials and often the majority of citizens are unwilling to pay for costly ecological land-use planning and implementation, even though a well-designed plan can prevent or ease many urban problems and save money in the long run.

- It's difficult to get municipalities in the same general area to cooperate in planning efforts. Thus an ecologically sound development plan in one area may be disrupted by unsound development in nearby areas.

**WAYS TO CONTROL LAND USE** Once a plan is developed, governments control the uses of various parcels of land by legal and economic methods. The most widely used approach is **zoning**, in which various parcels of land are designated for certain uses. Principal categories include commercial (various categories), residential (various categories), industrial, utilities, transport, recreation (parks and forest preserves), bodies of water, floodplains, and wildlife preserves. Zoning can be used to control growth and to protect areas from certain types of development.

## Ecological Land-Use Planning

**SOLUTIONS**

Ecological land-use planning is a complex process taking into account geological, ecological, economic, health, and social factors. Six basic steps are involved:

- *Make an environmental and social inventory.* Experts survey geological factors (soil type, fault lines, floodplains, water availability), ecological factors (forest types and quality, wildlife habitats, stream quality, pollution), economic factors (housing, transportation, utilities, industrial development), and health and social factors (disease and crime rates, ethnic distribution, illiteracy). A top priority is to identify and protect areas that are critical for preserving water quality, supplying drinking water, and reducing erosion.

- *Determine goals and their relative importance.* Experts, public officials, and the general public decide on goals and rank them in order of importance. For example, is the primary goal to encourage or to discourage further economic development and population growth? To preserve prime cropland from development? To reduce soil erosion?

- *Develop individual and composite maps.* Data for each factor surveyed in the environmental and social inventory are plotted on separate transparent plastic maps. The transparencies are then superimposed or combined by computer into three composite maps—one each for geological, ecological, and socioeconomic factors.

- *Develop a master composite.* The three composite maps are combined to form a master composite, which shows how the variables interact and indicates the suitability of various areas for different types of land use.

- *Develop a master plan.* The master composite (or a series of alternative master composites) is evaluated by experts, public officials, and the general public, and a final master plan is drawn up and approved.

- *Implement the master plan.* The plan is set in motion and monitored by the appropriate governmental, legal, environmental, and social agencies.

## Encouraging Ecologically Sound Development

**SOLUTIONS**

Local, state, and federal governments can take any of the following measures to protect cropland, forestland, wetlands, and other nonurban lands near expanding urban areas from degradation and ecologically unsound development:

- *Require an environmental impact analysis for proposed roads and development projects.*

- *Require developers to pay a fee that includes the full cost of additional services such as roads and water and sewer lines for all development projects.*

- *Tax land on the basis of its actual use as agricultural land or forestland rather than on the economically most profitable potential use.* This keeps farmers and other landowners from being forced to sell land to pay their tax bills.

- *Give tax breaks, or conservation easements, to landowners who agree to use land only for specified purposes, such as agriculture, wilderness, wildlife habitat, or nondestructive forms of recreation.*

- *Give subsidies to farmers who take highly erodible cropland out of production, or eliminate subsidies for farmers who farm such land or who convert wetlands to cropland.*

- *Purchase land development rights that restrict the way land can be used.*

- *Use land trusts to buy and protect ecologically valuable land.* Such purchases can be made by private groups such as the Nature Conservancy and the Audubon Society, and by local nonprofit, tax-exempt, charitable organizations, as well as by public agencies.

Zoning is useful, but it can be influenced or modified by developers because local governments depend on property taxes for revenue. Thus zoning often favors high-priced housing and factories, hotels, and other businesses. Overly strict zoning can discourage innovative approaches to solving urban problems.

In addition to zoning, local governments can control the rate of development by limiting the number of building permits, sewer hookups, roads, and other services, and use various methods to prevent ecologically unsound development (Solutions, above right).

**Q:** How much of the stratospheric ozone over the Antarctic is destroyed from September to December each year?

## Land-Use Planning in Oregon

Since the mid-1970s Oregon has had a comprehensive statewide land-use planning process based on three principles:

- *All rural land in Oregon has been permanently zoned, as forest, agricultural, or urban land.*

- *An urban growth line has been drawn around each community in the state, with no urban development allowed outside the boundary.*

- *Control over the process has been placed in state hands through the Land Conservation and Development Commission.*

Not surprisingly, this last principle has been the most controversial. It is based on the idea that public good takes precedence over private property rights—a well-established principle in most European countries that is generally opposed in the United States. The success of Oregon's plan, however, has helped people recognize that the land they own is not theirs alone to use in any way owners see fit.

Oregon's plan has worked because it is not designed to "just say no" to development. Instead it encourages certain kinds of development, such as dense, urban development.

Because of the plan, most of the state's rural areas remain undeveloped, and the state and many of its cities are consistently rated as some of the best places in the United States to live. Portland, for example, has plenty of greenways, open spaces, and affordable housing; a healthy inner city; and one of the country's best public transit systems. It has been voted the most livable U.S. city (1988), one of the top 10 cities in which to do business (1989), one of the best places to raise children (1990), and best in the Green Index that rates U.S. cities in terms of pollution, public health, and environmental health (1990).

Many urban areas in the United States have tried to curb urban expansion by using low-density residential zoning, usually by requiring each house to occupy its own large lot. However, instead of discouraging urban expansion, such low-density housing has forced developers to consume more open space. And, to accommodate new, outlying suburbs and towns, highways have been extended, further contributing to sprawling development.

Another problem is that zoning in the United States has been used to set up separate areas for residential, commercial, and industrial activities. Such compartmentalized zoning made sense in the smokestack days when factories polluted cities and few suburbs existed. But the end result has been to encourage urban sprawl and to separate homes, jobs, and shops by long distances, thus requiring increased car use. This practice has also broken up the sense of community found in integrated urban neighborhoods where most people can walk or cycle or take public transport to work or school and to buy groceries and other everyday items. Changing zoning laws to encourage such reintegration of homes, workplaces, and stores would reduce urban sprawl, energy waste, and loss of community.

Japan and western Europe have the world's most comprehensive land-use controls, and North America and Australia the weakest. In the United States, only Oregon has developed a comprehensive land-use plan (Solutions, left).

## 9-5 Making Urban Areas More Livable and Sustainable

**DOING MAINTENANCE AND REPAIRS** As philosopher–longshoreman Eric Hoffer observed, "History shows that the level achieved by a civilization can be measured by the degree to which it performs maintenance." America's older cities have enormous maintenance and repair problems—most of them aggravated by decades of neglect.

For example, when it rains in Chicago, sewage backs up into basements of about 25% of the homes. An estimated 46% of Boston's water supply and 25% of Pittsburgh's are lost through leaky pipes. Some 39% of America's bridges (55–68% in 11 states) are unsafe. About 56% of the paved highways in the United States are in poor or fair condition and need expensive repairs. Highways in western Europe are designed to last 40 years—twice as long as American roads.

Maintenance, repair, and replacement of existing U.S. bridges, roads, mass transit systems, water supply systems, sewers, and sewage treatment plants during the next decade could cost a staggering $2 trillion or more—an average expenditure of $2.1 million per minute. These huge bills from neglect are coming due in a time of record budget deficits, cutbacks in federal funds for building and maintaining public works, and

**Figure 9-17** The Riverwalk area in downtown San Antonio, Texas, which took 30 years to develop, is popular with the city's tourists and convention-goers.

strong citizen opposition to increases in federal, state, and local taxes.

**REVITALIZING EXISTING CITIES** Billions of dollars have been spent in decaying downtown areas to build new civic centers, museums, office buildings, parking garages, high-rise luxury hotels, and shopping centers. Montreal has built a large underground mall or "minicity" serviced by its subway system. Pittsburgh has rejuvenated its central-city area. Boston, Baltimore, San Francisco, Long Beach (California), Norfolk (Virginia), Portland, and New Orleans have revitalized their urban waterfront areas. San Antonio planted trees and built shops along a river canal (Figure 9-17).

These projects add beauty, preserve and reuse historic buildings, and help revive downtown areas. They provide white-collar jobs for suburbanites and generally safe and secure shopping and cultural facilities for urban residents and tourists. Although downtown revitalization can indirectly benefit the poor by providing additional tax revenues, such projects sometimes displace much-needed low-cost housing.

In many U.S. cities older neighborhoods are being revitalized by middle- and high-income residents who buy run-down houses at low prices, renovate them, and either live in them or sell them at high prices—a process called *gentrification*. This benefits the city economically by increasing property values and thus tax revenues, and by slowing the flight of businesses and

people to the suburbs, but it also displaces low-income residents.

A number of cities have set up *urban homesteading* programs to help middle- and low-income people purchase houses and apartment buildings abandoned by their owners or acquired by the city because of failure to pay taxes. The city sells these buildings to individuals or to cooperatives of low-income renters for $1–$100, or provides buyers with low-interest, long-term loans. The new owners must agree to renovate the buildings and live in them for at least three years. This approach has been particularly successful in Wilmington (Delaware), Detroit, and Baltimore.

**REVITALIZING PUBLIC HOUSING** America is increasingly becoming a nation of housing haves and have-nots. Many middle-income families cannot afford to buy a home. Several million poor people cannot get housing because since 1981 federal subsidies for low-income housing have been cut by 85%; in addition, over 2.5 million existing units were torn down, abandoned, or converted to high-rent apartments, luxury condominiums, and office buildings.

One way to ease the housing situation is to provide government aid for low-income tenants to renovate and manage many of the country's 1.3 million public housing units and 70,000 abandoned units (Individuals Matter, p. 251). More aid and lower interest rates would also help first-time low- and middle-income families buy homes. Tax provisions that reward property owners for building new structures but not for rehabilitating or maintaining existing ones need to be changed.

**CREATING URBAN ENTERPRISE ZONES** Some analysts call for increased federal aid to help revitalize poor urban areas. Others argue that federal aid is often wasted because it is controlled by distant bureaucrats who have little knowledge of the needs of local people. These analysts favor a program in which federal, state, and local tax breaks and other benefits are given to private companies that locate in economically depressed urban areas, hire the unemployed or disadvantaged, or build or rehabilitate low-income housing. Neighborhoods that qualify for such tax breaks are called *urban enterprise zones*.

Since 1978 urban enterprise zones have been established in 80 American cities in 37 states with mixed results. In most cases it is difficult to tell whether an increase in jobs is due to normal economic growth or to the lure of the zone.

Some companies lay off workers in one part of an urban area and hire new ones in an enterprise zone to qualify for tax breaks. Other companies have mostly brought along their old employees instead of hiring new employees from depressed areas. Moreover, tax breaks rarely are large enough to attract businesses to the worst urban neighborhoods, which have high crime rates and few trained workers. Another problem is that many of the minority poor in such areas lack the education and skills to take advantage of many of the new job opportunities.

Some enterprise zones have wasted huge sums of money. Another growing problem is political, with almost every member of Congress wanting a slice of the pie regardless of need or merit—assuring a pork barrel of failed programs. Properly managed, urban enterprise zones can help, but they put only a minor (and often expensive) dent in a huge problem.

**PRESERVING URBAN OPEN SPACE** Some cities have had the foresight to preserve moderate amounts of open space in the form of municipal parks. Central Park in New York City (Figure 9-18), Golden Gate Park in San Francisco, Fairmont Park in Philadelphia, and Lake Front Park in Chicago are examples of large urban parks in the United States.

Unfortunately, older cities that did not plan for such parks early in their development have little or no chance of getting them now. However, as newer cities expand they can develop large and medium-size parks.

Another way to provide open space and control urban growth is to surround a large city with a *greenbelt*—an open area used for recreation, sustainable

## Empowering People: Tenant-Owned Public Housing

**INDIVIDUALS MATTER** In 1981 the 3,500 tenants of the Kenilworth-Parkside public housing project in Washington, D.C., lived in a crime-ridden, drug-infested neighborhood. For three years they had no heat or hot water and the roofs of their apartments were caving in. Today residents have turned the once-squalid project into a safe, well-kept living space.

Things began turning around in 1982 when Kimi Gray, an unemployed welfare mother of five, persuaded housing authorities to let her and other tenants run the project. Gray was also able to get federal aid for renovation of all 464 units. Under her leadership the tenants evicted drug dealers, and at least one member of each family was required to take six weeks of training in home repairs, pest control, and personal budgeting. Residents took turns as hall and building captains.

Within a few years residents had cleaned up the area, made repairs, and restored utilities. Crime dropped sharply, rent collections rose 77%, administrative costs were reduced by 66%, welfare dependency fell from 85% to 2%, and teenage pregnancies were cut in half.

With federal aid the tenants have established a day-care center (only for tenants who are working or actively looking for work), several businesses, a treatment center for residents addicted to alcohol or other drugs, and a van shuttle that takes residents to jobs in the suburbs. The tenant-run management corporation now employs more than 100 people, 80% of them residents.

The government sold the project to the management corporation for $1. In 1990 tenants were allowed to apply money they formerly paid in rent to buy their units at discounted prices.

This project required $23 million in federal aid. In the long run, however, the money will be recovered by the lower administrative costs (already saving the government $5.7 million in operating expenses), elimination of most welfare payments, and taxes paid by tenants who now have jobs. Kimi Gray, who now has a college degree, has successfully trained tenant leaders in St. Louis, in Montgomery County (Maryland), and in other urban areas.

**Figure 9-18** Central Park in New York City.

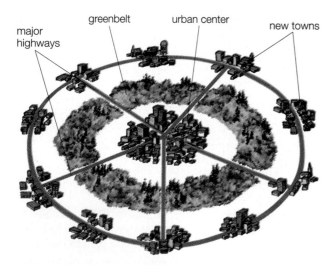

major highways  greenbelt  urban center  new towns

**Figure 9-19** A greenbelt around a large city. This arrangement can control urban growth and provide open space for recreation and other nondestructive uses. Satellite towns are sometimes built outside the belt. Rail systems transport people around the periphery or into the central city.

forestry, or other nondestructive uses (Figure 9-19). Satellite towns can be built outside the belt. Ideally the outlying towns and the central city are linked by an extensive public transport system. Many cities in western Europe, and Canadian cities such as Toronto and Vancouver, have used this approach. Another approach is to set up an *urban growth boundary*—a line surrounding a city beyond which new development is not allowed. Portland, Oregon, has used this approach with great success.

Since World War II the typical pattern of suburban housing development in the United States has been to bulldoze a tract of woods or farmland and build rows of standard houses on standard-sized lots. Many of these developments and their streets are named after the trees and wildlife they displaced: Oak Lane, Cedar Drive, Pheasant Run, Fox Fields. In recent years builders have increasingly used a new pattern, known as *cluster development*, which provides areas of open space within housing developments (Figure 9-20).

Some cities have converted abandoned railroad track lines and dry creek beds into bicycle, hiking, and jogging paths, often called *greenways*. At least 500 new greenway projects, developed largely by citizens' groups, are underway in the United States. Many German, Dutch, and Danish cities are connected by extensive networks of footpaths. Abandoned lots can be developed as community gardens, small plazas, and vest-pocket parks.

**BUILDING NEW CITIES AND TOWNS** Most urban problems will have to be solved in existing cities. However, building new cities and towns could take some of the pressure off overpopulated and stressed urban areas.

Great Britain has built 16 new towns and is building 15 more. New towns have also been built in Singapore, Hong Kong, Finland, Sweden, France, the Netherlands, Venezuela, Brazil, and the United States. There are three types: **(1)** *satellite towns*, located fairly close to an existing large city (Figure 9-19); **(2)** *free-*

252    Q: In tropical and temperate areas, how long does it take to renew 2.54 centimeters (1 inch) of topsoil?

*standing new towns*, located far from any major city; and **(3)** *in-town new towns*, located in existing urban areas. Typically new towns are designed for populations of 20,000–100,000 people (Case Study, right).

New towns rarely succeed without government financial support. Some don't succeed even then, primarily because of poor planning and management. In 1971 the Department of Housing and Urban Development (HUD) provided more than $300 million in federally guaranteed loans for developers to build 13 new towns in the United States. By 1980 HUD had to take title to nine of those projects, which had gone bankrupt, and HUD no longer funds new towns.

Private developers of new towns must put up large amounts of money to buy the land and install facilities and pay heavy taxes and interest charges for decades before they see profit. In the United States two privately developed new towns—Reston (Virginia) and Columbia (Maryland)—have been in financial difficulty since they were established two decades ago. However, their situations are gradually improving.

Recently a successful new town called Las Colinas was built 8 kilometers (5 miles) from the Dallas–Fort Worth Airport on land that was once a ranch. The community is built around an urban center, with a lake and water taxis to transport people across it. The town is laced with greenbelts and open spaces to separate high-rise office buildings, warehouses, and residential buildings. People working in high-rise buildings park their cars outside the core and take a computer-controlled personal transit system to their offices.

## CASE STUDY

# Tapiola, Finland

Tapiola, Finland, a satellite new town not far from Helsinki, is internationally acclaimed for its ecological design, beauty, and high quality of life for its residents. Designed in 1951, it is being built gradually in seven sections, with an ultimate projected population of 80,000. Today many of its 50,000 residents work in Helsinki, but the long-range goal is industrial and commercial independence.

Tapiola is divided into several villages separated by greenbelts. Each village consists of several neighborhoods clustered around a shopping and cultural center that can be reached on foot. Playgrounds and parks radiate from this center, and walkways lead to the various residential neighborhoods.

Each neighborhood has a social center and contains a mix of about 20% high-rise apartments and 80% single-family houses nestled among lush evergreen forests and rocky hills. Housing is not segregated by income. Because housing is clustered, more land is available for open space, recreation areas, and parks.

Industrial building and factories, with strict pollution controls, are located away from residential areas and screened by vegetation to reduce noise and visual pollution, but they are close enough so people can walk or bicycle to work. Finland plans to build six more new satellite towns around Helsinki.

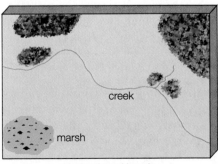

Undeveloped Land

Typical Housing Development

Cluster Housing Development

**Figure 9-20** Conventional and cluster developments as they would appear if constructed on the same land area. With cluster development, houses, town houses, condominiums, and two- to six-story apartments are built on part of the tract. The rest, typically 30% of the area, is left as open space, parks, and cycling and walking paths. Parking spaces and garages can also be clustered so that cars are not used within residential areas, with access only by walking, bicycling, or driving small electric or methane-powered golf carts.

A: 200–1,000 years depending on climate and soil type

## Improving Urban Life

**SOLUTIONS**

Since most people around the world now live, or will live, in urban areas, improving the quality of urban life in ways that also help sustain the earth should be an urgent priority. Ways to do this include:

### Economic Development and Population Regulation

- Reduce population growth (Section 8-3).
- Reduce the flow of people from rural to urban areas by increasing investments and social services in rural areas and by not giving higher food, energy, and other subsidies to urban dwellers than to rural dwellers.
- Recognize that increased urbanization and urban density is better than spreading people over the countryside, which would destroy more of the planet's biodiversity. The problem is not urbanization but hyper-urbanization and our failure to make cities more sustainable and livable.
- Maintain employment and plug dollar drains from local economies by setting up "buy local" programs, greatly improving energy efficiency, and instituting extensive recycling, reuse, and pollution prevention programs.
- Recruit only new businesses that meet unfulfilled needs and that won't compete with existing local businesses.

### Land Use and Maintenance

- Encourage well-planned compact growth to conserve energy, water, land, and wildlife resources: to arrest destructive sprawl; to create more diverse and socially integrated communities; to promote smaller, more affordable housing; and to take back urban areas from cars.
- Repair and revitalize existing cities.
- Stimulate the development of ecologically and economically sustainable new towns.
- Rely on comprehensive, regional ecological land-use planning and control (Solutions, p. 248).
- Give squatters legal title to land they have lived on, and provide them with support and low-cost loans to improve their communities.
- Plant lawns with low-maintenance groundcover vegetation and public areas with native plants to lessen the use of water, fertilizer, and pesticides.

- Plant large numbers of trees in greenbelts, on unused lots, and along streets to reduce air pollution and noise and to provide recreational areas and wildlife habitats.
- Establish greenbelts of undeveloped forestland and open space within and around urban areas (Figure 9-19), and preserve nearby wetlands and agricultural land.
- Restore natural and farm lands everywhere feasible, and at the same time protect and expand existing natural reserves and build wildlife corridors between such reserves.

### Transportation

- Discourage excessive dependence on motor vehicles within urban areas. Do this by providing efficient bus (traveling in express lanes) and trolley service, building bike lanes, charging single-occupant vehicles higher fees for tolls and parking, establishing express lanes solely for vehicles with three or more people, abolishing tax-free status for company-owned cars, giving businesses tax write-offs for providing employees with transit passes instead of free parking spaces, providing tax incentives

**MAKING CITIES MORE SUSTAINABLE** An important goal in coming decades should be to make urban areas more self-reliant, sustainable, and enjoyable places to live. As the era of cheap oil and gasoline comes to a close over the next few decades, urban sprawl and car-culture cities are likely to become unaffordable and unsustainable luxuries. In ecologically sustainable cities people would walk or use a bicycle or tricycle for most short trips and walk or bike to bus, metro, or trolley stops for longer urban trips. Rapid-rail transport between cities (Figure 9-16) would replace many long drives and short airplane flights.

Such ecologically healthy cities would be energy efficient, rely mostly on renewable energy resources, recycle or reuse almost everything (at least 80%), encourage rather than assault biodiversity, and use composting to grow food and to create rather than destroy soil. They would be based on good ecological design (Guest Essay, p. 256).

In a few decades people may be wondering why they allowed cars to dominate their lives and degrade the environment for so long, taking seriously the advice Lewis Mumford gave Americans over three decades ago: "Forget the damned motor car and build

Q: Worldwide, how much topsoil is eroded each year?

for individuals and businesses using car and van pooling or walking or cycling to work, and establishing car-free zones in downtown areas, with mass transit systems carrying people to and from the edges of these zones.

- End automobile subsidies. Make automobile owners pay for all their environmental and harmful social costs directly (up front) instead of indirectly in higher income, sales, and other taxes and higher insurance and health costs.

- Raise gasoline taxes sharply (with tax relief for the poor and lower middle class).

- Use at least half of the revenue for mass transit, high-speed rail networks (Figure 9-16), bike pedestrian paths, and improved auto fuel efficiency.

### Improving Energy Efficiency

- Get more energy from locally available resources (Chapter 17).

- Require all new cars to have fuel efficiencies of at least 17 kilometers per liter (40 miles per gallon) by 2000 and 21 kilometers per liter (50 miles per gallon) by 2010.

- Give tax rebates to businesses and individuals who use gas-sipping vehicles, and impose heavy taxes on those using gas guzzlers.

- Enact building codes that require new and existing buildings to be energy efficient and responsive to climate.

- Retrofit public buildings to obtain all or most of their energy from renewable sources.

### Water and Food

- Encourage water conservation by installing water meters in all buildings and raising the price of water to reflect its true cost.

- Establish small neighborhood water-recycling plants.

- Enact building codes that require water conservation in new and existing buildings and businesses.

- Grow food (with emphasis on sustainable organic methods) in abandoned lots, community garden plots, small fruit-tree orchards, rooftop gardens and greenhouses, apartment window boxes, school yards, and solar-heated fish ponds and tanks, and on some of the land in greenbelts (with careful controls).

### Pollution and Wastes

- Discourage industries that produce large quantities of pollution and that use large amounts of water or energy.

- Enact and enforce strict noise control laws to reduce stress from rising levels of urban noise.

- Give tax breaks and other economic incentives to businesses that recycle and reuse resources and that emphasize pollution prevention.

- Establish urban composting centers to convert yard and food wastes into soil conditioner and the effluents and sludge from sewage treatment plants into fertilizer for use on parks, roadsides, flower gardens, and forests.

- Recycle or reuse at least 80% of urban solid waste and some types of hazardous waste instead of burying it or burning it. Because solid wastes are concentrated in cities, collection costs are lower and recycling and reuse are more efficient than in less densely populated areas.

cities for lovers and friends." Each of us has an important role to play in making cities more enjoyable, affordable, and sustainable places to live (Solutions, p. 254).

Urban areas that fail to become more ecologically sustainable are inviting economic depression and increased unemployment, pollution, and social tension. We have no time to waste in making urban areas—where half of the world's people will live by 2000—better places to live and work in, with less stress on natural systems and people. Each of us has a vital role to play in converting this dream into reality.

*The city is not an ecological monstrosity. It is rather the place where both the problems and the opportunities of modern technological civilization are most potent and visible.*

PETER SELF

## The Ecological Design Arts

*David W. Orr*

*Since 1990 David W. Orr has been professor of environmental studies at Oberlin College. In 1979 he cofounded Meadowcreek, a nonprofit 600-hectare (1,500-acre) laboratory in north central Arkansas for the study of environmentally sound means of agriculture, forestry, renewable energy systems, architectural design, and livelihood. He served as its director until 1990. He has written numerous environmental articles and three books, including* Ecological Literacy *and* The Campus and the Biosphere *(see Further Readings). He is education editor for* Conservation Biology, *coeditor of the environmental policy series for* SUNY press, *and a member of the editorial advisory board of* Orion Nature Quarterly.

If *Homo sapiens* entered industrial civilization in an intergalactic design competition, it would be tossed out at the qualifying round. It doesn't fit. It won't last. The scale is wrong. And even its defenders admit that it's not very pretty. The most glaring design failures of industrial/technologically driven societies are the loss of diversity of all kinds, impending climate change, pollution, and soil erosion.

Industrial civilization, of course, wasn't designed at all. It was mostly imposed by single-minded individuals, armed with one doctrine of human progress or another, each requiring a homogenization of nature and society. These individuals for the most part had no knowledge of "ecological design arts." By this I mean the set of perceptual and analytic abilities, ecological wisdom, and practical wherewithal needed to make things that fit into a world of microbes, plants, animals, and entropy.

Good ecological design incorporates understanding about how nature works into the ways we design, build, and live. It is required in our designs of farms, houses, neighborhoods, cities, transportation systems, technologies, economies, energy policies, and just about anything that directly or indirectly requires energy or materials or governs their use.

When human artifacts and systems are well designed, they are in harmony with the ecological patterns in which they are embedded. When poorly designed, they undermine those larger patterns creating pollution, higher costs, and social stress. Bad design is not simply an engineering problem, although better engineering would often help. Its roots go deeper.

Good ecological design has certain common characteristics including right scale, simplicity, efficient use of resources, a close fit between means and ends, durability, redundancy, and resilience. They are often place-specific or, in John Todd's words, "elegant solutions predicated on the uniqueness of place." Good design also solves more than one problem at a time and promotes human competence (instead of addiction), efficient and frugal use of resources, and sound regional economies. Where good design becomes part of the social fabric at all levels, unanticipated positive side effects multiply. When people fail to design with ecological competence, unwanted side effects and disasters multiply.

The pollution, violence, social decay, and waste all around us indicate that we have designed things badly. Why? There are, I think, three primary reasons. First, as long as land and energy were cheap and the world was relatively empty, we did not have to master the discipline of good design. The result: sprawling cities, wasteful economies, waste dumped into the environment, bigger and less efficient automobiles and buildings, and conversion of entire forests into junk mail and Kleenex—all in the name of economic growth and convenience.

Second, design intelligence fails when greed, narrow self-interest, and individualism take over. Good design is a cooperative community process requiring people

## Critical Thinking

1. What conditions, if any, would encourage you to rely less on the automobile? Would you regularly travel to school or work by bicycle or motor scooter, on foot, by mass transit, or by a car or van pool? Explain.

2. Do you believe that cities should continue expanding into agricultural land? If not, how would you control this?

3. How is land use decided in your community? What roles do citizens play in this process?

4. Should squatters around cities of LDCs be given title to land they don't own or rent? Explain. What are the alternatives?

*5. Consult local officials to identify any floodplain areas in your community. How are these areas used?

*6. As a class or group project try to borrow one or more decibel meters from the physics or engineering department or from a local stereo or electronics repair shop. Make a survey of sound pressure levels at various times of day and at several locations, and

**Q:** Worldwide, how fast is soil eroding on farmland?

who share common values and goals that bring them together and hold them together. American cities with their extremes of poverty and opulence are products of people who believe they have little in common with one another. Greed, suspicion, and fear undermine good community and good design alike.

Third, poor design results from poorly equipped minds. Good design can only be done by people who understand harmony, patterns, and systems. Industrial cleverness, on the contrary, is mostly evident in the minutiae of things, not in their totality or in their overall harmony. Good design requires a breadth of view that causes people to ask how human artifacts and purposes fit within a particular culture and place. It also requires ecological intelligence, by which I mean an intimate familiarity with how nature works.

An example of good ecological design is found in John Todd's "living machines," which are carefully orchestrated ensembles of plants, aquatic animals, technology, solar energy, and high-tech materials to purify wastewater, but without the expense, energy use, and chemical hazards of conventional sewage treatment technology. Todd's living machines resemble greenhouses filled with plants and aquatic animals [Figure 23-2]. Wastewater enters at one end and purified water leaves at the other. In between, an ensemble of organisms driven by sunlight remove and use nutrients, break down toxics, and incorporate heavy metals in plant tissues.

Ecological design standards also apply to the making of public policy. For example, the Clean Air Act of 1970 required car manufacturers to install catalytic converters to remove air pollutants. Two decades later emissions per vehicle are down substantially, but since more cars are on the road, air quality is about the same—an example of inadequate ecological design. A sounder design approach to transportation would create better access among housing, schools, jobs, stores, and recreation areas; build better public transit systems; restore and improve railroads; and create bike trails and walkways.

An education in the ecological design arts would foster the ability to see things in their ecological context, integrating firsthand experience and practical competence with theoretical knowledge about how nature works. It would aim to equip learners to build households, institutions, farms, communities, corporations, and economies that (1) do not emit carbon dioxide or other heat-trapping gases, (2) operate on renewable energy, (3) preserve biological diversity, (4) recycle material and organic wastes, and (5) promote sustainable local and regional economies.

The outline of a curriculum in ecological design arts can be found in recent work in ecological restoration, ecological engineering, solar design, landscape architecture, sustainable agriculture, sustainable forestry, energy efficiency, ecological economics, and least-cost, end-use analysis. A program in ecological design would weave these and similar elements together around actual design objectives that aim to make students smarter about systems and about how specific things and processes fit in their ecological context. With such an education we can develop the habits of mind, analytical skills, and practical competence needed to sustain the earth for us and other species.

### Critical Thinking

1. Does your school offer courses or a curriculum in ecological design? If not, why?

2. Use the principles of good ecological design to evaluate how well your campus is designed and suggest ways to improve its design.

---

plot the results on a map. Also measure sound levels in a room with a stereo and from earphones at several different volume settings. If possible, measure sound levels at an indoor concert or a nightclub at various distances from the sound system speakers. Correlate your findings with those in Figure 9-14.

*7. As a class project evaluate land use and land-use planning by your school, draw up an improved plan based on ecological principles, and submit the plan to school officials.

*8. As a class project use the following criteria to rate your city on a green index from 0 to 100. Are existing trees protected and new ones planted throughout the city? Do you have parks to enjoy? Can you swim in nearby lakes and rivers? What is the quality of your water and air? Is there an effective noise pollution reduction program? Does your city have a recycling program, a composting program, a source reduction program, and a hazardous waste collection program with the goal of reducing the current solid waste output by 80%? Is there an effective mass transit system? Are there bicycle paths? Are all buildings required to meet high energy-efficiency standards? Is there an effective program for the sustainable use of locally available matter and energy resources and a buy-local program? How much of the energy is obtained from locally available renewable resources? Are environmental regulations for existing industry tough enough and enforced well enough to protect the citizens? Do local officials look carefully at an industry's environmental record and plans before encouraging it to locate in your city or county? Are land-use decisions made by using ecological planning with active participation by citizens? Is your city actively planning to improve the quality of life for all of its citizens now and in the future?

PART IV
# Ultimate Global Problems

*If we don't address the issues of global ecology, we won't have to worry about the other issues.*
CARLOS SALINAS DE GORTARI (President of Mexico)

## How Farmers and a Monkey Saved a Forest

It's early morning in a tropical forest in the Central American country of Belize (Figure 9-3). Suddenly loud roars that trail off into wheezing moans—territorial wake-up calls of black howler monkeys (Figure 10-1)—rouse everyone in or near the wildlife sanctuary by the Belize River. These long-tailed primates live in small troops headed by a dominant male. Vegetarians, they travel slowly among the treetops, feeding on leaves, flowers, and fruits.

This species is the centerpiece of an experiment recruiting peasant farmers to preserve nearby tropical forests and wildlife. The project is the brainchild of

Carol Farneti/Planet Earth Pictures

**Figure 10-1** Black howler monkey in a tropical forest in Belize. This is one of six howler monkey species in Latin America whose populations have declined as tropical forests in countries such as Guatemala and Mexico have been cleared. The black howler is one of the more than two-thirds of the world's 150 known species of primates threatened with extinction.

American Robert Horwich. Meeting in 1985 with the 300 people of Bermudian Landing, Robert suggested that the villagers establish a sanctuary that would benefit the local black howlers and themselves. He proposed that the farmers leave thin strips of forest along the edges of their fields to provide food for the howlers and let them travel through the sanctuary's patchwork of active garden plots and young and mature forest. Leaving strips of forest along the river, he noted, would also reduce soil erosion and river silting, yielding more fish for the villagers.

To date more than 100 farmers have done this, and the 47-square-kilometer (18-square-mile) sanctuary is now home for an estimated 1,100 black howlers. The idea has spread to seven other villages.

Now as many as 6,000 ecotourists visit the sanctuary each year to catch glimpses of its loudmouth monkeys and other wildlife. Villagers serve as tour guides, cook meals for the visitors, and lodge tourists overnight in their spare rooms. So long as ecotourism doesn't get so big that it destroys the howlers, this experiment can demonstrate the benefits of integrating ecology and economics by allowing local villagers to make money by helping sustain the forest and its wildlife.

Forests are home to 50–90% of Earth's species. They are also potentially renewable resources if used sustainably. However, forests—especially tropical forests and old-growth forests in the northwestern United States and southwestern Canada—are disappearing faster than any other biome as they are cleared for timber, paper pulp, fuelwood, cropland, livestock grazing, mining, reservoirs, and urbanization. They are also threatened by air pollution and by possible climate change that their destruction is helping to cause.

If these incredibly diverse and important forest biomes continue to vanish at the current rate, most will be gone within 30–50 years. Preventing further losses of these vital forms of Earth capital and helping to heal forests we have degraded are urgent priorities.

In this chapter we will answer the following questions:

- What are the major types of forests, and why are they such important ecosystems?
- How fast is tropical deforestation taking place, and why should we care about the problem?
- What are the causes of tropical deforestation and fuelwood shortages?
- What can be done to reduce tropical deforestation and fuelwood shortages?
- Why are the remaining old-growth forests in North America important, and what can be done to prevent their destruction?

## 10-1 Forests: Types and Importance

**TYPES OF FORESTS**  Since agriculture began about 10,000 years ago, human activities have reduced Earth's forest cover by at least one-third to about 34% of the world's land area (p. 259 and Figures 5-11, 5-22, 5-24, and 5-26). Forests are disappearing almost everywhere, although losses in Europe and North America have been partially offset by new forest growth.

**Old-growth forests** are virgin (uncut) and old second-growth forests that have not been seriously disturbed for several hundred years. They contain massive trees hundreds or even thousands of years old. Examples include forests of Douglas fir, western hemlock, giant sequoia (Figure 4-9), and coastal redwoods (Figure 2-7) in the western United States; loblolly pine in the Southeast; and 60% of the world's tropical forests.

The understory zones and other vegetation in old-growth forests provide ecological niches for a variety of wildlife (Figure 4-37). These forests also have large numbers of standing dead trees (snags) and fallen logs (boles), which are habitats for a variety of plants, animals, and microorganisms. Their decay returns nutrients to the soil.

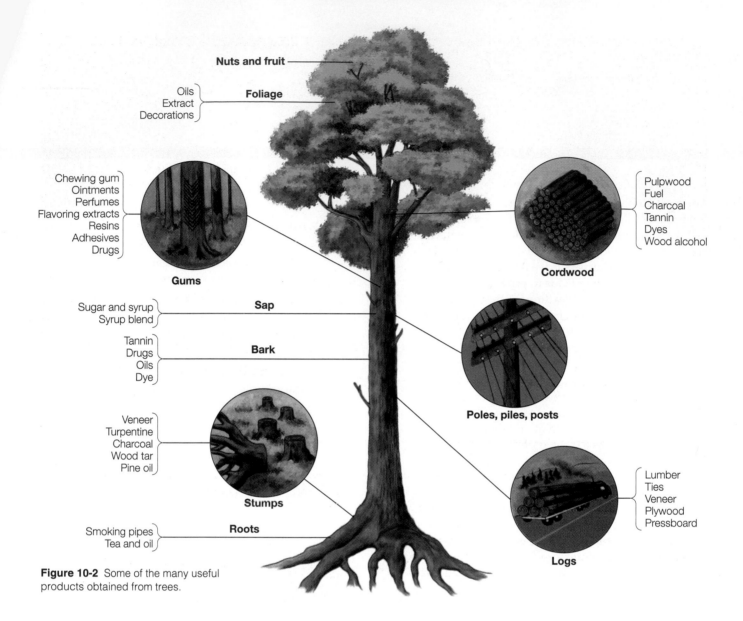

Nuts and fruit

Foliage
Oils
Extract
Decorations

Gums
Chewing gum
Ointments
Perfumes
Flavoring extracts
Resins
Adhesives
Drugs

Cordwood
Pulpwood
Fuel
Charcoal
Tannin
Dyes
Wood alcohol

Sap
Sugar and syrup
Syrup blend

Bark
Tannin
Drugs
Oils
Dye

Poles, piles, posts

Stumps
Veneer
Turpentine
Charcoal
Wood tar
Pine oil

Roots
Smoking pipes
Tea and oil

Logs
Lumber
Ties
Veneer
Plywood
Pressboard

**Figure 10-2** Some of the many useful products obtained from trees.

**Second-growth forests** are stands of trees resulting from secondary ecological succession after cutting (Figure 6-14). Most forests in the United States and other temperate areas are second-growth forests that grew back after virgin forests were logged or farms were abandoned. Some of these second-growth stands have remained undisturbed and are old-growth forests, but many are *tree farms*—intensively managed tracts of even-aged trees of one species (Figure 5-25). About 40% of tropical forests are second-growth forests.

**COMMERCIAL IMPORTANCE** Forests give us lumber for housing, biomass for fuelwood, pulp for paper, medicines, and many other products worth more than $300 billion per year (Figure 10-2). Many forestlands are also used for mining, grazing livestock, and recreation.

Worldwide about half of the timber cut each year is used as fuel for heating and cooking, especially in LDCs. Some of this is burned directly as firewood, and some is converted into charcoal, which is widely used as a fuel by urban dwellers in LDCs and by some industries. One-third of the world's annual harvest is sawlogs that are converted into building materials: lumber, plywood, hardboard, particleboard, and chipboard. One-sixth is converted into pulp used in a variety of paper products. Three countries—the United States, the Commonwealth of Independent States (CIS), and Canada—supply 53% of the world's commercial timber.

**ECOLOGICAL IMPORTANCE** Forested watersheds act as giant sponges, slowing down runoff and absorbing and holding water that recharges springs, streams, and groundwater. Thus they regulate the flow of water from mountain highlands to croplands and urban areas, and help control soil erosion, moderate flooding, and reduce the amount of sediment washing into streams, lakes, and reservoirs.

Q: On how much of the world's cropland is soil eroding faster than it forms?

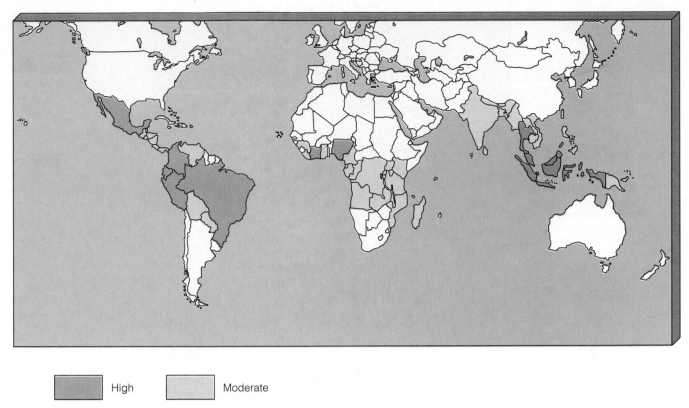

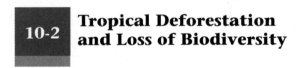
High        Moderate

**Figure 10-3** Countries rapidly losing their tropical forests. (Data from UN Food and Agriculture Organization)

Forests also influence local, regional, and global climates. For example, 50–80% of the moisture in the air above tropical forests comes from trees by transpiration and evaporation. If large areas of these lush forests are cleared, average annual precipitation drops; the region's climate gets hotter and drier; and its soils are depleted of already-scarce nutrients, baked, and washed away. Eventually this process can convert a diverse tropical forest into a sparse grassland or even a desert.

Forests are vital to the global carbon cycle (Figure 4-28) and act as a brake on a possible runaway greenhouse effect (Figure 5-10). Through photosynthesis trees remove carbon dioxide from and add oxygen to the air, explaining why they are called Earth's "lungs."

Forests provide habitats for more wildlife species than any other biome, making them the planet's major reservoir of biodiversity. They also buffer us against noise, absorb air pollutants, and nourish the human spirit.

According to one calculation a typical tree provides $196,250 worth of ecological benefits in the form of oxygen, air cleaning, soil fertility and erosion control, water recycling and humidity control, and wildlife habitats. Sold as timber the same tree is worth only about $590. As long as the lasting and renewable ecological benefits of forests are undervalued in the marketplace, we will continue to destroy and degrade these forests, and their long-term ecological services, for short-term economic gain.

## 10-2 Tropical Deforestation and Loss of Biodiversity

**SHRINKING TROPICAL FORESTS** Tropical forests, which cover about 6% of Earth's land area, grow near the equator in Latin America, Africa, and Asia (Figure 5-11). Just three countries—Brazil, Indonesia, and Zaire—contain more than half the world's total. Latin America has 90% of the world's tropical forests in the vast Amazon Basin, which runs though eight countries (Figure 9-3).

These forests consist of *tropical moist forests* or *rain forests* that receive rainfall almost daily and *tropical seasonal deciduous forests* with one or two dry seasons each year. Because the seasonal forests often have good soils and are easy to exploit, they have been under assault for centuries. Central America, for example, has lost 80% of its original tropical seasonal forests.

About 56% of the world's tropical forests have been cleared or damaged, and the annual rate of loss rose by 50% between 1981 and 1991 (Figure 10-3). Satellite scans indicate that these forests are vanishing

**Figure 10-4** Photo taken from the space shuttle *Discovery* in September 1988 shows smoke from fires burning cleared areas of tropical rain forests in South America's Amazon Basin. The white "clouds" are plumes of smoke, covering an area about three times the size of Texas. These fires may have accounted for 10% of all carbon dioxide entering the atmosphere in 1988. Mostly because of international pressure and an economic slowdown, the amount of forest land cleared in Brazil dropped about 30% between 1988 and 1990. Even so, Brazil accounts for a larger area of deforestation each year than any of the 62 tropical countries.

NASA

at a rate of at least 170,000 square kilometers (66,000 square miles) per year—equivalent to about 37 city blocks per minute or almost two football fields per second. An equal area of these forests is damaged every year.

Haiti has lost 98% of its original forest cover, the Philippines 97%, and Madagascar 84% (Case Study, p. 265). Only about 11% of the vast Amazon Basin forest has been cut (Figure 10-4), with 80% of this loss occurring since 1980. The green hemorrhage continues there, but the rate has slowed by almost one-third since 1987.

Most attention has focused on the Amazon Basin, but 95% of the once-vast rain forests on Brazil's Atlantic coast and 98% the coniferous Araucaria forests of the south have been devastated by logging and urban expansion. Only a few fragments are left. In 1990, under pressure from environmentalists, Brazil's president halted all cutting of native vegetation in the 13 states containing the remaining Atlantic coast rain forests.

Reforestation in the tropics scarcely deserves the name, with only 1 tree planted for every 10 trees cut; in Africa the ratio is 1 for every 29. If the current rate of loss continues, all remaining tropical forests (except for a few preserved and vulnerable patches) will be gone within 30–50 years, and much sooner in some areas (see cartoon, p. 266).

Q: Worldwide, how much land has become desertified during the past 50 years?

Madagascar, the world's fourth largest island, lies in the Indian Ocean off the East African coast (Figure 10-5). Because of its astounding biological diversity, this Texas-sized island is considered a crown jewel among Earth's ecosystems—a "biological superpower."

Most of its species have evolved in relative isolation for at least 40 million years, after the drift of Earth's lithospheric plates (Figure 7-5b) moved the island far enough from Africa's mainland to prevent migrations from Africa. The result is an estimated 160,000 species unique to this island, mostly in its vanishing eastern rain forests. Unique species include 80% of its 10,000 species of flowering plants (including 1,000 orchids), 66% of the world's species of chameleons (Figure 10-6), 800 butterfly species, half of the island's birds, and all its reptiles and mammals (Figure 10-7).

Madagascar's plant and animal species are also among the world's most endangered, mostly because of loss of habitat from slash-and-burn agriculture on poor soils fueled by rapid population growth. Since humans arrived about 1,500 years ago, 84% of its tropical seasonal forests and over 66% of its rain forests have been cut for cropland, fuelwood, and lumber, leaving blood-red gullies and streams (Figure 5-30) and vast eroded fields and hillsides. Madagascar is now the world's most eroded country.

Since 1984 the government, conservation organizations, and scientists worldwide have united to slow the island's plunge into wasteland. For such efforts to succeed, population growth—projected to triple between 1993 and 2025—will have to be slowed drastically, and local people will need to be involved in the planning and management of conservation areas, given ownership of land they occupy and trees

they plant, and encouraged to make a living from reforestation, ecotourism, and sustainable use of forest, wildlife, and soil resources.

The hour is late, but if fully supported and implemented, this inter-nationally funded effort can serve as a model for other areas. Even then, half of Madagascar's plant and animal species will probably be lost; however, doing nothing would be much worse.

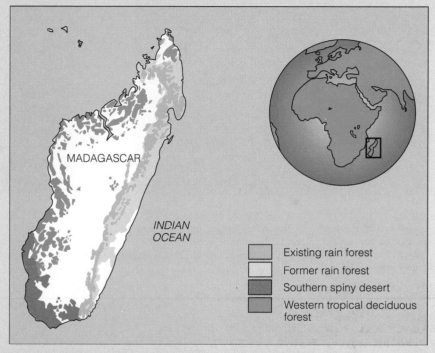

MADAGASCAR

INDIAN OCEAN

Existing rain forest
Former rain forest
Southern spiny desert
Western tropical deciduous forest

**Figure 10-5** Where is Madagascar?

Gérard Lacz/NHPA

**Figure 10-6** Parson's giant chameleon in a tropical forest in Madagascar. The largest of the chameleons, an adult Parson's can reach 70 centimeters (28 inches) in length. Among its prey are small birds. Madagascar is the only home for 60% of the world's known species of chameleons, some as small as a thumbnail.

Robert and Linda Mitchell

**Figure 10-7** Endangered ring-tailed lemur in Madagascar. Lemurs are the oldest distant relative of the human species. The 30 species of lemurs on this island are found nowhere else in the wild. Half of them are endangered.

Roy P. Fontaine/Photo Researchers, Inc.

William Grenfell/Visuals Unlimited

**Figure 10-8** Tropical forests are the planet's largest storehouse of biological diversity. Two of the species found there are the red uakari monkey (left) from the Amazon Basin in Peru and the keel-billed toucan from Belize in Central America (right). Most tropical forest species have specialized niches (Figure 4-37). This makes them highly vulnerable to extinction when their forest habitats are cleared or damaged.

Reprinted by permission of Tribune Media Services. (Color added)

**WHY SHOULD WE CARE ABOUT TROPICAL FORESTS?** Environmentalists consider what's happening to tropical forests one of the world's most serious environmental problems (Guest Essay, p. 288). These forests are homes to at least 50% (some estimate 90%) of Earth's total stock of species—most of them still unknown and unnamed. Biologist Edward O. Wilson estimates that at least 20% of tropical forest species could be gone by 2022, and as many as 50% by 2042, if current rates of tropical deforestation and degradation

continue. No extinction of this scale has occurred for 65 million years.

Rain forests teem with species of plants (Figures 4-11 and 5-23), fish, amphibians (Figure 4-34), birds (Figure 10-8, right), and above all, insects (Spotlight, p. 84). Rain forests also support many mammals, including nonhuman primates (p. 45 and Figures 10-1 and 10-8, left).

The world's tropical forests touch the daily lives of everyone on Earth through the products and ecological services they provide. These forests supply half of the world's annual harvest of hardwood and hundreds of food products (including coffee, tea, cocoa, spices, nuts, chocolate, and tropical fruits), and materials such as natural latex rubber, resins, dyes, and essential oils that can be harvested sustainably (Spotlight, p. 267).

The active ingredients for 25% of the world's prescription drugs are substances extracted from plants—most growing in tropical rain forests. Once the active component is isolated and identified, it can be synthesized for use, often at a lower cost than extracting it from harvested plants. Then the natural compound can be modified to produce an array of related chemi-

**Q:** How much of the planet's land is threatened by desertification?

**SPOTLIGHT**

Rubber tapping is one way to live off of tropical forests without destroying them. A rubber tapper cuts a diagonal groove through the bark of a live rubber tree and lets milky liquid latex trickle into a collecting cup (Figure 10-9). The latex, which is about 30% rubber, is processed to make rubber, and the scars heal without killing the tree. About 300,000 rubber tappers living in the Amazon Basin also gather Brazil nuts, fruits, and fibers in the forests, and cultivate small plots near their homes. Generally they hold no legal title to this government-owned land.

A 1988 study by a team of scientists showed that sustainable harvesting of such nonwood products as nuts, fruits, herbs, spices, oils, medicines, and latex rubber in Amazon rain forests over 50 years would generate twice as much revenue per hectare as timber production and three times as much as cattle ranching.

Chico Mendes, the rubber tapper shown in Figure 10-9, proposed that one-fourth of the Brazilian Amazon rain forest be set aside as *extractive reserves*—areas reserved for sustainable harvesting of potentially renewable commercial forest products by traditional resident populations. Such proposals are dangerous on the Brazilian frontier. Mendes was one of more than 1,500 rubber tappers, priests, lawyers, union officials, and other activists against rain forest destruction in Brazil who have been killed over the past 25 years, mostly by gunmen working for wealthy ranchers and cash-crop farmers trying to amass large land holdings. (The average price of a settler's life is $25.) Most of those homicides have not been investigated by Brazilian officials.

Because of the international outcry over Mendes' murder, however, Brazilian officials have established

14 extractive reserves covering about 0.8% of the Brazilian Amazon Basin and three new national parks since 1987. Environmentalists applaud these actions but fear that they are mostly window dressing calculated to weaken local and international pressures to protect much larger areas of the Amazon Basin from development. Evidence for this came in 1991 when Brazil's government reinstated tax breaks for cattle ranches and other destructive forms of development in the Amazon Basin, and cut funds for identifying and setting aside indigenous and extractive reserves by 80%.

Extractive reserves can help sustain some areas of tropical forests, but this approach is limited. Brazil's roughly 300,000 rubber tappers are greatly outnumbered by perhaps 6 million peasant farmers, ranchers, and loggers who make a living largely from destructive, unsustainable use of the land.

Local extractors of renewable forest resources often get little of the profit made from their efforts. For example, about $20 million worth of Brazil nuts are exported to the United States each year, but Brazil-nut gatherers get less than 3% of what the nuts sell for wholesale in New York City. Also, products such as latex rubber and nuts from extractive reserves often go through a pattern of surging demand, overexploitation of the resource, competition from other sources (such as lower-cost production in monoculture plantations of latex rubber) or substitutes (synthetic rubber), and eventual decline in both supply and demand.

As long as tropical forests and other forms of Earth capital are valued only for the resources that can be removed from them and not for the ecological services they provide, there is little hope they will be used sustainably.

Randall Hyman

**Figure 10-9** Rubber tapping is a potentially sustainable use of tropical forests. This photo, taken in 1987, shows Chico Mendes, leader of 70,000 Amazon rubber tappers, in his Brazilian home state of Acre, making a cut on a rubber tree. On December 22, 1988, he was murdered near his home in Xapuri by ranchers who opposed his internationally recognized efforts to protect Brazil's rain forests from land-clearing, colonization, and other destructive forms of development. In 1991 his assassins were convicted of murder but escaped from jail in 1993.

Figure 10-10 Rosy periwinkle found in the threatened tropical forests of Madagascar. Two compounds extracted from this plant have been used to successfully treat victims of two deadly cancers—lymphocytic leukemia (which used to be an almost certain death sentence for children) and Hodgkin's disease (mostly affecting young adults). Annual income from the sale of these two drugs exceeds $80 million—none of which is returned to Madagascar. Only a tiny fraction of tropical plants have been studied for such potential uses, and many will become extinct before we can study them.

## A Tree for All Seasons

**SPOTLIGHT**

What if there were a single plant that could quickly reforest bare land, provide fuelwood and lumber in dry areas, produce alternatives to toxic pesticides, treat numerous diseases, and help control population growth? There is—the neem tree, a relative of the mahogany tree. This remarkable tropical species, native to India and Burma, is ideal for reforestation because it can grow 9 meters (30 feet) tall in only six years! And it grows fastest on poor soil in semi-arid lands in Africa and Arabia. This drought-resistant tree can provide an abundance of fuelwood, lumber, and lamp oil.

It's also a natural pesticide—chemicals in its leaves can repel or kill over 200 insect species. And neem seeds and leaves have relieved so many different fevers, infections, and pains that the tree has been called a "village pharmacy." It's also a tooth brush—millions of Indians brush their teeth with a frayed neem twig. And it's a contraceptive—neem-seed oil evidently acts as a strong spermicide. Researchers are now trying to use a compound extracted from this oil to create a male birth control pill.

Figure 10-11 These are members of the Yanomami tribe in a tropical forest in Brazil's Amazon Basin. Earth's remaining tribal peoples, representing 5,000 cultures, are vanishing as their lands are taken over for economic development.

cals, many of which are useful drugs. This process has led to compounds used in birth control pills, tranquilizers, muscle relaxers, and life-saving drugs for treating malaria, leukemia and Hodgkin's disease (Figure 10-10), testicular and lung cancers, heart disease, high blood pressure, multiple sclerosis, venereal warts, and many other diseases. Commercial sales of these drugs account for more than $40 billion per year worldwide and $14 billion per year in the United States!

Seventy percent of the 3,000 plants identified by the National Cancer Institute (NCI) as sources of cancer-fighting chemicals come from tropical forests. Recently the NCI has found that an extract from a creeping vine from the canopies of rain forests in Cameroon inhibits the replication of the AIDS virus, and another potential anti-AIDS drug was discovered in a tropical plant from Samoa. While you are reading this page, a plant species that could cure a type of cancer, AIDS, or some other deadly disease might be wiped out forever. And some tropical tree species can be used for many purposes (Spotlight, above).

Most of the original strains of rice, wheat, and corn that supply more than half of the world's food

Q: What major food-producing country is doing the most to reduce soil erosion?

Over billions of years of evolution, plants, animals, and microorganisms—especially in tropical forests—have experienced astronomical numbers of mutations and genetic recombinations that have produced millions of unique chemicals that ward off predators, attract pollinators (Figure 5-23, left), or otherwise promote their—and possibly our survival. Collectively the world's wild organisms are far better synthesizers of organic molecules of practical use than all the world's chemists. Drug and biotech companies are stepping up "chemical prospecting" in tropical and other ecosystems to find unique genetic and chemical raw material before it is lost forever.

So far, the countries of origin have received little or none of the immense profits from the drugs and new genetic combinations developed from their raw material. Now these countries want a fair share of the profits as royalties or patent rights on products derived from organisms found on their turf. This threat to the profit margins and patented intellectual property

rights of drug and biotechnology companies is why the United States—alone—refused to sign an international biodiversity agreement at the 1992 Earth Summit in Rio de Janeiro. In 1993, however, President Clinton signed the agreement after stipulations were added to protect U.S. patent rights.

There is a legitimate debate over transferring patents to other countries without compensation for the huge investments necessary to develop new drugs and products. But returning 1–3% of the $8 billion made each year in the United States on sales of plant-derived drugs as royalties to the countries of origin would reward their contribution and still provide drug companies with ample profits.

Some U.S. companies have taken a promising approach along such lines. An example is the 1989 agreement between Merck & Co. and Costa Rica's National Biodiversity Institute (INBio), a private non-profit organization set up by biologists Daniel Janzen (Case Study, p. 280) and Rodrigo Gamez to survey and catalog Costa Rica's biodiversity. In the agreement Merck paid $1 million to INBio for locating and

collecting specimens of tropical plants, insects, and microbes that are possible sources of drugs or other commercial products, classifying them, and making extracts that are sent to Merck. Janzen also came up with the idea of training *parataxonomists*—students, teachers, bus drivers, and other ordinary people—in the art of collecting and identifying species. INBio is now helping Indonesia set up a similar institute.

If this chemical prospecting leads Merck to develop a marketable product, it will retain all patent rights but will pay INBio an undisclosed royalty (believed to be 1–3%). Ten percent of the up-front $1 million, and 50% of INBio's share of any royalties, will be invested in helping preserve Costa Rica's system of protected forests. Monsanto Corporation has contracted with the Missouri Botanical Garden to supply the company with several thousand tropical plant specimens. Critics of such plans, however, argue that some, if not most, of the money should go to local people or indigenous people whose land or knowledge provides the lead for a new medicine or biotech product.

were developed from wild tropical plants. Scientists believe that tens of thousands of strains of plants with potential value as food, including 2,450 edible fruits, await discovery in tropical forests.

Despite this immense potential less than 1% of the estimated 125,000 flowering plant species in the world's tropical forests (and less than 3% of the world's 220,000 such species) have been examined closely for their possible use as human resources. Destroying these forests and the species they contain for short-term economic gain is like throwing away a wrapped present or burning down an ancient library before you read the books (Spotlight, above).

More than 200 million indigenous people (4% of the world's population), representing 5,000 of the world's 6,000 cultures, live in environments ranging

from polar ice to tropical forests and rain forests (Figure 10-11). They get most of their food by hunting and gathering (Figure 2-5), trapping, herding of livestock, and sustainable slash-and-burn and shifting cultivation (Figure 2-6) (Spotlight, p. 270).

Many people believe that destruction of these reservoirs of biological and cultural diversity must be stopped because it is *wrong*. Otherwise, within a few decades we will see the premature extinction of numerous tribal cultures and millions of wild species with as much right to exist, or struggle to exist, as we do. In addition, the Environmental Policy Institute estimates that unless the destruction of tropical forests stops, the resulting loss of water and topsoil, along with flooding, will cause as many as a billion people to starve to death during the next 30 years.

## 10-3 Causes of Tropical Deforestation and the Fuelwood Crisis in LDCs

**RESOURCE EXTRACTION FOR SURVIVAL AND FOR MDCs** The underlying causes of the current massive destruction and degradation of tropical forests are:

- *Population growth and poverty.* These two factors combine to drive subsistence farmers and the landless poor to tropical forests to grow enough food to survive. To defuse social tensions from unfair land distribution or from the pressures of rapid population growth in existing agricultural areas, governments of some countries—such as Brazil, Indonesia, and Mexico—have encouraged

---

**SPOTLIGHT**

## Cultural Extinction

Tribal peoples living in tropical forests have used them sustainably for centuries. They have a deep regard for the natural world, as summarized by Ajaan Pongsak of the Dhammanaat Foundation reforestation project in Thailand:

*Our parents gave us life but the forest sustains it. From it we get the four necessities of life—food, clothing, shelter, and medicine. It balances the air we breathe, cleanses the water we drink, produces the soil we grow our crops in. It nourishes the spirit in the same way as it nourishes the body. We should be endlessly grateful to it—every grove, every tree, every leaf.*

Indigenous peoples are the primary guardians and sustainable users of vast, mostly undisturbed habitats that provide much of the planet's ecosystem services important to all life. They are stewards of 99% of Earth's genetic resources, and their homelands are sanctuaries for more threatened and endangered species than all the world's official wildlife reserves.

These peoples in tropical forests and other biomes, however, are seeing their lands bulldozed, cut, burned, mined, and flooded. They are being driven from their homelands by commercial resource extractors and landless peasants and forced to adopt new ways while reeling from shock and hunger. Often they are killed by foreign diseases to which they have no immunity. Those who resist are

often killed by ranchers, miners, and settlers.

About 500 years ago some 6 million tribal people lived in the Amazon Basin. Today there are only about 200,000, and many of them are threatened. In remote Amazon Basin rain forests of Brazil and Venezuela, the Yanomami—a Stone Age tribe now reduced to fewer than 20,000 people (9,000 in Brazil)—have been struggling for 20 years to preserve their land and way of life (Figure 10-11). Since 1985, 45,000–100,000 gold miners have invaded Yanomami territory in Brazil, bringing malaria and other diseases that killed some of the tribe's people. The miners carved more than 100 airstrips out of the rain forests, cleared and gouged out large tracts of land, turned streams into sewers, and poisoned nearby soil, water, and food webs with toxic mercury used to extract gold from gold ore.

In 1991 the governments of Brazil and Venezuela recognized an area of Amazon Basin forest about the size of South Dakota as the permanent homeland of the beleaguered Yanomami people. The governments, however, have not adequately protected the Yanomami land from thousands of new gold miners and other illegal intruders.

Besides being wrong—even genocidal—eliminating indigenous peoples represents a tragic loss of Earth wisdom and cultural diversity. These people know more about how to live sustainably in tropical forests (and in other bi-

omes) and what plants can be used as foods and medicines than anyone. Natives of the Amazon Basin rain forest, for example, use more than 1,300 plant species for curing various illnesses, and traditional healers in southeast Asia rely on as many as 6,500 medicinal plants. As we continue to deplete Earth's biodiversity, their knowledge of how to live sustainably will become the planet's most important resource.

Environmentalists and others, led by organizations such as Survival International and Cultural Survival, call upon governments to protect and honor the rights and Earth wisdom of remaining indigenous peoples by:

- Establishing a UN Declaration on the Rights of Indigenous Peoples enforceable by international law

- Mapping their homelands and granting them full ownership of their land, as well as mineral rights

- Protecting their lands from intrusion and illegal resource extraction

- Giving them legal control over and just compensation for marketable drugs and other products derived from their lands

- Creating an international organization to fight for their legal rights

We need to heed the words of Argentina's Guarani holyman Pae Antonio, "When the Indians vanish, the rest will follow."

---

Q: How much of the world's irrigated cropland has reduced yields because of soil salinization?

colonization of tropical forests by the poor by giving them title to land they clear (Figure 10-12).

■ *Massive foreign debt and policies of governments and international development and lending agencies.* LDCs are encouraged to borrow huge sums of money from MDCs to finance economic growth. To pay the interest on their debt, these countries often sell off their forests, minerals, oil, and other resources at low prices dictated by the international marketplace, mostly to support the affluent lifestyles of people in MDCs and the wealthy few in their own countries.

The process of destroying a tropical forest begins with a road (Figures 10-13 and 10-14). Once the forest becomes accessible it is doomed by:

■ *Unsustainable small-scale farming.* Colonists follow logging roads into the forest to plant crops on small cleared plots, build homes, and try to survive. With little experience many cut and burn too much forest to grow crops without allowing depleted soils to recover (Figure 2-6), ultimately destroying large tracts of forest.

Figure 10-13 Computer-enhanced satellite image of a 1,300-square-kilometer (500-square-mile) area of tropical rain forest north of Manaus in Brazil's Amazon Basin in 1991. Remaining old-growth forest is dark red, regenerating forest orange or light red, and recently deforested areas blue-green or white.

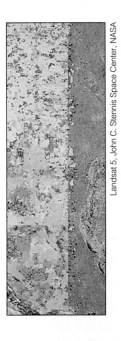

**Figure 10-12** Results of different forest policies in two bordering countries shown by this 1986 computer-enhanced satellite view of a portion of the border between Mexico (left) and Guatemala (right). Undisturbed forests are shown in red, lakes and rivers in dark blue, and cleared areas in white, light blue, and yellow. In the 1970s the Mexican government began giving settlers forestland they cleared and planted with corn. When the soil gave out the settlers turned to grazing cattle, resulting in almost complete loss of forest in this part of Mexico. Most forests in Guatemala, which doesn't have a settlement program, are still intact except for areas illegally cleared by Mexican farmers and cattle grazers (yellow areas).

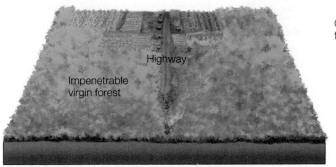

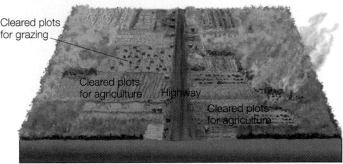

**Figure 10-14** Building roads into inaccessible tropical (and other) forests paves the way to destruction and degradation. Usually these roads are financed by international lending agencies controlled by MDCs. Much of the timber and other resources extracted from the forests are then exported to MDCs, often to help pay interest on debts to MDCs.

## Burgers, Ghost Ranching, and Tropical Forests

As satellite photos have shown, between 1965 and 1983 Central America lost two-thirds of its tropical forestland (Figure 10-3), much of it cleared to raise beef for export to the United States, Canada, and western Europe.

This imported beef is mixed with more fatty domestic cattle trimmings and sold mostly to fast-food chains and food-processing companies for use in hamburgers (which cuts the price of a quarter-pound burger by about 1¢), hot dogs, luncheon meats, chilies, stews, frozen dinners, and pet food. Since 1979 Central American beef exports to the United States have dropped by about two-thirds but in 1992 still amounted to about 44,000 metric tons (48,000 tons). The true cost of a quarter-pound hamburger made from cattle grazing on land that was once tropical forest is the destruction of 5 square meters (54 square feet) of the forest, an area

roughly the size of a small kitchen. Although beef eaters in MDCs are responsible for some of this deforestation, Latin Americans consume about 70% of the beef they produce.

Much of the land being cleared of trees is unsuited for grazing. After only 5–10 years, tropical pastures can no longer support cattle. When torrential rains and overgrazing turn the soils into eroded wastelands, ranchers move to another area and repeat the process. This destructive *shifting ranching* is often encouraged by government tax subsidies.

Brazil has over 135 million cattle—the world's fourth largest herd—but little Brazilian beef can be exported because of foot-and-mouth disease. The main reason for the explosive growth of cattle ranching in the Amazon Basin (Figure 10-15) is land speculation. Under Brazilian law anyone who clears an area of forest can claim the land. Grazing cattle (often on land cleared and abandoned by poor

farmers) allows ranchers (supported by government subsidies averaging $5.6 million per ranch) to claim large tracts of land and the mineral rights below it, and then sell both land and minerals for quick profits—something called *ghost ranching*. At least half of the 600 large ranches in the Brazilian Amazon Basin have never sent a cow to market, and about 30% are now abandoned. All told, cattle ranching has been responsible for about 60% of the deforestation in this basin. Despite lavish subsidies, the Amazon Basin has provided less than 0.1% of Brazil's income since 1975.

Environmental and consumer groups (especially the Rainforest Action Network in San Francisco) have organized boycotts of hamburger chains buying beef imported from Central America and other tropical countries. Many large chains claim they no longer buy beef from tropical countries, but it's difficult to substantiate such claims because, once the U.S. government inspects beef imports, the meat enters the domestic market with no origin labels.

Environmentalists call for a ban on all beef or beef products raised on cleared tropical forestland. This would encourage tropical countries to raise beef on existing rangeland (which could double or triple meat yields with improved management). They also urge governments to stop subsidizing ranchers for clearing tropical forestland.

**Figure 10-15** The hamburger connection. Large areas of tropical forests in Latin America have been converted into rangeland for grazing cattle. This rangeland in Brazil's Amazon Basin was once covered with trees.

R. Azoury/SIPA-Press

- *Cattle ranching.* Cattle ranches are often established on exhausted and abandoned cropland, with the ranchers often receiving government subsidies to make the ranches profitable (Spotlight, above).

- *Commercial logging.* Often LDCs sell timbering rights to foreign companies at prices far below the real worth of the timber to stimulate economic growth, pay interest on foreign debt, or buy wea-

pons. Cleared forests are not replanted and degraded ones are not restored because few, if any, of the costs of environmental degradation are included in the prices charged loggers or owners of tree or cash-crop plantations. Typically loggers take just the best large and medium trees, but topple up to 17 other trees for each one they remove. The falling trees damage many others, with up to 70% of them eventually dying from their injuries.

Q: What percentage of the world's irrigated cropland suffers from waterlogging?

## Japan: Ecovillain or Ecosavior?

Japan (Figure 8-15), with 124 million people squeezed into an area slightly larger than California, has few minerals or fossil fuels and a limited timber supply. Thus it must import vast quantities of raw materials. As Japan has developed into a leading economic power, its impact on the global environment has grown. It has a mixed environmental record.

On the negative side Japan:

- Has logged much of its forests, drained precious wetlands, destroyed offshore reefs, and built nuclear power plants in earthquake zones.

- Imports 60% of all tropical timber, resulting in the deforestation of vast tracts in Asia and displacement of indigenous peoples. Much of this wood is used to make throwaway items such as concrete molds, packing crates, and chopsticks (25 billion pairs per year). Because Asian tropical forests will be stripped of timber within 15 years, Japan is now looking to tropical forests in Brazil and other parts of Latin America.

- Has imported logs clear-cut from old-growth coniferous forests in Washington, Oregon, Alaska, and the Canadian province of Alberta at bargain prices.

- Has bought logging rights to clear-cut 63% of remaining old-growth coniferous forests in

Alberta, Canada, and plans to buy rights to cut the largely untapped forests of Siberia (which has half of the world's coniferous forests, in an area the size of the continental United States).

- Is the world's largest illegal importer of endangered and threatened species and products made from them.

- Uses a provision in the Convention on International Trade of Endangered Species to exempt itself from bans on imports of 10 endangered species.

- Continues to disobey an International Whaling Commission ruling and harvests about 300 minke whales per year for "scientific" purposes.

- Works hard to have the international ban on commercial whaling lifted.

- Used drift nets (Figure 14-16) in the Pacific Ocean until 1991. These nets—called "curtains of death" by environmentalists—are intended to catch mostly tuna and squid, but they also drown hundreds of thousands of dolphins, porpoises, seals, and seabirds, and can deplete stocks of commercially valuable fish. Environmentalists claim that drift nets are still used illegally, sometimes by boats flying other flags but financed by Japanese interests.

- Finances large-scale environmentally harmful projects such

as roads, dams, power plants, and mines in LDCs without requiring environmental impact assessments.

- Is the only MDC without a strong environmental movement.

On the positive side Japan:

- Is a leader in control of industrial and urban air pollution.

- Makes and sells the world's finest and most cost-effective incinerators and air pollution control scrubbers.

- Is the world's most energy-efficient country and has led the world in developing and selling fuel-efficient cars and energy-efficient industrial processes.

- Has one of the world's highest recycling rates, using a sophisticated resource recovery system.

- Slashed its birth rate during the 1960s and now has an annual population growth rate half that of the United States.

- Devotes more than $1 billion of its annual foreign aid budget to environmental projects in LDCs.

- Funds 14% of the UN Environment Programme.

- Assumed a major leadership role at the 1992 Earth Summit in Rio de Janeiro and committed at least $7 billion for environmental assistance to LDCs (compared to $1.2 billion pledged by the United States).

(continued)

---

Since 1950 the consumption of tropical lumber has risen 15-fold, with Japan now accounting for 60% of annual consumption (Case Study, above). Other leading importers of tropical hardwoods are the United States and Great Britain. As tropical timber in Asia is depleted in the 1990s, cutting will shift to Latin America and Africa. The World Bank estimates that by 2000 only 10 of the 33 countries now exporting tropical timber will have any left to ex-

port. Although timber exports to MDCs contribute to tropical forest depletion and degradation, over 80% of the trees cut in LDCs are used at home.

- *Raising of cash crops.* Immense plantations grow crops such as sugarcane, bananas, tea, and coffee, mostly for export to MDCs.

- *Growing of marijuana and cocaine-yielding coca.* Most of these drugs are smuggled into MDCs to supply the illegal drug trade.

- Ratified the international treaty to protect the ozone layer.

- Has supported international efforts to slow global warming.

- Plans to stabilize its carbon dioxide emissions at 1990 levels by 2000, even though it contributes only 5% of global $CO_2$ emissions (compared to 24% by the United States, which has not agreed to reduce its emissions).

- Unveiled a 100-year plan in 1990 to protect and restore Earth's natural functions, dominate global markets for new ecotechnologies, and lead the way in what it calls an era of global citizenry.

- Has launched a $28-million-per-year joint government–industry venture to find ways to remove $CO_2$ from industrial exhaust gases, genetically engineer fast-growing trees that will remove more $CO_2$ from the atmosphere than conventional trees and that can be used to reforest denuded areas, develop salt- and drought-resistant plants to help reverse desertification, formulate substitutes for chlorofluorocarbons, improve energy efficiency of cars and appliances, develop hydrogen-powered cars and super-energy-efficient buildings, improve solar cells and other

forms of renewable energy, and develop low-polluting fuel cells.

If Japan becomes a major force in helping sustain the earth, it can dominate one of the major areas of economic growth and jobs in the 1990s and beyond, make a hefty profit, turn its critics into admirers, and stimulate other MDCs to follow its lead. But critics caution that Japan's "technofix" approach to managing the entire planet for use by humans could backfire because of depletion of biodiversity and our lack of knowledge about the complex workings of nature.

**Figure 10-16** During the early 1980s up to 50,000 miners toiled at this gold mine in the Amazon Basin of Brazil. Once the gold was extracted, they moved on. The hole shown here is now flooded with water. Toxic mercury used here and at other mining sites to separate the gold from sand and gravel has poisoned nearby soil and water.

*Serra Pelada/SIPA-Press*

- *Mining operations.* Much of the extracted minerals, such as iron ore and bauxite (aluminum ore), are exported to MDCs. Widespread gold mining has been particularly damaging because it pollutes streams with toxic mercury (Figure 10-16).

- *Oil drilling and extraction.* Strips and patches of Amazonian forest have been destroyed by roads, pipelines, and shabby temporary boomtowns that

will be abandoned when the oil is gone. Most of this oil goes to MDCs (about half to the United States). Large amounts of oil have oozed into forests and waterways from leaky pipelines.

- *Damming of rivers and flooding of large areas of forest.* Water allowed to flow past the dams is used mostly to produce electricity (hydropower) often used in mining and smelting minerals exported to

Q: What percentage of your body weight consists of water?

Speech bubble: YO! AMIGO!! WE NEED THAT TREE TO PROTECT US FROM THE GREENHOUSE EFFECT!

MDCs. Several large dams in the Amazon Basin have flooded large areas of forest, and the 79 hydroelectric dams planned there over the next 20 years will flood an area the size of the state of Georgia—and displace many indigenous people.

The reasons for this massive deforestation vary in different regions. In Latin America the chief causes are cattle ranching, land speculation, settlement in the wake of road building, and unsustainable shifting agriculture. In Africa and Asia the main causes are unsustainable shifting agriculture, conversion to cash-crop agriculture, and, in dry forests, fuelwood cutting.

Government officials of most tropical countries argue that they must sell cash crops, timber, and minerals to MDCs at any price they can get to finance economic growth and to pay interest on loans from MDCs and international lending agencies. They contend that they are doing the same thing that the United States (see cartoon) and other MDCs did to help finance their economic growth. They resent being lectured by the United States, which has cleared 95% of the old-growth forests in the 48 lower states and is still cutting today. Indeed, much of the remaining old-growth forest in the United States is much more fragmented (Figure 10-17) than old-growth tropical forests in Brazil (Figure 10-13). They also note that much of the timber, beef, and mineral resources removed from tropical forests are exported to MDCs. Moreover, they argue that the MDCs are the biggest culprits in ozone depletion and projected climate change.

**THE FUELWOOD CRISIS IN LDCs** In many areas forests are being depleted for fuelwood faster than they are being replenished (Figure 10-18). Almost 70% of the people in LDCs rely on biomass as their primary fuel for heating and cooking. About 50% of this biomass comes from wood or charcoal, 33% from crop residues, and 17% from dung. Each year the energy

**Figure 10-17** Computer-enhanced satellite image of a 1,300-square-kilometer (500-square-mile) area of Mount Hood National Forest in Oregon in 1991. Old-growth forest patches are dark red, clear-cut old-growth forest regenerating as tree farms lighter red, and recently clear-cut areas blue-green and white. Most of the same area of Amazonian rain forest shown in Figure 10-13 is still relatively undisturbed, while this old-growth forest has been extensively cleared and fragmented into vulnerable patches.

provided by biomass is about equal to that from the oil supplied by OPEC nations.

City dwellers rely more on charcoal than on wood because charcoal's light weight makes it easier to transport from the countryside to the city. When wood is converted into charcoal, however, more than half the original energy content is lost. This means that villagers who move to a city will double their consumption of wood—if they can afford it.

By 1985 about 1.5 billion people—almost one out of every three persons on Earth—in 63 LDCs either could not get enough fuelwood to meet their basic needs or were forced to meet their needs by consuming wood faster than it was being replenished. The UN Food and Agriculture Organization projects a fuelwood crisis by the end of this century for 3 billion people in 77 LDCs.

Besides deforestation and accelerated soil erosion, fuelwood scarcity has other harmful effects. It places an additional burden on the poor, especially women,

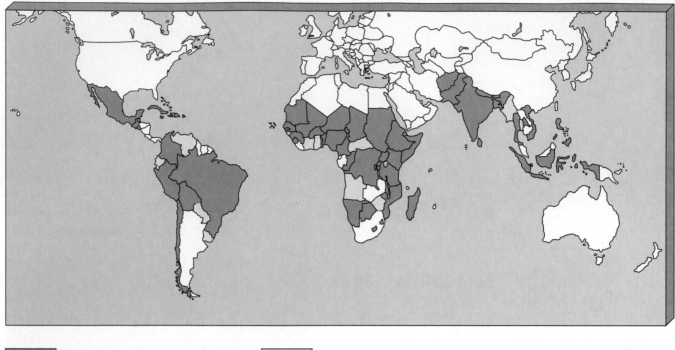

Acute scarcity and depletion in 1985          Deficits and scarcity by 2000

**Figure 10-18** Scarcity of fuelwood, 1985 and 2000 (projected). (Data from UN Food and Agriculture Organization)

Pierre A. Pittet/UN Food and Agriculture Organization

**Figure 10-19** Making fuel briquettes from cow dung in India. As fuelwood becomes scarce, more people collect and burn dung, depriving the soil of an important source of plant nutrients.

who must often walk long distances to gather fuel. Buying fuelwood or charcoal can take 40% of a poor family's meager income. And poor families who can't get enough fuelwood often burn dried animal dung and crop residues for cooking and heating (Figure 10-19). As a result, these natural fertilizers never reach the soil, cropland productivity is reduced, the land is degraded even more, and hunger and malnutrition increase.

<table>
<tr><td>10-4</td><td>**Solutions: Reducing Tropical Deforestation and Fuelwood Shortages**</td></tr>
</table>

**REDUCING THE DESTRUCTION AND DEGRADATION OF TROPICAL FORESTS** Environmentalists have suggested a number of ways to reduce tropical deforestation:

*Prevention*

- *Use remote-sensing satellites to find out how much of the world is covered with forest and how much has been deforested.* This could be done for about $5 million per year—equal to what the world spends for military purposes *every three minutes.*

- *Use economic indicators that include the environmental services provided by forests in their estimated value.* By failing to do this, conventional GNP indicators and cost-benefit analyses usually lead to overuse and depletion of forestlands for unsustainable short-term economic gain.

- *Establish a mandatory international labeling system to identify tropical (and other) timber grown and harvested sustainably.* So far only 0.1% of the world's tropical forests are managed sustainably.

- *Decrease the demand for tropical wood products in major consuming countries.* Do this by eliminating

Q: How much of Earth's enormous supply of water is available to us as usable fresh water?

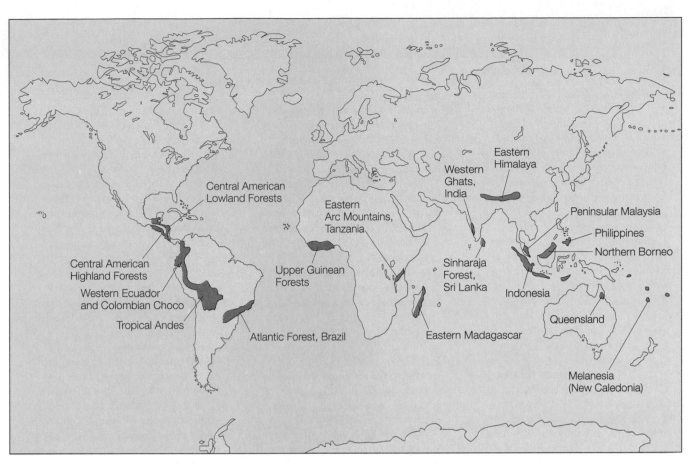

**Figure 10-20** Tropical forest "hot spots." These 17 areas, believed to be unusually rich storehouses of biodiversity, are being deforested rapidly. (Data from Norman Myers and Conservation International)

wasteful one-time uses of tropical woods (such as throwaway chopsticks and molds for concrete), substituting reusable products, and banning imports of tropical timber (as Germany has done since 1989). However, a drop in demand can reduce the market value of wood as well as the forest, leading governments to convert forests to higher-value and even more destructive purposes, such as cattle ranching or raising of cash crops for export.

- *Reform tropical timber-cutting regulations and practices.* This would involve charging more for timber-cutting concessions, making the contracts longer (70 years) to encourage conservation and reforestation, and requiring companies to post adequate bonds for reforestation and restoration.

- *Fully fund the Rapid Assessment Program (RAP).* This program sends tropical biologists to assess the biodiversity of "hot spots," forests and other habitats that are both rich in unique species and in imminent danger, with the goal of channeling funds and efforts toward immediate protection of these valuable ecosystems (Figure 10-20).

- *Offer tropical countries financial incentives to adopt sustainable environmental practices.* This would entail providing aid and debt relief for tropical countries that ban commercial logging, cattle ranching, and other destructive uses of virgin tropical forests, and that emphasize economically and ecologically sustainable harvesting of rubber, nuts, fruits, and other renewable forest resources (Spotlight, p. 267).

- *Use debt-for-nature swaps and conservation easements to encourage countries to protect areas of tropical forests or other valuable natural systems.* In a debt-for-nature swap, participating tropical countries act as custodians for protected forest reserves in return for foreign aid or debt relief (Case Study, p. 278). With conservation easements a country, private organization, or group of countries compensates individual countries for protecting selected forest areas. Currently less than 5% of the world's tropical forests are part of parks and preserves, many of which are protected only on paper.

- *Help settlers learn how to practice small-scale sustainable agriculture.*

**CASE STUDY**

In 1984 biologist Thomas Lovejoy suggested that debtor nations willing to protect part of their natural resources should be rewarded. In the **debt-for-nature swaps** Lovejoy proposed that a certain amount of foreign debt be canceled in exchange for spending a certain sum on better natural resource management. Typically a conservation organization buys a certain amount of a country's debt from a bank at a discount rate and negotiates the swap. A government or private agency must then agree to enact and supervise the conservation program.

In 1987 Conservation International, a private U.S. banking consortium, purchased $650,000 of Bolivia's $5.7-billion national debt from a Citibank affiliate in Bolivia for $100,000. In exchange for not having to pay back this part of its debt, the Bolivian government agreed to expand and protect 1.5 million hectares (3.7 million acres) of tropical forest around its existing Beni Biosphere Reserve in the Amazon Basin—containing some of the world's largest reserves of mahogany and cedar—from harmful forms of development. The government was to establish maximum legal protection for the reserve and create a $250,000 fund, with the interest to be used to manage the reserve.

The plan is supposed to be a model of how conservation of forest and wildlife resources can be compatible with sustainable economic development (Figure 10-21). Central to the plan is a virgin tropical forest to be set aside as a biological reserve and surrounded by a protective buffer of savanna used for sustainable grazing of livestock. Controlled commercial logging—as well as hunting and fishing by local natives—would be permitted in some parts of the forest but not in the mountain area above the tract, to protect the area's watershed and to prevent erosion.

As of 1993, six years after the agreement was signed, however, the Bolivian government still had not provided legal protection for the reserve. It also waited until April 1989 to contribute only $100,000 to the reserve management fund. Meanwhile, with government approval, timber companies have cut thousands of mahogany trees in the area, with most of this lumber exported to the United States. Also, the area's 5,000 native inhabitants were not consulted about the swap plan, even though they are involved in a land-ownership dispute with logging companies.

One lesson learned from this first debt-for-nature swap is that legislative and budget requirements must be met before the swap is executed. Another is that such swaps need to be carefully monitored by environmental organizations to be sure that paper proposals for sustainable development are not disguises for eventually unsustainable development.

Debt-for-nature swaps are a fine idea if they lead to real protection or restoration of some of Earth's remaining natural areas. However, simply drawing park boundaries on a map does little to protect endangered ecosystems. Parks set aside in the four countries—Ecuador, Costa Rica, Madagascar, and the Philippines—that accounted for 95% of the total funds generated so far for debt-for-nature swaps are being invaded illegally by miners, loggers, and the landless poor.

By 1992, 21 debt-for-nature swaps had eliminated more than $100 million of debt for 11 countries

- *Stop funding dams, tree and crop plantations, ranches, roads, and destructive types of tourism on any land now covered by old-growth tropical forests.*

- *Concentrate farming, tree and crop plantations, and ranching activities on cleared tropical forest areas in various stages of secondary ecological succession (Figure 6-14).*

- *Reforest 5 million square kilometers (about the size of the continental United States) of deforested land in tropical countries with fast-growing trees adapted to local conditions.*

- *Set aside extractive reserves for nonindigenous rural people and large protected areas for indigenous tribal peoples.*

- *Include indigenous tribal peoples, women, and private local conservation organizations in the creation and execution of tropical forestry plans.*

- *Give indigenous people title to tropical forestlands (and all minerals and other resources they contain) that they and their ancestors have lived on for centuries. The key stipulations here would be that these lands cannot be developed in unsustainable ways and cannot be sold. Countries such as Colombia and Ecuador have done this for native peoples, but the governments have retained the mineral rights—leaving the land and native cultures vulnerable to future exploitation.*

- *"Green" the multilateral development banks. This would mean preventing banks and international*

Q: How much of the world's cropland is irrigated?

at a cost of $17 million and generated over $65 million for conservation efforts in these countries. However, this amounts to only 0.008% of the $800-billion foreign debt of tropical countries. The impact of such transactions could be increased if such swaps were greatly expanded to include bilateral debt (between two nations) and multilateral debt (between one nation and the World Bank or a regional bank like the Inter-American Development Bank).

This method is a useful tool, but it cannot solve the debt problem or the environmental problems of LDCs. Critics also point out that such swaps legitimize the LDCs' $1.4-trillion debt at a time when environmentalists and debtor governments are urging that much of this debt be forgiven in return for agreements to reduce poverty, redistribute land, control population growth, and protect biodiversity and indigenous peoples in priority areas. Many of the debt swaps also support international (mostly corporate) control over debtor countries' development, while giving banks in MDCs a way to make good on part of essentially bad loans.

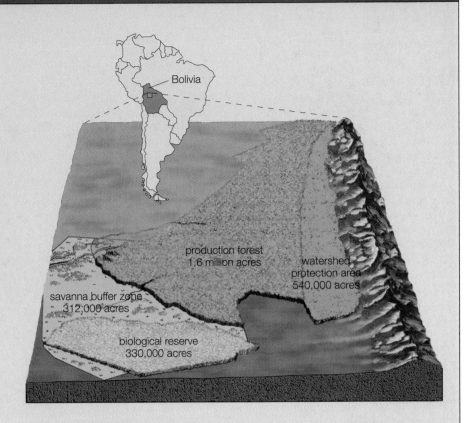

**Figure 10-21** Blending economic development and conservation in a 1.5-million-hectare (3.7-million-acre) tract in Bolivia. A U.S. conservation organization arranged a debt-for-nature swap to help protect this land from destructive development.

lending agencies (controlled by MDCs) from lending money for environmentally destructive projects—especially road building (Figure 10-14)—involving tropical forests by requiring a thorough environmental impact evaluation based on internationally accepted standards, and halting funding when abuse occurs.

- *Exert political and consumer pressure (boycotts) on MDC-based companies involved in destructive development projects in tropical forests.*

- *Pressure government officials to vote down parts of the international General Agreement on Tariffs and Trade (GATT) that weaken environmental protection in the name of free trade.* For example, under these provisions if a country wants to stop exporting of its timber or other resources, require a labeling system to certify sustainably produced timber, or ban the import of beef produced on cleared tropical forests, it can be accused of violating the principles of free trade.

- *Redistribute land more fairly inside and outside tropical forests.* In Latin America, for example, just 7% of all landowners control 73% of the continent's potential cropland. Currently many governments will grant title to forestland to those who clear it for cattle grazing, plantation agriculture, mining, or other forms of unsustainable development on nutrient-poor tropical soils. Traditional land uses, such as sustainable shifting cultivation (Figure 2-6) and collecting nontimber

Costa Rica (Figure 9-3), smaller in area than West Virginia, has a population of 3.2 million. Growing at 2.4% per year, its population is projected to reach 5.6 million by 2025.

Costa Rica is one of the leading LDCs in social indicators such as infant and maternal mortality, literacy, and life expectancy (two years longer than in the United States). Because the country abolished its army in 1949, it has been able to devote more funds and resources to health, education, and family planning. However, paying interest on its $2-billion foreign debt has reduced the amount of money available to fund social programs and conservation efforts. Currently half of the children in Costa Rica are malnourished.

Costa Rica was once almost completely covered with tropical forests. Between 1963 and 1983, however, politically powerful ranching families cleared much of the country's forests to graze cattle, with most of the beef exported to the United States and western Europe (Spotlight, p. 272). By 1983 only 17% of the country's original tropical forest remained, and soil erosion was rampant.

Despite widespread degradation tiny Costa Rica, like Madagascar (Case Study, p. 265), is a "superpower" of biodiversity, with an estimated 500,000 species of plants and animals. A single park in Costa Rica is home for more bird species than in all of North America.

Another bright note is that in the mid-1970s Costa Rica established a system of national parks and reserves that now protects 12% of its

land (6% of it in indigenous reserves), compared to only 1.8% protected in the lower 48 states of the United States. One reason for this was the establishment in 1963 of the Organization of Tropical Studies (OTS), a consortium of 44 U.S. and Costa Rican universities, with the goal of promoting research and education in tropical ecology. The resulting infusion of several thousand scientists has helped its leaders and people appreciate its great biodiversity. It also led to the establishment of INBio in 1989 to catalog the country's biodiversity (Spotlight, p. 269). The country plans to combine conservation and sustainable economic development, and to protect 25% of its land by the end of this century.

This strategy has paid off. By 1990 revenue from ecotourism was the country's second largest source of outside income, ahead of banana exports and closing fast on coffee exports.

In a rugged mountainous region with a tropical rain forest lies a centerpiece of Costa Rica's efforts—the Guanacaste National Park, which has been designated an international biosphere reserve. In the park's lowlands a small tropical seasonal forest is being restored and relinked to the rain forest on adjacent mountain slopes.

Daniel Janzen, professor of biology at the University of Pennsylvania, has helped galvanize international support and raised more than $10 million for this restoration project—the world's largest. Janzen is a leader in the growing field of rehabilitation and restoration of degraded ecosystems. He believes it will take about 20 years to convert unused grassland into a closed-

canopy forest; in perhaps 200 years it will look like the seasonal tropical forest that was once there; perhaps in 1,000 years it may come close to functioning like the earlier forest.

Janzen's vision is to make the nearly 40,000 people who live near the park an essential part of the restoration of 740 square kilometers (285 square miles) of degraded forest—a concept he calls *biocultural restoration*. By actively participating in the project, local residents will reap enormous educational, economic, and environmental benefits. Local farmers have been hired to plant large areas with tree seeds and with seedlings started in Janzen's lab.

Students in grade schools, high schools, and universities study the ecology of the park in the classroom and go on annual field trips to the park itself. There are educational programs for civic groups and tourists from Costa Rica and elsewhere. These visitors and activities will stimulate the local economy.

The project will also serve as a training ground in tropical forest restoration for scientists from all over the world. And research scientists working on the project will give guest lectures in classrooms and lead some of the field trips.

Janzen recognizes that in 20–40 years today's children will be running the park and the local political system. If they understand the importance of their local environment, they are more likely to protect and sustain its biological resources. He understands that education, awareness, and involvement—not guards and fences—are the best ways to protect ecosystems from unsustainable use.

forest products (Spotlight, p. 269), however, rarely qualify as "improvement." As a result, indigenous peoples and other forest dwellers often face eviction from lands long used sustainably so others can use them unsustainably.

- *Reduce poverty and the flow of the landless poor to tropical forests by slowing population growth.*

### Restoration

- *Rehabilitate degraded tropical forests and watersheds (Case Study, above).*

Q: What activity constitutes the largest global use of water withdrawn from surface or groundwater sources?

- *Enlist local peoples and institutions in programs to restore forests.*

## SOLUTIONS: REDUCING THE FUELWOOD CRISIS

LDCs can reduce the severity of the fuelwood crisis by planting more fast-growing fuelwood trees such as leucaenas and acacias, burning wood more efficiently, and switching to other fuels. Experience has shown that planting projects are most successful when local people, especially women, are involved in their planning and implementation. Programs work best when village farmers own the land or are given ownership of any trees they grow on village land. This gives them a strong incentive to plant and protect trees for their own use and for sale.

The governments of China, Nepal, Senegal, and South Korea have established successful tree-planting programs at the village level in selected areas. Typically these are joint ventures by the government and locally elected village forestry associations. Government foresters supply villagers with seeds or seedlings of fast-growing fuelwood trees and shrubs, and advise them on the planting and care of the trees; villagers do the planting. They are encouraged to plant these species in fields along with crops (agroforestry), on unused patches of land around homes and farmland, and along roads and waterways.

Fast-growing tree species used to establish fuelwood plantations, however, must be selected carefully to prevent harm to local ecosystems. For example, eucalyptus trees are being used to reforest areas threatened by desertification and to establish fuelwood plantations in some parts of the world. Because these species grow fast even in poor soils, this might seem like a good idea. But environmentalists see it as an ecological disaster. In their native Australia these trees thrive in areas with good rainfall. When planted in arid areas, however, the trees suck up so much of the scarce soil water that most other plants can't grow. Then farmers don't have fodder to feed their livestock and groundwater is not replenished. The eucalyptus trees also deplete the soil of nutrients and produce toxic compounds that accumulate in the soil because of low rainfall. In Karnata, India, villagers became so enraged over a government-sponsored project to plant these trees that they uprooted the saplings.

Another promising method is to encourage villagers to use the sun-dried roots of various common gourds and squashes as cooking fuel. These rootfuel plants, which regenerate themselves each year, produce large quantities of burnable biomass per unit of area on dry deforested lands. They also help reduce soil erosion and produce an edible seed that is high in protein.

New, more efficient and less polluting stoves can make use of locally available materials and provide both heat and light like the open fires they replace, and at the same time reduce indoor air pollution—a major health threat. Villagers in Burkina Faso in West Africa, for example, have been shown how to make a stove from mud and dung in half a day that cuts wood use by 30–70%. During the 1980s over 64 million efficient cookstoves were distributed in rural areas in LDCs, especially in Africa and India.

Despite encouraging success in some countries, most LDCs suffering from fuelwood shortages have inadequate forestry policies and budgets, and lack trained foresters. Such countries are cutting trees for fuelwood and forest products 10–20 times faster than new trees are being planted.

## 10-5 Deforestation in the United States and Canada

### ANCIENT FORESTS: A DISAPPEARING HERITAGE

More of the United States is forested today than in 1900, but most of this is second-growth forest outside of national parks and other reserves. About 90–95% of the untouched, temperate-zone old-growth forests that once covered much of what is now the lower 48 states have been cleared away (Figure 10-22), with most of what is left in fragmented sections on U.S. public lands in Washington, Oregon (Figure 10-17) and northern California. The huge conifers (Figures 2-7 and 4-9) that dominate much of this region often live for 500 years and can survive for as long as 3,500 years—17 times longer than the United States has been in existence.

The remnants of these ancient forests are rapidly being destroyed and fragmented for short-term economic gain—much faster, in fact, than the rain forests of Brazil (Figure 10-13). Each year enough old-growth trees are taken from the Pacific Northwest to fill a convoy of logging trucks that would almost encircle the planet. At current logging rates—the equivalent of about 129 football fields per day—all unprotected ancient forests in western Washington and Oregon will be gone by the year 2023.

### ECOLOGY OF OLD-GROWTH FORESTS IN THE NORTHWEST

In the Pacific Northwest it typically takes 350 years for an old-growth forest to reach its prime state of growth and diversity. These forests:

- Accumulate biomass more efficiently than any other ecosystem on Earth.
- Have the world's largest accumulation of dead standing trees (snags) and fallen dead trees

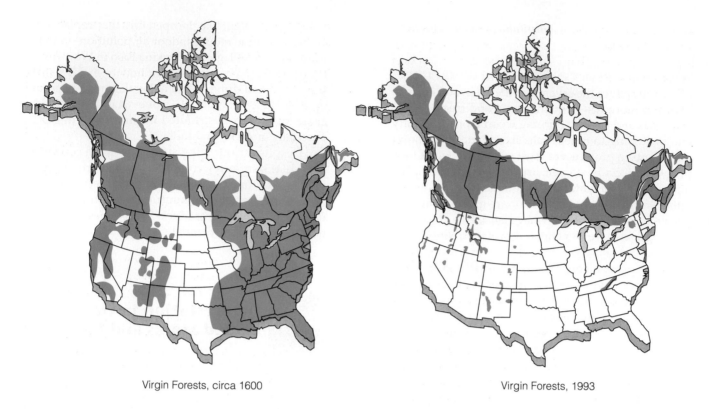

Virgin Forests, circa 1600

Virgin Forests, 1993

**Figure 10-22** Vanishing old-growth forests in the United States and Canada. Since 1600, 90–95% of the virgin forests that once covered much of the lower 48 states have been cleared away. Most of the remaining old-growth forests in the lower 48 states and Alaska are on public lands. In the Pacific Northwest about 80% of this forestland in 12 national forests is slated for logging. (Data from the Wilderness Society, the U.S. Forest Service, and *Atlas Historique du Canada*, Vol. 1, p. 198)

(boles), which decompose slowly over 200–400 years and recycle nutrients in the forest ecosystem.

- Are unusually rich in wildlife species for their latitude.

- Hold enough moisture to help protect against fires and floods and nourish nearby streams.

We know relatively little about how these complex old-growth forests work, but research has revealed that they survive by a complex network of cooperative or symbiotic relationships between their species (Spotlight, p. 283).

The survival of old-growth forests in the Pacific Northwest is also connected to the survival of salmon stocks in this region—a $1-billion-per-year sport and commercial fishing industry providing jobs for 62,000 people. The loss of salmon stocks in this region has been devastating. Several factors including damming of rivers, pollution, and overfishing are involved in this decline, but a key factor has been excessive logging on public lands throughout the region. Sediment in streams from the logging of old-growth forests and

associated road building smothers spawning beds and disrupts the feeding patterns of young salmon.

**CONTROVERSY OVER OLD-GROWTH DEFORESTATION** To officials of timber companies the giant living trees and rotting dead trees in old-growth forests are valuable resources that should be harvested for timber, profits, and jobs, not locked up to please environmentalists. They also note that the timber industry brings millions of dollars annually into the Pacific Northwest's economy and provides jobs for about 109,000 loggers and millworkers. Timber officials claim that protecting large areas of remaining old-growth forests on public lands will cost as many as 147,200 jobs and hurt the economy of logging and milling towns throughout the Pacific Northwest; by contrast, the Wilderness Society, Forestry Policy Center, and U.S. Fish and Wildlife Service put the job loss at 12,000-34,000.

Protecting old-growth forests on public lands from chain saws and bulldozers is not the main cause of past and projected job losses in the timber industry in this region. Other factors include automation,

Q: How much of the water withdrawn in the United States is used for irrigation?

export of raw logs overseas (depriving U.S. millworkers of jobs while providing jobs for millworkers in Japan, China, and South Korea), and timber imports from Canada.

It is illegal to export unprocessed (raw) logs from federal lands in the West, but timber companies get around this ban by a combination of legal loopholes and lax enforcement that enables them to export logs cut from their own private lands and then cut timber from publicly owned national forests for domestic sale—also an illegal practice. Even when violations are detected, the penalties are minuscule compared with the profits earned from violating the law.

Environmentalists charge the U.S. Forest Service with playing a key role in destroying old-growth forests on public lands. One reason is that Congress allows the Forest Service to use most of the money from timber sales in national forests to supplement its budget, with any financial losses passed on to taxpayers. This gives the Forest Service a powerful incentive to make timber sales on public lands its primary objective. Forest rangers who speak out against timber sales are likely to find themselves transferred or fired; those who build big timber sales programs tend to get promoted. Some dynamics of the U.S. economic system also stimulate timber companies to liquidate old-growth timber on their own lands and then turn to public lands (Case Study, p. 284).

To environmentalists America's remaining ancient forests on public lands are a treasure whose ecological, scientific, aesthetic, and recreational values far exceed the economic value of cutting them down for short-term economic gain. The fate of these forests is a national issue because these forests are owned by all the American people, not just the timber industry or the residents of a region. It is a global issue because these forests are important reservoirs of irreplaceable biodiversity and because U.S. treatment of its remaining old-growth forest sets a precedent for nations we are asking to preserve their old-growth forests, wetlands, and coral reefs.

The endangered spotted owl has become a symbol in the struggle between environmentalists and timber company owners over the fate of unprotected old-growth forests on public lands in the Pacific Northwest (Case Study, p. 285).

## SOLUTIONS: REDUCING OLD-GROWTH FOREST DESTRUCTION To reduce degradation and destruction of old-growth forests on federal lands, environmentalists propose that we:

- *Cut the annual harvesting of timber from federal public lands in half.*

**SPOTLIGHT**

# Survival Through Cooperation

The growth of the conifers in old-growth forests depends on a mutualistic relationship between the tree roots and a class of fungi, known as mycorrhizae, that infect their roots. Unable to carry out photosynthesis, these underground fungi attach themselves to tree roots to get the sugars they need. In return the fungi absorb water, nutrients, and oxygen from the soil and pass them along to the tree.

Antibiotic compounds in the fungi protect the tree from root-rot pathogens, and the sheath of fungus around the roots acts as a barrier to keep out some parasites. The fungi also produce chemicals that speed the growth of new root tips.

This root–fungus mutualistic relationship is dependent, in turn, upon symbiotic relationships with a number of the forest's small mammals, such as flying squirrels, voles, and mice. To reproduce, the fungus forms a fleshy collection of spores and other material—called truffles—which are important food sources for these mammals. The animals detect the truffles by their strong, cheesy smell, dig them up, and eat them. The spores themselves are not digested but are excreted in the animals' feces, thus spreading this important fungus throughout the forest.

Many of these animals need large decaying logs for protection from predators. Spotted owls and other predators also play a key role in the forest's complex ballet of interactions by controlling the populations of the small mammals so they won't dig up too many truffles.

Fragmenting these forests into small patches or clearing and replacing them with tree plantations and second-growth forests disrupts the vital network of symbiotic relationships that help sustain the complex, old-growth forest communities. Without snags and boles, for example, about 29% of the wildlife in old-growth forests would disappear.

These disappearing ancient forests are not renewable on a human time scale, despite the boast of the owner of a logging company that he could "replicate the forest, redo it like a farmer growing a crop and do it better than nature." No amount of crossbreeding, genetic engineering, or boasting can replace a 1,000-year-old Douglas fir that can be cut down with a chain saw in 10 minutes.

About 96% of California's original coastal redwood forests have been cut. The philosophy of such over-exploitation was summed up by Ronald Reagan when he was governor of California: "When you've seen one redwood tree, you've seen them all." Of the 4% of these forests left, about three-quarters are protected in parks (Figure 2-7).

Almost half of the remaining unprotected trees are owned by one company, Pacific Lumber. Until 1986 it was a model logging company: highly profitable, debt-free, with a $60-million surplus in its employee pension fund. To make its redwood forests last indefinitely, it had for decades selectively harvested individual trees no faster than they grew back.

That changed in 1986 when the company was taken over by Maxxam Corporation, headed by corporate raider Charles Hurwitz, in a leveraged buyout arranged by Ivan Boesky (later jailed for illegal financial dealings). In such a buyout investors borrow huge sums of money, usually through the sale of high-risk, or "junk," bonds, to buy a company they think is undervalued in the stock market. After using the company's assets as collateral for the borrowed funds, they obtain the cash needed to pay off the interest on the debt and the junk bonds by selling off the company's undervalued assets.

If the target is chosen correctly, the takeover can result in huge profits for the investors. Timber companies are often attractive takeover targets because their forest assets can be cut and converted quickly into cash that can be invested to take over other companies—a "rape-and-run" strategy.

After raising $900 million to buy up Pacific Lumber's stock, Hurwitz drained the surplus from the pension fund and sold off the company's welding division and office building for $417 million. Then he began liquidating the company's timberlands, estimated to be worth more than $1.4 billion, mainly by increasing the rate of logging by at least 30% and by switching from sustainable selective cutting to unsustainable clear-cutting of the company's old-growth redwoods. At the current rate of cutting, these redwoods will be gone in about 17 years, and the highest-value old-growth stands will be gone before 1995. Many long-time employees are working overtime to bring in larger harvests, but they fear that when the old redwoods are gone, their jobs will be gone, too.

These forests may get a reprieve. In 1991 Hurwitz was having a hard time paying off the junk bonds used to buy Pacific Lumber. He may sell the land to the state of California in return for relief of some of the company's debts—a form of financial blackmail that environmentalists call greenmail. Meanwhile other timber companies that had been sustaining their forests are being forced to liquidate (clear-cut) their timber assets to ward off being taken over. Environmentalists call for changes in tax laws and lending regulations to halt such rapid depletion of natural resources for short-term economic gain.

- *Ban clear-cutting* (and thinly disguised harvest methods that leave a few trees but amount to clear-cutting).

- *Sharply raise the price of timber sold from national forests and other public lands to include the environmental and social costs of harvesting this timber.*

- *Require use of sustainable forestry methods* that maintain the species and structural diversity of old-growth forests, leave snags and boles, and allow natural regeneration.

- *Give logging and milling towns grants and interest-free loans* to spur economic diversification and to help retrain displaced loggers and millworkers.

- *Provide dislocated timber workers and their families with financial assistance* for housing, job retraining, job searching, health insurance, and extended unemployment benefits.

- *Close loopholes in and strictly enforce the ban on exporting unprocessed logs* from the Pacific Northwest, and expand this ban to the entire United States to keep lumber mill jobs in the United States.

- *Tax exports of raw logs heavily (15–20%),* but leave exports of lumber, plywood, and other finished wood products untaxed.

- *Provide tax breaks and interest-free loans for revamping mills to cut smaller second-growth logs instead of large old-growth trees.*

- *Provide funds for extensive reforestation and restoration on denuded lands* to furnish alternative jobs for unemployed loggers and millworkers.

- *Allow individuals, environmental organizations, or other groups to buy conservation easements that prevent harvesting of the timber on designated areas of*

## Endangered Forests and the Spotted Owl

The threatened spotted owl (Figure 10-23) is a territorial bird that lives almost exclusively in forests of 200-year-old Douglas firs in western Oregon and Washington, mostly in 12 national forests. These nocturnal owls hunt flying squirrels, red-backed voles, and mice, and nest only in standing dead trees. Each nesting pair needs 900–1,800 hectares (2,300–4,500 acres) of old-growth forest. The species is vulnerable to extinction because of its low reproductive rates and the low survival rates of juveniles through their first five years. Only 2,000– 3,500 pairs remain.

Because the owl feeds at the top trophic level in old-growth forest food webs, it is an *indicator species*. If the owl's survival is threatened, probably dozens of other species are just as threatened.

In July 1990 the U.S. Fish and Wildlife Service added the spotted owl to the federal list of threatened species. This requires that its habitat be protected from logging or other practices that would decrease its chances of survival. The timber industry is looking for ways to get around the decision. They hope to persuade Congress to revise the Endangered Species Act to allow for economic considerations or to exempt some or most of the spotted owl's protected habitat from this law. They also contend that the owls do not require old-growth forest and can adapt to younger second-growth forests. Timber officials further claim that in 1991 the volume of wood withdrawn from harvest in Pacific Northwest national forests because of owl restrictions drove up lumber prices at least 30%.

A major problem is that the media and many politicians and citizens discuss this and other complex environmental problems on a simplistic we-versus-them basis. This disguises the fact that *the controversy over cutting of ancient forests*

**Figure 10-23** The threatened northern spotted owl lives secretively in old-growth forests of the Pacific Northwest. Environmentalists have used the Endangered Species Act as a tool to help achieve the much wider goal of preserving biodiversity by preventing further destruction of America's endangered old-growth forests.

Pat & Tom Leeson/Photo Researchers, Inc.

*in the Pacific Northwest isn't an owl-versus-jobs issue.* The owl and other threatened species—including the Pacific yew tree (source of a drug used to treat breast cancer) and the marbled murrelet (a robin-size seabird)—in these forests, and threatened salmon species downstream from these forests, are merely symbols of the broader clash between timber company owners who want to clear-cut most remaining old-growth stands in the national forests and environmentalists who want to protect them or at least allow only sustainable harvesting in some areas using selective cutting. The Endangered Species Act is the best tool environmentalists have to help them achieve this broader goal of protecting biodiversity by protecting fast-disappearing old-growth forest habitats. The truth is that both owls and humans are utterly dependent on healthy, diverse ecosystems. Timber jobs are disappearing for the same reasons the owls are: The ancient forests they depend on are almost gone.

Loggers, millworkers, and store owners who live in these communities are caught in the middle—pawns in a high-stakes game of corporate profit. They correctly fear for their jobs, but automation, export of raw logs (fueled by Japan's willingness to pay top dollar for these resources), and cutting of most remaining old-growth trees will also do away with their jobs.

Supporting sustainable use of public forests based on limited selective cutting, replanting and restoring of cleared areas, economic diversification, and tourism are the best ways logging-based communities can remain economically and ecologically healthy. The other part of the solution to this dilemma is to recognize that the owls, loggers, and environmentalists are not the problem. *We are all the problem.* We buy wood that is logged at such a low price that sustainable logging is not economically feasible. The marketplace is not signaling to us the real costs of destroying and degrading our forests because we don't insist that the prices of wood and wood products include their full short- and long-term environmental and social costs. Until we change the market system to include these real costs, we will continue to deplete Earth capital and eliminate potentially sustainable jobs.

---

**A:** 70–80% through evaporation or seepage into the ground before reaching crops

**Figure 10-24** Wangari Maathai, the first Kenyan woman to earn a Ph.D. (in anatomy) and to head a department (veterinary medicine) at the University of Nairobi, organized the internationally acclaimed Green Belt Movement in 1977. The goal of this widely regarded women's self-help community action group is to plant a tree for each of Kenya's 25 million people. She recruited 50,000 women to establish tree nurseries and to help farmers raise tree seedlings. Members of the group get a small fee for each tree that survives. By 1990 more than 10 million trees had been planted. The success of this project has sparked the creation of similar programs in more than a dozen other African countries. She and members of this group are true Earth heroes.

*old-growth forests on public lands.* In such *conservation-for-tax-relief swaps* purchasers would be allowed tax breaks for the funds they put up.

If we don't take steps like these, we won't save either jobs or remaining old-growth forests.

**DESTRUCTION OF OLD-GROWTH FORESTS IN WESTERN CANADA** One of every 10 jobs in Canada is related directly to forestry. Canada has lost 60% of its old-growth forests to logging, and less than 20% of what remains is in protected areas. Each year timber companies clear-cut about 270,000 hectares (667,000 acres) of old-growth forest (some containing trees up to 1,500 years old) in Texas-sized British Columbia for pulp and lumber or as whole logs sold cheaply to Japan and western European countries. Timber companies hold government licenses to clear-cut almost all of what remains—65% of this by a Japanese consortium. In a deal worked out behind closed doors, the province is providing the Japanese timber consortium $475 million in subsidies and charging almost nothing for the wood. The cutting will also displace Lubicon Cree—native people who have lived sustainably in these boreal forests for at least 10,000 years.

In Canada a timber company receives a free 20-year, usually automatically renewable, license to cut trees on government-owned forests but must pay a small tax on each tree cut down. If the Canadian government wants to withdraw part of the land covered by a timber-cutting license, it must pay the company the current value of the standing timber, usually millions of dollars.

Such generous concessions to timber companies explain why so little (5.6%) of British Columbia's old-growth forests is protected as parks and reserves. Environmentalists call for the Canadian government to protect 12% of the remaining old-growth forests in western Canada before most of what is worth saving is gone. One tool in this struggle may be declaring certain areas off limits to logging to protect the endangered marbled murrelet, a rare and secretive bird that nests in the treetops of some forest areas in British Columbia.

## 10-6 Solutions: Individual Action

**CHANGE BEGINS FROM THE BOTTOM UP** People throughout the world are working to protect forests. For example, Penan tribes people in Sarawak, Malaysia, have joined forces with environmentalists to halt destructive logging, which has reduced their population from 10,000 to less than 500. In Brazil 500 conservation organizations have formed a coalition to preserve the country's remaining tropical forests. In the United States, members of Earth First! have perched in the tops of giant Douglas firs and lain in front of logging trucks and bulldozers to prevent the felling of trees in national forests.

In Kenya, Wangari Maathai started the Green Belt Movement, a national self-help community action effort by 50,000 women and half a million schoolchildren to plant trees for firewood and to help hold the soil in place (Figure 10-24). This inspiring leader has said:

> *I don't really know why I care so much. I just have something inside me that tells me that there is a problem and I have got to do something about it. And I'm sure it's the same voice that is speaking to everyone on this planet, at least everybody who seems to be concerned about the fate of the world, the fate of this planet.*

For her heroic efforts to sustain the earth and fight for human rights, the Kenyan government closed down her Green Belt Movement offices (she moved the headquarters into her home) and jailed her twice. In 1992 she was severely beaten by police while leading a hunger strike pressing for the release of political prisoners.

Q: What percentage of the world's population live in areas that have prolonged droughts?

**INDIVIDUALS MATTER**

## The Chipko Movement

In the late fifteenth century Jambeshwar, the son of a village leader in northern India, developed 29 principles for living and founded a Hindu sect, called the Bishnois, based on a religious duty to protect trees and wild animals. In 1730, when the Maharajah of Jodhpur in northern India ordered that the few remaining trees in the area be cut down, the Bishnois forbade it. Women rushed in and hugged the trees to protect them, but the Maharajah's minister ordered the work to proceed anyway. According to legend 363 Bishnois women died on that day.

In 1973 some women in the Himalayan village of Gopeshwar in northern India started the modern Chipko (an Indian word for "hug" or "cling to") movement to protect the remaining trees in a nearby forest from being cut down to make tennis rackets for export. It began when Chandi Prasad Bhatt, a village leader, urged villagers to run into the forest ahead of loggers and "hold fast," or "chipko," to protect the trees (Figure 10-25), thus reviving the tradition started several hundred years earlier by the Bishnois.

When the loggers came, local women, children, and men rushed into the forests, flung their arms around trees, and dared the loggers to let the axes fall on their backs. They were successful, and their action inspired women in other Himalayan villages to protect their forests. As a result, the commercial cutting of timber in the hills of the Indian state of Uttar Pradesh has been banned.

Since 1973 the Chipko movement, whose slogan is quoted at the beginning of this chapter, has widened its efforts. Now the women—who still guard trees from loggers—also plant trees, prepare village forestry plans, and build walls to stop soil erosion.

The spreading actions of such Earth citizens should inspire us to help protect the earth. Sustaining the earth will come mostly from the bottom up by the actions of ordinary people, not from the top down.

**Figure 10-25** A member of the Chipko movement protecting a tree in northern India from being cut down for export. This is another example of a successful grass-roots group dedicated to sustaining the earth. Women are the driving force in this group.

In a like-spirited grass-roots movement, for two decades women and children in parts of India have gone into nearby forests, joined hands, and encircled trees to prevent commercial loggers from cutting them down (Individuals Matter, above).

*Forests precede civilizations, deserts follow them.*

FRANÇOIS-AUGUSTE-RENÉ DE CHATEAUBRIAND

## Tropical Forests and Their Species: Going, Going . . . ?

*Norman Myers*

**GUEST ESSAY** *Norman Myers is an international consultant in environment and development with emphasis on conservation of wildlife species and tropical forests. He has served as a consultant for many development agencies and research organizations, including the U.S. National Academy of Sciences, the World Bank, the Organization for Economic Cooperation and Development, various UN agencies, and the World Resources Institute. Among his recent publications (see Further Readings) are* The Sinking Ark *(1979),* Conversion of Tropical Moist Forests *(1980), A* Wealth of Wild Species *(1983),* The Primary Source *(1984),* The Gaia Atlas of Planet Management *(1992), and* The Gaia Atlas of Future Worlds *(1990).*

Tropical forests still cover an area roughly equivalent to the "lower 48" United States. Climatic and biological data suggest they could once have covered an area at least twice as large. So we have already lost half of them, mostly in the recent past.

Worse, remote-sensing surveys show that we are now destroying the forests at a rate of at least 1.25% per year, and we are grossly degrading them at a rate of at least another 1.25% per year—and both rates are accelerating rapidly. Unless we act now to halt this loss, within another few decades at most there could be little left except perhaps a block in central Africa and another in the western Amazon Basin. Even those remnants may not survive the combined pressures of population growth and land hunger beyond the middle of the next century.

This means that we are imposing one of the most broad-scale and impoverishing impacts that the biosphere has ever suffered in its 3.8 billion years of existence. Tropical forests represent the greatest celebration of nature to appear on the planet since the first flickerings of life. They are exceptionally complex ecologically, and they are remarkably rich biotically. Although they now cover only about 6% of Earth's land surface, they still are home for half, and perhaps three-quarters or more, of all species of plant and animal life. Thus elimination of these forests is by far the leading factor in the mass extinction of species that appears likely over the next few decades.

Already we are losing several species every day because of clearing and degradation of tropical forests. The time will surely come, and come soon, when we will be losing many thousands every year. The implications are profound, whether they be scientific, aesthetic, ethical—or simply economic. In medicine alone we benefit from myriad drugs and pharmaceuticals derived from tropical forest plants. The commercial value of these products worldwide can be reckoned at $40 billion each year.

By way of example, the rosy periwinkle [Figure 10-10] from Madagascar's tropical forests has produced two potent drugs used to treat Hodgkin's disease, leukemia, and other blood cancers. Madagascar has—or used to have—an estimated 10,000 plant species, 8,000 of which could be found nowhere else; but Madagascar has lost 93% of its virgin tropical forest [Figure 10-5]. The U.S. National Cancer Institute estimates that many plants in tropical forests might have potential in fighting various

## Critical Thinking

1. What difference could the loss of essentially all the remaining virgin tropical forests and old-growth forests in North America have on your life and on the lives of your descendants?

2. How might eating a hamburger from a fast-food chain indirectly be contributing to the destruction of virgin tropical forests? What, if anything, do you believe should be done about this?

3. Why do you agree or disagree with each of the proposals listed in Section 10-4 concerning protection of the world's tropical forests? Explain.

4. In the name of progress, the policies of various governments are virtually eliminating the cultures of remaining hunter-gatherers and other indigenous peoples by taking over their lands for growing

crops, cutting timber, grazing cattle, mining, building hydroelectric dams and reservoirs, and creating other forms of economic development. Some believe that these people should be given title to the land and minerals they and their ancestors have lived on for centuries, a decisive voice in formulating policies about resource management in their areas, and the right to be left alone by modern civilization. We have created protected reserves for endangered wild species, so why not create reserves for these endangered human cultures? What do you think? Explain.

5. Should all cutting on remaining old-growth forests in U.S. national forestlands be banned? Explain.

6. Why do you agree or disagree with each of the proposals listed in Section 10-5 for protecting old-growth forests on public lands in North America? Explain.

Q: What percentage of the world's population clash over rights to water?

cancers, provided pharmacologists can get to them before they are eliminated by chain saws and bulldozers.

We benefit in still other ways from tropical forests. One critical environmental service is the "sponge effect," by which the forests soak up rainfall during the wet season and then release it in regular amounts throughout the dry season. When tree cover is removed and this watershed function is impaired, the result is an annual regime of floods followed by droughts, which destroys property and reduces agricultural productivity. There is also concern that if tropical deforestation continues unabated, it could trigger local, regional, or even global changes in climate. Such climatic upheavals would affect the lives of billions of people, if not the whole of humankind.

All this raises important questions about our role in the biosphere and our relations with the natural world around us. As we proceed on our disruptive way in tropical forests, we—political leaders and the general public alike—give scarcely a moment's thought to what we are doing. We are deciding the fate of the world's tropical forests unwittingly, yet effectively and increasingly.

The resulting shift in evolution's course, stemming from the elimination of tropical forests, will rank as one of the greatest biological upheavals since the dawn of life. It will equal, in scale and significance, the development of aerobic respiration, the emergence of flowering plants, and the arrival of limbed animals, which took place over eons. Whereas those were enriching disruptions in the course of life on this planet, the loss of biodiversity associated with the destruction of tropical forests will be almost entirely an impoverishing phenomenon

brought about entirely by human actions. And it will all have occurred within the twinkling of a geologic eye.

In short our intervention in tropical forests should be viewed as one of the most challenging problems that humankind has ever encountered. After all, we are the first species ever to be able to look upon nature's work and to decide whether we should consciously eliminate it or leave much of it untouched.

So the decline of tropical forests is one of the great "sleeper" issues of our time—an issue with far more sweeping consequences that it might initially seem. Yet we can still save much of these forests and the species they contain. Should we not consider ourselves fortunate that we alone among all generations are being given the chance to preserve tropical forests as the most exuberant expression of nature in the biosphere—and thereby to support the right to life of many of our fellow species and their capacity to undergo further evolution without human interference?

### Critical Thinking

1. Should MDCs provide most of the money to preserve remaining tropical forests in LDCs? Explain.

2. What can you do to help preserve some of the world's tropical forests? Which, if any, of these actions do you plan to take?

# 11 Global Warming and Ozone Loss: Apocalypse Soon?

## 2040 A.D.: *Hard Times on Planet Earth**

Mary Wilkins sat in the living room of her underground home in Illinois (Figure 11-1). She looked at her calendar—July 4, 2040—and remembered the exciting Independence Day parades of her youth in the 1980s. There would be no parade or barbecue or fireworks today. People couldn't stay outside for long now because of the searing heat and intense ultraviolet radiation.

Many of her friends and millions of other Americans had long ago migrated to Canada for its cooler climate and more plentiful food supply after America's midwestern breadbasket dried up and California turned to desert. Her friend June had written recently wondering where to go now that Canadian farmland was drying up.

---

*\* Compare this fictional worst-case scenario with the hopeful scenario that opens Chapter 27.*

Just then a door opened. Her daughter Jane came out, dressed for work in a wide-brimmed straw hat, anti-UV sunglasses, long white gloves, and a lightweight floor-length duster. Behind her the shouts and squeals of the children playing Refugees and Border Patrol erupted. It had been a popular game since 2020 when the United States built a "Great Wall" along its border with Mexico in a mostly vain attempt to keep out millions of starving Latin Americans trying to find food and work in the north.

"They're playing that awful game again, Mother," said Jane. "Could you tell them a story or something?" Mary sighed as she went to corral the children. She felt sorry for them—their father killed fighting last summer's endless forest fire, their mother struggling to support them all on her job at the Refugee Center, and no place to play in the daytime except their underground bedroom.

With her sweaty grandchildren gathered around her chair, Mary began her favorite story. It was about the old days—before the Warming and severe ozone

**Figure 11-1** This earth-sheltered house in Will County, Illinois, could be like Mary Wilkins's 2040 house. Across the United States about 13,000 families have built earth-sheltered houses.

We, humanity, have finally done it: disturbed the
environment on a global scale.

THOMAS E. LOVEJOY

depletion—when school was not a TV set with lessons year-round, but let out in June, and kids could play outside all day during the summer. There were green parks to play in and green trees to climb, swimming pools full of water, and lakes and rivers everywhere. Sometimes it rained so much you actually got tired of it and wished it would go away. And in the winter cold white stuff called snow fell from the sky and could be gathered up in balls to throw at each other.

She also told them that almost everyone had a car. "What's a car?" asked Jessica, the oldest child. "Is it like the bus that Mommy rides to work?"

"Yes, only much smaller—just for one person or one family. It could go fast and ran on a fuel called gasoline—much too rare to be used anymore. You could go anywhere you wanted in your car, even to the drive-in for a hamburger."

"What's a hamburger, Grandma?" asked Jeffery, the youngest. "What's a drive-in?" asked Jessica. She patiently explained to them about drive-ins and how good hamburgers had tasted. "Why did people let things get so bad?" Jessica asked. Mary's eyes filled with tears as she took the child wordlessly in her arms. Why didn't we take the warnings of scientists in the 1980s seriously? she asked herself. Then she looked at Jessica and admitted, "Because we didn't want to believe anything bad could happen."

Although our species has existed for only an eye-blink of Earth's history, we are altering its atmosphere 10–100 times faster than the natural rate of change over the past 10,000 years. Global warming from our binge of fossil-fuel burning (Figure 3-8) and deforestation (Figure 10-3), and depletion of stratospheric ozone from our use of chlorofluorocarbons and other chemicals, are now global threats.

If these interconnected, largely invisible problems build until they cross threshold levels, there will be no place for us to hide from harmful effects that could last decades, perhaps hundreds of years. Preventing this ultimate tragedy of the commons will be our challenge into the twenty-first century. Otherwise, we or our children may end up living like Mary Wilkins and her family, or much worse.

This chapter will be devoted to answering the following questions:

- Can we really make Earth warmer, and if so what will a few degrees matter?
- What can we do about possible global warming?
- Why should we care about ozone depletion in the stratosphere?
- What can we do to slow ozone depletion?

## Global Warming or a Lot of Hot Air?

**11-1**

SOME THINGS WE KNOW ABOUT EARTH'S CLIMATE  In 1990 and 1992 the Intergovernmental Panel on Climate Change (IPCC) published reports by several hundred leading atmospheric scientists on the best available evidence about past climate change, the greenhouse effect, and recent changes in global temperatures. According to the panel's reports and other studies, this was the scientific consensus on these matters:

- Earth's climate is the result of complex interactions among the sun, atmosphere, oceans, land, and biosphere which we only partly understand (Section 5-2).
- Analysis of ocean and lake sediments, fossils of climate-sensitive organisms, rock strata, and air bubbles trapped in different levels of glacial ice indicates that Earth's average surface temperature has fluctuated considerably over geologic time, with several ice ages covering much of the planet with thick ice during the past 800,000 years (Figure 7-10). Each glacial period lasted about 100,000 years and was followed by a warmer interglacial period of 10,000–12,500 years. As the ice melted at the end of the last ice age, average sea levels rose about 100 meters (300 feet), changing the face of the earth.
- For the past 10,000 years we have enjoyed the relative warmth of the latest interglacial period, during which mean surface temperatures have

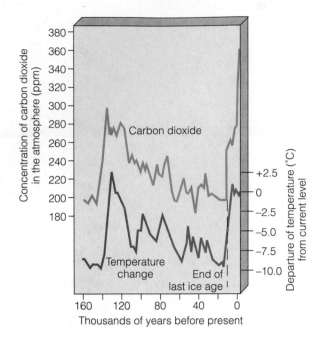

**Figure 11-2** Estimated variations in mean global surface temperature and average tropospheric carbon dioxide levels over the past 160,000 years. Since the last great ice age ended about 10,000 years ago, we have enjoyed a warm interglacial period. One factor that influences Earth's mean surface temperature is the greenhouse effect (Figure 5-10). Changes in tropospheric levels of carbon dioxide, a major greenhouse gas, correlate closely with changes in Earth's mean surface temperature and thus its climate, although other factors also influence global climate (Section 5-2).

fluctuated only 0.5–1°C (0.9–1.8°F) over 100- to 200-year periods. This relative climatic stability over thousands of years has saved us from drastic changes in the nature of soils and vegetation patterns, allowing large increases in food production and thus in population (Figure 2-4). However, even these small temperature changes have led to large migrations of peoples in response to changed agricultural and grazing conditions. If past climatic history is an accurate indicator, we should experience another ice age sometime in the next 2,500 years.

- The troposphere traps heat by a natural process called the *greenhouse effect* (Figure 5-10). This idea, proposed by mathematician Jean Fourier more than 100 years ago, has been confirmed by numerous laboratory experiments and atmospheric measurements, and is one of the most widely accepted scientific theories.

- The amount of heat trapped in the troposphere depends mostly on the concentrations of heat-trapping or *greenhouse gases*, and the length of time they stay in the atmosphere. The major greenhouse gases are water vapor, carbon dioxide, ozone, methane, nitrous oxide, and chloro-

fluorocarbons (CFCs). The high levels of greenhouse gases on Venus and the low levels on Mars demonstrate the fire-and-ice extremes of the greenhouse effect.

- Heat trapped by greenhouse gases in the atmosphere is what keeps the planet warm enough to allow us and other species to exist (Spotlight, p. 155).

- The two predominant greenhouse gases in the troposphere are water vapor, controlled by the hydrologic cycle (Figure 4-33), and carbon dioxide, controlled mostly by the global carbon cycle (Figure 4-28).

- Over the past 160,000 years levels of water vapor in the troposphere have remained fairly constant while those of $CO_2$ have fluctuated by a factor of two. Estimated changes in the $CO_2$ (as well as methane) content of the troposphere correlate closely with estimated variations in Earth's mean surface temperature (Figure 11-2).

- Measured atmospheric levels of certain greenhouse gases—$CO_2$, methane, nitrous oxide, and CFCs—have risen in recent decades (Figure 11-3).

- Most of the increased levels of these greenhouse gases have come from human activities—burning of fossil fuels, use of CFCs, agriculture, and deforestation.

- The United States is the largest emitter of all greenhouse gases (18.4% of global emissions), followed by the former Soviet Union (13.5%), China (9.1%), Japan (4.7%), India (4.1%), Brazil (3.9%), and Germany (3.4%). Among the industrialized countries the United States, Canada, and Australia have the highest per capita emissions of greenhouse gases.

- The United States is the largest emitter of $CO_2$ (with 18% of the total), followed by the former Soviet Union (14%), China (9%), Japan (5%), Brazil (4%), Germany (3%), India (2%), Great Britain (2%), Poland (2%), and Canada (2%).

- Since 1970 the oceans have absorbed more than a third (some estimate half) of the excess $CO_2$ we have added to the atmosphere.

- Deforestation is reducing Earth's ability to remove $CO_2$ through photosynthesis (Chapter 10). This may account for about 20–33% of the rise in $CO_2$ levels.

- Since 1860, when measurements began, the mean global temperature has risen 0.3–0.6°C (0.5–1.1°F) (Figure 11-4).

- Eight of the 13 years from 1980 to 1992 were the hottest in the 110-year recorded history of land-surface temperature measurements, and 1990 was the hottest of all.

Q: How much U.S. drinking water is withdrawn from groundwater?

**Figure 11-3** Increases in average concentrations of major greenhouse gases in the troposphere, mostly because of human activities. (Data from Electric Power Research Institute. Adapted and updated by permission from Cecie Starr and Ralph Taggart, *Biology: The Unity and Diversity of Life*, 6th ed., Belmont, Calif.: Wadsworth, 1992)

**a. Carbon dioxide (CO$_2$)** contributes about 55% to global warming from greenhouse gases produced by human activities. Industrial countries account for about 76% of annual emissions. The main sources are fossil-fuel burning (67%) and deforestation and other forms of land clearing and burning (33%). CO$_2$ stays in the atmosphere for about 500 years.

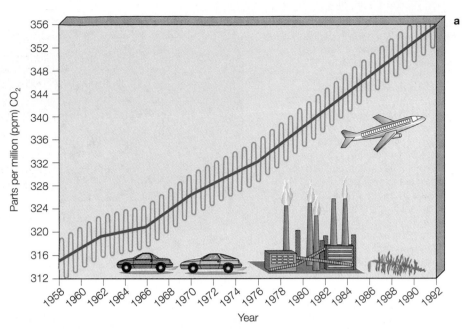

**b. Chlorofluorocarbons (CFCs)** are believed to be responsible for 24% of the human contribution of greenhouse gases. They also deplete ozone in the stratosphere. The main sources are leaking air conditioners and refrigerators, evaporation of industrial solvents, production of plastic foams, and aerosol propellants. CFCs take 10–15 years to reach the stratosphere and generally trap 1,500–7,000 times as much heat per molecule as CO$_2$ while they are in the troposphere. This heating effect in the troposphere may be partially offset by the cooling caused when CFCs deplete ozone during their 65- to 110-year stay in the stratosphere.

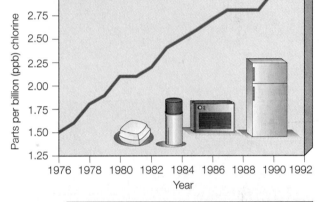

**c. Methane (CH$_4$)** accounts for about 18% of the increase in greenhouse gases. Methane is produced when bacteria break down dead organic matter in moist places that lack oxygen. These areas include swamps and other natural wetlands, rice paddies, landfills, and the digestive tracts of cattle, sheep, and termites. Production and use of oil and natural gas, and incomplete burning of organic materials (including biomass burning in the tropics), also are significant sources. CH$_4$ stays in the troposphere for 7–10 years. Each CH$_4$ molecule traps about 25 times as much heat as a CO$_2$ molecule.

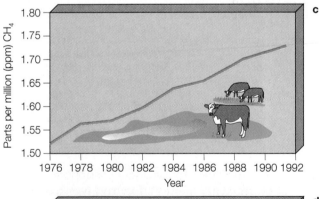

**d. Nitrous oxide (N$_2$O)** is responsible for 6% of the human input of greenhouse gases. Besides trapping heat in the troposphere it also depletes ozone in the stratosphere. It is released from nylon production, from burning of biomass and nitrogen-rich fuels (especially coal), and from the breakdown of nitrogen fertilizers in soil, livestock wastes, and nitrate-contaminated groundwater. Its life span in the troposphere is 140–190 years, and it traps about 230 times as much heat per molecule as CO$_2$.

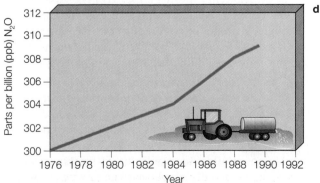

**A:** About 50% (96% in rural areas, 20% in urban areas)

**Figure 11-4** Changes in Earth's mean surface temperature between 1860 and 1990 (dark line). The yellow region shows global warming projected by various computer models of Earth's climate systems. Note that the computer projections roughly match the historically recorded change in temperature between 1860 and 1990. All current models suggest that global temperature will rise between now and 2050, a larger and more rapid change than any taking place within a 100- to 200-year period in the last 10,000 years and possibly the last 65 million years. Scientists admit that current models could underestimate or overestimate the amount of warming by a factor of two. (Data from National Academy of Sciences and National Center for Atmospheric Research)

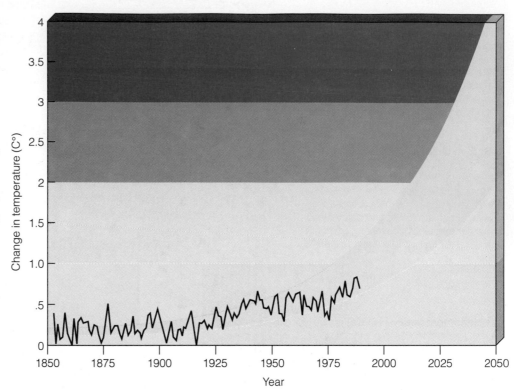

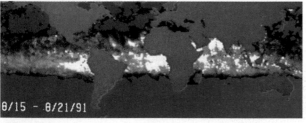

Larry Stowe/National Oceanic Atmospheric Administration

8/15 - 8/21/91

**Figure 11-5** Satellite view of sulfur dioxide and sulfuric acid aerosols in the atmosphere 12 weeks after the massive eruption of Mount Pinatubo in the Philippines in June 1991—the largest volcanic eruption of this century. These chemicals are expected to reflect incoming sunlight and lower average global temperatures up to 0.6°C (1°F) between 1992 and 1995 until the aerosols return to Earth's surface.

- So far any temperature changes possibly caused by an enhanced greenhouse effect have been too small to exceed normal short-term swings in mean atmospheric temperature caused by volcanic eruptions (Figure 11-5), El Niño–Southern Oscillations (Figure 5-9), air pollution, and other climatic factors.

- Warming or cooling by more than 2°C (4°F) over a few decades, instead of over centuries as has happened during the last 10,000 years, could be disastrous for Earth's ecosystems and for human economic and social systems. Such rapid climatic changes would alter conditions faster than some species, especially plants, could adapt or migrate.

These changes might also shift the areas where people could grow food. Some areas might become uninhabitable because of drought or floods following a rise in average sea levels.

- We don't know enough about how Earth works to make accurate projections about the possible effects of our inputs of greenhouse gases on global and regional climates and on the biosphere.

**COMPUTERS AS CRYSTAL BALLS: MODELING GREENHOUSE WARMING** To project the behavior of climatic and other complex systems, scientists develop mathematical models that simulate such systems and run them on computers (Spotlight, p. 219). How well the results correspond to the real world depends on the design of the model and on the accuracy of the data and assumptions used.

Current climate models (Figure 11-6) generally agree on how the global climate might change but disagree on changes for individual regions. Here are the main projections of the major climate models:

- Earth's mean surface temperature will rise 1.5–5.5°C (2.7–9.9°F) by 2050 if inputs of greenhouse gases continue to rise at the present rate (Figure 11-3). Even at the lower value, Earth would be warmer than it has been for 10,000 years (cartoon, p. 295).

- Air will warm more and sooner over land than over oceans because water takes longer to warm than land.

Q: How much of the groundwater withdrawn in United States is not replenished?

**Figure 11-6** Generalized model of the greenhouse effect and its possible consequences. The greenhouse effect itself (model 1) is well established. The increase in temperature resulting from higher concentrations of greenhouse gases (model 2) is projected by crude climate models. These models predict that average global temperature should rise 1.5–5.5°C (2.7–9.9°F) if atmospheric concentrations of greenhouse gases double. Because of uncertainties in the models, however, a particular model's projections could be off by a factor of two in either direction. Current models cannot project the specific climate changes (model 3) and their consequences (models 4–7) in various parts of the world.

- The Northern Hemisphere will warm more and faster than the Southern Hemisphere, mostly because the Southern Hemisphere has more ocean (Figure 5-27).

- Temperatures at middle and high latitudes should rise two to three times the global average, while temperatures near the equator will rise less than the global average.

- Soil will be drier in some middle latitudes, especially during summer in the Northern Hemisphere.

- More areas will have extreme heat waves and more forest and brush fires.

- The average sea level will rise 2–4 centimeters (0.8–1.6 inches) per decade.

So what's the big deal? Why should we worry about a possible rise of only a few degrees in the mean surface temperature of Earth? We often have that much change between June and July, or between yesterday and today. The key point is that we are not talking about normal swings in local weather, but about a projected *global* change in average climate from a thickening greenhouse blanket.

**A CLOUDY CRYSTAL BALL: THINGS WE DON'T KNOW** A model is only as good as the assumptions and data it's based on. Because we have only partial knowledge about how Earth's climate system works, our models are flawed. Scientists disagree on whether various factors in the system might dampen (negative feedback) or amplify (positive feedback) a temperature rise, how fast temperatures might climb, and what the effects will be on various areas.

Solar output varies by about 0.1%— apparently in 11-year, 80-year, and other cycles—which can cause

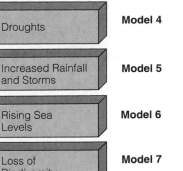

temporary warming or cooling on Earth and thus affect the projections of climate models. Some scientists believe that the oceans may help slow or prevent global warming (Spotlight, p. 296).

Polar ice might also speed up or slow global warming. The Greenland and Antarctic ice sheets act like enormous mirrors reflecting sunlight back into space. If warmer temperatures melted some of this ice and exposed darker ground or ocean that would absorb more sunlight, warming would be accelerated. Then more ice would melt, amplifying this positive feedback loop even more.

On the other hand, the early stages of global warming might actually increase the amount of Earth's water stored as ice. Warmer air would carry more water vapor, which could drop more snow on some glaciers, especially the gigantic Antarctic ice sheet. If snow accumulated faster than ice was lost, the ice sheet would grow, reflect more sunlight, and help

## Will the Oceans Save Us?

**SPOTLIGHT**

Oceans are the biggest factor in global warming because of their huge capacity to absorb heat and to remove $CO_2$ from the atmosphere. The amount of heat absorbed by the oceans depends on how long the heat takes to reach deeper layers—something we don't know.

Because $CO_2$ dissolves in water, the oceans now take up at least a third of the excess $CO_2$ we pump into the atmosphere. We don't know, however, if they can absorb more. Worse, global warming could mean they might dissolve less. If the oceans warm up enough, more $CO_2$ will bubble out of solution than dissolves—just as in a glass of ginger ale left out in the sun. If this happens, the additional $CO_2$ in the atmosphere will amplify and accelerate global warming.

If air warms just 2–3°C (4–5°F), it can hold 33% more water. Since water vapor is a potent greenhouse gas, this jump in its concentration in the atmosphere could also accelerate global warming.

On the other hand, warmer air might speed up photosynthesis by oceanic phytoplankton, which would absorb more $CO_2$ from the atmosphere and slow global warming. But warming or increased UV radiation from ozone depletion might decrease populations of these producers and amplify global warming.

Another possibility is that warmer air will evaporate more water from the oceans and create more clouds, which now cool the planet by 10–15°C (18–27°F). Depending on their type (thick or thin) and altitude, more clouds could contribute to either warming or cooling. We don't know which type might predominate and how this would vary in different parts of the world.

cool the atmosphere—perhaps within a thousand years ushering in a new ice age.

Some scientists suggest that air pollution can help slow global warming. Like volcanic eruptions (Figure 11-5), burning fossil fuels, especially coal and oil, injects huge quantities of tiny particles and gases such as sulfur dioxide that react in the troposphere to form tiny droplets of sulfuric acid in the atmosphere in a few days. Projected global warming might be offset partially by such particles and droplets because they reflect back some of the incoming sunlight. This fossil-fuel connection may explain why the air temperature of the heavily industrialized Northern Hemisphere dropped slightly between 1940 and 1970 when air pollutants were not controlled and there were few major

volcanic eruptions. It may also explain why there is more warming in the Northern Hemisphere at night (when the sun can't be reflected by pollutants) than during the day.

As usual, things aren't that simple. Aerosols in the lower troposphere can either warm or cool the air and surface below them, depending on the reflectivity (albedo) of the underlying surface. These contradictory and patchy effects, as well as improved air pollution controls, make it unlikely that these air pollutants could do much to counteract greenhouse warming in the next half century. Even if they did, levels of these pollutants, which already kill hundreds of thousands of people per year, need to be reduced.

We can put various plants in a controlled environmental chamber, double $CO_2$ levels, and see what happens. Some measurements suggest that more $CO_2$ in the atmosphere is likely to increase the rate of photosynthesis and thus stimulate the growth of plants such as wheat, corn, and rice, and some trees where $CO_2$ availability limits growth. This would help reduce $CO_2$ levels, but this stimulus will peter out as the $CO_2$ level rises and it is no longer a limiting factor. Also much of the increased plant growth could be negated by insects that breed more rapidly and year-round in warmer temperatures. Again we know very little about such possibilities. What plants do in environmental chambers may not happen in nature, where there are many other interacting variables.

Another possibility that could amplify global warming is the *population-food trap*. As humans try to expand food production to keep up with population growth, the resulting increase in land clearing, fertilizers, livestock, and fossil-fuel use would release more greenhouse gases. This positive feedback would increase global warming, which in turn could reduce food production. Some evidence suggests that fertilizing rice paddies to provide more food may reduce emissions of methane but increase emissions of nitrous oxide, a much more potent greenhouse gas (Figure 11-3).

Here is another wild card. In a warmer world huge amounts of methane tied up in arctic tundra soils and in muds on the bottom of the Arctic Ocean might be released if the blanket of permafrost covering tundra soils melts and the oceans warm considerably. Because methane is a potent greenhouse gas, this release could greatly amplify global warming. On the other hand, some scientists believe that bacteria in tundra soils would rapidly oxidize the escaping methane to $CO_2$, a less potent greenhouse gas. Again we don't know what might happen.

As the world warmed use of air conditioning would increase, contributing more heat to the troposphere. That would intensify and spread urban heat islands (Figure 9-13), causing people to use even more

**Q:** How much of the world's water is provided by desalination?

air conditioning. Using fossil fuels to produce more electricity to run air conditioners would add more $CO_2$ to the atmosphere, accelerating global warming.

Because of these and numerous other uncertainties in global climate models, their developers admit their projections might be off by a factor of two. In other words global warming during the next 50–100 years could be half the projected temperature increase in Figure 11-4—the best-case scenario—or double it—the worst-case scenario. The story at the beginning of this chapter was based on the worst-case scenario, but most scientists agree that even the best-case scenario is something we don't want to experience. As Pogo put it, "We have met the enemy and it is us."

## 11-2 Possible Effects of Global Warming

**FOOD PRODUCTION** A warmer troposphere would have different consequences for different peoples and species. Some places would get drier, and some wetter. Some would get hotter, and others cooler.

Food productivity could vary considerably, increasing in some areas and dropping in others, because of changes in the global distribution of heat and precipitation. Ice core analysis and other data indicate that the last time Earth's $CO_2$ levels were double 1860 levels, the area of the planet's arid and semiarid zones more than doubled in the middle and lower altitudes because there was more water in the atmosphere and less in the soil.

Water is a limiting factor in the growth of many crops, especially in drier areas. Two climate models project that, with warming from a doubling of $CO_2$ over 1988 levels, current "once-in-a-century" droughts would occur every other year across much of the world, thus having the potential to lower crop yields. Past evidence and computer models indicate that climate belts and thus tolerance ranges of plant species (including crops) would shift northward by 100–150 kilometers (60–90 miles) or 150 meters (500 feet) vertically (Figure 5-14) for each 1°C (1.8°F) rise in the global temperature.

Computer models have projected drops in the global yield of key food crops ranging from 30% to 70%. Drops in crop yields, however, might be offset by (1) increased irrigation, (2) increased growth because of higher $CO_2$ levels, (3) use of crop varieties better adopted to new conditions, (4) changed planting dates, and (5) crops grown at higher latitudes. Current greenhouse modeling and some field experiments suggest that these factors could lead to a more manageable 10% drop in global per capita food production with the projected rise in global temperature.

On the other hand, these factors might be offset by (1) lack of irrigation water in some areas, (2) increases in crop-eating insects and diseases (which will have better survival rates and more generations per season in food-growing areas with a warmer climate), (3) the high cost of moving food-growing areas to higher latitudes, and (4) thinner and poorer soils and increased ultraviolet radiation because of less stratospheric ozone at higher latitudes.

With current knowledge we can't predict where changes in crop-growing capacity might occur and how long such climate changes might last before shifting again. The possible result: a moving climatic target with a complex and shifting set of winners and losers.

Lakes, streams, and aquifers in some areas that have watered ecosystems, cropfields, and cities for centuries could shrink or dry up altogether, forcing entire populations to migrate to areas with adequate water supplies—if they could. We can't say with much certainty where this might happen.

**FORESTS AND BIODIVERSITY** Rapid climate change would also have severe impacts on natural ecosystems. Forest growth in temperate and subarctic regions would move toward the poles or to higher altitudes (Figure 5-14), if the forests could keep up with the rate of climate change. However, tree species can move only through the slow growth of new trees along forest edges where their seeds fall—typically about 0.9 kilometer (0.5 mile) per year or 9 kilometers (5 miles) per decade.

Thus, if climate belts moved faster than this or if migration was blocked by cities and other human barriers, entire forests of oak, beech (Figure 11-7), and other deciduous trees could wither and die. According to some studies 40% of the planet's boreal forests (Figure 5-11) might be killed off by a century of global warming.

Such diebacks would amplify the greenhouse effect as decaying trees released $CO_2$ into the air. According to Oregon State University scientists, projected drying from global warming could cause massive fires in up to 90% of North American forests, destroying wildlife habitats and injecting huge amounts of $CO_2$ into the atmosphere.

Large-scale forest diebacks would also cause mass extinction of species that couldn't migrate to new areas. And fish would die as temperatures soared in streams and lakes, and as lowered water levels concentrated pesticides.

Any shifts in regional climate would threaten many parks, wildlife reserves, wilderness areas, wetlands, and coral reefs—offsetting many current efforts

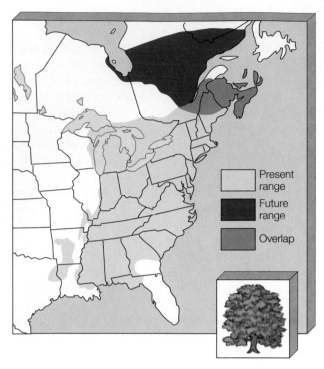

**Figure 11-7** According to one projection, if $CO_2$ emissions doubled between 1990 and 2050, beech trees, now common throughout the eastern United States, would be able to survive only in a greatly shrunken range in northern Maine and southeast Canada (shown in orange and red). (Data from Margaret B. Davis and Catherine Zabinski, University of Minnesota)

Legend:
- Present range
- Future range
- Overlap

to stem the loss of biodiversity. One study found, depending on which climate models were used, that 55–80% of the world's 243 UN Biosphere Reserves would not be able to support their current plant species during the next century. If this happens, the already serious bleeding of Earth's biodiversity would become a hemorrhage.

**SEA LEVELS** Water expands slightly when heated. This explains why global sea levels would rise if the oceans warmed, just as the fluid in a thermometer rises when heated. Since 1900 the world's average sea level has risen 10–20 centimeters (4–8 inches) and now appears to be rising about 2.5 centimeters (1 inch) per decade. Globally the extent of polar sea ice has shrunk about 16% in the last 15 years. If warming at the poles caused ice sheets and glaciers to melt even partially, the global sea level would rise even more. There is uncertainty, however, about how fast and how much the sea level might rise.

About one-third of the world's population and more than a third of the world's economic infrastructure are concentrated in coastal regions. Current models indicate that an increase in the average atmospheric temperature of 3°C (5°F) would raise the average global sea level by 0.2–1.5 meters (0.6–4.6 feet) over the next 50–100 years. If the Antarctic ice sheet gets larger because snow accumulation exceeds ice loss, the lower estimate (give or take 0.4 meter) is more likely by the year 2050.

A 1-meter (3-foot) rise would flood low-lying areas of major cities such as Shanghai, Cairo, Bangkok, Sydney, Hamburg, and Venice, as well as agricultural lowlands and deltas in Egypt, Bangladesh, India, and China, where much of the world's rice is grown. Scientists project that even a modest 0.3-meter (1-foot) rise in average sea level would:

- Flood coastal wetlands (including most mangrove swamps; Figure 5-33) and low-lying cities and croplands, flood and move barrier islands (Figure 5-36) farther inland, contaminate coastal aquifers with salt, and flood tanks storing oil and other hazardous chemicals in coastal areas. Coastal areas that were not flooded would still be at risk from higher tides and storm waves.

- Flood 30–70% of remaining coastal wetlands in the United States. Marshes might "migrate" inland if the 0.3-meter sea-level rise took place over 100 years or so. Attempts to protect buildings and roads with seawalls (Figure 5-37) would compound the loss of biodiversity by directing the full force of storm surges onto nearby wetlands.

- Flood low-lying U.S. cities such as New Orleans, New York, Atlantic City, Boston, Washington, D.C., Galveston, Charleston, Savannah, and Miami unless billions of dollars were spent to build and maintain extensive systems of dikes and levees.

- Push shorelines back about 30 meters (98 feet). Especially hard-hit would be the gradually sloping shorelines of North and South Carolina, which would move several kilometers inland.

- Greatly accelerate coastal erosion, resulting in shoreline losses of 3–30 meters (10–100 feet), depending on local conditions.

- Cut coral reefs off from adequate sunlight, causing them to lose vast amounts of algae, begin bleaching (Figure 4-1, right), and die.

One comedian jokes that she is planning to buy land in Kansas because it will probably become valuable beachfront property. Another boasts he isn't worried because he lives in a houseboat—the "Noah strategy." In a world of grim scenarios humor can release tension and help educate people about serious problems in less threatening ways.

**HUMAN HEALTH AND WEATHER EXTREMES**
A warmer world would affect human health by disrupting supplies of food and fresh water, displacing

Q: Worldwide, how much of the water withdrawn is unnecessarily wasted?

millions of people, and altering disease patterns in dangerous and unpredictable ways. The spread of tropical climates from the equator would bring malaria, encephalitis, yellow fever, dengue fever, and other insect-borne diseases to formerly temperate zones. Sea-level rise could spread infectious disease by flooding sewage and sanitation systems in coastal cities.

In a warmer world weather extremes, such as prolonged heat waves and droughts, would become common in many areas. As the upper layers of seawater warmed, hurricanes and typhoons would blow more frequently and fiercely. U.S. cities such as Miami, Galveston, Atlantic City, Charleston, and Ocean City, Maryland, (Figure 5-36) could be devastated by super-hurricanes. Even a slight warming of surface waters could intensify hurricanes in partially enclosed ocean basins like the Gulf of Mexico and the Bay of Bengal.

## 11-3 Solutions: Dealing with Global Warming

**DENIAL AND DELAY** Scientists urge that we mount a crash program to learn more about Earth's climate. Even with better understanding, which could take decades, our knowledge will be limited because the system is so incredibly complex. Thus science will never be able to offer the certainty that some decision makers want before making such tough decisions as phasing out fossil fuels and replacing deforestation with reforestation. Despite the need for better information, in 1992 NASA, citing lack of funds, proposed shutting down two satellites used to monitor global climate and ozone depletion—a disastrous possibility for scientists who rely on data from the satellites.

Many politicians and bureaucrats are dragging their feet, hoping they won't have to take drastic action. They hope some undiscovered property of the global climate system will absorb or correct for our input of greenhouse gases—a potentially deadly form of denial (Spotlight, right).

**SLOWING GLOBAL WARMING** Our crystal ball is still cloudy, but scientists have reached some consensus (Section 11-1) ) that possible global warming is scary. The good news, according to Gus Speth, president of the World Resources Institute, is that "even though climate change threatens to be bigger, more irreversible, and more pervasive than other environmental problems, it's also *controllable*, if we act now." According to recent studies by the National Academy of Science and the Congressional Office of Technology

### Deadly Denial

Our denial response to possible global warming is what psychologist Robert Ornstein calls the *boiled frog syndrome*. Imagine trying to alert a frog to danger as it sits in a pan of water very slowly being heated on the stove.

If the frog could talk it would say, "I'm a little warmer, but I'm doing fine." As the water gets hotter, we warn the frog that it will die, but it replies, "The temperature has been increasing for a long time, and I'm still alive. Stop worrying." Eventually the frog dies because it has no evolutionary experience of the lethal effects of boiling water and thus cannot perceive its situation as dangerous.

Suppose we sit like the frog denying the possibility of climate change until Earth's mean temperature rises to the point where it exceeds normal climatic fluctuations (which some climate scientists expect to happen within the next 5–20 years). Reacting then to improve energy efficiency, replace fossil fuels with renewable and perpetual energy resources, and starting massive reforestation will take another 40–50 years. By then much of the damage would already have been done, and the effects would last for hundreds if not thousands of years.

Instead of denial some scientists suggest that we adopt the *precautionary principle*, the idea that when dealing with unpredictable, risky, and irreversible environmental problems, it is often wise to take action before there is enough scientific knowledge to justify it.

Assessment, the United States could reduce its greenhouse gas emissions by 35–36% of 1990 levels using existing technology at low or no net cost, and by 48% at low to moderate cost.

The general guidelines for slowing global warming are to reduce our use of cars, coal, cattle, CFCs, and chain saws; increase our use of contraceptives; and replace deforestation with reforestation. There are a number of steps we can take to accomplish this.

### Prevention

- *Ban all production and uses of CFCs and other ozone-destroying chemicals by 1995.*

- *Cut current fossil-fuel use 20% by 2000 (35% in the United States), 50% by 2010, and 80% by 2030.*

- *Use energy more efficiently.* This is the quickest, cheapest, and most effective method to reduce emissions of $CO_2$ and other air pollutants during

## Energy Efficiency to the Rescue

**SOLUTIONS**

According to energy expert Amory Lovins (Guest Essay, p. 71) *the remedies for slowing global warming are things we should be doing already even if there were no threat of global warming.* He also argues that getting countries to sign treaties and agree to cut back and reallocate their use of fossil fuels in time to reduce serious environmental effects is difficult, if not almost impossible, and very costly. Climate models suggest that $CO_2$ emissions must be reduced by 80% to slow projected global warming to a safe rate. So far countries can't even agree to a 20% reduction.

According to Lovins improving energy efficiency would be the fastest, cheapest, and surest way to slash emissions of $CO_2$ and most other air pollutants within two decades using existing technology. This approach would save the world up to $1 trillion per year in reduced energy costs—as much as the annual global military budget.

Moreover, using energy more efficiently would reduce all forms of pollution, help protect biodiversity, and forestall arguments among governments about how $CO_2$ reductions should be divided up and enforced. This approach would also make the world's supplies of fossil fuel last longer, reduce international tensions over who gets the dwindling oil supplies, and give us more time to phase in alternatives to fossil fuels.

Greatly improving worldwide energy efficiency *now* is a money-saving, life-saving, Earth-saving, win-win offer that we should not refuse even if there were no possibility of climate change.

the next two to three decades (Solutions, above). According to the National Academy of Sciences this alone could lower U.S. greenhouse gas emissions by 10–40% at no net cost to the economy.

- *Shift over the next 30 years to perpetual and renewable energy resources that do not emit $CO_2$* (Chapter 17).

- *Transfer energy efficiency, renewable energy, pollution prevention, and waste reduction technologies to LDCs.*

- *Increase the use of nuclear power to produce electricity.* This is an option only if safer and cheaper reactors can be developed and if the problem of how to store nuclear waste safely for thousands of years can be solved (Section 18-4). However, improving energy efficiency is much quicker and safer, and reduces $CO_2$ emissions 2.5–10 times more than nuclear power per dollar invested.

- *Over a 10-year period phase out government subsidies for fossil fuels and nuclear power, and phase in carbon taxes on fossil fuels (especially coal and gasoline) based on their emissions of $CO_2$ and other air pollutants.* The tax revenue should be used to improve the energy efficiency of dwellings and heating systems for the poor in MDCs and LDCs, to provide them with enough energy to offset higher fuel prices, and to subsidize the transition to improved energy efficiency and perpetual and renewable energy resources.

- *Slash our use of coal.* Coal emits 60% more $CO_2$ per unit of energy produced than any other fossil fuel. To power their industrialization programs, China (with almost half of the world's coal reserves) plans to nearly double coal use in the next decade, and India plans to triple its use. MDCs must try to prevent this increase by helping these and other LDCs greatly improve their energy efficiency and shift from coal to perpetual and renewable energy sources.

- *Switch from coal to natural gas for producing electricity and high-temperature heat in countries that have ample supplies,* such as the United States and the CIS. Burning natural gas emits only half as much $CO_2$ per unit of energy as coal and emits far less of most other air pollutants as well. Because burning natural gas still emits $CO_2$, this transition method would merely buy some time to switch to an age of energy efficiency and renewable energy.

- *Capture methane gas emitted by landfills and use it as a fuel, and reduce leaks from natural gas distribution systems.*

- *Cut beef production to reduce fossil-fuel inputs into agriculture, $CO_2$ released because of deforestation for grazing land (Figure 10-15), and methane belched into the atmosphere by cattle.*

- *Halt unsustainable deforestation everywhere by 2000 and replace it with massive reforestation (Sections 10-4 and 10-5).*

- *Switch from unsustainable to sustainable agriculture (Section 14-6).* Worldwide, agriculture is now responsible for about 15% of the greenhouse gases we emit into the atmosphere.

- *Slow population growth (Section 8-3).* If we cut per capita greenhouse gas emissions in half but world population doubles, we're back where we started.

- *Develop win-win pacts between MDCs and LDCs.* In this "let's make a deal" strategy LDCs would agree to stop deforestation, protect biodiversity, slow population growth, enact fairer land distribution, and phase out coal burning. In return MDCs would forgive much of their foreign debt and help fund the transfer of modern energy efficiency, solar energy, pollution control and prevention, sustainable agriculture, and reforestation technologies to them. MDCs would also agree to make substantial cuts in their use of fossil fuels, abandon ozone-depleting chemicals, greatly improve energy efficiency, stop deforestation, shift to sustainable agriculture, and slow population growth.

### Cleanup

- *Develop better methods to remove $CO_2$ from the smokestack emissions of coal-burning power and industrial plants and from vehicle exhausts.* Currently available methods can remove only about 30% of the $CO_2$ and would at least double the cost of electricity. The recovered $CO_2$ must also be kept out of the atmosphere, but the effectiveness of doing so is unknown, and the costs are much higher than for other strategies, especially reforestation and improvements in energy efficiency.

- *Plant and tend trees.* This is important for restoring deforested and degraded land and for reducing soil erosion, but it's only a stopgap measure for slowing $CO_2$ emissions. To absorb the $CO_2$ we put into the atmosphere, we would have to plant and tend an average of 1,000 trees per person every year. Also, if the newly grown forests are cleared and burned by us or by massive forest fires caused by global warming, or if much of the new forest dies because of drought, most of the $CO_2$ removed would be released, accelerating global warming. Moreover, according to William Nordhaus, complete reforestation of the earth would offset only three years of $CO_2$ emissions from fossil fuels.

- *Remove $CO_2$ by using tanks and ponds of genetically engineered, photosynthesizing algae.* This would be very expensive and does not answer the question of what we would do with the mountains of dead algae slurry.

- *Fertilize the oceans with iron to stimulate the growth of marine algae.* This would be very expensive and could have potentially harmful effects on ocean ecosystems.

**ADJUSTING TO GLOBAL WARMING** Even if we stopped adding greenhouse gases to the atmosphere now, current models project that what we have already added could warm the earth by 0.5–1.8°C (0.9–3.2°F). Since many of the things we should do either will not be done or will be done too slowly, some analysts suggest that we should also begin preparing for the effects of long-term global warming. They suggest that we:

- *Breed food plants that need less water or can thrive in salty water.*

- *Build dikes to protect coastal areas from flooding, as the Dutch have done for centuries.*

- *Move storage tanks of hazardous materials away from coastal areas.*

- *Ban new or rebuilt construction on low-lying coastal areas.*

- *Stockpile one to five years' worth of key foods throughout the world as short-term insurance against disruptions in food production.*

- *Expand existing wilderness areas, parks, and wildlife refuges northward in the Northern Hemisphere and southward in the Southern Hemisphere, and create new wildlife reserves in these areas.*

- *Connect wildlife reserves by corridors that would allow mobile species to move with climate changes.*

- *Waste less water.*

All of the measures for slowing or responding to possible climate change discussed in this chapter would cost far less than the $12 trillion we have spent since 1945 to protect ourselves from the possibility of nuclear war. Global warming is an equally serious threat. Dealing with this threat will require action at the international, national, local, and individual levels (Individuals Matter, p. 302).

## 11-4 Letting in Deadly Rays: Ozone Depletion

**THE THREAT** Thanks to the evolution of photosynthetic, oxygen-producing bacterial cells, Earth has had a stratospheric sunscreen—the ozone layer—for the past 450 million years. However, an avalanche of evidence indicates that we are thinning this screen with our recent use of chlorine- and bromine-containing compounds (Figure 11-8).

Unlike global warming this threat is here now. It will have serious long-term effects on human health, animal life, and the sunlight-driven producer plants that support Earth's food chains and webs. It is too late to prevent much of the damage, which will worsen in years to come as chemicals we have already put into the atmosphere work their way up to the stratosphere and deplete ozone for decades. However, if we stop using these chemicals now, ozone levels might return to 1985 levels in about 100 years.

**FROM DREAM CHEMICALS TO NIGHTMARE CHEMICALS** How did we get into this mess? It started when Thomas Midgley, Jr., a General Motors

## What You Can Do to Reduce Global Warming

**INDIVIDUALS MATTER**

While the world's governments argue over what to do about projected global warming, we can take matters into our own hands:

- *Learn what adds $CO_2$ to the air and reduce those activities.* Each U.S. resident is responsible for an average of 16.7 metric tons (18.4 tons) of $CO_2$ emissions a year (mostly from burning fossil fuels)—six times more than the average citizen in an LDC.

- *Reduce your use of fossil fuels.* Driving a car that gets at least 15 kilometers per liter (35 miles per gallon), joining a car pool and using mass transit, and walking or bicycling where possible will reduce your emissions of $CO_2$ and other air pollutants, will save energy and money, and can improve your health.

- *Use energy-efficient light bulbs, refrigerators, and other appliances.*

- *Use solar energy to heat household space or water as much as possible.* When you can't use solar energy, use natural gas, not electricity.

- *Cool your house by using shade trees and available breezes* (Section 17-2).

- *Plant and care for trees to help absorb $CO_2$ and cool the globe.*

- *Prioritize all your purchases. Reduce resource use by buying only what you need; reuse; recycle; throw away only as a last resort.*

- *Buy products made from recycled materials.*

- *Lobby for laws aimed at encouraging energy efficiency, halting the harvest of old-growth stands in national forests* (Section 10-5), *and curbing emissions of greenhouse gases and other air pollutants.* In 1990 Connecticut was the first state to pass a global warming law. This legislation bans use of electric heating in new or renovated buildings after 1993 unless they met certain minimum energy standards.

- *Reject unpredictable technofixes for slowing possible global warming.* Examples include covering the oceans with white Styrofoam chips to help reflect more energy away from Earth's surface, dumping iron into oceans to stimulate the growth of marine algae that remove $CO_2$ from the atmosphere, unfurling a gigantic foil-faced sun shield in space, or injecting sunlight-reflecting sulfate particulates into the stratosphere to cool Earth's surface. Some of these schemes may prove feasible in the future, but for now our understanding of the ecosphere is too poor for us to anticipate all their potentially harmful side effects. And there are many better, quicker, and cheaper solutions.

---

chemist, discovered the first chlorofluorocarbon (CFC) in 1930 and chemists then made similar compounds to create a family of highly useful CFCs. The two most widely used are CFC-11 (trichlorofluoromethane, $CCl_3F$) and CFC-12 (dichlorofluoromethane, $CCl_2F_2$).

These amazingly useful, chemically stable, odorless, nonflammable, nontoxic, and noncorrosive compounds seemed to be dream chemicals. Cheap to make, they became popular as coolants in air conditioners and refrigerators, propellants in aerosol spray cans, cleaners for electronic parts such as computer chips, sterilants for hospital instruments, fumigants for granaries and ship cargo holds, and building blocks for the bubbles in Styrofoam, used for insulation and packaging.

But it was too good to be true. In 1974 chemists Sherwood Rowland and Mario Molina made calculations indicating that CFCs were lowering the average concentration of ozone in the stratosphere and creating a global time bomb. They shocked the scientific community and the $28-billion-per-year industry making these chemicals by calling for an immediate ban of CFCs in spray cans.

Here's what Rowland and Molina found: Spray cans, discarded or leaky refrigeration and air conditioning equipment, and the production and burning of plastic foam products release CFCs into the atmosphere. These molecules are too unreactive to be removed and, mostly through convection and random drift, rise slowly into the stratosphere—taking 10–20 years to make the journey. There, under the influence of high-energy ultraviolet (UV) radiation, they break down and release chlorine atoms, which speed up the breakdown of ozone ($O_3$) into $O_2$ and O. Each CFC molecule can last in the stratosphere for 65–110 years. During that time each chlorine atom in these molecules—like a gaseous Pac-Man—can convert as many as 100,000 molecules of $O_3$ to $O_2$. *Each time you use and throw away a polystyrene cup you are eventually adding over 1 billion CFC molecules to the stratosphere, which, while there, will destroy up to 100 trillion molecules of ozone!* These dream molecules have turned into a nightmare of global ozone terminators.

Rowland and Molina warned us in 1974, but it took 15 years of interaction between the scientific and political communities before countries agreed to start slowly

Q: What percentage of U.S. toilets leak?

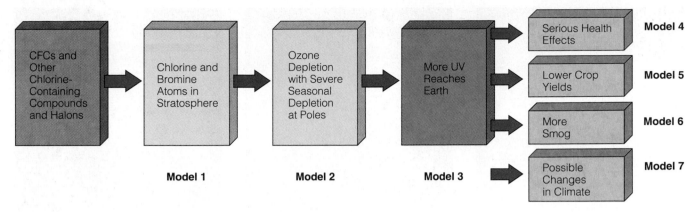

**Figure 11-8** Generalized model of ozone layer depletion and its effects. Models 1–3 have been confirmed. The extent of the effects in models 4–7 is still being studied.

phasing out CFCs.* The CFC industry was a powerful, well-funded adversary with lots of profits and jobs at stake. But through 15 years Rowland and Molina held their ground, expanded their research, and relentlessly explained the meaning of their calculations to other scientists, elected officials, and the press.

CFCs are not the only ozone eaters. Here are a few others that, like CFCs, are also greenhouse gases as they traverse the troposphere on their way to the stratosphere:

- Bromine-containing compounds called *halons* and *HBFCs*, used in fire extinguishers, and *methyl bromide*, a widely used pesticide. Each bromine atom destroys hundreds of times more ozone molecules than does a chlorine atom.

- *Carbon tetrachloride* (a cheap but highly toxic solvent) and *methyl chloroform*, or 1,1,1-trichloroethane (used as a cleaning solvent for clothes and metals and as a propellant in more than 160 consumer products, such as correction fluid, dry-cleaning sprays, spray adhesives, and other aerosols). Substitutes are available for virtually all uses of these two chemicals.

**OZONE HOLES AND OTHER SURPRISES** Each year the news about ozone loss seems to get worse. Often it takes scientists by surprise. The first surprise came in 1985 when researchers discovered that 50% (98% in some areas) of the ozone in the upper stratosphere over the Antarctic region was being destroyed during the Antarctic spring and early summer (September–December)—something not predicted by computer models (Figure 11-8). Since then this seasonal Antarc-

tic *ozone hole*—or *ozone thinning*—has expanded in most years and in 1992 covered an area three times larger than the continental United States (Figure 11-9).

Measurements soon showed us what was happening. Each sunless winter steady winds blow in a circular pattern over Earth's poles, creating *polar vortices*—swirling masses of bitter-cold air that trap a huge mass of air inside for several months. When water droplets in clouds enter these large circling streams of frigid air, they form tiny ice crystals. The surfaces of these ice crystals collect CFCs and other ozone-depleting chemicals, enabling them to destroy ozone much faster. The return of sunlight two to three months later triggers a weeks-long orgy of ozone depletion before the vortex breaks up. Huge clumps of ozone-depleted air then flow northward and linger over parts of Australia, New Zealand, and the southern tips of South America and Africa for a few more weeks, raising UV levels in these areas as much as 20%.

In 1988 scientists discovered that a similar but much smaller ozone thinning forms over the North Pole during the arctic spring and early summer (February–June) with an annual ozone loss of 10–25%. When this mass of air breaks up each spring, clots of ozone-depleted air flow southward to linger over parts of Europe, North America, and Asia. Mostly because it flows alternately over land and water, the North Pole's annual polar vortex is weaker, less stable, and somewhat warmer than the South Pole's vortex and thus loses less ozone. However, in 1991 NASA reported another surprise: The stratospheric ozone shield over heavily populated regions of North America, Europe, and Asia had fallen to record lows, decreasing twice as fast as scientists had projected only a few years earlier.

The worst is still to come. Scientists estimate that ozone losses over northern mid-latitudes will be 10–30% as ozone-destroying chemicals already in the troposphere drift slowly into the stratosphere. In 1992 atmospheric scientists warned that if rising levels of

---

* For a fascinating account of how corporate stalling, politics, economics, and science interact, see Sharon Roan's *Ozone Crisis: The 15-Year Evolution of a Sudden Global Emergency* (New York: John Wiley, 1989).

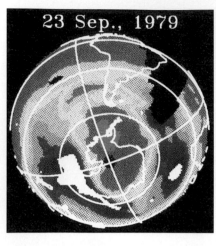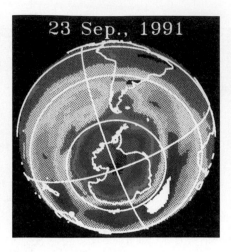

**Figure 11-9** Increase in the size of the seasonal ozone hole or area where the normal ozone concentration is cut at least by half (shown by shades of pink) in the upper stratosphere over the Antarctic region as measured by the Nimbus-7 satellite on September 23, 1979, 1991, and 1992. Since 1987 this area of thinning has been larger than the continental United States. In 1992—aided by sulfuric acid droplets formed as a result of the 1991 volcanic eruption of Mount Pinatubo (Figure 11-5)—the size of the hole increased to cover three times the area of the continental United States, and ozone levels above the South Pole fell to an all-time low.

greenhouse gases change the climate as projected over the next 50 years, this will alter the stratosphere over the Arctic so that it will experience severe ozone thinning like that now found over Antarctica.

**CONSEQUENCES: LIFE IN THE ULTRAVIOLET ZONE** Why should we care about ozone loss (see cartoon)? With less ozone in the stratosphere, more biologically harmful UV-B radiation will reach Earth's surface, giving us worse sunburns, earlier wrinkles,

more cataracts (a clouding of the eye lens that reduces vision and can cause blindness if not removed), and more skin cancers (Spotlight, p. 305).

Scientists estimate that a 10% drop in the average level of ozone in the stratosphere (likely within the next few decades and already happening part of the year in some places) would probably have the following effects:

- 300,000 more cases of basal-cell and squamous-cell cancers, 14,000 more malignant melanomas (leading

Q: How many of the world's plant species are edible?

## The Cancer You Are Most Likely to Get

Cases of skin cancer (Figure 11-10) and eye cataracts are soaring in Australia, New Zealand, South Africa, Argentina, and Chile, where the ozone layer is thin for several months after the mass of ozone-depleted air over the South Pole (Figure 11-9) breaks up and drifts northward.

Australian television stations now broadcast daily UV levels and warnings for fair-skinned Australians—with the world's highest rate of skin cancer—to stay inside during bad spells and to protect themselves from the sun's rays with hats, clothing, and sunscreens when they go out during daytime—required by law for school children. During their lifetime 2 of every 3 Australians will develop some kind of skin cancer, and 1 in 60 will be stricken with malignant melanoma.

In New Zealand school children are urged to wear hats and eat their lunches under the shade of trees. Chile, the only populous country located under the Antarctic ozone hole, has experienced a four-fold increase in malignant melanoma since 1980. Residents in southern Chile report seeing thousands of blind rabbits and sheep with cataracts. Levels of skin cancer and cataracts are also increasing rapidly in the United States. Some 600,000 Americans per year develop skin cancer, 90% because of overexposure to the sun.

Virtually anyone can get skin cancer, but those with fair and freckled skin, blonde or red hair, and light eye color run the highest risk. People who spend long hours in the sun or in tanning parlors (even more hazardous than direct sun) multiply their chances of developing skin cancer and having wrinkled, dry skin by age 40. Nor does a dark suntan prevent skin cancer. Dark-skinned people are almost immune to sunburn but do get skin cancer, although at a rate one-tenth that of Caucasians. Outdoor workers are particularly susceptible to skin cancer on the face, neck, hands, and arms.

Years of exposure to UV ionizing radiation in sunlight is the primary cause of basal-cell and squamous-cell skin cancers (Figures 11-10a and 11-10b),which make up 95% of all skin cancers. Typically there is a 20- to 30-year lag between UV exposure and development of these cancers. Caucasian children or adolescents who get only a single severe sunburn double their chances of getting these cancers.

Some 90–95% of these types of skin cancer can be cured if detected

(continued)

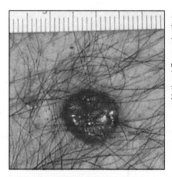

*National Cancer Institute*

**a** Basal-cell cancer

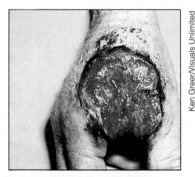

*Ken Greer/Visuals Unlimited*

**b** Squamous-cell cancer

*Ken Greer/Visuals Unlimited*

**c** Malignant melanoma

**Figure 11-10** Three types of skin cancer: **(a)** basal-cell cancer, **(b)** squamous-cell cancer, and **(c)** malignant melanoma. The incidence of these types of cancer is rising mostly because people are being exposed to more ultraviolet-B radiation as a result of depletion of the stratospheric ozone layer.

to 4,000 deaths), and 1.6 million more cataracts (many leading to blindness) each year worldwide as long as this level of depletion continued. The EPA estimates there will be 200,000 skin cancer deaths in the United States alone over the next 50 years.

- Suppression of the human immune system, which would reduce our defenses (regardless of skin pigmentation) against a variety of infectious diseases, an effect similar to that of HIV.

- An increase in eye-burning, highly damaging ozone, and acid deposition in the troposphere (Chapter 22). According to the EPA, each 1% loss of life-saving stratospheric ozone may cause a 0.7–2% gain in harmful ozone near the ground.

- Lower yields (about 1% for each 3% drop in stratospheric ozone) of vital crops such as corn, rice, soybeans, cotton, beans, peas, sorghum, and wheat, with losses totaling $2.5 billion per year

A: About 30,000

early enough, although their removal may leave disfiguring scars. (I have had three basal-cell cancers on my face because of "catching too many rays" in my younger years. I wish I had known then what I know now.)

Because melanoma spreads rapidly to other organs, it kills one-fifth of its victims (most under age 40) within five years despite surgery, chemotherapy, and radiation. Each year it kills about 100,000 people (including 7,000 Americans)—mostly Caucasian—but can often be cured if detected early enough. In the United States melanoma cases doubled between 1980 and 1990. It is now the most prevalent type of cancer among women ages 25–29. In 1980, 1 in 250 Americans developed melanoma. By 1991 the figure was 1 in 101, and by 2000 is projected to be 1 in 75.

Evidence suggests that people, especially Caucasians, who get three or more blistering sunburns before age 20 have five times more risk of contracting deadly malignant melanoma (Figure 11-10c) later in life than those who have never had severe sunburns. Other risk factors include a family history of the disease, being born with large brown moles, having irregular-shaped moles larger than a pencil

eraser, and exposure to radioactivity and certain chemicals (especially photographic chemicals).

To protect yourself, the safest course is to stay out of the sun and say no to tanning parlors. In other words, don't join the "bronzed age." Avoid direct sun between 10:00 A.M. and 3:00 P.M. when the sun's UV radiation is strongest. A beach umbrella can't fully protect you because sunlight is reflected from the sand. Clouds are deceptive because they let as much as 80% of the harmful UV radiation pass through.

When you are in the sun, wear tightly woven protective clothing (gauzy clothes and wet T-shirts don't protect you), a wide-brimmed hat, and sunglasses that protect against UV radiation (ordinary sunglasses may actually harm your eyes by dilating your pupils so that more UV radiation strikes the retina). Unfortunately, the world's poor people can't afford such glasses. People who take antibiotics or birth control pills are more susceptible to UV damage.

Apply sunscreen with a protection factor of 15 or more (25 if you have light skin) to all exposed skin, and reapply it after swimming or excessive perspiration. Children using a sunscreen with a protection

factor of 15 anytime they are in the sun from birth to age 18 decrease their chance of skin cancer by 80%. Babies under a year old should not be exposed to the sun at all. Before using a particular sunscreen, run a test patch to be sure that you are not allergic to its ingredients or that it doesn't have the reverse effect and amplify sun damage (something I recently learned the hard way). If you like the bronzed look, try some of the improved creams that give you a tanned appearance without spending long hours in the sun, but again, test them for any allergic reaction first.

Get to know your moles, and examine your skin surface at least once a month. The warning signs of skin cancer are a change in the size, shape, or color of a mole or wart (the major sign of malignant melanoma, which needs to be treated quickly), sudden appearance of dark spots on the skin, or a sore that keeps oozing, bleeding, and crusting over but does not heal. You should look out for precancerous growths—reddish-brown spots with a scaly crust. If you observe any of these signs, consult a doctor immediately. What are you doing to protect your skin and your life?

---

in the United States alone before the middle of the next century. Loblolly pine common in the southeastern United States is also sensitive to UV radiation.

■ Reduction in the growth of microscopic phytoplankton when UV-B radiation penetrates scores of meters below the surface of oceans. These tiny, floating producers form the base of ocean food chains and webs, and help remove $CO_2$ from the atmosphere.

■ A loss of perhaps $2 billion per year from degradation of paints, plastics, and other polymer materials in the United States alone.

In a worst-case scenario most people would have to avoid sun altogether (see cartoon and p. 290). Cattle could graze only at dusk. And farmers and other outdoor workers might measure their exposure to the sun in minutes.

In an ironic twist some air pollutants may decrease the amount of UV radiation reaching the surface and partly offset the effects of ozone depletion in urban areas of MDCs. Examples include sulfate aerosols from coal-burning power plants and ozone formed in smog. The presence of these dangerous chemicals in the troposphere may be the reason that the expected increase in UV radiation has not as yet been detected in urban areas in the United States and most other industrialized countries.

Q: How many plants feed most of the world's people?

"I MISS THE OZONE LAYER...."

## 11-5 Solutions: Protecting the Ozone Layer

**JUST SAY NO** We know what needs to be done: Stop producing any ozone-depleting chemicals now (global abstinence). After saying no, we will have to wait about 100 years for the ozone layer to return to 1985 levels and another 100–200 years for full recovery.

Substitutes are already available for most uses of CFCs, and others are being developed (Table 11-1, p.308, and Individuals Matter, right). CFCs in existing air conditioners, refrigerators, and other products must be recovered and in some cases reused until the substitutes are phased in.

HFCs and HCFCs may help ease the transition from CFCs for essential uses, but these chemicals themselves need to be banned as soon as possible—no later than 2005. Both categories contain greenhouse gases. And HCFCs contain some (but much less) chlorine and, if widely used, will still deplete ozone.

**CAN TECHNOFIXES SAVE US?** What about a quick fix from technology so we can keep on using CFCs? One suggestion is to collect the bad ozone at ground level over Los Angeles and other cities, and ship it up to the stratosphere. Unfortunately, even if we knew how to collect this dispersed and highly toxic ozone, it would take about 2½ times all of the energy used throughout the world every year from now on to do this. And just about as fast as we got the ozone there, our increased use of CFCs would start breaking much of it down.

Two atmospheric scientists have speculated that we might inject large quantities of ethane and propane into the stratosphere, where they might react with CFCs to remove the offending chlorine atoms. They estimate this would take only 1,000 jumbo-jet flights

**INDIVIDUALS MATTER**

## Ray Turner and His Refrigerator

Ray Turner, an aerospace manager at Hughes Aircraft in California, made an important low-tech, ozone-saving discovery by using his head—and his refrigerator. His concern for the environment led him to look for a cheap and simple substitute for the CFCs used as cleaning agents in the manufacture of most electronic circuit boards at his plant and elsewhere.

He started his search for a low-tech solution to a high-tech problem by looking in his refrigerator for a better circuit-board cleaner. He decided to put drops of various substances on a corroded penny to see whether any of them would remove the film of oxidation. Then he used his soldering gun to see if solder would stick to the cleaned surface of the penny, indicating that the film had been cleaned off.

First, he tried vinegar. No luck. Then he tried some ground-up lemon peel, also a failure. Next he tried a drop of lemon juice and watched as the solder took hold. The rest is history.

In the months that followed, Turner and a Hughes team perfected the technique, which is now used on several of the company's military projects. Other companies have also found substitutes for CFC cleaners, some of them citrus-based. AT&T, for example, is using a chemical found in cantaloupes, peaches, and plums to clean computer chips and circuit boards. But Turner's discovery was the first to meet the Department of Defense's rigid specifications for manufacturing military equipment. Since it was introduced, the new cleaning technique has reduced circuit-board defects by about 75% at Hughes. And Turner got a hefty bonus. Maybe you can find a solution to an environmental problem in your refrigerator.

over a critical 30-day period every year for several decades. But the scientists floating this possibility warn that the plan could backfire, accelerate ozone depletion, and have unpredictable effects on climate.

Others have suggested using tens of thousands of lasers to blast CFCs out of the atmosphere before they can reach the stratosphere. However, the energy requirements would be enormous and expensive, and decades of research would be needed to perfect the types of lasers needed—time we don't have. Also, no one knows the possible effects on climate, birds, planes, and whatever else might be there. Total abstinence is the only way, and the sooner the better.

**A:** 30 (mostly wheat, rice, corn, and potatoes)

## Table 11-1 CFC Substitutes

| Types | Pros | Cons |
|---|---|---|
| **HCFCs** (hydrochlorofluorocarbons) | Break down faster (2–20 years). Pose about 90% less danger to ozone layer. Can be used in aerosol sprays, refrigeration, air conditioning, foam, and cleaning agents. | Are greenhouse gases. Will still deplete ozone, especially if used in large quantities. Health effects largely unknown. HCFC-123 causes benign tumors in the pancreas and testes of male rats, and may be banned for use in aerosol sprays, foam, and cleaning agents. May lower energy efficiency of appliances. |
| **HFCs** (hydrofluorocarbons) | Break down faster (2–20 years). Do not contain ozone-destroying chlorine. Can be used in aerosol sprays, refrigeration, air conditioning, and foam. | Are greenhouse gases. Safety questions about flammability and toxicity still unresolved. May lower energy efficiency of appliances. Production of HFC-134a, a refrigerant substitute, yields an equal amount of methyl chloroform, a serious ozone depleter. |
| **Hydrocarbons** (such as propane and butane) | Cheap and readily available. Can be used in aerosol sprays, refrigeration, foam, and cleaning agents. | Can be flammable and poisonous. Some increase ground-level pollution. |
| **Ammonia** | Simple alternative for refrigerators; widely used before CFCs. | Toxic if inhaled. Must be handled carefully. |
| **Water and Steam** | Effective for some cleaning operations and for sterilizing medical instruments. | Creates polluted water that must be treated. Wastes water unless the used water is cleaned up and reused. |
| **Terpenes** (from the rinds of lemons and other citrus fruits) | Effective for cleaning electronic parts. | None. |
| **Helium** | Effective coolant for refrigerators, freezers, and air conditioners. | This rare gas may become scarce if use is widespread, but very little coolant is needed per appliance. |

**SOME SIGNS OF PROGRESS** The bright side is that some progress has been made since the surprise discovery of the Antarctic ozone hole. That event and public pressure forced political leaders in MDCs to begin taking action after over a decade of corporate stalling and political "foot dragging."

In 1987, 24 nations meeting in Montreal developed a treaty—commonly known as the Montreal Protocol—to cut emissions of CFCs (but not other ozone depleters) into the atmosphere by about 35% between 1989 and 2000. Meanwhile, some communities began thinking globally and acting locally (Solutions, p. 309).

In 1992, after more bad news about increased ozone thinning over much of the Northern Hemisphere in 1991, representatives of more than half the world's nations met in Copenhagen and agreed to **(1)** phase out production (except for essential uses) of CFCs, carbon tetrachloride, halons, HBFCs, and methyl chloroform by January 1996, **(2)** freeze consumption of HCFCs at 1991 levels and eliminate them by 2030, and **(3)** freeze methyl bromide production at 1991 levels by 1995.

The agreements reached so far are important symbols of global cooperation, but many scientists believe that they still do not go far enough fast enough and that we must expand and strengthen our efforts to provide environmental security (Guest Essay, p. 310). Meanwhile, we can respond to these global challenges by minimizing our individual impacts on the ozone layer (Individuals Matter, p. 309).

Some people have wondered whether there is intelligent life in other parts of the universe. Perhaps a better question at this point is whether there is intelligent life on Earth. If we can seriously deal with the interconnected planetary emergencies discussed in this chapter and the previous one, beginning *now*, then the answer is a hopeful yes. This means recognizing that *prevention* is the only safe (and in the long-run the least costly) way to deal with global environmental problems.

If we insist on decades more of discussion, research, denial, delay, and wasteful depletion of Earth's natural capital, however, the answer is a tragic no. We may even bring about extinction of our species—the first species, *Homo self-destructus*, to commit suicide—and take several million more species with us. The choice is ours. Not to decide is to decide.

Q: How much of Earth's land area is suitable for cultivation?

## Leadership by Newark, New Jersey

**SOLUTIONS**

In 1989 Newark, New Jersey, decided to do something about its contribution to ozone depletion by enacting an ordinance that:

- Prohibits the manufacture of any ozone-depleting chemical

- Requires refrigeration and air conditioner repair businesses to capture and reuse all CFCs

- Bans the retail sale of ozone-depleting coolants for refrigeration or air conditioning units

- Forbids the sale, purchase, or use of food-packaging materials made with any ozone-depleting substance

- Prohibits further use of building insulation containing any ozone-depleting chemicals

- Imposes up to $1,000 fines for each violation and for each day the ordinances are not complied with after a violator is cited

*The atmosphere is the key symbol of global interdependence. If we can't solve some of our problems in the face of threats to this global commons, then I can't be very optimistic about the future of the world.*

MARGARET MEAD

## Critical Thinking

1. What consumption patterns and other features of your lifestyle directly add greenhouse gases to the atmosphere? Which, if any, of those things would you be willing to give up to slow projected global warming and reduce other forms of air pollution?

2. Explain why you agree or disagree with each of the proposals for **(a)** slowing down emissions of greenhouse gases into the atmosphere listed in Section 11-3 and **(b)** adjusting to the effects of global warming listed in Section 11-2. Explain. What effects would carrying out these proposals have on your lifestyle and that of your descendants? What effects might not carrying out these actions have?

3. What consumption patterns and other features of your lifestyle directly and indirectly add ozone-depleting chemicals to the atmosphere? Which, if any, of those things would you be willing to give up to slow ozone depletion?

4. Should all uses of CFCs, halon, and other ozone-depleting chemicals be banned in the United States

## What You Can Do to Help Protect the Ozone Layer

**INDIVIDUALS MATTER**

- *Don't buy products containing CFCs, carbon tetrachloride, or methyl chloroform (1,1,1-trichloroethane on most ingredient labels). Read labels and seek out substitutes for these products. Write companies telling them why you are boycotting their products.*

- *Don't buy CFC-containing polystyrene foam insulation. Types of insulation that don't contain CFCs are extended polystyrene (commonly called EPS or beadboard), fiberglass, rock wool, cellulose, and perlite.*

- *Try to get your community to pass laws like Newark's (Solutions, left).*

- *Don't buy halon fire extinguishers. Instead, buy those using dry chemicals. If you already have a halon extinguisher, store it until a halon-reclaiming program is developed.*

- *Stop using all aerosol spray products, except in some necessary medical sprays. Even those not using CFCs and HCFCs (such as Dymel) emit hydrocarbons or other propellant chemicals into the air. Use roll-on and hand-pump products instead.*

- *Pressure legislators to ban all uses of CFCs, halons, methyl bromide, carbon tetrachloride, and methyl chloroform by 1995 (with no loopholes), and HCFCs by 2005 instead of by 2030.*

- *Pressure legislators not to exempt the military and space programs from any phaseout of ozone-depleting chemicals.*

- *Buy new refrigerators and freezers that use vacuum insulation (as in Thermos bottles) instead of rigid-foam insulation and that use helium as a coolant. (Such refrigerators are available from Cryodynamics, 1101 Bristol Road, Mountainside, NJ 07092. China has purchased 9 million of them.)*

- *If you junk a car, refrigerator, freezer, or air conditioner, make sure the coolant is removed and kept safely for reuse or destruction.*

- *Pressure legislators to require labels on all products containing or requiring CFCs, halon, or other ozone-depleting chemicals for their manufacture. Products using HCFCs should not be labeled as ozone or environmentally friendly.*

- *Have car and home air conditioners checked regularly for CFC leaks, and repair them.*

- *If you buy a car with an air conditioner, look for one that doesn't use CFCs. These should be available on some models in 1994 and on most models by 1995.*

- *Pressure legislators to establish a fund to help LDCs switch from ozone-depleting chemicals to safe substitutes.*

# Framing a Global Response to Environmental Threats

GUEST ESSAY

*Jessica Tuchman Mathews*

*Jessica Tuchman Mathews is currently vice president of the World Resources Institute, a highly respected center for policy research on global resource and environmental issues. Dr. Mathews has served as director of the Office of Global Issues on the President's National Security Council and on the editorial board of* The Washington Post. *In 1989 she published an influential article in* Foreign Affairs *calling for nations to redefine national security in terms of national and global environmental security.*

*National security* and *national sovereignty* must be redefined during the 1990s to accommodate new global environmental realities, just as they were redefined during the 1970s to accommodate global economic realities.

Intricately interconnected effects of the way we live—the buildup of greenhouse gases, the depletion of the ozone layer, and the loss of tropical forests and species—are shifting the center of gravity in international relations. These phenomena threaten national securities, defy solution by one or a few countries, and render national borders irrelevant. By definition, then, they pose a major challenge to national sovereignty.

One of the few clear things about the post–Cold–War era is that national security will increasingly depend on how resource, environmental, and demographic issues are resolved. It is no coincidence that control of Persian Gulf oil was central to this era's first international crisis.

Regional environmental decline is already threatening well-being and thereby political stability in many parts of the world. Eastern Europe's horrendous environmental degradation is undercutting attempts to rebuild its shattered economies. For instance, 95% of the water in Poland's rivers is unfit for human consumption, land is being withdrawn from cultivation because of contamination with toxic heavy metals, and air pollution causes heavy economic losses due to health costs and lost productivity. In LDCs natural resources such as farmland, forests, and fisheries are being ravaged while the number of people these resources must sustain is expected to grow by nearly 1 billion during the 1990s.

The fallout from global environmental trends goes far beyond economic and political arrangements. Unless the community of nations finds ways to reverse these trends, they will eventually shake not just the security of states but also the foundations of life. No one nation can succeed alone.

Dealing with the global environmental problems of tropical deforestation and species loss, climate change, and ozone depletion will require a rising level of collective international cooperation and management. Fortunately nations are beginning to act as though they understand their mutual interest in cooperation. The most spectacular demonstration of understanding was the agreement reached by 93 nations in 1990 and 1992 to phase out emissions of most ozone-destroying chemicals.

Turning this mutual interest into effective international management remains an elusive goal. Progress does not lie in a vain attempt to apply uniform environmental standards to nations whose members differ by 100-fold in per capita income and that have vastly different cultures, climates, religions, resources, and attitudes toward nature. Instead, it lies in institutional innovations as sweeping as those that inaugurated the post–World War II period.

The new international system must be designed to catalyze cooperation. Instead of the glacial pace required to negotiate treaties that set particular performance standards, we need fluid international processes that respond quickly to changes in scientific understanding and that set all nations moving in the same direction at whatever pace is realistic for each nation's circumstances.

Scientific theory and economic, political, and environmental concerns are all in a constant state of flux. Only a new institutional agility can keep international environmental governance closely attuned to these changing realities and ensure the best possible outcome.

## Critical Thinking

1. Do you agree that national security and national sovereignty must be redefined to include national and global environmental security? Explain.

2. What changes in the current interactions between nations do you believe must be made to catalyze international cooperation on global environmental problems? How would you bring about these changes?

and worldwide? Explain. Suppose this meant that air conditioning (especially in cars and perhaps in buildings) had to be banned or became five times as expensive. Would you still support such a ban?

5. In 1989 U.S. Senator (now Vice President) Albert Gore introduced a legislative package he calls the Strategic Environment Initiative (SEI), a worldwide program that would discourage and phase out older, inappropriate technologies, and replace them with a new generation of more environmentally benign technologies in MDCs and LDCs. The emphasis would be on improved energy efficiency, development of alternative fuels and energy sources based on solar energy, reforestation, comprehensive recycling and reuse, sustainable agriculture, and elimination of ozone-depleting chemicals. Do you support such a bill? What provisions, if any, would you add? What has happened to this proposal since it was first introduced in 1989?

*Our entire society rests upon—and is dependent upon—our water, our land, our forests, and our minerals. How we use these resources influences our health, security, economy, and well-being.*

JOHN F. KENNEDY

# 12 Soil Resources

## The Dust Bowl: Will It Happen Again?

Windy and dry, the vast grasslands of the Great Plains stretch across 10 states, from Texas through Montana and the Dakotas. Before settlers began grazing livestock and planting crops there in the 1870s, the deep and tangled root systems of native prairie grasses anchored the fertile topsoil in place. Plowing the prairie soil tore up these roots, and the agricultural crops planted annually in their place have less extensive root systems.

After each harvest the land was plowed and left bare for several months, exposing it to the fierce wind. Overgrazing also destroyed large expanses of grass, denuding the ground. The stage was set for severe wind erosion and crop failure, needing only a long drought to raise the curtain.

Such a drought arrived, lasting from 1926 to 1934. In the 1930s dust clouds created by hot, dry windstorms darkened the sky at midday in some areas (Figure 12-1). Rabbits and birds choked to death on the dust. During May 1934 a cloud of topsoil blown off the Great Plains blanketed the eastern United States as far as 2,400 kilometers (1,500 miles) away. Ships 322 kilometers (200 miles) in the Atlantic Ocean were dusted with midwestern topsoil. Journalists began calling the Great Plains the Dust Bowl (Figure 12-2).

Cropland equal in area to Connecticut and Maryland combined was stripped of topsoil, and an area the size of New Mexico was severely eroded. Thousands of displaced farm families from Oklahoma, Texas, Kansas, and other states migrated to California or to the industrial cities of the Midwest and East. Most found no jobs because the country was in the midst of the Great Depression.

In May 1934 Hugh Bennett of the U.S. Department of Agriculture (USDA) was pleading before a congressional hearing in Washington for new programs to protect the country's topsoil. Lawmakers took action when Great Plains dust began seeping into the hearing room.

Western History Collection, University of Oklahoma

**Figure 12-1** A daytime dust storm over Baca County, Colorado, in 1936 brought total darkness for half an hour.

In 1935 the United States established the Soil Conservation Service (SCS) under the Department of Agriculture. With Bennett as its first head, the SCS began promoting good conservation practices, first in the Great Plains states and later in every state. Soil conservation districts were formed throughout the country, and farmers and ranchers were given technical assistance in setting up soil conservation programs. But even these efforts could not stop human-accelerated erosion in the Great Plains. The basic problem is that much of the region is better suited for moderate grazing than for farming.

In 1975 the Council of Agricultural Science and Technology warned that severe drought could again create a dust bowl in the Great Plains. So far those warnings have been ignored. Depletion of groundwater in the Ogallala aquifer underlying the Great Plains (Figure 13-18) also threatens farming and ranching in parts of the Dust Bowl area. With global warming the region would become even drier and farming would have to be abandoned.

Unless you are a farmer, you probably think of soil as dirt—something you don't want on your hands, clothes, or carpet. However, your life and the lives of other organisms depend on soil, especially topsoil. Yet since the beginning of agriculture we have abused this vital, potentially renewable resource. Entire civilizations have collapsed because they mismanaged the topsoil that supported their populations.

Today we are abusing soil more than ever. Unless we protect this life-giving resource, Dust Bowl days may come again.

**Figure 12-2** The Dust Bowl of the Great Plains, where a combination of periodic severe droughts and poor soil conservation practices led to severe erosion of topsoil by wind in the 1930s.

The discussion in this chapter answers the following questions:

- What is soil, and what types are best for growing crops?
- Why should we worry about soil erosion?
- How can we control erosion and stop losing nutrients from topsoil?
- How is soil degraded by excessive salt buildup (salinization) and waterlogging?

##  12-1   What Is Soil?

**SOIL LAYERS AND COMPONENTS**   Pick up a handful of soil and notice how it feels and looks. **Soil** is a complex mixture of inorganic materials (clay, silt, pebbles, and sand), decaying organic matter, water, air, and billions of living organisms. Soil forms when life forms decay, when solid rock weathers and crumbles (Figure 7-9), and when sediments are deposited by erosion (Figure 12-3).

Mature soils are arranged in a series of zones called **soil horizons**, each with a distinct texture and composition that varies with different types of soils. A cross-sectional view of the horizons in a soil is called a **soil profile**. Most mature soils have at least three of the possible horizons (Figure 12-3).

The top layer, the *surface-litter layer* or *O-horizon*, consists mostly of freshly fallen and partially decomposed leaves, twigs, animal waste, fungi, and other organic materials. Normally it is brown or black in color. The *topsoil layer*, or *A-horizon*, is a porous mixture of partially decomposed organic matter (humus) and some inorganic mineral particles. Usually it is darker and looser than deeper layers. The roots of most plants and most of a soil's organic matter are concentrated in these two upper layers. As long as these layers are anchored by vegetation, soil stores water and releases it in a nourishing trickle instead of a devastating flood.

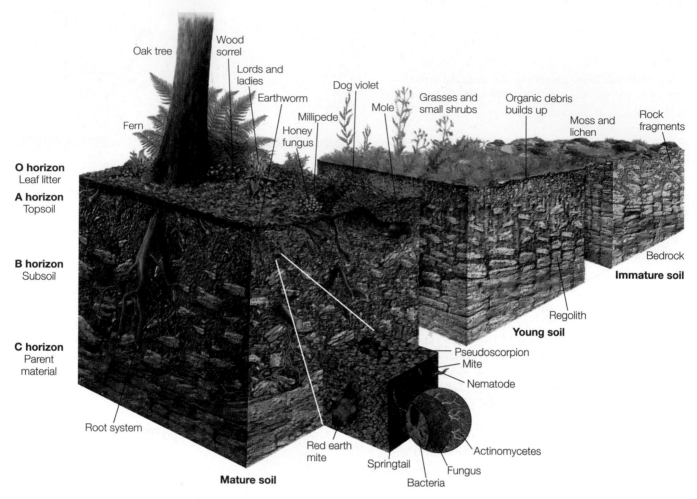

**Figure 12-3** Formation and generalized profile of soils. Horizons, or layers, vary in number, composition, and thickness, depending on the type of soil. (Adapted by permission of Macmillan Publishing Company from Derek Elsom, *Earth*, New York: Macmillan, 1992. Copyright © 1992 by Marshall Editions Developments Limited.)

The two top layers of most well-developed soils teem with bacteria, fungi, earthworms, and small insects (Figure 12-3). These layers are also home for burrowing animals such as moles and gophers. These soil dwellers interact in complex food webs (Figure 12-4).

Bacteria and other decomposer microorganisms are found by the billions in every handful of topsoil. They recycle the nutrients we and other organisms need by breaking down complex organic compounds in the upper soil layers into simpler inorganic compounds soluble in soil water. Soil moisture carrying these dissolved nutrients is drawn up by the roots of plants and transported through stems and into leaves (Figure 12-5).

Some organic litter in the two top layers is broken down into a sticky, brown residue of partially decomposed organic material called **humus**. Because humus is only slightly soluble in water, most of it stays in the topsoil layer. A fertile soil, producing high crop yields, has a thick topsoil layer with lots of humus.

Humus is an important soil material. It coats the sand, silt, and clay particles in topsoil and binds them together into clumps, giving a soil its *structure*. Humus also helps topsoil hold water and nutrients taken up by plant roots. Particles of humus and of clay tend to have a negative electrical charge on their surfaces. This allows them to attract positively charged nutrient ions such as potassium ($K^+$), calcium ($Ca^{2+}$), and ammonium ($NH_4^+$) strongly enough to keep them from being carried away as rainwater percolates downward through the topsoil.

Humus also provides spaces for the growth of nutrient-absorbing root hairs and a class of fungi, known as mycorrhizae, that are the mutualistic partners of some trees and other plants (Spotlight, p. 283).

Color tells us a lot about how useful a soil is for growing crops. For example, dark-brown or black topsoil is nitrogen-rich and high in organic matter. Gray, bright yellow, or red topsoils are low in organic matter and will need nitrogen fertilizer to support most crops.

**Q:** How much of the world's food is produced on irrigated cropland?

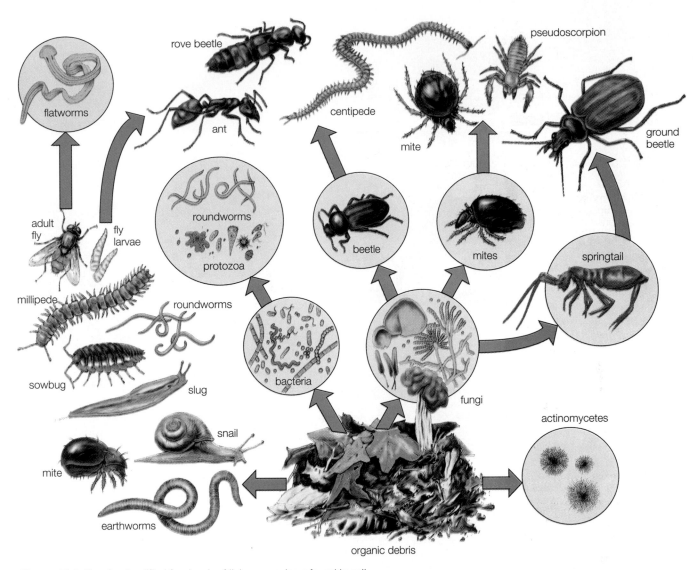

**Figure 12-4** Greatly simplified food web of living organisms found in soil.

The *B-horizon (subsoil)* and the *C-horizon (parent material)* contain most of a soil's inorganic matter. It is mostly broken-down rock, a varying mixture of sand, silt, clay, and gravel. The C-horizon lies on a base of unweathered parent rock called bed rock.

The spaces, or pores, between the solid organic and inorganic particles in the upper and lower soil layers contain varying amounts of air (mostly nitrogen and oxygen gas) and water. Plant roots need oxygen, concentrated in the topsoil, for respiration in their cells.

Some of the rain falling on the soil percolates through the soil layers and occupies many of the pores. This downward movement of water through soil is called **infiltration**. As the water seeps down, it dissolves and picks up various soil components in upper layers and carries them to lower layers—a process called **leaching**.

**SOIL TYPES** Soils develop and mature slowly (Figure 12-3). One maturation process is **humification**—in which organic matter in the upper soil layers becomes humus. In lower layers a soil matures through **mineralization**, in which decomposers turn organic materials into inorganic ones.

Mature soils vary widely from biome to biome in color, content, pore space, acidity (pH), and depth. Five important soil types or orders, each with a distinct profile, are shown in Figure 12-6. Most of the world's crops are grown on soils exposed when grasslands (Figure 5-21) and deciduous forests (Figure 5-24) are cleared.

**SOIL TEXTURE AND POROSITY** Soils vary in their content of *clay* (very fine particles), *silt* (fine particles), *sand* (medium-size particles), and *gravel* (coarse

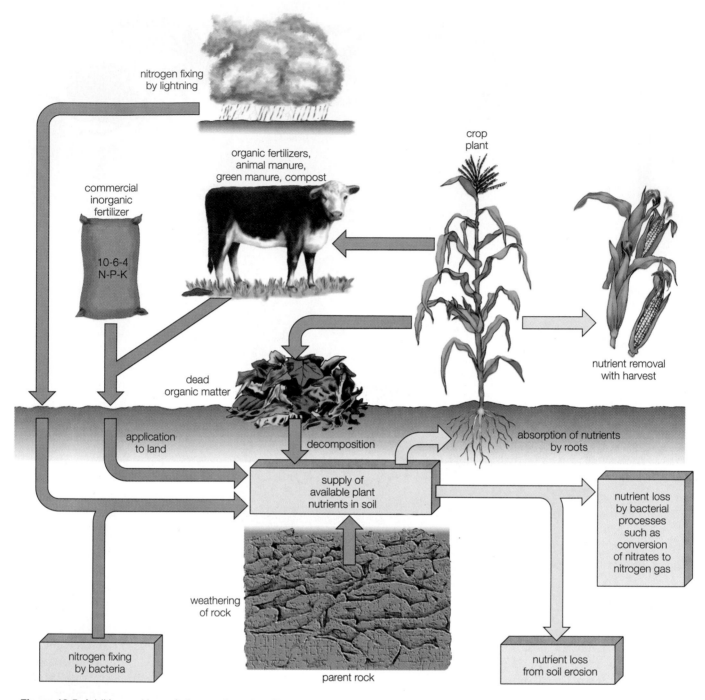

**Figure 12-5** Addition and loss of plant nutrients in soils.

to very coarse particles). The relative amounts of the different sizes and types of mineral particles determine **soil texture**. Figure 12-7 groups soils into textural classes according to clay, silt, and sand content. Soils containing a mixture of clay, sand, silt, and humus are called **loams**.

To get an idea of a soil's texture, take a small amount of topsoil, moisten it, and rub it between your fingers and thumb. A gritty feel means that it contains a lot of sand. A sticky feel means a high clay content, and you should be able to roll it into a clump. Silt-

laden soil feels smooth like flour. A loam topsoil, best suited for plant growth, has a texture between these extremes—a crumbly, spongy feeling with many of its particles clumped loosely together.

Soil texture helps determine **soil porosity**: a measure of the volume of pores or spaces per volume of soil and the average distances between those spaces. Typically 40–60% of the volume of soil consists of pore spaces that allow air and water to travel through the soil. A porous soil (with many pores) can hold more water and air than a less porous soil. The average size

**Q:** What percentage of Americans live on farms?

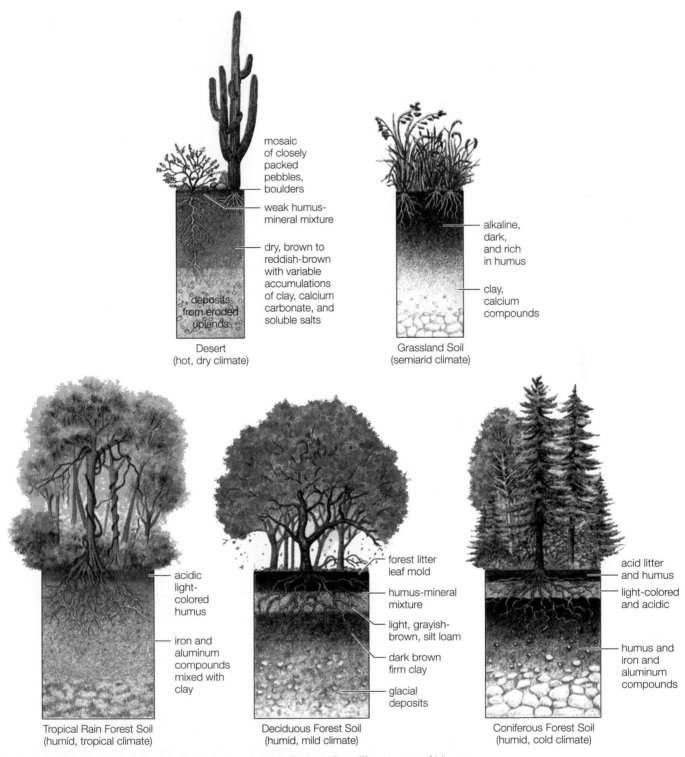

**mosaic of closely packed pebbles, boulders**

**weak humus-mineral mixture**

**dry, brown to reddish-brown with variable accumulations of clay, calcium carbonate, and soluble salts**

deposits from eroded uplands

Desert
(hot, dry climate)

**alkaline, dark, and rich in humus**

**clay, calcium compounds**

Grassland Soil
(semiarid climate)

**acidic light-colored humus**

**iron and aluminum compounds mixed with clay**

Tropical Rain Forest Soil
(humid, tropical climate)

**forest litter leaf mold**

**humus-mineral mixture**

**light, grayish-brown, silt loam**

**dark brown firm clay**

**glacial deposits**

Deciduous Forest Soil
(humid, mild climate)

**acid litter and humus**

**light-colored and acidic**

**humus and iron and aluminum compounds**

Coniferous Forest Soil
(humid, cold climate)

**Figure 12-6** Soil profiles of the principal soil types typically found in five different types of biomes.

of the spaces or pores in a soil determines **soil permeability**: the rate at which water and air move from upper to lower soil layers. Soil porosity is also influenced by **soil structure**: how the soil particles are organized and clumped together.

Soil texture, porosity, and permeability determine a soil's *water-holding capacity*, *aeration* or *oxygen content* (the ability of air to move through the soil), and *workability* (how easily it can be cultivated). Table 12-1 compares the main physical and chemical properties of sand, clay, silt, and loam soils.

Loams are the best soils for growing most crops because they hold lots of water but not too tightly for plant roots to absorb. Sandy soils are easy to work, but water flows through them rapidly because their pores are larger than those in most other soils. They are useful for growing irrigated crops or those with low water requirements, such as peanuts and strawberries.

The particles in clay soils are very small and easily compacted. When these soils get wet, they form large, dense clumps, explaining why wet clay can be molded into bricks and pottery. Clay soils are more porous and have a greater water-holding capacity than sandy soils, but the pore spaces are so small that these soils have a low permeability. Because little water can infiltrate to lower levels, the upper layers can easily become too waterlogged for most crops.

## SOIL ACIDITY (pH)
The acidity or basicity (alkalinity) of a soil is another factor determining the types of plants it can support. Acidity and basicity of substances in water solution are commonly expressed in terms of **pH** (Figure 12-8).

Soils vary in acidity, and the pH of a soil influences the uptake of soil nutrients by plants. Plants vary in the pH ranges they can tolerate. For example, wheat, spinach, peas, corn, and tomatoes grow best in slightly acidic soils; potatoes, berries, watermelons, azaleas, rhododendrons, chrysanthemums, and marigolds do best in very acidic soils; alfalfa and asparagus do best in neutral soils; and beans, beets, cabbage,

| Table 12-1 Useful Properties of Soils with Different Textures | | | | | |
|---|---|---|---|---|---|
| | Nutrient-Holding Capacity | Water Infiltration | Water-Holding Capacity | Aeration | Workability |
| **Clay** | Good | Poor | Good | Poor | Poor |
| **Silt** | Medium | Medium | Medium | Medium | Medium |
| **Sand** | Poor | Good | Poor | Good | Good |
| **Loam** | Medium | Medium | Medium | Medium | Medium |

**Figure 12-7** Soil texture depends on the percentages of clay, silt, and sand particles in the soil. Soil texture affects soil porosity—the average number and spacing of pores in a volume of soil. Loams— roughly equal mixtures of clay, sand, silt, and humus—are the best soils for growing most crops. (Data from Soil Conservation Service)

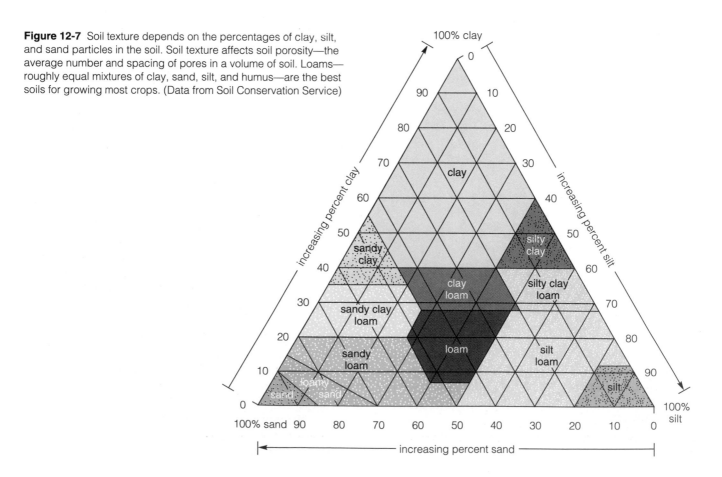

**Q:** In terms of total sales, what is the biggest U.S. industry?

cantaloupe, cauliflower, lettuce, onions, peas, squash, and irises do well in slightly alkaline soils.

When soils are too acidic, the acids can be partially neutralized by an alkaline substance such as lime. Because lime speeds up the decomposition of organic matter in the soil, however, manure or another organic fertilizer should also be added to maintain soil fertility.

In dry regions such as much of the western and southwestern United States, calcium and other alkaline compounds are not leached away by rain. Soils in such areas may be too alkaline (pH above 7.5) for some crops. If drainage is good irrigation can leach the alkaline compounds away. Adding sulfur, which is gradually converted into sulfuric acid by soil bacteria, also reduces soil alkalinity.

The burning of fossil fuels, especially coal, releases sulfur dioxide and nitrogen oxides, which form acidic compounds in the atmosphere. These compounds fall back to the earth as *acid deposition* (Section 22-2). As acidic rain or melted acidic snow infiltrates the soil, the hydrogen ions ($H^+$) in the acids are attracted to particles of minerals and humus in the topsoil layer, displacing some of the potassium ($K^+$), calcium ($Ca^{2+}$), magnesium ($Mg^{2+}$), and ammonium ($NH_4^+$) ions that were attached to those particles. The resulting loss in soil fertility can reduce crop and tree growth, and make them more vulnerable to drought, disease, and pests.

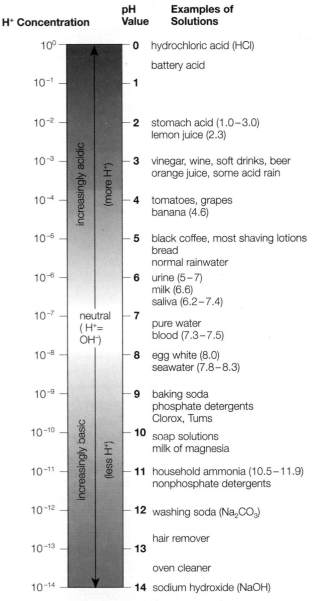

**Figure 12-8** The pH scale, used to measure acidity and alkalinity of water solutions. Values shown are approximate. A neutral solution has a pH of 7; one with a pH greater than 7 is basic, or alkaline; and one with a pH less than 7 is acidic. The lower the pH below 7, the more acidic the solution. Each whole-number drop in pH represents a 10-fold increase in acidity.

## 12-2 Soil Erosion

**NATURAL AND HUMAN-ACCELERATED EROSION** **Soil erosion** is the movement of soil components, especially surface-litter and topsoil, from one place to another. The two main movers are flowing water (Figure 12-9) and wind (Figures 5-1 and 12-1). Some soil erosion is natural (Section 7-2), but the roots of plants generally anchor the soil. In undisturbed vegetated ecosystems soil is not usually lost faster than it forms. However, farming, logging, building, overgrazing by livestock, four-wheeling off-road, and other

**Figure 12-9** Rill and gully erosion of vital topsoil from irrigated cropland in Arizona.

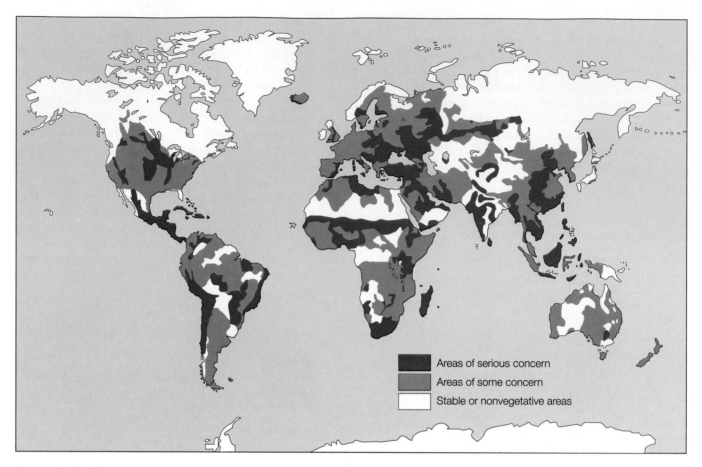

| | |
|---|---|
| ■ | Areas of serious concern |
| ▨ | Areas of some concern |
| □ | Stable or nonvegetative areas |

**Figure 12-10** Global soil erosion. (Data from World Resources Institute)

human activities that destroy plant cover leave the soil vulnerable to erosion.

Although wind causes some erosion, most is caused by moving water. Soil scientists distinguish three types of water erosion. **Sheet erosion** occurs when surface water moves down a slope or across a field in a wide flow and peels off uniform sheets, or layers, of soil. Because the topsoil disappears evenly, sheet erosion may not be noticeable until much damage has been done. In **rill erosion** the surface water forms fast-flowing little rivulets that cut small channels in the soil (Figure 12-9). In **gully erosion** rivulets of fast-flowing water join together and with each succeeding rain cut the channels wider and deeper until they become ditches or gullies (Figure 12-9). Gully erosion usually happens on steep slopes where all or most of the vegetation has been removed (Figure 1-3).

Losing topsoil makes a soil less fertile and less able to hold water. The resulting sediment, the largest source of water pollution, clogs irrigation ditches, boat channels, reservoirs, and lakes. Fish die. Water is cloudy and tastes bad. Flood risk increases. Rivers running brown with silt show Earth capital hemorrhaging away from the land (Figure 5-30).

Soil, especially topsoil, is classified as a renewable resource because it is continuously regenerated by natural processes. However, in tropical and temperate areas it takes 200–1,000 years for 2.54 centimeters (1 inch) of new topsoil to form, depending on climate and soil type. If topsoil erodes faster than it forms on a piece of land, the soil there becomes a nonrenewable resource. Annual erosion rates for farmland throughout the world are 20–100 times the natural renewal rate (Guest Essay, p. 332). Soil erosion is milder on forestland and rangeland than on cropland, but forest soil takes two to three times longer to restore itself than does cropland. Construction sites usually have the highest erosion rates by far.

**THE WORLD SITUATION** Today topsoil is eroding faster than it forms on about one-third of the world's cropland (Figure 12-10). In some countries more than half the land is affected, including Nepal (95%), Peru (95%), Turkey (95%), Lesotho (88%), Madagascar (79%), and Ethiopia (53%). In Africa soil erosion has increased 20-fold in the last three decades. A 1992 study by the World Resources Institute found that soil on more than 12 million square kilometers (5 million

**Q:** How many people on average does one U.S. farmer feed?

**Figure 12-11** Terracing of rice fields in Bali, Indonesia, reduces soil erosion. Terraces also increase the amount of land that can be used to grow crops on steep slopes, even mountainsides.

square miles) of land—an area the size of China and India combined—had been seriously eroded since 1945 (Figure 12-10). It also found that 89,000 square kilometers (34,000 square miles) of land scattered across the globe was too eroded to grow crops anymore.

Two-thirds of the seriously degraded lands are in Asia and Africa; Central America and the United States have each lost 25% of their productive cropland. Overgrazing is the worst culprit, accounting for 35% of the damage, with the heaviest losses in Africa and Australia. Deforestation causes 30% of Earth's severely eroded land and is most prevalent in Asia and South America (Figures 10-3 and 10-4). Unsustainable methods of farming account for 28% of such erosion, with two-thirds of the damage found in North America.

Each year we must feed 94 million more people with 24 billion metric tons (26 billion tons) less topsoil. This topsoil washing and blowing into the world's streams, lakes, and oceans each year would fill a train of freight cars long enough to encircle the planet 150 times. At that rate the world is losing about 7% of its topsoil from potential cropland each de-

cade—a serious problem for farmers and eventually for all of us. The situation is worsening as farmers in MDCs and LDCs plow marginal lands to feed themselves. But erosion is only the most obvious damage. Overcultivating robs the soil of nitrogen, phosphorus, and potassium (Figure 12-5).

In mountainous areas, such as the Himalaya on the border between India and Tibet, and the Andes near the west coast of South America, farmers have traditionally built elaborate systems of terraces (Figure 12-11). Terracing allowed them to cultivate steeply sloping land that would otherwise quickly lose its topsoil.

Today, however, some of these slopes are being farmed without terraces, leaving the soil too poor after 10–40 years to grow crops or generate new forest. Although most poor farmers know the risks of not terracing, many have too little time and too few workers to build terraces. They must plant crops or starve. The resultant loss of protective vegetation and topsoil also greatly intensifies flooding below these watersheds, as in Bangladesh (Case Study, p. 340).

For thousands of years people in tropical forests have successfully used shifting slash-and-burn

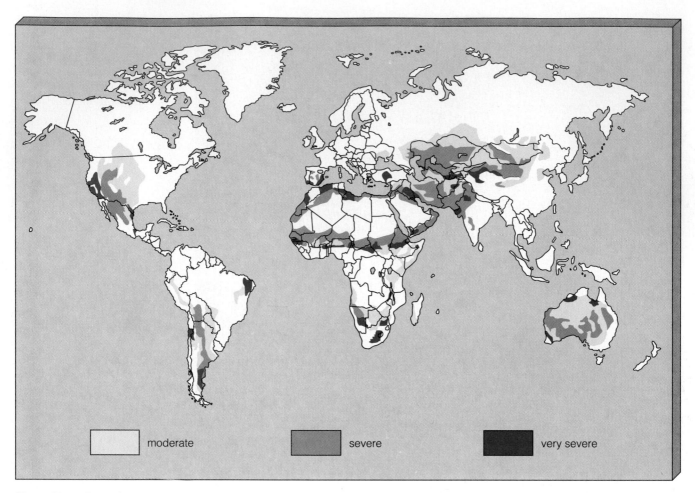

**Figure 12-12** Desertification of arid and semiarid lands. (Data from UN Environmental Programme and Harold E. Dregnue)

cultivation (Figure 2-6) to feed their small populations. In recent decades, however, growing population, mostly from forest immigrants, and poverty have forced many such farmers to reduce the fallow period of their fields to as little as 2 years, instead of the 10–30 years needed for the soil to regain its fertility. The result has been vanishing topsoil and soil nutrients.

Once-forested hills in many LDCs, such as Madagascar (Case Study, p. 265), have been stripped of trees by poor people for local fuelwood and timber exports. Because new trees are seldom planted in LDCs, the topsoil quickly washes away (Figure 5-30).

In MDCs many farmers have replaced traditional soil conservation practices with commercial inorganic fertilizers and irrigation water. However, a 10-fold increase in fertilizer use and a tripling of irrigated cropland between 1950 and 1992 have only temporarily masked the effects of erosion and nutrient depletion. For one thing, commercial inorganic fertilizer is not a complete substitute for naturally fertile topsoil. For another, irrigation is not a long-term solution. Soil

irrigated for years on end without sufficient drainage eventually becomes too waterlogged and salty to grow crops. Even with good drainage repeated irrigation leaches nutrients out of the soil.

**SPREADING DESERTIFICATION** Desertification is a process whereby the productive potential of arid or semiarid land falls by 10% or more and is caused mostly by human activities. *Moderate desertification* is a 10–25% drop in productivity, and *severe desertification* is a 25–50% drop. *Very severe desertification* is a drop of 50% or more, usually creating huge gullies and sand dunes.

Desertification is a serious and growing problem in many parts of the world (Figure 12-12). The regions most affected by desertification are all cattle-producing areas and include sub-Saharan Africa (between North Africa's barren Sahara and the plant-rich land to its south), the Middle East, western Asia, parts of Central and South America, the western half of the United States, and Australia (Case Study, p. 323).

**Q:** How much of the world's food and fiber are produced by U.S. farmers?

Within 200 years after English settlers arrived in Australia in the eighteenth century, they had destroyed most of the country's forest cover, eliminated or endangered 70% of its mammal species, caused widespread erosion and salting of the soil leading to desertification throughout much of the country (Figure 12-13), and decimated the once-sizable aboriginal population. Today 160 million sheep, 14% of the world's sheep population, overgraze much of the land. Topsoil is eroding 50 times faster than it did prior to 1788.

In 1859 Thomas Austin, longing for home pastimes, imported and released 24 English rabbits into the Australian countryside for hunting. Without any natural enemies the rabbits multiplied so rapidly that within 10 years they numbered in the millions, and like hordes of locusts they began munching their way across the continent. They ate crops, competed with livestock for grass, and destroyed wild vegetation, displacing and endangering many native animal species.

Australians tried without success to contain this plague of rabbits until the 1950s when they introduced a virus that killed off 99% of the rabbits. Now, however, the rabbits are back. Through natural selection the remaining 1% became resistant to the virus, began multiplying, and now number more than 200 million, causing about $75 million in damages per year to grazing land.

Farmers and ranchers attack the rabbits with guns, dogs, poison, and dynamite, but they keep multiplying. Australian scientists are using genetic engineering in a desperate attempt to develop stronger viruses before the country is again overrun.

In the 1930s someone came up with the bright idea of importing the South American cane toad to help control beetles that were devastating the sugarcane crop. Unfortunately the plump 0.5-kilogram (1-pound) toads stayed on the ground while the sugarcane beetles flew above, so they never met. Then the toads began multiplying. They now occupy 40% of Queensland and are moving into New South Wales and the Northern Territory. The poisonous toads are almost impossible to kill. Toads that are shot recover and hop away. The ones that are run over by a car simply swallow their squashed guts and limp away.

Even while introducing alien species, Australians also have been trying to kill off one of their most famous natives—the kangaroo. These animals are hated by farmers who claim they damage crops and by ranchers because they compete for forage with cattle and other livestock. Kangaroos are often hunted at night by truckloads of hunters armed with spotlights and automatic weapons. The skin and meat of these animals is used to make pet food, gold bags, handbags, and athletic shoes.

Australians are now trying to reverse some of the consequences of their centuries of destruction and thoughtless introductions of alien species. The government has abolished tax advantages for clearing land and replaced them with incentives for planting trees, preferably the native species they destroyed. They have a daunting task.

**Figure 12-13** Desertification in this arid outback region of Australia was caused by cattle overgrazing the vegetation. Livestock cropped plants so short that the vegetation died; trampling kept new seedlings from growing. Overgrazing is the biggest cause of desertification.

Greg Fyfe/Australasian Nature Transparencies

Moderate desertification can go unrecognized. For example, overgrazing has reduced the productivity of much of the grassland in the western United States. Yet most of the residents do not realize they live in a moderately desertified area.

Practices that leave topsoil vulnerable to erosion and drying include overgrazing (Figure 12-13); deforestation without reforestation (Figure 10-15); surface mining without land reclamation (Figures 7-22 and 10-16); irrigation techniques that lead to increased erosion, salt buildup, and waterlogged soil; farming on land with unsuitable terrain or soils; and soil compaction by farm machinery, cattle hoofs, and the impact of raindrops on denuded soil surfaces.

These destructive practices are linked to rapid population growth, high human and livestock densities, poverty, and poor land management. The consequences of desertification include worsening drought, famine, declining living standards, and swelling numbers of environmental refugees whose land is too eroded to grow crops or feed livestock.

It is estimated that 810 million hectares (2 billion acres)—an area the size of Brazil and 12 times the size of Texas—have become desertified during the past 50 years. The United Nations Environment Programme estimates that worldwide 63% of rangelands, 60% of rain-fed croplands, and 30% of irrigated croplands are threatened by desertification. The total area of this threatened land is 33 million square kilometers (13 million square miles)—about the size of North and South America combined. If present trends continue, desertification could threaten the livelihoods of 1.2 billion people by 2000.

Every year an estimated 60,000 square kilometers (23,000 square miles)—an area the size of West Virginia—of new desert are formed, and another 210,000 square kilometers (81,000 square miles)—an area the size of Kansas—lose so much topsoil and fertility that they are no longer able to be used for farming or grazing.

The most effective way to slow the march of desertification is to drastically reduce overgrazing, deforestation (Section 10-4), and destructive forms of planting, irrigation, and mining. In addition, reforestation will anchor the soil and hold water while providing fuelwood, slowing desertification, and reducing the threat of global warming.

The total cost of such prevention and rehabilitation would be about $141 billion, only 3½ times the estimated $42 billion annual loss in agricultural productivity from desertified land. Thus, once this potential productivity is restored, the cost of the program could be recouped in 3–4 years. So far, however, little has been done; only about one-tenth of the needed money has been provided.

**THE U.S. SITUATION** Vanishing topsoil and creeping desertification have become serious problems in parts of the United States (Figures 12-10 and 12-12). According to the Soil Conservation Service about one-third of the nation's original prime topsoil has been washed or blown into streams, lakes, and oceans, mostly as a result of overcultivation, overgrazing, and deforestation.

Soil on cultivated land in the United States is eroding about 16 times faster than it can form. And erosion rates are even higher in heavily farmed regions such as the Great Plains, which has lost one-third or more of its topsoil in the 150 years since it was first plowed. Parts of the western rangelands and the Great Plains are rapidly becoming deserts from overcultivation, overgrazing, and depletion of groundwater used for irrigation—a new Dust Bowl waiting to happen (Figure 12-2). Some of the country's most productive agricultural lands, such as those in Iowa, have lost about half their topsoil. California's soil is eroding 80 times faster than it can be formed.

Enough topsoil erodes away each day in the United States to fill a line of dump trucks 5,600 kilometers (3,500 miles) long. About 86% of it comes from land used to graze cattle or to raise crops to feed cattle. Each 0.5-kilogram (1-pound) steak produced by a feedlot steer causes about 16 kilograms (35 pounds) of eroded soil. The other 14% of eroded soil comes from land used to raise crops for human consumption. David Pimentel (Guest Essay, p. 332) estimates that the direct and indirect costs of soil erosion and runoff in the United States exceed $25 billion per year—an average loss of $2.9 million per hour!

Of the world's major food-producing countries, only the United States is reducing some of its soil losses. Even so, effective soil conservation is practiced on only about half of all U.S. agricultural land and on less than half of the most erodible cropland.

## 12-3   Saving the Soil

**CONSERVATION TILLAGE** Soil conservation involves reducing soil erosion, preventing depletion of soil nutrients, and restoring nutrients already lost by erosion, leaching, and overcropping (Figure 12-5). Most methods used to control soil erosion involve keeping the soil covered with vegetation.

In **conventional-tillage farming** the land is plowed and the soil is broken up and smoothed to make a

Q: What percentage of U.S. commercial energy is consumed by the agricultural system?

Soil Conservation Service

**Figure 12-14** Contoured rows planted with alternating crops (strip cropping) to reduce soil erosion on gently sloping land in Illinois.

planting surface. In areas such as the midwestern United States harsh winters prevent plowing just before the spring growing season. Thus cropfields are often plowed in the fall. This bares the soil during the winter and early spring months, leaving it vulnerable to erosion.

To lower labor costs, save energy, and reduce erosion, many U.S. farmers are trying **conservation-tillage farming** (or *minimum-tillage* or *no-till farming*). The idea is to disturb the soil as little as possible in planting crops. With minimum tillage special tillers break up and loosen the subsurface soil without turning over the topsoil, previous crop residues, and any cover vegetation. In no-till farming special planting machines inject seeds, fertilizers, and weed-killers (herbicides) into slits made in the unplowed soil.

Besides reducing soil erosion conservation tillage saves fuel, cuts costs, holds more water in the soil, keeps the soil from getting packed down, and allows more crops to be grown during a season (multiple cropping). Yields are at least as high as those from conventional tillage. Depending on the soil type this approach can be used for three to seven years before crop yields decline. At first, conservation tillage was thought to require more herbicides. However, a 1990 U.S. Department of Agriculture (USDA) study of maize production in the United States found no real difference in levels of herbicide use between conventional and conservation tillage systems.

Conservation tillage is now used on about one-third of U.S. croplands and is projected to be used on over half by 2000. The USDA estimates that using conservation tillage on 80% of U.S. cropland would reduce soil erosion by at least half. So far the practice is not widely used in other parts of the world.

**CONTOUR FARMING, TERRACING, STRIP CROPPING, AND ALLEY CROPPING** Soil erosion can be reduced 30–50% on gently sloping land by **contour farming**: plowing and planting crops in rows across, rather than up and down, the sloped contour of the land (Figure 12-14). Each row planted horizontally along the slope of the land acts as a small dam to help hold soil and slow the runoff of water.

**Terracing** can be used on steeper slopes. The slope is converted into a series of broad, nearly level terraces that run across the land contour, with short vertical drops from one terrace to another (Figure 12-11). Terracing retains water for crops at all levels and cuts soil erosion by controlling runoff. In areas of high rainfall diversion ditches must be built behind each terrace to permit adequate drainage.

In **strip cropping**, a row crop like corn alternates in strips with a soil-saving cover crop, such as a grass or a grass–legume mixture, which completely covers the soil and thus reduces erosion (Figure 12-14). The strips of cover crop trap soil that washes from the row crop, catch and reduce water runoff, and help keep pests and plant diseases from spreading from one strip to another. They can also help restore soil fertility if nitrogen-fixing legumes, such as soybeans or alfalfa, are planted in some of the strips.

Erosion can also be reduced by **alley cropping**, or **agroforestry**, a form of *intercropping* in which crops are planted between hedgerows of trees or shrubs that provide fruit or fuelwood (Figure 12-15). The hedgerow

**Figure 12-15** Alley cropping in Peru. Several crops are planted together in strips or alleys between trees and shrubs. The trees provide shade (which reduces water loss by evaporation) and help retain soil moisture and release it slowly.

P. A. Sanchez/North Carolina State University

**Figure 12-16** Windbreaks, or shelterbelts, on a farm in South Dakota. Besides reducing erosion, wind damage, and evaporation, they help hold soil moisture in place, supply some wood for fuel, and provide a habitat for wildlife.

Soil Conservation Service

trimmings can be used as mulch (green manure) for the crops and as fodder for livestock.

## GULLY RECLAMATION AND WINDBREAKS

Water runoff quickly creates gullies in sloping bare land (Figures 1-3 and 12-9). Such land can be restored by **gully reclamation**. Small gullies can be seeded with quick-growing plants such as oats, barley, and wheat for the first season, while deeper gullies can be dammed to collect silt and gradually fill in the chan-

nels. Fast-growing shrubs, vines, and trees can also be planted to stabilize the soil, and channels can be built to divert water from the gully and prevent further erosion.

Wind erosion can be reduced by **windbreaks**, or **shelterbelts**: long rows of trees planted to partially block the wind (Figure 12-16). These are especially effective if uncultivated land is kept covered with vegetation. Windbreaks also provide habitats for birds, pest-eating and pollinating insects, and other

Q: How many units of energy are required to put one unit of food energy on the table in the United States?

## Table 12-2 Land Capability Classification According to the Soil Conservation Service

| Class | Land Class Characteristics | Primary Uses | Secondary Uses | Conservation Measures |
|---|---|---|---|---|
| **Land Suitable for Cultivation** | | | | |
| I | Excellent, flat, well-drained land | Agriculture | Recreation Wildlife Pasture | None |
| II | Good land with minor limitations such as slight slope, sandy soil, or poor drainage | Agriculture Pasture | Recreation Wildlife | Strip cropping Contour farming |
| III | Moderately good land with important limitations of soil, slope, or drainage | Agriculture Pasture Watershed | Recreation Wildlife Urban industry | Contour farming Strip cropping Waterways Terraces |
| IV | Fair land, severe limitations of soil, slope, or drainage | Pasture Orchards Limited agriculture Urban industry | Pasture Wildlife | Farming on a limited basis Contour farming Strip cropping Waterways Terraces |
| **Land Not Suitable for Cultivation** | | | | |
| V | Rockiness, shallow soil, wetness, or slope prevents farming | Grazing Forestry Watershed | Recreation Wildlife | No special precautions if properly grazed or logged; must not be plowed |
| VI | Moderate limitations for grazing and forestry | Grazing Forestry Watershed Urban industry | Recreation Wildlife | Grazing or logging should be limited at times |
| VII | Severe limitations for grazing and forestry | Grazing Forestry Watershed Recreation Aesthetics Wildlife Urban industry | | Careful management required when used for grazing or logging |
| VIII | Unsuitable for grazing and forestry because of steep slope, shallow soil, lack of water, too much water | Recreation Aesthetics Watershed Wildlife Urban industry | | Not to be used for grazing or logging |

animals. Unfortunately many of the windbreaks planted in the upper Great Plains after the 1930s Dust Bowl disaster have been cut down to make way for large irrigation systems and farm machinery.

### LAND-USE CLASSIFICATION AND CONTROL
To encourage wise land use and reduce erosion, the U.S. Soil Conservation Service (SCS) has set up the classification system summarized in Table 12-2 and illustrated in Figure 12-17. An obvious anti-erosion strategy is to avoid planting crops or clearing vegetation on marginal land (classes V–VIII in Table 12-2 and Figure 12-17). The SCS basically relies on voluntary compliance with its guidelines through the almost 3,000 local and state soil and water conservation districts it has established and provides technical and economic assistance through the local district offices. However, the officials of the soil conservation associations usually represent the interests of local farmers and ranchers. This subjects them to intense pressure

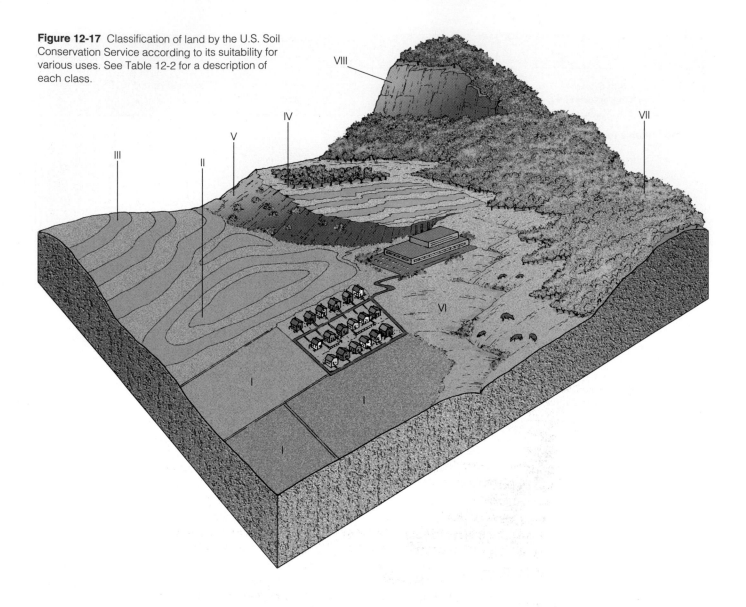

**Figure 12-17** Classification of land by the U.S. Soil Conservation Service according to its suitability for various uses. See Table 12-2 for a description of each class.

to make land-use decisions based on short-term economic gains, which can have harmful long-term environmental and economic impacts.

The bright note is the 1985 Farm Act. This act grants subsidies for farmers who take highly erodible cropland out of production and put it into a conservation reserve, and requires farmers to use soil-conserving techniques to reduce erosion on land still being cultivated (Spotlight, p. 329).

**MAINTAINING AND RESTORING SOIL FERTILITY** Fertilizers partially restore plant nutrients lost by erosion, leaching, and crop harvesting. (Figure 12-5). Three basic types of **organic fertilizer** are animal manure, green manure, and compost.

**Animal manure** includes the dung and urine of cattle, horses, poultry, and other farm animals. In China and South Korea human manure, sometimes called night soil, is used to fertilize crops in vegetable-growing greenbelts around cities. Animal manure improves soil structure, adds organic nitrogen, and stimulates beneficial soil bacteria and fungi. It is particularly useful on corn, cotton, potatoes, and cabbage.

Despite its effectiveness the use of animal manure in the United States has decreased. One reason is that separate farms for growing crops and raising animals have replaced most mixed animal-raising and crop-farming operations. Animal manure is available at feedlots near urban areas, but transporting it to rural crop-growing areas usually costs too much. Thus much of this valuable resource is wasted and can end up polluting nearby bodies of water. In addition, tractors and other motorized farm machinery have replaced horses and other draft animals that naturally added manure to the soil.

**Green manure** is fresh or growing green vegetation plowed into the soil to increase the organic matter

Q: How much of the world's cropland is used to grow livestock feed?

## Slowing Erosion in the United States

The 1985 Farm Act established a strategy to reduce soil erosion in the United States. In the first phase of this program farmers are given a subsidy for highly erodible land they take out of production and replant with soil-saving grass or trees for 10 years. The land in such a *conservation reserve* cannot be farmed, grazed, or cut for hay. Farmers who violate their contracts must pay back all subsidies, with interest. By 1992 more than 14 million hectares (35 million acres) of land had been placed in the conservation reserve, cutting soil erosion on U.S. cropland by almost one-third. If the program is expanded and adequately enforced, it could cut soil losses from U.S. cropland by 80%.

The second phase of the program required all farmers with highly erodible land to develop SCS-approved five-year soil conservation plans for their entire farms by the end of 1990. By 1995 these farmers must implement their plans or lose eligibility for any subsidies and loans.

A third provision of the Farm Act authorizes the government to forgive all or part of farmers' debts to the Farmers Home Administration if they agree not to farm highly erodible cropland or wetlands for 50 years. The farmers are required to plant trees or grass on this land or to convert it back into wetland.

In 1987, however, the SCS eased the standards that farmers' soil conservation plans must meet to keep them eligible for other subsidies. Environmentalists have also accused the SCS of laxity in enforcing the Farm Act's "swampbuster" provisions, which deny federal funds to farmers who drain or destroy wetlands on their property. Despite some weaknesses the 1985 Farm Act makes the United States the first major food-producing country to make soil conservation a national priority.

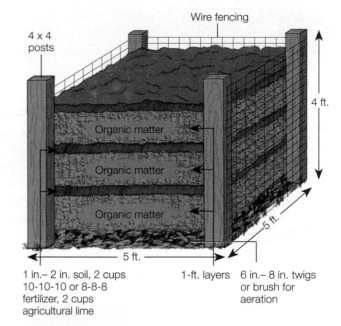

**Figure 12-18** A simple home compost bin can produce mulch for garden and yard plants. Starting with a layer of crossed branches helps aerate the pile, and a layer or two of cat litter or alfalfa meal will cut down on odors. The pile should be turned over every month or so, and covered with a tarp during the winter. A month or so before spring mix 1.3–8 centimeters (0.5 to 3 inches) of compost into the top 10 centimeters (4 inches) of soil. You can also have an odorless indoor compost pile in a plastic bag or garbage container.

and humus available to the next crop. It may consist of weeds in an uncultivated field, grasses and clover in a field previously used for pasture, or legumes such as alfalfa or soybeans grown to build up soil nitrogen.

**Compost** is a rich natural fertilizer and soil conditioner. It aerates soil, improves its ability to retain water and nutrients, helps prevent erosion, and prevents nutrients from being wasted in landfills. Farmers and home owners produce it by piling up alternating layers of carbohydrate-rich plant wastes (such as grass clippings, leaves, weeds, pine needles, hay, straw, and sawdust), and kitchen scraps (such as vegetable remains and egg shells), animal manure, and topsoil (Figure 12-18). This mixture provides a home for microorganisms that aid the decomposition of the plant and manure layers.

Today, especially in the United States and other industrialized countries, farmers rely on **commercial inorganic fertilizers**, which contain nitrogen (as ammonium ions, nitrate ions, or urea), phosphorus (as phosphate ions), and potassium (as potassium ions). Other plant nutrients may also be present in low or trace amounts. Farmers can have their soil and harvested crops chemically analyzed to determine the mix of nutrients that should be added.

Inorganic commercial fertilizers are easily transported, stored, and applied. Worldwide their use increased about 10-fold between 1950 and 1992. Today the additional food they help produce feeds one of every three persons in the world. Without them world food output would plummet an estimated 40%.

Commercial inorganic fertilizers have some disadvantages, however. They do not add humus to the soil. Unless animal manure and green manure are also added, the soil's content of organic matter and thus its ability to hold water will decrease, and the soil will

A: More than 50% (66% in the United States)

**Figure 12-19** Salinization and waterlogging of soil on irrigated land without adequate drainage lead to decreased crop yields.

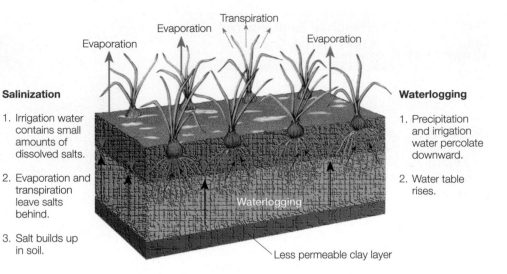

**Salinization**

1. Irrigation water contains small amounts of dissolved salts.

2. Evaporation and transpiration leave salts behind.

3. Salt builds up in soil.

**Waterlogging**

1. Precipitation and irrigation water percolate downward.

2. Water table rises.

Evaporation     Evaporation     Transpiration     Evaporation

Waterlogging

Less permeable clay layer

**Figure 12-20** Because of high evaporation, poor drainage, and severe salinization, white alkaline salts have displaced crops that once grew in this heavily irrigated land in Colorado.

Soil Conservation Service

become compacted and less suitable for crop growth. By decreasing its porosity, inorganic fertilizers also lower the oxygen content of soil and keep added fertilizer from being taken up as efficiently. In addition, most commercial fertilizers supply only 2 or 3 of the 20-odd nutrients needed by plants.

The widespread use of commercial inorganic fertilizers, especially on sloped land near streams and lakes, causes water pollution as well. Some of the nutrients in the fertilizers are washed into nearby bodies of water, where the resulting cultural eutrophication causes algae blooms that use up dissolved oxygen and kill fish. Rainwater seeping through the soil can leach nitrates in commercial fertilizers into groundwater. Drinking water drawn from wells containing high levels of nitrate ions can be toxic, especially for infants.

A third method for conserving soil nutrients is **crop rotation**. Corn, tobacco, and cotton can deplete the topsoil of nutrients (especially nitrogen) if planted on the same land several years in a row. Farmers using crop rotation plant areas or strips with corn, tobacco, and cotton one year. The next year they plant the same areas with legumes, whose root nodules (Figure 4-30) add nitrogen to the soil, or with crops such as oats, barley, rye, or sorghum. This method helps restore soil nutrients and reduces erosion by keeping the soil covered with vegetation. Varying the types of crops planted from year to year also reduces infestation by insects, weeds (especially if the land is planted in sorghum, which releases natural herbicides), and plant diseases.

Concern about soil erosion should not be limited to farmers. At least 40% of soil erosion in the United

Q: What percentage of U.S. cropland is used to produce fruits and vegetables?

States is caused by timber cutting, overgrazing, mining, and urban development carried out without proper regard for soil conservation.

## 12-4 Soil Contamination by Excess Salts and Water

**SALINIZATION** Some 18% of the world's cropland is now irrigated, producing about one-third of the world's food. Irrigated cropland is projected to at least double by 2020.

Irrigated land can produce crop yields two to three times those from rain-watered land, but irrigation has its downside. Irrigation water contains dissolved salts. In dry climates much of the water in this saline solution evaporates, leaving its salts, such as sodium chloride, behind in the topsoil. The accumulation of these salts, called **salinization** (Figure 12-19), stunts crop growth, lowers yields, and eventually kills crop plants and ruins the land (Figure 12-20).

It is estimated that salinization is reducing yields on one-fourth of the world's irrigated cropland. In Egypt, for example, where virtually all cropland is irrigated, half is salty enough to reduce yields. Worldwide 50–65% of all currently irrigated cropland will probably lose productivity from salting by 2000.

When irrigation water is repeatedly withdrawn from and returned to a stream as it flows from its source to its outlet (Figure 5-41), the salinity of the water steadily increases. Using this saltier water for irrigation accelerates salt buildup in the soil. Eventually the water becomes useless for irrigation. For example, by the time the Colorado River makes its way from its headwaters in the Rocky Mountains to Mexico, its salt concentration has increased 20-fold, and it cannot be used for crop irrigation. This problem is at the root of a long-standing dispute between Mexico and the United States that may be partially resolved by the recent opening of the Yuma Desalting Plant in Arizona.

Salts can be flushed out of soil by applying much more irrigation water than is needed for crop growth, but this practice increases pumping and crop-production costs, and wastes enormous amounts of water. Heavily salinized water can also be renewed by taking the land out of production for two to five years, installing an underground network of perforated drainage pipes, and flushing the soil with large quantities of low-salt water. This costly scheme only slows the salt buildup, however it does not stop the process. Flushing salts from the soil also makes downstream

## What You Can Do to Help Protect the Soil

**INDIVIDUALS MATTER** Here are some ways you can help protect the soil:

- *When building a home, save all the trees possible.* Require the contractor to disturb as little soil as possible, to set up barriers that catch any soil eroded during construction, and to save and replace any topsoil removed instead of hauling it off and selling it. Plant disturbed areas with fast-growing native ground cover (preferably not grass) immediately after construction is completed.

- *Landscape the area not used for gardening with a mix of wildflowers, herbs (for cooking and for repelling insects), low-growing ground cover, small bushes, and other forms of vegetation natural to the area.* This biologically diverse type of yard saves water, energy, and money, and reduces infestation of mosquitoes and other damaging insects by providing a diversity of habitats for their natural predators.

- *Set up a compost bin (Figure 12-18) and use it to produce mulch and soil conditioner for yard and garden plants.*

- *Use organic methods for growing vegetables and maintaining your yard.* This involves using organic fertilizers (mulch, green manure, and animal manure) and biological and cultural control of pests.

- *Pressure elected officials to establish and strictly enforce laws and policies that minimize soil erosion, salt buildup, and waterlogging.*

irrigation water saltier unless the saline water can be drained into evaporation ponds rather than returned to the stream or canal.

In the Indian state of Uttar Pradesh, farmers are rehabilitating salinized land by planting a salt-tolerant tree that lowers the water table by taking up water through its roots. Tube wells also lower water tables but are useful only in areas with an adequate groundwater supply.

**WATERLOGGING** Another disadvantage of irrigation is **waterlogging** (Figure 12-19). Farmers often apply heavy amounts of irrigation water to leach salts deeper into the soil. Without adequate drainage, however, water accumulates underground, gradually

# Land Degradation and Environmental Resources

*David Pimentel*

**GUEST ESSAY** *David Pimentel is professor of insect ecology and agricultural sciences in the College of Agriculture and Life Sciences at Cornell University. He has published over 350 scientific papers and 12 books on environmental topics including land degradation, agricultural pollution and energy use, biomass energy, and pesticides. He was one of the first ecologists to employ an interdisciplinary, holistic approach in investigating complex environmental problems.*

At a time when the world's human population is rapidly expanding and its need for more land to produce food, fiber, and fuelwood is also escalating, valuable land is being degraded through erosion and other means at an alarming rate. Soil degradation is of great concern because soil reformation is extremely slow. Worldwide annual erosion rates for agricultural land are about 20–100 times the average of 500 years (with a range of 220–1,000 years) required to renew 2.5 centimeters (1 inch) of soil in tropical and temperate areas—a renewal rate of about 1 metric ton of topsoil per hectare of land per year.

Erosion rates vary in different regions because of topography, rainfall, wind intensity, and the type of agricultural practices used. In China, for example, the average annual soil loss is reported to be about 40 metric tons per hectare (18 tons per acre) while the U.S. average is 18 metric tons per hectare (8 tons per acre). In states like Iowa and Missouri, however, annual soil erosion averages more than 35 metric tons per hectare (16 tons per acre).

Worldwide about 10 million hectares (25 million acres) of land—about the size of Virginia—are abandoned for crop production each year because of high erosion rates plus waterlogging of soils, salinization, and other forms of soil degradation. In addition, according to the UN Environment Programme, crop production becomes uneconomical on about 20 million hectares (49 million acres) each year because soil quality has been severely degraded.

Soil erosion also occurs in forestlands but is not as severe as that in the more exposed soil of agricultural land. However, soil erosion in managed forests is a primary concern because the soil reformation rate in forests is about two to three times longer than that in agricultural land. To compound this erosion problem, at least 24 million hectares (59 million acres) of forest are being cleared each year throughout the world, with much of the land used to grow food and raise cattle [Section 10-2].

The effects of agriculture and forestry are interrelated in other ways. Deforestation reduces fuelwood supplies and forces the poor in LDCs to substitute crop residue and manure for fuelwood. When these plant and animal wastes are burned instead of being returned to the land as ground cover and organic fertilizer, erosion is intensified and productivity of the land is decreased. These factors, in turn, increase pressure to convert more forestland into agricultural land, further intensifying soil erosion.

One reason soil erosion is not a high-priority concern among many governments and farmers is that it usually occurs so slowly that its cumulative effects may take decades to become apparent. For example, the removal of 1 millimeter (.04 inch) of soil is so small that it goes undetected. But over a 25-year period the loss would be 25 millimeters (1 inch)—taking about 500 years to replace by natural processes.

Besides reduced soil depth, soil erosion leads to reduced crop productivity because of losses of water, organic matter, and soil nutrients. A 50% reduction of soil organic matter on a plot of land has been found to reduce corn yields as much as 25%.

When soil erodes, vital plant nutrients such as nitrogen, phosphorus, potassium, and calcium are also lost. With U.S. annual cropland erosion rates of about 18 metric tons per hectare (8 tons per acre), an estimated $18 billion of plant fertilizer nutrients are lost annually.

raising the water table. Saline water then envelops the roots of plants and kills them.

Waterlogging is a serious problem in the heavily irrigated San Joaquin Valley of California, where soils contain a clay layer with a low permeability to water. Worldwide at least one-tenth of all irrigated land suffers from waterlogging, and the problem is getting worse.

Because soil is the base of life, soil depletion must be halted and replaced with soil rebuilding and conservation so that these vital, slowly renewable re-sources are used sustainably. Each of us has a role to play (Individuals Matter, p. 331).

*At some point, either the loss of topsoil from the world's croplands will have to be checked by effective soil conservation practices, or the growth in the world's population will be checked by hunger and malnutrition.*

LESTER R. BROWN

Q: Worldwide, how many people are underfed and undernourished?

Using fertilizers to replace these nutrients substantially adds to the cost of crop production.

Some analysts who are unaware of the numerous and complex effects of soil erosion have falsely concluded that the damages are relatively minor. For example, they report that soil loss causes an annual reduction in crop productivity of only 0.1–0.5% in the United States. However, we need to consider all the ecological effects caused by erosion, including reductions in soil depth, in availability of water for crops, and in soil organic matter and nutrients. When this is done, agronomists and ecologists report a 15–30% reduction in crop productivity—a key factor in increased levels of costly fertilizer and declining yields on some land despite high levels of fertilization. Because fertilizers are not a substitute for fertile soil, they can be applied only up to certain levels before crop yields begin to decline.

Reduced agricultural productivity is only one of the effects of soil erosion. In the United States water runoff is responsible for transporting about 3 billion metric tons (3.3 billion tons) of sediment (about 60% from agricultural land) each year to waterways in the lower 48 states. Off-site damages to U.S. water storage capacity, wildlife, and navigable waterways from these sediments cost an estimated $6 billion each year. Dredging sediments from U.S. streams, harbors, and reservoirs alone costs about $570 million each year. About 25% of new water storage capacity in U.S. reservoirs is built solely to compensate for sediment buildup.

When soil sediments that include pesticides and other agricultural chemicals are carried into streams, lakes, and reservoirs, fish production is adversely affected. These contaminated sediments interfere with fish spawning, increase predation on fish, and destroy fisheries in estuarine and coastal areas.

Increased erosion and water runoff on mountain slopes flood agricultural land in the valleys below, further decreasing agricultural productivity. Eroded land also does not hold water very well, again decreasing crop productivity. This effect is magnified in the 80 countries (with nearly 40% of the world's population) that experience frequent droughts. The rapid growth in the world's population, accompanied by the need for more crops and a projected doubling of water needs in the next 20 years, will only intensify water shortages, particularly if soil erosion is not contained.

Thus soil erosion is one of the world's critical problems and, if not slowed, will seriously reduce agricultural and forestry production, and degrade the quality of aquatic ecosystems. Solutions are not particularly difficult but are often not implemented because erosion occurs so gradually that we fail to acknowledge its cumulative impact until damage is irreversible. Many farmers have also been conditioned to believe that losses in soil fertility can be remedied by applying more fertilizer or by using more fossil-fuel energy.

The principal way to control soil erosion and its accompanying runoff of sediment is to maintain adequate vegetative coverage on soils [by various methods discussed in Section 12-3]. These methods are also cost-effective, especially when off-site costs of erosion are included. Scientists, policy makers, and agriculturists need to work together to implement soil and water conservation practices before world soils lose most of their productivity.

**Critical Thinking**

1. Some analysts contend that average soil erosion rates in the United States and the world are low and that the soil erosion problem can easily be solved with improved agricultural technology such as no-till cultivation and increased use of commercial inorganic fertilizers. Do you agree or disagree with this position? Explain.

2. What specific things do you believe elected officials should do to decrease soil erosion and the resulting water pollution by sediment in the United States?

# Critical Thinking

1. Why should everyone, not just farmers, be concerned with soil conservation?

2. Explain how the Dust Bowl phenomenon of the 1930s could happen again. How would you try to prevent a recurrence?

3. What are the main advantages and disadvantages of commercial inorganic fertilizers? Why should both inorganic and organic fertilizers be used?

*4. Visit rural or undeveloped areas near your campus, and classify the lands according to the system shown in Figure 12-17 and Table 12-2. Look for examples of land being used for purposes to which it is not best suited.

*5. As a class project evaluate soil erosion on your school grounds. Use this information to develop a soil conservation plan for your school, and present it to school officials.

## Water Wars in the Middle East

The next wars in the Middle East will probably be fought over water, not oil. Most water in this arid region comes from three shared river basins: the Jordan, the Tigris-Euphrates, and the Nile (Figure 13-1).

Arguments among Ethiopia, Sudan, and Egypt over access to water from the Nile River basin (Figure 13-2) are escalating rapidly. Ethiopia, which controls the headwaters of 80% of the Nile's flow, has plans to divert more of this water; so does Sudan. This could reduce the amount of water available to water-short Egypt, which is a desert except for the thin strip of irrigated cropland along the Nile and its delta. By 2025 Egypt's population is expected to double, increasing the demand for water. Its options are to go to war against Sudan and Ethiopia to get more water or to slash population growth and improve irrigation efficiency.

There is also fierce competition for water among Jordan, Syria, and Israel, which get most of their water from the Jordan River basin. The 1967 Arab-Israeli war was fought in part over access to this water.

Israel uses water more efficiently than any other country. Nevertheless, it is now using 95% of its renewable supply of fresh water, and the supply is pro-

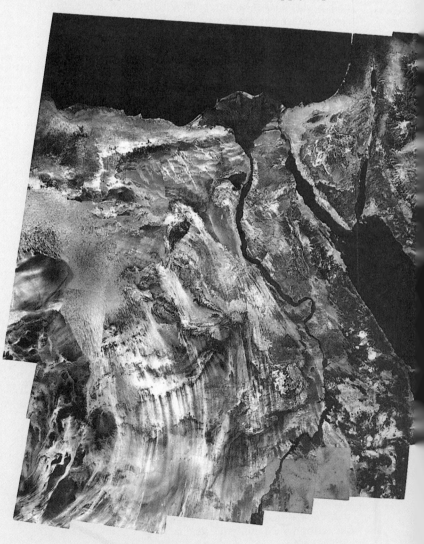

**Figure 13-1** Middle Eastern countries have some of the highest population growth rates in the world. Because of their dry climate, food production depends on irrigation. In the 1990s and beyond, conflicts among countries in this region over access to water may overshadow long-standing religious and ethnic clashes, as well as disputes over ownership of oil supplies.

*Our liquid planet glows like a soft blue sapphire in the hard-edged darkness of space. There is nothing else like it in the solar system. It is because of water.*

JOHN TODD

jected to fall 30% short of demand by 2000 because of increased immigration.

Turkey, by contrast, has abundant water. It plans to build 22 dams along the upper Tigris-Euphrates to generate huge quantities of electricity, irrigate a large area of land, and provide more than 3 million jobs in its most impoverished region. These dams will drastically reduce the flow of water to Syria and Iraq, which lie downstream. Indeed, the greatest threat to Iraq is a cutoff of its water supply by Turkey and Syria.

Turkey hopes to become the region's water superpower. It plans to build pipelines to transport and sell water to parched Saudi Arabia and Kuwait, and perhaps to Syria, Israel, and Jordan.

Clearly distribution of water resources will be a key issue in any future peace talks in this volatile region. The keys to resolving these water supply problems involve a combination of regional cooperation, reduced population growth, and improved water efficiency.

Fresh water is vital for agriculture, manufacturing, transportation, and countless other human activities— in the Middle East and everywhere on the planet. Water also plays a key role in sculpting the earth's surface, moderating climate, and diluting pollutants. In fact, without water, life as we know it could not exist.

**Figure 13-2** Mosaic of satellite images of the lower 1,400 kilometers (870 miles) of the Nile River. (GEOPIC/Earth Satellite Corporation)

In this chapter we will answer the following questions:

- What are water's unique physical properties?
- How much fresh water is available to us, and how much of this are we using?
- What are the world's water resource problems?
- How can we get more water, and how can we use it more efficiently?

## 13-1 Water's Unique Properties

We live on the water planet. A precious film of water—most of it salt water—covers about 71% of Earth's surface (Figure 5-27). Earth's organisms are made up mostly of water. For example, a tree is about 60% water by weight, you and most animals are about 65% water, and a jellyfish is more than 90% water.

Water has many unique—almost magical—properties compared with other molecules of similar weight. For example:

- *Water exists as a liquid over a wide temperature range.* Its high boiling point of 100°C (212°F) and its low freezing point of 0°C (32°F) mean that water remains a liquid in most climates on Earth.
- *Liquid water changes temperature very slowly because it can store a large amount of heat without a large change in temperature.* This high heat capacity prevents large bodies of water from warming or cooling rapidly, helps protect living organisms from the shock of abrupt temperature changes, moderates Earth's climate, and makes water an effective coolant for car engines, power plants, and other heat-producing industrial processes.
- *Liquid water has a very high heat of vaporization.* That is, it takes lots of heat to evaporate liquid water. Water's ability to absorb large amounts of heat as it changes into water vapor and to release this heat as the vapor condenses back to liquid

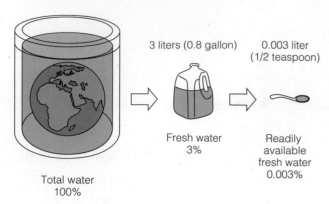

100 liters (26 gallons)

3 liters (0.8 gallon)

0.003 liter
(1/2 teaspoon)

Fresh water
3%

Readily
available
fresh water
0.003%

Total water
100%

**Figure 13-3** Only a tiny fraction of the world's water supply is available as fresh water for human use.

water is a primary factor in distributing heat throughout the world (Figure 5-6). This property makes evaporation of water an effective cooling process for plants and animals, explaining why you feel cooler when perspiration evaporates from your skin.

- *Liquid water dissolves a variety of compounds.* This enables water to carry dissolved nutrients throughout the tissues of living organisms, to flush waste products out of those tissues, to serve as an all-purpose cleanser, and to help remove and dilute the water-soluble wastes of civilization. However, water's superiority as a solvent also means that it is easily polluted by water-soluble wastes. Water is also a carrier of disease-causing bacteria and viruses.

- *Liquid water has an extremely high surface tension (attractive forces between molecules that cause the surface of a liquid to contract) and an even higher wetting ability (capacity to adhere to and coat a solid).* Together these properties allow water to rise through a plant from the roots to the leaves.

- *Liquid water is the only common substance that expands rather than contracts when it freezes.* Consequently ice has a lower density (mass per unit of volume) than liquid water. Thus ice floats on water, and bodies of water freeze from the top down instead of from the bottom up. Without this property lakes and streams in cold climates would freeze solid, and most current forms of aquatic life would not exist. Because water expands on freezing, it can also break pipes, crack engine blocks (which is why we use antifreeze), and fracture streets and rocks.

Water—the lifeblood of the ecosphere—is truly a wondrous substance that connects us to one another,

to other forms of life, and to the entire planet. Despite its importance water is one of the most poorly managed resources on earth. We waste it and pollute it. We also charge too little for making it available, encouraging even greater waste and pollution of this vital renewable resource.

**WORLDWIDE SUPPLY, RENEWAL, AND DISTRIBUTION** Only a tiny fraction of the planet's abundant water is available to us as fresh water. About 97% is found in the oceans and is too salty for drinking, irrigation, or industry (except as a coolant).

The remaining 3% is fresh water. About 2.997% is locked up in ice caps or glaciers, or is buried so deep that it costs too much to extract. Only about 0.003% of Earth's total volume of water is easily available to us in soil moisture, exploitable groundwater, water vapor, and lakes and streams. If the world's water supply were only 100 liters (26 gallons), our usable supply of fresh water would be only about 0.003 liter (one-half teaspoon) (Figure 13-3).

Fortunately this amounts to a generous supply that is continuously collected, purified, and distributed in the *hydrologic cycle* (Figure 4-33). This natural recycling and purification process provides plenty of fresh water as long as we don't overload it with slowly degradable and nondegradable wastes or withdraw water from underground supplies faster than it is replenished. Unfortunately we are doing both. Also, usable fresh water is unevenly distributed around the world. Differences in average annual precipitation divide the world into water "haves" and "have-nots."

As population and industrialization increase, water shortages in already water-short regions will intensify, and water wars may erupt (p. 334). Projected global warming (Section 11-2) also might cause changes in rainfall patterns and disrupt water supplies. No one knows what areas might be affected.

**SURFACE WATER** The fresh water we use comes from two sources: surface water and groundwater (Figure 13-4). Precipitation that does not soak into the ground or return to the atmosphere by evaporation or transpiration is called **surface water**. It forms streams, lakes, wetlands, and artificial reservoirs.

**Watersheds**, also called **drainage basins**, are areas of land that drain into bodies of surface water. Water

Q: Worldwide, how many people die each year from hunger-related causes?

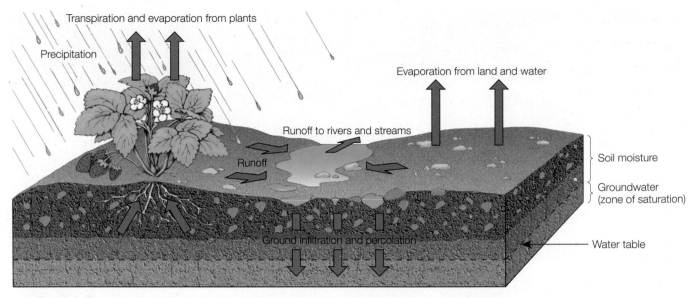

**Figure 13-4** Main routes of local precipitation: surface runoff into surface waters, ground infiltration into aquifers, and evaporation and transpiration into the atmosphere.

flowing off the land into these bodies is called **surface runoff**.

GROUNDWATER Some precipitation infiltrates the ground and fills the pores in soil and rock. The subsurface area where all available soil and rock spaces are filled by water is called the **zone of saturation**, and the water in these pores is called **groundwater** (Figure 13-4). The **water table** is the upper surface of the zone of saturation. It is the fuzzy and fluctuating dividing line between saturated soil and rock, where every available pore is full, and unsaturated (but still wet) rock and soil where the pores can absorb more water. The water table falls in dry weather and rises in wet weather.

The ability of soil or rock to hold water depends on its porosity and permeability (Table 12-1). Porous, water-saturated layers of sand, gravel, or bed rock through which groundwater flows and that can yield an economically significant amount of water are called **aquifers** (Figure 13-5).

Most aquifers are replenished naturally by precipitation, which percolates downward through soil and rock in what is called **natural recharge**. Any area of land through which water passes into an aquifer is called a **recharge area**. Groundwater moves from the recharge area through an aquifer and out to a discharge area (well, spring, lake, geyser, stream, or ocean) as part of the hydrologic cycle.

The direction of flow of groundwater from recharge areas to discharge areas depends on gravity, pressure, and friction. Normally groundwater moves from points of high elevation and pressure to points of lower elevation and pressure. This movement is quite slow, typically only a meter or so (about 3 feet) per year and rarely more than 0.3 meter (1 foot) per day. Thus most aquifers are like huge, slow-moving underground lakes.

There is 40 times as much groundwater as there is surface water. However, groundwater is unequally distributed, and only a small amount of it is economically exploitable.

If the withdrawal rate of an aquifer exceeds its natural recharge rate, the water table around the withdrawal well is lowered, creating a waterless volume known as a *cone of depression* (Figure 13-6). Any pollutant discharged onto the land above will be pulled directly into this cone and will pollute water withdrawn by the well.

Some aquifers, called *fossil aquifers*, get very little—if any—recharge. Often found deep underground, they are nonrenewable resources on a human time scale. Such aquifers underlie the Sahara and Kalahari deserts, the Great Artesian Basin in Australia, the central Asian basins, and the midwestern United States. Withdrawals from fossil aquifers amount to "water mining"—and if kept up will deplete these ancient deposits of liquid Earth capital.

WORLD AND U.S. WATER USE Two common measures of human water use are withdrawal and consumption. **Water withdrawal** is taking water from a groundwater or surface-water source to a place of use. **Water consumption** occurs when water that has been withdrawn is not returned to the surface water or groundwater from which it came so that it may be

A: 40 million (some say 20 million while others say 60 million)

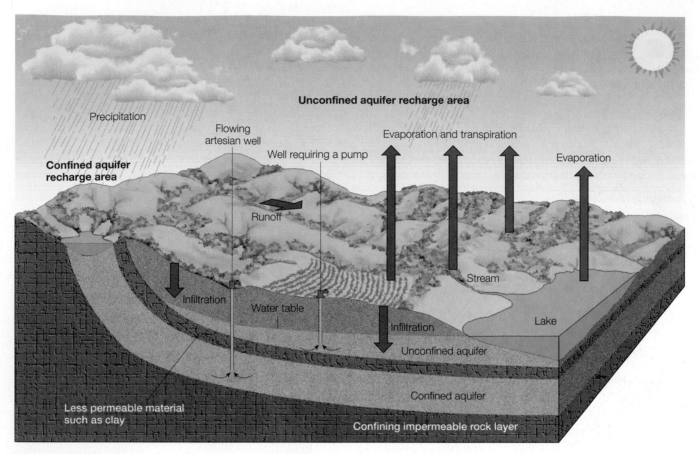

**Figure 13-5** The groundwater system. An *unconfined*, or *water table, aquifer* forms when ground-water collects above a layer of rock or compacted clay through which water flows very slowly (low permeability). A *confined aquifer* is sandwiched between layers that have low permeability, such as clay or shale. Groundwater in this type of aquifer is confined and under pressure.

**Figure 13-6** Drawdown of water table and cone of depression.

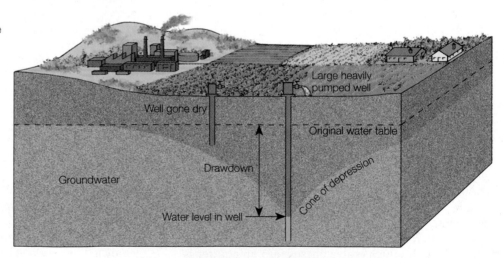

used again in that area. This usually occurs because the water has evaporated or transpired into the atmosphere. Worldwide about 60% of the water withdrawn is consumed.

Since 1950 the rate of global water withdrawal has increased almost fivefold and per capita use has tre-bled, largely to meet the food and other resource needs of the world's rapidly growing population. Water withdrawal rates are projected to at least double in the next two decades.

The United States has the highest per capita water withdrawal rate in the world, followed by Canada

Q: What is the chief cause of hunger, malnutrition, and premature death from hunger-related diseases?

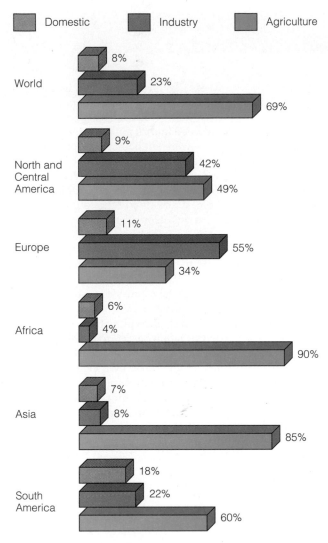

Figure 13-7 Water withdrawal by use and region. (Data from World Resources Institute)

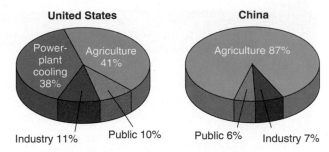

**Figure 13-8** Use of water in the United States and China. (Data from Worldwatch Institute and World Resources Institute)

In the western United States irrigation accounts for about 85% of all water use, and much of this water is used inefficiently. One reason for this is that federal subsidies make water so cheap that western farmers dependent on this water would lose money by investing in more efficient irrigation.

Worldwide about 23% of the water withdrawn is used for energy production (oil and gas production and power-plant cooling) and industrial processing, cleaning, and removal of wastes. Water withdrawal for energy production and industrial use is highest in Europe and North America (Figure 13-7), especially in the United States (Figure 13-8). The amount of water U.S. industry uses each year to cool, wash, circulate, and manufacture materials is equivalent to 30% of the water in the world's streams. Agricultural and manufactured products both require large amounts of water, much of which could be used more efficiently and reused. For example, it takes 380,000 liters (100,000 gallons) to make an automobile, 3,800 liters (1,000 gallons) to produce 454 grams (1 pound) of aluminum, and 3,000 liters (800 gallons) to produce 454 grams (1 pound) of grain-fed beef in a feedlot.

Domestic and municipal use accounts for about 8% of worldwide withdrawals and about 13–16% of withdrawals in industrialized countries (Figure 13-7). Increases in domestic and municipal water use and in industrial use are usually accompanied by an increase in wastewater. As population, urbanization, and industrialization grow, the volume of wastewater needing treatment will increase enormously.

## 13-3 Water Resource Problems

**TOO LITTLE WATER** Droughts—periods in which precipitation is much lower and evaporation much higher than normal—cause more damage and suffering

(with 20% of the world's freshwater supply), Australia, the CIS, Japan, and Mexico. Per capita water withdrawal rates in LDCs typically are 1–2% that in the United States. If every country were to withdraw as much water per person as the United States, we would be trying to withdraw more than the available supply.

Uses of withdrawn water also vary from one region to another (Figure 13-7) and from one country to another (Figure 13-8). Averaged globally, about 69% of the water withdrawn each year is used to irrigate 18% of the world's cropland, especially in the United States, the CIS, and Mexico. In Asia 82% of the water withdrawn is used to irrigate crops; in Africa the figure is 68%, in the United States 41%, and in Europe 30%. A large portion of irrigation water is wasted, with 70–80% of the water evaporating or seeping into the ground before reaching crops.

Bangladesh (Figure 8-15) is one of the world's most densely populated countries. Its 119 million people are packed into an area roughly the size of Wisconsin. Women bear an average of 4.9 children, and the population could reach 226 million by 2025. Bangladesh is also one of the world's poorest countries, with an average per capita income of about $180.

Most of the country consists of floodplains and shifting islands of silt formed by a delta at the mouth of three major rivers. Runoff from annual monsoon rains in the Himalaya of India, Nepal, Bhutan, and China flow down the rivers through Bangladesh into the Bay of Bengal.

The people of Bangladesh are used to moderate annual flooding during the summer monsoon season and depend on the floodwaters to grow rice, their primary source of food. The annual deposit of Himalayan soil in the delta basin also helps maintain soil fertility. However, severe flooding from excessive Himalayan runoff and from storm surges caused by cyclones in the Bay of Bengal has had disastrous consequences. In the past great floods occurred every 50 years or so, but during the 1970s and 1980s they came about every 4 years.

Bangladesh's flood problems begin in the Himalayan watershed. There a combination of rapid population growth, deforestation, overgrazing, and unsustainable farming on steep, easily erodible mountain slopes has greatly diminished the ability of the soil to absorb water (Figure 13-9). Instead of being absorbed and released slowly, water from the monsoon rain runs off the denuded Himalayan foothills carrying vital topsoil with it. This runoff, combined with heavier-than-normal monsoon rains, has caused severe flooding in Bangladesh.

In 1988, for example, a disastrous flood covered two-thirds of the country's land area for three weeks and leveled 2 million homes after the heaviest monsoon rains in 70 years. At least 2,000 people drowned and 30 million people—1 in 4—were left homeless. Hundreds of thousands more contracted cholera and typhoid fever from contaminated water and food supplies. At least a quarter of the country's crops were destroyed, costing at least $1.5 billion and causing thousands of people to die of starvation.

In their struggle to survive, the poor in Bangladesh have cleared many of the country's coastal mangrove forests (Figure 5-32) for fuelwood and crop cultivation. This deforestation has led to more severe flooding because these coastal wetlands shelter the low-lying coastal areas from storm surges. About five cyclones per year hit Bangladesh, mainly in the spring and autumn, and some can be devastating, with fierce winds whipping up waves as high as 9 meters (30 feet).

In 1970 as many as 1 million people drowned in one storm. Another

---

worldwide than any other natural hazard. Since the 1970s drought has killed more than 24,000 people per year and created swarms of environmental refugees (Figure 8-11). At least 80 arid and semiarid countries, where nearly 40% of the world's people live, experience years-long droughts.

In water-short areas many women and children must walk long distances each day, carrying heavy jars or cans, to get a meager supply of sometimes contaminated water. Areas likely to face increased water shortages in the 1990s and beyond include northern Africa, parts of India, northern China, much of the Middle East, Mexico, parts of the western United States, Poland, and much of the CIS.

Reduced precipitation, higher-than-normal temperatures, or both usually trigger a drought; rapid population growth and poor land use make it worse. Deforestation (Section 10-2), overgrazing (Figure 12-13), plowing prairies (Figure 12-1), and irrigating fields also can intensify the effects of drought. Unfortunately millions of poor people in LDCs have no choice but to try to survive on drought-prone land.

If global warming occurs as projected (Section 11-2), severe droughts may become more frequent in some areas of the world and jeopardize food production. Some water-starved cities may have to be abandoned.

*Water will be the burning foreign policy issue for water-short countries in the 1990s and beyond.* Almost 150 of the world's 214 major river systems are shared by 2 countries, and 50 by 3–10. This 40% of the world's population already clash over water (p. 334).

Competition between cities and farmers for scarce water is also escalating in regions such as the western United States and China. In northern China, for example, dozens of cities, including Beijing, already face acute water shortages, and water shortages are expected in 450 of China's 644 cities by the end of the century.

Some water-short areas can increase their supply by tapping into deep deposits of groundwater. A new

---

Q: What human activity has the most harmful overall environmental impact?

**Figure 13-9** When the Himalayan foothills in areas such as Nepal and northern India are deforested for timber and fuelwood, grazing livestock, and unsustainable farming, water from monsoon rains rushes down denuded slopes, eroding precious topsoil and flooding downstream areas such as Bangladesh.

surge killed 140,000 people in 1991. Flood damages and deaths in areas still protected by mangrove forests are much lower than in areas where the forests have been cleared. This problem can be solved only if Bangladesh, Bhutan, China, India, and Nepal all cooperate in reforestation efforts and flood control measures, and reduce their population growth.

energy-efficient pump using sonic waves to drive a piston and draw water up becomes more efficient the deeper you go. The pump can easily be powered by solar cells, a boon especially in rural areas without electricity. The initial cost is about half that of conventional systems and one-third that of a wind turbine. It is an excellent example of appropriate technology. However, withdrawing water from aquifers faster than they are replenished is not appropriate.

**TOO MUCH WATER** Some countries have enough annual precipitation but get most of it at one time of the year. In India, for example, 90% of the annual precipitation falls between June and September, the monsoon season. This downpour causes floods, waterlogs soils, leaches soil nutrients, and washes away topsoil and crops.

Hurricanes and typhoons can flood low-lying coastal areas. Prolonged rains anywhere can cause streams and lakes to overflow and flood the surrounding land, but low-lying river basins such as the Ganges River basin in India and Bangladesh are especially vulnerable.

In the 1970s floods killed more than 4,700 people per year and caused tens of billions of dollars in property damages—a trend that continued and even worsened in the 1980s and into the 1990s. In India, for example, flood losses doubled in the 1980s.

Floods, like droughts, are usually called natural disasters, but human activities have contributed to the sharp rise in flood deaths and damages since the 1960s. Cultivation of land, deforestation (Figure 10-3), overgrazing (Figure 12-13), and mining (Figure 10-16) have removed water-absorbing vegetation and soil (Case Study, p. 340). In Thailand loggers were banned from forests after catastrophic floods in 1988 buried entire villages in mud and logs from denuded hillsides.

Urbanization also increases flooding, even with moderate rainfall, by replacing vegetation and soil with highways, parking lots, and buildings that lead to rapid runoff of rainwater. If sea levels rise during the next century as projected, many low-lying coastal cities, wetlands, and croplands will be under water.

Flood damage can be prevented or reduced by reforestation, rechannelization, dams, artificial levees, and floodplain management (Section 7-5).

**WATER FAR FROM PEOPLE** In some countries the largest rivers, which carry most of the runoff, are far from agricultural and population centers where the water is needed. For example, South America has the largest annual water runoff of any continent, but 60% of the runoff flows through the Amazon River in remote areas where few people live (Figure 9-3).

Strategies for capturing some of this water and bringing water to people include building dams and reservoirs and using aqueducts to transfer water to other areas. These approaches, however, are expensive and have harmful environmental impacts in addition to their benefits, as discussed in Section 13-4.

**CONTAMINATED DRINKING WATER** Not only is water becoming more scarce in many parts of the world, its quality is also being degraded. Rivers in Poland (Case Study, p. 18), Latin America, and Asia are severely polluted, as are some in MDCs. Aquifers used as sources of drinking water in many MDCs and LDCs are becoming contaminated with pesticides, fertilizers, and hazardous organic chemicals. In China, for example, 41 large cities get their drinking water from polluted groundwater.

In its passage through the hydrologic cycle, water is polluted by:

- *Sediment* washed from the land into surface waters by natural erosion and farming activities (Figures 5-30 and 12-9), forestry, mining (Figure 10-16), grazing (Figure 10-15), and construction
- *Excess nutrients* from soil erosion, human and animal waste, and effluents from sewage treatment plants, causing algae blooms that use up dissolved oxygen and disrupt aquatic communities
- *Pathogens* (disease-causing bacteria and viruses) from sewage and livestock wastes
- *Hazardous chemicals* produced by industrialized societies

All four categories of waste are increasing because of rapid population growth, poverty, and industrialization. These forms of water pollution are discussed in Chapter 23.

According to the World Health Organization, 1.5 billion people don't have a safe supply of drinking water and 1.7 billion lack adequate sanitation facili-

ties. At least 5 million people die every year from waterborne diseases that could be prevented by clean drinking water and better sanitation. Most of the 13,700 who die each day from such diseases are children under age 5.

In 1980 the United Nations called for spending $300 billion to supply all of the world's people with clean drinking water and adequate sanitation by 1990. The $30-billion-per-year cost of this program is about what the world spends every 10 days for military purposes. Sadly only about $1.5 billion per year was actually spent.

**THE U.S. SITUATION** The United States has plenty of fresh water. But much of it is in the wrong place at the wrong time or is contaminated by agriculture and industry. The eastern states usually have ample precipitation, while many of the western states have too little. In the East the largest uses for water are energy production, cooling, and manufacturing. In the West the largest use by far is irrigation.

In many parts of the eastern United States the most serious water problems are flooding, some urban shortages, and pollution. For example, the 3 million residents of Long Island, New York, get their water from an aquifer that is becoming severely contaminated by industrial wastes, leaky septic tanks and landfills, and ocean water pulled into the aquifer when fresh water is withdrawn faster than it is naturally recharged.

The most serious water problem in the arid and semiarid areas of the western half of the country is a shortage of runoff caused by low precipitation, high evaporation, and recurring prolonged drought. In many areas water tables are dropping rapidly as farmers and cities deplete groundwater aquifers faster than they are recharged.

Many major urban centers, especially those in the West and Midwest, are located in areas that don't have enough water or are projected to have water shortages by 2000 (Figure 13-10). Experts project that present shortages and conflicts over water supplies will get much worse as more industries and people migrate west and compete with farmers for scarce water. These shortages could worsen even more if climate warms up as a result of an enhanced greenhouse effect (Figure 11-4). Because water is such a vital resource, you might find Figure 13-10 useful in deciding where to live in coming decades.

**METHODS FOR MANAGING WATER RESOURCES** One way to manage water resources is to increase the supply in a particular area by building dams and reservoirs, bringing in surface water from another area,

Q: How much of the world's cropland is used to grow livestock feed?

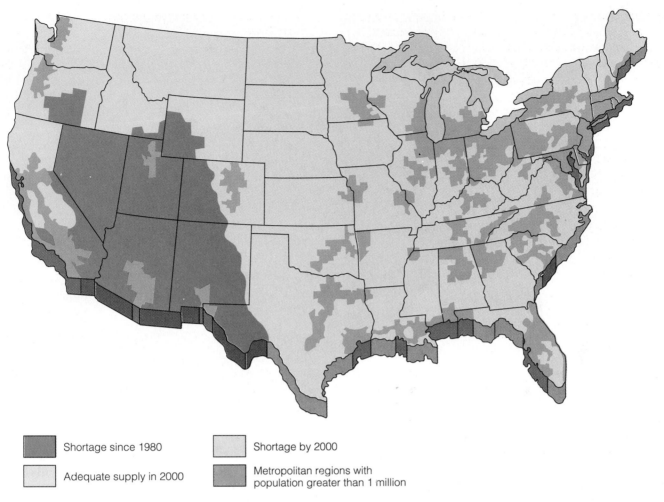

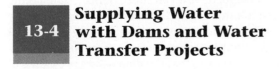 Shortage since 1980

Adequate supply in 2000

Shortage by 2000

Metropolitan regions with
population greater than 1 million

**Figure 13-10** Present and projected water deficit regions in the continental United States compared with present metropolitan regions having populations greater than 1 million. (Data from U.S. Water Resources Council and U.S. Geological Survey)

or tapping groundwater. The other approach is to improve the efficiency of water use.

LDCs rarely have the money to develop the water storage and distribution systems needed to increase their supply. Their people must settle where the water is. In MDCs people tend to live where the climate is favorable and bring in water from another watershed. Some even settle in a desert and expect water to be brought to them at a low price.

<table>
<tr><td>13-4</td><td>**Supplying Water with Dams and Water Transfer Projects**</td></tr>
</table>

**DAMS AND RESERVOIRS** Rainwater and water from melting snow can be captured and stored in large reservoirs created by damming streams. This water can be released as desired to produce hydroelectric power at the dam site, irrigate land below the dam, control flooding of land below the reservoir, and provide water carried by aqueduct to towns and cities. Reservoirs are also used for recreation activities such as swimming, fishing, and boating.

About 13.5% of the electrical power used in the United States is hydroelectric. This is a potentially renewable source of energy as long as droughts or long-term climate changes don't reduce water flow in the dam's basin. Large dams and reservoirs have benefits and drawbacks (Figure 13-11 and Case Study, p. 345). Building small dams, which have fewer destructive effects than large dams and reservoirs, is a useful way to trap water for irrigation.

Proposed dams in LDCs will cover vast areas with water and uproot millions of people. Despite protests by more than 50,000 villagers, the Indian government is going ahead with plans to build 30 large dams

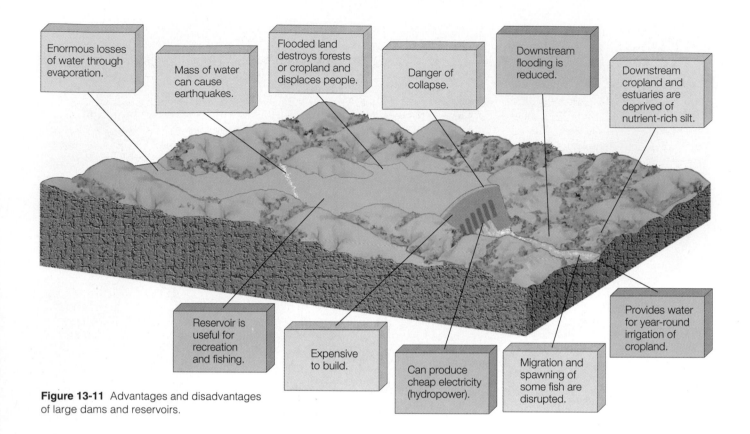

**Figure 13-11** Advantages and disadvantages of large dams and reservoirs.

The text boxes in the figure read:

- Enormous losses of water through evaporation.
- Mass of water can cause earthquakes.
- Flooded land destroys forests or cropland and displaces people.
- Danger of collapse.
- Downstream flooding is reduced.
- Downstream cropland and estuaries are deprived of nutrient-rich silt.
- Reservoir is useful for recreation and fishing.
- Expensive to build.
- Can produce cheap electricity (hydropower).
- Migration and spawning of some fish are disrupted.
- Provides water for year-round irrigation of cropland.

**Figure 13-12** The James Bay project in northern Quebec will alter or reverse the flow of 19 major rivers and flood an area the size of Washington State to produce hydropower for consumers in Quebec and the United States, especially in New York State. Phase I of this 50-year project is completed. Phase II is scheduled to begin but is being opposed by the indigenous Cree, whose ancestral hunting grounds would be flooded, and by environmentalists in Canada and the United States.

and thousands of smaller ones along the Namada River and 41 of its tributaries. The project will flood an estimated 4,000 square kilometers (1,500 square miles) of forests and farms, and displace 1 million people. In Brazil the $1-billion Balbina Dam across the Amazon River destroyed 2,400 square kilometers (930 square miles) of virgin tropical forest, displaced thousands of indigenous people, and killed millions of wild animals—all to supply only 80 megawatts of electricity.

These projects, however, are small compared to China's Three Gorges Project—the world's largest proposed hydroelectric dam and reservoir. When completed it will create a 590-kilometer-long (370-mile) lake on the Yangtze River. It will flood large areas of farmland and 800 factories and existing power stations, and displace 1.2 million people, including two cities each containing 100,000 people.

Faulty construction, earthquakes, floods, landslides, sabotage, or war can cause dams to fail, taking a terrible toll in lives and property. According to the Federal Emergency Management Agency the United States has about 1,300 unsafe dams in populated areas. The agency reported that the dam safety programs of most states are inadequate because of weak laws and budget cuts. A bright spot is Pennsylvania, which since 1986 has cut its number of unsafe dams from 203 to 40.

Q: What percentage of the world's commercial fish species have been overfished?

## Egypt's Aswan High Dam: Blessing or Disaster?

The billion-dollar Aswan High Dam on the Nile River in Egypt (Figure 13-1) shows what can happen when a major dam and reservoir project is built without adequate consideration of long-term environmental effects and costs. The dam was built in the 1960s to provide flood control and irrigation water for the lower Nile basin, and electricity for Cairo and other parts of Egypt. In arid Egypt all cropland must be irrigated.

Today the dam supplies about one-third of Egypt's electrical power, and it saved Egypt's rice and cotton crops during the droughts of 1972 and 1973. Year-round irrigation in the lower Nile basin has increased food production: Farmers now produce crops three times per year where before they could produce a crop only once a year. Irrigation has also brought about 405,000 hectares (1 million acres) of desert land under cultivation.

Since the dam opened in 1964, however, it has also had a number of harmful ecological effects. It ended the yearly flooding that had fertilized the Nile Delta with silt; now the river's silt accumulates behind the dam, filling up Lake Nasser. In addition, the annual flooding flushed mineral salts from the soil and swept away snails that carry flukes that cause schistosomi-asis—a painful, debilitating, and sometimes fatal disease.

Cropland in the Nile Delta basin now has to be treated with commercial fertilizer at a cost of over $100 million per year to make up for plant nutrients once available at no cost. Ironically the country's new fertilizer plants use up much of the electrical power produced by the dam. Also, because salts are no longer flushed from the soil, salinization (Figure 12-19) has offset three-fourths of the gain in food production from new, less productive land irrigated by water from the reservoir.

Because it contains less sediment, the Nile has eroded its bed and has undermined numerous bridges and smaller dams downstream. To remedy this problem, the government proposes to build ten barrier dams at a projected cost of $250 million—one-fourth of what the Aswan Dam cost. And without the Nile's annual discharge of sediment, the sea is eroding the delta and advancing inland, reducing productivity on large areas of agricultural land. This loss of productive land is increased by subsidence in the Nile Delta.

Now that nutrient-rich silt no longer reaches the river's mouth, Egypt's sardine, mackerel, shrimp, and lobster industries have all but disappeared. This has led to losses of approximately 30,000 jobs, mil-lions of dollars annually, and an important source of protein for Egyptians. Eventually, however, these losses are expected to be recovered by a new fishing industry based on taking bass, catfish, and carp from Lake Nasser behind the dam.

Flooding to create Lake Nasser uprooted 125,000 people. By 1970 the lake was supposed to hold enough water to meet the needs of Egypt and Sudan during a prolonged drought, but evaporation and seepage of water into the underlying sandstone have been much greater than projected. Even today the reservoir is only about half full, and most authorities believe that the level will not rise much more in the next 100 years. In addition, about 80% of the water flowing into Lake Nasser comes from Ethiopia. This vital source of water may be reduced by dams being built along the Nile by Ethiopia as well as by severe drought (p. 334).

Although it is in a low-risk area, the dam was jolted by a fairly severe earthquake in 1981. Scientists believe the quake was triggered by the weight of the water in Lake Nasser.

Some analysts believe that in the long run the benefits of the Aswan High Dam will outweigh its costs. Others consider it an economic and ecological disaster. What do you think?

**WATERSHED TRANSFERS** Tunnels, aqueducts, and underground pipes can transfer stream runoff collected by building dams and reservoirs from water-rich watersheds to water-poor areas. Two of the world's largest watershed transfer projects are the California Water Project (Case Study, p. 346) and the diversion of water from rivers feeding the Aral Sea in the CIS to irrigate cropland (Case Study, p. 347).

Another major watershed transfer project is the James Bay Project, a $60-billion, 50-year scheme to harness the wild rivers that flow into the James and Hud-son bays in Canada's Quebec Province to produce electric power for Canadian and U.S. consumers (Figure 13-12). If completed, it would **(1)** reverse or alter the flow of 19 giant rivers, **(2)** reshape a territory the size of France with more than 215 dams and dikes, **(3)** flood 176,000 square kilometers (68,000 square miles)—an area the size of Washington State or Germany—of boreal forest and tundra, and **(4)** displace thousands of indigenous Cree who have lived sustainably off James Bay by subsistence hunting, fishing, and trapping for 5,000 years.

In California the basic water problem is that 75% of the population lives south of Sacramento but 75% of the rain falls north of it. The California Water Project uses a maze of giant dams, pumps, and aqueducts to transport water from water-rich northern California to heavily populated areas of the state and to arid and semiarid agricultural regions (Figure 13-13). For decades northern and southern Californians have been feuding over how state water should be allocated under this project.

Southern Californians say they need more water from the north to support Los Angeles, San Diego, and other growing urban areas, and to grow crops. Agriculture uses 82% of all water withdrawn in California. Irrigation for just two crops, alfalfa and cotton, uses as much water as the residential needs of all 30 million Californians.

Opponents in the north say that sending more water south would degrade the Sacramento River, threaten fisheries, and reduce the flushing action that helps clean San Francisco Bay of pollutants. They also argue that much of the water already sent south is wasted and that making irrigation just 10% more efficient would provide enough water for domestic and industrial uses in southern California.

To supply agribusiness in California and other western states with cheap water, the Bureau of Reclmation has drained major rivers and lakes, and destroyed vast areas of wetland waterfowl habitat and salmon spawning habitat. Owens Lake has been virtually sucked dry and reduced to a salt flat, mostly to supply water for Los Angeles. Mono Lake activists are fighting the same fate.

Environmentalists believe that the federal government should not award new long-term water contracts that give many farmers and ranchers cheap, government-subsidized water for irrigating crops—especially grass for cows and "thirsty" crops such as rice, alfalfa, and cotton—that could be grown more cheaply in rain-fed areas. They also propose enacting state laws requiring cities wanting more water to pay farmers to install water-saving irrigation technology. Cities could then use the water saved. Mostly because of federal and state subsidies, the average price of water in California is 21% lower than that for the rest of the United States.

A related project is the federally financed $3.9-billion Central Arizona Project, which pumps water from the Colorado River uphill to Phoenix and Tucson (Figure 13-13). Because of this project Arizona has been able to reduce its dependence on groundwater from over 90% to about 65%. However, southern California, especially the arid and booming San Diego region, lost up to one-fifth of its water from the Colorado River, which Arizona has a legal right to divert.

If water supplies in California were to drop sharply because of projected global warming, water delivered by its huge distribution system would plummet as well. Most irrigated agriculture in California would have to be abandoned, and much of the population of southern California might have to move to areas with more water. The six-year drought that northern and southern California experienced between 1986 and 1992—which cost the state more than $4 billion in lost revenues—was a small taste of a possible future.

Groundwater is no answer. Throughout most of California it is already being withdrawn faster than it is replenished. Santa Barbara, Los Angeles, and several other southern California cities are planning experimental desalination plants—an option five to six times more costly than state-provided water. Improving irrigation efficiency and allowing farmers to sell their water allotments are much quicker and cheaper solutions.

**Figure 13-13** California Water Projects and Central Arizona Project for large-scale transfer of water from one watershed to another. Arrows show general direction of water flow.

Q: How much do farmers in MDCs get in government subsidies?

## The Aral Sea Ecological Disaster

The CIS states of Kazakhstan and Uzbekistan have the driest climate in Central Asia. Since 1960 enormous amounts of irrigation water have been diverted from the inland Aral Sea—a huge freshwater lake—and its two feeder rivers to grow cotton and food crops. The irrigation canal, the world's longest, stretches over 1,300 kilometers (800 miles).

The diversion has caused a regional ecological disaster, described by one CIS official as "ten times worse than the 1986 Chernobyl accident." The sea's salinity has tripled, its surface area has shrunk by 46%, and its volume has decreased by 69% (Figure 13-14). The two supply rivers are mere trickles. About 30,000 square kilometers (11,600 square miles) of former lake bottom have turned into desert, and the process continues.

All the native fish are gone, devastating the area's fishing industry, which once provided work for more than 60,000 people. Two major fishing towns are now surrounded by a desert containing stranded fishing boats and rusting commercial ships. Roughly half of the area's bird and mammal species have also disappeared.

Salt, dust, and dried pesticide residues have been carried as far as 300 kilometers (190 miles) away by the wind. As the salt spreads, it kills crops and trees, wildlife, and pastureland. This phenomenon has added a new term to our vocabulary of environmental ills: *salt rain*. Data indicate that the Aral Sea basin may be experiencing some of the worst salinization in the world.

These changes have also affected the area's already semiarid climate. The once-huge Aral Sea acted as a thermal buffer, moderating the heat of summer and the extreme cold of winter. Now there is less rain, summers are hotter, winters are colder, and the growing season is shorter.

Cotton and crop yields have dropped dramatically.

Local farmers have turned to herbicides, insecticides, and fertilizers to keep growing some crops. Many of these chemicals have percolated downward and accumulated to dangerous levels in the groundwater, from which most of the drinking water comes. The area has experienced soaring rates of hepatitis (up 7-fold since 1960), typhoid fever (up 30-fold since 1960), kidney disease, birth defects, intestinal infections, throat and other cancers, and respiratory and eye diseases. It also has the highest infant mortality rate in the CIS.

Ways to deal with this problem include (1) charging farmers more for irrigation water to reduce waste and encourage a shift to less water-intensive crops, (2) decreasing irrigation water quotas, (3) introducing water-saving technologies, (4) developing a regional integrated water management plan, (5) planting protective forest belts, (6) using underground water to supplement irrigation water and lower the water table to reduce waterlogging and salinization, (7) improving health services, and (8) slowing the area's rapid population growth (3% per year).

One gigantic scheme to save the Aral Sea involves reversing the direction of the Ob and Irtysh rivers in Siberia, which now flow into the Arctic Ocean, and channeling the water 2,400 kilometers (1,500 miles) south to refill the sea and provide more irrigation water. However, this project, with a start-up cost of $40 billion, has already been rejected three times because of the cost and possible environmental side effects, including possible regional climate changes that might affect the global climate.

In 1990 the former Soviet Union and the United Nations Environment Programme signed an agreement to save the Aral Sea. However, given the political and economic crises brought about by the breakup of the Soviet Union, the huge sums of money needed to do this will probably not be available.

**Figure 13-14** Once the world's fourth largest freshwater lake, the Aral Sea has been shrinking and getting saltier since 1960 because most of the water from the rivers that replenish it have been diverted to grow cotton and food crops. As the lake shrinks, it leaves a salty desert.

A: $300 billion per year ($17–22 billion per year in the United States)

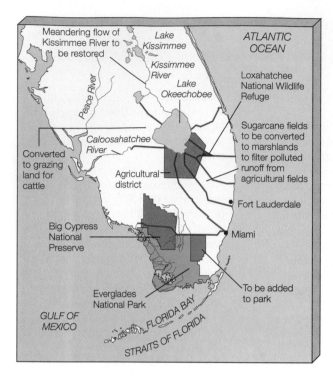

**Figure 13-15** The world's largest ecological restoration project is an attempt to undo and redo an engineering project that is destroying Florida's Everglades.

Phase I, which took 20 years and $16 billion to complete, reversed the flow of a major river and flooded an 11,000-square-kilometer (4,200-square-mile) area of northern Canadian forest. However, the resulting reservoir disrupted caribou migration routes and obliterated a primary calving ground of North America's largest caribou herd. In addition, when trees in flooded forests began decomposing, bacteria transformed mercury that had been tied up in rocks and soil into highly toxic methyl mercury, which has accumulated in the food web and contaminated fish that have been an important source of food for the Cree. It will take 20–30 years for the mercury levels in the fish to return to normal.

The second and much larger phase (Figure 13-12), scheduled to begin soon, would flood a wilderness area the size of New Hampshire that includes the world's largest breeding ground for waterfowl. However, this phase is being opposed in court by the Cree, whose ancestral hunting grounds would be flooded. They also contend that twice the amount of electricity that the project will eventually provide could be saved by an energy conservation program at one-fifth to one-tenth the cost. In 1990 the federal court of Canada ordered a full environmental impact assessment for this project, including public hearings. And in the summer of 1992, New York Governor Mario Cuomo

canceled a contract to buy electricity produced by phase II for use in New York. But the battle is not over.

**ECOLOGICAL RESTORATION: CAN WE SAVE THE EVERGLADES?** The Florida Everglades is a slow-flowing river 80 kilometers (50 miles) wide and generally only 15 centimeters (6 inches) deep. It begins south of Orlando in a series of spring-fed lakes that drain into the Kissimmee River, which until the 1960s meandered 160 kilometers (100 miles) through marshland to the vast, shallow Lake Okeechobee. From there it flows south through Everglades National Park to the estuary of Florida Bay (Figure 13-15).

As the thin layer of water trickles south to the Florida Bay, it creates a vast wetland with a variety of habitats. When the water reaches the Florida Bay it flows through coastal marshes and mangroves, which help protect the shoreline from storms. Without the Everglades rain distribution and aquifer recharge system, Miami and the rest of south Florida would be uninhabitable.

This waterlogged subtropical wilderness is a sanctuary for a staggering variety of wildlife, including many rare plants and animals, hundreds of species of wading birds and migratory waterfowl, and bald eagles roosting in cypress trees. It is a haven for 14 endangered or threatened species, including the American alligator (Figure 4-35), West Indian manatee (Figure 16-26), wood stork, green turtle, and highly endangered Florida panther (Figure 13-16).

Since the Civil War Americans have been draining, diking, filling, and converting much of the Everglades to farmlands, fruit groves, pastures, and cities to serve central and south Florida's exploding resident and tourist population. The result: Half of the original Everglades has been lost to development. The most devastating blow came in the 1960s when the U.S. Army Corps of Engineers transformed the meandering 103-mile-long Kissimmee River into a straight 84-kilometer (56-mile) canal—called "the dirty ditch" by environmentalists. The canal provided flood control by speeding the flow of water, but in the process it drained the water from large wetlands north of Lake Okeechobee, which farmers turned into cow pastures. South of the lake, water was drained to create a large agricultural zone used mostly to grow sugarcane and vegetables.

To help preserve the lower end of the system, the U.S. government established the Everglades National Park in 1947, which contains about 20% of the remaining Everglades (Figure 13-15). This didn't work because—as environmentalists had predicted—the massive plumbing and land development project to the north cut off much of the water flow needed to sustain the park's wildlife—making it the country's most

Q: What percentage of U.S. crops are grown using organic methods (no pesticides or commercial fertilizers)?

**Figure 13-16** The highly endangered Florida panther. Some 30 to 50 of these animals remain in the Everglades and in Big Cypress National Preserve. These nocturnal carnivores roam up to 130 square kilometers (50 square miles) to hunt deer, wild hogs, and small mammals. To reduce killing of these animals by cars, underpasses have been built along Interstate 75. A captive breeding program has transferred 5 breeding pairs from the wild to zoos with the goal of breeding 200 panthers for return to the wild by 2000—if a place can be found to return them to.

endangered national park. By the late 1960s the park had lost 80% of its marshlands, and populations of wading birds had plummeted 90% from 1930 levels. Florida Bay received less than one-fourth of the fresh water that once flowed from the Everglades estuary, increasing salinity and decreasing the productivity of one of the country's richest fisheries.

Falling water levels also began threatening Miami's water supply as more water was drawn from its aquifer than was replenished. This caused salt water to move inland, irreversibly contaminating supplies of drinking water in some areas of south Florida.

There were also serious ecological effects north and south of Lake Okeechobee. Nutrients from cow manure running off the new pastures shot down the straight Kissimmee canal and into Lake Okeechobee, spawning the explosive growth of algae and other vegetation that deplete the water of oxygen. North and south of Lake Okeechobee, nutrients flowing from pastures and cropland caused an explosive growth of cattails, fast-growing Meleleuca trees (deliberately introduced from Australia in the 1940s), and other non-native species that displaced native sawgrass. This takeover by exotic species has been slowly spreading south.

By the 1970s state and federal officials recognized that this massive plumbing project—especially converting the winding Kissimmee River to a straight canal—had been a serious ecological blunder. In 1976 the Florida legislature passed a bill calling for restoration of the Kissimmee River. After another 15 years of delay and haggling, the state and federal government

have agreed upon a massive ecological project to undo some of the damage—the most ambitious river restoration project ever undertaken (Figure 13-15). Its goals include:

- Filling in half of the Kissimmee canal
- Restoring the curving flow of over half of the Kissimmee River
- Altering highway construction to safeguard the endangered Florida panther (Figure 13-16)
- Reclaiming large areas of wetlands along the floodplain above and below Lake Okeechobee
- Constructing artificial marshes to filter pollutants out of agricultural drainage water
- Establishing stricter water-use and water quality regulations for farms
- Removing spillways and levees blocking water flow south of Lake Okeechobee
- Creating a large buffer area separating the agricultural areas south of Lake Okeechobee from Everglades National Park
- Adding land to the park's eastern border

This ambitious project will take at least 15 years and cost at least $800 million, with the federal government paying 75% of the tab and the state 25%. This reengineering project will not restore the Everglades to its natural state, but hopefully it will fix some of what was broken. This is another lesson from nature showing that prevention is best and cheapest.

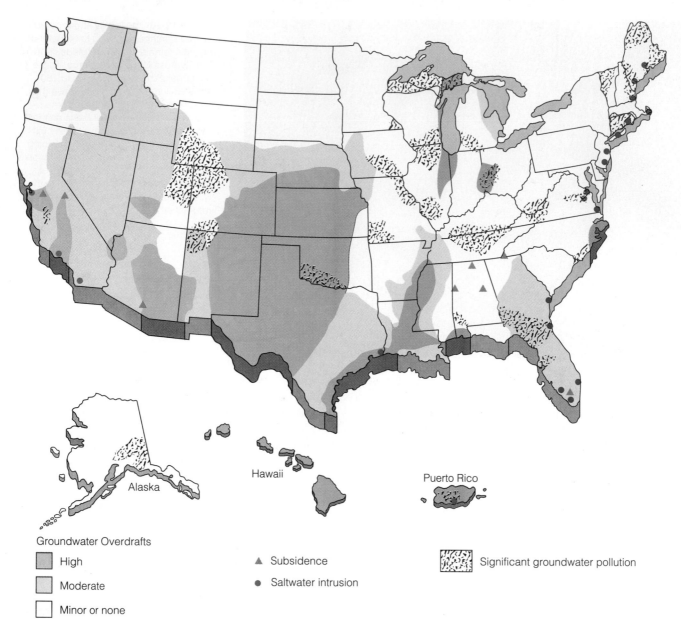

**Groundwater Overdrafts**

■ High

▲ Subsidence

▨ Significant groundwater pollution

■ Moderate

● Saltwater intrusion

□ Minor or none

**Figure 13-17** Areas of greatest aquifer depletion, subsidence, saltwater intrusion, and groundwater contamination in the United States. (Data from U.S. Water Resources Council and U.S. Geological Survey)

| 13-5 | **Other Ways to Supply Water** |

**TAPPING GROUNDWATER** In the United States 23% of all fresh water used is groundwater. About half of the country's drinking water (96% in rural areas and 20% in urban areas) and 40% of irrigation water are pumped from aquifers. In Florida, Hawaii, Idaho, Mississippi, Nebraska, and New Mexico, more than 90% of the population depends on groundwater for supplies of drinking water.

Overuse of groundwater can cause or intensify several problems: aquifer depletion, subsidence (sinking of land when groundwater is withdrawn; Figure 7-31), and intrusion of salt water into aquifers (Figure 13-17). Groundwater can also become contaminated from industrial and agricultural activities, septic tanks, and other sources. Because groundwater is the source of about 40% of the stream flow in the United States, groundwater depletion robs streams of water.

Currently about one-fourth of the groundwater withdrawn in the United States is not replenished. The most serious overdraft is in parts of the huge Ogallala Aquifer, extending from northern Nebraska to north-

**Q:** How much of the food produced in the United States is wasted?

The Ogallala (Figure 13-18)—the world's largest known aquifer— underlies the arid Great Plains. Water pumped from the Ogallala has helped transform much of a vast prairie into America's most productive farmland in an area too dry for rainfall farming. Although this aquifer is gigantic, it is essentially a nonrenewable fossil aquifer with an extremely slow recharge rate. Water is being pumped out at eight times its natural recharge rate, mostly for irrigation to supply 15% of the country's corn and wheat, 25% of its cotton, and 40% of its feedlot beef. Each time Americans eat hamburgers or steaks, they may contribute to this draining of Earth capital.

The withdrawal rate is 100 times the recharge rate for parts of the aquifer that lie beneath Texas, New Mexico, Oklahoma, and Colorado. At the present rate of withdrawal, water experts project that one-

fourth of the aquifer's original supply will be depleted by 2020—much sooner in areas where it is shallow. Then the area will become a desert. It will take thousands of years to replenish the aquifer. Depletion is encouraged by federal tax laws that allow farmers and ranchers to deduct the cost of drilling equipment and sinking of wells.

Long before the water is gone, the high cost of pumping water from a rapidly dropping water table will force many farmers to grow "water-miser" crops instead of profitable but "thirsty" crops such as cotton and sugar beets. Some farmers will go out of business. Total irrigated area is already declining in five of the seven states using this aquifer because water must be pumped from depths as great as 1,830 meters (6,000 feet).

If farmers in the Ogallala region conserved more water and switched to low-water crops, depletion of the aquifer could be delayed.

**Figure 13-18** The Ogallala, the world's largest known aquifer. If the water in this aquifer were above ground, it would be enough to cover the entire lower 48 states with 0.5 meter (1.5 feet) of water. This fossil aquifer, which is renewed very slowly, is being depleted to grow crops and raise cattle.

---

western Texas (Case Study, above). Aquifer depletion is also a serious problem in Saudi Arabia, northern China, Mexico City, Bangkok, and parts of India. For example, the demands of Mexico City's 16 million people (Case Study, p. 232) are lowering the water table of their main aquifer as much as 3.4 meters (11 feet) per year. And Saudi Arabia's remarkable increase in agricultural productivity is based on withdrawing water from fossil aquifers, with essentially negligible recharge rates, to irrigate crops in the desert. At the current rate the country's fossil groundwater will be exhausted by 2007.

Ways to slow groundwater depletion include (1) controlling population growth, (2) not growing water-thirsty crops in dry areas, (3) developing crop strains that require less water and are more resistant to heat stress, and (4) wasting less irrigation water.

When groundwater in an unconfined aquifer (Figure 13-5) is withdrawn faster than it is replenished, the water table drops and land overlying the aquifer can sink, or subside. This subsidence can damage pipelines, highways, railroad beds, and buildings (Figure 7-31).

When fresh water is withdrawn from an aquifer near a coast faster than it is recharged, salt water intrudes into the aquifer (Figure 13-19). Saltwater intrusion threatens to contaminate the drinking water of many towns and cities along the Atlantic and Gulf coasts (Figure 13-17) and in the coastal areas of Israel, Syria, and the Arabian Gulf states. Another growing problem in the United States and many other MDCs is groundwater contamination, which is discussed in Section 23-4.

**DESALINATION** Desalination—the removal of dissolved salts from ocean water or brackish (slightly salty) groundwater—is another way to increase freshwater supplies. Distillation and reverse osmosis are the two most widely used methods. *Distillation* involves heating salt water until it evaporates and condenses as fresh water, leaving salts behind in solid form. In *reverse osmosis* salt water is pumped at high pressure through a thin membrane whose pores allow water molecules but not dissolved salts to pass through.

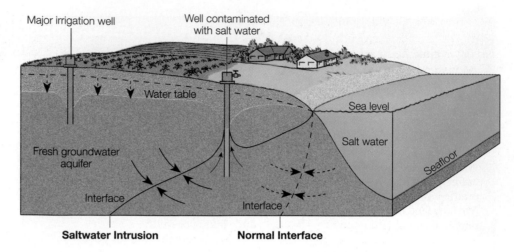

**Figure 13-19** Saltwater intrusion along a coastal region. When the water table is lowered, the normal interface (dotted line) between fresh and saline groundwater moves inland (solid line).

Major irrigation well

Well contaminated with salt water

Water table

Sea level

Salt water

Seafloor

Fresh groundwater aquifer

Interface

Interface

**Saltwater Intrusion**

**Normal Interface**

Although about 7,500 desalination plants are in operation in 120 countries, these plants provide less than 0.1% of the world's water. About two-thirds of these plants are treating sea water, and the rest brackish water. Desalination plants in the Middle East (especially Saudi Arabia and Kuwait) and North Africa produce about two-thirds of the world's desalinated water. Desalination is also used in parts of Florida. Soon Marin County (northern California) and Santa Barbara, San Diego, and Los Angeles may turn to desalination to supplement their water supplies.

Desalination, however, has a downside. It uses vast amounts of electricity and therefore costs three to five times more than water from conventional sources. Distributing the water from coastal desalination plants costs even more in terms of the energy needed to pump desalinated water uphill and inland. Moreover, desalination produces large quantities of brine with high levels of salt and other minerals that must go somewhere. Dumping the concentrated brine in the ocean near the plants might seem to be the logical solution, but this would increase the salt concentration and threaten food resources in estuarine waters. And if these wastes were dumped on the land, they could contaminate groundwater and surface water. There is no away.

Desalination can provide fresh water for coastal cities in arid regions, such as sparsely populated and oil-rich Saudi Arabia, where the cost of getting fresh water by any method is high. There is also interest in building desalination plants alongside power plants and using waste heat from the plants to drive the desalination process. However, desalinated water will probably never be cheap enough to use for irrigating conventional crops or to meet much of the world's demand for fresh water, unless efficient solar-powered methods can be developed. And the problem of what to do with the salt must be solved.

**CLOUD SEEDING AND TOWING ICEBERGS** Several countries, particularly the United States, have been experimenting for years with seeding clouds with chemicals to produce more rain over dry regions and snow over mountains. Cloud seeding involves injecting a large, suitable cloud with a powdered chemical such as silver iodide from a plane or from ground-mounted burners. Small water droplets in the cloud clump together around tiny particles of the chemical (condensation nuclei) and form drops or ice particles large enough to fall to Earth as precipitation.

Unfortunately, cloud seeding is not useful in very dry areas, where it is most needed, because rain clouds are rarely available. Also, large-scale use could change snowfall and rainfall patterns, and alter regional or even global climate patterns in unknown ways. Furthermore, widespread cloud seeding would introduce large amounts of the cloud-seeding chemicals into soil and water systems, possibly harming people, wildlife, and agricultural productivity. A final obstacle to cloud seeding is legal disputes over the ownership of water in clouds. For example, during the 1977 drought in the western United States, the attorney general of Idaho accused officials in neighboring Washington of "cloud rustling" and threatened to file suit in federal court.

There also have been proposals to tow massive icebergs to arid coastal areas (such as Saudi Arabia and southern California) and pump the fresh water from the melting bergs ashore. However, the technology for doing this is not available and the costs may be too high, especially for water-short LDCs.

**13-6** **Using Water More Efficiently**

**CURBING WASTE** Increasing the water supply in some areas is important, but soaring population, food needs, and industrialization, along with unpredictable

Q: How much of all U.S. land consists of public lands?

shifts in water supplies, will eventually outstrip this approach. It makes much more sense economically and environmentally to use water more efficiently.

Mohamed El-Ashry of the World Resources Institute estimates that *65–70% of the water people use throughout the world is wasted through evaporation, leaks, and other losses*. The United States—the world's largest user of water—does slightly better but still wastes 50% of the water it withdraws. El-Ashry believes that it is economically and technically feasible to reduce water waste to 15%, thus meeting most of the world's water needs for the foreseeable future.

Conserving water would have many other benefits. These include reducing the burden on wastewater plants and septic systems, decreasing pollution of surface water and groundwater, reducing the number of expensive dams and water transfer projects that destroy wildlife habitats and displace people, slowing depletion of groundwater aquifers, and saving energy and money needed to supply and treat water.

In many parts of the world farmers pay by the area of land they irrigate, regardless of how much water they use. Thus they have little incentive to conserve water.

A prime cause of water waste in the United States (and in most countries) is artificially low water prices. Cheap water is the only reason that farmers in Arizona and southern California can grow water-thirsty crops like alfalfa in the middle of the desert. It also enables people in Palm Springs, California, to keep their lawns and 74 golf courses green in a desert area.

Water subsidies are paid for by all taxpayers in higher taxes. Because these external costs don't show up on monthly water bills, consumers have little incentive to use less water or to install water-conserving devices and processes. Raising the price of water to reflect its true cost would be a powerful incentive for using water more efficiently.

The federal Bureau of Reclamation supplies one-fourth of the water used to irrigate land in the western United States under long-term contracts (typically 40 years) at greatly subsidized prices. During the 1990s hundreds of these long-term water contracts will come up for renewal. Sharply raising the price of federally subsidized water would encourage investments in improving water efficiency, and many of the West's water supply problems could be eased. Outdated laws governing access to and use of water resources also encourage unnecessary water waste (Spotlight, right).

Another reason for water waste in the United States is that the responsibility for water resource management in a particular watershed may be divided among many state and local governments rather than being handled by one authority. For example, the Chicago metropolitan area has 349 water supply

## Water Rights in the United States

**SPOTLIGHT**

Laws regulating surface-water access and use differ in the eastern and western parts of the United States. In most of the East water use is based on the doctrine of **riparian rights**. Basically this system of water law gives anyone whose land adjoins a flowing stream the right to use water from the stream as long as some is left for downstream landowners. However, as population and water-intensive land uses grow, there often is not enough water to meet the needs of all the people along a stream.

In the arid and semiarid West the riparian system does not work because large amounts of water are needed in areas far from major surface-water sources. In most of this region the principle of **prior appropriation** regulates water use. In this first-come, first-served approach, the first user of water from a stream establishes a legal right for continued use of the amount originally withdrawn. If there is a shortage, later users are cut off in order, one by one, until there is enough water to satisfy the demands of the earlier users. Some states have a combination of riparian and prior appropriation water rights.

To retain their prior appropriation rights, users within a particular state must withdraw a certain amount of water even if they don't need it—a use-it-or-lose-it approach—which discourages farmers from adopting water-conserving irrigation methods. However, this use-it-or-lose-it rule does not apply to water bodies shared by two or more states. Water allocation between states is determined by interstate compacts and court decrees.

Most groundwater use is based on common law, which holds that subsurface water belongs to whoever owns the land above such water. This means that landowners can withdraw as much as they want to use on their land.

When many users tap the same aquifer, that aquifer becomes a common-property resource. Unfortunately multiple users may remove water faster than it is replaced. The largest users have little incentive to conserve and can deplete the aquifer for everyone, creating another tragedy of the commons (Spotlight, p. 14).

Environmentalists and many economists call for a change in laws allocating rights to surface and groundwater supplies, with emphasis on *water marketing*. They believe that farmers and other users who save water through conservation or a shift to less water-thirsty crops should be able to sell or lease the water they save to industries and cities rather than losing their rights to this water.

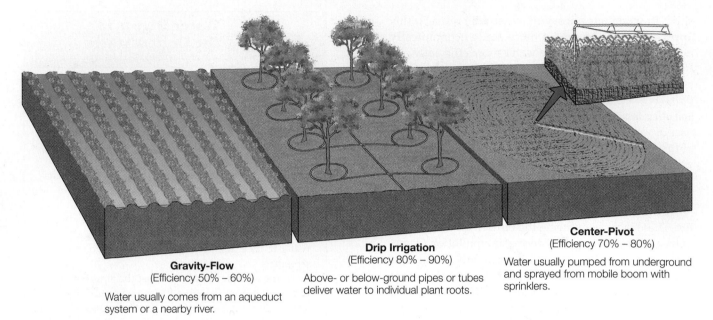

**Figure 13-20** Major irrigation systems.

**Gravity-Flow**
(Efficiency 50% – 60%)
Water usually comes from an aqueduct system or a nearby river.

**Drip Irrigation**
(Efficiency 80% – 90%)
Above- or below-ground pipes or tubes deliver water to individual plant roots.

**Center-Pivot**
(Efficiency 70% – 80%)
Water usually pumped from underground and sprayed from mobile boom with sprinklers.

systems, divided among some 2,000 local units of government over a six-county area.

In sharp contrast is the regional approach to water management used in England and Wales. The British Water Act of 1973 replaced more than 1,600 agencies with 10 regional water authorities based on natural watershed boundaries. Each water authority owns, finances, and manages all water supply and waste treatment facilities in its region. The responsibilities of each authority include water pollution control, water-based recreation, land drainage and flood control, inland navigation, and inland fisheries. Each water authority is managed by a group of elected local officials and a smaller number of officials appointed by the national government.

**REDUCING IRRIGATION LOSSES** Since irrigation accounts for 63% of water use and since almost two-thirds of that water is wasted, more efficient use of even a small amount of irrigation water frees water for other uses.

Most irrigation systems distribute water from a groundwater well or a surface canal by downslope or gravity flow through unlined field ditches (Figure 13-20). This method is cheap as long as farmers in water-short areas don't have to pay the real cost of making this water available. However, it delivers far more water than needed for crop growth, with only 50–60% of the water reaching crops because of evaporation, deep percolation (seepage), and runoff. Such

overwatering without adequate drainage also decreases crop yields by waterlogging and the buildup of salts in the soil (Figure 12-19).

Farmers can prevent seepage by placing plastic, concrete, or tile liners in irrigation canals. Lasers can also be used as a surveying aid to help level fields so that water gets distributed more evenly. Small check dams of earth and stone can capture runoff from hillsides and channel it to fields. Holding ponds can store rainfall or capture irrigation water for recycling to crops. Reforesting watersheds leads to a more manageable flow of irrigation water, instead of a devastating flood (Case Study, p. 340).

Many farmers served by the dwindling Ogallala Aquifer now use center-pivot sprinkler systems (Figure 13-20), with which 70–80% of the water reaches crops. Some farmers are switching to low-energy precision-application (LEPA) sprinklers. These systems bring 75–85% of the water to crops by spraying it closer to the ground and in larger droplets than does the center-pivot system. They also reduce energy use and costs by 20–30%. However, because of the high initial costs, sprinklers are used on only about 1% of the world's irrigated land.

In the 1960s highly efficient trickle or drip irrigation systems were developed in arid Israel. A network of perforated piping, installed at or below the ground surface, releases a trickle of water close to plant roots (Figure 13-20). This minimizes evaporation and seepage, and brings 80–90% of the water to crops. These systems are expensive to install but are economically

Q: Where is most of the federally owned and managed land in the United States?

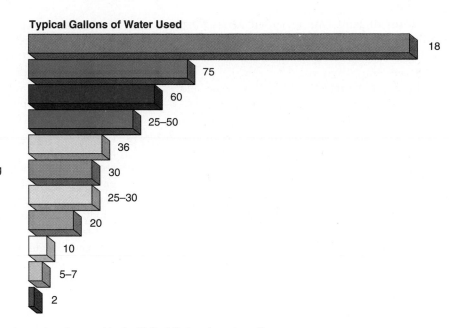

| Use | Typical Gallons of Water Used |
|---|---|
| Washing a car with hose running | 18 |
| Watering lawn for ten minutes | 75 |
| Washing machine at top level | 60 |
| Ten-minute shower | 25–50 |
| Average bath | 36 |
| Hand-washing dishes with water running | 30 |
| Dripping faucet (per day) | 25–30 |
| Shaving with water running | 20 |
| Automatic dishwasher | 10 |
| Toilet flush | 5–7 |
| Brushing teeth with water running | 2 |

**Figure 13-21** Some ways domestic water is used and wasted in the United States. An automatic or self-service car wash that recycles much of the water uses about 30 gallons of water per wash. Washing your car without the hose running takes about 15 gallons. (Data from American Water Works Association)

feasible for high-profit fruit, vegetable, and orchard crops and for home gardens. They would become cost-effective in most areas if water prices reflected the true cost of this resource.

Irrigation efficiency can also be improved by computer-controlled systems that monitor soil moisture and provide water only when necessary. Farmers can switch to more water-efficient, drought-resistant, and salt-tolerant crop varieties. In addition, farmers can use organic farming techniques, which produce higher crop yields per hectare and require only one-fourth of the water and commercial fertilizer of conventional farming. Since 1950 Israel has used many of these techniques to slash irrigation water waste by about 84%, while irrigating 44% more land.

As fresh water becomes scarce and cities consume water once used for irrigation, carefully treated urban wastewater could be used for irrigation. Effluents from sewage treatment plants are rich in nitrates and phosphates. Now these nutrients are often dumped into waterways where they overfertilize and disrupt aquatic ecosystems. It makes more sense to return them to the land to fertilize trees, crops, and other vegetation. For example, Israel now reuses 35% of its municipal wastewater, mostly for irrigation, and plans to reuse 80% of this flow by 2000.

**WASTING LESS WATER IN INDUSTRY** Manufacturing processes can use recycled water or be redesigned to save water. Japan and Israel lead the world in conserving and recycling water in industry. For example, a paper mill in Hadera, Israel, uses one-tenth as much water as most other paper mills do. Manufacturing aluminum from recycled scrap rather than virgin ores can reduce water needs by 97%.

In the United States industry is the largest conserver of water. However, the potential for water recycling in U.S. manufacturing has hardly been tapped because the cost of water to many industries is subsidized. A higher, more realistic price would stimulate additional water reuse and conservation in industry.

**WASTING LESS WATER IN HOMES AND BUSINESSES** Flushing toilets, washing hands, and bathing account for about 78% of the water used in a typical U.S. home. In the arid western United States and in dry Australia, lawn and garden watering can take 80% of a household's daily usage. Much of this water is wasted (Figure 13-21).

More than half the water supply in Cairo, Lima, Mexico City, and Jakarta disappears before it can be used, mostly from leaks. Leaky pipes, water mains, toilets, bathtubs, and faucets waste 20–35% of water withdrawn from public supplies in the United States. Because water is cheap, leaky faucets may often not be fixed, and large quantities of water are used to clean sidewalks and streets and to irrigate lawns and golf courses. Green lawns in an arid or semiarid area should be replaced with vegetation adapted to a dry climate—a form of landscaping called *xeriscaping*, from the Greek word *xeros*, meaning "dry." A xeriscape yard typically uses 30–80% less water than a conventional one.

Many cities offer no incentive to reduce leaks and waste. In New York City, for example, 95% of the residential units don't have water meters. Users are charged flat rates, with the average family paying less than $100 a year for virtually unlimited use of high-quality water. The same is true for one-fifth of all U.S. public water systems. And many apartment dwellers have little incentive to conserve water because their water use is included in their rent. In Europe no country charges households for the amount of water they use, although France and the Netherlands are considering doing so.

In Boulder, Colorado, the introduction of water meters reduced water use by more than one-third. Tucson, Arizona, whose laws require conserving and reusing water, consumes half as much water per capita as Las Vegas, another desert city where water conservation is still voluntary.

In some parts of the United States you can lease systems that purify and completely recycle wastewater from houses, apartments, or office buildings. Such a system can be installed in a small shed and serviced for a monthly fee about equal to that charged by most city water and sewer systems. In Tokyo all the water used in Mitsubishi's 60-story office building is purified for reuse by an automated recycling system.

A New Jersey office complex cut water consumption 62% with an on-site treatment and reuse system. A Michigan hotel saved about $750,000 over eight years in construction costs and water and sewer bills by installing water-saving toilets, faucets, and shower heads when it was built. In 1988 Massachusetts became the first state to require that all new toilets use no more than 6 liters (1.6 gallons) per flush. Since then 14 other states have followed suit and most have also adopted water-saving standards for new faucets and shower heads. A California water utility gives rebates for water-saving toilets and distributed free some 35,000 water-saving shower heads, cutting per capita water use 40% in only one year.

A low-flow shower head costing $20 saves about $66 a year in water and energy costs. Audits conducted by students in Brown University's environmental studies program showed that the school could save $44,000 a year by installing low-flow shower heads in dormitories.

In 1989 Mexico adopted nationwide water-efficiency standards for new household plumbing fixtures and appliances. Water-short Mexico City has launched a program to replace conventional toilets (which use about 16 liters per flush) with 6-liter models in all of its buildings. It also hiked water rates in 1990 to encourage residents to install water-saving devices. In Ontario, Canada, new toilets must meet a 6-liter per flush standard by 1996. The University of Arizona's Casa del Agua (House of Water) is a demonstration project in which a house and its grounds have been landscaped and fitted with water-saving and water-recycling devices. Rainfall is captured and used to irrigate plants and to provide water for some household uses. Gray water from bathtubs, showers, bathroom sinks, and clothes washers is stored, carefully treated, and reused for irrigation and other purposes. California has become the first state to legalize reuse of gray water to irrigate landscape. An estimated 50–75% of the water used by a typical house could be reused as gray water.

**FUTURE WATER MANAGEMENT GOALS** Sustainable use of Earth's water resources involves developing an integrated approach to managing water resources and water pollution throughout each watershed. It also means reducing or eliminating water subsidies so that market prices more closely reflect water's true cost.

Doing this will require us to recognize that the environment we now treat as separate parts—air, water, soil, life—is an interconnected whole. This will require unprecedented cooperation among communities, states, and countries. Each of us can play our part by reducing unnecessary water waste (Individuals Matter, p. 357).

*It is not until the well runs dry, that we know the worth of water.*

BENJAMIN FRANKLIN

## Critical Thinking

1. How do human activities increase the harmful effects of prolonged drought? How can these effects be reduced?

2. How do human activities contribute to flooding? How can these effects be reduced?

3. How can dams and reservoirs cause more flood damage than they prevent? Explain. Should all proposed large dam and reservoir projects be scrapped? Explain.

4. Should water prices for all uses in the United States be raised sharply to encourage water conservation?

**Q:** What percentage of land in the lower 48 states is covered by forests?

## How to Save Water and Money

**INDIVIDUALS MATTER**

- For existing toilets, reduce the amount of water used per flush by putting a tall plastic container weighted with a few stones into each tank, or buy and insert a toilet dam. Ask school officials to install toilet dams.

- Install water-saving toilets that use no more than 6 liters (1.6 gallons) per flush.

- Consider flushing toilets only when necessary, using the advice found on a bathroom wall in a drought-stricken area: "If it's yellow, let it mellow—if it's brown, flush it down."

- Install water-saving shower heads and flow restrictors on all faucets. Ask school officials to install these devices.

- Check frequently for water leaks in toilets and pipes and repair them promptly. A pinhole-sized leak can waste up to 640 liters (170 gallons) per month. A toilet must be leaking more than 940 liters (250 gallons) *a day* before you can hear the leak. To test for toilet leaks, add some water-soluble dye to the water in the tank but don't flush. If you have a leak, some color will show up in the bowl's water within a few minutes.

- Don't keep water running while brushing teeth, shaving, or washing.

- Try to wash only full loads; use the short cycle and fill the machine to the lowest possible water level.

- When buying a new washer, choose one that uses the least amount of water and fills up to different levels for loads of different sizes. Front-loading clothes washers use less water and energy than comparable top-loading models.

- Try to use an automatic dishwasher only for full loads; use the short cycle and let dishes air-dry to save energy and money.

- When washing many dishes by hand, don't let the faucet run. Instead, use one filled dishpan or sink for washing and another for rinsing.

- Keep a reusable jug of water in the refrigerator rather than running water from a tap until it gets cold enough to drink.

- Don't use a garbage disposal system—a large user of water. Instead, compost your food wastes.

- Wash your car from a bucket of soapy water and use the hose only for rinsing. Use a commercial car wash that recycles its water.

- Sweep walks and driveways instead of hosing them off.

- Reduce evaporation losses by watering lawns and gardens in the early morning or in the evening, rather than in the heat of midday or when windy. Better yet, landscape with native plants adapted to local average annual precipitation so that watering is unnecessary.

- Use drip irrigation systems and mulch on home gardens to improve irrigation efficiency and reduce evaporation.

- To irrigate plants, install a system to capture rainwater or collect, filter, and reuse normally wasted gray water from bathtubs, showers, sinks, and the clothes washer.

Explain. What effects might this have on the economy, on you, on the poor, and on the environment?

5. List 10 major ways to conserve water on a personal level. Which, if any, of these practices do you now use or intend to use?

*6. In your community:
   a. What are the major sources of the water supply?
   b. How is water use divided among agricultural, industrial, power-plant cooling, and public uses? Who are the biggest consumers of water?
   c. What has happened to water prices during the past 20 years? Are they too low to encourage water conservation and reuse?
   d. What water supply problems are projected?
   e. How is water being wasted?

# 14 Food Resources

## *Perennial Crops on the Kansas Prairie*

When you think about farms in Kansas you probably picture endless fields of wheat or corn plowed up and planted each year. By 2040 the picture might change, thanks to the pioneering work of the nonprofit Land Institute near Salina, Kansas (Figure 14-1).

The institute, founded by Wes and Dana Jackson, is experimenting with an ecological approach to agriculture on the midwestern prairie based on planting various *perennial* grasses, legumes, sunflowers, and grain crops in the same field rather than planting and replanting a single food crop each year. The institute's goal is to raise food by mimicking many of the natural conditions of the prairie. Its researchers want to sustain a variety of plants in a harsh environment with high winds, drought, floods, and extremes of heat and cold without losing fertile grassland soil.

In the natural grasslands of the midwest (Figure 5-18) soil is rarely left exposed to the wind and rain. Instead, it is protected and sustained by a community of perennials that grow together from year to year. These plants have deep roots that anchor the soil in place and enrich it with their own decaying tissues. The institute is attempting to duplicate this process by planting polycultures of edible perennial plants.

Institute researchers don't envision completely replacing the present production of annual monoculture crops with a diverse mix of perennials. But they do believe that perennial polyculture can be blended

**Figure 14-1** The Land Institute in Salina, Kansas. It is a farm, prairie laboratory, and school dedicated to changing the way we grow food by substituting a diverse mixture of edible perennial plants for traditional annual monoculture crops.

Terry Evans

with modern agriculture to reduce its massive environmental impact. Perennial polyculture is especially suitable for marginal land, leaving prime, flat land for annual crops.

By eliminating yearly soil preparation and planting, perennial polyculture requires much less labor than conventional monoculture farms and diversified organic farms growing annual crops. Perennial polyculture rewards farmers more for their wits, creative thinking, and caring for the land and less for routine drudgery and labor.

If it succeeds in learning how nature does it, the institute believes that the same basic ecological principles—such as the need for biodiversity and the importance of perennial plant roots to hold and enrich the soil—can be applied to agriculture in other biomes. And if the institute and similar groups doing such Earth-sustaining research succeed, by 2040 many people may be eating food made from *Maximilian sunflower* (which produces seeds with as much protein as soybeans), *eastern gamma grass* (a relative of corn with three times as much protein as corn and twice as much as wheat), *Illinois bundleflower* (a wild nitrogen-producing legume that can enrich the soil and whose seeds may serve as livestock feed), and *giant wild rye* (once eaten by Mongols in Siberia).

These discoveries will come none too soon. Global food production has increased substantially over the past two decades, but producing food and other agricultural products by conventional means uses more soil, water, plant, animal, and energy resources, and causes more pollution and environmental damage, than any other human activity. To feed the 8.5 billion people projected by 2025, we must produce and distribute as much food during the next 30 years as was produced since agriculture began about 10,000 years ago.

The discussion in this chapter answers several general questions:

- How is the world's food produced?
- What are the world's food problems?
- Can increasing crop yields and cultivating more land provide enough food?
- How much food can we get from catching more fish and cultivating fish in aquaculture farms and ranches?
- What can government policies, food aid, and land redistribution do to provide enough food?
- How can we design and shift to sustainable-Earth agricultural systems?

## 14-1 How Is Food Produced?

**PLANTS AND ANIMALS THAT FEED THE WORLD**
Of Earth's perhaps 30,000 plants with edible parts, we eat only about 30. Just 15 plants and 8 animal species supply 90% of our food. Four crops—wheat, rice, corn, and potato—make up more of the world's total food production than all others combined. Those four, and most of our other crops, are *annuals*, whose seeds must be replanted each year.

Grain provides about half the world's calories, with two out of three people eating mainly a vegetarian diet. As incomes rise, people consume more grain indirectly in the form of meat, eggs, milk, cheese, and other products of domesticated livestock. More than 70% of the protein in the typical American diet comes from animal products, with the remainder from plants; in China 89% comes from plants. Global meat production has nearly quadrupled since 1950.

**TYPES OF FOOD PRODUCTION** There are two major types of agricultural systems, industrialized and traditional (Spotlight, p. 360). **Industrialized agriculture** uses large amounts of fossil-fuel energy, water,

## Industrial Farmers

### Crop Production

Grow surplus food for sale by investing a large amount of money.

Plant hybrid seeds of a single crop variety on a large field (Figure 5-20).

Use high-tech equipment that is costly to buy, operate, repair, and replace.

Farm on flat, easily cultivated fields with fertile soil.

Increase yields with commercial fertilizers and irrigation (Figure 13-20).

Use chemicals to kill pest species as well as predators of pest species.

Keep a monoculture at an early stage of secondary ecological succession (Figure 6-14).

Cultivate with machinery powered by fossil fuels (Figure 5-20).

### Meat and Animal Product Production

Produce large quantities of a single meat or animal product for sale by investing a large amount of money.

Use feedlots to fatten hundreds to thousands of livestock in a small space (Figure 14-2). Feed animals antibiotics, and growth hormones to encourage rapid gain.

Produce fatty meat that most consumers like.

Burn fossil fuels to pump water, produce feed, and transport supplies and livestock, and plant, till, and harvest crops to feed livestock.

Produce large concentrations of animal wastes, which can contaminate nearby surface water or groundwater with nitrates, disease-causing bacteria, and excess plant nutrients.

## Traditional Subsistence Farmers

### Crop Production

Grow enough food to feed their families, investing little, if any, money.

Often plant a mix of naturally available crop seeds on a small plot (Figure 2-6).

Make or buy simple equipment that costs relatively little to run, repair, or replace.

Often farm on easily erodible, hard-to-cultivate, mountainous highlands, drylands with fragile soils, or tropical soils with low fertility.

Increase crop yields by using naturally available water and organic fertilizers.

Plant a mix of crops to provide habitats for natural predators of pest species (Figure 12-15).

Allow a mix of crops to imitate natural secondary ecological succession (Figure 6-14).

Cultivate by hand (Figure 14-4) or with help from draft animals.

### Meat and Animal Product Production

Produce enough meat and animal products to feed their families, investing little money.

Use natural grasslands and forests as sources of food and water for small groups of livestock. Often move flocks from one place to another to obtain enough food and water.

Produce lean meat, which is more healthful than fatty meat.

Use human and animal labor with little or no input of fossil fuels.

Return nutrient-rich animal wastes to the soil where the animals graze, use it as organic fertilizer, or burn it as fuel.

**Figure 14-2** Huge cattle feedlot near Coalinga, California. Most steers in the United States feed on the open range or on pasturelands for a year. Then they are brought to feedlots and fed for about 100 days on grain (mostly corn) laced with antibiotics (to prevent disease in the crowded conditions) to fatten them up before slaughter. Chickens and pigs may be kept in feedlots from birth to death. These feedlots increase production efficiency but also produce huge concentrations of animal wastes, which, without proper controls, can pollute groundwater and contribute to cultural eutrophication of nearby lakes and slow-moving streams.

Gene Daniels/National Archives/EPA Documerica

Q: What percentage of U.S. commercial forestland is found in national forests?

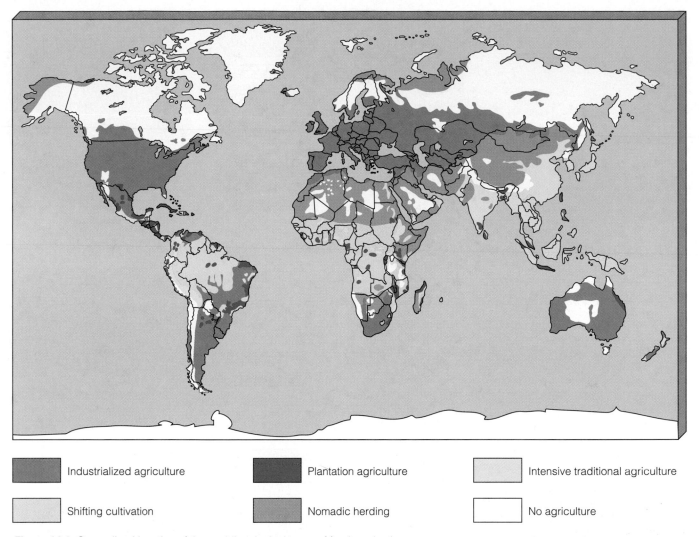

| | | |
|---|---|---|
| Industrialized agriculture | Plantation agriculture | Intensive traditional agriculture |
| Shifting cultivation | Nomadic herding | No agriculture |

**Figure 14-3** Generalized location of the world's principal types of food production.

commercial fertilizers, and pesticides to produce huge quantities of one crop or animal for sale. Industrialized agriculture, practiced on about 25% of all cropland, mostly in MDCs, has spread since the mid-1960s to some LDCs (Figure 14-3). **Plantation agriculture**, a form of industrialized agriculture, grows cash crops, such as bananas, coffee, and cacao, in tropical LDCs, mostly for sale to MDCs.

Traditional agriculture consists of two main types. **Traditional subsistence agriculture** produces enough crops or livestock for a farm family's survival and, in good years, a surplus to sell or put aside for hard times. Subsistence farmers use human labor and draft animals. Examples of this type of agriculture include shifting cultivation in tropical forests (Figure 2-6) and nomadic livestock herding. With **traditional intensive agriculture** farmers increase their inputs of human and draft labor, fertilizer, and water to get a higher yield per area of cultivated land to produce enough food to feed their families and perhaps a surplus for

sale (Figure 14-4). These forms of traditional agriculture are practiced by about 2.7 billion people—almost half the people on Earth—in LDCs.

The relative inputs of land, human and animal labor, fossil-fuel energy, and capital needed to produce one unit of food energy by various types of cultivation and herding are shown in Figure 14-5.

**INDUSTRIALIZED AGRICULTURE AND GREEN REVOLUTIONS** Farmers can produce more either by farming more land or by getting higher yields from existing cropland. Since 1950 most of the increase in global food production has come from raising the yield per hectare, the so-called **green revolution**. This involves planting monocultures of improved plants and lavishing fertilizer, pesticides, and water on them. Between 1950 and 1970 this approach dramatically increased crop yields in most MDCs—the *first green revolution* (Figure 14-6).

**Figure 14-4** Labor-intensive cultivation of rice in China. Biological pest control and hand weeding make pesticides unnecessary. Although China has greatly increased food production, intensive farming has eroded and depleted its soil, lowered water tables, and polluted its water with fertilizers. If China cannot bring its population under control (Section 8-4), widespread famine may return.

Then fast-growing dwarf varieties of rice and wheat, specially bred for tropical and subtropical climates, were introduced into several LDCs in the *second green revolution* (Figure 14-6). With enough fertilizer, water, and pesticides, yields of these new plants can be two to five times those of traditional wheat and rice varieties (Figure 14-7). And fast growth allows farmers to grow two or even three crops a year (multiple cropping) on the same land parcel.

Nearly 90% of the increase in world grain output in the 1960s, about 70% in the 1970s, and 80% of that in the 1980s resulted from this second green revolution. In the 1990s at least 80% of any increase is expected to come from green revolution techniques.

These increases depend heavily on fossil fuels to run machinery, produce and apply inorganic fertilizers and pesticides, and pump water for irrigation. Since 1950 agricultural use of fossil fuels has quadrupled, the number of tractors has quadrupled, irrigated area has tripled, use of commercial fertilizer has risen 10-fold, and use of pesticides has risen 32-fold. All told, green revolution agriculture now uses about 8% of the world's oil output.

These high inputs of energy, water, fertilizer, and pesticides have yielded dramatic results, but at some point additional inputs become useless because no more output can be squeezed from the land. In fact, yields may even start dropping because the soil

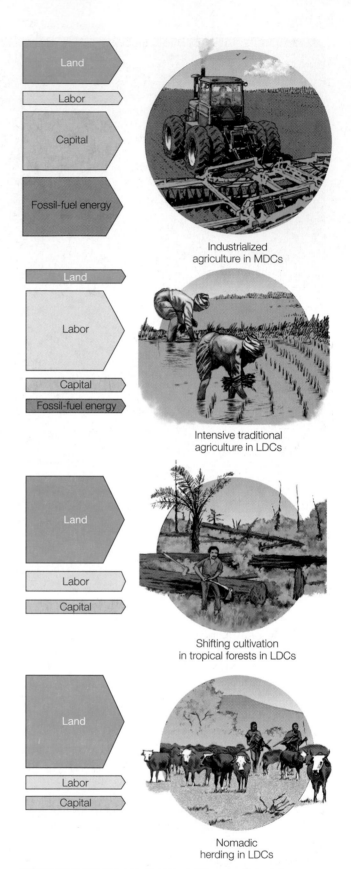

**Figure 14-5** Relative inputs of land, labor, capital, and fossil-fuel energy to the principal agricultural systems. An average of 60% of the people in LDCs are involved directly in producing food, compared with only 8% in MDCs (2% in the United States).

Q: What percentage of U.S. timber is harvested by clear-cutting?

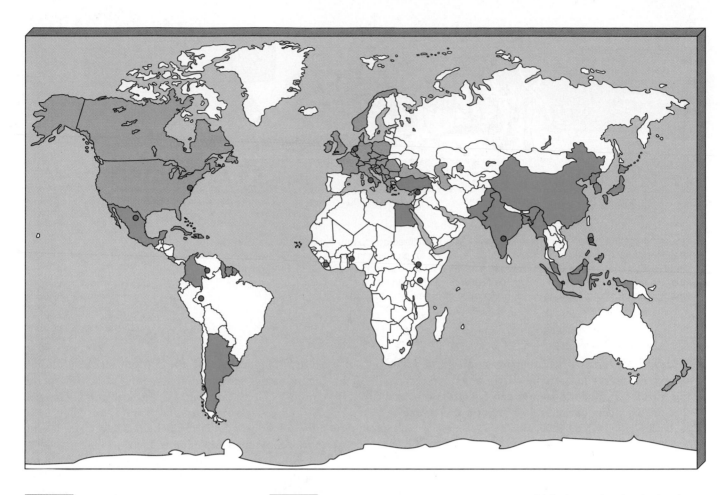

| 1st Green Revolution (MDCs) | 2nd Green Revolution (LDCs) | ● Major international agricultural research centers and seed banks |

**Figure 14-6** Countries whose crop yields per unit of land area increased during the two green revolutions. The first took place in MDCs between 1950 and 1970, and the second since 1967 in LDCs with enough rainfall or irrigation capacity. Thirteen agricultural research centers and genetic storage banks play a key role in developing high-yield crop varieties.

**Figure 14-7** Two parent strains of rice, PETA from Indonesia (center) and DGWG from China (right), were crossbred to yield IR-8 (left), a new, high-yield, semidwarf variety of rice used in the second green revolution. The shorter and stiffer stalks of the new varieties allow them to support larger heads of grain without toppling over.

International Rice Research Institute, Manila

**A: About 66% (33% in national forests)**

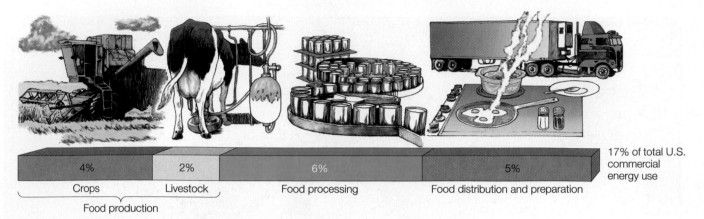

| 4% | 2% | 6% | 5% | 17% of total U.S. commercial energy use |
| Crops | Livestock | Food processing | Food distribution and preparation | |

Food production

**Figure 14-8** Commercial energy use by the U.S. industrialized agriculture system. About 20% of the total energy used directly on farms to produce crops is for pumping irrigation water. On average a piece of food eaten in the United States has traveled 2,100 kilometers (1,300 miles). Processing food also requires large amounts of energy. For example, supplying orange juice takes four times more energy than providing fresh oranges that contain the same amount of juice.

erodes, loses fertility, and becomes salty and water logged. Aquifers can be depleted, deserts can advance, and surface and groundwater can become polluted. And insect pests can develop genetic resistance to pesticides.

**INDUSTRIALIZED AGRICULTURE IN THE UNITED STATES** Since 1940 U.S. farmers have more than doubled crop production without cultivating more land. They have done this through industrialized agriculture coupled with a favorable climate and some of the world's most fertile and productive soils. Farming has become *agribusiness* as big companies and larger family-owned farms have taken control of most U.S. food production. The U.S. Department of Agriculture projects that 1% of U.S. farms will produce 50% of all food in the country by the year 2000.

Only 1.9% of the U.S. population lives on the country's 2.1 million farms, and only about 650,000 Americans work full-time at farming. Yet these people produce enough food to feed their fellow citizens better and for a lower percentage of their income than do farmers in any other country. Americans spend an average of 10–15% of their disposable income on food, while people in much of the world spend 40% or more. The poorest fifth of humankind typically spend 60–80% of their income on food and still don't have an adequate diet.

About 23 million people—9% of the population—are involved in the U.S. agricultural system, from growing and processing food, to distributing it, to selling it at the supermarket. In terms of total annual sales agriculture is the biggest industry in the United States—bigger than the automotive, steel, and housing industries combined. It generates about 18% of the country's GNP (farming, 2%; agricultural chemicals, 2%; and processing, marketing, and retail sales, 14%) and 19% of all jobs in the private sector, employing more people than any other industry.

U.S. farmland, called the "breadbasket" of the world, produces half the world's grain exports. In 1991 one U.S. farmer fed and clothed 128 people (94 at home and 34 abroad), up from 58 persons in 1976. Only 0.08% of the world's population working on U.S. farms produces about 25% of the world's food and fiber.

With only 4.7% of the world's population the United States is also the largest single beef producer (22% of global production). This $36-billion-per-year industry is the country's fourth largest, with 100,000 cows slaughtered every day. Since 1962 the number of American feedlots capable of holding 16,000 head of cattle has risen from 23 to 189 (Figure 14-2). The United States is also the world's largest producer of poultry and the third largest producer of pigs (after China and the European Community).

Although per capita beef consumption in the United States has declined, during a typical lifetime the average American consumes the meat of seven 500-kilogram (1,100-pound) steers. And despite producing enormous quantities of beef, the United States is also the world's largest beef importer, with many of the imports coming from Latin America (Spotlight, p. 272).

The industrialization of agriculture was made possible by the availability of cheap energy (Figure 1-11). Agriculture consumes about 17% of all commercial energy used in the United States each year (Figure

Q: How much of the U.S. Forest Service budget is devoted to timber sales?

## Some Consequences of Eating Meat

For thousands of years domesticated animals have played important roles in the human economy, providing food, fertilizer, fuel, clothing, and transport. Meat and meat products are good sources of high-quality protein, and to most people they also taste good. Traditionally, when both crops and livestock are grown on diversified farms, the livestock return nutrients to the soil as manure, provide draft power, and graze on fallow fields.

When cattle graze in reasonable numbers on naturally occurring range grass, they help maintain grass productivity and use a resource we can't eat. Range-fed cattle are also leaner than grain-fed animals, so their meat has less of the cholesterol and fat harmful to human health. Furthermore, range cattle are an important source of income and protein for many people in LDCs. With care to avoid overgrazing, livestock grazing can be beneficial.

During the past 50 years, however, the livestock population has exploded. There has also been a growing trend toward factory-style production of large numbers of livestock in feedlots (Figure 14-2).

Here are some impacts of this livestock boom:

### Resource Use

- More than half of the world's cropland grows livestock feed.
- The land used to feed 1 meat eater could feed 20 pure vegetarians.
- Livestock consume about 38% of the world's grain, and that consumption is growing twice as fast as people's grain consumption. Pigs and chickens account for two-thirds of this consumption, and dairy and beef cattle much of the remaining third.
- Over 70% of the grain consumed in the United States is fed to livestock, compared to only 2% in India and sub-Saharan Africa.
- Almost two-thirds of U.S. cropland is used to produce livestock feed; only 2% is used to produce vegetables eaten by people.
- One-third of the world's fish catch is converted into fish meal and fed to livestock in MDCs.
- About 40% of the commercial inorganic fertilizer used in the United States is applied to cornfields used to produce livestock feed.

- Livestock use more than half the water withdrawn each year in the United States, with most of this water used to irrigate crops fed to livestock and to wash manure away. The water used to produce the meat on a 455-kilogram (1,000-pound) grain-fed steer would float a battleship.
- A person switching from a typical meat-based diet to a pure vegetarian diet saves 5.3 million liters (1.4 million gallons) of water a year—enough to fill 2 Olympic-size pools.
- If everyone in the United States switched to a pure vegetarian diet, the country's oil imports could be cut by 60%.
- Almost half the energy used in American agriculture goes into the livestock sector.

### Damage to the Environment

- About 85% of U.S. topsoil loss is directly associated with livestock grazing.
- Overgrazing of sparse vegetation and trampling of the soil by too many cattle and other livestock is the major cause of desertification in arid and semiarid areas (Figures 12-12 and 12-13).

(continued)

14-8). Most of this energy comes from oil, followed by natural gas used for drying and producing inorganic fertilizers. The prices of these fossil fuels are expected to rise in coming decades (Case Study, p. 15, and Section 18-1).

Most plant crops in the United States provide more food energy than the energy used to grow them. However, raising livestock requires much more fossil-fuel energy than the animals provide in food energy. If we include crops and livestock, U.S. farms currently use about 3 units of fossil-fuel energy to produce 1 unit of food energy.

Energy efficiency is much worse if we look at the whole system. Considering the energy used to grow, store, process, package, transport, refrigerate, and cook all plant and animal food, an average of about 10 units of nonrenewable fossil-fuel energy are needed to put 1 unit of food energy on the table. By comparison, every unit of energy from the human labor of subsistence farmers provides at least 1 unit of food energy and, with traditional intensive farming, up to 10 units of food energy (Figure 14-5).

The meat-based diet of Americans and people in other MDCs has an enormous impact on resource use, environmental degradation, and pollution (Spotlight, above). Suppose everyone in the world ate a typical meat-based American diet produced by industrialized agriculture. If the world's known oil reserves were

- Cutting down tropical forests in South America and converting them to short-lived pastures for cattle to raise beef for export to MDCs and for domestic use have destroyed vast areas of these storehouses of biodiversity (Figure 10-15).

**Pollution**

- Cattle belch out 12–15% of all the methane released into the atmosphere (Figure 11-3).

- Some of the nitrogen in commercial inorganic fertilizer used to produce livestock feed is converted to nitrous oxide, another greenhouse gas (Figure 11-3).

- Nitrogen in manure escapes into the atmosphere as gaseous ammonia ($NH_3$), a pollutant that contributes to acid deposition.

- Meat accounts for 55% of the pesticide residues in the U.S. diet, compared to 6% from vegetables, 4% from fruits, and 1% from grains.

- Livestock in the United States produce 114 metric tons (125 tons) of excrement every second—21 times more than that produced by the country's human population. If returned to the soil in modest amounts manure is a valuable organic fertilizer, but it is a pollutant if allowed to enter surface waters.

- Only about half of the livestock waste produced in the United States is recycled to the soil. This leaves farmers with high fertilizer bills and livestock producers with high waste disposal costs.

- Livestock wastes and sediment from land eroded by livestock account for about half the water pollution in the United States.

We don't necessarily need to give up eating meat, but we should produce most of it sustainably.

Sustainable production of meat will require:

- Reducing the number of livestock animals in many areas

- Producing crops and livestock together in areas where such diversified farming systems have disappeared, and encouraging them where they survive

- Raising the price of agricultural inputs (such as soil, water, and fertilizer) and products to reflect their true environmental costs

- Slowing and eventually halting human population growth (Section 8-3) to reduce the demand for food.

Chemistry may come to the rescue of those who like the taste of beef but don't like its harmful health and ecological effects. In 1992 USDA researchers announced that they had identified the natural substance that gives beef its meaty taste and synthesized it in the lab. The substance, a chain of eight amino acids, called BMP (beefy-meaty-peptide), has a shelf life of at least two years. Soon it may be used to give cheap cuts of meat the deeper flavor of more expensive beef and to make imitation beef with little or no saturated fat and cholesterol.

---

used only to produce this food, those reserves would be gone in less than 12 years. If humans stopped eating meat and other factors stayed the same, the world's oil reserves would last 260 years.

Industrialized farming in the United States and elsewhere has made remarkable gains in food production. However, to many environmentalists it is a non-sustainable way to produce food because it is built upon depleting and degrading the soil, water, and genetic diversity upon which the entire system depends, and fails to take into account these ecosystem services in the value of food crops.

## EXAMPLES OF TRADITIONAL AGRICULTURE

Farmers in LDCs grow about 20% of the world's food on about 75% of its cultivated land (Figure 14-3). Many traditional farmers imitate nature by simultaneously growing several crops on the same plot, or **interplanting**. This biological diversity reduces the chances of losing most or all of their year's food supply to pests, flooding, drought, or other disasters. Common inter-planting strategies include:

- **Polyvarietal cultivation**, in which a plot is planted with several varieties of the same crop.

- **Intercropping**, in which two or more different crops are grown at the same time on a plot for example, a carbohydrate-rich grain that uses soil nitrogen alongside a protein-rich legume that puts it back.

- **Agroforestry**, or **alley cropping**, a variation of intercropping in which crops and trees are planted together—for example, a grain or legume crop planted around fruit-bearing orchard trees or in rows between fast-growing trees or shrubs that can be used for fuelwood or for adding nitrogen to the soil (Figure 12-15).

- **Polyculture**, a more complex form of intercropping in which many different plants maturing at

Q: Between 1978 and 1992, how much money did the Forest Service lose on timber sales?

various times are planted together (Case Study, right). If cultivated properly, these plots can provide food, medicines, fuel, and natural pesticides and fertilizers on a sustainable basis.

 ## 14-2 World Food Problems

**GOOD AND BAD NEWS ABOUT FOOD PRODUCTION** Between 1950 and 1990 world grain production more than tripled and per capita production rose by almost 50%. During the same period average food prices adjusted for inflation dropped by 25%, and the amount of food traded in the world market quadrupled.

Despite these impressive achievements in food production, population growth is outstripping food production where 2 billion people live. Since 1978 food production has lagged behind population growth in 69 of the 102 LDCs for which data are available. And the annual rate of increase in global food production dropped from a high of 3.5% between 1966 and 1976 to about 2.2% between 1980 and 1990—barely above the rate of population growth in LDCs. In 22 African countries per capita food production has dropped 28% since 1960 and may drop another 30% during the next 25 years (Case Study, p. 368). More than 100 countries now regularly import food from the United States, Canada, Australia, Argentina, western Europe, and a few other surplus producers.

**NUTRITION** People who cannot grow or buy enough food to give themselves 2,700 calories per day for men and 2,000 per day for women suffer from **undernutrition**. To maintain good health and disease resistance, however, people need not only a certain number of calories but also food with the proper amounts of protein (41 grams per adult per day), carbohydrates, fats, vitamins, and minerals. People who are forced to live on a low-protein, high-starch diet of grains such as wheat, rice, or corn often suffer from **malnutrition**, or deficiencies of protein and other key nutrients. Many of the world's desperately poor people suffer from both undernutrition and malnutrition.

According to the World Health Organization about 1.3 billion people—1 out of 4 and 1 in 3 children—are underfed and undernourished (a low estimate is around 0.8 billion). Each year 40 million people—half of them children under age 5—die prematurely from undernutrition, malnutrition, or normally nonfatal infections and diseases worsened

**CASE STUDY**

## Small-Scale, Sustainable Polyculture*

In the Philippines many subsistence-farming families feed themselves by small-scale polyculture. Typically they plant a small plot with a mixture of fast-maturing grains and vegetables, slow-maturing perennials such as papayas and bananas, and slow-maturing tubers such as cassava, taro, and sweet potatoes.

Root systems at different depths in the soil capture nutrients and moisture efficiently, and minimize the need for fertilizer (usually chicken manure) and irrigation water. Year-round plant coverage protects the soil from wind and water erosion.

The various habitats for natural predators means that crops don't need to be sprayed with insecticides to control pests. In addition, weeds have trouble competing for nutrients with the multitude of crop plants and thus can be removed fairly easily by hand with no herbicide use.

Various crops are harvested throughout the year, so there is always something to eat or sell. Crop diversity also provides insurance against bad weather: Even if one crop fails because of too much or too little rain, another crop may survive or even thrive. This approach also spreads the work throughout the year.

Although most of the crops produced in this system have little market value because they are high in starch and low in protein, a typical family can supply most of the food they need without borrowing money. By contrast, although small-scale farmers using mechanized, green revolution agriculture can produce surplus crops to sell, many of them must borrow so much money to establish and maintain their crops that they go bankrupt. They then lose their land and can no longer feed their families by farming.

*This Case Study is based on research by geographer David L. Clawson at the University of New Orleans (see Further Readings).

by malnutrition. Some put the annual death toll at 20 million, while others put it at 60 million. The World Health Organization estimates that diarrhea alone kills at least 5 million children under age 5 each year. *Every 5–10 days hunger-related causes kill as many people as the atomic bomb killed at Hiroshima.*

Chronically undernourished and malnourished individuals are disease-prone and too weak to work

In 1970 Africa was essentially self-sufficient in food. Since then there has been a tragic breakdown of the continent's life support systems; thousands die each day from malnutrition or related diseases. Since 1985 one of every four Africans has been fed with grain imported from abroad—a dependence likely to increase.

Per capita food production is lowest south of the Sahara Desert, where 76% of the continent's people live (Figure 14-9). There, about 160 million people—30% of the population—suffer from chronic hunger and malnutrition, worsening year by year.

Several interacting factors are to blame:

- Africa's population growth is the fastest of any continent (Figure 8-3), with 1 million more mouths to feed every three weeks. At current rates Africa's population will more than double by 2025 (Figure 8-5).

- Because of its generally flat topography and dry climate, Africa has less surface water than most other regions, and groundwater is often deep underground and thus expensive to obtain.

- Rainfall can vary by as much as 40% from year to year, and prolonged droughts are common for two-thirds of Africa's land.

- The green revolution has largely bypassed Africa (Figure 14-6),

mostly because of a lack of water, suitable soil, and money. About 30% of Africa is covered by desert or has soil too sandy for crops (Figure 5-11).

- Good soils are being lost by overgrazing, deforestation (Figure 10-3), soil erosion, and desertification (Figure 12-12).

- There is an acute shortage of fuelwood, which provides 80% of Africa's energy (Figure 10-18). Since 29 trees are cut for each 1 replanted, by 2000 half of Africa's population may not have enough wood for heating and cooking.

- A parasitic disease carried by the tsetse fly that can infect people and livestock has blocked the

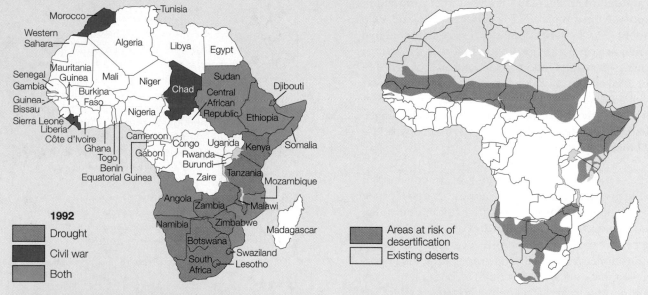

**Figure 14-9** Prolonged cyclical droughts, rapid population growth, land misuse, war, misguided government policies, ineffective water and soil resource management, and increased desertification plague many African countries and cause millions of premature deaths each year.

productively or think clearly. As a result, their children are also underfed and malnourished (Spotlight, p. 370, left). If these children survive to adulthood, many are locked in a tragic malnutrition–poverty cycle in which these conditions are often passed on to succeeding generations (Figure 14-11, p. 371).

Officials of the United Nations Children's Fund (UNICEF) estimate that between half and two-thirds of childhood deaths from nutrition-related causes could be prevented at an average annual cost of only $5–$10 per child—10–19¢ per week. This life-saving program would involve the following simple measures:

**Q:** Who is the world's largest road construction agency?

development of agriculture in over 10 million square kilometers (4 million square miles) of Africa's semiarid land (Figure 14-10). The bite of this insect can infect people and livestock with incurable sleeping sickness and transmit the wasting disease nagana to livestock. A $120-million eradication program has been proposed, but many scientists doubt it can succeed. Others point out that developing this land would cause extinction of many forms of wildlife and contribute to the planet's growing biodiversity crisis.

■ Food distribution systems are poor.

■ To prevent urban unrest, governments often keep food prices low, giving rural farmers little incentive to grow more crops.

■ Social unrest and frequent wars make it difficult to grow and distribute food.

■ Increasing dependence on food imports has helped raise Africa's foreign debt eightfold to $210 billion—equal to nearly half the continent's annual income. The interest alone on the debt is $9 billion per year.

Unless African governments and donors of foreign aid address these problems, the likelihood of reducing environmental degradation and famine is slight. Despite massive problems, here are a few seeds of hope:

■ In Burkina Faso farmers in the Yatengo province line the contours of their cropland with stones, which serve as minidams to hold back water to irrigate the land uphill while letting enough water through to keep the land below from drying out.

■ In Niger a 320-kilometer (200-mile) long windbreak of trees has been planted in the Majii Valley to diminish wind erosion.

■ Kenya's national soil conservation program, begun in 1974, is regarded as one of the most successful in Africa.

■ In Kenya soil erosion has been slowed and fuelwood increased by the Green Belt Movement started in the 1970s, which has planted more than 10 million trees (Figure 10-24).

■ In Nigeria the International Institute of Tropical Agriculture has developed new varieties of cassava, yams, and sweet potatoes that give high yields without fertilizers or pesticides.

■ In East Africa improved varieties of cowpeas, maize, sorghum, and millet are being planted.

■ In Zimbabwe new seed varieties and increased use of fertilizer more than trebled maize yields between 1978 and 1985.

If these and other projects can be nurtured and expanded and coupled with population control, much of Africa can have a sustainable future instead of becoming an international basket case of famine, disease, and ecological deterioration.

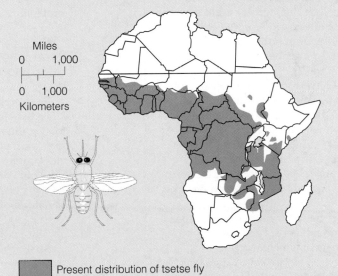

Miles
0    1,000

0    1,000
Kilometers

■ Present distribution of tsetse fly

**Figure 14-10** Range of the tsetse fly in Africa. Its bite can infect people with incurable sleeping sickness and transmit a fatal disease to livestock. Official records show 20,000 cases of sleeping sickness each year, but many more probably go unreported.

■ Immunizing against childhood diseases such as measles

■ Encouraging breastfeeding

■ Preventing dehydration from diarrhea by giving infants a solution of a fistful of sugar and a pinch of salt in a glass of water

■ Preventing blindness by giving people a vitamin A capsule twice a year at a cost of about 75¢ per person

■ Providing family-planning services to help mothers space births at least two years apart

■ Increasing female education, with emphasis on nutrition, sterilization of drinking water, and child care

## Nutritional-Deficiency Diseases

The two most common nutritional-deficiency diseases are marasmus and kwashiorkor. **Marasmus** (from the Greek, "to waste away") occurs when a diet is low in both calories and protein. Most victims are nursing infants of undernourished mothers or children who do not get enough food after being weaned. A marasmic child has a thin body, a bloated belly, shriveled skin, wide eyes, and an old-looking face (Figure 1-7). If the child is treated in time with a balanced diet, most of these effects can be reversed.

**Kwashiorkor** (meaning "displaced child" in a West African dialect) is a severe protein deficiency occurring in infants and children ages 1–3, usually after the arrival of a new baby deprives them of breast milk. The displaced child's diet changes to grain or sweet potatoes, which provide enough calories but not enough protein. Such children are lethargic and irritable, and have a bloated abdomen. They suffer from diarrhea, lose their hair, and may have liver damage. If caught soon enough, most of the effects can be cured with a balanced diet. Otherwise, even if they survive, their growth will be stunted and they may be mentally retarded.

Each of us must have a small daily intake of vitamins that cannot be made in the human body. Although balanced diets, vitamin-fortified foods, and vitamin supplements have slashed the number of vitamin-deficiency diseases in MDCs, millions of cases occur each year in LDCs. For example, each year more than 500,000 children in LDCs are partially or totally blinded because their diet lacks vitamin A.

Other nutritional-deficiency diseases are caused by the lack of certain minerals. For example, too little iron causes anemia, which in turn causes fatigue, makes infection more likely, increases a woman's chances of dying in childbirth, and increases an infant's chances of dying from infection during its first year of life. In tropical regions of Asia, Africa, and Latin America iron-deficiency anemia affects about one-tenth of the men, more than half of the children, two-thirds of the pregnant women, and about half of the other women.

Too little iodine in the diet can cause goiter, an abnormal enlargement of the thyroid gland in the neck, which leads to deafness if untreated. It affects up to 80% of the population in the mountainous areas of Latin America, Asia, and Africa, where soils are deficient in iodine and people have no access to iodine-rich seafood.

## Food Additives

In the United States at least 2,800 chemicals are deliberately added to processed foods, with sales of these food additives amounting to $4.5 billion per year. Some food additives extend shelf life and prevent food poisoning, but most are added to improve appearance and thus sales.

In 1958 the first federal laws were passed requiring that the safety of any new food additive be established by the manufacturer and approved by the Food and Drug Administration (FDA) before the additive was put into common use. Today the manufacturer of a new additive must conduct extensive toxicity testing, costing up to a million dollars, and submit the results to the FDA for evaluation.

However, these federal laws do not apply to the hundreds of additives in use before 1958. Instead of conducting expensive, time-consuming tests, the FDA drew up a list of the food additives in use in 1958 and asked several hundred experts for their professional opinions on the safety of these substances. A few substances were deleted, and in 1959 a list of the remaining 415 additives was published as the "generally recognized as safe," or GRAS (pronounced "grass"), list. Since 1959 further testing has led the FDA to ban several substances on the original GRAS list.

Federal law prohibits the deliberate use of any food additive shown to cause cancer in test animals or in people. This requirement is absolute, allowing for no extenuating circumstances or consideration of benefits versus risks. However, since 1958 the FDA has used this law to ban only nine chemicals.

The food industry would like to see this absolute prohibition removed, and some scientists and politicians want it modified to allow for a consideration of benefits versus risks. Other scientists believe it should be strengthened and expanded to include additives that cause birth defects or genetic mutations in test animals or in people. These critics cite the FDA's infrequent use of the law as evidence that it is too weak.

While 15% of the people in LDCs suffer from severe undernutrition and malnutrition, about 15% of the people in MDCs—including at least 34 million Americans—suffer from **overnutrition**. This is an excessive intake of food, especially fats, that can cause obesity (excess body fat) in people who do not suffer from physiological disorders that promote obesity.

Q: How much of the world's wastepaper was recycled in 1992?

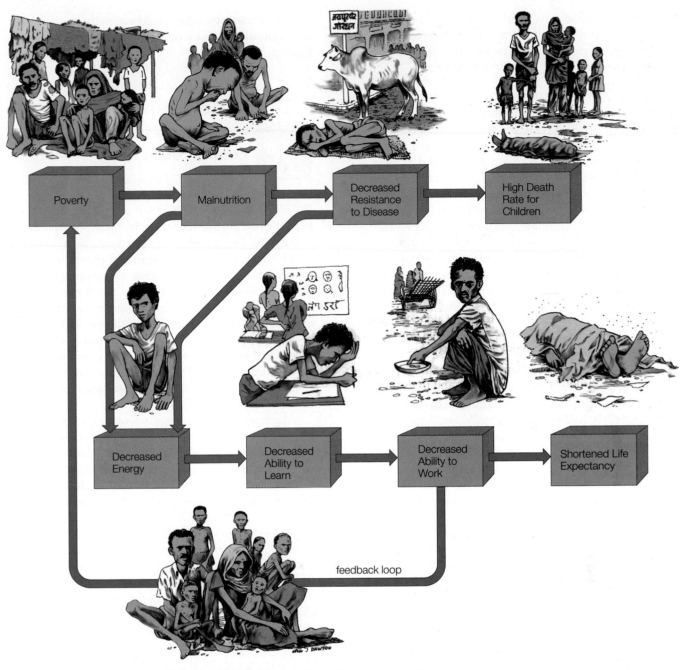

**Figure 14-11** Interactions among poverty, malnutrition, and disease form a tragic cycle that tends to perpetuate such conditions in succeeding generations of families.

Overnourished people exist on diets high in calories, cholesterol-containing saturated fats (especially from red meat), salt, sugar, and processed foods, and low in unprocessed fresh vegetables, fruits, and fiber. Partly because of these dietary choices, overweight people have significantly higher than normal risks of diabetes, high blood pressure, stroke, heart disease, kidney disease, arthritis, and some types of cancer. Overnutrition is associated with at least two-thirds of the deaths in the United States each year. A study of thousands of Chinese villagers indicates that the healthiest diet for humans is nearly vegetarian, with only 10–15% of calories coming from fat, in contrast to the typical meat-based diet in which 40% of the calories come from fats.

There is also concern over possible harmful effects from some of the chemicals, called **food additives**, that are added to processed foods for sale in grocery stores and restaurants. Additives retard spoilage; enhance flavor, color, and texture; or provide missing vitamins or other nutrients (Spotlight, p. 370, right). The presence of synthetic chemical additives does not necessar-

A: About 33% (39% in the United States)

ily mean that a food is harmful, however, and the fact that a food is completely natural is no guarantee that it is safe. A number of natural or totally unprocessed foods contain potentially harmful substances.

**FOOD SUPPLY AND DISTRIBUTION** The world produces more than enough food to meet the basic needs of every person on Earth. Indeed, if distributed equally, the grain currently produced worldwide would be enough to give 6 billion people—the projected world population for the year 1998—a meatless subsistence diet. Food is not distributed equally among the world's people, however, nor will it be, because of differences in soil, climate, political and economic power, and average income throughout the world.

By contrast, if everyone ate the diet typical of a person in an MDC, with 30–40% of the calories coming from animal products, the current world agricultural system would support only 2.5 billion people. That is less than half the present population and only one-fourth of the 10 billion people projected sometime in the next century (Figure 1-1).

Increases in global food production and food production per person often hide wide differences in food supply and quality among and within countries. For example, nearly half of India's population is too poor to buy or grow enough food to meet basic needs, and an estimated two-thirds of its land is threatened by erosion, water shortages, and salinization. This, coupled with a current population growth rate of 18 million per year, means that India might again suffer from famine in the 1990s and beyond.

Similarly in fertile, urbanized southern Brazil the average daily food supply per person is high, but in Brazil's semiarid northeastern interior many people are severely underfed. Overall almost two out of three Brazilians suffer from malnutrition.

Food is also unevenly distributed within families. In poor families the most food goes to men working outside the home. Children (ages 1–5) and women (especially pregnant women and nursing mothers) are the most likely to be underfed and malnourished.

MDCs also have pockets of poverty and hunger. For example, a 1985 report by a task force of doctors estimated that at least 20 million people (12 million children and 8 million adults)—1 out of every 11 Americans and 1 out of 8 American children—were hungry, mostly because of cuts in food stamps and other forms of government aid since 1980. A 1991 study revealed that one out of eight U.S. families with children under age 12 experiences hunger due to poverty.

**ENVIRONMENTAL EFFECTS OF PRODUCING FOOD** Agriculture—both industrialized and traditional—has a greater impact on air, soil, and water

resources than any other human activity, as discussed throughout this book and summarized in the Spotlight, p. 373.

## 14-3 Increasing World Food Production

**INCREASING CROP YIELDS** Agricultural experts expect most future increases in food production to come from increased yields per hectare on existing cropland, from improved strains of plants, and from expansion of green revolution technology to other parts of the world. One promising development, after over 40 years of research, is *triticale*, a new cereal grain produced by crossing wheat with rye. Triticale can flourish in poor soils and in both cold and hot climates, and is now being grown in 32 countries. However, triticale is subject to some diseases, and its genetic resistance to various other diseases could break down as its use spreads.

Agricultural scientists are working to create new green revolutions—or *gene revolutions*—by using genetic engineering and other forms of biotechnology (Pro/Con, p. 167). Over the next 20–40 years they hope to breed high-yield plant strains that are more resistant to insects and disease, thrive on less fertilizer, make their own nitrogen fertilizer as do legumes (Figure 4-30), do well in slightly salty soils, withstand drought, and use solar energy more efficiently during photosynthesis. Even only occasional breakthroughs could generate enormous increases in global crop production before the middle of the next century. However, several factors have limited the success of the green and gene revolutions so far—and may continue to do so:

- Without huge doses of fertilizer and water, most green revolution crop varieties produce yields no higher and often lower than those from traditional strains; that is why the second green revolution has not spread to many arid and semiarid areas (Figure 14-6). Without good soil, water, and weather, new genetically engineered crop strains could fail.

- Continuing to increase inputs of fertilizer, water, and pesticides eventually produces no further increase in crop yields as the J-shaped curve of crop productivity reaches its limits and is converted to an S-shaped curve.

- Without careful land use and environmental controls (Section 12-3), degradation of water and soil

Q: How much of the world's wastepaper could be recycled by 2000?

## Harmful Environmental Impacts of Industrialized and Traditional Agriculture

### Industrialized Agriculture

■ Soil erosion and loss of soil fertility through poor land use, failure to practice soil conservation techniques, and too little use of organic fertilizers (Section 12-3)

■ Reduction in the number and diversity of nutrient-recycling soil microorganisms (Figure 12-4) from heavy use of pesticides and commercial inorganic fertilizers and from soil compaction by large tractors and other farm machinery

■ Salinization and waterlogging of heavily irrigated soils (Figures 12-19 and 12-20)

■ Air pollution caused by dust blown from cropland that is not kept covered with vegetation (Figure 12-12) and from overgrazed rangeland (Figure 12-13)

■ Air pollution from droplets of pesticides sprayed from planes or ground sprayers

■ Air pollution from extraction, processing, transportation, and combustion of fossil fuels used in industrialized agriculture (Figure 14-8)

■ Pollution of estuaries and deep ocean zones with oil from offshore wells and tankers and from improper disposal of oil, the main fossil fuel used in industrialized agriculture

■ Pollution of streams, lakes, and estuaries, and killing of fish and shellfish from pesticide runoff

■ Depletion of groundwater aquifers by excessive withdrawals for irrigation (Figures 13-6 and 13-17)

■ Pollution of groundwater caused by leaching of water-soluble pesticides, nitrates from commercial inorganic fertilizers, and salts from irrigation water

■ Overfertilization of lakes and slow-moving rivers caused by runoff of nitrates and phosphates in commercial inorganic fertilizers, livestock wastes, and food-processing wastes

■ Sediment pollution of surface waters caused by erosion and runoff from farm fields and animal feedlots

■ Loss of genetic diversity in plants caused by clearing biologically diverse grasslands and forests (Section 10-2) and often replacing them with monocultures (Figure 5-20).

■ Endangerment and extinction of wildlife from loss of habitat when grasslands and forests are cleared and wetlands are drained for farming

■ Threats to human health from nitrates in drinking water and pesticides in drinking water, food, and the atmosphere

### Traditional Subsistence and Intensive Agriculture

■ Soil erosion and rapid loss of soil fertility caused by clearing and cultivating steep mountain highlands without terracing (Figure 12-11), using shifting cultivation in tropical forests without leaving the land fallow long enough to restore soil fertility (Figure 2-6), overgrazing of rangeland (Figure 12-13), deforestation to provide cropland or fuelwood, and destruction of mangroves (Figure 5-33), and coastal wetlands

■ Increased frequency and severity of flooding in lowlands when mountainsides are deforested (Case Study, p. 340)

■ Desertification caused by cultivation of marginal land with unsuitable soil or terrain, overgrazing, deforestation, and failure to use soil conservation techniques (Figure 12-12)

■ Air pollution caused by dust blown from cropland not kept covered with vegetation and from overgrazed rangeland

■ Sediment pollution of surface waters caused by erosion and runoff from farm fields, overgrazed rangeland, and deforested land (Figure 5-30)

■ Endangerment and extinction of wildlife caused by loss of habitat when grasslands and forests are cleared for farming

■ Threats to human health from flooding intensified by poor land use (Case Study, p. 340) and from human and animal wastes discharged or washed into irrigation ditches and sources of drinking water

can limit the long-term ecological and economic sustainability of green and gene revolutions.

■ The cost of genetically engineered crop strains is too high for most of the world's subsistence farmers in LDCs.

■ The severe and increasing loss of Earth's biodiversity from deforestation, destruction and degradation of other ecosystems, and replace-

ment of a diverse mixture of natural crop varieties with monoculture crops limits the potential of future green and gene revolutions (Spotlight, p. 374).

**NEW FOOD SOURCES** Some analysts recommend greatly increased cultivation of various nontraditional

## Loss of Genetic Diversity

Scientists can crossbreed varieties of animal and plant life (Figure 14-7), and genetic engineers can move genes from one organism to another, but they need the genetic materials in Earth's existing species to work with. The UN Food and Agriculture Organization estimates that by the year 2000 two-thirds of all seed planted in LDCs will be of uniform strains. This genetic uniformity increases the vulnerability of food crops to pests and diseases. This, plus widespread species extinction, severely limits the potential of future green and gene revolutions.

In the mid-1970s, for example, a valuable wild corn species was barely saved from extinction. When this strain was discovered, only a few thousand stalks survived in three tiny patches in south central Mexico that were about to be cleared by squatter cultivators and commercial loggers. This wild species is the only known perennial strain of corn. Crossbreeding it with commercial varieties could reduce the need for yearly plowing and sowing, which would reduce soil erosion, water use, and energy use.

Even more important, this wild corn has a built-in genetic resistance to four of the eight major corn viruses. Bringing this strain's immunity to commercial corn strains could save $500 million per year. Furthermore, this wild corn grows in cooler and damper habitats than established commercial strains. Crossbreeding in these genetic traits could expand the potential corn land by up to 10%. Overall the genetic benefits from this wild plant could total several billion dollars per year.

The loss of genetic diversity is a global problem. In Indonesia, for example, 1,500 local varieties of rice have disappeared in the past 15 years. In India, which once had 30,000 varieties of rice, more than 75% of the rice production now comes from 10 varieties. In the United States 71% of the corn fields are planted with only 6 varieties, and 50% of the wheat fields are planted with just 9 varieties. In other words we are rapidly shrinking the world's genetic "library" just when we need it more than ever.

Wild varieties of the world's most important plants can be collected and stored in gene banks, agricultural research centers (Figure 14-6), and botanical gardens; however, space and money severely limit the number of species that can be preserved there. Moreover, many cannot be stored successfully in gene banks, and power failures, fires, or unintentional disposal of seeds can cause irrevocable losses. Also, stored plant species stop evolving and thus are less fit for reintroduction to their native habitats, which may now have changed.

Because of these limitations ecologists and plant scientists warn that the only effective way to preserve the genetic diversity of most plant and animal species is to protect representative ecosystems throughout the world from agriculture and other forms of development.

---

plants to supplement or replace such staples as wheat, rice, and corn. One of many possibilities is the winged bean, a protein-rich legume now common only in New Guinea and Southeast Asia (Figure 14-12). Other examples are the sugar apple of South America, protein-rich seeds of the grain amaranth (which grows well in cool, dry climates); the groundnut (a high-protein tuber eaten by Native Americans); cocyam (a native plant of West Africa and Latin America that is as nutritious as the potato); and the Amazonian babassu palm (which gives the world's highest known yield of vegetable oil). Insects are also important potential sources of protein, vitamins, and minerals (Figure 14-13).

Scientists have identified many plants and insects that could be used as sources of food. The problem is getting farmers to cultivate such crops and convincing consumers to try new foods.

Most crops we depend on are tropical annuals. Each year the land is cleared of all vegetation, dug up, and planted with their seeds. David Pimentel (Guest Essay, p. 332) and plant scientists at the Land Institute in Salina, Kansas, believe we should rely more on polycultures of perennial crops, which are better adapted to regional soil and climate conditions than most annuals (p. 358). This would eliminate the need to till soil each year, greatly reducing energy use. It would also save water and reduce soil erosion and sediment water pollution. On the other hand, widespread use of perennials would reduce the profits of agribusinesses selling annual seeds, fertilizers, and pesticides, explaining why they don't favor this approach. Thus research into and development of such crops must be carried out by governments and private groups.

If not overharvested certain wild animals could be an important source of food. Prolific Amazon river turtles, for example, are used as a source of protein by local people. Another delicacy is the green iguana—the "chicken of the trees." If managed properly these large, tasty lizards can yield up to 10 times as much meat as cattle on the same amount of land. In

Q: How much of U.S. public rangeland is in unsatisfactory (fair or poor) condition?

**Figure 14-12** The winged bean, a protein-rich annual plant from the Philippines, is only one of many unfamiliar plants that could become important sources of food and fuel. Its edible winged pods, spinachlike leaves, tendrils, and seeds contain as much protein as soybeans, and its edible roots contain more than four times the protein of potatoes. Its seeds can be ground into flour or used to make a caffeine-free beverage that tastes like coffee. Indeed, this plant yields so many different edible parts that it has been called a "supermarket on a stalk." Because of nitrogen-fixing nodules in its roots, this fast-growing plant needs little fertilizer.

Indonesia the piglike babirosa is an important source of meat.

**CULTIVATING MORE LAND** Humankind grows crops on about 11% of Earth's land area (excluding Antarctica and the Greenland icecap) and raises livestock on nearly 25%. The rest either is covered by ice, is too dry or too wet, is too hot or too cold, is too steep, or has unsuitable soils. People already live on or use, to varying degrees, 66% of the world's land—89% if severe deserts and frozen tundra are excluded.

Theoretically the world's cropland could be more than doubled by clearing tropical forests and irrigating arid land (Figure 14-14). About 83% of the world's potential new cropland is in the remote rain forests of South America and Africa, primarily in Brazil (Figure 9-3) and Zaire (Figure 14-9). Clearing rain forests to grow crops and graze livestock, however, has disastrous consequences, as discussed in Chapter 10. And in Africa potential cropland in savanna (Figure 5-17) and other semiarid land cannot be used for farming or livestock grazing because it is infested by 22 species of the tsetse fly (Figure 14-10).

Researchers hope to develop new methods of intensive cultivation in tropical areas. But some scientists argue that it makes more ecological and economic sense to combine the ancient method of shifting cultivation followed by fallow periods long enough to restore soil fertility (Figure 2-6) with various forms of interplanting. Scientists also recommend plantation cultivation of rubber trees (Figure 10-9), oil palms, and banana trees, which are adapted to tropical climates and soils.

**Figure 14-13** In South Africa, "Mopani"—emperor moth larvae—are among several insects eaten. Kalahari Desert dwellers eat cockroaches. Lightly toasted butterflies are a favorite food in Bali. French-fried ants are sold on the streets of Bogotá, Colombia, and Malaysians love deep-fried grasshoppers. Most of these insects are 58–78% protein by weight—three to four times as protein rich as beef, fish, or eggs.

**A:** About 50% in 1990 (compared with 84% in 1936)

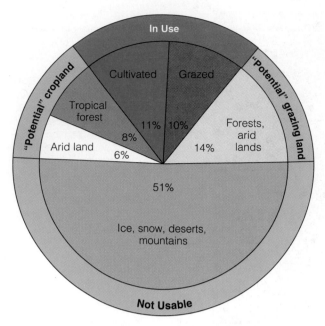

**Figure 14-14** Classification of Earth's land. Theoretically we could double the amount of cropland by clearing tropical forests and irrigating arid lands. However, converting this marginal land into cropland would destroy valuable forest resources, reduce Earth's biodiversity, and cause serious environmental problems, usually without being cost-effective.

Much of the world's potentially cultivable land lies in dry areas, especially in Australia and Africa (Figure 14-9). Large-scale irrigation in these areas would be very expensive, requiring large inputs of fossil fuel to pump water long distances. Irrigation systems would deplete groundwater supplies and the land would need constant and expensive maintenance against erosion, groundwater contamination, salinization, and waterlogging.

There are signs that irrigation limits are being reached in land now under cultivation. Between 1950 and 1980 the world's irrigated cropland almost tripled, increasing the average irrigated area per person by 52%. However, growth in irrigated area fell behind population growth during the 1980s, leading to an 8% drop in the irrigated area per person—a trend that is continuing in the 1990s.

Thus much of the new cropland that could be developed would be on marginal land requiring expensive inputs of fertilizer, water, and energy. Furthermore, these possible increases in cropland would not offset the projected loss of almost one-third of today's cultivated cropland from erosion, overgrazing, waterlogging, salinization, mining, and urbanization. Since 1979, for example, China, India, and the CIS—three of the world's largest food producers—have each lost about 13% of their grain-producing cropland from these effects.

Pollution is also reducing yields on existing cropland. In the United States ozone pollution in the troposphere reduced harvests of crops by at least 5% during the 1980s. Other air pollutants, such as sulfur dioxide and nitrogen oxides, have also damaged crops. Yields of some crops and populations of marine phytoplankton that support fish and shellfish used as food have been reduced by depletion of ozone in the stratosphere (Figure 11-9).

Finally, if current population projections are accurate, the global average of 0.28 hectare (0.69 acre) of cropland per capita in 1992 is expected to decline to 0.17 hectare (0.42 acre) by 2025.

**DO THE POOR BENEFIT?** Increasing per capita food production is a big task, but making sure the food reaches the hungry is an even bigger one. Whether present and future green or gene revolutions reduce hunger among the world's poor depends on how the technology is applied.

In LDCs the resource most available to agriculture is human labor. When green revolution techniques are used to increase yields of traditional labor-intensive agriculture on existing or new cropland in countries with equitable land distribution, the poor benefit, as has occurred in China. Most poor farmers, however, don't have enough land, money, or credit to buy the seed, fertilizer, irrigation water, pesticides, equipment, and fuel that the new plant varieties need. This means that the second green revolution (Figure 14-6) has bypassed more than 1 billion poor people in LDCs—four times the U.S. population.

Switching to industrialized agriculture makes LDCs heavily dependent on large, MDC-based multinational corporations for expensive supplies, increasing the LDCs' foreign debts. It also makes their agricultural and economic systems more vulnerable to collapse from increases in oil and fertilizer prices and from environmental degradation. In addition, mechanization displaces many farm workers, thus increasing rural-to-urban migration and overburdening the cities.

## 14-4 Catching or Raising More Fish

**HARVESTING FISH AND SHELLFISH** **Fishing** is a form of hunting in which fish and shellfish are the prey. People do **commercial fishing** for profit, **subsis-**

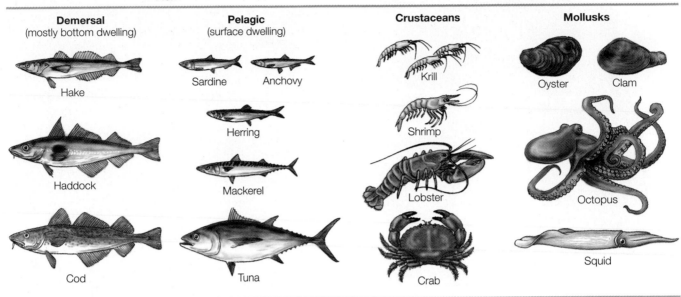

**Figure 14-15** Some major types of commercially harvested marine fish and shellfish.

tence fishing to get food for survival, and **sport fishing** in which **game fish** are caught mostly for recreation.

Concentrations of particular aquatic species suitable for commercial harvesting in a given ocean area or inland body of water are called **fisheries**. Worldwide people get an average of 20% of their animal protein directly from fish and shellfish, and another 5% indirectly from livestock fed with fish meal. In most Asian coastal and island regions fish and shellfish supply 30–90% of people's animal protein.

About 86% of the annual commercial catch of fish and shellfish comes from the ocean. Ninety-nine percent of this comes from plankton-rich waters (mostly estuaries and upwellings) within 370 kilometers (200 nautical miles) of the coast. However, this vital coastal zone is being disrupted and polluted at an alarming rate (Case Study, p. 139).

Only about 40 of the world's 20,000 species of fish are harvested in large quantities. Just six groups—cod, herring, jack, redfish, mackerel, and tuna—account for nearly two-thirds of the annual commercial marine fish catch. Some commercially important marine species of fish and shellfish are shown in Figure 14-15.

**Marine demersal species** feed mostly on or near ocean bottoms, usually within a small range. Examples include cod, flounder, haddock, sole, lobster, crawfish, and crab. **Marine pelagic species** usually feed near the surface and often migrate over a wide area. Most are fast, active swimmers with torpedo-shaped bodies. Examples are tuna, herring, pilchard

(whose young we know as sardines), anchovy, mackerel, squid, and salmon. Most fish are either marine or freshwater species. However, some pelagic species are **anadromous**. They hatch in streams, move to the ocean, and return to fresh water to spawn. This group includes salmon, sturgeon, smelt, and shad.

To obtain large catches, modern commercial fishing boats use sonar, radar, temperature measurement (often transmitted to modern high-tech boats via satellite), and other electronic devices to find schools of fish. Some larger boats and fishing fleets use helicopters and aerial photography to spot large schools of fish. Lights and electrodes are used to attract fish. Because modern fishing boats are motorized the energy input per unit of food energy from marine species is enormous. The harvesting method used depends on the species (Figure 14-16 and Spotlight, p. 379).

## COMMERCIAL FISH CATCH AND OVERFISHING

Between 1950 and 1970 the weight of the commercial fish catch grew by about 7% per year and increased more than threefold during that time (Figure 14-17). Since then the rate of growth has slowed, and the marine catch may soon reach the estimated sustainable yield. Fishery experts estimate that subsistence fishing adds about 25% to the world's officially reported commercial catch.

Although the total fish catch has grown, the per capita fish catch has declined in most years since 1970 because the human population has grown faster than

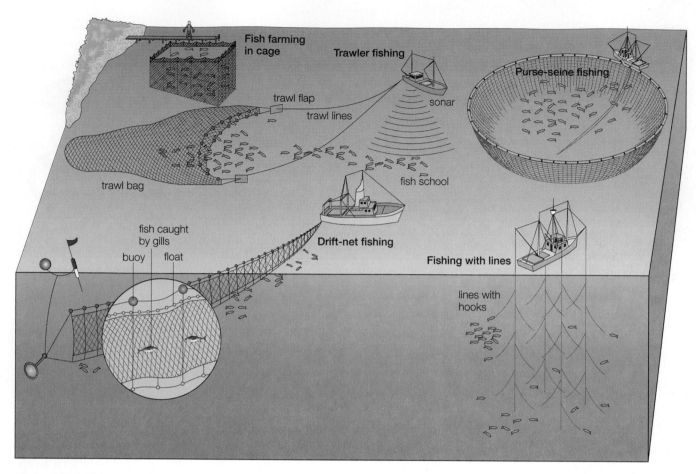

**Figure 14-16** Major commercial fishing methods used to harvest marine species.

**Figure 14-17** World fish catch—worth $4.2 billion in 1992. About one-third of the annual marine catch is used to feed animals and fertilize croplands. Scientists estimate that the sustainable yield of the world's marine fishery is 100 million metric tons (110 million tons), which may be reached or exceeded soon. If this yield is exceeded, key fish stocks will be depleted and yields will drop sharply. (Data from UN Food and Agriculture Organization)

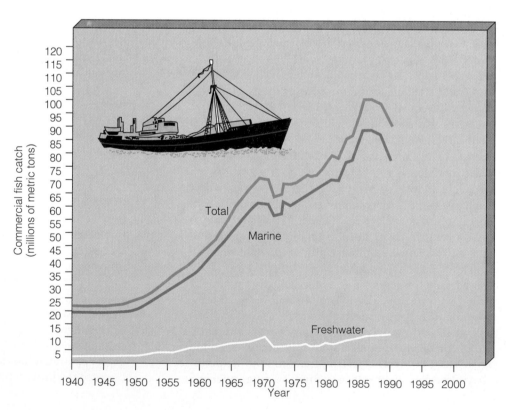

Q: How much do 30,000 U.S. ranchers with permits to graze on public lands get in federal subsidies?

Some fishing boats, called trawlers, catch demersal fish by dragging a funnel-shaped net held open at the neck along the ocean bottom (Figure 14-16). The large mesh of the net allows most small fish to escape. This method, known as **trawler fishing**, is intended to catch cod and other bottom-feeding fish and bottom-dwelling shrimp. However, thousands of harp seals drown each year in cod nets, and at least 12,000 endangered and threatened sea turtles die each year in Atlantic and Gulf Coast shrimp nets.

Pelagic species, such as tuna, which feed in schools near the surface or in shallow areas, are often caught by **purse-seine fishing**. After a school is found, it's surrounded by a purse-seine net (Figure 14-16). The bottom of the net is then closed to trap the fish, and the catch is hauled aboard. Nets used to capture yellowfin tuna in the eastern tropical Pacific Ocean also kill large numbers of dolphins. They swim on the surface of the water above schools of yellowfin tuna, which make up 5% of the global tuna catch.

To reduce the slaughter, Congress passed the Marine Mammal Protection Act in 1972. This law required the U.S. tuna fleet to reduce the number of dolphin kills from an estimated 400,000 per year to 20,500 per year by modifying purse-seine nets so that dolphins can escape and by having outside observers on all boats to monitor dolphin kills. The good news is that tuna boats flying the American flag now kill fewer than 1,000 dolphins a year.

The bad news is that at least 100,000 dolphins are still being killed each year by foreign boats selling their catch worldwide, including in the United States. Also, some U.S. vessels evade the regulations by reflagging their boats and operating from foreign ports.

To prevent this, environmentalists pushed Congress to amend the Marine Mammal Protection Act in 1985 and 1988 to specify that tuna imported to the United States had to be caught in ways that limited dolphin kills to numbers comparable to what the U.S. fleet was allowed. In 1990 Mexico challenged this policy as an unfair trade practice that violated the General Agreement on Tariffs and Trade (GATT), a treaty among 103 countries aimed at expanding world trade by eliminating barriers to free trade. In 1991 a GATT resolution panel of judges ruled that U.S. rules governing tuna fishing amounted to an unfair and illegal trade barrier.

Environmentalists have long warned that certain provisions in GATT are aimed at allowing corporations to get around, restrict, or eliminate environmental regulations at the local, state, and national level in the name of free trade. They are pressuring Congress to modify GATT to eliminate such loopholes.

The world's major marine fishing countries—especially Japan, South Korea, Taiwan, and the CIS—have large fishing fleets that can stay out for months or even years and can or freeze their catches at sea.

Most of these fleets use **drift-net fishing** to capture massive quantities of fish, mostly pelagic, at various depths (Figure 14-16). Weighted at the bottom and floated at the top, these monster nets drift in the water and catch fish when their gills become entangled in the nylon mesh. Each net descends as much as 15 meters (50 feet) deep and is up to 65 kilometers (40 miles) long. Almost anything that comes in contact with these nearly invisible "curtains of death" becomes entangled. Between 1980 and 1991 an estimated 1,800 fishing vessels from Japan, South Korea, and Taiwan used drift-net fishing in international waters. Each night of the fishing season, the fleet's nets could more than encircle the world.

Every country that has used drift nets in its own waters has eventually banned them. In 1990 the UN General Assembly called for a moratorium on drift-net fishing in international waters after June 1992. Under intense international pressure Japan and Taiwan reluctantly agreed to cease fishing with drift nets by the end of 1992, and South Korea may follow suit.

The ban, however, has numerous loopholes and no effective mechanism for monitoring, enforcement, and punishment. Indeed, enforcement over vast ocean areas is impractical, and compliance is voluntary. In 1992 the Sea Shepherd Society revealed that some Japanese shipowners intend to defy the ban. Other Japanese owners are having their drift-net vessels fly the flag of other nations, such as Vanuatu in the South Pacific, which plan to defy the ban. Japan also plans to continue buying drift-net fish from other countries not honoring the ban. And even if this method of harvesting is effectively banned, large numbers of "ghost nets"—pieces of netting that are lost at sea—will kill marine animals until the nets sink with the weight of decomposing bodies.

Environmentalists believe that the only effective way to reduce drift-net fishing and tuna caught by purse-seine fishing is to mount U.S. and global boycotts of fish caught in these ways. This tactic, led by the Earth Island Institute, caused companies selling canned tuna in the United States to stop buying tuna caught by purse-seine or drift-net methods. Consumer power works and does not violate GATT agreements.

Environmentalists are also pushing Congress to require all companies selling tuna and other fish in the United States (which consumes 40% of the world's canned tuna) to have labels on their products indicating that purse-seine and drift-net fishing were not used. Environmentalists hope to spread this practice to other countries.

the fish catch (Figure 14-18). Because of overfishing, pollution, and population growth, the world catch per person is projected to drop back to the 1960 level by 2000.

Fish are potentially renewable resources—as long as the annual harvest leaves enough breeding stock to renew the species for the next year. Ideally an annual **sustainable yield** figure—the size of the annual catch that could be harvested indefinitely without a decline in the population of a species—should be established for each species to avoid depleting the stock. However, determining sustainable yields is difficult. Counting aquatic populations isn't easy because they disappear beneath the water. And sustainable yield values shift from year to year because of changes in climate, pollution, and other factors. Many marine sci-

entists believe that the annual harvest for each species should be based on an **optimum yield**—the catch that can be economically harvested on a sustained basis—which is usually less than the sustainable yield.

**Overfishing** is taking so many fish that too little breeding stock is left to maintain numbers—that is, when the sustainable yield is exceeded. Prolonged overfishing leads to **commercial extinction**: So few of a species is left that it's no longer profitable to hunt them. Fishing fleets then move to a new species or to a new region, hoping that the overfished species will eventually recover.

Since the early 1980s overfishing has caused declines in the yields of nearly one-third of the world's fisheries and the collapse of 42 valuable fisheries, including 42% of the species commercially fished in U.S. coastal waters. Examples include cod and herring, Atlantic salmon, red snapper, Atlantic bluefin tuna, Alaska king crab, and Peruvian anchovy (Case Study, p. 381).

In 1982 the UN Convention on the Law of the Sea was signed by 159 countries in an effort to reduce overfishing. This treaty gives all coastal countries the legal right to control fishing by their own and foreign fishing fleets within 364 kilometers (200 nautical miles) of their coasts. However, 22 countries, including the CIS, the United States, Germany, and the United Kingdom, refused to ratify the treaty. They disagreed with provisions that consider mineral and living resources in the open ocean as belonging to the entire world, so that MDCs would have to share them, or profits made from them, with LDCs.

**AQUACULTURE** Aquaculture, in which fish and shellfish are raised for food, supplies about 10% of the world's commercial fish harvest. There are two basic

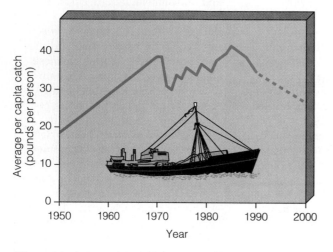

**Figure 14-18** Per capita world fish catch has declined since the mid-1980s and is projected to drop further by the end of this century. (Data from United Nations and Worldwatch Institute)

**Figure 14-19** Harvesting silver carp on an aquaculture farm in China.

Q: How much of the money taken in by private concessionaires operating in national parks is paid in user fees to the federal government?

In 1953 Peru began fishing for anchovies off its western coast. The size of the fishing fleet increased rapidly. The tiny fish were processed into fish meal and sold to MDCs as livestock feed. Between 1965 and 1971 Peruvian anchovies made up about 20% of the world's commercial fish catch.

The bonanza was short-lived, however. Biologists with the UN Food and Agriculture Organization warned that during seven of the eight years between 1964 and 1971 the anchovy harvest exceeded the estimated sustainable yield. Peruvian fishery officials ignored those warnings. The enormous anchovy populations depend on the rich nutrient upwelling near the Peruvian coast (Figure 5-8), but at unpredictable intervals the productivity of the upwellings drops sharply because of a natural weather change called the El Niño–Southern Oscillation, or ENSO (Figure 5-9). The anchovies, as well as other fish, seabirds, and marine mammals in food webs based on phytoplankton, then die back.

Disaster struck in 1972 when a strong ENSO arrived. The anchovy population, already decimated by overfishing, could not recover from the effects of the ENSO, and the annual yield plummeted (Figure 14-20). By putting short-term profits above a long-term anchovy fishery, Peru lost a major source of income and jobs, and had to increase its foreign debt.

The country has made some economic recovery by harvesting the Peruvian sardine, which took over the niche once occupied by the anchovy. Catches of mackerel, bonita, and hake have also increased. And since 1983 the Peruvian anchovy fishery has shown some recovery (Figure 14-20).

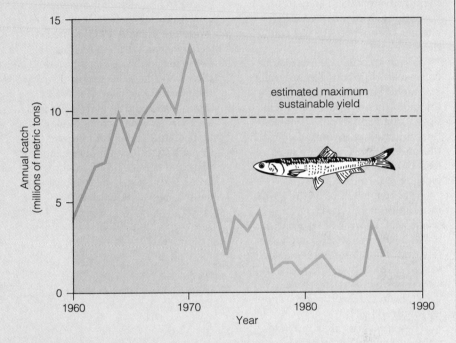

**Figure 14-20** Peruvian anchovy catch, showing the combined effects of overfishing and a natural climate change, known as the El Niño–Southern Oscillation, that occurs every few years. (Data from UN Food and Agriculture Organization)

types of aquaculture. **Fish farming** involves cultivating fish in a controlled environment, usually a pond, and harvesting them when they reach the desired size (Figure 14-19). **Fish ranching** involves holding species in captivity—usually in fenced-in areas or floating cages (Figure 14-16) in coastal lagoons and estuaries—for the first few years of their lives and then harvesting the adults when they return to spawn. Ranching is useful for such anadromous species as ocean trout and salmon (Spotlight, p. 382).

Almost three-fourths of the world's annual aquaculture catch comes from 71 LDCs. Species cultivated in LDCs include carp (Figure 14-19), tilapia, milkfish, clams, and oysters, which feed on phytoplankton and other aquatic plants. These are usually raised in small freshwater ponds or underwater cages. Aquaculture supplies 60% of the fish eaten in Israel, 40% in China, and 22% in Indonesia.

In MDCs aquaculture is used mostly to stock lakes and streams with game fish and to raise expensive fish and shellfish. This benefits sport anglers and is highly profitable for aquaculture business, but it does little to increase food and protein supplies for the poor.

About 40% of the oysters and most of the catfish, crayfish, and rainbow trout consumed as food in the United States is supplied by U.S.-based fish farms. Farmed tilapia (similar to sole) is being pushed as the fish of the future.

Aquaculture has several advantages. First, it can produce high yields per unit of area. Second, little fuel

# Salmon Ranching and Farming

Salmon divide their lives between fresh water and salt water (Figure 14-21). They hatch in freshwater streams, develop for a year or two, and then migrate to the ocean to feed. When they reach sexual maturity after two to six years at sea, they return to the gravel beds of their birth streams to spawn. Apparently each stream has unique chemical properties the fish can detect.

*Salmon ranching*, a form of aquaculture, modifies this natural cycle by hatching salmon eggs in hatcheries and then keeping the hatchlings (called fry) in pens or tanks for about two years until they reach the smolt stage. Then they're released into nearby streams for their journey to the ocean.

After two to six years the 1% or more of smolts that survive and reach sexual maturity return to breed in streams where they were released. They can then be harvested by placing nets across the streams or by diverting them through chutes directly into canneries (Figure 14-21).

These practices are a threat to wild salmon, whose populations in many areas have already been reduced sharply by hydropower dams along their migration routes, pollution, sediment from logged lands, and overfishing. Ranch salmon that escape interbreed with wild ones, reducing the genetic variability of the species and their ability to survive in particular

streams to which they have become finely adapted by evolution.

Japan is the world leader in salmon ranching, followed by the CIS and the United States. Salmon ranching is also becoming popular in Iceland, Canada, Sweden, and France.

Another aquaculture approach is *salmon farming*, in which salmon are raised in huge floating cages and pens in coastal areas (Figure 14-16). Although this method is more expensive than salmon ranching because the salmon must be fed all their lives, the extra cost is offset by the much lower rate of loss of the newly hatched fish. Norway is the leader in salmon farming, followed by Scotland, Ireland, Chile, and Canada. Atlantic salmon are the principal species raised in salmon farms because they take to captivity better than Pacific salmon.

**Figure 14-21** Normal (left) and modified (right) life cycle of an anadromous salmon species.

is needed, so yields and profits are not closely tied to the price of oil, as they are in commercial marine fishing. Also, aquaculture is usually labor-intensive and can provide much-needed jobs.

There are problems, however. For one thing, large-scale aquaculture requires considerable capital and scientific knowledge, which are in short supply in LDCs. For another, scooping out huge ponds for fish

and shrimp farming in Ecuador, the Philippines, Panama, Indonesia, Honduras, and other LDCs has destroyed ecologically important mangrove forests (Figure 5-32). Also, fish in aquaculture ponds can be killed by pesticide runoff from nearby croplands, and bacterial and viral infections can also limit yields. Finally, without adequate pollution control, waste outputs from shrimp farming and other large-scale aqua-

Q: How much of all U.S. land area is protected as wilderness?

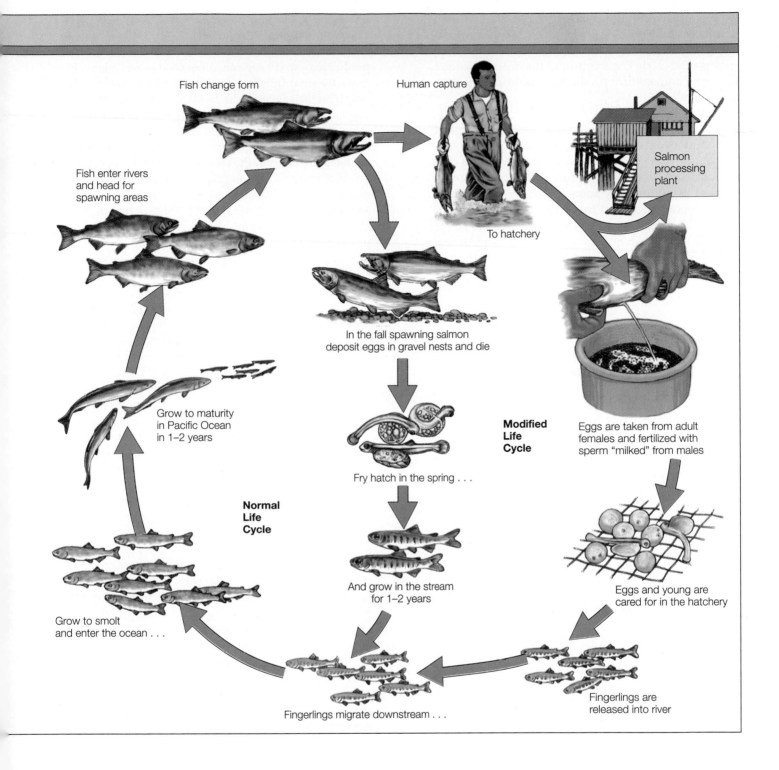

Fish change form

Human capture

Salmon processing plant

To hatchery

Fish enter rivers and head for spawning areas

In the fall spawning salmon deposit eggs in gravel nests and die

Eggs are taken from adult females and fertilized with sperm "milked" from males

**Modified Life Cycle**

Grow to maturity in Pacific Ocean in 1–2 years

Fry hatch in the spring . . .

**Normal Life Cycle**

Eggs and young are cared for in the hatchery

And grow in the stream for 1–2 years

Grow to smolt and enter the ocean . . .

Fingerlings are released into river

Fingerlings migrate downstream . . .

culture operations can contaminate nearby estuaries, surface water, and groundwater.

**CAN THE ANNUAL CATCH BE INCREASED SIGNIFICANTLY?** Some scientists believe that the world fish catch can be expanded by harvesting more squid, octopus, Antarctic krill, and other unconventional species. However, this would have unpredictable effects on ocean food webs. Heavier harvesting of shrimplike krill, for example, could decimate the populations of certain whales and other krill-eaters (Figure 4-21). Also, food scientists have been unable to make krill palatable for humans; thus for now it is used for livestock feed.

However, the fish catch could be increased by cutting waste. Currently one-fifth of the annual catch is wasted, mainly from throwing back potentially useful fish taken along with desired species. More refrigerated storage at sea to prevent spoilage would also increase the catch. Experts project that freshwater and saltwater aquaculture production could also be doubled during the 1990s.

Other fishery experts believe that further increases in the marine catch are limited by overfishing and by pollution and destruction of estuaries. Another limiting factor is the projected rise in oil prices—and thus of boat fuel—sometime before 2015. Unless more seafood is produced by aquaculture, consumers may find seafood prices too high. Health inspections of seafood also need to be increased. Unlike other forms of meat more than 80% of the seafood eaten in the United States is sold without being inspected for bacterial and chemical contamination.

## 14-5 Agricultural Policy, Food Aid, and Land Reform

### GOVERNMENT AGRICULTURAL POLICIES

Agriculture is a risky business. Whether farmers have a good or a bad year is determined by factors over which they have little control—weather, crop prices, crop pests and disease, interest rates, and the global market. Because of the need for reliable food supplies, despite such variability, most governments provide various forms of assistance to farmers.

Governments have several choices. They can:

- *Keep food prices artificially low,* which makes consumers happy but means that farmers may not be able to make a living

- *Give farmers subsidies* to keep them in business and encourage them to increase food production

- *Eliminate most or all price controls and subsidies,* allowing market competition to be the primary factor determining food prices and thus the amount of food produced

Most governments in LDCs have concentrated their limited financial resources on the cities and on industrial development, neglecting farming and rural areas. Many of them keep food prices in cities lower than in the countryside to prevent political unrest. This discourages farmers from producing enough to feed the country's population, and the government must use limited funds or go into debt to buy imported food. With food prices lower in the cities more rural people migrate to urban areas, aggravating urban problems and unemployment, and increasing the chances of political unrest.

Governments can stimulate crop and livestock production—and keep consumer food prices relatively low—by guaranteeing farmers a minimum yearly return on their investment. In MDCs government price supports and other subsidies for agriculture total more than $300 billion per year ($17–22 billion per year in the United States). However, if government subsidies are too generous and the weather is good, farmers may produce more food than can be sold. Food prices and profits then drop because of the surplus. Large amounts of food become available for export or as food aid to LDCs, depressing world food prices. The low prices reduce the financial incentive for farmers to increase domestic food production. Moreover, the taxes citizens pay to provide these agricultural supports more than offset the lower food prices.

The U.S. agricultural system produces so much food that the government pays farmers not to produce food on one-fourth of U.S. cropland or buys up and stores unneeded crops. This encourages farmers to produce even more (often on marginal land), wastes taxpayer dollars, and serves as a form of welfare for wealthy farmers. In 1989 nearly 60% of federal farm subsidies went to the wealthiest 25% of U.S. farms.

Some analysts call for eliminating all federal subsidies, say over five years, and letting farmers respond to market demand. Only those who were good farmers and financial managers would be able to stay in business. However, any phaseout of farm subsidies in the United States or any other country should be coupled with increased aid for the poor, who would suffer the most from any increase in food prices.

Instead of eliminating all subsidies, many environmentalists believe that we should refocus them by rewarding farmers and ranchers who protect the soil, conserve water, reforest degraded land, protect and restore wetlands, and conserve wildlife. Those who didn't would receive no subsidies.

Environmentalists also warn that the current GATT negotiations to deregulate global trade in agricultural and related products would doom most small- and medium-scale farming operations around the world, many of which practice sustainable diversified farming. They would be replaced by larger-scale monoculture farming and feedlots that are much more environmentally destructive. This agreement would also reduce or eliminate all farm subsidies, weaken environmental and health safety standards, and undermine local, state, and national authority. However, eliminating trade barriers (with adequate environmental protection) could help LDCs, which now lose an estimated $100 billion per year in agricultural sales because of such barriers by MDCs.

Q: How much of the U.S. gross national product is derived from wildlife resources?

**INTERNATIONAL AID** Between 1945 and 1985 the United States was the world's largest donor of nonmilitary foreign aid to LDCs; since 1986 Japan has taken over that role. This aid is used mostly for agriculture and rural development, food relief, population planning, health care, and economic development. Private charity organizations such as CARE and Catholic Relief Services and funds from benefit concerts and record sales, provide over $3 billion per year of additional foreign aid.

Besides helping other countries, foreign aid stimulates economic growth and provides jobs in the donor country. For example, 70¢ of every dollar the United States gives directly to other countries is used to purchase American goods and services. Today 21 of the 50 largest buyers of U.S. farm goods are countries that once received free U.S. food.

Despite the humanitarian benefits and economic returns of such aid, the percentage of the U.S. GNP used for nonmilitary foreign aid to LDCs has dropped from a high of 1.6% in the 1950s to only 0.2% since 1980 (0.19% in 1990)—an annual average of only $30 per American. Since 1980, 16 other MDCs have allocated a higher percentage of their GNP for nonmilitary foreign aid to LDCs than has the United States.

A controversial form of international aid is food relief. Some people call for greatly increased food relief for starving people from government and private sources, while others question the value of such aid (Pro/Con, right).

**SOLUTIONS: LAND REFORM** An important step in reducing world hunger, malnutrition, poverty, and land degradation is land reform. This usually means a redistribution of land, giving the landless rural poor in LDCs ownership or free use of enough land to produce their food and, ideally, enough surplus to provide some income.

Such reform would increase agricultural productivity in LDCs and reduce the need to farm and degrade marginal land. It would also help reduce migration of poor people to overcrowded urban areas by creating employment in rural areas. To date China and Taiwan have had the most successful land reform programs.

The world's most unequal land distribution is in Latin America, where 7% of the population owns 93% of the farmland. Most of this land is used for export crops such as sugar, tea, coffee, bananas, or beef, or is left idle on huge estates. Of course land reform is difficult to institute in countries where government leaders are unduly influenced by wealthy and powerful landowners.

## Food Relief

**PRO/CON**

Most people view food relief as a humanitarian effort to prevent people from dying prematurely. However, some analysts contend that giving food to starving people in countries with high population growth rates does more harm than good in the long run. By not helping people grow their own food, they argue, food relief can condemn even greater numbers to premature death in the future.

Biologist Garrett Hardin (Guest Essay, p. 226) has suggested that we use the concept of *lifeboat ethics* to decide which countries get food aid. His basic premise is that there are already too many people in the lifeboat we call Earth. Thus, if food aid is given to countries that are not reducing their population, this simply adds more people to an already-overcrowded lifeboat. Sooner or later the boat will sink and most of the passengers will drown.

Large amounts of food aid can also depress local food prices, decrease food production, and stimulate mass migration from farms to already-overburdened cities. In addition, food aid discourages the government from investing in rural agricultural development to enable the country to grow enough food for its population on a sustainable basis.

Another problem is that much food aid does not reach hunger victims. Transportation networks and storage facilities are inadequate, so that some of the food rots or is devoured by pests before it can reach the hungry. Also, typically, some of the food is stolen by officials and sold for personal profit. And some must often be given to officials as bribes for approving the unloading and transporting of the remaining food to the hungry.

Critics of food relief are not against foreign aid. Instead, they believe that such aid should be given to help countries control population growth and grow enough food to feed their population using sustainable agricultural methods (Section 14-6). Temporary food aid, they believe, should be given only when there is a complete breakdown of an area's food supply because of natural disaster. What do you think?

## 14-6 Solutions: Sustainable-Earth Agriculture

**CHARACTERISTICS** To environmentalists the key to reducing world hunger, poverty, and the harmful environmental impacts of both industrialized and

# Mazunte: A Farming and Fishing Ecological Reserve in Mexico

*Alberto Ruz Buenfil*

*Alberto Ruz Buenfil, an international environmental activist, writer, and performer, is the founder of a land-based ecovillage in the mountains of Mexico, called Huehuecoytl. His articles on ecology and alternative living have appeared in publications from the United States, Canada, Mexico, Japan, and Europe. His book* Rainbow Nation Without Borders: Toward an Ecotopian Millennium *(New Mexico: Bear, 1991) has been published in English, Italian, and Spanish.*

The Pacific coasts of southern Mexico, especially the shores of the state of Oaxaca, are the main sites for turtle nesting, reproduction, and conservation. They also contain some of Mexico's last reserves of wetlands.

Only recently have we begun recognizing the ecological values of wetlands, deltas, and coastal ecosystems [Case Study, p. 139]. They provide habitats for a rich diversity of wildlife, maintain water supplies, protect shorelines from erosion, and play a role in regulating the global climate.

Previously places like swamps, marshes, and bogs have been considered wastelands to be drained, filled, and turned into "productive land," especially for constructing and developing urban and tourist areas. During the last few decades the coasts of Oaxaca have not escaped such exploitation, especially after business interests discovered the paradiselike beaches of Mazunte, Zipolite, San Agustinilo, Puerto Angel, and Puerto Escondido, and the magnificent bays of Hautulco.

The villages of Mazunte and San Agustinilo were founded in the late 1960s, basically to bring in cheap labor from neighboring indigenous villages and to provide workers for a slaughterhouse producing products from various species of turtles nesting in the area.

Nearly 200 families of indigenous farmers became fishermen and employees for the new turtle meat factory, which was fully operational in the 1970s and 1980s. According to some of these workers nearly 2,000 turtles were killed and quartered every day during those years, with no law to protect them. At night dozens of poachers came to collect turtle eggs from their nests.

In the 1980s this situation came to the attention of two of the first environmental organizations to speak up in defense of species, forests, and natural resources in Mexico. They began denouncing the massacre of the area's turtles and pointed out the danger that some of the species might be exterminated. With support from other international organizations they campaigned for almost 10 years, until a 1990 presidential decree made it illegal to exploit the turtles and led to the closing of San Agustinilo's turtle slaughterhouse.

The Mexican government provided some funds, boats, and freezers to compensate for the loss of jobs. However, only about 5% of the indigenous population benefited from this compensation. Since then most of the people have been living on the verge of starvation. What had seemed to be an important environmental victory turned into a nightmare for a large population of indigenous people. Understandably these people had no use for ecologists or environmentalists.

In 1990 a group called ECOSOLAR A.C. began efforts to change this situation by implementing a plan for sustainable development of the coast of Oaxaca. They were successful in obtaining funding for this project from different national and international institutions. By 1992 the members of this small but effective group had been able to:

- Make a detailed study of the bioregion, which is being used to define the possible uses of different areas with the participation of the local people

traditional agriculture (Spotlight, p. 373) is to develop a variety of **sustainable-Earth agricultural systems**. This involves combining the wisdom of traditional agricultural systems with new techniques that take advantage of local climates, soils, resources, and cultural systems. Here are some general guidelines:

- *Don't rob the soil of nutrients and waste water, and return whatever is taken from the earth.* This means not trying to grow water-thirsty crops in arid and semiarid areas; raising water prices to encourage water conservation; using irrigation systems that minimize water waste, salinization, and waterlogging; planting and not destroying windbreaks (Figure 12-16); limiting livestock grazing on arid and semiarid areas; maintaining vegetative cover

on cropland; using no-till cultivation; using organic fertilizers, crop rotation, and intercropping to increase the organic content of soils; and not cultivating marginal land (Figure 12-17).

- *Design the agricultural system to fit the environment (soil, water, climate, and pest populations) of the region.* This involves trying to answer three questions: What vegetation was here? What would nature put here? How can we work with nature in this place to produce food sustainably?

- *Encourage systems featuring a diverse mix of crops and livestock, instead of monoculture production of a single crop or livestock type.* Emphasize increased use of perennial polyculture and other forms of intercropping (p. 358 and Case Study, p. 367).

Q: How much of the world's population relies on plants or plant extracts for medicines?

- Create a system of credits to help native inhabitants build better houses and small family-run restaurants, and manufacture hammocks for rent or sale to visitors looking for an almost untouched, rustic vacation site

- Begin building systems for drainage, water collection, and latrines using low-impact technology and local materials and workers, as well as home nurseries for local seeds, reforestation, and wildlife preservation

- Work with the community to promote Mazunte as a center for ecotourism, a place where visitors can experience unique ecosystems containing alligators, turtles, and hundreds of species of birds and fishes

In only two years the native inhabitants of Mazunte and other neighboring communities have completely changed their opinion and perspective about ecology and environmentalists. In May 1992 Mazunte hosted the second annual gathering of "Earth Keepers," involving nearly 150 representatives of 35 organizations from 20 different countries.

For one week these specialists shared their practical knowledge with the local people. They used their health skills to help the community set up an alternative clinic of healing arts, their skills in permaculture and organic agriculture to improve local hatcheries and home nurseries, and their skills in ecotechnology to build biodigestors for producing natural fertilizers from biomass and a village recycling center located at the school. In addition, artistic and cultural activities took place every night in the Center for Biological Investigations, which the people of Mazunte want to turn into Mexico's first Marine Turtles Museum. Run by local people, it will attract and educate visitors from around the world.

A few days after the event concluded, the village of Mazunte called a general meeting attended by 150 heads of family to discuss the invasion and destruction of the zone needed to protect turtle nesting shores. Out of that meeting came a "Declaration of Mazunte," requesting that competent higher authorities and the president of Mexico put an immediate end to such destruction, which violates the earlier presidential decree forbidding the annihilation of turtles in Mexico.

The community went further and declared that their village and neighboring environments be considered Mexico's first *farming and fishing ecological reserve*. Its goals would be to protect the area's forests, water sources, wetlands, wildlife, shores, beaches, and scenic places, and to "establish new forms of relationship between humans and nature, for the well-being of today's and tomorrow's generations." This declaration has been presented to the government of Mexico and to many national and international organizations.

Mazunte is taking the lead in showing how cooperation between local people and environmental experts can lead to ecologically sustainable communities that benefit local people and wildlife. This model can show farmers and indigenous communities everywhere how they can live sustainably on Earth and turn things around in a short time. It is a message of hope and empowerment for people seeking a better world for themselves and others.

### Critical Thinking

1. What lessons have you learned from this essay that could be applied to your own life?

2. Could the rapid change toward sustainability brought about by environmentalists and local people in Mazunte be accomplished in your own community?

- *Whenever possible, rely on locally available, renewable biological resources, and use them in ways that preserve their renewability.* Examples include using organic fertilizers from animal and crop wastes (green manure and compost), planting fast-growing trees to supply fuelwood and add nitrogen to the soil, building simple devices for capturing and storing rainwater for irrigating crops, and cultivating crops adapted to local growing conditions.

- *Greatly reduce the use of fossil fuels in agriculture by using locally available perpetual and renewable energy resources such as sun, wind, and flowing water, and by using more organic fertilizer instead of commercial inorganic fertilizer.*

- *Emphasize biological pest control instead of chemical pesticides* (Section 24-5).

- *Provide economic incentives for farmers using sustainable-Earth agricultural systems.*

- *Encourage local people to grow food for local people, and let them plant what they want, instead of encouraging export of cash crops that reduces food available to local people.*

- *Promote trading patterns and kinds of foreign aid that encourage local self-reliance* (Guest Essay, above).

- *Slow—even stop—human population growth* (Section 8-3).

- *Encourage land reform and sustainable rural development.*

## What You Can Do to Promote Sustainable-Earth Agriculture

**INDIVIDUALS MATTER**

- *Waste less food.* An estimated 25% of all food produced in the United States is wasted; it rots in the supermarket or refrigerator, or is scraped off the plate and into the garbage in households and restaurants.

- *Eat lower on the food chain.* This can be done by reducing or eliminating meat consumption, which would reduce the environmental impact associated with raising cattle (Spotlight, p. 365).

- *Don't feed your dog or cat canned meat products.* Balanced grain pet foods are available and are better for your pet.

- *Reduce the use of pesticides on agricultural products by asking grocery stores to stock fresh produce and meat produced by organic methods* (without the use of commercial fertilizers and pesti-

cides).* Support legislation that will set standards for labeling and certification of organic foods. About 0.5% of U.S. farmers grow about 3% of the country's crops using organic methods.

- *Use sustainable-Earth cultivation techniques to grow some of your own food.* This can be done in a backyard plot, a window planter, a rooftop garden, or a cooperative community garden. Planting a living-room-size garden (with about $35 in supplies) can give you fresh vegetables worth about $250—a better return than almost any financial investment you can make.

- *Fertilize your crops primarily with organic fertilizer produced in a compost bin* (Figure 12-18).

- *Use drip irrigation to water your crops* (Figure 13-20).

* A *Consumer's Organic Mail-Order Directory* of farmers and wholesalers who sell organically grown food by mail can be obtained for $9.95 (plus $2.50 postage) from California Action Network, P.O. Box 464, Davis, CA 95617.

- *Control pests by a combination of cultivation and biological methods* (Section 24-5).

- *Think globally, eat locally.* Whenever possible eat food that is locally grown and in season. This supports your local economy, gives you more influence over how the food is grown (organic or conventional methods), saves energy from having to transport food over long distances, and reduces the use of fossil fuels and pollution. Each year nearly $21 billion is spent just moving food in the United States. If you deal directly with local farmers, you can also save money.

- *Pressure elected officials to develop and encourage sustainable-Earth agricultural systems in the United States and throughout the world.*

- *Support efforts to slow down—even stop—human population growth* (Section 8-3).

---

**MAKING THE TRANSITION IN MDCs** In MDCs such as the United States a shift to sustainable-Earth agriculture will not be easy. It would be opposed by agribusiness, by successful farmers with large investments in industrialized agriculture, and by specialized farmers unwilling to learn the demanding art of farming sustainably.

However, this shift could be brought about over 10–20 years by:

- *Greatly increasing government support of research and development of sustainable-Earth agricultural methods and equipment.* At present only about 1% of the Department of Agriculture's annual research budget is used for this purpose.

- *Setting up demonstration projects in each county so that farmers can see how sustainable systems work.*

- *Establishing training programs for farmers, county farm agents, and Department of Agriculture personnel in sustainable-Earth agriculture.*

- *Establishing college curricula for sustainable-Earth agriculture.*

- *Giving subsidies and tax breaks to farmers using sustainable-Earth agriculture and to agribusiness companies developing products for this type of farming.* For example, Iowa taxes fertilizers and pesticides, and uses the revenues to support research into and development of sustainable agriculture. Minnesota provides low-interest loans for farmers engaged in sustainable agriculture. Austria, Denmark, Finland, Germany, Norway, and Sweden offer three- to five-year subsidies for farmers converting to sustainable agriculture.

- *Reducing the average size of U.S. farms so that farmers can monitor and manage them for sustainability.* Reducing the average size of U.S. farms from the current 187 hectares (461 acres) back to 1960 levels of 121 hectares (300 acres) would allow more sustainable management of farms and create over 1 million jobs—2 million if the farms were organic.

**Q:** How many of the medicines sold in the world have active ingredients extracted from wildlife (mostly plants)?

Each of us has a role to play in bringing about a shift from unsustainable to sustainable agriculture at the local, national, and global levels (Individuals Matter, p. 388).

*The need to bring birthrates well below death rates, increase food production while protecting the environment, and distribute food to all who need it is the greatest challenge our species has ever faced.*

Paul and Anne Ehrlich

## Critical Thinking

1. What are the biggest advantages and disadvantages of **(a)** labor-intensive subsistence agriculture, **(b)** energy-intensive industrialized agriculture, and **(c)** sustainable-Earth agriculture?

2. Summarize the advantages and limitations of each of the following proposals for increasing world food supplies and reducing hunger over the next 30 years: **(a)** cultivating more land by clearing tropical forests and irrigating arid lands, **(b)** catching more fish in the open sea, **(c)** producing more fish and shellfish with aquaculture, and **(d)** increasing the yield per area of cropland.

3. Should price supports and other federal subsidies paid to U.S. farmers out of tax revenues be eliminated? Explain. Try to consult one or more farmers in answering this question.

4. Is sending food to famine victims helpful or harmful? Explain. Are there any conditions you would attach to sending such aid? Explain.

5. Should tax breaks and subsidies be used to encourage more U.S. farmers to switch to sustainable-Earth farming? Explain.

*6. If possible visit a nearby conventional industrialized farm and an organic farm. Compare soil erosion and other forms of land degradation, use and costs of energy, use and costs of pesticides and inorganic fertilizer, use and costs of natural pest control and organic fertilizer, yields per hectare for the same crops, and overall profit per hectare for the same crops.

## Who's Afraid of the Big Gray Wolf?

Anne Gray, a park ranger in spectacular Yellowstone National Park, sat bolt upright in her sleeping bag. She was sure she had heard the primal howl of wolves echoing across the valley. After shaking herself awake, she realized it had been a dream.

Soon it may be a reality, however. Either the endangered gray wolf, *Canis lupus* (Figure 15-1), will return to the Yellowstone area on its own, or the U.S. Fish and Wildlife Service may reintroduce it by 1994. The proposal has pitted environmentalists against ranchers and hunters, transforming a biological and land-use question into a hot political issue.

At one time the gray wolf ranged over most of North America. Between 1850 and 1900, 2 million wolves were shot, trapped, poisoned, and even drenched with gasoline and set afire by ranchers, hunters, and government employees. The idea was to make the West and the Great Plains safe for livestock and for big game animals prized by hunters.

In the Yellowstone area most wolves had been purged by the late 1920s, and the last few survivors were gone by the 1940s. By the 1960s the gray wolf was found mostly in Alaska and Canada with a few hundred left in Minnesota. By 1992 about 50 wolves naturally recolonized Montana by crossing over from Canada. The species is now listed as endangered in all 48 lower states except Minnesota (with 1,550–1,750 wolves) where it is listed as threatened.

**Figure 15-1** The gray wolf, an endangered species in the lower 48 states (except in Minnesota, where it is listed as threatened). Efforts to return this species to its former habitat in the Yellowstone National Park area are vigorously opposed by ranchers, who fear the wolves will kill some of their sheep, and by hunters, who fear that the wolves will kill big-game animals.

Tom J. Ulrich/Visuals Unlimited

Ecologists now recognize the important role these predators once played in the Yellowstone ecosystem. They culled herds of bison, elk, and mule deer, which in recent years have proliferated, devastating some of the area's vegetation and threatening the niches of other forms of wildlife. They killed only for food, usually taking weaker animals, and thereby strengthened the genetic pool of the survivors.

In 1987 the U.S. Fish and Wildlife Service proposed that wolves be reintroduced to the Yellowstone ecosystem, which includes two national parks, seven national forests, and other federal and state land in Wyoming, Idaho, and Montana. The plan calls for introducing 10 breeding packs, each containing about 100 wolves, in three recovery areas.

The proposal immediately brought outraged howls from ranchers who feared the wolves would attack their cattle and sheep and from hunters alarmed that the wolves would kill their prized big game animals. An enraged rancher said that the idea is "like reintroducing smallpox."

Park Service officials said that they would trap or shoot any wolves roaming outside the park to feast on livestock and that ranchers would be reimbursed for lost stock from a private $100,000 fund established by Defenders of Wildlife. However, these promises fell on deaf ears, and since then ranchers and hunters have been able to delay the plan.

The wolves may have a better chance to survive if enough of them make it back to Yellowstone on their own. Then, as an endangered species, they will be fully protected, at least legally. If they are relocated to the area, they will be treated as an "experimental" population. Then if they venture outside the park they can be killed by ranchers. Some ranchers and hunters say that, either way, they'll take care of the wolves quietly— what they call the shoot, shovel, and shut up solution.

Protection and reintroduction of the gray wolf to Yellowstone is at bottom a land-use issue. Forests, rangelands, parks, and wilderness, which serve as homes for wildlife are coming under increasing stress from population growth and economic development worldwide. Protecting these vital oases of biodiversity from damage, using them sustainably, and healing those we have damaged are important challenges.

This chapter is devoted to answering the following questions:

- What types of public lands are in the United States, and how are they used?
- How should forest resources be managed and conserved?
- Why are rangelands important, and how should they be managed?
- What problems do parks face, and how should parks be managed?
- Why is wilderness important, and how much should be preserved?

## 15-1 U.S. Public Lands: This Land Is Your Land

**PUBLIC LANDS: AN OVERVIEW** No nation has set aside so much of its land—about 42%—for public use and enjoyment and for wildlife as the United States. Almost one-third of the country's land is managed by the federal government; 73% of it is in Alaska and another 22% is in the western states. The allowed uses of these public lands vary (Spotlight, p. 392).

Between 1970 and 1992 the area of land in all public land systems except the national forests increased significantly (2.7-fold in the National Park System, 3-fold in the National Wildlife Refuge System, and 9-fold in the National Wilderness Preservation System). Most of the additions, by President Carter just before he left office in 1980, are in Alaska. Since then little land has been added to the systems.

**HOW SHOULD PUBLIC LANDS BE USED?** Federally administered public lands contain much of the country's commercial timber (40%), grazing land (54%), and energy resources (especially shale oil, uranium, coal, and geothermal energy) and most of its copper, silver, asbestos, lead, molybdenum, beryllium, phosphate, and potash. For over a century private individuals and corporations have exploited

### Multiple-Use Lands

**National Forest System** These 156 forests (Figure 15-2) and 19 grasslands are managed by the Forest Service. Except for wilderness areas (15%) this land is managed using two principles. **(1)** The *principle of sustainable yield* states that a potentially renewable resource should not be harvested or used faster than it is replenished; **(2)** The *principle of multiple use* allows a variety of uses on the same land at the same time. Today national forests are used for timbering (the dominant use in most cases), mining, grazing, farming, oil and gas extraction, recreation, sport hunting, sport and commercial fishing, and conservation of watershed, soil, and wildlife resources. Off-road vehicles are usually restricted to designated routes.

**National Resource Lands** These grasslands, prairies, deserts, scrub forests, and other open spaces in the western states and Alaska are managed by the Bureau of Land Management under the principle of multiple use. Emphasis is on providing a secure domestic supply of energy and strategic minerals and on preserving rangelands for livestock grazing under a permit system. Some of these lands that have not been disturbed by roads are being evaluated for designation as wilderness areas.

### Moderately Restricted–Use Lands

**National Wildlife Refuges** These 503 refuges (Figure 15-2) and other ranges are managed by the Fish and Wildlife Service. About 24% of this land is designated as wilderness. Most refuges protect habitats and breeding areas for waterfowl and big game to provide a harvestable supply for hunters. A few protect specific endangered species from extinction. These lands are not officially managed under the principle of multiple use. Nevertheless, sport hunting, trapping, sport and commercial fishing, oil and gas development, mining (old claims only), logging, grazing, and farming are permitted as long as the Department of the Interior finds such uses compatible with the purposes of each unit.

### Restricted-Use Lands

**National Park System** These 359 units include 50 major parks (mostly in the West) and 309 national recreation areas, monuments, memorials, battlefields, historic sites, parkways, trails, rivers, seashores, and lakeshores (Figure 15-2). All are managed by the National Park Service. Its goals are to preserve scenic and unique natural landscapes, preserve and interpret the country's historic and cultural heritage, protect wildlife habitats and wilderness areas within the parks, and provide certain types of recreation. National parks may be used only for camping, hiking, sport fishing, and boating. Motor vehicles are permitted only on roads. In national recreation areas these same activities plus sport hunting, mining, and oil and gas drilling are allowed. About 49% of National Park System land is designated as wilderness.

**National Wilderness Preservation System** These 474 roadless areas lie within the national parks, national wildlife refuges, and national forests. They are managed by the National Park Service, the Fish and Wildlife Service, and the Forest Service, respectively. These areas are to be preserved essentially untouched "for the use and enjoyment of the American people in such a manner as will leave them unimpaired for future use and enjoyment as wilderness." Wilderness areas are open only for recreational activities such as hiking, sport fishing, camping, nonmotorized boating, and, in some areas, sport hunting and horseback riding. Roads, logging, grazing, mining, commercial activities, and buildings are banned, except where they predate the wilderness designation. Motorized vehicles, boats, and equipment are banned except for emergencies, but aircraft may land in Alaskan wilderness.

**Figure 15-2** National forests, parks, and wildlife refuges managed by the U.S. federal government. (Data from U.S. Geological Survey)

Q: What percentage of the world's estimated plant species have been evaluated for their medical uses?

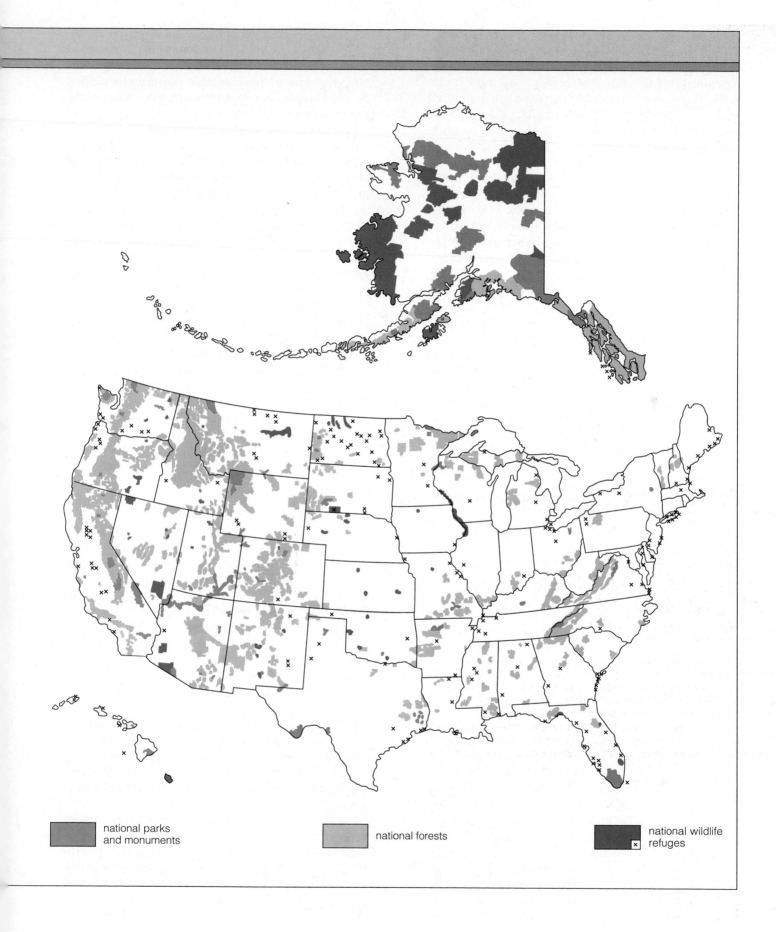

national parks and monuments

national forests

national wildlife refuges

many of these resources, often at below-market prices. This bonanza, long disputed (Section 2-5), is now more controversial than ever.

Since 1980 federal agencies managing these lands have yielded to pressure for increased grazing, road building, logging, mining, resort development, and oil and natural gas drilling. These activities have brought erosion, air and water pollution, deforestation, over-grazing, noise, and loss of habitat and biodiversity.

There are two major schools of thought on managing public lands. *Preservationists* seek to protect large areas from mining, timbering, and other forms of resource extraction so they can be enjoyed today and passed on unspoiled to future generations. Members of the *wise-use* school see all public lands as resources to be used wisely to enhance economic growth and national strength, and to provide the greatest benefit to the greatest number of people. This should be done by managing these lands more efficiently and scientifically for sustainable yield and multiple use.

Resource extractors accuse preservationists of wanting to keep us from using resources that could benefit people now. Preservationists say wise-users pay lip service to the concepts of sustainable yield and wise multiple use but, unless carefully regulated (which is hard to do), end up practicing unwise multiple abuse instead.

## 15-2 Forest Management and Conservation

**FOREST RESOURCES IN THE UNITED STATES**
Though forests cover about one-third of the lower 48 states (Figure 5-12), most of their virgin forests have been cut (Figure 10-22) and what remains is threatened (Section 10-5). U.S. forests provide habitats for more than 80% of the country's wildlife species and are the prime setting for outdoor recreation.

Nearly two-thirds of this forestland is capable of producing commercially valuable timber. Since 1950 the United States has met the demand for wood and wood products without serious depletion of its commercial forestlands. Most of the country's other forestland has no commercial value or is set aside as parks, wildlife refuges, or wilderness. About 55% of the wood cut in the United States is used for construction, 20% is burned as fuel, and 25% is pulped to make paper and cardboard—much of which ends up in landfills.

For three centuries the United States was self-sufficient in wood. Since 1940, however, the country

has been a net importer of wood, and the gap is widening even though the United States cuts more wood than any other country. The United States exports a large volume of irreplaceable old-growth timber, mostly to Japan, but imports much more. Most of the imports come from Canada, the world's greatest wood exporter (44% of world lumber exports).

The reason for this import–export gap is not higher per capita consumption of wood, which is half of what it was in 1900 (Figure 3-8), but population growth, which has tripled since 1900.

**TYPES OF FOREST MANAGEMENT** Whereas agricultural crops can be harvested annually or even more often, trees take 20–1,000 years to mature, depending on the species. There are two basic forest management systems: even-aged and uneven-aged.

With **even-aged management** trees in a given stand are maintained at about the same age and size. Even-aged management begins with the cutting of all or most trees from an area. Then the site is replanted naturally or artificially all at once. Once the trees in such a tree farm (Figure 5-25) reach maturity, the entire stand is harvested and the area replanted. Growers emphasize single species (monocultures) of fast-growing softwoods to get the best return on their investment in the shortest time. Crossbreeding and genetic engineering can improve both the quality and the quantity of tree farm wood. Tree farms need close supervision, fertilizers, and pesticides to protect the monoculture from diseases and insects.

With **uneven-aged management** trees in a given stand are maintained at many ages and sizes to foster natural regeneration. Here the goals are biological diversity, long-term production of high-quality timber, a reasonable economic return, and multiple use. Mature trees are selectively cut, with clear-cutting used only on small patches of species that benefit from it.

**THE MANAGEMENT PROCESS** Forest management consists of a cycle of decisions and events between planting and harvesting called a *rotation*. The most important steps in a rotation include taking an inventory of the site, developing a forest management plan, building roads into the site, preparing the site for harvest, harvesting commercially valuable timber, and regenerating and managing the site until the next harvest.

The volume of wood produced by a forest varies as it goes through different stages of growth and ecological succession (Figure 15-3). If the goal is to produce the most fuelwood or fiber for paper production in the shortest time, the forest is usually harvested on a short rotation cycle before the growth rate peaks (point A of Figure 15-3). Harvesting at the peak

Q: How much is a Kenyan elephant worth during its lifetime in ecotourist income?

growth rate gives the maximum yield of wood per unit of time (point B of Figure 15-3). If the goal is high-quality wood for fine furniture or veneer, managers use longer rotations to develop larger, older-growth trees (point C of Figure 15-3).

## ROAD BUILDING AND TREE HARVESTING

Logging roads make timber accessible. Unhappily that's not all they do. They cause erosion and sediment pollution of waterways and expose forests to pests, diseases, and alien wildlife. Their most serious impact, however, is the chain of events they start (Figure 10-14). In many LDCs they open up once-impenetrable forests to farmers, miners, and ranchers who cut, damage, or flood large areas of trees, and to hunters who deplete wild animal species.

Once loggers can reach a forest, the harvesting method they use depends on whether the stand is uneven- or even-aged (Figure 15-4). It also depends on the tree species being harvested, the nature of the site, and the objectives and resources of the owner.

In **selective cutting** intermediate-aged or mature trees in an uneven-aged forest are cut singly or in small groups, creating gaps not much larger than those from natural treefall (Figure 15-4a). This reduces crowding, encourages the growth of younger trees, maintains an uneven-aged stand with trees of different species and sizes, and allows trees to grow back naturally. In addition, selective cutting lowers the fire hazard because less wood debris (slash) is left after harvest. If done properly it also helps protect the site from soil erosion and wind damage.

Selective cutting does have certain drawbacks. For example, it's costly unless the trees removed are quite valuable; and maintaining a good mixture of tree ages, species, and sizes takes planning and skill. Nor is it useful for species whose seedlings require full sun. Also, reopening roads and trails periodically for selective harvests can erode certain soils.

An unsound type of selective cutting is *high grading*, or *creaming*, which removes the most valuable trees. This practice, common in many tropical forests, ends up injuring one-third to two-thirds of the remaining trees.

**Shelterwood cutting** removes all mature trees in a series of cuttings, stretched out over about 10 years (Figure 15-4b). This technique can be applied to even- or uneven-aged stands. The first cut removes most mature canopy trees, unwanted tree species, and diseased, defective, and dying trees. This opens the forest floor to light and leaves enough mature trees to cast seed and to shelter growing seedlings. Some years later after enough seedlings take hold, a second cut removes more canopy trees, though some of the best mature trees are left to shelter the young trees. After these are well established, a third cut removes the

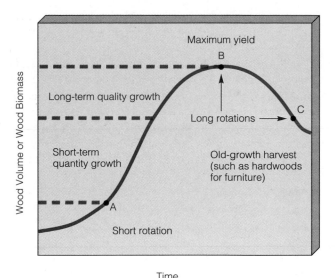

**Figure 15-3** Rotation cycle of forest management.

remaining mature trees, and the even-aged stand of young trees then grows to maturity. Sometimes this form of harvesting is done in only two cuts.

This method allows natural seeding from the best seed trees and keeps seedlings from being crowded out. It leaves a fairly natural-looking forest that can be used for a variety of purposes and also helps reduce soil erosion and provides a good habitat for wildlife. The danger is that loggers may take too many trees in the first cut. Shelterwood cutting is also more costly and takes more skill and planning than clear-cutting.

**Seed-tree cutting** harvests nearly all the stand's trees in one cutting, leaving a few uniformly distributed seed-producing trees to regenerate a new crop (Figure 15-4c). After the new trees have become established, the seed trees may be harvested. By allowing several species to grow at once, seed-tree cutting leaves an aesthetically pleasing forest, useful for recreation, deer hunting, erosion control, and wildlife conservation. Leaving the best trees for seed can also lead to genetic improvement in the new stand.

**Clear-cutting** is the removal of all trees from a given area in a single cutting. The clear-cut area may be a whole stand (Figures 15-4d and 15-5), a strip (Figure 15-4e), or a series of patches. After all trees are cut, the site is reforested naturally from seed released by the harvest, or artificially as foresters broadcast seed over the site or plant genetically superior seedlings raised in a nursery. If clear-cut areas are small enough, seeding may occur from nearby uncut trees.

Currently almost two-thirds of the annual U.S. timber harvest and about one-third of the cutting in national forests is clear-cut. On the positive side clear-cutting increases timber yield per hectare, reduces

**A: $1 million**

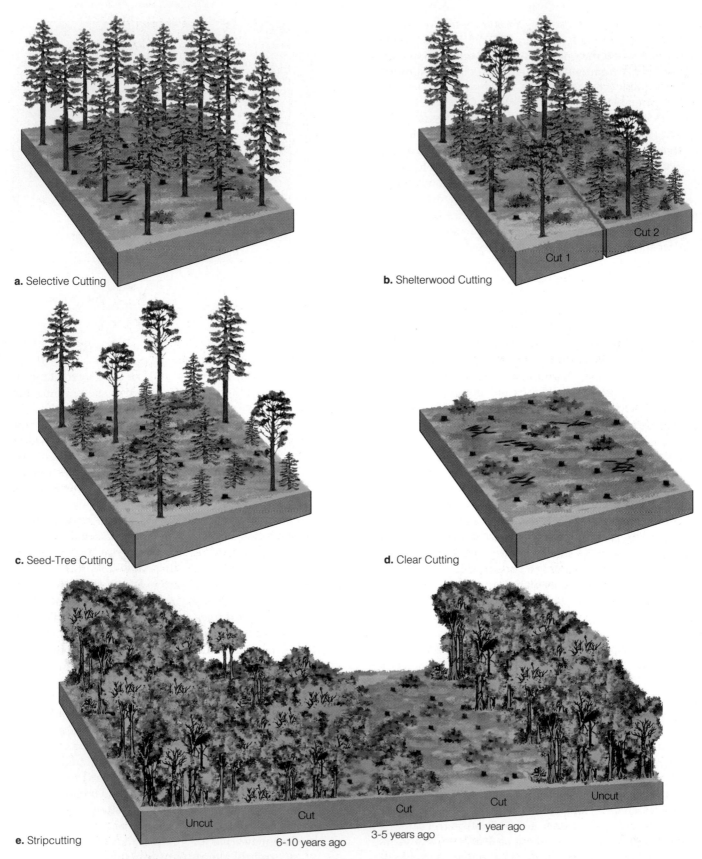

**a.** Selective Cutting

**b.** Shelterwood Cutting

Cut 1

Cut 2

**c.** Seed-Tree Cutting

**d.** Clear Cutting

**e.** Stripcutting

Uncut

Cut

6-10 years ago

Cut

3-5 years ago

Cut

1 year ago

Uncut

**Figure 15-4** Tree harvesting methods.

Q: How many of Earth's species are believed to become extinct each year because of human activities?

road building, permits reforesting with genetically improved stocks of fast-growing trees, and shortens the time needed to establish a new stand of trees (Figure 15-3). It also requires much less skill and planning than other harvesting methods, and usually gives timber companies the maximum economic return.

On the negative side clear-cutting leaves ugly, unnatural forest openings (Figures 15-4d and 15-5) and eliminates any potential recreational value. It also destroys wildlife habitats and thus reduces biodiversity. Furthermore, trees in stands bordering clear-cut areas are more vulnerable to windstorms, and large-scale clear-cutting on steep slopes leads to severe soil erosion, sediment water pollution, flooding (Case Study, p. 340), and landslides. Finally, the heavy logging equipment compacts the soil and reduces its productivity, so that such slopes often become barren wastelands.

Some tree species grow best in full or moderate sunlight in large clearings. Such sun-loving species are usually harvested by shelterwood cutting, seed-tree cutting, or clear-cutting. Proper clear-cutting is appropriate for some sun-loving species, such as the Douglas fir. "Proper" means cutting small areas not on steep slopes and making sure that the area is replanted and protected until the next harvest. The problem is that timber companies have a built-in economic incentive to use large-scale clear-cutting, often on species that could be harvested by less environmentally destructive methods.

A variation of clear-cutting is **whole-tree harvesting**, in which a machine cuts trees at ground level or uproots entire trees. These trees are usually transported to a chipping machine in which huge blades reduce the wood to small chips in about one minute. This approach is used primarily to harvest stands for use as pulpwood or fuelwood chips.

Many foresters and ecologists oppose whole-tree harvesting because it removes all tree materials, including standing dead timber and fallen logs, which deprives the soil of plant nutrients and removes numerous wildlife habitats (Figure 4-16). Research is underway to determine how whole-tree harvesting methods might be modified to reduce such harmful environmental effects. Meanwhile, as roads are built and logging operations spread, remaining uncut areas become endangered habitat islands in a sea of degraded lands (Figure 10-17).

Another variation of clear-cutting is **strip logging** (Figure 15-4e), which can allow a sustainable timber yield from forests without the widespread destruction often associated with conventional clear-cutting. A strip of trees is clear-cut along the contour of the land, with the corridor narrow enough to allow natural regeneration within a few years. After regeneration

**Figure 15-5** Forest Service clear-cut in Oregon. All trees in the area are removed and the area is usually reseeded.

another strip is cut above the first, and so on. This allows a forest area to be clear-cut in narrow strips over several decades with minimal damage.

**PROTECTING FORESTS FROM PATHOGENS AND INSECTS** In a healthy and diverse forest, tree diseases and insect populations are usually controlled by interaction with other species. Thus they rarely get out of control and seldom destroy many trees. However, a biologically simplified tree farm is vulnerable to attack by pathogens and insects.

The most destructive tree diseases are caused by parasitic fungi. In the United States three deadly tree diseases were introduced accidentally from other countries: chestnut blight (from China), Dutch elm disease (from Asia via Europe), and white-pine blister rust (from Europe). Chestnut blight has almost eliminated the once-abundant and valuable chestnut tree from eastern hardwood forests, while Dutch elm disease has killed more than two-thirds of the elm trees in the United States.

A few insect species can wreak havoc, especially in tree farms or simplified forests where their natural predators may not exist. For example, bark beetles bore channels through the layer beneath the bark of spruce, fir, and pine trees, and the numerous channels loosen the bark. These insects have killed large expanses of forest in the western and southern United States. The larvae of leaf eaters, such as spruce budworm and gypsy moth larvae, eat the needles or leaves of trees. Repeated attacks over several years can kill trees by eliminating the foliage they need to carry out photosynthesis and produce food. In diverse forests populations of such leaf-eating insects are usually kept under control by predator populations.

A: 4,000–36,000 (11–99 per day)

**Figure 15-6** Destructive crown fire in Yellowstone National Park during the summer of 1988. Since 1972 Park Service policy has been to allow most lightning-caused fires to burn themselves out, as long as they don't threaten human lives, park facilities, private property, or endangered wildlife. The Park Service's intention is to allow fire to play its important role in forest succession and regeneration. After fires ravaged parts of Yellowstone National Park during the hot, dry summer of 1988, some people called for a reversal of this policy. Biologists, however, contend that damage was more widespread than it should have been because the previous policy of fighting all fires had allowed the buildup of flammable ground litter and small plants.

Biodiversity is the best and cheapest defense against tree diseases and insects. Other methods include banning imported timber that might introduce harmful new parasites, removing infected trees or clear-cutting infected areas and burning all debris, treating diseased trees with antibiotics, developing disease-resistant tree species, applying pesticides (Section 24-1), and using integrated pest management (Section 24-5).

**A NEW LOOK AT FIRE** Occasional natural fires set by lightning are an important part of the ecological cycle of many forests. Some species actually need occasional fires. For example, the seeds of the giant sequoia (Figure 4-9) and the jack pine are released or germinate only after being exposed to intense heat.

Forest ecosystems can be affected by different types of fires. Some, called *surface fires*, usually burn only undergrowth and leaf litter on the forest floor. These fires kill seedlings and small trees but spare most mature trees. Most wild animals can escape.

In forests where ground litter accumulates rapidly, a surface fire every five or so years burns away flammable material and helps prevent more destructive crown and ground fires. Surface fires also release valuable mineral nutrients tied up in slowly decomposing litter and undergrowth, increase the activity of underground nitrogen-fixing bacteria, stimulate the germination of certain tree seeds, and help control pathogens and insects. Some wildlife species—deer, moose, elk, muskrat, woodcock, and quail, for example—depend on occasional surface fires to maintain their habitats and to provide food in the form of vegetation that sprouts after fires.

Some extremely hot fires, called *crown fires*, may start on the ground but eventually burn whole trees and leap from treetop to treetop (Figure 15-6). They usually occur in forests where all fire has been prevented for several decades, allowing deadwood, leaves, and other flammable ground litter to build up. These rapidly burning fires can destroy all vegetation, kill wildlife, and lead to accelerated erosion.

Sometimes surface fires go underground and burn partially decayed leaves or peat (Figure 7-14). Such *ground fires*, most common in northern peat bogs, may smolder for days or weeks before being detected and are difficult to extinguish.

Protecting forest resources from fire involves four approaches: prevention, prescribed burning, presuppression, and suppression. Methods of *prevention* of forest fires include requiring burning permits and closing all or parts of a forest to travel and camping during periods of drought and high fire danger. The most important—and the cheapest—prevention method, however, is education. The Smokey-the-Bear educational campaign of the Forest Service and the National Advertising Council, for example, has prevented countless forest fires in the United States, saving many lives and avoiding billions of dollars in losses. However, ecologists contend that by allowing litter buildup in some forests, prevention increases the likelihood of highly destructive crown fires (Figure 15-6). For that reason many fires in national parks and wilderness areas are now allowed to burn as part of the natural ecological cycle of succession and regeneration (Figures 6–14 and 15-7).

*Prescribed burning* in some forests can effectively prevent crown fires by reducing litter buildup. These surface fires are also used to control outbreaks of tree disease and pests. These fires are started only by well-trained personnel when weather and forest conditions are ideal for control and proper intensity of burning.

National Park Service

Jim Peaco/National Park Service

**Figure 15-7** Secondary ecological succession in action. The fires that raged in parts of Yellowstone National Park during the summer of 1988 affected less than 0.1% of the park's area so badly that it won't recover. The bulldozers used to fight the fires did more damage to the park's delicate soils than the searing heat. Ash from the fire provided mineral nutrients for new plant growth, and within a few weeks after the fire, grasses and other small pioneer plants, such as these wild lupines, took over the charred fields. In 1989 park visits rose by about 20%, and business was booming in surrounding towns.

Prescribed fires are also timed to keep levels of air pollution as low as possible.

*Presuppression* involves trying to detect a fire at an early stage and reducing its spread and damage. To help confine fires and allow access by fire-fighting equipment, vegetation is cleared to form firebreaks and fire roads, and brush and trees are cleared along existing roads. Helicopters and small airplanes are used to detect small fires before they get out of control. Helicopters are also used to carry fire fighters to remote areas.

Once a wildfire starts fire fighters have a number of methods for fire *suppression*. They use specially designed bulldozers and breaker plows to establish firebreaks. They pump water onto the fire from tank trucks and drop water or fire-retarding chemicals from aircraft. Trained personnel use controlled backfires to create burned areas to confine fires.

**PROTECTING FORESTS FROM AIR POLLUTION AND CLIMATE CHANGE** Air pollution is a growing threat to many forests, especially in MDCs. Forests at high elevations and downwind from urban and industrial centers are exposed to air pollutants that can harm trees, especially conifers. Besides doing direct harm, prolonged exposure to multiple air pollutants makes trees much more vulnerable to drought, diseases, and insects.

Large-scale forest damage from air pollution has hit Poland, Czechoslovakia, Great Britain, France, Germany, Switzerland, Scandinavia, and parts of eastern North America. The solution is to slash emissions of the offending pollutants from coal-burning power plants, industrial plants, and motor vehicles (Section 22-4).

In coming decades an even greater threat to forests, especially temperate and boreal forests, may come from projected regional climate changes brought about by projected global warming (Section 11-1). Possible ways to slow down projected global warming are discussed in Section 11-3.

**SOLUTIONS: SUSTAINABLE-EARTH FORESTRY**
To timber companies sustainable forestry means getting a sustainable yield of commercial timber in as short a time as possible—a practice known as cut-and-run management among its critics. This usually means clearing diverse forests and replacing them with intensively managed tree farms (Figure 5-25).

To environmentalists this does not qualify as sustainable use (Pro/Con, p. 400). They call for widespread use of sustainable-Earth forestry, which recognizes that a biologically diverse forest ecosystem is the best protection against erosion, flooding, sediment water pollution, loss of biodiversity, and tree loss from fire, wind, insects, and diseases.

Such sustainable-Earth forest management emphasizes:

- Recycling more paper to reduce the demand for pulpwood

- Growing timber on long rotations, generally about 100–200 years, depending on the species and the soil quality (point C, Figure 15-3)

A: At least 25%

- Practicing selective cutting of individual trees or small groups of most tree species (Figure 15-4a)

- Minimizing fragmentation (Figure 10-17) of remaining larger blocks of forest

- Taking extreme precautions to protect topsoil, upon which all present and future forest productivity depends

- Using road building and logging methods that minimize soil erosion and compaction, including use of small, lightweight logging equipment

- Practicing strip logging (Figure 15-4e) instead of conventional clear-cutting, clear-cutting only in patches of less than 6 hectares (15 acres), and banning all clear-cutting on land that slopes more than 15–20°.

- Leaving standing dead trees (snags) and fallen timber (boles) to maintain diverse wildlife habitats and to be recycled as nutrients

- Leaving slash (wood debris) to help restore soil fertility, unless it causes too much buildup of dry fuel on the ground or hinders seeding of some desirable species

- Relying on natural controls to protect forests from most diseases and pests

- Controlling occasional severe pest outbreaks by using natural predators (biological control) and integrated pest management (Section 24-5)

Sustainable-Earth forestry does not mean that tree farms or even-aged management should never be used, but it does mean that their use should be severely limited on public land, especially in old-growth forests (Section 10-5). On private land such forestry practices should be designed to prevent excessive soil erosion and water pollution from runoff of sediment, fertilizers, and pesticides.

**MANAGING NATIONAL FORESTS** About 22% of the commercial forest area in the United States is located within the 156 national forests managed by the U.S. Forest Service (Spotlight, p. 392). These forestlands serve as grazing lands for more than 3 million cattle and sheep each year, support multimillion-dollar mining operations, contain a network of roads eight times longer than the entire U.S. interstate highway system, and receive more recreational visits than any other federal public lands.

The Forest Service—with an annual budget of around $2 billion and roughly 39,000 full-time employees—is required by law to manage national forests according to the principles of sustained yield and multiple use, a nearly impossible task. For example, timber company officials complain that they aren't

## Monocultures or Mixed Cultures?

**PRO/CON**

Most commercial foresters believe that tree farms are the best way to meet the increasing demand for wood and wood products and to increase short-term profits for timber companies. They contend that intensively managed forests can be harvested and regenerated in ways that conserve these potentially renewable resources for future generations. In addition, high yields from tree farms can reduce pressure to clear old-growth forests. Planting a tree farm is also the quickest way to reforest damaged land, preventing soil erosion and desertification.

However, the German experience between 1840 and 1918 shows that widespread monoculture forestry is not the way to go. Around 1840 German foresters decided to clear-cut diverse natural forests and replace them with pine and spruce plantations to increase the output of wood per hectare. These trees were harvested every 20–30 years to provide low-quality timber and pulp. Deciduous hardwood and true fir species nearly became extinct.

Yields increased for a time, but the monoculture plantations depleted the soil of plant nutrients. After the second or third generation the yield of the pine and spruce stands dropped and the general quality of the wood fell off. Many trees were stunted or fell victim to pests, disease, or wind.

After 1918 German foresters shifted to a more natural type of forestry management. Monoculture stands were replaced by uneven-aged mixtures of commercially valuable species. Instead of clear-cutting, loggers selectively harvested only certain economically important trees in a stand. The result was an increase in timber production and an improvement in soil quality. Today German foresters are appalled to see the United States and other countries making the same mistakes their predecessors made in sacrificing long-term, sustainable productivity for short-term gain.

allowed to buy and cut enough timber on public lands, especially in remaining old-growth forests in California and the Pacific Northwest (Section 10-5). Environmentalists charge that the Forest Service has allowed timber harvesting to become the dominant activity in most national forests and has turned the multiple-use policy into one of multiple abuse (Spotlight, p. 401).

When many private timber reserves were gone by the 1940s, cutting in the national forests surged and

Q: What is the greatest threat to wild species?

## How Should National Forests Be Used?

Environmentalists are alarmed at Forest Service proposals to double the timber harvest on national forests between 1986 and 2030 (see cartoon). To accomplish this the Forest Service—already the world's biggest road-building agency—plans to build a vast network of new roads in the forests by 2030. If this proposal is carried out, the system of roads in the national forests will be 14 times longer than the entire U.S. interstate highway system. Environmentalists charge that at least one-fifth of the proposed new roads are deliberately designed to keep those areas out of the National Wilderness Preservation System.

Environmentalists and the General Accounting Office have also accused the Forest Service of poor financial management of public forests. By law the Forest Service must sell timber for no less than the cost of reforesting the land it was harvested from. However, the cost of access roads is not included in this price but is provided as a subsidy to logging companies. Logging companies also get the timber itself for less than they would normally pay a private landowner.

Studies have shown that between 1978 and 1992 national forests lost at least $4.2 billion (some sources say $7 billion) from timber sales. With interest this added at least $5.9 billion to the

national debt. The Forest Service claims it made a $179-million profit in 1991, but economists dismiss this claim as absurd, estimating a $100-million loss instead when all costs are accounted for.

One glaring example of poor financial management is the logging operation in Alaska's Tongass National Forest, which is three times the size of Massachusetts and is the world's last remaining largely intact temperate rain forest. During the 1980s the Forest Service lost as much as $383 million in timber sales in this forest. Until 1990 Congress and the Forest Service gave two timber companies 50-year contracts to cut giant trees in this old-growth forest. The companies paid the government slightly more than $2 per tree while selling each tree in Japan for hundreds of dollars.

In 1990 Congress passed the Tongass Timber Reform Act, which

directed the Forest Service to stop the practice of taking only the most valuable old-growth stands (high-grading) and to get fair prices for any timber cut. However, none of this has been done. High-grading not only continues but is expected to accelerate in the next 20 years. Furthermore, the U.S. Treasury is expected to continue losing $20 million per year by selling timber in this forest unless enough citizens protest to their elected representatives.

Environmentalists oppose taxpayer subsidies for private timber companies because they encourage the cutting of old-growth timber on public lands (Section 10-5) and discourage the recycling of wastepaper. Representatives of the timber industry argue that such subsidies help taxpayers by keeping lumber and paper prices down. What do you think should be done?

© 1992 by Chip Bok/Creative Syndicate. (Color added)

hasn't slowed down since. Today the national forests are managed primarily for timber production, with private timber companies bidding for rights to cut in areas designated by the Forest Service. A drive through most national forests might give the illusion of traveling through a primeval forest because the Forest Service leaves thin buffers of uncut trees along the roads, but a flight over these forests will reveal that many of the trees have been clear-cut (Figure 10-17).

Environmentalists point out that almost three-fourths of the Forest Service budget is devoted directly or indirectly to the sale of timber, making it little more than a taxpayer-subsidized logging agency. The agency keeps most of the money it makes on timber sales, while any losses are passed on to taxpayers. Since logging increases its budget, the Forest Service has a powerful built-in incentive to encourage timber sales. Local county commissioners also exert tremendous pressure on members of Congress and Forest Service officials to keep the volume of timber cutting high because counties get 25% of the gross receipts from national forests within their boundaries.

National forest managers who sell lots of timber are promoted; those who don't or who warn that national forests are being harvested unsustainably are usually demoted and transferred to obscure jobs. The situation is so bad that 1,500 of the 39,000 Forest Service employees have formed the Association of Forest Service Employees for Environmental Ethics to oppose what they see going on in the nation's forests.

**SOLUTIONS: REFORMING FEDERAL FOREST MANAGEMENT** Forestry experts and environmentalists have suggested several ways to reduce exploitation of publicly owned timber resources and provide true multiple use of national forests as required by law:

- *Ban all timber cutting in national forests and fund the Forest Service completely from user fees for recreation.* The Forest Service estimates that recreational user fees, based on what national-forest users say they would be willing to pay, would generate $5 billion per year—three times what it earns from timber sales.

- *Until a total ban is enacted, cut the present annual harvest of timber from national forests in half instead of doubling it as proposed by the timber industry.*

- *Prevent at least 50% of remaining old-growth timber in any national forest from being cut.*

- *Build no more roads in national forests.*

- *Require that timber from national forests be sold at a price that includes the costs of road building, site preparation, and site regeneration.*

- *Require that all timber sales in national forests yield a profit for taxpayers based on the fair market value of the timber harvested using realistic accounting methods.*

- *Don't use money from sales of timber in national forests to supplement the Forest Service budget.*

- *Eliminate the provision that returns 25% of the gross receipts from national forests to counties containing the forests or base such returns only on recreational user-fee receipts.*

**SOLUTIONS: RECYCLING WASTEPAPER** The United States leads the world in total and per capita consumption—and waste—of paper. Each American throws away paper equivalent to an average of four trees per year.

Overpackaging—including double packages and oversized containers—is a major contributor to paper use and waste. Nearly $1 of every $10 spent for food in the United States goes for throwaway packaging. Junk mail also wastes enormous amounts of paper.* Each year the U.S. work force throws away enough office and writing paper to build a 4-meter-high (12-foot) wall stretching from New York City to Los Angeles.

Environmentalists estimate that at least 50% of the world's wastepaper (mostly newspapers, corrugated board and paperboard, office paper, and computer and copier paper) could be recycled by 2000. During World War II, when recycling was a national priority, the United States recycled about 45% of its wastepaper compared to 39% in 1992 (up from 25% in 1989). Some other countries do better, including the Netherlands (53%), Japan (50%), Mexico (45%), Germany (41%), and Sweden (40%). Recycling Sunday newspapers alone would save 500,000 trees per week. Currently only about 10% of U.S. newspapers are printed on paper containing some recycled fibers.

Apart from saving trees, recycling (and reusing) paper has a number of benefits. First, it saves energy, because it takes 30–64% less energy to produce the same weight of recycled paper as to make the paper from trees. Second, recycling paper reduces air pollution from pulp mills by 74–95%, lowers water pollution by 35%, conserves large quantities of water, saves landfill space, and creates five times more jobs than harvesting trees for pulp. Third, recycling paper helps prevent groundwater contamination from the toxic ink left after paper rots in landfills over a 30- to 60-year period. Finally, recycling paper can save money. In 1988, for example, American Telephone and Telegraph earned more than $485,000 in revenue and saved $1.3 million in disposal costs by collecting and recycling high-grade office paper.

Separating paper from other waste materials is a key to increased recycling. Otherwise paper becomes so contaminated that wastepaper dealers won't buy it.

In the United States tax subsidies and other financial incentives make it cheaper to make paper from trees than from recycled wastepaper—except in Florida, where virgin newsprint is taxed. Widely fluctuating prices and weak demand for recycled paper products also make recycling wastepaper a risky venture. Loans and tax credits to companies that invest in paper-recycling equipment could ease this risk, which is discouraging communities from recycling paper just when consumer interest in doing so has soared.

---

* To reduce your junk mail by about 75%, write to Mail Preference Service, Direct Marketing Association, 11 West 42nd Street, P.O. Box 3861, New York, NY 10163-3861. They will remove your name from the mailing lists of most large companies.

Q: How much of the original U.S. tall-grass prairies have been destroyed?

## Recycled Paper Hype and Tradeoffs

True or false: Buying recycled paper products will reduce solid waste. The answer is, not necessarily. Only products made from *postconsumer waste*—intercepted on its way from consumer to landfill—will do that.

Most recycled paper is actually made from *preconsumer waste*—scraps and cuttings recovered from paper and printing plants. Since the paper industry has always recycled this waste, it has never contributed to landfill problems. In the past it was not even called recycled paper because the industry believed no one would buy it. Now this paper is labeled "recycled" as a marketing ploy, giving the false impression that people who buy such products (sometimes at higher prices) are helping the solid waste problem. Until government guidelines prohibit such misleading labels, we cannot expect to see much high-grade paper made from postconsumer waste. Most "recycled"

paper has no more than 10% postconsumer waste, but some brands of toilet paper contain 90–100% postconsumer waste.

Any pre- or post-consumer recycled fibers in paper products, however, cut down on the harvesting of trees (most grown in plantations) and the resulting pollution and degradation.

Studies by Greenpeace have shown that the recycling process weakens paper fiber, making it more suitable for boxes, cereal cartons, and the like than for the demands of high-speed printing. This book is printed on acid-free recycled paper containing the maximum amount of recycled fiber possible to create paper resilient enough for high-speed printing presses without being prohibitively expensive.

More affordable printing-stock paper with higher percentages of preconsumer and postconsumer waste may be available within a few years. New methods of de-inking (removing ink from old paper to

make pulp) and crisscrossing and layering recycled fibers to make paper stronger are improving the quality of recycled paper. And some German and Japanese companies are beginning to produce paper with a high postconsumer waste content without using chlorine (which adds toxic dioxins to the environment; p. 555) to bleach the fibers. So far, however, the demand for such paper greatly exceeds the supply and prices are high. We will use such paper as soon as it is available and its price does not significantly increase the price of this textbook.

Meanwhile, we go further than simply using the best available recycled paper. Each year the publisher and I donate money to organizations that protect existing tropical forests and to tree-planting organizations so that at least two trees are planted for each one used in printing this book. As for the additional paper I use in publishing this book, I see that 50 trees are planted for each tree used.

---

With stronger demand recycled paper would be cheaper and the price paid for wastepaper would rise. One way to increase demand would be to require that federal and state governments use recycled paper products as much as possible. Such a federal law already exists, needing only to have its many loopholes closed.

Even with the best of intentions, governments, businesses, and individuals may be fooled by claims about recycled paper products. Moreover, as usual, there are tradeoffs (Spotlight, above).

Nevertheless we can all do something to slow down the rate at which trees are converted to paper. Teachers can have their students write on both sides of the paper to reduce unnecessary paper waste and increase environmental awareness. We can use both sides of the sheet when copying (now done automatically in some copiers). We can plant and tend trees, and work to protect existing old-growth forests (Sec-

tion 10-5). We can buy recycled paper products made from as much postconsumer waste as possible, and we can pressure elected officials to see that at least 50% of the paper produced is recycled by 2000.

**15-3 Rangelands**

**THE WORLD'S RANGELAND RESOURCES** Almost half of Earth's ice-free land is **rangeland**: land that supplies forage or vegetation (grasses, grasslike plants, and shrubs) for grazing (grass-eating) and browsing (shrub-eating) animals and that is not intensively managed. Most rangelands are grasslands in areas too dry for unirrigated crops (Figure 5-11).

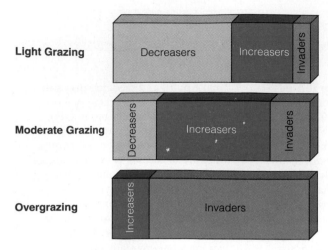

**Figure 15-8** Effects of grazing on three major types of grassland plants. Grass species depleted with moderate grazing are *decreasers*. Those that multiply with heavy grazing are *increasers*. *Invaders* are plants that colonize an area because of overgrazing or other changes in rangeland conditions.

*Soil Conservation Service*

**Figure 15-9** Overgrazed (left) and lightly grazed rangeland (right).

About 42% of the world's rangeland is used for grazing livestock. Much of the rest is too dry, cold, or remote from population centers to be grazed by large numbers of livestock animals.

About 34% of the total land area of the United States is rangeland. Most of this is short-grass prairies in the arid and semiarid western half of the country (Figure 5-19). About 52% of the nation's rangeland is privately owned, and 43% is owned by the general public and managed by the federal government, mostly by the Forest Service and the Bureau of Land Management (Figure 15-2). The remaining 5% is owned by state and local governments.

## RANGELAND VEGETATION AND LIVESTOCK

Most rangeland grasses have deep, complex root systems (Figure 12-6) that not only anchor the plants but sustain them through several seasons. If the leaf tip of most plants is eaten the leaf stops growing, but the blades of rangeland grass grow from the base. As long as only its upper half is eaten and its lower half, or *metabolic reserve* remains, rangeland grass is a renewable resource that can be grazed again and again. Range plants do vary in their ability to recover, however, and grazing changes the balance of plant species in grassland communities (Figure 15-8).

In addition to vast numbers of wild herbivores, the world has about 10 billion domesticated animals. About 3 billion of these are *ruminants*, mostly cattle (1.5 billion), sheep, and goats that can digest the cellulose in grasses. Three-fourths of these animals forage on rangeland vegetation before being slaughtered for meat, while the rest are fattened on grain in feedlots (Figure 14-2) before slaughter. Seven billion pigs,

chickens, and other livestock are *nonruminants*. They cannot feed on rangeland vegetation and eat mostly cereal grains grown on cropland.

Each type of grassland has a ruminant **carrying capacity**: the maximum number of ruminants that can graze a given area without destroying the metabolic reserve needed for grass renewal. Carrying capacity is influenced by season, range conditions, climatic conditions, past grazing use, soil type, kinds of grazing animals, and amount of grazing.

**Overgrazing** occurs when too many animals graze too long and exceed the carrying capacity of a grassland area. It lowers the productivity of vegetation and changes the number and types of plants in an area (Figure 15-8). Large populations of wild ruminants can overgraze rangeland in prolonged dry periods, but most overgrazing is caused by excessive numbers of domestic livestock feeding too long in a particular area (Figures 12-13 and 15–9).

Heavy overgrazing compacts the soil, which diminishes its capacity to hold water and to regenerate soil, converts continuous grass cover into patches of grass, and thus exposes the soil to erosion, especially by wind. Then woody shrubs such as mesquite and prickly cactus invade and take over. Figure 15-9 compares normally grazed and severely overgrazed grassland. Overgrazing is the major cause of desertification in arid and semiarid lands. Dune buggies, motorcycles, and other off-road vehicles also damage or destroy rangeland vegetation. There is some interest in

Q: Worldwide, how much money is made each year from illegal trade in wildlife and wildlife products?

raising wild herbivores as a source of meat in arid and semiarid rangelands, especially in Africa, and to reduce overgrazing by livestock (Solutions, right).

## CONDITION OF THE WORLD'S RANGELANDS

*Range condition* is usually classified as excellent (more than 80% of its potential forage production), good (50–80%), fair (21–49%), and poor (less than 21%). Except in North America no comprehensive survey of rangeland conditions has been done. However, data from surveys in various countries indicate that most of the world's rangelands have been degraded to some degree (Figure 12-12).

In 1936, 84% of public rangeland in the United States was rated as being in unsatisfactory (fair or poor) condition. With better government management, by 1990 the percentage of unsatisfactory range had dropped to about 50%—a considerable improvement although there's still a long way to go. Environmentalists point out, however, that overall estimates of rangeland condition obscure the severe damage to certain heavily grazed areas, especially vital riparian zones (Spotlight, p. 406).

**MANAGING RANGELANDS** The primary goal of rangeland management is to maximize livestock productivity without overgrazing rangeland vegetation. The most widely used method to prevent overgrazing is to control the **stocking rate**—the number of a particular kind of animal placed on a given area—so it doesn't exceed carrying capacity. Determining the carrying capacity of a range site is difficult and costly. And, as noted, that capacity changes because of drought, invasions by new species, and other environmental factors.

Not only the numbers but the distribution of grazing animals over a rangeland must be controlled to prevent overgrazing. Ranchers can control distribution by fencing off damaged rangeland, rotating livestock from one grazing area to another, providing supplemental feeding at selected sites, and locating water holes and salt blocks in strategic places.

**Continuous grazing** is year-long or season-long grazing on a given area. It's used in many range areas with favorable climatic conditions, especially in the southwestern United States. This method is popular because it's easy to manage and reduces costs by requiring little livestock handling and fencing, but it has several disadvantages. Left to their own devices, livestock tend to overgraze flat areas and areas near water supplies (Spotlight, p. 406). They also can overgraze desirable species of forage grass, prompting invasion by less desirable forms of vegetation (Figure 15-8).

Another common grazing system is **deferred-rotation grazing**, which involves moving livestock

## Wild-Game Ranching

**SOLUTIONS**

Some ecologists have suggested that wild herbivores, such as eland, oryx, and Grant's gazelle, could be raised on ranches on grasslands such as tropical savanna (Figure 5-17). Because many wild herbivores have a more diversified diet than cattle, they can make more efficient use of available vegetation and thus reduce the potential for overgrazing. In addition, they need less water than cattle and are more resistant than cattle to animal diseases found in savanna grasslands. These animals also handle much of their own predator control because of long evolutionary experience with lions, leopards, cheetahs, and wild dogs.

Since 1978 David Hopcraft has carried out a successful game-ranching experiment on the Athi Plains near Nairobi, Kenya. The ranch is stocked with various native grazers and browsers, including antelope, zebras, giraffes, and ostriches. Cattle once raised for comparison purposes, are being phased out and may be replaced with native Cape buffalo. The yield of meat from the native herbivores has been rising steadily, the condition of the range has improved, and costs are much lower than those for raising cattle in the same region.

Other game ranches have been developed in Zimbabwe, Zambia, South Africa, and Botswana. If beef eaters develop a taste for wild game raised on ranches, desertification from excessive nomadic herding in Sub-Saharan Africa could be reduced (Figure 12-12). Game ranching of native deer and antelope might also help reverse overgrazing and desertification in the western United States, especially with government subsidies to replace those now given for raising cattle.

between two or more range areas. This allows perennial grasses to recover from the effects of grazing. This method requires closer management than continuous grazing, but is usually a better way to protect and improve range quality.

A more expensive and less widely used method of rangeland management is to suppress the growth of unwanted plants by herbicide spraying, mechanical removal, or controlled burning. A cheaper and more effective way to remove unwanted vegetation is controlled, short-term trampling by large numbers of livestock.

Growth of desirable vegetation can be increased by seeding and applying fertilizer, but this method

## Endangered Riparian Zones

**Riparian zones** are thin strips of lush vegetation along streams. Although they make up less than 1% of the western U.S. landscape, they have important ecological functions. They help prevent floods and help keep streams from drying out during droughts by storing and releasing water slowly from spring runoff and summer storms. They also provide habitats, food, water, and shade for wildlife, acting as centers of biodiversity in the arid and semiarid western lands. Studies of riparian zones in southeast Oregon, Wyoming, Arizona, and New Mexico have shown that 75–80% of wildlife depend on these green patches during some or all of their life cycles.

Because cattle need lots of water, if allowed, they will concentrate around riparian zones and feed there until the grass and shrubs are gone. The result: Riparian vegetation is destroyed by trampling and by overgrazing.

The denuded banks erode, making the streams wider and shallower, and muddying the water with sediment. The sediment, as well as the depletion of dissolved oxygen when the hot sun warms the shallower water, threatens cold-water fish such as wild trout. The water from spring snow melts and occasional summer storms rush off the compacted and denuded riparian land, adding to floods and speeding the drying up of streams during drought.

It takes only a few cows to degrade a riparian zone, and these habitats crucial to arid-land ecology are now in the worst condition ever. According to Hugh Harper, a former grazing-management specialist with the Bureau of Land Management, 98% of livestock use in the West occurs around riparian areas. A 1988 General Accounting Office Report concluded that "poorly managed livestock grazing is the major cause of degraded riparian habitat on federal rangelands." Arizona and New Mexico have already lost 90% of their riparian areas, primarily to grazing.

Despite the threat to soil and wildlife, little has been done to protect riparian zones on public land from livestock or to repair the damage. Ranching interests are influential, and there has been little pressure from the public to protect these vital areas on public lands.

sands of predators have been shot, trapped, and poisoned by ranchers, farmers, and federal predator control officials. In 1990, for example, $29.4 million in federal funds plus $15 million in state funds were spent to kill 250,000 wild animals, mostly coyotes and prairie dogs (because horses and cows sometimes break their legs when they step into the burrows of these animals) but also black bears and mountain lions. Several hundred pet dogs and domestic cats were also accidentally trapped or poisoned. Federally subsidized predator control programs reduced gray wolf (p. 390) and grizzly bear populations to the point where they are endangered species. Now more federal dollars are being spent by the U.S. Fish and Wildlife Service to protect and help revive them. Experience has shown that killing predators is an expensive and often short-lived solution—and one that can even make matters worse (Pro/Con, p. 407).

**SOLUTIONS: SUSTAINABLE MANAGEMENT OF PUBLIC RANGELAND** Some 30,000 U.S. ranchers hold what are essentially lifetime permits to graze about 4 million livestock (3 million of them cattle) on Bureau of Land Management (BLM) and National Forest Service rangelands in 16 western states. About 10% of these permits are held by small livestock operators. The other 90% belong to wealthy individuals and corporations such as Union Oil, Getty Oil, and the Vail Ski Corporation.

Permit holders pay the federal government a grazing fee for this privilege. Since 1981 grazing fees on public rangeland have been set by Congress at only one-fourth to one-eighth the going rate for leasing comparable private land. This means that taxpayers give the 2% of U.S. ranchers with federal grazing permits subsidies amounting to about $150 million a year—the difference between the fees collected and the actual value of the grazing on this land.

The economic value of a permit is included in the overall worth of the ranches, can be used as collateral for a loan, and is usually automatically renewed every 10 years—allowing permit holders in effect to treat and view federal land as part of their ranches. It's not surprising that politically influential permit holders have fought so hard to block any change in this system.

The public subsidy does not end with low grazing fees, however. Taxpayers also foot the bill for items such as fencing, water pipelines, stock ponds, weed control, livestock predator control, clearing of undesirable vegetation, and planting of grass for livestock. Overall the government collects only about $1 in grazing fees for every $3 spent on range management.

When erosion, lowered recreational values, loss of biodiversity, and other hidden environmental costs are factored in, it's estimated that taxpayers are

usually costs too much. Reseeding is an excellent way to restore severely degraded rangeland, however.

Another aspect of range management for livestock is predator control. For decades hundreds of thou-

Q: What is the world's toughest environmental law?

Coyotes (*Canis latrans*) are smaller relatives of wolves. These omnivores live on a diet of small rodents (especially mice and rabbits), animal carcasses, and various plants. They live in small packs but unlike wolves usually hunt alone or in pairs. They are prolific and highly adaptable animals.

A controversial issue in the western United States is the effect coyotes have on livestock, especially sheep. On the one hand, sheep ranchers claim that coyotes kill large numbers of sheep on the open range and should be exterminated (Figure 15-10). On the other hand, many wildlife experts maintain that although coyotes kill some sheep, their net effect is to increase rangeland vegetation for livestock and wild herbivores.

The ranchers' view has prevailed, and since 1940 western ranchers and the U.S. Department of the Interior have waged a controversial war against livestock predators. Elimination of the wolves allowed the coyote population to expand in numbers and range. Because coyotes are so prolific, adaptable, and crafty, environmentalists contend that any attempt to control them is doomed to failure. They also argue that it would cost taxpayers much less to pay ranchers for each sheep or goat killed by a coyote than to spend $29 million per year on predator control.

Some range ecologists argue that the coyote may even benefit some grazing animals by helping to control populations of smaller herbivores (especially rabbits) that compete with large herbivores such as cattle or deer. Unlike deer and cattle, sheep (especially lambs) are small enough to be killed by coyotes. The question is whether the increase in sheep production from improved vegetation is greater than the number of sheep killed by the coyote. We don't know.

Environmentalists suggest that a combination of fences, repellents, and trained guard dogs be used to keep predators away. With these methods, for example, sheep producers in Kansas have one of the country's lowest rates of livestock losses to coyotes.

In 1986 Department of Agriculture researchers reported that predation can be sharply reduced by penning young lambs and cattle together for 30 days and then allowing them to graze together on the same range. When predators attack, cattle butt and kick them and in the process protect themselves and the sheep. Llamas and donkeys, also tough fighters against predators, can be used in the same way to protect sheep.

Environmentalists point out that most coyotes and other predators do not prey on livestock. Instead of trying to kill all predators, they suggest concentrating on killing or removing the rogue individuals. Despite strong opposition from environmentalists, however, the federal predator control program continues to receive funding because of the political power of ranchers and farmers who see the coyote and other predators as threats to their livelihood.

**Figure 15-10** For decades ranchers in the western United States have waged war on the coyote because of its reputation for killing livestock, as shown by these coyote carcasses lashed to a fence in California. Each year thousands of coyotes are poisoned, trapped, or shot in the western United States. This predator control program mostly for the benefit of a few ranchers and hunters is paid for by all U.S. taxpayers.

## The Green Cowboy

Wyoming rancher Jack Turnell is a new breed of cowboy who gets along with environmentalists and talks about riparian ecology and biodiversity as fluently as he talks about cattle. According to Jack, "I guess I have learned how to bridge the gap between the environmentalists, the bureaucracies, and the ranching industry."

He grazes cattle on his 32,000-hectare (80,000-acre) ranch south of Cody, Wyoming, and on 16,000 hectares (40,000 acres) of Forest Service land where he has grazing rights. For the first decade after he took over the ranch, he punched cows the conventional way. Even though he went to college he had never heard the word *riparian* or learned anything about the ecology of range grasses.

This rancher disagrees with the proposals by environmentalists to raise grazing fees and even remove sheep and cattle from public rangeland. He believes that if ranchers are kicked off the public range, ranches like his will be sold to developers and chopped up into vacation sites, irreversibly destroying the range for wildlife and livestock.

At the same time, he believes that ranches can be operated in more ecologically sustainable ways. To demonstrate this he began systematically rotating his cows away from the riparian areas, stopped using most fertilizers and pesticides, and crossed his Hereford and Angus cows with a French breed that does not like to congregate around water. Most of his ranching decisions are now made in consultation with range and wildlife scientists, and changes in range condition are carefully monitored with photographs.

The results have been impressive. Riparian areas on his rangeland and on Forest Service land are lined with willow trees and other plant life, providing lush habitats for an expanding population of wildlife including antelope, deer, moose, elk, bear, and mountain lions. And Jack makes more money because the better-quality grass puts more meat on his cattle. He frequently talks to cattle groups about sustainable range management, some of whom think he has lost his marbles.

Some environmentalists believe that all commercial grazing of livestock on public lands should be phased out over a 10- to 15-year period. They also contend that the water-poor western range is not a very good place to raise livestock (cattle and sheep), which require a lot of water. Forage is produced at a slow rate, droughts are frequent, and animals can only be grazed part of the year. And a century of public grazing has taken a heavy toll on the land and wildlife.

Ranchers counter that meat produced on rangeland that is not otherwise usable for food production represents a net increase in available food. They point out that when livestock are fattened on corn and other grains, this uses land that could be producing more grains for direct human consumption. Some range scientists point out that while cattle have played a significant role in degrading western rangeland, other factors are also involved. They include climate change, farming, and deliberate burning of rangelands. All these factors combine to alter range vegetation. However, excessive cattle grazing may have tipped the balance toward desertification, especially in dry areas (Figure 12-12).

Some environmentalists agree that with proper management ranching on western rangeland is a potentially sustainable operation and that encouraging such ranching keeps the land from being broken and converted to developments. To achieve this they call for curbing overgrazing and destruction of vital riparian zones on western public rangeland by:

- *Greatly reducing the number of livestock grazing on these lands.*

- *Excluding livestock grazing from riparian areas.*

- *Banning grazing on poor-condition rangeland until it recovers.*

- *Ending federal predator control for livestock.*

- *Giving top priority to protecting and restoring riparian areas.*

- *Greatly increasing funds for restoration of degraded rangeland.*

- *Sharply raising grazing fees to a fair market value.* This would promote lower livestock numbers, improve rangeland management practices, save taxpayer dollars, and drive marginal or irresponsible operators out of business.

- *Giving family ranchers with small ranches grazing fee discounts.* This would help them stay in business and keep their ranches from being converted to real estate developments. Ranchers with large operations who artificially divide their holdings to qualify would not get discounts.

- *Abolishing grazing advisory boards.* These boards work with local BLM officials to develop allot-

providing 30,000 ranchers with an annual subsidy of about $2 billion—an average of $66,700 per rancher—to produce only 3% of the country's beef. This explains why many critics charge that the public lands grazing programs are little more than "cowboy welfare," mostly for well-to-do ranchers.

Q: What is the best way to prevent wildlife extinction from human activities?

Dr. M.P. Kahl/Bruce Coleman Ltd.

**Figure 15-11** Mount Kilimanjaro in Tanzania as seen from Amboseli National Park, Kenya.

ment management plans and advise on budget expenditures. This gives ranchers undue influence on BLM officials and leads to about 96% of the allotted funds being spent on grazing instead of for other uses. Other multiple-use public lands (Spotlight, p. 392) have no such boards.

- *Replacing the current noncompetitive grazing permit system with a competitive bidding system.* If the bids did not reflect the current market value of the forage, no permit would be issued. The current system gives ranchers with essentially lifetime permits an unfair economic advantage over ranchers who can't get such government subsidies. Competitive bidding would let free enterprise work and allow conservation and wildlife groups to obtain grazing permits. They could then decide to graze wild animals such as elk or bison on the land or not graze it at all.

- *Imposing stricter restrictions on grazing permit holders.* Livestock grazing would be allowed only on range in good or excellent condition, under strictly controlled conditions to prevent overgrazing. Permits would extend for only three to five years, and failure to live up to the permit requirements would lead to automatic cancellation. Ranchers with permits would share equally with the government the cost of capital improvements related to livestock grazing.

- *Subsidizing experimental programs of game ranching of native deer and antelope* (Solutions, p. 405).

- *Banning soil-damaging off-road vehicles (ORVs)— called "wheeled locusts" by some environmentalists— from public lands.*

The problem is that western ranchers wield enough political power to block any changes they don't like in grazing policies. Ranchers, ORV organizations, mining interests, oil companies, and other exploiters of resources on western public lands have mounted a well-funded effort, called the "wise-use movement," to see that proposals like the ones just listed are not enacted by elected officials. A few ranchers, however, have demonstrated that rangeland can be grazed sustainably (Individuals Matter, p. 408).

## 15-4 National Parks

**PARKS AROUND THE WORLD** Today there are over 1,100 national parks of more than 1,000 hectares (2,500 acres) in more than 120 countries (Figure 15-11). Together, they cover an area equal to that of Alaska, Texas, and California combined. This important achievement in the global conservation movement was spurred by the creation of the first public national park system in the United States in 1912 (Section 2-5).

**Figure 15-12**
Yosemite National Park, California. In 1992, 275 million visits were made to U.S. national parks.

M.P.L. Fogden/Bruce Coleman Ltd.

The U.S. National Park System is dominated by 50 national parks, most of them in the West (Figure 15-2). These repositories of majestic beauty and biodiversity have been called America's crown jewels (Figure 15-12) and are supplemented by state, county, and city parks (Figure 9-18). Most state parks are located near urban areas and thus are used more heavily than national parks. Nature walks, guided tours, and other educational services by U.S. Park Service employees have given many visitors a better appreciation for and understanding of nature.

**STRESSES ON PARKS** Parks everywhere are under siege. In LDCs parks are often invaded by local people who desperately need wood, cropland, and other resources. Poachers kill animals to sell rhino horns, elephant tusks, and furs. Park services in these countries have too little money and staff to fight these invasions, either by force or by education. Also, most of the world's national parks are too small to sustain many of their larger animal species.

Success is the biggest problem of national and state parks in the United States (and other MDCs). Because of increased numbers of people, roads, and

cars, and growing affluence, annual recreational visits to National Park System units have increased more than 12-fold, and visits to state parks 7-fold, since 1950. The recreational use of state and national parks and other public lands is expected to double again by 2020.

During the peak summer season, the most popular national and state parks are often choked with cars and trailers, and plagued by noise, traffic jams, litter, vandalism, poaching, deteriorating trails, polluted water, and crime. Many visitors to heavily used parks leave the city to commune with nature only to find the parks more congested, noisy, and stressful than where they came from.

Park Service rangers now spend an increasing amount of their time on law enforcement instead of on resource conservation and management; many even wear body armor. Since 1976 the number of federal park rangers—about 3,200—has not changed, while the number of visitors to park units has risen by 75 million and is expected to rise by another 162 million in the next 20 years. Many overworked rangers, earning an average salary of less than $20,000 and living in substandard housing, are leaving for better-paying

**410**

Q: How much of the earth's land surface has been set aside to protect wildlife?

jobs. Some who stay depend on food stamps, welfare, parental assistance, or second jobs to support their families.

Wolves, bears, and other large predators in and near various parks have all but vanished because of excessive hunting, poisoning by ranchers and federal officials (Pro/Con, p. 407), and the limited size of most parks. As a result, populations of prey species they once controlled have exploded, destroying vegetation and crowding out other species.

Alien species are moving into parks. Wild boars (imported to North Carolina in 1912 for hunting) are threatening vegetation in parts of the Great Smoky Mountains National Park. The Brazilian pepper tree has invaded Florida's Everglades National Park (Figure 13-15). Mountain goats in Washington's Olympic National Park trample native vegetation and accelerate soil erosion.

The greatest danger to many parks today, however, is from human activities. Wildlife and recreational values are threatened by mining, logging, grazing, coal-burning power plants, water diversion, and urban development. Polluted air drifts hundreds of kilometers to kill trees in California's Sequoia National Park (Figure 4-9) and blur the awesome vistas at Arizona's Grand Canyon. According to the National Park Service, air pollution affects scenic park views more than 90% of the time.

But that's not all. Mountains of trash wash ashore daily at Padre Island National Seashore in Texas. Water use in Las Vegas threatens to shut down geysers in the Death Valley National Monument. And unless a massive ecological restoration project works, Florida's Everglades National Park may dry up (Figure 13-15).

**SOLUTIONS: PARK MANAGEMENT** Some park managers, especially in LDCs, are developing integrated management plans that combine conservation practices with sustainable development of the park and surrounding areas (Figure 10-21). In such a plan the inner core and especially vulnerable areas of the park are protected from development and treated as wilderness. Controlled numbers of people are allowed to use these areas only for hiking, nature study, ecological research, and other nondestructive recreational and educational activities.

In other buffer areas surrounding the core, controlled commercial logging, sustainable grazing by livestock, and sustainable hunting and fishing by local people are allowed. Money spent by park visitors adds to local income. By involving local people in developing park management plans, managers help them see the park as a vital resource they need to protect and sustain rather than ruin (Case Study, p. 280).

Park managers can also survey the land surrounding a park to identify areas where development might threaten the park's wildlife. Sometimes these areas can be added to the park. If not, managers may be able to persuade developers or local people to use less threatened areas for certain types of development.

While these integrated management plans look good on paper, they cannot be carried out without the support of nearby landowners and users or money for land acquisition, enforcement, and maintenance. Moreover, the protected inner core may be too small to sustain some of the park's larger animal species.

In the United States national parks are managed under the principle of natural regulation—as if they are wilderness ecosystems that, if left alone, will sustain themselves. Many ecologists consider this a misguided policy: Most parks are far too small to even come close to sustaining themselves and even the biggest ones cannot be isolated from the harmful effects of nearby activities.

**SOLUTIONS: AN AGENDA FOR U.S. NATIONAL PARKS** The National Park Service has two goals that increasingly conflict: (1) to preserve nature in parks, and (2) to make nature more available to the public. The Park Service must accomplish these goals with a small budget at a time when park usage and external threats to the parks are increasing.

In 1988 the Wilderness Society and the National Parks and Conservation Association suggested a blueprint for the future of the U.S. National Park System:

- *Educate the public about the urgent need to protect, mend, and expand the system.*

- *Establish the National Park Service as an independent agency.* This would make it less vulnerable to the shifting political winds of the Interior Department.

- *Significantly increase the number and pay of park rangers.*

- *Acquire new parkland near threatened areas and add at least 75 new parks within the next decade.* About half of the most important types of ecosystems in the United States are not protected in national parks.

- *Locate most commercial park facilities (such as restaurants, hotels, and shops) outside park boundaries.*

- *Raise the fees charged to private concessionaires who operate lodging, food, and recreation services inside national parks to at least 22% of their gross receipts.* The present maximum return for taxpayers is only 5% and the average is only 2.5% of the $1.5 billion they take in annually. Many large concessionaires have long-term contracts by which they pay the government as little as 0.75% of their gross receipts.

- *Halt concessionaire ownership of facilities in national parks, which makes buying buildings back very expensive.*

- *Wherever feasible, place visitor parking areas outside the park areas.* Use low-polluting vehicles to transport visitors to and from parking areas and within the park.

- *Limit visitors to damaged areas within parks until they recover.*

- *Greatly expand the Park Service budget for maintenance and for science and conservation programs.* Currently only 1% of national park funding goes for environmental research. The national parks face a $2.2-billion backlog of maintenance and repairs.

- *Make buildings and vehicles in national and state parks educational showcases.* These facilities and vehicles could "model" improvements in energy efficiency and the latest developments in the use of energy from the sun, wind, flowing water, and Earth's interior heat (geothermal energy).

- *Require the Park Service, Forest Service, and Bureau of Land Management to develop integrated management plans so activities in nearby national forests don't degrade national parklands and wilderness areas within the parks.*

## 15-5 Wilderness Preservation

**HOW MUCH WILD LAND IS LEFT?** According to the Wilderness Act of 1964, **wilderness** consists of those areas "where the earth and its community of life are untrammeled by man, where man himself is a visitor who does not remain." President Theodore Roosevelt summarized what we should do with wilderness: "Leave it as it is. You cannot improve it."

The Wilderness Society estimates that a wilderness area should contain at least 400,000 hectares (1 million acres). Otherwise, it can be affected by air, water, and noise pollution from nearby mining, oil and natural gas drilling, timber cutting, industry, and urban development.

A 1987 survey sponsored by the Sierra Club revealed that only about 34% of Earth's land area is undeveloped wilderness in blocks of at least 400,000 hectares (Figure 15-13). About 30% of these remaining wildlands are forests, many of which are threatened

tropical forests (Section 10-2). Tundra, ice-covered land, and desert make up most of the rest. Only about 20% of the wild lands identified in this survey are protected. Environmentalists urge that remaining wilderness be protected by law everywhere, with efforts focused first on the most endangered spots in wilderness- and species-rich countries (Figure 10-20).

**WHY PRESERVE WILDERNESS?** We need wild places where we can experience the beauty of nature and observe natural biological diversity. We need places where we can enhance our mental and physical health by getting away from noise, stress, and large numbers of people. Wilderness preservationist John Muir advised:

> *Climb the mountains and get their good tidings. Nature's peace will flow into you as the sunshine into the trees. The winds will blow their freshness into you, and the storms their energy, while cares will drop off like autumn leaves.*

Even those who never use wilderness may want to know it is there, a feeling expressed by novelist Wallace Stegner:

> *Save a piece of country . . . and it does not matter in the slightest that only a few people every year will go into it. This is precisely its value . . . we simply need that wild country available to us, even if we never do more than drive to its edge and look in. For it can be a means of reassuring ourselves of our sanity as creatures, a part of the geography of hope.*

Wilderness areas provide recreation for growing numbers of people. Wilderness also has important ecological values. It provides undisturbed habitats for wild plants and animals, protects diverse biomes from damage, and provides a laboratory in which we can discover more about how nature works. It is a biodiversity bank and an eco-insurance policy. In the words of Henry David Thoreau: "In wildness is the preservation of the world."

To sustainable-Earth environmentalists the most important reason for protecting and expanding the world's wilderness areas is an ethical one: Wilderness should be preserved because the wild species it contains have a right to exist without human interference.

**U.S. WILDERNESS PRESERVATION SYSTEM**
In the United States preservationists have been trying to keep wild areas from being developed since 1900. On the whole they have fought a losing battle (Section 2-5). Not until 1964 did Congress pass the Wilderness Act, which allows the government to protect undeveloped tracts of public land from development as part of the National Wilderness Preservation System (Spotlight, p. 392).

Q: How many unwanted dogs and cats are killed by U.S. animal shelters each year because of pet overpopulation?

Only 4% of U.S. land area is protected as wilderness, with almost three-fourths of it in Alaska. Only 1.8% of the land area of the lower 48 states is protected, most of it in the West. Almost half of the wilderness east of the Mississippi is in the threatened Florida Everglades National Park (Figure 13-15) and Minnesota's Boundary Waters Canoe Area. Of the 413 wilderness areas in the lower 48 states, only 4 are larger than 400,000 hectares. Furthermore, the present wilderness preservation system includes only 81 of the country's 233 distinct ecosystems. Like the national parks, most wilderness areas in the lower 48 states are habitat islands in a sea of development.

There remain almost 40 million hectares (100 million acres) of public lands that could qualify for designation as wilderness.

*Wilderness recovery areas* could be created by closing roads in large areas of public lands, restoring habitats, allowing natural fires to burn, and reintroducing species that have been driven from such areas. However, resource developers lobby elected officials and government agencies to build roads in national forests and other areas being evaluated for inclusion in the wilderness system so that they can't be designated as wilderness and strongly oppose the idea of wilderness recovery areas.

**WILDERNESS MANAGEMENT** To protect the most popular areas from damage, wilderness managers must designate areas where camping is allowed and limit the number of people hiking or camping at any one time. Managers have increased the number of wilderness rangers to patrol vulnerable areas and enlisted volunteers to pick up trash discarded by thoughtless users.

Historian and wilderness expert Roderick Nash suggests that wilderness areas be divided into three categories. The easily accessible, popular areas would be intensively managed and have trails, bridges, hiker's huts, outhouses, assigned campsites, and extensive ranger patrols. Large, remote wilderness areas would be used only by people who get a permit by demonstrating their wilderness skills. The third category—biologically unique areas—would be left undisturbed as gene pools of plant and animal species, with no human entry allowed.

**NATIONAL WILD AND SCENIC RIVERS SYSTEM**
In 1968 Congress passed the National Wild and Scenic Rivers Act. It allows rivers and river segments with outstanding scenic, recreational, geological, wildlife, historical, or cultural values to be protected in the National Wild and Scenic Rivers System. These waterways are to be kept free of development. They may not be widened, straightened, dredged, filled, or dammed along the designated lengths. The only activities

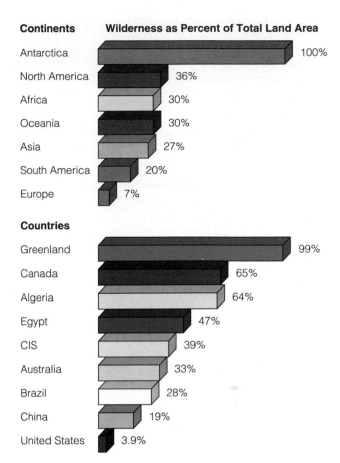

**Figure 15-13** Wilderness areas by major geographical regions. (Data from J. Michael McCloskey and Heather Spalding, "A Reconnaissance-Level Inventory of the Wilderness Remaining in the World," Sierra Club, 1987)

allowed are camping, swimming, nonmotorized boating, sport hunting, and sport and commercial fishing. New mining claims are permitted in some areas, however.

Currently only 0.3% of the country's 6 million kilometers (3.5 million miles) of waterways in about 150 stretches are protected by the Wild and Scenic Rivers System. In contrast, 17% of the length of the country's wild rivers has been tamed and altered by dams (Figure 13-11). Environmentalists have urged Congress to add 1,500 additional eligible river segments to the system by 2000. If that goal is achieved, about 2% of the country's river systems would be protected. Environmentalists want none of the candidate rivers to be developed in any way that might affect their ecological integrity. Environmentalists also urge that a permanent federal administrative body be established to manage the Wild and Scenic Rivers System and that states develop their own wild and scenic river programs.

A: 15 million—an average of 41,000 per day

## What You Can Do to Help Sustain Parks and Wilderness

**INDIVIDUALS MATTER**

- *Don't harm or remove anything if you visit a park or wilderness area, and don't leave anything there. "Leave it better than we found it" should be our motto.*

- *Support efforts to protect large areas of the world's remaining undeveloped lands and wild rivers as wilderness.*

- *Lobby elected officials to take a number of immediate actions.* These include protecting old-growth forests on public lands, reducing or banning timber harvests in national forests, requiring that taxpayers get a fair return on all timber harvesting, livestock grazing, and mining on public lands, eliminating subsidies for cutting virgin timber, and adopting a program for recycling at least half of the wastepaper in the United States by the year 2000.

- *Support efforts to protect, expand, and mend the National Park System and to get a much fairer return from concessionaires who operate services in park units.*

- *Support efforts to increase the budget for maintenance and repair of federal and state parks.*

**NATIONAL TRAILS SYSTEM** In 1968 Congress passed the National Trails Act, which protects scenic and historic hiking trails in the National Trails System. However, no designated scenic or historic trail is complete because the Trails System has a low priority and gets little funding.

To fulfill the promise of the Trails Act, environmentalists propose that the Trails System be managed by a single agency. Armed with a comprehensive study of present and future trail needs, the agency should plan to develop a countrywide network of trails in the next decade.

## 15-6 Solutions: Individual Action

Sustaining existing forests, rangelands, wilderness, and parks, and rehabilitating damaged areas are important tasks. This will cost a great deal of money and require strong support from the public and

## Creating a Global Earth Conservation Corps

**SOLUTIONS** Earth Conservation Corps (ECC), expanded versions of the Peace Corps, could be created. Such groups could be funded by the government or by the private sector. They could be a source of full-time or part-time jobs and satisfaction for people of all ages. These Earth citizens could:

- Restore damaged forests, grassland, cropland, rangeland, watersheds, wetlands, and strip-mined lands

- Plant trees in rural and urban areas

- Create and maintain national, state, and local parks and trails

- Reduce soil erosion

- Help establish and maintain wildlife refuges for endangered plants and animals

- Help the poor restore abandoned or dilapidated urban housing

- Help the poor insulate and weatherize housing

- Build new energy- and resource-efficient housing for the poor

- Convert abandoned urban lots to community gardens, playgrounds, and vest-pocket parks

Would you be willing to participate in such an Earth-sustaining venture?

changes in individual lifestyles (Individuals Matter, above left). However, it will cost our civilization much more if we do not protect and rehabilitate these resources. Creating Earth Conservation Corps throughout the world would help (Solutions, above right).

The task of protecting Earth's biodiversity and restoring lands we have damaged is enormous, but it can be done if you and enough other people care.

*Health is the capacity of the land for self-renewal. Conservation is our effort to understand and preserve this capacity.*

ALDO LEOPOLD

## Critical Thinking

1. Should private companies cutting timber from national forests continue to be subsidized by federal

Q: How much of the world's energy is provided by perpetual and renewable resources?

payments for reforestation and for building and maintaining access roads ? Explain.

2. Explain why you agree or disagree with the proposals on page 408 for providing more sustainable use of western public rangeland.

3. Should cattle be banned from grazing on western public rangeland? Explain.

4. Should trail bikes, dune buggies, and other ORVs be banned from public rangeland to reduce damage to vegetation and soil? Explain. Should such a ban also include national forests, national wildlife refuges, and national parks? Explain.

5. Explain why you agree or disagree with each of the proposals listed on pages 411–412 concerning the U.S. National Park System.

6. Should more wilderness areas and wild and scenic rivers be preserved in the United States, especially in the lower 48 states? Explain.

7. Should most U.S. Forest Service and Bureau of Land Management public land be reclassified as wilderness and restored as natural wildlife habitat? Explain.

*8. Investigate paper recycling in your community and by your school. Try to find answers to the following questions:
   a. What percentage of the paper used by your school is recycled?
   b. What percentage of the paper used in your community is recycled?
   c. What percentage of the newsprint in local or nearby newspapers is made from recycled materials? What percentage of this comes from postconsumer waste?
   d. What percentage of the paper products bought by your school contains recycled fibers? What percentage of this comes from postconsumer waste?
   e. What percentage of the paper products bought by local government agencies contains recycled fibers? What percentage of this comes from postconsumer waste?

## The Passenger Pigeon: Gone Forever

In the early 1800s bird expert Alexander Wilson watched a single migrating flock of passenger pigeons darken the sky for over four hours. He estimated that this flock was more than 2 billion birds strong, 386 kilometers (240 miles) long, and 1.6 kilometers (1 mile) wide.

By 1914 the passenger pigeon (Figure 16-1) had disappeared forever. How could this species of bird that was once the most common in North America become extinct in only a few decades?

The answer is people. The main reasons for the extinction of this species were uncontrolled commer-

**Figure 16-1** Passenger pigeons, extinct in the wild since 1900. The last known passenger pigeon died in the Cincinnati Zoo in 1914. (No. 1= male; No. 2= female)

John James Audubon/The New-York Historical Society

cial hunting and loss of the bird's habitat and food supply as forests were cleared for farms and cities.

Passenger pigeons were good to eat, their feathers made good pillows, and their bones were widely used for fertilizer. They were easy to kill because they flew in gigantic flocks and nested in long, narrow colonies. People would capture one pigeon alive, sew its eyes shut, and tie it to a perch called a stool. Soon a curious flock would land beside this "stool pigeon." The birds would then be shot or ensnared by nets that might trap more than 1,000 birds at once.

Beginning in 1858 passenger pigeon hunting became a big business. Shotguns, traps, artillery, and even dynamite were used. Birds were suffocated by burning grass or sulfur below their roosts. Live birds were used as targets in shooting galleries. In 1878 one professional pigeon trapper made $60,000 by killing 3 million birds at their nesting grounds near Petoskey, Michigan.

By the early 1880s commercial hunting had ceased because only a few thousand birds were left. At that point recovery of the species was doomed because the females laid only one egg per nest. On March 24, 1900, in Ohio, a young boy shot the last known passenger pigeon in the wild. The last passenger pigeon on Earth, a hen named Martha after Martha Washington, died in the Cincinnati Zoo in 1914. Her stuffed body is now on view at the National Museum of Natural History in Washington, D.C.

Sooner or later all species become extinct, but humans have become a primary factor in the premature extinction of more and more species as we march relentlessly across the globe. Every day at least 10 and perhaps as many as 140 species become extinct because of our activities. The loss rate may soon reach several hundred species per day.

Many biologists consider this epidemic of extinction an even more serious problem than depletion of stratospheric ozone or global warming (Chapter 11) because it is happening faster and it is irreversible. Stemming this hemmorhage of biodiversity, protecting wildlife habitats throughout the world, and restoring species that we have decimated are planetary emergencies.

This chapter will be devoted to answering the following questions:

- Why should we care about wildlife?
- What human activities and natural traits endanger wildlife?
- How can we prevent premature extinction of species?
- Can game animals be managed sustainably?
- Can freshwater and marine fish be managed sustainably?

## 16-1 Why Preserve Wild Species?

**WHY NOT LET THEM DIE?** Millions of species have vanished over Earth's long history, so why should we worry about losing a few more? Does it matter that the California condor (Figure 16-2), the black rhinoceros (Figure 4-43), the spotted owl (Figure 10-23), the loggerhead turtle (Figure 16-3), or some unknown plant or insect in a tropical forest becomes extinct mostly because of us? The answer is yes.

Some species are of great economic and medical importance to us and we can't predict which ones. Each species is a unique and irreplaceable product of millions of years of evolution. Each species is of scientific interest and each makes some sort of contribution to its ecosystem. Some are keystone species whose demise can take other species with them. Furthermore, some believe every species has an inherent right to exist and does not need to be of value to us to justify its existence.

### ECONOMIC AND MEDICAL IMPORTANCE

Wild species that are actually or potentially useful to people are called **wildlife resources**. About 10% of the U.S. gross national product comes directly from such resources.

**Figure 16-2** California condor. The few California condors still in the wild were collected in 1985 to become part of a $1.5-million-per-year captive breeding program. By January 1993 there were 57 of these birds in the Los Angeles Zoo and the San Diego Wild Animal Park and another 8 had been released to their natural habitat north of Los Angeles. This species is especially vulnerable to extinction because of its low reproduction rate, the long period (seven years) needed to reach reproductive age, the failure of parents scared away from the nest by noise or human activities to hatch chicks, and the need for a large, undisturbed habitat.

**Figure 16-3** Endangered loggerhead turtle lying on a beach in Bahia State, Brazil. Of the world's 270 known turtle species, 42% are rare or are threatened with extinction.

**Figure 16-4** The nine-banded armadillo is used in leprosy research.

**Figure 16-5** Many species of wildlife, like this bird of paradise in a New Guinea forest, are a source of beauty and pleasure. This species is vulnerable to extinction because it can't mate unless a throng of males assemble and "strut their stuff" in front of females. When numbers decline this is not possible.

Q: What is the largest untapped energy source in the United States?

**Figure 16-6** Wildlife tourism, or ecotourism, in which tourists visit areas to see and photograph wildlife, is an important source of revenue for LDCs with unique, protected wildlife resources. Here tourists are observing wildlife in Serengeti National Park in Tanzania.

G. Cubitt/FPG International

Some 90% of today's food crops were domesticated from wild tropical plants. Agricultural scientists and genetic engineers will need to use existing wild plant species, most of them still unknown, to develop new crop strains (Section 14-3), and some may become important sources of food (Figure 14-12). Wild animal species are a largely untapped food source (Solutions, p. 405). Wild plants and plants domesticated from wild species also supply rubber (Figure 10-9), oils, dyes, fiber, paper, lumber, and other useful products (Figure 10-2).

Nitrogen-fixing microbes in the soil and root nodules (Figure 4-30) supply nitrogen to grow food crops worth almost $50 billion per year worldwide ($7 billion in the United States). Pollination by birds and insects is essential to many food crops, including 40 U.S. crops valued at approximately $30 billion per year.

About 75% of the world's population relies on plants or plant extracts for medicines. Prescription and nonprescription drugs worth $40 million per year—roughly half of the medicines used in the world, and 25% of those used in the United States—have active ingredients extracted from wild species (Figure 10-10). Only about 5,000 of the estimated 250,000 plant species have been studied thoroughly for their possible medical uses. In addition, over 3,000 antibiotics—including penicillin and tetracycline—are derived from microorganisms.

Many animal species are used to test drugs, vaccines, chemical toxicity, and surgical procedures, and in studies of human health and disease. For example, elephants under stress are used to study heart disease. The nine-banded armadillo (Figure 16-4) is being used to study leprosy and prepare a vaccine for it. Mice, rats, chimpanzees, and rhesus monkeys are used to test for possible cancer-causing agents and toxic chemicals. However, animal welfare advocates protest the use of animals in medical and biological research and teaching.

Most scientists accept the principle that experimental animals must not be subjected to avoidable distress or discomfort, but they contend that some animal research is vital for the welfare of people, pets, and livestock. Under intense pressure from animal rights groups, scientists are trying to find testing methods that minimize animal suffering or, better yet, do not use animals at all. Promising alternatives for some purposes include cell and tissue cultures, simulated tissues and body fluids, and bacteria. Computer-generated models can be used to estimate the toxicity of a compound from knowledge of its chemical structure and properties. Computer simulations and videotapes, plastic models with removable organs, and high-resolution graphics can replace many live-animal demonstrations for biology and veterinary students. However, scientists point out that such techniques cannot replace all animal research.

**AESTHETIC AND RECREATIONAL IMPORTANCE**
Wild plants and animals are a source of beauty, wonder, joy, and recreational pleasure for many people (Figure 16-5). Wild **game species** provide recreation in the form of hunting, fishing, observation, and photography. Each year almost 50% of Americans and 84% of Canadians participate in bird watching, photography, and other nondestructive outdoor recreational activities involving wildlife.

Wildlife tourism, sometimes called *ecotourism*, generates as much as $12 billion in revenues each year. It is especially important to the economy of some LDCs, such as Kenya, Rwanda, and Tanzania (Figure 16-6). Each year, for example, almost 700,000 visitors pass through Kenya's national parks and protected

## How "Green" Is Your Ecotour?

Ecotourism can either protect or harm ecosystems and cultures. Before taking an ecotour find out how "green" it really is by getting answers (preferably in writing) to several questions:

- Are yearly totals of tourists from all tours limited enough to protect the area from environmental damage?

- What precautions are taken to reduce the tour's environmental impact on local ecosystems?

- How much time is spent in the field versus the city or traveling in a vehicle?

- Will you be using scarce fuel (such as wood, which involves forest depletion)?

- Where will the tour's waste and garbage go?

- What percentage of the people involved in planning, organizing, and guiding the tour are local? Are any of the guides trained naturalists?

- Is most of the lodging and food provided by local people, or will you be staying in nationally or internationally owned accommodations?

- Does the tour respect local customs and culture?

- What percentage of the tour costs does the tour company donate to local environmental and social projects?

Kenya has developed national guidelines for ecotourism. All revenue raised by Kenyan national parks and reserves remains under the jurisdiction of the Kenyan Wildlife Service and is used mostly to provide better conservation of the protected areas. The government requires that tourist lodges give Kenyans preferential employment treatment for all but the most senior positions and use Kenyan food products as much as possible. Furthermore, every game-lodge visitor pays a $5 tax that is put into a trust fund for local use. Parks without lodges deposit a percentage of gate receipts into local trusts. Money from these trusts is used to fund schools and hospitals, and to compensate local landowners.

areas, spending nearly half a billion dollars and making ecotourism the country's leading industry. A wildlife economist has estimated that in Kenya one male lion living to age 7 generates $515,000 in tourist dollars. By contrast, if killed for its skin, the lion would bring only about $1,000. Similarly each of Kenya's

20,000 elephants brings in about $20,000 per year in tourist income. Over a lifetime of 60 years a Kenyan elephant is worth close to $1 million in tourist revenue.

Another example of a country that has benefited from ecotourism is Rwanda, where tourism is largely responsible for saving the nation's mountain gorillas from extinction by poaching and habitat loss. A wildlife reserve created by Dian Fossey—who was murdered by a poacher because of her efforts to protect the mountain gorilla—has become an international attraction and contains 150 of the country's 320 remaining gorillas. The reserve has brought $4 million annually into the area surrounding the gorillas' home—giving local people an important incentive to protect the gorillas. However, civil war is threatening the gorillas' habitat, and their survival is uncertain.

Ecotourism is a boon to many countries. However, care must be taken to ensure that ecotourists do not damage or disturb wildlife and ecosystems, especially in popular or particularly sensitive areas (Spotlight, left).

## SCIENTIFIC AND ECOLOGICAL IMPORTANCE

Each species has scientific value because it can help scientists understand how life has evolved and will continue to evolve on this planet. We need to protect wild species from premature extinction because our survival and the survival of other species depends on the vital ecosystem services provided by wild species. They supply us and other species with food from the soil and the sea, recycle nutrients essential to agriculture, and help maintain soil fertility. They also produce oxygen and other gases in the atmosphere, moderate Earth's climate, help regulate water supplies, and store solar energy. Moreover, they detoxify poisonous substances, break down organic wastes, control potential crop pests and disease carriers, and make up a vast gene pool from which we and other species can draw. Although we tend to focus on plants and large animals, it is the numerous small organisms—bacteria, fungi, and insects—that dominate the structure and functioning of natural ecosystems.

**ETHICS** The reasons given so far for preserving wild species are based on their actual or potential usefulness for people. Many biologists believe that wild species will continue to vanish until we replace this human-centered (anthropocentric) view of wildlife and the environment with either a life-centered (biocentric) or an ecosystem-centered (ecocentric) view (Section 27-2).

According to various *biocentric worldviews* each wild species has an inherent right to exist—or to struggle to exist—equal to that of any other species. Thus it is ethically wrong for us to hasten the extinction of any species. Some go further and assert that each individual organism—not just each species—has a right to survive without human interference, just as each human being has the right to survive.

Some people distinguish between the survival rights of plants and those of animals, mostly for practical reasons. Poet Alan Watts, for example, once said that he was a vegetarian "because cows scream louder than carrots." Other people distinguish among various types of animals. For instance, they think little about killing a fly, mosquito, cockroach, or sewer rat. Unless they are strict vegetarians, they also think little about having others kill domesticated animals in slaughterhouses to provide them with meat, leather, and other products. These same people, however, might deplore the killing of wild animals such as deer, squirrels, or rabbits.

Various *ecocentric worldviews* stress the importance of preserving the whole rainbow of biodiversity by protecting entire ecosystems rather than individual species or organisms. It recognizes that saving wildlife means saving the places where they live. This view is based on Aldo Leopold's ethical principle that something is right when it tends to maintain Earth's life support systems for us and other species, and wrong when it doesn't.

## 16-2 How Species Become Depleted and Extinct

**THE RISE AND FALL OF SPECIES** Extinction is a natural process (Section 6-3). As the planet's surface and climate have changed over the 4.6 billion years of its existence, species have disappeared and new ones have evolved to take their places (Figure 7-32).

This rise and fall of species has not been smooth. Evidence indicates that there have been several periods when mass extinctions reduced Earth's biodiversity, and other periods, called radiations, when the diversity of life increased and spread (Figure 6-12). These periods of mass extinction and radiation were caused by climate change, continental drift, interactions of life with nonliving parts of the ecosphere, and other environmental factors.

**EXTINCTION OF SPECIES TODAY: FATAL SUBTRACTION** Imagine you are driving on an interstate highway at a high speed. You notice that your two passengers are passing the time unscrewing bolts, screws, and other parts of your car at random, and throwing them out the window. How long will it be before they remove enough parts to cause a crash?

This urgent question is one that we as a species should be asking ourselves. As we tinker with the only home for us and other species, we are rapidly removing parts of Earth's natural biodiversity upon which we and other species depend in ways we know little about. We are not heeding Aldo Leopold's warning: "To keep every cog and wheel is the first precaution of intelligent tinkering."

Past mass extinctions took place slowly enough to allow new forms of life to arise as adaptations to an ever-changing world. This process started to change about 40,000 years ago when the latest version of our species came on the scene. Since agriculture began about 10,000 years ago, the extinction rates have soared as human settlements have expanded worldwide.

It is hard to document extinctions, since most go unrecorded. Biologists estimate that during 1993 at least 4,000 and as many as 36,000 species became extinct; the figure could reach 50,000 species per year by 2000. These scientists warn that if deforestation (especially of tropical forests), desertification, and destruction of wetlands and coral reefs continue at their present rates, we could easily lose at least a quarter, and conceivably half, of Earth's species within the next few decades. This massive bleeding of life from the planet will rival some of the great natural mass extinctions of the past.

There are three important differences between the present mass extinction and those of the past:

- *The present crisis is the first to be caused by a single species—our own.* By using 40% of Earth's terrestrial net primary productivity (Figure 4-27), we are crowding out other terrestrial species (Figure 16-7). What will happen to wildlife and the services they provide for us if our population doubles in the next 40 years and we use as much as 80% of the planet's terrestrial net primary productivity?

- *The current wildlife holocaust is taking place in only a few decades rather than over thousands to millions of years.* Such rapid extinction cannot be balanced by speciation because it takes 2,000–100,000 generations for new species to evolve.

- *For the first time plant species are disappearing as fast as animal species.* Plant extinctions are more important ecologically than animal extinctions because most animal species depend directly or indirectly on plants for food. The fate of our species and millions of others could depend on the survival of numerous known and unknown species of plants, insects that pollinate plants, and decomposers.

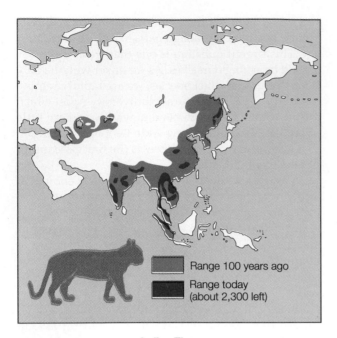

**Indian Tiger**

Range 100 years ago

Range today
(about 2,300 left)

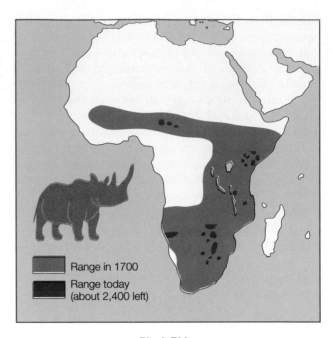

**Black Rhino**

Range in 1700

Range today
(about 2,400 left)

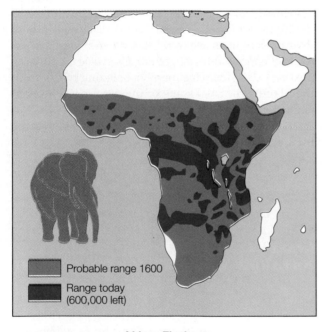

**African Elephant**

Probable range 1600

Range today
(600,000 left)

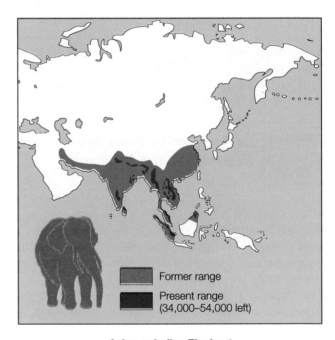

**Asian or Indian Elephant**

Former range

Present range
(34,000–54,000 left)

**Figure 16-7** Reduction in the range of several species, mostly through a combination of habitat loss and hunting. What will happen to these and millions of other species if the global human population doubles in the next few decades? (Data from International Union for the Conservation of Nature and World Wildlife Fund)

## ENDANGERED AND THREATENED SPECIES

Species heading toward extinction are classified as either endangered or threatened. An **endangered species** has so few individual survivors that the species could soon become extinct over all or most of its natural range. Examples are the white rhinoceros in Africa (about 4,000 left), the California condor in the United States (only 7 in the wild; Figure 16-2), the giant panda in central China (1,000 left; Figure 4-36), the snow leopard in central Asia (2,500 left; Figure 16-8), the black rhinoceros in Africa (4,000 left; Figure 16-7), and the rare swallowtail butterfly (Figure 16-9).

Q: How much money could be saved if the United States got serious about improving energy efficiency?

E. A. James/Natural History Photographic Agency

**Figure 16-8** The snow leopard, found in Central Asia, is endangered because it has been hunted and killed for its fur.

A **threatened species** is still abundant in its natural range but is declining in numbers and likely to become endangered. Examples are the bald eagle (Figure 2-10) and the grizzly bear.

Some species are more vulnerable than others to premature extinction (Table 16-1). One trait that affects the survival of species under different environmental conditions is their reproductive strategy. Species that take years to mature and have few offspring are especially at risk. Generally in times of stress r-strategist species have an advantage over many K-strategist species (Section 6-2).

Each animal species has a critical population density and size below which survival may be doubtful because males and females have a hard time finding each other. Once a population falls below its critical size, it continues to decline, even if the species is protected, because its death rate exceeds its birth rate. The remaining small population can easily be wiped out by fire, flood, landslide, disease, or some other single catastrophe. Some species, such as bats, are vulnerable

John Markham/Bruce Coleman Ltd.

**Figure 16-9** The swallowtail butterfly was pushed almost to extinction in Great Britain but is now hanging on, mostly in protected nature reserves.

to extinction for a combination of reasons (Case Study, p. 425).

Many wild species are not in danger of extinction, but their populations have been diminished locally or regionally. Such species may be a better indicator of the condition of entire ecosystems than endangered and threatened species. They can serve as early warnings so that we can prevent species extinction rather than responding to emergencies.

**HABITAT LOSS AND FRAGMENTATION** Quite simply, the greatest threat to most wild species is losing their homes. We routinely interrupt migration routes and destroy breeding areas and food sources. About 50% of the world's land area is devoted directly or indirectly to agriculture (Figure 14-3), some 20% to commercial forests, and another 25% to human settlements. This leaves only about 5% for all wild terrestrial species, and overpopulation may double within a few decades (Figure 1-1).

Tropical deforestation (Figure 10-3) is the greatest killer of species followed by destruction of coral reefs (Case Study, p. 135) and wetlands and plowing of grasslands (Figure 5-20). Wildlife habitat loss is quite high in a number of countries including Vietnam (80%), the Philippines (79%), Madagascar (75%; Case Study, p. 265), Burma (71%), and Ethiopia (70%)

In the United States 98% of the tall-grass prairies (Figure 5-18) have been plowed, half of the wetlands drained (Spotlight, p. 144), 90–95% of old-growth forests cut (Figure 10-22), and overall forest cover reduced by 33%. At least 500 native species have been driven to extinction and others (Figures 16-2 and

## Table 16-1 Characteristics of Extinction-Prone Species

| Characteristic | Examples |
|---|---|
| Low reproduction rate | Blue whale, polar bear, California condor, Andean condor, passenger pigeon, giant panda, whooping crane |
| Specialized feeding habits | Everglades kite (eats apple snail of southern Florida), blue whale (krill in polar upwellings), black-footed ferret (prairie dogs and pocket gophers), giant panda (bamboo), koala (certain eucalyptus leaves) |
| Feed at high trophic levels | Bengal tiger, bald eagle, Andean condor, timber wolf |
| Large size | Bengal tiger, lion, elephant, Javan rhinoceros, American bison, giant panda, grizzly bear |
| Limited or specialized nesting or breeding areas | Kirtland's warbler (6- to 15-year-old jack pine trees), whooping crane (marshes), orangutan (only on Sumatra and Borneo), green sea turtle (lays eggs on only a few beaches), bald eagle (prefers forested shorelines), nightingale wren (only on Barro Colorado Island, Panama) |
| Found in only one place or region | Woodland caribou, elephant seal, Cooke's kokio, many unique island species |
| Fixed migratory patterns | Blue whale, Kirtland's warbler, Bachman's warbler, whooping crane |
| Preys on livestock or people | Timber wolf, some crocodiles |
| Behavioral patterns | Passenger pigeon and white-crowned pigeon (nest in large colonies), redheaded woodpecker (flies in front of cars), Carolina parakeet (when one bird is shot, rest of flock hovers over body), Key deer (forages for cigarette butts along highways—it's a "nicotine addict") |

Pedro Ramirez, Jr./U.S. Fish and Wildlife Service

**Figure 16-10** The whooping crane, shown in its winter refuge in Texas, is an endangered species in North America. Its low reproduction rate and fixed migration pattern make it vulnerable to extinction. Once, it lived throughout most of North America, but illegal shooting and habitat loss reduced its numbers to only 16 by 1941. Thanks to a $5-million-per-year habitat protection and captive breeding program directed by the U.S. Fish and Wildlife Service, about 217 birds survive today, including 142 in the wild. By the mid-1990s wildlife officials hope to release 15–20 birds annually into the wild.

16-10) to near extinction mostly because of habitat loss. Furthermore, much of the remaining wildlife habitat is being fragmented (Figure 10-17) and polluted at an alarming rate.

Many rare and threatened species live in vulnerable, specialized habitats, such as islands or single trees

Peter Lowry/Missouri Botanical Gardens

**Figure 16-11** Island species are especially vulnerable to extinction. The endangered *Symphonia* clings to life on Madagascar (Figure 10-5), where 90% of the original vegetation has been destroyed.

in tropical forests. For example, on Madagascar hundreds of unique species are threatened with extinction (Figure 16-11 and Case Study, p. 265). Hawaii is fast becoming the global extinction "capital" because of increasing population and development. Generally the smaller an island is and the farther it is from a source of potential colonizing species, the fewer species it supports.

However, any habitat surrounded by a different one is, in effect, an island for the species that live there. Human settlements, roads, and clear-cut areas (Figure

**Q:** How much of the U.S. gross national product is spent to obtain energy?

## Bats: A Bad Rap

Despite their variety (950 species) and worldwide distribution, bats have several traits that expose them to extinction from human activities. Not only do bats reproduce slowly, but many nest in huge cave colonies, where people can easily destroy them by blocking the entrances. And once the population of a bat species falls below a certain level, it may not recover because of its slow reproductive rate.

Bats play significant ecological roles and are also of great economic importance. They help control many crop-damaging insects and other pest species, such as mosquitoes and rodents (Figure 16-12). About 70% of all bat species feed on night-flying insects, making them the primary controls for such insects.

Other species eat pollen; still others eat certain fruits. Because of this specialized feeding, they are the chief pollinators for certain trees, shrubs, and other plants. They also spread plants throughout tropical forests by excreting undigested seeds. If these keystone species are eliminated from an area, dependent plants will disappear. Examples of bat-pollinated species in the United States are the giant saguaro cactus (Figure 4-10) and agaves (plants of the desert Southwest used in making fiber rope and

tequila). In Southeast Asia a cave-dwelling, nectar-eating bat species is the only known pollinator of durian trees, whose fruit is worth $120 million per year. If you enjoy bananas, cashews, dates, figs, avocados, or mangos, you can thank bats. Likewise, you can thank bats if you have benefited from surgical bandages or kapok-filled life preservers, hemp rope, and hundreds of other commercially important materials.

Bat research has contributed to the development of birth control and artificial insemination methods, to drug testing, to studies of disease resistance and aging, to vaccine production, and to development of navigational aids for the blind.

People mistakenly fear bats as filthy, aggressive, rabies-carrying blood-suckers. But most bat species are harmless to people, livestock, and crops. Like cats bats clean themselves thoroughly, and they are shy and nonaggressive. Rabies is rare in bats, and a rabid bat is rarely aggressive. The few people who are bitten are those who foolishly pick up a sick bat, which bites in self-defense, as almost any sick wild animal would.

In the United States only 10 people have died of bat-transmitted disease in four decades of record keeping. More Americans die each year from falling coconuts. Only three species of bats (none of them

found in the United States) feed on blood, drawn mostly from cattle or wild animals. These bat species can be serious pests to domestic livestock but rarely affect humans.

Because of unwarranted fears of bats and misunderstanding of their vital ecological roles, several species have been driven to extinction and others are threatened. Americans spend millions of dollars annually to exterminate bats. By contrast, in Europe and the CIS, where their benefits are recognized, bats receive legal protection. We need to see bats as valuable allies—not enemies.

**Figure 16-12** Endangered ghost bat carrying a mouse in tropical northern Australia. This carnivorous night-feeding bat is harmless to people. Bats are considered keystone species in many ecosystems because of their roles in pollinating plants, dispersing seeds, and controlling insect and rodent populations.

10-17) break wildlife habitats into patches, or "habitat islands," that may be too small to support the minimum breeding populations of species. Most national parks and other protected areas are habitat islands. A rule of thumb is that the number of species is cut in half with each 10-fold decrease in habitat area. Freshwater lakes are also examples of habitat islands. They are especially vulnerable when nonnative species are introduced.

Migrating species face a double habitat problem. Nearly half of the 700 U.S. bird species spend two-thirds of the year in the tropical forests of Central or South America or the Caribbean islands and return to North America during the summer to breed. This includes some of the continent's most popular songbirds, such as thrushes, warblers, vireos, tanagers, and flycatchers. A U.S. Fish and Wildlife study showed that between 1978 and 1987 populations of 44 species of insect-eating, migratory songbirds in North America declined, with 20 species showing drops of 25–45% (Figure 16-13). The main culprits are logging of tropical forests in their winter habitats (Figure 10-3) and fragmentation of their summer forest habitats in North America. As farms, freeways, and suburbs intrude,

**Figure 16-13** Many species of migratory North American songbirds, such as the wood thrush, are suffering serious population declines because of loss of their winter tropical forest habitats in Latin America and the Caribbean islands, and fragmentation of their summer habitats in North America. The wood thrush population, found over most of the eastern United States during the summer, declined 31% between 1978 and 1987. Three-fourths of the world's bird species are declining in population or threatened with extinction.

**Figure 16-14** In Yemen rhino horns are carved into ornate dagger handles like these, which sell for $500–$12,000. In China and other parts of Asia powdered rhino horn is used for medicinal purposes and as an alleged aphrodisiac. All five species of rhinoceros are threatened with extinction because of poachers, who kill them for their horns, and loss of habitat. Efforts to protect these species from extinction are under way, but only about 12,000 rhinos remain in the wild today.

they not only remove trees and break forests into patches but also create more "edge" habitat for opossums, skunks, squirrels, chipmunks, raccoons, and blue jays that feast on the eggs and young of migrant songbirds, and for parasitic cowbirds that take over their nests. Three-fourths of the world's 9,000 known bird species are declining in numbers or are threatened with extinction, mostly because of habitat loss and fragmentation.

**COMMERCIAL HUNTING AND POACHING** Killing animals to provide enough food for survival is called **subsistence hunting**. **Sport hunting** is the hunting of animals for recreation (or for extra food). **Commercial hunting** involves killing animals to sell their meat, fur, or other parts. Illegal commercial hunting or fishing is called **poaching**.

Today subsistence hunting is rare because of the decline in hunting-and-gathering societies (Spotlight, p. 270). Sport hunting is closely regulated in most countries, and game species are endangered only where protective regulations do not exist or are not enforced. No animal in the United States, for instance, has become extinct or endangered because of regulated sport hunting.

However, legal and illegal commercial hunting has driven many species, such as the American bison (p. 28), to or over the brink of extinction This continues today. Bengal tigers are in trouble because a tiger

fur coat sells for $100,000 in Tokyo. A mountain gorilla is worth $150,000, an ocelot skin $40,000, an imperial Amazon macaw $30,000, a snow leopard skin $14,000 (Figure 16-8), and rhinoceros horn as much as $28,600 per kilogram (Figure 16-14). Only about 300 Siberian tigers are left, mostly because these and other tigers are killed for their furs and their bones, which are ground up and used in Chinese medicines. To poachers such riches far outweigh the risk of fines and the much smaller risk of jail.

Poachers slaughter elephants for their valuable ivory tusks (Figure 16-15). Trade in ivory and habitat loss have reduced African elephant numbers from 2.5 million in 1970 to about 609,000 today. In January 1990 members of the 119-nation Convention on International Trade in Endangered Species (CITES, pronounced sigh-teez) banned international trade in African elephant products. Although seven countries exempted themselves from the ban, the bottom has dropped out of the worldwide ivory market. Environmentalists now fear, however, that poachers will start killing

Q: What country has the highest industrial energy efficiency?

Figure 16-15 Vultures feeding on an elephant carcass in Tanzania. Poachers killed it to cut off its ivory tusks, which are used to make jewelry, piano keys, ornamental carvings, and art objects. The 1990 international ban on the trade of ivory from African elephants may save this species.

Figure 16-16 Increasing numbers of bull walruses found in the Bering Sea off the coast of Alaska are being killed illegally for their ivory tusks. A pair of tusks is worth $800–$1,500 on the black market. Walruses are easy to kill because they spend the summer on ice floes. Hunters (mostly Inuit) in small boats shoot the slow-moving mammals and use the liver, heart, and other parts for food (legally allowed); some also sever the head with a chain saw and illegally sell the tusks. With an estimated population of 250,000 in the Pacific, the walrus is not endangered now but may soon be if hunting for their tusks continues.

Alaska's walruses for their tusks (Figure 16-16). Salespeople in the CIS are also touting ancient ivory from long-dead mammoths preserved in Siberia's snow.

As more species become endangered, the demand for them on the black market soars, hastening their extinction. Poaching is also increasing in the United States, especially in the West (Spotlight, right).

**PREDATOR AND PEST CONTROL** People deliberately try to exterminate species that compete with

## Poaching in the United States: The New Killing Fields

SPOTLIGHT

Figure 16-17 The peregrine falcon is endangered in the United States, mostly because of DDT. The insecticide caused their young to die before hatching because the eggshells were too thin to protect them. In 1975 only about 120 peregrine falcons were left in the lower 48 states; today there are about 1,400. Most of them were bred in captivity and then released into the wild in a $6-million-per-year recovery program. However, some of these birds are illegally shot or captured for sale on the black market. Peregrine falcons also die because of loss of habitat in their South American wintering grounds.

Poaching is increasing in the United States, especially in national parks and wilderness areas, where hunters kill endangered bighorn sheep or grizzly bear. A few renegades violate hunting laws, but much of the illegal killing and trapping is done by professional poachers for markets.

According to the U.S. Fish and Wildlife Service a poached gyrfalcon sells for $120,000, a bighorn sheep head for $10,000–$60,000, a large saguaro cactus (Figure 4-10) for $5,000–$15,000, a peregrine falcon (Figure 16-17) for $10,000, a polar bear for $6,000, a grizzly bear for $5,000, a mountain goat for $3,500, a bald eagle (Figure 2-10) for $2,500, and a 29-gram (1-ounce) bear gallbladder (used in Asia for medicinal purposes) for $5,000.

Most poachers are not caught. The Fish and Wildlife Service has only 200 special agents, with only 22 agents covering one-third of the country where extensive poaching occurs. Some judges have begun imposing heavy fines and even prison terms on flagrant violators, but most poachers get off lightly.

them for food and game. For example, U.S. fruit farmers killed off the Carolina parakeet around 1914 because it fed on fruit crops. The species was easy prey because when one member of a flock was shot, the rest

**Figure 16-18** The Utah prairie dog is a threatened species in the United States, mostly because of widespread poisoning by ranchers and government agencies since 1929.

**Figure 16-19** The black-footed ferret is nearly extinct in North America because most of the prairie dogs (Figure 16-18) that made up 90% or more of its diet have been eliminated. By 1985 no black-footed ferrets were left in the wild. Between 1985 and 1992, however, the captive population grew from 18 to 325. Since 1991, 129 have been released to a favorable habitat in north central Wyoming, but at least 30 of them have died. Over the next decade there are plans to reintroduce the ferrets to nine other areas throughout the West, with the goal of eventually building a wild population of about 1,500 animals.

**Figure 16-20** Collectors of exotic birds may pay $10,000 for a threatened hyacinth macaw smuggled out of Brazil. These high prices help doom such species to eventual extinction. However, in its lifetime a single macaw might yield $165,000 in tourist revenues. Worldwide over 5 million live wild birds are captured and sold legally each year, and 2.5 million more are captured and sold illegally.

**Figure 16-21** The black lace cactus is one of many U.S. plants that are endangered because of development and collectors.

of the birds hovered over its body, making themselves easy targets.

As animal habitats shrink, African farmers kill large numbers of elephants to keep them from trampling and eating food crops. Since 1929 U.S. ranchers and government agencies have poisoned prairie dogs because horses and cattle sometimes step into the burrows and break their legs. This poisoning has killed 99% of North America's prairie dogs (Figure 16-18). It has also nearly wiped out the black-footed ferret (Figure 16-19), which preyed on the prairie dog.

**PETS AND DECORATIVE PLANTS** Each year millions of birds are captured for export, mostly to Europe, Japan, and the United States. Over 40 species, mostly parrots, are endangered because of this wild-bird trade. About 25 million American households have exotic birds as pets, 85% of them imported (Fig-

ure 16-20). And for every bird that reaches a pet shop, legally or illegally, as many as 10 others die during capture or in transport.

Some exotic plants, especially orchids and cacti, are also endangered because they are gathered, often

**Q:** How could the United States eliminate the need to import oil?

**Bioaccumulation** is the retention or buildup of non-biodegradable or slowly biodegradable chemicals in the body. Toxic metals such as lead and mercury, chlorine-containing hydrocarbons such as DDT and PCBs, and some radioactive isotopes are readily absorbed into the body but excreted very slowly if at all. Some of these substances accumulate in fatty tissue, and others in bones or organs.

Bioaccumulation is compounded in a food chain. Figure 16-22 shows the **biological amplification** (also called *biological magnification*) for DDT in a five-step estuary food chain. If each phytoplankton organism in such a food chain retains one unit of DDT from the water, a small fish eating thousands of zooplankton (which feed on the phytoplankton) will store thousands of units of DDT in its fatty tissue. Then a large fish that eats 10 of the smaller fish will receive and store tens of thousands of units, and a bird (or a human) that eats several large fish will ingest hundreds of thousands of units.

High concentrations of DDT or other slowly biodegraded, fat-soluble organic chemicals can directly kill the organisms, reduce their ability to reproduce, or make them more vulnerable to diseases, parasites, and predators.

During the 1950s and 1960s populations of ospreys, cormorants, brown pelicans (Figure 2-8), and bald eagles (Figure 2-10) plummeted. These birds feed mostly on fish at the top of aquatic food chains and webs, and thus ingest large quantities of biologically amplified DDT in their prey. Prairie falcons, sparrow hawks, Bermuda petrels, and peregrine falcons (Figure 16-17) also died off when they ate animal prey containing DDT, such as rabbits, ground squirrels, and other crop-damaging small mammals.

Research has shown that the culprit was DDE, a breakdown product of DDT, accumulating in the bodies of the affected birds. This chemical reduces the amount of calcium in the shells of their eggs. The fragile shells break and the unborn chicks die.

Since the U.S. ban on DDT in 1972, most of these species have made a comeback. In 1980, however, DDT levels were again rising in peregrine falcons and ospreys. These species may be picking up biologically amplified DDT and other banned pesticides in Latin America, where they winter. In those countries the use of such chemicals is still legal. Illegal use of DDT and other banned pesticides in the United States may also play a role.

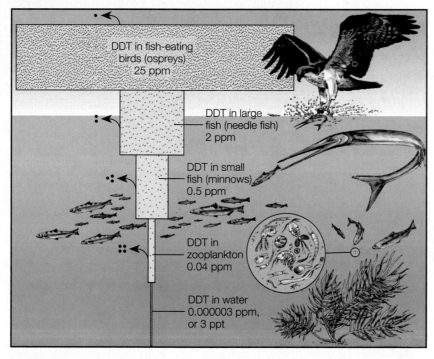

DDT in fish-eating birds (ospreys)
25 ppm

DDT in large fish (needle fish)
2 ppm

DDT in small fish (minnows)
0.5 ppm

DDT in zooplankton
0.04 ppm

DDT in water
0.000003 ppm, or 3 ppt

**Figure 16-22** DDT concentrations in the fatty tissues of organisms were biologically amplified about 10 million times in this food chain of an estuary near Long Island Sound. Dots represent DDT, and arrows show small losses of DDT through respiration and excretion.

illegally (Figure 16-21), and then sold to collectors and used to decorate houses, offices, and landscapes. A collector may pay $5,000 for a single rare orchid. A single rare mature crested saguaro cactus can earn cactus rustlers as much as $15,000. To thwart the cactus rustlers, Arizona has put 222 species under state protection with penalties of up to $1,000 and jail sentences of up to one year. However, only seven people are assigned to enforce this law over the entire state, and the fines are too small to discourage poaching.

**POLLUTION AND CLIMATE CHANGE** Toxic chemicals degrade wildlife habitats, including wildlife refuges, and kill some plants and animals. Slowly degradable pesticides, especially DDT and dieldrin, have caused populations of some bird species to decline (Spotlight, above). And wildlife in even the

**Figure 16-23** The very aggressive brown tree snake is normally found in eastern and northern Australia, Indonesia, and New Guinea. It has been introduced from Australia into Guam, where it has wiped out many native species of birds.

best-protected and best-managed reserves may be depleted in a few decades because of climatic change caused by projected global warming (Section 11-1).

**INTRODUCED SPECIES** Travelers sometimes pick up plants and animals intentionally or accidentally, and introduce them to new geographical regions. Many of these alien species provide food, game, and aesthetic beauty, and help control pests in their new environments. Some alien species, however, have no natural predators and competitors in their new habitats, which allows them to dominate their new ecosystem and reduce the populations of many native species (Case Study, p. 432 and Figure 16-23). Eventually such aliens can displace or wipe out native species (Table 16-2).

One example is the kudzu vine with its beautiful purple flowers. In the 1930s this import from Japan was planted in the southeastern United States to help control soil erosion. It does control erosion, but it is so prolific and hard to kill that it engulfs hills, trees, houses, roadsides, stream banks, utility poles, patches of forest, and anything else in its path (Figure 16-24). According to the U.S. Department of Agriculture it costs an estimated $50 million annually in lost farm and timber production. Currently kudzu is confined by climate to the South, but it could spread as far north as the Great Lakes by 2040 if projected global warming occurs. Although kudzu is considered a menace in the United States, Asians use a powdered kudzu starch in beverages, gourmet confections, and herbal remedies. A Japanese firm is building a large kudzu farm and processing plant in Alabama, and will ship the extracted starch to Japan where demand exceeds supply.

**Figure 16-24** Kudzu taking over a field and trees near Lyman, South Carolina. It can grow 0.3 meter (1 foot) per day and is now found from East Texas to Florida and as far north as southeastern Pennsylvania. Kudzu can't be stopped by being dug up or burned. Grazing by goats and repeated doses of herbicides can destroy it, but goats and herbicides also destroy other plants, and herbicides can contaminate water supplies.

Another example is wild African bees, which were imported to Brazil in 1959 with the false hope that they would increase honey production. Since then these bees have moved northward into Central America and recently reached Texas. They are now heading north at 240 kilometers (150 miles) per year, though they will be stopped eventually by cold winters in the central United States. These "killer" bees displace domestic honeybees and reduce the honey supply. Although they are not the killer bees portrayed in some horror movies, they are aggressive and unpredictable, and have killed animals and even humans.

**Table 16-2 Damage Caused by Plants and Animals Imported into the United States**

| Name | Origin | Mode of Transport | Type of Damage |
|------|--------|-------------------|----------------|
| **Mammals** | | | |
| European wild boar | Russia | Intentionally imported (1912), escaped captivity | Destroys habitat by rooting; damages crops |
| Nutria (cat-sized rodent) | Argentina | Intentionally imported, escaped captivity (1940) | Alters marsh ecology; damages levees and earth dams; destroys crops |
| **Birds** | | | |
| European starling | Europe | Intentionally released (1890) | Competes with native songbirds; damages crops; transmits swine diseases; causes airport nuisance |
| House sparrow | England | Intentionally released by Brooklyn Institute (1853) | Damages crops; displaces native songbirds |
| **Fish** | | | |
| Carp | Germany | Intentionally released (1877) | Displaces native fish; uproots water plants; lowers waterfowl populations |
| Sea lamprey (Figure 4-42) | North Atlantic Ocean | Entered via Welland Canal (1829) | Wiped out lake trout, lake whitefish, and sturgeon in Great Lakes |
| Walking catfish | Thailand | Imported into Florida | Destroys bass, bluegill, and other fish |
| **Insects** | | | |
| Argentine fire ant | Argentina | Probably entered via coffee shipments from Brazil (1918) | Damages crops; destroys native ant species |
| Camphor scale insect | Japan | Accidentally imported on nursery stock (1920s) | Damaged nearly 200 plant species in Louisiana, Texas, and Alabama |
| Japanese beetle | Japan | Accidentally imported on irises or azaleas (1911) | Defoliates more than 250 species of trees and other plants, including many of commercial importance |
| **Plants** | | | |
| Water hyacinth | Central America | Intentionally introduced (1884) | Clogs waterways; shades out other aquatic vegetation |
| Chestnut blight (fungus) | Asia | Accidentally imported on nursery plants (1900) | Killed nearly all eastern U.S. chestnut trees; disturbed forest ecology |
| Dutch elm disease (fungus) | Europe | Accidentally imported on infected elm timber used for veneers (1930) | Killed millions of elms; disturbed forest ecology |

From *Biological Conservation* by David W. Ehrenfeld. Copyright © 1970 by Holt, Rinehart & Winston, Inc. Modified and reprinted by permission.

**POPULATION GROWTH, AFFLUENCE, AND POVERTY** The underlying causes of extinction and population reduction of wildlife are human population growth and economic systems and policies that fail to value the environment and its vital ecosystem services, and thus promote unsustainable exploitation. As our population grows we clear, occupy, and damage more land to supply food, fuelwood, timber, and other resources.

Paradoxically both affluence and poverty contribute to extinction. Increasing affluence and economic growth lead to greater average resource use per person, which is a prime factor in taking over wildlife habitats (Figure 1-16). In LDCs the combination of rapid population growth and poverty push the poor to cut forests, grow crops on marginal land, overgraze grasslands, deplete fish species, and poach endangered animals.

A: Improve the energy efficiency of motor vehicles

**CASE STUDY**

The fast-growing water hyacinth is native to Central and South America. In 1884 a woman took one from a New Orleans exhibition and planted it in her back yard in Florida. Within 10 years the plant, which can double its population in two weeks, had become a public menace. Unchecked by natural enemies and thriving in Florida's nutrient-rich waters, water hyacinths rapidly displaced native plants, clogging many ponds, streams, canals, and rivers, first in Florida and later in the southeastern United States (Figure 16-25).

Mechanical harvesters and herbicides have failed to keep the plant in check. Grazing Florida manatees, or sea cows (Figure 16-26), control water hyacinths better than mechanical or chemical methods. However, these gentle and playful herbivores are threatened with extinction. Slashed by powerboat

**Figure 16-25** The fast-growing water hyacinth was intentionally introduced into Florida from Latin America in 1884. Since then this plant, which can double its population in only two weeks, has taken over waterways in Florida and other southeastern states.

Heather Angel/Biofotos

---

**16-3**

## Solutions: Protecting Wild Species from Extinction

**WORLD CONSERVATION STRATEGY** In 1980 the International Union for Conservation of Nature and Natural Resources (IUCN), the UN Environment Programme, and the World Wildlife Fund developed the World Conservation Strategy, a long-range plan for conserving the world's biological resources. This plan was expanded in 1991. Its primary goals are to:

- Maintain essential ecological processes and life support systems on which human survival and economic activities depend, mostly by combining wildlife conservation with sustainable development (Figure 10-21)

- Preserve species diversity and genetic diversity

- Ensure that any use of species and ecosystems is sustainable

- Minimize the depletion of nonrenewable resources

- Improve the quality of human life

Q: What two countries have the toughest standards for energy efficiency in homes and other buildings?

propellers, entangled in fishing gear—even hit on the head by oars—they reproduce too slowly to recover from these assaults and loss of habitat.

Scientists have introduced water hyacinth–eaters to help control its spread. They include a weevil from Argentina, a water snail from Puer-to Rico, and the grass carp, a fish from the former Soviet Union. These species can help, but water snails and grass carp also feed on other, desirable aquatic plants.

The good news is that water hyacinths have several beneficial uses. For example, they absorb toxic chemicals in sewage treatment lagoons. They can be fermented into a biogas fuel similar to natural gas, added as a mineral and protein supplement to cattle feed, and applied to the soil as fertilizer. They can also be used to clean up polluted ponds and lakes—if their growth can be kept under control.

Florida Marine Research Institute/Florida Department of Natural Resources

**Figure 16-26** The Florida manatee, or sea cow, one of America's most endangered species. Despite a $15 million-per-year recovery program, only about 1,000 of these gentle animals are left in the sluggish and increasingly polluted bays and streams of southern and central Florida.

- Include women and indigenous peoples in the development of conservation plans

- Monitor the sustainability of development

- Promote an ethic that includes protection of plants and animals as well as people

- Encourage recognition of the harmful environmental effects of armed conflict and economic insecurity

- Encourage rehabilitation of degraded ecosystems upon which humans depend for food and fiber

So far 40 countries have planned or established national conservation programs (the United States is not one of them). If MDCs provide enough money and scientific assistance, this conservation strategy offers hope for slowing the loss of biodiversity. Ultimately, however, no conservation strategy can protect the planet's biodiversity unless governments act to reduce poverty, control population growth, slow global warming, and reduce the destruction and degradation of tropical and old-growth forests, wetlands, and coral reefs.

## The Endangered Species Act

**SPOTLIGHT**

The Endangered Species Act of 1973 is one of the world's toughest environmental laws. It authorizes the National Marine Fisheries Service (NMFS) to identify and list endangered and threatened ocean species; the Fish and Wildlife Service (FWS) identifies and lists all other endangered and threatened species. These species cannot be hunted, killed, collected, or injured in the United States.

Any decision by either agency to list or unlist a species must be based only on biology, without economic considerations. The act also forbids federal agencies to carry out, fund, or authorize projects that would jeopardize an endangered or threatened species, or destroy or modify its critical habitat—the land, air, and water necessary for its survival.

Between 1970 and 1992 the number of species found only in the United States that have been placed on the official endangered and threatened list rose from 92 to 750.

Also on the list are 529 species found elsewhere.

Getting listed is only half the battle. Next, the FWS or the NMFS is supposed to prepare a plan to help it recover. However, because of a lack of funds, recovery plans have been developed and approved for only about 61% of the endangered or threatened U.S. species, and half of those plans exist only on paper. Only 6 species have recovered enough to be unlisted, but 238 of the 750 listed species are stable and recovering. On the losing end, 7 listed domestic species have become extinct.

The annual federal budget for endangered species is less than what beer companies spend on two 30-second TV commercials during the Super Bowl. At this level of funding it will take the FWS up to 48 years to evaluate the almost 3,500 species (about 1,500 of them severely imperiled) now proposed for listing. Wildlife experts estimate that at least 400 of them will vanish while they wait, as did 34 species

awaiting listing between 1980 and 1990.

The act requires that all commercial shipments of wildlife and wildlife products enter or leave the country through one of nine designated ports. Many illegal shipments slip by, however, because the 60 FWS inspectors can physically examine only about one-fourth of the 90,000 shipments that enter and leave the United States each year (Figure 16-27). Even if caught, many violators are not prosecuted, and convicted violators often pay only a small fine.

In 1990 Secretary of the Interior Manuel Lujan (whose department is responsible for wildlife protection) proposed changes that would weaken the Endangered Species Act. He suggested that economic factors be considered in evaluating species for listing and in carrying out federally funded projects that threaten the critical habitats of endangered or threatened species. However, between 1987 and 1991 just 19 of more than 7,000 projects

---

**METHODS FOR PROTECTING BIODIVERSITY AND MANAGING WILDLIFE** There are three basic approaches to managing wildlife and preserving biodiversity. The *species approach* is based on protecting endangered species by identifying them, giving them legal protection, preserving and managing their critical habitats, propagating them in captivity, and reintroducing them in suitable habitats. The *ecosystem approach* aims to preserve balanced populations of species in their native habitats, establish legally protected wilderness areas and wildlife reserves, and eliminate alien species. The *wildlife management approach* manages game species for sustained yield by regulating hunting, establishing harvest quotas, developing population management plans, and using international treaties to protect migrating game species such as waterfowl.

 **16-4**

## Solutions: Protecting Endangered Species

**TREATIES AND LAWS** Several international treaties and conventions help protect wild species. One of the most far-reaching is the 1975 Convention on International Trade in Endangered Species (CITES). This treaty, now signed by 119 countries, lists 675 species that cannot be commercially traded as live specimens or wildlife products because they are endangered or threatened.

However, enforcement of this treaty is spotty, convicted violators often pay only small fines, and member countries can exempt themselves from protection of any listed species. Also, much of the $5-billion-per-

434     Q: How much of the heat in U.S. homes and other buildings escapes through closed windows?

**Figure 16-27** Confiscated products made from endangered species. Because of a lack of funds and inspectors, probably no more than one-tenth of the illegal wildlife trade in the United States is discovered. The situation is even worse in most other countries.

evaluated by the FWS were blocked or withdrawn as a result of the Endangered Species Act.

Environmentalists and many members of Congress argue that the Endangered Species Act should be strengthened—not weakened. Besides greatly increasing funding for federal endangered species programs, they would mandate deadlines for developing and implementing recovery plans for ecosystems containing threatened, endangered, and candidate species, and would require federal officials to develop conservation plans for whole ecosystems to help prevent future declines in species not yet listed as threatened or endangered. They would also allow citizens to file lawsuits immediately if an endangered species faces serious harm or extinction.

year illegal trade in wildlife and wildlife products goes on in countries such as Singapore that have not signed the treaty. Other centers of illegal animal trade are Argentina, Indonesia, Spain, Taiwan, and Thailand.

The United States controls imports and exports of endangered wildlife and wildlife products with two important laws. The Lacey Act of 1900 prohibits transporting live or dead wild animals or their parts across state borders without a federal permit. The Endangered Species Act of 1973, amended in 1982 and 1988, makes it illegal for Americans to import or trade in any product made from an endangered or threatened species unless it is used for an approved scientific purpose or to enhance the survival of the species (Spotlight, p. 434).

The federal government has primary responsibility for managing migratory species, endangered species, and wildlife on federal lands. States are responsible for the management of all other wildlife.

Funds for state game management programs come from the sale of hunting and fishing licenses and from federal taxes on hunting and fishing equipment. Two-thirds of the states also have provisions on state income tax returns that allow individuals to contribute money to state wildlife programs. Only 10% of all government wildlife dollars, however, are spent to study or benefit nongame species, which make up nearly 90% of the country's wildlife species.

**WILDLIFE REFUGES** Since 1903, when President Theodore Roosevelt established the first U.S. federal wildlife refuge at Pelican Island, Florida, the National Wildlife Refuge System has grown to 503 refuges

## Should We Develop Oil and Gas in the Arctic National Wildlife Refuge?

The Arctic National Wildlife Refuge on Alaska's North Slope (Figure 16-28) contains more than one-fifth of all the land in the U.S. wildlife refuge system and has been called the crown jewel of the system. During all or part of the year it is home for more than 160 animal species, including caribou, musk oxen, snowy owls, grizzly bears, arctic foxes, and migratory birds (including as many as 300,000 snow geese). It is also home for about 7,000 Inuit (Eskimos) who depend on the caribou for a large part of their diet.

Its coastal plain, the most biologically productive part of the refuge, is the only stretch of Alaska's arctic coastline not open to oil and gas development. The big oil companies hope to change this because they believe that the area *might* contain oil and natural gas deposits. Since 1985 they have been urging Congress to open 607,000 hectares (1.5 million acres) along the coastal plain to drilling—an area roughly two-thirds the size of Yellowstone National Park.

Environmentalists oppose this idea and want Congress to designate the entire coastal plain as wilderness. They cite Interior Department estimates that there is only a 19% chance of finding as much oil as the United States consumes every six months. Even if the

oil does exist, environmentalists do not believe the potential degradation of any portion of this irreplaceable wilderness area would be worth it, especially considering that improvements in energy efficiency would save far more oil at a much lower cost (Section 17-2).

Officials of oil companies claim they have developed Alaska's Prudhoe Bay oil fields without significant harm to wildlife and that the area they want to open to oil and gas development is less than 1.5% of the entire coastal plain region—equivalent in size to Dulles International Airport in Washington, D.C., in an area approximately the size of South Carolina.

However, the huge 1989 oil spill from the tanker *Exxon Valdez* in

Alaska's Prince William Sound cast serious doubt on such claims (Case Study, p. 606). Moreover, a study leaked from the Fish and Wildlife Service in 1988 revealed that oil drilling at Prudhoe Bay has caused much more air and water pollution than was anticipated before drilling began in 1972. According to this study oil development in the coastal plain could cause the loss of 20–40% of the area's 180,000-member caribou herd, 25–50% of the remaining musk oxen, 50% or more of the wolverines, and 50% of the snow geese that live there part of the year. A 1988 EPA study also found that "violations of state and federal environmental regulations and laws are occurring at an unacceptable rate" in the Prudhoe Bay area.

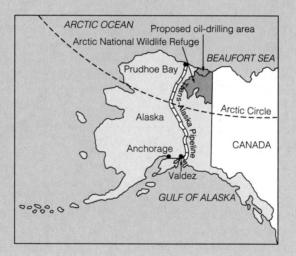

**Figure 16-28** Proposed oil-drilling area in Alaska's Arctic National Wildlife Refuge. (Data from U.S. Fish and Wildlife Service)

(Figure 15-2). About 85% of the area included in these refuges is in Alaska.

Over three-fourths of the refuges are wetlands for protection of migratory waterfowl. Most species on the U.S. endangered list have habitats in the refuge system, and some refuges have been set aside for specific endangered species. These have helped Florida's Key deer, the brown pelican (Figure 2-8), and the trumpeter swan to recover. Environmentalists urge the establishment of more refuges for endangered plants.

Congress has not established guidelines (such as multiple use or sustained yield) for management of the National Wildlife Refuge System, as it has for other public lands. As a result, the Fish and Wildlife Service has allowed many refuges to be used for hunting, fishing, trapping, timber cutting, grazing, farming, oil and gas development (Pro/Con, above), mining, military air exercises, power and air boating, and off-road vehicles. Currently, for example, more than 50% of the refuges are open to hunting, 56% to fishing, and 18%

to trapping. A 1990 report by the General Accounting Office found that activities considered harmful to wildlife occur in nearly 60% of the nation's wildlife refuges. In addition, a 1986 FWS study estimated that one in five federal refuges is contaminated with chemicals from old toxic-waste dump sites (including military bases) and runoff from nearby agricultural land. For example, massive waterfowl deaths in the Kesterson National Wildlife Refuge in California's San Joaquin Valley in 1982 have been blamed on runoff of selenium-tainted irrigation water.

Private groups play an important role in conserving wildlife in refuges and other protected areas. For example, since 1951 the Nature Conservancy has preserved over 1 million hectares (2.5 million acres) of forests, marshes, prairies, islands, and other areas of unique ecological or aesthetic significance in the United States.

## GENE BANKS, BOTANICAL GARDENS, AND ZOOS

Botanists preserve genetic information and endangered plant species by storing their seeds in gene banks—refrigerated, low-humidity environments. Scientists urge that many more such banks be established, especially in LDCs; however, some species can't be preserved in gene banks, and maintaining the banks is very expensive.

The world's 1,500 botanical gardens and arboreta hold about 90,000 plant species. However, these sanctuaries have too little storage capacity and too little funding to preserve most of the world's rare and threatened plants.

Worldwide 500 zoos house about 540,000 individual animals, many of them from species not threatened or endangered. Zoos and animal research centers are increasingly being used to preserve some individuals of critically endangered animal species.

Two techniques for preserving such species are egg pulling and captive breeding, with the long-term goal of reintroducing the species into protected wild habitats. *Egg pulling* involves collecting eggs laid in the wild by critically endangered bird species and hatching them in zoos or research centers. For *captive breeding* some or all individuals of a critically endangered species still in the wild are captured for breeding in captivity.

Captive breeding programs at zoos in Phoenix, San Diego, and Los Angeles saved the nearly extinct Arabian oryx (Figure 16-29). This large antelope species once lived throughout the Middle East. By the early 1970s, however, it had been hunted to extinction in the wild by people riding in jeeps and helicopters, and wielding rifles and machine guns. Since 1980 small numbers of oryx bred in captivity have been returned to the wild in protected habitats in the Mid-

**Figure 16-29** The Arabian oryx barely escaped extinction in 1969 after being overhunted in the deserts of Oman and Jordan (Figure 13-1). Captive breeding programs saved this antelope species from extinction. Some have been reintroduced into protected habitats in the Middle East, with the wild population now about 120. These desert animals survive in an arid environment by licking the dew that accumulates at night on rocks and on one another's hair.

dle East. Endangered U.S. species now being bred in captivity include the California condor (Figure 16-2), the peregrine falcon (Figure 16-17), and the black-footed ferret (Figure 16-19). Endangered golden lion tamarins bred at the National Zoo in Washington, D.C., have been released in Brazilian rain forests.

Unfortunately, keeping populations of endangered animal species in zoos and research centers is limited by lack of space and money. The captive population of each species must number 100–500 to avoid extinction through accident, disease, or loss of genetic variability through inbreeding. Moreover, caring for and breeding captive animals is very expensive. Thus the world's zoos now contain only 20 endangered species of animals with populations of 100 or more individuals. It is estimated that today's zoos and research centers have space to preserve healthy and sustainable populations of only 925 of the 2,000 large vertebrate species that could vanish from the planet. It is doubtful that the more than $6 billion needed to care for these animals for 20 years will be available.

Because of limited funds and trained personnel, only a few of the world's endangered and threatened species can be saved by treaties, laws, wildlife refuges, and zoos. That means that wildlife experts must decide which species out of thousands of candidates

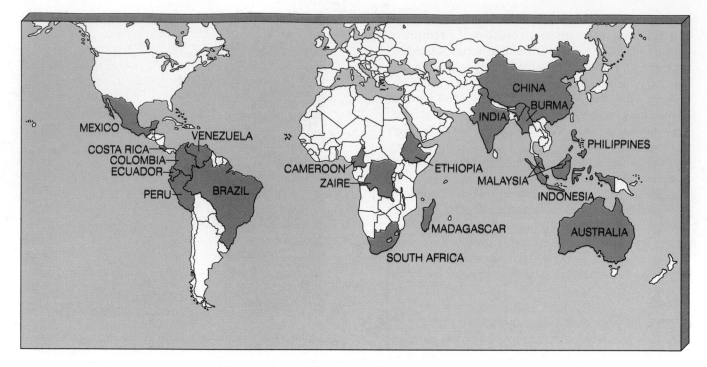

**Figure 16-30** Earth's megadiversity countries. Environmentalists believe that efforts should be concentrated on preserving repositories of biodiversity in these countries. (Data from Conservation International and the World Wildlife Fund)

should be saved. Many experts suggest that the limited funds for preserving threatened and endangered wildlife be concentrated on those species that **(1)** have the best chance for survival, **(2)** have the most ecological value to an ecosystem, and **(3)** are potentially useful for agriculture, medicine, or industry.

## Solutions: Protecting Entire Ecosystems

16-5

### HOW MUCH SHOULD BE PROTECTED?

Most wildlife biologists believe that the best way to preserve biodiversity is through a worldwide network of reserves, parks, wildlife sanctuaries, and other protected areas. According to Aldo Leopold, "A species must be saved *in many places* if it is to be saved at all."

By 1993 there were about 7,000 nature reserves, parks, and other protected areas throughout the world—occupying 4.9% of Earth's land surface. That is an important beginning, but environmentalists say that a minimum of 10% of the globe's land area is needed. Moreover, many existing reserves are too

small to protect their populations of wild species and receive little actual protection.

**BIOREGIONS AND BIOSPHERE RESERVES** Many conservation biologists believe that the best way to protect biodiversity is by using an integrated approach called *bioregional management*. A **bioregion** is a land area or life territory with distinctive soils, land forms, watersheds, microclimates, native plants and animals, and other biological and physical characteristics. Sometimes a bioregion is also defined by its human inhabitants, who give it a unique cultural identity. California has identified 11 bioregions and is beginning to use this concept to manage its public lands and waters.

In 1981 UNESCO proposed that at least one, and ideally five or more, *biosphere reserves* be set up in each of Earth's 193 biogeographical zones. Each reserve should be large enough to prevent gradual species loss, as occurs on most isolated islands, and should be designed to combine both conservation and sustainable use of natural resources. To date more than 300 biosphere reserves have been established in 76 countries.

A well-designed biosphere reserve has three zones: **(1)** a *core area* containing an important ecosystem that has had little, if any, disturbance from human activities; **(2)** a *buffer zone*, where activities and

Q: How much money does switching from an incandescent bulb to a fluorescent bulb save?

uses are managed in ways that help protect the core; and **(3)** a second *buffer* or *transition zone*, which combines conservation and sustainable forestry, grazing, agriculture, and recreation. Buffer zones can also be used for education and research.

Research indicates that in some areas several medium-sized, interconnected reserves may offer more protection for wildlife than a single large one. If the population of a species in one reserve is wiped out due to fire, epidemic, or some other disaster, the species might still survive in the other reserves. Conservation biologists also suggest establishing protected corridors between reserves to help support more species and allow migrations when environmental conditions in a reserve deteriorate.

So far most biosphere reserves fall short of the bioregional ideal. Most were imposed on existing national parks and reserves with little emphasis on expanding them to encompass bioregions. Also, too little funding has been provided for their protection and management.

Conservationist Norman Myers (Guest Essay, p. 288) proposes extending all key parks and reserves northward in the Northern Hemisphere (and southward in the Southern Hemisphere) and providing a network of corridors to allow migration of animal species and some plant species if global warming occurs (Section 11-1). Otherwise, he argues, existing parks and reserves will become death traps instead of sanctuaries.

An international fund to help LDCs protect and manage bioregions and biosphere reserves would cost $100 million per year—about what the world spends on arms every 90 minutes. Since there won't be enough money to protect all of the world's biodiversity, environmentalists believe that efforts should be focused on the megadiversity countries (Figure 16-30). In the United States environmentalists have urged Congress to pass an Endangered Ecosystems or Biodiversity Protection Act as an important step toward preserving the country's biodiversity.

 **16-6** **Wildlife Management**

**MANAGEMENT APPROACHES** **Wildlife management** entails **(1)** manipulating wildlife populations (especially game species) and habitats for their welfare and for human benefit, **(2)** preserving endangered and threatened wild species, and **(3)** enforcing wildlife laws.

The first step in wildlife management is to decide which species are to be managed in a particular area—a source of much controversy. Ecologists stress preserving biodiversity. Wildlife conservationists are concerned about endangered species. Bird-watchers want the greatest diversity of bird species. Hunters want large populations of game species for harvest during hunting season. In the United States most wildlife management is devoted to producing surpluses of game animals and game birds.

After goals have been set, the wildlife manager must develop a management plan. Ideally the plan is based on principles of ecological succession (Section 6-4), wildlife population dynamics (Section 6-2), and an understanding of the cover, food, water, space, and other habitat requirements of each species to be managed. The manager must also consider the number of potential hunters, their success rates, and the regulations available to prevent excessive harvesting.

This information is difficult, expensive, and time-consuming to obtain. In practice it involves much guesswork and trial and error, which is why wildlife management is as much an art as a science. Management plans must also be adapted to political pressures from conflicting groups and to budget constraints.

**MANIPULATION OF VEGETATION AND WATER SUPPLIES** Wildlife managers can encourage the growth of plant species that are the preferred food and cover for a particular animal species by controlling the ecological succession of vegetation in various areas (Figure 6-14).

Animal wildlife species can be classified into four types according to the stage of ecological succession at which they are most likely to be found: early-successional, mid-successional, late-successional, and wilderness (Figure 16-31). *Early-successional species* find food and cover in weedy pioneer plants. These plants invade an area that has been cleared of vegetation for human activities and then abandoned, as well as areas devastated by mining, fires, volcanic lava, or glaciers (Figure 6-13).

*Mid-successional species* are found around abandoned croplands and partially open areas created by logging of small stands of timber, controlled burning, and clearing of vegetation for roads, firebreaks, oil and gas pipelines, and electrical transmission lines. Such openings of the forest canopy promote the growth of vegetation favored by mid-successional mammal and bird species. They also increase the amount of edge habitat, where two communities such as a forest and a field come together. This transition zone allows animals such as deer to feed on vegetation in clearings and quickly escape to cover in the nearby forest.

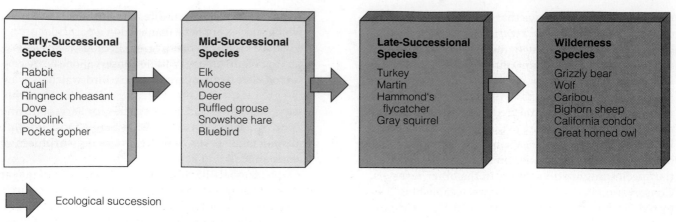

**Figure 16-31** Preferences of some wildlife species for habitats at different stages of ecological succession.

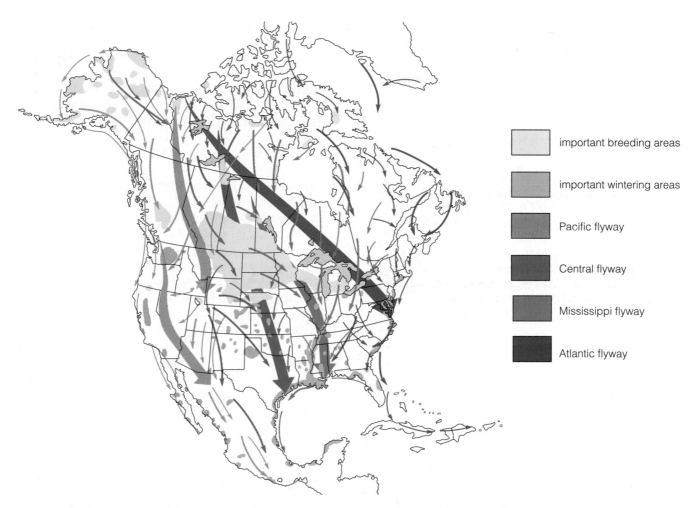

**Figure 16-32** Principal breeding and wintering areas and fall migration flyways used by migratory waterfowl in North America.

*Late-successional species* need old-growth and mature forest habitats to produce the food and cover on which they depend. These animals require the protection of moderate-sized, old-growth forest refuges.

*Wilderness species* flourish only in fairly undisturbed, mature vegetation communities, such as large areas of old-growth forests, tundra, grasslands, and deserts. They can survive only in large wilderness areas and wildlife refuges.

Various types of habitat improvement can be used to attract a desired species and encourage its population growth, including planting seeds, transplanting

Q: How much of the world's electricity could solar cells supply by 2050?

## Sport Hunting Controversy in the United States

Sport hunters, hunting groups, and state game officials believe that Americans should be free to hunt as long as they obey state and local game regulations, and don't damage wildlife resources. They argue that carefully regulated sport hunting is needed because we have eliminated most of the natural predators of deer and other large game animals. Without hunting, populations of game species will exceed the carrying capacity of their habitats and destroy vegetation they and other species need.

Sport hunting provides recreational pleasure for millions of people (16 million in the United States) and stimulates local economies. Its defenders also point out that sales of hunting licenses and taxes on firearms and ammunition have provided more than $1.6 billion since 1937 to buy, restore, and maintain wildlife habitats and to support wildlife research in the United States.

Environmental groups such as the Sierra Club and Defenders of Wildlife support carefully controlled sport hunting as a way of preserving biological diversity by helping prevent depletion of other native species of plants and animals. But some individuals and groups, such as the Humane Society, oppose sport hunting because they believe it inflicts unnecessary pain and suffering on animals, few of which are killed to supply food needed for survival. In addition, the Humane Society argues that sport hunting tends to reduce the genetic quality of remaining wildlife populations because hunters are most likely to kill the largest and strongest animals. By contrast, natural predators tend to improve population quality by eliminating weak and sick individuals.

Opponents of hunting also argue that game managers deliberately create a surplus of game animals by eliminating their natural predators, such as wolves (Figure 15-1). The game managers then claim that the surplus must be harvested by hunters to prevent habitat degradation or starvation of the game. Instead of eliminating natural predators, say opponents, wildlife managers should reintroduce them to eliminate the need for sport hunting. However, supporters of hunting point out that populations of many game species, such as deer, are so large that predators like the wolf cannot possibly control them. Also, because most wildlife habitats are fragmented, introduction of predators can lead to the loss of nearby livestock.

certain types of vegetation, building artificial nests, and setting prescribed burns. Wildlife managers often create or improve ponds and lakes in wildlife refuges to provide water, food, and habitat for waterfowl and other wild animals.

**POPULATION MANAGEMENT BY SPORT HUNTING** Most MDCs use sport hunting laws to manage populations of game animals although sport hunting is controversial (Pro/Con, left). Licensed hunters are allowed to hunt only during certain months of the year so as to protect animals during mating season. Hunters can use only certain types of hunting equipment, such as bows and arrows, shotguns, and rifles, for a particular type of game. Limits are set on the size, number, and sex of animals that can be killed, and on the number of hunters allowed in a game refuge.

Close control of sport hunting is difficult. Accurate data on game populations may not exist and may cost too much to get. People in communities near hunting areas, who benefit from money spent by hunters, may push to have hunting quotas raised.

**MANAGEMENT OF MIGRATORY WATERFOWL** In North America migratory waterfowl such as ducks, geese, and swans nest in Canada during the summer. During the fall hunting season they migrate to the United States and Central America along generally fixed routes called **flyways** (Figure 16-32).

Canada, the United States, and Mexico have signed agreements to prevent habitat destruction and overhunting of migratory waterfowl. However, since 1972 the estimated breeding population of North American ducks has dropped 38%, mostly because of prolonged drought in key breeding areas and degradation and destruction of wetland and grassland breeding habitats by farmers. What wetlands remain are used by dense flocks of ducks and geese (Figure 6-1), whose crowding makes them more vulnerable to diseases and to predators such as skunks, foxes, coyotes, minks, raccoons, and hunters. Waterfowl in wetlands near croplands are also exposed to pollution from pesticides and other chemicals in irrigation runoff.

Wildlife officials manage waterfowl by regulating hunting, protecting existing habitats, and developing new habitats, as well as by building artificial nesting sites, ponds, and nesting islands. More than 75% of the federal wildlife refuges in the United States are wetlands used by migratory birds. Local and state agencies and private conservation groups such as Ducks Unlimited, the Audubon Society, and the Nature Conservancy have also established waterfowl refuges.

In 1986 the United States and Canada agreed to spend $1.5 billion over a 16-year period, with the goal of almost doubling the continental duck-breeding

**Figure 16-33** Pilot whales, which are not now endangered, being butchered in the Faeroe Islands of the Baltic Sea between the coasts of Sweden and the CIS. The whaling industry has pushed most of the dozen or so species of great whales to commercial extinction through overharvesting.

population. The key elements in this program will be the purchase, improvement, and protection of additional waterfowl habitats in five priority areas.

Since 1934 the Migratory Bird Hunting and Conservation Stamp Act has required waterfowl hunters to buy a duck stamp each season they hunt. Revenue from these sales goes into a fund to buy land and easements for the benefit of waterfowl.

## 16-7 Fishery Management and Protecting Marine Biodiversity

**FRESHWATER FISHERY MANAGEMENT** The goals of freshwater fish management are to encourage the growth of populations of desirable commercial and sport fish species and to reduce or eliminate populations of less desirable species. A number of techniques are used:

- Regulating the timing and length of fishing seasons
- Setting the size and number of fish that can be taken
- Requiring commercial fishnets to have a large enough mesh to prevent harvesting of young fish
- Building reservoirs and farm ponds, and stocking them with game fish
- Fertilizing nutrient-poor lakes and ponds
- Protecting and creating spawning sites and cover spaces
- Protecting habitats from buildup of sediment and other forms of pollution, and removing debris
- Preventing excessive growth of aquatic plants
- Using small dams to control water flow
- Controlling predators, parasites, and diseases by improving habitats, breeding genetically resistant fish varieties, and using antibiotics and disinfectants
- Using hatcheries to restock ponds, lakes, and streams with species such as trout and salmon

**MARINE FISHERY MANAGEMENT** By international law the offshore fishing zone of coastal countries extends to 370 kilometers (200 nautical miles or 230 statute miles) from their shores. Foreign fishing vessels can take certain quotas of fish within such zones, called **exclusive economic zones**, only with government permission. Ocean areas beyond the legal jurisdiction of any country are known as the **high seas**. Any limits on the use of the living and mineral common-property resources in these areas are set by international maritime law and international treaties.

Managers of marine fisheries use several techniques to help prevent commercial extinction and allow depleted stocks to recover. Fishery commissions, councils, and advisory bodies with representatives from countries using a fishery can set annual quotas and establish rules for dividing the allowable catch among the participating countries. These groups may limit fishing seasons and regulate the type of fishing gear that can be used to harvest a particular species; fishing techniques such as dynamiting and poisoning, for example, are outlawed. Fishery commissions may also make it illegal to keep fish below a certain size, usually the average length of the particular fish species when it first reproduces.

**Q:** How much of the world's electricity is supplied by hydropower?

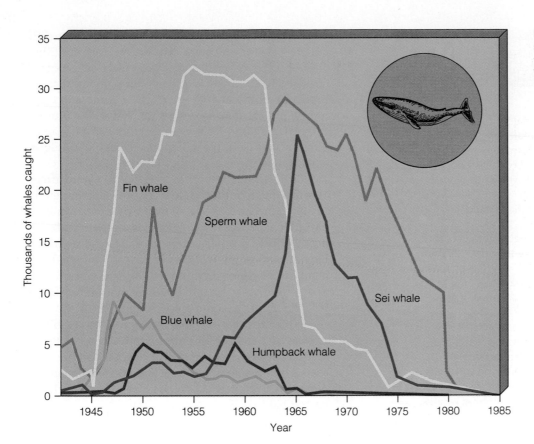

**Figure 16-34** Whale harvests, showing the signs of overharvesting. (Data from International Whaling Commission)

*Fin whale*

*Sperm whale*

*Blue whale*

*Humpback whale*

*Sei whale*

Thousands of whales caught

35 30 25 20 15 10 5 0

1945 1950 1955 1960 1965 1970 1975 1980 1985

Year

In addition, food and game fish species, such as the striped bass along the Pacific and Atlantic coasts of the United States, can be introduced. Finally, artificial reefs can be built from boulders, construction debris, and automobile tires to provide food and cover for commercial and game fish species. About 400 such reefs have been established off U.S. coasts, and Japan has set aside $1 billion to create 2,500 of them.

As voluntary associations, however, fishery commissions don't have any legal authority to compel member states to follow their rules. Nor can they compel all countries fishing in a region to join the commission and submit to its rules. Furthermore, it is difficult to estimate the sustainable yields of various marine species.

**DECLINE OF THE WHALING INDUSTRY** *Cetaceans* are an order of mammals ranging in size from the 0.9-meter (3-foot) porpoise to the giant 15- to 30-meter (50- to 100-foot) blue whale. They can be divided into two major groups: toothed cetaceans and baleen whales.

*Toothed cetaceans*, such as the porpoise, sperm whale, and killer whale, bite and chew their food. They feed mostly on squid, octopus, and other marine animals. *Baleen whales*, such as the blue, gray, humpback, and finback, are filter feeders. Instead of teeth they have several hundred horny plates made of baleen, or whalebone, which hang down from their upper jaw. These plates filter plankton, especially shrimplike krill (Figure 4-21) smaller than your thumb, from seawater. Baleen whales are the most abundant group of cetaceans.

In 1900 an estimated 4.4 million whales swam the ocean; today only about 1 million are left (Figure 16-33). Overharvesting has caused a sharp drop in the population of almost every whale species with commercial value (Figure 16-34) because whales are more vulnerable to biological extinction than are fish species. The populations of 8 of the 11 major species of whales once hunted by the whaling industry have been reduced to commercial extinction (Case Study, p. 444).

In 1946 the International Whaling Commission (IWC) was established to regulate the whaling industry. Since 1949 the IWC has set annual quotas to prevent overfishing and commercial extinction. However, these quotas often were based on inadequate scientific information or were ignored by whaling countries. Without any powers of enforcement the IWC has been unable to stop the decline of most whale species.

In 1970 the United States stopped all commercial whaling and banned all imports of whale products,

## Near Extinction of the Blue Whale

**CASE STUDY**

The blue whale is the world's largest animal. Fully grown it's more than 30 meters (100 feet) long—longer than three train boxcars—and weighs more than 25 adult elephants. The adult has a heart the size of a Volkswagen "Beetle" car, and some of its arteries are so big that a child could swim through them.

Blue whales spend about eight months of the year in Antarctic waters. There they find an abundant supply of shrimplike krill, which they filter daily by the trillions from seawater. During the winter months they migrate to warmer waters where their young are born.

Once an estimated 200,000 blue whales roamed the Antarctic Ocean. Today the species has been hunted to near biological extinction for its oil, meat, and bone (Figure 16-34). This decline was caused by a combination of prolonged overfishing and certain natural characteristics of blue whales. Their huge size made them easy to spot. They were caught in large numbers because they grouped together in their Antarctic feeding grounds. Also, they take 25 years to mature sexually and have only one offspring every 2–5 years—a reproduction rate that makes it hard for the species to recover once its population falls to a low level.

Blue whales haven't been hunted commercially since 1964 and have been classified as an endangered species since 1973. Despite this protection some marine experts believe that too few blue whales—perhaps less than 5,000—remain for the species to recover. Within a few decades the blue whale could disappear forever.

mostly because of pressure from environmentalists and the general public. Since then many environmental groups and governments have called for a permanent ban on all commercial whaling, leading the IWC to halt commercial whaling. Since 1986, however, Japan, Norway, and Iceland have been allowed to kill several hundred whales per year for "scientific" purposes. Environmentalists believe that killing whales for such purposes is a sham and that a total ban on whaling should be imposed and vigorously enforced. However, in 1992 four nations—Iceland, Norway, Greenland, and Denmark—quit the IWC and announced their intention to resume commercial whaling, with most of the meat sold to Japan.

**PROTECTING MARINE BIODIVERSITY** It is difficult to protect marine biodiversity. For one thing, shore-hugging species are adversely affected by coastal development and the accompanying massive inputs of sediment and other wastes from land (Case Study, p. 139). This poses a severe threat to biologically diverse and highly productive coastal ecosystems such as coral reefs (Figure 4-1), marshes (Figure 5-31), and mangrove swamps (Figure 5-33).

Protecting marine biodiversity is also difficult because much of the damage is not visible to people. In addition, the seas are viewed by many as an inexhaustible source of resources and as capable of absorbing an almost infinite amount of waste and pollution. Finally, most of the world's ocean area lies outside the legal jurisdiction of countries and thus is an open-access resource subject to overexploitation because of the tragedy of the commons (Spotlight, p. 14).

Protecting marine biodiversity requires countries to enact and enforce tough regulations to protect coral reefs, mangrove swamps, and other coastal ecosystems from unsustainable use and abuse. Also, much more effective international agreements are needed to protect biodiversity in the open seas.

## 16-8 Solutions: Individual Action

We are all involved, at least indirectly, in the destruction of wildlife any time we buy or drive a car, build a house, consume almost anything, and waste electricity, paper, water, or any other resource. All those activities contribute to the destruction or degradation of wildlife habitats or to the killing of one or more individuals of some plant or animal species.

Modifying our consumption habits is a key goal in protecting wildlife, the environment, and ourselves (Individuals Matter, p. 445). This also involves supporting efforts to reduce deforestation, projected global warming, ozone depletion, population growth, and poverty—the greatest threats to Earth's wildlife and to the human species.

During our short time on this planet we have gained immense power over what species—including our own—live or die. We named ourselves the wise (*sapiens*) species. In the next few decades we will learn whether we are indeed a wise species. If we eliminate ourselves and take millions of other species down with us, we will be mourned by no one, and what's left will go cycling on without us.

## What You Can Do to Protect Wildlife Resources and Preserve Biodiversity

**INDIVIDUALS MATTER**

- *Improve the habitat on a patch of the earth in your immediate environment, emphasizing the promotion of biological diversity.*

- *Refuse to buy furs, ivory products, reptile-skin goods, tortoiseshell jewelry, rare orchids or cacti, and endangered or threatened animal species.*

- *Leave wild animals in the wild.*

- *Consider reducing or eliminating your consumption of meat (especially beef) and not using leather.*

- *Refuse to buy canned tuna unless it is labeled as caught by dolphin-safe methods, and boycott all fish products caught using drift nets (Figure 14-16).*

- *Support efforts to ensure that test animals are treated humanely and that their use is reduced to a minimum.*

- *Have a pet dog or cat spayed or neutered. Each year U.S. pounds and animal shelters have to put to sleep about 15 million unwanted dogs and cats because of pet overpopulation.*

- *Learn about endangered species found in or near the area where you live, and work to ensure their protection and recovery.*

- *Reduce habitat destruction and degradation by recycling paper, cans, plastics, and other household items. Better yet, reuse items and sharply reduce your use of throw-away items.*

- *Support efforts to sharply reduce the destruction and degradation of tropical forests (Section 10-2) and old-growth forests (Section 10-5), slow global warming (Section 11-3), and reduce ozone depletion in the stratosphere (Section 11-5).*

- *Pressure elected officials to pass laws requiring larger fines and longer prison sentences for wildlife poachers and to provide more funds and personnel for wildlife protection.*

- *Pressure Congress to pass a national biodiversity act and to develop a national conservation program as part of the World Conservation Strategy.*

- *Encourage the development of an international treaty to preserve biodiversity.*

---

*A greening of the human mind must precede the greening of the Earth. A green mind is one that cares, saves, and shares. These are the qualities essential for conserving biological diversity now and forever.*

M. S. SWAMINATHAN

## Critical Thinking

1. Discuss your gut-level reaction to this statement: "It doesn't really matter that the passenger pigeon is extinct and that the blue whale, the whooping crane, the California condor, the rhinoceros, and the grizzly bear are endangered mostly because of human activities." Be honest about your reaction, and give arguments for your position.

2. Make a log of your own consumption and use of food and other products for a single day. Relate your consumption to the increased destruction of wildlife and wildlife habitats in the United States, in tropical forests, and in aquatic ecosystems.

3. **a.** Do you accept the ethical position that each *species* has the inherent right to survive without human interference, regardless of whether it serves any useful purpose for humans? Explain.
   **b.** Do you believe that each *individual* of an animal species has an inherent right to survive? Explain. Would you extend such rights to individual plants and microorganisms? Explain.

4. Do you believe that the use of animals to test new drugs and vaccines and the toxicity of chemicals should be banned? Explain. What are the alternatives? Should animals be used to test cosmetics?

5. Are you for or against sport hunting? Explain.

*6. Identify examples of habitat destruction or degradation in your local community that have had harmful effects on the populations of various wild plant and animal species. Develop a management plan for the rehabilitation of these habitats and wildlife.

# 17 Perpetual and Renewable Energy Resources

## Goodbye Oil and Smog, Hello Hydrogen

When oil is gone or what's left costs too much to use, what will fuel our vehicles, our industries, and our buildings? Science fiction writer Jules Verne told us as early as 1874, in *The Mysterious Island*. Chemist John Bockris of Texas A&M has been telling us for 30 years, and Joan Ogden and colleagues at Princeton's Center for Energy and Environmental Studies are telling us now. They say the fuel of the future is hydrogen gas ($H_2$).

We need to solve three big problems, however, to make hydrogen one of our primary energy resources. First, what is the best way to get it, because there is very little around? Many energy experts give the answer Jules Verne predicted, that it will come from something we have plenty of: water, split by electricity into gaseous hydrogen and oxygen (Figure 17-1).

The electricity to split water might come from coal-burning and nuclear power plants, but this subjects us to the harmful environmental effects associated with using these fuels (Chapter 18). According to Bockris, Ogden, and other visionaries, in the long run the energy to produce hydrogen must come from the sun. This means we have to develop solar-cell technology or solar energy concentrators to the point where the energy they produce can decompose water at an affordable cost. Japanese and German scientists are hard at work on this. American scientists are too, but they have been hampered by a 90% cut in federal research and development funds in this area since 1980.

The second problem is that it's difficult to store enough hydrogen gas in a car for it to run very far. One solution is to react the hydrogen with metals that release the gas when heated. Chemists are working to perfect this process. If they succeed, instead of pumping gas you'll drive up to a fuel station, pull out a metal rack, replace it with a new one charged with

**Figure 17-1** Crater Lake in Oregon. Hydrogen, the possible fuel of the future, can be made by passing electric current through one of Earth's most abundant resources: water. When burned in a car engine, furnace, or energy-efficient fuel cell (Figure 3-16), the byproduct is water vapor—thereby eliminating most of the world's air pollution problems.

Jack Carey

metallic hydrogen, and zoom away. We don't need to invent hydrogen-powered cars. Mercedes, BMW, and Mazda already have prototypes being tested on the roads. Hydrogen-powered submarines cruised the deep as early as 1988, and Mercedes hydrogen-powered buses could be on the streets of Hamburg, Germany, by 1997. Another solution is to burn hydrogen in energy-efficient fuel cells that produce electricity to run cars and heat buildings and water.

Designing the technology for hydrogen-fueled cars, factories, and home furnaces and appliances is the easy part. The biggest problem is economic and political. It involves figuring out how to replace an economy based largely on oil with entirely new production and distribution facilities and jobs. It means convincing investors and energy companies with strong vested interests in fossil and nuclear fuels that they should risk lots of capital on hydrogen.

If we can make the transition to an energy-efficient solar-hydrogen age, we can say goodbye to smog, oil spills, acid rain, and nuclear energy, and perhaps to the threat of global warming. The reason is simple. When hydrogen burns in air it reacts with oxygen gas to produce water vapor—not a bad thing to have coming out of our tailpipes, chimneys, and smokestacks. If clean solar-hydrogen technology comes on line soon enough, it could help heavily populated LDCs raise their living standards without severely disrupting Earth's life support systems.

Our choices at this point are crucial because it takes at least 50 years and huge investments to phase in new energy alternatives (Figure 3-8). The research and development and the economic rewards and penalties we provide today will determine the energy choices and levels of pollution and possible global warming we will have in 2045.

What is our best immediate energy option? Cutting energy waste by improving energy efficiency (Guest Essay, p. 71). What is our best long-term energy option? Some experts think it is hydrogen, along with energy from the sun, wind, flowing water, biomass, and heat stored in Earth's interior. These perpetual and renewable energy options are evaluated in this chapter. Others favor nonrenewable fossil fuels and nuclear power—options evaluated in the next chapter.

These are the questions answered in this chapter:

- How should we evaluate energy alternatives?
- What are the benefits and drawbacks of the following energy alternatives?
  a. Improving energy efficiency
  b. Using solar energy to heat buildings and water and to produce electricity
  c. Using flowing water and solar energy stored as heat in water to produce electricity
  d. Using wind to produce electricity
  e. Burning plants and organic waste (biomass) for heating buildings and water, for producing electricity, and for transportation (biofuels)
  f. Extracting heat from Earth's interior (geothermal energy)
  g. Producing hydrogen gas and using it to make electricity, heat buildings and water, and propel vehicles

## 17-1 Evaluating Energy Resources*

**QUESTIONS TO ASK** Because of the roughly 50 years to develop and phase in new energy resources on a large scale, we need to plan for the short term (1995–2005), the intermediate term (2005–2015), and the long term (2015–2045). First, we must decide how much we need, or want, of different kinds of energy, such as low- and high-temperature heat, electricity, and transport fuels. This involves finding the best type and quality of energy for each task (Figure 3-9). Then, we must factor in the cost and environmental impact of each source. This involves answering several questions for each energy alternative:

---

* I suggest that you review Sections 3-3, 3-6, 3-7, and 3-8 before studying this and the next chapter.

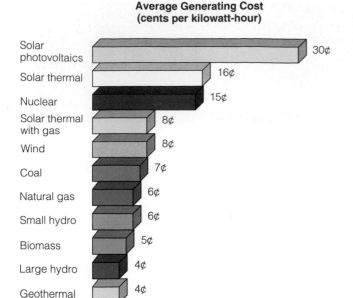

**Average Generating Cost
(cents per kilowatt-hour)**

| Technology | Cost |
|---|---|
| Solar photovoltaics | 30¢ |
| Solar thermal | 16¢ |
| Nuclear | 15¢ |
| Solar thermal with gas | 8¢ |
| Wind | 8¢ |
| Coal | 7¢ |
| Natural gas | 6¢ |
| Small hydro | 6¢ |
| Biomass | 5¢ |
| Large hydro | 4¢ |
| Geothermal | 4¢ |

**Figure 17-2** Generating costs of electricity per kilowatt-hour by various technologies in 1989. By 2000 costs per kilowatt-hour for wind are expected to fall to 5¢, solar thermal with gas assistance to 6¢, and solar photovoltaic to 10¢. Costs for other technologies are projected to remain about the same. (Data from U.S. Department of Energy, Council for Renewable Energy Education, and Investor Responsibility Research Center)

- How much will be available during the short, intermediate, and long term?

- What is the net useful energy yield (Figure 3-19)?

- How much will it cost to develop, phase in, and use?

- How will using it affect the environment?

The key question decision makers and individuals should ask is *What energy choices will do the most to sustain the earth for us, for future generations, and for the other species living on this planet?* Getting government officials, energy company executives, and ordinary people to consider this ethical question is probably the most difficult challenge we face.

**THE SOLAR AGE: BUILDING A SOLAR ECONOMY**
Potentially the largest sources of energy worldwide are perpetual and renewable energy from the sun, wind, flowing water, biomass, and Earth's internal heat. Such energy resources—primarily hydropower and biomass—already supply 17% of the world's energy and 9% of the energy used in the United States (Figure 3-7). About 92% of the known reserves and potentially available energy resources in the United States are perpetual and renewable. The other 8% of potentially available domestic energy resources are coal (5%), oil (2.5%), and uranium (0.5%). Developing these mostly untapped resources could meet 50–80%

of projected U.S. energy needs by 2030 or sooner, and virtually all energy needs if coupled with improvements in energy efficiency.

Such development would save money, create jobs, eliminate the need for oil imports, cause less pollution and environmental damage per unit of energy used, and increase economic, environmental, and military security. In the United States geothermal power plants, wood-fired (biomass) power plants, hydropower plants, wind farms, and solar thermal power plants can produce electricity more cheaply than can new nuclear power plants, and with far fewer federal subsidies (Figure 17-2). According to the Minnesota Department of Energy each dollar spent on renewable energy generates $2.33–$2.92 worth of local economic activity versus only 64¢ for imported oil.

With an aggressive development program, perpetual and renewable energy resources could meet 50–80% of the world's projected energy demand by 2030 or sooner and cut greenhouse gas emissions enough to stabilize projected climate changes. The use of these—or any energy resources—however, must be coupled with improving energy efficiency.

**17-2  Solutions: Improving Energy Efficiency**

**DOING MORE WITH LESS** The easiest, fastest, and cheapest way to get more energy with the least environmental impact is to cut energy waste (Figure 3-15). There are two general ways to achieve this goal:

- *Reduce energy consumption.* Examples include walking or biking for short trips, using mass transit, putting on a sweater instead of turning up the thermostat, and turning off unneeded lights.

- *Improve energy efficiency.* Examples of doing more with less include insulating houses and buildings, tuning car engines, and switching to, or developing, more energy-efficient cars, houses, heating and cooling systems, appliances, lights, and industrial processes (Figure 3-16).

Reducing energy use and waste would make nonrenewable fossil fuels last longer, buying time to phase in perpetual and renewable energy resources. It would also ease international tensions and improve national and global military and economic security; it would decrease dependence on oil imports (almost 50% in the United States) and lessen the need for military intervention in the oil-rich but politically unstable Middle East.

Q: What is the most promising fuel for replacing oil and other fossil fuels?

**Table 17-1 Energy Use and Conservation in the United States and Sweden**

| Use or Method | United States | Sweden |
|---|---|---|
| Per capita use | 230,000 kcal/day | 150,000 kcal/day |
| Perpetual and renewable sources | 9% | 27% |
| Transportation | High | One-fourth of United States |
|   Country size | Large | Small |
|   Cities | Dispersed | Compact |
|   Mass transit use | Low | High |
|   Average car fuel economy | Poor | Good |
|   Gasoline taxes | Low | High |
|   Tariffs on oil imports | Low | High |
| Industrial energy efficiency | Fairly low | High |
| Nationwide energy-efficiency building codes | No | Yes |
| Municipally owned district heating systems | None | 30% of population |
| Emphasis on electricity for space heating | High (half of new homes) | High (half of new homes) |
| Domestic hot water | Most kept hot 24 hours per day in large tanks | Most supplied as needed by instant tankless heaters |
| Refrigerators | Mostly large, frost-free | Mostly smaller, non-frost-free, using about one-third the electricity of U.S. models |
| Long-range national energy plan | No | Yes |
| Government emphasis and expenditures on energy efficiency and renewable energy | Low | High |
| Government emphasis and expenditures on nuclear power | High | Low (to be phased out) |

Improving energy efficiency would reduce environmental damage because less of each energy resource would provide the same amount of useful energy. Also, it would add no carbon dioxide to the atmosphere and would be the cheapest and quickest way to slow projected global warming (Solutions, p. 300) and remove the need for nuclear power. It would not mean freezing in the dark or having to drive small, unsafe vehicles.

Using energy more efficiently would also save money, provide more jobs, and promote more economic growth per unit of energy than do other alternatives. According to Amory Lovins (Guest Essay, p. 71), cumulative savings from improvements in energy efficiency since the first Arab oil embargo in 1973 total nearly $1 trillion. *If the world really got serious about improving energy efficiency, we could save $1 trillion per year—about 5% of the gross global product.*

The United States wastes as much energy as two-thirds of the world's population consumes. The largest and cheapest untapped supplies of energy in the United States are not in Alaska or offshore reserves but in energy-wasting buildings, factories, and vehicles.

Lovins also argues that by using existing technology the U.S. economy could run on one-fourth as much energy as it now uses. The necessary $50-billion-per-year investment would yield a net savings of at least $200 billion per year. This investment would also create many jobs, lower production costs, and make the United States more competitive in the international marketplace. Currently the United States spends about 11% of its GNP on energy, while Japan spends only 5%. That gives Japanese goods an automatic 6% cost advantage.

Japan, Sweden, and most industrialized western European countries use an average of one-third to two-thirds less energy per person than Americans (Table 17-1). One reason for the difference is that those countries place greater emphasis on improving energy efficiency than the United States does. Another is that most cities in those countries are more compact and closer together than U.S. cities. If the United States were as energy efficient as Japan, France, or Sweden, it would need no imported oil.

Why isn't the United States in hot pursuit of improving energy efficiency? There are several reasons. One is the political influence of oil, coal, nuclear

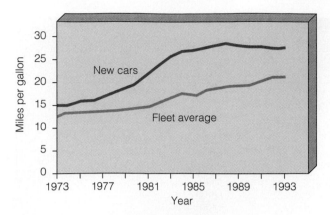

**Figure 17-3** Average fuel efficiency in new cars and all cars in the United States between 1973 and 1992. (Data from U.S. Department of Energy and Environmental Protection Agency)

power, and automobile companies with their emphasis on short-term profits regardless of the long-term economic and environmental consequences. Other reasons include a glut of low-cost fossil fuels, the failure of elected officials to require that external costs of using fossil and nuclear fuels be included in their market prices, and sharp cutbacks in federal support since 1980 for improvements in energy efficiency and development of perpetual and renewable resources.

Consumers must also learn to evaluate the true costs of homes, cars, and appliances using life-cycle costs instead of the initial purchase price:

$$\frac{\text{life-cycle}}{\text{cost}} = \frac{\text{purchase}}{\text{price}} + \left( \frac{\text{yearly}}{\text{energy cost}} \times \text{lifetime} \right)$$

Basing purchases on life-cycle costs not only saves money but helps sustain the earth.

**INDUSTRY** Industrial processes consume 36% of the energy used in the United States. Even though U.S. industry currently uses 70% as much energy to produce the same amount of goods as in 1973, it still wastes enormous amounts. Furthermore, since 1986 overall U.S. industrial energy efficiency has scarcely improved. Japan has the world's highest overall industrial energy efficiency, followed closely by the former West Germany and by Sweden (Table 17-1).

Industries that use enough high-temperature heat or steam and electricity could save energy and money by installing *cogeneration units*, already widely used in western Europe. These units recover about two-thirds of the energy wasted in a conventional boiler and use it to produce both heat and electricity. By 2000 cogeneration could produce more electricity than all the U.S. nuclear power plants, and do it much more cheaply. Cogeneration could also supply energy for local heating and cooling systems by piping hot or chilled water or steam to nearby buildings as is done in Sweden and

Denmark. In Germany new micro-cogeneration units allow restaurants, apartment buildings, and other buildings to produce their own electric power.

About 60–70% of the electricity used in U.S. industry drives electric motors. Most of them run at full speed with their output "throttled" to match their task—somewhat like driving with the gas pedal to the floor and using the brake to slow the car down. Each year a heavily used electric motor consumes 10 times its purchase cost in electricity—the equivalent of using $120,000 worth of gasoline each year to fuel a $12,000 car. According to Amory Lovins it would be cost-effective to scrap virtually all such motors and replace them with adjustable-speed drives. Within a year the costs would be paid back.

Switching to high-efficiency lighting would be another energy saver for industry. Industries could also use computer-controlled energy management systems to turn off lighting and equipment in nonproduction areas and to make adjustments during periods of low production.

Yet another way to save energy in industry would be to increase recycling and reuse and to make products that last longer and are easy to repair and recycle (Section 19-4). Despite the potential energy savings, federal support for research and development in industrial energy efficiency was cut nearly 60% between 1981 and 1992.

**TRANSPORTATION** One-fourth of the commercial energy consumed in the United States is used to move people and goods. Americans have 35% of the world's cars and drive about as far each year as the rest of the world's motorists combined. About one-tenth of the oil consumed in the world carries U.S. motorists to and from work, 75% of them driving alone.

Today transportation consumes 65% of all oil used in the United States—up from 50% in 1973. Burning gasoline and other transportation fuels accounts for about 33–35% of total U.S. emissions of carbon dioxide, while leaking vehicle air conditioners put out 75% of chlorofluorocarbon emissions. Thus the best ways to cut world oil consumption, slow ozone depletion in the stratosphere, slow projected global warming, and reduce air pollution would be to improve the fuel efficiency of vehicles (Figure 17-3), ride mass transit more often (Figure 17-4), and haul freight more efficiently.

An estimated 10–20% of the travel for commuting, business trips, and shopping in the United States could be eliminated by telecommunications. Fax messages reduce the need for overnight delivery services. Some state governments and private companies are encouraging a transition to increased use of the "electronic home office." Energy and time can also be saved by increased use of computerized home delivery services that allow people to shop from the home.

Q: How long will the world's oil reserves last at the current consumption rate?

Between 1973 and 1985 the average fuel efficiency doubled for new American cars, and rose 54% for all cars on the road (Figure 17-3). The modest $200–$400 added to the price of the average car was more than offset by savings at the gas pump. These improvements now save American consumers about 5 million barrels of oil per day and nearly $40 billion per year, but existing technology could save considerably more. The entire U.S. car fleet averaged 8.5 kilometers per liter (kpl), or 20 miles per gallon (mpg), in 1992, compared to 16 kpl (37 mpg) in Italy—with a gasoline tax of 95¢ per liter ($3.58 per gallon) to encourage fuel efficiency. Moreover, since 1987, U.S. fuel efficiency has declined for new cars because Congress relaxed fuel standards (Figure 17-3).

According to the U.S. Office of Technology Assessment new U.S. cars—which averaged 12 kpl (27.5 mpg) in 1992—could easily average 15 kpl (35 mpg) by 2001 and 19 kpl (45 mpg) or higher by 2010. New light trucks—pickups, minivans, and four-wheel-drive sport vehicles—could go from 8.5 kpl (20 mpg) to 14 kpl (33 mpg) within 10 years.

Improvements such as more efficient engines and more lightweight materials would raise the fuel efficiency of the U.S. automotive fleet to 15 kpl (35 mpg) by 2000, eliminate oil imports, and save more than $50 billion per year in fuel costs. Buyers of fuel-efficient cars would get back any extra purchase costs—probably about $500 per car—in fuel savings in about a year. From then on they would be saving money on fuel. According to a 1991 poll 80% of Americans favored raising the average fuel economy for new automobiles to 19 kpl (45 mpg) by 2000, but Congress—under pressure from the president and automobile and energy companies—was unwilling to do this.

In 1992 U.S. consumers could buy Chevrolet's Geo Metro XFi (built by Suzuki), which has a fuel efficiency of 25/22 kpl (58/53 mpg) for highway/city driving, and the Honda Civic Hatchback VX with a fuel efficiency of 23/20 kpl (55/48 mpg). In fact, the technology has existed since the mid-1980s to build even more fuel-efficient cars (Solutions, p. 452).

Electric cars might help reduce dependence on oil, especially for urban commuting and short trips. All major U.S. car companies have prototype electric cars and minivans, some available by 1995. They are extremely quiet, need little maintenance, and produce no air pollution, except indirectly from the generation of the electricity needed to recharge their batteries. If solar cells could be used for recharging, this environmental impact would be eliminated. Another possibility is to produce electricity to power the car using fuel cells powered by solar-produced hydrogen (p. 446).

On the negative side the batteries in current electric cars have to be replaced about every 40,000 kilometers (25,000 miles) at a cost of about $1,500. This

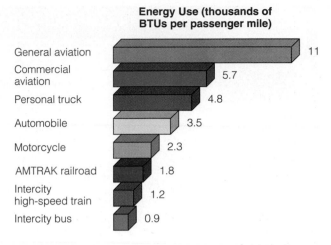

**Energy Use (thousands of BTUs per passenger mile)**

| Type | BTUs |
| --- | --- |
| General aviation | 11 |
| Commercial aviation | 5.7 |
| Personal truck | 4.8 |
| Automobile | 3.5 |
| Motorcycle | 2.3 |
| AMTRAK railroad | 1.8 |
| Intercity high-speed train | 1.2 |
| Intercity bus | 0.9 |

**Figure 17-4** Energy efficiency of various types of domestic passenger transportation.

requirement, and the electricity costs for daily recharging, mean double the operating cost of gasoline-powered cars. If longer-lasting batteries that hold a higher charge density and last 160,000 kilometers (100,000 miles) can be developed, operating costs would be reduced and performance would increase.

Another way to stretch the world's shrinking oil supply would be to shift more freight from trucks and planes to trains and ships. Currently trucks burn 59% of the energy used to move freight in the United States. General Motors has developed a new truck trailer that converts to a railcar without unloading. This truck–rail combination would use 80% less fuel than trucks alone for hauls of more than 322 kilometers (200 miles).

Manufacturers could also raise the fuel efficiency of new transport trucks 50% with improved aerodynamic design, turbocharged diesel engines, and radial tires. And truck companies could slash energy waste and increase income by not letting trucks come back empty from their destination.

With regard to planes and ships Boeing's new 777 jet will use about half the fuel per passenger seat of a 727. Existing advanced diesel engine technology could improve the fuel efficiency of ships by 30–40% over the next few decades.

**BUILDINGS** Sweden and South Korea have the world's toughest standards for energy efficiency in homes and other buildings. The average Swedish home consumes about one-third as much energy as an average American home of the same size. Indeed, many homes in the United States are so full of leaks that their heat loss in cold weather and heat gain in hot weather is equivalent to having a large, window-sized hole in the wall of the house.

A: 42 years (undiscovered oil might add another 40 years)

Fuel-efficient cars will take decades to develop, and will be sluggish, small, and unsafe. Wrong! Since 1985 at least 10 companies, including Volvo, Volkswagen, Renault, Peugeot, Honda, Mazda, Toyota, and General Motors, have had peppy prototype cars that meet or exceed current safety and pollution standards, with fuel efficiencies of 29–59 kpl (67–138 mpg). If they were mass-produced, their slightly higher costs would be more than offset by their fuel savings.

One such ecocar is Volvo's LCP 2000 (Figure 17-5), which would be in production today if the consumer demand were there. Its super-charged diesel engine averages 35 kpl (81 mpg) on the highway and 27 kpl (62 mpg) in the city. Using better design and lighter but stronger

materials (magnesium, aluminum, and plastics), it exceeds U.S. crash standards. It carries four passengers in comfort and quiet, resists corrosion better than most of today's cars, and accelerates from 0 to 97 kilometers per hour (kph), or 0 to 60 miles per hour (mph), in 11 seconds—better than average.

This car also meets California's air pollution emission standards—the tightest in the world. Over its lifetime the LCP 2000 would use about half the energy of a conventional car its size. It can run on several different fuels, including diesel fuel and vegetable oil. The Volvo LCP 2000 is also designed for easy assembly and for recycling of its materials when it is taken off the road.

Another ecocar is General Motors' sleek, roomy, four-passenger Ultralite car (Figure 17-6). This pro-

totype gets 36/19 kpl (85/45 mpg) using off-the-shelf technology. What's more, the Ultralite zooms from 0 to 97 kph (0 to 60 mph) in 7.8 seconds, has a 217-kph (135-mph) top speed, and is equipped with four air bags. Its body is made from lightweight carbon-fiber composites that won't dent, scratch, or corrode. The car's 3-cylinder, 2-stroke engine is much more efficient than conventional 4-stroke engines. Furthermore, with 200 fewer parts than a conventional engine, it costs about $400 less to make and saves consumers in maintenance expenses.

We can have roomy, peppy, safe, gas sippers, but only if consumers begin demanding them and buying them. In 1992 there were more than 25 car models on the market with fuel efficiencies of at least 17 kpl (40 mpg), but they made up only 5% of U.S. car sales.

**Figure 17-5** Volvo's LCP 2000 prototype car. Developed in 1985, this gas-sipping vehicle can run on various fuels, including diesel, a diesel–gasoline mixture, and vegetable oil—which means the driver could carry a bottle of vegetable oil along as an emergency source of fuel.

**Figure 17-6** Ultralite concept car built by General Motors. It is fast and much safer than existing cars, and when driven at 81 kph (50 mph) gets 43 kpl (100 mpg).

The 110-story, twin-towered World Trade Center in Manhattan is a monument to energy waste. It uses as much electricity as a city of 100,000 people for about 53,000 employees. Since its windows don't open to take advantage of natural warming and cooling, its heating and cooling systems must run around the clock.

By contrast, Atlanta's 17-story Georgia Power Company building uses 60% less energy than conventional office buildings. The largest surface of the

building faces south to capture solar energy. Each floor extends over the one below, which blocks out the higher summer sun to cut air conditioning costs but allows warming by the low winter sun. Energy-efficient lights focus on desks rather than illuminating entire rooms. Employees working during nonbusiness hours use an adjoining three-story building so the larger structure doesn't have to be heated or cooled just for them. The Georgia Power model and other

Q: How long could *all* known and projected U.S. oil deposits supply the world and the U.S. at current consumption?

## Houses That Save Money and Energy

Energy experts Amory and Hunter Lovins have built a large passively heated, superinsulated, partially earth-sheltered home in Old Snowmass, Colorado, where winter temperatures can drop to –40°C (–40°F) (Figure 17-7). This structure, which also houses the research center for the Rocky Mountain Institute—an office used by 40 people—gets 99% of its space and water heating and 95% of its daytime lighting (through superwindows) from the sun. It uses one-tenth the usual amount of electricity and less than half the usual amount of water for a structure of its size. Total energy savings repaid the cost of its energy-saving features after 10 months and are projected to pay for the entire facility in 40 years.

In energy-efficient houses of the near future, microprocessors will monitor indoor temperatures, sunlight angles, and people's location, and send heat or cooled air where it is needed. Windows and insulated shutters will automatically open and close to take advantage of solar energy and breezes as well as reduce heat loss from windows at night and on cloudy days. Sensors will turn off lights in unoccupied rooms or dim lights when sunlight is available.

Researchers have developed "smart windows" that change electronically from clear, which lets sunlight and heat in on cold days, to reflective, which deflects sunlight when the house gets too warm. Superinsulating windows (R-8 to R-10), already here, mean that a house can have as many windows as the owner wants in any climate without much heat loss. And improved superinsulating windows (R-12 or better) should soon be available. Thinner insulation material will allow roofs to be insulated to R-100 and walls to R-43, far better than in today's best superinsulated houses.

Small-scale cogeneration units that run on natural gas or liquefied petroleum gas (LPG), and that can supply a home with all its space heat, hot water, and electricity needs, are already available. The units are no larger than a refrigerator and make less noise than a dishwasher. Except for an occasional change of filters and spark plugs, they are nearly maintenance-free. Typically this home power and heating plant pays for itself in four to five years.

Soon homeowners may be able to get all the electricity they need from rolls of solar cells attached like shingles to a roof or applied to window glass as a coating. Such cells have already been developed by Japanese and German firms. In addition, the Bomin company of Germany has developed a solar-powered hydrogen system that can meet all the energy needs of a home, an apartment building, or a small village or housing development at an affordable price. A windproof panel of solar collectors automatically tracks the sun, concentrating sunlight at a fixed focus to temperatures as high as 500°C (932°F). The collected heat is stored in metal powders (hydrides) that release hydrogen gas, which burns cleanly to provide energy for cooking, lighting, heating, and cooling. This system has an energy efficiency greater than that of electric power plants.

In 1989 Albers Technologies Corporation of Arizona patented a home air conditioner that uses water, not CFCs or HCFCs, as a coolant, draws half the electricity of a conventional unit, and costs about the same as conventional models with the same cooling capacity.

**Figure 17-7** The Rocky Mountain Institute in Colorado. This facility is a center for the study of energy efficiency and sustainable use of other energy sources. It is also an example of energy-efficient passive solar design.

existing cost-effective technologies could double the energy efficiency of U.S. buildings by 2010, cut carbon emissions in half, and save $100 billion per year (Solutions, above).

Building a **superinsulated house** can improve the efficiency of residential space heating and cooling by more than 75%, and save on lifetime energy costs (Figure 17-8). Such a house is heavily insulated and nearly

A: 1.7 years for the world, 10 years for the United States

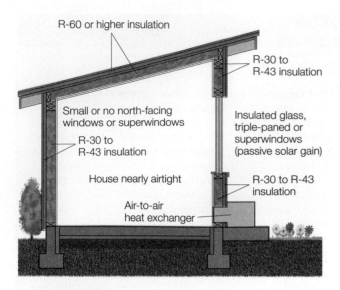

**Figure 17-8** Major features of a superinsulated house.

airtight. Heat from direct solar gain, appliances, and human bodies warms the house, which requires little or no auxiliary heating. An air-to-air heat exchanger prevents buildup of indoor air pollution.

To keep prices low for buyers, builders often skimp on energy-saving features. When lifetime costs are considered, however, these energy-inefficient houses cost owners 40–50% more. A superinsulated house costs about 5% more to build than a conventional house, but this extra cost is paid back by energy savings within five years and can save a homeowner $50,000–$100,000 over 40 years. Sadly less than 1% of new homes in the United States are superinsulated, mostly because of a lack of consumer demand. Moreover, builders and owners of rental housing have little incentive to make their units energy efficient when renters pay the utility bills.

Setting higher energy-efficiency standards and requiring a building's estimated annual and lifetime energy consumption to be revealed to buyers would help correct these problems. Rebates for buying high-efficiency appliances and houses (and cars), lower hookup fees for gas or electric service, and lower electricity rates for energy-efficient buildings would also help.

Many energy-saving features can be added to existing homes, a process called *retrofitting*. Simply increasing insulation above ceilings can reduce heating and cooling loads. The homeowner usually recovers initial costs in two to six years and thereafter saves money each year. Caulking and weatherstripping around windows, doors, pipes, vents, ducts, and wires also save energy and money. Environmentalists urge that all existing public buildings in the United States be retrofitted to improve energy efficiency and

that all new public buildings be required to meet high energy-efficiency standards.

One-third of the heat in U.S. homes and buildings escapes through closed windows—equal to the energy in all the oil flowing through the Alaskan pipeline every year. During hot weather these windows also let heat in, increasing the use of air conditioning. A single-pane glass window has an insulating value of only R-1. (The R-value of a material is its resistance to heat flow.)

Even double-glazed windows have an insulating value of only R-2, and triple-glazed only R-4 to R-6. Two U.S. firms and a Canadian firm now sell "superinsulating" R-8 to R-10 windows (a normal outside wall has an insulating value of about R-11), which pay for themselves in lower fuel bills within two to four years and then save money every year thereafter. Insulating curtains or quilts are also available that can be used to retrofit existing windows with R-values of 4–5.

Building codes could be changed to require that all new houses use 80% less energy than conventional houses of the same size, as has been done in Davis, California (p. 228). Finally, laws could require that existing houses be insulated and weatherproofed to certain standards before being sold, as required in Portland, Oregon, for example.

**LIGHTS AND APPLIANCES** Using the most energy-efficient lights (Solutions, p. 455) and appliances available would also save energy and money.* Similarly, if the most energy-efficient appliances now available were installed in all U.S. homes over the next 20 years, the energy savings would equal the estimated energy content of Alaska's entire North Slope oil fields. Currently home refrigerators consume about 7% of the electricity used in the United States. If all U.S. households used the most efficient frost-free refrigerator now available, eighteen 1,000-megawatt power plants could be shut down. The SunFrost refrigerator, for example, which costs $2,400, uses 85% less electricity than the average model. By spending $1,000 more on such a refrigerator, a consumer saves about $2,550 in life-cycle costs. Meanwhile, consumers can reduce the energy use of an existing refrigerator by taping about $25 worth of foil-faced rigid insulation on the outside of its sides and doors; the payback time for this would be about one year.

---

*Each year the American Council for an Energy-Efficient Economy (ACEEE) publishes a list of the most energy-efficient major appliances mass produced for the U.S. market. To obtain a copy send $3 to the council at 1001 Connecticut Ave. N.W., Suite 530, Washington, DC 20036. Each year they also publish *A Consumer Guide to Home Energy Savings*, available in bookstores or from the ACEEE for $8.95.

Q: How much new oil must be discovered and developed to continue using oil at the current rate?

SOLUTIONS

One-fourth of the electricity produced in the United States goes for lighting. Since conventional incandescent bulbs are only 5% efficient and last only 750–1,500 hours, they waste enormous amounts of energy and money, and add to the heat load of houses during hot weather (Figure 17-9). About half the air conditioning in a typical U.S. office building is used to remove the internal heat gain from inefficient lighting.

Socket-type fluorescent light and new E-lamp (electronic lamp) bulbs that use one-fourth as much electricity as conventional bulbs are now available. Although they cost about $10–$20 per bulb, they last 10–20 times longer than conventional incandescent bulbs and save three times their cost over their long life (Figure 17-9). For example, replacing a 75-watt incandescent bulb with an 18-watt compact fluorescent or E-lamp bulb cuts electricity consumption by 75%. Students in Brown University's environmental studies program showed that the school could save more than $40,000 per year just by replacing the incan-

descent light bulbs in exit signs with fluorescents.

E-lamp bulbs, available in 1995, use high-frequency radio waves to generate electricity. They last even longer than compact fluorescent bulbs because there is no electrode to burn out. Furthermore, they are smaller than compact fluorescents, making them usable in existing light fixtures, and unlike compact fluorescents work with a dimmer switch.

Efficient lighting could save U.S. businesses $15–20 billion per year in electricity bills. In 1991 the EPA launched Green Lights, a voluntary program to encourage corporations, government agencies, colleges, hospitals, and other institutions to install energy-efficient lighting. The Boeing Corporation in Seattle found it could save $1 million per year, and Columbia University is saving $2 million per year.

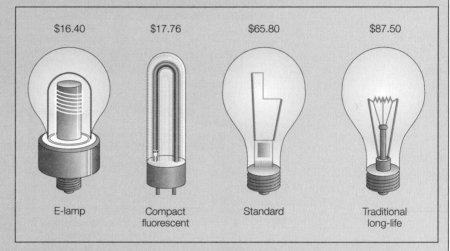

| $16.40 | $17.76 | $65.80 | $87.50 |

| E-lamp | Compact fluorescent | Standard | Traditional long-life |

**Figure 17-9** Cost of electricity for comparable light bulbs used for 10,000 hours. (Data from Electric Power Research Institute)

Similar savings are possible with high-efficiency stoves, water heaters, air conditioners, and clothes dryers. Microwave ovens can cut electricity use for cooking by 25–50% (but not if used for defrosting food). New microwave clothes dryers being developed use 15% less energy than conventional electric dryers and 28% less energy than gas units, while virtually eliminating wrinkles. Dryers with moisture sensors cut energy use by 15%. Front-loading washers use 50% less energy than top-loading models and cost no more.

Department of Energy 1990 standards for major household appliances should save consumers roughly $40 billion by 2015 and eliminate the need for eight large power plants. Such standards, however, need to be upgraded every two or three years to reflect advances in technology. They also need to be developed for lighting, windows, and plumbing fixtures.

**Solutions: Direct Solar Energy for Heat and Electricity**

17-3

**HEATING SPACE AND WATER** Buildings and water can be heated by solar energy using two methods: passive and active. A **passive solar heating system** captures sunlight directly within a structure and converts it into low-temperature heat for space heating (Figure 17-10). Superwindows, greenhouses, and sunspaces face the sun to collect solar energy by direct gain. Thermal mass (heat-storing capacity)—such as walls and floors of concrete, adobe, brick, stone, salt-treated timber, or tile—stores collected solar energy as heat and releases it slowly throughout the day and night. Some systems also store heat in water-filled glass or plastic

**Figure 17-10** Three examples of passive solar design.

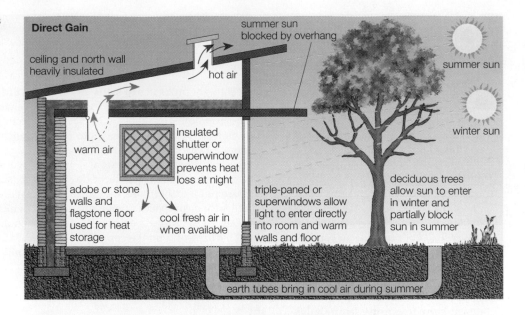

**Direct Gain**

ceiling and north wall heavily insulated

summer sun blocked by overhang

hot air

warm air

insulated shutter or superwindow prevents heat loss at night

adobe or stone walls and flagstone floor used for heat storage

cool fresh air in when available

triple-paned or superwindows allow light to enter directly into room and warm walls and floor

summer sun

winter sun

deciduous trees allow sun to enter in winter and partially block sun in summer

earth tubes bring in cool air during summer

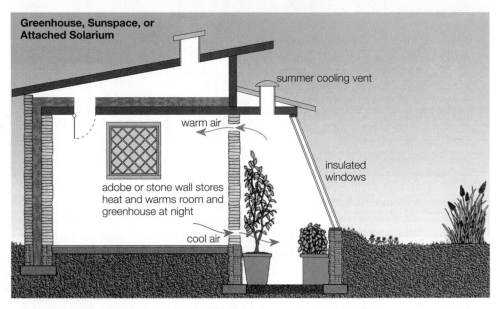

**Greenhouse, Sunspace, or Attached Solarium**

summer cooling vent

warm air

insulated windows

adobe or stone wall stores heat and warms room and greenhouse at night

cool air

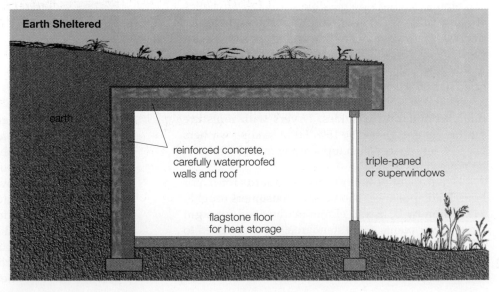

**Earth Sheltered**

earth

reinforced concrete, carefully waterproofed walls and roof

triple-paned or superwindows

flagstone floor for heat storage

Q: What would happen if the harmful effects of using oil were included in its market price and government subsidies were removed?

**Figure 17-11** Earth-sheltered houses, such as this one in Colorado, can look like any ordinary house inside. Passive solar design and skylights admit more daylight than most conventional houses (Figure 11-1). On a life-cycle cost basis, earth-sheltered houses are cheaper than conventional aboveground houses of the same size because of lower heating and cooling costs, no exterior maintenance or painting, and lower fire insurance rates. These structures also provide more privacy, quiet, and security from break-ins, fires, earthquakes, hurricanes, tornadoes, and ordinary storms.

columns, black-painted barrels filled with water, and panels or cabinets containing heat-absorbing chemicals.

Buildup of moisture and indoor air pollutants is minimized by an air-to-air heat exchanger, which supplies fresh air without much heat loss or gain. A small backup heating system may be used but is not necessary in most climates.

Today over 250,000 homes and 17,000 nonresidential buildings in the United States, including earth-sheltered homes (Figures 11-1, 17-10, and 17-11), have passive solar designs. However, that is a small fraction of the 80 million U.S. homes.

With available or developing technologies, passive solar designs can provide at least 80% of a building's heating needs and at least 60% of its cooling needs (Solutions, pp. 453 and 458).

Roof-mounted passive solar water heaters can supply all or most of the hot water for a typical house

### Passive Solar Water Heating System

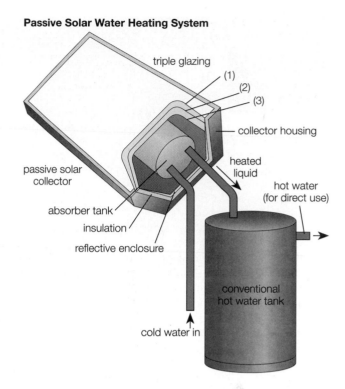

### Active Solar Water Heating System

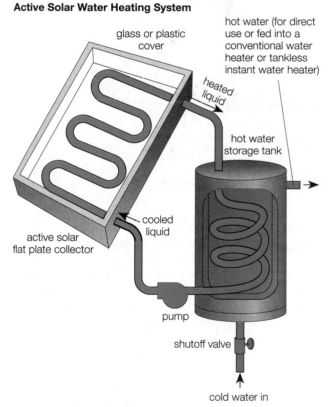

**Figure 17-12** Passive and active solar water heaters.

(Figure 17-12). A particularly promising model, called the Copper Cricket, sells for $2,200. Inexpensive passive solar cookers are used in an increasing number of rural villages in LDCs.

A: It would be too expensive to use and would be phased out.

Engineer and builder Michael Sykes has designed a solar envelope house that is heated and cooled passively by solar energy and the slow storage and release of energy by massive timbers and the earth beneath the house (Figure 17-13). The front and back sides of this house are double walls of heavy timber impregnated with salt to increase the ability of the wood to store heat. The space between these two walls, plus the basement, forms a convection loop or envelope around the inner shell of the house.

Solar energy enters through windows or a greenhouse on the side of the house facing the sun, circulates around the loop, is stored in the heavy timber, and is released slowly during the day and at night. In summer roof vents release heated air from the convection loop throughout the day. At night these roof vents, with the aid of a fan, draw air into the loop, which passively cools the house.

The interior temperature of the house typically stays within 2° of 21°C (70°F) year-round, without any conventional cooling or heating system. In cold or cloudy climates a small wood stove or vented natural gas heater in the basement can be used as a backup to heat the air in the convection loop.

Timber kits are available for sale so that people can construct their own solar envelope houses. Because of the extra timber involved, initial costs are higher than for conventional houses. However, they are recovered severalfold by not having the initial cost and lifetime bills of a conventional heating and cooling system. Furthermore, all timber comes precut, which enables quick assembly. Buyers can save money by erecting the inner and outer shells themselves, which requires little experience and few tools. And Sykes plants 50 trees for each one used in providing builders with his timber kits.

For his Enertia design he has received both the Department of Energy's Innovation Award and the North Carolina Governor's Energy Achievement Award.

**Figure 17-13** Solar envelope house that is heated and cooled passively by solar energy and Earth's thermal energy. This patented Enertia design needs no conventional heating or cooling system in most areas. It comes in a precut kit engineered and tailored to the buyer's design goals.

Enertia Building Systems, Inc. Rte. 1, Box 67, Wake Forest, NC, 27587

In hot weather, passive cooling can be provided by blocking the high summer sun with deciduous trees, window overhangs, or awnings (Figure 17-10). For example, one large tree has the cooling power of five average air conditioners running 20 hours per day. Also, windows and fans take advantage of breezes and keep air moving, and a reflective insulating foil sheet suspended in the attic will block heat from radiating down into the house.

At a depth of 3–6 meters (10–20 feet) the soil temperature stays at about 5–13°C (41–55°F) all year long in cold northern climates and about 19°C (67°F) in warm southern climates. Earth tubes—simple plastic (PVC) plumbing pipes with a diameter of 10–15 cen-

Q: Who has the world's largest reserves of natural gas?

timeters (4–6 inches)—buried at this depth can pipe cool and partially dehumidified air into an energy-efficient house at a cost of a few dollars per summer (Figure 17-10). Four to five of these pipes are buried about 0.3–0.6 meter (1–2 feet) apart to create a low-tech geothermal cooling field. The pipes run under the house into a distribution box connected to the structure's conventional heating and cooling duct system.

For a large space two or three of these geothermal cooling fields running in different directions from the house can be installed. When heat degrades the cooling effect from one field, homeowners can switch to another. During cold months these geothermal cooling fields are renewed naturally for use during the summer. Initial construction costs (mostly for digging) are high, but operating and maintenance costs are extremely low. People allergic to pollen and molds should add an air purification system, but they would also need to do that with a conventional cooling system.

Solar-powered air conditioners have been developed but thus far are too expensive for residential use. In Reno, Nevada, however, some buildings are kept cool throughout the hot summer through the use of large, insulated tanks of water chilled by cool nighttime air that keep indoor temperatures comfortable during the day.

In an **active solar heating system**, specially designed collectors absorb solar energy, with a fan or a pump used to supply part of a building's space-heating or water-heating needs. Several connected collectors are usually mounted on a roof with an unobstructed exposure to the sun (Figure 17-12).

Active solar collectors can also supply hot water. Over 1.3 million active solar hot-water systems have been installed in the United States, especially in the sunshine states of California, Florida, and the Southwest. The main barrier to their widespread use is an initial cost of $1,800–$5,000—although the Pacemaker unit from Solar Development in Riviera Beach, Florida, costs only $700. In Cyprus, Jordan, and Israel, active solar water heaters supply 25–65% of the hot water for homes. About 12% of houses in Japan and 37% in Australia also use such systems.

Solar energy for low-temperature heating of buildings is free and is naturally available on sunny days; the net useful energy yield is moderate (active) to high (passive). Both active and passive technology are well developed and can be installed quickly. No carbon dioxide is added to the atmosphere, and environmental impacts from air and water pollution are low. Land disturbance is also minimal because passive systems are built into structures and active solar collectors are usually placed on rooftops.

On a life-cycle cost basis good passive solar and superinsulated design is the cheapest way to heat a home or a small building in regions where sunlight is available more than 60% of the time (Figure 17-14). Such a system usually adds 5–10% to the construction cost, but the life-cycle cost of operating such a house is 30–40% lower.

Active systems cost more than passive systems over their lifetime because they use more materials, need more maintenance, and eventually deteriorate and must be replaced. However, retrofitting is often easier with an active solar system. Environmentalists urge that existing public buildings be made energy efficient and retrofitted for renewable energy and that all new public buildings be highly energy efficient and make maximum use of perpetual and renewable energy.

There are disadvantages. Higher initial costs discourage buyers who are not used to considering life-cycle costs or who move every few years. With present technology active solar systems usually cost too much for heating most homes and small buildings, but improved designs and mass-production techniques could change that. Some people also consider active solar collectors sitting on rooftops or in yards ugly.

Most passive solar systems require that windows and shades be opened and closed to regulate heat flow and distribution, but this can be done by inexpensive microprocessors. Owners of passive and active solar systems also need "solar rights," laws against building structures that block access to sunlight. Such legislation is often opposed by builders of high-density developments.

## HIGH-TEMPERATURE HEAT AND ELECTRICITY

Several systems are in operation that draw on solar energy to generate electricity and high-temperature heat. In one such system huge arrays of computer-controlled mirrors, called heliostats, track the sun and focus sunlight on a central heat-collection tower (Figure 17-15) or on oil-filled pipes running through the middle of curved solar collectors (Figure 17-16). This concentrated sunlight can generate temperatures high enough for industrial processes or for producing steam to run turbines and generate electricity. Molten salt stores solar heat to produce electricity at night or on cloudy days. By 2030 or earlier other designs with parabolic dishes (shaped like TV satellite dishes) that track the sun and focus sunlight onto a single point may produce electricity at a cost of about 5¢ per kilowatt-hour.

Today these plants are used mainly to supply reserve power for daytime peak electricity loads, especially in sunny areas with a larger demand for air conditioning. Backed up by small natural gas turbines, solar-thermal plants occupying less than 1% of the Mojave Desert could probably supply Los Angeles

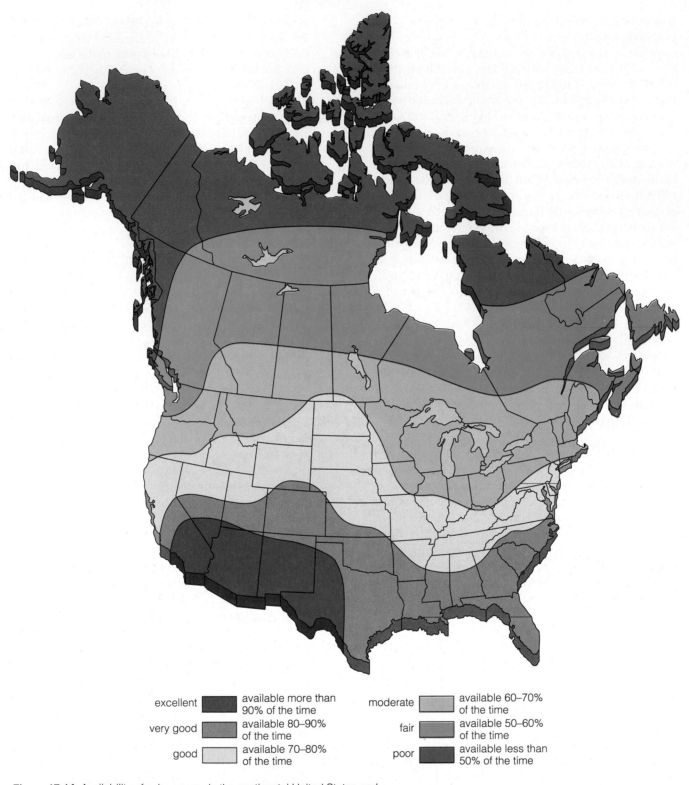

| | | | | |
|---|---|---|---|---|
| excellent | | available more than 90% of the time | moderate | available 60–70% of the time |
| very good | | available 80–90% of the time | fair | available 50–60% of the time |
| good | | available 70–80% of the time | poor | available less than 50% of the time |

**Figure 17-14** Availability of solar energy in the continental United States and Canada. (Data from U.S. Department of Energy, National Wildlife Federation, and Environment Canada)

Q: How long will proven reserves of natural gas last at current consumption rates?

Figure 17-15 Solar furnace near Odeillo in the Pyrenees Mountains of southern France. A field of curved, computer-driven mirrors (not shown in this photo) tracks the sun and reflects sunlight onto the giant parabolic collector, producing temperatures high enough to melt metals.

with electricity. They could also produce hydrogen gas for fuel (p. 446 and Section 17-8) and convert some hazardous wastes into less harmful substances.

The impact of solar power plants on air and water is low. They can be built in 1–2 years, compared to 5–15 years for coal-fired and nuclear power plants. Thus builders would save millions in interest on construction loans. Solar power plants need large collection areas but use one-third less land than a coal-burning plant (when the land used to extract coal is included) and 95% less land per kilowatt-hour than most hydropower projects. However, deserts may not have enough water for the cooling towers that recondense spent steam.

**PHOTOVOLTAIC CELLS** Solar energy can be converted directly into electrical energy by **photovoltaic cells**, commonly called **solar cells**. Most solar cells consist of layers of purified silicon, which can be made from inexpensive, abundant sand. When traces of gallium arsenide or cadmium sulfide are added, the resulting semiconductor emits electrons and produces a small amount of electrical current when struck by sunlight (Figure 17-17).

Today solar cells supply electricity for at least 30,000 homes worldwide (20,000 in the United States) and for whole villages in LDCs, including 6,000 in India. Most of these homes and villages are in remote areas without power lines. However, a Dutch scientist has shown that equipping each house in an Indonesian village with solar cells to operate efficient lights

Figure 17-16 The world's largest solar power facility, in California's Mojave Desert. Mirrored parabolic troughs focus sunlight on oil-filled tubes; the concentrated heat absorbed by the oil produces steam, which is used to run an electricity-generating turbine. Small natural gas turbines run the facility on cloudy days. This solar–natural gas fuel mix produces less than one-sixth as much carbon dioxide per kilowatt-hour of electricity as does a normal coal-fired plant. Unfortunately, because solar energy receives only a tiny fraction of the federal and state subsidies given to fossil fuels and nuclear energy, the companies running this facility declared bankruptcy in 1992. With an even economic playing field, however, this plant could produce electricity more cheaply than a coal-burning or nuclear power plant.

A: 80 years for the world, 60 years for the United States

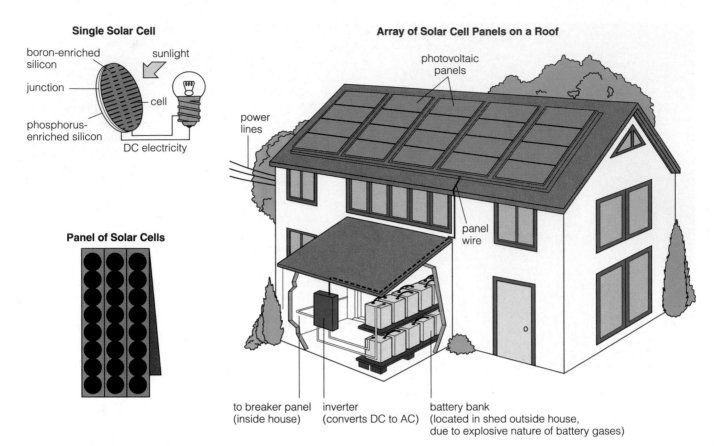

**Single Solar Cell**

boron-enriched silicon

sunlight

junction

cell

phosphorus-enriched silicon

DC electricity

**Panel of Solar Cells**

**Array of Solar Cell Panels on a Roof**

photovoltaic panels

power lines

panel wire

to breaker panel (inside house)

inverter (converts DC to AC)

battery bank (located in shed outside house, due to explosive nature of battery gases)

**Figure 17-17** Use of photovoltaic (solar) cells to provide DC electricity for an energy-efficient home; any surplus can be sold to the local power company. Prices should be competitive sometime in the 1990s. In 1990 a Florida builder began selling tract houses that get all of their electricity from roof-mounted solar cells. Although the solar-cell systems account for about one-third of the cost of each house, the savings in electric bills will pay this off over a 30-year mortgage period. Sanyo, a Japanese company, has incorporated solar cells into roof shingles.

and appliances was so cost effective that the villagers would save money by not hooking up to a power line running right past the village.

Solar cells are also used to switch railroad tracks and to supply power for water wells and irrigation pumps, battery chargers, calculators, portable laptop computers, ocean buoys, lighthouses, and offshore oil-drilling platforms in the sunny Persian Gulf. In 1992 Sanyo, a Japanese company, began producing a room air conditioner powered mostly by solar cells. Recently Swiss scientists have developed transparent solar panels that generate electricity from sunlight filtering through windows at a cost one-tenth to one-fifth the price of conventional solar cells.

Because a single solar cell produces a tiny amount of electricity, many cells are wired together in a panel providing 30–100 watts (Figure 17-17). Several panels, in turn wired together and mounted on a roof or on a rack that tracks the sun, produce electricity for a home or a building.

Massive banks of such cells can also produce electricity at a small power plant (Figure 17-18). By 2030

such solar electricity could drop to 4¢ per kilowatt-hour, making it fully cost-competitive. In 1991 Texas Instruments and Southern California Edison developed new low-cost solar-cell roof panels (Figure 17-19). These should cut the cost of solar electricity for the grid from 30¢ per kilowatt-hour (Figure 17-2) to 14¢ per kilowatt-hour, about what Southern California Edison now charges residential customers at peak hours. Pacific Gas & Electric considers solar cells cost-effective now and is starting to order more of them.

With an aggressive program starting now, by 2010 solar cells could supply 17% of the world's electricity—as much as nuclear power does today—at a lower cost and much lower risk, and 30% (50% in the United States), by 2050. That would eliminate the need to build any large-scale power plants and would allow many existing nuclear and coal-fired plants to be phased out.

Despite this enormous potential the U.S. government cut its research and development budget for solar cells 76% between 1981 and 1990, while the U.S. share of the worldwide solar-cell market fell from 75%

**Q:** Who has the world's largest coal reserves?

U.S. Department of Energy

**Figure 17-18** This power plant near Sacramento, California, uses photovoltaic cells to produce electricity. The nuclear power plant in the background has been closed down. Today at least two dozen U.S. utility companies are using photovoltaic cells in their operations. As the price of such electricity drops, usage will increase dramatically.

to 32%. During that same period Japan tripled expenditures in this area and saw its share of the global solar-cell market grow from 15% to 37%. And in 1989 a U.S. company that was the world's largest manufacturer of solar cells was sold to German interests. Unless federal and private research efforts on photovoltaics are increased sharply, the United States will lose out on a huge global market (at least $5 billion per year by 2010) and may have to import photovoltaic cells from Japan, Germany, Italy, and other countries that are investing heavily in this promising technology. If the federal government were to order $500 million worth of solar cells over five years, the U.S. industry could expand. Because of the assured sales and resulting mass-production cost efficiencies, the price of these cells could drop sharply.

Solar cells are reliable and quiet, have no moving parts, and should last 30 years or more if encased in glass or plastic. They can be installed quickly and easily. Maintenance consists of occasional washing to keep dirt from blocking the sun's rays. Small or large solar-cell packages can be built, and they can be easily expanded or moved as needed. Solar cells can be located in deserts and marginal lands, alongside interstate highways, in yards, and on rooftops.

Solar cells produce no carbon dioxide during use. Air and water pollution during operation is extremely low, air pollution from manufacture is low, and land disturbance is very low for roof-mounted systems. The net useful energy yield is fairly high and rising with new designs.

Southern California Edison

**Figure 17-19** New photovoltaic cells that look like metallic sandpaper cost half as much to manufacture as existing solar cells. They are made by sprinkling tiny silicon beads on an aluminum surface. Used as roof panels they should meet a house's electrical needs at a cost competitive with conventional electric power.

There are certain drawbacks. The present costs of solar-cell systems are high but should become competitive in 5–15 years and are already cost-competitive in some situations. Their use could be limited if gallium or cadmium becomes scarce. Moderate levels of water pollution from chemical wastes introduced through the manufacturing process could be a problem without effective pollution controls. Also, some people find racks of solar cells on rooftops or in yards unsightly.

## 17-4 Solutions: Electricity from Moving Water and from Heat Stored in Water

**HYDROELECTRIC POWER** Hydroelectric power, or hydropower, supplies about 20% of the world's electricity and 6% of its total commercial energy. Hydropower supplies Norway with essentially all its electricity, Switzerland with 74%, Austria with 67%, and LDCs with 50%.

In *large-scale hydropower projects* high dams are built across large rivers to create large reservoirs (Figure 13-11). The stored water then flows through huge pipes at controlled rates, spinning turbines and producing electricity. In *small-scale hydropower projects* a low dam with no reservoir, or only a small one, is built across a small stream. Since natural water flow generates the electricity, output can vary with seasonal changes in stream flow.

Falling water can also be used to produce electricity in *pumped-storage hydropower systems*, which are used mainly to supply extra power during times of peak electrical demand. When demand is low, usually at night, pumps using surplus electricity from a conventional power plant pump water uphill from a lake or a reservoir to another reservoir at a higher elevation. When a power company temporarily needs more electricity than its other plants can produce, water in the upper reservoir is released. The water flows through turbines and generates electricity on its downward trip back to the lower reservoir. This can be an expensive way to produce electricity, however, and cheaper alternatives are available. Another possibility may be to use solar-powered pumps to raise water to the upper reservoir.

Much of the hydropower potential of North America and Europe has been developed. By contrast, Africa has tapped only 5% of its hydropower potential, Latin America 8%, and Asia 9%, although many potential sites are far from where the electricity is needed. Many large-scale hydroelectric dams are being built or planned in Brazil, China, India, and other LDCs. By 2000 China, for example, with one-tenth of the world's hydropower potential, may become the world's largest producer of hydroelectricity. China has also built almost 100,000 small dams to produce electricity for villages. Brazil has identified 136 potential hydropower sites, of which 70 are in the Amazon—already threatened with deforestation.

Currently the United States is the world's largest producer of hydroelectricity, which supplies 10% of its electricity and 3–5% of all commercial energy. However, the era of large dams is ending in the United States because construction costs are high, few suitable sites are left, and environmentalists oppose many of the proposed projects due to their harmful effects. Any new large supplies of hydroelectric power in the United States will be imported from Canada, which gets more than 70% of its electricity from hydropower.

According to the U.S. Army Corps of Engineers, retrofitting abandoned small and medium-sized hydroelectric sites, and building new small-scale hydroelectric plants on suitable sites, could supply as much electricity as forty-seven 1,000-megawatt power plants. However, since 1985 the development of small-scale hydropower in the United States has fallen off sharply due to low oil prices, loss of federal tax credits, and opposition to some projects from local residents and environmentalists.

Hydropower has a moderate to high net useful energy yield and fairly low operating and maintenance costs. Hydroelectric plants rarely need to be shut down, and they emit no carbon dioxide or other air pollutants during operation. They have lifespans 2–10 times those of coal and nuclear plants. Large dams also help control flooding and supply a regulated flow of irrigation water to areas below the dam.

However, hydropower also has adverse effects on the environment (Figure 13-11). The reservoirs of large-scale projects flood huge areas, destroy wildlife habitats, uproot people, decrease natural fertilization of prime agricultural land in river valleys below the dam, and decrease fish harvests below the dam (Case Study, p. 345). And small hydroelectric projects can threaten recreational activities and aquatic life, disrupt the flow of wild and scenic rivers, and destroy wetlands. Also, during drought periods these plants produce little if any power. Furthermore, most of the electricity produced by these projects can be supplied at a lower cost and with less environmental impact by switching to industrial cogeneration and by improving the energy efficiency at existing big dams.

**TIDAL POWER** Twice a day water flows in and out of coastal bays and estuaries in high and low tides. In perhaps two to three dozen places in the world, a bay mouth is narrow enough, and the difference in water height between high and low tide large enough, that the kinetic energy in these daily tidal flows can be used economically to spin turbines to produce electricity. Currently two large tidal energy facilities are operating, one at La Rance, France, and the other in Canada in the Bay of Fundy. China has built several small tidal plants.

The benefits of tidal power include a free energy source (the moon's gravitational attraction), low operating costs, and a moderate net useful energy yield. Also, no carbon dioxide is added to the atmosphere, air pollution is low, and little land is disturbed. However, most analysts expect tidal power to make only a

Q: How long will the world's proven reserves of coal last at current consumption rates?

tiny contribution to world electricity supplies. There are few suitable sites, construction costs are high, and the output of electricity varies daily with tidal flows, which means there must be a backup system. In addition, the dam and power plant can be damaged by storms and their metal parts are easily corroded by seawater. Finally, the disruption of normal tidal flows may also disturb aquatic life in coastal estuaries—including organisms passing through the turbines.

**WAVE POWER** The kinetic energy in ocean waves, created primarily by wind, is another potential source of electricity. Japan, Norway, Great Britain, Sweden, the United States, and the former Soviet Union have all built small experimental plants to evaluate this form of hydropower. None of these plants has produced electricity at a competitive price, but some designs show promise.

Most analysts expect wave power to make little contribution to world electricity production, except in a few coastal areas with the right conditions. Construction costs are moderate to high, and the net useful energy yield is moderate. Also, equipment could be damaged or destroyed by saltwater corrosion and severe storms.

**OCEAN THERMAL ENERGY CONVERSION** Ocean water stores huge amounts of heat from the sun, especially in tropical areas. Japan and the United States have been studying the technological and economic feasibility of using the large temperature differences between the cold deep waters and the sun-warmed surface waters of tropical oceans to produce electricity in *ocean thermal energy conversion* (OTEC) plants anchored to the bottom of tropical oceans in suitable sites. Despite 50 years of work, the technology is still in the research and development stage.

The energy source for OTEC is limitless at suitable sites, no costly energy storage and backup system is needed, and the floating power plant requires no land area. Nutrients brought up when water is pumped from the ocean bottom might nourish schools of fish and shellfish.

However, most energy analysts believe that the large-scale extraction of energy from ocean thermal gradients may never compete economically with other energy alternatives. For one thing, construction costs would be high—two to three times those of comparable coal-fired plants. For another, operating and maintenance costs would be high as well because of corrosion of metal parts by seawater and fouling of heat exchangers by algae and barnacles. Plants could also be damaged by hurricanes. Other problems include a limited number of sites and a low net useful energy yield; possible disruption of coral reef communities and other aquatic life by pumping large volumes of deep-ocean water to the surface; and the release of large quantities of dissolved carbon dioxide into the atmosphere.

**SOLAR PONDS** *Saline solar ponds*—usually located near inland saline seas or lakes in areas with ample sunlight—can be used to produce electricity. The bottom layer of water in such a pond stays on the bottom when heated because it has a higher salinity and density (mass per unit volume) than the top layer. Heat accumulated during the daytime in the bottom layer can be used to produce steam that spins turbines, generating electricity. An experimental saline solar-pond power plant on the Israeli side of the Dead Sea has been operating successfully for several years. By 2000 Israel plans to build several plants around the Dead Sea to supply electricity for air conditioning and for desalinating water. Several experimental saline solar ponds have also been built in the United States, Australia, India, and Mexico.

*Freshwater solar ponds* can be used for water and space heating. A shallow hole is dug and lined with concrete, and covered with fiberglass insulation panels. A number of large, black plastic bags, each filled with several centimeters of water, are placed in the hole. The top of the pond is then covered with the panels, which let sunlight in and keep most of the heat stored in the water during the daytime from being lost to the atmosphere. When the water in the bags has reached its peak temperature in the afternoon, a computer turns on pumps to transfer hot water from the bags to large, insulated tanks for distribution.

Both saline and freshwater solar ponds require no energy storage and backup systems, emit no air pollution, and have a moderate net useful energy yield. Furthermore, freshwater solar ponds can be built in almost any sunny area and have moderate construction and operating costs. With adequate research and development solar ponds could supply 3–4% of U.S. energy needs within 10 years.

## 17-5 Solutions: Electricity from Wind

Worldwide, by 1993, there were over 20,000 wind turbines, most grouped in clusters called *wind farms* (Figure 17-20), which fed power to a utility grid and produced 2,700 megawatts of electricity. Most are in California (17,000 machines) and Denmark (which gets about 2% of its electricity from wind turbines). Most are located in windy mountain passes and ridges

**Figure 17-20** Wind farm in California.

and along coastlines, which generally have strong and steady winds. Sweden has installed an offshore wind power plant. In 1991 new wind-farm projects were announced in northern Germany and in Iowa and the U.S. Department of Energy has identified 37 states with enough wind to support commercial power generation. In inner Mongolia 2,000 small wind turbines provide electricity for lighting, TV sets, electrified fences, and other purposes.

California wind farms in mountain passes (Figure 17-21) produce enough electricity to meet the residential power needs of San Francisco. Potentially the state could increase its use of wind to produce electricity 4- to 20-fold by 2000, yet California is only the fourteenth windiest state in the United States. The island of Hawaii gets about 8% of its electricity from wind, and the use of wind power is spreading to the state's other islands such as Oahu.

Wind power experts project that by the middle of the next century wind power could supply more than 10% of the world's electricity and 10–25% of the electricity used in the United States. U.S. government studies indicate that one-fourth of the country's current electric power could be supplied by wind farms installed on the windiest 1.5% of the land area of the continental United States.

However, the development of this energy resource in the United States has slowed since 1986, when federal tax credits and most state tax credits for wind power were eliminated. Also, the federal budget for research and development of wind power was cut by 90% between 1981 and 1990. Today Danish companies, with tax incentives and low-interest loans from their government, have taken over the lion's share of the global market for manufacturing wind turbines. In 1992 European countries spent almost 20 times more on wind-energy development than did the United States.

Wind power has a number of benefits. It is an unlimited source of energy at favorable sites, and large wind farms can be built in only three to six months. With a moderate to fairly high net useful energy yield, these systems emit no carbon dioxide or other air pollutants during operation; they need no water for cooling; and their manufacture and use produce little water pollution. The land occupied by wind turbines can be used for grazing cattle and other purposes, while the leases to use the land for wind turbines can provide extra income for farmers and ranchers. Wind power (with much lower subsidies) also has a significant cost advantage over nuclear power (Figure 17-2) and should become competitive with coal in many areas between 1993 and 2000, especially if the environmental costs are factored in.

However, wind power is economical only in areas with steady winds. When the wind dies down, backup electricity from a utility company or from an energy storage system becomes necessary; backup power

Q: How long will proven U.S. coal reserves last at current consumption rates?

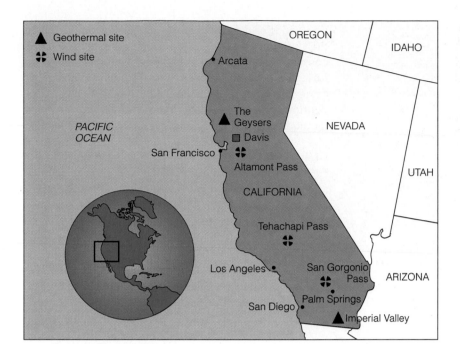

could also be provided by linking wind farms with a solar-cell or hydropower system or with efficient natural gas turbines. Other drawbacks to wind farms include visual pollution and noise, although these can be overcome with improved design and location in isolated areas. Large wind farms might also interfere with the flight patterns of migratory birds in certain areas.

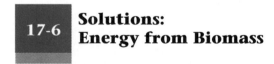

## Solutions: Energy from Biomass

**BIOMASS AS A VERSATILE FUEL**  Biomass is organic plant matter produced by solar energy through photosynthesis. It includes wood, agricultural wastes (including manure, Figure 10-19), and garbage. Some of this plant matter can be burned as solid fuel or converted into more convenient gaseous or liquid *biofuels* (Figure 17-22). Biomass, mostly from the burning of wood and manure to heat buildings and cook food, supplies about 11% of the world's energy—4–5% in Canada and the United States—and about half of the energy used in LDCs.

Various types of biomass fuels can be used for heating space and water, producing electricity, and propelling vehicles. Biomass is a renewable energy resource as long as trees and plants are not harvested faster than they grow back—a requirement that is not being met in most places (Section 10-2). Also, no net increase in atmospheric levels of carbon dioxide occurs as long as the rate of removal and burning of trees and plants and loss of below-ground organic matter does not exceed the rate of replenishment. Burning biomass fuels adds much less sulfur dioxide and nitric oxide to the atmosphere per unit of energy produced than does the uncontrolled burning of coal, and thus it requires fewer pollution controls.

However, it takes a lot of land to grow biomass fuel—about 10 times as much land as solar cells need to provide the same amount of electricity. Without effective land-use controls and replanting, widespread removal of trees and plants can deplete soil nutrients and cause excessive soil erosion, water pollution, flooding, and loss of wildlife habitat. Biomass resources also have a high moisture content (15–95%), which lowers their net useful energy. The added weight of the moisture makes collecting and hauling wood and other plant material fairly expensive and reduces the net useful energy yield.

**ENERGY PLANTATIONS**  One way to produce biomass fuel is to plant large numbers of fast-growing trees (especially cottonwoods, poplars, sycamores, and leucaenas), shrubs, and water hyacinths in *biomass energy plantations*. After being harvested these "BTU bushes" can be burned directly, converted into burnable gas, or fermented into fuel alcohol.

Plantations of oil palms and varieties of Euphorbia plants, which store energy in hydrocarbon compounds, can be established and harvested, and their oil-like material extracted and either refined to produce gasoline or burned directly in diesel engines.

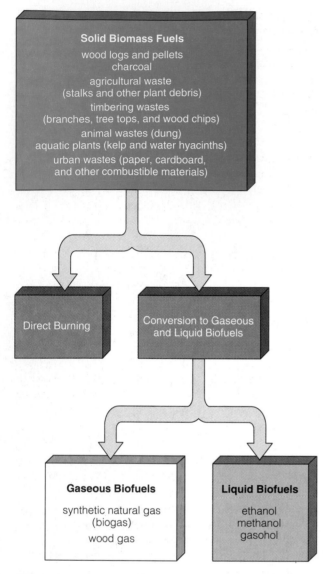

**Solid Biomass Fuels**

wood logs and pellets
charcoal
agricultural waste
(stalks and other plant debris)
timbering wastes
(branches, tree tops, and wood chips)
animal wastes (dung)
aquatic plants (kelp and water hyacinths)
urban wastes (paper, cardboard,
and other combustible materials)

Direct Burning

Conversion to Gaseous
and Liquid Biofuels

**Gaseous Biofuels**

synthetic natural gas
(biogas)
wood gas

**Liquid Biofuels**

ethanol
methanol
gasohol

**Figure 17-22** Principal types of biomass fuel. Biomass is any plant matter that stores the sun's energy through photosynthesis.

Such plantations can be located on semiarid land not needed to grow crops, although lack of water can limit productivity. They can also be planted to reduce soil erosion and can help restore degraded lands. In Sioux City, Iowa, buses are running on a fuel made from vegetable oils such as soybean or canola.

There are several drawbacks to this form of biomass fuel. The industrialized approach to biomass production usually requires large areas of land as well as heavy use of pesticides and fertilizers, which can pollute drinking water supplies and harm wildlife. Conversion of large forested areas into monoculture energy plantations also reduces biodiversity. In addition, in some areas biomass plantations might compete with food crops for prime farm land. For example, to produce enough liquid fuels to replace all of the gaso-

line and diesel fuel currently consumed each year in the United States would require planting energy crops on more land than the country now devotes to agriculture. Furthermore, these crops are likely to have low or negative net useful energy yields, as do most conventional crops grown by industrialized agricultural methods.

**BURNING WOOD AND WOOD WASTES** Almost 70% of the people living in LDCs heat their dwellings and cook their food by burning wood or charcoal. However, at least 1.1 billion people in LDCs cannot find, or are too poor to buy, enough fuelwood to meet their needs, and that number may increase to 2.5 billion by 2000 (Figure 10-18).

Sweden leads the world in using wood as an energy source, mostly for district heating plants. In the United States small wood-burning power plants located near sources of their fuel can produce electricity a little more cheaply than burning coal. Wood-fired power plants provide 23% of the electricity used in Maine and about 4% of the electricity used in New England.

The forest products industry (mostly paper companies and lumber mills) consumes almost two-thirds of the fuelwood used in the United States. Homes and small businesses burn the rest. The largest consumer of fuelwood is New England, where wood is plentiful. The amount of firewood used in the United States each year would be enough to build a wall 30 meters (100 feet) high from New York City to San Francisco. Total energy use from wood in the United States (and elsewhere) is difficult to estimate because most of this fuel is not sold in traditional markets but is probably at least 3% of total U.S. energy use.

Wood has a moderate to high net useful energy yield when collected and burned directly and efficiently near its source. However, burning wood has a number of drawbacks. In urban areas where wood must be hauled from long distances, it can cost homeowners more per unit of energy produced than oil and electricity. Harvesting and burning wood also can cause accidents. For example, each year in the United States over 10,000 people are injured by chain saws, and several hundred people are killed in house fires caused by improperly located or poorly maintained or operated wood stoves.

Although burning wood produces virtually no emissions of sulfur dioxide, it does release carbon monoxide, solid particulate matter, hydrocarbons, and unburned residues that pollute indoor and outdoor air. According to the EPA wood burning causes as many as 820 cancer deaths a year in the United States. In London, South Korean cities, and some areas of Colorado and Oregon, wood fires have been banned or limited to reduce air pollution. Since 1990 the EPA has required all new wood stoves sold in the United States

Q: How much of the world's electricity is produced by burning coal?

to emit at least 70% less particulate matter than earlier models.

Fireplaces can also be used for heating but usually result in a net loss of energy from a house. The draft of heat and gases rising up the fireplace chimney exhausts warm air and pulls in cold air from cracks and crevices throughout a house. Fireplace inserts with glass doors and blowers help but still waste energy compared with an efficient wood-burning stove. Energy loss can be reduced by closing off the room and cracking a window so that the fireplace won't draw much heated air from other rooms. A better solution is to run a small pipe from outside into the front of the fireplace so it gets the air it needs during combustion.

### BURNING AGRICULTURAL AND URBAN WASTES
In agricultural areas crop residues (such as stalks left after harvest and processing refuse) and animal manure can be collected and burned or converted into biofuels, as can coconut shells, peanut and other nut hulls, cherry pits, and cotton stalks. By 1985, for example, Hawaii was burning *bagasse*, the residue left after sugarcane harvesting and processing, to supply almost 10% of its electricity (58% on the island of Kauai and 33% on the island of Hawaii). Brazil gets 10% of its electricity from burning bagasse and plans to use this crop residue to produce 35% of its electricity by 2000.

This approach makes sense when residues are burned in small power plants located near areas where the residues are produced. Otherwise, it takes too much energy to collect, dry, and transport the residues to power plants. Some ecologists argue that it makes more sense to use crop residues to feed livestock, retard soil erosion, and fertilize the soil, but the ash from these biomass power plants can sometimes be used as fertilizer. The same is true for manure, which can be dried and burned as a fuel—as millions of people in LCDs do (Figure 10-19).

An increasing number of cities in Japan, western Europe, and the United States have built incinerators that burn trash and use the energy released to produce electricity or to heat nearby buildings (Section 19-3). For example, New England obtains about 2% of its electricity from 20 trash-burning plants. However, this approach has been limited by opposition from citizens concerned about emissions of toxic gases and disposal of toxic ash. Some analysts argue that more energy is saved by composting or recycling paper and other organic wastes than by burning them (Section 19-4).

### CONVERTING BIOMASS INTO BIOFUELS
Plants, organic wastes, sewage, and other forms of solid biomass can be converted by bacteria and various chemical processes into gaseous and liquid biofuels (Figure 17-22). Examples include *biogas* (a mixture of 60%

methane, the principal component of natural gas, and 40% carbon dioxide), *liquid ethanol* (ethyl, or grain alcohol), and *liquid methanol* (methyl, or wood alcohol).

In China anaerobic bacteria in more than 6 million *biogas digesters* (500,000 of them improved models built in the 1980s) convert organic plant and animal wastes into methane fuel for heating and cooking. After the biogas has been separated, the solid residue is used as fertilizer on food crops or, if contaminated, on trees. India has about 750,000 biogas digesters in operation, half of them built since 1986 (Figure 17-23). When they work, biogas digesters are very efficient. However, they are slow and unpredictable—a problem that could be corrected with development of more reliable models.

Methane gas, produced by anaerobic decomposition of organic matter in landfills, can be collected by pipes inserted into the ground, separated from other gases, and burned as a fuel. Eighty-two U.S landfills currently recover methane, but 2,000–3,000 U.S. landfills have the potential for large-scale methane recovery. Burning this gas instead of allowing it to escape into the atmosphere helps slow projected global warming because methane causes roughly 25 times as much atmospheric global warming per molecule as carbon dioxide (Figure 11-3c).

Methane can also be produced by anaerobic digestion of manure from animal feedlots (Figure 14-2) and sludge from sewage treatment plants. In California a plant burning cattle manure from nearby feedlots supplies electricity for as many as 20,000 homes. However, environmentalists believe that applying manure to the land would probably save more natural gas (used to produce inorganic fertilizer) than is saved by burning the manure.

Some analysts believe that liquid ethanol and methanol could replace gasoline and diesel fuel when oil becomes too scarce and expensive. Ethanol can be made from sugar and grain crops (sugarcane, sugar beets, sorghum, and corn) by fermentation and distillation. For example, since 1987 ethanol made by fermentation of surplus sugarcane has supplied about half the automotive fuel in Brazil, helped Brazil cut its oil imports, and created an estimated 575,000 full-time jobs. However, the government has spent $8 billion to subsidize the country's ethanol industry, and in recent years ethanol production has been curtailed because of financial difficulties.

Gasoline mixed with 10–23% pure ethanol makes *gasohol*, which burns in conventional gasoline engines and is sold as super unleaded or ethanol-enriched gasoline. Gasohol now accounts for about 8% of gasoline sales in the United States—25–35% in Illinois, Iowa, Kentucky, and Nebraska. The ethanol used in gasohol is made mostly by fermenting corn. Excluding federal taxes it costs about $1.60 per gallon to

A: 44% (56% in the United States)

**Figure 17-23** This biogas digester converts animal dung into a methane-rich gas that can be burned for cooking, space heating, and other purposes.

produce, compared to about 50¢ per gallon for gasoline, but new, energy-efficient distilleries could make this fuel competitive with other forms of unleaded gasoline without federal tax breaks.

Growing grains to make alcohol fuel could cut into cropland needed to grow food. For example, about 40% of the entire U.S. corn harvest would be needed to make enough ethanol to meet just 10% of the country's demand for automotive fuel.

Another alcohol, methanol, can be produced from wood, wood wastes, agricultural wastes (such as corncobs), sewage sludge, garbage, coal, or natural gas at a cost of about $1.10 per gallon—more than twice the cost of producing gasoline. Table 17-2 gives the advantages and disadvantages of using ethanol, methanol, and several other fuels as alternatives to gasoline.

## 17-7 Solutions: Geothermal Energy

Heat contained in underground rocks and fluids is an important source of energy. Over millions of years this **geothermal energy** from the earth's mantle (Figure 7-2) is transferred to underground concentrations of dry steam (steam with no water droplets), wet steam (a mixture of steam and water droplets), and hot water

trapped in fractured or porous rock at various places in the earth's crust (Figure 3-6). If geothermal sites are close to the surface, wells can be drilled to extract the dry steam, wet steam (Figure 17-24), or hot water. This thermal energy can be used for space heating and to produce electricity or high-temperature heat for industrial processes.

Currently about 20 countries are extracting energy from geothermal sites and supplying enough heat to meet the needs of over 2 million homes in a cold climate and enough electricity for over 1.5 million homes. The United States accounts for 44% of the geothermal electricity generated worldwide. The most accessible, high-temperature geothermal sites in the United States lie in the West, especially in California and the Rocky Mountain states. Iceland, Japan, New Zealand, and Indonesia are among the countries with the greatest potential for tapping geothermal energy.

Geothermal reservoirs can be depleted if heat is removed faster than it is renewed by natural processes. Thus geothermal resources are nonrenewable on a human time scale, but the potential supply is so vast that it is often classified as a potentially renewable energy resource. There are four sources of this type of geothermal energy: dry-steam reservoirs, wet-steam reservoirs, hot-water reservoirs, and geopressurized brines.

*Dry-steam reservoirs* are the preferred geothermal resource, but they are also the rarest. A large dry-steam well near Larderello, Italy, has been an important

Q: How much of global emissions of carbon dioxide come from burning coal?

## Table 17-2 Evaluation of Alternatives to Gasoline

| Advantages | Disadvantages |
|---|---|
| **Compressed Natural Gas** | |
| Fairly abundant domestic and global supplies | Cumbersome fuel tank required |
| Low emissions of hydrocarbons, CO, and $CO_2$ | Expensive engine modification required ($2,000) |
| Currently inexpensive | One-fourth the range |
| Vehicle development advanced | New filling stations required |
| Reduced engine maintenance | Nonrenewable resource |
| Well suited for fleet vehicles | |
| **Electricity** | |
| Renewable if not generated from fossil fuels or nuclear power | Limited range and power |
| Zero vehicle emissions | Batteries expensive |
| Electric grid in place | Slow refueling (6–8 hours) |
| Efficient and quiet | Power-plant emissions if generated from coal or oil |
| **Reformulated Gasoline (Oxygenated Fuel)** | |
| No new filling stations required | Nonrenewable resource |
| Low to moderate emission reduction of CO | Dependence on imported oil perpetuated |
| No engine modification required | Possible high cost to modify refineries |
| | No emission reduction of $CO_2$ |
| | Higher cost |
| | Water resources contaminated by leakage and spills |
| **Methanol** | |
| High octane | Large fuel tank required |
| Emission reduction of $CO_2$ (total amount depends on method of production) | One-half the range |
| | Corrosive to metal, rubber, plastic |
| Reduced total air pollution (30–40%) | Increased emissions of potentially carcinogenic formaldehyde |
| | High $CO_2$ emissions if generated by coal |
| | High capital cost to produce |
| | Hard to start in cold weather |
| **Ethanol** | |
| High octane | Large fuel tank required |
| Emission reduction of $CO_2$ (total amount depends on distillation process and efficiency of crop growing) | Much higher cost |
| | Corn supply limited |
| Emission reduction of CO | Competition with food growing for cropland |
| Potentially renewable | Less range |
| | Smog formation possible |
| | Corrosive |
| | Hard to start in cold weather |
| **Solar-Hydrogen** | |
| Renewable if produced using solar energy | Nonrenewable if generated by fossil fuels or nuclear power |
| Lower flammability | Large fuel tank required |
| Virtually emission-free | No distribution system in place |
| Zero emissions of $CO_2$ | Engine redesign required |
| Nontoxic | Currently expensive |

source of power for Italy's electric railroads since 1904. Two other large sites are the Matsukawa field in Japan and the Geysers steam field about 145 kilometers (90 miles) northwest of San Francisco (Figure 17-21). Currently 28 plants economically tap energy from the Geysers field, supplying more than 6% of northern California's electricity, largely without government subsidies.

However, in 1991 the U.S. Geological Survey estimated that the amount of heat trapped in California's rock that could be extracted for power generation was about half the amount estimated in 1978.

*Wet-steam reservoirs* are more common than dry-steam reservoirs but are more difficult and more expensive to convert to electricity. The world's largest

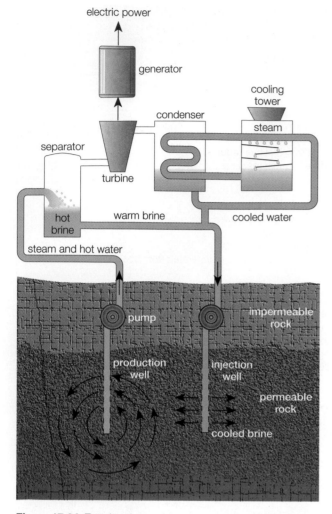

**Figure 17-24** Tapping the earth's heat or geothermal energy in the form of wet steam to produce electricity.

wet-steam power plant is in Wairaki, New Zealand; others operate in Mexico, Japan, El Salvador, Nicaragua, and parts of the CIS. Four small-scale wet-steam demonstration plants in the western United States produce electricity at a cost equivalent to paying $40 per barrel for oil, about twice the current price of oil.

*Hot-water reservoirs* are more common than dry-steam or wet-steam reservoirs. Almost all the homes, buildings, and food-producing greenhouses in Reykjavik, Iceland (population 85,000), are heated by hot water drawn from geothermal wells under the city. In Paris, France, the equivalent of 200,000 dwellings are heated the same way. At 180 locations in the United States, mostly in the West, hot-water reservoirs have been used for years to heat homes and farm buildings and to dry crops.

*Geopressurized brines* are underground reservoirs of high-temperature, high-pressure water, usually trapped deep under continental shelf beds of shale or

clay. With present drilling technology they would supply geothermal energy and natural gas at a cost equal to paying $30–$45 a barrel for oil.

There are also three virtually perpetual sources of geothermal energy: *molten rock* (magma), found near the earth's surface (in volcanoes, for example); *hot dry-rock zones*, where molten rock that has penetrated the earth's crust heats subsurface rock to high temperatures; and low- to moderate-temperature *warm-rock reservoir deposits*, which could be used to preheat water and run heat pumps for space heating and air conditioning. According to the National Academy of Sciences the energy potentially recoverable from such reservoirs would meet U.S. energy needs at current consumption levels for 600–700 years, but costs may be too high.

The biggest advantages of geothermal energy include a vast and sometimes renewable supply of energy for areas near reservoirs, moderate net useful energy yields for large and easily accessible reservoir sites, far less carbon dioxide emission per unit of energy than fossil fuels, and competitive cost of producing electricity (Figure 17-2).

A serious limitation of geothermal energy is the scarcity of easily accessible reservoir sites. Geothermal reservoirs must also be carefully managed or they can be depleted within a few decades. Furthermore, geothermal development in some areas can destroy or degrade forests or other ecosystems. In Hawaii, for example, environmentalists are fighting the construction of a large geothermal project in the only lowland tropical rain forest left in the United States.

Without pollution control, geothermal energy production causes moderate to high air pollution from hydrogen sulfide, ammonia, mercury, boron, and radioactive materials. It also causes moderate to high water pollution from dissolved solids (salinity) and runoff of toxic compounds of heavy metals such as arsenic and mercury. Noise, odor, and local climate changes can also be problems. With proper controls, however, most experts consider the environmental effects of geothermal energy to be less, or no greater, than those of fossil-fuel and nuclear power plants.

## 17-8 Solutions: The Solar-Hydrogen Age

Perpetual and renewable energy resources will make increasingly important contributions to world energy supplies. However, solar and wind energy are diffuse

**Q:** What would happen if coal's harmful effects were included in its market price and government subsidies were removed?

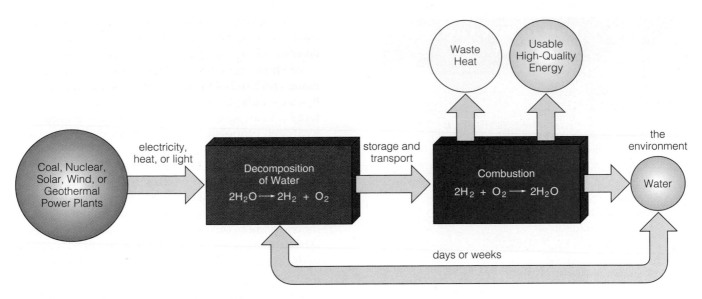

**Figure 17-25** The hydrogen energy cycle. The production of hydrogen gas requires electricity, heat, or solar energy to decompose water, thus leading to a negative net useful energy yield. However, hydrogen is a clean-burning fuel that can be used to replace oil and other fossil fuels and nuclear energy. Using solar energy to produce hydrogen from water could provide an antidote to our fossil-fuel addiction, eliminate most air pollution, and greatly reduce the threat of global warming.

and intermittent, suitable for many purposes but not for running an entire economy.

A way around this is to convert renewable energy to a gaseous fuel that is easy to store and transport—such as hydrogen gas ($H_2$) (p. 446 and Table 17-2). Hydrogen is produced easily by passing electrical current through water, which decomposes into oxygen and hydrogen gases (Figure 17-25).

When hydrogen burns it combines with oxygen gas in the air and produces nonpolluting water vapor. Hydrogen has about 2.5 times the energy by weight of gasoline, making it an especially attractive aviation fuel.

Hydrogen gas is much easier to store than electricity. It can be stored in a pressurized tank or in metal hydrides, metal powders that absorb gaseous hydrogen and release it when heated for use as a fuel in a car, a furnace, or an electricity-producing fuel cell (with energy efficiencies of up to 60%; Figure 3-16). Currently fuel cells are expensive but this could change with more research and mass production. Unlike gasoline solid metallic hydrogen compounds will not explode or burn if a vehicle's tank is ruptured in an accident. Years' worth of hydrogen could be stored in depleted oil or gas wells or other underground areas.

Several experimental cars, a bus in Utah, and a large jet airplane in the former Soviet Union have been running on hydrogen fuel for several years. A fleet of 20 Mercedes-Benz hydrogen-powered test cars have logged more than 800,000 kilometers (500,000 miles).

Hydrogen could be phased in gradually by mixing it with natural gas as reserves of this fuel are gradually depleted. The sunny U.S. Southwest could supply much of the country with electricity produced by solar power (Figures 17-16 and 17-18) or with hydrogen produced by solar power. The gas could then be carried by pipeline to areas where it is needed. Small industrial hydrogen pipelines have been used for decades in several countries.

Currently it would cost about $1.40 to produce hydrogen gas with the energy found in 3.8 liters (1 gallon) of gasoline. However, the current price of gasoline does not include its numerous pollution and health costs, which add at least 50¢ per gallon to its true cost. Thus even today hydrogen is cheaper than gasoline and other fossil fuels when the overall societal costs are considered.

Because of the first and second energy laws (Section 3-6), hydrogen production by any method will take more energy than is released when it is burned, making its net useful energy yield negative. That means that its widespread use depends on having an abundant and affordable supply of some other type of environmentally acceptable energy.

Using fossil fuels (especially coal and oil) or nuclear fuels to produce hydrogen would be too expensive and would cause serious environmental problems. The key to the hydrogen revolution is the development of affordable methods of using solar energy to produce electricity that in turn can be used to make hydrogen gas. If this can be accomplished, we

A: It would be too expensive to use and would be phased out.

## How to Save Energy and Money

- Don't use electricity to heat space or water (unless it is provided by affordable solar cells or hydrogen).

- Insulate new or existing houses heavily, caulk and weatherstrip to reduce air infiltration and heat loss, and use energy-efficient windows. Add an air-to-air heat exchanger to minimize indoor air pollution.

- Obtain as much heat and cooling as possible from natural sources—especially sun, wind, geothermal energy, and trees (windbreaks and natural shading).

- Buy the most energy-efficient homes, lights, cars, and appliances available, and evaluate them only in terms of lifetime cost.

- Consider walking or riding a bicycle for short trips and busses or trains for intermediate trips.

- During cold weather dress more warmly indoors, humidify air, and use fans to distribute heat so that the thermostat setting can be lowered (saves 3% for each °F decrease).

- Turn down the thermostat on water heaters to 43°–49°C (110°–120°F) and insulate hot water pipes.

- Lower the cooling load on an air conditioner by increasing the thermostat setting (saves 3–5% for each °F increase), installing energy-efficient lighting, using floor and ceiling fans, and whole-house window or attic fans to bring in outside air (especially at night when temperatures are cooler).

- Turn off lights and appliances when not in use.

search and development has been minuscule. By contrast, the Japanese and German governments have been spending seven to eight times more on hydrogen research and development than the United States. Germany and Saudi Arabia have each built a large solar-hydrogen plant, and Germany and the CIS have entered into an agreement for the joint development of hydrogen propulsion technology for commercial aircraft.

Sometime in the 1990s a German firm also plans to market solar-hydrogen systems that would meet all the heating, cooling, cooking, refrigeration, and electrical needs of a home, as well as providing hydrogen fuel for one or more cars. Within a few years BMW plans to introduce hydrogen-powered automobiles, with the hydrogen produced by home generators leased from the company. Germany has also built a 193-kilometer (120-mile) pipeline that transports hydrogen produced from fossil fuels for use in industry. And in Japan, in 1992, Mazda unveiled a prototype car that runs on hydrogen released slowly from metal hydrides heated by the car's radiator coolant. By 2000 hydrogen cars could be cost-competitive with gasoline cars if gas prices rise to about 53¢ per liter ($2 per gallon)—half the current price in some European countries.

Large-scale funding of hydrogen research is generally opposed by powerful U.S. oil companies, electric utilities, and automobile manufacturers, because a solar-hydrogen revolution represents a serious threat to their short-term economic well-being. Supporting the necessary research and providing the subsidies needed to usher in the solar-hydrogen revolution in the United States will require considerable political pressure by individuals to counteract the powerful economic interests temporarily threatened by such a change. Without such development Americans will be buying most of their solar-hydrogen equipment and fuel cells from Germany and Japan, and will lose out on a huge global market and source of domestic jobs.

can make the transition to a *solar-hydrogen economy* over the next 50 years, using natural gas to help us make the shift.

A *solar-hydrogen revolution* over the next 50 years would eliminate the air and water pollution caused by extracting, transporting, and burning fossil fuels, and would reduce the threat of global warming. It would also reduce the threat of wars over dwindling oil supplies. Furthermore, nuclear power could be phased out. Finally, individuals would be able to produce most, if not all, of their own energy, instead of having to rely on oil and utility companies.

Despite the enormous potential of hydrogen as a fuel, U.S. government funding for solar-hydrogen re-

 ## 17-9 Solutions: Developing a Personal Energy Plan

While elected officials, energy company executives, and environmentalists argue over the key components of a national energy strategy, many individuals have taken energy matters into their own hands. With or without tax credits, they are taking steps to increase energy efficiency and save money.

Some are building passively heated and cooled solar homes. Others are building superinsulated

Q: How much of the world's electricity is supplied by nuclear power?

dwellings or are adding passive or active solar heating to existing homes. Each of us can develop a personal energy strategy that improves personal and national security, saves money, and helps sustain the earth (Individuals Matter, p. 474).

Countries that have the vision to change from unsustainable to sustainable energy strategies will be rewarded with increased security—not just military security but also economic, energy, and environmental security. Those that do not will suffer the consequences.

*In the long run, humanity has no choice but to rely on renewable energy. No matter how abundant they seem today, eventually coal and uranium will run out. The choice before us is practical: We simply cannot afford to make more than one energy transition within the next generation.*

DANIEL DEUDNEY AND CHRISTOPHER FLAVIN

## Critical Thinking

1. What are the most important things an individual can do to save energy in the home and in transportation (see Individuals Matter, p. 474)? Which, if any, of these do you do? Which, if any, do you plan to do? When?

2. Should the United States institute a crash program to develop solar photovoltaic cells and solar-produced hydrogen fuel? Explain.

3. Explain why you agree or disagree with the ideas that the United States can get most of the electricity it needs by (a) developing solar power plants, (b) using direct solar energy to produce electricity in photovoltaic cells, (c) building new, large hydroelectric plants, (d) building ocean thermal electric power plants, (e) building wind farms, (f) building power plants fueled by wood, crop wastes, trash, and other biomass resources, (g) tapping dry-steam, wet-steam, and hot-water geothermal deposits, (h) tapping molten rock (magma) geothermal deposits, and (i) improving energy efficiency by 50%.

4. Explain why you agree or disagree with the following propositions:
   a. The United States should cut average per capita energy use by at least 50% over the next 20 years.
   b. A mandatory energy conservation program should form the basis of any U.S. energy policy to help provide economic, environmental, and military security.
   c. To solve world and U.S. energy supply problems, all we need do is recycle some or most of the energy we use.

*5. Make an energy-use study of your school or dorm, and use the findings to develop an energy-efficiency improvement program. Present your plan to school officials.

A: 17% (5% of the world's total commercial energy use)

## *Bitter Lessons from Chernobyl*

Chernobyl is a chilling word, recognized around the globe as the site of the worst nuclear disaster ever. On April 25, 1986, a series of explosions in a nuclear power plant flung radioactive debris and dust high into the atmosphere to encircle the planet (Figure 18-1). Here are some of the consequences of this disaster, which was caused by human error and poor design:

- 31 people died shortly after the accident from massive radiation exposure and 239 people were hospitalized with acute radiation sickness.

- 135,000 people were evacuated within a few days; 125,000 more were evacuated in 1991, and 2.2 million more may need to be moved.

- 576,000 people were exposed to dangerous radioactivity; some may suffer from cancers (especially thyroid cancer and leukemia).

- 4 million people, mostly in the Ukraine and Belarus and in northern Europe, may suffer health effects. A Ukrainian health official estimates that 6,000–8,000 people in the Ukraine have died as a result of the accident.

- The total cost of the accident will reach at least $358 billion.

These figures boggle the mind. We cannot take them in. We need to hear individual stories to comprehend the enormity of the event.

When people were evacuated from the region around Chernobyl, they weren't clearing out a few apartment buildings and farms until the danger passed. This danger would not pass for many centuries. People were forced to abandon their radioactive cats and dogs. They had to say goodbye, with little or no notice, to lush green wheatfields and blossoming apple trees, to land their families had farmed for generations, to cows and goats that would be shot because the grass they ate was radioactive. Fleeing a danger they could not see or understand, leaving their possessions behind, most would never return.

**Figure 18-1** Heat-sensing satellite view of the Chernobyl nuclear power plant in Ukraine. The red area near the center shows intense heat from the reactor that exploded in 1986.

© CNES 1991/Spot Image Corporation

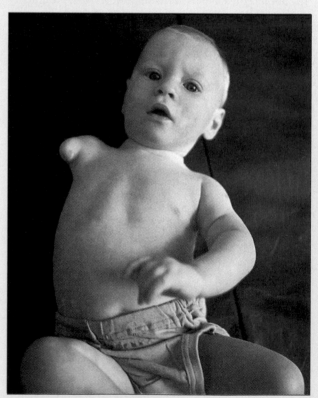

Wojtek Laski/Sipa-Press

**Figure 18-2** This young boy has birth defects that doctors believe were caused by his mother's exposure to radioactivity from the 1986 Chernobyl nuclear power plant accident.

What "health effects" have people experienced? Seven thousand children, victims of leukemia, are being treated at the regional hospital in Minsk, and untold others, born after Chernobyl, have birth defects and other problems (Figure 18-2). The accident has also been blamed for the birth in 1992 of three children without eyes in northern Norway. As world-famous gymnast Olga Korbut reported in 1991:

*I was . . . in Minsk when Chernobyl happened, and they didn't tell us for three or four days. . . . We were all outdoors, because it was close to the May 1 celebration, and we were planting gardens and enjoying the spring. If they had told us Chernobyl had happened, we would have stayed inside. . . . It has been five years. . . , but people are still very frightened . . . and very angry. Our food and water supply is contaminated, and we suffer sicknesses from radiation. Now we have headaches all the time, and we always feel . . . weary. . . .*

*When I went into the schools in Byelorussia, I learned that the first-graders have never been in the forest. . . because the trees were so contaminated. . . . When children want to see what nature used to be like, they go into a little courtyard inside the building, and the teacher says, "This is a bird and this is a tree," and they are plastic. Isn't that sad?*

Others must speak for the penguins of Antarctica, where radioactive snow fell 20 months after Chernobyl; for the reindeer of Lapland, whose food was so contaminated with radioactive cesium-137 that thousands had to be destroyed; or for the sheep of the English Lake District, where as late as 1990 some lambs were too radioactive to be sold. The primary lesson of Chernobyl is that a major nuclear accident anywhere is a nuclear accident everywhere.

What role should nuclear energy play in the future? After Chernobyl our answer to this question takes on renewed importance. Will we have to continue depending mostly on the other nonrenewable energy resources, the fossil fuels? If so, how long will the various fossil fuels last, and how can we reduce their environmental impact? And perhaps most important of all, how can we develop a sustainable-Earth energy strategy?

In this chapter we will seek answers to the following questions:

- How can the following energy alternatives help us?
  **a.** oil
  **b.** natural gas
  **c.** coal
  **d.** conventional nuclear fission
  **e.** breeder nuclear fission
  **f.** nuclear fusion

- What are the best energy options?

## 18-1 Oil

**CONVENTIONAL CRUDE OIL** **Petroleum**, or **crude oil**, is a gooey liquid consisting mostly of hydrocarbon compounds with small amounts of oxygen, sulfur, and nitrogen compounds. Crude oil and natural gas are often trapped together deep within Earth's crust (Figure 3-6). The crude oil is dispersed in pores and cracks in rock formations.

**Primary oil recovery** involves drilling a well and pumping out the oil that flows into the bottom of the well. After the flowing oil has been removed, water can be injected into nearby wells to force some of the remaining heavy oil to the surface, a process known as **secondary oil recovery**.

For each barrel of crude oil removed by primary and secondary recovery, two barrels of *heavy oil* are usually left. As oil prices rise, it may become economical to remove about 10% of this heavy oil by **enhanced**, or **tertiary, oil recovery**. Steam or carbon dioxide gas can be used to force some of the heavy oil into the well cavity for pumping to the surface. However, enhanced oil recovery is expensive: It takes the energy in one-third of a barrel of oil to retrieve each barrel of heavy oil.

Most crude oil travels by pipeline to a refinery. There it is heated and distilled to separate it into gasoline, heating oil, diesel oil, asphalt, and other components (Figure 18-3). Some of the resulting products,

477

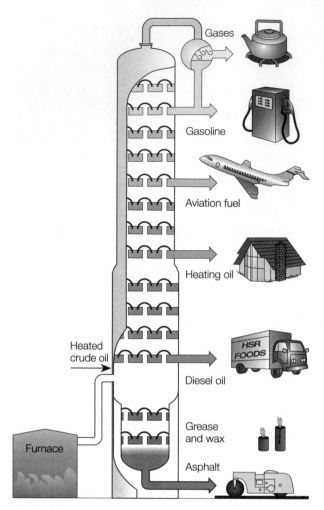

Gases

Gasoline

Aviation fuel

Heating oil

Heated
crude oil

Diesel oil

Grease
and wax

Furnace

Asphalt

**Figure 18-3** Refining of crude oil. Components are removed at various levels, depending on their boiling points, in a giant distillation column.

called **petrochemicals**, are used as raw materials in industrial chemicals, fertilizers, pesticides, plastics, synthetic fibers, paints, medicines, and many other products.

**HOW LONG WILL SUPPLIES LAST?** Oil is the lifeblood of the global economy. Oil *reserves* are identified deposits from which oil can be extracted profitably at present prices with current technology (Figure 7-17). The 13 countries that make up the Organization of Petroleum Exporting Countries (OPEC) have 67% of these reserves (25% in Saudi Arabia). Geologists believe that the Middle East also contains most of the world's undiscovered oil. Therefore, OPEC is expected to have long-term control over world oil supplies and prices

Although output has been falling since 1988, the CIS remains the world's largest oil producer, followed

by the United States. Mostly because of aging and poorly maintained production facilities (with as much as 20% of the production spilling out of leaky pipes and storage tanks), the CIS may be forced to import oil by 1995 unless it cuts domestic production by reducing spillage, increasing energy efficiency, or raising prices—all unlikely in the current economic and political climate.

With only 4% of the world's oil reserves the United States uses nearly 30% of the oil extracted worldwide each year, 63% of it for transportation. The rest is used by industry (24%), residences and commercial buildings (8%), and electric utilities (5%). In 1992 about 46% of U.S. oil was imported, and this amount is projected to rise (Figure 1-12).

Figure 18-4 shows the locations of the largest crude oil fields in the United States and Canada. Despite an upsurge in exploration and test drilling, U.S. oil extraction has declined since 1985. Moreover, over half of the country's biggest oil fields are 80% depleted, and the net useful energy yield for most domestic new oil is low and falling. Sabotage of the vulnerable Trans-Alaska oil pipeline—which the Department of Defense says is impossible to protect—could disrupt the entire U.S. economy.

At present consumption rates the world's crude oil reserves will be depleted in 42 years, and there may be enough undiscovered oil to last another 40 years (Figure 18-5). U.S. reserves will be depleted by 2018 at today's consumption rate and by 2010 if usage rises 2% per year.

Some analysts argue that rising oil prices will stimulate exploration, and that the earth's crust may contain 100 times more oil than generally thought. Such oil, if it exists, lies 10 kilometers (6 miles) or more below the surface—about twice the depth of today's deepest wells. Most geologists, however, do not believe this oil exists. These same analysts also believe we can extract and upgrade heavy oils from oil shale, tar sands, and existing wells at affordable prices.

Other analysts argue that such optimistic projections about future oil supplies ignore the consequences of exponential use of oil. Consider the following, assuming we continue to use crude oil at the current rate:

- Saudi Arabia, with the largest known crude oil reserves, could supply all the world's oil needs for only 10 years.

- The estimated reserves under Alaska's North Slope—the largest ever found in North America—would meet world demand for only 6 months and U.S. demand for 3 years.

- All estimated, undiscovered, recoverable deposits of oil in the United States could meet world

Q: How many sites in the United States are contaminated with radioactive materials?

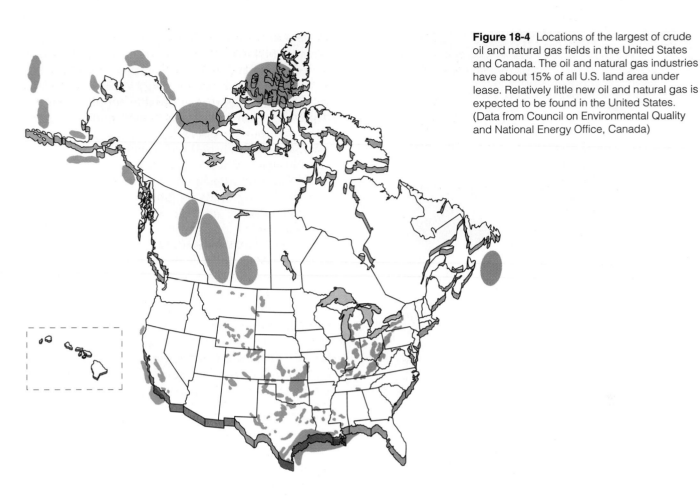

**Figure 18-4** Locations of the largest of crude oil and natural gas fields in the United States and Canada. The oil and natural gas industries have about 15% of all U.S. land area under lease. Relatively little new oil and natural gas is expected to be found in the United States. (Data from Council on Environmental Quality and National Energy Office, Canada)

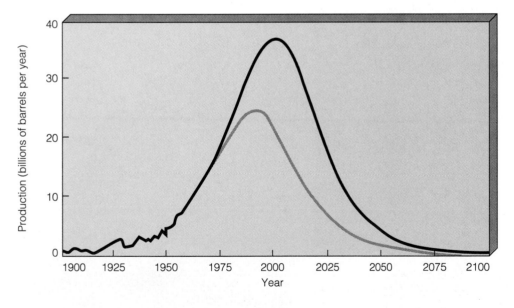

**Figure 18-5** The end of the petroleum age is in sight. These two curves show that the world's known petroleum reserves will be 80% depleted between 2025 and 2035 depending on how fast this oil is used. (Data from M. King Hubbert)

demand for only 1.7 years and U.S. demand for 10 years.

In short, those who rely on new discoveries to supply the world with oil must bring in a new Saudi Arabian supply *every 10 years* just to keep on using oil at the current rate. Moreover, if the economies of LDCs grow, the rate of oil use will probably exceed current rates and deplete supplies much faster.

**Figure 18-6** Oil shale and the shale oil extracted from it. Big U.S. oil shale projects have been canceled because of excessive cost.

**PROS AND CONS OF CONVENTIONAL OIL**  Oil is a versatile fuel, still cheap (Figure 1-11), easily transported within and between countries, and from some deposits high in net useful energy yield (Figure 3-19). Oil's fatal flaw is that affordable supplies may be depleted within 35–80 years. In addition, burning it releases carbon dioxide, which could alter global climate, and other air pollutants such as sulfur oxides and nitrogen oxides, which damage people, crops, trees, fish, and other species. Oil spills and leakage of toxic drilling muds pollute water, and the brine solution injected into oil wells can contaminate groundwater.

Indeed, if all the harmful environmental effects of using oil were included in its market price and current government subsidies were removed, oil would be too expensive to use and would be replaced by less harmful and cheaper perpetual and renewable energy resources.

**HEAVY OIL FROM OIL SHALE**  **Oil shale** is a fine-grained rock (Figure 18-6) that contains a solid, waxy

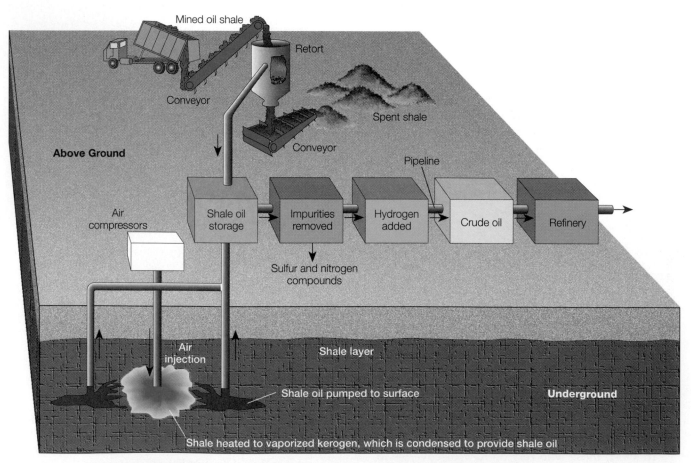

**Figure 18-7**  Aboveground and underground (*in situ*) methods for producing synthetic crude oil from oil shale.

Q: How much will it cost U.S. taxpayers to clean up contaminated nuclear weapons production facilities?

mixture of hydrocarbon compounds called **kerogen**. After being removed by surface or subsurface mining, the shale is crushed and heated to vaporize the kerogen (Figure 18-7). The kerogen vapor is condensed, forming heavy, slow-flowing, dark-brown **shale oil**. Before shale oil can be sent by pipeline to a refinery, it must be heated to increase its flow rate and processed to remove sulfur, nitrogen, and other impurities.

The shale oil potentially recoverable from U.S. deposits—mostly on federal lands in Colorado, Utah, and Wyoming—could probably meet the country's crude oil demand for 41 years at current use levels. Canada, China, and the CIS also have big oil shale deposits.

Environmental problems may limit production, however. Shale oil processing requires lots of water, which is scarce in the semiarid locales of the richest deposits. Furthermore, converting kerogen to processed shale oil and burning it release more carbon dioxide per unit of energy than do processing and burning conventional oil; nitrogen oxides and sulfur dioxide are also released. Moreover, aboveground mining of shale oil tears up the land, leaving mountains of shale rock (which expands like popcorn when heated). Finally, salts, cancer-causing substances, and toxic metal compounds can be leached from the processed shale rock into nearby water supplies.

One solution is to extract shale oil underground, known as *in situ* (in-place) *processing* (Figure 18-7). However, this method is too expensive with present technology and puts out more sulfur dioxide than does surface processing.

Shale oil yields less net useful energy than conventional oil because it takes the energy from almost half a barrel of conventional oil to extract, process, and upgrade one barrel of shale oil (Figure 3-19). Further-

more, shale oil yields fewer useful products at the refinery.

**HEAVY OIL FROM TAR SAND** **Tar sand** (or oil sand) is a mixture of clay, sand, water, and **bitumen**, a gooey, black, high-sulfur heavy oil. Tar sand is usually removed by surface mining and heated with pressurized steam until the bitumen fluid softens and floats to the top. The bitumen is purified and chemically upgraded into a synthetic crude oil suitable for refining (Figure 18-8). So far it is not technically or economically feasible to mine underground deposits of tar sand or to extract bitumen underground.

The world's largest known deposits of tar sands—the Athabasca Tar Sands— lie in northern Alberta, Canada. Heavy oil in these deposits is estimated to exceed the proven oil reserves of Saudi Arabia. Other large deposits are in Venezuela, Colombia, and the CIS, and smaller deposits exist in the United States, mostly in Utah. If all U.S. deposits were developed, they would supply all U.S. oil needs at the current usage rate for only about three months at a price of $48–$62 per barrel.

Since 1985 two plants have supplied almost 12% of Canada's oil by processing tar sands at below average cost. Economically recoverable deposits can supply all of Canada's projected oil needs for about 33 years at today's consumption rate, but they would meet the world's present oil needs for only about 2 years.

Environmentalists charge that Canada's synthetic crude oil is so cheap ($12–$15 per barrel) because the tar-sand processors need not control their air pollution emissions. The plants have also created huge waste disposal ponds. Cleaning up these toxic sites is another external cost not included in the price of Canadian tar-sand oil.

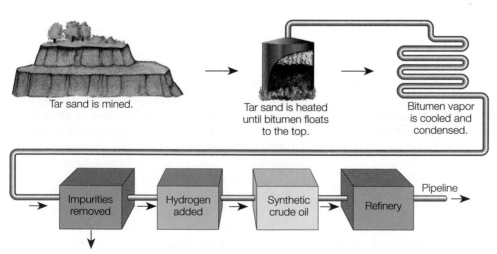

**Figure 18-8** Generalized summary of how synthetic crude oil is produced from tar sand.

Tar sand is mined.

Tar sand is heated until bitumen floats to the top.

Bitumen vapor is cooled and condensed.

Impurities removed

Hydrogen added

Synthetic crude oil

Refinery

Pipeline

Producing synthetic crude oil from tar sands has several disadvantages. The net useful energy yield is low because it takes the energy in almost one-half a barrel of conventional oil to extract and process one barrel of bitumen and upgrade it to synthetic crude oil. Also, large quantities of water are needed for processing, and upgrading bitumen to synthetic crude oil releases sulfur dioxide, hydrogen sulfide, and toxic metal particles.

Figure 18-9 Large quantities of energy are wasted when natural gas found with oil is burned off, as in this Saudi Arabian oil field. This is done because the cost of collecting and using the natural gas is more than the price it can be sold for in the oil-rich Middle East. Burning this high-quality fuel adds carbon dioxide and other pollutants to the atmosphere, but burning causes less projected global warming than allowing the methane to escape into the atmosphere.

## 18-2 Natural Gas

**TYPES, DISTRIBUTION, AND USES** In its underground gaseous state **natural gas** is a mixture of 50–90% by volume of methane ($CH_4$) and smaller amounts of heavier gaseous hydrocarbons such as propane ($C_3H_8$) and butane ($C_4H_{10}$).

*Conventional natural gas* lies above most reservoirs of crude oil (Figure 3-6). Some of this is burned off and wasted when the target is oil (Figure 18-9). *Unconventional natural gas* is found by itself in other underground sources, including coal seams, Devonian shale rock, deep underground deposits of tight sands, and deep geopressurized zones that contain natural gas dissolved in hot water. It is not yet economically feasible to get natural gas from unconventional sources, but the extraction technology is being developed rapidly.

When a natural gas field is tapped, propane and butane gases are liquefied and removed as **liquefied petroleum gas (LPG)**. LPG is stored in pressurized tanks for use mostly in rural areas not served by natural gas pipelines. The rest of the gas (mostly methane) is dried to remove water vapor, cleaned of hydrogen sulfide and other impurities, and pumped into pressurized pipelines for distribution.

At a very low temperature of –184°C (–300°F) natural gas can be converted to **liquefied natural gas (LNG)**. This highly flammable liquid can then be shipped to other countries in refrigerated tanker ships.

CIS countries, with 40% of the world's natural gas reserves, are the world's largest extractors of natural gas. Other countries with large proven natural gas reserves are Iran (14%), the United States (5%), Qatar (4%), Algeria (4%), Saudi Arabia (3%), and Nigeria (3%). Geologists expect to find more natural gas, especially in unexplored LDCs.

Most U.S. natural gas reserves are located in the same areas as crude oil (Figure 18-4). About 95% of the natural gas used in the United States is domestic; the other 5% is imported by pipeline from Canada. Algeria and some of the CIS countries use pipelines to supply Europe with natural gas. More pipelines are planned. The United Kingdom plans to shut down many of its coal mines and to use more natural gas.

About 82% of the natural gas consumed in the United States is used to heat residential and commercial buildings and for drying and other purposes in industry. The rest is used to produce electricity (15%) and to power vehicles (3%) (Table 17-2). Natural gas is the fuel of choice for most new power plants, and energy conversion efficiencies in new combined-cycle units can approach 45%.

Q: Which country has the world's largest number of sites contaminated with radioactive materials?

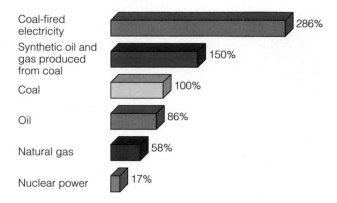

**Figure 18-10** Carbon dioxide emissions per unit of energy produced by various fossil fuels and nuclear energy as percentages of those produced by coal.

**PROS AND CONS** Natural gas has a number of advantages over other nonrenewable energy sources. It burns hotter and produces less air pollution than any other fossil fuel. It produces virtually no sulfur dioxide or particulate matter. Burning natural gas does produce carbon dioxide, but the amount per unit of energy produced is half that of coal and two-thirds that of oil (Figure 18-10). Methane, the major component of natural gas, is a greenhouse gas that is more potent per molecule than is carbon dioxide in causing global warming (Figure 11-3c); however, little of the methane in the atmosphere comes from extraction and use of natural gas. And extracting natural gas is much less damaging to the environment than coal extraction.

So far natural gas has been cheaper than oil. Known reserves and undiscovered, economically recoverable deposits of conventional natural gas in the United States are projected to last 60 years, and world supplies at least 80 years, at present consumption rates. It is estimated that conventional supplies of natural gas, as well as unconventional supplies available at higher prices, will last about 200 years at the current rate, and 80 years if usage rates rise 2% per year.

Natural gas can be transported easily over land by pipeline and has a high net useful energy yield. Moreover, it burns cleanly and efficiently in furnaces, stoves, water heaters, dryers, boilers, incinerators, motor vehicles (with almost 1 million vehicles on the road), fuel cells, heat pumps, air conditioners, and refrigerators.

New natural-gas-burning turbines, working like jet engines, can be used to produce electricity. Compared to coal-fired systems equipped with the latest pollution control devices, these turbines cost 50% less to build and 25% less to operate, are much more energy-efficient, and emit 65–85% less nitrogen oxides and 65% less carbon dioxide. Natural gas can also be burned cleanly and efficiently in cogenerators to pro-

duce high-temperature heat and electricity, and small amounts burned with coal in boilers can reduce emissions of nitrogen oxides by 50–75%.

One problem with natural gas is that it must be converted to liquid form (LNG) before it can be shipped by tanker from one country to another overseas. This is expensive and dangerous—huge explosions could kill many people and cause much damage in urban areas near LNG loading and unloading facilities. Conversion of natural gas into LNG also reduces the net useful energy yield by one-fourth. And extracting natural gas has many of the air and water pollution and land disruption problems associated with oil.

If large amounts of natural gas can be extracted from nonconventional deposits at affordable prices, natural gas may be a key option in making an orderly transition from oil to perpetual and renewable energy over the next 50 years. Hydrogen gas produced from water by solar-generated electricity (Section 17-8) could be mixed gradually with natural gas to help smooth the shift to a solar-hydrogen economy.

## 18-3 Coal

**TYPES, DISTRIBUTION, AND USES** Coal is a solid formed in several stages as plant remains are subjected to intense heat and pressure over many millions of years. It is a complex mixture of organic compounds, 30–98% (commonly 70–80%) carbon by weight, plus varying amounts of water and small amounts of nitrogen and sulfur.

Three types of increasingly harder coal are formed over the eons: lignite, bituminous coal, and anthracite (Figure 7-14). Peat, formed in the first stage, is not a coal. It is burned in some places but has a low heat content. Low-sulfur coal (lignite and anthracite) produces less sulfur dioxide when burned than does high-sulfur (bituminous) coal. Anthracite is the most desirable type of coal because of its high heat content and low sulfur content.

About 68% of the world's proven coal reserves and 85% of the estimated undiscovered coal deposits are located in the United States, the CIS, and China. Coal now provides 76% of China's commercial energy, making China the third largest emitter of carbon dioxide in the world (after the United States and the CIS).

Most U.S. coal fields occur in 17 states (Figure 18-11). Anthracite makes up only 2% of U.S. coal reserves; about 45% is high-sulfur bituminous coal with a high fuel value, found mostly in the East,

**Figure 18-11** Major coal fields in the United States and Canada. (Data from Council on Environmental Quality and Geological Survey of Canada)

mainly in Kentucky, West Virginia, Pennsylvania, Ohio, and Illinois. About 55% of U.S. coal reserves are found west of the Mississippi River. Most of these deposits contain low-sulfur bituminous coal and lignite. Lignite has a low energy content. These deposits are far from the heavily industrialized and populated East, where most coal is consumed.

About 60% of the coal extracted in the world, and 80% in the United States, is burned to produce steam for generating electrical power. The rest is either converted to coke (burned to make steel) or burned to produce steam for various manufacturing processes. Coal is used to generate 44% of the world's electricity and make 75% of its steel. Coal supplies 56% of the elec-

Q: Does using nuclear power add carbon dioxide to the atmosphere?

tricity generated in the United States; the rest is produced by nuclear energy (20%), natural gas (11%), hydropower (9%), oil (3%), and geothermal and solar energy (1%).

**PROS AND CONS OF SOLID COAL** Coal is the most abundant conventional fossil fuel in the world and in the United States. Identified world reserves of coal should last about 220 years at current usage rates and 65 years if usage rises 2% per year. The world's unidentified coal reserves are projected to last about 900 years at the current rate and 149 years if the usage rate increases 2% per year. Identified U.S. coal reserves should last about 300 years at the current consumption rate, and unidentified U.S. coal resources could extend those supplies for perhaps 100 years, at a much higher average cost.

Coal has a high net useful energy yield (Figure 3-19). In countries with adequate supplies, burning solid coal is the cheapest way to produce high-temperature heat and electricity. However, the low costs do not include requiring the best air pollution control equipment on all plants or reclaiming of all land surface mined for coal (Figure 7-24). If all of coal's harmful environmental costs were included in its market price and government subsidies were removed, coal would become so expensive that it would generally be replaced by cheaper and less environmentally harmful perpetual and renewable energy resources.

Coal has a number of other drawbacks. Since 1900 underground mining in the United States has killed more than 100,000 miners and permanently disabled at least 1 million—and mining safety laws in most countries are much weaker than those in the United States. Another 250,000 or more retired U.S. miners suffer from black lung disease, a form of emphysema caused by prolonged breathing of coal dust and other particulate matter.

Coal mining harms land as well as people. Underground mining causes subsidence when a mine shaft collapses during or after mining. For example, over 800,000 hectares (2 million acres) of land, much of it in central Appalachia, has subsided because of underground coal mining. Surface mining causes severe land disturbance (Figures 7-22 and 7-23) and soil erosion. In arid and semiarid areas the land cannot be fully restored. Surface and subsurface coal mining also can severely pollute nearby streams and groundwater from acids and toxic metal compounds (Figure 7-25). Furthermore, once coal is mined it is expensive to move from one place to another; and because it is solid it cannot be used as a fuel for cars and trucks.

Coal is the dirtiest fossil fuel. Although chemical "cleaning" can remove some of coal's sulfur before combustion, without expensive pollution control devices, burning coal produces much more sulfur dioxide, nitrogen oxides, and particulate matter than any other fossil fuel. These pollutants contribute to acid deposition, corrode metals, and harm trees, crops, wild animals, and people. Each year, for example, air pollutants from coal burning kill between 5,000 and 200,000 people in the United States and cause at least 50,000 cases of respiratory disease and several billion dollars in property damage.

Because coal produces more carbon dioxide per unit of energy than do other fossil fuels (Figure 18-10), burning more coal accelerates projected global warming (Section 11-1). This problem alone may keep much of the world's coal from being mined and burned.

New ways have been developed to burn coal more cleanly and efficiently. One is *fluidized-bed combustion*, which slashes emissions of sulfur and nitrogen oxides (Figure 18-12). Successful small-scale fluidized-bed combustion plants have been built in Great Britain, Sweden, Finland, the CIS, Germany, and China. In the United States commercial fluidized-bed combustion boilers are expected to begin replacing conventional coal boilers in the mid-1990s.

**CONVERTING SOLID COAL INTO GASEOUS AND LIQUID FUELS** Coal can also be converted into gaseous or liquid **synfuels**. **Coal gasification** (Figure 18-13) is the conversion of solid coal into **synthetic natural gas (SNG)**. **Coal liquefaction** is the conversion of solid coal into a liquid fuel such as methanol or synthetic gasoline.

Synfuels can be transported by pipeline. They produce much less air pollution than solid coal. Synfuels can be burned to produce high-temperature heat and electricity, heat houses and water, and propel vehicles.

However, synfuels also have low net useful energy yields (Figure 3-19). A synfuel plant costs much more to build and run than an equivalent coal-fired power plant fully equipped with air pollution control devices. In addition, widespread use of synfuels would accelerate the depletion of world coal supplies because 30–40% of the energy content of coal is lost in the conversion process. It would also lead to greater land disruption from surface mining because producing a unit of energy from synfuels uses more coal than does burning solid coal. Producing synfuels requires huge amounts of water. Burning synfuels releases larger amounts of carbon dioxide per unit of energy than does burning coal (Figure 18-10).

A big factor holding back large-scale production of synfuels in the United States is their high cost. Most analysts expect synfuels to play only a minor role as an energy resource in the next 30–50 years.

A: Yes, but it produces only one-sixth as much per unit of electricity as a coal-burning plant.

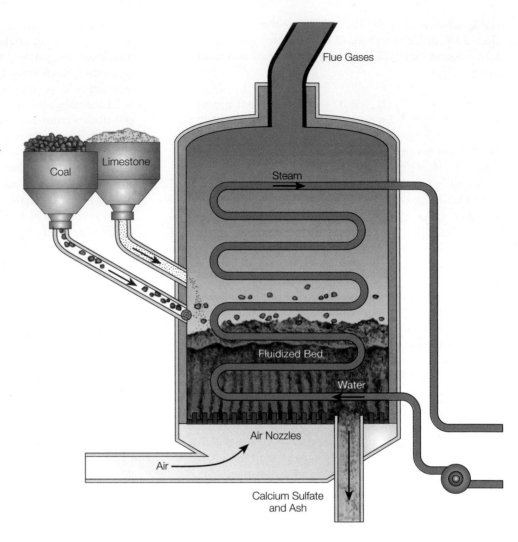

**Figure 18-12** Fluidized-bed combustion of coal. A stream of hot air is blown into a boiler to suspend a mixture of powdered coal and crushed limestone. This removes most of the sulfur dioxide, sharply reduces emissions of nitrogen oxides, and burns the coal more efficiently and more cheaply than conventional combustion methods.

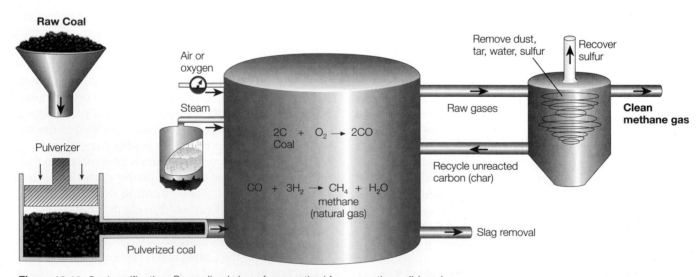

**Figure 18-13** Coal gasification. Generalized view of one method for converting solid coal into synthetic natural gas (methane).

**Q:** Nuclear weapons existing today could kill everyone in the world how many times over?

# Conventional Nuclear Fission

**A FADING DREAM** In the 1950s, when the development of controlled nuclear energy was just beginning, researchers predicted that by the end of the century 1,800 nuclear power plants would supply 21% of the world's commercial energy and 25% of that used in the United States. By 1993, after 45 years of development and enormous government subsidies, about 420 commercial nuclear reactors in 25 countries were producing only 17% of the world's electricity and less than 5% of its commercial energy. By 2000 nuclear power will supply less than one-tenth of the electricity it was once projected to produce.

In western Europe plans to build more nuclear power plants have come to a halt, except in France, which with 56 nuclear power plants got 75% of its electricity from nuclear power in 1993 and plans to up that figure to 90% by 2000. In 1993 Japan's 42 commercial nuclear reactors supplied 24% of the country's electricity, and 10 additional reactors now being built are expected to bring the total to 50% sometime after 2000. Since 1987, however, the government has been unable to find new sites for nuclear plants, mostly due to rising public opposition since the Chernobyl accident in 1986 (p. 476).

No new nuclear power plants have been ordered in the United States since 1978, and 119 previous orders have been canceled. In 1993 the 109 licensed commercial nuclear power plants in the United States generated about 20% of the country's electricity, a percentage that is expected to fall over the next two decades when many of the current reactors reach the end of their useful life.

What happened to nuclear power? The answer is billion-dollar construction cost overruns, high operating costs, frequent malfunctions, false assurances and cover-ups by government and industry officials, over forecasts of electricity uses, poor management, Chernobyl (p. 476), and public concerns about safety, costs, radioactive waste disposal.

**HOW DOES A NUCLEAR FISSION REACTOR WORK?** When the nuclei of atoms such as uranium-235 and plutonium-239 are split by neutrons in a nuclear fission chain reaction, energy is released and converted mostly into high-temperature heat (Figure 3-12). The rate at which this happens can be controlled in the nuclear fission reactor of a nuclear power plant; the heat generated can be used to spin a turbine and produce electricity.

*Light-water reactors (LWRs)* like the one shown in Figure 18-14 generate about 85% of the world's electricity (100% in the United States) produced by nuclear power plants. Key parts of an LWR are the core, control rods, moderator, and coolant. The core of an LWR typically contains 35,000–40,000 long, thin fuel rods bundled in 180 fuel assemblies of around 200 rods each. Each fuel rod is packed with pellets of uranium oxide fuel the size of a pencil eraser.

About 97% of the uranium in each fuel pellet is uranium-238, a nonfissionable isotope; the other 3% (versus 0.7% in nature) is uranium-235, which is fissionable. The concentration of uranium-235 in the ore is increased (enriched) from 0.7% to 3% by removing some of the uranium-238 to create a suitable fuel. The uranium-235 in each fuel rod produces energy equal to that in three railroad carloads of coal over its lifetime of about three to four years.

Control rods are made of materials such as boron or cadmium that absorb neutrons. The rods are moved in and out of the reactor core to regulate the rate of fission and thus the amount of power the reactor produces. All reactors use some material, known as a moderator, to slow down the neutrons emitted by the fission process so that the chain reaction can be kept going.

Some 75% of the world's commercial reactors use ordinary water, called light water, as a moderator. Thus the interior of most commercial reactors is somewhat like a swimming pool with a large number of movable vertical fuel rods and control rods hanging in it. The moderator in about 20% of the world's commercial reactors (50% of those in the CIS, including the ill-fated Chernobyl reactor) is solid graphite, a form of carbon. Graphite-moderated reactors can also be used to produce fissionable plutonium-239 for use in nuclear weapons. The moderator in the rest, mostly in Canada, is heavy water ($D_2O$).

A coolant circulating through the reactor's core removes heat to keep fuel rods and other materials from melting and to produce steam for generating electricity. Most water-moderated and some graphite-moderated reactors use water as a coolant; the few gas-cooled reactors use an unreactive gas such as helium or argon for cooling.

Even after control rods have been inserted to stop all nuclear fission in the reactor core, the fission products produced continue to give off radioactivity and heat. To prevent a *meltdown*—which could release enormous quantities of highly radioactive materials into the environment—huge amounts of water must be kept circulating through the core to cool it.

Nuclear power plants, each with one or more reactors, are only one part of the nuclear fuel cycle (Figure 18-15). In evaluating the safety and economy

A: 60 (20 if current arms reduction proposals are carried out)

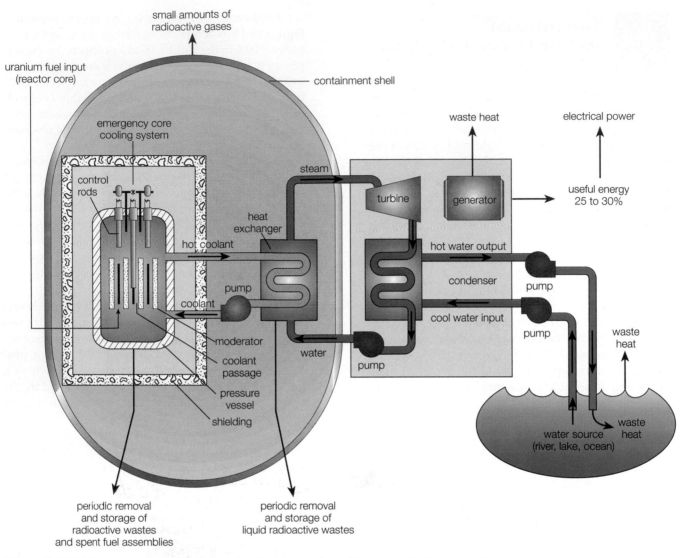

small amounts of radioactive gases

uranium fuel input (reactor core)

containment shell

emergency core cooling system

control rods

heat exchanger

hot coolant

steam

waste heat

electrical power

turbine

generator

useful energy 25 to 30%

pump

coolant

hot water output

condenser

pump

moderator

coolant passage

pressure vessel

shielding

water

cool water input

pump

pump

waste heat

pump

waste heat

water source (river, lake, ocean)

waste heat

periodic removal and storage of radioactive wastes and spent fuel assemblies

periodic removal and storage of liquid radioactive wastes

**Figure 18-14** Light-water-moderated-and-cooled nuclear power plant with a pressurized water reactor.

of nuclear power, we need to look at the entire cycle, not just the nuclear plant itself.

After three to four years in a reactor the concentration of fissionable uranium-235 in a fuel rod becomes too low to keep the chain reaction going, or the rod becomes damaged from exposure to ionizing radiation. Each year about one-third of the spent fuel assemblies in a reactor are removed and stored in large, concrete-lined pools of water at the plant site.

After they have cooled for several years and lost some of their radioactivity, the spent fuel rods are sealed in shielded, supposedly crash-proof casks. They can be transported by truck or train to storage pools away from the reactor, to a nuclear waste repository or dump, or to a fuel-reprocessing plant (Figure 18-15). At a reprocessing plant remaining uranium-235 and plutonium-239 produced as a by-product of the

fission process are removed and sent to a fuel fabrication plant. Such plants also handle and ship weapons-grade plutonium-239.

If the fuel is processed to remove plutonium and other radioactive isotopes with long half-lives (Table 3-1), the remaining radioactive waste must be safely stored for at least 10,000 years. Otherwise, the rods must be stored safely for at least 240,000 years—several times as long as our species has been around.

Commercial fuel-reprocessing plants have been built in France, Great Britain, Japan, and Germany, but all have had severe operating and economic problems. The United States has delayed development of commercial fuel-reprocessing plants because of policy concerns (terrorist diversion of bomb-grade material), high construction and operating costs, and adequate domestic supplies of uranium.

Q: Can switching to increased use of nuclear power in the United States save much oil?

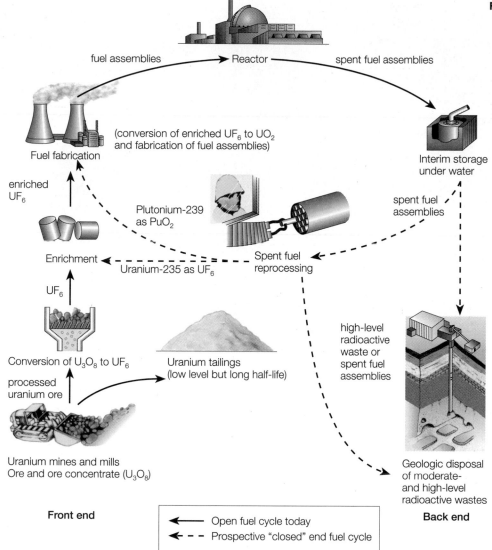

**Figure 18-15** The nuclear fuel cycle.

fuel assemblies → Reactor → spent fuel assemblies

(conversion of enriched UF$_6$ to UO$_2$ and fabrication of fuel assemblies)

Fuel fabrication

enriched UF$_6$

Plutonium-239 as PuO$_2$

Enrichment

Uranium-235 as UF$_6$

UF$_6$

Spent fuel reprocessing

Conversion of U$_3$O$_8$ to UF$_6$

processed uranium ore

Uranium tailings (low level but long half-life)

Uranium mines and mills
Ore and ore concentrate (U$_3$O$_8$)

Interim storage under water

spent fuel assemblies

high-level radioactive waste or spent fuel assemblies

Geologic disposal of moderate- and high-level radioactive wastes

**Front end**

**Back end**

← Open fuel cycle today
←--- Prospective "closed" end fuel cycle

**HOW SAFE ARE NUCLEAR POWER PLANTS?** To greatly reduce the chances of a meltdown or other serious reactor accident, commercial reactors in the United States (and most countries) have many safety features:

■ Thick walls and concrete and steel shields surrounding the reactor vessel

■ A system for automatically inserting control rods into the core to stop fission under emergency conditions

■ A steel-reinforced concrete containment building to keep radioactive gases and materials from reaching the atmosphere after an accident

■ Large filter systems and chemical sprayers inside the containment building to remove radioactive dust from the air and further reduce chances of radioactivity reaching the environment

■ Systems to condense steam released from a ruptured reactor vessel and prevent pressure from rising beyond the holding power of containment building walls

■ An emergency core-cooling system to flood the core automatically with huge amounts of water within one minute to prevent meltdown of the reactor core

■ Two separate power lines servicing the plant and several diesel generators to supply backup power for the huge pumps in the emergency core-cooling system

■ An automatic backup system to replace each major part of the safety system in the event of a failure

Such elaborate safety systems make a complete reactor core meltdown very unlikely. However, a

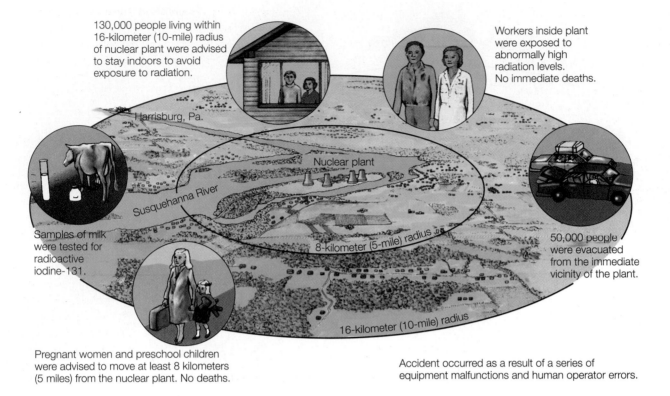

130,000 people living within 16-kilometer (10-mile) radius of nuclear plant were advised to stay indoors to avoid exposure to radiation.

Workers inside plant were exposed to abnormally high radiation levels. No immediate deaths.

Harrisburg, Pa.

Nuclear plant

Susquehanna River

8-kilometer (5-mile) radius

16-kilometer (10-mile) radius

Samples of milk were tested for radioactive iodine-131.

50,000 people were evacuated from the immediate vicinity of the plant.

Pregnant women and preschool children were advised to move at least 8 kilometers (5 miles) from the nuclear plant. No deaths.

Accident occurred as a result of a series of equipment malfunctions and human operator errors.

**Figure 18-16** Three Mile Island in eastern Pennsylvania, where a nuclear accident occurred on March 29, 1979, as a result of a series of operator errors and equipment malfunctions.

partial or complete meltdown or explosion is possible, as Chernobyl (p. 476) and Three Mile Island taught us. On March 29, 1979, one of the two reactors at the Three Mile Island (TMI) nuclear plant near Harrisburg, Pennsylvania lost its coolant water because of a series of mechanical failures and human operator errors not anticipated in safety studies, and the reactor's core became partially uncovered (Figure 18-16). At least 70% of the core was damaged, and about 50% of it melted and fell to the bottom of the reactor. Unknown amounts of ionizing radiation escaped into the atmosphere, 50,000 people were evacuated, and another 50,000 fled the area on their own. Investigators discovered that if a valve had stayed stuck open for another 30–60 minutes, there would have been a complete meltdown.

No one can be shown to have died immediately because of the accident. So far, a dozen studies, mostly by federal and state officials, have found no links between the estimated radiation release and subsequent cancers, birth defects, and other ailments. However, long-term health effects on workers and nearby residents are still being debated. Data published on the radiation released during the accident are contradictory and incomplete.

Partial cleanup of the damaged TMI reactor, which continues, has cost $1 billion so far, more than

the $700-million construction cost of the reactor. In addition, about $187 million of taxpayers' money has been spent by the Department of Energy on the TMI cleanup. Plant owners have also paid out $25 million to over 2,100 people who filed lawsuits for damages.

Although many studies of nuclear safety have been made since 1957, none has been officially accepted, and no safety study of the entire nuclear fuel cycle has been conducted. The Nuclear Regulatory Commission (NRC) estimates that there is a 15–45% chance of a complete core meltdown at a U.S. reactor during the next 20 years. The commission also found that 39 U.S. reactors have an 80% chance of containment failure from a meltdown or a tremendous gas explosion. Scientists in Germany and Sweden project that worldwide there is a 70% chance of another serious core-damaging accident within the next 5.4 years. Especially risky are 13 nuclear reactors in Russia, Lithuania, and Belarus with a Chernobyl-type design. Environmentalists urge that these and 10 other poorly designed and operated nuclear plants in eastern Europe be shut down.

A 1982 study by the Sandia National Laboratory estimated that a possible, but highly unlikely, *worst-case accident* in a reactor near a large U.S. city might cause 50,000–100,000 immediate deaths, 10,000–40,000 subsequent deaths from cancer, and $100–$150 billion in damages. Most citizens and businesses suffering injuries or property damage from a major nuclear accident would get little if any financial reimbursement because combined government–nuclear industry insurance covers only 7% of the estimated damage from such a worst-case accident. Nuclear critics also contend that plans for dealing with major nuclear accidents in the United States are inadequate.

There is widespread lack of confidence in the ability of the Nuclear Regulatory Commission and the Department of Energy to enforce nuclear safety in commercial and military nuclear facilities. Congressional hearings in 1987 uncovered evidence that high-level NRC staff members destroyed documents and obstructed investigations of criminal wrongdoing by utilities, suggested ways utilities can evade commission regulations, and provided utilities and their contractors with advance notice of surprise inspections. Some NRC field supervisors also harassed and intimidated lower-level NRC inspectors who cited utilities for too many violations.

Since 1986 government studies and once-secret documents have revealed that most of the nuclear weapons production facilities supervised by the Department of Energy (DOE) have been operated with gross disregard for the safety of their workers and people in nearby areas. Since 1957 these facilities have released huge quantities of radioactive particles into the air and dumped tons of radioactive waste and toxic substances into flowing creeks and leaking pits without telling local residents.

Senator John Glenn of Ohio summed up the situation: "We are poisoning our own people in the name of national security." Lois Camp, who lives near the Hanford, Washington, facility and who suffers from uterine cancer and has trouble swallowing, says, "I feel like they used us as guinea pigs, and I don't feel like they cared one iota what happened to us or our families."

In 1992 the EPA estimated there may be as many as 45,000 sites in the United States contaminated with radioactive materials, 20,000 of these sites belonging to the DOE and the Department of Defense. The General Accounting Office and the DOE estimate that it will cost taxpayers at least $270 billion over 30 years to clean up these facilities, which may expose cleanup workers to dangerous levels of radiation. Stung by 50 years of secrecy and lies by government officials, some believe that the full story has yet to come out and will be even worse. Some doubt that the necessary cleanup funds will be provided by Congress.

This tragic situation in the United States pales in comparison to the legacy of nuclear waste and contamination in the former Soviet Union. Mayak, a plutonium production facility in southern Russia, has spewed out two and a half times as much radiation as Chernobyl into the atmosphere and into the nearby Techa River and Lake Karachay. Today the lake is so radioactive that standing on its shores for about an hour would be fatal. Around the shores of Novaya Zemyla off the coast of Russia, 15 defunct nuclear-powered submarines have been dumped (at least three of them loaded with nuclear fuel), along with as many as 17,000 containers of radioactive waste. If released by corrosion, radioactivity from these submarines and containers would threaten Russian citizens in these areas as well as many people living along the northern shores of Finland, Sweden, and Norway.

**WHAT CAN WE DO WITH RADIOACTIVE WASTES?**
Each part of the nuclear fuel cycle (Figure 18-15) produces solid, liquid, and gaseous radioactive wastes with various half-lives (Table 3-1). Those classified as *low-level radioactive wastes* give off small amounts of ionizing radiation, usually for a long time. From the 1940s to 1970 most low-level radioactive waste produced in the United States (and most other countries) was dumped into the ocean in steel drums; Great Britain and Pakistan still dispose of their low-level wastes in this way. Since 1970 low-level radioactive wastes from U.S. military activities have been buried in government-run landfills.

Today low-level waste materials from commercial nuclear power plants, hospitals, universities, industries, and other producers are put in steel drums and shipped to regional landfills run by federal and state governments (Figure 18-17). Three of the six landfills for these wastes have been closed because of radioactive contamination of groundwater and nearby property. Attempts to build new regional dumps for low-level radioactive waste have met with fierce public opposition.

According to the EPA all landfills eventually leak. The best-designed low-level radioactive landfills may not leak for several decades, just about the time the companies running them will no longer be liable for leaks and problems. After that, any problems would be passed on to future generations.

In June 1990 the Nuclear Regulatory Commission proposed that most of the country's low-level radioactive waste be removed from federal regulation and handled like ordinary trash (dumped in landfills, incinerated, reused, or recycled into consumer products). According to the NRC exposure to radiation from these unregulated wastes would kill 2,500 Americans per year—1 out of every 100,000 citizens. Other estimates show as many as 12,412 more cancer deaths per year (see cartoon). Several environmental groups successfully opposed this NRC policy.

*High-level radioactive wastes* give off large amounts of ionizing radiation for a short time and small amounts for a long time. Most high-level radioactive

A: It would be too expensive to use and would be phased out.

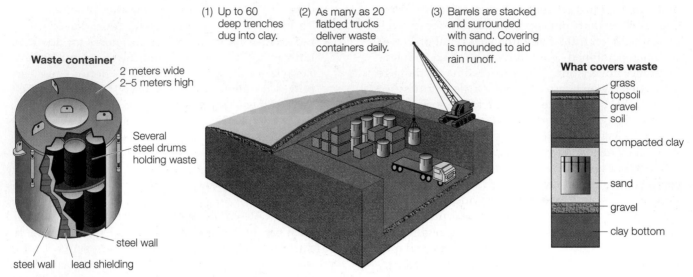

(1) Up to 60 deep trenches dug into clay.

(2) As many as 20 flatbed trucks deliver waste containers daily.

(3) Barrels are stacked and surrounded with sand. Covering is mounded to aid rain runoff.

**Waste container**

2 meters wide
2–5 meters high

Several steel drums holding waste

steel wall

steel wall  lead shielding

**What covers waste**

grass
topsoil
gravel
soil

compacted clay

sand

gravel

clay bottom

**Figure 18-17** Proposed low-level radioactive waste landfill. At least 56% (some say 80%) of U.S. low-level radioactive waste comes from nuclear power plants and 31% from industry. Less than 2% comes from the medical community. Since all landfills leak, some environmentalists believe that low-level radioactive waste should be stored in carefully designed aboveground buildings, located at nuclear power plant sites, which produce most of the wastes and which have the expertise to manage these wastes. (Data from Atomic Industrial Forum)

wastes are spent fuel rods from commercial nuclear power plants and an assortment of wastes from nuclear weapons plants.

Each year there are about 3 million shipments of radioactive materials across the United States, over 1,000 of them consisting of highly radioactive spent fuel. Currently most of this spent fuel is being stored at reactor sites in specially designed cooling ponds, but some plants are running out of storage space. The DOE eventually wants to ship this waste to a moni-

tored retrievable storage (MRS) facility. There the wastes would be consolidated for eventual transfer to a permanent disposal site. However, proposed locations for MRS sites have been vigorously opposed by citizens and state officials.

After 38 years of research and debate, scientists still don't agree on a safe method of storing these wastes (Case Study, p. 493). Regardless of the storage method, most citizens strongly oppose the location of a low-level or high-level nuclear waste disposal facility anywhere near them (Case Study, p. 494).

In 1991 the DOE proposed that the handling of low- and high-level nuclear waste be turned over to the private sector, arguing that this would reduce government accountability and regulation, and lower budget expenditures. This move would also limit public access to information about nuclear waste by avoiding the disclosure requirements faced by government agencies.

There has also been strong citizen opposition to proposals for high-level radioactive waste depositories in Europe, Canada, and Japan. None of the European countries is in a hurry to find a permanent disposal site. For example, Sweden, which generates almost 50% of its electricity in 12 nuclear power plants to be phased out by 2010, has developed a centralized interim storage facility. Fuel is expected to be stored there for at least 40 years. A permanent storage site will probably not be chosen until 2006. The Netherlands and Great Britain also plan interim storage of their radioactive wastes for at least 50 years before deciding on a more permanent solution.

**Q:** Is nuclear fusion the answer to our energy problems?

Some scientists believe that the long-term safe storage or disposal of high-level radioactive wastes is technically possible. Others disagree, pointing out that it is impossible to show that any method will work for the 10,000–240,000 years of fail-safe storage needed for such wastes. Here are some of the proposed methods and their possible drawbacks:

■ *Bury it deep underground.* This favored strategy is under study by all countries producing nuclear waste. Spent fuel rods would be reprocessed to remove very long-lived radioactive isotopes. The remainder would be fused with glass or a ceramic material and sealed in metal canisters for burial in a deep underground salt, granite, or other stable geological formation that is earthquake resistant and waterproof (Figure 18-18). However, according to a 1990 report by the National Academy of Sciences, "use of geological information—to pretend to be able to make very accurate predictions of long-term site behavior—is scientifically unsound."

■ *Shoot it into space or into the sun.* Costs would be very high, and a launch accident, such as the explosion of the space shuttle *Challenger,* could disperse high-level radioactive wastes over large areas of the earth's surface. This strategy has been abandoned for now.

■ *Bury it under the Antarctic ice sheet or the Greenland ice cap.* The long-term stability of the ice sheets is not known. They could be destabilized by heat from the wastes, and retrieval of the wastes would be difficult or impossible if the method failed. This strategy has also been abandoned for now.

■ *Dump it into descending subduction zones in the deep ocean* (Figure 7-6). Again, our geological knowledge is incomplete; wastes might eventually be spewed out somewhere else by volcanic activity. Also, waste containers might leak and contaminate the ocean before being carried downward, and retrieval would be impossible if the method did not work. This method is under active study by a consortium of 10 countries.

■ *Change it into harmless, or less harmful, isotopes.* Currently there is no way to do this. Even if a method were developed, costs would probably be extremely high, and resulting toxic materials and low-level, but very long-lived, radioactive wastes would still have to be disposed of safely. This method is under active study by the United States, France, Japan, and the CIS.

Critics of nuclear power are appalled that the nuclear industry has built hundreds of nuclear reactors and weapons facilities without finding an acceptable way to deal with radioactive wastes. Even if every nuclear power plant and weapons facility were shut down today, future generations would be saddled with the costs and risks of dealing with their radioactive wastes for millennia.

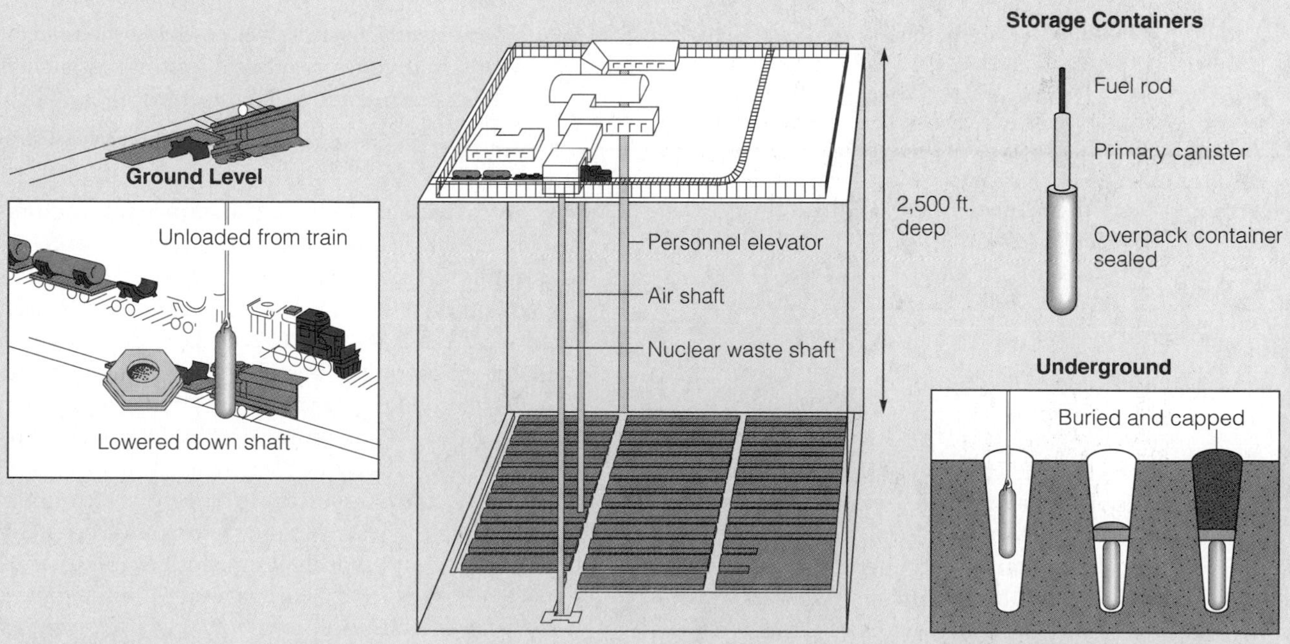

**Storage Containers**

Fuel rod

Primary canister

Overpack container sealed

**Ground Level**

Unloaded from train

Lowered down shaft

Personnel elevator

Air shaft

Nuclear waste shaft

2,500 ft. deep

**Underground**

Buried and capped

**Figure 18-18** Proposed general design for deep-underground permanent storage of high-level radioactive wastes from commercial nuclear power plants in the United States. (Source: U.S. Department of Energy)

# The Search for a Radioactive Waste Depository

The U.S. government planned to open an underground depository for storing high-level radioactive waste from commercial reactors in a salt formation near Lyons, Kansas, by 1987. That site was abandoned when it was shown that water could leak in and cause the salt to rapidly eat away spent fuel containers and release radioactive materials into groundwater.

In 1982 Congress passed the Nuclear Waste Policy Act. It set a timetable for the DOE to choose a site and build the country's first deep-underground repository for storage of high-level radioactive wastes from commercial nuclear reactors. In 1985 the DOE announced plans to build the first repository (Figure 18-18) on federal land in the Yucca Mountain desert region, 160 kilometers (100 miles) northwest of Las Vegas, Nevada. Construction on the $10-billion project was supposed to begin in 1998, and the facility was scheduled to open by 2003.

In 1990, however, the DOE moved the opening date to at least 2010, and there is a strong possibility that the facility may never open. A young, active volcano is only 11 kilometers (7 miles) away, and according to the DOE's own data there are 32 active earthquake faults on the site itself. Yucca Mountain's many rock fractures also suggest that water flowing through the site could leach out radioactive wastes and carry them 5 kilometers (3.1 miles) or more from the site in 400–500 years.

Meanwhile, the DOE has also asked Congress for permission to build an aboveground interim storage facility for high-level radioactive wastes— a sort of halfway house for wastes awaiting permanent disposal. Some critics fear the temporary facility could become the permanent site, with the DOE declaring the problem solved.

## WHAT CAN WE DO WITH WORN-OUT NUCLEAR PLANTS?

The useful operating life of today's nuclear power plants is supposed to be 40 years, but many plants are aging faster than anticipated. After many years of bombardment by neutrons released by nuclear fission (Figure 3-12), the walls of a reactor's pressure vessel become brittle and thus more likely to crack, thereby exposing the highly radioactive reactor core (Figure 18-14). Moreover, decades of pressure and temperature changes gradually weaken tubes in the reactor's steam generator, which can crack, releasing contaminated water. Finally, corrosion of pipes and valves throughout the system can cause them to crack. Because so many of its parts become radioactive, a nuclear plant cannot be abandoned or demolished by a wrecking ball the way a worn-out coal-fired power plant can.

Decommissioning nuclear power plants and nuclear weapons plants is the last step in the nuclear fuel cycle. Three methods have been proposed, each of which involves shutting down the plant, removing the spent fuel from the reactor core, draining all liquids, flushing all pipes, and sending all radioactive materials to an approved waste storage site yet to be built:

- *Immediate dismantling.* This involves decontaminating and taking the reactor apart after shutdown, and shipping all radioactive debris to a radioactive waste burial facility. This method promptly rids the plant site of radioactive materials and is the least expensive option. However, it exposes work crews to the highest level of radiation and results in the largest volume of radioactive waste.

- *Mothballing.* This involves putting up a barrier and setting up a 24-hour security system to keep out intruders for 30–100 years before dismantling. This method permits radioactive isotopes with short half-lives to decay, reducing the threat to work crews and the volume of contaminated waste.

- *Entombment.* This involves covering the reactor with reinforced concrete and putting up a barrier to keep out intruders. This method allows for radioactive decay but passes a dangerous legacy on to future generations.

Worldwide more than 25 commercial reactors (10 in the United States) have been retired and await decommissioning. Another 228 large commercial reactors (20 in the United States) are scheduled for retirement between 2000 and 2012. By 2030 all U.S. reactors will have to be retired based on the life of their operating licenses. Many reactors may have to be retired early because of structural problems or lack of profitability.

Utility company officials currently estimate that dismantling a typical large reactor should cost about $170 million, and mothballing about $225 million, but most analysts place the cost around $1 billion per reactor. So far U.S. utilities have only $3.5 billion set aside for decommissioning more than 100 reactors. The balance of the cost could be passed along to ratepayers and taxpayers, adding to the already high cost of electricity produced by nuclear fission. Politicians and nuclear industry officials may be tempted to mothball retired plants, passing dismantlement costs and problems on to the next generation.

**CAN WE SLOW THE SPREAD OF NUCLEAR WEAPONS?** Since 1958 the United States has been giving away and selling to other countries various forms of nuclear technology. Today at least 14 other countries sell nuclear technology in the international marketplace.

For decades the U.S. government denied that the information, components, and materials used in the nuclear fuel cycle could be used to make nuclear weapons. In 1981, however, a Los Alamos National Laboratory report admitted, "There is no technical demarcation between the military and civilian reactor and there never was one"—something environmentalists had been saying for years.

To date 135 countries have signed the 1968 Nuclear Nonproliferation Treaty, agreeing to forgo building nuclear weapons in return for help with commercial nuclear power. However, nuclear facilities belonging to India, Israel, South Africa, Argentina, Brazil, Pakistan, and other countries that have not signed the treaty are not monitored.

*We live in a world with enough nuclear weapons to kill everyone on Earth 60 times over—20 times over if current nuclear arms reduction proposals are carried out.* By the end of this century 60 countries—one of every three in the world—will have either nuclear weapons or the knowledge and capability to build them, with the fuel material and knowledge coming mostly from research and commercial nuclear reactors.

A sophisticated terrorist group might also be able to obtain enough material to make a small atomic bomb. Spent reactor fuel is so highly radioactive that theft is unlikely, but plutonium separated at commercial and military reprocessing plants (Figure 18-15) is much less radioactive and can be handled fairly easily. Although plutonium shipments are heavily guarded, plutonium could be stolen from nuclear weapons or reprocessing plants, especially by employees.

It takes only about 10 kilograms (22 pounds) of plutonium to make an atomic bomb the size of the one dropped by the United States on Nagasaki, Japan, at the end of World War II. As little as 3 kilograms (7 pounds) of plutonium or uranium-233, or about 20 kilograms (45 pounds) of enriched uranium-235, could blow up a large building (such as the World Trade Center) or a small city block, and contaminate a much larger area with radioactive materials for centuries. However, those who would steal plutonium need not bother to make atomic bombs; they could simply use a conventional explosive charge to disperse the pluto-

nium into the atmosphere from atop any tall building. Dispersed in that way 1 kilogram (2.2 pounds) of plutonium oxide powder theoretically would contaminate 8 square kilometers (3 square miles) with dangerous levels of radioactivity for several hundred thousand years. Or they could put plutonium in a city's water supply.

One way to reduce the diversion of plutonium fuel from the nuclear fuel cycle would be to contaminate it with other substances that make it useless in weapons. Thus far, however, no one has found a way to do this. The best ways to slow the spread of bomb-grade material are to abandon civilian reprocessing of power-plant fuel, develop substitutes for highly enriched uranium in research reactors, and tighten international safeguards.

**CAN WE AFFORD NUCLEAR POWER?** After the United States dropped atomic bombs on Hiroshima and Nagasaki, killing over 200,000 people and ending World War II, the scientists who developed the bomb and the elected officials responsible for its use were determined to show that the peaceful uses of atomic energy could outweigh the immense harm it had done. One part of this "Atoms for Peace" program was to use nuclear power to produce electricity.

Initially U.S. utility companies were skeptical. However, they began developing nuclear power plants in the late 1950s because the Atomic Energy Commission promised them that nuclear power would produce electricity at a much lower cost than coal and other alternatives, and because the government paid about a quarter of the cost of constructing the first group of commercial reactors. Also, after insurance companies refused to cover more than a small part of the possible damages from a nuclear power-plant accident, Congress passed the Price-Anderson Act, which protected the nuclear industry and utilities from significant liability to the general public in case of accidents. It was an offer utility company officials could not resist. Today many wish they had.

Nuclear power is an expensive way to boil water to produce electricity, even when it is heavily subsidized. Despite massive subsidies new nuclear power plants produce electricity at an average of about 13¢ per kilowatt-hour—the equivalent of burning oil costing over $100 per barrel to produce electricity. These costs do not include most of the costs of storing radioactive wastes and decommissioning worn-out plants. All methods of producing electricity in the United States except solar-photovoltaic and solar-thermal plants have average costs below those of new nuclear power plants (Figure 17-2). The newest and last U.S. nuclear plant took 20 years to build and cost $11 billion—14 times the original estimate.

# Should More Nuclear Power Plants Be Built in the United States?

Since the Three Mile Island accident the U.S. nuclear industry and utility companies have financed a $20-million-per-year public relations campaign by the U.S. Council for Energy Awareness. Its goals are to improve the industry's image, resell nuclear power to the American public, and downgrade the importance of solar energy, conservation, geothermal energy, wind, and hydropower as alternatives.

Most ads use the argument that the United States needs more nuclear power to reduce dependence on imported oil and improve national security. The truth is that since 1979 only about 5% (3% in 1991) of the electricity in the United States has been produced by burning oil, and 95% of that is residual oil that can't be used for other purposes. Even if all electricity in the United States came from nuclear power—which would require about 500 nuclear plants—this would reduce U.S. oil consumption by less than 5%. The nuclear industry also does not point out that half of the uranium used for nuclear fuel in the United States is imported.

The nuclear industry also claims that nuclear power, unlike coal burning, adds no greenhouse-enhancing carbon dioxide to the atmosphere. Nuclear power plants themselves don't release $CO_2$, but processing of uranium fuel (Figure 18-15) produces about one-sixth the $CO_2$ per unit of electricity as that from a coal-burning plant (Figure 18-10). To offset just 5% of current global $CO_2$ emissions would require nearly doubling the worldwide nuclear power capacity at a cost of more than $1 trillion. To replace all existing coal plants with nuclear plants would cost at least $5.3 trillion and increase the number of nuclear reactions from 420 to 5,000.

According to the Rocky Mountain Institute, if we hope to reduce $CO_2$ emissions using the least-cost methods, then investing in energy efficiency and renewable energy resources are at the top of the list and nuclear power is at the bottom (Guest Essay, p. 71).

The nuclear industry hopes to persuade governments and utility companies to build hundreds of new "second-generation" plants using standardized designs, most with passive "fail-safe" safety features. Supposedly they are safer and can be built more quickly (three to five years).

However, according to *Nucleonics Week*, an important nuclear industry publication, "experts are flatly unconvinced that safety has been achieved—or even substantially reduced—by the new designs."

Furthermore, none of the new designs solves the problem of what to do with nuclear waste and the problem of using nuclear technology and fuel to build nuclear weapons. Indeed, these problems would become more serious if the number of nuclear plants increased from a few hundred to several thousand.

---

In the United States, with 81 different designs among the country's 109 operating commercial reactors, poor planning and management and stricter safety regulations since the TMI accident have increased costs and lengthened construction time. Currently a new U.S. nuclear power plant would cost three times as much to build as equivalent coal-fired plants with the latest air pollution control equipment. New nuclear plants in France and Japan cost about half as much per kilowatt of power to build as those in the United States because they are better planned and use standardized designs.

Banks and other lending institutions have become leary of financing new U.S. nuclear power plants. The TMI accident showed that utility companies could lose $1 billion worth of equipment in an hour and at least $1 billion more in cleanup costs, even without any known harmful effects on public health. Abandoned reactor projects have cost U.S. utility investors over $100 billion since the middle 1970s. *Forbes* magazine has called the failure of the U.S. nuclear power pro-gram "the largest managerial disaster in U.S. business history." In fact, no U.S. utility company is planning to build any new nuclear power plants because they are no longer a cost-effective or wise investment even with massive government subsidies.

Is nuclear power dead in the United States and most other MDCs? You might think so because of its high costs and tremendous public opposition, but the DOE and energy agencies in many other MDCs continue to push for nuclear power instead of safer and more cost-effective alternatives (Spotlight, above).

**PROS AND CONS** On the one hand, nuclear plants don't release particulate matter, sulfur dioxide, or nitrogen oxides into the atmosphere, as do coal-fired plants. Also, water pollution and disruption of land are low to moderate if the entire nuclear fuel cycle operates normally. Moreover, multiple safety systems greatly decrease the likelihood of a catastrophic accident releasing deadly radioactive material into the environment.

Q: What is the value of hard-rock minerals removed from U.S. public lands?

On the other hand, construction and operating costs for nuclear power plants in the United States and most countries are high and rising, even with enormous government subsidies. And even though standardized designs and mass production can bring construction costs down, electricity can still be produced by safer methods at equal or lower cost. Also, although major accidents are infrequent, a combination of mechanical failure and human errors (p. 476), sabotage, or shipping accidents could again release deadly radioactive materials into the environment.

The net useful energy yield of nuclear-generated electricity is probably low, especially if the entire nuclear fuel cycle (Figure 18-15) is included. Scientists disagree over how high-level radioactive wastes should be stored; some doubt that an acceptably safe method can ever be developed. Also, some carbon dioxide and other pollutants are released as part of the nuclear fuel cycle.

Today's military and commercial nuclear energy programs commit future generations to storing dangerous radioactive wastes for thousands of years even if nuclear fission power is abandoned tomorrow. The existence of nuclear power technology also helps spread knowledge and materials that can be used to make nuclear weapons. For these reasons many people believe that it is unethical, uneconomical, and unnecessary to use nuclear power to generate electricity.

## 18-5 Breeder Nuclear Fission and Nuclear Fusion

BREEDER NUCLEAR FISSION Fissionable uranium-235, used in conventional fission reactors, comes from natural uranium ore (Figure 3-3). At its present rate of use the world's supply of uranium should last for at least 100 years and perhaps 200 years. Some nuclear power proponents urge the development and widespread use of **breeder nuclear fission reactors**, which generate more nuclear fuel than they consume by converting nonfissionable uranium-238 into fissionable plutonium-239. Since breeders would use over 99% of the uranium in ore deposits, the world's known uranium reserves would last for 1,000 years and perhaps several thousand years.

However, if the safety system of a breeder reactor should fail, the reactor could lose some of its liquid sodium coolant. This could cause a runaway fission chain reaction and perhaps a small nuclear explosion with the force of several hundred kilograms of TNT.

Such an explosion could blast open the containment building, releasing a cloud of highly radioactive gases and particulate matter. Leaks of flammable liquid sodium also can cause fires, as has happened with all experimental breeder reactors built so far.

Since 1966 small experimental breeder reactors have been built in the United Kingdom, the former Soviet Union, Germany, Japan, and France. In December 1986 France opened a $3-billion commercial-size breeder reactor. Not only did it cost three times the original estimate to build, but the little electricity it produced was twice as expensive as that generated by France's conventional fission reactors. In 1987, shortly after the reactor began operating at full power, it began leaking liquid sodium coolant and was shut down. Repairs may be so expensive that the reactor is never put back into operation.

Tentative plans to build full-size commercial breeders in Germany, the CIS, the United Kingdom, and Japan have been abandoned because of the French experience and an excess of electric-generating capacity. Also, the experimental breeders already built produce only about one-fourth of the plutonium-239 needed to replace their own fissionable material. If this problem is not solved, it will take 100–200 years for breeders to begin producing enough plutonium to fuel a significant number of other breeders.

NUCLEAR FUSION Scientists hope someday to use controlled nuclear fusion (Figure 3-13) to provide an almost limitless source of high-temperature heat and electricity. For 48 years research has focused on the D-T nuclear fusion reaction in which two isotopes of hydrogen—deuterium (D) and tritium (T)—fuse at about 100 million degrees. Another possibility is the D-D fusion reaction, in which the nuclei of two deuterium atoms fuse together at even higher temperatures. If developed it would run on virtually unlimited heavy water ($D_2O$) fuel, obtained from seawater at a cost of about 10¢ per gallon.

After almost five decades of research, however, high-temperature nuclear fusion is still at the laboratory stage. Deuterium and tritium atoms have been forced together using electromagnetic reactors the size of 12 locomotives, 120-trillion-watt laser beams, and bombardment with high-speed particles. So far, none of these approaches has produced more energy than it uses. And in 1989 two chemists claimed to have achieved D-D nuclear fusion at room temperature using a simple apparatus, but subsequent experiments did not substantiate their claims.

If researchers eventually can get more energy out than they put in, the next step would be to build a small fusion reactor and then scale it up to commercial size—one of the most difficult engineering problems ever undertaken. Also, the estimated cost of a

A: $4–$6 billion per year

commercial fusion reactor is several times that of a comparable conventional fission reactor.

If things go right, a commercial nuclear fusion power plant might be built by 2030. Even if everything goes right, however, energy experts don't expect nuclear fusion to be a significant energy source until 2100, if then. Meanwhile, we can produce and save more electricity than we need using several other quicker, cheaper, and safer methods.

## 18-6 Solutions: A Sustainable-Earth Energy Strategy

**OVERALL EVALUATION OF ENERGY ALTERNATIVES** Table 18-1 summarizes the major advantages and disadvantages of the energy alternatives discussed in this and the preceding chapter, with emphasis on their potential in the United States. Energy experts argue over these and other projections, and new data and innovations may affect the status of certain alternatives, but the table does provide a useful framework for making decisions based on presently available information. Three conclusions can be drawn:

- The best short-term, intermediate, and long-term alternatives are a combination of improved energy efficiency and greatly increased use of locally available perpetual and renewable energy resources (Chapter 17).

- Future energy alternatives will probably have low to moderate net useful energy yields and moderate to high development costs. Since there is not enough financial capital to develop all energy alternatives, projects must be chosen carefully.

- We cannot and should not depend mostly on a single nonrenewable energy resource such as oil, coal, natural gas, or nuclear power.

**ECONOMICS** Cost is the biggest factor determining which commercial energy resources are widely used by consumers. Governments throughout the world use three basic economic and political strategies to stimulate or dampen the short-term and long-term use of a particular energy resource:

- *Not attempting to control the price.* Use depends on open, free-market competition (assuming all other alternatives also compete in the same way).

- *Keeping prices artificially low.* This encourages its use and development.

- *Keeping prices artificially high.* This discourages its use and development.

Each approach has certain advantages and disadvantages.

**FREE-MARKET COMPETITION** Leaving energy pricing to the marketplace without any government interference is appealing, in principle. However, a free market is rarely allowed in practice because of government intervention. For example, in the United States (and most other countries) the energy marketplace is greatly distorted by huge government subsidies and tax breaks that make the prices of fossil fuels and nuclear power artificially low. At the same time, improving energy efficiency and solar alternatives receive much lower subsidies and tax breaks, creating an uneven economic playing field.

Despite these inequities many solar technologies already produce electricity and heat more cheaply than can nuclear energy and fossil fuels; and these prices are coming down (Figure 17-2). If the current energy alternatives were competing in a true free market in which prices included their external costs to society, use of nuclear power and fossil fuels (especially coal) would decline dramatically within two decades or less.

A problem with the free-market concept is its emphasis on today's prices to enhance short-term economic gain. This inhibits long-term development of new energy resources, which can rarely compete in their development stages without government support.

**KEEPING ENERGY PRICES ARTIFICIALLY LOW: THE U.S. STRATEGY** Many governments, including the United States, give tax breaks and other subsidies, pay for long-term research and development, and use price controls to keep prices for particular energy resources artificially low. This approach encourages the development and use of those energy resources getting favorable treatment. It also helps protect consumers (especially the poor) from sharp price increases and can help reduce inflation. Because keeping prices low is popular with consumers, this practice often helps leaders in democratic societies get reelected and helps keep leaders in nondemocratic societies from being overthrown.

However, this approach also encourages waste and rapid depletion of an energy resource (such as oil) by making its price artificially low relative to its true value and projected long-term supply. This strategy discourages the development of those energy alternatives not getting at least the same level of subsidies and price control. And once an energy industry gets government subsidies, it usually has enough clout to

Q: What royalties do companies and individuals removing hard-rock minerals from U.S. public lands pay the federal government?

maintain that support long after it becomes unproductive. Moreover, the industry often fights subsidies for development of competing energy alternatives.

According to Harold Hubbard, former director of the Solar Energy Research Institute, government subsidies in 1990 were $26 billion for fossil fuels, $19 billion for nuclear power, and only $5 billion for renewable energy sources and for improving energy efficiency. Furthermore, many of the harmful pollution and health costs of using fossil fuels and nuclear power are not included in their market prices. A 1990 study by the American Solar Energy Society estimated that in the United States these hidden costs amount to at least $109 billion per year. Thus the marketplace is heavily distorted in favor of fossil fuels and nuclear power.

**KEEPING ENERGY PRICES ARTIFICIALLY HIGH: THE WESTERN EUROPEAN STRATEGY** Governments keep the price of an energy resource artificially high by withdrawing existing tax breaks and other subsidies or by adding taxes on its use. This encourages improvements in energy efficiency, reduces dependence on imported energy, and decreases use of an energy resource (like oil) that has a limited future supply. High gasoline and oil import taxes have been imposed by many European governments and by Japan. That is one reason those countries use about half as much energy per person as the United States (Table 17-1).

Increasing taxes on energy use can contribute to inflation and dampen economic growth. It also puts a heavy economic burden on the poor unless some of the energy tax revenues are used to help low-income families offset increased energy prices and to stimulate labor-intensive forms of economic growth, such as improving energy efficiency. On the other hand, it helps balance government budgets.

One popular myth is that higher energy prices wipe out jobs. Actually low energy prices increase unemployment because farmers and industries find it cheaper to substitute machines run on cheap energy for human labor. Raising energy prices stimulates employment because building solar collectors, adding insulation, and carrying out most forms of improving energy efficiency are labor-intensive activities.

**WHY THE UNITED STATES HAS NO COMPREHENSIVE LONG-TERM ENERGY STRATEGY** After the 1973 oil embargo Congress was prodded to pass several laws dealing with the country's energy problems. Most energy experts agree, however, that those laws do not represent a comprehensive energy strategy.

One reason is the complexity of energy issues as revealed in this and the preceding chapter. But the biggest problem is that the nature of the American political system makes it difficult to develop policies to deal with long-term problems (Chapter 26). Each law reflects political pressures of the moment and a maze of compromises among competing groups representing industry, environmentalists, and consumers. Such laws are difficult to repeal or modify drastically until their long-term harmful consequences reach crisis proportions.

The Energy Policy Act of 1992:

- Extends tax benefits to solar and wind-energy industries
- Provides a 1.5¢-per-kilowatt-hour subsidy to utilities for electricity produced by use of perpetual or renewable energy resources
- Increases taxes on employer-paid parking and cuts taxes on commuters who use public transportation
- Encourages improvements in energy efficiency by requiring utilities to look for the least-costly ways to balance the demand and supply for electricity
- Requires that 75% of federally purchased cars and light-duty trucks run on fuels such as natural gas, propane, ethanol, methanol, or hydrogen by 1999
- Requires greater energy efficiency in federal buildings
- Requires mandatory efficiency standards for new electric motors, lighting, commercial heating and cooling equipment, shower heads, toilets, and urinals
- Prohibits oil and gas drilling in the Arctic National Wildlife Refuge
- Removes restrictions on the use of Canadian natural gas
- Gives independent oil and gas producers in the United States a $1.1-billion tax break over five years
- Reduces public participation in nuclear power plant licensing and speeds up construction of nuclear power plants by requiring only one instead of two public hearings (one prior to construction and another before the plant starts up)

**SOLUTIONS: A SUSTAINABLE-EARTH ENERGY FUTURE FOR THE UNITED STATES** Communities (p. 46) and individuals are taking energy matters into their own hands (Individuals Matter, p. 475). At the same time, citizens will have to exert intense pressure from the bottom up on elected officials to develop a national energy policy based on much greater improvements in energy efficiency and a more

A: None

**Table 18-1  Evaluation of Energy Alternatives for the United States (shading indicates favorable conditions)**

| Energy Resources | Estimated Availability | | | Estimated Net Useful Energy of Entire System | Projected Cost of Entire System | Actual or Potential Overall Environmental Impact of Entire System |
|---|---|---|---|---|---|---|
| | Short Term (1995–2005) | Intermediate Term (2005–2015) | Long Term (2015–2045) | | | |
| **Nonrenewable Resources** | | | | | | |
| Fossil Fuels | | | | | | |
| Petroleum | High (with imports) | Moderate (with imports) | Low | High but decreasing | High for new domestic supplies | Moderate |
| Natural gas | High (with imports) | Moderate (with imports) | Moderate (with imports) | High but decreasing | High for new domestic supplies | Low |
| Coal | High | High | High | High but decreasing | Moderate but increasing | Very high |
| Oil shale | Low | Low to moderate | Low to moderate | Low to moderate | Very high | High |
| Tar sands | Low | Fair? (imports only) | Poor to fair (imports only) | Low | Very high | Moderate to high |
| Synthetic natural gas (SNG) from coal | Low | Low to moderate | Low to moderate | Low to moderate | High | High (increases use of coal) |
| Synthetic oil and alcohols from coal | Low | Moderate | High | Low to moderate | High | High (increases use of coal) |
| Nuclear energy | | | | | | |
| Conventional fission (uranium) | Low to moderate | Low to moderate | Low to moderate | Low to moderate | Very high | Very high |
| Breeder fission (uranium and thorium) | None | None to low (if developed) | Moderate | Unknown, but probably moderate | Very high | Very high |
| Fusion (deuterium and tritium) | None | None | None to low (if developed) | Unknown, but may be high | Very high | Unknown (probably moderate to high) |
| Geothermal energy (some are renewable) | Low | Low | Moderate | Moderate | Moderate to high | Moderate to high |
| **Perpetual and Renewable Resources** | | | | | | |
| Improving energy efficiency | High | High | High | Very high | Low | Decreases impact of other sources |
| Hydroelectric | | | | | | |
| New large-scale dams and plants | Low | Low | Very low | Moderate to high | Moderate to very high | Low to moderate |

Q: How much damage have mining activities done to U.S. public lands?

| Energy Resources | Estimated Availability | | | Estimated Net Useful Energy of Entire System | Projected Cost of Entire System | Actual or Potential Overall Environmental Impact of Entire System |
| --- | --- | --- | --- | --- | --- | --- |
| | Short Term (1995–2005) | Intermediate Term (2005–2015) | Long Term (2015–2045) | | | |

**Perpetual and Renewable Resources** (continued)

Hydroelectric (continued)

| Energy Resources | Short Term | Intermediate Term | Long Term | Net Useful Energy | Projected Cost | Environmental Impact |
| --- | --- | --- | --- | --- | --- | --- |
| Reopening abandoned small-scale plants | Moderate | Moderate | Low | Moderate | Moderate | Low to moderate |
| Tidal energy | Very low | Very low | Very low | Moderate | High | Low to moderate |
| Ocean thermal gradients | None | Low | Low to moderate (if developed) | Unknown (probably low to moderate) | High | Unknown (probably moderate to high) |

Solar energy

| Energy Resources | Short Term | Intermediate Term | Long Term | Net Useful Energy | Projected Cost | Environmental Impact |
| --- | --- | --- | --- | --- | --- | --- |
| Low-temperature heating (for homes and water) | High | High | High | Moderate to high | Moderate | Low |
| High-temperature heating | Low | Moderate | Moderate to high | Moderate | High initally, but probably declining fairly rapidly | Low to moderate |
| Photovoltaic production of electricity | Low to moderate | Moderate | High | Fairly high | High initially but declining fairly rapidly | Low |
| Wind energy | Low | Moderate | Moderate to high | Fairly high | Moderate | Low |
| Geothermal energy (low heat flow) | Very low | Very low | Low to moderate | Low to moderate | Moderate to high | Moderate to high |
| Biomass (burning of wood and agricultural wastes) | Moderate | Moderate | Moderate to high | Moderate | Moderate | Moderate to high |
| Biomass (urban wastes for incineration) | Low | Moderate | Moderate | Low to fairly high | High | Moderate to high |
| Biofuels (alcohols and biogas from organic wastes) | Low to moderate | Moderate | Moderate to high | Low to fairly high | Moderate to high | Moderate to high |
| Hydrogen gas (from coal or water) | Very low | Low to moderate | Moderate to high | Variable but probably low | Variable | Variable, but low if produced with solar energy |

rapid transition to a mix of perpetual and sustainable energy resources. Environmentalists support the following actions to achieve these goals:

- *Raise the contribution of perpetual and renewable energy resources to the country's domestic energy production from 10% in 1993 to at least 40% by 2020.*

- *Reduce the use of coal and oil at least 50% by 2020.*

- *Use natural gas as an interim fuel during the transition toward cleaner, sustainable energy resources.*

- *Build no new nuclear reactors and accelerate the decommissioning of existing plants.* This would involve funding a modest research and development program for building and testing a few prototype advanced nuclear reactors in case they are needed after 2020. It would also mean putting off any decision to build commercial versions of such plants until 2020 when the effectiveness of efforts to improve energy efficiency and shift to perpetual and renewable energy sources could be evaluated—if such policies have been made the foundation of a national energy strategy.

- *Phase out most government subsidies for fossil fuels and nuclear energy, and phase in such subsidies for improvements in energy efficiency and development of perpetual and renewable energy resources over the next decade.*

- *Add taxes on fossil fuels (especially coal) that reflect their full external costs to society.* The tax revenues should be used to improve energy efficiency, encourage use of perpetual and renewable energy resources, and provide energy assistance to poor and lower-middle-class Americans. The public might accept these higher taxes if income or other taxes were lowered as carbon taxes were raised.

- *Give tax credits or government rebates for purchases of gas-sipping vehicles.* Similar tax credits or rebates could be given for those building and buying energy-efficient buildings and those buying energy-efficient appliances. This could be accomplished by using *freebates*, a self-financing mechanism that charges fees to purchasers of inefficient products and uses those funds to provide rebates to buyers of energy-efficient products. This approach relies on market forces and requires no new government taxes or subsidies. Adding high taxes on gas-guzzling vehicles might also be an option.

- *Greatly increase required fuel efficiency standards for cars and trucks.*

- *Strengthen federal energy efficiency standards for commercial and residential appliances, and establish energy-efficient building standards for all new and existing buildings.*

- *Require all federal and state facilities to meet the highest feasible standards for energy efficiency.*

- *Buy renewable-energy systems for new government facilities and retrofit existing government buildings with such systems wherever possible.*

- *Require that all government support for energy alternatives be determined by least-cost analysis.* Such analysis would be based on life-cycle costs of each system and would include estimates of all major external costs. Government subsidies would be subtracted from estimated costs so that energy resources could be compared on an equal economic basis.

- *Modify electric-utility regulations so that the utilities are required to produce electricity on a least-cost basis, are permitted to earn money for their shareholders by reducing electricity demand, and are allowed rate increases based primarily on improvements in energy efficiency.* Then the goal of utility companies would be to maximize production of what Amory Lovins calls energy- and money-saving "negawatts" instead of megawatts.

- *Have prices of all energy sources and energy-consuming products reflect their true social and environmental costs.*

Energy experts estimate that implementing these policies now could save money, create a net gain in jobs, improve competitiveness in the global marketplace, slow projected global warming, and sharply reduce air and water pollution. This sustainable-energy path could raise the percentage of energy obtained from perpetual and renewable energy resources in the United States to as high as 50% by 2020.

A few countries and states are leading the way in making the transition from the age of oil to the age of energy efficiency and renewable energy. Brazil and Norway get more than half their energy from hydropower, wood, and alcohol fuel. Israel, Japan, the Philippines, and Sweden plan to rely on renewable and perpetual sources for most of their energy. California has become the world's showcase for solar and wind power. What are you, your local community, and your state doing to save energy and money and to shift to renewable and perpetual energy sources?

*Nuclear fission energy is safe only if a number of critical devices work as they should, if a number of people in key positions follow all their instructions, if there is no sabotage, no hijacking of the transport, if no reactor fuel processing plant or repository anywhere in the world is situated in a region of riots or guerrilla activity, and no revolution or war—even a "conventional" one—takes*

Q: How much in subsidies do U.S. taxpayers give to the nonfuel mining industry?

*place in these regions. No acts of God can
be permitted.*

HANNES ALFVEN (Nobel Laureate, Physics)

# Critical Thinking

1. Explain why you agree or disagree with the ideas that the United States can get **(a)** most of the oil it needs by extracting and processing heavy oil left in known oil wells, **(b)** most of the oil it needs by extracting and processing heavy oil from oil shale deposits, **(c)** most of the oil it needs by extracting heavy oil from tar sands, and **(d)** most of the natural gas it needs from unconventional sources.

2. Coal-fired power plants in the United States cause an estimated 5,000–200,000 deaths per year, mostly from atmospheric emissions of sulfur oxides, nitrogen oxides, and particulate matter. These emissions also damage many buildings and some forests and aquatic systems.
   a. Should air pollution emission standards for *all* new and existing coal-burning plants be tightened significantly? Explain.
   b. Do you favor a U.S. energy strategy based on greatly increased use of coal-burning plants to produce electricity? Explain. What are the alternatives?

3. Explain why you agree or disagree with each of the following proposals made by the nuclear power industry:
   a. The licensing time for new nuclear power plants in the United States should be halved (from an average of 12 years) so they can be built at lower cost and can compete more effectively with coal-burning plants and other energy-producing facilities or technologies.
   b. A large number of new, better-designed nuclear fission power plants should be built in the United States to reduce dependence on imported oil and slow down projected global warming.
   c. Federal subsidies to the commercial nuclear power industry (already totaling $1 trillion) should be continued so it does not have to compete in the open marketplace with other energy alternatives receiving no, or smaller, federal subsidies.
   d. A comprehensive program for developing the nuclear breeder fission reactor should be developed and funded largely by the federal govern-
   ment to conserve uranium resources and keep the United States from being dependent on other countries for uranium supplies.

4. Explain why you agree or disagree with the following proposals by various energy analysts:
   a. Federal subsidies for all energy alternatives should be eliminated so that all energy choices can compete in a true free-market system.
   b. All government tax breaks and other subsidies for conventional fuels (oil, natural gas, coal), synthetic natural gas and oil, and nuclear power should be removed and replaced with subsidies and tax breaks for improving energy efficiency and developing solar, wind, geothermal, and biomass energy alternatives.
   c. Development of solar and wind energy should be left to private enterprise with little or no help from the federal government, but nuclear energy and fossil fuels should continue to receive large federal subsidies.
   d. To solve present and future U.S. energy problems, all we need to do is find and develop more domestic supplies of oil, natural gas, and coal, and increase dependence on nuclear power.
   e. A heavy federal tax should be placed on gasoline and imported oil used in the United States.
   f. Between 2000 and 2020 the United States should phase out all nuclear power plants.
   g. All low-level radioactive wastes should be stored in aboveground buildings at nuclear power plant sites. The cost of doing this would be offset by allowing utilities to charge for all such wastes shipped to the plants for storgae. This would help to defuse controversy over location of regional and state landfills for these wastes.

*5. Throughout the United States there are 42 nuclear reactors operating on college campuses. Does your campus have a nuclear reactor? If so, find out how large it is, what it is used for, and who is in charge of operating it. Has it had any safety problems? Do you believe that nuclear reactors should be allowed on college campuses? Explain.

*6. How is the electricity in your community produced? How has the cost of that electricity changed since 1970? Do your community and your school have a plan for improving energy efficiency? If so, what is this plan, and how much money has it saved during the past 10 years? If there is no plan, develop one and present it to the appropriate officials.

A: About $500 million per year ($560 million in 1992)

## The Great Terrain Robbery

Want to get rich at taxpayers' expense? You can if you know how to make use of a little-known mining law passed in 1872 to encourage mining of gold, silver,

**Figure 19-1** Contamination of Bear Trap Creek in Montana from gold mining.

lead, copper, uranium, and other hard-rock minerals on public lands. While oil, coal, and logging companies and ranchers have to pay to obtain resources from public lands, miners can extract hard-rock minerals and even get the land almost free of charge.

The Mining Law of 1872, adopted during the presidency of Ulysses S. Grant, was originally designed to promote rapid development of the western frontier, and it did. But the Wild West era is long gone, and environmentalists argue that repeal of the "last great land giveaway" is long overdue.

Under the outdated 1872 law any person or corporation can assume legal ownership of any public land not classified as wilderness or park simply by "patenting" it. This involves declaring their belief that the land contains valuable hard-rock minerals, spending $500 to improve the land for mineral development, filing a claim, and then paying the federal government $6–$12 per hectare ($2.50–$5.00 per acre). Since 1872 the government has sold public land under this law equal in area to Connecticut.

The law does not require that patented property be mined. Land speculators have often purchased such properties at 1872 prices and then sold it for thousands of times what they paid. In 1992 Manville Corporation was in the process of patenting for $10,000 about 809 hectares (2,000 acres) of federal land in Montana that contained an estimated $32 billion of platinum and palladium. Other patent owners have developed sites as casinos, homes, ski resorts, golf courses, and vacation-home tracts.

Miners operating under this law annually remove mineral resources worth $4–$6 billion. They pay no royalties, which could amount to $200–$450 million per year. According to Senator Dale Bumpers, "the 1872 mining law is a license to steal and the biggest scam in America."

Miners can ravage the land and dump toxic chemicals with little likelihood of having to reclaim the disrupted land and water. Some of the nation's richest mines on former public lands have gaping holes, scarred hillsides, mountainous piles of tailings and waste rock, and water polluted with acids, cyanide, arsenic, and mercury (Figure 19-1). Estimated cleanup costs—to be paid by the government—range between

$11 billion and $50 billion depending on whether groundwater and toxic waste impacts are included.

Environmentalists have fought without success to repeal the 1872 law. They would end the practice of granting title to public lands for actual or imaginary hard-rock mining, require mining companies to pay a royalty on any hard-rock minerals they extract from federal land, and make them responsible for restoring the land and cleaning up environmental damage caused by their activities. They would also give government officials the power to forbid mining operations that conflict with recreation, wildlife conservation, groundwater protection, and other public land resource values.

Mining companies claim that charging royalties for minerals taken from public lands will force them to do their mining in other countries, which would cost American jobs and reduce tax revenues. They also argue that their average cost for patenting land under the 1872 law is about $42,000 per hectare ($17,000 per acre). Environmentalists counter that mining companies would still make a reasonable profit on minerals they get from public lands and that threats to move operations elsewhere are a rarely implemented scare tactic. For example, gold costs miners about $30 per ounce to extract but can be sold for at least $320 per ounce. Even with a 12.5% royalty—what offshore oil and gas leases pay—mining companies can turn a hefty profit.

Mineral resources are a foundation of modern civilization. Countries without domestic fuel and nonfuel mineral deposits must buy or trade for them, or stay at a low standard of living. Most countries with such resources, including the United States, subsidize their development even though such subsidies promote waste, environmental degradation, and more rapid resource depletion. Realistically, if the world is to have adequate and affordable nonfuel mineral supplies into the future without severely damaging the environment, we must manage these finite resources more efficiently through a combination of reduced use and much more reuse and recycling.

In this chapter we will seek answers to the following questions:

- How fast are nonfuel mineral supplies being used up?
- What are the environmental limits of using such resources?
- How can we increase supplies of key minerals?
- How can we stretch supplies of key minerals ?

## 19-1 Mineral Supplies and Environmental Impacts

**HOW FAST ARE SUPPLIES BEING USED UP?**
We know how to find and extract more than 100 nonrenewable minerals from the earth's crust (Section 7-4). We convert these raw materials into everyday items we use and then discard, reuse, or recycle.

Worldwide the demand for mineral commodities is soaring because both population and per capita consumption are rising (Figure 1-16). Concentrations of nonrenewable mineral resources formed millions of years ago are being depleted in decades. The future supply of such resources depends on two factors: **(1)** the actual or potential supply and **(2)** the rate at which that supply is being used.

We never completely run out of any mineral. But a mineral becomes economically depleted when finding, extracting, transporting, and processing the remaining deposits cost more than the results are worth. At that point we have five choices: recycle or reuse existing supplies, waste less, use less, find a substitute, or do without.

Most published supply estimates for a given resource refer to *reserves*: known deposits from which a usable mineral can be extracted profitably at current prices (Figure 7-17). **Depletion time** is the time it takes to use a certain portion—usually 80%—of the reserves of a mineral at a given rate of use. When experts disagree about depletion times, they are using different assumptions about supply and rate of use (Figure 19-2).

The shortest depletion time assumes no recycling or reuse and no increase in reserves (curve A, Figure 19-2). A longer depletion time assumes that recycling will stretch existing reserves and that better mining technology, higher prices, and new discoveries will, say, double the reserves (curve B, Figure 19-2). An even longer depletion time assumes that new discoveries will expand reserves, say, 5- or 10-fold, and that recycling, reuse, and reduced consumption will extend supplies (curve C, Figure 19-2). Finding a substitute for a resource dictates a whole new set of depletion curves for the new resource.

Some minerals are more important than others. Minerals essential to the economy of a country are called **critical minerals**, and those necessary for national defense are called **strategic minerals**. The definition of "critical" or "strategic" may vary from country to country or from time to time.

## WHO HAS THE WORLD'S NONFUEL MINERAL RESOURCES?
Nonfuel mineral resources are unevenly distributed in the world. The CIS, the United States, Canada, Australia, and South Africa supply most of the world's 20 most important nonfuel minerals.

No industrialized country is self-sufficient in mineral resources, although the former Soviet Union came close and was a major exporter of critical and strategic minerals. By contrast, in addition to lacking coal, oil, and timber resources, Japan has virtually no metals. Japan depends on resource imports, which it upgrades to finished products and then sells abroad to buy the resources it needs to sustain its economy. Most western European countries depend heavily on minerals from Africa.

## THE U.S. SITUATION
Because of mineral and energy wealth, the United States became the world's richest and most powerful nation in less than 200 years. However, this meteoric rise had a price: the rapid depletion of many of its energy (especially oil) and nonfuel mineral resources (such as lead, aluminum ore, and iron ore). Each year the United States needs more than 4.8 billion metric tons (5.2 billion tons) of new fuel and nonfuel minerals—19 metric tons (21 tons) per American—just to maintain the present standard of living in its largely throwaway economy (Figures 3-15 and 3-20).

The United States will never again be self-sufficient in oil or in many key metals. Massive resource consumption and unsustainable depletion of much of its domestic nonrenewable Earth capital has also cost the country millions of jobs. Even though it is the world's largest producer of nonfuel minerals, the

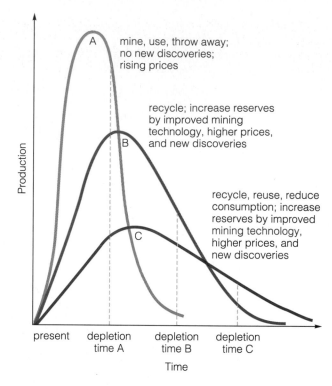

**Figure 19-2** Depletion curves for a nonrenewable resource, such as aluminum or copper, using three sets of assumptions. Dashed vertical lines show when 80% depletion occurs.

United States must import 50% or more of 24 of its 42 most important nonfuel minerals. Some are imported because they are used faster than they can be produced from domestic supplies, others because foreign ore deposits are higher grade and cheaper to extract than remaining U.S. reserves.

Figure 19-3 shows U.S. reserves for 20 important nonfuel minerals to 2000 and their major foreign sources. Most U.S. mineral imports come from reliable and politically stable countries. However, experts are concerned about four strategic minerals—manganese, cobalt, platinum, and chromium–for which the United States has little or no reserves and depends on imports from potentially unstable countries in the CIS and Africa (South Africa, Zambia, Zaire). As the American Geological Institute notes, "Without manganese, chromium, platinum, and cobalt, there can be no automobiles, no airplanes, no jet engines, no satellites, and no sophisticated weapons—not even home appliances."

The United States stockpiles critical and strategic minerals to cushion against short-term supply interruptions and price jumps. These supplies are supposed to last through a three-year conventional war (minus the amounts available from domestic and secure foreign sources), but most of them would not.

Q: How much of the world's solid waste is produced by the United States?

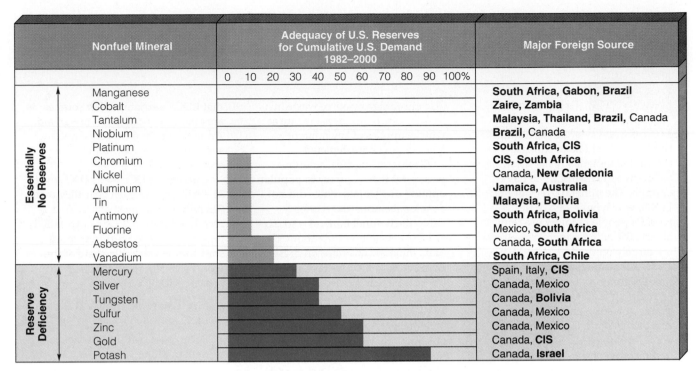

**Figure 19-3** Evaluation of the supply of selected nonfuel minerals in the United States, 1982–2000, and major foreign sources of these minerals. Foreign sources subject to potential interruption of supply by political, economic, or military disruption are shown in boldface print. (Data from U.S. Geological Survey)

As more and more minerals are imported, industries and jobs related to extracting and processing them are lost. If export income does not exceed the cost of imports (as it now does not), the United States faces a worsening trade balance, a soaring national debt, and a weakened dollar.

**WILL THERE BE ENOUGH?** Experts disagree about how long affordable supplies of key nonfuel minerals will last. Geologists and environmentalists tend to see Earth's supply of minerals as finite because of their uneven distribution and because the two laws of energy set minimum grades of ore that can be processed without spending more money than they are worth or causing unacceptable environmental damage. Economists, by contrast, tend to see mineral supplies as essentially infinite because we can improve technologies for finding and processing minerals—or find substitutes (Guest Essay, p. 24).

Meanwhile, many LDCs fear that MDCs will gobble up most of the world's resources for their own economic growth, before these poorer countries can develop (Spotlight, p. 508).

**ENVIRONMENTAL IMPACTS** The greatest danger from high levels of resource consumption may not be the exhaustion of resources but the damage that their extraction and processing do to the environment. Mining (Section 7-4) and processing minerals are among the most environmentally damaging of all human activities (Figure 7-21).

Each year an estimated 27 billion metric tons (30 billion tons) of nonfuel minerals and overburden are taken from the earth's crust. The minerals industry accounts for 5–10% of world energy use, making it a major contributor to air and water pollution and to greenhouse gases. As more remote, deeper deposits are mined, even more energy will be needed to dig bigger holes and transport the ore farther.

The *grade* of an ore—its percentage of metal content—largely determines the environmental impact of metal mining. Generally we use the more accessible and higher-grade ores first. As they are depleted, it takes more money, energy, water, and other materials to exploit lower-grade ores. Environmental impacts increase accordingly (Figure 7-21).

In the United States, nonfuel mining produces at least six times more solid waste than all municipal garbage. These mining wastes often contain hazardous substances. At least 48 of the 1,211 sites on the Superfund hazardous-waste cleanup list (Section 21-4) are former mining operations. The situation is much

To LDCs and to some resource analysts, asking whether we will have enough affordable minerals really means asking whether MDCs will have enough. The mineral needs of the LDCs, which have 78% of the world's people but now use only about 20% of the mineral resources, are largely ignored.

MDCs argue that when they buy nonfuel minerals from LDCs, they are helping fund the LDCs' economic development. Multinational companies point out that mines they develop in LDCs mean jobs and income for those countries.

LDCs respond that they typically get such low prices for their resources that their long-term economic development is jeopardized. MDC-based companies end up with most of the profits and, in extracting minerals, often cause severe environmental degradation and pollution in LDCs. Moreover, economic growth in mineral-exporting LDCs is stunted when they borrow money from MDCs to buy expensive finished products. Low mineral prices

also encourage resource waste in MDCs, which increases the rate at which supplies of key nonrenewable resources are depleted.

Geologist Eugene Cameron points out that, contrary to popular opinion, the United States did not develop its industrial economy using the nonfuel mineral resources of LDCs. As late as 1979 about 97% of its mineral consumption drew on domestic supplies. Today mineral imports have increased, but about 62% come from other MDCs (Figure 19-3).

However, critics counter that U.S. mineral imports are so enormous that the 38% it gets from LDCs gives the United States and other large-volume buyers, such as Japan and western European countries, considerable influence over the market price of such resources. LDCs fear that as the United States becomes more dependent on imports, its influence over mineral prices will grow as well.

Politics also plays a key role in mineral prices. If an LDC opposes a mineral-importing MDC's policies, the MDC may cut off imports from

that LDC (assuming other sources are available) or stop its foreign aid. An LDC that does not succumb to such "economic blackmail" faces economic ruin.

Currently LDCs owe MDCs over $1.4 trillion, and each year they owe $43 billion in interest alone. To correct this situation, LDCs have called for economic changes that would shift a more equitable share of the world's wealth to them. Their proposals include:

- Much more aid from MDCs to LDCs

- Forgiveness of some of their debt to MDCs

- Removal of trade barriers in MDCs against some LDC products

- Higher prices for minerals, timber, and other LDC exports

- Greater LDC influence over the decisions of international lending institutions, such as the World Bank and the International Monetary Fund

So far MDCs have generally opposed this program.

worse in mineral-producing LDCs, most with nonexistent or ineffective environmental regulations.

Today's low mineral prices do not include the full costs of forests denuded (Figure 10-16), land gouged (Figures 7-20 and 7-22) or eroded, rivers dammed and land flooded to supply electricity for metal processing (Figure 13-11), displaced and poisoned indigenous peoples (Figure 10-11), air polluted and vegetation destroyed by it (Figure 7-26), and water pollution (Figures 7-25 and 19-1). For example, smelting of copper and other nonferrous (noniron) metals accounts for about 8% of human-related emissions of sulfur dioxide each year. As a result, dead zones surround the Sudbury, Ontario, nickel smelter in Canada (Figure 7-26), the Copper Hill smelter in Tennessee, and the Severonikel nickel smelter in Russia.

## 19-2 Increasing Mineral Resource Supplies: The Supply-Side Approach

**ECONOMICS AND RESOURCE SUPPLY** Geologic processes determine how and where a mineral resource is concentrated in the earth (Sections 7-2 and 7-3). Economics determines what part of the known supply will be used (Figure 7-17).

According to standard economic theory, in a competitive free market a plentiful resource is cheap because supply exceeds demand, but when a resource becomes scarce its price rises—stimulating exploration and development of better mining technology. Rising prices will make it profitable to mine ores of ever-

Q: What is the largest source of solid waste in the United States?

## Mines in Antarctica

Antarctica (Figure 19-4) is the coldest, driest, windiest, iciest, and most remote, of Earth's seven continents. The ice that covers 98% of the continent contains 90% of Earth's ice and 70% of its fresh water.

Antarctica helps regulate the global climate and sea level. In winter parts of the sea freeze and the continent doubles in size; in the summer it shrinks when some of the ice pack melts and huge icebergs break off the edges of the ice shelf. This frozen ice mass draws heat out of the tropics and sends cold air and water northward (Figure 5-5), while its cold waters help drive ocean circulation (Figure 5-3). Were

large amounts of Antarctic ice to melt because of an enhanced greenhouse effect (Section 11-1), global average sea levels would rise significantly.

Antarctica's cold coastal waters teem with marine life because of an abundant supply of dissolved oxygen and continuous summer sunlight. Moreover, the water is rich in nutrients brought up from the ocean depths by currents. These nutrients support an abundance of marine phytoplankton, eaten by multitudes of shrimplike krill, which in turn support many other forms of life (Figure 4-21). That explains why Antarctica is home to 85 million penguins (Figure 19-5), 80 million seabirds (the world's

largest gathering), 12 species of whales, half of Earth's seal population, and 200 species of fish.

Some of Antarctica's aquatic life may be susceptible to jumps in ultraviolet radiation levels from the human-caused seasonal ozone hole over much of the continent (Figure 11-9). Another threat to its aquatic life is overfishing of the slowly reproducing krill. The greatest threat to its wildlife and pristine beauty, however, comes from pressure to develop the continent's mineral resources. Many geologists believe that the continent and its offshore waters may contain significant amounts of oil, natural gas, coal, cobalt, chromium, and

(continued)

---

lower grades and will motivate the search for substitutes. However, this theory may no longer apply to MDCs. In the United States, for example, industry and government control supply, demand, and prices of minerals to such a large extent that a competitive free market does not exist.

Most mineral prices are artificially low because countries subsidize development of their domestic mineral resources. In the United States, for instance, mining companies get depletion allowances amounting to 5–22% of their gross income, depending on the mineral. In addition, the companies can deduct much of their costs for finding and developing mineral deposits. Moreover, the U.S. mining industry gets another big federal subsidy through virtual giveaways of federal lands and hard-rock minerals (p. 504).

Over the last decade these mining subsidies have cost U.S. taxpayers $5 billion ($560 million in 1992 alone). The U.S. Treasury could gain about $2 billion over the next five years if the mineral industry were taxed on the same basis as other industries. Taxing rather than subsidizing the extraction of nonfuel mineral resources would create incentives for more efficient resource use, encourage recycling and reuse, and provide governments with revenue.

Another problem is that the cost of nonfuel mineral resources is only a small part of the final cost of goods. Thus scarcity does not raise the market prices

of products very much, so industries and consumers have no incentive to reduce demand in time to avoid economic depletion of the minerals. Low mineral prices, made possible by ignoring the harmful environmental costs of mining and processing (Figure 7-21), encourage waste, pollution, and environmental damage. And mining companies and manufacturers have little incentive to reduce resource waste and pollution as long as they can pass many of the harmful environmental costs of their production on to society.

An economic factor limiting production of nonfuel minerals is investment capital. With today's fluctuating mineral markets and rising costs, investors are wary of tying up large sums for long periods with no assurance of a reasonable return.

**FINDING NEW LAND-BASED MINERAL DEPOSITS** Geologic exploration guided by better knowledge, satellite surveys, and other new techniques will increase present reserves of most minerals. Although most of the easily accessible, high-grade deposits are already known, new discoveries will be mostly in unexplored areas of LDCs.

Antarctica may contain large mineral deposits. However, mining this harsh land may be too expensive. Moreover, environmentalists believe we should protect this last remaining large wilderness area on the planet from development (Pro/Con, above).

---

A: Mining of nonfuel minerals, creating waste equal to six times the garbage produced by the entire population    CHAPTER 19

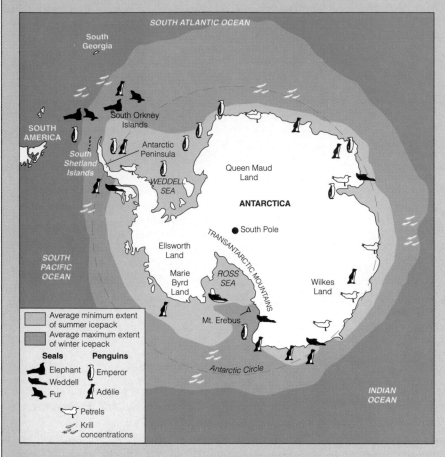

**Figure 19-4** The ice-covered continent of Antarctica makes up 10% of Earth's land mass. It is the world's last great wilderness.

**Figure 19-5** A huge colony of king penguins on an island off Antarctica. King penguins are only one of 35 species of penguins found in this region of the world.

manganese. No one knows, however, whether these minerals are there or whether it would be physically possible and economically profitable to exploit them.

Seven countries have unresolved ownership claims to parts of Antarctica and its offshore waters, and 26 countries operate 69 scientific research stations there. This entitles them to vote on treaties governing how the continent is to be used. According to a 1959 treaty signed by these and other nations, Antarctica remains a demilitarized, nuclear-free zone dedicated to the peaceful pursuit of knowledge and the free exchange of scientific information. Today the Antarctic Treaty System has 26 voting and 13 non-voting members.

In 1977 these 39 countries agreed not to explore for or develop minerals in Antarctica until they could develop a treaty regulating such activities. In 1988, after six years of negotiations, the 26 voting nations completed an international treaty called the Convention on the Regulation of Antarctic Mineral Resources (CRAMA), which would allow some mineral development.

Environmentalists, however, want Antarctica set aside as a permanent World Park, or International Wilderness Reserve, in which only scientific research and carefully controlled tourism (now 4,000 visitors a year) would be allowed. In 1989 France and Australia announced that they backed the World Park idea and would not ratify the treaty. Other countries, including Great Britain, the United States, Germany, and Japan, opposed a permanent ban on mineral development.

In 1991 the 39 nations involved with Antarctica worked out a compromise treaty that would ban mining there for 50 years, at which time a two-thirds majority of the 26 nations signing the treaty would be needed to lift the ban.

Q: How much of the solid waste produced in the United States is municipal solid waste (garbage)?

Exploring for new resources takes a lot of capital and is a risky venture. Typically, if geologists identify 10,000 possible deposits of a given resource, only 1,000 sites are worth exploring; only 100 justify drilling, trenching, or tunneling; and only 1 will become a producing mine or well. Even if large new supplies are found, no nonrenewable mineral supply can stand up to continued exponential growth in its use.

**IMPROVING MINING TECHNOLOGY AND MINING LOW-GRADE ORE** Some analysts say that all we need to do to increase supplies of any mineral is to extract lower grades of ore. They point to new earth-moving equipment, new techniques for removing impurities, and other technological advances during the past few decades.

For example, in 1900 the average copper ore mined in the United States was about 5% copper by weight; today it is 0.4%—and copper costs less (adjusted for inflation). Technological improvements also increased world copper reserves 500% between 1950 and 1980, and future advances may let us use even lower-grade ores of some metals (Solutions, right).

Several factors limit the mining of lower-grade ores, however. As ever-poorer ores are mined, we reach a point where it costs more to mine and process such resources than they are worth, unless we have a virtually inexhaustible source of cheap energy. Availability of fresh water also may limit the supply of some mineral resources, because large amounts of water are needed to extract and process most minerals. Many mineral-rich areas lack fresh water.

Finally, exploitation of lower-grade ores may be limited by the environmental impact of waste material produced during mining and processing (Figures 7-20 and 7-21). At some point the costs of land restoration and pollution control exceed the current value of the minerals, unless we continue to pass these harmful costs on to society and to future generations.

**MINING THE OCEANS** Ocean mineral resources are found in three areas: seawater, sediments and deposits on the shallow continental shelf, and sediments and nodules on the deep-ocean floor. Most of the chemical elements found in seawater occur in such low concentrations that recovering them takes more energy and money than they are worth. Only magnesium, bromine, and sodium chloride are abundant enough to be extracted profitably at present prices with current technology.

Continental shelf deposits and placer deposits are already significant sources of sand, gravel, phosphates, and nine other nonfuel mineral resources. Offshore wells also supply large amounts of oil and natural gas.

The deep-ocean floor may be a future source of manganese and other metals. For example, at a few

## Mining with Microbes

**SOLUTIONS**

One emerging prospect for improving mining technology is the use of microorganisms for in-place (*in situ*) mining, which would remove desired metals from ores while leaving the surrounding environment relatively undisturbed. This method would also reduce the air pollution associated with the smelting of metal ores (Figure 7-26) and water pollution associated with using hazardous chemicals such as cyanides to extract gold (Figure 19-1).

Once an ore deposit had been identified and deemed economically viable, wells would be drilled into it and the ore fractured. Then the ore would be inoculated with either natural or genetically engineered bacteria to extract the desired metal. Next the ore would be flooded with water, which would be pumped to the surface, where the desired metals would be removed. Thus metal production would become essentially biological, with little energy input compared with current extraction technologies.

In 1990 a gold-mining plant using microbes went into operation in Colorado. It uses *Thiobacillus ferrooxidans*, a natural bacterium, to extract gold that is embedded in iron sulfide ore and that is uneconomical to extract by conventional methods. The bacteria consume the sulfur and iron in the ore, leaving gold in a form that is easily extracted by current technology. The plant is expected to produce gold at about $240 per ounce, well below the current market price.

Microbiological processing of ores, however, is slow. It can take decades to remove the same amount of material that conventional methods can remove within months or years. So far biological methods are economically feasible only with low-grade ore (such as gold), for which conventional techniques are too expensive.

Some people have expressed concern about potential harm from genetically engineered organisms (Pro/Con, p. 167). However, proponents of mining biotechnology point out that these organisms get their energy from chemical sources, not from living or formerly living organisms as do genetically engineered organisms used in agriculture and medicine. Consequently, they argue, the risks are several orders of magnitude lower than those from other genetically engineered organisms.

sites manganese-rich nodules have been found in large quantities. These cherry- to potato-sized rocks contain 30–40% by weight manganese, used in certain steel alloys. They also contain small amounts of other

## The Materials Revolution

**SOLUTIONS**

Scientists and engineers are rapidly developing new materials—in particular, ceramics and plastics—for metals being used in engines. Ceramics have many advantages over conventional metals. For example, they are harder, stronger, lighter, and longer-lasting than many metals. Also, they withstand intense heat and do not corrode. Because they can burn fuel at higher temperatures than metal engines, ceramic engines can boost fuel efficiency by 30–40%. We also have ceramic knives, scissors, batteries, fishhooks, and artificial limbs.

Within a few decades we may have high-temperature ceramic superconductors in which electricity flows without resistance. That may lead to faster computers, more efficient power transmission, and affordable electromagnets for propelling magnetic levitation trains (Figure 9-16). To date Japanese scientists have filed more patent applications for such superconductors than the rest of the world combined.

Plastics also have advantages over many metals. High-strength plastics and composite materials strengthened by lightweight carbon and glass fibers are likely to transform the automobile (Figures 17-5 and 17-6) and aerospace industries. They cost less to produce than metals because they require less energy, don't need painting, and are easily molded into any shape. Many cars now have plastic body parts, which reduce weight and boost gas mileage. Planes and cars made almost entirely of plastics—held together by new superglues—may be common in the next century. New plastics and gels are also being developed to provide superinsulation without taking up much space.

The materials revolution is also transforming medicine. So-called biomaterials, made of new plastics, ceramics, glass composites, and alloys, are being used in artificial skin, arteries, organs, and joints.

strategically important metals, such as nickel, copper, and cobalt. These nodules might be sucked up from the ocean floor by pipe or scooped up by a continuous cable with buckets to a mining ship. However, most of these nodule beds occur in international waters. Their development has been put off indefinitely because of squabbles over who owns them.

Iron, manganese, copper, and zinc also occur in sulfide deposits around hydrothermal vents found at certain locations on the deep-ocean floor. However, concentrations of metals in most of these deposits are too low to be valuable mineral resources.

Environmentalists recognize that seabed mining would probably cause less harm than mining on land. They are concerned, however, that removing seabed mineral deposits and dumping back unwanted material will stir up ocean sediments, which could destroy seafloor organisms and have unknown effects on poorly understood ocean food webs. Surface waters might also be polluted by the discharge of sediments from mining ships and rigs.

**FINDING SUBSTITUTES** Some people believe that even if supplies of key minerals become very expensive or scarce, human ingenuity will find substitutes. They point to the current materials revolution in which silicon and other abundant elements are being substituted for scarce metals in many uses (Solutions, left).

Substitutes can undoubtedly be found for many scarce mineral resources, but the search is costly, and phasing a substitute into a complex manufacturing process takes time. Also, while a vanishing mineral is being replaced, people and businesses dependent on it may suffer economic hardships as its price soars. Moreover, finding substitutes for some key materials—such as helium, phosphorus for phosphate fertilizers, manganese for making steel, and copper for wiring motors and generators—may be hard, if not impossible. Finally, some substitutes are inferior to the minerals they replace. For example, aluminum could replace copper in electrical wiring, but producing aluminum takes much more energy than producing copper, and aluminum wiring is more of a fire hazard than copper wiring.

## 19-3 Wasting Resources: Solid Waste and the Throwaway Approach

**SOURCES OF SOLID WASTE** With only 4.7% of the world's population, the United States produces 33% of the **solid waste**: any unwanted or discarded material that is not a liquid or a gas. The United States—the world's most material nation—generates about 10 billion metric tons (11 billion tons) of solid waste per year—an average of 40 metric tons (44 tons) per person. While garbage produced directly by households and businesses is a significant problem, about 98.5% of the solid waste in the United States comes from mining, oil and natural gas production, agriculture,

Q: How much municipal solid waste per person is produced in the United States?

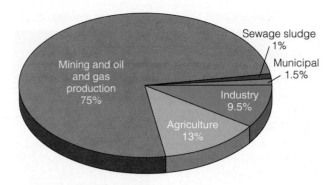

**Figure 19-6** Sources of the 10 billion metric tons (11 billion tons) of solid waste produced each year in the United States. Some 65 times as much solid waste is produced by mining and industrial activities as by household garbage. (Data from Environmental Protection Agency and U.S. Bureau of Mines)

and industrial activities (Figure 19-6). Although individuals don't generate this waste directly, they are responsible indirectly through the products they consume.

Most mining waste is left piled near mine sites and can pollute the air, surface water, and groundwater. Abandoned and unrestored metal and coal surface mines in the United States cover an area about the size of Indiana. That figure does not include the many abandoned sand and gravel pits or stone quarries. Although mining waste is the single largest category of U.S. solid waste, the EPA has done little to regulate its disposal, mostly because Congress has specifically exempted mining wastes from regulation as a hazardous waste. In LDCs there is even less regulation of mining procedures and wastes.

Most industrial solid waste—such as scrap metal, plastics, paper, fly ash removed by air pollution control equipment in industrial and electrical power plants, and sludge from industrial waste treatment plants—is buried or incinerated at the plant site where it was produced.

The remaining 1.5% of solid waste produced in the United States is **municipal solid waste** from homes and businesses in or near urban areas. The estimated 178 million metric tons (196 million tons) of municipal solid waste—often referred to as garbage—produced in the United States in 1993 would fill a bumper-to-bumper convoy of garbage trucks encircling the earth almost six times (Spotlight, right). This amounts to 700 kilograms (1,540 pounds) per person annually—two to three times that in most other MDCs (except Canada) and many times that in LDCs.

The biggest component in U.S. landfills is paper and paperboard (38% by volume), followed by plastic (18%), metals (14%), yard waste (11%), food (4%), glass (2%), and other materials (13%). About 17% of these potentially usable resources is recycled or composted.

**What It Means to Live in a Throwaway Society**

SPOTLIGHT

U.S. consumers throw away:

- Enough aluminum to rebuild the country's entire commercial airline fleet every three months
- Enough glass bottles to fill the 412-meter-high (1,350-foot) towers of the New York World Trade Center every two weeks
- Enough tires to encircle the earth almost three times each year
- Enough disposable plates and cups to serve a meal to everyone in the world six times per year
- About 2 billion disposable razors, 1.6 billion throwaway ballpoint pens, and 500 million disposable cigarette lighters each year
- About 2.5 million nonreturnable plastic bottles each hour
- Some 14 billion catalogs plus 38 billion pieces of junk mail per year.

And this is only part of the 1.5% of solid waste labeled as municipal in Figure 19-6.

The other 83% is hauled away and dumped (66%) or burned (17%) at a cost of about $30 billion per year (projected to rise to $75 billion by 2000).

Litter is also a source of solid waste. For example, helium-filled balloons are often released into the atmosphere at ball games and parties. When the helium escapes or the balloons burst, they become litter. Fish, turtles, seals, whales, and other aquatic animals die when they ingest balloons falling into oceans and lakes. This practice also implies that it is acceptable to litter, waste helium (a scarce resource) and energy (used to separate helium from air), and kill wildlife (even if we switched to balloons that biodegraded within six weeks).

**DEALING WITH SOLID WASTE** There are two ways to deal with the mountains of solid waste we produce: *waste management* and *pollution (waste) prevention*. Waste management is a *throwaway* or *high-waste approach* that encourages waste production and then attempts to manage the wastes in ways that will reduce environmental harm—mostly by burying them or burning them.

Sooner or later, however, even the best-designed waste incinerators release some toxic substances into the atmosphere and leave a toxic residue that must

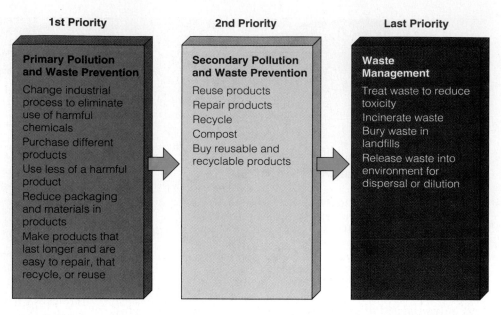

**Figure 19-7** Priorities for dealing with material use and waste. So far these priorities are not being followed, with most efforts devoted to waste management (bury or burn). (Environmental Protection Agency and National Academy of Sciences).

| 1st Priority | 2nd Priority | Last Priority |
|---|---|---|
| **Primary Pollution and Waste Prevention**<br><br>Change industrial process to eliminate use of harmful chemicals<br>Purchase different products<br>Use less of a harmful product<br>Reduce packaging and materials in products<br>Make products that last longer and are easy to repair, that recycle, or reuse | **Secondary Pollution and Waste Prevention**<br><br>Reuse products<br>Repair products<br>Recycle<br>Compost<br>Buy reusable and recyclable products | **Waste Management**<br><br>Treat waste to reduce toxicity<br>Incinerate waste<br>Bury waste in landfills<br>Release waste into environment for dispersal or dilution |

be disposed of—usually in landfill. Even the best-designed landfills leak wastes into groundwater. And eventually we run out of affordable or politically acceptable sites for landfills and incinerators.

The basic problem is that modern economic systems give higher rewards to those who produce waste instead of those who try to use resources more efficiently. We give timber, mining, and energy companies tax write-offs and other subsidies to cut trees and to find and mine copper, oil, coal, and uranium. At the same time, we seldom subsidize companies and businesses that recycle copper or paper, use oil or coal more efficiently, or develop renewable alternatives to fossil fuels. That tilts the economic playing field against waste prevention.

Pollution or waste prevention is a *low-waste approach* that sees solid wastes as resources or wasted solids that we should be recycling, reusing, or not using in the first place (Figures 3-21 and 19-7). The low-waste approach involves teaching people to see trash cans and dumpsters as resource containers, and trash as a concentrated urban ore that needs to be mined for useful materials for recycling. With this approach the economic system is used to discourage waste production and encourage pollution and waste prevention.

The main goal of the low-waste approach is not to reduce the volume of solid waste and make landfills last longer. Instead, it is to reduce the depletion of resources and decrease the pollution and environmental degradation caused by resource extraction, processing, and use (Figure 7-21). This prevention approach has a hierarchy of goals (Figure 19-7): **(1)** *Reduce* waste and pollution by preventing its creation; **(2)** *reuse* as many things as possible; **(3)** *recycle and compost* as

much waste as possible; **(4)** *incinerate or treat* waste that can't be reduced, reused, recycled, or composted; and **(5)** *bury* what is left in state-of-the-art landfills after the first four goals have been met.

**19-4** **Solutions: Pollution and Waste Prevention and Reuse**

**REDUCING WASTE AND POLLUTION** By reducing unnecessary waste of nonrenewable mineral resources, plastics, and paper, pollution and waste prevention can extend supplies even more dramatically than recycling and reuse. Cutting waste generally saves more energy and virgin resources than recycling, and reduces the environmental impacts of extracting, processing, and using resources (Figure 7-21). Table 19-1 compares the throwaway resource system of the United States, a resource recovery and recycling system, and a sustainable-Earth, or low-waste, resource system.

Manufacturers can conserve resources by using less material per product and by redesigning manufacturing processes to use fewer resources and produce less waste. Lighter cars, for example, save nonfuel mineral resources as well as energy and can still meet or exceed federal safety standards for all cars (Figures 17-5 and 17-6). Fiber optic technology slashes the use of copper wire in telephone transmission lines.

One of the best ways to reduce municipal solid waste and pollution is to cut down on unnecessary

514

**Table 19-1 Three Systems for Handling Discarded Materials**

| Item | For a High-Waste Throwaway System | For a Moderate-Waste Resource Recovery and Recycling System | For a Low-Waste Sustainable-Earth System |
|------|-----------------------------------|--------------------------------------------------------------|-------------------------------------------|
| Glass bottles | Dump or bury | Grind and remelt; remanufacture; convert into building materials | Ban all nonreturnable bottles; reuse bottles |
| Bimetallic "tin" cans | Dump or bury | Sort, remelt | Limit or ban production; use returnable bottles |
| Aluminum cans | Dump or bury | Sort, remelt | Limit or ban production; use returnable bottles |
| Cars | Dump | Sort, remelt | Sort, remelt; tax cars getting less than 17 kilometers per liter (40 miles per gallon) |
| Metal objects | Dump or bury | Sort, remelt | Sort, remelt; tax items lasting less than 10 years |
| Tires | Dump, burn, or bury | Grind and revulcanize or use in road construction; incinerate to generate heat and electricity | Recap usable tires; tax or ban all tires not usable for at least 96,000 kilometers (60,000 miles) |
| Paper | Dump, burn, or bury | Incinerate to generate heat | Compost or recycle; tax all throwaway items; eliminate overpackaging |
| Plastics | Dump, burn, or bury | Incinerate to generate heat or electricity | Limit production; use returnable glass bottles instead of plastic containers; tax throwaway items and packaging |
| Yard wastes | Dump, burn, or bury | Incinerate to generate heat or electricity | Compost; return to soil as fertilizer; use as animal feed |

packaging, which makes up about 50% by volume and 30% by weight of municipal waste. Packaging accounts for 50% of all paper produced in the United States, 90% of all glass, 11% of all aluminum, and 3% of all energy used. Americans and Canadians use twice as much packaging per person as Europeans. Some U.S. manufacturers have reduced the weight of some of their packaging bottles and cartons by 10–30%, but much more needs to be done. Ideally, packaging should be minimal, returnable, refillable, or reusable. At the least, it should be recyclable and made from the greatest possible amount of postconsumer recycled materials.

Another low-waste approach is to make products that last longer. Today many items are intentionally designed to make repair, reuse, or recycling too costly if not impossible—a way to increase sales of new items. To reduce waste manufacturers can use modular design, which now allows circuits in computers, television sets, and other electronic devices to be replaced easily and quickly, without having to replace the entire item. We also need to encourage the development of remanufacturing industries that disassemble, repair, and reassemble used and broken items. Several European auto manufacturers, for example, are designing their cars for easy disassembly, reuse,

and recycling of various parts, and are trying to minimize the use of nonrecyclable or hazardous materials.

**REUSABLE CONTAINERS** Recycling, though an important step, still reinforces the throwaway mentality. A much more important step is *reuse* in which a product is used again and again in its original form.

One example is the refillable glass beverage bottle. In 1964, 87% of beer and soda containers in the United States were refillable glass bottles, but since then most local bottling companies have been bought up or driven out of business by aluminum and large soft-drink companies. Refillable glass bottles now make up only 11% of the market, and only 10 states even have returnable bottles.

Refillable glass bottles can be used 50 times or more. Collected and filled at local bottling plants, they reduce transportation and energy costs, and create local jobs. Moreover, studies by Coca-Cola and Pepsi-Co of Canada show that 0.5-liter (16-ounce) bottles of their soft drinks cost one-third less in refillable bottles.

To encourage use of refillable glass bottles, Ecuador has a beverage container deposit fee that is 50% higher than the cost of the drink. This has been so successful that bottles as old as 10 years continue to circulate. Sorting is not a problem because only two

A: Enough to rebuild the country's commercial airline fleet every three months

**Figure 19-8** Energy used to make a 400-milliliter (12-fluid-ounce) beverage container. (Data from Argonne National Laboratory)

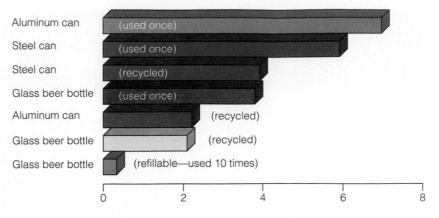

| | |
|---|---|
| Aluminum can | (used once) |
| Steel can | (used once) |
| Steel can | (recycled) |
| Glass beer bottle | (used once) |
| Aluminum can | (recycled) |
| Glass beer bottle | (recycled) |
| Glass beer bottle | (refillable—used 10 times) |

**Energy Used (thousand BTUs)**

**Figure 19-9** An example of good Earth-keeping. A reusable string bag (or a cloth or canvas bag) can be used to carry groceries and other purchases. This eliminates the need for throwaway paper and plastic bags, both of which are environmentally harmful even if they are recycled.

sizes of glass bottles are allowed. In Finland 95% of the soft drink, beer, wine, and spirits containers are refillable, and in Germany 73% are refillable.

Refillable glass bottles are the most energy-efficient beverage containers on the market (Figure 19-8).

Denmark has led the way by banning all beverage containers that can't be reused. Reuse is much easier if containers for products that can be packaged in reusable glass are available in only a few sizes, as required in Norway and Denmark.

Most plastic bottles can't be refilled because the Food and Drug Administration requires that refillable containers be sterilized, and most plastic can't take the heat. Furthermore, some plastics—unlike glass and aluminum—tend to absorb minute quantities of what they contain. However, since 1989 Coca-Cola and PepsiCo have been selling reusable PET plastic bottles in Europe and South America, where local bottling plants still exist in large numbers. The bottles can be refilled 20–30 times.

Another reusable container is the metal or plastic lunch box that most workers and schoolchildren once used. Today many people carry their lunches in throwaway paper or plastic bags. At work people can have their own reusable glasses, cups, dishes, utensils, cloth napkins, and towels, and can use handkerchiefs instead of tissues. In 1989 a social studies class at a New Jersey high school persuaded the school board to switch from Styrofoam lunch trays to washable dishes. The students then raised enough money to buy and protect 121 hectares (300 acres) of rain forest in Belize. In Germany outdoor festivals increasingly use washable plates, glasses, and cutlery.

Also reusable are plastic or metal garbage cans and wastebaskets, which might better be called *resource containers*. Using these containers to separate wastes for recycling and rinsing them out as needed would eliminate the need for throwaway plastic liner bags, which waste oil (because they are made from petrochemicals) and contribute to the solid waste problem.

You can carry reusable baskets, canvas or plastic grocery bags, or string containers (Figure 19-9) when you shop for groceries or other items. Several

**Q:** How many tires do Americans throw away each year?

## Paper or Plastic?

You've just paid for your groceries and you're offered a choice: plastic or paper bags. Which do you choose?

The answer is neither. Both are environmentally harmful, and the question of which is the more damaging has no clear-cut answer. On the one hand, plastic bags are made from nonrenewable fossil fuels, degrade slowly in landfills, and harm wildlife (Figure 19-10), and producing them pollutes the environment.

On the other hand, the brown paper bags in most supermarkets are made from virgin paper. Even those that supposedly contain some recycled fiber use mostly preconsumer paper waste (Spotlight, p. 403). Papermaking uses trees, pollutes the air and water, and releases toxic dioxins. On a weight basis plastic bags take less energy to make and transport and less landfill space than paper bags. Paper bags, however, break down faster in landfills and produce fewer toxic substances. Moreover, unlike the oil used to make plastic bags, the wood used to make paper bags is a potentially renewable resource. Also, the technology for recycling paper is more advanced than that for plastics, and recycled paper can be used in a greater variety of products.

Don't fall for labels claiming paper and plastic bags are recyclable. Just about anything is in theory recyclable. What counts is whether it is, in fact, recycled.

So don't choose between paper and plastic. Instead, bring your own reusable (cloth or string) bags, or at least save and reuse any paper or plastic bags you get.

**Figure 19-10** Before the discarded plastic beverage can yoke was removed, this Hawaiian monk seal was slowly starving to death. Each year plastic waste dumped from ships and left as litter on beaches threatens the lives of millions of marine animals and seabirds that ingest such debris, become entangled in it, or choke on it.

Doris Alcorn/National Marine Fisheries

---

can be folded up and kept in your handbag, pocket, or car (Spotlight, above).

**THE DIAPER DILEMMA** What should we do about diapers? Some favor reusable cloth diapers instead of disposable diapers, but this issue has no clear-cut resolution.

Disposable diapers may make life easier, but they also add to the trash load. The 18 billion disposable diapers used each year in the United States take up 2–4% by volume of municipal solid waste and take 200–500 years to degrade in landfills. Even the new biodegradable diapers take 100 years to break down in a landfill. Production of disposable diapers uses trees, consumes plastic resources (about a third of each diaper is plastic), and creates air and water pollution.

U.S. sales of disposable diapers bring in $4 billion per year. But the annual life-cycle bill (not including the pollution cost of their manufacture) for their disposal is $3.9 billion. Thus, to cover environmental costs directly, the retail price of disposable diapers would have to be doubled.

Cloth diapers can be washed and reused 80–200 times, and then retired into lint-free rags, which keeps the roughly 10,000 disposable diapers the average baby uses before becoming toilet trained from reaching landfills. Cloth diapers also save trees and money. For example, the disposable diapers needed for one baby cost about $1,533. A cloth diaper service costs about $975, and washing cloth diapers at home costs about $283.

Does the choice seem simple? Consider this: Laundering cloth diapers produces 9 times as much air pollution and 10 times as much water pollution as disposable diapers do in their lifetime. Over their lifetime cloth diapers also consume 6 times more water and 3 times more energy than disposables.

So the choice between disposable diapers and reusable cloth diapers is not clear-cut. Many people opt for cheaper cloth diapers and use disposable ones for trips or at child-care centers that won't allow use of cloth diapers.

**TIRES** There are now 2–3 billion used tires heaped in landfills (Figure 19-11), old mines, abandoned houses, and other dump sites throughout the United States, and the pile grows by about 280 million tires per year. About 7% are recycled or reused, 9% are

---

A: 220 million—enough to encircle the earth almost three times

**Figure 19-11** Tires at a landfill in North Carolina illustrate the throwaway mentality prevalent in the United States and other affluent countries.

R. Calentine/Visuals Unlimited

incinerated to produce energy, and 5% are exported. The remaining 79% (about 220 million tires per year) are landfilled, stockpiled, or dumped illegally.

Tire dumps are fire hazards and breeding grounds for mosquitoes. In 1989 there were at least 87 large tire fires in the United States that burned for weeks or months, polluting the air with soot, carbon dioxide, and particles of toxic metals such as cadmium, lead, zinc, and arsenic. Water sprayed onto the burning tires can carry the oil and other toxic substances with it, and pollute nearby surface water and groundwater.

Rather than being dumped, used tires can be put to a number of uses. In Westley, California, for example, a power plant burns tires to generate enough electricity for 15,000 homes, using state-of-the-art air pollution controls. Next to the plant sits the world's largest pile of tires, at least 42 million of them. Still other companies convert used tires into heating oil and high-octane compounds that can substitute for lead in gasoline by heating the tires in the absence of oxygen in a sealed reactor (pyrolysis). Other companies use pulverized tires to make resins for products ranging from car bumpers, garbage cans, and doormats to road-building materials. If asphalt pavement were required to contain at least 20% rubber by 1997, this could create a market for 70–100 million tires per year in the United States.

Discarded tires can be reused for the foundations and walls of low-cost passive solar homes (Spotlight, p. 519). And some worn-out tires have been reused to build artificial reefs to attract fish.

Tire life can be extended by retreading, although modern radial tires are difficult and expensive to retread. Instead of investing in new equipment, many U.S. retreaders went out of business. Before radials were invented, 60% of tires were retreaded; now it's around 20%. On the other hand, radial tires can last longer and improve fuel efficiency.

Individuals can reduce the number of tires they use by buying longer-lasting brands, rotating and balancing tires every 9,700–13,000 kilometers (6,000–8,000 miles), using mass transportation, and doing more walking and biking.

Reuse extends resource supplies and reduces energy use and pollution even more than recycling. A popular bumper sticker reads "Recyclers do it more than once." A better version might be "Recyclers do it more than once, but reusers do it the most."

## 19-5 Solutions: Composting and Recycling

**COMPOSTING** Biodegradable solid waste from slaughterhouses and food-processing plants, kitchen and yard waste, manure from animal feedlots (Figure 14-2), wood, and municipal sewage sludge can be mixed with soil and decomposed by aerobic bacteria to produce **compost**, a sweet-smelling, dark brown humus that is rich in organic matter and soil nutrients. It can be used as an organic soil fertilizer or conditioner, as topsoil, or as a landfill cover for golf courses,

Q: What are the two biggest components of municipal solid waste in U.S. landfills?

# Sailing Through Life in an Earthship

When is a ship not a ship? When it's an Earthship. Because then it's a house with three thick walls made from dirt-packed used tires partly buried in the ground and the other wall facing the sun with a slanted glass wall to capture solar energy (Figure 19-12). To Earthship architect Michael Reynolds such houses are ships. Though the houses are rooted in the earth, he sees them as vessels designed to sail right through whatever the future may bring—climate changes, soaring energy costs, recession, and even famine—as well as through peace and prosperity.

Earthship houses can be built for as little as $2 per square meter ($20 per square foot), and the owners can live well on small incomes. You can build one yourself , using things that someone else has thrown away—tires and aluminum cans. Once the house is up, depending on the features you choose to build in, you will pay little for electricity, heating, cooling, and water heating. You can

even grow your own food in the greenhouse created by the sun-facing glass wall that also captures solar energy for heating.

These passive solar houses are not unlike the one built by Amory and Hunter Lovins (Figure 17-7) and use the same principles as Michael Sykes's solar envelope house (Figure 17-13). The big difference is that Earthship walls are built from tires that most tire dealers are glad to give away or even pay you to haul off. To build the walls, steel-belted radial tires are filled with dirt and layered in staggered courses like bricks. Dirt (from excavated soil) is packed tight inside (usually with a sledgehammer) and between them to make the wall rock solid; then it's finished with a coat of plaster or adobe. These walls are so thick and strong that they qualify as structural bearing walls, which means you need no other footings or foundations—a big money-saver. A 140-square-meter (1,500-square-foot) Earthship uses 500–700 tires, which can be filled with dirt and pounded rock

hard by two people in less than a month.

Once heated by the sun, the walls have so much thermal mass that they stay warm for a long time, steadily radiating that warmth into the spaces they enclose. Their huge thermal mass allows them to be built in areas without enough sunlight for conventional solar homes (Figure 17-14). If, as Reynolds prefers, the whole house is partly underground on the three sides not facing the sun, an Earthship can maintain a steady mean temperature of 18–21°C (65–70°F) in such outside temperature extremes as those in Taos, New Mexico, ranging from 38°C (100°F) in summer to –34°C (–30°F) in winter.

Some of the inner walls can be built of another type of solid waste that is often thrown away—aluminum beverage cans—imbedded in cement mortar. Like the tires, they are packed with dirt to provide thermal mass. Living in an Earthship is a great way to live more gently on the earth while saving money.

Pamela Freund/Solar Survival Architecture

Solar Survival Architecture

**Figure 19-12** A completed Earthship house (left) and one during construction (right) in Taos, New Mexico.

parks, forests, roadway medians, and the grounds around public buildings.

Compost can be produced from biodegradable solid waste in large plants. This approach is used in many European countries, including the Netherlands, Germany, France, Sweden, and Italy, and in states such as Minnesota and Oregon. Odors can be controlled by enclosing the facilities and filtering the air

## Lorie Parker

**INDIVIDUALS MATTER**

In 1983 Lorie Parker, a long-time environmental activist, wrote an idealized recycling law based on voluntary participation for a college class project and then persuaded a legislator to introduce her proposed law as a state bill. To her surprise, it became Oregon's 1986 Recycling Opportunity Act.

Two years later she was invited to administer the law as state manager of waste reduction. The first priority of the program she created and administers is to reduce the amount of waste generated. The next priority is to reuse material for its original purpose, then to recycle what cannot be reused. Energy is recovered by burning materials that cannot be reused or recycled, as long as incineration does not degrade the quality of air, water, or land resources. Only as a last resort is landfilling used.

inside, but residents near large composting plants still complain of unacceptable odors. In 1991 a $30-million composting plant in Dade County, Florida, that accepted mixed solid waste was forced to close because of odor problems.

Households can use backyard compost bins (Figure 12-18) for food and yard wastes. Seattle, for example, promotes backyard composting by using a network of volunteer composting experts to help people get started. Apartment dwellers can compost by using indoor bins in which a special type of earthworm converts food waste into humus.

Composting yard waste could cut U.S. solid waste by almost 18%. By 1993 about 5% of U.S. yard waste was composted, with Minnesota, New Jersey, Wisconsin, and Michigan leading the way. By 1993 almost 2,300 U.S. cities had yard waste composting systems, and the number is growing rapidly.

**CLOSING THE LOOP** Recycling, already widely used in many countries, is also becoming widespread in the United States. In 1992 about 17% of municipal solid waste was recycled or composted, and a 30% recovery rate seems within reach by 2000. Japan already recycles 40% of its municipal solid waste.

Environmentalists believe we can do much better. In a recent pilot study 100 families in East Hampton, New York, achieved an 84% recycling rate for their household trash. This shows that a 60–80% recycling and composting rate is possible. Seattle, Washington, recycled 45% of its municipal solid waste in 1992 and

plans to recycle 60% by 1998. At least 10 smaller U.S. communities have done even better than Seattle. By contrast, New York City recycles only 6% of its garbage, and Tucson, Arizona, only 0.02%.

Twenty-nine states have set recycling goals ranging from 15% to 46% by 2000. By 1992 Washington led the way by recycling 34% of its municipal solid waste, and four other states—Minnesota, New Jersey, Massachusetts, and Michigan—recycled 25–35% of such waste. Five states—Maine, Washington, New York, California, and Iowa—plan to recycle 50% of their municipal solid waste by 2000, and New Jersey has set a 60% recycling goal. In 1986 Oregon passed a Recycling Opportunity Act designed to slash the amount of waste by making recycling available to all citizens (Individuals Matter, left). By 1992 over 4,000 communities (up from 600 in 1989) containing a third of the U.S. population had curbside recycling programs—60% of them voluntary and the rest involuntary. However, more than half the states recycle less than 5% of the mass of their municipal solid waste.

Resources can be recycled by high- or low-technology methods. In *high-technology materials recovery facilities (MRFs)* machines shred and automatically separate mixed urban waste to recover glass, iron, aluminum, and other valuable materials (Figure 19-13). These materials are then sold to manufacturers as raw materials, and the remaining paper, plastics, and other combustible wastes are recycled or burned. The resulting heat produces steam or electricity to run the recovery plant and to sell to nearby industries or homes.

By 1993 the United States had more than 220 MRFs and at least 60 more in the planning stages. However, such plants are expensive to build and maintain. Furthermore, once trash is mixed it takes a lot of money and energy to separate it. It makes much more sense economically for consumers to separate trash into recyclable and reusable categories before it is picked up.

With *low-technology resource recovery* homes and businesses put different kinds of waste materials—usually glass, paper, metals, and plastics—into separate containers. Studies have shown that once people start doing this, it takes no more time than putting garbage into one container. Compartmentalized city collection trucks, private haulers, or volunteer recycling organizations pick up the segregated wastes and sell them to scrap dealers, compost plants, and manufacturers.

A key to the low-technology approach is not to mix wastes so we don't have to spend so much money to separate them. When toxic and nontoxic materials are mixed, we have to treat the resulting mixture as toxic; when smelly and nonsmelly wastes are mixed, everything becomes smelly. And if we mix the useless with the useful, what we get tends to be useless.

**Q:** What percentage of U.S. glass beverage bottles are refillable?

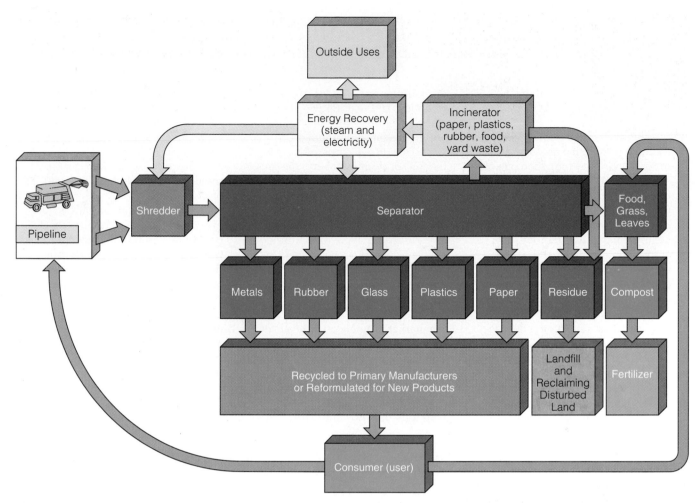

**Figure 19-13** Generalized materials recovery facility used to sort mixed wastes for recycling and burning to produce energy. Because such plants depend on high volumes of trash to be economical, they discourage reuse and waste reduction.

The low-technology approach produces little air and water pollution, reduces litter, and has low start-up costs and moderate operating costs. It also saves more energy (5% of U.S. energy use) and provides more jobs for unskilled workers than high-technology resource recovery plants, and creates three to six times more jobs per unit of material than landfilling or incineration. Another advantage is that collecting aluminum (Case Study, p. 522), paper, glass, plastics (Case Study, p. 523), and other materials for recycling is an important source of income for volunteer service organizations and for many people, especially the homeless and the poor in MDCs and LDCs (Figure 19-14).

According to resource expert Paul Connett, communities should set up *resource parks* containing:

- A reuse and repair center
- A hazardous-waste drop-off and exchange area where consumers and businesses could take toxic wastes, batteries, and used motor oil, and reuse items others have turned in

- A drop-off area for used tires
- A composting area and instructions for people wishing to do backyard composting
- A section for handling commercial waste
- A recycling center where separated household paper, cardboard, aluminum, glass, plastics, and iron and other metallic wastes are dropped off and upgraded (if needed) for sale to recycled materials processors
- A drop-off area for reusables and repairables such as appliances, furniture, clothing, and books
- A flea market where reusables and repairables could be sold

Low-tech recycling and reuse programs can sometimes save communities money, but this should not be the deciding factor in whether they are established. Just as we don't expect landfills to make a profit for a community, we should not expect or require that resource recovery programs make a net profit. Instead,

Strip-mining its ore and using enormous amounts of electricity to convert the ore to metal make aluminum production one of the world's most damaging industries. The world aluminum industry uses nearly as much electricity as is used for all purposes in Africa. On the other hand, using lightweight aluminum in vehicles and aircraft and in moving parts of machinery and many building products saves energy by replacing heavier metals. These uses are beneficial, but environmentalists consider the increasing use of aluminum for packaging (31% in the United States)—mostly in beverage cans—unnecessary and environmentally unacceptable, even when the metal in these products is recycled. Aluminum producers disagree.

Worldwide the recycling rate for aluminum in 1991 was about 33% (30% in the United States). Recycling aluminum produces 95% less air pollution and 97% less water pollution, and requires 95% less energy (Figure 19-8), than mining and processing aluminum ore.

In 1991, 62% (compared to 15% in 1972) of aluminum beverage cans in the United States were recycled at more than 10,000 recycling centers set up by the aluminum industry, other private interests, and local governments. People who returned the cans got about a penny per can for their efforts, earning about $900 million. Within six weeks the average recycled aluminum can had been melted down and was back on the market as a new can. Makers of aluminum cans saved $566 million and the energy equivalent of 20 million barrels of oil. (The electricity used to produce one aluminum can from virgin ore would keep a 100-watt light bulb burning for 100 hours.)

Despite this progress about 38% of the 83 billion aluminum cans produced in 1991 in the United States were still thrown away. If these cans were laid end-to-end, they would wrap around the earth more than 120 times. These discarded cans contain more aluminum than most countries use for all purposes, and each discarded aluminum can represents almost indestructible solid waste.

Recycling aluminum cans is great, but many environmentalists believe that aluminum cans could be replaced by refillable glass bottles—a switch from recycling to reuse. One way to encourage this change would be to place a heavy tax on nonrefillable containers and no tax on reusable glass bottles. Environmentalists also believe that unnecessary use of aluminum could be reduced by not giving the aluminum industry huge electric power subsidies, which hide the true environmental cost of using this metal. Meanwhile, they urge consumers not to buy beverages in aluminum cans and to buy reusable glass containers when they are available.

**Figure 19-14** In many cities in LDCs as much as 25% of the collected municipal waste is recycled by scavengers removing useful and salable materials from dump sites. Here Philippine slum-dwellers are scavenging for useful materials in Manila's main dump.

SIPA-Press

Q: What are the best ways to deal with solid waste?

## Plastics

Plastics are synthesized from petrochemicals (chemicals produced from oil). The plastics industry is among the leading producers of hazardous waste.

Plastics now account for about 8% by weight and 20% by volume of municipal solid wastes in the United States. In landfills toxic cadmium and lead compounds used as binders can leach out of plastics and ooze into groundwater and surface water. And when plastics are thrown away as litter, they can harm wildlife (Figure 19-10). Plastics account for about 60% of the debris found on U.S. beaches.

Most plastics used today are nondegradable or take 200–400 years to degrade. When a plastic product is labeled as biodegradable or recyclable, this statement is true but also misleading. Without sunlight photodegradable plastics take decades to break down, and even biodegradable plastics take decades to partially decompose in landfills because of a lack of oxygen and moisture. Furthermore, the residues

from the breakdown of many plastics could contaminate groundwater supplies and also might harm animals that swallow them.

In theory nearly all plastics could be recycled; in 1992, however, about 2.5% by weight of all plastic wastes and 5% of plastic packaging (including 14% of plastic bottles) used in the United States were recycled. Plastics are more difficult to recycle than glass or aluminum because there are so many different types of plastics. Thus, for recycling to work most plastic trash must be sorted into different categories—a costly procedure. The plastics industry has plastics recycling programs in almost 2,500 U.S. communities, but most recycling of plastics doesn't make economic sense with current technology.

Since most of the raw materials used to make plastics comes from petroleum and natural gas, recycling would help reduce unnecessary waste of these energy resources. However, as long as the true environmental costs of producing, using, and throwing away plastic are not included in product

prices, it will usually be cheaper to make new plastic than to recycle it. For example, if environmental costs are added, the true cost of a PVC-plastic box containing 100 metal screws is $7.44, not $2.99. The true cost for the same screws in a paperboard box would be $3.29, and in a recycled paperboard box $3.18.

The $140-billion-per-year U.S. plastics industry has established the Partnership for Plastics Progress (also known as P3) and the American Plastics Council. These groups spend $50 million per year on ads promoting the value of plastics to society. Critics argue, however, that the main purposes of these organizations are to keep us buying more plastic containers, utensils, and other mostly throwaway items and to fight any laws banning or limiting the use of throwaway plastic items.

Environmentalists recognize the importance of plastics in many products but believe that its widespread use in throwaway beverage and food containers should be sharply reduced and replaced with less harmful and wasteful alternatives such as reusable glass bottles.

we should see this approach as providing more benefits to a community and to the environment than landfills and incinerators.

There are two types of recycling: primary and secondary. The most desirable type is *primary*, or *closed-loop, recycling*, in which products are recycled to produce new products of the same type—newspaper into newspaper and aluminum cans into aluminum cans, for example. The less desirable type is *secondary*, or *open-loop, recycling*, in which waste materials are converted into different products. This does not reduce the use of resources as much as the first type of recycling. For example, primary recycling reduces the use of virgin materials in making a product by 20–90%; secondary recycling reduces it only 25% at most.

In 1991 Germany enacted the world's toughest packaging law, designed to reduce the amount of waste being landfilled or incinerated. The goal is to

recycle or reuse 65% of the nation's packaging by 1995, including 90% of metals and glass, and 80% of paper, board, and plastics. Product distributors must take back their boxes for reuse or recycling. And incineration of packaging, even if it is used to generate power, is not allowed.

**BEVERAGE CONTAINER DEPOSIT BILLS** Beverage container deposit laws can be used to decrease litter and encourage recycling of nonrefillable glass, metal, and plastic containers. Consumers pay a deposit on each beverage container they buy. The deposits are refunded when empty containers are turned in to retailers, redemption centers, or reverse vending machines, which return cash for empty beverage cans and bottles.

Container deposit laws have been adopted in Sweden, Norway, the Netherlands, the CIS, Ecuador, and parts of Australia, Canada, and Japan. Such laws have been proposed in almost every U.S. state but have been enacted in only 10, containing about 20% of the population. Maine has the toughest law. Studies by state and federal agencies show that such laws decrease litter, reduce the use of mineral resources, extend the life of landfills, increase recycling, save energy, reduce air and water pollution, and create jobs. Almost all plastic beverage bottles, most glass bottles, and the majority of aluminum cans that are recycled come from deposit-bill states.

Environmentalists and 73% of Americans polled favor a federal deposit law. So far, however, a well-funded lobby of steel, aluminum, and glass companies, metalworkers' unions, supermarket chains, and brewers and soft-drink bottlers has effectively opposed it. For example, ad campaigns financed by Keep America Beautiful—formed in the 1960s by some of America's largest corporations, including beverage producers, waste management companies, and other groups opposing deposit laws—have helped prevent passage of such laws in a number of states. These groups favor litter-recycling laws, which levy a tax on industries whose products may end up as litter or in landfills. Revenues from the tax are used to set up and maintain statewide recycling centers. By 1992, seven states, containing about 14% of the U.S. population, had this type of law.

Environmentalists point out that litter laws are waste management approaches that provide some money to clean up litter. By contrast, container deposit laws are pollution and waste prevention approaches that reward consumers who return containers and that can make people aware of the need to shift to refillable containers. This is a main reason that companies making nonrefillable containers oppose such laws.

**OBSTACLES TO RECYCLING** Several factors hinder recycling (and reuse) in the United States. One is that Americans have been conditioned by advertising and upbringing to accept a throwaway lifestyle. Another is that many of the environmental and health costs of items are not reflected in their market prices, so consumers have little incentive to recycle, reuse, or reduce their use of throwaway products.

Another serious problem is that the logging, mining, and energy industries get huge tax breaks, depletion allowances, cheap access to public lands (p. 504), and other subsidies to encourage them to extract virgin resources as quickly as possible. By contrast, recycling industries get few tax breaks or other subsidies. Finally, the lack of large, steady markets for recycled materials makes recycling a risky boom-and-bust business that attracts little investment capital.

Communities and businesses leaped into recycling with little emphasis on creating a demand for recycled products. Thus, the supply of waste materials collected for recycling has often exceeded the demand, lowering the prices paid for such materials. To help correct this situation, in 1992 the National Recycling Coalition established a campaign to get businesses to buy recycled material and to pump up the demand for products made from recycled materials. Beginning with 25 large U.S. corporations—including McDonald's, 3M, Sears, and Coca-Cola, the coalition hopes to recruit 5,000 companies for the campaign by 1994.

**OVERCOMING THE OBSTACLES** Studies suggest that with a vigorous program by 2000 the United States could reuse, recycle, and compost 60–80% by weight of the municipal solid waste resources it now throws away by instituting the following measures:

- *Deny landfill or incinerator permits until a community or state has achieved 60% recycling rate and has established a program to reduce waste output per person by 20% over 1990 levels.*
- *Pass a national beverage container deposit law.*
- *Require that all soda and beer bottles have a few standardized sizes, forms, and colors so that any bottler can refill any returned bottles.*
- *Add a tax on virgin materials.*
- *Tax manufacturers on the amount of waste they generate by having them pay a tax or fee equal to the cost of landfilling or incineration.*
- *Include a waste disposal fee in the price of all disposable items so that market prices of items reflect what it costs to dispose of them.*
- *Provide economic incentives for recycling waste oil, plastics, tires, and CFCs used as coolants in refrigerators and air conditioners.*
- *Require labeling of products made with recycled materials to show the percentages used and the percentage from postconsumer waste.*
- *Give tax breaks on products that are easy to repair, reuse, or recycle (primary only) and tax products that are not.*
- *Provide federal and state subsidies and tax credits for secondary-materials industries and for municipal recycling and waste reduction programs. New York, North Carolina, Florida, Oregon, and Wisconsin give tax breaks to businesses that use secondary materials or buy recycling equipment.*
- *Cut federal and state subsidies for primary-materials industries.*
- *Lower or eliminate the sales tax on products made with postconsumer recycled materials.*
- *Guarantee a large market for recycled items and stimulate the recycling industry by passing laws requiring*

Q: What are the worst ways to deal with solid waste?

federal, state, and local governments to purchase products with the highest feasible percentage of recycled materials. Twenty-two states have such laws, with varying effectiveness because of loopholes.

- *Use advertising and education to discourage the throwaway mentality.*

- *Require consumers to sort household wastes for recycling, or give them financial incentives for recycling.*

- *Establish national standards for calculating and comparing municipal recycling rates.* This would make it more difficult to inflate or distort figures.

- *Encourage municipal and backyard composting by banning the disposal of yard wastes in landfills.*

- *Establish standardized ecolabeling for all products.* Such labeling programs should use a "cradle-to-grave" or life-cycle approach, in which the cumulative environmental impacts of products at the extraction, production, use, and disposal stages are taken into account (Figure 7-21). By 1993 a Green Seal, life-cycle labeling system set up by a U.S. environmental and consumer group had set standards for 35 household items. In Canada a government agency has established an Environmental Choice labeling system using cradle-to-grave analysis. Japan and several other countries also have ecolabeling systems, but so far they are not based on life-cycle analysis.

Recycling municipal solid waste is important, but it only puts a small dent in the overall solid-waste problem. For example, if everyone in the United States recycled all of their personal solid waste, 98.5% of the nation's solid waste would still remain (Figure 19-6).

Moreover, recycling is not a solution to the throwaway society. Although recycling usually saves energy and reduces pollution, it still takes energy to recycle materials.

## 19-6 Last Resorts: Incineration and Burial

**BURNING SOLID WASTE** In *trash-to-energy incinerators* trash is burned as a fuel to produce steam or electricity, which can be sold or used to run the incinerator. Most are *mass-burn incinerators*, which burn mixed trash without separating out hazardous materials (such as batteries) and noncombustible materials that can interfere with combustion conditions and pollute the air. Denmark and Sweden burn 50% of their solid waste to produce energy, compared with 17% in the United States.

## Incineration in Japan and the United States

**SPOTLIGHT**

Newer Japanese incinerators are more strictly controlled than those built in the United States. In Japan hazardous wastes and unburnable materials that would pollute the air are removed before wastes are incinerated, which also greatly reduces the amount and toxicity of the remaining ash.

Furthermore, to protect Japanese workers, bottom ash and fly ash are removed by conveyor belt and transported to carefully designed and monitored hazardous-waste landfills in sealed trucks. Before disposal the ash is often solidified in cement blocks. In the United States most ash is simply dumped into conventional landfills.

Newer Japanese incinerators also are equipped with air pollution control devices that remove 95–99% of potential air pollutants, compared with 90% removal in the United States. In Japan violations of air standards are punishable by large fines, plant closings, and—in some cases—jail sentences for company officials. In the United States monitoring is not as strict and punishment for violations is much less severe. However, government figures on air pollution from Japanese incinerators may be misleading because only a few air pollutants emitted by incinerator stacks are monitored. For example, dioxin is not monitored or regulated because it is not considered a problem. The United States also lacks a national standard for dioxin emissions, although some states have standards.

Japanese incinerator workers must have an engineering degree, and they spend 6–18 months learning how the incinerator works and undergo closely supervised on-site training. U.S. incinerator workers need no degrees and get far less training. Incineration in the United States is also plagued by faulty equipment and human errors that have exposed workers and people in surrounding areas to dangerous levels of air pollution.

Incinerating solid waste kills germs and reduces the volume of waste going to landfills by about 60% (not 90% as usually cited). However, incinerators are costly to build, operate, and maintain, and they create very few long-term jobs. Moreover, even with advanced air pollution control devices, incinerators put highly toxic dioxins and furans, and tiny particles of lead, cadmium, mercury, and other toxic substances that can cause cancers and nervous system disorders, into the atmosphere. And without continuous maintenance and good operator training and supervision (Spotlight, above), the air pollution control equipment

A: Burial and incineration

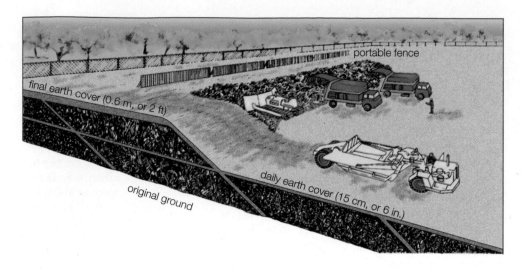

**Figure 19-15** A sanitary landfill. Wastes are spread in a thin layer and then compacted with a bulldozer. A scraper (foreground) covers the wastes with a fresh layer of clay or plastic foam at the end of each day. Portable fences catch and hold windblown debris.

portable fence

final earth cover (0.6 m, or 2 ft)

daily earth cover (15 cm, or 6 in.)

original ground

on incinerators often fails, so that emission standards are exceeded.

Incinerators produce residues of toxic *fly ash* (lightweight particles removed from smokestack emissions by air pollution control devices) and less toxic *bottom ash*; approximately 10% is fly ash, and 90% bottom ash. Usually the two types of ash are mixed and disposed of in ordinary landfills. Although the amount of material to be buried is greatly reduced, its toxicity is increased. And because incinerator ash is a powder, toxic materials left after the solid waste is burned can be leached into groundwater much faster than can bulkier toxic materials in conventional solid waste placed in a landfill.

Environmentalists have pushed Congress and the EPA to classify incinerator ash as hazardous waste, disposable only in landfills designed to handle hazardous waste, as is done in Japan. To date, however, no action has been taken, largely because waste management companies claim it would make incineration too expensive. Environmentalists counter that if the companies can't properly dispose of the toxic ash they produce, they shouldn't be in the incineration business.

In 1992 there were 140 trash-to-energy incinerators operating in the United States. With no new nuclear power plants being built, large construction companies, backed by the Department of Energy and the National Center for Resource Recovery (an offshoot of industry-formed Keep America Beautiful), decided they could keep making money by building large incinerators.

Since 1985, however, over 73 new incinerator projects have been blocked, delayed, or canceled because of public opposition and high costs—the same thing that happened to nuclear power. Of the 70 plants still in the planning stage, most face stiff opposition, and many may not be built as communities discover that recycling, reuse, composting, and waste reduction are cheaper and safer alternatives that can handle up to 80% of municipal waste.

Environmentalists oppose heavy dependence on incinerators because it encourages people to continue tossing away paper, plastics, and other burnable materials. Many existing incinerators have 20- to 30-year contracts with cities to supply them with a certain volume of trash, which makes it hard for cities to switch to large-scale recycling, composting, reuse, and pollution prevention. In 1992, however, Rhode Island became the first state to ban solid waste incineration because of its threats to the health and safety of Rhode Islanders, especially children, and its unacceptably high cost.

**GARBAGE GRAVEYARDS** About 69% by weight of the municipal solid waste in the United States is buried in sanitary landfills, compared with 98% in Australia, 93% in Canada, 90% in Great Britain, 54% in France, 44% in Sweden, 18% in Switzerland, and 17% in Japan. A **sanitary landfill** is a garbage graveyard in which wastes are spread out in thin layers, compacted, and covered daily with a fresh layer of clay or plastic foam (Figure 19-15).

The world's largest landfill is in Fresh Kills on Staten Island. It is as big as 16,000 baseball diamonds and is the final resting place for 80% of New York City's trash. It is as tall as a 15-story building, and when it reaches its capacity, probably around 2005, it will be as tall as a 50-story building. Fresh Kills opened in the early 1970s, before the EPA required stricter standards for new sanitary landfills. As a result, it has no liner, and each day 3.8 million liters (1 million gallons) of contaminated leachate oozes into groundwater beneath Fresh Kills. Fortunately, Staten Island residents do not rely on groundwater to meet their water needs.

Q: What happens to U.S. municipal solid waste?

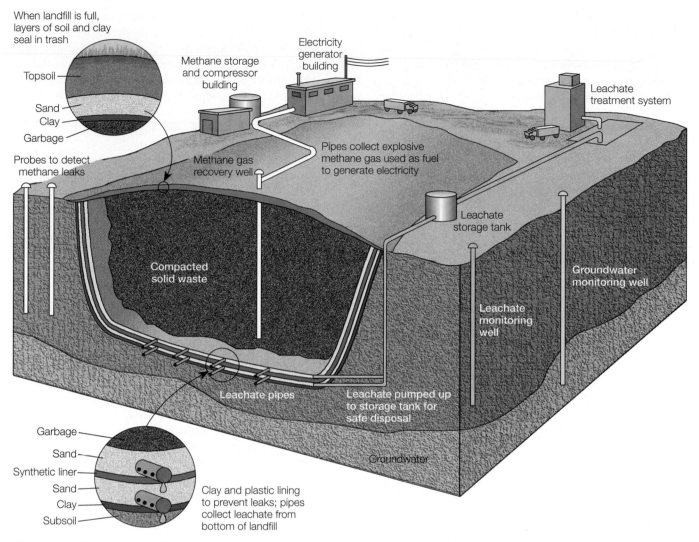

When landfill is full, layers of soil and clay seal in trash

Topsoil
Sand
Clay
Garbage

Probes to detect methane leaks

Methane storage and compressor building

Methane gas recovery well

Electricity generator building

Pipes collect explosive methane gas used as fuel to generate electricity

Leachate treatment system

Leachate storage tank

Compacted solid waste

Groundwater monitoring well

Leachate monitoring well

Leachate pipes

Leachate pumped up to storage tank for safe disposal

Groundwater

Garbage
Sand
Synthetic liner
Sand
Clay
Subsoil

Clay and plastic lining to prevent leaks; pipes collect leachate from bottom of landfill

**Figure 19-16** A modern state-of-the-art sanitary landfill designed to eliminate or minimize environmental problems that plague older landfills. Unfortunately, only a few municipal landfills in the United States have such state-of-the-art design, and 85% of U.S. landfills are unlined. Furthermore, even state-of-the-art landfills will eventually leak, passing contamination and cleanup costs on to the next generation.

Modern state-of-the-art landfills are lined with clay and plastic before being filled with garbage (Figure 19-16). The site must be geologically suitable. The bottom is covered with an impermeable liner usually made of several layers of clay, thick plastic, and sand. This liner collects leachate (rainwater that is contaminated as it percolates down through the solid waste) and is supposed to keep it from leaking into groundwater. Collected leachate ("garbage juice") is pumped from the bottom of the landfill, stored in tanks, and sent either to a regular sewage treatment plant or to an on-site treatment plant. When the landfill is full, it is covered with clay, sand, gravel, and topsoil to prevent water from seeping in. Several wells are drilled around the landfill to monitor any leakage of leachate into nearby groundwater. Methane gas produced by anaerobic decomposition in the sealed landfill is col-

lected and burned to produce steam or electricity. As of 1993 all landfills in the United States must meet such standards, forcing operators to either upgrade or close their operations.

Sanitary landfills offer certain benefits. No air-polluting open burning is allowed. Odor is seldom a problem, and rodents and insects cannot thrive. Sanitary landfills should be located so as to reduce water pollution from leaching, but that is not always done. Moreover, a sanitary landfill can be put into operation quickly, has low operating costs, and can handle a huge amount of solid waste. And after a landfill has been filled, the land can be graded, planted, and used as a park, a golf course, a ski hill, an athletic field, a wildlife area, or some other recreation area.

However, landfills also have drawbacks. While they operate they cause traffic, noise, and dust. Most also emit toxic gases. In addition, paper and other biodegradable wastes break down very slowly in today's compacted and water- and oxygen-deficient landfills. For example, newspapers dug up from some landfills are still readable after 30 or 40 years, and hot dogs, carrots, and chickens that have been dug up after 10 years have not rotted (Figure 19-17). Biodegradable plastics also take decades to decompose in landfills. Thus, they are largely a waste of money and can discourage recycling and less use of plastics (Case Study, p. 523).

The underground anaerobic decomposition of organic wastes at landfills produces toxic hydrogen sulfide gas, explosive methane gas, and smog-forming volatile organic compounds that escape into the air.

**Figure 19-17** Hot dogs and rolls after 10 years in a sanitary landfill. The idea that a landfill is a large compost pile in which things biodegrade fairly rapidly is a myth. Decomposition in modern landfills is slow because the garbage is tightly packed and exposed to little moisture and essentially no light.

Landfills can be equipped with vent pipes to collect these gases and the collected methane burned to produce steam or electricity (Figure 19-16). A single large landfill can provide enough methane to meet the energy needs of 10,000 homes. Besides saving energy, using the methane gas from all large landfills worldwide would lower atmospheric emissions of methane and help reduce projected global warming from greenhouse gases.

Contamination of groundwater and nearby surface water is another serious problem, especially for thousands of older unlined and abandoned landfills. When rain filters through a landfill it leaches out inks, water-soluble metal compounds, and other toxic materials. This produces a contaminated *leachate* that seeps from the bottom of unlined landfills or cracks in the lining of lined landfills. Only 11% of U.S. landfills collect leachate, and only 25% monitor groundwater. Even when leachate is collected it is rarely treated to render it harmless. Moreover, 86% of the landfills studied have contaminated groundwater. Once groundwater is contaminated it is extremely difficult—often impossible—to clean up (Section 23-4). And while modern double-lined landfills (Figure 19-16) delay the release of toxic leachate into groundwater below landfills, they do not prevent it. Landfills also deprive present and future generations of valuable resources, and encourage waste production instead of pollution prevention and waste reduction.

Within the next 10 years half of the landfills in the United States (40% of those in Canada) will be filled and closed; within 20 years 80% will probably be closed. The Netherlands has already run out of landfill sites, and Japan will run out by 2005. Few new landfills are being built in the United States. Either there are no geologically and environmentally acceptable sites, costs to build or upgrade landfills to new

**Figure 19-18** There is no away. In 1987 the barge *Mobro* tried to dump 2,900 metric tons (3,190 tons) of garbage from Islip, Long Island. It was refused permission to unload in North Carolina, Florida, Louisiana, the Bahamas, Mexico, and Honduras. After 164 days and a 9,700-kilometer (6,000-mile) journey, it came back to New York City where it was barred from docking. After staying in the harbor for three months, its garbage was incinerated in Brooklyn; the resulting 364 metric tons (400 tons) of ash was shipped back to Islip for burial in a local landfill. The publicity from this event catalyzed Islip into developing a recycling program, and by 1989 the town was recycling 35% of its solid waste. This has saved the community $2 million per year and extended the life of its landfill.

Q: What country recycles the largest amount of its municipal solid waste?

## What You Can Do to Reduce Waste and Save Money

- *Buy less by asking yourself whether you really need a particular item.* Instead of shopping until you drop, see if you can drop some of your shopping.

- *Buy things that last, keep them as long as possible, and then have them repaired if possible.*

- *Buy things that are reusable or recyclable, and be sure to reuse and recycle them.*

- *Buy beverages in refillable glass containers instead of cans or throwaway bottles.*

- *Use plastic or metal lunch boxes and metal or plastic garbage containers without throwaway plastic liners.*

- *Wrap sandwiches in biodegradable wax paper or put them in reusable plastic containers; and store food in the refrigerator in reusable containers instead of aluminum foil or plastic wrap.*

- *Use rechargeable batteries.*

- *Carry groceries and other items in a reusable basket, a canvas or string bag, or a small cart.* Ideally, stores would not provide paper or plastic bags, or would charge for them, as is done in the Netherlands.

- *Skip the bag when you buy only a quart of milk, a loaf of bread, or anything you can carry out with your hands.*

- *Use sponges and washable cloth napkins, dish towels, and handkerchiefs instead of paper ones.*

- *Don't use throwaway paper and plastic plates and cups, eating utensils, razors, pens, lighters, and other disposable items when reusable or refillable versions are available.*

- *Avoid red or yellow packaging, the kind most likely to contain toxic cadmium and lead.*

- *Buy recycled goods, especially those made by primary recycling, and then recycle them.*

- *Recycle all newspaper, glass, and aluminum, and any other items accepted for recycling in your community.*

- *If you plan to build a house, consider building a highly energy-efficient and less costly structure built mostly from discarded tires, aluminum cans, bottles, and clay* (Figure 19-12).

- *Avoid using throwaway plastic items.*

- *Reduce the amount of junk mail you get.* This can be accomplished by writing to Mail Preference Service, Direct Marketing Association, 11 West 42nd St., P.O. Box 3681, New York, NY 10163-3861, or by calling (212) 768-7277, and asking that your name not be sold to large mailing-list companies. Of the junk mail you do receive, recycle as much of the paper as possible.

- *Push for mandatory trash separation and recycling programs in your community and schools.*

- *Support legislation that would ban the transport of garbage from one state or country to another.* This would promote recycling, reuse, and waste reduction, as well as make individuals more responsible for and aware of the wastes they produce.

- *Push for use of washable, reusable dishes and silverware in school and business cafeterias.*

- *Ask stores, communities, and colleges to install reverse vending machines that give you cash for each reusable or recyclable container you put in.*

- *Buy food items in large economy-size cans or packages or in bulk to reduce packaging.*

- *Buy products in concentrated form whenever possible.*

- *Choose items that have the least packaging or, better yet, no packaging ("nude products").*

- *Don't buy helium-filled balloons, and urge elected officials and administrators to ban balloon releases except for atmospheric research and monitoring.* Mass releases of helium balloons are now banned in Florida, Connecticut, Tennessee, and Virginia.

- *Compost your yard and food wastes* (Figure 12-18), *and pressure local officials to set up a community composting program.*

- *Share, barter, trade, or donate items you no longer need.*

- *Pressure managers of businesses and schools to set up recycling systems and to buy products made from recycled materials.*

- *Photocopy and write on both sides of the page.*

- *Don't litter.*

---

stricter federal standards are too high, or construction is prevented by citizens who want their trash hauled away but don't want a landfill anywhere near them.

Some cities without enough landfill space are shipping their trash to other states or other countries, especially LDCs. However, a few of these states and some LDCs are refusing to accept it (Figure 19-18).

**WHAT CAN INDIVIDUALS DO?** Adopt the three Rs of Earth care: Reduce, Reuse, Recycle. Think of recycling as a first and important baby step in helping sustain the earth. Then move to reuse as part of environmental adolescence. Finally, reach environmental maturity by sharply reducing the amount of waste you produce (Individuals Matter, above).

A: Japan (50%)

We will always produce some waste, but we can produce much less. To prevent pollution and reduce waste, we must understand and live by three key principles: *Everything is connected; there is no away for the wastes we produce; and dilution is not the solution to most pollution.* As Paul Connett puts it, "We must start handling our discarded materials as if the future mattered."

*Solid wastes are only raw materials we're too stupid to use.*

ARTHUR C. CLARKE

# Critical Thinking

1. Explain why you agree or disagree with each of the following propositions:
   a. The competitive free market will control the supply and demand of mineral resources.
   b. New discoveries will provide all the raw materials we need.
   c. The ocean will supply all the mineral resources we need.
   d. We will not run out of key mineral resources because we can always mine lower-grade deposits.
   e. When a mineral resource becomes scarce, we can always find a substitute.
   f. When a nonrenewable resource becomes scarce, all we have to do is recycle it.

2. Use the second law of energy (thermodynamics) to analyze each of the following processes. Which, if any, could be profitable without subsidies?
   a. Extracting most minerals dissolved in seawater
   b. Recycling minerals that are widely dispersed
   c. Mining increasingly lower-grade deposits of minerals
   d. Using inexhaustible solar energy to mine minerals
   e. Continuing to mine, use, and recycle minerals at increasing rates
   f. Building high-tech materials recovery plants (Figure 19-13) to separate mixed wastes for recycling

3. Explain why you support or oppose the following:
   a. Eliminating all tax breaks and depletion allowances for extraction of virgin resources by mining industries
   b. Passing a national beverage container deposit law
   c. Requiring that all beverage containers be reusable
   d. Requiring all households and businesses to sort recyclable materials for curbside pickup in separate containers
   e. Requiring consumers to pay for plastic or paper bags at grocery and other stores to encourage the use of reusable shopping bags

4. Compare the throwaway, recycling, and sustainable-Earth (or low-waste) approaches to waste disposal and resource recovery and conservation for (a) glass bottles, (b) "tin" cans, (c) aluminum cans, (d) plastics, (e) yard wastes, and (f) food wastes (see Table 19-1). Which approach do you favor? Which approach do you use in your own lifestyle?

*5. Keep a list for a week of the solid waste you throw away. What percentage is materials that could be recycled, reused, or burned for energy?

*6. Determine whether (a) your school and your city have recycling programs; (b) your school sells soft drinks in throwaway cans or bottles; (c) your school bans release of helium-filled balloons at sporting events and other activities; and (d) your state has, or is contemplating, a law requiring deposits on all beverage containers.

*7. What happens to solid waste in your community? How much is landfilled? Incinerated? Composted? Recycled? What technology is used in local landfills and incinerators? What leakage and pollution problems have local landfills or incinerators had? Does your community have a recycling program? Is it voluntary or mandatory? Does it have curbside collection? Drop-off centers? Buy-back centers? What is the annual cost of the recycling program?

# PART VI
# Pollution

*I am utterly convinced that most of the great environmental struggles will be either won or lost in the 1990s, and that by the next century it will be too late to act.*

THOMAS E. LOVEJOY

## The Greatest Threat to Human Health

What is roughly the size of a 30-caliber bullet, can be bought almost anywhere, and kills about 8,200 people every day? A cigarette (Figure 20-1).

*Cigarette smoking is the single most preventable major cause of death and suffering among adults.* Each cigarette you smoke reduces your average life span by about 10 minutes. The World Health Organization estimates that tobacco kills at least 3 million people each year from heart disease, lung cancer, other cancers, bronchitis, emphysema, and stroke. By 2050 the death toll from smoking-related diseases is projected to be 12 million annually—an average of 33,000 per day.

In 1992 smoking killed about 435,000 Americans—an average of 1,190 per day (Figure 20-1). This death toll is equivalent to three jumbo jets crashing every day with no survivors but with little or no outcry. In the United States about 30% of all cancers and 85% of lung cancer cases are related to smoking.

Nicotine is not an illegal drug. Yet it kills more people each year in the United States than all illegal drugs, alcohol (the second most harmful drug), automobile accidents, suicide, and homicide combined.

It is also highly addictive. A British government study showed that adolescents who smoke more than one cigarette have an 85% chance of becoming smokers. Some 75% of smokers who quit start smoking again within six months, about the same relapse rate as for recovering alcoholics and heroin addicts.

Studies show that passive smoke (inhaled by nonsmokers) is also a killer, causing up to 40,000 premature deaths in the United States a year (3,000 of them from lung cancer). Nonsmokers regularly exposed to passive smoke have a 30% greater chance of developing heart disease, lung cancer, or other respiratory ill-

American Cancer Society

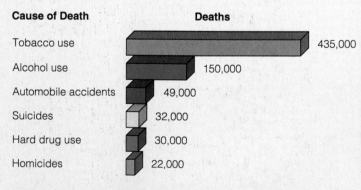

| Cause of Death | Deaths |
|---|---|
| Tobacco use | 435,000 |
| Alcohol use | 150,000 |
| Automobile accidents | 49,000 |
| Suicides | 32,000 |
| Hard drug use | 30,000 |
| Homicides | 22,000 |

**Figure 20-1** Deaths in the United States from tobacco use and other causes in 1992. Smoking is by far the nation's leading cause of preventable death, causing more premature deaths each year than all the other categories in this figure combined. (Data from National Center for Health Statistics)

nesses than do nonsmokers who avoid frequent exposure to smoke. According to a 1992 study by the EPA, each year secondhand smoke contributes to 150,000–300,000 respiratory infections like bronchitis and pneumonia in American children, triggers 8,000–26,000 new cases of asthma in children, and aggravates symptoms in 400,000–1 million children with asthma.

Smoking costs the United States at least $65 billion per year (and perhaps as much as $95 billion) in expenses related to premature death, disability, medical treatment, increased insurance costs, and lost productivity because of illness (accounting for 19% of all absenteeism in industry). These harmful social costs amount to at least $3.00 per pack of cigarettes sold.

Many health experts urge that this amount of tax be added to the price of a pack of cigarettes. This high cost would discourage smoking among U.S. teenagers (3,000 of whom start smoking each day) and require people choosing to smoke to pay for the resulting harmful costs now borne by society as a whole—a user-pays approach. This would raise about $50 billion per year, which could be used to help finance a better national health-care system.

Only about 25% of the U.S. population smokes, down from 42% in 1966. By 2000 the percentage may be 14%. To make up for declining sales, American tobacco companies have targeted other countries—especially LDCs—with sales outside the U.S. tripling since 1985.

The companies give away free cigarettes where teenagers are found, including high schools, video arcades, and rock concerts. Cigarettes are also touted in cartoons and in logos on jeans and T-shirts. Ads falsely imply that almost all Americans smoke and that smoking, like wearing jeans and eating pizza, is a way to be American. It works. In many Latin American cities 50% of teenagers smoke, with some starting as early as age 7.

All of us face certain hazards to our health and well-being; some of them—like smoking—are avoidable, but others are not. When we evaluate the risks we face, the key questions we need to ask are whether the risks of damage from each hazard outweigh the short- and long-term benefits, and how can we reduce the hazards and minimize the risks.

This chapter will seek answers to these questions:

- What types of hazards do people face?
- What chemical hazards do people face, and how can they be measured?
- How harmful is ionizing radiation?
- What types of disease threaten people living in LDCs and in MDCs?
- How can risks be estimated and managed?
- What risks can lead to cancer, and how can they be reduced?

## 20-1 Types of Hazards

**HAZARDS AND RISK** A **hazard** is any substance or action that can cause injury, disease, economic loss, or environmental damage—in short, a danger. **Risk** is the possibility of suffering harm from a hazard. It is expressed in terms of **probability**—a mathematical statement about how likely it is that something will happen. **Risk assessment** involves using data, assumptions, and models to estimate the probability of harm to human health or to the environment that may result from exposures to specific hazards.

**COMMON HAZARDS** Here are some hazards that people face:

- *Cultural hazards.* These include unsafe living and working conditions (Spotlight, p. 534), smoking, poor diet, drugs, drinking, driving, criminal assault, unsafe sex, and poverty (Spotlight, p. 10).
- *Chemical hazards.* These result from harmful chemicals in air (Chapter 22), water (Chapter 23), food (Spotlight, p. 370, and Chapter 24), and soil.
- *Physical hazards.* These include ionizing radiation, noise (Figure 9-14), fires, floods (Case Study,

## Working Can Be Hazardous to Your Health

**SPOTLIGHT**

Roughly one-fourth of U.S. workers risk illness from routine exposure to one or more toxic compounds. The National Institute for Occupational Safety and Health estimates that as many as 100,000 deaths per year—at least half from cancer—are linked to workers' exposure to toxic agents in the United States. The most dangerous occupation is farming, followed by construction, mining, and factory work.

Most work-related illnesses and premature deaths could be prevented by stricter laws and by enforcement of existing laws governing exposure of workers to ionizing radiation and dangerous chemicals. However, political pressure by industry officials has hindered effective enforcement of these laws.

Industry representatives argue that U.S. industries have some of the world's safest workplaces and that stricter health and safety standards would cut profits and reduce competitiveness in the global marketplace. If such standards are enacted, they claim, they would have to shut down U.S. plants and move to countries where health and safety standards—and wages—are lower.

Environmentalists call this form of job blackmail "greenmail." They believe that pollution taxes and more of a company's profits could and should be used for improving worker health and safety standards, as is done in many Japanese, Scandinavian, and German industries.

A growing number of workers are becoming involved in the environmental movement because they and their families have more to lose than most people from poorly enforced or weak environmental and occupational health and safety laws. These workers often feel they must accept high health risks to keep their jobs so they can feed themselves and their families. They see themselves and their families as victims of greenmail.

p. 340), drought, tornadoes, hurricanes, landslides, earthquakes (Figure 7-1), and volcanic eruptions (Figure 7-30).

■ *Biological hazards.* These are disease-causing bacteria and viruses, pollen, parasites, and animals such as pit bulls and rattlesnakes.

## 20-2 Chemical Hazards

**DOSE AND RESPONSE** The amount of a potentially harmful substance ingested, inhaled, or absorbed through the skin is called the **dose**, and the amount of resulting health damage is called the **response**. Whether a chemical is harmful depends on (1) how big the dose is during a certain amount of time, (2) how often an exposure occurs, (3) who is exposed (adult or child, for example), and (4) how well the body's detoxification system (liver, lungs, and kidneys) works. If the body gets a large dose in a short time, its repair mechanisms can be overwhelmed. The same total dose spread over a much longer time might cause little harm. On the other hand, some substances—such as lead—accumulate in the body so that the total dose over a long time can be harmful, even fatal.

An *acute effect* is an immediate or rapid reaction to an exposure. It can range from dizziness or a rash to death. A *chronic effect* is a long-lasting effect from exposure to a harmful substance. It can result from a single large or small dose or many doses over a long period of time. Examples include kidney and liver damage.

**TYPES OF CHEMICAL HAZARDS** The main types of chemical hazards are toxic substances, hazardous substances, carcinogens, mutagens, and teratogens. Toxins are poisons of biological origin, but the term *toxic* covers poisons in general. **Toxic chemicals** are generally defined as substances fatal to over 50% of test animals at stated concentrations. Many are *neurotoxins*, which attack nerve cells. Nerve gases, potassium cyanide, heroin, chlorinated hydrocarbons (DDT, PCBs, dioxins), organophosphate pesticides (Malathion, Parathion), carbamate pesticides (Sevin, Zeneb), and various compounds of arsenic, mercury, lead, and cadmium are all neurotoxins. Most toxic chemicals are discharged into the environment by industrial and agricultural activities, but others occur naturally, such as hemlock, botulinus toxin, and cobra venom.

**Hazardous chemicals** are literally dangerous chemicals. They cause harm because they are flammable or explosive, irritate or damage the skin or lungs (such as strong acidic or alkaline substances; Figure 12-8), interfere with or prevent oxygen uptake and distribution (asphyxiants such as carbon monoxide and hydrogen sulfide), or induce allergic reactions of the immune system (allergens).

In **cancer** certain cells multiply uncontrollably and invade surrounding tissue. Anything, be it chemicals,

Q: What percentage of new U.S. aluminum drink cans are recycled?

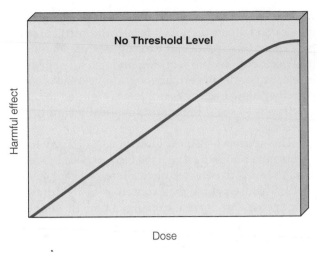

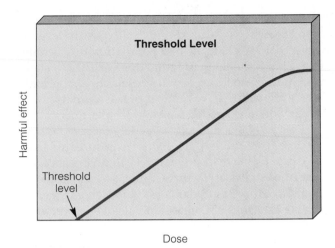

**Figure 20-2** Different hypothetical dose-response curves. The curve on the left represents harmful effects that occur with increasing doses of a chemical or ionizing radiation. No dose is considered to be safe. The curve on the right shows the response of exposure to a chemical or ionizing radiation in which harmful effects appear only when the dose is above a certain threshold level. There is considerable uncertainty and controversy over which of these models applies to various harmful agents because of the difficulty in estimating the response to very low doses.

ionizing radiation, or viruses, that causes or promotes the growth of a malignant (cancerous) tumor is a **carcinogen**. If not detected and treated in time, many cancerous tumors **metastasize**; that is, they release malignant cells that travel in body fluids to various parts of the body, and start new tumors there—making treatment much more difficult.

A **mutagen** is an agent, such as a chemical or ionizing radiation, that causes *mutations*—changes in the DNA molecules of the genes that can be transmitted from parent to offspring. A few mutations are beneficial and some are neutral, but many are harmful. For example, manic depression, cystic fibrosis, hemophilia, sickle-cell anemia, Down syndrome, and some types of cancer are the result of harmful inheritable mutations.

Any chemical, ionizing agent, or virus that causes birth defects during the growth and development of the human embryo is a **teratogen**. Chemicals known to cause birth defects in laboratory animals include PCBs, thalidomide, and metals such as arsenic, cadmium, lead, and mercury.

Some people have the mistaken idea that all natural chemicals are safe and all synthetic chemicals are harmful. In fact, many synthetic chemicals are quite safe if used as intended, and a great many natural chemicals are deadly.

Avoiding or minimizing exposure to harmful or potentially harmful chemicals is not easy. According to the National Academy of Sciences only about 10% of the 70,000 chemicals in commercial use have been thoroughly screened for toxicity and only 2% have been

adequately tested to determine whether they are carcinogens, teratogens, or mutagens. Only 2% of cosmetic ingredients, 5% of food additives, 10% of pesticides, and 18% of drugs used in medicines have been thoroughly tested. Furthermore, each year about 1,000 new chemicals are introduced into the marketplace with little knowledge about their potentially harmful effects.

Even if we determine the biggest risks associated with a particular technology or chemical, we know little about its possible interactions with other technologies and chemicals or about the effects of such interactions on human health and ecosystems. Moreover, some chemicals and radioactive isotopes build up in the body.

**SOLUTIONS: WHAT IS TOXIC** Determining the level at which a substance poses a health threat is done by laboratory investigations (*toxicology*) and by studies of human populations (*epidemiology*). Both approaches are difficult and costly, and both have certain limitations.

Toxicity is usually determined by tests on live laboratory animals (especially mice and rats), bacteria, and cell and tissue cultures. Tests are run to develop a **dose-response curve**, which shows the effects of various doses of a toxic agent on a group of test organisms (Figure 20-2). The results are extrapolated for low doses on the test organisms and then extrapolated to humans.

An experiment to assess acute effects often involves determining the **lethal dose**: the amount of material per unit of body weight of the test organism that kills all of the test population in a certain time. Then the dose is reduced until an exposure level is found that kills half the test population in a certain time. This is the **median lethal dose** or **$LD_{50}$**, a standard measurement in toxicity research. Using high dose levels reduces the number of test animals needed, cuts the time needed to obtain results, and lowers costs. Because it is difficult to get data on responses to low doses, the results of high dose exposures are usually extrapolated to low dose levels. Experiments evaluating the effects of low to medium doses might look for changes in tissue damage, blood chemistry, or enzyme activities in the test animals over a period of several months.

There are problems with animal tests. Extrapolating test animal data from high to low dose levels is uncertain and controversial. According to the *linear dose-response model* any dose of ionizing radiation or of a toxic chemical is harmful, and the harm rises as the dose increases until it reaches a saturation level (Figure 20-2, left). With the *threshold dose-response model* there is a threshold dose below which no detectable harmful effects occur, presumably because the body can repair the damage caused by low doses of some substances (Figure 20-2, right). It's very difficult, however, to establish which of these models applies at low doses.

Some scientists challenge the validity of extrapolating data from test animals to humans because human physiology and metabolism differ from those of the test animals. Others counter that such tests work fairly well, especially for revealing cancer risks, when the correct experimental animal is chosen. However, animal tests take two to five years and cost from $200,000 to $2 million per substance. Furthermore, they are coming under increasing fire from animal rights groups. As a result, scientists are looking for substitute methods.

Also controversial are bacteria and cell and tissue culture tests for toxic agents. One of the most widely used bacterial tests, the Ames test, is considered an accurate predictor of whether a substance is mutagenic; it is also quick (two weeks) and cheap ($1,000–$1,500 per substance). Some believe this test will also detect carcinogens, but the evidence for this is controversial. Cell and tissue culture tests have similar uncertainties, take several weeks to months, and cost about $18,000 per substance.

Chronic toxicity is much harder to assess than acute toxicity. The problem is establishing that a particular substance is responsible for chronic effects when people are exposed to hundreds, even thousands, of potentially harmful substances over a long period of time.

Another approach to testing for toxicity and determining the agents causing diseases such as cancer is *epidemiology*—an attempt to find out why some people get sick and others do not. Typically the health of people exposed to a particular toxic agent from an industrial accident, people working under high exposure levels, or people in certain geographic areas is compared with the health of people not exposed to these conditions to see if there are statistically significant differences.

This approach also has limitations. For many toxic agents not enough people have been exposed to high enough levels to detect statistically significant differences. Because people are exposed to many different toxic agents and disease-causing factors throughout their lives, it is often impossible to link an observed epidemiological effect with exposure to a particular toxic agent. And because epidemiology can be used only to evaluate hazards to which people have already been exposed, it is rarely useful for predicting the effects of new technologies or substances.

*Thus all methods for estimating toxicity levels have serious limitations, but they are also all we have.* To take this uncertainty into account and minimize harm, standards for allowed exposure to toxic substances and radiation are typically set at levels 10, 100, or even 1,000 times lower than the estimated harmful level.

This still may not be enough to protect some people, particularly those vulnerable to a particular hazard because of an allergic reaction or acute sensitivity. Ideally all products likely to be inhaled, ingested, or absorbed would list their ingredients so that people allergic to or sensitive to certain substances could avoid exposure.

## 20-3 Ionizing Radiation: A Physical Hazard

**HOW MUCH ARE WE EXPOSED TO?** Ionizing radiation, a form of electromagnetic radiation (Figure 3-5), has enough energy to damage body tissues. Examples of ionizing radiation are X rays, ultraviolet radiation from the sun and sunlamps (Spotlight, p. 305), neutrons emitted by nuclear fission (Figure 3-11) and nuclear fusion (Figure 3-13), and alpha, beta, and gamma radiation from radioactive isotopes (Figure 3-10).

Each year people are exposed to some ionizing radiation from natural or background sources and from human activities (Figure 20-3). Sources of natural ionizing radiation include cosmic rays from outer space, radioactive radon-222 (Case Study, p. 573), soil, rocks, air, water, and food.

Among human activities nuclear power plants provide low exposure, as long as they are operating properly. However, nuclear accidents can be disastrous, killing people and contaminating large areas and making them uninhabitable (p. 476).

Most nonnatural ionizing radiation comes from medical X rays and from diagnostic tests and treatment using radioactive isotopes. The federal government estimates that one-third of the X rays taken each year in the United States are unnecessary. If your doctor or dentist proposes an X ray or a diagnostic test involving radioisotopes, ask why it is necessary, how it will help find what is wrong and influence possible treatment, and what less risky tests might be available.

**EFFECTS** Exposure to ionizing radiation can damage cells in two ways. One is to alter genes and chromosomes by causing mutations in DNA molecules. This *genetic damage* shows up as a genetic defect in immediate offspring or several generations later. The other is to damage tissues, causing harm during the victim's lifetime. Examples of this *somatic damage* include burns, miscarriages, eye cataracts, and cancers (bone, thyroid, breast, skin, and lung). Most scientists assume that the dose-response curve for radioactivity is linear (Figure 20-2, left), but others believe there may be a threshold level (Figure 20-2, right) because of the body's ability to repair some of the damage.

Exposure to a large dose of ionizing radiation over a short time can be fatal—as the victims of Nagasaki, Hiroshima, and Chernobyl (p. 476) remind us. Small doses over a long period of time cause less damage than the same total dosage given all at once. However, a 1990 study by the U.S. National Academy of Sciences concluded that the likelihood of getting cancer from exposure to a low dose of radiation is three to four times higher than previously thought.

Some scientists believe that the current limit on occupational exposure to low-level radiation needs to be reduced by at least a factor of 10, and perhaps by a factor of 1000. Evidence supporting this conclusion comes from a 1991 study revealing that white male workers at Tennessee's Oak Ridge National Laboratory exposed to radiation well below permissible levels had a 63% higher death rate from leukemia than all U.S. white males. In 1993 the United Kingdom enacted limits on occupational and public exposure to radiation that are much more stringent than those in the United States.

The effects of ionizing radiation also vary with the type, penetrating power, source (outside or inside the body), and half-life of the radioisotope (Table 3-1). Alpha particles lack the penetrating power of beta particles (Figure 3-10) but have more energy. Thus alpha-emitting isotopes are particularly dangerous when breathed in or taken in from food or water. Alpha par-

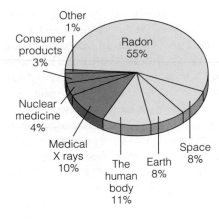

Natural sources 82%

Human-generated 18%

**Figure 20-3** Natural and human contributions to the average annual dose of ionizing radiation received by the U.S. population. Most studies indicate that there is no safe dose of ionizing radiation. (Data from National Council on Radiation Protection and Measurements)

ticles outside the body can cause skin cancer but cannot penetrate the skin and reach vital organs. Because beta particles can penetrate the skin, a beta emitter outside the body can damage internal organs. Generally radioisotopes with intermediate half-lives (Table 3-1) pose the greatest threat to human health; they stay around long enough to reach the human body and decay fast enough to cause considerable damage while they are around.

The effects of radioactive isotopes also depend on where they accumulate in the body and to what degree their concentrations can be biologically amplified in food chains and webs (Spotlight, p. 429). For example, iodine-131, a beta and gamma emitter with a half-life of 8 minutes, accumulates in the thyroid gland where it can cause cancer. Strontium-90, a beta emitter with a half-life of 28 years, is chemically similar to calcium and accumulates in bone tissue, where it can cause leukemia (cancer of the bone marrow tissue). Rapidly growing tissues of the developing embryo are extremely sensitive. In 1993 the World Health Organization reported that thyroid cancer in children in the Chernobyl area increased 80% since the 1986 accident (p. 476) and childhood leukemia increased 1.5 times.

According to the National Academy of Sciences exposure over an average lifetime to average levels of ionizing radiation from natural and human sources causes about 1% of all fatal cancers and 5–6% of all normally encountered genetic defects in the U.S. population. Some analysts believe these estimates are too low. Either way, any unnecessary increase in emissions of or exposure to ionizing radiation from human activities should be avoided.

A: 2.5% by weight (5% of plastic packaging, 14% of plastic bottles)

**Figure 20-4** Unsafe water supply in Nigeria. Transmissible disease from drinking contaminated water is the leading killer, especially of young children, in LDCs.

## 20-4 Biological Hazards: Disease in MDCs and LDCs

**TYPES OF DISEASE** A **transmissible disease** is caused by a living organism—often a bacterium, virus, or parasitic worm—and can be spread from one person to another. The infectious agents are spread by air, water (Figure 20-4), food, body fluids, and, in some cases, insects and other nonhuman carriers (called *vectors*). Examples are sexually transmitted diseases (Case Study, p. 539), malaria (Case Study, p. 540), schistosomiasis, elephantiasis, sleeping sickness, and measles.

Diseases such as cardiovascular (heart and blood vessel) disorders, most cancers, diabetes, bronchitis, emphysema, and malnutrition (Spotlight, p. 370) often have multiple (often unknown) causes, tend to develop slowly and progressively over time, are not caused by living organisms, and do not spread from one person to another. They are classified as **nontransmissible diseases**.

**DISEASE IN LDCS** Poverty is the underlying cause of lower average life expectancy and higher infant mortality (Figure 8-10) in LDCs, as well as for poor people in MDCs. The overcrowding, unsafe drinking water (Figure 20-4), poor sanitation, and malnutrition associated with poverty increase the spread of transmissible diseases, which account for about 40% of all deaths in LDCs (8% in MDCs). The hot, wet climates of tropical and subtropical LDCs also increase the chances of infection, because disease organisms can thrive year-round (Case Study, p. 540).

With adequate funding, significant improvements in human health care in LDCs can be made (Solutions, p. 542).

**DISEASE IN MDCS** As a country industrializes and makes the *demographic transition* (Figure 8-18), it also makes an *epidemiological transition*, in which the infectious diseases of childhood become less important and the chronic diseases of adulthood (heart disease and stroke, cancer, and respiratory conditions) become more important in determining mortality.

Each year about 2.3 million people die in the United States: 37% from heart attacks, 22% from cancer, 7% from strokes, 5% from accidents, and the remaining 29% from a variety of causes. In the United States and other MDCs most deaths are a result of environmental and lifestyle factors rather than infectious agents invading the body. Except for auto accidents, these deaths result from chronic diseases (heart attack, cancer, stroke) that take a long time to develop, have multiple causes, and are largely related to location (urban or rural), work environment, diet, smoking (p. 532), exercise, sexual habits (Case Study, p. 539), and alcohol or other harmful drugs.

Changing these harmful lifestyle factors could prevent 40–70% of all premature deaths, one-third of all cases of acute disability, and two-thirds of all cases of chronic disability. Currently about 95% of the money spent on health care in the United States is used to *treat* rather than to *prevent* disease.

Q: What percentage of U.S. municipal solid waste could be recycled, composted, or reused?

## Sex Can Be Hazardous to Your Health

**CASE STUDY**

Sexually transmitted diseases (STDs) are passed on during sexual activity. Many can also be transmitted from mother to infant during birth, from one intravenous (IV) drug user to another on shared needles, and by exposure to infected blood.

Worldwide there are about 250 million new infections and 750,000 deaths from STDs each year. By 2000 the number of deaths per year from STDs is expected to reach 1.5 million—an average of 4,100 per day. In the United States STDs strike about 12 million people (8 million of them under age 25) per year (Figure 20-5). The number of new reported cases of most STDs has risen every year since 1981.

Major STDs caused by bacteria include *chlamydia* (which affects as many as 45% of sexually active U.S. teenagers and college students), *gonorrhea*, and *syphilis*. These diseases can be treated with antibiotics if caught in time.

Major STDs caused by viruses include *genital warts* (which may infect 10–12 million Americans), *genital herpes* (which may infect 20% of sexually active persons in the United States), *hepatitis B*, and *acquired immune deficiency syndrome* or *AIDS* (which develops from the HIV virus). These viral diseases—with the possible exception of genital warts—are presently incurable.

Since 1981 AIDS—a fatal disease transmitted primarily by sexual contact—has become a serious global health threat. The World Health Organization estimated that by August 1992 at least 13 million people worldwide (62% of them in sub-Saharan Africa) had been infected with HIV—many of them unknowingly. Every 15–20 seconds someone in the world—80% of them in LDCs—is infected with HIV. By 2000 48–120 million people are expected to be infected, with the largest proportion (42%) in Asia. Heterosexual transmission accounts for about 90% of the new infections worldwide and about 6% in the United States (12% among those ages 13–24).

Within 10 years 95% of those with this virus develop AIDS. There is as yet no cure for AIDS, although drugs may help some infected people live longer. By August 1992 an estimated 2.7 million people had AIDS (69% of them in Africa and 16% in the United States), and 2.5 million had died from the disease (100,000 in 1992 alone). By 2000 as many as 24 million people are expected to have AIDS—almost a 10-fold increase in only 8 years—and the annual death toll may reach 400,000.

In the United States about 1 million people (some estimate up to 3 million) are infected with HIV, 227,000 have AIDS, and 160,000 have died from the disease. Each day about 150 Americans die from AIDS, with the disease being the sixth leading cause of death among young people ages 15–24.

You can slash the risk of contracting an STD by:

- Not having sex with another person
- Having sex only with one uninfected partner in a strictly monogamous relationship
- Using a good-quality latex (not lambskin) condom plus a spermicide when engaging in sex

In addition to the above you can cut the risk of contracting AIDS by:

- Not having sex with anyone known or suspected to be an IV drug user
- Not injecting drugs

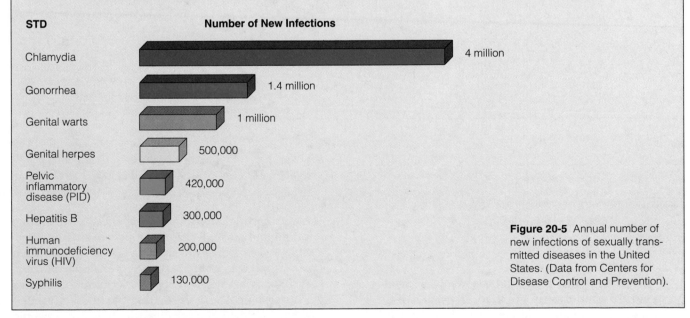

**STD** — **Number of New Infections**

- Chlamydia — 4 million
- Gonorrhea — 1.4 million
- Genital warts — 1 million
- Genital herpes — 500,000
- Pelvic inflammatory disease (PID) — 420,000
- Hepatitis B — 300,000
- Human immunodeficiency virus (HIV) — 200,000
- Syphilis — 130,000

**Figure 20-5** Annual number of new infections of sexually transmitted diseases in the United States. (Data from Centers for Disease Control and Prevention).

## CASE STUDY

## Malaria

About 40% of the world's people live in malaria-prone tropical and subtropical regions (Figure 20-6). There are 200–300 million new cases each year—about 90% of them in sub-Saharan Africa (Figure 14-9). Some 1–2 million of these people (some estimate as many as 5 million) die each year—more than half

of them children under age 5. Malaria's intermittent symptoms include fever and chills, anemia, an enlarged spleen, severe abdominal pain and headaches, extreme weakness, and greater susceptibility to other diseases.

Malaria is caused by four species of protozoa of the genus *Plasmodium*. Most cases of the disease are transmitted when an un-

infected female of any one of 60 species of *Anopheles* mosquito bites an infected person, ingesting blood that contains the parasite, and then bites an uninfected person. When this happens *Plasmodium* parasites move from the mosquito into the bloodstream, multiply in the liver, and then enter blood cells to continue multiplying (Figure 20-7). Malaria can also be transmitted

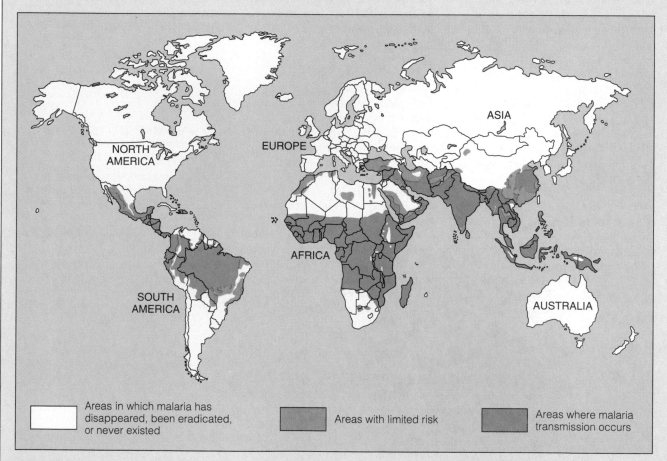

Areas in which malaria has disappeared, been eradicated, or never existed

Areas with limited risk

Areas where malaria transmission occurs

**Figure 20-6** Malaria threatens about 40% of the world's population. (Data from World Health Organization)

## 20-5 Risk Analysis

**ESTIMATING RISKS** **Risk analysis** involves identifying hazards and evaluating their associated risks (*risk assessment*), ranking risks (comparative risk analy-

sis), using this and other information to determine options and make decisions about reducing or eliminating risks (*risk management*), and informing decision makers and the public about risks (*risk communication*).

Risk assessment involves determining the types of hazards involved, estimating the probability that each hazard will occur, estimating how many people

Q: What percentage of U.S. landfills are lined to help prevent groundwater contamination?

by blood transfusions or sharing needles. This cycle repeats itself until immunity develops, treatment is given, or the victim dies.

During the 1950s and 1960s the spread of malaria was sharply curtailed by draining swamplands and marshes, by spraying breeding areas with insecticides, and by using drugs to kill the parasites in the bloodstream.

Since 1970, however, malaria has come roaring back. Most of the malaria-carrying *Anopheles* mosquitoes have become genetically resistant to most of the insecticides used. Worse, the *Plasmodium* parasites have become genetically resistant to the common antimalarial drugs. Irrigation ditches—breeding grounds for mosquitoes—have proliferated and malaria-control budgets have been cut in the mistaken belief that the disease is under control.

Researchers are working to develop new antimalarial drugs and vaccines, and biological controls for *Anopheles* mosquitoes, but such approaches are underfunded, in the early stages of development, and more difficult than originally thought. Recently scientists have found that a chemical (quinghaosu) extracted from tropical wormwood can successfully combat the skyrocketing number of quinine-resistant malaria strains. The Chinese have used this chemical to treat malaria for nearly 1,000 years.

The World Health Organization estimates that only 3% of the money spent worldwide each year on biomedical research is devoted to malaria and other tropical diseases, even though more people suffer and die worldwide from these diseases than from all others combined.

Prevention offers the best approach to slowing the spread of malaria. Methods include increasing water flow in irrigation systems to prevent mosquito larvae from developing (an expensive and wasteful use of water), using mosquito nets dipped in a nontoxic insecticide (permethrin) in windows and doors of homes, cultivating fish that feed on mosquito larvae, clearing vegetation around houses, and planting trees that soak up water in low-lying marsh areas where mosquitoes thrive.

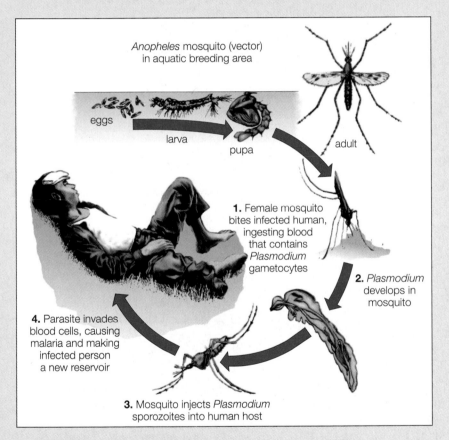

*Anopheles* mosquito (vector) in aquatic breeding area

eggs
larva
pupa
adult

1. Female mosquito bites infected human, ingesting blood that contains *Plasmodium* gametocytes

2. *Plasmodium* develops in mosquito

4. Parasite invades blood cells, causing malaria and making infected person a new reservoir

3. Mosquito injects *Plasmodium* sporozoites into human host

**Figure 20-7** The life cycle of malaria.

are likely to be exposed to it, and how many may suffer serious harm. Probabilities based on past experience, animal and other tests, and epidemiological studies are used to estimate risks from older technologies and products (Section 20-1). For new technologies and products much more uncertain statistical probabilities, based on models rather than actual experience, must be calculated. Table 20-1 is an example of *comparative risk analysis* and summarizes the greatest ecological and health risks identified by a panel of scientists acting as advisers to the U.S. Environmental Protection Agency.

The more complex a technological system and the more people needed to design and run it, the harder it

A: About 15%

## Improving Health Care in LDCs

**SOLUTIONS**

The health of people in LDCs can be improved dramatically, quickly, and cheaply by providing:

- Contraceptives (Figure 8-7), sex education, and family-planning counseling.
- Better nutrition, prenatal care, and birth assistance for pregnant women. At least 500,000 women in LDCs die each year of mostly preventable pregnancy-related causes, compared with 6,000 in MDCs.
- Better nutrition for children (Spotlight, p. 370).
- Greatly improved postnatal care (including the promotion of breastfeeding) to reduce infant mortality.
- Immunization against tetanus, measles, diphtheria, typhoid, and tuberculosis.
- Oral rehydration for diarrhea victims (a simple solution of water, salt, and sugar).
- Antibiotics for infections.
- Clean drinking water and sanitation facilities to the third of the world's population that lacks them.

Extending such primary health care to all the world's people would cost an additional $10 billion per year, a mere 4% of what the world spends every year on cigarettes or devotes every four days to military spending.

---

### Table 20-1 Greatest Ecological and Health Risks

**High-Risk Ecological Problems**

Global climate change

Stratospheric ozone depletion

Wildlife habitat alteration and destruction

Species extinction and loss of biodiversity

**Medium-Risk Ecological Problems**

Acid deposition

Pesticides

Airborne toxic chemicals

Toxic chemicals, nutrients, and sediment in surface waters

**Low-Risk Ecological Problems**

Oil spills

Groundwater pollution

Radioactive isotopes

Acid runoff to surface waters

Thermal pollution

**High-Risk Health Problems**

Indoor air pollution

Outdoor air pollution

Worker exposure to industrial or farm chemicals

Pollutants in drinking water

Pesticide residues on food

Toxic chemicals in consumer products

Data from Science Advisory Board, *Reducing Risks*, Washington, DC, Environmental Protection Agency, 1990. Items in each category are not listed in rank order.

---

is to calculate the risks. The overall reliability of any technological system is the product of two factors:

$$\frac{\text{system}}{\text{reliability (\%)}} = \frac{\text{technology}}{\text{reliability}} \times \frac{\text{human}}{\text{reliability}} \times 100$$

With careful design, quality control, maintenance, and monitoring, a highly complex system such as a nuclear power plant, a space shuttle, or an early warning system for nuclear attack can achieve a high degree of technology reliability. However, human reliability is almost always much lower than technology reliability and is virtually impossible to predict; to be human is to err.

Suppose, for example, that the technology reliability of a nuclear power plant is 95% (0.95) and that the human reliability is 75% (0.75). Then the overall system reliability is only 71% ($0.95 \times 0.75 \times 100 = 71\%$). Even if we could make the technology 100% reliable (1.0), the overall system reliability would still be only 75% ($1.0 \times 0.75 \times 100 = 75\%$).

This crucial dependence of even the most carefully designed systems on unpredictable human reliability helps explain essentially "impossible" tragedies like the Three Mile Island and Chernobyl nuclear power plant accidents (p. 476) and the explosion of the space shuttle *Challenger*.

Poor management, poor training, and poor supervision increase the chances of human errors. Maintenance workers or people who monitor warning panels in the control rooms of nuclear power plants (Figure 20-8) get bored because most of the time nothing goes wrong. They may fall asleep on duty (as has happened

Q: According to the EPA, how many U.S. landfills will eventually leak?

U.S. Department of Energy

**Figure 20-8** Control room of a nuclear power plant. Watching these indicators is such a boring job that government investigators have found some operators asleep, and in one case they found the control room empty.

in control rooms at several U.S. nuclear plants) or falsify maintenance records because they think the system is safe without their help. They may be distracted by personal problems or illness. And managers may order them to take shortcuts that increase short-term profits or make the managers look more efficient and productive.

One way to make a system more foolproof or "fail-safe" is to move more of the potentially fallible elements from the human side to the technical side. However, chance events such as a lightning bolt can knock out automatic control systems. And no machine or computer program can completely replace human judgment in assuring that a complex system operates properly and safely. Also, the parts in any automated control system are manufactured, assembled, tested, certified, and maintained by fallible human beings.

**RISK–BENEFIT ANALYSIS** The key question is whether the estimated short- and long-term benefits of using a particular technology or product outweigh the estimated short- and long-term risks of other alternatives. One method for making such evaluations is **risk–benefit analysis**. It involves estimating the short- and long-term societal benefits and risks involved, and then dividing the benefits by the risks to find a **desirability quotient**:

$$\text{desirability quotient} = \frac{\text{societal benefits}}{\text{societal risks}}$$

Assuming that benefits and risks can be calculated accurately (a big assumption), here are several possibilities:

1. $\text{large desirability quotient} = \dfrac{\text{large societal benefits}}{\text{small societal risks}}$

   **Example:** *X rays.* Use of X rays (a form of ionizing radiation) to detect bone fractures and other medical problems has a large desirability quotient, if the dose is no larger than needed, less harmful procedures are not available, and doctors do not overprescribe them. Other examples in this category include mining, most dams, and airplane travel. Proponents of nuclear power plants place nuclear technology in this category.

2. $\text{small desirability quotient} = \dfrac{\text{large societal benefits}}{\text{much larger societal risks}}$

   **Example:** *Coal-burning power plants and nuclear power plants* (Sections 18-3 and 18-4, respectively).

3. $\text{uncertain desirability quotient} = \dfrac{\text{potentially large benefits}}{\text{potentially large risks}}$

   **Example:** *Genetic engineering* (Pro/Con, p. 167). Some see biotechnology as a way to increase food supplies, degrade toxic wastes, eliminate certain genetic diseases and afflictions, and make enormous amounts of money. Others fear that, without strict controls, it could do great harm.

**PROBLEMS WITH RISK ASSESSMENT** Calculation of desirability quotients, as well as other ways of evaluating or expressing risk, is extremely difficult, imprecise, and controversial. Here are some of the key problems and issues:

- *Are risk evaluators overconfident about the reliability of current scientific and technical knowledge and models?*

- *Will some technologies benefit one group of people (population A) while imposing a risk on another (population B, often the poor and lower middle class)?* Who should decide which population to favor?

- *Should estimates emphasize short-term risks, or should more weight be put on long-term risks?* Who decides this?

- *Should the primary goal of risk analysis be to determine how much harm is acceptable (the current approach) or to figure out how to do the least damage (a prevention approach)?*

- *Who should do a particular risk–benefit analysis or risk assessment?* Should it be the corporation or government agency that develops or manages the technology, or some independent laboratory or panel of scientists? For an outside evaluation who chooses the people to do the study? Who pays the bill and thus can influence the outcome by denying the lab, agency, or experts future business?

- *Once a risk-assessment study is done, who reviews the results?*—Is it a government agency? Independent scientists? The general public?

- *Should cumulative impacts of various risks be considered, or should risks be considered separately, as is usually done?* For example, suppose a pesticide is found to have a risk of killing one in a million people from cancer—the current EPA limit. Cumulatively, however, effects from 40 such pesticides might kill 40—or even 400—of every 1 million people. Is this acceptable?

To some the most important question concerns risk analysis. Some see it as a useful and much-needed tool. Others see it as a way to justify premeditated murder in the name of profit. According to Peter Montague (Guest Essay, p. 41), "The explicit aim of risk assessment is to convince people that some number of citizens *must* be killed each year to maintain a national lifestyle based on necessities like Saran Wrap, throwaway cameras, and lawns without dandelions." Risk evaluator Mary O'Brien says, "Risk assessment is industry's attempt to make the intolerable appear tolerable." Such critics accuse industries of favoring risk analysis because so little is known about health risks from pollutants and because the data that do exist are controversial. This allows risk–benefit analysis to be crafted to support almost any conclusion and then labeled "scientific decision making." The huge uncertainties in risk–benefit analysis also allow industries to delay regulatory decisions for decades by challenging data in the courts.

Despite the inevitable uncertainties involved, proponents argue that risk analysis is a useful way to organize available information, identify significant hazards, focus on areas that need more research, and stimulate people to make more informed decisions about health and environmental goals and priorities.

However, those who must make decisions based on risk assessments should be aware of their serious limitations. They should recognize that politics, economics, bias, and value judgments are involved at every step of the risk-analysis process. At best risk assessments yield only a range of probabilities and uncertainties based on different assumptions—not the precise numbers that decision makers want.

**MANAGING RISK** **Risk management** includes the administrative, political, and economic actions taken to decide whether and how a particular societal risk is to be reduced to a certain level, and at what cost. It is integrated with risk assessment. Risk management involves trying to answer the following questions:

- Which of the vast number of risks facing society should be evaluated and managed with the limited funds available?

- In what sequence or priority should the risks be evaluated and managed?

- How reliable is the risk–benefit analysis or risk assessment carried out for each risk?

- How much risk is acceptable? How safe is safe enough?

- How much money will it take to reduce each risk to an acceptable level?

- How much will each risk be reduced if available funds are limited, as is usually the case?

- How will the risk management plan be communicated to the public, monitored, and enforced?

Risk managers must make difficult decisions based on inadequate and uncertain scientific data with potentially grave consequences for human health and the environment, and large economic effects on industry and consumers. Each step in this process involves value judgments and trade-offs to find some reasonable compromise between conflicting political, economic, and environmental interests.

**RISK PERCEPTION AND COMMUNICATION**
Most of us do poorly in assessing the risks from the hazards that surround us, and we tend to be full of contradictions. For example, many people deny or shrug off the high-risk nature of activities such as motorcycling (1 death per 50 participants), smoking (1 death in 600 by age 35 for a pack-a-day smoker), a car crash (1 in 5,000 with a seat belt versus 1 in 2,500

**Q:** What environmental and lifestyle factor causes the most death and suffering?

**Figure 20-9** The Mississippi River between Baton Rouge and New Orleans, Louisiana, is lined with oil refineries and petrochemical plants. Along this corridor, known as "Cancer Alley" because of its abnormally high cancer rates, tons of carcinogenic and mutagenic chemicals leak into groundwater or are discharged into the river. In 1988 an environmental alliance of black and white residents protested chemical dumping in their communities and groundwater by marching the 137 kilometers (85 miles) from Baton Rouge to New Orleans.

without), parachuting (1 in 4,000), and rock climbing (1 in 5,000). Yet these same people may be terrified about the possibility of dying in a commercial airplane crash (1 in 800,000), in a train crash (1 in 20 million), in a shark attack (1 in 300 million), or from drinking water with the EPA limit of trichloroethylene (1 in 2 billion).

Being bombarded with news about people killed or harmed by various hazards distorts our sense of risk. *The real news each year is that 99% of the people on Earth didn't die.* However, that's not what we see on TV or hear about every day.

The public generally sees a technology or a product to be riskier than do the experts (Table 20-1) when:

- *It is relatively new or complex rather than familiar.* Examples might include genetic engineering or nuclear power as opposed to dams or automobiles.

- *It is mostly involuntary instead of voluntary.* Examples might include nuclear power plants, nuclear weapons, industrial pollution, or food additives as opposed to smoking, drinking alcohol, or driving.

- *It is viewed as unnecessary rather than as beneficial or necessary.* Examples might include CFC and hydrocarbon propellants in aerosol spray cans or food additives used to increase sales appeal as opposed to cars or firearms for self-defense.

- *It involves a large, well-publicized death toll from a single catastrophic accident rather than the same or even larger death toll spread out over a longer time.* Examples might include a severe nuclear power plant accident, or industrial explosion, or a plane

crash as opposed to coal-burning power plants, automobiles, or malnutrition in LDCs.

- *It involves unfair distribution of the risks.* For example, citizens are outraged when government officials decide to put a hazardous-waste landfill or incinerator in or near their neighborhood even when the decision is based on risk–benefit analysis. This is usually seen as politics, not science.

- *It is poorly communicated* (Guest Essay, p. 548). Does the decision-making agency or company seem trustworthy and concerned or dishonest, unconcerned, and arrogant (Exxon after the *Valdez* oil spill, the Nuclear Regulatory Agency and the nuclear industry since the Three Mile Island accident)? Does it involve the community in the decision-making process from start to finish and reveal what's going on before the real decisions are made? Does it understand, listen to, and respond to community concerns, or does it let the public blow off steam at a few public meetings while decisions are made behind closed doors?

- *It is promoted by people who ignore ethical and moral concerns.* Spouting numbers and talking about trade-offs seem very callous when the risk involves the health of people and other species and environmental quality.

- *It does not involve a sincere search for and evaluation of alternatives.*

People who believe their lives and the lives of their children are being threatened because they live near an actual or proposed chemical plant (Figure 20-9), toxic-waste dump, or waste incinerator don't care that experts say the chemical is likely to kill only one in a million people in the general population. Only a few of those million people live or will live near the plant, dump, or incinerator as they do. And that one might be their child. To them it is a personal threat, not a statistical abstraction.

## 20-6 Risk Factors and Cancer

**CANCER INCIDENCE AND CURE RATES** Currently nearly 500,000 people die each year from cancer in the United States (nearly one in four deaths) and 1 million new cases are diagnosed annually. Worldwide 1 of every 10 deaths is due to cancer.

The good news is that almost 50% of Americans under age 75 who get cancer can now be cured (surviving and cancer-free five or more years after treatment) compared with only 38% in 1960. Five-year survival rates for some types of cancers now range from 66% to 88%, thanks to a combination of early detection and improved surgical, radiation, and drug treatments.

**CANCER RISK FACTORS** According to the World Health Organization environmental and lifestyle factors play a key role in causing or promoting up to 80% of all cancers. Major sources of carcinogens are cigarette smoke (35–40% of cancers), diet (20–30%), occupational exposure (5–15%), and environmental pollutants (1–10%). About 10–20% of cancers are believed to be caused by inherited genetic factors or by certain viruses (such as papilloma virus in cervical cancer and hepatitis B in liver cancer).

Cancer risks can be greatly reduced by working and living in safer environments, not smoking or being around smokers (p. 532 and Solutions, right), drinking in moderation (no more than two beers or drinks per day) or not at all, eating a healthful diet (Solutions, p. 547), and shielding oneself from the sun (Spotlight, p. 305). According to experts 60% of all cancers could be prevented by such lifestyle changes.

The poor may have little choice about living and working in dangerous places. But even those who have choices may not change. One problem is that 10–40 years may elapse between the initial exposure to a carcinogen and the appearance of detectable symptoms. Healthy teenagers and young adults have trouble believing that their smoking, drinking, eating, and other lifestyle habits today could kill them before age 50. Such denial can be deadly.

## Reducing the Health Impacts of Smoking

**SOLUTIONS**

The good news is that smoking—the single greatest human health hazard, is preventable. To reduce this hazard the American Medical Association and many health experts call for:

- Banning cigarette advertising in the United States.

- Forbidding the sale of cigarettes and other tobacco products to anyone under age 21, with strict penalties for violators.

- Banning all cigarette vending machines.

- Classifying nicotine as an addictive and dangerous drug and placing its use under the jurisdiction of the Food and Drug Administration.

- Eliminating all federal subsidies to U.S. tobacco farmers and tobacco companies.

- Taxing cigarettes at about $3.00 per pack (instead of the current 51¢, the second lowest in the world) to discourage smoking and to make smokers pay the costs now borne by society as a whole. This would bring in at least $60 billion per year in revenues and would reduce smoking and money spent on health care. In Denmark, by contrast, a pack of cigarettes costs almost $6, $4 of which is tax; cigarette taxes are $3.09 per pack in Norway, $3.25 in Canada, and $3.24 in Great Britain.

- Forbidding U.S. officials to pressure other governments to import American tobacco or tobacco products. Since 1985 the federal government has threatened trade sanctions against countries that place tariffs and other restrictions on American tobacco products. Thus, the U.S. government is coercing other governments into allowing imports of a hazardous (but legal) drug from America while trying to halt the flow of illegal drugs into the United States.

## 20-7 Solutions: Reducing Health Risks

The most effective and cheapest way to reduce the risks we face from chemical and biological hazards is pollution prevention. We can do this on a personal

Q: Worldwide, how many people die prematurely each year of causes related to smoking?

## The Prudent Diet

**SOLUTIONS**

Improper diet plays a key role in an estimated 20–30% of all cancer deaths. The National Academy of Sciences, the surgeon general, and the American Heart Association advise that the risk of certain types of cancer (lung, stomach, colon, and esophageal), heart disease, and diabetes can be significantly reduced by a daily diet that cuts down on certain foods and includes others. The guidelines are:

- Limit total fat intake to 25% or less of total calories, with no more than 10% from saturated fats and the remaining 15% divided about equally between polyunsaturated (safflower oil and corn oil) and monounsaturated fats (olive oil).

- Limit protein (particularly meat) to 15% of total calories, or about 171 grams (6 ounces) per day (about the amount in one hamburger).

- Limit alcohol consumption to 15% of total caloric intake—no more than two drinks, glasses of wine, or beers per day. Pregnant women should not consume any alcohol.

- Limit cholesterol consumption to no more than 300 milligrams per day, the goal being to keep blood cholesterol levels below 200 milligrams per deciliter.

- Limit sodium intake to no more than 6 grams (about 1 teaspoon of salt) per day to help lower blood pressure, which should not exceed 140 over 90.

- Eat more poultry, fish, beans, whole grains, cereals, fruits, and vegetables, and much less red meat (which recently was linked to a higher risk of colon cancer) and processed foods.

- Achieve and maintain the ideal body weight for your frame size and age by a combination of diet and 20 minutes of exercise at least three days per week.

in order to survive. At the local, national, and global levels we must become involved politically to ensure that people are not involuntarily exposed to unnecessary health hazards by insisting that pollution prevention be the centerpiece of all environmental, health, and economic policy.

*Not all waste and pollution can be eliminated. . . . What is absolutely crucial, however, is to recognize that pollution prevention should be the first choice and the option against which all other options are judged. The burden of proof imposed on individuals, companies, and institutions should be to show that pollution prevention options have been thoroughly examined, evaluated, and used before lesser options are chosen.*

JOEL HIRSCHORN

## Critical Thinking

1. Should standards for allowed pollution levels be set to protect the most sensitive person or only the average person in a population? Explain. Should we have zero pollution levels for all hazardous chemicals? Explain.

2. Do you believe that smoking is the single greatest threat to human health? Explain why you agree or disagree.

3. Explain why you agree or disagree with each of the following proposals:
   a. All advertising of cigarettes and other tobacco products should be banned.
   b. All smoking should be banned in public buildings and commercial airplanes, buses, subways, and trains.
   c. All government subsidies to tobacco farmers and the tobacco industry should be eliminated.
   d. Cigarettes should be taxed at about $3.00 per pack so that U.S. smokers alone pay for the health and productivity losses now borne by society as a whole.

4. Do you believe that health and safety standards in the workplace should be strengthened and enforced more vigorously even if this causes a loss of jobs because companies transfer operations to countries with weaker standards? Explain.

5. Do you believe that standards for allowed exposure of workers and the general public to ionizing radiation produced by human activities should be reduced? Explain. If you agree, how would you accomplish this?

6. How would you go about reducing the overall threat to human health from AIDS and other STDs?

level by becoming more informed about the relative risks of various hazards and by making lifestyle choices—choosing not to smoke or be around smokers, to practice safe sex, to follow a healthy diet coupled with some exercise, and to protect our eyes and skin from the sun.

We must also work to see that the poor have such choices instead of being forced to face serious hazards

## Public Confidence in Industry and Government: A Crisis in Environmental Risk Communication

**GUEST ESSAY**

*Vincent T. Covello*

*Vincent T. Covello is professor of environmental sciences in the School of Public Health at Columbia University and director of Columbia University's Center for Risk Communication in New York City. Before these appointments he was director of the Risk Assessment Program at the National Science Foundation and a senior scientist for the White House Council on Environmental Quality. He is on the editorial board of several scientific journals and is the past president of the Society for Risk Analysis. He has written or edited over 25 books and 75 articles on environmental risk management. Two of his most recent books are* Effective Risk Communication *(Plenum, 1989) and* Principles and Methods for Analyzing Health and Environmental Risks *(Council on Environmental Quality, 1988).*

Obtaining reliable scientific information about environmental risk is a matter of intense concern to the public. In the United States the majority of people see industry and government as the most knowledgeable about those risks. Yet at the same time most Americans view industry and government as two of the least trustworthy sources of information about the risks of chemicals, radiation, and potential environmental hazards.

Several factors have contributed to this crisis in communication between industry and government and concerned citizens. They include:

- *Disagreements among scientific experts.* Because of different assumptions, data, and methods, experts in industry and government disagree and engage in highly visible debates about the reliability, validity, and interpretation of risk-assessment results. While such debates may advance scientific knowledge, they can undermine confidence in the ability of industry and government to resolve critical questions.

- *Lack of resources for risk assessment and management.* Most people don't buy explanations that the generation of health and environmental data about risks is constrained by financial, technical, statutory, legal, or other limitations.

- *Lack of adequate coordination among responsible authorities.* Regulatory agencies are rarely required to develop coherent, coordinated, consistent, and interrelated plans, programs, and guidelines for assessing and managing risks. This fragmentation often leads to jurisdictional conflicts about which agency or level of government has the ultimate responsibility for assessing and managing the risk in question, and in many cases to competing estimates of risk.

- *Lack of attention to and priority for risk communication.* Many industry and government officials are poor communicators. Their complex language and jargon-ridden statements often make them look unresponsive, dishonest, or evasive. They aggravate the problem by ignoring the special pitfalls of risk

---

What things do you do in your own life to reduce your risk of getting a sexually transmitted disease?

7. Do you believe that risk–benefit analysis should be used as the primary method to evaluate and manage risks? Explain.

8. Assume you have been appointed to a technology risk–benefit assessment board. Explain why you would approve or disapprove of widespread use of each of the following: **(a)** abortion pills (now used in France and China); **(b)** effective sex stimulants; **(c)** drugs to retard the aging process; **(d)** drugs that

would let people get high but are physiologically and psychologically harmless; **(e)** electrical or chemical methods that would stimulate the brain to eliminate anxiety, fear, unhappiness, and aggression; **(f)** genetic engineering to produce people with superior intelligence, strength, and other traits.

*9. Conduct a survey to determine the major physical, chemical, and biological hazards to human health at your school. Develop a plan for preventing or reducing these hazards, and present the results of your survey and plan to school officials.

Q: How many Americans die because of exposure to other people's smoke (secondhand smoke)?

communication, including using quantitative risk numbers in public presentations inappropriately, attacking the credibility of environmental or consumer activists, using risk- and cost-benefit studies inappropriately, and comparing risks for activities the public sees as different.

- *Insensitivity to the information needs and concerns of the public.* Risk experts and the general public frequently look at risks differently. For example, experts tend to focus on the numbers, while laypeople consider a complex array of factors such as voluntariness (choice), familiarity, effects on children, effects on future generations, benefits, origin (natural or from human activities), and fairness.

Public trust and confidence in industry and government will be restored only when people are convinced that industry and government officials share their concerns about environmental risks; that they are scientifically, technologically, and managerially competent; that they are honest, fair, and open; and that they are personally committed to eliminating risks or reducing them to an absolute minimum. Even more basic, trust and credibility will be restored only when industry and government officials recognize, accept, and involve the public as a legitimate partner in making decisions about risk.

Such a partnership also places demands on citizens, who must be open-minded and willing to take the time to learn about risk issues. A guiding principle of risk communication in a democracy is that people and communities have a right to participate in decisions that affect their lives, their property, and the things they value. The goal of risk communication in a democracy should be to produce an informed public that is involved, interested, reasonable, thoughtful, solution-oriented, and collaborative. It should not be to defuse public concerns or to replace needed action.

## Critical Thinking

1. In general do you believe information provided by government or industry officials about environmental risks? Explain why you do or don't. Whom do you trust as sources of such information? Why?

2. Are you willing to learn about and participate in making decisions about environmental risks? Explain. Have you ever done so? Why or why not?

## There Is No Away: The Love Canal Tragedy

In 1977 the residents of Love Canal, a suburb of Niagara Falls, New York, discovered that "out of sight, out of mind" can be hazardous to your health and peace of mind. Toxic industrial wastes buried decades earlier bubbled to the surface, found their way into groundwater, and ended up in people's backyards and basements.

Between 1942 and 1953 Hooker Chemicals and Plastics Corporation (now owned by Occidental Chemical) sealed its chemical wastes into steel drums and dumped them into an old canal excavation (called Love Canal after its builder, William Love). In 1953 Hooker Chemicals covered the dump site with clay and topsoil, and sold it to the Niagara Falls school board for $1.

An elementary school, playing fields, and 949 homes were built in the 10-square-block Love Canal area (Figure 21-1, left). Residents began complaining to city officials in 1976 about chemical smells and chemical burns their children received playing in the canal area, but they were ignored. In 1977 chemicals began leaking from the badly corroded steel drums into storm sewers, gardens, basements of homes next to the canal, and the school playground.

Alarmed residents, led by Lois Gibbs (a mother galvanized into action when her children came down with one illness after another; Guest Essay, p. 564), conducted an informal health survey. They found an unusually high incidence of birth defects, miscarriages, assorted cancers, and nerve, respiratory, and kidney disorders among people who lived near the canal.

Continued pressure from residents and unfavorable publicity eventually led state officials to conduct a preliminary health survey and tests. They found that pregnant women living near the canal had a miscarriage rate four times higher than average. They also found that the air, water, and soil of the canal area and the basements of nearby houses were contaminated with several toxic and carcinogenic chemicals.

In 1978 the state closed the school, permanently relocated the 238 families whose homes were closest to the dump, and fenced off the area around the canal. Two years later, after protests from outraged families still living fairly close to the landfill, President Jimmy Carter declared Love Canal a federal disaster area and had the remaining families relocated.

The school and 239 homes within a block and a half of the canal were torn down. All remaining homes, except 60 whose owners decided to stay, were purchased by the state. The dump site was covered

**Figure 21-1** The Love Canal housing development near Niagara Falls, New York, was built near a hazardous-waste dump site. The photo on the left shows the area when it was abandoned in 1980. The photo on the right shows the area in 1990, when people were allowed to buy the remaining houses and move back into the area despite protests from environmentalists.

NY State Department of Environmental Conservation

with a new clay cap and surrounded by a drain system that pumps leaking wastes to a new treatment plant. By 1991 the total cost for cleanup and relocation had reached $275 million.

In June 1990 the EPA declared the area—renamed Black Creek Village—safe and allowed state officials to begin selling 236 dilapidated and boarded-up houses at 10–20% below market value (Figure 21-1, right). Yet the dump has not been cleaned up but only fitted with a drainage system, and even the EPA acknowledges that it will leak again sooner or later. To environmentalists, selling the houses in Love Canal sends a message from the government that chemical dumps make good homes for people who can't afford to live in a healthier neighborhood.

The long-term health effects on Love Canal residents of exposure to hazardous chemicals remain unknown, but psychological damage to the evacuated families is enormous. For the rest of their lives they will worry about the possible effects of the chemicals on themselves and their children and grandchildren.

The Love Canal incident is a vivid reminder that we can never really throw anything away, that wastes don't stay put, and that preventing pollution is much safer, easier, and cheaper than trying to clean it up.

J. Goerg/NY State Department of Environmental Conservation

This chapter is devoted to answering the following questions:

- What is hazardous waste, and how much is produced?
- What are the hazards from lead and dioxins?
- What can we do about hazardous waste?
- What is done with hazardous waste in the United States?

## 21-1 Hazardous Waste: Types and Production

**WHAT IS HAZARDOUS WASTE?** According to the Environmental Protection Agency, **hazardous waste** is any discarded material that **(1)** contains one or more of 39 toxic, carcinogenic, mutagenic, or teratogenic compounds at levels that exceed established limits; **(2)** is flammable; **(3)** is reactive or unstable enough to explode or release toxic fumes; or **(4)** is capable of corroding metal containers such as tanks, drums, and barrels.

However, this narrow official definition of hazardous wastes (mandated by Congress) does not include:

- Radioactive wastes (Section 18-4).
- Hazardous and toxic materials discarded by households (Table 21-1).
- Mining wastes.
- Oil- and gas-drilling wastes, routinely discharged into surface waters or dumped into unlined pits and landfills.
- Liquid waste containing hydrocarbons (80% of all liquid hazardous waste). The EPA allows it to be burned as fuel in cement kilns and industrial furnaces with little regulation.
- Cement kiln dust produced when liquid hazardous wastes are burned in the kilns—a practice classified as recycling by the EPA but called dangerous "sham recycling" by environmentalists.

| Table 21-1 | Common Toxic and Hazardous Household Materials |
|---|---|

**Cleaning Products**

Disinfectants

Drain, toilet, and window cleaners

Oven cleaners

Bleach and ammonia

Cleaning solvents and spot removers

Septic tank cleaners

**Paint and Building Products**

Latex and oil-based paints

Paint thinners, solvents, and strippers

Stains, varnishes, and lacquers

Wood preservatives

Acids for etching and rust removal

Asphalt and roof tar

**Gardening and Pest Control Products**

Pesticide sprays and dusts

Weed killers

Ant and rodent killers

Flea powder

**Automotive Products**

Gasoline

Used motor oil

Antifreeze

Battery acid

Solvents

Brake and transmission fluid

Rust inhibitor and rust remover

**General Products**

Dry-cell batteries (mercury and cadmium)

Artist paints and inks

Glues and cements

Data from Science Advisory Board, *Reducing Risks*, Washington, DC, Environmental Protection Agency, 1990. Items in each category are not listed in rank order.

- Municipal incinerator ash, which if classified as hazardous waste would be so expensive to ship to and bury in special landfills that the whole waste incineration industry would collapse.

- Wastes from the thousands of small businesses and factories that generate less than 100 kilograms (220 pounds) of hazardous waste per month.

- Waste generated by the military, except at 116 sites so toxic that they are on the EPA's list of priority sites to be cleaned up. U.S. military installations produce more hazardous waste each year (about a ton per minute) than the top five U.S. chemical companies combined. Studies by the Department of Defense have identified over 17,482 contaminated sites at 1,855 military bases in every state.

Environmentalists call these omissions "linguistic detoxification" designed to save industries money and mislead the public. They urge that all excluded categories be designated hazardous—a decision that would quickly shift the emphasis and innovation from waste management and pollution control to reducing waste and preventing pollution, which would save lots of money.

**HOW MUCH IS PRODUCED?** The EPA estimates that at least 5.5 billion metric tons (6 billion tons) of hazardous waste are produced each year in the United States—an average of 21 metric tons (23 tons) per person. However, only 6%, or 350 million metric tons (385 million tons), of the total is legally defined as hazardous waste and subject to government regulation. Thus *94% of the country's hazardous waste is not regulated by hazardous-waste laws.* The U.S. leads the world in total and per capita hazardous-waste production, and this amount is growing (Spotlight, p. 553).

A serious problem facing the United States and most industrialized countries is what to do about hazardous chemicals leaking from thousands of abandoned waste dumps (Figures 21-1 and 21-2). One-third of the usable land area that used to be called the Soviet Union is considered a hazardous-waste diaster zone.

## 21-2 Case Studies: Lead and Dioxins

**LEAD: WE HAVE POISONED OUR CHILDREN**
Atmospheric emissions of lead from human sources are 28 times greater than those from natural sources. And emissions of lead into the soil and aquatic ecosystems from human activities are almost three times those emitted into the atmosphere.

Q: How many U.S. workers die prematurely from exposure to toxic substances?

## Exponential Growth in Synthetic Organic Chemicals

Between 1945 and 1993 the U.S. chemical industry produced 5–6 trillion kilograms (12 trillion pounds) of synthetic organic chemicals. Many of these chemicals degrade slowly in the environment and are hazardous to our health as well as that of other species. Some of these chemicals are biologically amplified in food chains and webs (Figure 16-22).

If the annual production of these chemicals continues to grow at its current rate of 6.5%, in only 11 years we will produce another 5–6 trillion kilograms; and in a typical lifetime of 70 years the quantity of these chemicals will increase 90-fold. That is why J-curves of potentially harmful chemical production can literally bury us.

Only about 1% by weight of the toxic chemicals produced by the U.S. chemical industry is treated and converted into harmless chemicals. To destroy the other 99% of these wastes would cost about $20 billion per year. Since the annual profit of the entire U.S. chemical industry is about $2 billion, it obviously cannot afford to destroy its own wastes. That is why the government continues to allow the release of these toxic chemicals into the environment and why pollution prevention is the best remedy.

**Figure 21-2** Leaking barrels in a hazardous-waste dump near Washington, D.C. Such dumps are now illegal in the United States and many MDCs. However, there are tens of thousands of older dumps, and some illegal dumping still occurs in MDCs. In most LDCs there is little regulation of hazardous wastes, and the United States and many other MDCs export hazardous wastes to other countries. Eight out of ten Americans live near an active or abandoned hazardous-waste site.

We take in small amounts of lead in the air we breathe, the food we eat, and the water we drink. This lead builds up in our bodies. Once lead enters the blood only about 10% is excreted. The rest is stored in the bones, where its half-life is 20 years. Even at very low levels it damages the central nervous system, especially in young children. Pregnant women can also transfer dangerous levels of lead to their unborn children.

Each year 12,000–16,000 American children (mostly poor and nonwhite) under age 9 are treated for acute lead poisoning, and about 200 die. About 30% of the survivors suffer from palsy, partial paralysis, blindness, and mental retardation.

Children under age 6 with levels greater than 10 micrograms of lead in each tenth of a liter (about half a cup) of blood are especially vulnerable. To achieve this blood level, a child would need to ingest lead equal to that in only one-third of a granule of sugar a day—something easily done by touching soil or house dust contaminated with lead and sucking the thumb. Such lead levels can damage the brain and central ner-

vous system, lower IQ scores, impair memory and reaction time, stunt growth, interfere with the body's use of vitamin D and hemoglobin production (needed for red blood cells to carry oxygen), and cause high blood pressure, partial hearing loss, hyperactivity, irritability, and behavior problems. Some scientists believe that there is no minimum threshold for safe exposure of children and fetuses to lead.

According to a 1986 EPA study *88% of all children in the United States under age 6 have unsafe blood levels of lead that may retard their mental, physical, and emotional development*. This epidemic affects children of every socioeconomic background, but those in poor families and minority groups suffer most.

The following are the greatest sources of lead in the United States:

- *Lead particles injected into the atmosphere that settle onto the soil and become outdoor or indoor dust*. Children ingest this lead as they play in contaminated soil or dust in carpeting, toys, or the floor, and then put their thumbs or hands in their mouths. The major sources of atmospheric lead particles today are solid-waste and hazardous-waste incinerators, lead smelters, furnaces burning used motor oil, and battery manufacturing plants. Leaded gasoline has been phased out, but the massive amounts of indestructible lead particles that fell out of the atmosphere for 50 years before the ban contaminate land almost everywhere. In countries that have not banned leaded gasoline, it is the largest atmospheric source of lead.

A: Up to 100,000 per year

## Protecting Children from Lead Poisoning

**SOLUTIONS**

Because it's impossible to hospitalize and treat the 88% of American children with unsafe blood levels of lead, the only option is to reduce lead exposure. Ways to do this include:

- Setting lead standards to protect children and fetuses

- Requiring that all U.S. children be tested for lead by age 1, and establishing a lead-screening program to test all children under age 6

- Establishing community programs for identifying and preventing childhood lead poisoning

- Eliminating leaded paint and contaminated dust in housing

- Testing all community sources of drinking water, especially in schools and homes, for lead contamination, and removing the contamination or providing alternate sources of drinking water

- Running water for several minutes each morning from all taps used as a source of drinking water—saving the water in containers and using it for watering flowers or other plants that are not sources of food

- Banning the use of lead solder in plumbing pipes and in food cans, and removing lead from municipal drinking water systems within 7 years instead of the current 21 years

- Making sure children wash their hands thoroughly before eating

- Requiring that all ceramic ware used to cook, store, or serve food produced domestically or imported be lead free

- Banning incineration of municipal solid waste and hazardous waste—the largest new source of lead

- Mounting a global campaign to reduce lead poisoning in LDCs

- Banning leaded gasoline throughout the world

Doing these things will cost lots of money (an estimated $50 billion in the United States). But the alternative is to keep poisoning and mentally handicapping almost 90% of the children.

- *Interior paint in 52%, or 57 million, of the houses built before 1978, when use of lead compounds in interior and exterior paint was banned.* These houses are a major source of lead poisoning for children ages 1–3, who inhale lead dust from cracking and peeling paint or ingest it by sucking their thumbs, putting contaminated toys in their mouths, or gnawing on window sills or furniture. People living in houses or apartments built before 1980 should have samples of the paint analyzed for lead by the local health department or by a private testing laboratory (cost: $100–$450).*

- *Groundwater contaminated by lead leached from landfills.* Over 3,000 sources of community drinking water are believed to be contaminated in this way.

- *Drinking water contaminated by plumbing containing lead solder.* According to the EPA nearly one in eight Americans in 819 tested communities drinks tap water containing unsafe levels of lead leached by acidic or soft water from solder and connectors used with copper piping in plumbing systems. Homeowners with copper pipes or joints should have the local water department or a private laboratory (cost: $20–$100) test their tap water for lead. And before buying or renting an existing house or apartment, prospective buyers or renters should have its water (that has been standing in pipes for at least 12 hours) tested for lead. In 1991 the EPA ordered removal of lead from municipal drinking water systems but gave the country's largest municipalities up to 21 years to do the job.

- *Lead solder used to seal the seams on food cans.* This applies especially to acidic foods such as tomatoes and citric juices. This type of solder has been sharply reduced in U.S. food cans but may be found in cans of imported foods.

- *Imported cups, plates, pitchers, leaded glass crystal, and other items used to cook, store, or serve food, especially acidic foods and hot liquids and foods.* Before using such items, test them for lead content.[†]

- *Vegetables and fruits grown on soil contaminated by lead.* This applies especially to cropland or home gardens near highways, incinerators, and smelters. Careful washing should remove at least half of this lead.

- *Burning comic strips, Christmas wrapping paper, or painted wood, in wood stoves and fireplaces.*

According to the Centers for Disease Control and Prevention and the Department of Health and Human

---

* If you find lead paint in your home, send a postcard to U.S. Consumer Product Safety Commission, Washington, DC 20207, and ask for the free pamphlet *What You Should Know About the Lead-Based Paint in Your Home.* Two home kits for testing paint for lead are sold by HybriVet Systems (800-262-LEAD) and Frandon Enterprises (800-359-9000).
[†] A simple home test for lead content of up to 100 items of dishware is available for $24.50 from Frandon Enterprises, 511 N. 48th St., Seattle, WA 98103. Commercial testing costs about $60 per item; contact American Council of Independent Laboratories, 1725 K Street N.W., Washington, DC 20006 (202-887-5872) for a testing lab near you.

Q: What percentage of the 70,000 chemicals in commercial use have been thoroughly screened for toxicity?

Services, *lead is the number one environmental health threat to children in the United States* and should be a matter of the highest priority (Solutions, p. 554).

**DIOXINS: UNRAVELING A COMPLEX HEALTH THREAT** **Dioxins** are a family of 75 different chlorinated hydrocarbon compounds formed as by-products in chemical reactions involving chlorine and hydrocarbons, usually at high temperatures. One of these compounds, TCDD, sometimes simply called dioxin, is the most harmful and most widely studied.

TCDD and other dioxins result from the burning of chlorine-containing wastes in municipal and hazardous waste incinerators and cement kilns, chlorine-bleaching of pulp and paper, and the manufacture of certain herbicides (for example, 2,4,5-T), many plastics (for example, PVC), and many chlorinated hydrocarbon chemicals. Dioxins persist in the environment, especially in soil and human fatty tissue, and can apparently be biologically amplified to higher levels in food webs.

Researchers studying the health effects of TCDD in the early 1970s were puzzled because it produced different effects in different species, as well as different effects in the same species at various doses. Also, epidemiological studies of people exposed to TCDD found a variety of health effects, including various cancers, but no consistent effects.

In 1991 representatives of the paper industry claimed that the inconsistent results of health studies exonerated TCDD and other dioxins, and pushed the EPA for a reassessment of the health risks of dioxin. This strategy may have backfired, however, when the preliminary results of the EPA's reevaluation cleared up some of the mysteries and indicated that dioxin was an even greater health threat than previously thought. These results also suggested that two major studies industry scientists cited as evidence that TCDD did not cause cancer were based on fraudulent data.

This new review showed that TCDD does indeed cause cancer in humans but, unlike most carcinogens, does not damage DNA. Instead, TCDD promotes cancer by activating DNA already damaged by other carcinogens. This explains why researchers found a variety of cancers rather than a single type, as is usually the case with most carcinogens.

This review also revealed that TCDD's immunological, developmental, and neurological effects at very low exposure levels may pose an even greater threat to human health than its cancer-promoting ability. Studies on mice revealed that minuscule doses of TCDD disrupted and suppressed the immune system—making the test animals (and presumably humans) more vulnerable to a variety of diseases. For example, a viral infection that rarely kills a normal mouse was fatal to mice injected with trace amounts of TCDD.

## Reducing Dioxin Production

**SOLUTIONS**

To reduce the threat from dioxins, environmentalists call for:

- Phasing out the use of chlorine in manufacturing.
- Banning the use of chlorine for bleaching wood pulp and substituting oxygen or other non-chlorine processes. Sweden, for example, has banned the sale of chlorine-bleached disposable diapers. Both Austria and Sweden use unbleached (slightly brown) coffee filters, toilet paper, milk cartons, and other paper products.
- Banning all incineration of chlorine-containing chemicals.

Equally worrisome, TCDD was found to be an environmental hormone that imitates naturally occurring sex and growth hormones. These potent natural chemicals travel in the bloodstream to trigger the different stages of fetal growth, determine male and female characteristics, and initiate bodily changes during puberty. Male mice and rats exposed to low levels of TCDD had reduced levels of the male sex hormone testosterone, which caused delayed sexual development, feminization, and reduced sex drive and sperm counts—a result described by one researcher as chemical castration. And rhesus monkeys exposed to TCDD before birth showed reduced memory and performance on mental tasks, and were more aggressive than unexposed monkeys.

Tainted foods such as fish, mother's milk, milk from cows eating grass growing in contaminated soil, and crops grown in contaminated soil are the major sources of exposure to dioxins for the general population. Americans routinely eat food containing 7–120 times more TCDD than the EPA considers safe, depending on whose data is accepted regarding dioxin contamination in the food chain. Industries producing dioxins as by-products face an avalanche of lawsuits and possible bankruptcy as long as the EPA classifies low-level exposures to dioxin as a serious human health threat. This classification also threatens to halt the burning of hazardous wastes in incinerators and cement kilns, which the EPA has sanctioned as an important way to deal with such wastes. With so much at stake, there is intense industry pressure to discredit and water down this health reassessment of dioxins, even while environmentalists call for action to reduce the health threats of dioxins (Solutions, above).

A: 10%

## Pollution Prevention Pays

Some U.S. firms have found that pollution prevention saves them money. In 1974 the Minnesota Mining and Manufacturing Company (3M) produced tons of hazardous waste and single-handedly accounted for 2% of all industrial emissions of air pollutants in the United States. In 1975 the company, which makes 60,000 different products in 100 manufacturing plants, began a Pollution Prevention Pays (3P) program. It redesigned equipment and processes, used fewer hazardous raw materials, identified hazardous chemical outputs and recycled or sold them as raw materials to other companies, and began making nonpolluting products.

By 1993 3M's overall waste production was down by one-third, and emissions of air pollutants by 70%—and the company had saved over $600 million in waste disposal costs. By 2000 it plans to reduce overall generation of waste by 50% and environmental releases of hazardous and nonhazardous waste to air, water, and land by 90% of 1987 levels.

An EPA study of 28 firms engaged in waste reduction found that 54% got their investment back within a year or less and 93% got it back within three years. The key is to get everyone in the company thinking about ways to reduce waste and pollution by making it a top corporate priority. However, most firms have little incentive to reduce their output of waste because waste management costs them only about 0.1% of the total value of their output.

North Carolina has taken the lead in encouraging pollution prevention with a program that offers technical assistance, a database of information, and matching grants to companies and communities wanting to implement such projects. California, New York, Pennsylvania, Illinois, Wisconsin, Minnesota, and Tennessee also have pollution prevention programs—something every state should have. What is your state doing?

## 21-3 Solutions: Dealing with Hazardous Waste

**WHAT ARE OUR OPTIONS?** There are five basic options for dealing with hazardous wastes: **(1)** Don't make them in the first place (pollution prevention) or use less harmful substitutes (Table 21-2), **(2)** recycle or reuse them (pollution prevention if done within production processes or on site but waste management otherwise), **(3)** detoxify them, **(4)** burn them, and **(5)** hide them by putting them into a deep well, pond, pit, or landfill, or by dumping them in the ocean.

**POLLUTION PREVENTION, RECYCLING, AND REUSE** Despite much talk about preventing pollution, the order of priorities for dealing with hazardous waste in the United States is the reverse of what prominent scientists say it should be (Figure 21-3). Prevention—the most desirable option—involves substituting safer chemicals, reformulating products, modifying production processes, improving operations and maintenance, and practicing closed-loop recycling and reuse of wastes on site (Solutions, left). No country has an effective pollution prevention program for hazardous waste, but countries like Denmark, the Netherlands, Germany, and Sweden are all far ahead of the United States in this area. And in 1992, 13 European nations agreed in principle to eliminate all discharges and emissions of chemicals that are toxic, persistent, or likely to bioaccumulate in food chains and webs. In short, these nations made a binding commitment to try to achieve "zero discharge" of persistent toxic substances.

Effective pollution prevention requires assuming that any waste or pollutant is potentially harmful unless proven otherwise. This *precautionary principle* is the inverse of the waste management approach, in which wastes are assumed to be benign until proven harmful.

After preventing pollution the next most desirable options are recycling and reuse (Figure 21-3), currently applied to only 7% of legally regulated U.S. hazardous waste. Yet the EPA devotes less than 1% of its waste management budget to encouraging prevention, reuse, and recycling of such waste. Required annual reporting of legally regulated toxic emissions by industry has helped promote these options. However, waste-disposal and mining companies and government facilities and power plants are not required to report their annual emissions.

**DETOXIFICATION AND INCINERATION** The next priority in hazardous-waste management is to convert any remaining waste into less hazardous or nonhazardous materials (Figure 21-3). Conversion methods include spreading biodegradable wastes on the land, using heat, chemical, or physical methods, using natural or bioengineered bacteria to break them down, and burning them on land or at sea in incinerators.

Denmark has the world's most comprehensive and effective hazardous-waste detoxification program. Each municipality has at least one facility that accepts

## Table 21-2 Alternatives to Some Common Household Chemicals

| Chemical | Alternative | Chemical | Alternative |
|---|---|---|---|
| Deodorant | Sprinkle baking soda on a damp wash cloth and wipe skin. | General surface cleaner | Mixture of vinegar, salt, and water. |
| Oven cleaner | Baking soda and water paste, scouring pad. | Bleach | Baking soda or borax. |
| Toothpaste | Baking soda. | Mildew remover | Mix ½ cup vinegar, ½ cup borax, and warm water. |
| Drain cleaner | Pour ½ cup salt down drain, followed by boiling water; or pour 1 handful baking soda and ½ cup white vinegar and cover tightly for one minute. | Disinfectant and general cleaner | Mix ½ cup borax in 1 gallon hot water. |
| Window cleaner | Add 2 teaspons white vinegar to 1 quart warm water. | Furniture or floor polish | Mix ½ cup lemon juice and 1 cup vegetable or olive oil. |
| Toilet bowl, tub, and tile cleaner | Mix a paste of borax and water; rub on and let set one hour before scrubbing. Can also scrub with baking soda and a brush. | Carpet and rug shampoos | Sprinkle on cornstarch, baking soda, or borax and vacuum. |
| Floor cleaner | Add ½ cup vinegar to a bucket of hot water; sprinkle a sponge with borax for tough spots. | Detergents and detergent boosters | Washing soda or borax and soap powder. |
| Shoe polish | Polish with inside of a banana peel, then buff. | Spray starch | In a spray bottle, mix 1 tablespoon cornstarch in a pint of water. |
| Silver polish | Clean with baking soda and warm water. | Fabric softener | Add 1 cup white vinegar or ¼ cup baking soda to final rinse. |
| Air freshener | Set vinegar out in an open dish. Use an opened box of baking soda in closed areas such as refrigerators and closets. To scent the air, use pine boughs or make sachets of herbs and flowers. | Dishwasher soap | 1 part borax and 1 part washing soda. |
| | | Pesticides (indoor and outdoor) | Use natural biological controls. |

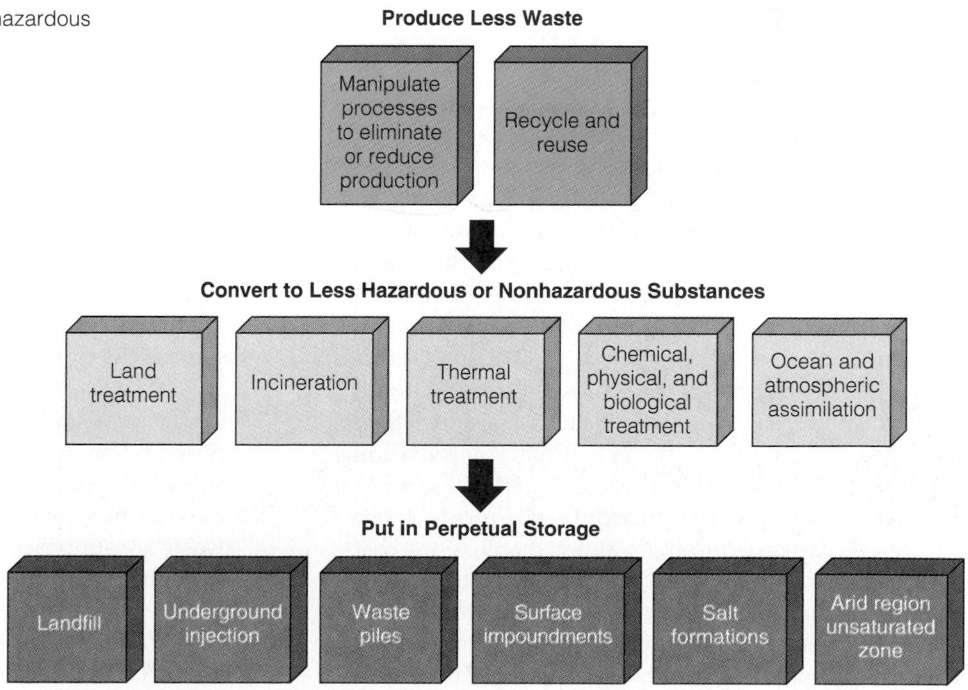

**Figure 21-3** Priorities for dealing with hazardous waste. (National Academy of Sciences)

**Produce Less Waste**

Manipulate processes to eliminate or reduce production | Recycle and reuse

**Convert to Less Hazardous or Nonhazardous Substances**

Land treatment | Incineration | Thermal treatment | Chemical, physical, and biological treatment | Ocean and atmospheric assimilation

**Put in Perpetual Storage**

Landfill | Underground injection | Waste piles | Surface impoundments | Salt formations | Arid region unsaturated zone

**A:** About 1%

## Is Incineration the Answer?

Generators of hazardous waste like incinerators. Incineration generally is affordable, and anything can be burned legally. Burning gets rid of the waste and any legal liability at the same time. Once wastes are mixed and burned it is virtually impossible to trace the resulting toxic ash or pollution to any one cutomer of the incinerator company. And the EPA likes hazardous-waste incineration because it gives the appearance of solving the hazardous-waste problem in a way favored by industry.

However, after making an extensive study of hazardous-waste incineration, Peter Montague (Guest Essay, p. 41), an expert in this field, has concluded that it is an out-of-control technology that should be banned. He and other environmentalists point out that the incinerators release toxic air pollution (especially small particles of metals such as lead and mercury that cannot be removed by scrubbers and other devices), create new toxic air pollutants like dioxins,

and leave a highly toxic ash to be disposed of in landfills that even the EPA says will eventually leak.

EPA incinerator regulations require 99.99% destruction or removal of all burned hazardous wastes and 99.9999% destruction of especially hazardous wastes such as dioxins and PCBs. However, tests show that the actual rate falls between 79.23% and 99.99% (although operators almost always claim the higher figure). Assuming that 99.99% of the 7% of U.S. hazardous wastes that are incinerated are destroyed, this still puts 2.5 million kilograms (5.4 million pounds) of hazardous waste into the environment each year. The actual amount released is much higher.

Furthermore, a 1992 memo by the EPA's director of solid waste admitted that no U.S. hazardous-waste incinerators can destroy 99.999% of the most hazardous chemicals as required by law. Technically, all U.S. hazardous-waste incinerators violate federal law and should be shut down. The EPA, however, continues allowing them to operate.

Most of the pollutants move

downwind from the incinerators where people can breathe them or eat food contaminated by them. Even a videotape produced by Keep America Beautiful (the voice of the waste management industry) admits that incinerators aren't safe enough.

According to EPA hazardous-waste expert and whistle-blower William Sanjour, EPA incinerator regulations don't work because

*the regulations require no monitoring of the outside air in the vicinity of the incinerator. Because operators maintain the records, they can easily cheat. . . . Government inspectors are poorly trained and have low morale and high turnover. . . . Government inspectors typically work from nine to five Monday through Friday. So if there is anything particularly nasty to burn, it will be done at night or on weekends. When complaints come in . . . the inspector may visit the plant but rarely finds anything. The enforcement officials tend to view the incinerator operator as their client and the public as a nuisance. . . . There is no reward to inspectors for finding serious violations.*

paints, solvents, and other hazardous wastes from households. Toxic waste from industries is delivered to 21 transfer stations throughout the country. All waste is then transferred to a large treatment facility where 75% of the waste is detoxified and the rest is buried in a carefully designed and monitored landfill.

Biological treatment of hazardous waste, or *bioremediation*, may be the wave of the future. In this process bacteria secrete enzymes that break down large complex molecules into smaller molecules they can absorb. The end result is cell mass and carbon dioxide. If toxin-munching bacteria can be found or engineered for specific hazardous chemicals, these substances can be fed to them at less than half the cost of disposal in landfills, and only one-third the cost of on-site incineration. Although, releasing genetically engineered microorganisms into the environment is expensive and controversial (Pro/Con, p. 167), stud-

ies indicate that most wastes can be digested better and more cheaply by naturally occurring microbes.

The EPA estimates that 60% of U.S. hazardous waste could be incinerated. With proper air pollution controls and highly trained personnel, the agency considers incineration as a potentially safe, if expensive, disposal method. However, environmentalists and some EPA scientists disagree (Spotlight, above).

**LAND DISPOSAL** Most U.S. hazardous waste is disposed of by deep-well injections (Pro/Con, p. 559), surface impoundments, and secured landfills (Figure 21-4). Ponds, pits, or lagoons used to store hazardous waste are supposed to be sealed with a plastic liner on the bottom. Solid wastes settle to the bottom and accumulate, while water and other volatile compounds evaporate into the atmosphere. According to the EPA, however, 70% of these storage basins have no liners,

## Is Deep-Well Disposal of Hazardous Waste a Good Idea?

**PRO/CON**  With deep-well disposal, liquid hazardous wastes are pumped under pressure through a pipe into dry, porous geologic formations or into fracture zones of rock far beneath aquifers tapped for drinking and irrigation water. In theory these liquids soak into the porous rock material and are isolated from overlying groundwater by essentially impermeable layers of rock.

This method is simple and cheap. Also, it is less visible (because it is usually done on company land) and less carefully regulated than other disposal methods. Its use is increasing rapidly as other methods are legally restricted or become too expensive.

If sites are chosen according to the best geological and seismic data, deep wells may be a reasonably safe way of disposing of fairly dilute solutions of organic and inorganic waste. With proper site selection and care, it may be safer than incineration. Also, if some use eventually were found for the waste, it could be pumped back to the surface.

However, the Office of Technology Assessment and many environmentalists believe that current regulations for geologic evaluation, long-term monitoring, and long-term liability if wells contaminate groundwater are inadequate and may allow injected wastes to:

- Spill or leak at the surface and leach into groundwater

- Escape into groundwater from corroded pipe casing or leaking seals in the well

- Migrate down or horizontally from the porous layer of rock where they are transmitted to aquifers through existing fractures or new ones caused by earthquakes or even by stresses from the introduction of the wastes

Until this method is more carefully evaluated and regulated, environmentalists believe that its use should not be allowed to increase.

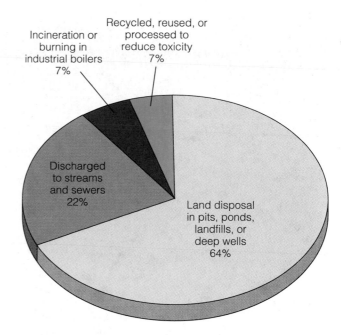

**Figure 21-4**  Management of hazardous waste in the United States. Even the best-designed landfills (Figure 19-16) eventually leak. Relying on landfills, deep wells, and incinerators for solid- and hazardous-waste disposal takes politicians off the hook today by passing contamination and cleanup costs on to the next generation. (Data from Worldwatch Institute)

and as many as 90% may threaten groundwater. Eventually all liners leak, and wastes will percolate into groundwater. Also, major storms or hurricanes can cause overflows. Moreover, volatile compounds, such as hazardous organic solvents, can evaporate into the atmosphere and eventually contaminate surface water and groundwater in other locations.

About 5% of the legally regulated hazardous waste produced in the United States is concentrated, put into drums, and buried either in one of 21 specially designed and monitored commercial hazardous-waste landfills (Figure 19-16) or in one of 35 landfills run by companies to handle their own waste. Sweden goes further and buries its concentrated hazardous wastes in underground vaults (Figure 21-5). Ideally such landfills should be located in geologically and environmentally secure places, and carefully monitored for leaks.

However, both the EPA and the Office of Technology Assessment have concluded that even the best-designed landfill will eventually leak because the liners leak: They can be ripped or punctured during installation or by burrowing animals, or dissolved by chemical solvents. Hazardous-waste engineer Peter Montague (Guest Essay, p. 41) examined four hazardous-waste landfills equipped with the latest synthetic plastic liners and found they all leaked within one year.

When current and future commercial hazardous-waste landfills do leak and threaten water supplies, many of their operators will declare bankruptcy. Then the EPA will put the landfills on the Superfund list, and taxpayers will pick up the tab for cleaning them

**Figure 21-5** Swedish method for handling hazardous waste. Hazardous materials are placed in drums, which are embedded in concrete cubes and then stored in an underground vault.

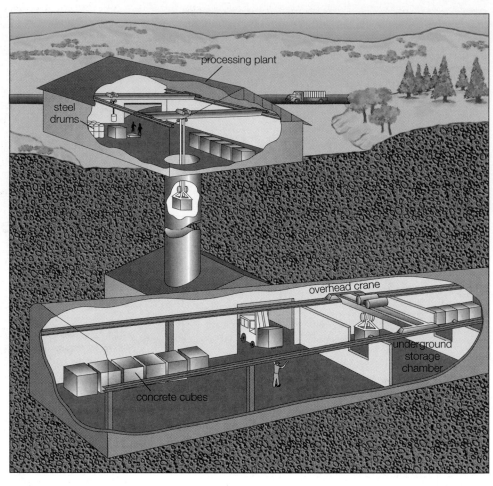

up. As EPA hazardous-waste expert William Sanjour points out:

> *The real cost of dumping is not borne by the producer of the waste or the disposer, but by the people whose health and property values are destroyed when the wastes migrate onto their property and by the taxpayers who pay to clean it up. . . . It is better for liners to leak sooner than later, because then there will be responsible parties that they can get to clean it up. Liners don't protect communities. They protect the people who put the waste there and the politicians who let them put the waste there, because they are long since gone when the problem comes up.*

Some engineers and environmentalists have proposed storing hazardous wastes aboveground in large, two-story, reinforced concrete buildings until better technologies are developed. The first floor would contain no wastes but would have inspection walkways so people could check for leaks from above. Any leachate would be collected, treated, solidified, and returned to the storage building. Such buildings would last for many decades, perhaps as long as a cen-

tury. Proponents believe this *in-sight* approach would be cheaper and safer than *out-of-sight* landfills or incinerators for many hazardous wastes.

There is also growing concern about accidents during some of the more than 500,000 shipments of hazardous wastes (mostly to landfills and incinerators) in the United States each year. Between 1980 and 1990 alone, for example, there were 13,476 toxic-chemical accidents, causing 309 deaths, over 11,000 injuries, and evacuation of over 500,000 people. Few communities have the equipment and trained personnel to deal adequately with hazardous-waste spills.

**GRASS-ROOTS ACTION** Traditionally incinerators, landfills, or treatment plants for hazardous wastes have been located in communities populated by African Americans, Asian Americans, Hispanics, and poor whites. And a 1992 study revealed that government cleanup of hazardous-waste sites in white areas was 20% faster than in communities where people of color live. Such actions have been condemned as a mixture of environmental racism (Guest Essay, p. 566) and economic discrimination.

Q: Worldwide, how many people die from sexually transmitted diseases?

Now people of color, the poor, and middle-class whites have joined together in a loose-knit coalition known as the grass-roots movement for environmental justice (Figure 20-9). As a result, it is now nearly impossible to site new dumps and incinerators anywhere. This coalition offers the following guidelines for achieving environmental justice for all:

- *Don't compromise our children's futures by cutting deals with polluters and regulators.* Environmental justice should not be bought or sold.

- *Hold polluters and elected officials who go along with them personally accountable because what they are doing is wrong.*

- *Don't fall for the argument that protesters against hazardous-waste landfills, incinerators, and injection wells are holding up progress in dealing with hazardous wastes.* Instead, recognize that the best way to deal with waste and pollution is not to produce so much of it. After that has been done we can decide what to do with what is left—a strategy supported by the National Academy of Sciences (Figure 21-3).

- *Oppose all hazardous-waste landfills, deep-disposal wells, and incinerators.* This will sharply raise the cost of dealing with hazardous materials and encourage waste producers and elected officials to get serious about pollution prevention. The goal of politically powerful waste management companies is to have us produce more and more hazardous (and nonhazardous) waste so they can make higher profits. In 1992 the total revenues in the burgeoning hazardous-waste business were $18 billion (compared to $0.5 billion in 1977), and by 2000 are expected to reach $43 billion.

- *Recognize that there is no such thing as "safe" disposal of hazardous waste.* For such materials the goal should be "Not in Anyone's Backyard" (NIABY) or "Not on Planet Earth" (NOPE).

- *Ban release of any toxic chemical that bioaccumulates or has a half-life greater than eight weeks into any medium (water, air, sediment, soil, or living things).* Thirteen European nations have agreed to do this.

- *Oppose the increasingly powerful waste-management industrial complex, which rewards with high-paying jobs EPA officials who write and enforce regulations favorable to the complex's interests and which hinders more effective and less costly recycling, reuse, and prevention of hazardous waste.*

- *Pressure elected officials to pass legislation requiring that unwanted industries and waste facilities be distributed more widely instead of being concentrated in poor and working-class neighborhoods, many populated mostly by minorities.*

- *Ban all hazardous-waste exports from one country to another* (Spotlight, p. 562).

Politically and economically powerful waste management companies (often with government support) are fighting back. For example, they are offering financial incentives to entice Native Americans to allow hazardous-waste facilities on their reservations, which are exempt from state and local laws. And in 1991 the Department of Energy began trying to find a Native American tribe willing to have a retrievable storage facility for nuclear waste located on its land in return for government compensation.

These companies are also trying (sometimes successfully) to get state legislatures to strip communities of veto power over siting waste landfills, incinerators, and treatment plants. They are also urging Congress and the courts to prevent states from blocking such decisions and to leave such matters up to the EPA. Another tactic is to propose a number of possible locations for a hazardous (or radioactive) landfill or incinerator, with the goal of getting communities to dilute their efforts by fighting one another (a divide-and-conquer strategy).

## 21-4 Hazardous-Waste Regulation in the United States

**RESOURCE CONSERVATION AND RECOVERY ACT** In 1976 the U.S. Congress passed the Resource Conservation and Recovery Act (RCRA, pronounced rick-ra), amending it in 1984. This law requires the EPA to identify hazardous wastes and set standards for their management, and provides guidelines and financial aid for states to establish waste management programs. The law also requires all firms that store, treat, or dispose of more than 100 kilograms (220 pounds) of hazardous wastes per month to have a permit stating how such wastes are to be managed.

To reduce illegal dumping, hazardous-waste producers granted disposal permits by the EPA must use a "cradle-to-grave" system to keep track of waste transferred from point of origin to approved off-site disposal facilities. However, the EPA and state regulatory agencies do not have enough people to review the documentation of more than 750,000 hazardous-waste generators and 15,000 haulers each year, let alone to detect and prosecute offenders.

If caught violators are subject to large fines. However, environmentalists argue that the fines are still

A: 750,000 per year

# Ash to Cash: The International Hazardous-Waste Trade

To save money and to get around regulations and local opposition, cities and waste disposal companies in the United States and other MDCs legally ship vast quantities of hazardous waste to other countries. Most legal U.S. exports of hazardous wastes go to Canada and Mexico, but at least nine African countries have also accepted them.

These shipments can take place without EPA approval because U.S. hazardous-waste laws allow exports for "recycling." Sometimes exported wastes labeled as materials to be recycled are dumped after reaching their destination.

U.S. companies are also exporting hazardous waste and jobs by moving highly polluting smelters and manufacturing plants to countries with weak or poorly enforced pollution control laws and with workers willing to work for lower wages under dangerous conditions. A glaring example is the growing number of U.S. and other foreign factories located along Mexico's northern border. Mexico has some strong environmental laws, but enforcement is lax. Most host countries, hungry for jobs and foreign capital, turn a blind eye to unsafe and polluting practices.

There is also a growing illegal trade in hazardous wastes across international borders. There are too few customs inspectors, and they are not trained to detect such shipments. Hazardous wastes have also been mixed with wood chips or sawdust and shipped as burnable material.

Waste disposal firms can charge high prices for picking up hazardous wastes. If they can then dispose of them—legally or illegally—at low costs, they pocket huge profits. Officials of poor LDCs find it hard to resist the income (often in the form of bribes) from receiving these wastes.

Currently at least 83 countries have banned imports of hazardous waste, and some have adopted a "return to sender" policy when illegal waste shipments are discovered. Environmentalists and some members of Congress call for the United States to ban all exports of hazardous waste (including radioactive waste). They would also ban exports of pesticides and drugs not approved for use in the United States, and classify violations as criminal acts. They argue that exporting hazardous wastes to other countries (or to other states) encourages the throwaway mentality and discourages pollution prevention. Also, toxic exports may come back to haunt the exporters. For instance, they may contaminate soil or fertilizer used to grow food that is imported by the exporting countries.

In 1989, 105 countries meeting in Basel, Switzerland, drew up the Basel Convention, which establishes principles to be enforced by international law that would control shipments of toxic waste across national borders. However, some countries and international law experts say that the pact is too vague and full of loopholes to stop the international trade in hazardous wastes.

An effective U.S. or worldwide ban on all hazardous-waste exports would help, but would not end illegal trade in these wastes. The potential profits are simply too great. The only real solution to the hazardous-waste problem is to stop most hazardous waste from being produced (Solutions, p. 556).

too low—sending polluters the clear message that crime pays. They believe that people who deliberately, or through negligence, illegally release harmful chemicals into the environment should be subject to jail terms because such acts can harm and even kill people.

Operators of EPA-licensed hazardous-waste landfills must prevent leakage, use at least three wells to monitor the quality of groundwater around the sites, and report any contamination to the EPA. When a landfill reaches capacity and is closed, the operators must cover it with a leakproof cap and monitor the nearby groundwater for 30 years; they are financially responsible for cleanup and damages from leaks for 30 years. Environmentalists consider that provision a serious weakness in the law because leaks from most landfills may not be detected or revealed to the public until after 30 years, passing the hazards and the cleanup costs on to succeeding generations.

Recycled chemical wastes are exempted from control under RCRA. Using this loophole the EPA (under pressure from producers and handlers of hazardous waste) allows liquid hazardous wastes to be mixed with fuel and burned in industrial boilers, industrial furnaces, and cement kilns, and calls it "recycling." Because these combustion facilities don't have to meet the permit requirements and emission standards of EPA-licensed hazardous-waste incinerators, this increasingly common practice pollutes the air with toxic metals and other hazardous chemicals. And the resulting toxic ash can be mixed with cement (which can then be used in the walls of buildings and in pipes used to deliver drinking water) instead of having to be disposed of in EPA-licensed hazardous-waste land-

Q: Worldwide, what is the main cause of new HIV infections?

fills. RCRA also allows hazardous wastes to be "recycled" into pesticides as "inert" ingredients.

In 1984 Congress amended RCRA to minimize or eliminate land disposal of 450 regulated hazardous wastes by May 1990 unless the EPA determined that land disposal was an acceptable or the only feasible approach. Even then each chemical was to be detoxified to the fullest extent possible before land disposal. However, instead of requiring treatment, EPA regulations issued in 1990 allowed industries to dilute hazardous wastes by mixing them with other wastes and then injecting the mixture into deep wells—a practice environmentalists say violates the 1984 RCRA amendments. The EPA recommends that most of the several million tons of hazardous waste per year no longer landfilled be incinerated—a decision that pleases the incinerator industry but angers environmentalists (Spotlight, p. 558).

In 1992 the EPA proposed to exempt any waste containing toxins below certain concentrations from regulation, without requiring the industry in question to produce laboratory analyses or data to support its claim. This rule, based on EPA risk–benefit analysis, would exempt up to 66% of presently defined hazardous waste from federal regulation, pollute the drinking water of at least 13,200 people getting their water from wells within 1.6 kilometers (1 mile) of landfills receiving exempt waste, and create as many as 1,681 new "Superfund" sites requiring expensive cleanup. According to the EPA the financial benefits to industries from this rule outweigh its estimated harmful effects.

SUPERFUND The 1980 Comprehensive Environmental Response, Compensation and Liability Act is commonly known as the Superfund program. This law (plus amendments in 1986 and 1990) established a $16.3-billion fund, financed jointly by federal and state governments and by taxes on chemical and petrochemical industries, to clean up inactive hazardous-waste dump sites and leaking underground tanks that threaten human health and the environment. The EPA is authorized to collect fines and sue the owners of abandoned sites and tanks (if they can be found and held responsible) to recover up to three times the cleanup costs.

The EPA has identified 34,000 potentially hazardous-waste sites but has stopped looking for new ones, even though the General Accounting Office estimates that there are between 103,000 and 425,000 such sites. And if the 17,482 known toxic sites at military bases are included, there are potentially 51,482–442,482 hazardous-waste sites in the United States.

So far the EPA has placed more than 1,200 sites on a National Priority List for cleanup because they threaten nearby populations. By 1992, however, after spending at least $7.5 billion of taxpayers' money, the EPA had declared only 64 sites clean or stabilized and had removed only 24 from the priority list. Only $2.4 billion was spent on site-specific activities, with the rest used for outside consultants, administration, management, and litigation. And according to a 1989 report by the Office of Technology Assessment (OTA), about 75% of the cleanups are unlikely to work over the long term.

The EPA estimates the cost of cleaning up the current 1,211 National Priority sites at $40 billion. The OTA and the Waste Management Research Institute estimate that the final list could include at least 10,000 priority sites, with cleanup costs of up to $1 trillion, not counting legal fees. Cleaning up toxic military dumps will cost another $100–$200 billion and take at least 30 years; cleaning up contaminated Department of Energy sites used to make nuclear weapons will cost an additional $100–$360 billion and take 30–50 years.

It is hard to imagine a more convincing reason for emphasizing pollution prevention (Figure 21-3). The OTA estimates that it costs 10–100 times more to clean up hazardous-waste contamination than it does to prevent the original releases into the environment.

Are the fears of the more than 40 million people living near identified hazardous-waste sites justified? According to a 1992 study by the National Academy of Sciences, we don't know. The study concluded that the federal government has no comprehensive inventory of waste sites, no program for discovering new sites, insufficient data for determining safe exposure levels, questionable methods for assessing the public health danger at Superfund and other hazardous-waste sites, an inadequate system for identifying sites that require immediate action, and no plan to clean up sites using more cost-effective approaches.

In the meantime real people are living near thousands of real hazardous-waste dumps. These victims of environmental injustice are trapped in a toxic nightmare that fills them with fear and has made any property they own essentially worthless. We need to clean up these sites and see that no new ones are created (Individuals Matter, p. 564).

*Rather than stop the poisons at the source, those who have violated the environment have tried to control the effects. And they have . . . put the poisonous wastelands nearest the black, the brown, and the poor—the line of least resistance. . . . But because we live in one big room called Planet Earth, what may be the backyard of a family farmer or a black, brown, or poor person today, affects everybody as soon as the winds blow or the waters flow.*

JESSE JACKSON

## What You Can Do to Reduce Hazardous Wastes

**INDIVIDUALS MATTER**

- Use pesticides and other hazardous chemicals only when absolutely necessary, and in the smallest amount possible.

- Use rechargeable batteries and recycle them when their useful life is over. Every year Americans throw away 2.7 million nonrechargeable batteries that can contaminate groundwater with mercury and other toxic metals. If you must use nonrechargeable batteries (which cost much more money on a life-cycle basis), use alkaline batteries offered by some companies that are 99.999% mercury free.

- Use less hazardous (and usually cheaper) cleaning products (Table 21-2). Three inexpensive chemicals—baking soda, vinegar, and borax—can be used for most cleaning and clothes bleaching. Baking soda can also be used as a deodorant and a toothpaste.

- Do not flush hazardous chemicals down the toilet, pour them down the drain, bury them, throw them away in the garbage, or dump them down storm drains.* Consult your local health department or environmental agency for safe disposal methods.

- Take used motor oil, transmission fluid, brake fluid, and car batteries to a local auto service center or to a hazardous-waste collection center for recycling. Just 0.9 liter (1 quart) of motor oil can pollute 94,340 liters (250,000 gallons) of drinking water.

- Encourage engineering schools to thoroughly train all students in waste reduction and pollution prevention,

\* See the *Household Hazardous Waste Wheel*, Environmental Hazards Management Institute, 10 Newmarket Road, P.O. Box 932, Durham, NH 03824 ($3.75), and *Earth Wise Household Inventory Sheet*, available from Earth Ways, P.O. Box 682, Belmar, NJ 07719 ($2). You can make a household inventory of hazardous and wasteful items by using the *Household Inventory Worksheet: A Blueprint for Safer Homes*, also available from Earth Ways ($2).

and to set up retraining programs in these areas for existing engineers.

- Support legislation requiring that all government agencies favor products that produce the least amount of wastes and pollutants.

- Support legislation that would encourage pollution prevention and waste reduction. This would include recycling 80% of the country's municipal solid waste by 2010, cutting industrial hazardous-waste production 50% over 1990 levels by 2000, and placing a 10-year moratorium on the burning of solid and hazardous wastes in incinerators, industrial boilers, and cement kilns and on placing hazardous wastes in landfills and deep injection wells.

- Support legislation banning shipments of hazardous waste to other countries or from one state to another.

- Support legislation requiring that all products be labeled with simple, easily understood hazardous waste symbols or codes.

## We Have Been Asking the Wrong Questions About Wastes

*Lois Marie Gibbs*

**GUEST ESSAY**

*In 1977 Lois Marie Gibbs was a housewife living near the Love Canal, New York, toxic dump site (p. 550). She had never engaged in any sort of political action until toxic chemicals began oozing from the dump site into front yards and basements. Then she organized her neighborhood and became the president and major strategist for the Love Canal Homeowners Association. This dedicated grass-roots political action by "amateurs" brought hazardous-waste issues to national prominence and spurred passage of the federal Superfund legislation to help clean up abandoned hazardous-waste sites. Lois Gibbs then moved to Washington, D.C., and formed Citizens' Clearinghouse for Hazardous Wastes, an organization that has helped over 7,000 community grass-roots organizations protect themselves from hazardous wastes. Her story is told in her autobiography,* Love Canal: My Story *(State University of New York Press, 1982), and was also the subject of a CBS movie,* Lois Gibbs: The Love Canal, *which aired in 1982. She is an inspiring example of what an ordinary citizen can do to change the world.*

Just about everyone knows our environment is in danger. One of the most serious threats is the massive amount of waste put into the air, water, and ground every year. All across the United States and around the world, there are thousands of places that have been, and continue to be, polluted by toxic chemicals, radioactive waste, and just plain garbage.

For generations the main question people have asked is, "Where do we put all this waste? It's got to go somewhere." That is the wrong question, as has been shown by a series of experiments in waste disposal and by the simple fact that there is no away [Section 3-4].

We tried dumping our waste in the oceans. That was wrong. We tried injecting it into deep, underground wells. That was wrong. We've been trying to build landfills that don't leak. That doesn't work. We've been trying to get rid of waste by burning it in high-tech incinerators. That only produces different types of pollution, such as air pollution and toxic ash. We've tried a broad range of "pollution" controls. But all that does is allow legalized, high-tech pollution. Even

Q: How many people are expected to be infected with HIV by 2000?

recycling, which is a very good thing to do, suffers from the same problem as all the other methods: It addresses waste *after* it has been produced.

For many years people have been assuming that "it's got to go somewhere," but now many people, especially young people, are starting to ask, "Why?" Why do we produce so much waste? Why do we need products and services that have so many toxic by-products? Why can't industry change the way it makes things so that it stops producing so much waste?

These are the *right* questions. When you start asking them, you start getting answers that lead to *pollution prevention* and *waste reduction* instead of simply *pollution control* and *waste management*. People, young and old, who care about pollution prevention are challenging our use and disposal of enormous amounts of polystyrene (Styrofoam) plastic each year. They are challenging companies to stop making products with gases that destroy the ozone layer [Section 11-4] and contribute to the threatening possibility of global warming [Section 11-1]. They are asking why so many goods are wrapped in excessive, throwaway packaging. They are challenging companies that sell pesticides, cleaning fluids, batteries, and other hazardous products to either remove the toxins from those products or take them back for recovery or recycling, rather than disposing of them in the environment. They are demanding alternatives to throwaway materials in general.

Since 1988 hundreds of student groups have contacted my organization to get help and advice in taking these effective types of actions. Many of these groups begin by working to get polystyrene food packaging out of their school cafeterias and out of local fast-food restaurants.

Oregon students even took legal action to get rid of cups and plates made from bleached paper, because the paper contains the deadly poison dioxin. They were asking the right questions—and getting the right answer—when they demanded the school systems switch to reusable cups, plates, and utensils.

Dozens of student groups have joined with local environmental and grass-roots organizations in their communities to get toxic-waste sites cleaned up or to stop new toxic-waste sites, radioactive waste sites, or waste incinerators from being built.

Waste issues are not simply environmental issues. They are all tied up with economics. Our economy is geared to producing and then disposing of waste. *Somebody* is making money from every scrap of waste and has a vested interest in leaving things the way they are. Environmentalists and industry officials constantly argue about what's called "cost–benefit analysis" [Section 25-2]. Simply stated, this poses the question of whether the benefit of controlling pollution or waste will be greater than the cost. This is another example of the wrong question. The right question is, "Who will benefit and who will pay the cost?"

Waste issues are also issues of *justice* and *fairness*. Again, there's a lot of debate between industry officials and environmentalists, especially those in federal and state environmental agencies, about what they call "acceptable risk." Simply stated, that means industry officials and environmentalists will decide people's exposure to toxic chemicals. Unfortunately they hardly ever ask the people who are actually going to be exposed how they feel about it. Instead, industry officials debate and ask one another how much people will be exposed to. Again, this is the wrong question: It's simply not fair to expose people to chemical poisons without their consent.

Risk analysts often say, "But there's only a one in a million chance of increased death from this toxic chemical." That may be true. But suppose I took a pistol and went to the edge of your neighborhood and began shooting. There's probably only a one in a million chance that I'd hit somebody. But would you give me permission, would you give me a license, to do that? As long as we don't stand up for our rights and demand that "bullets" in the form of hazardous chemicals not be "fired" in our neighborhoods, we are giving environmental regulators and waste producers a license to kill a certain number of us without our even being consulted.

When you study environmental issues, remember that they are not abstract issues that only happen somewhere else. We *all* have to live, breathe, and survive in this environment. We have all learned that decisions made for us or by us in the past have come back to haunt us. Likewise, today's decisions will affect all of us tomorrow and far into the future.

From my personal experience I know that decisions to dump wastes at Love Canal and in thousands of other places in the past were not made simply on the basis of the best available scientific knowledge. The same holds true for decisions made about how to manage the wastes we produce today and how to produce less waste.

Instead, the world we live in is shaped by decisions based on money and power. If you really want to understand what's behind any given environmental issue, the first question you should ask is, "Who stands to profit from this?" Then ask, "Who is going to pay the price?" You can then identify both sides of the issue and decide whether you want to be part of the problem or part of the solution.

## Critical Thinking

1. What changes would you be willing to make in your own lifestyle to prevent pollution and reduce waste?

2. What political and economic changes, if any, do you believe must be made so that we shift from a waste production and waste management society to a pollution prevention and waste reduction society? What actions, if any, are you taking to bring about such social changes?

## Environmental Justice for All

*Robert D. Bullard*

GUEST ESSAY *Robert D. Bullard is a professor of sociology at the University of California, Riverside. For more than a decade he has worked on and conducted research in the areas of urban land use, housing, community development, industrial facility siting, and environmental justice. His scholarship and activism have made him one of the leading experts on environmental racism—the systematic selection of communities of color for waste facilities and polluting industries. He is the author of four books and more than three dozen articles, monographs, and scholarly papers that address equity concerns. His book* Dumping in Dixie: Race, Class, and Environmental Quality *(Westview Press, 1990) has become a standard text in the field. His most recent book is* Confronting Environmental Racism *(South End Press, 1993).*

Despite widespread media coverage and volumes written on the U.S. environmental movement, environmentalism and social justice have seldom been linked. Nevertheless, an environmental revolution is now taking shape in the United States that combines the environmental and social justice movements into one framework.

The struggles of politically and economically disenfranchised groups epitomize this new revolution. People of color (African Americans, Latinos, Asians, Pacific Islanders, and Native Americans), working-class people, and poor people in the United States suffer disproportionately from industrial toxins, dirty air and drinking water, unsafe work conditions, and the location of noxious facilities such as municipal landfills, incinerators, and toxic-waste dumps. Despite the government's attempts to level the playing field, all communities are not created equal.

Environmental inequities are created and maintained by institutional agreements—policies and practices that favor one group over another. The environmental justice movement attempts to dismantle exclusionary zoning ordinances, discriminatory land-use practices, differential enforcement of environmental regulations, disparate siting of risky technologies, and the dumping of toxic waste on the poor and people of color in the United States and in LDCs.

All communities are not treated as equals when it comes to resolving environmental and public health concerns either. Over 300,000 farm workers (over 90% of whom are people of color) and their children are poisoned by pesticides sprayed on crops in the United States. Some 3–4 million children (many of them African Americans or Latinos living in the inner city) are poisoned by lead-based paint in old buildings, lead-soldered pipes and water mains, lead-tainted soil contaminated by industry, and air pollutants from smelters. Lead poisoning is considered the number one environmental health problem facing children in the United States. Yet little has been done over the past 20 years to rid the nation of this preventable childhood hazard.

All communities do not bear the same burden or reap the same benefits from industrial expansion. This is true in the case of the mostly African American Emelle, Alabama (home of the nation's largest hazardous-waste landfill); Navajo lands in Arizona where uranium is mined; and the 2,000 factories known as *maquiladores*, located just across the U.S. border in Mexico.

Communities, states, and regions that contain hazardous-waste disposal facilities (importers) receive far fewer economic benefits (jobs) than the geographic locations that generate the wastes (exporters). Nationally 60% of African Americans and 50% of Latinos live in communities with at least one uncontrolled toxic-waste site. Three of the five largest hazardous-waste landfills are located in communities that are predominantly African American or Latino.

## Critical Thinking

1. Would you oppose locating a hazardous-waste landfill, treatment plant, deep-injection well, or incinerator in your community? Explain. If you oppose these disposal facilities, how should the hazardous waste generated in your community and state be managed?

2. Give your reasons for agreeing or disagreeing with each of the following proposals for dealing with hazardous waste:
   a. Reduce the production of hazardous waste and encourage recycling and reuse of hazardous materials by levying a tax or fee on producers for each unit of waste generated.
   b. Ban all land disposal of hazardous waste to encourage recycling, reuse, and treatment and to protect groundwater from contamination.
   c. Provide low-interest loans, tax breaks, and other financial incentives to encourage industries producing hazardous waste to recycle, reuse, treat, destroy, and reduce generation of such waste.
   d. Ban the shipment of hazardous waste from the United States to any other country.
   e. Ban the shipment of hazardous waste from one state to another.

Q: How many people are expected to have full-blown AIDS by 2000?

The marginal status of many people of color in the United States makes them prime actors in the movement for environmental and social justice. For example, the organizing theme of the 1991 First National People of Color Environmental Summit held in Washington, D.C., was justice, fairness, and equity. More than 650 delegates from all 50 states, as well as Puerto Rico, Mexico, Chile, Colombia, and the Marshall Islands, participated in this historic four-day gathering.

Environmental justice does not stop at the U.S. borders. Environmental injustices exist from the *favelas* of Rio de Janeiro [photo, p. 201] to the shantytowns of Johannesburg. Activists are challenging the "business-as-usual" environmentalism that is generally practiced by the more privileged wildlife and conservation-oriented groups in the industrial world. They are also questioning the wasteful and nonsustainable development models being exported to the developing world.

It is no mystery why grass-roots environmental justice groups in Louisiana's "Cancer Alley" [Figure 20-9], Chicago's southside, and Los Angeles's East and South Central neighborhoods are attacking the institutions they blame for their underdevelopment, disenfranchisement, and poisoning. Some people see these threats to their communities as a form of genocide.

Many of these environmental problems are imbedded in the struggle against oppression and dehumanization that exists in the larger society. Grass-roots leaders are demanding justice. Today their battle cry is "No justice, no peace." Residents of communities such as West Dallas and Texarkana (Texas), West Harlem (New York), Rosebud (South Dakota), Kettleman City (California), and Sunrise, Lions, and Wallace (Louisiana) see their struggle for environmental justice as a life-and-death matter. Unfortunately their stories of environmental racism are not piped into the nation's living rooms during the nightly news, nor are they blasted across the front pages of national newspapers and magazines. To a large extent the communities that are the victims of environmental injustice remain "invisible" to the larger society.

The quest for environmental justice is a social movement that parallels the larger mainstream environmental movement. The environmental justice movement is led, planned, and to a large extent funded by individuals who are not part of the established environmental community or the "Big 10" environmental organizations. Most environmental justice groups are small and operate with resources generated from the local community.

For too long these groups and their leaders have been "invisible" and their stories muted. This is changing as these grass-roots groups are forcing their issues onto the nation's environmental agenda.

The United States has a long way to go in achieving environmental justice for all its citizens. Many decision-making boards and commissions still do not reflect the racial, ethnic, and cultural diversity of the country. And token inclusion of persons of color on boards and commissions does not necessarily mean that their voices will be heard or their cultures respected. The ultimate goal of any inclusion strategy should be to democratize the decision-making process and empower disenfranchised people to speak and do for themselves.

### Critical Thinking

1. Does your lifestyle and political involvement help promote or reduce environmental racism in society as a whole and in the community where you live?

2. How would you go about helping prevent polluting factories and hazardous-waste facilities from being located in or near communities made up largely of people of color, working-class people, and poor people?

*3. What hazardous wastes are produced at your school? What happens to them?

*4. Are there any active or abandoned hazardous-waste dumps in your community? Where are they located? What has been dumped there? Do they have one or more liners? Has there been any testing to determine whether wastes have leaked from the sites? What were the results of the tests? Who owns the sites?

## When Is a Lichen Like a Canary?

Nineteenth-century coal miners took canaries with them into the mines—not for their songs but for that moment when they stopped singing. Then the miners knew the air was going bad, and it was time to get out of the mine.

Nowadays we use sophisticated equipment to monitor air quality, but living things like lichens (Figure 22-1) still have a role in warning us of bad air. A lichen consists of fungus and alga living together, usually in a mutually beneficial (mutualistic) partnership. Typically the fungus absorbs moisture that the alga needs, secretes acids that help the lichen stay attached to the rock or tree, and dissolves minerals from the rock that both the fungus and alga need. The alga, in turn, carries out photosynthesis and supplies itself and the fungus with carbohydrates.

With more than 20,000 known species, lichens can live almost anywhere—on rocks, trees, bare soil, buildings, gravestones, and even sun-bleached bones—and some survive for more than 4,000 years.

These hearty pioneer species are good air pollution detectors because they are always absorbing air as a source of nourishment. They store everything the air brings their way, whether they need it or not.

Certain lichen species are sensitive to specific air-polluting chemicals. Old man's beard (*Usnea trichodea*; Figure 22-1, right) and yellow *Evernia* lichens, for example, sicken or die in the presence of too much sulfur dioxide, while *Ramalina* lichens from California are damaged by nitrate and fluoride salts.

Lichens also vary in their vulnerability to specific pollutants. Thus they can be used to determine levels of pollution by a single compound and to monitor

**Figure 22-1** Red and yellow crustose lichen (left) growing on slate rock in the foothills of the Sierra Nevada near Merced, California, and *Usnea trichodea* lichen (right) growing on a larch tree in Gifford Pinchot National Forest, Washington. Various species of lichens can be used to detect levels of specific air pollutants and to track down their sources.

Kenneth W. Fink/Ardea London

Milton Rand/Tom Stack & Associates

*I thought I saw a blue jay this morning. But the smog was so bad that it turned out to be a cardinal holding its breath.*

MICHAEL J. COHEN

those levels over time. For sulfur dioxide, for example, *Usnea trichodea* is the most sensitive, *Evernia* is moderately sensitive, and the crusty European lichen *Lecanora conizaeoides* practically thrives in its presence.

Since lichens are widespread, long-lived, and reliably anchored in their spots, they can also be used to track pollution to its source. The scientist who discovered sulfur dioxide pollution on Isle Royale in Lake Superior, where no car or smokestack had ever intruded, used *Evernia* lichens to point the finger northward to coal-burning facilities at Thunder Bay, Canada. Conversely healthy lichens on damaged trees of Germany's Black Forest got French coal-burning power plants off the hook in the 1970s and allowed investigators to focus on the true culprit: nitrogen oxides from car exhausts. The result was Germany's first auto emission standards, which went into effect in 1992.

When the Chernobyl nuclear power plant disaster (p. 476) spread radioactive clouds across the northern reaches of Scandinavia, cesium-137 particles were absorbed by the lichens carpeting Lapland. The area's Saami people depend on reindeer meat for food, and the reindeer feed on lichens. After Chernobyl more than 70,000 reindeer had to be killed and the meat discarded because it was too radioactive to eat. However, scientists helped the Saami relocate their reindeer herds by analyzing lichens to pinpoint the most contaminated areas.

Last, but not least, lichens replace electronic monitoring stations that would cost more than $100,000 each. This is not so much a triumph of nature over technology, but a partnership between the two, for technicians use highly sophisticated methods to analyze lichens for polluting chemicals and measure their rates of photosynthesis. The happy result, in any case, is a bad-air warning system that is definitely better than canaries, for it can warn us in advance, even before any visible damage to the lichen itself.

Because we all must breathe air from a shared global atmospheric commons, air pollution anywhere is a potential threat elsewhere, and in some cases everywhere. Although lichens can alert us to the danger, as with all forms of pollution, the only real solution is prevention.

This chapter is devoted to answering the following questions:

- What are air pollutants, and where do they come from?
- What is smog?
- What is acid deposition?
- What are the harmful effects of air pollutants?
- How can we prevent and control air pollution?

## 22-1 Outdoor and Indoor Air Pollution

**TYPES AND SOURCES OF OUTDOOR AIR POLLUTION** Earth's atmosphere is layered like an onion (Figure 5-2). The layer that concerns us most is the one we live in—the troposphere. As clean air moves across Earth's surface, it collects the products of natural events (volcanic eruptions and dust storms) and human activities (emissions from cars and smokestacks). These potential pollutants, called **primary pollutants,** mix with the churning air in the troposphere, and some may react with one another or with the basic components of air to form new pollutants, called **secondary pollutants** (Figure 22-2). Long-lived pollutants travel far before they return to the earth as particles, droplets, or chemicals dissolved in precipitation.

Table 22-1 lists the major classes of pollutants found in outdoor air. Outdoor pollution in industrialized countries comes mostly from five groups of primary pollutants: carbon oxides, nitrogen oxides (mostly NO and $NO_2$, or $NO_x$), sulfur oxides (mostly $SO_2$ and $SO_3$), volatile organic compounds (mostly hydrocarbons), and suspended particles (Figure 22-3), all produced primarily by combustion of fossil fuels. Air pollution is not new (Spotlight, p. 571), but it has mushroomed since the Industrial Revolution.

In MDCs most pollutants enter the atmosphere from the burning of fossil fuels in power plants and

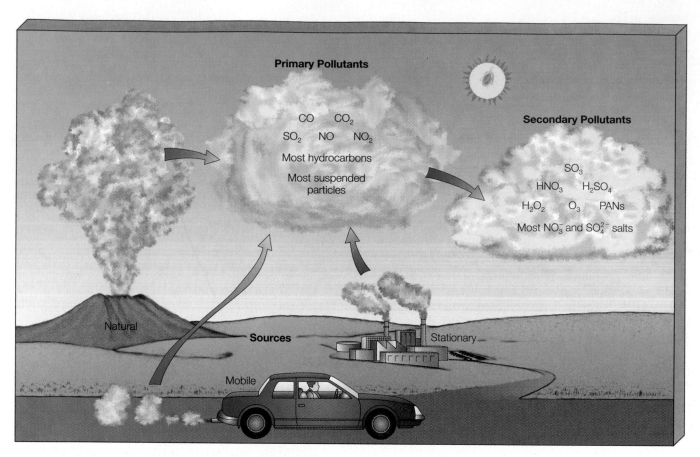

**Figure 22-2** Primary and secondary air pollutants.

**Table 22-1  Major Classes of Air Pollutants**

| Class | Examples |
|---|---|
| Carbon oxides | Carbon monoxide (CO), carbon dioxide ($CO_2$) |
| Sulfur oxides | Sulfur dioxide ($SO_2$), sulfur trioxide ($SO_3$) |
| Nitrogen oxides | Nitric oxide (NO), nitrogen dioxide ($NO_2$), nitrous oxide ($N_2O$) (NO and $NO_2$ are often lumped together and labeled as $NO_x$) |
| Volatile organic compounds | Methane ($CH_4$), propane ($C_3H_8$), benzene ($C_6H_6$), chlorofluorocarbons (CFCs) |
| Suspended particles | Solid particles (dust, soot, asbestos, lead, nitrate and sulfate salts), liquid droplets (sulfuric acid, PCBs, dioxins, pesticides) |
| Photochemical oxidants | Ozone ($O_3$), peroxyacyl nitrates (PANs), hydrogen peroxide ($H_2O_2$), aldehydes |
| Radioactive substances | Radon-222, iodine-131, strontium-90, plutonium-239 (Table 3-1) |
| Toxic compounds | Trace amounts of at least 600 toxic substances (many of them volatile organic compounds), 60 of them known carcinogens |

factories (*stationary sources*) and in motor vehicles (*mobile sources*). People who live near or downwind from steel and chemical plants, metal smelters (Figure 7-26), paper plants, oil refineries and petrochemical plants, coal-burning power plants, and hazardous-waste and city-trash incinerators have the highest risk from these pollutants. In car-clogged cities like Los Angeles, São Paulo, London, and Mexico City (Figure

Q: How many Americans die from AIDS?

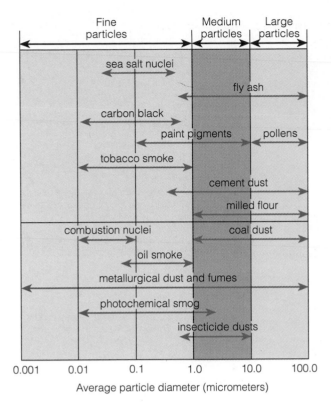

Fine particles | Medium particles | Large particles

sea salt nuclei
fly ash
carbon black
paint pigments | pollens
tobacco smoke
cement dust
milled flour
combustion nuclei | coal dust
oil smoke
metallurgical dust and fumes
photochemical smog
insecticide dusts

0.001  0.01  0.1  1.0  10.0  100.0
Average particle diameter (micrometers)

**Figure 22-3** Suspended particles are found in a wide variety of types and sizes. (1 micrometer = 0.001 millimeter = 0.00004 in.)

9-4) motor vehicles are responsible for 80–88% of the air pollution.

**TYPES AND SOURCES OF INDOOR AIR POLLUTION** If you are reading this book indoors, you may be inhaling more air pollutants with each breath than if you had been outside. As many as 150 dangerous chemicals, in concentrations 10–40 times higher than those outdoors, occur in the typical American home (Table 21-1 and Figure 22-4).

The health risks from exposure to such chemicals are magnified because people spend 70–90% of their time indoors. In 1990 the EPA placed indoor air pollution at the top of the list of 18 sources of cancer risk. At greatest risk are smokers, the young, the old, the sick, pregnant women, people with breathing or heart problems, and factory workers.

Pollutants found in buildings produce dizziness, headaches, coughing, sneezing, nausea, burning eyes, chronic fatigue, and flulike symptoms—the "sick building syndrome." According to the EPA, at least one-fifth of all U.S. buildings are considered "sick"—costing the nation $60 billion a year in absenteeism and reduced productivity. Some indoor pollutants cause disease and premature death. According to the

## Air Pollution in the Past

**SPOTLIGHT**

As early as 1273, Edward I of England banned the burning of coal in London to reduce air pollution. Obviously his ban did not become permanent. More than 500 years later, the famous English poet Shelley observed, "Hell must be much like London, a smoky and populous city."

In 1911 more than 1,100 Londoners died from the effects of coal smoke. The authors of a report on this disaster coined the word *smog* for the deadly mixture of smoke and fog blanketing the city. An even worse yellow fog killed 4,000 Londoners in 1952, and disasters in 1956, 1957, and 1962 killed 2,500 more. As a result, London took a page from the book of Edward I and passed strong air pollution control measures.

The first U.S. air pollution disaster occurred in 1948, when fog laden with sulfur dioxide and suspended particulate matter stagnated for five days over the town of Donora in Pennsylvania's Monongahela Valley south of Pittsburgh. About 6,000 of the town's 14,000 inhabitants fell ill, and 20 of them died. This killer fog resulted from a combination of mountainous terrain surrounding the valley and stable weather conditions that trapped and concentrated deadly pollutants emitted by the community's steel mill, zinc smelter, and sulfuric acid plant.

In 1963 high concentrations of air pollutants accumulated in the air over New York City, killing about 300 people and injuring thousands. Other episodes during the 1960s in New York, Los Angeles, and other large cities led to much stronger air pollution control programs in the 1970s.

EPA and public health officials, cigarette smoke (p. 532), radioactive radon-222 gas (Case Study, p. 573), asbestos (Pro/Con, p. 575), and formaldehyde are the four most dangerous indoor air pollutants.

As many as 20 million Americans suffer from chronic breathing problems, dizziness, rashes, lethargy, headaches, sore throat, sinus and eye irritation, and nausea caused by daily exposure to low levels of formaldehyde emitted (outgassed) from common building materials and household items (Figure 22-4). Formaldehyde is used in plywood, particleboard, paneling, and (worst) medium-density fiberboard, which in turn are used in countertops, kitchen cabinets, subflooring, and about 90% of the furniture sold in the

A: 55,000 per year (150 per day) in 1992

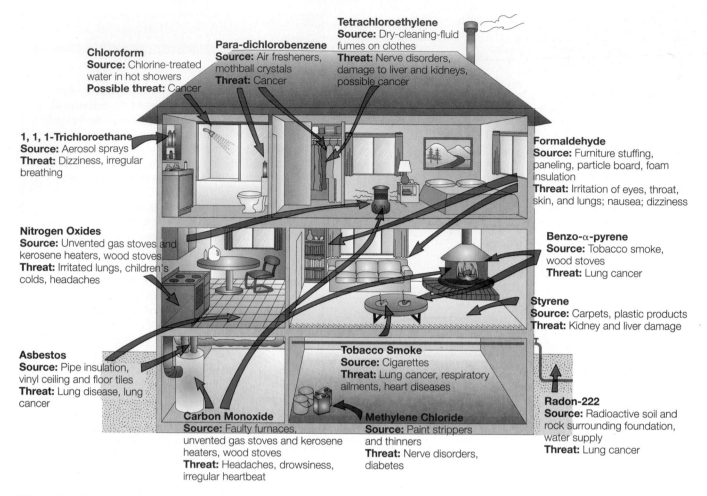

**Chloroform**
**Source:** Chlorine-treated water in hot showers
**Possible threat:** Cancer

**Para-dichlorobenzene**
**Source:** Air fresheners, mothball crystals
**Threat:** Cancer

**Tetrachloroethylene**
**Source:** Dry-cleaning-fluid fumes on clothes
**Threat:** Nerve disorders, damage to liver and kidneys, possible cancer

**1, 1, 1-Trichloroethane**
**Source:** Aerosol sprays
**Threat:** Dizziness, irregular breathing

**Formaldehyde**
**Source:** Furniture stuffing, paneling, particle board, foam insulation
**Threat:** Irritation of eyes, throat, skin, and lungs; nausea; dizziness

**Nitrogen Oxides**
**Source:** Unvented gas stoves and kerosene heaters, wood stoves
**Threat:** Irritated lungs, children's colds, headaches

**Benzo-α-pyrene**
**Source:** Tobacco smoke, wood stoves
**Threat:** Lung cancer

**Styrene**
**Source:** Carpets, plastic products
**Threat:** Kidney and liver damage

**Asbestos**
**Source:** Pipe insulation, vinyl ceiling and floor tiles
**Threat:** Lung disease, lung cancer

**Tobacco Smoke**
**Source:** Cigarettes
**Threat:** Lung cancer, respiratory ailments, heart diseases

**Carbon Monoxide**
**Source:** Faulty furnaces, unvented gas stoves and kerosene heaters, wood stoves
**Threat:** Headaches, drowsiness, irregular heartbeat

**Methylene Chloride**
**Source:** Paint strippers and thinners
**Threat:** Nerve disorders, diabetes

**Radon-222**
**Source:** Radioactive soil and rock surrounding foundation, water supply
**Threat:** Lung cancer

**Figure 22-4** Some important indoor air pollutants. (Data from Environmental Protection Agency)

United States. Other formaldehyde sources include drapes, upholstery, urea-formaldehyde foam insulation (now banned), adhesives in carpeting and wallpaper, and permanent-press clothing. Chronic low-level exposure to formaldehyde can cause cancer.

According to the EPA at least half the mobile homes (also called manufactured homes) in the United States have formaldehyde levels high enough to cause harmful symptoms. The EPA estimates that as many as 2 out of every 10,000 persons who live in mobile homes for more than 10 years will develop cancer from formaldehyde exposure. Many new condominiums, town houses, and tract houses also have formaldehyde pollution problems.

Severe indoor air pollution, especially from particulate matter, occurs inside the dwellings of many poor rural people in LDCs. The burning of wood, dung, and crop residues in open fires or in unvented or poorly vented stoves for cooking and heating (in temperate and cold areas) exposes the people, especially women and young children, to very high levels of indoor air pollution. Partly as a result, respiratory illnesses are a major cause of death and illness in most LDCs.

## 22-2 Smog and Acid Deposition

**SMOG: CARS + SUNLIGHT = TEARS** Photochemical smog is a mixture of primary and secondary pollutants that forms when some of the primary pollutants interact under the influence of sunlight (Figure 22-6). The resulting mix of more than 100 chemicals is dominated by ozone, a highly reactive gas that harms most living organisms.

Virtually all modern cities have photochemical smog, but it is much more common in cities with sunny, warm, dry climates and lots of motor vehicles.

Q: Worldwide, how many people have malaria?

Radon-222 is a colorless, odorless, tasteless, naturally occurring radioactive gas produced by the radioactive decay of uranium-238. Small amounts of uranium-238 are found in most soil and rock, but this isotope is much more concentrated in underground deposits of uranium, phosphate, granite, and shale.

When radon gas from such deposits seeps upward through the soil and is released outdoors, it disperses quickly in the atmosphere and decays to harmless levels. However, when the gas is drawn into buildings through cracks, drains, and hollow concrete blocks, or seeps into water in underground wells over such deposits, it can build up to high levels (Figure 22-5). Stone and other building materials obtained from radon-rich deposits can also be a source of indoor radon contamination.

Radon-222 gas quickly decays into solid particles of other radioactive elements that can be inhaled, exposing lung tissue to a large amount of ionizing radiation from alpha particles (Figure 3-10). Repeated exposure to these radioactive particles over 20–30 years can cause lung cancer, especially in smokers. According to studies by the EPA and the National Research Council, for example, 10,000–15,000 of the 130,000–140,000 new cases of lung cancer each year in the United States may be caused by prolonged exposure to radon or to radon acting together with smoking. Radon and its airborne decay products account for an estimated 55% of the current radiation dose of the U.S. population (Figure 20-3).

According to the EPA average radon levels above 4 picocuries (one-trillionth of a curie, used to measure radioactivity) per liter of air in a closed house are considered unsafe. However, some researchers

cite evidence suggesting that radon becomes dangerous only if indoor levels exceed 20 picocuries per liter—above the government safety limit set for workers who handle radioactive materials. In Canada, Sweden, and Norway, for example, authorities have set the "danger level" for radon at 20 picocuries per liter of air.

EPA indoor radon surveys suggest that 4–5 million U.S. homes may have annual radon levels above 4 picocuries per liter of air and 50,000–100,000 homes may have levels above 20 picocuries per liter. Unsafe levels can build up easily in a superinsulated or airtight home unless the building has an air-to-air heat exchanger to change indoor air without losing much heat. According to a 1992 EPA survey of 1,000 schools, one school in five has levels of radon gas higher

than 4 picocuries per liter, exposing an estimated 11 million students and teachers to this health threat.

When groundwater in or near radon-laden rock is withdrawn, heated, and used for showers and for washing clothes and dishes, it releases radon-222. Some research indicates that the risk from waterborne radon released indoors may be even higher than that from airborne radon. Homeowners with wells thus should have their water tested for radon.

Because radon "hot spots" can occur almost anywhere, it's impossible to know which buildings have unsafe levels of radon without carrying out tests. In 1988 the EPA and the U.S. Surgeon General's Office recommended that everyone living in a detached house, a town house, or a mobile home, or on the first three

(continued)

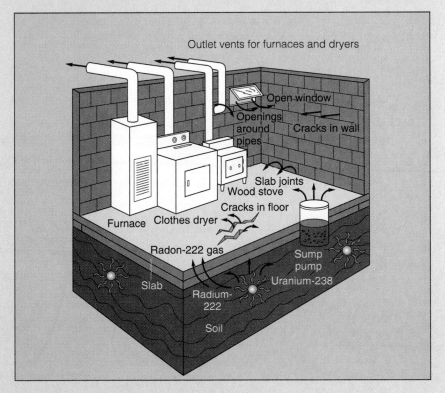

**Figure 22-5** Sources and paths of entry for indoor radon-222 gas. (Data from Environmental Protection Agency)

floors of an apartment building, test for radon.* By 1992, however, only 9% of U.S. households had conducted such tests (at $20– $100 per home). If testing reveals an unacceptable level, you can consult the free EPA publication *Radon Reduc-*

* For information see "Radon Detectors: How to Find Out If Your House Has a Radon Problem," *Consumer Reports*, July 1987. Ideally radon detectors should be left in the main living area a full year.

*tion Methods* for ways to reduce radon levels and health risks.

In Sweden no house can be built until the lot has been tested for radon. If the reading is high (above 20 picocuries per liter), the builder must follow government-mandated construction procedures to ensure that the house won't be contaminated. Environmentalists urge enactment of a similar building code for new construction in the United States.

Other recommendations include having an existing house or building lot tested for radon before you purchase it and insisting that contractors construct new houses using EPA-approved techniques that prevent harmful buildup of radon but add $1,000–$1,500 to the construction cost.

Has the building where you live or work been tested for radon?

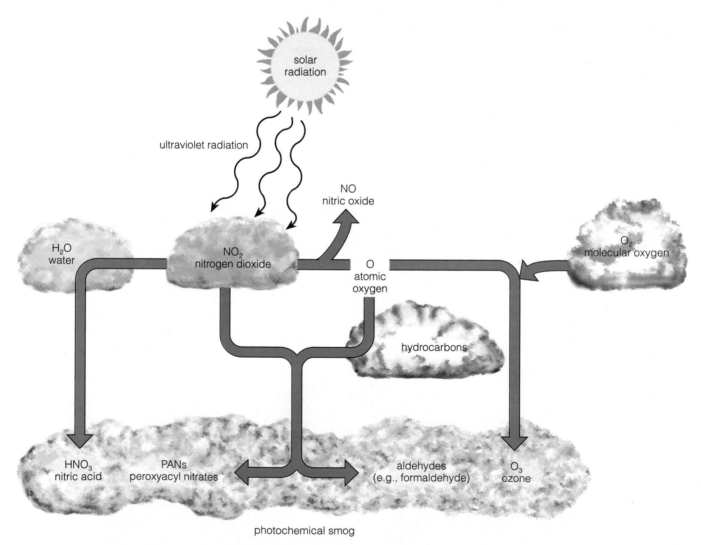

**Figure 22-6** Simplified scheme of the formation of photochemical smog. The severity of smog is generally associated with atmospheric concentrations of ozone at ground level.

Q: How many people die from malaria each year?

## What Should Be Done About Asbestos?

Asbestos is a group of minerals that sometimes crystallize as fibers. Chrysotile, the most abundant type of asbestos, forms curly white fibers; another type, amphibole, crystallizes as sharp needles.

Between 1900 and 1986 over 28 million metric tons (31 million tons) of asbestos (80–95% of it chrysotile) were used in the United States for hundreds of purposes. Much of it was sprayed on ceilings and walls of schools and other public and private buildings for fireproofing, soundproofing, insulation of heaters and pipes, and wall and ceiling decoration. The EPA banned those uses in 1974.

Unless completely sealed within a product, asbestos easily crumbles into a dust of fibers tiny enough to become suspended in the air and to be inhaled into the lungs, where they remain for many years. Prolonged exposure to asbestos fibers can cause asbestosis (a chronic lung condition that eventually makes breathing nearly impossible), lung cancer, and mesothelioma (an inoperable cancer of the chest cavity lining). Smokers exposed to asbestos fibers have a much greater chance of dying from lung cancer than do nonsmokers exposed to such fibers. Some evidence suggests that the greatest risk for contracting mesothelioma comes from prolonged

exposure to amphibole asbestos fibers, but other researchers challenge these studies.

Most of these diseases occur in people exposed for years to high levels of asbestos fibers. This group includes asbestos miners, insulators, pipe fitters, shipyard employees, auto mechanics (from brake linings), and workers in asbestos-producing factories. More than 350,000 former U.S. workers have come down with asbestos-caused diseases, and each year an estimated 10,000 people—mostly U.S. industrial and construction workers exposed to high levels of asbestos fibers for years—die prematurely from asbestos-related diseases. Asbestos manufacturing companies in the United States have been swamped with health claims from workers, and some have been driven into bankruptcy.

In 1989 the EPA ordered a ban on almost all remaining uses of asbestos such as brake linings, roofing shingles, and water pipes in the United States by 1997. Representatives of the asbestos industry in the United States and Canada (which produces most of the asbestos used in the United States) challenged the ban in court, contending that with proper precautions these asbestos products can be safely used and that the costs of the ban outweigh the benefits. In 1991 a federal appeals court overturned the EPA ban.

In 1986 Congress passed the Asbestos Hazards Emergency Response Act, which required all schools to have a qualified inspector check for asbestos and submit plans for containment or removal by May 8, 1989. In 1988 the EPA estimated that one of every seven commercial and public buildings in the United States contains asbestos that has crumbled or could crumble and release fibers. Removal of asbestos from such buildings could cost $50–$150 billion.

Critics of this law contend that the health benefits of asbestos removal from schools, homes, and other buildings are not worth the costs, unless measurements (not just visual inspection) show that the buildings have a high level of airborne asbestos fibers. They call for sealing, wrapping, and other forms of containment instead of removal of most asbestos, and point out that improper removal can release more asbestos fibers than sealing off asbestos that is not crumbling.

The EPA estimates that half of all asbestos-removal projects, and three-fourths of those in schools, have been done improperly. After spending billions on removal, there is now general agreement that asbestos should not be removed from buildings where it has not been damaged or disturbed, but should be sealed or wrapped to minimize release of fibers.

---

Los Angeles (Figure 22-7), Denver, Salt Lake City, Sydney, Mexico City (Figure 9-4), and Buenos Aires all have serious photochemical smog problems. The hotter the day, the higher the levels of ozone and other components of photochemical smog.

Nitrogen oxides are key ingredients needed to form photochemical smog. As vehicle traffic increases in the morning, $NO_x$ levels rise and begin reacting with volatile organic compounds—mostly hydrocarbons, which are released by vehicles, gas stations, oil refineries, dry cleaners, print shops, and vegetation—in the presence of sun-

light to yield photochemical smog. On a sunny day the smog builds up to peak levels by early afternoon, irritating people's eyes and respiratory tracts. People with asthma and other respiratory problems, and healthy people who exercise outdoors between 11 AM and 4 PM, are especially vulnerable.

Thirty years ago cities like London, Chicago, and Pittsburgh burned large amounts of coal and heavy oil, which contain sulfur impurities, in power plants and factories and for space heating. During winter such cities suffered from **industrial smog**, consisting mostly

Normal pattern

Thermal inversion

J. Scowen/FPG

**Figure 22-7** Thermal inversion traps pollutants in a layer of cool air that cannot rise to carry the pollutants away. The photograph shows a Los Angeles freeway covered with an orange haze of photochemical smog at twilight. Because of its topography Los Angeles has frequent thermal inversions, many of them prolonged during the summer months.

of a mixture of sulfur dioxide (Figure 22-8), suspended droplets of sulfuric acid formed from some of the sulfur dioxide, and a variety of suspended solid particles. Today in most parts of the world coal and heavy oil are burned only in large boilers with reasonably good pollution control or with tall smokestacks, so industrial smog, sometimes called *gray-air smog*, is rarely a problem. However, in China, the Ukraine, and some eastern European countries, such as Poland (Case Study, p. 18), large quantities of coal are still burned with inadequate pollution controls.

## LOCAL CLIMATE, TOPOGRAPHY, AND SMOG

The frequency and severity of smog in an area depend on the local climate and topography, the density of the population, the amount of industry, and the fuels used in industry, heating, and transportation. In areas with high average annual precipitation, rain and snow help cleanse the air of pollutants. Winds also help sweep pollutants away and bring in fresh air but may transfer some pollutants to distant areas.

Hills and mountains tend to reduce the flow of air in valleys below and allow pollutant levels to build up at ground level. Buildings in cities also slow wind speed and reduce dilution and removal of pollutants.

During the day the sun warms the air near the earth's surface. Normally this heated air expands and rises, carrying low-lying pollutants higher into the troposphere. Colder, denser air from surrounding high-pressure areas then sinks into the low-pressure area created when the hot air rises (Figure 22-7). This continual mixing of the air helps keep pollutants from reaching dangerous levels near the ground.

**Q:** How many women in LDCs die each year of preventable pregnancy-related causes?

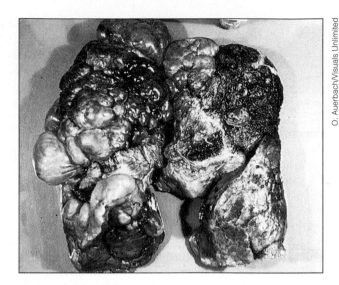

**Figure 22-12** Normal appearance of human lungs (left) and appearance of the lungs of a person who died from emphysema (right). Prolonged smoking and exposure to air pollutants can cause emphysema in anyone, but about 2% of emphysema cases are caused by a defective gene that reduces the elasticity of the air sacs in the lungs. Anyone with this hereditary condition, for which testing is available, should not smoke and should not live or work in a highly polluted area.

Cigarette smoking (p. 532) is responsible for the largest human exposure to *carbon monoxide* (CO), but CO is also released outdoors mostly by motor vehicles and indoors by kerosene heaters and faulty heating systems. CO reduces the ability of blood to carry oxygen, which impairs perception and thinking, slows reflexes, and causes headaches, drowsiness, dizziness, and nausea. It also can trigger heart attacks and angina attacks in people with heart disease, damage the development of fetuses and young children, and aggravate the condition of people suffering from chronic bronchitis, emphysema, and anemia. Exposure to high levels of CO causes collapse, coma, and even death.

Suspended particles (Figure 22-3) aggravate bronchitis and asthma. Long-term breathing of such particles damages lung tissues, contributing to development of chronic respiratory disease, cancer, and premature illness and death. Fine particles are especially hazardous because they are small enough to penetrate the body's natural defenses against air pollution. They can also bring with them droplets or other particles of toxic or cancer-causing pollutants that become attached to their surfaces.

Sulfur dioxide causes constriction of the airways in people with asthma. Chronic exposure causes a condition similar to bronchitis. Sulfur dioxide and suspended particles react to form far more hazardous acid sulfate particles, which are inhaled more deeply into the lungs than $SO_2$ and remain there for long periods.

Nitrogen oxides, especially $NO_2$, can irritate the lungs, aggravate the condition of people suffering from asthma or chronic bronchitis, cause conditions similar to chronic bronchitis and emphysema, and increase susceptibility to respiratory infections such as the flu and common colds (especially in young children). Recent preliminary evidence from test animals indicates that nitrogen dioxide may encourage the spread of cancer, especially deadly melanoma (Figure 11-10c), throughout the body.

Many volatile organic compounds (such as benzene and formaldehyde) and particulates (such as lead, cadmium, PCBs, and dioxin) can cause mutations, reproductive problems, or cancer. Volatile organic compounds also contribute to ground-level ozone formation.

Inhaling ozone, found in photochemical smog (Figure 22-6), causes coughing, chest pain, shortness of breath, and eye, nose, and throat irritation. It also aggravates chronic diseases—such as asthma, bronchitis, emphysema, and heart trouble—and reduces resistance to colds and pneumonia. Outdoor exercise in areas where ozone concentrations exceed the safe level (0.12 parts per million per hour) amplifies these effects. Many U.S. cities frequently exceed safe levels, especially during warm weather.

No one knows how many people die prematurely from respiratory or cardiac problems caused or aggravated by air pollution. In the United States estimates of deaths related to outdoor air pollution range from 50,000 to 188,000, and between 150,000 and 350,000 per year if indoor air pollution is included. Millions more fall ill and lose work time. According to the EPA and the American Lung Association, air pollution costs the

A: Up to 80% (smoking, 35–40%; diet, 20–30%; work, 5–15%; and pollution 1–10%)

## The World's Most Polluted City

The air pollution capital of the world may be Cubatao, a heavily industrialized city an hour's drive south of São Paulo, Brazil (Figure 9-3). This city of 100,000 people lies in a coastal valley that has frequent thermal inversions.

Scores of factories spew thousands of tons of pollutants per day into the frequently stagnant air. More babies are born deformed in Cubatao than anywhere else in Latin America. Residents call the area "the valley of death."

In one recent year, 13,000 of the 40,000 people living in the downtown core area suffered from respiratory disease. One resident says, "On some days, if you go outside, you will vomit." The mayor refuses to live in the city.

Most residents would like to live somewhere else, but they need the jobs available in the city and cannot afford to move. The government has begun some long overdue efforts to control air pollution, but it has a long way to go. Meanwhile, the poor continue to pay the price of this form of economic progress: poor health and premature death.

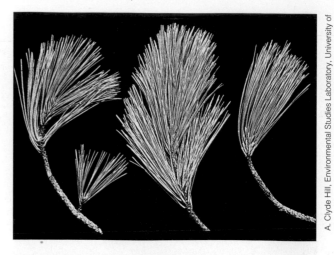

**Figure 22-13** Injury to ponderosa pine needles from exposure to ozone and other pollutants in photochemical smog.

United States at least $150 billion annually in health care and lost work productivity, with $100 billion of that caused by indoor air pollution.

The World Health Organization estimates that worldwide about 1.3 billion people—one person in four—mostly in LDCs, live in cities where air is unhealthy to breathe (Spotlight, above). The global death toll from air pollution is estimated to be at least four times that in the United States.

**DAMAGE TO PLANTS** Some gaseous pollutants—sulfur dioxide, nitrogen oxides, PANs, and especially ozone—damage leaves of crop plants and trees directly when they enter leaf pores (Figure 22-10). Chronic exposure of leaves and needles to air pollutants can break down the waxy coating that helps prevent excessive water loss and damage from diseases, pests, drought, and frost. Such exposure also interferes with photosynthesis and plant growth, reduces nutrient uptake, and causes leaves or needles to turn yellow or brown and drop off (Figure 22-13). Spruce, fir, and other conifers, especially at high elevations, are most vulnerable to air pollution because of their long life spans and the year-round exposure of their needles to polluted air.

Prolonged exposure to high levels of multiple air pollutants from smelters can kill all trees and most other vegetation in an area (Figure 7-26). However, the effects may not be visible for several decades, when large numbers of trees suddenly begin dying off because of depletion of soil nutrients and increased susceptibility to pests, diseases, fungi, and drought (Figure 22-10). This phenomenon, known as *Waldsterben* (forest death), has turned whole forests of spruce, fir, and beech into stump-studded meadows. The five European countries with the highest percentages of coniferous forest damage are Poland (75%), the former Czechoslovakia (71%; photo, p. 531), Greece (64%), Great Britain (64%), and Germany (60%). The overall productivity of European forests has been reduced by 16% because of air pollution, causing damages of roughly $30 billion per year.

Similar diebacks in the United States have occurred mostly on high-elevation slopes facing moving air masses and dominated by red spruce. The most seriously affected areas are in the Appalachian Mountains, which extend from Georgia to New England. Air pollution is also implicated in the recent dieback of sugar maples in Canada and the northeastern United States. In addition, ozone is suspected as the main cause of the reduced growth rate observed in commercial yellow pine forests in the southern United States.

Air pollution, mostly by ozone, also threatens some crops—especially corn, wheat, soybeans, and peanuts—and is reducing U.S. food production by 5–10%. In the United States estimates of economic losses to agriculture as a result of air pollution range from $1.9 billion to $5.4 billion per year.

**DAMAGE TO AQUATIC LIFE** High acidity (low pH) can severely harm the aquatic life in freshwater lakes with low alkaline content or in areas where surrounding soils have little acid-neutralizing capacity. Much

Q: How much of the U.S. hazardous waste is regulated by federal laws?

**Table 22-2  Harmful Effects of Air Pollution on Materials**

| Material | Effects | Principal Air Pollutants |
|---|---|---|
| Stone and concrete | Surface erosion, discoloration, soiling | Sulfur dioxide, sulfuric acid, nitric acid, particulate matter |
| Metals | Corrosion, tarnishing, loss of strength | Sulfur dioxide, sulfuric acid, nitric acid, particulate matter, hydrogen sulfide |
| Ceramics and glass | Surface erosion | Hydrogen fluoride, particulate matter |
| Paints | Surface erosion, discoloration, soiling | Sulfur dioxide, hydrogen sulfide, ozone, particulate matter |
| Paper | Embrittlement, discoloration | Sulfur dioxide |
| Rubber | Cracking, loss of strength | Ozone |
| Leather | Surface deterioration, loss of strength | Sulfur dioxide |
| Textile | Deterioration, fading, soiling | Sulfur dioxide, nitrogen dioxide, ozone, particulate matter |

of the damage to aquatic life in the Northern Hemisphere is a result of *acid shock*. It is caused by the sudden runoff of large amounts of highly acidic water and toxic aluminum into lakes and streams when snow melts in the spring or when heavy rains follow a drought. The aluminum leached from the soil and lake sediment kills fish by clogging their gills.

At least 16,000 lakes in Norway and Sweden contain no fish, and 52,000 more have lost most of their acid-neutralizing capacity because of excess acidity. In Canada some 14,000 acidified lakes are almost fishless, and 150,000 more are in peril.

In the United States about 9,000 lakes are threatened with excess acidity, one-third of them seriously. Most are concentrated in the Northeast and the upper Midwest—especially Minnesota, Wisconsin, and the upper Great Lakes—where 80% of the lakes and streams are threatened by excess acidity. Over 200 lakes in New York's Adirondack Mountains are too acidic to support fish, and in California pollution from automobile exhaust and industries is threatening life in lakes in the Sierra Nevada.

Acidified lakes can be neutralized by treating them or the surrounding soil with large amounts of limestone, but liming has its problems. It is an expensive—and only temporary—solution. Moreover, it can kill some types of plankton and aquatic plants, and can harm wetland plants that need acidic water. It is also tricky to use correctly. If you put lime into the water, it can be diluted and made ineffective by the next rain. If you pour it on the ground so each rain will wash a new supply into a stream or lake, it is hard to know how much of the chemical to put where.

**DAMAGE TO MATERIALS** Each year air pollutants cause billions of dollars in damage to various materials (Table 22-2). The fallout of soot and grit on build-

**Figure 22-14** This marble monument on a church in Surrey, England, has been damaged by exposure to acidic air pollutants.

ings, cars, and clothing requires costly cleaning. Air pollutants break down exterior paint on cars and houses, and deteriorate roofing materials. Irreplaceable marble statues, historic buildings, and stained-glass windows throughout the world have been pitted and discolored by air pollutants (Figure 22-14).

Damage to buildings in the United States from acid deposition alone is estimated at $5 billion per year.

## 22-4 Solutions: Preventing and Controlling Air Pollution

**U.S. AIR POLLUTION LEGISLATION** In the United States Congress passed the Clean Air acts in 1970, 1977, and 1990 giving the federal government considerable power to control air pollution, with federal regulations enforced by each state. These laws required the EPA to establish national ambient air quality standards (NAAQS) for seven outdoor pollutants: suspended particulate matter, sulfur oxides, carbon monoxide, nitrogen oxides, ozone, hydrocarbons, and lead. Each standard specifies the maximum allowable level, averaged over a specific time period, for a certain pollutant in outdoor (ambient) air.

The EPA was required to establish:

- *Primary ambient air quality standards.* These are designed to protect human health, with a margin of safety for the elderly, infants, and other vulnerable persons. According to the 1977 act each of the 247 air quality control regions established by the EPA across the country was supposed to meet all primary standards by 1982, with some extensions possible to 1987; however, many areas failed to meet the deadlines. The 1990 act requires 87 cities that have not met primary standards for ozone to meet them between 1993 and 1999, and 8 severely polluted cities to do so by 2005–2007. Los Angeles was given until 2010, although it must meet even tougher state standards.

- *Secondary ambient air quality standards.* These are designed to maintain visibility and to protect crops, buildings, and water supplies. No deadlines were set for their attainment, however.

- *A prevention-of-significant-deterioration policy.* This policy maintains air quality in regions where the air is cleaner than required by the NAAQS for suspended particulate matter and sulfur dioxide. Otherwise, industries could move into those areas and gradually degrade air quality to the national standards for these two pollutants.

- *National emission standards.* These apply to the 600 or more air pollutants that are toxic in trace amounts. By 1990 the EPA had established emission standards for only 7 of them: arsenic, as-

bestos, benzene, beryllium, mercury, vinyl chloride, and radioisotopes. The 1990 act requires industries to use the best available technology to reduce the industrial emissions of 189 toxic chemicals by 90% between 1995 and 2003.

More specifically, the Clean Air Act of 1990 requires coal-burning power plants (responsible for 70% of U.S. $SO_2$ emissions) to cut their 1991 annual $SO_2$ emissions roughly in half and their $NO_x$ emissions by one-third by 2000.

To help reduce $SO_2$ emissions, the 1990 act allows utilities to buy and sell $SO_2$ pollution rights. With this *emissions trading policy* each utility has a specified limit on their annual $SO_2$ emissions. A utility that emits less $SO_2$ than its limit would receive pollution credits. The utility could then use its credits to avoid reductions in $SO_2$ emissions in some of its other facilities, bank them for future expansions, or sell them to other utilities, private citizens, or environmental groups. Instead of the government dictating how each utility should meet its emissions target, this approach lets the marketplace determine the cheapest, most efficient way to get the job done. If this market-based approach works for reducing $SO_2$ emissions, it could be applied to other air and water pollutants.

Some environmentalists see this as an improvement over the current regulatory approach, which they argue has not led to significant enough reductions in most air pollution emissions after more than 20 years of effort. Others argue that it continues to set a bad example by legally sanctioning the right to pollute, especially if the annual legal pollution limits are not lowered as companies find better ways to reduce emissions. Moreover, if in trading pollution rights a *net* reduction in pollution does not result, no real progress has been achieved.

Congress also set a timetable for achieving reductions in emissions of carbon monoxide, hydrocarbons, and nitrogen oxides from motor vehicles. These standards forced automakers to build cars that emit six to eight times fewer pollutants than did the cars of the late 1960s. The 1990 act requires a reduction in hydrocarbon emissions by 35% and nitrogen oxide emissions by 60% for all new cars by 1994. By 2003 stricter emission standards for new cars will go into effect, and auto-emission controls will be required to last for 160,000 kilometers (100,000 miles).

The 1990 act also requires oil companies to sell cleaner-burning gasoline or other fuels in the nine dirtiest cities (Baltimore, Chicago, Hartford, Houston, Los Angeles, Milwaukee, New York, Philadelphia, and San Diego) by 1995 and to sell at least 150,000 electric or other clean-fuel vehicles in California by 1996, and at least 300,000 by 1999.

Q: What percentage of U.S. children under age 6 have unsafe levels of lead in their blood?

Although the Clean Air Act of 1990 is a good start, environmentalists point to a number of deficiencies in the law. These include:

- Failing to sharply increase the fuel efficiency standards for cars and light trucks, which would cut oil imports and air pollution more quickly and effectively than any other method, and would also save consumers enormous amounts of money

- Failing to classify the ash from municipal trash incinerators as hazardous waste, thus encouraging incineration instead of pollution prevention as a solution to solid- and hazardous-waste reduction

- Giving municipal trash incinerators 30-year permits, which locks the nation into hazardous air pollution emissions and toxic waste from incinerators well into the twenty-first century, and undermines pollution prevention, recycling, and reuse

- Setting weak standards for air pollution emissions from incinerators, thus allowing unnecessary emissions of mercury, lead, dioxins, and other toxic pollutants (Section 21-2)

- Setting municipal recycling goals at a token 25% (which the law allows the EPA and states to waive) instead of an achievable 60%, which undermines recycling and reuse, and encourages reliance on burying and burning solid and hazardous wastes

- Doing essentially nothing to reduce emissions of carbon dioxide and other greenhouse gases (Section 11-2)

- Failing to ban CFCs and other ozone-depleting chemicals by 1995 (Section 11-4)

- Continuing to rely almost entirely on pollution cleanup rather than preventing pollution

**TRENDS IN U.S. OUTDOOR AIR QUALITY** Since 1970 the United States has significantly reduced pollution from five of the six major outdoor air pollutants (Figure 22-15). Emissions of nitrogen oxides have increased somewhat because of a combination of insufficient automobile emission standards and a growth in both the number of motor vehicles and the miles traveled. This has also led to increases in ozone levels in many major urban areas.

Without the 1970 standards emissions of pollutants shown in Figure 22-15 would be 130–315% higher today. Even so, in 1991 at least 86 million people lived in areas that exceeded at least one air pollution standard.

A serious problem is that most U.S. air pollution control laws are based on pollution cleanup rather than pollution prevention. The only air pollutant with a sharp drop in its atmospheric level was lead, which was virtually banned in gasoline. This shows the effectiveness of the pollution prevention approach. If the current 4% annual growth in the miles vehicles travel in the United States continues, annual emissions of nitrogen dioxide, carbon monoxide, and hydrocarbons will rise about 45% between 1995 and 2009 without stricter controls.

Using emission standards to improve air quality on a global scale, especially in LDCs, is a daunting task. Even when emission standards are set, the economic means to comply with them is often lacking and enforcement is weak.

### SOLUTIONS: SULFUR DIOXIDE ($SO_2$) EMISSIONS FROM STATIONARY SOURCES

#### Prevention

- *Burning low-sulfur coal.* This would be especially useful for new power and industrial plants located near deposits of such coal.

- *Removing sulfur from coal.* This would be fairly inexpensive. Current methods (mostly washing) remove 20–50%, but scientists hope to develop bacteria capable of removing sulfur more efficiently and cheaply. Sulfur removed must also be dealt with.

- *Converting coal to a liquid or gas fuel* (Figure 18-13). The major drawback is a low net energy yield (Figure 3-19).

- *Removing sulfur during fluidized-bed combustion of coal* (Figure 18-12). This would remove up to 90% of the $SO_2$ and reduce $CO_2$ by 20%. It should be commercially available for small- to medium-sized plants by the mid-1990s; the sulfur removed must be dealt with.

- *Removing sulfur during limestone-injection multiple burning of powdered coal* (Figure 22-16). This is still in the development and testing stage; the sulfur removed must be dealt with.

- *Improving energy efficiency and shifting to less polluting fuels, especially solar-produced hydrogen gas* (Table 18-1).

#### Dispersion or Cleanup

- *Using smokestacks tall enough to pierce the thermal inversion layer* (Figure 22-7). This would decrease pollution near power or industrial plants but increase pollution levels in downwind areas (Figure 22-9).

- *Removing pollutants after combustion using a flue gas scrubber* (Figure 22-17d). This would remove 70–95% of $SO_2$ and 99.9% of suspended particulate

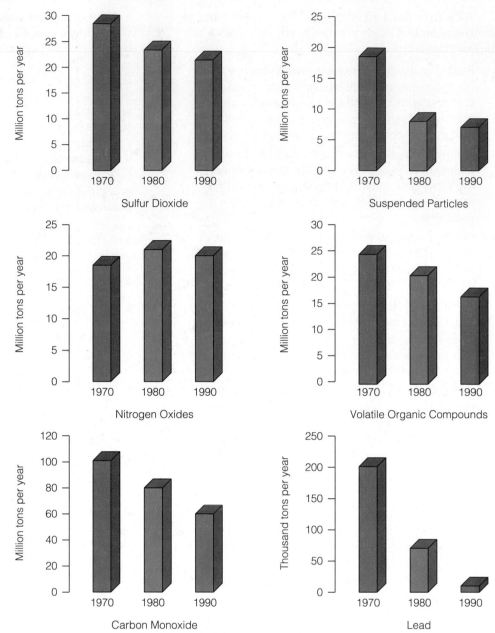

**Figure 22-15** Trends in emissions of six major outdoor pollutants in the United States, 1970–1990. (Data from Environmental Protection Agency)

matter (but not the more harmful fine particles). It can be used in new plants and added to most existing large plants; however, it is expensive and leaves sludge that must be disposed of safely.

- *Removing $SO_2$ after combustion using organic amine salt scrubbers.* This would remove 99% of $SO_2$ and be about one-third cheaper than flue gas scrubbing. Organic amine salt can be regenerated by heating. It is still being developed.

- *Taxing each unit of $SO_2$ emitted.* This would encourage development of more efficient and cost-effective methods of emissions control; however, it is opposed by industry because it costs more than

tall smokestacks and requires polluters to bear more of the costs now passed on to society. In 1990 France became the first nation to impose such a tax; Sweden is considering such a tax.

By 1985 the former Soviet Union and 22 European countries had signed a treaty agreeing to reduce their annual $SO_2$ emissions from 1980 levels by at least 30% by 1993; 4 countries agreed to 70% cuts. Between 1983 and 1993 the former West Germany cut $SO_2$ emissions by 85%. Although the United States did not sign the agreement, it has subsequently passed legislation that will reduce $SO_2$ emissions some 35% between 1995 and 2000 and 55% over a longer time frame.

**Q:** Does the dioxin TCDD cause cancer in humans?

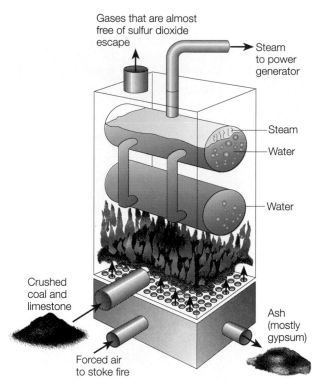

Gases that are almost free of sulfur dioxide escape

Steam to power generator

Steam

Water

Water

Crushed coal and limestone

Ash (mostly gypsum)

Forced air to stoke fire

**Figure 22-16** Limestone injection multiple burning (LIMB). Crushed limestone is injected into a boiler burning powdered coal at a lower temperature than normal burners. The limestone combines with sulfur dioxide to produce a solid ash (mostly gypsum).

**SOLUTIONS: NITROGEN OXIDE (NO$_x$) EMISSIONS FROM STATIONARY SOURCES** So far little emphasis has been placed on reducing NO$_x$ emissions from stationary sources because control of SO$_2$ and particulates was considered more important. Now it is clear that NO$_x$ emissions are a major contributor to acid deposition and that they increase tropospheric levels of ozone and other photochemical oxidants that can damage crops, trees, and materials. The following approaches can be used to decrease NO$_x$ emissions from stationary sources:

### Prevention

■ *Removing NO$_x$ during fluidized-bed combustion* (Figure 18-12). This would remove 50–75%.

■ *Removing NO$_x$ during limestone-injection multiple burning* (Figure 22-16). This would remove 50–60% but is still being developed.

■ *Reducing NO$_x$ emissions by decreasing combustion temperatures*. This well-established technology would reduce production of these gases by 50–60%. However, this may reduce energy conversion efficiency, thereby increasing CO$_2$ emissions.

■ *Improving energy efficiency and shifting to less-polluting fuels, especially solar-produced hydrogen gas* (Table 18-1).

### Dispersion or Cleanup

■ *Using tall smokestacks.*

■ *Taxing each unit of NO$_x$ emitted.*

■ *Removing NO$_x$ after combustion by reburning.* This would remove 50% or more but is still under development for large plants.

■ *Removing NO$_x$ after combustion by reacting with isocyanic acid (HCNO).* Removes up to 99%, but it will not be available commercially for at least 10 years.

■ *Removing NO$_x$ after combustion in flue gas scrubbers* (Figure 22-17d). This would remove 70–90% but is expensive and produces sludge that must be disposed of safely.

In 1988 representatives from 24 countries, including the United States, signed an agreement that would freeze NO$_x$ emissions at 1987 levels by 1995. Twelve western European countries agreed to cut NO$_x$ emissions by 30% between 1987 and 2007. Global emissions of NO$_x$ are expected to rise in coming years as energy demand and number of vehicles in LDCs rise.

### SOLUTIONS: PARTICLE EMISSIONS FROM STATIONARY SOURCES

#### Prevention

■ *Converting coal into a gas or liquid* (Figure 18-13). This would be expensive and low in net energy yield (Figure 3-19).

■ *Not burning coal.*

■ *Improving energy efficiency and shifting to less polluting fuels, especially solar-produced hydrogen gas* (Table 18-1).

#### Dispersion or Cleanup

■ *Using tall smokestacks.*

■ *Taxing each unit of particulate matter emitted.*

■ *Removing particulates from stack exhaust gases.* This approach is widely used in electric power and industrial plants. Several methods are in use: electrostatic precipitators (Figure 22-17a), baghouse filters (Figure 22-17b), cyclone separators (Figure 22-17c), and wet scrubbers (Figure 22-17d). Of these, only baghouse filters, remove many of the more hazardous fine particles (Figure 22-3). Also, all produce hazardous materials that must be disposed of safely, and except for cyclone separators all methods are expensive.

A:  No, but it can promote cancer.

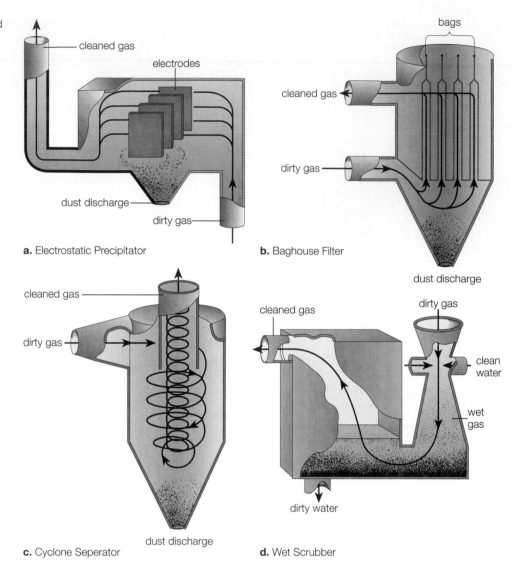

**Figure 22-17** Four commonly used methods for removing particulates from the exhaust gases of electric power and industrial plants. The wet scrubber is also used to reduce sulfur dioxide emissions.

cleaned gas

electrodes

dust discharge

dirty gas

**a.** Electrostatic Precipitator

bags

cleaned gas

dirty gas

**b.** Baghouse Filter

dust discharge

cleaned gas

dirty gas

**c.** Cyclone Seperator

dust discharge

cleaned gas

dirty gas

clean water

wet gas

dirty water

**d.** Wet Scrubber

## SOLUTIONS: MOTOR VEHICLE EMISSIONS

### Prevention

- *Relying more on mass transit, bicycles, and walking* (Section 9-3).

- *Shifting to less polluting automobile engines.* Examples include the stratified charge engine, the hydrogen-powered engine (Section 17-8), and the electric motor—if the additional electricity needed to charge batteries is produced by renewable energy resources that generate little air pollution.

- *Shifting to less polluting fuels, especially solar-produced hydrogen gas* (Table 18-1).

- *Improving fuel efficiency.* This would be the quickest and most cost-effective approach (Section 17-2).

- *Modifying the internal combustion engine to reduce emissions.* Burning gasoline using a lean, or more air-rich, mixture would reduce carbon monoxide

and hydrocarbon emissions but increase $NO_x$ emissions; a lean-burn engine that reduces $NO_x$ emissions by 75–90% may be available in about 10 years.

- *Raising annual registration fees on older, more polluting, gas-guzzling cars, or offering owners cash payments or rebates to retire such cars.* Cars built before 1975 account for only 7% of the miles all cars in the United States travel but produce 25% of the country's automobile emissions. Getting them off the road would result in a much greater reduction in auto emissions at a lower cost than trying to remove the last few percentage points worth of emissions from new cars.

- *Taxing the manufacturer for each new car based on the amount of key pollutants emitted by the engine according to EPA tests.*

- *Giving subsidies to automakers for each low- or nonpolluting, energy-efficient car they sell.*

**Q:** What are the most serious potential dangers from low-level exposure to TCDD?

- *Giving buyers federally subsidized rebates when they buy low- or nonpolluting, energy-efficient cars, and charging them fees when they buy more polluting, energy-inefficient cars.* Revenues from the fees would be used to provide the rebates.

- *Restricting driving in downtown areas.*

### Cleanup

- *Using emission control devices.* This is the most widely used approach. However, current catalytic converters are poisoned by the lead in leaded gasoline (still used in most countries, especially LDCs), work for only about 80,000 kilometers (50,000 miles), and increase carbon dioxide emissions; improved catalytic converters, which should be available in few years, could decrease pollutants further and work for up to 160,000 kilometers (100,000 miles).

- *Requiring car inspections twice a year.* For cars exceeding the standards, an emission charge based on the grams of pollutants emitted per kilometer and the number of kilometers driven since the last inspection would be imposed. This would encourage drivers not to tamper with emission control devices and to keep them in good working order. Currently the emission control systems on at least 50% of the U.S. car and light-truck fleet have been disconnected or are not working properly.

- *Establishing emission standards for light-duty trucks.* These vehicles currently are not effectively regulated by U.S. air pollution control laws.

**SOLUTIONS: TROPOSPHERIC OZONE ($O_3$)** Most $O_3$ in the troposphere results from photochemical smog, which forms when $NO_x$ and hydrocarbons interact with sunlight (Figure 22-6). Thus decreasing $O_3$ levels involves using the solutions already discussed for $NO_x$ emissions from stationary sources and for motor vehicles emissions.

It also involves decreasing hydrocarbon emissions from cars, which produce part of the pollutants that cause smog, and from a variety of hard-to-control sources, such as oil-based paints, aerosol propellants, dry-cleaning plants, and gas stations, which along with vegetation emit much of the rest.

Despite strict air pollution control laws, $O_3$ levels in the United States have been rising. Currently one of every four persons in the United States is routinely exposed to $O_3$ concentrations that exceed standards set under the Clean Air Act.

In 1989 California's South Coast Air Quality Management District Council proposed a drastic program to reduce $O_3$ levels and photochemical smog in the Los Angeles area. This plan would:

- *Require 10% of new cars sold in California by 2003 to emit no air pollutants.*

- *Outlaw drive-through facilities to keep vehicles from idling in lines.*

- *Substantially raise parking fees and assess high fees for families owning more than one car.* This would discourage automobile use and encourage car and van pooling and use of mass transit.

- *Strictly control or relocate industries that release large quantities of hydrocarbons and other pollutants.* These include petroleum-refining, dry-cleaning, auto-painting, printing, baking, and trash-burning plants.

- *Find substitutes for or ban use of consumer products that release hydrocarbons.* These include aerosol propellants, paints, household cleaners, and barbecue starter fluids.

- *Eliminate gasoline-burning engines over two decades by converting trucks, buses, chain saws, outboard motors, and lawn mowers to run on electricity or on alternative fuels* (Table 18-1).

- *Require gas stations to use a hydrocarbon-vapor recovery system on gas pumps and to sell alternative fuels.*

The plan may be defeated by public opinion when residents begin to feel the economic pinch from such drastic changes. Proponents argue, however, that the economic impact of not carrying out such a program will cost consumers and businesses much more. Such measures are a glimpse of what most cities will have to do as people, cars, and industries proliferate.

**SOLUTIONS: INDOOR AIR POLLUTION** For many people indoor air pollution poses a greater threat to health than does outdoor air pollution. Yet the EPA spends $200 million per year trying to reduce outdoor air pollution and only $5 million per year on indoor air pollution.

To sharply reduce indoor air pollution, it's not necessary to establish mandatory indoor air quality standards and monitor the more than 100 million homes and buildings in the United States. Instead indoor air pollution reduction can be achieved by:

- *Modifying building codes to prevent radon infiltration, or requiring use of air-to-air heat exchangers or other devices to change indoor air at regular intervals.*

- *Requiring exhaust hoods or vent pipes for appliances burning natural gas or another fossil fuel.*

- *Setting formaldehyde emission standards for building materials, furniture, and carpets.*

- *Equipping workstations with small, adjustable fresh air inputs (much like those on commercial aircraft).*

A: Immunological, developmental, and neurological effects

## What You Can Do About Air Pollution

**INDIVIDUALS MATTER**

To reduce your exposure to indoor air pollutants:

- *Test for radon and taking corrective measures as needed (Case Study, p. 573).*

- *Install air-to-air heat exchangers or regularly ventilate your house by opening windows.*

- *Test indoor air for formaldehyde at the beginning of the winter heating season when the house is closed up. The cost is $200–$300.\**

- *Don't buy synthetic wall-to-wall carpeting, furniture, and other products containing formaldehyde; use "low-emitting formaldehyde" or nonformaldehyde building materials.*

- *Reduce indoor levels of formaldehyde and several other toxic gases by using houseplants. Examples are the spider or airplane plant (the most effective), golden*

\* To locate a testing laboratory in your area, write to Consumer Product Safety Commission, Washington, DC 20207, or call (301) 492-6800.

pothos, syngonium, philodendron (especially the elephant-ear species), chrysanthemum, ligustrum, photina, variegated liriope, and Gerbera daisy. About 20 plants can help clean the air in a typical home. Plants should be potted with a mixture of soil and granular charcoal (which absorbs organic air pollutants).

- *Test your house or workplace for asbestos fiber levels if it was built before 1980.\* If airborne asbestos levels are too high, hire an independent consultant—not an asbestos-removal firm—to advise you on what to do. (The typical charge is $500 or more, but this could save you asbestos-removal costs of $10,000–$100,000.) Don't buy a pre-1980 house without having its indoor air tested for asbestos.*

- *Attach whole-house electrostatic air cleaners and charcoal filters to cen-*

\* To get a free list of certified asbestos laboratories that charge $25–$50 to test a sample, send a self-addressed envelope to NIST/NVLAP, Building 411, Room A124, Gaithersburg, MD 20899, or call the EPA's Toxic Substances Control Hotline at (202) 554-1404.

*tral heating and air conditioning equipment. Humidifiers, however, can load indoor air with bacteria, mildew, and viruses.*

- *Change air filters regularly, clean air conditioning systems, and empty dehumidifier water trays frequently.*

- *Don't store gasoline, solvents, or other volatile hazardous chemicals inside a home or attached garage.*

- *Don't use commercial room deodorizers or air fresheners (Table 21-2).*

- *Don't use aerosol spray products.*

- *Don't smoke. If you must smoke, do it outside or in a closed room vented to the outside.*

- *Have people take off their shoes when entering your house. This greatly reduces indoor levels of toxic lead dust (Section 21-2) and pesticides picked up by shoe bottoms, which transfer them to floors and especially to indoor carpets.*

- *Make sure that wood-burning stoves, fireplaces, and kerosene- and gas-burning heaters are properly installed, vented, and maintained.*

---

- *Finding substitutes for potentially harmful chemicals in aerosols, cleaning compounds, paints, and other products used indoors (Table 21-2).*

In LDCs significant reductions in respiratory illnesses would occur if governments gave the poor simple stoves that burn biofuels more efficiently (which would also reduce deforestation) and that are vented outside.

### SOLUTIONS: PROTECTING THE ATMOSPHERE

Protecting our commonly shared atmosphere, and the health of people and other organisms, will require the following significant changes throughout the world:

- *Integrate air pollution, water pollution, energy, land-use, and population regulation policies.*

- *Emphasize pollution prevention rather than pollution control.* Widespread use of solar-produced hydro-

gen fuel (p. 446 and Section 17-8) would eliminate most air pollution.

- *Improve energy efficiency (Section 17-2).*

- *Reduce use of fossil fuels, especially coal and oil.*

- *Shift to perpetual and renewable energy resources.*

- *Emphasize distribution of low-emission and better-vented cookstoves in rural areas of LDCs.*

- *Discourage automobile use (Section 9-5). Increase recycling and reuse, and reduce the production of all forms of waste.*

- *Develop air quality strategies based on the air flows and pollution sources for an entire region instead of the current piecemeal, city-by-city approach.*

- *Slow population growth (Section 8-3).*

- *Include the social costs of air pollution and other forms of pollution in the market prices of goods and services.*

Q: What are the two most desirable ways to deal with hazardous waste?

Without this, industries, utilities, and individuals will have little incentive to reduce the amount of pollution they generate.

■ *Recognize that all nations and all individuals have a responsibility to protect the atmosphere—a regional and global common property resource shared by all* (Individuals Matter, p. 590).

As population and consumption rise we generate new air pollution faster than we can clean up the old, even in MDCs with strict air pollution control laws. This shows the need for slowing population growth and relying on pollution prevention.

*We are in somewhat the same position in regard to polluted air as the fish are to polluted water.*

ALLAN V. KNEESE

# Critical Thinking

1. Evaluate the pros and cons of the following statement: "Since we have not proven absolutely that anyone has died or suffered serious disease from nitrogen oxides, present federal emission standards for this pollutant should be relaxed."

2. What topographical and climate factors either increase or help decrease air pollution in your community?

3. Should all tall smokestacks be banned? Explain.

4. Should all remaining uses of asbestos be banned in the United States? Explain.

*5. Do buildings in your school contain asbestos? If so, what are the indoor levels? Should this asbestos be removed? What are the current indoor levels of asbestos fibers in any buildings from which asbestos has been removed within the past five years? If indoor asbestos testing has not been done, talk with school officials about having it done.

*6. Have dormitories and other buildings on your campus been tested for radon? If so, what were the results? What has been done about areas with unacceptable levels? If this testing has not been done, talk with school officials about having it done.

## Learning Nature's Ways to Purify Sewage

Natural wetlands have a great—but not unlimited—capacity to cleanse. They can be used to treat urban sewage, but many have been overwhelmed by pollution or destroyed by development (Case Studies, p. 131 and 144). An exciting, low-tech, low-cost alternative to expensive waste treatment plants is to create an artificial wetland, as the residents of Arcata, California (Figure 17-21), did.

In this coastal town of 15,000, some 63 hectares (155 acres) of wetlands have been constructed between the town and the adjacent Humboldt Bay (Figure 23-1) (the process was a variant of that used to restore degraded natural marshes; p. 146). The marshes, fashioned on land that was once a dump, act as an inexpensive, natural waste treatment plant. The project was completed in 1974 for $3 million less than the estimated cost of a conventional treatment plant.

Here's how it works. First, sewage from sewers is held in sedimentation tanks where the solids settle out. This resulting sludge is removed and processed for use as fertilizer. The liquid is pumped into oxidation ponds where the wastes are broken down by bacteria. After a month or so the water is released into the artificial marshes, where it is further filtered and cleansed by plants and bacteria. Although the water is clean enough to discharge directly into the bay, state law requires that it first be chlorinated. So the town chlorinates the water and then dechlorinates it before sending it into the bay, where oyster beds thrive.

Some water from the marshes is piped into the city's salmon hatchery. Arcata hopes to establish a salmon-ranching operation as well (Figure 14-21) and turn its marsh treatment plant into a moneymaker.

Figure 23-2 At the Providence, Rhode Island, Solar Sewage Plant, biologist John Todd is demonstrating how ecological waste engineering in a greenhouse can be used to purify wastewater. Todd and others are carrying out research to perfect such solar aquatic systems based on working with nature.

**Figure 23-1** Marsh sewage treatment area in Arcata, California.

*Brush your teeth with the best toothpaste. Then rinse your mouth with industrial waste.*

TOM LEHRER

The marshes and lagoons are an Audubon Society bird sanctuary and provide habitats for thousands of otters, seabirds, and marine animals. The treatment center is a city park and attracts many tourists. The town even celebrates its natural sewage treatment system with an annual "Flush with Pride" festival. Over 150 cities and towns in the United States now use natural and artificial wetlands for treating sewage.

Can you use natural processes for treating wastewater if there isn't a wetland available or enough land to build one? According to ecologist John Todd you can—just set up a greenhouse lagoon and use sunshine the way nature does (Figure 23-2). The process begins when sewage flows into a greenhouse containing rows of large aquarium tanks covered with plants such as water hyacinths, cattails, and bulrushes. In these tanks algae and microorganisms decompose wastes into nutrients absorbed by the plants. Decomposition is speeded up by sunlight streaming into the greenhouse, and toxic metals are absorbed into the tissues of trees to be transplanted outside. Then the water passes through an artificial marsh of sand, gravel, and bulrush plants that filters out algae and organic waste. Next the water flows into aquarium tanks where snails and zooplankton consume microorganisms and are themselves consumed by crayfish, tilapia, and other fish that can be eaten or sold as bait. After 10 days the now clear water flows into a second artificial marsh for final filtering and cleansing. When working properly such solar-aquatic treatment systems have produced water fit for drinking.

These natural alternatives to building expensive treatment plants may not solve the waste problems of large cities. But they can help and are an attractive alternative for small towns, the edges of urban areas, and rural areas.

Water pollution is connected with air pollution, land-use practices, and the number of people, farms, and industries producing sewage. Solving water pollution must be integrated with air pollution, energy, land-use, and population policies that emphasize pollution prevention. Otherwise, we will continue shifting potential pollutants from one part of the ecosphere to another until threshold levels of damage are exceeded as more people produce more wastes.

In this chapter we will seek answers to the following questions:

- What pollutes water, where do the pollutants come from, and what effects do they have?
- What are the water pollution problems of streams, lakes, oceans, and groundwater?
- How can we prevent and reduce water pollution?
- What can you do about water pollution?

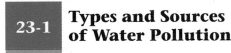

## 23-1 Types and Sources of Water Pollution

**PRINCIPAL WATER POLLUTANTS** The eight most common types of water pollutants are:

- *Disease-causing agents.* These include bacteria, viruses, protozoa, and parasitic worms that enter water from domestic sewage and animal wastes (Table 23-1). In LDCs they are the biggest cause of sickness and death, prematurely killing an average of 25,000 people each day—half of them children under age 5. A good indicator of the quality of water for drinking or swimming is the number of colonies of *coliform bacteria* present in a 100-milliliter (0.1-quart) sample of water. The World Health Organization recommends a coliform bacteria count of 0 colonies per 100 milliliters for drinking water, and the EPA recommends a maximum level for swimming water of 200 colonies per 100 milliliters.

- *Oxygen-demanding wastes.* These are organic wastes that can be decomposed by aerobic (oxygen-requiring) bacteria. Large populations of bacteria supported by these wastes can deplete water of dissolved oxygen (Figure 23-3), causing fish and other forms of oxygen-consuming aquatic life to die. The quantity of oxygen-demanding wastes in water can be determined by measuring the **biological oxygen demand (BOD)**: the amount of dissolved oxygen needed by aerobic

**Table 23-1  Common Diseases Transmitted to Humans Through Contaminated Drinking Water**

| Type of Organism | Disease | Effects |
|---|---|---|
| Bacteria | Typhoid fever | Diarrhea, severe vomiting, enlarged spleen, inflamed intestine; often fatal if untreated |
| | Cholera | Diarrhea, severe vomiting, dehydration; often fatal if untreated |
| | Bacterial dysentery | Diarrhea; rarely fatal except in infants without proper treatment |
| | Enteritis | Severe stomach pain, nausea, vomiting; rarely fatal |
| Viruses | Infectious hepatitis | Fever, severe headache, loss of appetite, abdominal pain, jaundice, enlarged liver; rarely fatal but may cause permanent liver damage |
| Parasitic protozoa | Amoebic dysentery | Severe diarrhea, headache, abdominal pain, chills, fever; if not treated can cause liver abscess, bowel perforation, and death |
| | Giardia | Diarrhea, abdominal cramps, flatulence, belching, fatigue |
| Parasitic worms | Schistosomiasis | Abdominal pain, skin rash, anemia, chronic fatigue, and chronic general ill health |

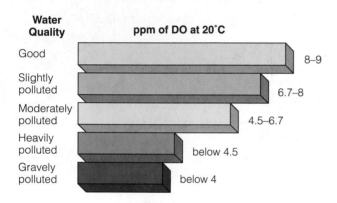

**Figure 23-3** Water quality and dissolved oxygen (DO) content in parts per million (ppm) at 20°C (68°F). The solubility of oxygen decreases as the water temperature increases. Only a few species of fish can survive in water with fewer than 4 ppm of dissolved oxygen.

decomposers to break down the organic materials in a certain volume of water over a five-day incubation period at 20°C (68°F).

- *Water-soluble inorganic chemicals.* These consist of acids, salts, and compounds of toxic metals such as mercury and lead. High levels of these chemicals can make water unfit to drink, harm fish and other aquatic life, depress crop yields, and accelerate corrosion of equipment that uses water.

- *Inorganic plant nutrients.* These are water-soluble nitrates and phosphates that can cause excessive growth of algae and other aquatic plants, which then die and decay, depleting water of dissolved oxygen and killing fish. Excessive levels of nitrates in drinking water can reduce the oxygen-carrying capacity of the blood and kill unborn children and infants, especially those under three months of age.

- *Organic chemicals.* These include oil, gasoline, plastics, pesticides, cleaning solvents, detergents,

and many other chemicals that threaten human health and harm fish and other aquatic life.

- *Sediment or suspended matter.* These are insoluble particles of soil and other solids that become suspended in water mostly when soil is eroded from the land (Figure 5-30). By weight this is by far the biggest water pollutant. It clouds water and reduces photosynthesis, disrupts aquatic food webs, and carries pesticides, bacteria, and other harmful substances. Sediment that settles out destroys feeding and spawning grounds of fish, and clogs and fills lakes, artificial reservoirs, stream channels, and harbors.

- *Radioactive isotopes that are water soluble or capable of being biologically amplified to higher concentrations as they pass through food chains and webs.* Ionizing radiation from such isotopes can cause birth defects, cancer, and genetic damage (Section 20-3).

- *Heat absorbed by water that is used to cool electric power plants.* The resulting rise in water temperature lowers dissolved oxygen content and makes aquatic organisms more vulnerable to disease, parasites, and toxic chemicals.

Total damage from water pollution in the United States is estimated to cost $20 billion per year.

**POINT AND NONPOINT SOURCES  Point sources** discharge pollutants at specific locations through pipes, ditches, or sewers into bodies of surface water. Examples include factories, sewage treatment plants (which remove some but not all pollutants), active and abandoned underground coal mines (Figure 7-25), gold mines (Figure 19-1), offshore oil wells (Figure 3-6), and oil tankers. Because point sources are at specific places (mostly in urban areas), they are fairly easy to identify, monitor, and regulate. In MDCs many

Q: What are the three least desirable ways of handling hazardous waste?

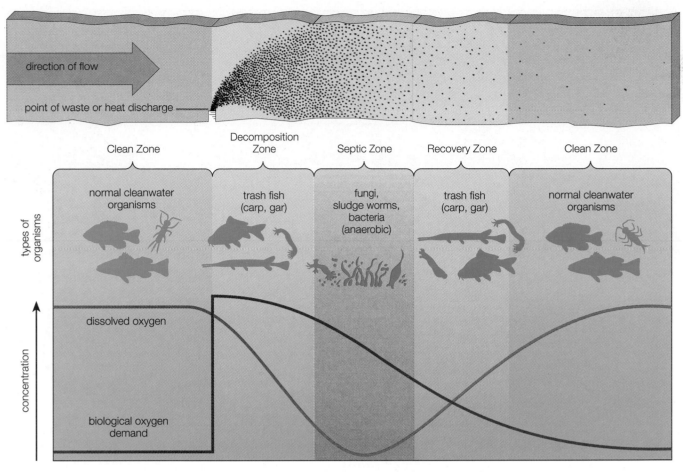

timo or distanco downctroam

**Figure 23-4** The oxygen sag curve (orange) versus oxygen demand (blue). Depending on flow rates and the amount of pollutants, streams can recover from oxygen-demanding wastes and heat if they are given enough time and not overloaded.

industrial discharges are strictly controlled, whereas in LDCs such discharges are largely uncontrolled.

**Nonpoint sources** are sources that cannot be traced to any single discharge. They are usually large, poorly defined areas that pollute water by runoff, subsurface flow, and deposition from the atmosphere. Land examples include runoff of chemicals into surface water and seepage into the ground from croplands, livestock feedlots (Figure 14-2), logged forests (Figure 15-5), streets, lawns, septic tanks, construction sites, parking lots, and roadways.

In the United States nonpoint pollution from agriculture—mostly in the form of sediment, inorganic fertilizer, manure, salts dissolved in irrigation water, and pesticides—is responsible for an estimated 64% of the total mass of pollutants entering streams and 57% of those entering lakes. Little progress has been made in the control of nonpoint water pollution because of the difficulty and expense of identifying and controlling discharges from so many diffuse sources.

## 23-2 Pollution of Streams and Lakes

**STREAMS** Flowing streams—including large ones called *rivers*—recover rapidly from degradable oxygen-demanding wastes and excess heat by a combination of dilution and bacterial decay. This recovery process works as long as streams are not overloaded with these pollutants and as long as their flow is not reduced by drought, damming, or diversion for agriculture and industry. Slowly degradable and nondegradable pollutants are not eliminated by these natural dilution and degradation processes.

This breakdown of degradable wastes by bacteria depletes dissolved oxygen, which reduces or eliminates populations of organisms with high oxygen requirements until the stream is cleansed. The depth and width of the resulting *oxygen sag curve* (Figure 23-4), and thus the time and distance a stream takes to

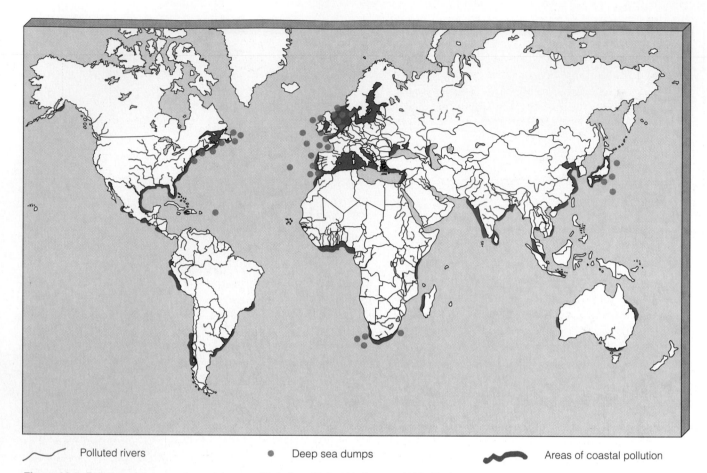

| ⌇ | Polluted rivers | ● | Deep sea dumps | ⌇ | Areas of coastal pollution |

**Figure 23-5** Pollution of rivers and coastal areas. (Data from United Nations and U.S. Environmental Protection Agency)

recover, depend on the stream's volume, flow rate, temperature, and pH level, and on the volume of incoming degradable wastes. Similar oxygen sag curves can be plotted when heated water from power plants is discharged into streams.

The types of pollutants, flow rates, dilution capacity, and recovery time vary widely with different river basins and in the three major parts of a river as it flows from its headwaters to its wider and deeper middle sections and finally to an ocean or lake (Figures 5-41 and 23-5). River basins differ greatly in size, climate, topography, geology, vegetation, wetlands, and land use—all of which influence flow rate and pollutant load.

Requiring each city to withdraw its drinking water downstream rather than upstream (as is done now) would dramatically improve water quality as the stream flows toward the sea. Each city would be forced to clean up its own waste outputs rather than pass them downstream. However, upstream users, who have the use of fairly clean water without high cleanup costs, fight this pollution prevention approach.

**STREAM WATER QUALITY** Water pollution control laws enacted in the 1970s have greatly increased the number and quality of wastewater treatment plants in the United States and in many other MDCs. Laws have also required industries to reduce or eliminate point source discharges into surface waters. These efforts have enabled the United States to hold the line against increased pollution of most of its streams by disease-causing agents and oxygen-demanding wastes. That is an impressive accomplishment, considering the rise in economic activity and population since the laws were passed.

One success story is the cleanup of Ohio's Cuyahoga River, which was so polluted that in 1969 it caught fire as it flowed through the city of Cleveland. That prompted city and state officials to pass laws limiting the discharge of wastes by industries into the river and sewage systems and to upgrade sewage treatment facilities. Today the river has made a comeback and is widely used by boaters and anglers.

According to a 1990 survey of 36% of the total river kilometers in the United States, 37% did not meet standards that permit uses such as fishing or swim-

596

Q: How are 71% of official U.S. hazardous wastes handled?

ming. The truth is we know relatively little about stream quality because water quality in 64% of U.S. stream kilometers has not been measured. And many existing monitoring stations are not located in places designed to assess the presence or absence of pollutants from their drainage basins. Furthermore, even this limited monitoring does not measure toxics and ecological indicators of water quality. Further improvements in the quality of U.S. streams will require more widespread monitoring and enforcement of existing standards for discharges from point sources, as well as massive efforts to reduce inputs from nonpoint sources.

Pollution control laws have also led to improvements in dissolved oxygen content in many streams in Canada, Japan, and most western European countries since 1970. A spectacular cleanup has occurred in Great Britain. In the 1950s the Thames River was little more than a flowing anaerobic sewer, but after more than 30 years of effort, $250 million of British taxpayers' money, and millions more spent by industry, the Thames has made a remarkable recovery. Commercial fishing is thriving, and many species of waterfowl and wading birds have returned to their former feeding grounds.

Despite progress in improving stream quality in most MDCs, large fish kills and contamination of drinking water still occur. Most of these disasters are caused by accidental or deliberate releases of toxic inorganic and organic chemicals by industries, malfunctioning sewage treatment plants, and nonpoint runoff of pesticides from cropland. For example, a 1986 fire at a Sandoz chemical warehouse in Switzerland released large quantities of toxic chemicals into the Rhine River, which flows through Switzerland, France, Germany, and the Netherlands before emptying into the North Sea. The chemicals killed much aquatic life, forced temporary shutdowns of drinking-water plants and commercial fishing, and offset improvements made in the river's water quality between 1970 and 1986. The river is now making a slow comeback.

Available data indicate that pollution of streams from huge discharges of sewage and industrial wastes is a serious and growing problem in most LDCs, where waste treatment is practically nonexistent (Figure 23-5). Numerous streams in the CIS and in eastern European countries such as Poland are severely polluted (Case Study, p. 18). Currently more than two-thirds of India's water resources are polluted, and the Ganges River, which receives untreated sewage and industrial wastes from millions of people in 114 cities, has caught fire twice. Of the 78 streams monitored in China, 54 are seriously polluted. In Latin America and Africa most streams passing through urban or industrial areas are severely polluted.

**LAKES AND ARTIFICIAL RESERVOIRS** In lakes and reservoirs dilution is often less effective than in streams because these bodies of water frequently contain stratified layers (Figure 5-38) that undergo little vertical mixing. Stratification also reduces levels of dissolved oxygen, especially in the bottom layer. In addition, lakes and reservoirs have little flow, further reducing dilution and replenishment of dissolved oxygen. The flushing and changing of water in lakes and large artificial reservoirs can take from 1 to 100 years, compared with several days to several weeks for streams.

Thus lakes are more vulnerable than streams to contamination by plant nutrients, oil, pesticides, and toxic substances that can destroy bottom life and kill fish. Atmospheric fallout and runoff of acids is a serious problem in lakes vulnerable to acid deposition (Figure 22-11). Many toxic chemicals also enter lakes and reservoirs from the atmosphere. Surveys in 1988 and 1989 found that 56% of U.S. lakes and reservoirs checked did not meet the EPA standards set for them.

In any body of water some synthetic organic compounds and toxic metals such as lead and mercury are not biodegraded, and others are biodegraded very slowly. Concentrations of some chemicals, such as DDT (Figure 16-22), PCBs (Figure 23-6), some radioactive isotopes, and some mercury compounds can be biologically amplified as they pass through food webs.

Lakes receive inputs of nutrients and silt from the surrounding land basin as a result of natural erosion and runoff. Some of these become more eutrophic over time (Figure 5-39), but others don't because of differences in the surrounding waterbasin. Near urban or agricultural areas the input of nutrients to a lake can be greatly accelerated by human activities, a process known as **cultural eutrophication**. It is caused mostly by nitrate- and phosphate-containing effluents from sewage treatment plants, runoff of fertilizers and animal wastes, and accelerated erosion of nutrient-rich topsoil (Figure 23-7).

During warm weather this nutrient overload produces dense growths of organisms such as algae, cyanobacteria, water hyacinths, and duckweed (Figure 23-8). Dissolved oxygen in the surface layer of water near the shore, and in the bottom layer, is depleted when large masses of algae die, fall to the bottom, and are decomposed by aerobic bacteria. This depletion can kill fish and other oxygen-consuming aquatic animals. If excess nutrients continue to flow into a lake, the bottom water becomes foul and almost devoid of animals, as anaerobic bacteria take over and produce smelly decomposition products such as hydrogen sulfide and methane.

About one-third of the 100,000 medium to large lakes and about 85% of the large lakes near major population centers in the United States suffer from some

A: Buried in deep wells, ponds, pits, or landfills (64%) and incinerated (7%)

**Figure 23-6** Biological amplification of PCBs (polychlorinated biphenyls) in an aquatic food chain in the Great Lakes. Most of the 209 different PCBs are insoluble in water, soluble in fats, and resistant to biological and chemical degradation—properties that result in their bioaccumulation in the tissues of organisms and their biological amplification in food chains and webs. The long-term health effects on people exposed to low levels of PCBs are unknown. However, in laboratory animals high doses of PCBs produce liver and kidney damage, gastric disorders, birth defects, bronchitis, miscarriages, skin lesions, hormonal changes, and tumors. Some studies indicate that most of these harmful effects are caused by polychlorinated dibenzofurans (commonly called furans) found as contaminants in some PCBs. In the United States and Canada PCBs have been banned since 1976. Prior to that, however, millions of metric tons of these chemicals were released into the environment, many of them ending up in bottom sediments of lakes, streams, and oceans.

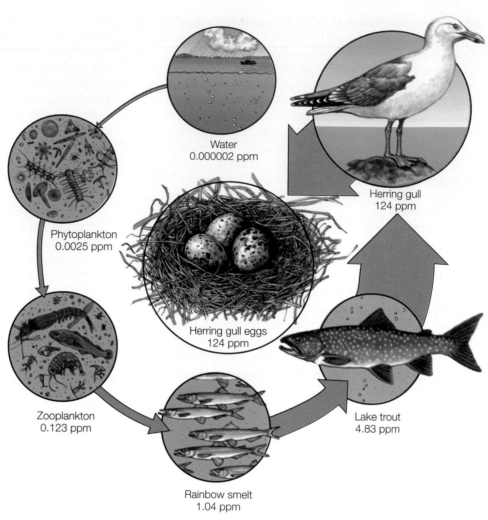

Water
0.000002 ppm

Phytoplankton
0.0025 ppm

Zooplankton
0.123 ppm

Rainbow smelt
1.04 ppm

Herring gull eggs
124 ppm

Lake trout
4.83 ppm

Herring gull
124 ppm

**Figure 23-7** Principal sources of nutrient overload, or cultural eutrophication, in lakes, ponds, slow-flowing streams, and estuaries. The amount of nutrients from each source varies, depending on the types of human activities taking place in each airshed and watershed.

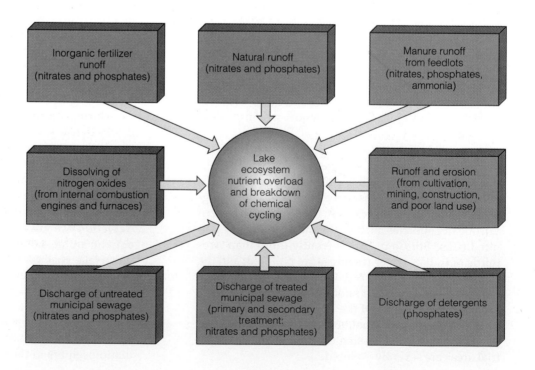

Inorganic fertilizer runoff
(nitrates and phosphates)

Natural runoff
(nitrates and phosphates)

Manure runoff
from feedlots
(nitrates, phosphates, ammonia)

Dissolving of
nitrogen oxides
(from internal combustion engines and furnaces)

Lake ecosystem nutrient overload and breakdown of chemical cycling

Runoff and erosion
(from cultivation, mining, construction, and poor land use)

Discharge of untreated municipal sewage
(nitrates and phosphates)

Discharge of treated municipal sewage
(primary and secondary treatment:
nitrates and phosphates)

Discharge of detergents
(phosphates)

Q: What percentage of official U.S. hazardous wastes are recycled or reused?

W. A. Banaszweski/Visuals Unlimited

**Figure 23-8** Cultural eutrophication in a lake in the northeastern United States. Plant nutrients from agriculture and domestic sources have stimulated growth of algae and aquatic plants. Levels of dissolved oxygen (Figure 23-3) drop when these excess algae and plants die and are decomposed by aerobic bacteria, which in turn can kill fish and other aquatic life, and lower the aesthetic and recreational values of the lake. Hot weather and drought, which lower water levels, can accelerate this process.

degree of cultural eutrophication (Case Study, p. 600). A quarter of China's lakes are classified as eutrophic.

## SOLUTIONS: CONTROLLING CULTURAL EUTROPHICATION

### Prevention

- *Using advanced waste treatment* (Section 23-5). This would remove 90% of phosphates from effluents of sewage treatment and industrial plants before they reach a lake.

- *Banning or setting low limits on phosphates in household detergents and other cleaning agents.* This would reduce the amount of phosphate reaching sewage treatment plants.

- *Controlling land use and using sound soil conservation practices* (Sections 9-4 and 12-3, respectively). This would reduce runoff of fertilizers, manure, and soil from nonpoint sources.

- *Protecting coastal and inland wetlands.* These filter and retain nutrients flowing off the land (Case Study, p. 139, Spotlight, p. 144, and p. 592).

### Cleanup

- *Dredging bottom sediments to remove excess nutrient buildup.* However, this is impractical in large, deep lakes and not very effective in shallow lakes. Also, dredging often reduces water quality by stirring up toxic pollutants in bottom sediments, and it can increase water salinity and changes wildlife habitats. In addition, the

dredged material is often simply dumped into the ocean.

- *Removing or harvesting excess weeds.* Not only does this disrupt some forms of aquatic life, it is also difficult and expensive in large lakes.

- *Controlling nuisance plant growth with herbicides and algicides.* However, the chemicals can pollute water and kill off animals and desirable plants (Section 24-3).

- *Pumping air through lakes and reservoirs to avoid oxygen depletion.* This is expensive, however.

As with other forms of pollution, prevention is more effective and usually cheaper in the long run than pollution control. If excessive inputs of limiting plant nutrients stop, a lake can usually return to its previous state. However, prevention methods have to be tailored to each situation based on the limiting factor principle (Section 4-2).

For example, because phosphorus is the limiting factor in most freshwater lakes, its control should be emphasized; it is also easier to control than nitrogen. There is disagreement, however, over whether phosphorus inputs should be lowered by banning or limiting phosphates in laundry detergents and other cleaning agents, by removing phosphates from wastewater at sewage treatment plants, or both. Studies of over 400 bodies of water indicate that the total phosphate load must be reduced by at least 20% to produce a detectable effect on water quality.

Currently eight states (Indiana, Maryland, Michigan, Minnesota, New York, Vermont, Virginia, and

# The Great Lakes: Pollution and Alien Invaders

CASE STUDY

The five interconnected Great Lakes contain at least 95% of the surface fresh water in the United States and 20% of the world's fresh surface water (Figure 23-9). The Great Lakes basin is home for about 40 million people, making up about 30% of the Canadian population and 13% of the U.S. population. The lakes supply drinking water for 35 million people.

About 40% of U.S. industry and half of Canadian industry are located in this watershed. Great Lakes tourism generates $16 billion annually, with $4 billion of that from sport fishing.

Despite their enormous size these lakes are vulnerable to pollution from point and nonpoint sources because less than 1% of the water entering the Great Lakes flows out to the St. Lawrence River each year. In addition to land runoff these lakes

also receive large quantities of acids, pesticides, and other toxic chemicals by deposition from the atmosphere—often blown in from hundreds or thousands of kilometers away.

By the 1960s many areas of the Great Lakes were suffering from severe cultural eutrophication, huge fish kills, and contamination from bacteria and other wastes. The impact on Lake Erie was particularly intense because it is the shallowest of

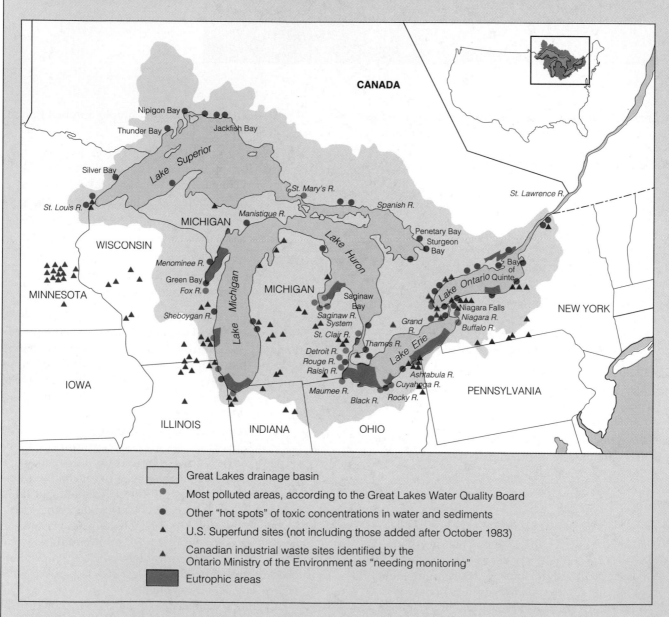

**Figure 23-9** The Great Lakes basin. (Data from Environmental Protection Agency)

Legend:
- Great Lakes drainage basin
- Most polluted areas, according to the Great Lakes Water Quality Board
- Other "hot spots" of toxic concentrations in water and sediments
- U.S. Superfund sites (not including those added after October 1983)
- Canadian industrial waste sites identified by the Ontario Ministry of the Environment as "needing monitoring"
- Eutrophic areas

Q: How many sites in the United States contain potentially hazardous wastes?

the Great Lakes, it has the smallest volume of water, its drainage basin is heavily industrialized, and it has the largest human population. Many bathing beaches had to be closed, and by 1970 the lake had lost nearly all its native fish.

Since 1972 a $20-billion pollution control program, carried out jointly by Canada and the United States, has significantly decreased levels of phosphates, coliform bacteria, and many toxic industrial chemicals in the Great Lakes. Algal blooms have also decreased, dissolved oxygen levels and sport and commercial fishing have increased, and most swimming beaches have been reopened.

These improvements were brought about mainly by new or upgraded sewage treatment plants and improved treatment of industrial wastes. Also, phosphate detergents, household cleaners, and water conditioners were banned or their phosphate levels were lowered in many areas of the Great Lakes drainage basin—a prevention approach.

The most serious pollution problem today is contamination from toxic wastes flowing into the lakes (especially Lake Erie and Lake Ontario) from land runoff, streams, and atmospheric deposition. Toxic chemicals such as PCBs have built up in food chains and webs (Figure 23-6) and have contaminated many types of fish caught by anglers. They also have caused birth defects, reproductive problems, and brain, liver, and kidney damage in birds, river otters, and other animals feeding on contaminated fish. Half the PCBs in Lake Michigan, and 90% of those in Lake Superior, are blown in from industries and other sources hundreds or even thousands of kilometers away.

A survey by Wisconsin biologists revealed that one in four fish taken from the Great Lakes is unsafe for consumption. Children under age 16 and pregnant women are advised not to eat any salmon, trout, or other fatty fish from many areas of the Great Lakes. Other people are advised not to eat such fish more than once per week and not to consume more than 2.3 kilograms (5 pounds) of Great Lakes fish per year.

In 1991 the U.S. government passed a law requiring accelerated cleanup of the lakes, especially of 42 toxic hot spots, and an immediate reduction in emissions of toxic air pollutants in the region. However, meeting these goals may be delayed by lack of federal and state funds. Furthermore, recent studies indicate that much of the input of toxic chemicals—more than 50% in Lake Superior, for example—comes from the atmosphere, a source not covered by the agreement. Meanwhile, environmentalists call for a ban on the use of chlorine as a bleach in the pulp and paper industry around the Great Lakes, a ban on all new incinerators in the area, and an immediate ban on toxic discharge into the lakes of 70 toxic chemicals that threaten human health and wildlife.

Pollution is not the only problem. Since the 1800s the Great Lakes have been invaded by numerous alien species that have sharply reduced populations of commercial and sport fish, and caused other problems. Canals built in the early 1800s allowed the lakes to be invaded by the sea lamprey, a parasite that attaches itself to the body of soft-skinned fish and sucks out blood and other body fluids (Figure 4-42). Between the 1920s and the mid-1950s a combination of large populations of sea lampreys and overfishing devastated populations of commercially valuable lake trout, whitefish, and herring. In 1954 a selective poison was found that could kill the larvae of sea lampreys. By 1962 the poison had caused a sharp drop in sea lamprey populations, and a $10-million-per-year program has kept them under control.

Since the 1980s, however, the sea lamprey has been breeding in large rivers near the lakes that are hard to treat with poisons. Unless other control methods are developed, the sea lamprey may again decimate populations of desirable game and commercial fish in the Great Lakes.

In 1986 an alien species—the *zebra mussel*—arrived when a commercial ship from Europe discharged its freshwater ballast into the St. Clair River near Detroit. The water contained tiny larvae of zebra mussels. Since then the tiny mussels, with no known natural enemies, have run amok. They clog irrigation pipes, shut down water intake systems for power plants and city water supplies, foul beaches, and grow in huge masses on boat hulls, piers, and other surfaces.

These invaders feed on algae, phytoplankton, and zooplankton, which cuts into the food supply of other animals, including various fish species. On the positive side the mussel's voracious appetite for algae has improved water clarity, which allows aquatic plants to thrive as more sunlight penetrates into deeper water. And they may also be filtering some of the toxic pollutants from lake water. This removal, however, is only temporary because the toxins are released when the mussel dies.

This alien species costs the Great Lakes basin at least $500 million per year, and the costs could reach $5 billion by 2000. Even worse, the zebra mussel is expected to spread uncontrollably and dramatically alter freshwater communities throughout the United States. By 1992 it had migrated as far as Tennessee to the south and Montreal to the north; it is expected to adapt to the warmer waters of Texas and Florida by 2000.

There is even worse news. In 1991 another larger and potentially more destructive species—the *quagga mussel*—invaded the Great Lakes, probably brought in by a Russian freighter. It can survive at greater depths and tolerate more extreme temperatures than the zebra mussel. There is concern that it may eventually colonize areas such as the Chesapeake Bay and waterways in parts of Florida.

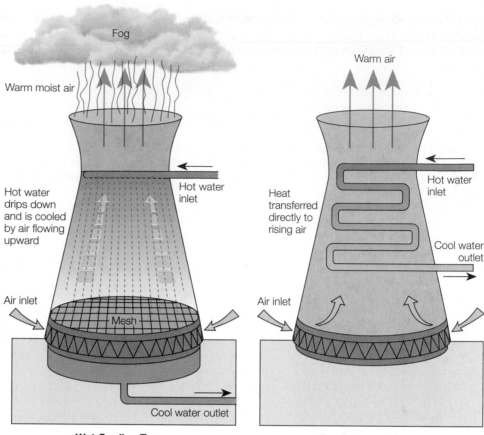

**Figure 23-10** Cooling towers transfer heat from cooling water to the atmosphere. Most new power plants use wet cooling towers because dry cooling towers cost two to four times more to build.

Fog

Warm moist air

Warm air

Hot water inlet

Hot water drips down and is cooled by air flowing upward

Heat transferred directly to rising air

Hot water inlet

Cool water outlet

Air inlet

Mesh

Air inlet

Cool water outlet

**Wet Cooling Tower**

**Dry Cooling Tower**

Wisconsin), many U.S. cities, and many regions in Canada have banned the use of phosphate detergents. The prevention approach has contributed greatly to reducing cultural eutrophication in the Great Lakes and other areas, and has saved taxpayers money.

In some lakes and in coastal waters and estuaries, nitrogen is the limiting factor. It is much harder to control nitrogen than phosphorus because nitrates are more water soluble and run off from large areas of land.

### THERMAL POLLUTION OF STREAMS AND LAKES

Because power plants are only 32–36% efficient, two-thirds of the energy in the fuel they burn is converted to heat that must be dissipated into the environment, usually water. The cheapest and easiest method is to withdraw cool water from a nearby body of surface water, pass it through the plant, and return the heated water to the same body of water (Figure 18-14). Almost half of all water withdrawn in the United States each year is for cooling electric power plants.

This process has several drawbacks, however. For one thing many fish die on intake screens used to prevent fish and debris from clogging the heat exchanger pipes. For another large inputs of heated water from a single plant or a number of plants using the same lake or slow-moving stream can have harmful effects on aquatic life. This is called **thermal pollution**. Removal of vegetation that shades water in streams can also cause thermal pollution (Spotlight, p. 406).

Warmer temperatures lower dissolved oxygen content by decreasing the solubility of oxygen in water. Warmer water also causes aquatic organisms to increase their respiration rates and consume oxygen faster, and it increases their susceptibility to disease, parasites, and toxic chemicals. Discharge of heated water near the shore of a lake also may disrupt spawning and kill young fish. Moreover, fish and other organisms adapted to a particular temperature range can be killed from **thermal shock**: the effect of sharp changes in water temperature when a power plant first opens or shuts down for repair.

Although some scientists call excess heat added to aquatic systems thermal pollution, others—emphasizing the beneficial uses of heated water—call it **thermal enrichment**. They point out that heated water lengthens the commercial fishing season and reduces winter ice cover in cold areas. Warm water from power plants can also be used for irrigation to extend the growing season in frost-prone areas and cycled through aquaculture pens (Figure 14-19) to speed the growth of commercially valuable fish and shellfish.

Q: How many sites in the United States are on the EPA's list for cleanup?

For example, waste hot water is used to cultivate oysters in aquaculture lagoons in Japan and in New York's Long Island Sound, and to cultivate catfish and redfish in Texas.

In addition, the hot water can be used to heat nearby buildings and greenhouses, and to desalinate ocean water, and it can be run under sidewalks to melt snow. However, because of dangers from air pollution and release of radioactivity, most electric power plants are located too far from aquaculture operations, buildings, and industries to make thermal enrichment economically feasible.

## SOLUTIONS: REDUCING THERMAL WATER POLLUTION

### Prevention

- *Using and wasting less electricity* (Section 17-2).
- *Limiting the amount of heated water discharged into the same body of water.*

### Control by Dilution

- *Returning the heated water at a point away from the ecologically vulnerable shore zone.*
- *Transferring the heat from the water to the atmosphere by means of wet or dry cooling towers* (Figure 23-10).
- *Discharging the heated water into shallow ponds or canals, allowing it to cool, and reusing it as cooling water.* This method is useful where enough affordable land is available.

## 23-3   Ocean Pollution

### THE DEEP OCEAN AS THE ULTIMATE SINK

The oceans are the ultimate sink for much of the waste matter we produce. This is summarized in the African proverb "Water may flow in a thousand channels, but it all returns to the sea."

Oceans can dilute, disperse, and degrade large amounts of raw sewage, sewage sludge, oil, and some types of industrial waste, especially in deep-water areas. Marine life has also proved to be more resilient than some scientists had expected, leading them to suggest that it is generally safer to dump sewage and most other hazardous wastes into the deep ocean than to bury them on land or burn them in incinerators.

Other scientists dispute this idea, pointing out that we know less about the deep ocean than we do about outer space. Instead of throwing our wastes into the ocean and hoping for the best, we should keep toxics out of sewers (prevention) and return valuable nitrogen and phosphorus nutrients to the soil. Marine explorer Jacques Cousteau has warned that "the very survival of the human species depends upon the maintenance of an ocean clean and alive, spreading all around the world. The ocean is our planet's life belt."

**OVERWHELMING COASTAL AREAS**   Coastal areas —especially wetlands and estuaries (Case Study, p. 604), mangrove swamps (Figure 5-32), and coral reefs (Figures 4-1 and 5-29)—bear the brunt of our enormous inputs of wastes into the ocean (Figure 23-5). This is not surprising because half the world's population lives on or close to the coast and another quarter lives within 80 kilometers (50 miles) of the sea. Ocean pollution comes from many sources including rivers carrying pollutants from industries, cities, and farms (44%), deposition from the atmosphere (33%), shipping (12%), deliberate dumping (10%), and oil and gas production (1%).

In most coastal LDCs and in some coastal MDCs, untreated municipal sewage and industrial wastes are often dumped into the sea without treatment. The most polluted seas are off the densely populated coasts of Bangladesh, India, Pakistan, Indonesia, Malaysia, Thailand, and the Philippines. About 85% of the sewage from large cities along the Mediterranean Sea, which has a coastal population of 200 million people during tourist season, is discharged into the sea untreated, causing widespread beach pollution and shellfish contamination.

In the United States about 35% of all municipal sewage ends up virtually untreated in marine waters. Most U.S. harbors and bays are badly polluted from municipal sewage, industrial wastes, and oil. They may still be pleasing to look at from shore, but scuba divers talk of swimming through clouds of half-dissolved feces and of bay and harbor bottoms covered with foul and toxic sediment known as "black mayonnaise." They see lobsters and crabs covered with mysterious burn holes and fish with cancerous sores and rotting fins.

Each year fully one-third of the area of U.S. coastal waters around the lower 48 states is closed to shellfish harvesters because of pollution and habitat disruption. In 1991 there were more than 2,000 beach closings in 14 coastal states, mostly because of bacterial contamination from inadequate and overloaded sewage treatment systems. Even worse, many more would be closed if their waters were tested. Ten coastal states do not test regularly for contamination of coastal waters. For example, while New Jersey tests its beach waters weekly, Maryland and Connecticut test coastal waters just once a month, and Rhode Island tests some

## Chesapeake Bay: An Estuary in Trouble

CASE STUDY

Chesapeake Bay (Figure 23-11) is the largest estuary in the United States, and one of the world's most productive. It is the largest source of oysters in the United States and the largest producer of blue crab in the world. The bay is also important for shipping, recreational boating, and sport fishing. Between 1940 and 1993 the number of people living in the Chesapeake Bay area grew from 3.7 million to 15 million and by 2000 may reach 18 million.

The estuary receives wastes from point and nonpoint sources scattered throughout a huge drainage basin that includes 9 large rivers and 141 smaller streams and creeks in parts of six states. The bay has become a huge pollution sink because it is quite shallow—with an average depth of less than 7 meters (23 feet)—and because only 1% of the waste entering it is flushed into the Atlantic Ocean.

Levels of phosphate and nitrate plant nutrients have risen sharply in many parts of the bay, causing algal blooms and oxygen depletion. Studies have shown that point sources, primarily sewage treatment plants, contribute about 60% by weight of the phosphates. Nonpoint sources, mostly runoff from urban, suburban, and agricultural land and deposition from the atmosphere, are the origin of about 60% by weight of the nitrates. Air pollutants account for nearly 30% of the nitrogen entering the estuary. In addition, large quantities of pesticides run off cropland and urban lawns, and industries discharge large amounts of toxic wastes, often in violation of their discharge permits. Commercial harvests of oysters, crabs, and several important fish have fallen sharply since 1960 because of a combination of overfishing, pollution, and disease.

Since 1983 more than $700 million in federal and state funds has been spent on a Chesapeake Bay cleanup program that will ultimately cost several billion dollars. Since 1987 nitrogen and phosphorus from nonpoint sources dropped about 7%, but goals for the year 2000 are unlikely to be met.

Phosphate-containing detergents and cleaning agents will probably have to be banned throughout the six-state drainage basin. Forests and wetlands around the bay must also be protected from development. To add to its problems, the bay will soon be invaded by zebra mussels. Halting the deterioration of this vital estuary will require the prolonged, cooperative efforts of citizens, officials, and industries throughout its entire watershed, with much greater emphasis on pollution prevention.

**Figure 23-11** Chesapeake Bay. The largest estuary in the United States is severely degraded as a result of water pollution from point and nonpoint sources in six states and deposition of pollutants from the atmosphere.

---

beaches only at the beginning of the summer. Maine has the strictest limits on bacteria; New York is the most lax.

Cultural eutrophication affects coastal as well as inland waters. Runoff of sewage and agricultural wastes into coastal waters introduces large quantities of nitrogen and phosphorus, which can cause explosive growth of algae. These algal blooms—called red, brown, or green tides, depending on the color—damage fisheries, reduce tourism, and poison seafood, and have been reported in coastal areas around the world. Moreover, when the algae die and decompose, coastal waters are depleted of oxygen, and fish and other species die. Currently a 7,800-square-kilometer (3,000-square-mile) biologically depleted zone exists in the Gulf of Mexico, near the mouth of the Mississippi River.

**OCEAN DUMPING** Dumping of industrial waste off U.S. coasts has stopped, although it still takes place in a number of MDCs and LDCs. However, barges and ships legally dump large quantities of dredge spoils, materials (often laden with toxic metals) scraped from the bottoms of harbors and rivers to maintain shipping channels, off the Atlantic, Pacific, and Gulf coasts at 110 sites (Figure 23-5).

In addition, many countries, including Great Britain, dump large quantities of **sewage sludge**, a gooey mixture of toxic chemicals, infectious agents, and settled solids removed from wastewater at sewage treatment plants, into the ocean. This practice was banned in the United States as of 1992 by the Ocean Dumping Ban Act of 1988. Some elected officials and scientists oppose this ban, however, arguing that ocean disposal, especially in the deep ocean, is safer and

Q: What percentage of the estimated hazardous waste produced in the United States is regulated by law?

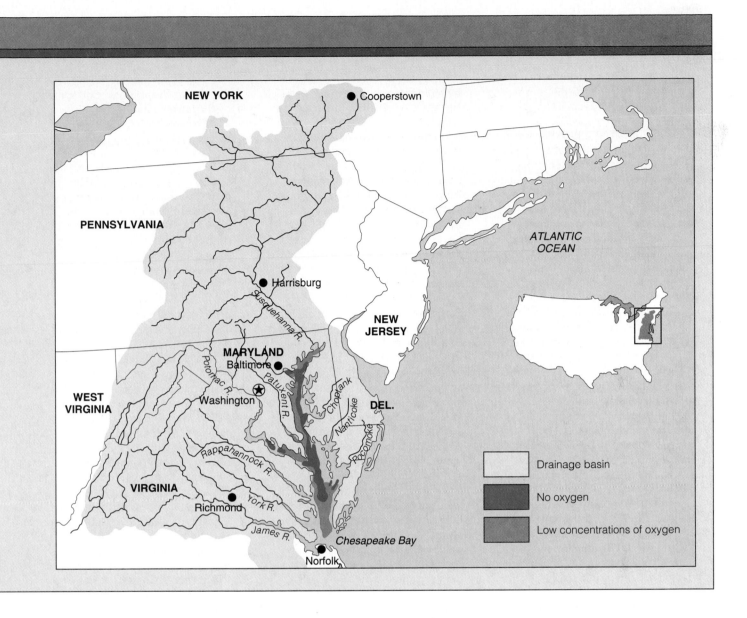

Drainage basin

No oxygen

Low concentrations of oxygen

cheaper than land dumping and incineration, especially for areas like New York City where there are not enough suitable sites for landfills or incinerators.

Ships also dump large amounts of their garbage at sea because it is free; the alternative is paying $500–$1,000 per ship for garbage disposal when they dock. Countries could ban such dumping in waters under their control, and an international treaty could ban garbage dumping in international waters, but such bans would be hard to enforce. Furthermore, most shipowners would save money by dumping at sea and risking small fines if caught.

The United States is responsible for about one-third of all the trash thrown or washed into the world's oceans. Each year as many as 2 million seabirds and more than 100,000 marine mammals, including whales, seals (Figure 19-10), dolphins, sea

lions, and sea turtles die when they ingest or become entangled in plastic cups, bags, six-pack yokes, drift nets (Figure 14-16), ropes, and other debris.

Since 1985 ocean dumping of radioactive waste in the open sea beyond the limits of national jurisdiction has been banned by an international agreement. However, Great Britain and Pakistan dispose of low-level radioactive wastes in coastal areas under their jurisdiction. And in 1992 it was learned that for decades the former Soviet Union had been dumping large quantities of high- and low-level radioactive wastes into the Arctic Ocean and tributaries that flow into this ocean.

OIL POLLUTION Crude petroleum (oil as it comes out of the ground) and refined petroleum (fuel oil, gasoline, and other processed petroleum products;

Crude oil from Alaska's North Slope fields near Prudhoe Bay is carried by pipeline to the port of Valdez and then shipped by tanker to the West Coast (Figure 23-12). Just after midnight on March 24, 1989, the *Exxon Valdez*, a tanker more than three football fields long, went off course in a 16-kilometer-wide (10-mile) channel in Prince William Sound near Valdez and hit submerged rocks on a reef, creating the worst oil spill ever in U.S. waters.

The rapidly spreading oil slick coated more than 1,600 kilometers (1,000 miles) of shoreline, almost the length of the shoreline between New Jersey and South Carolina. The oil killed between 300,000 and 695,000 birds (including 144 bald eagles), up to 5,500 sea otters, 30 seals, 23 whales, and unknown numbers of fish, making this the deadliest oil spill ever in terms of estimated bird and marine mammal deaths. The real toll on wildlife will never be known, however, because most of the dead animals sank and decomposed without being counted. Some of these animal populations are recovering, but others, such as sea otters and murres, may take decades to recover.

Knowledge of the true extent of the damage, based on data collected by hundreds of scientists and on projections about the rate and extent of recovery, is not available to the public because of lawsuits that may take years to resolve. Furthermore, because Prince William Sound was not extensively studied by biologists prior to the accident, there is little baseline data about its wildlife.

In the early 1970s environmentalists had predicted that a large, damaging spill might occur in these waters, made treacherous by icebergs, submerged reefs, and violent storms. Environmentalists urged that Alaskan oil be brought to the lower 48 states by pipeline over land to reduce potential damage. Officials of Alyeska, a company formed by the seven oil companies extracting oil from Alaska's North Slope, countered that a pipeline would take too long to build and that a large spill was "highly unlikely." They also assured Congress they would be at the scene of any accident within 5 hours and have enough equipment and trained people to clean up any spill.

When the Valdez spill occurred, Alyeska and Exxon officials did not have enough equipment and personnel, and did too little too late. After initial attempts to downplay the incident, Exxon responded to intense pressure from government officials and the public by mounting a $2.5-billion cleanup program and promptly establishing a claims process, even though no law required it; the federal government and the Alaskan state government spent another $500 million on the cleanup. However, some parts of the cleanup effort did more harm than good. For example, the use of high-pressure water to clean beaches killed coastal plants and animals. Also, beach cleaning crews and their equipment consumed more than three times the amount of oil spilled by the tanker. And Exxon shipped 27,000 metric tons (30,000 tons) of oil-contaminated solid waste to an Oregon landfill.

In 1990 the National Transportation Safety Board ruled that the accident was the result of drinking by the captain, a fatigued and overworked crew, and inadequate traffic control by the Coast Guard. Despite the fact that between 1984 and 1989 the captain (now retired) had been arrested for drunken driving three times and had lost his license to drive a car, he was still in charge of one of Exxon's largest tankers, carrying a $20-million cargo.

In 1991 Exxon pleaded guilty to federal felony and misdemeanor charges, and agreed to pay the federal government and the state of Alaska $1 billion in fines and civil damages. After tax write-offs and inflation adjustments, Exxon will end up paying about $500 million in fines, with the rest being absorbed by taxpayers through lost tax revenue. Exxon still faces some $59 billion in lawsuits from the Alaskan fishing industry, landowners, cannery workers, Native Americans, and other injured parties.

This multibillion-dollar accident might have been prevented if Exxon had spent $22.5 million to fit the tanker with a double hull. In the early 1970s Interior Secretary Rogers Morton told Congress that all oil tankers using Alaskan waters would have double hulls, but under pressure from oil companies the requirement was later dropped. Today virtually all merchant ships

Figure 18-3) are accidentally or deliberately released into the environment from a number of sources. Tanker accidents (Case Study, above) and blowouts (oil escaping under high pressure from a borehole in the ocean floor) at offshore drilling rigs get most of the publicity, but more oil is released by normal operation of offshore wells and from washing out and releasing only ballast water from tankers and from pipeline and storage tank leaks than from well blowouts or tanker accidents. A 1993 Friends of the Earth study estimated that each year U.S. oil companies unnecessarily spill, leak, or waste oil equal to that of 1,000 *Exxon Valdez*

Q: How much more does it cost to clean up contamination by hazardous waste than to prevent it?

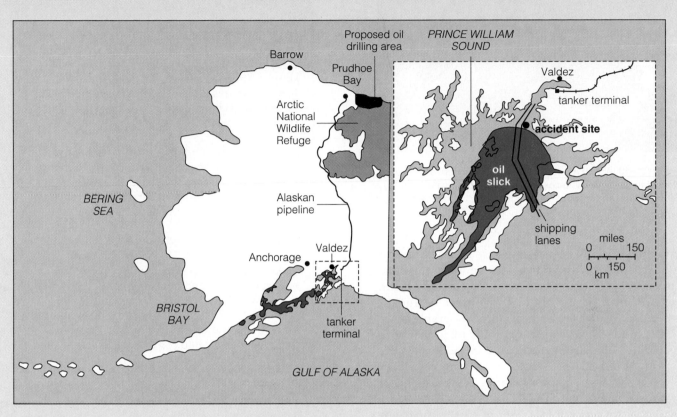

**Figure 23-12** Site of the oil spill in Alaska's Prince William Sound from the tanker *Exxon Valdez* on March 24, 1989.

have double hulls—except oil tankers. Furthermore, a 1992 report by Shell Petroleum indicated that 20% of the world's oil tanker fleet was suitable only for "the scrapyard."

According to Jay Hair, president of the National Wildlife Federation, "This is a classic example of corporate greed. Big oil, big lies. Big lie number one was, 'Don't worry, be happy; nothing's going to happen at Valdez.' Big lie number two was,

'We're doing such a good job with the environment at the North Slope we ought to be allowed into the Arctic National Wildlife Refuge' " (Pro/Con, p. 436).

Others must share the blame for this tragedy. State officials had been lax in monitoring Alyeska, and the Coast Guard did not effectively monitor tanker traffic because of inadequate radar equipment and personnel. American consumers also get some of the blame: Their

unnecessarily wasteful use of oil and gasoline (Section 17-2) is the driving force behind the search for more domestic oil but without adequate environmental safeguards.

This spill also highlighted the importance of pollution prevention. Even with the best technology and fast response by well-trained people, scientists estimate that no more than 10–15% of the oil from a major spill can be recovered.

tankers, or more oil than Australia uses. Although natural oil seeps also release large amounts of oil into the ocean at some sites, most ocean oil pollution comes from activities on land. Almost half (some experts estimate 90%) of the oil reaching the oceans is waste oil dumped onto the land or into sewers by cities, indi-

viduals, and industries. Each year 20 times the amount of oil spilled by the tanker *Exxon Valdez* is improperly disposed of (dumped or burned) by Americans changing their own motor oil.

The effects of oil on ocean ecosystems depend on a number of factors: type of oil (crude or refined),

A: 10–100 times more

**Figure 23-13** A seabird coated with crude oil from an oil spill. Most of these birds die unless the oil is removed with a detergent solution, and many die even after the oil is removed.

amount released, distance of release from shore, time of year, weather conditions, average water temperature, and ocean currents. Volatile organic hydrocarbons in oil immediately kill a number of aquatic organisms, especially in their more vulnerable larval forms. In warm waters most of these toxic chemicals evaporate within a day or two, but in cold waters this may take up to a week.

Some other chemicals form tarlike globs or mousse that floats on the surface. This floating oil coats the feathers of birds (Figure 23-13), especially diving birds, and the fur of marine mammals such as seals and sea otters. This oily coating destroys the animals' natural insulation and buoyancy, and many drown or die of exposure from loss of body heat.

The globs of oil are broken down by bacteria over several weeks or months, although they persist much longer in cold polar waters. Heavy oil components that sink to the ocean floor or wash into estuaries can smother bottom-dwelling organisms such as crabs, oysters, mussels, and clams or make them unfit for human consumption because of their oily taste and smell. Some oil spills have killed reef corals.

Research shows that most forms of marine life recover from exposure to large amounts of crude oil within three years. However, recovery from exposure to refined oil, especially in estuaries, may take 10 years or longer. The effects of spills in cold waters (such as Alaska's Prince William Sound and Antarctic waters) and in shallow enclosed gulfs and bays (such as the Persian Gulf) generally last longer.

Oil slicks that wash onto beaches can have a serious economic impact on coastal residents, who lose income from fishing and tourist activities. Oil-polluted beaches washed by strong waves or currents are cleaned up after about a year, but beaches in sheltered areas remain contaminated for several years. Estuaries

## Groundwater Contamination in Woburn, Massachusetts

**CASE STUDY**  Like many U.S. cities Woburn, Massachusetts, relies on wells to supply drinking water for its 37,000 inhabitants. For decades this industrial town has been home to factories and chemical plants making pesticides, glues, dry-cleaning fluids, leather, and other products.

For years these companies dumped their wastes at a site that was less than 0.8 kilometer (0.5 mile) from two of the town's wells. In the late 1970s tests showed that water from those two wells contained hazardous levels of a number of toxic synthetic organic chemicals.

The wells were closed, but people's health had already been affected. The rate of childhood leukemia in Woburn is two to three times the national average, and 19 children have died from the disease. A study by the Harvard School of Medicine linked the deaths to two industrial solvents, trichloroethylene and perchloroethylene, which had leaked into community wells.

and salt marshes (Figure 5-31) suffer the most damage and cannot effectively be cleaned up.

## 23-4  Groundwater Pollution and Its Prevention

**GROUNDWATER CONTAMINATION** Groundwater (Figure 13-5) is a prime source of water for drinking and irrigation. However, this vital form of Earth capital is easy to deplete and pollute because it is renewed so slowly. On a human time scale groundwater contamination can be considered permanent.

While highly visible oil spills get lots of media attention, a much greater threat to human health is the out-of-sight pollution of groundwater. Laws protecting groundwater are weak in the United States and nonexistent in most countries.

Results of limited testing of groundwater in the United States are alarming. In a 1982 survey the EPA found that 45% of the large public water systems served by groundwater were contaminated with synthetic organic chemicals that posed potential health

Q: According to the EPA, which are the three most dangerous indoor air pollutants in the United States?

Somewhere between 6 million and 15 million underground tanks are used throughout the United States to store petroleum, gasoline, solvents, and other hazardous chemicals. Of these 2 million are large commercial tanks used by refineries, airports, and gasoline stations; the remainder are small tanks, such as home-heating fuel tanks.

The EPA estimates that at least 1 million tanks are leaking their contents into groundwater. Leaks occur from improper installation, corrosion (most are bare steel tanks designed to last only 20–40 years), cracking (fiberglass tanks), and overfilling. Just as all landfills will eventually leak, so will all underground tanks.

The estimated amount of gasoline and other hazardous chemicals leaking from these tanks each year equals the volume of oil spilled by the *Exxon Valdez* tanker (Case Study, p. 606). A slow gasoline leak of just 4 liters (1 gallon) per day can seriously contaminate the water supply for 50,000 people. Such slow leaks usually remain undetected until someone discovers that a well is contaminated.

Determining the extent of a leak can cost $25,000–$250,000. Cleanup costs run from $10,000 for a small spill to $250,000 or more if the chemical reaches an aquifer.

Replacing a leaking tank adds an additional $10,000–$60,000. Legal fees and damages to injured parties can run into the millions.

As of 1993 the EPA requires all new tanks to have a leak detection system, and discovered leaks must be stopped right away. New tanks must also be made of noncorrosive material such as fiberglass. Since 1993 new tanks holding petroleum products or any of 701 hazardous chemicals listed under the Superfund law have had to have overfill and spill prevention devices and double walls or concrete vaults to help prevent leaks into groundwater (already required in 13 states for some or all tanks). Also, each owner of a commercial underground tank must carry at least $1 million in liability insurance—a requirement that has driven many independent gasoline stations out of business.

Even with the new regulations the EPA projects that 62,000 private water wells and 4,700 public water wells have been or will be contaminated by leaks from underground tanks. In 1986 Congress passed legislation placing a tax on motor fuel to create a $500-million trust fund for cleaning up leaking underground tanks. However, this is a drop in the bucket compared to estimated costs of only partial cleanup of such spills, which could run as high as $32 billion.

Environmentalists believe these regulations are too little too late and do little to deal with the millions of older tanks that are "toxic time bombs." Some tanks, especially near large refineries, have been leaking for years but have received little publicity. For example, the estimated amount of oil that has leaked from Chevron's storage tanks in El Segundo, California, is 18 times the amount released by the *Exxon Valdez* incident. In Brooklyn, New York, a Mobil Oil tank has leaked 1.5 times more oil than was spilled by the *Exxon Valdez*.

Environmentalists call for stricter training and certification for tank installers, as is done in Maine and Massachusetts. They also believe that monitoring systems should be required for all underground tanks, not just new ones. In addition, operators of older tanks should be required to carry enough liability insurance to cover cleanup and damage costs, and should be liable for leaks from abandoned tanks.

Twenty years ago the former West Germany instituted such a program, which has been quite successful in reducing leaks from underground tanks. Most business owners in the United States oppose such regulations, believing they are too costly.

Some analysts call for aboveground storage of hazardous liquids so that leaks can be easily collected and detected.

---

threats (Case Study, p. 608). Another EPA survey in 1984 found that two-thirds of the rural household wells tested violated at least one federal health standard for drinking water. The most common contaminants were pesticides and nitrates from fertilizers (which cause a life-threatening blood disorder in infants during their first year). A 1990 study found that more than 4.5 million Americans were drinking water from wells containing excessive levels of nitrates. The EPA has documented groundwater contamination by 74 pesticides in 38 states. About 1% of the wells tested in 1990 had pesticide residues at levels that might cause health problems.

Crude estimates indicate that while only 2% by volume of all U.S. groundwater is contaminated, up to 25% of usable groundwater is contaminated, and in some areas as much as 75% is contaminated. In New Jersey, for example, every major aquifer is contaminated. In California pesticides contaminate the drinking water of more than 1 million people. In Florida, where 92% of the residents rely on groundwater for drinking, over 1,000 wells have been closed.

**SOURCES OF CONTAMINATION** Groundwater can be contaminated from a number of sources, including underground storage tanks (Pro/Con, above),

---

A: Cigarette smoke, radon, and formaldehyde

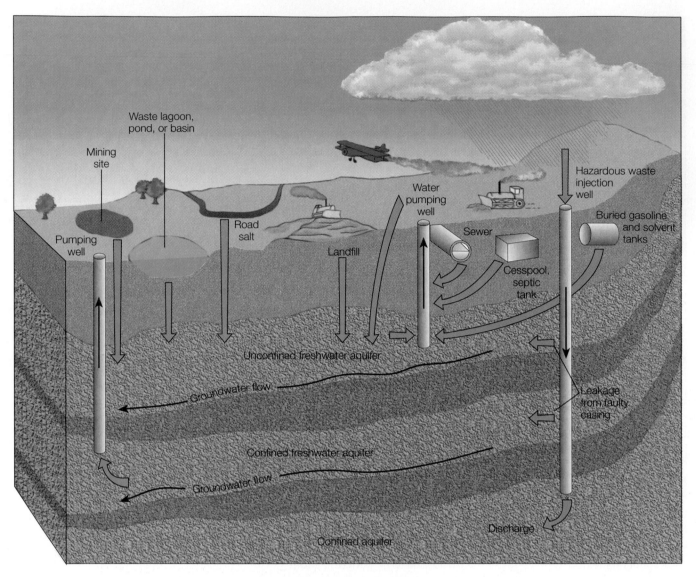

**Figure 23-14** Principal sources of groundwater contamination in the United States.

landfills, abandoned hazardous waste dumps, deep wells used to dispose of liquid hazardous wastes (Pro/Con, p. 559), and industrial-waste storage lagoons located above or near aquifers (Figure 23-14). An EPA survey found that one-third of 26,000 industrial-waste ponds and lagoons have no liners to prevent toxic liquid wastes from seeping into aquifers. One-third of those sites are within 1.6 kilometers (1 mile) of a drinking-water well.

**VULNERABILITY TO POLLUTION**  As contaminated water percolates through the soil into aquifers, some bacteria and most suspended solid pollutants are removed. However, this process can be overloaded by large volumes of wastes, and its effectiveness varies with the type of soil. Furthermore, no soil is effective in filtering out viruses and many synthetic organic chemicals.

When groundwater becomes contaminated, it does not cleanse itself, as surface water tends to (Figure 23-4). Because groundwater flows are slow and not turbulent, contaminants are not effectively diluted and dispersed. Also, groundwater has fairly small populations of decomposing bacteria, and its cold temperature slows down decomposition reactions. That means it can take hundreds to thousands of years for contaminated groundwater to cleanse itself of degradable wastes, and nondegradeable wastes will be there permanently.

Because groundwater is not visible, there is little awareness of it and little public outcry against its contamination—"out of sight, out of mind"—until wells and public water supplies must be shut down. By then,

**Q:** What is the most dangerous indoor air pollutant in LDCs?

pollution thresholds have been exceeded and it is too late (Case Study, p. 608).

**SOLUTIONS** Groundwater pollution is much more difficult to detect and control than surface water pollution. Monitoring groundwater pollution is expensive (up to $10,000 per monitoring well), and many monitoring wells must be drilled.

Pumping polluted groundwater to the surface, cleaning it up, and returning it to the aquifer is usually prohibitively expensive—$5–$10 million or more for a single aquifer. Recent attempts to pump and treat contaminated aquifers show that it may take decades, even hundreds of years, of pumping before all of the contamination is forced to the surface.

Thus the only effective way to protect groundwater resources is to prevent contamination by:

- *Banning virtually all disposal of hazardous wastes in sanitary landfills and deep injection wells (Figure 23-14)*

- *Monitoring aquifers near existing sanitary and hazardous-waste landfills, underground tanks, and other potential sources of groundwater contamination (Figure 23-14)*

- *Controlling application of pesticides and fertilizers by farmers and homeowners much more strictly*

- *Requiring that people who use private wells for drinking water have their water tested once a year*

- *Establishing pollution standards for groundwater*

- *Emphasizing aboveground storage of hazardous liquids—an in-sight, in-mind approach that allows rapid detection and collection of leaks*

## 23-5 Solutions: Preventing and Controlling Surface-Water Pollution

**NONPOINT-SOURCE POLLUTION** Although most U.S. surface waters have not declined in quality since 1970, they also have not improved. The primary reason has been the absence until recently of any national strategy for controlling water pollution from nonpoint sources coupled with population growth in humans and in livestock animals and economic growth (Figure 1-15).

The leading nonpoint source of water pollution is agriculture (Spotlight, p. 373). Farmers can sharply reduce fertilizer runoff into surface waters and leaching into aquifers by not using excessive amounts of fertilizer and by using none on steeply sloped land.

They can use slow-release fertilizers and alternate their plantings between row crops and soybeans or other nitrogen-fixing plants to reduce the need for fertilizer (Figure 12-14). Farmers should also be required to plant buffer zones of permanent vegetation between cultivated fields and nearby surface water.

Farmers can also reduce pesticide runoff and leaching by applying pesticides only when needed. They can reduce the need for pesticides by using biological pest control or integrated pest management (Section 24-5). Nonfarm uses of inorganic fertilizers and pesticides—on golf courses, yards, and public lands, for example—could be sharply reduced.

Livestock growers can control runoff and infiltration of manure from feedlots and barnyards by managing animal density, planting buffers, and not locating feedlots on land that slopes toward nearby surface water. Diverting the runoff into detention basins would allow this nutrient-rich water to be pumped and applied as fertilizer to cropland or forestland.

Critical watersheds should also be reforested. Besides reducing water pollution from sediment, reforestation would reduce soil erosion and the severity of flooding (Case Study, p. 340) and help slow projected global warming (Section 11-1) and loss of Earth's precious biodiversity (Chapter 16).

**POINT-SOURCE POLLUTION** In many LDCs and in some MDCs, sewage and waterborne industrial wastes are discharged without treatment into the nearest waterway or into wastewater lagoons (p. 592). In Latin America less than 2% of urban sewage is treated. Only 15% of the urban wastewater in China receives treatment. Treatment facilities in India cover less than a third of the urban population.

In MDCs most wastes from point sources are purified to varying degrees. In rural and suburban areas with suitable soils, sewage from each house is usually discharged into a **septic tank** (Figure 23-15). About 25% of all homes in the United States are served by septic tanks.

In urban areas most waterborne wastes from homes, businesses, factories, and storm runoff flow through a network of sewer pipes to wastewater treatment plants. Some cities have separate lines for stormwater runoff, but in 1,200 U.S. cities the lines for these two systems are combined because it is cheaper. When rains cause combined sewer systems to overflow, they discharge untreated sewage directly into surface waters.

When sewage reaches a treatment plant, it can undergo up to three levels of purification, depending on the type of plant and the degree of purity desired. **Primary sewage treatment** is a mechanical process that uses screens to filter out debris such as sticks, stones, and rags. Then suspended solids settle out as

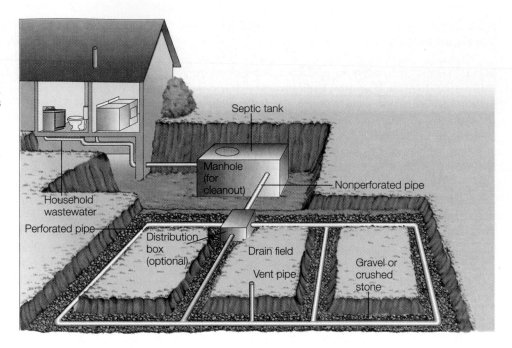

**Figure 23-15** Septic tank system used for disposal of domestic sewage and wastewater in rural and suburban areas. This system traps greases and large solids, and discharges the remaining wastes over a large drainage field. As these wastes percolate downward, the soil filters out some potential pollutants, and soil bacteria decompose biodegradable materials. To be effective septic tank systems must be properly installed in soils with adequate drainage, not placed too close together or too near well sites, and pumped out when the settling tank becomes full.

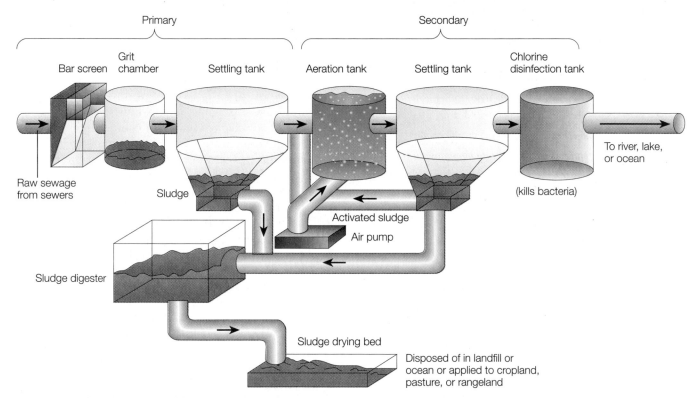

**Figure 23-16** Primary and secondary sewage treatment.

sludge in a settling tank (Figure 23-16). Improved primary treatment uses chemically treated polymers to remove suspended solids more thoroughly.

**Secondary sewage treatment** is a biological process in which aerobic bacteria are used to remove up to 90% of biodegradable, oxygen-demanding organic wastes (Figure 23-16). Some plants use *trickling filters*, where aerobic bacteria degrade sewage as it seeps through a bed of crushed stones covered with bacteria and protozoa. Others use an *activated sludge process*, in which the sewage is pumped into a large tank and mixed for several hours with bacteria-rich

Q: How much air pollution is emitted into the atmosphere each year by a typical motor vehicle in the United States?

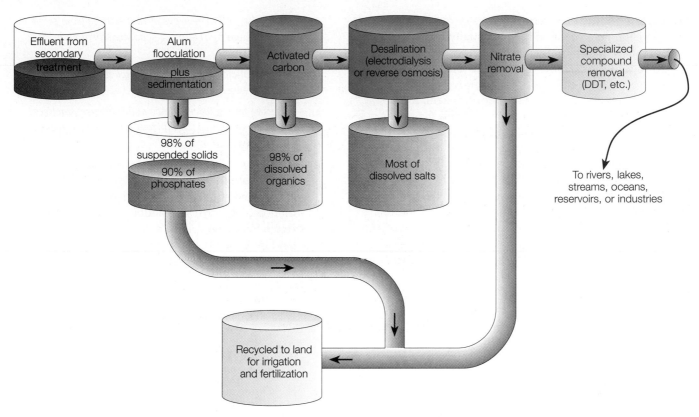

**Figure 23-17** Advanced sewage treatment. Often only one or two of these processes are used to remove specific pollutants in a particular area. This expensive method is not widely used.

sludge and air bubbles to increase degradation by microorganisms. The water then goes to a sedimentation tank, where most of the suspended solids and microorganisms settle out as sludge. The sludge produced from either primary or secondary treatment is broken down in an anaerobic digester and incinerated, dumped in the ocean or a landfill, or applied to land as fertilizer.

In the United States all communities served by wastewater treatment plants must use combined primary and secondary treatment. After such treatment, however, wastewater still contains about 3–5% by weight of the oxygen-demanding wastes, 3% of the suspended solids, 50% of the nitrogen (mostly as nitrates), 70% of the phosphorus (mostly as phosphates), and 30% of most toxic metal compounds and synthetic organic chemicals. Virtually none of any long-lived radioactive isotopes and persistent organic substances such as pesticides is removed.

**Advanced sewage treatment** is a series of specialized chemical and physical processes that remove specific pollutants left in the water after primary and secondary treatment (Figure 23-17). Types of advanced treatment vary depending on the specific contaminants to be removed. Without advanced treatment, sewage treatment plant effluents contain enough nitrates and phosphates to contribute to accelerated eutrophication of lakes, slow-moving streams, and coastal waters (Figures 23-5 and 23-7). Advanced treatment is rarely used because the plants cost twice as much to build and four times as much to operate as secondary plants. However, despite the cost it is used for more than a third of the population in Finland, the former West Germany, Switzerland, and Sweden, and to a lesser degree in Denmark and Norway.

Before water is discharged after primary, secondary, or advanced (tertiary) treatment, it is disinfected to remove water coloration and to kill disease-carrying bacteria and some, but not all, viruses. The usual method is *chlorination*. However, chlorine can react with organic materials in water to form small amounts of chlorinated hydrocarbons, some of which cause cancers in test animals. Disinfectants such as ozone and ultraviolet light are being used in some places, but they cost more than chlorination.

Sewage treatment produces a toxic gooey sludge that must be disposed of or recycled as fertilizer to the land. About 54% by weight of all U.S. municipal sludge is applied to farmland, forests, highway medians, and degraded land as fertilizer, and 9% is composted. The rest is dumped in conventional landfills (which can contaminate groundwater) or incinerated

A: 0.9 metric ton (1 ton)

(which can pollute the air with traces of toxic chemicals; also, the resulting toxic ash is usually buried in a landfill that will eventually leak).

Sewage sludge—sometimes called "black gold" or "Metrogro"—is rich in humus and improves soil structure more than commercial inorganic fertilizers. Experiments show that the sludge can provide all the nitrogen and phosphorus needed to grow corn at about one-fourth the cost of commercial inorganic fertilizer.

Before it is applied to land, sewage sludge can be heated to kill harmful bacteria, as is done in Switzerland and parts of Germany; it can also be treated to remove toxic metals and organic chemicals before application, but that can be expensive. The best and cheapest solution is to prevent such toxins from reaching sewage treatment plants. However, untreated sludge can be applied to land not used for crops or livestock. Examples include forests, surface-mined land, golf courses, lawns, cemeteries, and highway medians.

Conventional sewage treatment has helped reduce pollution of surface water, but it can eventually be overwhelmed by more people producing more wastes. Between 1972 and 1992 Americans spent more than $75 billion on sewage treatment plants. However, by 1992 the amount of organic wastes reaching the country's surface waters was about the same as in 1972 because sewage production grew as fast as sewage treatment. In LDCs and in many areas of MDCs, natural or created ecosystems may be the cheapest and best way to purify wastewater (p. 592).

**PURIFICATION OF DRINKING WATER** Treatment of water for drinking by urban residents is much like wastewater treatment. Areas depending on surface water usually store it in a reservoir for several days to improve clarity and taste by allowing the dissolved oxygen content to increase and suspended matter to settle out.

The water is then pumped to a purification plant, where it is treated to meet government drinking-water standards. Usually it is run through sand filters, then through activated charcoal, and then disinfected. In areas with very pure sources of groundwater, little, if any, treatment is necessary.

**SOLUTIONS: PROTECTING COASTAL WATERS**
The most important suggestions for preventing excessive pollution of coastal waters and for cleaning them up include the following:

*Prevention*
- *Eliminating the discharge of toxic pollutants into coastal waters from both industrial facilities and municipal sewage treatment plants.*

- *Eliminating all discharges of raw sewage from sewer line overflows by requiring separate storm and sewer lines in cities.*

- *Banning all ocean dumping of sewage sludge and hazardous dredged materials.*

- *Enacting and enforcing laws and land-use practices that sharply reduce runoff from nonpoint sources in coastal areas.*

- *Protecting sensitive marine areas from all development by designating them as ocean sanctuaries. In 1993 federal and state officials decided to spend $38.7 million of the civil suit settlement funds from the Exxon Valdez oil spill to buy and preserve coastal land in Alaska that was slated for logging.*

- *Regulating coastal development to minimize its environmental impact, and eliminating subsidies and tax incentives that encourage harmful coastal development (Case Study, p. 139).*

- *Instituting a national energy policy based on energy efficiency and renewable energy resources to reduce dependence on oil (Section 18-6).*

- *Prohibiting oil drilling in ecologically sensitive offshore and nearshore areas (Pro/Con, p. 436)*

- *Collecting used oils and greases from service stations and other sources, and reprocessing them for reuse.* Currently more than 90% of the used oil collected for "recycling" is burned as fuel, releasing lead, chromium, arsenic, and other pollutants into the air.

- *Requiring all existing oil tankers to have double hulls, double bottoms, or other oil-spill prevention measures by 1998.* Recent studies by the National Academy of Sciences and the Coast Guard concluded that double hulls are the best and most cost-effective way to prevent or minimize oil spills.

- *Greatly increasing the financial liability of oil companies for cleaning up oil spills, thus encouraging pollution prevention.*

- *Routing oil tankers as far as possible from sensitive coastal areas.*

- *Having Coast Guard vessels guide tankers out of all harbors and enclosed sounds and bays.*

- *Banning the rinsing of empty oil tanker holds and the dumping of oily ballast water into the sea.*

- *Banning discharge of garbage from vessels into the sea, and levying large fines on violators.*

- *Instituting a nationwide program to collect and safely dispose of household hazardous wastes, and educating consumers to use cheaper and safer alternatives to most common household chemicals (Section 21-3 and Table 21-2).*

Q: How many Americans die prematurely each year because of air pollution?

- *Adopting a nationwide tracking program to ensure that medical waste is safely disposed of.*

### Cleanup

- *Greatly improving oil-spill cleanup capabilities.* However, according to a 1990 report by the Office of Technology Assessment, there is little chance that large spills can be effectively contained or cleaned up.

- *Upgrading all coastal sewage treatment plants to at least secondary treatment, or developing alternative methods for sewage treatment* (p. 592).

 ## 23-6 U.S. Water Pollution Control Laws

**IS YOUR WATER SAFE TO DRINK?** Only about 54 countries, most of them in North America and Europe, have safe drinking water. Currently about 89% of the U.S. population get their drinking water from approximately 200,000 public water supply systems. The other 11%, mainly in rural areas, get their drinking water from private wells.

The Safe Drinking Water Act of 1974 requires the EPA to establish national drinking-water standards, called *maximum contaminant levels,* for any pollutants that "may" have adverse effects on human health. This act has helped improve drinking water in much of the United States, but there is still a long way to go. At least 700 potential pollutants are found in municipal drinking-water supplies. Of the ones that have been tested, 97 cause cancers, 82 cause mutations, 28 are toxic, and 23 promote tumors in test animals. As of 1993 the EPA had set maximum contaminant levels for only 84 chemicals, although it is required by Congress to set standards for 108 contaminants by 1995.

Privately owned wells in suburban and rural areas are not required to meet federal drinking water standards. The biggest reasons are the cost of testing each well regularly (at least $1,000) and ideological opposition to mandatory testing and compliance by some homeowners.

A survey by the National Wildlife Federation found that only 2% of the roughly 100,000 violations of federal drinking-water standards and of water-testing and -reporting requirements, which affected 40 million people, were subject to enforcement action and fines. In 94% of the cases, people were not notified when their drinking water either was contaminated or had not been adequately tested. The EPA's inspector general also reported that the agency was failing to enforce regulations covering 140,000 noncommunity water systems, such as those in restaurants and hospitals, serving 36 million people. More money is spent on military bands each year than on the EPA's enforcement of the Safe Drinking Water Act.

Contaminated wells and concern about possible contamination of public drinking-water supplies have created a boom in the number of Americans drinking bottled water or adding water purification devices to their home systems. This has created enormous profits for both legitimate companies and con artists in these businesses (Spotlight, p. 616).

**SOLUTIONS: CONTROLLING SURFACE-WATER POLLUTION** The Federal Water Pollution Control Act of 1972, renamed the Clean Water Act of 1977 when it was amended (along with amendments in 1981, 1987, and 1993), and the 1987 Water Quality Act form the basis of U.S. efforts to control pollution of the country's surface waters. The goal of these laws is to make all U.S. surface waters safe for fishing and swimming. Since 1972 U.S. taxpayers and the private sector have spent more than $541 billion on water pollution control—nearly all of it on end-of-pipe controls on municipal and industrial discharges from point sources mandated by these laws.

These acts require the EPA to establish *national effluent standards* and to set up a nationwide system for monitoring water quality. The effluent standards limit the amounts of certain conventional and toxic water pollutants that can be discharged into surface waters from factories, sewage treatment plants, and other point sources. Each point-source discharger must get a permit specifying the amount of each pollutant that a facility can discharge.

As a result of the Clean Water Act most U.S. cities have secondary sewage treatment plants. In 1989, however, the EPA found that more than 66% of sewage treatment plants have water quality or public-health problems, and studies by the General Accounting Office have shown that most industries sometimes violate regulations. Also, 500 cities ranging from Boston to Key West, Florida, have failed to meet federal standards for sewage treatment plants, and 34 East Coast cities simply screen out large floating objects from their sewage before discharging it into coastal waters. According to the EPA $12 billion is needed to improve sewage treatment plants that don't meet federal standards, and $88 billion more is needed for new wastewater treatment facilities.

**SOLUTIONS: FUTURE WATER QUALITY GOALS** Once we stop overloading aquatic systems with pollutants, they recover amazingly fast. Doing this requires

## Is Drinking Bottled or Home-Treated Water the Answer?

In 1992 Americans spent $2.5 billion on bottled water, at costs about 1,500 times more than that of tap water. Many bottled-water drinkers are getting ripped off. More than one-third of the bottled water comes from the same sources used to supply tap water.

Bottled water is regulated by the Food and Drug Administration (FDA), not the EPA, and the FDA requires bottlers to check for only 23 of the 30 chemicals municipal water systems must test for. Only bottled water marketed over state lines must meet all federal drinking-water standards, and testing is required every one to four years, depending on the contaminant, except for bacteria, which are tested for weekly. FDA inspectors check bottling plants only every two to three years. Mineral water is not regulated by the FDA or any other agency. In 1993, however, the FDA proposed establishing standards and requiring testing for 50 possible contaminants in bottled water.

To be safe, consumers should purchase bottled water only from companies that have their water frequently tested and certified, ideally by EPA-certified laboratories. Copies of their past year's tests, as well as information on the source of their water, can be obtained and then compared with test results from the source of public drinking water to determine whether the bottled water is worth it.

Before buying bottled water the consumer should also determine whether the bottler belongs to the International Bottled Water Association (IBWA) and adheres to its testing requirements. The IBWA requires its members to test for 181 contaminants and sends an inspector from the National Sanitation Foundation, a private lab, to bottling plants annually to check all pertinent records and make sure the plant is run cleanly.

Several processes can be used in devices for treating home drinking water, each with certain advantages and disadvantages:*

- *Activated-carbon filters* ($200–$2,500). This process removes most synthetic organic chemicals, chlorine, and radon if the filter is changed regularly; however, it does not remove bacteria, viruses, nitrates and other dissolved salts, and toxic metals such as lead and mercury. Also, unless the filter is changed regularly and kept scrupulously clean, it can serve as a breeding ground for disease-causing bacteria.

- *Reverse-osmosis* ($600–$1,000). This process removes most particulates and dissolved solids and some volatile synthetic organic chemicals. However, it does not remove radon, arsenic, chloroform, and phenol; some models don't do well in removing bacteria and viruses; filters must be changed regularly; calcium must be removed by a water softener; and water must have a pH level below 8. In addition, this process wastes 15 liters (4 gallons) of water for each 4 liters (1 gallon) it produces.

- *Distillation* ($200–$700). This process removes toxic metals, radioactive contamination, and nonvolatile organic compounds, and kills bacteria. However, it does not remove volatile organic chemicals (like chloroform) or radon, it is expensive to operate, it uses lots of energy, it produces flat-tasting water, and it is a slow process with low output. Also, the equipment must be cleaned and serviced regularly.

- *Ultraviolet light*. UV light kills most bacteria and some viruses but does not remove other pollutants.

- *Water softeners* ($1,000). These remove dissolved minerals and prevent scales in water pipes and equipment, but they do not remove bacteria, viruses, and most other toxic substances.

Machines that combine several approaches can remove most pollutants if they are properly maintained at a cost of at least $100 per year. Before buying expensive purifiers, consumers should have their water tested by local health authorities or private labs to find out what contaminants, if any, need to be removed, and then buy a unit that does the job.

Buyers should be suspicious of door-to-door salespeople, telephone appeals, and scare tactics. They should carefully check out companies selling such equipment and demand a copy of purifying claims made by EPA-certified laboratories.

*See *Consumer Reports*, January 1990, pp. 27–43, for an evaluation of water treatment equipment.

---

that we shift from pollution cleanup to pollution prevention. To make such a shift we must truly accept that the environment—air, water, soil, life—is an interconnected whole. Without an integrated approach to all forms of pollution, we will continue to shift environmental problems from one part of the environment to another.

Individuals can contribute to bringing about this change in the way we view and act in the world by reducing their contributions to water pollution (Individuals Matter, p. 617).

*The reason we have water pollution is not basically the paper or pulp mills. It is, rather, the*

Q: Worldwide, how many people live in cities where outdoor air is unhealthy to breathe?

## What You Can Do About Water Pollution

**INDIVIDUALS MATTER**

- *Use and waste less water (Individuals Matter, p. 356).*

- *Use less harmful substances instead of commercial chemicals for most household cleaners (Table 21-2).*

- *Use low-phosphate, phosphate-free, or biodegradable dishwashing liquid, laundry detergent, and shampoo.*

- *Don't use water fresheners in toilets.*

- *Use manure or compost instead of commercial inorganic fertilizers to fertilize garden and yard plants.*

- *Use biological methods or integrated pest management to control garden, yard, and household pests (Section 24-5).*

- *Don't pour pesticides, paints, solvents, oil, or other products containing harmful chemicals down the drain or on the ground.* Contact your local Health Department about disposal.

- *Recycle old motor oil and antifreeze at an auto service center or auto parts center that has an oil recycling program.*

- *If you get water from a private well or suspect that municipal water is contaminated, have it tested by an EPA-certified laboratory for lead, nitrates, trihalomethanes, radon, volatile organic compounds, and pesticides.*

- *Run water from taps for several minutes every morning before using the water for drinking or cooking. Save it and use it to water plants.*

- *If you have a septic tank, monitor it yearly and have it cleaned out every three to five years by a reputable contractor so that it won't contribute to groundwater pollution. Do not use septic tank cleaners,* which contain toxic chemicals that can kill bacteria important to sewage decomposition and that can contaminate groundwater if the system malfunctions.

- *Support ecological land-use plan-*

*ning in your community (Solutions, p. 248, left).*

- *Get to know your local bodies of water and form community watchdog groups to help monitor, protect, and restore them.*

- *Support efforts to clean up riverfronts and harbors.* San Antonio's restoration of the San Antonio River to create a riverwalk (Figure 9-17) brings in 1 million tourists and $6.6 billion per year. Cities such as Boulder, Colo.; Boise, Idaho; Portland, Ore.; Berkeley, Calif.; Boston, Lowell, and Groton (p. 658), Mass.; Baltimore, Md.; Chattanooga, Tenn.; and London, England have achieved ecological and economic benefits from restoration of urban waters.

- *Support tougher water and air pollution control laws and their enforcement at the local, state, and federal levels with emphasis on pollution prevention.*

*social side of humans—our unwillingness to support reform government, to place into office the best-qualified candidates, to keep in office the best talent, and to see to it that legislation both evolves from and inspires wise social planning with a human orientation.*

STEWART L. UDALL

## Critical Thinking

1. Why is dilution not always the solution to water pollution? Give examples and conditions for which this solution is, and is not, applicable.

2. How can a stream cleanse itself of oxygen-demanding wastes? Under what conditions will this natural cleansing system fail?

3. Should all dumping of wastes in the ocean be banned? Explain. If so, where would you put the wastes instead? What exceptions would you permit, and why?

4. Why will banning ocean dumping alone not stop ocean pollution?

5. Should the injection of hazardous wastes into deep-underground wells be banned? Explain. What would you do with these wastes?

*6. In your community:
   a. What are the principal nonpoint sources of contamination of surface water and groundwater?
   b. What is the source of drinking water?
   c. How is drinking water treated?
   d. What contaminants are tested for?
   e. Has drinking water been analyzed recently for the presence of synthetic organic chemicals, especially chlorinated hydrocarbons? If so, were any found, and are they being removed?
   f. How many times during each of the past five years have levels of tested contaminants violated federal standards? Was the public notified about the violations?

# 24 Pesticides and Pest Control

## Along Came a Spider

The longest war in human history is our war against insects. This war was declared about 10,000 years ago, when we first got serious about agriculture, and we are no closer to winning today than we were then. In fact, the multitudes of insects that share our fondness for rice and corn, cotton and wheat, and beans and apples seem to be gaining on us.

In 1962 biologist Rachel Carson warned against relying on synthetic chemicals to kill insects and other species we deem pests. Chinese farmers have recently decided it's time to change strategies. Instead of spraying their rice and cotton fields with poison, they began to build little straw huts here and there around the fields in the fall.

If this sounds crazy, it was crazy like a fox. These farmers were giving aid and comfort to insects' worst enemy, one that has hunted them for millions rather than thousands of years: the spider. The little huts were for hibernating spiders. Protected from the worst of the cold, far more of them would awaken next spring. Ravenous after their winter fast, they would scuttle off into the fields to stalk their insect prey.

Even without human help the world's 30,000 known species of spiders kill far more insects every year than insecticides do (Figure 24-1). No more than 2% of all the insecticide sprayed on a field finds its target, but every spider gets insect meals—or it does not live to reproduce. Spraying a field with pesticides is like using saturation bombing. It kills almost everything—the target pests and often the spiders and other species that help control those pests. Recruiting spiders for our war against insects is like sending in heat-sensing missiles to hit specific targets.

**Figure 24-1** Biological control of pests by spiders—insects' worst enemies. Most spiders, like the crab spider (right) and the wolf spider (above) are harmless to humans and play an important role in keeping insects in check.

Apparently spiders are not only dedicated insect killers but astonishingly patient. Unlike ladybugs or wasps they do not abandon a field if the hunting turns poor, but wait, even for weeks, until the next wave of insects arrives.

Entomologist Willard H. Whitcomb found that leaving strips of weeds around cotton and soybean fields provides the kind of undergrowth favored by insect-eating wolf spiders (Figure 24-1). He also sings the praises of one type of banana spider, which lives in warm climates and can keep a house clear of cockroaches. In Maine Daniel Jennings of the U.S. Forest Service uses spiders to help control the spruce budworm, which devastates the Northeast's spruce and fir forests. Spiders also attack the much-feared gypsy moth, which devastates tree foliage.

The idea of encouraging populations of spiders in fields, forests, and even houses scares most people because spiders have gotten bad press. Also, perhaps because of their eight legs and numerous eyes, they look like dangerous space aliens instead of the helpful and mostly harmless creatures they are. Although a few species of spiders are dangerous to people, such as the black widow and brown recluse, the vast majority—including the ferocious-looking wolf spider—are harmless to humans. Even the giant tarantula rarely bites people, and its venom is too weak to harm us and other large mammals.

As biologist Thomas Eisner puts it, "Bugs are not going to inherit the earth. They own it now. So we might as well make peace with the landlord." As we seek new ways to coexist with the real rulers of the planet, we would do well to be sure spiders are in our corner.

This chapter looks first at the conventional chemical approach to pest control and then discusses alternatives based on working with nature. Some of these —like using spiders and other natural predators to kill pest insects—are not new. Their virtues merely need to be rediscovered. Others—such as genetically engineering food crops to resist specific pests—did not exist a mere decade ago.

This chapter will answer the following questions:

- What types of pesticides are used?
- What are the pros and cons of using chemicals to kill insects and weeds?
- How well is pesticide usage regulated in the United States?
- What alternatives are there to using pesticides?

## 24-1 Pesticides: Types and Uses

**POPULATION CONTROL IN NATURE** As Emerson's quote opening this chapter reminds us, there are no pests in nature. Classifying something as a **pest** is a human judgment about any species that competes with us for food, messes up lawns, destroys wood in houses, spreads disease (Case Study, p. 540), or is simply a nuisance.

About 99% of the species of plants, animals, and microbes benefit agriculture and other sectors of the economy. In diverse ecosystems populations of species, including the less than 1% we have classified as pests, are kept in control by their natural enemies (predators, parasites, and disease organisms)—another crucial type of Earth capital. When we simplify ecosystems we upset these natural checks and balances that keep any one species from taking over for very long. Then we have to figure out ways to protect crops, tree farms, and lawns from "pests" that nature used to control at no charge.

Mostly we have done this by developing a variety of **pesticides** (or *biocides*): chemicals to kill organisms we consider undesirable. Common types of pesticides include **insecticides** (insect-killers), **herbicides** (weed-killers), **fungicides** (fungus-killers), **nematocides** (roundworm-killers), and **rodenticides** (rat- and mouse-killers).

However, humans didn't invent the use of chemicals to repel or kill other species. Plants have been developing chemicals to ward off or poison herbivores

that feed on them for 225 million years. This is a never-ending, ever-changing process: Herbivores overcome various plant defenses through natural selection; then the plants use natural selection to develop new defenses. Monarch butterflies (Figure 4-5), golden toads (Figure 4-34), and bombardier beetles also wage chemical warfare against their predators.

Chemical warfare is only one of many ways species protect themselves or increase their chances of getting enough food. Other strategies include protective shells (Figure 16-3), thick bark (Figure 4-9), thorns (Figure 4-10), camouflage (Figure 4-39), division of resources through specialization to avoid direct competition (Figures 4-37 and 4-38), and cooperating with other species through mutualism (Figure 4-43) and commensalism (Figure 4-44).

The result of these dynamic interactions between predator and prey species is what biologists call *coevolution* (Section 6-3). The lesson to be learned from nature is that long-term survival requires a kaleidoscope of strategies and the ability to change from one to another as needed.

Early hunters and gatherers (Figure 2-5) survived by letting nature do the work and then taking enough plants and animals to survive, but not so many as to upset nature's built-in checks and balances. Early farmers practiced sustainable slash-and-burn and shifting cultivation on a small-scale basis (Figure 2-6), often growing a mixture of crops (Case Study, p. 367) to provide enough food and to mimic nature by using biodiversity to keep pest populations under control.

**FIRST-GENERATION PESTICIDES AND REPELLENTS** As the human population grew and agriculture spread, people began looking for better ways to protect their crops, mostly by using chemicals to kill or repel insects. For example, sulfur was used as an insecticide well before 500 B.C. By the fifteenth centu-

Q: How much is U.S. food production reduced by air pollution?

doorways and patios and by hanging a series of polyethylene strips in front of entry doors (like the ones you see on some grocery store coolers); grow sweet basil in the kitchen; place sweet clover in small bags made of mosquito netting and hang them around the room; hang nontoxic flypaper (made by applying honey to strips of yellow paper) from the ceiling; don't use pest strips, which expose people to potentially hazardous chemicals.

### Termites

- Make sure that the soil around and under your home is well drained and that crawl spaces are dry and well ventilated; remove scrap wood, stumps, sawdust, cardboard, firewood, and other sources of cellulose close to the house; replace heavily damaged or rotted sills, joists, or flooring; fill holes in concrete or masonry with mortar grout.

- In new construction install a termite shield between the foundation and floor joists, and don't let untreated wood touch soil.

- Inspect for damage each year, and if infestation is discovered apply a heat lamp for 10 minutes to any infested area; nematodes (tiny parasitic worms) can also be used; for a large infestation have your house treated by a professional using one of the new termicides such as Dursban, Torpedo, or Dragnet. Safer treatments include freezing termites to death by pouring liquid nitrogen into walls and infested areas, using a growth regulator to transform young termites into soldiers instead of workers needed to feed a colony, using antibiotics to kill the wood-digesting microorganisms that live inside termites, and using heat treatments and low-voltage electric shocks to kill them.

### Fleas

- Keep fleas off pets by using flea-repellent green-dye soaps and by feeding them brewer's yeast or vitamin B.

- Vacuum often, and toss a couple of mothballs into the vacuum cleaner bag to kill fleas sucked into the bag.

- Dust your pet with flea powders made from eucalyptus, sage, tobacco, wormwood, bay leaf, or vetiver.

- Mix essential oils such as citronella, cedarwood, eucalyptus, pennyroyal, orange, sassafras, geranium, clove, or mint with water, and use for pet dips and shampoos.

- Do not use flea collars or flea preparations containing synthetic insecticides, which contain chemicals that can cause cancer, nerve damage, and mutations in pets, and which may be a hazard to humans (especially small children).

### Garden Pests

- Use natural predators (Figure 24-1).

- Mix up and spray garden plants with one or more of the following solutions: Steep one handful of tobacco in warm water for 24 hours (handle with care); mix 2–3 very hot peppers, ½ onion, and 1 clove of garlic in water, boil, let sit for two days, and strain; mix 2 tablespoons of garlic juice, 1 teaspoon of rubbing alcohol, and 1 ounce of diatomaceous earth in 4 quarts of water; mix 2 tablespoons of liquid soap in 1 quart of water or 2 ounces of dry soap in 1 quart of water.

---

ry A.D. toxic compounds of arsenic, lead, and mercury were being applied to crops as insecticides, an approach that was abandoned in the late 1920s when the increasing number of human poisonings and fatalities encouraged a search for less toxic substitutes. However, traces of these nondegradable toxic metals are still being taken up by tobacco, vegetables, and other crops grown on soil dosed with them long ago.

In the seventeenth century nicotine sulfate, extracted from tobacco leaves, came into use as an insecticide. In the mid-1800s two more natural pesticides were introduced. One was pyrethrum, obtained from the heads of chrysanthemum flowers; the other was rotenone, from the root of the derris plant and other tropical forest legumes. These *first-generation pesticides* were mainly natural substances borrowed from plants that had been at war with insects for eons.

For hundreds of years people have taken another lesson from nature and used chemicals to repel insects.

Such repellents include red pepper (ants) and garlic and lemon oils (fleas, mosquito larvae, houseflies, and other insects). Today natural repellents and predators are becoming more popular to control common household pests (Solutions, p. 620). Plants can also be used to attract beneficial insects.*

**SECOND-GENERATION PESTICIDES** A major pest control revolution began in 1939, when entomologist Paul Mueller discovered that DDT (dichlorodiphenyltrichloroethane), a chemical known since 1874, was a potent insecticide. DDT soon became the world's most-used pesticide, and Mueller received the Nobel Prize in 1948. DDT was the first of the so-called *second-generation pesticides*. Since 1945 chemists have developed many such synthetic organic pesticides for use

---

* See Robert Kourik. 1993. "Flower Power." *Garbage* May/June, 26–31.

in crop fields, homes, gardens, tree farms, lawns, and golf courses.

Worldwide about 2.3 million metric tons (2.5 million tons) are used yearly—0.45 kilogram (1 pound) for each person on Earth. About 75% of these chemicals are used in MDCs, but use in LDCs is soaring.

In the United States about 600 biologically active (pest-killing) ingredients and 1,475 inert (non-pest-killing) ingredients are mixed to make some 35,000 different pesticide products. Between 1964 and 1981 pesticide use in the United States almost tripled, but it has leveled off at around 500 million kilograms (1.1 billion pounds) per year, or about 2 kilograms (4.4 pounds) per person per year—over four times the global average. Pesticides are big business, with annual sales in the United States alone of more than $4.6 billion and global sales of about $20 billion.

In 1991 herbicides accounted for 84% of all pesticides used by U.S. farmers, insecticides 14%, and fungicides 2%. Four crops—corn, cotton, wheat, and soybeans—account for about 70% of the insecticides and 80% of the herbicides used on crops in the United States. Fungicides are used primarily to treat seeds and to protect fruits, potatoes, and vegetables from fungal diseases during growth and after harvest.

About 30% of the pesticides used in the United States are to rid houses, gardens, lawns, parks, playing fields, swimming pools, and golf courses of unwanted pests. The average U.S. homeowner applies three to six times more pesticide per hectare than do farmers. Pesticides are added to products as diverse as paints, some shampoos, carpets, mattresses, and contact lenses.

**TYPES OF PESTICIDES** Some pesticides, called *broad-spectrum agents*, are toxic to many species. A broad-spectrum herbicide, for example, might be used to kill all the plants growing at a construction site. Other pesticides, called *selective* or *narrow-spectrum agents*, are effective against a narrowly defined group of organisms. Pesticides vary in their *persistence*, the length of time they stay deadly and unchanged in the environment.

The major classes of insecticides are:

- *Chlorinated hydrocarbons.* These are broad-spectrum agents that kill insects by causing convulsions, paralysis, and death. Examples include DDT, aldrin, dieldrin, toxaphene, lindane, chlordane, methoxychlor, kepone, and mirex. By the mid-1970s the use of DDT and other persistent chlorinated hydrocarbon insecticides (except lindane) had been banned or severely restricted in the United States and most other MDCs, mostly because of their persistence (2–15 years). They also threaten wildlife (Figures 2-8, 2-10, and 16-17) and people by building up in tissue and by biological amplification in food chains and webs (Figure 16-22). However, many of these compounds are still produced in the United States and exported to other countries, mostly LDCs, where they have not been banned.

- *Organophosphates.* These are broad- and narrow-spectrum agents that kill insects by deactivating a chemical involved in transmitting nerve impulses. Examples include malathion, parathion, methyl parathion, diazinon, TEPP, DDVP, and mevingphos. A few organophosphates are also used as fungicides and herbicides. Persistence generally is low to moderate (normally 1–12 weeks), although some can last several years. However, because organophosphates break down fast, farmers may apply them more often so that in effect they linger in the environment as long as the persistent chlorinated hydrocarbons they replaced. Organophosphates can easily contaminate water supplies because they are water-soluble. And while they do not bioaccumulate and are not biologically amplified, they are highly toxic to humans and other animals, and account for most human pesticide poisonings and deaths. Malathion is widely used because it is less toxic to mammals than other organophosphates.

- *Carbamates.* These are broad- and narrow-spectrum agents that kill insects by deactivating a chemical involved in transmitting nerve impulses. Examples include carbaryl (Sevin), propoxur, carbofuran, aldicarb, maneb, zineb, and methomyl. They have a low persistence (days to weeks), do not bioaccumulate, and are not biologically amplified. Their toxicity for humans and other animals ranges from low to high; unfortunately they are highly toxic to honeybees. Carbamates are among the world's most widely spread pesticides, with some also used as fungicides and herbicides.

- *Botanicals.* These are a group of broad- and narrow-spectrum agents produced naturally by plants, or by chemical modifications of such natural substances. Examples of natural botanicals include rotenone, pyrethrum, and camphor. Synthetic botanicals include several pyrethroids (chemically similar to naturally occurring pyrethrum) and rotenoids (variations of rotenone). Botanicals have a low persistence (days to weeks), are effective at a low dose, do not bioaccumulate, are not biologically amplified, and have low to moderate toxicity for humans and other animals. Most are expensive.

- *Microbotanicals.* These are a diverse array of microorganisms, including bacteria, fungi, and pro-

Q: Worldwide, how many people don't have a safe supply of drinking water?

tozoans, that selectively kill insects, usually by producing certain toxins. Examples include *Bacillus thuringensis* (caterpillars) and *Bacillus popilliae* (beetles). They have a low persistence (days to weeks), are effective at a low dose, do not bioaccumulate, are not biologically amplified, and have low toxicity for humans and other animals.

The major classes of herbicides are:

- *Contact chemicals.* These kill foliage by interfering with photosynthesis. Examples include atrazine, simazine, and paraquat. They have low persistence, do not bioaccumulate, are not biologically amplified, and have low to high (paraquat) toxicity for humans and other animals.

- *Systemic chemicals.* These create excess growth hormones, thereby killing plants, which cannot get enough nutrients to sustain their runaway growth. Examples include phenoxy compounds such as 2,4-D, 2,4,5-T, and Silvex; substituted ureas such as diruon, norea, and feuron; and other nitrogen-containing compounds such as daminozide (Alar), alachlor (Lasso), and glyphosate (Roundup). Most have low persistence, do not bioaccumulate, are not biologically amplified, and have low to moderate toxicity for humans and other animals. In the United States and most MDCs, 2,4,5-T and Silvex have been banned because of their potentially harmful effects on humans.

- *Soil sterilants.* These kill soil microorganisms essential to plant growth; most also act as systemic herbicides. Examples include trifualin, diphenamid, dalapon, and butylate. Most have low persistence, do not bioaccumulate, are not biologically amplified, and have low to moderate toxicity for humans and other animals.

*Fungicides*, chemicals used to prevent fungal spore germination and stop plant diseases, are among the most widely used pesticides in the United States. Examples include captan, mancozeb, maneb, zeneb, pentachorphenol, methyl bromide, carbon bisulfide, benomil, and chlorothalonil. Generally they have low persistence, do not bioaccumulate, are not biologically amplified, and have low to high toxicity for humans and other animals.

*Fumigants* are used to kill nematodes, fungi, insects, and other pests in soil, grain, and fruits. Examples include carbon tetrachloride, ethylene dibromide, dibromochloropropane, carbon disulfide, and methyl bromide. Most are persistent, can bioaccumulate, are highly toxic to humans and other animals, and can cause nerve damage, sterility, cancer, and birth defects in humans.

## 24-2 The Case for Pesticides

Proponents of pesticides believe that the benefits outweigh the harmful effects. They point out the following benefits:

- *Pesticides save lives.* Since 1945 DDT and other chlorinated hydrocarbon and organophosphate insecticides have probably prevented the premature deaths of at least 7 million people from insect-transmitted diseases such as malaria (carried by the *Anopheles* mosquito; Figure 20-7), bubonic plague (rat fleas), typhus (body lice and fleas), and sleeping sickness (tsetse fly).

- *They increase food supplies and lower food costs.* About 55% of the world's potential human food supply is lost to pests before (35%) or after (20%) harvest. In the United States 37% of the potential food supply is destroyed by pests before and after harvest (13% by insects, 12% by plant pathogens, and 12% by weeds). Without pesticides these losses might be worse, and food prices would rise (by 30–50% in the United States according to pesticide company officials).

- *They increase profits for farmers.* Pesticide companies estimate that every $1 spent on pesticides leads to an increase in U.S. crop yields worth approximately $4 but drops to about $2 if the harmful costs of pesticide use are included.

- *They work faster and better than alternatives.* Pesticides can control most pests quickly and reasonably cheaply, have a long shelf life, are easily shipped and applied, and are safe when handled properly. When genetic resistance occurs farmers can use stronger doses or switch to other pesticides.

- *The health risks of pesticides are insignificant compared with their health and other benefits.* According to Elizabeth Whelan, director of the American Council on Science and Health (ACSH), which presents the position of the pesticide industry, "The reality is that pesticides, when used in the approved regulatory manner, pose no risk to either farm workers or consumers." ACSH and pesticide-industry scientists argue that the health-risk studies done by the companies (required by law) and by independent researchers are worst-case scenarios. They also point out that the EPA sets maximum allowable levels of pesticide residues in food far below the levels likely to harm people. They call the pesticide health-scare news stories distorted science and irresponsible reporting, and point out

**Figure 24-2** In the cotton fields of the southern United States boll weevils can produce as many as six generations in one growing season. Attempts to control the cotton boll weevil account for at least 25% of the insecticides used in the United States. However, farmers are now increasing their use of natural predators and other biological methods to control this major pest.

that about 99.99% of the pesticides we eat are natural chemicals produced by plants.

■ *Safer and more effective products are continually being developed.* Company scientists are developing pesticides, such as botanicals and microbotanicals, that are safer to users and less damaging to the environment. Genetic engineering also holds promise (Pro/ Con, p. 167). However, research and development and government-approval costs for a single pesticide have risen from $6 million in 1976 to more than $40 million today, making pesticides more costly.

Scientists continue to search for the ideal pest-killing chemical. It would:

■ Kill only the target pest

■ Harm no other species

■ Disappear or break down into something harmless after doing its job

■ Not cause genetic resistance in target organisms

■ Be cheaper than doing nothing

Unfortunately no known pesticide meets all these criteria, and most don't even come close.

## 24-3 The Case Against Pesticides

**CREATING RESISTANT PESTS, SUPERPESTS, AND NEW PESTS** Over three decades after Rachel Carson's warning, we are beginning to get the message

that trying to eradicate insects and other pests with massive chemical warfare won't work because insects outnumber us, outbreed us, and rapidly develop immunity through natural selection to the chemicals we throw at them. Just when we think we've killed them off with our arsenal of chemicals, they come back stronger than before. Because pesticides are designed to kill organisms, they can also harm nontarget species, including us.

Spraying a field with a pesticide kills most of the pests. However, a few individuals of the target species survive to reproduce because they were missed or because they have genes that protect them from that poison. Each time the resistant survivors are sprayed, the next generation contains a higher percentage of resistant organisms—natural selection in action. And most pest species can produce hordes of offspring in a short time. For example, the boll weevil (Figure 24-2), a major cotton pest, lays thousands of eggs and produces a new generation every 21 days.

Most insects develop genetic resistance to a widely used chemical poison within 5–10 years, and much sooner in tropical areas. Weeds and plant-disease organisms also become resistant, but more slowly.

Since 1950 more than 500 major insect pests have developed genetic resistance to one or more insecticides. At least 20 species—called *superpests*—are now apparently immune to all widely used insecticides. By 2000 virtually all major insect pest species will probably show some genetic resistance. Natural predators can also develop genetic resistance to pesticides, but most predators can't reproduce as fast as their insect prey.

Likewise, about 273 of the more than 500-odd major weed species are resistant to one or more herbicides, and genetic resistance in weeds is expected to increase significantly as herbicides become more popular. Pesticide use has also led to genetic resistance in 150 plant pathogens (fungi and bacteria causing plant diseases) and in 10 species of rodents (mostly rats).

Because of genetic resistance, most widely used insecticides no longer protect people from insect-transmitted diseases in many parts of the world, leading to even more serious outbreaks of disease. Genetic resistance is the primary reason for the almost 40-fold increase in malaria since 1970 in tropical and subtropical countries (Case Study, p. 540).

Many insecticides are broad-spectrum poisons that kill not only the target pest species but also natural predators and parasites that may have been maintaining the pest species at a reasonable level. With wolf spiders (Figure 24-1), wasps, predatory beetles, and other natural enemies out of the way, a rapidly reproducing insect pest species can make a strong comeback within days or weeks after initially being controlled.

Q: Worldwide, how many people die every year from preventable waterborne diseases?

Wiping out natural predators can also unleash new pests whose populations the predators had previously held in check. That was the case with the cotton boll worm. As cotton farmers repeatedly applied huge doses of insecticides to control the boll weevil (Figure 24-2), they also destroyed the natural predators of the boll worm. Without predators the boll worm became a major pest.

These problems show why using large quantities of broad-spectrum chemical poisons to kill and control pest populations eventually fails and ends up costing more than it saves (Spotlight, right).

**MOBILITY AND BIOLOGICAL AMPLIFICATION OF PERSISTENT PESTICIDES** Pesticides don't stay put. According to the U.S. Department of Agriculture no more than 2% (and often less than 0.1%) of the insecticides applied to crops by aerial spraying (Figure 24-3) or ground spraying reach the target pests, and less than 5% of herbicides applied to crops reach the target weeds. Pesticides not reaching target pests end up in the soil, air, surface water, groundwater, bottom sediment, food, and nontarget organisms, including humans and animals—even penguins in the Antarctic (Figure 19-5). Concentrations of fat-soluble, slowly degradable insecticides such as DDT can be biologically amplified thousands to millions of times in food chains and webs (Figure 16-22).

Pesticide waste can be reduced by using recirculating sprayers, covering spray booms to reduce drift, and using rope-wick applicators (which deliver herbicides directly to weeds and cut their use by 90%).

**THREATS TO WILDLIFE** During the 1950s and 1960s populations of fish-eating birds such as the osprey, cormorant, brown pelican (Figure 2-8), and bald eagle (Figure 2-10) plummeted. A chemical derived from DDT, biologically amplified in food webs (Spotlight, p. 429), made their eggshells so fragile that the birds could not reproduce. Also hard hit were such predatory birds as the prairie falcon, sparrow hawk, and peregrine falcon (Figure 16-17), which help control rabbits, ground squirrels, and other crop-eaters (Spotlight, p. 429).

Each year some 20% of U.S. honeybee colonies are wiped out by pesticides and another 15% are damaged, costing farmers at least $206 million per year from reduced pollination of vital crops. Pesticide runoff from cropland is a leading cause of fish kills worldwide. According to the U.S. Fish and Wildlife Service pesticides menace about 20% of the endangered and threatened species in the United States.

**THREATS TO HUMAN HEALTH FROM PESTICIDE HANDLING AND MANUFACTURE** All of us are routinely and unavoidably exposed to pesticides in the air

## The Pesticide Treadmill

**SPOTLIGHT**

When genetic resistance develops, pesticide sales representatives usually recommend more frequent applications, stronger doses, or a switch to new (usually more expensive) chemicals to keep the resistant species under control, rather than suggesting nonchemical alternatives. That puts farmers on a **pesticide treadmill**, whereby they pay more and more for a pest control program that does less and less good.

A 1989 study by David Pimentel (Guest Essay, p. 332), an expert in insect ecology, based on data from more than 300 agricultural scientists and economists, concluded that:

- Although the use of synthetic pesticides has increased 33-fold since 1942, the United States loses more of its crops to pests today (37%) than in the 1940s (31%). Losses attributed to insects almost doubled from 7% to 13% despite a 10-fold increase in the use of synthetic insecticides; losses to plant diseases rose from 10% to 12%, and losses to weeds dropped from 14% to 12%.

- The estimated environmental, health, and social costs of pesticide use in the United States range from $4 billion to $10 billion per year.

- Alternative pest control practices (Section 24-5) could halve the use of chemical pesticides on 40 major crops in the United States without reducing crop yields.

- A 50% cut in pesticide use in the United States would raise retail food prices by only about 0.2%, but would raise average income for farmers about 9%.

we breathe, the water we drink, the foods we eat, and many consumer products we use. These pesticides, which can also be absorbed through the skin, generally affect the central nervous system. Although their toxic effects can be acute or chronic, more is known about their acute effects on people exposed to fairly large doses.

As many as 4.5 million agricultural workers (including farmers, pesticide mixers and appliers, and field hands), and 350,000 workers in chemical plants are exposed to relatively high levels of pesticides. The World Health Organization estimates that at least 1 million people (including 313,000 farm workers in the United States) are accidentally poisoned by pesticides each year; 4,000–20,000 of them die. At least half of them—and 90% of those killed—are farm workers in

**A:** At least 5 million (mostly children under age 5)

**Figure 24-3** Crop duster spraying an insecticide on grapevines south of Fresno, California. Aircraft are used to apply about 65% of the pesticides used on cropland in the United States. Only 0.1%–2% of insecticides reach their target pests.

LDCs, where educational levels are low, warnings few, and pesticide regulations lax or nonexistent. The actual number of pesticide-related illnesses among farm workers in the United States and throughout the world is probably greatly underestimated because of poor records, lack of doctors and reporting in rural areas, and faulty diagnoses. U.S. farm workers are excluded from the Occupational Safety and Health Act, governing workplace health and safety standards.

In the United States about 67,000 cases of nonfatal pesticide poisoning, most involving children, are reported each year, and about 200 people per year die from pesticide poisoning. Most of these poisonings happen in or around the home. Another 10,000 people in the United States get some form of pesticide-related cancer each year. Many of these people are farmers, pesticide plant workers, pesticide appliers, crop pickers, and home gardeners, all repeatedly exposed to much higher levels of pesticides than the rest of society. Accidents and unsafe practices in pesticide plants

can expose workers, their families, and sometimes the general public to harmful levels of pesticides or raw chemicals used to make them (Case Study, p. 627).

**THREATS TO HUMAN HEALTH FROM PESTICIDE RESIDUES** According to the FDA 1–3% of the food purchased in the United States has levels of one or more pesticides that are above the legal limit. These levels could well be higher because the tests now used can detect only about one-third of the more than 600 active ingredients approved for use in U.S. pesticides. Pesticide residues are especially likely to be found in tomatoes, grapes, apples, lettuce, oranges, potatoes, beef, and dairy products.

In 1987 the National Academy of Sciences reported that the active ingredients in 90% of all fungicides, 60% of all herbicides, and 30% of all insecticides in use in the United States may cause cancer in humans. According to the *worst-case estimate* in this study, exposure to pesticides in food causes 4,000–20,000 cases of cancer per year in the United States. In 1987 the EPA ranked pesticide residues in foods as the third most serious environmental health threat in the United States in terms of cancer risk.

Cancer is only one possible harmful effect of long-term exposure to low levels of pesticides. Some scientists are becoming increasingly concerned about possible genetic mutations, birth defects, nervous-system disorders, and effects on the immune and endocrine systems from such exposure. The EPA requires tests for some of these effects on new pesticides, but critics argue that the studies are not thorough enough for new pesticides and that most of the more than 600 older chemicals still in widespread use have been poorly evaluated for such effects. Also, when a pesticide is tested, it is the active pest-killing ingredients—not the breakdown products—that get most of the attention. However, a 1993 National Cancer Institute study found that women with high blood levels of DDE (a breakdown product of DDT) had four times the risk of breast cancer that women with low blood levels of DDE had.

Nor is food the only risk. Many people may actually be exposed to much higher levels of pesticides from community spraying programs used to control mosquitoes or other insect pests; from pesticide-sprayed lawns, parks, golf courses, and roadsides; and from living near sprayed croplands, rangelands, and forests.

Still controversial are the effects on U.S. soldiers who were exposed to Agent Orange, a 50-50 mixture of the herbicides 2,4-D and 2,4,5-T (banned for use in the United States since 1985) sprayed as a defoliant during the Vietnam War. Some 35,000 Vietnam veterans have filed claims with the Veterans Administration for disabilities allegedly caused by exposure to Agent Orange. The Veterans Administration and the

**Q:** What is the largest source of U.S. water pollution?

defoliant manufacturers, however, deny any connection between the medical disorders and Agent Orange. Various studies have led to conflicting and inconclusive results. In 1984 the manufacturers agreed to a $180-million out-of-court settlement with about 9,300 Vietnam veterans, without admitting any guilt or connection between the disorders and exposure to the herbicide.

## 24-4 Pesticide Regulation in the United States: Is the Public Adequately Protected?

Because of the potentially harmful effects of pesticides on wildlife and people, Congress passed the Federal Insecticide, Fungicide, and Rodenticide Act (FIFRA) in 1972. This law, which was amended in 1975, 1978, and 1988, requires that all commercial pesticides be approved for general or restricted use by the EPA. However, pesticide companies evaluate the biologically active ingredients in their products.

Since 1972 the EPA has used this law to ban the use, except for emergencies, of over 50 previously approved pesticides because of potential health hazards. The banned chemicals include most chlorinated hydrocarbon insecticides, several carbamates and organophosphates, and the herbicides 2,4,5-T and Silvex.

FIFRA also required the EPA to reevaluate the more than 600 active ingredients approved for use in pre-1972 pesticide products to determine whether any of them caused cancer, birth defects, or other health risks. However, so far, less than 10% of these active ingredients have been fully tested and evaluated for potential health problems.

According to the National Academy of Sciences federal laws regulating the use of pesticides in the United States are inadequate and poorly enforced by both the EPA and the Food and Drug Administration (FDA). The Academy also concluded that up to 98% of the potential risk of developing cancer from pesticide residues on food grown in the United States would be eliminated if EPA standards were as strict for pre-1972 pesticides as they are now.

In addition, many of the 1,475 so-called inert or biologically inactive ingredients in pesticides clearly can harm humans as well as wildlife. In fact, because "inert" ingredients make up 80–99% by weight of a pesticide product, they can pose a higher health risk than some active ingredients.

Inert ingredients can be chemicals such as carbon tetrachloride that have been banned as active ingredients, cadmium and lead compounds, such toxic solvents as methylene chloride and xylene, or hazardous

## A Black Day in Bhopal

**CASE STUDY**

December 2, 1984, will long be a black day on the Indian calendar. The world's worst industrial accident occurred on that date at a Union Carbide pesticide plant in Bhopal. Some 36 metric tons (40 tons) of highly toxic methyl isocyanate (MIC) gas, used in the manufacture of carbamate pesticides, leaked from an underground storage tank. When water accidentally entered the tank, its cooling system failed, which caused the reaction mixture to overheat and explode. Once in the atmosphere some of the toxic MIC was converted to even more deadly hydrogen cyanide gas.

According to Indian officials about 5,100 people were killed (2,600 from direct exposure to MIC and another 2,500 from the aftereffects). The estimates of serious injuries such as blindness or lung damage range from 10,000 (Union Carbide) to 200,000 (Indian officials).

The Indian Supreme Court ordered Union Carbide to pay a $470-million settlement, but dismissed criminal charges against the company. However, the Indian government has challenged the ruling, arguing that the settlement was inadequate and that the court had no constitutional right to dismiss the criminal charges. In 1991 the court upheld the settlement amount but allowed criminal charges to be refiled. Indian officials claim the accident was caused by negligence, while Union Carbide officials claim that it was due to sabotage. In any event, so far Union Carbide officials have refused to appear in Indian courts to stand trial and support their claim.

Union Carbide could probably have prevented this tragedy, which cost at least $570 million in cleanup and damage settlements, to say nothing of the human losses, by spending no more than $1 million to improve plant safety.

chemical wastes (known to cause cancers, mutations, or birth defects in test organisms) the EPA allows to be "recycled" into pesticides. Since 1987 the EPA has been evaluating these inert ingredients and thus far has labeled 100 of them "of known or potential toxicological concern" but has not banned their use. It has described another 800–900 as inadequately tested for their risk to humans.

FIFRA allows the EPA to leave inadequately tested pesticides on the market and to license new chemicals without full health and safety data. It also gives the EPA unlimited time to remove a chemical even when its health and environmental risks are

A: Agriculture (responsible for about two-thirds)

## The Circle of Poison

Pesticide companies can make and export pesticides banned or severely restricted—or never approved—in the United States. On average, 15 metric tons (17 tons) of such pesticides are shipped from the United States to other countries *each hour*.

But what goes around, as they say, comes around. In what environmentalists call a *circle of poison*, residues of some of these banned or unapproved chemicals return to the United States on imported items such as coffee, cocoa, pineapples, and out-of-season melons, tomatoes, and grapes. More than one-fourth of the produce (fruits and vegetables) consumed in the United States is grown overseas.

Environmentalists have urged Congress—without success—to break the deadly circle. They believe it is morally wrong for the United States to export pesticides known to damage human health and to allow food with residues of those pesticides to be imported for U.S. consumers.

for citizen suits against the EPA for not enforcing the law, an essential tool to ensure government compliance.

Each year FDA inspectors check less than 1% (about 12,000 samples) of domestic and imported food for pesticide contamination (Spotlight, left). Furthermore, the FDA's turnaround time for food analysis is so long that half of the food has been sold and eaten before the contamination is detected. Even when contaminated food is found, the growers and importers are rarely penalized.

### 24-5 Solutions: Other Ways to Control Pests

**CULTIVATION PRACTICES** Chemistry is not the only answer to pests. Other strategies, some of them ancient, are:

- *Rotating crops.* This involves changing crops planted in a field each year so that one crop's pests don't have time to multiply uncontrollably.

- *Planting rows of hedges or trees in and around crop fields.* These hinder insect invasions and provide habitats for their natural enemies.

- *Adjusting planting times.* This helps ensure that major insect pests either starve or get eaten by their natural predators.

- *Growing crops in areas where their major pests do not exist.*

- *Switching from monocultures to modernized versions of intercropping, agroforestry, and polyculture.* Plant diversity helps control pests (Section 14-6).

- *Removing diseased or infected plants and stalks and other crop residues that harbor pests.*

- *Using photodegradable plastic to keep weeds from sprouting between crop rows.*

- *Using denser planting patterns.* This crowds out weeds among some crops.

- *Mowing weeds instead of using herbicides.*

- *Using vacuum machines that gently remove harmful bugs from plants.*

Unfortunately to increase profits, qualify for government subsidies—and to avoid bankruptcy—many U.S. farmers feel they cannot use these cultivation methods.

**BUILDING IN RESISTANCE** Plants and animals that are genetically resistant to certain pest insects, fungi, and diseases can be developed. However, resistant varieties usually take a long time (10–20 years) and lots of money to develop by conventional methods.

shown to outweigh its economic benefits. The built-in appeals and other procedures often keep a dangerous chemical on the market for up to 10 years.

The EPA can ban a chemical immediately in an emergency. Until 1990, however, the law required the EPA to use its already severely limited funds to compensate pesticide manufacturers for their remaining inventory and for all storage and disposal. Because compensation costs for a single chemical could exceed the agency's annual pesticide budget, the only economically feasible solution was for the EPA to allow existing stocks of a dangerous chemical to be sold. One of the 1988 amendments to FIFRA shifted some of the costs of storing and disposing of banned pesticides from the EPA to the manufacturers.

Environmentalists welcome the 1988 amendments, but point out that the law still has many weaknesses and loopholes. One loophole allows the sale in the United States of insecticides (especially dicofol and chlorobenilate) containing as much as 15% DDT by weight, classified as an impurity. These products, along with others smuggled in (mostly from Mexico), are believed to be responsible for increased DDT levels since 1988 in some vulnerable forms of wildlife and in some fruits and vegetables grown and sold in the United States (especially in California). Also, this law is the only major environmental statute that does not provide

Q: What is the largest source of water pollution from oil?

Moreover, insects and plant diseases can develop new strains that attack the once-resistant varieties, forcing scientists to continually develop new resistant strains. Genetic engineering is now being used to speed the process (Figure 24-4 and Pro/Con, p. 167).

**NATURAL ENEMIES** Predators (Figures 24-1 and 24-5), parasites, and pathogens (disease-causing bacteria and viruses) can be encouraged or imported to regulate pest populations. Worldwide more than 300 biological pest control projects have been successful, especially in China. In Nigeria crop-dusting planes release parasitic wasps instead of pesticides to fight the cassava mealybug. Farmers get a $178 return for every $1 they spend on the wasps. In the United States natural enemies have been used to control more than 70 insect pests, and biological control is catching on as more farmers seek alternatives to chemical warfare.

Other examples of biological control include the use of:

- *Guard dogs or llamas to protect livestock from predators.*

- *Geese for weeding orchards, eating fallen and rotting fruit (often a source of pest problems), and controlling grass in gardens and nurseries.* Geese also warn of approaching predators or people by honking loudly.

- *Chickens to control insects and weeds after plants are well established.*

- *Birds to eat insects.* Farmers and homeowners can provide habitats and nesting sites that attract woodpeckers, purple martins, chickadees, barn swallows, nuthatches, and other insect-eating species.

- *Spiders to eat insects* (Figure 24-1).

- *Allelopathic plants that naturally produce chemicals toxic to their weed competitors or that repel or poison their insect pests.* For example, certain varieties of barley, wheat, rye, sorghum, and Sudan grass will suppress weeds in gardens or orchards. Peppermint can be planted around houses to repel ants (it is also a natural mouth freshener and a cooking spice).

Biological control has several advantages. It hones in on the target species and is nontoxic to other species, including people. Once a population of natural predators or parasites is established, pest control can often be self-perpetuating. Development of genetic resistance is minimized because pest and predator species interact and change together (coevolution). In the United States biological control has saved farmers an average of $25 for every $1 invested.

No method of pest control is perfect, of course. Years of research may be needed to understand how a

**Figure 24-4** Genetic engineering against pest damage. Both tomato plants were exposed to destructive caterpillars. The normal plant's leaves are almost gone (left), while the genetically altered plant (right) shows little damage.

**Figure 24-5** Biological control of pests. An adult convergent ladybug (right) is consuming an aphid (left).

particular pest interacts with its various enemies and to choose the best biological control agent. Biological agents can't always be mass produced, and farmers find that they're slower to act and harder to apply than pesticides. Also, biological agents must be protected from pesticides sprayed in nearby fields. Some may even become pests themselves; others (such as praying mantises) devour beneficial as well as pest insects.

**BIOPESTICIDES** Biopesticides are now a $100-million-per-year business in the United States. Botanicals such as synthetic pyrethroids are an increasingly popular method of pest control, and scientists are busy looking for new plant toxins to synthesize for mass production. One promising new synthetic botanical is a modified seed extract from the neem tree (Spotlight, p. 268). The neem-related botanical stops more than 100 insect species from feeding, repels them from

**Figure 24-6** Infestation of a steer by screwworm fly larvae. A fully grown steer can be killed in 10 days from thousands of maggots feeding on a single wound.

treated plants, and is harmless to pets and humans. An extract from the bark, wood, and roots of the papaw tree (midwestern United States) kills numerous insects in their adult and larval stages.

Microbes are also being drafted for the insect wars. For example, *Bacillus thuringensis (Bt)* toxin is a registered pesticide sold commercially as a dry powder. One of the thousands of strains of this common soil bacterium will kill a specific pest. Now a *Bacillus thuringensis* gene has been transferred to cotton plants. These plants then produce a protein that disrupts the digestive system of pests; insects that bite the plant die within hours. The bad news is that genetic resistance to some Bt toxins is already developing.

**BIRTH CONTROL** Males of some insect pest species can be lab-raised, sterilized by radiation or chemicals, and then released in hordes in an infested area to mate unsuccessfully with fertile wild females. This technique works best if the females mate only once, if the infested area is isolated so that it can't be repopulated with nonsterilized males, and if the insect pest population has already been reduced to a fairly low level by weather, pesticides, or other factors. Success is also increased if only the "sexiest"—the loudest, fastest, and largest—males are sterilized.

The case of the screwworm fly, a major livestock pest in South and Central America and the southern United States, illustrates both the benefits of and the drawbacks to this birth control method. This metallic blue-green insect, twice as big as the common housefly, deposits its eggs in open wounds of cattle and deer. Within hours the larvae begin feeding on the animal's flesh (Figure 24-6). A severe infestation of this pest can kill a mature steer within 10 days.

The Department of Agriculture used the sterile-male approach to essentially eliminate the screwworm

**Figure 24-7** A lemon infested with red scale mites. Pheromones are now being used to help control populations of red scale mites.

fly from the southeastern states between 1962 and 1971. In 1972, however, the pest made a dramatic comeback, infesting 100,000 cattle and causing serious losses until 1976, when a new strain of sterile males brought the situation under temporary control. To prevent resurgences of this pest, new strains of sterile male flies have to be released every few years. This approach is also being used on fruit flies in Florida.

Problems with this approach include the difficulties involved in knowing the mating times and behaviors of each target insect, and releasing enough sterile males to do the job. This approach is also expensive.

**INSECT SEX ATTRACTANTS** In many insect species, when a female is ready to mate she releases a minute amount (typically about one-millionth of a gram) of a chemical sex attractant called a *pheromone*. These pheromones, extracted from insects or synthesized in the laboratory, can be used to lure pests into traps or to attract their natural predators into crop fields (usually the more effective approach). Worldwide more than 50 companies sell about 250 pheromones to control pests (Figure 24-7).

These chemicals attract only one species, work in trace amounts, have little chance of causing genetic resistance, and are not harmful to nontarget species. However, it is costly and time-consuming to identify, isolate, and produce the specific sex attractant for each pest or natural predator species.

Q: How much water can be contaminated by 0.9 liter (1 quart) of oil?

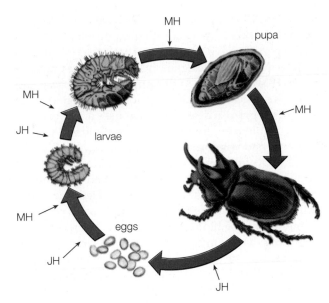

Agricultural Research Service/USDA

**Figure 24-8** For normal growth, development, and reproduction, certain juvenile hormones (JH) and molting hormones (MH) must be present at genetically determined stages in the typical life cycle of an insect. If applied at the right time, synthetic hormones can be used to disrupt the life cycle of insect pests.

**Figure 24-9** Chemical hormones can prevent insects from maturing completely and make it impossible for them to reproduce. The stunted tobacco hornworm (left) was fed a compound that prevents its larvae from producing molting hormones (MH); a normal tobacco hornworm is shown on the right.

**INSECT HORMONES** Hormones are chemicals, produced by an organism and sent through its bloodstream to control its growth and development. Each step in the insect life cycle is regulated by the timely release of juvenile hormones (JH) and molting hormones (MH) (Figure 24-8).

These chemicals can be extracted from insects or synthesized in the laboratory. When applied at certain stages in an insect's life cycle, they cause the insect to die before it can reach maturity and reproduce (Figure 24-9). For example, compounds found in the neem tree's oils disrupt the production of growth hormones in more than 200 insect species and thus prevent the insects from reproducing.

Insect hormones have the same advantages as sex attractants, but they take weeks to kill an insect, are often ineffective with a large infestation, and sometimes break down before they can act. Also, they must be applied at exactly the right time in the target insect's life cycle. Moreover, they sometimes affect the target's predators and other nonpest species, and they can kill crustaceans if they get into aquatic ecosystems. Finally, like sex attractants they are difficult and costly to produce.

**ZAPPING FOODS WITH RADIATION** Gamma irradiation (Figure 3-10) of certain foods is being touted by the nuclear power and food industries for killing insects and preventing them from reproducing in certain foods after harvest, extending the shelf life of some perishable foods, and destroying parasitic worms (such as trichinae in pork) and bacteria (such as salmonellae, which infect 51,000 Americans and kill 2,000 each year).

Since 1986 the FDA has approved low doses of gamma radiation for spices, fruits, vegetables, white potatoes, wheat and wheat flour, pork, nuts, seeds, teas, and chicken (half of those sold in the United States contain salmonella). It may soon be approved for use on seafood. Irradiated foods are already sold in 33 countries, including Japan, Canada, Brazil, Israel, and some western European countries.

Marketing surveys show that U.S. consumers will not buy food if it is labeled as irradiated. Thus foods sold in the United States that have been exposed to radiation bear a characteristic logo and a label stating that the product has been *picowaved*, which consumer advocates say will mean little to many consumers. Even this misleading label is not required for prepared or packaged food that contains irradiated ingredients, or for food sold in restaurants and cafeterias.

**A:** 940,000 liters (250,000 gallons)

## Should Food Be Irradiated?

**PRO/CON**

According to the FDA and the World Health Organization over 1,000 studies show that foods exposed to low doses of ionizing radiation are safe for human consumption.

However, critics argue that it's too soon to see long-term effects, which might not show up for 30–40 years. Moreover, some studies have suggested that consuming irradiated food may be harmful. For example, a 1984 EPA study tied food irradiation to increased production of aflatoxin, a deadly carcinogen.

Irradiated food does have certain known drawbacks. For one thing, irradiating food destroys some of its vitamins (especially A, C, E, and B complex) and other nutrients. Present levels of irradiation do not destroy the deadly spore-enclosed botulinus bacteria, but they do destroy the microbes that give off the rotten odor warning of its presence. Furthermore, some microorganisms can mutate when exposed to radiation, possibly creating new and more dangerous forms of botulism.

Besides concern over food safety, irradiation poses serious occupational and environmental hazards to workers in irradiation plants and related industries. Environmentalists consider current safety standards at such plants inadequate.

Environmentalists and consumer advocates argue that Americans want fresh, wholesome food, not old, possibly less nutritious food made to appear fresh and healthy by irradiation. Instead of using radiation to reduce salmonella in chickens, for example, they believe the government should adopt and enforce tighter inspection standards, especially since thorough cooking kills salmonella anyway. They call for consumers to pressure elected officials to halt food irradiation, strictly regulate all irradiation facilities, and require that any food product containing irradiated ingredients clearly state so.

Proponents respond that irradiation of food is likely to reduce health hazards to people by—among other things—making pesticides unnecessary and that its potential benefits greatly exceed the risks. Meanwhile, New York, New Jersey, and Maine have prohibited the sale and distribution of irradiated food, as have Germany, Denmark, Sweden, Australia, and New Zealand.

A food does not become radioactive when it is irradiated, just as being exposed to X rays does not make the body radioactive. The technology, however, is controversial (Pro/Con, above).

**SUSTAINABLE SOLUTIONS: INTEGRATED PEST MANAGEMENT** An increasing number of pest control experts believe that the best way to control crop pests is a carefully designed **integrated pest management (IPM)** program. In this approach each crop and its pests are evaluated as an ecological system. Then a control program is developed that uses a mix of cultivation, biological, and chemical methods in proper sequence and with proper timing.

The overall aim of IPM is not eradication of pest populations but maintenance at just below economically damaging levels (Figure 24-10). Fields are carefully monitored. When a damaging level is reached, farmers first use biological and cultivation controls, including vacuuming up harmful bugs. Small amounts of insecticides (mostly botanicals or microbotanicals) are applied when absolutely necessary; varying the chemicals helps to slow development of genetic resistance. This approach allows farmers to avoid the pesticide treadmill while minimizing chemical hazards to human health, wildlife, and the environment.

The experiences of countries such as China, Brazil, Indonesia, and the United States have shown that a well-designed IPM program can reduce pesticide use and pest control costs by 50–90%. IPM can also reduce preharvest pest-induced crop losses by 50%, improve crop yields, reduce inputs of fertilizer and irrigation water, and slow the development of genetic resistance because pests are zapped less often and with lower doses of pesticides. Thus IPM is an important form of pollution prevention that reduces risks to wildlife and human health.

However, IPM requires expert knowledge about each pest–crop situation and is slower acting than conventional pesticides. Moreover, methods developed for a given crop in one area may not apply to another area with slightly different growing conditions. And although long-term costs are typically lower than the costs of using conventional pesticides, initial costs may be higher.

Use of IPM is hindered by government subsidies of conventional chemical pesticides and by opposition of agricultural chemical companies, whose sales would drop sharply. In addition, farmers get most of their information about pest control from pesticide salespeople and from U.S. Department of Agriculture (USDA) county farm agents, few of whom have adequate training in IPM. The small number of IPM advisers and consultants is overwhelmed by the army of pesticide sales representatives.

For widespread use IPM will have to be developed and introduced to farmers by federal and state agencies. Currently, however, only about $16 million (1%) of the USDA's research and education budget is spent on IPM. Pesticide companies, by contrast, spend

Q: What percentage of U.S. rural wells tested violate at least one federal drinking water standard?

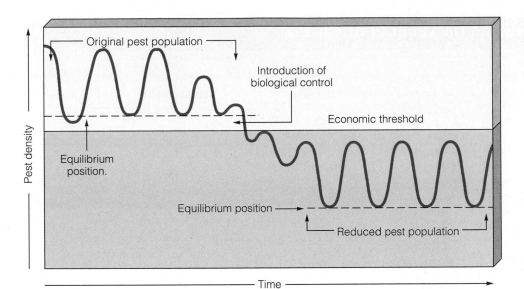

Original pest population

Introduction of
biological control

Economic threshold

Equilibrium
position.

Equilibrium position

Reduced pest population

Pest density

Time

**Figure 24-10** The goal of biological control and integrated pest management is to keep each pest population just below the size at which it causes economic loss.

$1.7 billion annually on research and development worldwide.

Environmentalists urge the USDA to promote integrated pest management by:

- Adding a 2% sales tax on pesticides to fund IPM research and education

- Setting up a federally supported demonstration IPM project on at least one farm in every county

- Training USDA field personnel and county farm agents in IPM so they can help farmers use this alternative

- Providing federal and state subsidies and perhaps government-backed crop-loss insurance to farmers who use IPM or other approved alternatives to pesticides

- Gradually phasing out subsidies to farmers depending almost entirely on pesticides once effective IPM methods have been developed for major pest species

Indonesia has led the way in the pest management revolution. In 1986 the Indonesian government banned the use of 57 pesticides on rice and launched a nationwide program to switch to IPM. The results were dramatic: Between 1987 and 1992 pesticide use dropped by 65%, rice production rose by 15%, and the country now saves about $120 million per year on pesticides—enough to cover the cost of its IPM program. Sweden cut its pesticide use by 50% between 1985 and 1990, and hopes to halve it again by 1997. Denmark, the Netherlands, and the Canadian province of Ontario have passed legislation to reduce pesticide use by 50% over the next 5–15 years.

 **24-6**

## Changing the Attitudes of Consumers and Farmers

Several attitudes tend to support the widespread use of pesticides and lock us into the pesticide treadmill:

- The only good bug is a dead bug.

- Insistence on perfect, unblemished fruits and vegetables, even though a few holes or frayed leaves do not significantly affect the taste, nutrition, or shelf life of such produce.

- Without these chemicals, there wouldn't be enough to eat and food prices would soar. However, studies show that halving pesticide use in the United States by using alternative forms of pest management would not lower crop yields, would raise food prices only slightly, and would reduce the health, environmental, and social costs of pesticides to consumers by $2–$5 billion per year (Spotlight, p. 625).

- Obsession with the perfect lawn. About 40% of U.S. lawns are treated with pesticides, typically at levels three to six times higher per acre than farmland. These chemicals can cause headaches, dizziness, nausea, and eye trouble, and more acute effects in sensitive individuals, including children who play on treated lawns and parks. Of the 40 pesticides commonly used by the lawn care industry, 12 are suspected human carcinogens, 10 may cause birth defects, 3 can affect reproduction, 9 can damage liver and kidneys, 20 can cause short-term nervous system damage, and 29 cause rashes or skin disease.

A: 66% (mostly contaminated by pesticides or nitrates from fertilizers)

## What You Can Do About Pesticide Use

**INDIVIDUALS MATTER**

- Buy organically grown produce that has not been treated with synthetic fertilizers, pesticides, or growth regulators.

- Urge your supermarket manager to carry organic produce that is certified to be free of pesticide residues by independent testing laboratories.

- Avoid buying imported produce, which generally contains more pesticide residues than domestic fruits and vegetables. Show your concern and influence supermarket buying decisions by asking managers where their produce comes from.

- Don't insist on perfect-looking fruits and vegetables. These are more likely to contain high levels of pesticide residues.

- Buy produce in season. It is less likely to be treated with fungicides and other chemicals to preserve its appearance during storage.

- Get rid of most pesticide residues by carefully washing and scrubbing all fresh produce in soapy water, discarding the outer leaves of lettuce and cabbage, and peeling thick-skinned fruits.

- Grow some or all of your own fruits and vegetables using organic methods or integrated pest management.

- Use pesticides in your home only when absolutely necessary, and use them in the smallest amount possible. Try natural alternatives first (Solutions, p. 620).

- Dispose of unused pesticides safely. Contact your local health department or environmental agency for safe disposal methods.

- Fix all leaking pipes and faucets. They waste water and provide moisture that attracts ants and roaches.

- Keep native plants on all or most of the land around your house not used for gardening. This type of yard keeps mosquitoes and other insects down by providing habitats for their natural predators.

- Don't cut grass shorter than 8 centimeters (3 inches). Taller grass provides more habitats for natural predators of pests, shades weeds out, and holds moisture in the soil.

- Don't use synthetic pesticides on your lawn, and avoid overfertilizing.

- If you hire a lawn-care company, choose one that uses organic methods.* And get its claims in writing.

- Urge elected officials to revise FIFRA to better protect human health and the environment from the harmful effects of pesticides.

- Urge elected officials to ban exports of pesticides not approved for use in the United States.

* For the names of lawn companies that don't use toxic chemicals, write Lorens Tronet, Executive Director of Lake Country Defenders, Box 911, Lake Zanich, IL 60047, or the Bio-Integral Resource Center, Box 7414, Berkeley, CA 94707. Also, consult *Success with Lawns Starts with Soil*, Ringer Research Corp., 6860 Flying Cloud Drive, Eden Prairie, MN 55344.

---

Educating farmers and consumers to change their attitudes, and urging elected officials to change U.S. agricultural and pesticide policies, would help reduce unnecessary pesticide use and economic loss and the resulting risks to human health and wildlife (Individuals Matter, above).

*We need to recognize that pest control is basically an ecological, not a chemical, problem.*

ROBERT L. RUDD

## Critical Thinking

1. Should DDT and other pesticides be banned from use in malaria control efforts throughout the world? Explain. What are the alternatives?

2. Environmentalists argue that because essentially all pesticides eventually fail and can pose health risks, their use should be minimized, and farmers should be given economic incentives for switching to integrated pest management. Explain why you agree or disagree with this proposal.

3. How can the use of insecticides increase the number of insect pest problems.

4. Debate the following resolution: Because DDT and the other banned chlorinated hydrocarbon pesticides pose no demonstrable threat to human health and have saved millions of lives, they should again be approved for use in the United States.

5. Should certain types of foods used in the United States be irradiated? Explain.

6. What changes, if any, do you believe should be made in the Federal Insecticide, Fungicide, and Rodenticide Act regulating pesticide use in the United States?

7. Should U.S. companies be allowed to export to other countries pesticides, medicines, and other chemicals that have been banned or severely restricted in the United States? Explain.

*8. How are bugs and weeds controlled in your yard and garden? On the grounds of your school and the public schools, parks, and playgrounds where you live? Consider mounting efforts to have integrated pest management and organic fertilizers used on school and public grounds. Do the same thing for your yard and garden.

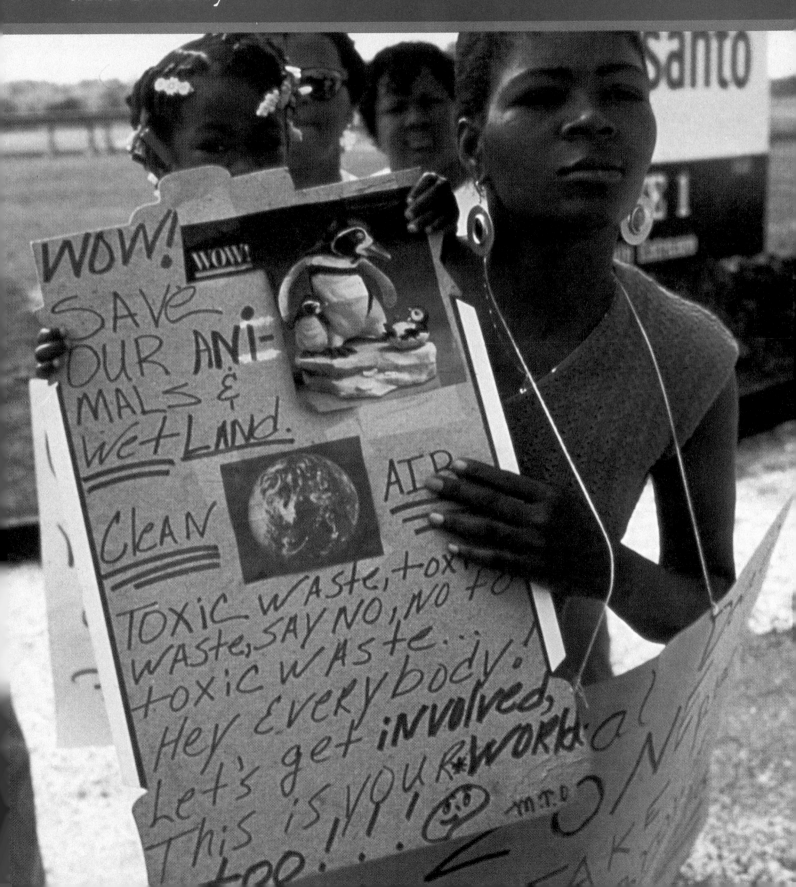

# PART VII

# Environment and Society

*When it is asked how much it will cost to protect the environment, one more question should be asked: How much will it cost our civilization if we do not?*
GAYLORD NELSON

# 25 Economics and Environment

## To Grow or Not to Grow: Is That the Question?

In the American Northwest the timber-based economy is in trouble, and recent efforts to save old-growth forests and the northern spotted owl (Figure 10-23) have run into an economic buzz-saw. Embattled loggers and environmentalists alike have too often framed their positions in either-or terms: "Trees or jobs." "Owls or people." What we really need to ask is "How can we have trees *and* jobs? How can we save the owls and the forests without putting people out of work? What happens to jobs after all the trees are cut?"

The same types of polarized positions apply to the question of economic growth in general. On the one hand, some economists and investors argue that we must have unlimited economic growth to create jobs, satisfy people's economic needs and wants,

*As important as technology, politics, law, and ethics are to the pollution question, all such approaches are bound to have disappointing results, for they ignore the primary fact that pollution is primarily an economic problem, which must be understood in economic terms.*

LARRY E. RUFF

clean up the environment, and help eliminate poverty. They see the earth as an essentially unlimited source of raw materials and the environment as an infinite sink for wastes. Any resource or environmental limits can be overcome by technological innovation. They see environmentalists as putting endangered species above endangered people, threatening jobs, and opposing economic growth.

On the other hand, environmentalists and some economists argue that economic systems depend on resources and services provided by Earth's natural processes (Figure 25-1). A healthy economy is ultimately dependent on a healthy planet. If they are right, we must replace the economics of unlimited growth with the economics of sustainability.

The question then is not so much "To grow or not to grow?" but "How can we grow without plundering the planet?" or "How can we grow as if Earth matters for our children and grandchildren?" These questions have more complex answers than do simplistic, either-or questions. They might lead us to change our whole pattern of subsidies and tax breaks—to stop rewarding harmful, resource-gobbling forms of economic growth and start rewarding more benign and sustainable forms of growth such as recycling, reuse, pollution prevention, energy efficiency, renewable energy, pollution prevention, population control, ecological restoration, and Earth education. One of the basic lessons of economics is that we get what we reward.

According to an ancient Chinese proverb, "Unless we change the direction we are going, we are likely to get where we are going." To most conventional economists, where we are heading is wonderful and no change in direction is needed. To most environmentalists and some environmental economists (Guest Essay, p. 656), we are headed in a dangerous and unsustainable direction and have only a few decades to change course.

**Figure 25-1** Earth, air, fire, water, life—the basic components of Earth capital for us and other species.

In this chapter we will seek answers to the following questions:

- What are economic goods and resources, and how are they provided?
- How should we measure economic growth?
- How can economics be used to improve environmental quality?
- How can we sharply reduce poverty?
- How can we shift from an Earth-plundering to an Earth-sustaining economy?

## 25-1 Economic Goods, Resources, and Systems

**ECONOMIC GOODS, NEEDS, AND WANTS** An **economic good** is any material item or service that gives people satisfaction. Economic goods—food, clothing, water, oxygen, shelter, health care, education—that you must have to survive and to stay healthy are your **economic needs.** Anything beyond those is an **economic want.** What you believe you need and want is influenced by the customs and conventions of the society in which you live, your level of affluence, and advertising.

**ECONOMIC RESOURCES** The kinds of capital used in an economy to produce material goods and services, and thus to sustain economic growth, are called economic resources. They fall into three groups:

- **Earth capital** or **natural resources**: resources produced by Earth's natural processes. They include the planet's air, water, and land; nutrients and minerals in the soil and deeper in the earth's crust; wild and domesticated plants and animals (biodiversity); and nature's dilution, waste disposal, pest control, and recycling services.
- **Manufactured capital**: items manufactured from Earth capital. These include economic goods and

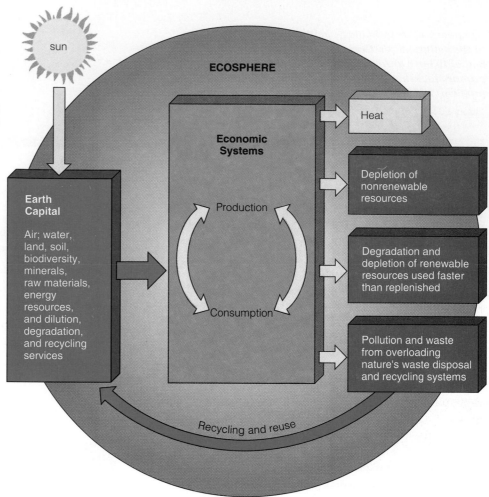

**Figure 25-2** Environmentalists see all economies as artificial subsystems dependent on resources and services provided by the sun and the ecosphere. A consumer society devoted to unlimited economic growth to satisfy ever-expanding wants assumes that ecosphere resources and services are essentially infinite or that our technological cleverness will allow us to overcome any ecosphere limits.

services bought by consumers, tools, machinery, equipment, factory buildings, and transportation and distribution facilities.

- **Human capital**: people's physical and mental talents. Workers sell their time and talents for wages. Managers take responsibility for combining Earth capital, manufactured capital, and workers to produce an economic good. Entrepreneurs and investors put up the monetary capital needed to produce an economic good in the hope of making a profit on their investment.

**PRIVATE-, COMMON-, AND PUBLIC-PROPERTY RESOURCES** Any resource to which access can be controlled because it is owned by an individual or a group is a **private-property resource.** People tend to maintain and improve resources they own.

A **common-property resource** is one to which people have virtually free and unmanaged access and for which each user can subtract from or degrade the supply available to other users. Most are potentially renewable resources. The ultimate common-property

resource is the ecosphere, which supports all life and all economic activity (Figures 4-3 and 25-2).

Because it is difficult, and in some cases impossible, to restrict access to common-property resources, they can easily be polluted (air, international waters, groundwater, the ozone layer) or overharvested (whales, bison, migratory birds) and be converted from renewable into slowly renewable or nonrenewable resources (environmental damage and extinction)—the tragedy of the commons (Spotlight, p. 14). One way to protect such resources involves cooperation instead of government regulation, although enforcement for most common-property resources is difficult. Another way is to get users to agree voluntarily to limit their consumption of common-property resources so they are used on a sustainable basis instead of being depleted or degraded.

Other resources, called **public-property resources,** fall between private- and common-property resources. That is, they are owned jointly by all people of a country, state, or locality but are managed by the government. Examples include national and state forests,

Q: How many U.S. underground tanks storing gasoline and other hazardous chemicals are leaking?

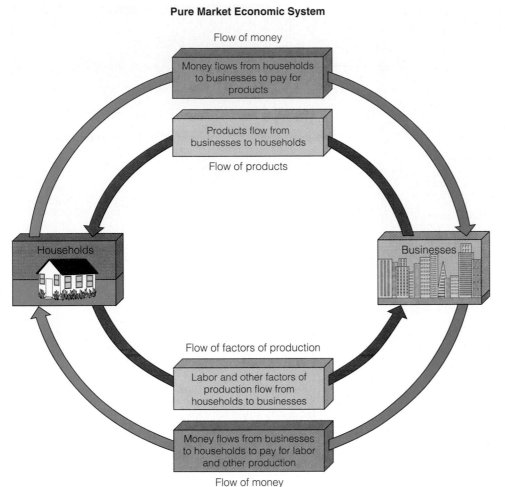

**Pure Market Economic System**

Flow of money

Money flows from households to businesses to pay for products

Products flow from businesses to households

Flow of products

Households

Businesses

Flow of factors of production

Labor and other factors of production flow from households to businesses

Money flows from businesses to households to pay for labor and other production

Flow of money

**Figure 25-3** In a pure market economic system economic goods and money would flow in a closed loop between households and businesses. People in households spend money to buy goods that firms produce, and firms spend money to buy factors of production (natural capital, manufactured capital, and human capital). In many economics textbooks this and other economic systems are depicted, as here, as if they were self-contained and thus not dependent on the ecosphere—a model that reinforces the idea that unlimited growth of any kind is sustainable.

wildlife refuges, parks, and national wilderness areas (Spotlight, p. 392). Governments are under continual pressure to sell these resources to individuals (convert them to private-property resources) or to give individuals access to their timberlands, grazing lands, minerals, energy resources, and recreational areas at below normal market prices (Section 2-5).

**TYPES OF ECONOMIC SYSTEMS** An **economy** is a system of production, distribution, and consumption of economic goods. In **economic systems** individuals, businesses, and societies decide what goods and services to produce, how to produce them, how many to produce, how to distribute them, and what to buy and sell. The form these decisions take indicates the type of economic system a given society follows.

In a **traditional economic system** people use past customs and traditions to make economic decisions. Often these systems are **subsistence economies**, in which families, tribes, or other groups produce only enough goods to meet their basic needs, with little or no surplus for sale or trade.

In a **pure command economic system**, or **centrally planned economy**, all economic decisions are made by the government. This system is based on the belief that government control and ownership of the means of production is the most efficient way to produce, use, and distribute scarce resources.

In a **pure market economic system**, also known as **pure capitalism**, all economic decisions are made in *markets*, where buyers (demanders) and sellers (suppliers) of economic goods freely interact without government or other interference. All economic resources are owned by private individuals and private institutions, rather than by the government. All buying and selling is based on **pure competition**, in which no seller or buyer is powerful enough to control the supply, demand, or price of a good and all sellers and buyers have full information about and access to the market.

Economists often represent pure capitalism as a circular flow of economic goods and money between households and businesses operating essentially independently of the ecosphere (Figure 25-3). By contrast, environmentalists emphasize the dependence of this

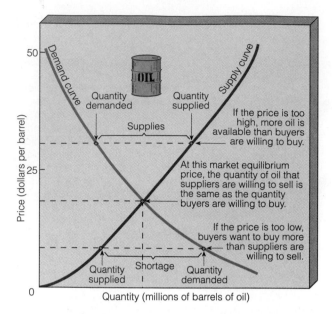

**Figure 25-4** Supply, demand, and market equilibrium for gasoline in a pure market system. If price, supply, and demand are the only factors involved, the market equilibrium point occurs where the demand and supply curves intersect.

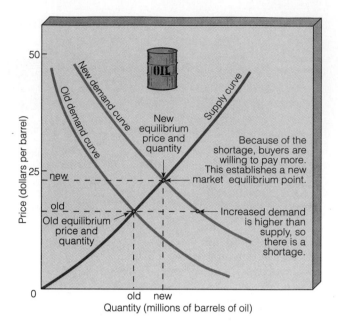

**Figure 25-5** Short-term effects of a rising demand for gasoline because of more drivers, a switch to less fuel-efficient cars, more spendable income for travel, or less use of mass transit. If the demand fell because of fewer drivers, a switch to more fuel-efficient cars, less spendable income for travel, or increased use of mass transit, the original demand curve would shift to the left. The decreased demand would create a temporary surplus, stimulating sellers competing for consumers' money to charge less, until the price reaches a new market equilibrium point.

or any other economic system on the ecosphere (Figure 25-2).

In a pure capitalism system a company has no legal allegiance to a particular nation, no obligation to supply any particular good or service, and no obligation to provide jobs, safe workplaces, or environmental protection. The company's only obligation is to produce the highest possible short-term economic return (profit) for the owners or stockholders whose capital the company is using to do business. Alfred Kahn, head of the Council on Wage and Price Stability under President Carter, put it bluntly: "No one in his or her right mind would argue that the competitive market system takes care of protecting the environment—it does not."

Economic decisions in a pure market system are governed by interactions of demand, supply, and price. Buyers want to pay as little as possible for an economic good, and sellers want to set as high a price as possible so as to maximize profits. **Market equilibrium** occurs when the quantity supplied equals the quantity demanded, and the price is no higher than buyers are willing to pay and no lower than sellers are willing to accept. If price, supply, and demand are the only factors involved, the demand and supply curves for an economic good intersect at the *market equilibrium point* (Figure 25-4).

However, factors other than price can shift the original demand curves (Figure 25-5) and supply curves (Figure 25-6). These factors upset the market equilibrium and establish new equilibrium points.

## MIXED ECONOMIC SYSTEMS: THE REAL WORLD

In reality all countries have **mixed economic systems** that fall somewhere between the pure market and pure command systems, as well as containing some elements of traditional systems. Pure market economies don't exist because they have flaws that require government intervention in the marketplace to:

- Prevent one seller or buyer (*monopoly*) or one group of sellers or buyers (*oligopoly* or *cartel*) from dominating the market and thus controlling supply or demand and price. (The goal of almost every business lobbyist in Washington and in other capitals of market economy countries is to subvert free-market competition by getting a subsidy or tax break.)

- Provide national security, education, and other public goods

- Redistribute some income and wealth, especially to people unable to attain their basic needs

- Protect people from fraud, trespass, theft, and bodily harm

- Protect the health and safety of workers and consumers

- Ensure economic stability by trying to control cycles of boom and bust that afflict a pure market system

Q: What can be done when groundwater becomes contaminated?

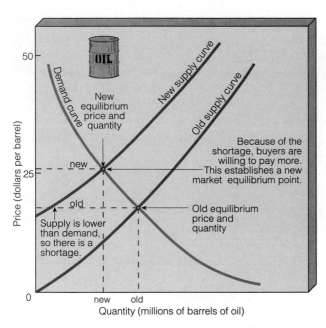

**Figure 25-6** Short-term effects of a dropping gasoline supply, which might occur if the cost of finding, extracting, and refining oil increases or if existing oil deposits are economically depleted. Also, if oil producers expect higher prices in the future, they may cut production with the hope of making larger profits later. A parallel situation occurs if the supply increases: The original supply curve shifts to the right, reflecting a temporary surplus; then competition stimulates sellers to charge less, and the price moves down to a new market equilibrium point.

- Help compensate owners for large-scale destruction of assets by floods, earthquakes, hurricanes, and other natural disasters (Section 7-5)

- Prevent or reduce pollution

- Prevent or reduce depletion of natural resources, which are undervalued in market economies

- Manage public land resources (Chapter 15)

Pure command economies don't exist either. Experience has shown that governments cannot efficiently control all economic activity from the top down. Recently eastern European countries and the former Soviet Union have moved away from command economic systems and toward market approaches.

## 25-2 Economic Growth and External Costs

**ECONOMIC GROWTH AND GROSS NATIONAL PRODUCT** Virtually all economies seek **economic growth**: an increase in the capacity of the economy to provide goods and services for final use. Such growth

is accomplished by maximizing the flow of matter and energy resources (throughput) by population growth (more consumers), more consumption per person, or both. Nature is seen as a "superstore" stocked with an infinite supply of goods to be used to meet the needs and ever expanding wants of a consumer society.

Economic growth is usually measured by the increase in a country's **gross national product (GNP)**: the market value in current dollars of all goods and services produced by an economy for final use during a year (an indicator introduced in the late 1940s). To get a clearer picture of economic output, economists use the **real GNP**: the GNP adjusted for *inflation* (any increase in the average price level of final goods and services). And to show how the average person's slice of the economic pie is changing, economists use the **real GNP per capita**: the real GNP divided by the total population. If population expands faster than economic growth, the real GNP per capita falls. However, this statistic can hide the fact that the wealthy few have enormous slices and the many poor have crumbs.

**GNP, QUALITY OF LIFE, AND ENVIRONMENTAL DEGRADATION: FAULTY RADAR** We are urged to buy and consume more and more so the GNP will rise, making the country and the world a better place for everyone (see cartoon). The truth is that GNP indicators are poor measures of social well-being, environmental health, and even economic health because:

- *They hide the negative impact on humans and the rest of the ecosphere of producing many goods and services.* For example, each year in the United States the estimated $150 billion in health care expenses and other damages caused by air pollution raise the GNP and GNP per capita. So do the funeral expenses for the 150,000–350,000 Americans killed prematurely each year from air pollution. The $2.2 billion that Exxon spent partially cleaning up the oil spill from the *Exxon Valdez* tanker (Case Study, p. 606) pushed up the GNP, as did the $1 billion spent because of the Three Mile Island nuclear accident (Figure 18-16), the $275 million spent dealing with toxic wastes at Love Canal (p. 550), and old-growth forest destruction.

- *They take no account of depletion and degradation of natural resources, upon which all economies ultimately depend.* A country can be headed toward ecological bankruptcy—exhausting its mineral resources, eroding its soils, polluting its water, cutting down its forests, destroying its wetlands and estuaries, and depleting its wildlife and fisheries—yet have a rapidly rising GNP.

- *They hide or underestimate some positive effects on society.* For example, more energy-efficient light bulbs, appliances, and cars reduce electric and

A: Usually nothing

gasoline bills and pollution, but these register as a drop in GNP. GNP indicators also do not include the labor we put into volunteer work, the health care we give loved ones, the food we grow for ourselves, or the cooking, cleaning, and repairs we do for ourselves.

■ *They tell us nothing about economic justice.* They don't tell us how resources, income, or the harmful effects of economic growth (pollution, waste dumps, land degradation) are distributed among the people in a country. UNICEF suggests that countries should be ranked not by average GNP per capita but by average income of the lowest 40% of their people. The environmental justice movement calls not only for a fairer distribution of income but also for a fairer distribution of the harmful effects of economic growth instead of concentrating these effects on the poor and on minority groups (Guest Essay, p. 566).

Russell Petersen, former head of the White House Council on Environmental Quality, summed up the problem with using GNP as a guideline for progress:

*If we produce a million dollars worth of carcinogens, this weighs as much on the GNP scale as a million dollars worth of antibiotics. If we hire a housekeeper, this counts in the GNP, but when one's spouse manages the household, this doesn't count. Teaching counts, but learning doesn't. GNP gives no measure of the hungry, the unemployed, the sick, the ill-housed, the illiterate, the oppressed, the frightened, the unhappily employed, or those who have reached the highest level of fulfillment. Furthermore, it does not measure the waste of*

*resources, the spending of our natural capital such as oil, or the befoulment of our life support systems.*

**SOLUTIONS: BETTER INDICATORS** Economists have never claimed that GNP indicators are a good measure of social and environmental health, but governments, businesses, and the media use them that way. Environmentalists and some economists believe that GNP indicators should be replaced or supplemented with indicators that measure the quality of life and our harmful impacts on the ecosphere. Such indicators exist, though they are not widely used.

In 1972, for example, economists William Nordhaus and James Tobin developed an indicator called *net economic welfare (NEW)* to estimate the annual change in quality of life in a country. They calculate a price tag for pollution and other "negative" goods and services included in the GNP, and subtract them from the GNP to give the NEW (NEW or good GNP = total GNP – bad GNP), as is done in Japan. Dividing a country's NEW by its population gives the *per capita NEW.*

Since 1940 the real NEW per capita in the United States has risen at about half the rate of the real GNP per person. And since 1968, in fact, the gap between these two indicators has been widening, suggesting that for 25 years things have been getting worse for most people in the United States. Economist David Pearce estimates that pollution and natural resource degradation subtract 1–5% from the GNP of MDCs and 5–15% for LDCs, and that in general these percentages are rising.

In 1989 economist Robert Repetto and other researchers at the World Resources Institute proposed

Q: What percentage of the world's potential food supply is lost to pests?

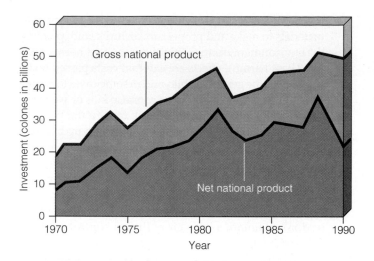

**Figure 25-7** GNP and NNP (net national product) for Costa Rica, 1970–1990. The NNP was calculated by adjusting the GNP to include depletion of the country's forests, soils, and fisheries. If depletion of coal, mineral ores, and other nonrenewable resources had been included, its NNP would have grown even more slowly. (Data from World Resources Institute)

that depletion or destruction of natural resources be included as a factor in GNP to calculate a country's *net national product (NNP)*. They developed a fairly simple model for doing this and have applied it to Indonesia and Costa Rica (Figure 25-7). Australia, France, Canada, the Netherlands, and Norway have been compiling inventories of their natural resources and how these stocks change over time, but have not used them to adjust GNP.

The United Nations Development Programme has devised a *human development index (HDI)* to estimate average quality of life in different countries. It is an aggregate of three indicators: life expectancy at birth, literacy rates, and real GNP per person. In 1990 the five countries with the highest HDI were Japan, Sweden, Switzerland, Holland, and Canada. Mostly because of its illiteracy rate, the United States placed nineteenth. This indicator would be greatly improved by including sex inequalities (which would drop Japan to number 17), income distribution, and environmental degradation. Even limited indicators of human development reveal that life quality can be improved by cooperation, education, and a more equitable distribution of land and resource wealth instead of relying on unrestricted economic growth to boost per capita income (Case Study, right).

Economists Herman E. Daly (Guest Essay, p. 656) and John B. Cobb, Jr., have developed an *index of sustainable economic welfare (ISEW)* and applied it to the United States (Figure 25-8). This comprehensive indicator of well-being measures per capita GNP adjusted for inequalities in income distribution, depletion of nonrenewable resources, loss of wetlands, loss of

## Kerala: Improving Life Quality Without Conventional Economic Growth

**CASE STUDY** The state of Kerala in southwest India (Figure 8-15) has shown how quality of life can be improved without emphasizing economic growth. By conventional measures it is one of the world's poorest areas, with a per capita income of less than $200 (compared to $330 for India and $870 for all LDCs) and 18% unemployment. Yet in terms of life quality it has some of the highest scores among LDCs.

Life expectancy is 68 years compared with 63 years in LDCs and 59 years in India. Infant mortality is 27 per 1,000 births compared with 77 for LDCs and 91 for India. And the total fertility rate is 2.3 in Kerala compared with 3.7 for MDCs and 3.9 in India. Almost 94% of Kerala's citizens can read or write compared with less than 50% (29% for women) for the rest of India. It is the sole Indian state where women are as literate as men, and in Kerala women have far more rights than in the rest of India.

Kerala's high educational level has attracted industrial jobs, but so far not at the expense of its natural environment. It is one of the world's most densely populated places, with a population larger than California's squeezed into one-tenth the area. Yet, forest still covers 29% of its area—the third highest rate in India and well ahead of other states with half its population. Since 1960 a land reform program has meant that 90% of the people own the land on which their house stands.

Kerala also leads India in the quality of its roads, schools, hospitals, public housing, drinking water, sanitation, immunization programs, and nutrition programs for infants and pregnant and lactating women. Its 29 million people have access to free or inexpensive medical care, and all households can buy rice and certain basic commodities at subsidized prices.

These gains in life quality and social justice are the results of decades of political struggles. Many observers see culturally diverse Kerala as a shining example of how people can help themselves by choosing self-reliance and economic redistribution of local wealth (mostly by land reforms) over conventional economic growth and dependence on outside loans.

farmland from soil erosion and urbanization, the cost of air and water pollution, and estimates of long-term environmental damage from ozone depletion and possible global warming.

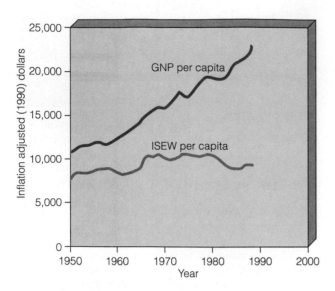

**Figure 25-8** Comparison of GNP and ISEW (index of sustainable economic welfare) per person in the United States, 1950–1988. After rising by 42% between 1950 and 1976, the ISEW fell 12% between 1977 and 1988. (Data from Herman E. Daly, John B. Cobb, Jr., and Clifford W. Cobb)

In poor countries, where such information is not available, grain consumption per person provides a rough estimate of life quality. Ideally this indicator should also take into account how much of the grain was produced unsustainably by depleting groundwater, destroying forests, and eroding soils.

None of these new economic, social, and environmental indicators is perfect. Without them, however, we know too little about what is happening to people, the environment, and the planet's natural resource base; what needs to be done; and what types of policies work. In effect, we are trying to guide national and global economies through treacherous waters at ever-increasing speed using faulty radar.

Because changing the indicators used by countries and the UN is so difficult, governments, economists, and the media should work together to widely publish several Earth indicators.

**INTERNAL AND EXTERNAL COSTS** All economic goods have both internal and external costs. For example, the price you pay for a car reflects the costs of the factory, raw materials, labor, marketing, shipping, and company and dealer profits. After you buy the car, you must pay for gasoline, maintenance, and repair. All these direct costs, paid for by the seller and the buyer of an economic good, are called **internal costs.**

Making, distributing, and using any economic goods also involve **externalities**. These are social costs or benefits not included in the market price of an economic good or service. For example, if a car dealer builds an aesthetically pleasing showroom and grounds, that is an **external benefit** to people who enjoy the sight at no cost.

On the other hand, extracting and processing raw materials to make and propel cars disturbs land, pollutes the environment, reduces biodiversity, and harms people. These harmful effects are **external costs** passed on to workers, to the general public, and in some cases to future generations. Air pollution from cars also kills or weakens some types of trees (Figure 22-10), raising the price of lumber and paper. In addition, taxes may go up because the public demands that the government regulate the pollution and degradation associated with producing and operating cars. You add to the external costs when you throw trash out of a car, drive a gas-guzzler (which adds more air pollution than a more efficient car), disconnect or don't maintain a car's air pollution control devices, drive with faulty brakes, or don't keep your motor tuned.

Because these harmful costs aren't included in the market price, you don't connect them with the car or type of car you are driving. As a consumer and taxpayer, however, you pay these hidden costs sooner or later in the form of higher taxes, higher health costs, higher health insurance premiums, and higher cleaning and maintenance bills. Good health, clean air and water, biodiversity, and quality of life aren't free. It's just that their costs are hidden from the marketplace.

To progrowth economists external costs are minor defects in the flow of production and consumption (Figure 25-3) that can be cured from the profits made from more economic growth (Guest Essay, p. 24). To environmentalists the rising number of harmful externalities is a warning sign that our economic systems are stressing the ecosphere (Guest Essays, pp. 26 and 656 and Figure 25-7) and need to be restructured.

**SOLUTIONS: FULL-COST PRICING** As long as people are rewarded for using up resources and polluting, few will volunteer to commit economic suicide by changing. Suppose you own a company and believe it's wrong to subject your workers to hazardous conditions and to pollute the environment any more than can be handled by Earth's natural processes. If you voluntarily improve safety conditions for your workers and install pollution controls but your competitors don't, your product will cost more and you will be at a competitive disadvantage. Your profits will decline, and sooner or later you may go bankrupt and your employees lose their jobs.

Under current economic systems a tree has economic value only when it is cut down and converted to lumber or paper. Thus it makes economic sense to cut down a forest and use the profits to reward investors, to cut down more forests, or to invest in other businesses when the forests dwindle (Case Study, p. 284). The external costs of doing this—loss of biodiversity, soil erosion, air and water pollution, and loss of jobs in areas depleted of timber—are passed on to society at large or to future generations.

**Q:** What percentage of U.S. crops are lost to pests?

A general way to deal with the problem of harmful external costs is for the government to add taxes, pass laws, or use other devices that force producers to include all or most of this expense in the market price of economic goods. Then that price would be the **full cost** of those goods: internal costs plus short- and long-term external costs. Full-cost pricing involves *internalizing the external costs*. This requires government action because few companies will increase their cost of doing business unless their competitors have to do it as well.

What would happen if we adopted this policy? Economic growth would be redirected. We would increase the beneficial parts of the GNP, decrease the harmful parts, increase production of beneficial goods, raise the net economic welfare, and help sustain the earth. Preventing pollution would become more profitable than controlling it; and waste reduction, recycling, and reuse would be more profitable than waste management.

You would pay more for most things because their market prices would be closer to their true costs, but everything would be "up front." External costs would no longer be hidden. You would also have the information you need to make informed economic decisions (as called for by the theory behind a true free-market economy) about the effects of your lifestyle on the planet's life-support systems.

Moreover, real market prices wouldn't always be higher, and some things might even cost less. Internalizing external costs stimulates producers to find ways to cut costs by inventing more resource-efficient and less harmful methods of production, and to offer less harmful *green products*. Jobs would be lost in Earth-degrading businesses, but at least as many—probably more—jobs would be created in Earth-sustaining businesses. We get what we reward.

As external costs are internalized, governments must reduce income and other taxes, and withdraw subsidies once used to hide and pay for these external costs. Otherwise consumers will face higher market prices without tax relief—a policy guaranteed to fail.

Full-cost pricing makes so much sense you might be wondering why it's not more widely done. One reason is that many producers of harmful and wasteful goods fear they would have to charge so much that they couldn't stay in business or would have to give up government subsidies that have helped hide the external costs. And why should they want to change a system that's been so good to them? Another reason is that it's difficult to internalize external costs because it's not easy to put a price tag on all the harmful effects of making and using an economic good. People disagree on the values they attach to various costs and benefits. However, making difficult choices about how resources should be used and distributed is what economics and politics are all about.

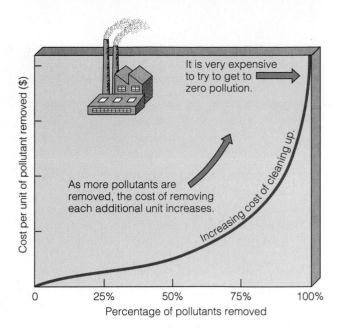

**Figure 25-9** The cost of removing each additional unit of pollution rises exponentially, which explains why it is usually cheaper to prevent pollution than to clean it up.

## 25-3 Solutions: Using Economics to Improve Environmental Quality

**COST-BENEFIT ANALYSIS** One of the chief tools corporations and governments use in making economic decisions is cost-benefit analysis. This controversial approach (Pro/Con, p. 646) involves comparing the estimated short-term and long-term costs (losses) and benefits (gains) resulting from various alternatives in making economic decisions.

**CONTROL OR PREVENTION?** Shouldn't our goal be zero pollution? Ideally, yes. In the real world, not necessarily. First, nature can handle some of our wastes, as long as we don't destroy, degrade, or overload these natural processes. But ideally toxic products that cannot be degraded by natural processes or that break down very slowly in the environment should not be produced or used except in small amounts with special permits.

Second, as long as we continue to rely on pollution control we can't afford zero pollution for any but the most harmful substances. We can remove a certain percentage of the pollutants in air, water, or soil, but when we remove more the price per unit rises sharply (Figure 25-9).

Beyond a certain point the costs will be greater than the harmful effects of pollution. As a result, some businesses could go bankrupt, and some people could

Compared with blundering ahead totally in the dark, cost-benefit analyses have obvious benefits. Used properly, they can be reasonable guides for action. At the very least, they can often indicate the cheapest way to go.

However, like many other things, cost-benefit analyses can be misused and even do great harm. It is important to understand that such analyses are only as good as the data and the assumptions used to arrive at both costs and benefits.

One problem with cost-benefit analysis is the use of **discount rate:** an estimate of how much economic value a resource will have in the future compared with its present value. Suppose a stand of redwood trees has a current market value of $1 million. At a zero discount rate it will still be worth $1 million 50 years from now, while at a 10% discount rate (normally used by most businesses and the U.S. Office of Management and Budget), it will be worth only $10,000 and should be cut down. Thus the choice of discount rate is a primary factor affecting the outcome of any cost-benefit analysis.

Proponents of high discount rates argue that inflation will make the value of their earnings less in the future than now. They also fear that innovation or changed consumer preferences will make a product or service obsolete. Proponents also assume that economic growth through technological progress will automatically raise average living standards in the future. Why, then, should the current generation pay higher prices and taxes to benefit future generations who will be better off?

Environmentalists question this belief, pointing out that current economic systems are based upon depleting the natural capital that supports them (Figure 25-2). High

discount rates worsen this situation by encouraging such rapid exploitation of natural resources for immediate payoffs that sustainable use is virtually impossible. They believe that unique and scarce resources should be protected by having a 0% or a negative discount rate, and that rates of 1–3% would make it profitable to use other resources sustainably or slowly. Thus, the choice of discount rate is an *ethical decision* about our responsibility to future generations.

Another problem with cost-benefit analysis, is determining who benefits and who is harmed. In the United States, for example, an estimated 100,000 Americans die each year from exposure to hazardous chemicals and other safety hazards at work, and an additional 400,000 are seriously injured from such exposure. In many other countries (especially LDCs) the situation is much worse. Is that a necessary or an unnecessary (and unethical) cost of doing business?

A serious limitation of cost-benefit analysis is that many things we value cannot be reduced to dollars and cents. How do we put meaningful price tags on human life, good health, clean air and water, accidents that are prevented, beautiful scenery, wilderness, the northern spotted owl (Case Study, p. 285), and the ability of natural systems to dilute and degrade some of our wastes and to replenish timber, fertile soil, and other vital potentially renewable resources?

The dollar values we assign to such things will vary widely because of different assumptions, discount rates, and value judgments, leading to a wide range of projected costs and benefits. For example, monetary values assigned to a human life vary from nothing to about $7 million, but typically range from $200,000–$500,000.

Because these and other estimates of costs and benefits are so

variable, figures can easily be weighted to achieve the desired outcome by proponents or opponents of a proposed project or action. For example, faced with regulation in 1971, the oil industry estimated that phasing out leaded gasoline in the United States would cost $7 billion per year until the task was completed, although actual costs were only $150–$500 million per year. Similarly, an industry-sponsored study estimated that compliance with a standard to protect workers from vinyl chloride would cost $65–$90 billion, but less than $1 billion was actually needed to comply with the standard.

In short, cost-benefit analyses are useful only if decision makers and the public realize their limitations and use them as only one of several guides for making economic decisions. To avoid possible abuses, environmentalists and economists suggest the following guidelines:

- Require all studies to use uniform standards.

- Clearly state all assumptions.

- Show all projected costs, with their estimated range of values based on each set of assumptions.

- Estimate the short- and long-term benefits and costs to all affected population groups.

- Estimate the effectiveness of the project or form of regulation, instead of assuming (as is often done) that all projects and regulations will be executed with 100% efficiency and effectiveness.

- Open the evaluations to public review and challenge.

- Do not use cost-benefit analysis as the sole method of determining environmental, health, resource, or consumer protection policies.

Q: What percentage of insecticides applied to U.S. crops reach the target pests?

lose jobs, homes, and savings (Case Study, p. 17). If we don't go far enough, the harmful external effects will cost more than pollution reduction.

How do we achieve this balance? Theoretically we plot a curve of the estimated economic costs of cleaning up pollution and a curve of the estimated social (external) costs of pollution. Adding the two curves together, we get a third curve showing the total costs. At the lowest point on this third curve is the balance point or *optimal level of pollution* (Figure 25-10).

On a graph this looks neat and simple, but environmentalists and business leaders often disagree in their estimates of the harmful costs of pollution. Furthermore, this approach assumes that we know which substances are harmful and how much each part of the environment can absorb—things we don't know and most likely will never know.

Some environmentalists believe that this approach is doomed to fail. They argue that as long as population and per capita resource use continue to rise, any gains based on pollution control will eventually be overwhelmed (Figure 1-15). Instead of spending a lot of money and time setting and enforcing standards, arguing over "optimal" levels, and cleaning up chemicals we release into the environment, they argue we should start rewarding people for preventing pollution (Guest Essay, p. 41) and penalizing those who don't.

These environmentalists also call for reversing the present assumption that a chemical or new technology is safe until it is shown to be harmful. By contrast, if a chemical or new technology was considered potentially harmful until shown to be safe, and this was coupled with full-cost pricing (mostly by removing subsidies and imposing taxes on harmful items), emphasis would shift from costly pollution cleanup to more effective pollution prevention.

Critics argue that this approach would wreck the economy, putting large numbers of people out of work. Proponents counter that our present course will further deplete the Earth capital upon which our economies and survival depend, wrecking the environment and thus the economy, putting even more people out of work, and killing large numbers of people.

In 1992 the ministers of 13 European nations (Belgium, Denmark, Finland, France, Germany, Great Britain, Iceland, Ireland, the Netherlands, Norway, Portugal, Spain, and Sweden) made a binding commitment to try to achieve zero discharge of persistent toxic substances. In doing this they replaced the *safe-until-shown-harmful* approach to pollution control with the *harmful-until-shown-safe* approach.

**REGULATION OR MARKET FORCES?** Controlling or preventing pollution and reducing resource waste require government intervention in the marketplace. This can be done either by *regulation* or by *market forces*.

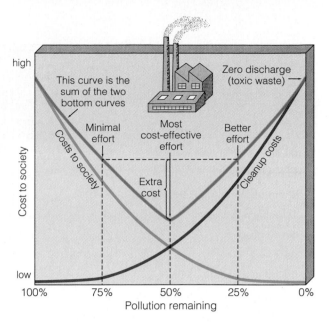

**Figure 25-10** Finding the optimal level of pollution.

*Regulation* is a *command-and-control* approach that involves passing and enforcing laws that set pollution standards, establish deadlines and penalties, regulate harmful activities, ban the release of toxic chemicals into the environment, and require that certain resources be protected from use or from unsustainable use.

Ways to use market forces to improve environmental quality and reduce resource waste are:

- *Providing subsidies that encourage desirable behavior.*

- *Withdrawing subsidies that encourage harmful behavior, such as waste production and energy efficiency.*

- *Granting tradable pollution and resource use rights.* This would be done by setting a total limit for a pollutant or resource use and allocating that total among manufacturers or users by permit. Permit holders not using their entire allocation could keep it as a credit against future expansion, use it in another part of their operation, or sell it to other companies. Tradable rights could also be established between countries to preserve biodiversity and to reduce emissions of greenhouse gases, ozone-destroying chemicals, lead, and other chemicals with regional or global effects.

- *Enacting green taxes.* This could include taxes on each unit of pollution discharged into the air or water, each unit of hazardous or nuclear waste produced, each unit of specified virgin resources used, each unit of fossil fuel used, each unit of pesticide used, and each unit of solid waste produced. To allow economic adjustment, such eco-taxes should be phased in over 5–10 years. At the same time, income tax and other taxes would be

**Table 25-1 Economic Solutions to Pollution and Resource Waste**

| Solution | Internalizes External Costs | Innovation | International Competitiveness | Administrative Costs | Increases Government Revenue |
|---|---|---|---|---|---|
| Regulation | Partially | Can encourage | Decreased* | High | No |
| Subsidies | No | Can encourage | Increased | Low | No |
| Withdrawing harmful subsidies | Yes | Can encourage | Decreased* | Low | Yes |
| Tradable rights | Yes | Encourages | Decreased* | Low | Yes |
| Green taxes | Yes | Encourages | Decreased* | Low | Yes |
| User fees | Yes | Can encourage | Decreased* | Low | Yes |
| Pollution-prevention bonds | Yes | Encourages | Decreased* | Low | No |

* Unless more cost-effective and productive technologies are developed.

reduced so that low- and middle-income people and businesses (especially small businesses) would not be penalized.

- *Charging user fees.* Users would pay fees to cover all or most costs for grazing livestock, extracting lumber and minerals from public lands, and using water provided by government-financed projects.

- *Requiring businesses to post a pollution-prevention bond when they open a plant, incinerator, or landfill.* After a reasonable time the deposit (with interest) would be returned *minus* the estimated environmental costs.

Each of these approaches has advantages and disadvantages (Table 25-1). Studies estimate that the current U.S. bill for environmental protection—over $120 billion per year—based mostly on regulation, could be cut by one-third to one-half with a mix of market-based policies.

## 25-4 Solutions: Reducing Poverty

**THE TRICKLE-DOWN APPROACH** **Poverty** is usually defined as not being able to meet one's basic economic needs (Spotlight, p. 10). According to the World Bank any person with an income of less than $370 per year—roughly $1 per day—is poor. Currently 1.2 billion people—one of every five persons on the planet—in LDCs are poor, and this number is projected to rise to 1.3 billion by 2000 and 1.5 billion by 2025.

Most economists believe that a growing economy is the best way to help the poor. Economic growth can lead to new businesses and expansion of existing ones. This creates more jobs and enables more of the in-

creased wealth to reach workers, and provides more tax revenue for helping the poor help themselves—the so-called *trickle-down hypothesis.*

The facts, however, suggest that either the hypothesis is wrong or it has not been applied. Instead of trickling down, most of the benefits of economic growth have flowed up since 1950 to make the top fifth of the world's people much richer and the bottom fifth poorer; most of those in between have lost or gained only slightly in real income per capita (Figure 1-6).

**ENCOURAGING SELF-RELIANT DEVELOPMENT** Critics contend that most so-called development has mainly benefited the affluent in LDCs and MDCs at the expense of the poor (especially the rural poor and indigenous people who are displaced from their land). These critics believe that dealing with the interrelated problems of poverty, environmental degradation, and population growth requires new forms of development based on Mahatma Gandhi's concept of *antyodaya*: putting the poor and their environment first, not last.

They believe that more beneficial economic development can be achieved by:

- *Protecting what works.* This involves learning where and how people are living sustainably, and not disrupting their lives and cultures.

- *Fostering individual and community self-reliance.* This can be accomplished by promoting fairer distribution of land and income, encouraging cooperation among community members, using locally controlled technologies and resources whenever possible, relying on sustainable use of local and regional renewable resources whenever possible, keeping the fruits of economic activities in local communities, creating local jobs, and

Q: Since 1945 how many premature deaths from insect-transmitted diseases have been prevented by using insecticides?

reducing dependence on outside suppliers, banks, and aid donors (Case Study, p. 643).

- *Involving local residents—including women—and private nongovernmental organizations (NGOs) in the planning and execution of all projects.* This means asking the poor what they need, giving it to them, putting them in charge, and telling others about what works.

- *Making use of local wisdom, skills, and resources.* The poor know far more about poverty, survival, environmental sustainability, local needs, and what will work locally than do outside bureaucrats or experts.

- *Learning from other cultures about sustainable living and sharing this knowledge with people in other LDCs and in MDCs.*

**REDUCING POVERTY** Sharply reducing poverty requires governments of most LDCs to make drastic, difficult, and controversial policy changes. They include:

- *Shifting more of the national budget to aid the rural and urban poor.*

- *Giving villages, villagers, and the urban poor title to common lands and to crops and trees they plant on common lands.*

- *Redistributing some of the land owned by the wealthy to the poor.* This has already been done in South Korea, China, and Kerala (Case Study, p. 643).

- *Spending more money on education, health care, family planning, clean drinking water, and sanitation for the poor in rural villages and in urban slums.*

- *Extending full human rights to women.* Special emphasis would be given to poor women, who usually have few rights.

MDCs and the rich in LDCs are also urged to play a key role in reducing poverty and see this as a vital investment in global environmental and economic security for everyone. The fortunate need to heed the words of John F. Kennedy: "If a free society cannot save the many who are poor, it cannot save the few who are rich." Controversial ways to do this include:

- *Forgiving at least 60% of the $1.35 trillion that LDCs owe to MDCs and international lending agencies.* These loans can't be repaid and interest payments are depleting Earth capital without improving the position of the poor (Figure 1-6). UNICEF blames the death of 500,000 children a year on the debt burden of the LDCs. Most of this debt could be written off over a decade. But some of it can be forgiven in exchange for agreements by the governments of LDCs to increase expenditures for rural development, family planning, health care, Earth-sustaining education, land redistribution, protection of

biodiversity, ecological restoration, and sustainable use of renewable resources. Debtor LDCs—which between 1982 and 1990 increased their debt by 61%—now pay creditors almost $12.5 billion per month in interest and principal—as much as all LDCs spend per month on health and education. This deprives their people of basic necessities and has provided private banks and the governments of MDCs with six times the assistance the U.S. provided to rebuild Europe after World War II.

- *Increasing the nonmilitary aid to LDCs from MDCs to 2% (and ideally to 5%) of the annual GNP of the MDCs (compared to 0.5% in 1992 and 0.15% for the United States).* This aid would go directly to the poor to help them become more self-reliant rather than more dependent on MDCs.

- *Establishing an international tax on all global arms sales (favored by 86% of Americans).* All proceeds would go to reduce poverty.

- *Shifting most international aid from large-scale projects to small projects targeted to benefit local communities of the poor.* Examples are community woodlots, rural cookstove industries, urban bicycle factories, solar cells for pumping water and providing electricity in rural areas, soil conservation and integrated pest management for small farmers, improved energy efficiency in dwellings and factories, low-cost housing, biogas digesters (Figure 17-23), environmental restoration, recycling materials, and factories for making solar cells and energy-efficient lights.

- *Requiring international lending agencies to use an environmental and social impact statement (developed by standardized guidelines) to evaluate any proposed development project.* No project should be supported unless its net environmental impact is favorable, most of its benefits go to the poorest 40% of the people affected, and the local people it affects are involved in planning and executing the project. All projects should be carefully monitored, and further funding halted immediately when environmental safeguards are not followed.

- *Lifting trade barriers that hinder the export of commodities from LDCs to MDCs.* Trade barriers in rich countries cost LDCs about $100 billion annually in lost sales and depressed prices. But trade policies should benefit the environment, workers, and the poorest 40% of humanity (Spotlight, p. 650).

- *Having governments throughout the world cooperate in tracking the movement of capital by wealthy elites in LDCs to MDCs.* Owners of that capital would be required to pay taxes on it and on any income it generates to help finance the economic recovery of their homelands.

## GATT: Solution or Problem?

The 1948 General Agreement on Tariffs and Trade (GATT) regulates over 90% of all world trade. Since 1986 the United States and 107 other GATT nations have been meeting to extend the treaty by abolishing all barriers to trade between them. The 1989 Free Trade Agreement (FTA) between Canada and the United States and the proposed North American Free Trade Agreement (NAFTA) between Canada, the United States, and Mexico have similar goals. Proponents argue that this will benefit LDCs whose products are often at a competitive disadvantage because of trade barriers erected by MDCs.

On the surface this sounds good, but critics see some serious drawbacks. For one thing, some trade "barriers" are not about profits and prices. They are designed to protect workers and consumers—and the environment. If trade becomes completely free—that is, if these protections are removed along with all other trade restrictions—the results could be disastrous.

In fact, such problems may have started. For example, British Columbia ended a government-funded tree-planting program because the

United States (under pressure from U.S. lumber companies) argued that it was an unfair subsidy to Canada's timber industry and violated the 1989 agreement. Canada also had to relax its regulations on pesticides to bring them in line with the weaker ones in the United States (Section 24-4).

Also, the Canadian timber industry is urging its government to challenge a U.S. law requiring the use of recycled fiber in newsprint as a trade barrier. And in 1991 a secret GATT panel of judges ruled that the U.S. requirement that tuna imported to the U.S. had to be caught in dolphin-sparing ways was an unfair and illegal trade barrier.

Without a massive public outcry against anti-environmental portions of GATT, NAFTA, and FTA, this is only a sampling of what is to come. Government bans on the export of raw logs to slow the destruction of rain forests or ancient forests could be overturned. Germany could be forced to repeal its law requiring recycling of all beverage containers. Countries could not restrict imports of hazardous wastes, banned medicines, and dangerous pesticides. International moratoriums on harvesting whales and bans on trading ivory to protect elephants could be overturned.

An LDC banning dirty industries could be accused of violating free trade. Indeed, Lawrence Summers, Vice President and Chief Economist of the World Bank, asked in a 1991 memorandum, "Shouldn't the World Bank be encouraging more migration of dirty industries to the less developed countries?"—noting that many people in LDCs don't live long enough to get cancer from exposure to toxic chemicals. GATT would also pit small and fledgling business against large multinational and transnational companies in the name of free trade.

Environmentalists applaud lifting restrictions that put LDCs at a disadvantage in the global marketplace. But they oppose any part of a trade agreement that restricts a country's freedom to set higher environmental, health, worker safety, or resource depletion standards than other countries. They believe that *a trade agreement should be judged on how it benefits the environment, workers, and the poorest 40% of humanity*. They argue that free trade will harm the environment unless internalizing the harmful costs of commodities by full-cost pricing and zero discharge of hazardous materials are key parts of any agreements.

---

- *Shifting to sustainable-Earth economic systems in MDCs over the next 40–50 years, and aiding LDCs in making this transition (Section 25-5).*

- *Establishing policies that will encourage MDCs and LDCs to slow population growth and stabilize their populations as soon as possible.*

## 25-5 Solutions: Making the Transition to a Sustainable-Earth Economy

**SUSTAINABLE-EARTH ECONOMIES: A NEW VISION**
What's wrong with today's economies? Most econo-

mists, business leaders, and government officials would answer, not much. They believe any problems caused by current market-based economic systems can be cured by further unlimited growth in an expanded global economy built around less—not more—government interference into economic matters. To them the best way to sustain the earth and its people is to free the market and let it work on a global basis.

Environmentalists and some economists, including Herman Daly (Guest Essay, p. 656), Kenneth Boulding, Nicholas Georgescu-Roegen, Joseph Vogel, E. J. Mishan, E. F. Schumacher, and John Gowdy, disagree with this analysis. They agree with what Aldo Leopold said in 1948: "Our bigger-and-better society is now like a hypochondriac, so obsessed with its own economic health as to have lost the capacity to remain

Q: Worldwide, how many people are poisoned each year by pesticides?

healthy." They believe that current economic systems are unsustainable because they:

- *Are based on unlimited economic growth that squanders Earth capital and promotes or does not discourage population growth (more consumers)*
- *Are guided by faulty indicators that hide unsustainable forms of growth*
- *Promote dependency rather than self-reliance in LDCs*
- *Exploit people and the environment by not sharing enough land and Earth income to sharply reduce poverty*

These environmentalists and economists believe that we must convert today's unsustainable economies to *sustainable-Earth economies* over the next 40–50 years. This new vision of economics would:

- *Encourage helpful and sustainable forms of growth, and discourage harmful and unsustainable forms.* Goals would be to cut pollution 75% and recycle or reuse 75% of all materials by 2010. This involves recognizing that economics is a subsystem of the ecosphere (Figure 25-2) and integrating economics and ecology in deciding the types of growth we should have—thinking eco-logically.
- *Be guided by economic, social, and environmental indicators that distinguish between harmful and helpful forms of growth (Section 25-2).*
- *Use full-cost pricing in which the externalities are included in the market prices of all goods and services.* This could be accomplished by withdrawing Earth-degrading subsidies, adding Earth-sustaining subsidies, and using a mix of regulation, tradable pollution and resource use rights, green taxes, and user fees (Table 25-1).
- *Place essentially infinite value on Earth capital so that it is not depleted.*
- *Shift from overconsumption by the affluent and underconsumption by the poor to sustainable consumption by all.*
- *Slow human population growth and then gradually reduce population in all countries.*
- *Greatly reduce poverty by meeting the basic needs of all (Section 25-4).*
- *Require all federal, state, and local agencies to purchase products with the highest feasible percentage of postconsumer recycled materials and energy efficiency, and to minimize use of disposable products.*
- *Require all products to be audited for environmental impact from cradle to grave, and to carry green labels summarizing this information in easily understandable form.* Such audits would be conducted using a standardized set of guidelines. Product labels would also rate energy efficiency (for energy-consuming products) and list any hazardous substances and the percentage of postconsumer recycled materials they contain.
- *Not allow the concepts of free trade and the global marketplace to restrict the freedom of any country or region to impose higher environmental, consumer, worker safety, or resource depletion standards than found in other countries (Spotlight, p. 650).*
- *Encourage decentralization of production, as well as local and regional economic self-reliance, instead of excessive dependence on the global marketplace.* This would involve making better use of locally and regionally available matter and energy resources, sustaining and increasing local jobs, and keeping money circulating in local economies instead of flowing to large multinational and transnational companies.
- *Repair past damage and create jobs by using local people to replant forests and grasslands, restore soil fertility, and rehabilitate streams and wetlands.*
- *Require any company offering stock for sale to provide potential investors with a brief summary of the environmental and social impact of the company and its products.*
- *Require that stockholders and lenders be provided with a summary of the environmental and social impact of any proposed corporate takeover, with independent analysts preparing these impact statements.*
- *Lower discount factors to lengthen the time frame of economic decisions by businesses and governments.*

**GREENING BUSINESS: MAKING SUSTAINING THE EARTH PROFITABLE** Even if one believes that sustainable-Earth economics is desirable, is it possible to make such a drastic change in the way people think and act? Some environmentalists, economists, and business leaders say it's not only possible but imperative. For example, in 1992 a group of business leaders, including the heads of Chevron, Dow, DuPont, Mitsubishi, and Ciba-Geigy, concluded that the current industrial system based on unlimited economic growth is not sustainable. Instead, they claim we must immediately make "environmental considerations . . . a part of the decision-making processes of all government agencies, all business enterprises, and in fact all people."

Proponents believe that the transition to sustainable economies can be made within 40–50 years. This would involve gradually changing the system of economic rewards and penalties in today's mixed-market economies so that the highest profits and largest source of jobs lie in Earth-sustaining economic activities. However, without the active participation of forward-looking business leaders, there is little hope of making the transition to an Earth-sustaining global economy.

A: At least 1 million (with 4,000–20,000 deaths)

## Jobs and the Environment

The idea that improvements in environmental quality will cost us jobs is simply not true. Jesse Jackson, a champion for workers, the poor, and minorities, has said, "There are two things we must know about environmental clean-up: It benefits jobs, and it benefits health. . . . But workers are intimidated by being asked: Do you want a job or lungs? . . . So after years of dedication they spend their savings and benefits on chemotherapy because they've had to make the unreal and unfair trade between lungs and jobs." Similarly, timber industry workers in the Northwest are told they must choose between owls and their jobs.

Telling workers that they must choose between their jobs and a cleaner environment is *environmental blackmail* or *greenmail*. It is a false choice used by some business and political leaders to weaken unions, undermine improvements in worker safety and health, create fear, pit workers against environmentalists, and hide the real causes of most job losses.

Studies have shown that the major reasons for job loss in the United States are unsustainable use of potentially sustainable resources (clear-cutting old-growth forests), rapid depletion of nonrenewable resources (oil and minerals), automation, declining sales because of

more efficient and innovative competitors, higher energy costs without improvements in energy efficiency, cheaper labor in other countries, decline of unsustainable "sunset" industries, failure to modernize or to invest in emerging "sunrise" industries, decreased research and development by government and business, and a reduction in defense contracts. A Bureau of Labor study found that only 0.1% of jobs lost in the United States in 1988 were lost because of environmental factors.

Studies also reveal that only a few U.S. industries have been driven abroad by environmental regulations. Most are declining, technologically inefficient industries in two categories: **(1)** makers of toxic chemicals that failed to invest in developing safer substitutes or technologies, and **(2)** mining or smelting industries that extract and process virgin minerals such as copper, lead, and zinc. Relocations in this second category are largely the result of depletion of high-quality domestic reserves or some countries' requirements that minerals mined there also be processed there.

Jobs can be lost in any economy as businesses decline or disappear because of changes in technologies or markets and resource substitution. This can have tragic impacts on individuals and on communities dependent on sunset businesses.

The real issues are whether a country and investors are investing in new technologies and sunrise businesses so more jobs are created than are lost, and whether people losing their jobs are retrained and helped financially until they can find new jobs. In 1993 the U.S. pollution control industry employed 3 million people and was growing fast.

Some of the growth businesses of the future include environmental consulting and auditing, environmental monitoring, ecological restoration, energy-efficient products and processes, green products, recycling, pollution control technology, solar-cell technology, solar thermal electricity (Figure 17-16), gas and wind turbines, hot-rock geothermal energy, cogeneration, better insulation, improved batteries and heat storage, agricultural biotechnology, integrated pest management, sustainable agriculture, superconductors, light-rail transit, magnetic levitation and other high-speed trains (Figure 9-16), fuel-efficient vehicles, hydrogen as an energy source, bike-path construction, fuel cells, precision fabrication, improved materials and production processes, energy audits and weatherization of buildings, design and information technologies, education, retraining, preventive medicine, and better contraception.

Promoting investments in such Earth-sustaining businesses will

---

Because profits drive market-based economic systems, such a shift is feasible. The problem is that those in power got there because of the old reward system, and changing the reward rules could threaten their position. Most people believe that the only way out of this dilemma is for coalition of citizens, workers, and forward-looking business and political leaders to force those in power either to work toward sustaining rather than plundering the earth or to lose their power.

With this approach, over the next 10–20 years *all* government subsidies encouraging resource depletion, waste, pollution, and environmental degradation would be phased out and replaced with taxes on such

activities. During that same period new government subsidies would be phased in for businesses built around reducing waste, recycling and reuse, preventing pollution, improving energy efficiency, and using renewable energy.

Because these plans would be well publicized and would take effect over 10–20 years, businesses would have time to adjust. The transition would also lead to a net increase in jobs because most Earth-sustaining businesses are more labor intensive than Earth-degrading businesses (Spotlight, above).

Critics claim that such a change won't happen because it would be opposed by people whose subsidies

Q: What is the most serious drawback to using chemicals to control pests (especially insects)?

create a variety of planet-friendly jobs requiring low-, moderate-, and high-level skills. For example, not only does recycling produce more jobs per unit of solid waste than either landfills or incinerators, but collecting and sorting materials for recycling creates low-skill jobs in local communities. In the United States twice as many people are employed in aluminum recycling as in aluminum production, and increasing the aluminum recycling rate to 75% would create 350,000 more jobs. Collecting and refilling reusable containers also creates many more jobs per dollar of investment than using throwaway containers, and most of the jobs are created in local communities.

The Center for the Biology of Natural Systems estimates that weatherizing all U.S. low-income housing units would create 6–7 million job years (a job year is the number of employees multiplied by the length of employment). Most of these would be low-skill jobs in or near urban areas, which are suffering the worst unemployment. Giving large tax breaks and zero- or low-interest loans for improving the energy efficiency of homes and appliances or switching to solar heating and to solar cells for producing electricity would create a huge number of jobs, reduce energy waste and air pollution, and help

the lower and middle classes. Large numbers of jobs could also be created by establishing a global network of Civilian Conservation Corps supported by government funds, private enterprise, or both.

Investments in building public transit and light-rail systems, and in manufacturing the needed rail cars and buses, produce 50% more jobs per dollar than new highway construction. A 1992 study by the Council for an Energy-Efficient Economy estimated that improving the fuel economy of new cars in the United States to 17 kilometers per liter (40 miles per gallon) by 2000 would lead to a net gain of 70,000 jobs by spurring development of new technology and by putting more money in the hands of consumers.

Wind farms (Figure 17-20) and solar thermal facilities (Figure 17-16) require two to five times as many workers per unit of electricity generated as do nuclear or coal-fired plants. Reforestation, ecological restoration, sustainable agriculture, and integrated pest management are all labor-intensive activities requiring low to moderate skills.

A congressional study concluded that investing $115 billion per year in solar energy and improving energy efficiency would eliminate about 1 million jobs in oil, gas, coal, and electricity production but

would create 2 million new jobs. And investment of the money saved by reducing energy waste could create another 2 million jobs.

A study by the Council on Economic Priorities estimates that each $1 billion spent on military goods and services in the United States creates 28,000 jobs. The same expenditure would create 32,000 jobs in public transit, 57,000 jobs in personal consumption industries, and 71,000 jobs in education.

Although a host of new jobs would be created in a sustainable-Earth economy, jobs will be lost in some industries, regions, and communities. Ways to ease the transition include (1) providing tax breaks to make it more profitable for companies to keep or hire more workers instead of replacing them with machines, (2) using incentives to encourage location of sunrise industries in hard-hit communities and helping such areas diversify their economic base, and (3) providing income and retraining assistance for workers displaced from environmentally destructive businesses (a *Superfund for Workers* as proposed by the U.S. Oil, Chemical, and Atomic Workers Union). Government and business leaders who continue to force a false choice between jobs and a healthy environment may end up with neither.

were being eliminated and whose activities were being taxed. However, investors and businesspeople have just as much interest in sustaining the earth as anyone else. Forward-looking investors and corporate executives recognize that Earth-sustaining businesses with good environmental management will prosper as the environmental revolution proceeds. They see environmental responsibility to their workers, customers, and society as part of a broadening concept of total quality.

**IMPROVING ENVIRONMENTAL MANAGEMENT**
A vital element in greening business is for schools

training economists, business leaders, and lawyers to educate their students and those already in these professions about how the earth works, what we are doing to it, how things are connected, how we need to change the way we think and do business, and what the principles of good environmental management are (Spotlight, p. 654).

**INVESTING IN THE FUTURE AND THE EARTH**
Japanese and German political and business leaders see sales of environmental goods and services—already a more than $250-billion-per-year business—as a major source of new markets, income, and jobs in the

## What Is Good Environmental Management?

**SPOTLIGHT**

Good environmental management requires:

- Providing leadership, beginning with the corporate board of directors
- Giving a clear statement of corporate environmental principles and objectives with the full backing of the board
- Making a commitment to quality; correcting defects before products are sold; providing a safe and healthy workplace; preventing pollution and waste; recycling and reusing materials within the production process; disposing of hazardous waste safely; using energy-efficient production methods; using renewable resources at sustainable rates; protecting biodiversity; marketing products that are safe, durable, energy-efficient, and easy to recycle; and asking all employees to find innovative and better ways of accomplishing these objectives
- Involving employees, environmental groups, customers, and members of local communities in developing and evaluating corporate environmental policies and strategies for improvement, and evaluating progress
- Making improving environmental quality and worker safety and health a major priority for every employee
- Conducting an annual cradle-to-grave environmental audit of all operations and products with a detailed strategy for making improvements, and publicizing the results to employees and stockholders
- Applying the same environmental and safety and health standards to company facilities and workers everywhere in the world
- Helping customers safely distribute, store, use, and dispose of or recycle company products (including picking them up and transporting them to remanufacturing plants)
- Recognizing that carrying out these policies is the best way to encourage innovation, expand markets, improve profit margins, develop happy and loyal customers, attract and keep the best-qualified employees, and help sustain the earth—a win-win strategy.

next century. They know that environmental standards and concerns are rising everywhere, and will continue to do so as the environmental revolution gains momentum. Environmental protection is one of the world's major growth industries, with the fastest economic growth occurring in cleaner production technologies (Guest Essay, p. 41 and Section 21-3), solar energy, and recycled materials processing.

Stricter environmental standards in their own countries have paid off in a cleaner environment and the development of cutting-edge technologies that can be sold at home and abroad. Indeed, each time a cleaner technology is developed it allows other countries to raise environmental standards. This increases sales for the companies developing the technology.

In 1977 the German government started the Blue-Angel product-labeling program to inform consumers about products that cause the least environmental harm. Since 1985 a more complete cradle-to-grave environmental audit of products has been available in *Okotest* (Ecotest)—the environmental equivalent of *Consumer Reports* magazine. The result has been a torrent of new environmentally friendly products that gives German producers a competitive edge in the rapidly growing global market for such products.

During the 1970s—the first green decade—the United States led the world in promoting improvements in environmental quality. Since 1980, however, the view that environmental protection weakens the economy has cost the United States its leadership in many environmental areas and marketplaces, with the gap being filled by Japan, Germany, and several other western European countries.

For example, air pollution regulations established in the mid-1970s in the United States were not strengthened until 1990, mostly because of opposition by industry and utilities. After 12 years of bickering the United States decided to make a 50% cut in sulfur dioxide emissions from its power and industrial plants by 2000. Meanwhile Germany required all its power and industrial plants to cut emissions 90% by 1990. Now German companies are selling the United States (which buys 70% of its air pollution control equipment from foreign companies) and the rest of the world cutting-edge technologies for reducing such emissions.

Mostly because of stricter air pollution regulations, German companies sell the world's cleanest and most efficient gas turbines, and have developed the world's first steel mill that uses no coal to make steel. In addition, Germany has cut energy waste and air pollution by requiring large and medium industries and utilities to use cogeneration. This technology is being sold globally. One reason German workers make 25% more than the average American worker is that German industries use half as much energy per unit of production as U.S. firms.

Germany has also revolutionized the recycling business. German car companies are required to pick up and recycle all domestic cars they make. Bar-coded parts and predesigned disassembly plants can dismantle an auto for recycling in 20 minutes. Such "take-back"

Q: According to environmentalists, what is the weakest U.S. environmental law?

requirements are being extended to almost all products to reduce use of energy and virgin raw materials. Germany plans to sell its newly developed recycling technologies to other countries. According to Carl Hahn, chairman of Volkswagen, "We must adopt the cyclical processes on which the whole of nature is based."

The German government has also supported research and development aimed at making Germany the world's leader in solar-cell technology and hydrogen fuel (p. 446), which it expects will provide a rapidly increasing share of the world's energy. Meanwhile between 1980 and 1990 the United States drastically cut back government-sponsored research in these areas and saw its share of the worldwide solar-cell market fall from 75% to 32%. And in 1989 a German company bought a U.S. company that is the world's largest manufacturer of solar cells.

Finally, Germany provides about $1 billion per year in green foreign aid to LDCs. Much of the aid is designed to stimulate demand for German technologies such as solar-powered lights, solar cells, and wind-powered water pumps.

The worst-led companies and countries will resist environmental improvement in last-gasp efforts to squeeze profits from Earth-degrading activities. Although 93% of the U.S. population favors the United States taking the lead in solving global environmental problems, the country invests only 4% of its GNP in future growth, compared to 8% in Germany and 16% in Japan. Government and business leaders that don't take advantage of the enormous opportunities for Earth-centered profits will be saddled with dying industries, inefficient economies, rising trade deficits, job losses, and falling standards of living. Companies that fail to invest in a green future may not have a future.

**SOME TRAPS: SUSTAINABLE DEVELOPMENT AND GREEN CONSUMERISM** Lately there has been much talk and excitement about the concept of **sustainable development** that emphasizes growth in the quality of life instead of the quantity of economic goods and that does not use up or degrade Earth's natural capital for future generations. Unfortunately the term *sustainable development* has been so overused that it is in danger of becoming meaningless. People have jumped on the sustainability bandwagon and used the term to promote or justify sanitized versions of growth as usual. We need to carefully analyze any proposals put forth under the sustainability banner.

For example, buying green products and boycotting harmful or wasteful products reduce our environmental impact and stimulate companies to make less harmful products. *Green consuming* buys some time, but it is not a cure-all.  If population and per capita consumption (even if it's all green) continue ris-

### What You Can Do to Promote Earth-Sustaining Living

**INDIVIDUALS MATTER**

- *Ask yourself whether you really need this product.* Recognize that even green consuming is still consuming, much of it devoted to filling harmful and unsatisfying wants.
- *When possible, buy durable, reusable products that are used rather than new.*
- *When that is not possible, buy recyclable products made from recycled materials or renewable resources. Also, be sure that what's left over after use is recycled.*
- *Buy the product with the least packaging.*
- *Boycott harmful products.**
- *Buy products that have been evaluated and approved from cradle to grave by a credible agency.* These include Green Seal or Green Cross in the United States, Blue Angel in Germany, Environmental Choice in Canada, and Eco-Mark in Japan. Because of gaps in data and funding, these new indicators are not perfect, but they are a start.
- *Help elect local, state, and national officials who make sustaining the earth (and thus people) their top priority.*
- *Invest in green funds and companies.†*
- *Try to work for or start green companies, or work to turn companies green.*
- *Participate in, invest in, and support environmentally responsible production by locally owned, operated, and controlled enterprises to reduce the hemorrhaging of capital, energy, resources, and jobs from local economies.*

\* For information on boycotted products, subscribe to *National Boycott News*, 6506 28th Avenue N.E, Seattle, WA 98115 ($10.00 per year).

† For information on green investing, contact The Social Investment Forum, 711 Atlantic Avenue, Boston, MA 02111.

ing, the environmental benefits of such consumption may eventually be overwhelmed (Figure 1-16).

**EARTH-SUSTAINING LIVING: CONSUMING LESS AND LIVING BETTER** Some environmentalists urge us to move beyond green consuming to *Earth-sustaining living* (Individuals Matter, above) by:

- Emphasizing consumption that meets basic needs—a balanced diet, decent housing, clean air and water, sanitation, Earth-sustaining education, health care, and a safe and fulfilling way to have

## The Steady State Economy in Outline

*Herman E. Daly*

**GUEST ESSAY** *Herman E. Daly is senior economist at the Environmental Department of the World Bank. Before joining the World Bank in 1989, he was alumni professor of economics at Louisiana State University. He has been a member of the Committee on Mineral Resources and Environment of the National Academy of Sciences, and has served on the boards of advisers of numerous environmental organizations. He is co-founder and associate editor of the journal* Ecological Economics *(Elsevier). He has written many articles and several books including* Steady-State Economics *(2nd ed., 1991),* Economics, Ecology, and Ethics *(1980), and with co-author John Cobb, Jr., For the Common Good: Redirecting the Economy Towards Community, the Environment, and a Sustainable Future *(1989). He is one of a small but growing number of economists seriously thinking about sustainable-Earth economics.*

The steady state economy is basically a physical concept with important social and moral implications. It is defined as a constant stock of physical wealth and people. This wealth and population size is maintained at some desirable, chosen level by a low rate of throughput of matter and energy resources so the longevity of people and goods is high.

Throughput is roughly equivalent to GNP, the annual flow of new production. It is the cost of maintaining the stocks of final goods and services by continually importing high-quality matter and energy resources from the environment, and exporting waste matter and low-quality heat energy back to the environment [Figure 3-20].

Currently we try to maximize the growth of the GNP, but the reasoning just given suggests that we should relabel it gross national cost or GNC. We should minimize it, subject to maintaining stocks of essential items. For example, if we can maintain a desired, sufficient stock of cars with a lower throughput of iron, coal, petroleum, and other resources, we are better off, not worse.

To maximize GNP throughput for its own sake is absurd. Physical and ecological limits to the volume of throughput suggest that a steady state economy will be necessary eventually. Less recognizable but probably more stringent social and moral limits suggest that a steady state economy will become desirable long before it becomes a physical necessity.

For example, the development and use of nuclear reactors to produce electricity is heavily subsidized by the government. Since the mid-1970s the growth of this technology has declined sharply—not because of a shortage of uranium fuel, but because of social and economic limits. Poor management, excessive costs, and serious accidents such as the one at the Chernobyl nuclear plant [p. 476] have seriously undermined public support of this technology.

Nuclear plants exist only because of huge government subsidies. If the nuclear power industry were forced to operate in an open market without government subsidies, it would probably never have been developed because of its low return on investment. Attempts to revive the nuclear industry now by providing more subsidies—as some have advocated, arguing that nuclear power is needed to reduce the rate of projected global warming—will further waste enormous amounts of limited economic and human resources. Furthermore, it will do little to slow global warming compared with other, more cost-effective alternatives [Spotlight, p. 495].

these things—instead of an ever-growing list of material wants

- Seeing improved energy efficiency, pollution prevention, waste reduction, and environmental protection as needs, not luxuries

- Seeking fulfillment in love, friendship, cooperation, sharing, and caring for others and the earth rather than in things bought in the marketplace

Is this unrealistic? Too idealistic? Risky? Perhaps. However, it may be more unrealistic and dangerous to maintain our present course. As Mohandas Gandhi reminds us, "When we take more than we need, we are simply taking from each other, borrowing from the future, or destroying the environment and other species."

*There is something fundamentally wrong in treating the earth as if it were a business in liquidation.*

HERMAN E. DALY

## Critical Thinking

1. The primary goal of all current economic systems is to maximize growth by maximizing the production and consumption of economic goods. Do you agree with that goal? Explain. What are the alternatives?

2. Do you believe that cost-benefit analysis should be used to make all decisions about how limited federal, state, and local government funds are to be used? Explain. If not, what decisions should not be made in this way?

Once we have attained a steady state economy at some level of stocks, we are not forever frozen at that level. Moral and technological changes may make it both possible and desirable to grow (or decline) to a different level. Growth, however, will be seen as a temporary process necessary to move from one steady state level to another, not as an economic norm. This requires a substantial shift in present economic thought. Most current economic ideas and models must be replaced or drastically modified. Most economists strongly resist this radical change in the way they think and act.

The greatest challenges facing us today are:

- For physical and biological scientists to define more clearly the limits and interactions within ecosystems and the ecosphere (which determine the feasible levels of the steady state), and to develop technologies more in conformity with such limits

- For social scientists to design institutions that will bring about the transition to a steady state and permit its continuance

- For philosophers, theologians, and educators to stress the neglected traditions of stewardship and distributive justice that exist in our cultural and religious heritage

The last item is of paramount importance because the problem of sharing a fixed amount of resources and goods is much greater than that of sharing a growing amount. Indeed, this has been the primary reason for giving top priority to growth. If the pie is always growing, it is said there will always be crumbs—and the hope of a slice—for the poor. This avoids the moral question of a more equitable distribution of the world's resources and wealth.

The kinds of economic institutions needed to make this transition follow directly from the definition of a steady state economy. We need an institution for maintaining a constant population size within the limits of available resources. For example, economic incentives can be used to encourage each woman or couple to have no more than a certain number of children, or each woman or couple could be given a marketable license to have a certain number of children, as economist Kenneth Boulding has suggested.

We also need an institution for maintaining a constant stock of physical wealth and limiting resource throughput. For example, the government could set and auction off transferable annual depletion quotas for key resources. Finally, there must be an institution to limit inequalities in the distribution of the constant physical wealth among the constant population in a steady state economy. For example, there might be minimum and maximum limits on personal income and maximum limits on personal wealth.

Many such institutions could be imagined. The problem is to achieve the necessary global and societal (macro) control with the least sacrifice of freedom at the individual (micro) level.

### Critical Thinking

1. Does a steady state economy imply technological stagnation? Explain.

2. Which might end up with more restrictions on human freedom: a growing population (consumers) and economy or a stable population and a steady-state economy? Explain.

3. Do you favor internalizing the external costs of pollution and unnecessary resource waste? Explain. How might it affect your lifestyle? Wildlife?

4. If a particular investment in resource exploitation will make the relatively well-off richer and the poor and middle class poorer, should the investment be made? Explain.

5. **a.** Do you believe that we should establish optimal levels or zero discharge levels for most of the chemicals we release into the environment? Explain. What effects would adopting zero discharge levels have on your life and lifestyle?

   **b.** Do you believe that all chemicals we release or propose to release into the environment should be assumed to be potentially harmful until proven otherwise? Explain. What effects would adopting this principle have on your life and lifestyle?

6. Do you favor making a shift to a sustainable-Earth economy? Explain. How might this affect your lifestyle? The lifestyle of any children you choose to have?

7. Do you agree or disagree with the proposals some environmentalists have made for sharply reducing poverty listed on pages 648–650? Explain.

*8. Make a list of all the economic goods you use, and then identify those that meet your basic needs and those that satisfy your wants. Identify any economic wants you would be willing to give up. Identify those you believe you should give up but are unwilling to give up. Identify wants that you hope to satisfy in the future. List what you believe will make you happy and improve the quality of your life. Relate the results of this analysis to your personal impact on the environment. Compare your results with those of your classmates.

## *Rescuing a River*

When Marion Stoddart first moved to Groton, Massachusetts, on the Nashua River in the early 1960s, the riverside location was nothing to brag about. In fact, the Nashua was considered one of the nation's filthiest rivers. Industries and towns along the 92-kilometer-long (57-mile) river had used it as a dump for decades. Sludge piled up at every dam. Dead fish bobbed on its waves, and at times the water was red, green, or blue from pigments discharged by paper mills.

Marion Stoddart was appalled. Instead of thinking nothing could be done, she committed herself to restoring the Nashua and establishing public parklands along its banks. She didn't start by filing lawsuits or organizing demonstrations. Rather, she created a careful cleanup plan and approached state officials with it in 1962. They laughed, but she was not deterred and began practicing the most time-honored skill of politics—one-on-one persuasion. She identified the power brokers in the riverside communities and began to educate them, win them over, and get them to cooperate in cleaning up the river.

One of her converts was William Flynn, former mayor of Fitchburg, a town whose paper mills were a major source of the Nashua's pollution. When she got the state to ban open dumping in the river, one factory threatened to close down rather than help pay for cleanup facilities. Flynn helped Stoddart persuade Fitchburg paper mills to cooperate with authorities in building a wastewater treatment plant.

**Figure 26-1** Earth citizen Marion Stoddart canoeing down the Nashua River near Groton, Massachusetts. She spent over two decades spearheading successful efforts to have this river cleaned up.

*A technological society has two choices. First, it can wait until catastrophic failures expose systemic deficiencies, distortions, and self-deceptions. . . . Second, a culture can provide social checks and balances to correct for systemic distortions prior to catastrophic failures.*

MAHATMA GANDHI

When promised federal matching funds for building the treatment plant failed to arrive, Stoddart got 13,000 signatures on a petition to President Nixon. The funds arrived in a hurry.

Stoddart's next success was getting a federal grant to beautify the river. She hired high school dropouts to clear away mounds of debris. When the cleanup was completed, she persuaded communities along the river to create some 2,400 (6,000 acres) hectares of riverside park and woodland along both banks.

Now, over two decades later, the Nashua is still clean. Several new water treatment plants have been built, and a citizens' group founded by Stoddart keeps watch on water quality. The river's waters support many kinds of fish and other wildlife, and are used for canoeing (Figure 26-1) and other kinds of recreation.

The project is considered a model for other states and is testimony to what a committed individual can do to change the world by getting people to work together.

For her efforts Stoddart has been named by the UN Environment Programme as an outstanding worldwide worker for the environment. She might say, however, that the blue and canoeable Nashua is itself her best reward.

**Politics** is the process by which individuals and groups try to influence or control the policies and actions of governments, whether local, state, national, or international. Politics is concerned with who has power over the distribution of resources and benefits—who gets what, when, and how. Thus it plays a significant role in regulating the world's economic systems, influencing economic decisions (Chapter 25), and persuading people to work together toward a common goal, as Marion Stoddart did.

We are at a turning point. Some say we can keep on doing business and politics as usual. Others argue that the old ways of doing business and politics are so threatening to our environmental, economic, and military security that we must have the wisdom and courage to reshape them into Earth-sustaining economic and political systems based on how nature works.

This chapter will be devoted to seeking answers to the following questions:

- How does a democratic government work?
- How can people bring about change?
- How is environmental policy made in the United States?
- How can the U.S. political system be improved?
- How can we improve global environmental policy?

## 26-1 How Government Works in a Democracy

**DEMOCRATIC GOVERNMENT** Democracy is literally government "by the people." Pure democracy is rare, found, for example, in New England towns and a few Swiss cantons (states). In what we call *representative democracy* today, people govern through elected officials and representatives. In a *constitutional democracy* a constitution provides the basis of governmental authority and limits governmental power through free elections and freely expressed public opinion.

The U.S. Constitution with its Bill of Rights aimed to promote majority rule while protecting the fundamental rights of individuals and minorities. That was done by dividing political power between the state and federal governments, and among the three branches of the federal government—legislative, executive, and judicial (Figure 26-2). Political power at the state level is also divided among executive, legislative, and judicial branches.

The elected members of the U.S. Congress make up the **legislative branch** of government (Figure 26-2). Congress's primary function is to develop, approve, and oversee **policy**—a planned course of action on a specific problem or topic. Proposed legislation is introduced by one or more legislators (co-sponsors) as a *bill* in Congress and must follow a certain path before it can become a law (Figure 26-3). Any legislation passed by Congress or a state legislature is

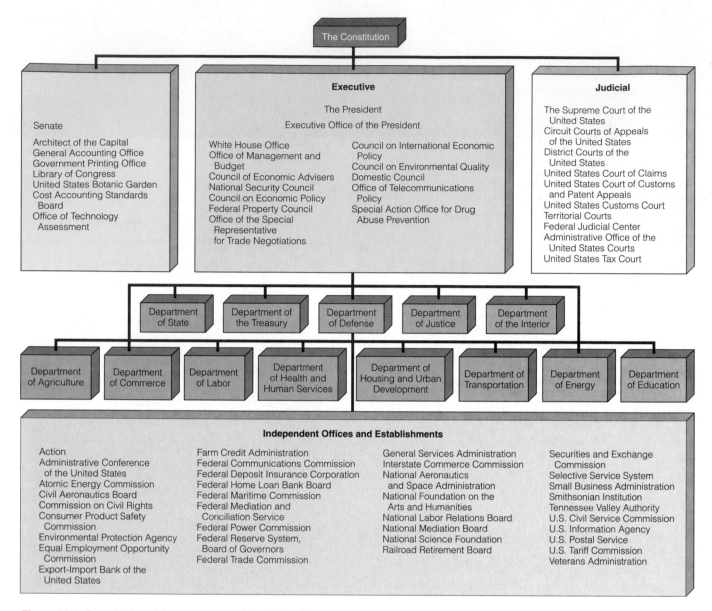

**Figure 26-2** Organization of the government of the United States.

called a **statutory law**. Congress also establishes, funds, and monitors the activities of the various administrative agencies of government.

The **executive branch** consists of an elected president and vice president and the various agencies of government established by Congress. The primary role of most federal agencies is to develop **regulations** for implementing laws passed by Congress. The real power of the presidency, however, rests on the president's leadership ability in persuading Congress to adopt certain policies or persuading the people to influence Congress to adopt these policies. An effective leader at any level of society—including the presidency—consistently acts according to clearly defined values or principles (Spotlight, p. 662).

Developing and adopting a budget for spending limited tax revenue is the most important thing members of the executive and legislative branches do. Someone once said that the way to understand human history is to study budgets. Developing a budget involves answering two key questions: **(1)** What resource use and distribution problems will be addressed? and **(2)** How much limited tax revenue will be used to address each problem?

The **judicial branch** consists of the Supreme Court and the lower federal courts established by Congress (Figure 26-2). Members of the Supreme Court are nominated by the President and, if confirmed by a majority vote of the Senate, serve for life. The Supreme Court is the final interpreter of all matters involving

Q: How many U.S. cancer deaths each year are caused by exposure to pesticide residues in foods?

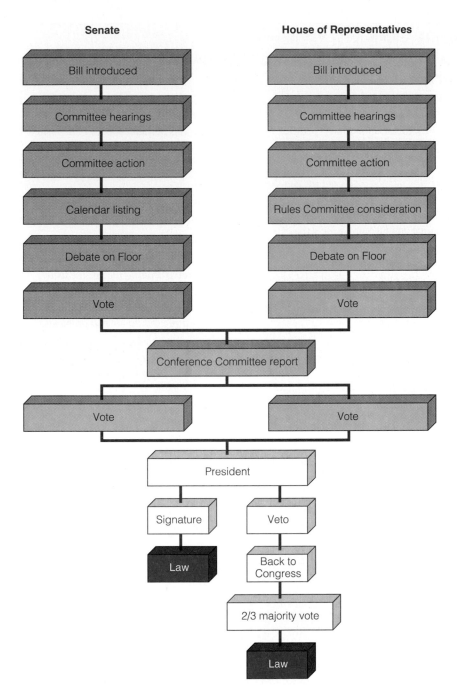

**Figure 26-3** How a bill introduced into Congress becomes a law.

**Senate**

- Bill introduced
- Committee hearings
- Committee action
- Calendar listing
- Debate on Floor
- Vote

**House of Representatives**

- Bill introduced
- Committee hearings
- Committee action
- Rules Committee consideration
- Debate on Floor
- Vote

Conference Committee report

- Vote
- Vote

President

- Signature → Law
- Veto → Back to Congress → 2/3 majority vote → Law

the U.S. Constitution, federal statutes, and treaties. To resolve disputes in the absence of applicable statutory law, courts at all levels use **common law**, a large body of unwritten principles and rules based on thousands of past court decisions.

**POWER GROUPS AND SOCIAL CHANGE IN REP-RESENTATIVE DEMOCRACIES** People in and outside of government who run modern democracies—the so-called *elites* or *power groups*—come largely from the upper levels of society. In passing laws, developing budgets, and formulating regulations, government

decision makers must deal with pressure from many competing interest groups, each asking for laws favorable to its cause, for resources or money or relief from taxes, or for bureaucratic regulations in line with its goals.

Some special-interest groups are *profit-making organizations* such as corporations and are run by elites, while others are *nonprofit, nongovernmental organizations (NGOs)*. Some NGOs, such as educational institutions, labor unions, and mainstream environmental organizations, are also run by elites. Other NGOs, usually smaller ones operating at the grass-roots level, are

The principles that should guide effective leaders can be boiled down to a few rules distilled mostly from the world's religions and ethical systems:

- *Don't hurt people; help them out. See ordinary people as real people with real needs, not as voting blocs, consumers, or statistics. See all people as unique, special, and precious.*

- *Don't hurt the Earth; help sustain it, and explain to people why we need to do this.*

- *Never insulate yourself from ordinary people and from nature.*

- *Don't lie.*

- *Don't support any action that steals from this generation or future generations.*

- *Be humble.*

- *Admit your mistakes, learn from them, and try again.*

- *Surround yourself with good people. They can make up for your weaknesses and tell you when* they think you are wrong and why. Always listen to them, and talk to some ordinary people, before making a decision.

- *Have the courage to try new things.*

- *Bring out the best—not the worst—in people.*

- *Lead by keeping hope and dreams alive, not by sowing the seeds of despair, fear, and hate.*

- *Help people believe in themselves, become more self-reliant, and cooperate with one another and with the earth to achieve a sustainable future.*

- *Emphasize cooperation, fairness, and peace, not competition, dominance, and violence.*

- *Always act out of love for people and the earth.*

- *Never do to others what you wouldn't want done to you.*

- *Have the courage to stand up for and strive to live by these principles.*

Writer Kurt Vonnegut has suggested a prescription for choosing Earth-sustaining leaders:

*I hope you have stopped choosing abysmally ignorant optimists for positions of leadership. . . . The sorts of leaders we need now are not those who promise ultimate victory over Nature, but those with the courage and intelligence to present what appear to be Nature's stern, but reasonable surrender terms:*

1. *Reduce and stabilize your population.*

2. *Stop poisoning the air, the water, and the topsoil.*

3. *Stop preparing for war and start dealing with your real problems.*

4. *Teach your kids, and yourselves too, while you're at it, how to inhabit a small planet without killing it.*

5. *Stop thinking science can fix anything, if you give it a trillion dollars.*

6. *Stop thinking your grandchildren will be OK no matter how wasteful or destructive you may be, since they can go to a nice new planet on a spaceship. That is really mean and stupid.*

---

run by ordinary citizens. Well-organized and well-funded interest groups usually have the most influence.

Most political decisions are made by bargaining, accommodation, and compromise between leaders of competing elites. The overarching goal of government by competing elites is maintaining the overall stability of the system by making only gradual changes and not questioning or changing the rules of the game or the fundamental societal beliefs that gave them political or economic power.

Political systems in constitutional democracies are designed for just such gradual change to promote economic and political stability. Indeed, rapid change in the United States, for example, is curbed by the system of checks and balances that distributes power among the three branches of government and among federal, state, and local governments. One disadvantage of this design is that such governments mostly react to crises instead of acting to prevent them. Ralph Waldo Emerson once said, "Democracy is a raft which will never sink, but then your feet are always in the water." In other words, there is what amounts to a built-in bias against policies for protecting the environment because they often call for preventing instead of reacting to crises, require integrated planning into the future, and sometimes call for fundamental changes in societal beliefs that can threaten the power of existing elites in government and business.

Democracy is designed to limit the abuse of power, but this is a constant struggle against the dark side of human nature (Spotlight, p. 663).

Some analysts believe that the U.S. political-economic system is working reasonably well and no fundamental changes need to be made. Others think that the system needs to be changed in ways that improve its ability to deal with, anticipate, or prevent the growing number of interlocking regional, national, and

Q: What percentage of U.S. lawns are treated with pesticides?

global environmental, economic, and social problems we face today.

## 26-2 Influencing Environmental Policy

### THE IMPORTANCE OF INDIVIDUAL INITIATIVE

A major theme of this book is that individuals matter. History shows that significant change comes from the bottom up, not the top down. Without grass-roots political action by millions of individual citizens and organized groups, the air you breathe and the water you drink today would be much more polluted.

Leaders with vision can lead only when they have the support of the people. Leaders without vision or courage must be pushed to lead by the people or else replaced with better leaders. Individuals can influence and change government policies in constitutional democracies by:

- *Voting for candidates and ballot measures.*

- *Contributing money and time to candidates running for office.*

- *Lobbying, writing, or calling elected representatives asking them to pass or oppose certain laws, establish certain policies, and fund various programs* (Individuals Matter, p. 664).

- *Using education and persuasion, both important vehicles by which to convince ordinary people and the elites who hold power to bring about specific changes or to change certain societal beliefs.*

- *Exposing fraud, waste, and illegal activities in government (whistle blowing).*

- *Filing lawsuits.*

- *Participating in grass-roots activities.*

- *Using consumer buying power to help convert brown corporations into green corporations* (Individuals Matter, pp. 529 and 655).

**LEADERSHIP** There are three types of environmental leadership:

- *Leading by example.* Individuals can use their own life and lifestyle to show others that change is possible and beneficial.

- *Working within existing economic and political systems to bring about environmental improvement, often in new, creative ways.* Individuals can influence political elites by campaigning and voting for pro-Earth candidates and by communicating with

## Getting and Keeping Power: The Dark Side

SPOTLIGHT

People in power (up front and behind the scenes) use several classic tactics to stay on top:

- *Divide and conquer.* This involves keeping people and interest groups fighting with one another so they can't get together on anything important.

- *Use a real or trumped-up enemy to divert people's attention and energy from the real issues.*

- *Mount smear and fear campaigns.*

- *Intimidate and weaken.* This is accomplished by infiltrating opposing groups, slapping them with nuisance lawsuits, and having opponents arrested and given large fines or jail sentences.

- *Threaten or use violence.* If charismatic leaders become too effective, intimidate or assassinate them.

- *Delay and decay.* This means setting up legal and bureaucratic roadblocks to forestall change and tire reformers out.

- *Practice paralysis-by-analysis.* This involves delaying action by appointing blue ribbon panels to study problems and make recommendations, paying little attention to their advice, and calling for more research (sometimes needed, but also used as an excuse for inaction).

- *Don't collect data, or keep it secret, and claim nothing can be done about a problem because of a lack of information.*

These often effective tactics represent the dark side of human nature and politics. They can be countered only by the efforts of individuals and leaders at all levels of society who bring out the good in people (Spotlight, p. 662). Because of the built-in bias against significant change from the top down, such change must occur from the bottom up, forced by people working together to insist that those in power either change or lose power. As grass-roots populist Jim Hightower (Guest Essay, p. 680) puts it:

*To move America from greed to greatness we must once again tap into the genius and gumption of the… workaday majority of Americans who sweat, plow, invent, repair, teach, construct, nurse, and do the myriad of other productive tasks that sustain society from the bottom up. You can't keep a tree alive by fertilizing it at the top. … We want a government that quits doing things for us. But neither do we want a government that does things for us. We want a government that is us, that involves us and empowers us so we can do for ourselves and do for the country.*

## Communicating with Elected Officials

### INDIVIDUALS MATTER

Here are some guidelines for communicating effectively with elected officials:

- Find out their names and addresses, and write or call them.*

- When you write a letter use your own words, be brief and courteous, cover only one subject, and ask the elected official to do something specific (such as co-sponsoring, supporting, or opposing certain bills†). Give reasons for your position, explain its impact on you and your district, try to offer alternatives, share any expert knowledge you have, and ask for a response. Be sure to include your name and return address.

- After a vote supporting your position write your representative (and others) a short note of thanks.‡

- Call and ask to speak to a staff member who works on the issue you are concerned about: the White House, (202) 456-1414; the U.S. Senate, (202) 224-3121; the House of Representatives, (202) 456-1414.

- Once a desirable bill is passed, write or call the president about not vetoing it and the members of the appropriations committee asking that enough money be appropriated to implement the law.

- Monitor and influence action at the state and local levels, where all federal and state laws are either ignored or enforced. As Thomas Jefferson said, "The execution of laws is more important than the making of them."

- Get others who agree with your position to write or call.

* Each year the League of Women Voters (1730 M St. N.W., Washington, DC 20036) publishes *When You Write to Washington*, which lists all elected federal officials and includes a list of all committee members and chairpersons.

†If possible, identify the bill by number (for example, "H.R. 123" or "S. 313" for federal legislation). You can get a free copy of any federal bill or committee report by writing to the House Document Room, U.S. House of Representatives, Washington, DC 20515, or the Senate Document Room, U.S. Senate, Washington, DC 20510. Call or write your state representative to find out how to get copies of state bills and committee reports.

‡ Each year the League of Conservation Voters (P.O. Box 500, Washington, DC 20077; 202-785-VOTE) publishes an *Environmental Scorecard* rating all members of Congress on how they voted on environmental issues

---

elected officials. They can also choose an environmental career (Individuals Matter, p. 665).

- *Challenging the system and basic societal values, and proposing and working for better solutions to environmental problems.* Leadership is more than being against something. It also involves showing people a better way to accomplish various goals.

All three types of leadership are needed to work with the earth and should be guided by the principles of good leadership (Solutions, p. 662). Find the one or more types of leadership you are most comfortable with, and become such a leader or work with such leaders.

**MAINSTREAM ENVIRONMENTAL GROUPS** There are many types of environmental groups working at the local, state, national, and international levels (Appendix 1). Mainstream environmental groups are active mostly at the national level and to a lesser extent at the state level. Often they form coalitions to work together on issues. Some mainstream organizations funnel substantial funds to local activists and projects, while others devote their funds to education and lobbying at the national level. A few organizations do both. Some organizations concentrate on education and research. Still other groups provide information, training, and help for localities and grass-roots organizations.

Mainstream groups do important work within the system but must guard against being subverted by that system. If they become too dependent on high salaries, budgets, and the trappings of Washington power brokers, they can end up spending a disproportionate amount of time and money on fundraising.

Because environmental groups compete for members, money, and status, some have accepted money from their corporate opponents who have lots of influence money to spread around. This is a standard ploy used by corporate lobbyists to influence politicians (campaign contributions), the media (advertising), and any organizations that oppose their positions.

All of the 10 largest national environmental organizations—the "Group of 10"—encourage corporate donations, and in 1990 six had corporate executives as board members, trustees, or council members. Proponents of this policy argue that it is a way to influence industry, while opponents believe it is a way for corporations to unduly influence the environmental organizations. However, the net effect has been to cause some internal divisiveness within these environmental organizations and to drive a wedge between them and many grass-roots activists.

As a national organization grows, it often needs managerial leaders who concentrate on organizational

## Environmental Careers

Besides committed Earth citizens, the environmental movement needs dedicated professionals working to help sustain the earth. You will find career opportunities in a large number of fields: sustainable forestry and range management; parks and recreation; air and water quality control; solid-waste and hazardous-waste management; urban and rural land-use planning; ecological restoration; and soil, water, fishery, and wildlife conservation and management.

Environmental careers can also be found in education, planning, health and toxicology, geology, ecology, conservation biology, chemistry, climatology, population dynamics and regulation (demography), law, accounting, journalism and communication, engineering, design and architecture, energy conservation and analysis, renewable-energy technologies, hydrology, consulting, activism and lobbying, economics, diplomacy, development and marketing, and law enforcement (pollution detection and enforcement teams). You can also run for an elected office on an environmental platform.

Many employers are now scrambling for environmentally educated graduates. They are especially interested in people with scientific and engineering backgrounds and in people with double majors (business and ecology, for example) or double minors.

For details on these careers, consult the Environmental Careers Organization (formerly the CEIP Fund), *The Complete Guide to Environmental Careers* (Covelo, CA: Island Press, 1990), and Nicholas Basta, *The Environmental Career Guide* (New York: Wiley, 1991). The Environmental Careers Organization (286 Congress St., Dept. GM, Boston, MA 02110; 617-426-4375) places college students and recent college graduates as interns in short-term, paid professional positions with corporations, consulting firms, government agencies, and nonprofit organizations.

For a superb guide to career planning and job searches in any field, see Richard Nelson Bolles, *What Color Is Your Parachute?* (Berkeley, CA: Ten Speed Press, published annually).

Other sources of information on jobs in the environmental field are:

- *Earth Work,* published monthly by the Student Conservation Association, P.O. Box 550, Charlestown, NH 03603; (603) 826-4301

- *Environmental Job Opportunities,* published 10 times per year by the Institute for Environmental Studies, 550 North Park St., 15 Science Hall, Madison, WI 53706

- *National Directory of Internships,* published annually by the National Society of Internships and Experiential Education, 3509 Haworth Drive, Suite 207, Raleigh, NC 27609-7229; (919) 787-3263

---

stability, funding, budgets, operating procedures, and staff training. These leaders can lose touch with ordinary people and nature. Green groups should hire people with experience as grass-roots activists and require all managers and lobbyists to spend one of every four years working in local communities, learning about natural areas, or both. They should adopt a decentralized management system, promote open communication and better self-evaluation of the organization, increase employee decision-making, and place more emphasis on customer (member) satisfaction.

Mainstream environmental groups play an important role and need financial support and volunteer work from individuals. However, individuals should check out a group before joining or donating money or time. Each group should publish an annual outside audit listing all salaries and executive perks, sources of all income and percentages from each category (members, corporations, environmental foundations, corporate foundations), ways money is spent, and percentage of income going to member groups at state and local levels and to action projects outside of Washington.

### GRASS-ROOTS ENVIRONMENTAL GROUPS

The base of the environmental movement in the United States and in other countries consists of thousands of grass-roots groups of citizens who have organized to protect themselves from pollution and environmental damage at the local level (Individuals Matter, p. 666). NGOs are growing, in both numbers and influence, especially in LDCs. The United States has almost 7,000 environmental NGOs.

The motto of such NGOs is *think globally and act locally*. They take to the streets, forests, oceans, and other front-line sites to defend the parts of the earth from abuse, make harmful activities economically unattractive, and raise public awareness of environmental abuse and the need for change.

The activist group Greenpeace is the world's largest environmental group with 2.2 million members

---

(up from 30,000 in 1980) in 26 countries. Greenpeace members have risked their lives by putting small boats between whales and the harpoon guns of whaling ships, and placing themselves between seals and the clubs of hunters. Others have dangled from a New York bridge to stop traffic and protest a garbage barge heading out to sea (Figure 19-18), hung banners to protest the dumping of toxic wastes into rivers by industries and sewage treatment plants (Figure 26-4), skydived from the smokestacks of coal-burning power plants to protest acid rain, and sneaked into plants to document illegal pollution and dumping.

Some environmental activists engage in *nonviolent civil disobedience* by disobeying laws they believe to be unjust. They chain themselves to the tops of trees to keep loggers from cutting them down or drive spikes into trees and label the trees (the spikes don't hurt the trees but they do shatter saw blades, which could hurt loggers or millworkers). They block bulldozers with their bodies (Figure 26-5), obstruct illegal whaling ships, and dye the fur of harp seals to keep them from being killed for their fur. They photograph or video-tape illegal activities involving pollution, mistreat-ment of animals, drift-netting (Spotlight, p. 379), har-vesting of whales (Sea Shepherd Society), and harvesting of trees and wildlife.

Other citizens have worked to restore wetlands (p. 146), save forests (p. 260), and restore degraded rivers (p. 658). In the United States people of color, working-class people, and poor people, who often bear the brunt of pollution and environmental degra-dation, have formed a growing coalition known as the *grass-roots movement for environmental justice* (Figure 20-9 and Guest Essay, p. 566) to change the system. Some unions and nonunionized workers are also forming coalitions with environmental groups to improve worker safety and health.

A small number of more militant activists engage in *monkeywrenching* or *ecotage*, aimed at thwarting environmental destruction. They practice nonviolence against humans and other living things, and strategic violence against inanimate objects. Examples include sabotaging bulldozers and other equipment used to build logging roads; pulling up survey stakes for log-ging roads and power lines; sinking whaling ships (docked in harbor) that illegally harvested whales in international waters (Sea Shepherd Society); and breaking into laboratories and rescuing experimental animals, and sometimes destroying equipment and files (People for the Ethical Treatment of Animals).

Monkeywrenchers and activists practicing civil disobedience are labeled by their opponents as ecoter-rorists and criminals. These activists counter that those who pollute the air and water, cut down irreplaceable ancient forests, and drive species to extinction are the true ecoterrorists. They believe with Ralph Nader that

## Effective Grass-Roots Action

**INDIVIDUALS MATTER**

John W. Gardner, former cabi-net official and founder of Common Cause, summarized the basic rules for effective political action by grassroots organizations:

- *Have a full-time continuing organization.*
- *Limit the number of targets and hit them hard.* Most groups dilute their effectiveness by taking on too many issues.
- *Organize for action, not just for study, discussion, or education.* This means limiting regular meet-ings, titles, and minutes. It also means having a group coordinator, a series of task forces with a project leader, a press and communications con-tact, legal and professional advisers, and a small group of dedicated workers.
- *Form alliances with other organizations on a partic-ular issue.*
- *Communicate your positions in an accurate, concise, and moving way.*
- *Persuade and use positive reinforcement.* This means complimenting individuals and organi-zations when they do something you like, and not resorting to personal attacks. Because most political influence is wielded behind the scenes through one-on-one conversations, this also involves respecting opponents' beliefs and working *with* them to achieve your goals. Usu-ally it's best not to bring up something at a pub-lic meeting unless you have the votes lined up ahead of time.
- *Concentrate much of your effort at the state and local level.*

"pollution is violence with a seriousness of harm exceeding that of crime in the streets. . . . The first pri-ority is to deprive the polluters of their unfounded legitimacy. Too often they assume a conservative, patriotic posture when in reality they are radical destroyers of the nation's resources and the most fun-damental rights of people."

Some mainstream environmentalists fear that mil-itant activists, especially if they break the law, could cause a public backlash against all environmental efforts. Hard-won environmental laws might be weak-ened or even repealed. Other environmentalists argue that leaders of mainstream environmental groups need the militants nipping at their heels to keep them

Q: What percentage of the USDA's research and education budget is spent on integrated pest management?

**Figure 26-4** Greenpeace activists protesting discharge of toxic waste from the "Pig's Eye" sewage treatment plant in St. Paul, Minnesota. This plant is the largest contributor of toxic chemicals into the Mississippi River north of St. Louis.

**Figure 26-5** Earth First! activists blocking a logging road in the Siskiyou National Forest in Oregon.

honest. They also argue that we need a full spectrum of groups working on the maze of environmental issues using an array of tactics.

Many local grass-roots organizations are unwilling to compromise or negotiate. Instead of dealing with environmental goals and abstractions, they are fighting immediate threats to their lives, the lives of their children and grandchildren, and the value of their property. They want pollution and environmental degradation stopped and prevented rather than merely controlled. They are inspired by the words of eco-activist Edward Abbey: "At some point we must draw a line across the ground of our home and our being, drive a spear into the land, and say to the bull-dozers, earthmovers, and corporations, 'this far and no further.' "

**THE ANTI-ENVIRONMENTAL MOVEMENT** A number of businesses, especially in Japan and Germany, recognize that participating in the environmental revolution not only helps the earth but can also increase profits, stimulate innovation, create jobs, and increase government tax revenue (Section 25-5). A small but growing number of U.S. political and business leaders also see improving environmental quality as a way to stimulate innovation, increase profits, and create jobs while helping sustain the earth (Section 25-3). However, a number of corporations attempt to ensure that

## Browns vs. Greens: The Wise-Use Movement

Since 1988 several hundred local and regional grass-roots groups in the United States have formed a national anti-environmental coalition called the *wise-use movement*. Much of their money comes from developers and from timber, mining, oil, coal, and ranching interests.

The announced goal of this movement is to "eradicate the environmental movement in the United States within a decade." Its specific goals are to:

- Cut all old-growth forests in the national forests and replace them with tree plantations
- Gut the Endangered Species Act so that economic factors override preservation of endangered and threatened species
- Eliminate government restrictions on wetlands development
- Open all public lands—including national parks and wilderness areas—to mineral and energy production

- Open three-fourths of the land in the National Wilderness Preservation System for mineral and energy production, off-road vehicles (ORVs), developed campsites, and commercial development
- Do away with the National Park Service and launch a 20-year construction program of new concessions in national parks to be run by private firms
- Create a national mining system that will continue mining on public lands under the provisions of the 1872 Mining Law (p. 504)
- Recognize private rights to mining claims, water, grazing permits, and timber contracts on public lands, and not raise fees for these activities
- Provide civil penalties against anyone who legally challenges economic action or development on federal lands
- Allow pro-industry (wise-use) groups or individuals to sue as

"harmed parties" on behalf of industries threatened by environmentalists

Leaders of this anti-environment movement raise funds and whip up support by branding all environmentalists as antipeople, anti-Christian, antijob, and anti-growth radical extremists who are crippling the U.S. economy, robbing land-owners of the right to do what they want with their land, and trying to lock up all natural resources and remove people from all public lands in the United States. When accused of using wild exaggeration and false smear tactics against environmentalists to raise money and spread distrust, hate, and fear, Ron Arnold, an expert rabble rouser and leader for the wise-use movement said, "Facts don't really matter. In politics, perception is reality."

Most groups in the anti-environmental movement use deceptive names and are funded by various corporate interests or conservative

environmental laws and regulations do little to damage corporate profit margins by:

- *Making donations to the election campaigns of politicians favoring their positions.* A run for federal office costs $10 million–$150 million, with most of the money coming from corporate PACs (political action committees).

- *Putting lobbyists in Washington and in state capitals.*

- *Getting industry-friendly people appointed to regulatory agencies.* The goal is to develop regulations that limit the liability of large corporations and protect them from free-market competition.

- *Making donations or giving research grants to environmental organizations to influence how far they go.*

- *Influencing the media by threatening to withdraw advertising income if they probe too deeply.*

- *Setting up and publicizing showcase environmental and resource conservation projects while continuing to do most of their business as usual.*

- *Adopting the latest environmental buzzwords to give the appearance of change.* Some environmentalists call this practice *ecopornography*, pointing to the exploitation of buzzwords such as sustainable development, pollution prevention, recycling, reuse, resource reduction, and biodegradable products.

- *Establishing industry-funded grass-roots groups with Earth-friendly names* (Spotlight, above).

- *Using the green menace scare tactic.* Branding environmentalists as radical, communist, anti-American terrorists who threaten jobs (Case Study, p. 285), the economy, national security, and traditional values instead of people who are trying to make the planet a safer, better, and more just place to live. Conservative political columnist George Will has described environmentalists as "a green tree with red roots ... dressed up as compassion for the planet."

- *Intimidating and disrupting environmental activists.* Fire whistle-blowers in industries and govern-

foundations.* Some examples are Center for the Defense of Free Enterprise (strategic planning, education, and implementation center for the wise-use movement, run by Allan Gottlieb and Ron Arnold and partially funded by the Moonies—Sun Myung Moon's Unification Church), National Center for Constitutional Studies (a partially Moonie-funded, right-wing group that has supported slavery, state restrictions on free speech, and abolition of all national forest and parks), Alliance for America (umbrella organization for 125 anti-environmental groups), Environmental Conservation Association (farmers, industries, and developers seeking to water down wetlands protection), U.S. Council for Energy Awareness (nuclear power industry), America the Beautiful (packaging industry), Partnership for Plas-

* See *The Greenpeach Guide to Anti-Environmental Organizations* (1993, Odonian Press, Box 7776, Berkeley, CA 94707—$7) and *Fronting for Big Business in America* by Andy Friedman and Mark Megalli, Essential Information, P.O. Box 19405, Washington, DC 20036.

tics Progress (plastics industry), American Council on Science and Health (food and pesticide industries), People for the West (mining industry), Sahara Club (promotes dirt biking in wilderness areas; one of its leaders tells audiences to "throw environmentalists off the bridge; water optional"), and Citizens for the Environment (industry-backed education group used to counter environmental ideas with claims such as recycling doesn't save forests, packaging prevents waste, and global warming and ozone depletion are hoaxes).

Leaders of such groups often train local citizens to lead the fight—hiding a group's true motives from unsuspecting ordinary citizens who are under economic stress and who feel that most politicians, government officials, and environmentalists don't listen to them or care about their needs.

Recently, there has been an all-out effort to cast doubt on the scientific underpinnings of environmental problems by misusing science.

Industry representatives, hoping to avoid regulation, say that we should not worry about risks from various chemicals or from ozone depletion and global warming because they are only unproven scientific theories. This falsely implies that science yields absolute proof or truth instead of certain levels of confidence (high, medium, or low) in its findings. When anyone talks about a theory (a widely tested and accepted scientific hypothesis) as being proven or not proven, we should take our minds and run.

The wise-use movement could have three unintended beneficial effects on the environmental movement: It may **(1)** increase membership in and support for environmental groups, **(2)** force mainstream environmental organizations to work more at the grass-roots level to meet the needs of ordinary people (Guest Essays, pp. 386 and 680), and **(3)** stimulate environmental scientists to educate the public and the media about the of limitations of scientific evidence (Section 3-1).

ment; sue individuals and environmental groups; persuade government officials to put activists under surveillance, and arrest or harass effective environmental activists.

Environmentalists also have an obligation to refrain from environmental overkill. They need to point out and oppose environmental proposals and policies and government regulations that go too far and cost too much (Spotlight, p. 671).

## 26-3 Environmental Policy in the United States

**THE ENVIRONMENTAL POLICY PROCESS** Figure 26-6 summarizes the primary forces in environmental policy-making at the federal level. Similar factors are found at the state level.

The first step in establishing environmental policy (or any other policy) is to persuade lawmakers that a problem exists and that the government has a responsibility to find solutions to the problem. This might be initiated by dramatic events (reaction-to-crisis politics), the president or Congress (Guest Essay, p. 680), or an increase in awareness of the need to keep environmental problems from reaching crisis levels.

Once over that hurdle, lawmakers try to pass laws to deal with the problem (Figure 26-3). Most environmental bills are evaluated by as many as 10 committees in both the House and the Senate. Effective proposals are often weakened by this fragmentation and by lobbying from groups opposing the bill. And even if a tough environmental law is passed, Congress must appropriate enough funds to implement and enforce the legislation.

Next, regulations designed to implement the law are drawn up by the appropriate government department or agency (Figure 26-2). Groups favoring or opposing the law try to influence how the regulations are written and enforced. Some of the affected parties

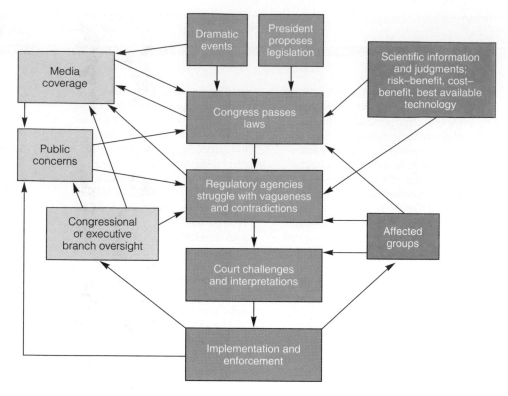

**Figure 26-6** Primary forces involved in making environmental policy at the federal level in the United States.

may challenge the final regulations in court. Then the agency implements and enforces the approved regulations. Proponents or affected groups may take the agency to court for failing to implement and enforce the regulations or for enforcing them too rigidly.

## PASSING ENVIRONMENTAL LEGISLATION

Environmentalists, with backing from many other citizens and members of Congress, have pressured Congress to enact a number of important federal environmental and resource protection laws, as discussed throughout this text and listed in Appendix 3.

These laws seek to protect the environment by the following approaches:

- *Setting standards for pollution levels or limiting emissions or effluents for various classes of pollutants* (Federal Water Pollution Control Act and Clean Air Act)

- *Screening new substances for safety before they are widely used* (Toxic Substances Control Act)

- *Requiring comprehensive evaluation of the environmental impact of an activity before it is undertaken by a federal agency* (National Environmental Policy Act)

- *Setting aside or protecting various ecosystems, resources, and species from harm* (Wilderness Act and Endangered Species Act)

- *Encouraging resource conservation* (Resource Conservation and Recovery Act and National Energy Act)

Most states have modeled their environmental and resource conservation laws after federal laws, and have established state environmental agencies similar to those at the federal level. Some states, such as California, have adopted more stringent air pollution laws and standards than the federal ones.

## IMPLEMENTING ENVIRONMENTAL LAWS

The interpretation and implementation of laws passed by federal and state legislatures are turned over to bureaucracies and the courts. The EPA, created by administrative reorganization in 1970, is responsible for enforcing most federal environmental laws, for administering the Superfund to clean up abandoned toxic-waste sites, and for awarding grants for local sewage treatment plants. Other environmental protection and resource management tasks are handled by other agencies or offices (Figure 26-2).

Some environmental laws contain glowing rhetoric about goals but little guidance about how to meet these goals. In other cases the laws specify general principles for setting regulations such as the following:

- *No unreasonable risk*—for example, food regulations in the Food, Drug, and Cosmetic Act

**Q:** What is the best way to prevent or reduce pollution?

# Distortion, Overkill, and Overregulation

In supporting, opposing, or executing various policies people on both sides of environmental issues have sometimes distorted facts and misused science, and some government officials have imposed excessive or unjust regulations and costs. Here are a few examples of environmental overkill:

- *Stating that acid rain is causing widespread destruction of forests and aquatic life in lakes and streams.* While tree diebacks and acidic lakes are serious problems (especially in parts of Europe), acid deposition is only one factor in a mix of poorly understood natural and human-related interactions (Figure 22–10). Decreasing our release of sulfur dioxide and nitrogen oxides into the atmosphere (Section 22-4) would improve human health (Section 22-3) and reduce health costs and costly corrosion and damage to materials (Table 22-2), regardless of their roles in degrading forests and streams.

- *Requiring that all forms of asbestos be removed from buildings.* Evidence suggests that some types of asbestos fibers may be more harmful to humans than others (Pro/Con, p. 575). Thus, monitoring air levels of each type of fiber in buildings containing asbestos is important. However, experience has shown that removal of asbestos that is not crumbling or releasing fibers can raise levels of asbestos fibers inside buildings yet cost enormous amounts of money. In 1992 the EPA reversed its policy of requiring asbestos removal in most buildings (largely because of court rulings against this approach), but only after billions of dollars had been spent.

- *Stating that global warming is occurring now.* So far, any change in average global temperature has been too small to distinguish from normal climate fluctuations (Figure 11-4). The real issues are how global climate might change in the future, what roles our inputs into the atmosphere have, and how climate might change in specific regions—all controversial and poorly understood issues (Sections 11-1 and 11-2). Remedies for slowing possible global warming include improving energy efficiency (Section 17-2), reducing fossil fuel use, increasing our reliance on perpetual and renewable energy resources (Chapter 17), protecting forest biodiversity (Chapter 10), restoring degraded ecosystems, and planting trees. Most environmentalists believe we should be doing these things regardless of the possibility of global warming (or cooling).

- *Not becoming informed about the degree of potential harm from various risks and not trying to rank risks as best we can.* Risk analysis is a difficult, uncertain, and controversial undertaking (Section 20-5). Failure to evaluate and rank risks (Table 20-1), to effectively communicate such information to the public, and to involve the public in risk management decisions can lead to more risk and regulation than necessary and waste money.

- *Thinking we can save the earth or planet.* We are absolutely dependent on the earth, but earth's existence and functioning does not depend on us. We can temporarily impair some of Earth's natural processes at local, regional, and perhaps global levels. We can cause the premature extinction of species. But the earth is resilient and adaptable and will continue functioning and changing with or without us. What is at stake is not the earth but the quality of life for most human beings and—if we should go too far—the existence of our species. The question is whether our unwillingness to work with Earth's natural processes could set in motion the mostly unpredictable forces that would cause our species (and other species) unnecessary suffering or premature extinction. People with different worldviews answer this question differently (Chapter 27).

- *Excessive and too costly government regulations.* In a world whose many people have conflicting goals, laws and regulations are necessary to help protect environmental quality, health, security, and individual freedom. However, the regulatory approach can waste enormous amounts of limited funds with minimal results. An example is the Superfund cleanup of hazardous waste dumps. Billions of dollars have been spent for lawyers and consultants (Section 21-4), with few dumps being cleaned up. Indeed, the technological impossibility and expense of returning some dumps to pristine conditions (Figure 25-9) illustrate the need for hazardous waste prevention. Superfund cleanup liability has forced some small landowners and owners of small businesses into bankruptcy while larger industries involved in creating toxic waste sites have the money and lawyers to escape or negotiate fines and liability. Some have paid small fines and then received government contracts to clean up messes they created. The longer they take the more money they make. This once promising law has failed, mostly because a growing and powerful waste management industry (with many of their executives former high-level EPA employees) has been able to control the EPA and develop regulations favorable to the industry (Guest Essay, p. 677). Complex and changing wetlands preservation regulations have produced a similar disparity of treatment

(continued)

---

between small landowners and larger property owners and developers. Many ordinary citizens justifiably fear loss of their jobs, failure of their small businesses, or loss or devaluation of their property through the actions of government regulators who have little knowledge of local conditions, problems, and alternative solutions. This fear makes them ripe for the scare tactics and rhetoric of groups whose primary goals are to protect their own economic and political power. (Spotlight, p. 668).

Those who support equitable and worthwhile policies and laws should root out environmental overkill from all sides and oppose excessive, unfair, and wasteful forms of government regulation. This applies especially to regulations and policies that place an undue burden on the poor and minorities (Guest Essay, p. 566), workers, and small business and property owners who make up the bulk of the population. This is one reason why an increasing number of environmentalists emphasize pollution and waste prevention over complex and costly pollution control and waste management (Sections 25-2 and 25-3 and Table 25-1).

Both preventive (front-of-pipe) and regulatory (end-of-pipe) approaches are needed, but so far about 95% of our efforts have been stop-gap regulatory approaches. The key question is how we can produce less waste, pollution, and environmental degradation while developing sustainable economies (Sections 25-3 and 25-5). The beauty of this approach is that it can save individuals, businesses, and government (taxpayers) money and reduce health risks that are difficult and expensive to evaluate and regulate. Insisting that we shift our emphasis to the front end of the pipe is an issue everyone can work on.

- *No risk*—for example, the Delaney clause, which prohibits the deliberate use of any food additive shown to cause cancer in test animals or people, and the zero discharge goals of the Safe Drinking Water Act and the Clean Water Act

- *Risk-benefit balancing* (Section 20-5)—for example, pesticide regulations (Section 24-4)

- *Standards based on best available technology*—for example, the Clean Air, Clean Water, and Safe Drinking Water acts

- *Cost-benefit balancing* (Pro/Con p. 646)—for example, the Toxic Substances Control Act and Executive Order 12291, which gives the Office of Management and Budget the power to delay indefinitely, or even veto, any federal regulation not proven to have the least cost to society

**USING THE COURTS** Almost every major environmental regulation is challenged in court by industry, environmental organizations, or both. In any court case the **plaintiff** is the individual, group of individuals, corporation, or government agency bringing the charges, and the **defendant** is the individual, group of individuals, corporation, or government agency being charged.

In a **civil suit** the plaintiff seeks to collect damages for injuries to health or for economic loss, to have the court issue a permanent injunction against any further wrongful action, or both. Such suits may be brought by an individual or a clearly identified group. A **class action suit** is a civil suit filed by a group, often a public interest or environmental group, on behalf of a larger number of citizens who allege similar damages but who need not be listed and represented individually.

The effectiveness of environmental lawsuits is limited by several factors:

- *Permission to file a damage suit is granted only if the harm to an individual plaintiff is clearly unique or different enough to be distinguished from that to the general public.* For example, you could not sue the Department of the Interior for actions leading to the commercialization of a wilderness area on the grounds that you do not want your taxes used to harm the environment, because the harm to you could not be separated from that to the general public. However, if the government damaged property you own, you would have grounds to sue.

- *Bringing any suit is expensive.* According to EPA employee and whistle-blower Hugh Kaufman (Guest Essay, p. 677), "The citizens are armed with rubber bands and chewing gum against major polluters armed with the best-paid engineers and lawyers in the country. It ain't a fair fight."

Q: How many of the world's people live in absolute poverty?

- *Public interest law firms cannot recover attorneys' fees unless Congress has specifically authorized such recovery in the law they have sued to enforce.*

- *It is often difficult for the plaintiff to prove that the defendant is liable and responsible for a harmful action.* For example, suppose that one company is charged with harming individuals by polluting a river. If hundreds of other industries and cities dump waste into that river, establishing that the defendant company is the culprit will be very difficult, requiring costly scientific testing, research, and expert testimony.

- *The court, or series of courts if the case is appealed, may take years to reach a decision.* During that time the defendant may continue the allegedly damaging action unless the court issues a temporary injunction against the action until the case is decided.

- *Plaintiffs sometimes abuse the system by bringing frivolous suits that delay and run up the costs of projects.*

In recent years corporations and developers have begun filing *strategic lawsuits against public participation (SLAPPs)* against individuals and activist environmental groups. Such suits are designed to waste the time of and drain funds from private citizens and environmental groups, and keep citizens from becoming involved. More than three-fourths of SLAPPs (which range from $100,000 to $100 million, but average $9 million) lose in court, but only after about three years of struggle.

Some citizen activists have fought back with countersuits and have been awarded damages. For example, a Missouri woman who was sued for criticizing a medical-waste incinerator won an $86.5-million judgment against the incinerator's owner. Even with such awards corporations generally save money by filing suits to intimidate and deter citizens from exercising their constitutional right to oppose actions they believe are wrong.*

Despite such handicaps, however, proponents of environmental law have accomplished a great deal since the 1960s. More than 100 public interest law firms and groups (Appendix 1) now specialize partly or totally in environmental and consumer law. In addition, hundreds of other lawyers and scientific experts participate in environmental and consumer law cases as needed.

---

* Free information on SLAPPs can be obtained from the SLAPP Resource Center, University of Denver College of Law, 1900 Olive St., Denver, CO 80220; 303-871-6266. Citizen's Clearinghouse for Hazardous Waste (Appendix 1) has a SLAPP Back Fact Pack available for $3.29.

# 26-4 Solutions: Improving the U.S. Political System

**MAKING GOVERNMENT MORE EFFECTIVE** In the United States a representative serves for two years, the president four, and a senator six. Because those hoping to get reelected must devote much of their time and energy—especially during the last year of their term—to this task, they have that much less time to solve problems.

Some analysts thus call for amending the Constitution to make these terms longer and limit the number of terms. Presidents (and vice presidents) might serve for a single, nonrenewable six-year term. Representatives might have a maximum of two four-year terms, and senators two six-year terms. California, Colorado, and Oklahoma have already passed term limits for state legislators.

Most analysts and citizens agree that the U.S. political system is based more on *money votes* than on *citizen votes*—one reason so many Americans don't bother to vote. Even those who do vote feel they're often simply choosing between the perceived lesser of two evils. Some see election finance reform as a partial solution (Solutions, p. 674, left).

**IMPROVING BUREAUCRACIES** In its pioneer stages a small, vigorous bureaucratic agency with dynamic leadership can do some good. However, over the years an agency can become rigid and more concerned with expanding its budget than with carrying out its original mandate. Also, it may become friendly with the industries it regulates.

Another problem is that responsibility for managing the nation's environmental and resource policy is divided among many federal and state agencies. This often leads to contradictory policies, duplicated efforts, and wasted funds, while preventing an effective integrated approach to linked problems. Several suggestions have been made for reducing the severity of these problems (Solutions, p. 674, right).

**LEVELING THE LEGAL PLAYING FIELD** Suggestions to help make the legal playing field more level for citizens include:

- *Allowing citizens to sue violators of environmental laws for treble damages.*

- *Awarding attorney fees in successful citizen suits.*

- *Letting citizens sue government officials for damages caused by failure to do their duty.*

- *Raising fines for violating environmental laws and punishing more violators with jail sentences.* Polls

---

## Election Finance Reform

**SOLUTIONS**

One suggestion for reducing undue influence by powerful special interests would be to let the people (taxpayers) alone finance all election campaigns. Candidates could not use any of their own funds or accept donations from any other individuals, groups, or parties, with *absolutely no exceptions*. Nor could incumbents use free mailing, staff employees, or other privileges to aid their election campaigns. Violators of this Public Funding Elections Act would be barred from the campaign or removed from office. Finally, all campaigns would be limited to eight weeks before an election.

Elected officials could then spend their time governing instead of raising money and catering to powerful special interests. Office seekers would not have to be wealthy, and public service could become a way to help the country and the world, not a lifelong profession or as a route to wealth and power. Special-interest groups would be heard because of the validity of their ideas, not the size of their pocketbooks.

The problem is how to get members of Congress (and state legislators) to pass a virtually foolproof plan that would put them on equal financial footing with their challengers and possibly decrease their chances of getting reelected.

## Reforming Bureaucracies

**SOLUTIONS**

Suggestions for improving the responsiveness of elected officials and government agencies to the people include:

- *Passing a sunset law that automatically terminates any government agency or program after, say, six years.* After five years the General Accounting Office and an outside commission would evaluate each agency and program, and recommend to Congress whether it should remain terminated or be reinstated, reorganized, or assigned a new mission. If renewal was recommended, the evaluating bodies would list suggested improvements with deadline dates for implementation.

- *Tying job tenure of political appointees and senior and middle-level managers to performance based on annual evaluation.*

- *Putting all elected officials in the executive and legislative branches on incentive pay.* Their pay would rise or fall based on how well they prevented problems from reaching a crisis level, how well they integrated their policies with other agencies, and how much waste they cut.

- *Rewarding whistle-blowers.* This would involve providing better job protection, government-paid legal expenses, and incentives (higher pay, promotion, cash rewards up to $100,000, well-publicized award ceremonies) for whistle-blowers who exposed fraud, waste, or illegal activities in government.

- *Slowing the revolving door.* This would mean prohibiting all political appointees and senior executive managers (including lawyers) of any regulatory or oversight agency from accepting any form of direct or indirect compensation from any person or group regulated by their agency for a period of five years after they left government service. Violators would be subject to large fines, jail sentences, or both.

- *Combining the EPA and all other environmental agencies into a cabinet-level Department of the Environment.* This would give the secretary of the department greater influence on policy, help consolidate environmental concerns, and allow a more integrated approach to policy development and environmental management.

show that 84% of Americans consider damaging the environment a serious crime. In California environmental crimes are felonies, punishable by jail sentences and seizure of personal property and bank accounts to pay fines.

- *Regulating SLAPP suits.* This would involve establishing rules and procedures for identifying and dismissing frivolous SLAPP suits within a few weeks rather than years, allowing defendants who win their cases to recover attorneys' fees from the plaintiffs, and making it easier for them to file SLAPP-back suits.

**REDUCING FUTURE SHOCK** Perhaps the greatest challenge we face is to use or modify political systems to anticipate and prevent serious long-term problems, many of them global. We cannot predict the future, but we can look at trends and project an array of possible results. Using these alternative futures or scenarios, we can evaluate possible outcomes of adopting various policies (Spotlight, p. 675).

Q: How much money have LDCs borrowed from MDCs?

## Thinking for Tomorrow

**SOLUTIONS**

In 1985 then-Senator Al Gore proposed that the federal government establish an Office of Critical Trends Analysis (OCTA) in the executive branch to help guide public- and private-sector decision making. OCTA would identify and analyze major economic, environmental, social, and political trends, use them in models to project the long-term effects of existing and proposed government policies, and outline alternative futures for the next 20 years. An OCTA report in easily understandable language would be published every four years and widely distributed to government officials, business leaders, universities, the media, and citizens to help "futurize" decision making at all levels of society. OCTA would also hold press conferences and workshops throughout the country to present its findings and get feedback for improving projections. It could also evaluate proposed legislation for positive and negative effects on economic and environmental sustainability. State governments could set up similar offices.

Since the 1960s this approach to analyzing complex systems, anticipating problems, and developing strategies has been widely used by systems analysts and professional futurists in the Department of Defense and in businesses. The challenge is to see that the best possible futuristic thinking and analysis are incorporated into all government economic and political decision making (Solutions, above).

### EXPANDING THE CONCEPT OF SECURITY

Countries have legitimate *national security* interests, but without adequate soil and water and clean air, no nation can be secure. Thus national security ultimately depends on *global environmental security* based on sustainable use of the ecosphere. Countries are also legitimately concerned with *economic security*. However, because all economies are supported by the ecosphere (Figure 25-2), economic security also depends on environmental security, which in turn depends on eliminating hunger, preventable disease, and poverty.

Ideally national, state, and local governments would have a security council of advisers divided equally among concerns about environmental, economic, and military security. Any major decision would involve integrating ideas from all three areas.

A growing number of people are calling for all countries to make environmental security a focus of government and diplomacy at all levels. They agree with President and General Dwight D. Eisenhower's warning in the 1960s:

*Every gun that is made, every warship launched, every rocket fired, signifies in the final sense a theft from those who are hungry and are not fed, those who are cold and are not clothed. This world in arms is not spending money alone. It is spending the sweat of its laborers, the genius of its scientists, and the hopes of its children.*

## 26-5 Global Environmental Policy

**PROGRESS AT THE INTERNATIONAL LEVEL**
Since the United Nations Conference on the Human Environment was held in Stockholm, Sweden, in 1972, some progress has been made at addressing environmental issues at the global level. Today 115 nations have environmental protection agencies, and more than 170 international environmental treaties have been signed. These treaties cover a range of subjects including endangered species, ozone depletion, ocean pollution, global warming, biodiversity, acid deposition, preservation of Antarctica, and export of hazardous waste.

The 1972 conference also created the United Nations Environment Programme (UNEP) to negotiate environmental treaties and help implement them. In 1992 the second United Nations Conference on the Human Environment was held in Rio de Janeiro, Brazil (Solutions, p. 676).

Despite some progress in developing international environmental policies, environmental diplomacy moves at a snail's pace. Also, most existing environmental treaties are fairly weak, rarely demand monitoring and annual national reports to see what progress has been made, and don't include effective provisions for updating. Even Norway—a leader on international environmental issues—is likely to fall short of its commitments in 12 of the 27 major international environmental agreements it has signed.

**SOLUTIONS: IMPROVING GLOBAL ENVIRONMENTAL PROTECTION** Suggestions for improving environmental protection at the global level include:

- *Expanding the role and budget of the United Nations Environmental Programme in negotiating environmental treaties and in monitoring and overseeing their*

# The 1992 Rio Earth Summit

**SOLUTIONS**

In June 1992 more than 100 heads of state, thousands of officials, and more than 1,400 accredited NGOs from 178 nations, met in Brazil to develop plans for addressing environmental issues. The official results included:

- An Earth Charter, a nonbinding statement of broad principles for guiding environmental policy
- Agenda 21, an action plan for developing the planet sustainably during the twenty-first century
- A broad statement of principles on how to protect forests
- A convention on climate change (signed by 154 nations)
- A convention on protecting biodiversity (signed by 153 nations, but not by the United States)
- Establishment of the UN Commission on Sustainable Development, composed of high-level government representatives, to carry out and oversee implementation of these agreements

There were also failures:

- The convention on climate change lacks the targets and timetables for stabilizing carbon dioxide emissions favored by all major industrial countries except the United States (which only signed the treaty when such items were eliminated).
- The forest-protection statement was so watered down that most environmentalists consider it almost useless.

- The United States failed to sign the biodiversity treaty, which attempts to protect biodiversity and calls for rural communities and indigenous peoples in LDCs whose wildlife genetic resources were used to develop biotechnology products to receive royalties or free access to the technology. President Bush claimed the treaty would make the U.S. biotechnology industry less competitive and undermine the legal protection of biotechnology ideas and products. However, in 1993 President Clinton signed the agreement but only after provisions were added to protect U.S. patent rights.
- Officials largely avoided addressing the issues of population and its relation to poverty and economic development, fairer distribution of Earth's wealth and income, forgiving much of the massive debt of LDCs, giving LDCs preferential access to modern environmental and energy-saving technology, creating an international tax on carbon emissions, and the environmental and economic justice impacts of free trade.
- Countries did not commit even the minimum amount of money conference organizers said was needed to begin implementing Agenda 21.
- A treaty on reversing desertification (Section 12-2) was not developed, mainly because of opposition by the United States.
- The United States was sharply criticized for its views and lack

of leadership at a time when other MDCs and LDCs desperately needed such leadership.

Does this mean that the conference was a failure? No, for two reasons. First, it gave the world a forum for talking about and seeking solutions to environmental problems. Much more could and should have been done, but at least there is a basis for future action and for building on the meeting's work.

Second, paralleling the official meeting was a Global Forum that brought together more than 7,000 other NGOs from 175 countries at a site just 40 kilometers (25 miles) from the summit site. The forum involved about 18,000 participants and more than 200,000 visitors. These NGOs worked behind the scenes to influence official policy, formulated their own agendas for sustaining the earth and eliminating poverty, learned from one another, and developed a series of new global networks, alliances, and projects. Many of these groups are staying in touch by radio, TV, fax machines, computer networks such as Eco-Net, electronic conferences, personal computers, and a forthcoming global citizens TV satellite channel.

In the long run these newly formed networks and alliances may play the greatest role in monitoring, supporting, and determining whether the commitments and plans developed by the formal conference are carried out and strengthened.

*implementation.* Satellites could be used to monitor loss of forest cover, illegal drift-netting (Spotlight, p. 379), tuna fishing, and other activities covered under international agreements.

- *Requiring regular compliance reports from countries signing environmental treaties.*

- *Establishing an International Environmental Court to settle disputes between nations over violations of international agreements.* International organizations and NGOs would have the right to initiate suits, and nations would be required to respond and to recognize the court.

Q: How many children die prematurely each year because of the debt burden of LDCs?

**GUEST ESSAY**

Hugh Kaufman

Lynn Moorer

Hugh Kaufman, a former captain in the United States Air Force, has been an engineer in the U.S. Environmental Protection Agency since its inception in 1970. In the 1970s he was the agency's chief investigator of hazardous-waste sites. He helped develop all federal laws for the EPA in the waste disposal field, including the Resource Conservation and Recovery Act and the Superfund law (Section 21-4). He is known as the agency's whistle-blower; his testimony before Congress exposed Love Canal and thousands of other hazardous sites, and led to the removal of former EPA Administrator Anne Burford and the incarceration of former EPA Assistant Administrator Rita Lavelle. Besides his official duties in EPA's Superfund program, he helps grass-roots groups and state officials around the country "fight environmental battles." One of the people he has worked with is Lynn Moorer. She is a former journalist who heads Citizens for Nebraska, a statewide grass-roots organization focusing on nuclear-, hazardous-, and solid-waste issues.

No environmental problem provides clearer examples of people's false assumptions about how the system works than waste (air, water, and land pollution) issues. For those wanting to protect the financial and environmental health of their communities, the following practical advice is offered about key fallacies and realities about how the world really works.

**Fallacy**: Industry has an incentive to prevent pollution.

**Reality**: As long as industry can continue to pass the costs and liabilities of pollution on to citizens and the waste business can continue to reap its phenomenally high rate of return on investment, as current national

(continued)

- *Having heads of all countries (not just the rich countries) meet together in an annual Earth Summit.*

- *Creating an Environmental Security Council as part of the United Nations. Its mission would be to discuss environmental issues, seek solutions to environmental problems, coordinate UN responses to environmental issues, and respond to environmental emergencies.*

- *Providing LDCs with funding to facilitate transfer of the latest environmental and most resource-efficient technologies.*

- *Seeing a major role of state department heads and professional diplomats as engaging in environmental diplomacy.*

- *Greening international lending agencies such as the World Bank and the International Monetary Fund.* This might involve having them shift most of their investment to small-scale grass-roots projects, having local people and NGOs participate in a meaningful way in the planning and implementation of all projects, opening agency documents to public scrutiny, and requiring environmental impact assessments and monitoring for all projects.

**EARTH POLITICS** Can we sustain the earth at the global, regional, and global levels? Yes—if we care enough to make the necessary commitment and in the process discover that understanding and caring for the earth is a never-ending source of joy and inner peace. We must become *Earth conservers*, not *Earth wasters*.

Earth or ecosphere politics, economics, and living are based on the green vision that sustaining the Earth is not a special interest. It is the ultimate interest of all people and all nonhuman species whose existence depends on our actions. This means learning to work together to sustain each local neighborhood and community, to help heal the ecological and social wounds we have inflicted, and to see that everyone's basic needs are met.

Environmentalists believe that no goal is more important, more urgent, or more worthy of our time, energy, creativity, and money. Making this new cultural change will be controversial and, like all significant change, will be neither predictable nor orderly.

In working with the earth we should be guided by historian Arnold Toynbee's observation: "If you make the world ever so little better, you will have done splendidly, and your life will have been worthwhile," and by George Bernard Shaw's reminder that "indifference is the essence of inhumanity."

*Unless we change direction, we are likely to end up where we are headed.*

ANCIENT CHINESE PROVERB

policies make possible, industry has no incentive to prevent pollution. While labeling citizens who oppose projects "NIMBYs" (Not In My Backyard), the industries are anxious to get the projects' liabilities out of their own backyards.

**Fallacy**: Industry spends most of its pollution control budget on engineering and technical research and development to reduce pollution and waste.

**Reality**: Most industry expenditures in pollution control go toward attorneys, lobbying, and PR efforts to kill proposals that would reduce pollution. In fact, more times than not, the business of pollution control has almost no science or technology to it. Instead, industry officials engage in word games, or " semantic detoxification," to obscure the real problems of pollution, sanitize risks, and conceal their failure to control and reduce risks.

**Fallacy**: The industrial sector wields the greatest influence in the governmental decision-making process because its positions are based upon scientifically and technically derived data and rigorous independent analysis.

**Reality**: As our nation's best-financed lobbying power and largest election campaign contributor, the industrial sector has the greatest influence on who is elected and reelected to political office, and on the decisions of elected officials. For the same reason industry has the most control over environmental policy in general and governmental mechanisms that permit pollution. (Thus, the fox has the most influence on how the chicken coop is guarded.)

As an example of a political directive from a pro-industry group overriding federal environmental policy, the President's Council on Competitiveness instructed the EPA administrator in 1990 to delete the agency's recycling requirement for incinerators. The incinerator industry had complained that since recycling would limit the burning of high-Btu, low-cost paper in incinerators, their profits would be hurt. Reducing waste is not good for the waste management business.

**Fallacy**: Environmental protection costs jobs and drains the economy.

**Reality**: Once projects are reviewed carefully, implementation of environmental protection strategies usually creates jobs [Spotlight, p. 652]. For example, the system of mandatory deposits on reusable beverage containers, in place in the United States through the end of World War II, was more labor-intensive and created less pollution than the throwaway, contained system in widespread use today.

**Fallacy**: The driving forces in the siting of waste dumps, incinerators, deep wells, and other projects with the potential to cause significant environmental impacts, or in correcting problems (such as abandoned waste dumps) that have significant environmental impact, are technology, meteorology, hydrology, and geology.

**Reality**: The driving force in siting projects and correcting hazardous situations is the sociology of the potentially affected area [Guest Essay, p. 566]. For example, despite highly productive farmland, a high water table, and wide seasonal temperature changes, Nebraska has been targeted to "host" one of the nation's first regional dumps for low-level radioactive waste. Nebraska's sociological characteristics, however, put it at the top of the list for such an unpopular dump. Nebraska has a unicameral (single house) legislature in which only 25 votes are needed to pass laws, and its rural people, with limited access to information, have shown little stamina for substantive participation in the political process. The state produces little nuclear waste.

**Fallacy**: The government's scientific conclusions can be trusted to be derived from risk and economic analyses that are objectively developed and accurately reported.

**Reality**: The government ignores significant factors in scientifically peer-reviewed studies that are used as a foundation for national environmental policy. An EPA risk-assessment study released in 1991, for example, "loaded the dice" by ignoring groundwater contamination as an environmental risk of waste disposal; thus one of its most significant impacts was dismissed. As a result, the EPA model concluded that waste disposal presents a low environmental risk for the nation.

**Fallacy**: Government environmental officials have environmental protection as their goal.

**Reality**: Avoidance of pain and perpetuating or increasing their position and power drive most government officials. Those who can deliver the most pain to officials have the greatest power in directing the government bureaucracy. On balance the incentive that proves most powerful is to keep polluters polluting and resource extractors extracting.

**Fallacy**: There is little citizens can do to influence significantly or to prevent projects and policies that cause major environmental problems.

Q: Will improving U.S. environmental quality cause a net gain or a net loss of jobs?

**Reality**: Grass-roots pressure has been shown to be an effective way to affect both government and industry. One important lever is the ballot box (other levers are discussed in the following paragraphs). An organized cadre of citizens can effectively influence elections for local and county officials, state legislators, and members of the U.S. Congress. Citizen organizations statewide can influence state officials and members of Congress.

In Nebraska, for example, Republican Governor Kay Orr lost a tight race for reelection in 1990 when conservative Republican farmers and ranchers opposed her promotion of a nuclear waste dump and other waste disposal projects in the state. Grass-roots political action by concerned citizens also played a key role in this political defeat.

**Fallacy**: Government regulators are the only ones with any real, substantial leverage on industry, through the system of permits and enforcement. At best citizens can testify at permit hearings and hope they receive adequate and unbiased coverage of their views.

**Reality**: Citizens can exert significant leverage by using several tactics: **(1)** concentrating leverage and activities on strategic projects, **(2)** actively and continuously watch-dogging policymakers (elected and appointed) and industrial representatives, **(3)** knowing the fine print of relevant laws, **(4)** seeking direct, "in-the-face" accountability of officials, **(5)** making face-to-face contact with policymakers through personal visits (including unannounced ones) to their offices, **(6)** corresponding with elected and appointed officials, sharing information, formulating proposed policies, and requesting information, data, and records using Freedom of Information laws, **(7)** participating in public meetings and hearings of governmental bodies, and **(8)** encouraging volunteer participation on task forces and committees created to advise policy-making bodies.

**Fallacy**: Since you can trust your government officials to do the right thing, there is no reason to watch their actions carefully.

**Reality**: Democracy is not a spectator sport. Officials' feet must be held to the fire by continuous citizen monitoring and involvement. The most effective citizen involvement in government begins after an election or at the passage of a new law. The potential leverage citizens can exert is severely diminished if their activity is evident only at election time. Continuous monitoring and involvement, however, take time and stamina—commodities that are often in short supply. Government and industry officials are aware of this reality and often defuse citizen action by a wear-them-down-and-they'll-go-away strategy and other tactics [Spotlight, p. 663].

**Fallacy**: Stopping an environmentally or financially ruinous project in your community will not positively affect policy because the promoters will just move down the road and force the project on your neighbors.

**Reality**: Empowered citizens who "plug the toilets" by blocking big polluting projects and refusing to be patsies exert significant leverage in forcing government to pursue better environmental policies. Strong opposition everywhere also costs polluting industries money and time, wears them down, and can eventually make pollution prevention and waste reduction more economically attractive than fighting thousands of individual political and legal battles. Once enough monkey wrenches are successfully embedded in the policy mechanism, the system is forced to address pollution prevention and waste reduction head-on.

## Critical Thinking

1. Do you disagree with any of the fallacy–reality items in this essay? If so, list them, and explain why you disagree. Can you add any other fallacy–reality items to this list?

2. As a class use the fallacy–reality items given in this essay (plus any additions or deletions) to develop a political strategy for opposing an environmentally harmful pollution, waste management, or land-use project in your community, and put this plan into action.

## If I Were President*

*Jim Hightower*

**GUEST ESSAY** *Jim Hightower is a populist, author, radio commentator, and political sparkplug who has spent more than two decades battling Washington and Wall Street on behalf of consumers, children, working families, environmentalists, and just-plain-folks who sustain society from the ground up. As Texas commissioner of agriculture from 1983 to 1991, he saw that Texas enacted the country's most stringent certification standards for organically grown food as well as a law that provided migrant workers with a right to know about the pesticides they were exposed to. He regularly travels the country working with local citizens and offering inspiration as a "Johnny Appleseed of grass-roots democracy."*

Let's just do it.

No more Presidential Commissions on Environmental Evasion. We know what needs to be done. Indeed, the "Blueprint for the Environment," a federal action plan laid out by the environmental community in 1988, still serves nicely as a point-by-point program in a gamut of environmental issues. Having never been used, it remains perfectly fresh.

What's been missing is any real presidential commitment to the environment. To get America moving on a pro-Earth agenda requires some heavy-duty pushing, pulling, and maybe a bit of shoving by a president. I'll take five approaches to moving our agenda.

* Used with permission from Jim Hightower and *Environmental Action*.

*First*, I'll go to the people. You can't have a mass movement without the masses, so the place to start is out in the countryside, using the presidential campaign as a mechanism for rallying a mandate for environmental action. The people are way ahead of politicians and pundits in wanting strong action and leadership on these issues, We know this from the polls, the breadth and intensity of local environmental activism, and simply from chatting with Americans at Chat and Chew cafes throughout the land.

In my campaign, I'd ask them for the political power needed to implement the three central issues of my campaign: a pro-Earth agenda, economic regeneration, and social justice. A presidential campaign can invigorate, organize, and focus a national pro-Earth constituency, bringing it to bear on Washington and Wall Street, starting at the opening bell when I assumed office.

*Second*, I'll use the presidential "Bully pulpit" (to borrow Theodore Roosevelt's adroitly-coined phrase) to propound a new ethic of environmental responsibility. As surely as Reagan preached greed from the White House, I'll preach conservation, regeneration, and accountability.

I'll challenge status quo assumptions. For example, we must challenge the assumption that pollution and environmental degradation by industry are "externalities." This allows corporations to take no responsibility for environmental costs, passing them on to society rather than putting them on their own balance sheets. Where's the disincentive to pollute if you don't have to pay? Indeed, this gives a competitive advantage to those who don't give a damn.

## Critical Thinking

1. What do you believe are the greatest strengths and weaknesses of the system of government in your country related to protecting the environment and helping sustain the earth? What substantial changes, if any, would you make in this system?

2. Do you agree or disagree with the idea that the most important form of patriotism is primary loyalty to working with the earth, and that any action harming the earth is unpatriotic and wrong? Explain.

3. Do you agree or disagree with proposals made to improve the U.S. political system through extending term lengths for elected officials, setting term limits, reforming election campaign financing, reforming government agencies, improving the legal system, practicing futurized thinking and decision making, and expanding the concept of security? Explain.

4. Do you believe that militant activist environmental groups that practice illegal monkey wrenching or ecotage against nonliving objects serve a useful role? Explain.

5. Suppose a presidential candidate ran on a platform calling for the federal government to phase in a tax on gasoline over 5–10 years to the point where gasoline would cost $3–$5 dollars per gallon (as is the case in Japan and most western European countries). The candidate argues that this tax increase is necessary to encourage conservation of oil and gasoline, to reduce air pollution, and to enhance future economic, environmental, and military security. Some of the tax revenue would be used to provide tax relief or other aid to all people with incomes below a certain level (the poor and lower middle class), who would be hardest hit by such a consumption tax. Would you vote for this candidate who promises to triple the price of gasoline? Explain.

6. Do you agree or disagree with each of the major goals of the anti-environmental movement (Spotlight, p. 668)? Explain.

Q: Which countries currently lead in the development of new environmental goods and services?

In presidential speeches and actions, I'll try to instill in the public mind and in public policy the assumption that polluters and degraders must put the messes on their own tabs. I will also make clear our society will have to just say no to production of things we cannot recycle, reuse, or manage safely, from foam coffee cups to nuclear waste.

*Third*, I'll invest in the green conversion of our economy. In defiance of conventional wisdom, this approach properly assumes that environmentalism is not anti-business, it is business. Converting our economy from Earth pollution to Earth solution—including conservation, alternative energy, sustainable agriculture, pollution prevention, toxic cleanup, and ecological restoration—will spawn thousands of new inventions and hundreds of new industries and huge numbers of new jobs. And it will open to American "bioneers" a long-term worldwide growth market in Earth-sustaining processes and products. This approach to economic regeneration will call forth not the speculators and spoilers, but the genius and gumption of the workaday people of our country.

*Fourth*, I'll offer a plan and process for global ecological security. If we can muster the good will and resources to restore Kuwait to its royal family and protect access of the United States and its allies to Middle East oil, then we can surely do as much to protect and restore the health of this old Earth for future generations.

This will not be an effort to batter down the economic aspirations of any nation or region, but rather I will promote new ways for all people to participate fully in a global economy that is in harmony with global environmental security. In addition to such daunting problems as $CO_2$ emissions and population growth, it is also time to confront multinational conglomerates and the world's greedy elites with their globe-hopping exploitation both of low-income people and of the environment, all under the false rubric of "free trade" [Spotlight, p. 650]. I believe it is presidential cowardice to avoid engaging in this Herculean struggle any longer.

*Fifth*, I will act locally while thinking globally. We need a president who will set a personal example. Why not an organic garden on the Ellipse, biological controls for White House roaches and Rose Garden aphids, energy-saving fluorescent lights and windows throughout the people's house, solar cells for producing some of the electricity, a presidential bicycle to compensate however slightly for the excess of Air Force One, a comprehensive White House recycling program, and other efforts to make the presidency as Earth-friendly as possible.

Being a leader requires putting yourself first on the line, then asking others to join you. Let's do it.

## Critical Thinking

1. Would you campaign for, vote for, and actively support a president running on the platform proposed in this Guest Essay? Explain. Do you think a candidate running on such a platform could be elected? Explain.

2. List any items you would delete or add to those proposed by Jim Hightower, and explain why.

---

7. Do you agree or disagree with the suggestions made on pages 675–677 for improving environmental protection at the international level? Explain.

*8. A 1990 national survey by the Roper Organization found that while 78% of Americans believe that a major national effort is required for environmental improvement (ranking it fourth among national priorities), only 22% were making significant efforts to improve the environment. The poll identified five categories of citizens: **(1)** *true-blue greens* (11%), who are involved in a wide range of environmental activities; **(2)** *greenback greens* (11%), who don't have time to be involved but who will pay more for a cleaner environment; **(3)** *grousers* (24%), who aren't involved in environmental action mainly because they don't see why they should be if everybody else isn't; **(4)** *sprouts* (26%), who are concerned but who don't believe individual action will make much difference; and **(5)** *basic browns* (28%), who are the most apathetic and least involved or who are strongly opposed to the environmental movement. Which category do you belong to? As a class, conduct a similar poll on your campus.

*9. Use a combination of the major trends you see in society, possible new trends, and your imagination to construct three different scenarios of what the world might be like in 2020. Identify the scenario you favor, and outline a program for achieving this alternative future. Compare your scenarios with those of your classmates.

*10. Conduct a survey of environmental education programs at your school and in your community. Develop a plan for making environmental or Earth education a priority at your school and in your community. Present your plan to school officials and the local school board, and call for public meetings to discuss this issue.

*11. Try to find and evaluate misuse of science on both sides of environmental issues.

## 2040 A.D.: Green Times on Planet Earth*

Mary Wilkins sat in the living room of the passive solar earth-sheltered house (Figure 11-1) she shared with her daughter Jane and her family. From habit she glanced at the electronic calendar powered by a tiny solar cell, but she knew it was July 4, 2040—Independence Day.

She walked into the greenhouse and gazed out at the large blue and green Earth flag (Figure 27-1) they proudly flew beside the American flag. She recalled the day in 2025 when President Elizabeth Jordan had declared that July 4 would also celebrate global independence from fossil and nuclear fuels.

Her eyes shifted to her grandchildren, Jessica and Donnie, running and hollering as they played tag on the neighborhood commons. She heard the hum of solar-powered pumps trickling water to rows of

*Compare this hopeful scenario with the worst-case scenario that opens Chapter 11.

organically grown vegetables and glanced at the fish in the aquaculture and waste treatment tanks. She was glad the tanks provided fish year-round, but it was much more fun to take her grandchildren fishing at the pond she had helped restore 15 years ago as part of a neighborhood wetlands project with help from their Bioregional Advisory Council.

Things began changing rapidly in 2000 with the formation of the Earth Coalition. Environmentalists with a diversity of worldviews and agendas agreed to stop bickering with one another and work together to help sustain the Earth. They finally decided to live by two of nature's most fundamental lessons: **(1)** Sustainability depends on cooperation and **(2)** a diversity of strategies is necessary to achieve sustainability.

She returned to the cavelike coolness of her earth-sheltered house and began putting the finishing touches on the children's costumes for this afternoon's pageant in Aldo Leopold Park. It would honor Earth heroes who began the Age of Ecology in the twentieth century and those who continued this tradition in the twenty-first. Mary smiled when she

*Alone in space, alone in its life-supporting systems, powered by inconceivable energies, mediating them to us through the most delicate adjustments, wayward, unlikely, unpredictable, but nourishing, enlivening, and enriching in the largest degree—is this not a precious home for all of us? Is it not worth our love?*

BARBARA WARD AND RENÉ DUBOS

thought of Jessica's delight at being chosen to play Rachel Carson, heroine of the 1960s skit.

Mary finished her seam and leaned back with a sigh of satisfaction. She closed her eyes and remembered being a frightened 20-year-old college student in 1995 when everything had seemed out of control. She had decided then to join the Earth Conservation Corps (ECC) after graduation.

Even in her most idealistic dreams she had never guessed she would see a halt in the hemorrhaging of global biodiversity; no more wars over oil; the end of nuclear power plants and nuclear weapons; the disappearance of most air pollution when energy from the sun, wind, and hydrogen replaced fossil and nuclear fuels; and the replacement of most cars with walking, bicycles, tricycles, and MAGLEV trains. World population had stabilized at 8 billion in 2030 and then begun a slow decline. And the rate of global warming had slowed significantly. She was glad that her husband Tim, whom she met while working in the ECC in Brazil, had lived long enough to see most of these changes.

Two hours later she, Jane, and her son-in-law Gene watched with pride as 40 beautiful children honored the leaders of the Age of Ecology. At the end Jessica stepped forward and said, "Today we have honored many Earth heroes, but the real heroes are the ordinary people in this audience and throughout the world who worked to help sustain the earth. Thank you grandma, mom, dad, and everyone here for giving us such a wonderful gift. We promise to leave the earth even better for our children and grandchildren and all living creatures." There wasn't a dry eye in the audience.

We are at a critical turning point—a time to make critical choices and act on them. One option is to start on a path toward a world like the one just described. Another option is to keep on our present path, which could result in a world like the one described on page 290. The choice is ours. Not to decide is to decide.

**Figure 27-1** Growing numbers of people are pledging allegiance to the planet that keeps them alive. They see themselves as common citizens of One Earth who represent every culture, every race, every species, and every living creature in this and future generations. Some display the Earth Flag as a symbol of their commitment to sustaining the earth. (Courtesy of Earth Flag Co., 33 Roberts Road, Cambridge, MA 02138)

This chapter will answer the following questions:

- What worldviews underlie today's industrialized societies?
- What are some Earth wisdom worldviews?
- What ethical guidelines can be used to sustain the earth?
- How can we live sustainably?
- How can we bring about a sustainability revolution?

# 27-1 Worldviews in Industrial Societies

**HOW SHALL WE LIVE?** As a powerful species what should our role on Earth be? What obligations do we have to all members of the human species? To other species? To future generations? What is "progress"?

Some people believe growth-driven economic and political systems in industrialized countries are ultimately unsustainable and destructive to ourselves and to the earth, which nurtures all life. They are searching for better visions and beliefs to live by, and better ways to organize human societies. They also yearn for leaders who genuinely care about people and the earth, who inspire us and bring out our good qualities.

At the same time, people differ over how serious our environmental problems are and over what should be done about them. One of the reasons they disagree is that they have different *worldviews*. Worldviews come in many flavors. But they can be divided into two groups according to whether they put humans at the center of things or not. Two examples are the human-centered (anthropocentric) *planetary management worldview* that underlies most industrial societies and the *Earth wisdom* (ecocentric or life-centered) *worldview* summarized inside the front cover.

## HUMAN-CENTERED WORLDVIEWS

Human-centered worldviews prevail in most industrial societies today. According to the *planetary management worldview*, as the planet's most important and dominant species we can and should manage the planet mostly for our benefit. Other species have only *instrumental value*; that is, their value depends on whether they are useful to us or not. These are the basic beliefs of this 40-year-old worldview:

- *We are the planet's most important species, and we are apart from and in charge of the rest of nature.*
- *There is always more and it's all for us.* Earth has an unlimited supply of resources to which we gain access through use of science and technology.
- *All economic growth is good, more economic growth is better, and the potential for economic growth is unlimited.*
- *A healthy environment depends on a healthy economy.*
- *Our success depends on how well we can understand, control, and manage the planet for our benefit.*

There are several versions of this worldview. Some people belong to what might be called the *"no-problem" school*. Economic and population growth are good, and more growth is better. There are no serious environmental, population, or resource problems—or if there are economic growth and technology will fix them (Guest Essay, p. 24).

Another group believes that the best way to manage the planet is through a *free-market global economy with minimal government interference*. They would convert essentially all public-property resources to private-property resources and let the marketplace, governed by free-market competition (pure capitalism), decide essentially everything (Section 25-1).

Still another group believes we have serious environmental, resource, and population problems that we must deal with by becoming better and more responsible planetary managers. These people follow the pragmatic principle of *enlightened self-interest*: Better Earth care is better self-care. They believe we can sustain our species by using a mixture of market-based competition, better technology, and government intervention to promote sustainable forms of economic growth, prevent abuse of power in the marketplace, and protect and manage public- and common-property resources (Section 25-1). Many people with this belief adopt a *spaceship-Earth strategy*, in which Earth is seen as a spaceship—a complex machine that we can understand, dominate, change, and manage to prevent environmental overload and provide a good life for everyone.

Another group with a human-centered worldview advocates the principle of *stewardship* in managing the earth. According to this principle, because of our supe-rior intellect and power or because of our moral or religious beliefs, we have an ethical responsibility to manage and care for all species and ecosystems.

This belief goes beyond enlightened self-interest. We are to be caring and responsible managers or stewards who tend the earth as if it were a garden. We can and should make the world a better place for ourselves and other species through love, care, and knowledge.

## 27-2 Ecocentric or Life-Centered Worldviews

**WILL ANY HUMAN-CENTERED WORLDVIEW WORK?** Some people believe that any human-centered worldview—even stewardship—is unsustainable (Spotlight, p. 685). They suggest that our worldviews must be expanded to recognize *inherent* or *intrinsic value* to all forms of life (that is, value regardless of their potential or actual use to us). This means that all species have an inherent right to live and flourish or at least to struggle to exist—to play their roles in evolution.

Proponents of such *life-centered* or *ecocentric* worldviews believe that as long as we see ourselves as the "top-dog" species, we will continue to eliminate species that are not useful to us instead of recognizing biodiversity as a vital element of Earth capital for all life. They also believe that any human-centered worldview will fail because it wrongly assumes we have or can gain enough knowledge to become effective managers or stewards of Earth. In the words of Aldo Leopold, "We are only fellow voyagers with other creatures in the odyssey of evolution." We can compare the life of astronauts on spaceships with what life might be like on spaceship Earth under a system of planetary management. The astronauts have virtually no individual freedom. To stay alive they must adhere to a rigid daily schedule of monitoring, maintenance, and repair of their simple, unresilient, short-lived, human-designed life support systems, with everything dictated by a central command (ground control). Managing Earth as a stripped-down spaceship leaves little room for human freedom, novelty, adaptability, or long-term sustainability.

Catholic theologian Thomas Berry calls the industrial-consumer society built upon the human-centered, planetary management worldview the "supreme pathology of all history":

*We can break the mountains apart; we can drain the rivers and flood the valleys. We can turn the most luxuriant forests into throwaway paper products. We can tear apart the great grass cover of the western plains,*

Q: What is the world's largest environmental group?

## Can We Manage the Planet?

Will our ongoing romance with unlimited economic growth turn out to be a fatal attraction—causing a fatal depletion of Earth capital? Critics of all human-centered worldviews say yes. They believe that the unhindered free-market approach won't work because it is based on mushrooming losses of Earth capital and focused on short-term benefits regardless of the long-term harmful consequences.

Because market economies are geared to maximize short-term profits, they are programmed to ignore long-term protection of the global commons (Pro/Con, p. 646). Unrestricted free enterprise can work only if we are not dependent on Earth capital or if Earth capital is infinite—both considered invalid assumptions by proponents of life-centered worldviews.

These same critics also contend that the spaceship-Earth and garden versions of planetary manage-

ment—even guided by wise stewardship—won't work. To them, thinking of Earth as a spaceship or a garden—simplified human constructs—that we can understand, manage, and redesign for our use with limited knowledge and only an eyeblink of experience is an arrogant, simplistic, and dangerous way to view an incredibly complex and ever-changing planet that is the result of billions of years of evolution.

For example, we don't even know how many species live on Earth, much less what their roles are and how they interact with one another and their nonliving environment. We have only an inkling of what goes on in a handful of soil, a meadow, a patch of forest, a pond, or any other part of the earth. We are like technicians who think they can build and repair car motors after thirty seconds of superficial training.

As biologist David Ehrenfeld puts it, "In no important instance

have we been able to demonstrate comprehensive successful management of the world, nor do we understand it well enough to manage it even in theory." David Orr (Guest Essay, p. 256) says we are losing rather than gaining the knowledge and wisdom needed to adapt creatively to continually changing environmental conditions:

*On balance, I think, we are becoming more ignorant because we are losing cultural knowledge about how to inhabit our places on the planet sustainably, while impoverishing the genetic knowledge accumulated through millions of years of evolution. . . . Most research is aimed to further domination of the planet. Considerably less of it is directed at understanding the effects of domination. Less still is aimed to develop ecologically sound alternatives that enable us to live within natural limits.*

These are sobering thoughts for those who see planetary management as the solution to our problems.

---

*and pour toxic chemicals into the soil and pesticides onto the fields, until the soil is dead and blows away in the wind. We can pollute the air with acids, the rivers with sewage, the seas with oil—all this in a kind of intoxication with our power for devastation. . . . We can invent computers capable of processing ten million calculations per second. And why? To increase the volume and speed with which we move natural resources through the consumer economy to the junk pile or the waste heap. . . . If, in these activities, the topography of the planet is damaged, if the environment is made inhospitable for a multitude of living species, then so be it. We are, supposedly, creating a technological wonderworld. . . . But our supposed progress . . . is bringing us to a wasteworld instead of a wonderworld.*

**ECOCENTRIC WORLDVIEWS: WORKING WITH THE PLANET** There are many ecocentric or life-centered worldviews, several of them overlapping in some of their beliefs. Humans must, of course, manage parts of the environment to survive and flourish. However, ecocentric worldviews call for us to work

with the rest of nature by learning and using mechanisms that nature has evolved for promoting sustainability and adaptability (Solutions, p. 169).

One ecocentric or **Earth wisdom worldview** has the following beliefs, which are the opposite of the planetary management worldview beliefs:

- *Nature exists for all of Earth's species, not just for us, and we are not apart from or in charge of the rest of nature.* We need the earth, but the earth does not need us.

- *There is not always more, and it's not all for us.* Earth's resources are limited, should not be wasted, and should be used sustainably for us and all species.

- *Some forms of economic growth are beneficial and some are harmful.* Our goals should be to design economic and political systems that encourage Earth-sustaining forms of growth and discourage or prohibit Earth-degrading forms, and to see that the benefits of such growth are distributed equitably among all people (social and economic

justice) and sexes (gender justice), and across generations (intergenerational justice).

- *A healthy economy depends on a healthy environment.* Our survival, life quality, and economies are totally dependent on the rest of nature (Earth capital, Figure 25-2).

- *Our success depends on learning to cooperate with one another and with the rest of nature instead of trying to dominate and manage Earth for our own use.* Because nature is so incredibly complex and always changing, we will never have enough information and understanding to manage the planet.

The roots of this worldview can be traced back to the ways of life of many tribal peoples (Spotlight, p. 270), and to principles articulated by Saint Francis of Assisi, Benedict Spinoza, Henry David Thoreau, Ralph Waldo Emerson, John Muir, Aldo Leopold, Rachel Carson, Alan Watts, Gary Snyder, Charles Reich, Theodore Roszak, Arne Naess (developer of what is called the *deep ecology worldview*), Bill Devall, George Sessions, and others, and embodied in Taoism and Zen Buddhism. Various ecocentric worldviews also emphasize beliefs of the ecofeminist, social ecology, and social and environmental justice movements.

**ECOFEMINISM** The term *ecofeminism* was coined in 1974 by the French writer Françoise d'Eaubonne, when she called upon women to lead an ecological revolution to save the planet. Ecofeminism now in-

cludes a rainbow of views on the relationships of women to the earth and to male-dominated societies (patriarchies).

Most ecofeminists agree that we need a life-centered worldview, but they believe that the main cause of our crisis of sustainability isn't just human-centeredness but specifically male-centeredness (*androcentrism*). They argue that the rise of male-dominated societies and worldviews since the beginning of agriculture is primarily responsible for our violence against nature and for the oppression of women and minorities. According to one hypothesis, when humans began the cultural change from hunting and gathering (Section 2-2) to agriculture (Section 2-3), there was competition for ownership and control of land and water sources, and domination of people (slavery) to obtain and exploit these resources. To survive females had to give up most of the power they had once shared with males to male warriors who could protect them and their children from aggressors.

This led to a shift from thinking of nature as a nurturing mother to thinking of nature as a foe to be conquered (see cartoon). In addition to being military warriors, men (and some women) have become economic warriors who gain power by using and generating income and wealth from as much Earth capital as possible.

As evidence of male domination, ecofeminists note that women do 65% of the world's work (including more than half of that associated with growing

Q: MDCs give what percentage of their GNPs to LDCs as nonmilitary aid?

food, gathering fuelwood, and hauling water), earn less than 10% of all wages, own less than 1% of all property, and in most societies have far fewer rights than do men. Also, to become primary players in the male power-and-domination game, most women are forced to take on male characteristics and become "honorary men" (an example is Margaret Thatcher, former prime minister of England, admired for her male-like use of power).

Most ecofeminists believe that women are more nurturing and closer to nature than men, although they recognize individual exceptions. Some ecofeminists attribute this to biological qualities in women related to carrying a fetus, giving birth, and suckling and protecting their offspring. Others believe the differences arise from the way young girls are culturally conditioned. Still other ecofeminists suggest that oppression by men has driven women (and minorities) closer to nature and made them more compassionate. As oppressed members of society, women have considerable experience in dealing with interpersonal conflicts, bringing people together, acting as caregivers, and identifying emotionally with injustice, pain, and suffering—vital qualities needed to heal the rift between women and men and between humans and the earth.

Ecofeminists argue that women should be seen as having intrinsic worth independent of their usefulness to men, given the same rights as men, allowed to have their views heard and respected, and treated as equal partners. They do not want just a fair share of the patriarchal pie; they want to work with men to bake an entirely new pie designed to heal the rift between humans and nature and end oppression based on sex, race, class, and cultural and religious beliefs. And in doing this, they do not want to be given token roles or co-opted into the male power game.

Ecofeminists are not alone in calling for us to encourage the rise of *life-centered persons* who emphasize the best human characteristics: gentleness, caring, compassion, nonviolence, cooperation, and love.

**SOCIAL ECOLOGY AND SOCIAL AND ENVIRONMENTAL JUSTICE** According to anarchist philosopher Murray Bookchin, the ecological crisis we face is due to the power of our hierarchical and authoritarian social, economic, and political structures, and the use of various technologies to dominate people and nature. In other words it has been caused by industrialized societies driven by the conventional planetary management worldview.

To solve the ecological crisis, Bookchin believes we must adopt a *social ecology worldview*. It would involve decentralizing our political and economic systems and corporations, and altering the types of technology we use. We need to create better versions of democratic community, new forms of Earth-sustaining production, and new types of ecotechnology that are smaller in scale, that consume fewer resources and Earth capital, and that are geared to the carrying capacities of local ecological regions.

The movement for social and environmental justice (Guest Essay, p. 566) is related to the social ecology movement. It involves a coalition of people of color, working people, and poor people in the United States. Currently many of these individuals are politically and economically disenfranchised (*social injustice*), and they are also disproportionately exposed to industrial toxins, dirty air and drinking water, unsafe work conditions, and toxic and hazardous wastes (*environmental injustice*).

Members of this group work within the system to protest and dismantle socially unjust rules and practices, and to change the system to prevent such discrimination. Most environmental justice groups are small and operate at the community level, and are led and funded mostly by individuals who are not part of the established environmental community.

<table>
<tr><td>27-3</td><td>**Earth Ethics: Living Within Earth's Means**</td></tr>
</table>

**ECOCENTRIC ETHICS** Ecocentrists believe that all levels and forms of life—individual organisms, species, and ecosystems—should be allowed to play their roles in the ecosphere. Some ecocentrists emphasize the right to life for all individuals of each species, unless those individuals are needed to meet absolute human necessities (not frivolous wants). For example, some say it's okay to kill animals or plants that harm us or compete with us for food. Others say it's okay to kill domesticated animals for food but not to kill wild animals except when necessary for survival and when no other alternatives are available. All ecocentrists agree, however, that we should not inflict unnecessary suffering on any animal we raise or hunt for food or use for scientific or other purposes.

Other ecocentrists believe in a species-centered approach, mainly because each species is an irreplaceable unit of evolution. They claim we have the right to kill or use individuals of wild species to meet vital needs or to protect ourselves from harm, but not the right to cause the premature extinction of any wild species.

Still others take a broader *ecosystem-centered* approach. They believe that the best way to ensure the survival of both individuals and species is to protect the wild ecosystems that support them. Preserving an

## Earth's Ten Commandments

**SOLUTIONS**

Earth thinker Ernest Callenbach has suggested the following ethical guidelines for working with the earth:

- *Thou shalt love and honor the Earth for it blesses thy life and governs thy survival.*
- *Thou shalt keep each day sacred to the Earth and celebrate the turning of its seasons.*
- *Thou shalt not hold thyself above other living things nor drive them to extinction.*
- *Thou shalt give thanks for thy food to the creatures and plants that nourish thee.*
- *Thou shalt limit thy offspring for multitudes of people are a burden to the Earth.*
- *Thou shalt not kill nor waste Earth's riches on weapons of war.*
- *Thou shalt not pursue profit at Earth's expense but strive to restore its damaged majesty.*
- *Thou shalt not hide from thyself or others the consequences of thy actions upon the Earth.*
- *Thou shalt not steal from future generations by impoverishing or poisoning the Earth.*
- *Thou shalt consume material goods in moderation so all may share Earth's bounty.*

**ETHICAL GUIDELINES** People differ in the ethical guidelines making up their worldviews. Some are *universalists* who believe that certain absolute, eternal, unchanging ethical rules apply to all people and cultures—as do many of the world's dominant religions. Others are *relativists* or *situational ethicists* who believe that ethical rules are not fixed and may change with particular situations, persons, species, or societies.

At its core Earth ethics involves a respect for all life and the processes that sustain it. Such respect implies limits on our actions: There are things we should not do, not because they cannot be done but because doing them shows a disrespect for life. There is nothing wrong with humans exploiting their environment—every living thing must get resources from its environment to survive. The problem is knowing how far to go.

Developing ethical guidelines for putting beliefs into action is a perilous and controversial undertaking, but many people believe it is a necessary one. Such guidelines can help us decide what to do when faced with hard choices. Ethicists, theologians, and philosophers have developed ethical guidelines for living sustainably on Earth; some of them are listed inside the back cover. Ernest Callenbach has stated them more simply and eloquently (Solutions, left). Such guidelines can be used by people with a human-centered stewardship worldview or with a life-centered Earth wisdom worldview.

Working with the earth requires each of us to make a personal commitment to strive to live an environmentally ethical life—not because it is mandated by law but because it is the right thing to do. It is our responsibility to ourselves, our children and grandchildren, our neighbors, and the earth.

## 27-4 Solutions: Ways to Live Sustainably

**EVALUATING SUSTAINABILITY PROPOSALS** *Sustainability* has become a buzzword. Hundreds of programs have been introduced or proposed in its name—some useful and some questionable or harmful. Lester Brown (Guest Essay, p. 43) has a simple test for any sustainability proposal: "Does this policy or action lower carbon emissions? Does it reduce the generation of toxic wastes? Does it slow population growth? Does it increase Earth's tree cover? Does it cut CFC emissions? Does it reduce air pollution and acid rain? Does it reduce radioactive waste generation? Does it lead to less soil erosion? Does it protect the planet's biodiversity?"

endangered or threatened species in a zoo, botanical garden, or other artificial environment is better than doing nothing, but not enough to maintain the full evolutionary potential for adaptation to unpredictable changes in environmental conditions through speciation. Ecosystem preservation is a *prevention* approach. Protecting endangered species is an emergency response necessitated mostly by our failure to protect ecosystems.

Ecocentrism is a profoundly prohuman belief that celebrates humanity's special qualities and achievements. Opposing a human-centered worldview (anti-anthropocentric) does not mean that one is against humans (misanthropic). Rather, ecocentrists call for us to expand our sense of compassion, caring, and love to all individuals, species, and ecosystems—not just humans—including future generations of all forms of life. To them, recognizing the intrinsic value of all life is the best way to serve and love people.

Others say we don't need to be ecocentrists to value life. Human-centered stewardship also calls for us to value individuals, species, and ecosystems as part of our responsibility as Earth's caretakers.

Q: How much do trade barriers in MDCs cost LDCs each year?

Others would ask further: Does it deplete Earth capital? Does it diminish cultural diversity? Does it reduce poverty, hunger, and disease? Does it promote individual and community self-reliance? Does it prevent pollution? Does it reduce resource waste? Does it save energy? Does it transfer the most resource-efficient and environmentally benign technologies to LDCs? Does it provide a fairer distribution of wealth and income between rich and poor people?

The search for sustainability presumes that we know or can discover what is sustainable: levels and thresholds of environmental carrying capacity for the world and regions. Long-term sustainability also involves preserving biodiversity as the primary way to maintain the potential for adaptability to changing conditions. Unfortunately it appears that we cannot even come close to having such information. Thus, many environmentalists believe we should follow the *precautionary principle*. This would involve slowing and then stabilizing our population size, preventing pollution, using resources more efficiently, and living off Earth income.

**USING APPROPRIATE TECHNOLOGY** Earth wisdom and stewardship worldviews do not reject science and technology. Instead, they insist that they be used in appropriate, just, and humane ways to protect—not to degrade and destroy—life on Earth.

**Appropriate technology** is typically fairly simple, locally adaptable, Earth-friendly, resource-efficient, culturally suitable technology that depends mostly on local resources and labor; that can be easily expanded, reduced, moved, and repaired; and that affects only a fairly small number of people when it fails.

People designing such technologies often use nature as a model (Guest Essay, p. 256). This approach to design, for example, would see a house as a *bioshelter* that is built mostly of natural or used materials, uses the sun and Earth for heating and cooling (Figures 11-1, 17-7, 17-10, 17-13, and 19-12), composts or recycles the wastes of its inhabitants, and has ecologically sustainable systems for growing most or all of its inhabitants' food. The same *design-with-nature* concepts can be applied to neighborhoods and local communities.

**PROMOTING EARTH EDUCATION** Environmentalists urge us to make Earth education the core of all education in schools and public discourse (Guest Essay, p. 698). Conventional, reductionist, discipline-oriented education is a useful and important way of breaking down and understanding some of Earth's complexity. However, our formal educational systems and public media should expose us to holistic, integrated, inter- and multidisciplinary thinking as an equally important component of Earth education (Spotlight, right).

## My Philosophy of Education

**SPOTLIGHT** After 36 years of teaching and writing textbooks, I believe that the main goals of an education should include the following:

- *Developing respect for all life.*
- *Understanding what we know about how the earth works and sustains itself* (Solutions, p. 169).
- *Understanding connections.* These include connections within nature, between people and the rest of nature, among all people (regardless of race, sex, age, and creed), between generations, among the problems we face, and among the solutions to these problems.
- *Understanding and evaluating one's worldview.*
- *Becoming a wisdom seeker instead of an information vessel.* We need to learn how to sift through mountains of facts and ideas and find the nuggets of knowledge and wisdom that are useful and worth knowing. Viewed this way, the goal of education is not to learn as much as possible but to learn as little as possible. We need an *Earth wisdom revolution* that enriches our minds and lives, not an information revolution that clogs our brains and dims our capacity to care and share—a form of cultural lobotomy that hinders us from fully participating in the Great Dance of Life. Currently we are using information mostly to dominate, deplete, and degrade the earth.
- *Learning to evaluate and resist advertising.* Most of the $256 billion spent worldwide on advertising each year (an average of $48 per person or $448 per American) is designed to accelerate Earth degradation by making us unhappy with what we have. Learning to detect ecopornography and psychological manipulation (beginning in elementary school) by analyzing TV and print ads is a superb way to teach critical thinking.
- *Learning to live sustainably in a place.* This would be a piece of Earth to which we are rooted or emotionally attached and whose ecological integrity, sustainability, and adaptability we feel driven to nurture and defend.
- *Fostering a desire to make the world a better place and to act on this desire.* As David Orr (Guest Essay, p. 256) puts it, education should help students "make the leap from I know to I care to I'll do something." Education that sedates us and reduces our capacity for passionate action against what we believe is wrong is a failure.

A: About $100 billion

## Emotional Learning

Formal education is important, but Aldo Leopold, Henry David Thoreau, Gary Snyder, and many others believe it's not enough. Such Earth thinkers and many religious thinkers believe that the essence, rhythms, and pulse of the earth within and around us can only be experienced at the deepest level by our senses and feelings—our emotions. They urge us to take the time to escape the cultural and technological "body armor" we use to insulate ourselves from nature and experience nature directly. They suggest that we reenchant our senses and kindle a sense of awe, wonder, and humility by standing under the stars, sitting in a forest, taking in the majesty and power of an ocean, or experiencing a stream, lake, or other part of untamed nature. We might pick up a handful of soil and try to sense the teeming microscopic life forms in it that keep us alive. We might look at a tree, a mountain, a rock, or a bee and try to sense how they are a part of us, and we a part of them.

These religious thinkers and Earth philosophers encourage us to stop attaching more importance to dollars that we can't eat, breathe, and drink than to the sun, land, air, water, plants, bacteria, and other organisms that really keep us alive. Michael J. Cohen suggests that each of us recognize who we really are by saying:

*I am a desire for water, air, food, love, warmth, beauty, freedom, sensations, life, community, place, and spirit in the natural world. These pulsating feelings are the Planet Earth, alive and well within me. I have two mothers: my human mother and my planet mother, Earth. The planet is my womb of life.*

They call for us to recognize that the technological cocoon we enclose ourselves in and the feeling of self-importance we hold as a species have given us a severely distorted picture of what is really important. As Catholic theologian Thomas Berry put it:

*So long as we are under the illusion that we know best what is good for the earth and for ourselves, then we will continue our present course, with its devastating consequences for the entire earth community. . . . We need only listen to what the Earth is telling us. . . . The time has come when we will listen, or we will die.*

Experiencing nature emotionally allows us to get in touch with our deepest self, which has sensed from birth that when we destroy and degrade the natural systems that support us, we are attacking ourselves. As ecowarrior Dave Foreman puts it:

*When a chain saw slices into the heart-wood of a two-thousand-year-old Coast Redwood, it's slicing into my guts. When a bulldozer rips through the Amazon rain forests, it's ripping into my side. When a . . . whaler fires an exploding harpoon into a great whale, my heart*

*is blown to smithereens. I am the land, the land is me. Why shouldn't I be emotional, angry, passionate? Madmen and madwomen are wrecking this beautiful, blue-green, living Earth. . . . We must love Earth and rage against her destroyers. . . . The Earth is crying. Do we hear? . . . We can't be perfect, but we can act.*

Many psychologists believe that consciously or unconsciously we spend much of our lives in a search for roots—something to anchor us in a bewildering and frightening sea of change. As philosopher Simone Weil observed, "To be rooted is perhaps the most important and least recognized need of the human soul."

Earth philosophers say that to be rooted, each of us needs to find a *sense of place*—a stream, a mountain, a yard, a neighborhood lot, or any piece of the earth we feel truly at one with. It can be a place where we live or a place we occasionally visit and experience in our inner being. When we become part of a place, it becomes a part of us. Then we are driven to defend it from harm and to help heal its wounds.

Emotionally experiencing our connectedness with the earth leads us to recognize that the healing of the earth and the healing of the human spirit are one and the same. We need to discover and tap into the green fire that burns in our hearts and use this as a force for working with the earth. This is living life at its fullest.

---

Making Earth education the center of the learning process will not be an easy task because most teachers and members of the educational establishment are trained to think primarily in terms of disciplines and vigorously guard their turfs. Shifting the focus of our education system involves the following:

- *Declaring the next decade the Earth Education Decade.* Government, private foundations, and educa-

tional institutions would mount a massive effort to have Earth education materials developed by our best Earth thinkers and then distributed throughout the educational system and the media.

- *Exposing all teachers, media people, and corporate and government leaders to Earth education.* This would involve the use of summer workshops, visiting

Q:  What percentage of the jobs lost in the United States in 1988 was due to environmental factors?

teachers, team teaching, week-long retreats, and other devices.

- *Inserting examples of holistic Earth thinking into teaching materials at all levels beginning in kindergarten.*

- *Requiring every student graduating from high school, college, and any professional school to take one or more courses in Earth education.*

- *Developing and widely using measures of ecological literacy.*

- *Setting up a dual-track specialist-holistic system.* Disciplinary thinking would remain important, but a parallel teaching and research track would be established for those wishing to pursue holistic, integrated, interdisciplinary education, and would give equal rewards (salaries, promotion, grants, tenure, and respect) to people in each track. We also need to encourage interaction between the two tracks.

**LISTENING TO THE EARTH** In 1948 Aldo Leopold said, "We can be ethical only in relation to something we can see, feel, understand, love, or otherwise have faith in." To Leopold and many other environmentalists, sustaining the earth requires not only a new or better way of thinking but also a commitment to experiencing and listening to the Earth with our senses and our hearts (Solutions, p. 690).

**LISTENING TO CHILDREN: BOTTOM-UP EDUCATION** Children are much more concerned about sustaining the earth than most adults because they know we are dumping a giant mess in their laps. Thus, we also need to take the time to listen—truly listen—to children. If they haven't gone too far in school, so that their creativity and sense of wonder are intact, they can see things quite clearly and tell the unvarnished truth.

Most children understand that much of what we are doing to the earth (and thus to them) is stupid and wrong, and they don't buy the excuses we give for not changing the way we do things (Solutions, right). Sadly many lose or suppress such insights as they move through educational systems and are exposed to advertising that brainwash them into becoming obedient participants in Earth-consuming, Earth-degrading societies.

We usually think of education as a top-down process—parents to children and teachers to students. The truth is that many adults are so confused or discouraged about what we are doing to one another and the earth that they need reeducating and reenergizing. One of the best ways to reform society and our educational system is a bottom-up approach in which children start educating parents and teachers about

## Learning from Jessica

**SOLUTIONS**

Jessica is my wonderful adopted granddaughter. When she is not in school she and my Earthmate Peggy—who since birth has been tuned in to nature—spend a lot of time enjoying and investigating nature while I sit here writing books about it.

Most nights at bedtime Jessica and I act out an Earth story. These are exercises in which we look for connections in nature, try to understand the consequences of what we are doing to nature, and try to come up with practical solutions to problems we uncover.

Do this with almost any young child and you will learn that they understand far more about how things really work and should work than you would dream. When Jessica deduces the implications of what we are doing (often with amazing speed), her simple and penetrating response is typically, "That is stupid, mean, and wrong." When you ask most young children to find ways out of the problems we have created, they come up with a range of possible solutions. And they don't understand why we haven't done these things because they seem so obvious and because we say we love them.

I've spent decades trying to understand how nature works and what we should do to help sustain the earth. Jessica intuitively understands most of this, gives simpler explanations than I do (she has less cultural baggage ), and constantly teaches me.

One of my greatest fears is that in becoming "educated" she will unlearn this real knowledge and wisdom. Thank you, Jessica, for helping me learn about and care for the earth. I hope you never lose your caring heart and Earth wisdom.

what's really important. Children have passion, honesty, a sense of wonder, and energy; adults have driver's licenses, influence, and the vote.

**LIVING BIOREGIONALLY** Another aid to working with the earth is to understand the geographic area where you live as part of a natural region or bioregion, a unique life territory with its own soils, landforms, watersheds, microclimates, native plants and animals, and other distinctive natural characteristics. A bioregion is ultimately governed by nature's laws and processes, not by our laws or the territorial lines we draw on maps. The large bioregions of North America include the Ozarks, the Sonora Desert, Appalachia,

Cascadia (the Pacific Northwest), and the Maritimes (northern Maine and eastern Canada). These can be divided into smaller bioregions and into individual watersheds, mountain ranges, and vegetation zones.

Bioregional living is an attempt to understand and live sustainably within the natural cycles, flows, and rhythms of a particular place. It means becoming "dwellers in the land," who establish an ecologically and socially sustainable pattern of existence within it by adapting ourselves to a place.

Most attempts at bioregional living involve *reinhabitation*: learning to live-in-place in an area that has been injured and disrupted through human exploitation. The first step is to learn as much as we can about how our bioregion works, what networks of symbiotic and synergistic relationships sustain its human and nonhuman inhabitants, what we have done to disrupt those relationships, and whether and how people lived sustainably in this region in the past. This involves asking, What was this region like before we came? What might nature put there if we were not present? How can we begin healing the wounds we have inflicted on our bioregion?

At the individual level it means being able to answer basic questions about where we live. Where does our water come from? Where does our energy come from? What kinds of soils are under our feet? How long is the growing season? What types of wildlife are our neighbors? Where does our food come from? Where does our waste go?

**LIVING MORE SIMPLY** An Earth wisdom worldview does not mean unplugging everything, moving to the country, growing all our food, or becoming a modern hunter-gatherer. The world is far too populated and developed for that, even if we wanted to. Instead, it involves learning how to live more sustainably—to live simply so that others, human and nonhuman, may simply live.

Some affluent people in MDCs are adopting a lifestyle of *voluntary simplicity*, based on doing and enjoying more with less by learning to live more simply but richly. They are realizing that buying more products and luxuries to satisfy artificially created wants doesn't provide security, freedom, or joy—what Paul Wachtel calls "the poverty of affluence." As humorist Will Rogers put it, "Too many people spend money they haven't earned to buy things they don't want to impress people they don't like." Although attaining happiness through material acquisition is denounced by every major religion and philosophy, it is preached incessantly by advertising.

Voluntary simplicity is based on Mahatma Gandhi's *principle of enoughness*: "The earth provides enough to satisfy every person's need but not every person's greed. . . . Civilization, in the real sense of the term, consists not in the multiplication, but in the deliberate and voluntary reduction of wants." It calls for an end to *overconsumption*, in which people consume more than they need at the expense of those who do not have what they need and at the expense of Earth capital. It means asking oneself, "How much is enough?" Because affluent people are conditioned by advertising to want more and more (cartoon, p. 642), and often think of such wants as vital needs, it's easy for need to slide into greed.

Voluntary simplicity means eliminating unnecessary consumption and waste of matter resources and energy resources (Individuals Matter, p. 529); trading or bartering time and skills to meet basic needs; growing as much of our own food as possible; obtaining used items or building things that last to meet basic needs; recycling, reusing, maintaining, and repairing things we need; and giving away or sharing things we don't need (Spotlight, p. 694). It also means getting as much of what we need from local resources and people, and striving for as much individual, neighborhood, and local community self-sufficiency, as possible. However, voluntary simplicity by those who have more than they really need should not be confused with the *forced simplicity* of the poor, who do not have enough to meet their basic needs for food, clothing, shelter, clean water and air, and good health.

**AVOIDING COMMON TRAPS** It's easy to fall into some common traps or offer typical excuses that lead to indifference and inaction. These include:

- *Gloom-and-doom pessimism.* This is the belief that nothing can be done.

- *Blind faith in experts and leaders.* This is the belief that someone is in charge who knows what to do and will do it without steady pressure and help from ordinary citizens.

- *Blind technological optimism.* This is the belief that we will always be able to come up with scientific and technological solutions to our problems.

- *The view of modern industrial society as the pinnacle of human achievement.* Critics argue that any society that is so busy damaging its life support systems cannot be regarded as being successful or as representing progress.

- *Fatalism.* This is the belief that we have no control over our actions and the future.

- *The "why bother" syndrome.* In other words, "Even if I share, care, and get involved, most other people won't, so why should I waste my time and energy trying to make the world a better place?"

Q: How many people are employed by the U.S. pollution control industry?

- *Extrapolation to infinity.* This is the belief that "if I can't change the entire world quickly, I won't try to change any of it." This attitude is reinforced by modern society's emphasis on instant gratification and quick results with as little effort as possible.

- *Paralysis-by-analysis.* This involves searching for the perfect worldview, philosophy, and solutions before doing anything. We need to reflect on our worldview and analyze proposed solutions to problems, but we will never have all the information we need.

- *Faith in simple, easy answers.* We should be guided by philosopher and mathematician Alfred North Whitehead, who advised, "Seek simplicity and distrust it, " and by writer and social critic H. L. Mencken, who warned, "For every problem there is a solution—simple, neat, and wrong." We have dug ourselves into a deep hole. We can and must work together to dig our way out, but it won't be simple or easy.

All of these traps represent various forms of *denial* that enable us to avoid facing up to problems and the need for change. We must break the chains of denial, despair, and fear, and find the courage and vision to choose better lifestyles and explore new cultural paths. Otherwise, we are courting disaster and misusing or not using the special qualities evolution has bestowed on the human species.

**BECOMING EARTH CITIZENS** The good news is that we can choose to sustain the earth and lead more meaningful and joyful lives. In "Individuals Matter" boxes throughout this book, I have listed specific actions various environmentalists believe we should take. No one can come close to doing them all, and you may disagree with some of them. Here are the items at the top of my list:

- *Respect all life, and fight to protect the inherent right of all life to exist.*

- *Learn all you can about how nature works, about how human nature and power work, and about the connections between things.*

- *Listen to and learn from nature and from children.*

- *Evaluate the beneficial and harmful consequences of your lifestyle and profession on the earth today and for the future.*

- *Lead by example.* People are most influenced by what we do, not by what we say.

- *Live more richly and tread more lightly on the earth by living more simply.*

- *Become politically active at the local, national, and global levels.* Theodore Roszak suggests that our common political agenda for the good of the planet should be to "Scale down. Slow down. Democratize. Decentralize." Working with the earth is not the exclusive province of liberals, conservatives, capitalists, socialists, or other groups. Becoming politically active, regardless of one's political persuasion, involves becoming a *true (Earth) conservative* by working to conserve and help sustain the life support system for ourselves and all life. We may disagree on what needs to be done or how to do it, but we can try to find those things we can work on together. This can lead to better understanding and mutual respect instead of mistrust, fear, and anger.

- *Do the little things based on thinking globally and acting locally.* Each small measure you take is important, sensitizes you to Earth-sustaining acts, and leads to more such acts. No one can do everything, but each of us can do something to help sustain the earth.

- *Think and act nationally and globally.* This means targeting the big polluters (industries, industrialized agriculture, governments) and big problems (ozone depletion, biodiversity loss, possible climate change) through political action, economic boycotts, and selective consumption.

- *Get to know, care about, and defend a piece of Earth.* As poet-philosopher Gary Snyder puts it, "find our place on the planet, dig in, and take responsibility from there."

- *Work with others to sustain and heal the Earth, beginning in your neighborhood and community.*

- *Personally help at least one person or family in need to the point where they can help themselves.* Do this with love, not condescension.

- *Provide quality parenthood for any child you choose to have or adopt.*

- *Don't try to do everything.* Focus your energy on the few things that you feel most strongly about and that you can do something about.

- *Don't use guilt and fear to motivate other people, and don't allow other people to do this to you.* We need to nurture, reassure, understand, and love, rather than threaten, one another.

- *Have fun and take time to enjoy life.* Don't get so intense and serious that you can't laugh every day and enjoy wild nature, beauty, friendship, and love.

I am writing this book deep in the midst of beautiful woods in Eco-Lair, a structure that Peggy, my wife and Earthmate, and I designed to work with nature. This ongoing experiment is a low-tech, low-cost example of sustainable-Earth design and living.

In 1980 we purchased a 1954 school bus from a nearby school district for $150 and sold the tires for the same price that we paid for the bus. We built an insulated foundation, rented a crane for two hours to lift the gutted bus onto the foundation, placed heavy insulation around the bus, and added a wooden outside frame. The interior is paneled with wood, some of it from the few trees we carefully selected for removal (Figure 27-2). Most visitors don't know the core of the structure is a school bus unless we tell them.

We attached a solar room—a passive solar collector with double-paned conventional sliding glass windows (for ventilation)—to the entire south side of the bus structure (Figure 27-2). Thick concrete floors and filled concrete blocks on the lower half of the interior wall facing the sun absorb and slowly release solar energy collected during the day. The solar room serves as a year-round sitting and work area. It contains a small kitchen with a stove and a heavily insulated refrigerator that run on liquefied petroleum gas (LPG). We plan to replace the windows with new superinsulated windows, which were not available at the time of construction.

The room collects enough solar energy for about 60% of the space heating needs during the cold months. The rest of the heat is provided by a continuous loop system of water preheated by solar collectors and, when necessary, heated further by a tankless instant water heater fueled by LPG.

Our compact fluorescent light bulbs last an average of six years and use about 75% less electricity than conventional bulbs. For the time being we are buying electricity from the power company, but we hope to get our electricity from roof-mounted photovoltaic panels (Figure 17-17 and 17-19) within a few years. Present electricity bills run around $30 per month ($18 is the minimum charge regardless of how much electricity we use), compared with $100 or more for conventional structures of the same size.

In moderate weather open windows capture breezes. During the hot and humid North Carolina summers additional cooling is provided by earth tubes (Figure 17-10). When a small variable-speed fan is turned on, outside air at a temperature of 35°C (95°F) is drawn slowly through the buried tubes (which are surrounded by earth at about 16°C or 60°F), entering the structure at about 22°C (72°F). This natural air conditioning costs about $1 per summer for running the fan.

Several large oak trees and other deciduous trees in front of the solar room give us additional passive cooling during summer, and drop their leaves to let the sun in during

Evan Kruppenbach

**Figure 27-2** Eco-Lair is where I work. It is a low-tech, low-cost, ongoing experiment in saving energy and money. A south-facing room (shown in the photo on the left) collects solar energy passively and distributes it to a well-insulated, reused 1954 school bus. Active solar collectors are shown on the left, and a passive solar water heater is shown near the ground on the right. The photo on the right shows the interior of the refurbished school bus. The computer and desk at the far end are located where the hood and motor of the bus used to be. The large cabinet on the left folds down and serves as a double bed. The bus windows on the right can be opened as needed to allow heat collected in the attached solar room to flow into the bus space. The floor vent seen in the lower righthand corner of the photo brings in Earth-cooled air during hot weather through buried earth tubes.

Q: In the United States how many jobs are created by $1 billion of military expenditures?

winter. A used conventional central air conditioning unit (purchased for $200) is our backup. It can be turned on for short periods (typically no more than 15–30 minutes per day) when excessive pollen or heat and humidity overwhelm our immune systems and the earth tubes. Life always involves some tradeoffs.

Eco-Lair is surrounded by natural vegetation, including flowers and low-level ground cover adapted to the climate of the area. This means there is no grass to cut and no lawn mower to push, repair, feed with gasoline, and listen to. Peggy added plants that repel various insects, so we have few insect pest problems. The surrounding trees and other vegetation also provide habitats for various species of insect-eating birds. When ants, mice, and other creatures find their way inside, we use natural alternatives to repel and control them (Solutions, p. 620).

We save with water-saving faucets, a water-saving shower head, and a low-flush toilet. We have also experimented with a waterless composting toilet that gradually converts waste and garbage scraps into a dry, odorless powder that can be used as a soil conditioner.

We compost kitchen wastes and recycle them to the soil. Paper, tin cans, and nonrefillable glass bottles go to a local recycling center, along with most of the small amount of plastics we use. We try never to use energy-intensive aluminum cans and plastic bags, choosing refillable glass bottles and reusable cloth bags instead. Extra furniture, clothes, and other items we have accumulated or salvaged over the years are stored in three other old school buses and recycled to family, friends, and people in need. For most household chemicals we use more Earth-friendly and also cheaper substitutes (Table 21-2, p. 557). We use recycled toilet paper made completely from post-consumer paper waste and recycled paper for my office.

Recently we have built an affordable, energy-efficient house, which we call Eco-Habitat. We bought a 130-square-meter (1,400-square-foot) manufactured home with enough insulation and energy-saving features to qualify for a discount on our electric bill from our electric utility company. The cost of the unit, which was made in a factory and set up on the lot in two days, was $29,000. Then we added more roof insulation and built a second roof over the original one to give us a 3-meter-wide (10-foot) covered porch around the entire house.

Part of the porch on the south side was glassed in to provide a passive solar collector and solar room. Another glassed-in room was added to the north side for use in warm weather. Half of the remaining porch was screened and the rest left open. Any part of the porch could be enclosed in the future to expand the house at little cost. We replaced the gas furnace that came with the house with a system using tankless water heaters fueled by LPG.

This modification cost $25,000 and gave us 177 square meters (1,900 square feet) of enclosed space, excluding the screened and open porch areas. Thus we ended up with an energy-efficient house at a cost of $30 per square meter ($28 per square foot), or $54,000 total—less than half the cost per unit of area of a conventional house (excluding the cost of land). The overall cost—including land, well, and septic system—of the project was about $80,000.

Because I work at home, I do little driving. Our primary car is a four-door, automatic-transmission version of a GEO Metro that gets 18 kpl (42 mpg). (Peggy has back problems that prevent her from using the even more energy-efficient manual-shift model.) It is peppy and has more interior room than most midsized cars; its only drawback is that it doesn't have air bags. Our backup transportation is a much less fuel-efficient 4-wheel-drive vehicle need-

ed mostly when bad weather transforms the 1.6-kilometer (1-mile) dirt road leading to Eco-Lair and Eco-Habitat into a muddy or icy mess.

We wish cars like the Volvo LCP 2000 (Figure 17-5) or GM's Ultralite (Figure 17-6) were available. Eventually we hope to be able to buy a vehicle that runs on hydrogen gas produced by solar photovoltaic cells.

We buy most of our food from the grocery store but are growing more of it in raised organic gardening beds. For health and environmental reasons we have greatly reduced our meat consumption. For ethical reasons we should be strict vegetarians but have not gone that far.

We feel a part of the piece of land we live on and love. We feel that its trees, flowers, deer, squirrels, owls, hummingbirds, songbirds, and other wildlife are a part of us, and we a part of them. As temporary caretakers of this small portion of the biosphere, we feel obligated to pass it on to future generations with its ecological integrity, adaptability, and sustainability preserved.

Our latest project involves wetland restoration. We built a spillway over a creek to allow water to collect and form a 0.8 hectare (2-acre) wetland that we have stocked with fish to provide a source of protein (aquaculture). The wetland is also an emergency source of water in case of fire. It is wonderful to see various plants and animals filling the niches in this newly formed aquatic habitat.

Most of our political activities involve thinking globally but acting locally. We also give money to many environmental and conservation organizations working at local, state, national, and global levels.

Working with nature gives us great joy and a sense of purpose. It also saves us money. Our attempt to work with nature is in a rural area, but people in cities can also have high-quality lifestyles that conserve resources and work with nature (see Further Readings).

**SOLUTIONS**

The Earth strategy I envision would involve the following components:

- *Getting environmentalists to stop bickering, come together, and develop a positive vision of working with the earth for all life.* This vision would consist of some general principles they could agree on, but more importantly it would foster inspiring, practical, and easily understandable stories, myths, and positive scenarios of what life could be like if we changed our ways. These visions would be presented in adults' and children's books, educational materials, novels, movies, videos, TV programs, poems, neighborhood and town meetings, and any other device that would expose the general public to these ideas.

- *Accepting and living by the diversity principle, and forming a massive Earth Coalition for change* (Figure 27-3). This would mean agreeing that there is no best way to sustain the earth and encouraging different groups, cultures, and people with various worldviews and political and religious beliefs to try what they think will work. However, diversity without a commitment to cooperation and to a core of commonly held basic values or principles can lead to massive cultural strife and breakdown. Diverse groups would have to set aside their differences and form a coalition dedicated to the overarching goals of working with the earth and with one another.

- *Spending much more time working at the grass-roots level and leading by example to help empower ordinary people to bring about change at the local level.* People have to see an inspiring vision translated into changes that improve and empower their own lives. They need to see environmentalists as dedicated and caring people who are willing to get their hands dirty. So far, ordinary people see most environmentalists as intellectual, elitist adversaries who are trying to tell them how to live without really listening to their problems and solutions, and who are unwilling to roll up their sleeves and work with them. For an inspiring example of what can be done in a short time, see the Guest Essay on page 386.

I urge you to pick the part or parts of the Earth Coalition you feel most comfortable with, and get involved by jumping into the exhilarating and frustrating arena of life. In the words of Robert Fulghum:

> *I do not want to talk about what you understand about this world. I want to know what you will do about it. I do not want to know what you hope. I want to know what you will work for. I do not want your sympathy for the needs of humanity, I want your muscle. As the wagon driver said when they came to a long, hard hill, "Them that's going on with us, get out and push. Them that ain't, get out of the way."*

---

**27-5** | **Coming Together: A Personal View**

**THERE IS NO BEST ANSWER** The more I learn about Earth and connections in nature, the more I realize how little we know. In my ongoing search for beliefs and values I have concluded that *there is no single correct or best culture, worldview, or type of society.*

Indeed, one of nature's most important lessons is that preserving diversity or a rainbow of possibilities or potentialities is the best way to adapt to Earth's largely unpredictable, ever-changing conditions and thus achieve long-term sustainability. Each human culture, religion, and worldview provides different experiences, wisdom, and insights for working with the earth.

My limited study of human history makes me wary of a monolithic or global worldview, ecoreligion, or world government. Various originally well-intended political, philosophical, and religious beliefs have led to much evil, injustice, suffering, killing, and abuse of power. We need competent, dedicated, caring believers in making the world a better place to live, but not "true believers" who insist that their way is the only way. Out of this thinking, I propose an *Earth strategy* (Solutions, above).

**BRINGING ABOUT A SUSTAINABILITY REVOLUTION** Every community needs a *hundred seedlings of sustainability* and every country needs thousands of *sustainability seedlings* that are spotlighted, nurtured, and transplanted so they can grow into *millions of sustainability seedlings* intertwined in a global network.

Q: In the United States how many jobs are created by $1 billion of expenditures on education?

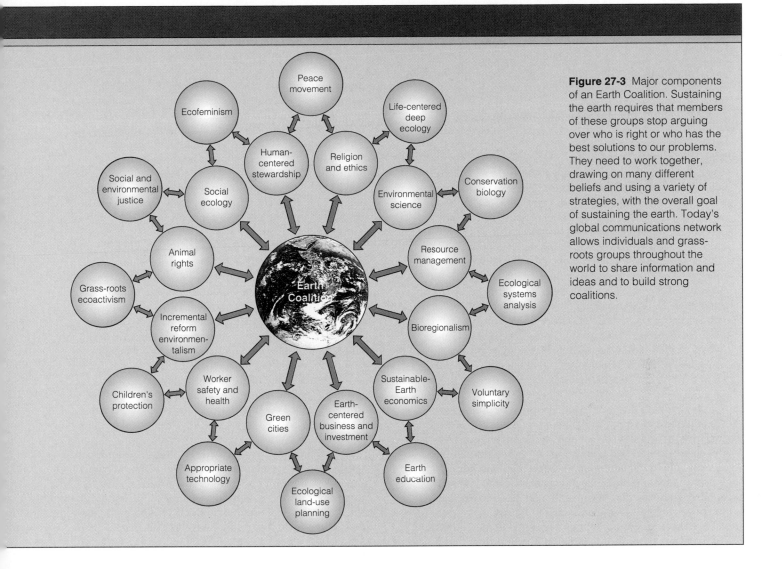

**Figure 27-3** Major components of an Earth Coalition. Sustaining the earth requires that members of these groups stop arguing over who is right or who has the best solutions to our problems. They need to work together, drawing on many different beliefs and using a variety of strategies, with the overall goal of sustaining the earth. Today's global communications network allows individuals and grass-roots groups throughout the world to share information and ideas and to build strong coalitions.

These seedlings of hope and change can show us how to live sustainably on this wondrous planet.

We need to recognize that love of other people and of all life is our least used and most renewable resource—as well as our most powerful force for change. Each of us can convert this love into acts of caring, beginning with the people around you and the place where you live: Care about the air, water, soil; care about wild plants, wild animals, wild places; care about all people in this generation and generations to come. Let this caring be your guide for doing and you will find true fulfillment and true wealth.

Rejoice in our connections with all human beings and with all other forms of life—past, present, and future—in the magnificent tapestry of evolution that produces a diversity of solutions to ever-changing environmental conditions. Delight in being part of this unfolding drama.

We need to see Earth's life-sustaining processes as a beautiful kaleidoscope of patterns, rhythms, and connections whose very complexity and multitude of possibilities remind us that cooperation, sharing, honesty, humility, responsibility, respect for all life, and love must be the guidelines for our behavior toward one another and the earth.

*The main ingredients of an environmental ethic are caring about the planet and all of its inhabitants, allowing unselfishness to control the immediate self-interest that harms others, and living each day so as to leave the lightest possible footprints on the planet.*

ROBERT CAHN

# Envisioning a Sustainable Society

*Lester W. Milbrath*

**GUEST ESSAY** *Lester W. Milbrath is director of the Research Program in Environment and Society and professor emeritus of political science and sociology at the State University of New York at Buffalo. During his distinguished career he has served as director of the Environmental Studies Center at SUNY/Buffalo (1976–1987) and taught at Northwestern University, Duke University, the University of Tennessee, National Taiwan University in Taipei, and Aarhus University in Denmark. He has also been a visiting research scholar at the Australian National University and Mannheim University in Germany. His research has focused on the relationship among science and society and citizen participation in environmental policy decisions, with emphasis on environmental perceptions, beliefs, attitudes, and values. He has written numerous articles and books. His most recent book,* Envisioning a Sustainable Society: Learning Our Way Out *(1989), summarizes a lifetime of studying our environmental predicament and is considered one of the best analyses of what we can do to help sustain the earth.*

The 1992 "Earth Summit" at Rio popularized the goal of sustainable development. Most of the heads of state meeting there believed that goal could be achieved by developing better technology and by writing better laws, agreements, and treaties—and enforcing them better. Unfortunately their approach was flawed and will not achieve sustainability because they do not understand the nature of the crisis in our earthly home.

Try this thought experiment: Imagine that, suddenly, all the humans disappeared but all the buildings, roads, shopping malls, factories, automobiles, and other artifacts of modern civilization were left behind. What then? After three or four centuries buildings would have crumbled, vehicles would have rusted and fallen apart, plants would have recolonized fields, roads, parking lots, even buildings. Water, air, and soil would gradually clear up; endangered species would flourish. Nature would thrive splendidly without us.

That mental experiment makes it clear that we do not have an environmental crisis; we have a crisis of civilization. Heads of state meeting at the Earth Summit neither understood nor dealt with civilization's most crucial problems: Humans are reproducing at such epidemic rates that world population will double to 10–11 billion in 45 years; resource depletion and waste generation will

triple or even quadruple over that period; waste discharges are already beginning to change the way the biosphere works; climate change and ozone loss will reduce the productivity of ecosystems just when hordes of new humans will be looking for sustenance and will destroy the confidence people need in order to invest in the future.

Without intending to, we have created a civilization that is headed for destruction. Either we learn to control our growth in population and in economic activity or nature will use death to control it for us.

Present-day society is not capable of producing a solution because it is disabled by the values our leaders constantly trumpet: economic growth, jobs, consumption, competitiveness, power, and domination. Societies pursuing these goals cannot avoid depleting their resources, degrading nature, poisoning life with wastes, and upsetting biospheric systems. *We have no choice but to change; resisting change will make us victims of change.*

But how do we transform to a sustainable society? My answer, which I believe is the only answer, is that *we must learn our way.* Nature, and the imperatives of its laws, will be our most powerful teacher as we learn our way to a new society. Most crucially, we must learn how to think about values.

Life in a viable ecosystem must become the core value of a sustainable society; that means all life, not just human life. Ecosystems function splendidly without humans (or any animals for that matter), but human society would die without viable ecosystems. Individuals seeking life quality require a well-functioning society living in well-functioning ecosystems. We must give top priority to our ecosystems, and second priority to our societies.

A sustainable society would affirm love as a primary value and extend it not only to those near and dear but to people in other lands, to future generations, and to other species. A sustainable society emphasizes partnership rather than domination, cooperation over competition, love over power. A sustainable society affirms justice and security as primary values.

A sustainable society would encourage self-realization, helping people to become all they are capable of being, rather than spending and consuming, as the key to a fulfilling life. A sustainable society would make long-lasting products to be cherished and conserved. People would learn a love of beauty and simplicity.

Q: Which two countries plan to be the world leaders in solar-cell and hydrogen-fuel technology?

A sustainable society would utilize both planning and markets as basic and supplementary information systems. Markets fail us because they cannot anticipate the future nor make moral choices between objects and between policies. Markets also cannot provide public goods—such as schools, parks, and environmental protection—which are just as important for life quality as private goods.

A sustainable society would continue further development of science and technology because we need practical creative solutions that are environmentally sound as well as economically feasible. However, we should recognize that those who control science and technology can use them to dominate all other creatures; we must learn to develop social controls of science and technology to make our society more sustainable. We should not allow the deployment of powerful new technologies that can induce sweeping changes in economic patterns, lifestyles, governance, and social values without careful forethought regarding their long-term impact.

Conscious social learning would become the dynamic of social change in a sustainable society—not only to deal with pressing problems but also to realize a vision of a good society. Meaningful and lasting social change occurs when nearly everyone learns the necessity of change and the value of working toward it.

Ecological thinking is different from most thinking that guides modern society. For example, these key maxims derived from the law of conservation of matter, the laws of thermodynamics, and the workings of ecosystems are routinely violated in contemporary thinking and discourse: (1) *Everything must go somewhere (there is no away)*; (2) *energy should not be wasted because all use of energy produces disorder in the environment*; (3) *we can never do just one thing (everything is connected)*; and (4) *we must constantly keep asking, "and then what?"* Every schoolchild and every adult should learn these simple truths; we need to reaffirm the tradition that knowledge of nature's workings and a respect for all life are basic to a true education. We should require such environmental education of all students as we now require every student to study history.

Ecological thinking recognizes that a proper understanding of the world requires people to learn how to think holistically, systematically, and futuristically. Because everything is connected to everything else, we must learn to anticipate second-, third-, and higher-order consequences for any contemplated major societal action. A society learning to be sustainable would redesign government to maximize its ability to learn. It would use the government learning process to promote social learning. It would require that people who govern listen to citizens not only to keep the process open for public participation but also to cultivate mutual learning between officials and citizens.

In the recognition that our health and welfare are vitally affected by how people, businesses, and governments in other lands behave, a sustainable society would strive for an effective planetary politics. It would encourage transnational social movements and political parties. It would nurture planetwide social learning, possibly leading eventually to a world society with a world government.

Learning our way to a new society cannot occur, however, until enough people become aware of the need for major societal change. So long as contemporary society is working reasonably well, and leaders keep telling us society is on the right track, the mass of people will not listen to a message urging significant change. For that reason urgently needed change will probably be delayed, and conditions on our planet are likely to get worse before they can get better. Nature will be our most powerful teacher, especially when biospheric systems no longer work the way they used to. In times of great system turbulence, social learning can be extraordinarily swift.

Our species has the gift of thought—an ability to recall the past and envision the future. Once we have a vision of the future, every decision becomes a moral decision. Even the decision not to act becomes a moral judgment. Those who understand what is happening to the only home for us and other species are not free to shrink from the responsibility to help make the transition to a sustainable society.

## Critical Thinking

1. Do you agree or disagree that we can only learn our way to a sustainable society? Explain.

2. Do you think we will learn our way to a sustainable society? Explain. What role, if any, do you intend to play in this process?

# Critical Thinking

1. What obligations, if any, concerning the environment do you have to future generations? How many generations ahead do we have responsibilities to? List the most important environmental benefits and harmful conditions passed on to you by the previous two generations.

2. Describe your worldview. Has taking this course changed your worldview? How?

3. Do you agree with the cartoon character Pogo that "we have met the enemy and he is us"? Explain. Criticize this statement from the viewpoint of the poor. Criticize it from the viewpoint that large corporations and government are the really big polluters and resource depleters and degraders.

4. a. Would you accept employment on a project that you knew would kill or harm people? Degrade or destroy a wild habitat? Explain.
   b. If you didn't have to work for a living, what would you do with your time?
   c. Could you live without an automobile? Explain.
   d. Could you live without TV? Explain.
   e. If you won $10 million in a lottery, how would you spend the money?
   f. Which specific issues do you feel strongly enough about to send a letter to a newspaper editor or to your elected officials?
   g. Which specific issues do you feel strongly enough about to spend time on? How much time?
   h. If you were granted three wishes, what would they be?
   i. If you knew you were going to die and had an opportunity to address everyone in the world for 10 minutes, what would you say?

5. What benefits do you receive from the world's environmental, social, and economic injustices?

6. How do you feel about (a) carving huge faces of people in mountains, (b) carving your initials into a tree, (c) driving an off-road motorized vehicle in a desert, grassland, or forest, (d) using paper towels, tissues, napkins, and plates, (e) wearing furs, (f) hunting for recreation, (g) fishing for recreation, (h) cutting or buying a cut tree for use as a decoration at Christmas or other celebrations, (i) having tropical fish, birds, snakes, or other wild animals as pets?

# Epilogue

This book is based on several theses:

- The ecosphere is not only more complex than we think but also more complex than we can ever think.

- In Garrett Hardin's terms, the basic principle of ecology is "that everything and everyone are all interconnected." Because we can never even come close to knowing how everything is connected, we must function in the ecosphere with a sense of humility and cooperation instead of arrogance and domination. Accepting this will require that our patterns of living become life-centered or Earth-centered instead of merely human-centered.

- Everything we have, or will have, comes directly or indirectly from the sun and Earth. To accept this dependence is to recognize that we cannot sustain ourselves by depleting Earth's capital. To deny this dependence is a recipe for disaster.

- Because of the law of conservation of matter, we can never really throw anything away. Because of the first law of thermodynamics, we can't get something for nothing. And because of the second law of thermodynamics, virtually every action we take has some undesirable present or future impact on the environment. Taken together these laws imply that any society built upon a rapidly growing population attempting to maximize resource use is unsustainable.

- Because population, resource use, pollution, and environmental degradation are increasing exponentially, we have the power to disrupt Earth's life support systems for ourselves and many other species. There is increasing evidence that we have already surpassed the planet's carrying capacity for humans in various parts of the world.

- Without environmental security there can be no lasting or meaningful economic or military security.

- We are at a turning point. Like it or not, we are immersed in the frightening, exciting, and controversial birth pangs of another *mindquake*—a new cultural revolution known as the *Environmental* or *Earth Wisdom Revolution*. We are nearing the limits of the Industrial Revolution and the 40-year-old planetary-management version of this cultural change and must rediscover our roots by again learning from nature.

- The *East-West* polarization is being replaced by a *North-South* or *Rich-Poor* clash over how Earth's limited resources should be shared as population and resource consumption rise, and the related *Green-Brown* clash between proponents of various versions of the *planetary management* and *Earth wisdom worldviews* (see inside front cover and Chapter 27). These issues will dominate our political and economic lives for decades.

- We need to shift to sustainable-Earth societies built around population stabilization, Earth-sustaining forms of economic growth, efficient use of resources, sustainable use of renewable resources, greater reliance on solar energy, pollution prevention, waste reduction, preservation of biological and cultural diversity, and Earth ethics. We have about 50 years to bring about this new cultural shift based on learning how to work with the earth.

- It is not too late. There is time to deal with the complex, interacting problems we face and to make a transition to a variety of dynamic, sustainable-Earth societies if enough of us really care. It's not up to "them," it's up to "us." Don't wait.

# Publications, Environmental Organizations, and Federal and International Agencies

## PUBLICATIONS

The following publications can help you keep well informed and up to date on environmental and resource problems. Subscription prices, which tend to change, are not given.

**African Wildlife News**   African Wildlife Foundation, 1717 Massachusetts Ave. NW, Washington, DC 20036

**Alternate Sources of Energy**   Alternate Sources of Energy, Inc., 107 South Central Ave., Milaca, MN 56353

**Ambio: A Journal of the Human Environment**   Royal Swedish Academy of Sciences, Box 50005, S-104 05 Stockholm, Sweden

**American Biology Teacher**   Journal of the National Association of Biology Teachers, 11250 Roger Bacon Dr., Room 319, Reston, VA 22090

**American Forests**   American Forestry Association, 1516 P St. NW, Washington, DC 20005

**American Journal of Alternative Agriculture**   9200 Edmonston Rd., Suite 117, Greenbelt, MD 20770

**Amicus Journal**   Natural Resources Defense Council, 40 W. 20th St., New York, NY 10011

**Annual Review of Energy**   Department of Energy, Forrestal Building, 1000 Independence Ave. SW, Washington, DC 20585

**Audubon**   National Audubon Society, 950 Third Ave., New York, NY 10022

**Audubon Activist**   National Audubon Society, 950 Third Ave., New York, NY 10022

**Biologue**   National Wood Energy Association, 1730 North Lynn St., Suite 610, Arlington, VA 22209

**BioScience**   American Institute of Biological Sciences, 730 11th St. NW, Washington, DC 20001

**Buzzworm: The Environmental Journal**   P.O. Box 6853, Syracuse, NY 13217-7930

**The CoEvolution Quarterly**   P.O. Box 428, Sausalito, CA 94965

**Common Sense on Energy and Our Environment**   P.O. Box 215, Morrisville, PA 19067

**Conservation Biology**   Blackwell Scientific Publications, Inc., 52 Beacon St., Boston, MA 02108

**Demographic Yearbook**   Department of International Economic and Social Affairs, Statistical Office, United Nations Publishing Service, United Nations, NY 10017

**Earth**   Kalmbach Publishing Co., 21027 Crossroads Circle, Waukesha, WI 53187

**Earth First!**   P.O. Box 5176, Missoula, MT 59806

**Earth Island Journal**   Earth Island Institute, 300 Broadway, Suite 28, San Francisco, CA 94133

**Earth Journal: Environmental Almanac and Resource Directory**   Buzzworm, Inc., 2305 Canyon Blvd., Suite 206, Boulder, CO 80302 (Published annually)

**Earthword**   Ecos Institute, 1550 Bayside Dr., Corona del Mar, CA 92625

**Earth Work**   Student Conservation Association, Dept. 1PR, P.O. Box 550, Charlestown, NH 03603

**The Ecologist**   MIT Press Journals, 55 Hayward St., Cambridge, MA 02142

**Ecology**   Ecological Society of America, Dr. Duncan T. Patten, Center for Environmental Studies, Arizona State University, Tempe, AZ 85281

**E Magazine**   P.O. Box 5098, Westport, CT 06881

**Endangered Species Update**   School of Natural Resources, University of Michigan, Ann Arbor, MI 48109

**Environment**   Heldref Publications, 4000 Albemarle St. NW, Washington, DC 20016

**Environment Abstracts**   Bowker A&I Publishing, 245 W. 17th St., New York, NY 10011 (in most libraries)

**Environmental Action**   6930 Carroll Park, 6th Floor, Takoma Park, MD 20912

**Environmental Almanac**   Annual compilation by the World Resources Institute (published by Houghton Mifflin, Boston)

**Environmental Engineering News**   School of Civil Engineering, Purdue University, West Lafayette, IN 47907

**Environmental Ethics**   Department of Philosophy, University of North Texas, Denton, TX 76203

**Environmental History Review**   American Society for Environmental History, Center for Technology Studies, New Jersey Institute of Technology, Newark, NJ 07102

**Environmental Opportunities**   Sanford Berry, P.O. Box 969, Stowe, VT 05672 (jobs)

**The Environmental Professional**   National Association of Environmental Professionals, Subscription Office, P.O. Box 15210, Alexandria, VA 22309

**Environmental Science & Technology**   American Chemical Society, 1155 16th St. NW, Washington, DC 20402

**Environmental Values**   The White Horse Press, 10 High St., Knapwell, Cambridge CB38NR, UK

**EPA Journal**   Environmental Protection Agency Order from Government Printing Office, Washington, DC 20402

**Everyone's Backyard**   Citizens' Clearinghouse for Hazardous Waste, P.O. Box 926, Arlington, VA 22216

**Family Planning Perspectives**   Planned Parenthood–World Population, 666 Fifth Ave., New York, NY 10019

**Forest & Conservation History**   Forest History Association, Duke University Press, 701 Vickers Ave., Durham, NC 27701

**The Futurist**   World Future Society, P.O. Box 19285, Twentieth Street Station, Washington, DC 20036

**Garbage: The Practical Journal for the Environment**   P.O. Box 56520, Boulder, CO 80321-6520

**Greenpeace Magazine**   Greenpeace USA, 1436 U St. NW, Washington, DC 20009

**Harrowsmith**   Ferry Road, Charlotte, VT 05445

**In Business: The Magazine for Environmental Entrepreneuring**   Subscription Dept., 419 State Ave., Emmaus, PA 18049

**In Context**   Box 11470, Bainbridge Island, WA 98110

**INFORM Reports**   INFORM, 381 Park Avenue South, New York, NY 10016

**International Environmental Affairs**   University Press of New England, 17½ Lebanon St., Hanover, NH 03755

**International Wildlife**   National Wildlife Federation, 8925 Leesburg Pike, Vienna, VA 22184

**Issues in Science and Technology**   National Academy of Sciences, 2101 Constitution Ave. NW, Washington, DC 20077-5576

**Journal of Agricultural and Environmental Ethics**   Room 039, MacKinnon Building, University of Guelph, Guelph, Ontario, Canada N1G 2W1

**Journal of the American Public Health Association**   1015 18th St. NW, Washington, DC 20036

**Journal of Environmental Education**   Heldref Publications, 4000 Albemarle St. NW, Suite 504, Washington, DC 20016

**Journal of Environmental Health**   National Environmental Health Association, 720 S. Colorado Blvd., Suite 970, Denver, CO 80222

**Journal of Environmental Science and Health**   Marcel Dekker Journals, P.O. Box 10018, Church Street Station, New York, NY 10249

**Journal of Forestry**   Society of American Foresters, 5400 Grosvenor Lane, Bethesda, MD 20814

**Journal of Pesticide Reform**   P.O. Box 1393, Eugene, OR 97440

**Journal of Range Management**   Society for Range Management, 1839 York St., Denver, CO 80206

**Journal of Soil and Water Conservation**   Soil and Water Conservation Society, 7515 Northeast Ankeny Rd., Ankeny, IA 50021

**Journal of the Water Pollution Control Federation**   601 Wythe St., Alexandria, VA 22314

**Journal of Wildlife Management**   Wildlife Society, 5410 Grosvenor Lane, Bethesda, MD 20814

**Mother Jones**   P.O. Box 50032, Boulder, CO 80322

**National Geographic**   National Geographic Society, P.O. Box 2895, Washington, DC 20077-9960

**National Parks and Conservation Magazine**   National Parks and Conservation Association, 1015 31st St. NW, Washington, DC 20007

**National Wildlife**   National Wildlife Federation, 1400 16th St. NW, Washington, DC 20036

**Natural Resources Journal**   University of New Mexico School of Law, 1117 Stanford NE, Albuquerque, NM 87131

**Natural Resources News** School of Natural Resources, University of Michigan, Ann Arbor, MI 48109

**Nature** 711 National Press Building, Washington, DC 20045

**Nature Conservancy News** 1815 North Lynn St., Arlington, VA 22209

**The New Farm** Rodale Research Center, Emmaus, PA 18049

**New Internationalist** P.O. Box 1143, Lewiston, NY 14092-9984

**New Scientist** 128 Long Acre, London, WC 2, England

**Newsline** Natural Resources Defense Council, 122 E. 42nd St., New York, NY 10168

**Not Man Apart** Friends of the Earth, 530 7th St. SE, Washington, DC 20003

**Ocean Watch** The Oceanic Society, 1536 16th St., NW, Washington, DC 20036

**OIKO: The Alternative Environmental Digest** P.O. Box 115, Greenwood, VA 22943

**One Person's Impact** P.O. Box 751, Westborough, MA 01581

**Organic Gardening & Farming Magazine** Rodale Press, Inc., 33 E. Minor St., Emmaus, PA 18049

**Orion Nature Quarterly** P.O. Box 3000, Denville, NJ 07834-9797

**Planetary Citizen** Stillpoint Publishing, Meetinghouse Rd., Box 640, Walpole, NH 03608

**Pollution Abstracts** Cambridge Scientific Abstracts, 7200 Wisconsin Ave., Bethesda, MD 20814 (found in many libraries)

**Popline** The Population Institute, 107 2nd St. NE, Suite 207, Washington, DC 20002

**Population and Vital Statistics Report** United Nations Environment Programme, North American Office, Publication Sales Section, United Nations, New York, NY 10017

**Population Bulletin** Population Reference Bureau, 1875 Connecticut Ave. NW, Suite 520, Washington, DC 20009

**Population-Environment Balance Data** 1325 G St. NW, Suite 103, Washington, DC 20005

**Rachel's Hazardous Waste News** Environmental Research Foundation, P.O. Box 4878, Annapolis, MD 21403

**Rainforest News** P.O. Box 140681, Coral Gables, FL 33115

**Real World: The Voice of Ecopolitics** 91 Nuns Moor Road, Newcastle Upon Tyne NE4 9BA, UK

**Renewable Energy News** Solar Vision, Inc., 7 Church Hill, Harrisville, NH 03450

**Renewable Resources** 5430 Grosvenor Lane, Bethesda, MD 20814

**Rocky Mountain Institute Newsletter** 1739 Snowmass Creek Rd., Snowmass, CO 81654

**Science** American Association for the Advancement of Science, 1333 H St. NW, Washington, DC 20005

**Science News** Science Service, Inc., 1719 N St. NW, Washington, DC 20036

**Scientific American** 415 Madison Ave., New York, NY 10017

**Sierra** 730 Polk St., San Francisco, CA 94108

**Solar Age** Solar Vision, Inc., 7 Church Hill, Harrisville, NH 03450

**Solar Today** American Solar Energy Society, 2400 Central Ave., Unit B-1, Boulder, CO 80301

**State of the Environment** OECD Publications and Information Center, 1750 Pennsylvania Ave., Suite 1207, Washington, DC 20006 (published annually)

**State of the States** Renew America, 1001 Connecticut Ave. NW, Suite 719, Washington, DC 20036 (published annually)

**State of the World** Worldwatch Institute, 1776 Massachusetts Ave. NW, Washington, DC 20036 (published annually)

**Statistical Yearbook** Department of International Economic and Social Affairs, Statistical Office, United Nations Publishing Service, United Nations, New York, NY 10017

**Talking Leaves** 1430 Willamette St., Suite 367, Eugene, OR 97401

**Technology Review** Room E219-430, Massachusetts Institute of Technology, Cambridge, MA 02139

**Transition** Laurence G. Wolf, ed., Department of Geography, University of Cincinnati, Cincinnati, OH 45221

**The Trumpeter Journal of Ecosophy** P.O. Box 5883, Victoria, BC, Canada V8R 6S8

**Vegetarian Journal** P.O. Box 1463, Baltimore, MD 21203

**Vegetarian Times** P.O. Box 570, 141 S. Oak Park St., Oak Park, IL 60603

**Wild Earth** Cenozoic Society, Inc., 68 Riverside Drive, Apt. 1, Canton, NY 13617

**Wilderness** The Wilderness Society, 1400 I St. NW, 10th Floor, Washington, DC 20005

**Wildlife Conservation** New York Zoological Society, 185th St. and Southern Boulevard, Bronx, NY 10460

**World Rainforest Report** Rainforest Action Network, 300 Broadway, Suite 298, San Francisco, CA 94133

**World Resources** World Resources Institute, 1735 New York Ave. NW, Washington, DC 20006 (published every two years)

**World Watch** Worldwatch Institute, 1776 Massachusetts Ave. NW, Washington, DC 20036

**Worldwatch Papers** Worldwatch Institute, 1776 Massachusetts Ave. NW, Washington, DC 20036

**Yearbook of World Energy Statistics** Department of International Economic and Social Affairs, Statistical Office, United Nations Publishing Service, United Nations, New York, NY 10017

**Z Magazine** The Institute for Social and Cultural Communications, 116 Botolph St., Boston, MA 02115

# ENVIRONMENTAL AND RESOURCE ORGANIZATIONS

For a more detailed list, see *Conservation Directory* (published annually by the National Wildlife Federation, 1400 16th St. NW, Washington, DC 20036); *Your Resource Guide to Environmental Organizations* (Irvine, CA: Smiling Dolphin Press, 1991); *National Environmental Organizations* (published annually by US Environmental Directories, Inc., P.O. Box 65156, St. Paul, MN 55165); and *World Directory of Environmental Organizations* (California Institute of Public Affairs, P.O. Box 10, Claremont, CA 91711).

**Acid Rain Foundation** 1410 Varsity Dr., Raleigh, NC 27606

**African Wildlife Foundation** 1717 Massachusetts Ave. NW, Washington, DC 20036

**Air Pollution Control Association** P.O. Box 2861, Pittsburgh, PA 15230

**Alan Guttmacher Institute** 2010 Massachusetts Ave. NW, 5th Floor, Washington, DC 20036

**Alliance for Animals** P.O. Box 909, Boston, MA 02103

**Alliance for Chesapeake Bay** 6600 York Rd., Baltimore, MD 21212

**Alliance for Environmental Education** 10751 Ambassador Drive, Suite 201, Manassas, VA 22110

**Alliance to Save Energy** 1925 K St. NW, Washington, DC 20006-1401

**American Cetacean Society** P.O. Box 2639, San Pedro, CA 90731-0943

**American Conservation Association, Inc.** 30 Rockefeller Plaza, Room 5402, New York, NY 10112

**American Council for an Energy Efficient Economy** 1001 Connecticut Ave. NW, Suite 535, Washington, DC 20013

**American Farmland Trust** 1920 N St. NW, Suite 400, Washington, DC 20036

**American Fisheries Society** 5410 Grosvenor Lane, Suite 110, Bethesda, MD 20814

**American Forestry Association** 1516 P St. NW, Washington, DC 20005

**American Geographical Society** 156 Fifth Ave., Suite 600, New York, NY 10010

**American Humane Society** 9725 E. Hampden Ave., Denver, CO 80231

**American Institute of Biological Sciences, Inc.** 730 11th St. NW, Washington, DC 20001

**American Rivers** 801 Pennsylvania Ave. SE, Suite 303, Washington, DC 20003

**American Society for Environmental History** Department of History, Oregon State University, Corvallis, OR 97331

**American Society for the Prevention of Cruelty to Animals (ASPCA)** 441 E. 92nd Street, New York, NY 10128

**American Solar Energy Society** 859 W. Morgan St., Raleigh, NC 27603

**American Water Resources Association** 5410 Grosvenor Lane, Suite 220, Bethesda, MD 20814

**American Wilderness Alliance** 7500 E. Arapahoe Rd., Suite 114, Englewood, CO 80112

**American Wildlife Association** 1717 Massachusetts Ave. NW, Washington, DC 20036

**American Wind Energy Association** 1730 N. Lynn St., Suite 610, Arlington, VA 22209

**Animal Rights Information and Education Service** P.O. Box 332, Rowayton, CT 06583

**Appropriate Technology International** 1331 H St. NW, Washington, DC 20005

**Association of Forest Service Employees for Environmental Ethics (AFSEE)** P.O. Box 11615, Eugene, OR 97440-9958

**Bat Conservation International** P.O. Box 162603, Austin, TX 78716

**Bio-Integral Resource Center** P.O. Box 7414, Berkeley, CA 94707

**Bioregional Project (North American Bioregional Congress)** Turtle Island Office, 1333 Overhulse Rd. NE, Olympia, WA 98502

**Carrying Capacity** 1325 G St. NW, Washington, DC 20005

**CEIP Fund, Inc.** 68 Harrison Ave., Boston, MA 02111

**Center for Conservation Biology** Department of Biological Sciences, Stanford University, Stanford, CA 94305

**Center for Environmental Information** 46 Prince Rd., Rochester, NY 14607

**Center for Holistic Resource Management** 5820 4th St. NW, Albuquerque, NM 87107

**Center for Marine Conservation** 1725 DeSales St. NW, Suite 500, Washington, DC 20036

**Center for Plant Conservation** P.O. Box 299, St. Louis, MO 63166

**Center for Science in the Public Interest** 1875 Connecticut Ave. NW, Suite 300, Washington, DC 20009

**Chesapeake Bay Foundation** 162 Prince George St., Annapolis, MD 21401

**Chipko** P.O. Silyara via Ghansale, Tehri-Garwhal, Utar Pradesh, 249155 India

**Citizens' Clearinghouse for Hazardous Waste** P.O. Box 6806, Falls Church, VA 22040

**Clean Water Action Project** 1320 18th St. NW, Washington, DC 20036

**Clean Water Fund** 317 Pennsylvania Ave. SE, 3rd Floor, Washington, DC 20005

**Coastal Society** 5410 Grosvenor Lane, Suite 110, Bethesda, MD 20814

**Concern, Inc.** 1794 Columbia Rd. NW, Washington, DC 20009

**Conservation Foundation** 1250 24th St. NW, Suite 500, Washington, DC 20037

**Conservation International** 1015 18th St. NW, Suite 1000, Washington, DC 20036

**Council for Economic Priorities** 30 Irving Pl., New York, NY 10003

**Cousteau Society** 930 W. 21st St., Norfolk, VA 23517

**Critical Mass Energy Project** 215 Pennsylvania Ave. SE, Washington, DC 20003

**Cultural Survival** 11 Divinity Ave., Cambridge, MA 02138

**Defenders of Wildlife** 1244 19th St. NW, Washington, DC 20036

**Ducks Unlimited** One Waterfowl Way, Long Grove, IL 60047

**Earth First!** 305 N. Sixth St., Madison, WI 53704

**Earth Island Institute** 300 Broadway, Suite 28, San Francisco, CA 94133

**EarthSave Foundation** P.O. Box 949, Felton, CA 95018

**Earthwatch** P.O. Box 403N, 680 Mt. Auburn St., Watertown, MA 02272

**Ecological Society of America** 9650 Rockville Pike, Bethesda, MD 20814

**Elmwood Institute** P.O. Box 5805, Berkeley, CA 94705

**Energy Conservation Coalition** 1525 New Hampshire Ave. NW, Washington, DC 20036

**Environmental Action, Inc.** 6930 Carroll Park, Suite 600, Takoma Park, MD 20912

**Environmental Defense Fund, Inc.** 257 Park Ave. South, New York, NY 10010

**Environmental Education Coalition** Pocono Environmental Education Center, Box 1010, Dingmans Ferry, PA 18328

**Environmental and Energy Study Institute** 122 C St. NW, Suite 700, Washington, DC 20001

**Environmental Law Institute** 1616 P St. NW, Suite 200, Washington, DC 20036

**Environmental Policy Institute** 218 D St. SE, Washington, DC 20003

**Farralones Institute** 15920 Coleman Valley Rd., Occidental, CA 95465

**Fish and Wildlife Reference Service** 5430 Grosvenor Lane, Suite 110, Bethesda, MD 20814

**Food First (Institute for Food and Development Policy)** 145 9th St., San Francisco, CA 94103

**Freshwater Foundation** P.O. Box 90, 2500 Shadywood Rd., Navarre, MN 55392

**Friends of Animals** 11 W. 60th St., New York, NY 10023

**Friends of the Earth** 218 D St. SE, Washington, DC 20003

**Friends of Trees** P.O. Box 1466, Chelan, WA 98816

**Fund for Animals** 200 W. 57th St., New York, NY 10019

**Global Greenhouse Network** 1130 17th St. NW, Suite 530, Washington, DC 20036

**Global Tomorrow Coalition** 1325 G St. NW, Suite 1010, Washington, DC 20005

**Greenhouse Crisis Foundation** 1130 17th St. NW, Suite 630, Washington, DC 20036

**Greenpeace, Canada** 427 Bloor St., West Toronto, Ontario M5S 1X7

**Greenpeace, USA, Inc.** 1436 U St. NW, Washington, DC 20009

**Green Seal** 1733 Connecticut Ave. NW, Washington, DC 20009

**Human Ecology Action League, Inc.** P.O. Box 66637, Chicago, IL 60666

**Humane Society of the United States, Inc.** 2100 L St. NW, Washington, DC 20037

**INFORM** 381 Park Ave. South, New York, NY 10016

**Institute for Alternative Agriculture** 9200 Edmonston Rd., Suite 117, Greenbelt, MD 20770

**Institute for Earth Education** P.O. Box 288, Warrenville, IL 60555

**Institute for Local Self-Reliance** 2425 18th St. NW, Washington, DC 20009

**International Alliance for Sustainable Agriculture** 1201 University Ave. SE, Suite 202, Minneapolis, MN 55414

**International Association of Fish and Wildlife Agencies** 444 North Capitol St. NW, Suite 534, Washington, DC 20001

**International Council for Outdoor Education** P.O. Box 17255, Pittsburgh, PA 15235

**International Institute for Energy Conservation** 420 C St. NE, Washington, DC 20002

**International Planned Parenthood Federation** 105 Madison Ave., 7th Floor, New York, NY 10016

**Izaak Walton League of America** 1401 Wilson Blvd., Level B, Arlington, VA 22209

**Land Institute** Route 3, Salina, KS 67401

**Land Trust Alliance** 900 17th St. NW, Suite 410, Washington, DC 20006

**League of Conservation Voters** 1707 L St. NW, Suite 550, Washington, DC 20036

**League of Women Voters of the U.S.** 1730 M St. NW, Washington, DC 20036

**Mineral Policy Center** 1325 Massachusetts Ave. NW, Suite 550, Washington, DC 20005

**National Association of Biology Teachers** 11250 Roger Bacon Dr., Room 19, Reston, VA 22090

**National Audubon Society** 950 Third Ave., New York, NY 10022

**National Center for Urban Environmental Studies** 516 North Charles St., Suite 501, Baltimore, MD 21201

**National Clean Air Coalition** 801 Pennsylvania Ave. SE, Washington, DC 20003

**National Coalition Against the Misuse of Pesticides** 701 E St. SE, Suite 200, Washington, DC 20001

**National Coalition for Marine Conservation** P.O. Box 23298, Savannah, GA 31403

**National Environmental Health Association** 720 S. Colorado Blvd., South Tower, Suite 970, Denver, CO 80222

**National Geographic Society** 17th and M St. NW, Washington, DC 20036

**National Park Foundation** P.O. Box 57473, Washington, DC 20037

**National Parks and Conservation Association** 1776 Massachusetts Ave. NW, Suite 200, Washington, DC 20036

**National Recreation and Park Association** 2775 S. Quincy St., Suite 300, Arlington, VA 22206

**National Recycling Coalition** 1101 30th St. NW, Suite 304, Washington, DC 20007

**National Science Teachers Association** 1742 Connecticut Ave. NW, Washington, DC 20009

**National Solid Waste Management Association** 1730 Rhode Island Ave. NW, Suite 100, Washington, DC 20036

**National Toxics Campaign** 29 Temple Pl., 5th Floor, Boston, MA 02111

**National Wildlife Federation** 1400 16th St. NW, Washington, DC 20036

**National Wood Energy Association** 1730 N. Lynn St., Suite 610, Arlington, VA 22209

**Natural Resources Defense Council** 40 W. 20th St., New York, NY 10011, and 1350 New York Ave. NW, Suite 300, Washington, DC 20005

**Nature Conservancy** 1814 N. Lynn St., Arlington, VA 22209

**New Alchemy Institute** 237 Hatchville Rd., East Falmouth, MA 02536

**North American Association for Environmental Education** P.O. Box 400, Troy, OH 45373

**Nuclear Information and Resource Service** 1424 16th St. NW, Suite 601, Washington, DC 20036

**Oceanic Society** 218 D St. SE, Washington, DC 20003

**People for the Ethical Treatment of Animals (PETA)** Box 42516, Washington, DC 20015

**Permaculture Association** P.O. Box 202, Orange, MA 01364

**Permaculture Institute of North America** 4649 Sunnyside Ave. N, Seattle, WA 98103

**Pesticide Action Network** 965 Mission St., Suite 514, San Francisco, CA 94103

**Physicians for Social Responsibility** 639 Massachusetts Ave., Cambridge, MA 02139

**Planetary Citizens** 325 9th St., San Francisco, CA 94103

**Planet/Drum Foundation** P.O. Box 31251, San Francisco, CA 94131

**Planned Parenthood Federation of America** 810 Seventh Ave., New York, NY 10019

**Population Crisis Committee** 1120 19th St. NW, Washington, DC 20036-3605

**Population-Environment Balance** 1325 G St. NW, Suite 1003, Washington, DC 20005

**Population Institute** 107 2nd St. NE, Suite 207, Washington, DC 20002

**Population Reference Bureau** 1875 Connecticut Ave. NW, Suite 520, Washington, DC 20009-5728

**Public Citizen** 215 Pennsylvania Ave. SE, Washington, DC 20003

Rachel Carson Council   8940 Jones Mill Rd., Chevy Chase, MD 20815

RAIN   2270 NW. Irving, Portland, OR 97210

Rainforest Action Network   3450 Sansome St., Suite 700, San Francisco, CA 94111

Rainforest Alliance   270 Lafayette St., Suite 512, New York, NY 10012

Rainforest Defense Fund   P.O. Box 2104, Cambridge, MA 02238

Rainforest Foundation   P.O. Box 757, Plainville, CT 06062

Renewable Natural Resources Foundation   5430 Grosvenor Lane, Bethesda, MD 20814

Renew America   1400 16th St. NW, Suite 710, Washington, DC 20036

Resources for the Future   1616 P St. NW, Washington, DC 20036

Rocky Mountain Institute   1739 Snowmass Creek Rd., Snowmass, CO 81654

Rodale Research Center   222 Main St., Emmaus, PA 18098

Safe Energy Communication Council   1717 Massachusetts Ave. NW, Suite LL215, Washington, DC 20036

Save America's Forests   4 Library Court SE, Washington, DC 20003

Save the Whales, Inc.   P.O. Box 2397, 1426 Main St., Unit E, Venice, CA 90291

Scientists' Institute for Public Information   355 Lexington Ave., New York, NY 10017

Sea Shepherd Conservation Society   1314 2nd St., Santa Monica, CA 90401

Sierra Club   730 Polk St., San Francisco, CA 94109, and 408 C St. NE, Washington, DC 20002

Smithsonian Institution   1000 Jefferson Dr. SW, Washington, DC 20560

Social Investment Forum   C.E.R.E.S. Project, 711 Atlantic Ave., Boston, MA 02111

Society of American Foresters   5400 Grosvenor Lane, Bethesda, MD 20814

Society for Conservation Biology   Department of Wildlife Ecology, University of Wisconsin, Madison, WI 53706

Soil and Water Conservation Society   7515 NE. Ankeny Rd., Ankeny, IA 50021

Student Conservation Association, Inc.   P.O. Box 550, Charlestown, NH 03603

Student Environmental Action Coalition (SEAC)   217 A Carolina Union, University of North Carolina, Chapel Hill, NC 27599

Survival International   2121 Decatur Pl. NW, Washington, DC 20008

Treepeople   12601 Mulholland Dr., Beverly Hills, CA 90210

Union of Concerned Scientists   26 Church St., Cambridge, MA 02238

U.S. Public Interest Research Group   215 Pennsylvania Ave. SE, Washington, DC 20003

Water Pollution Control Federation   601 Wythe St., Alexandria, VA 22314

The Wilderness Society   900 17th St. NW, Washington, DC 20006

Wildlife Conservation International (WCI)   New York Zoological Society, 185th St. and Southern Blvd., Bronx, NY 10460

Wildlife Society   5410 Grosvenor Lane, Bethesda, MD 20814

Windstar Foundation   2317 Snowmass Creek Rd., Snowmass, CO 81654

Woods Hole Research Center   P.O. Box 296, Woods Hole, MA 02543

Work on Waste   82 Judson St., Canton, NY 13617

World Future Society   4916 St. Elmo Ave., Bethesda, MD 20814

World Resources Institute   1709 New York Ave. NW, 7th Floor, Washington, DC 20006

Worldwatch Institute   1776 Massachusetts Ave. NW, Washington, DC 20036

Worldwide   1250 24th St. NW, Suite 500, Washington, DC 20037

World Wildlife Fund   1250 24th St. NW, Suite 500, Washington, DC 20037

Zero Population Growth   1400 16th St. NW, Suite 320, Washington, DC 20036

## ADDRESSES OF FEDERAL AND INTERNATIONAL AGENCIES

Agency for International Development   State Building, 320 21st St. NW, Washington, DC 20523

Bureau of Land Management   U.S. Department of Interior, 18th and C Sts., Room 3619, Washington, DC 20240

Bureau of Mines   2401 E St. NW, Washington, DC 20241

Bureau of Reclamation   Washington, DC 20240

Congressional Research Service   101 Independence Ave. SW, Washington, DC 20540

Conservation and Renewable Energy Inquiry and Referral Service   P.O. Box 8900, Silver Spring, MD 20907 (800-523-2929)

Consumer Product Safety Commission   Washington, DC 20207

Council on Environmental Quality   722 Jackson Pl. NW, Washington, DC 20006

Department of Agriculture   14th St. and Jefferson Dr. SW, Washington, DC 20250

Department of Commerce   14th St. between Constitution Ave. and E St. NW, Washington, DC 20230

Department of Energy   Forrestal Building, 1000 Independence Ave. SW, Washington, DC 20585

Department of Health and Human Services   200 Independence Ave. SW, Washington, DC 20585

Department of Housing and Urban Development   451 7th St. SW, Washington, DC 20410

Department of the Interior   18th and C Sts. NW, Washington, DC 20240

Department of Transportation   400 7th St. SW, Washington, DC 20590

Environmental Protection Agency   401 M St. SW, Washington, DC 20460

Federal Energy Regulatory Commission   825 N. Capitol St. NE, Washington, DC 20426

Fish and Wildlife Service   Department of the Interior, 18th and C Sts. NW, Washington, DC 20240

Food and Agriculture Organization (FAO) of the United Nations   101 22nd St. NW, Suite 300, Washington, DC 20437

Food and Drug Administration   Department of Health and Human Services, 5600 Fishers Lane, Rockville, MD 20852

Forest Service   P.O. Box 96090, Washington, DC 20013

Government Printing Office   Washington, DC 20402

Inter-American Development Bank   1300 New York Ave. NW, Washington, DC 20577

International Union for Conservation of Nature and Natural Resources (IUCN), World Conservation Union   Avenue du Mont-Blanc, CH-1196 Gland, Switzerland

International Whaling Commission   The Red House, 135 Station Rd., Histon, Cambridge CB4 4NP, England 02203 3971

Marine Mammal Commission   1625 I St. NW, Washington, DC 20006

National Academy of Sciences   2101 Constitution Ave. NW, Washington, DC 20418

National Aeronautics and Space Administration   400 Maryland Ave. SW, Washington, DC 20546

National Cancer Institute   9000 Rockville Pike, Bethesda, MD 20892

National Center for Appropriate Technology   3040 Continental Dr., Butte, MT 59701

National Center for Atmospheric Research   P.O. Box 3000, Boulder, CO 80307

National Marine Fisheries Service   U.S. Dept. of Commerce, NOAA, 1335 East-West Highway, Silver Spring, MD 20910

National Oceanic and Atmospheric Administration   Rockville, MD 20852

National Park Service   Department of the Interior, P.O. Box 37127, Washington, DC 20013

National Science Foundation   1800 G St. NW, Washington, DC 20550

National Solar Heating and Cooling Information Center   P.O. Box 1607, Rockville, MD 20850

National Technical Information Service   U.S. Department of Commerce, 5285 Port Royal Rd., Springfield, VA 22161

Nuclear Regulatory Commission   1717 H St. NW, Washington, DC 20555

Occupational Safety and Health Administration   Department of Labor, 200 Constitution Ave. NW, Washington, DC 20210

Office of Ocean and Coastal Resource Management   1825 Connecticut Ave., Suite 700, Washington, DC 20235

Office of Surface Mining Reclamation and Enforcement   1951 Constitution Ave. NW, Washington, DC 20240

Office of Technology Assessment   U.S. Congress, 600 Pennsylvania Ave. SW, Washington, DC 20510

Organization for Economic Cooperation and Development   2001 L St. NW, Suite 700, Washington, DC 20036 (U.S. office)

Soil Conservation Service   P.O. Box 2890, Washington, DC 20013

Solar Energy Research Institute   1617 Cole Blvd., Golden, CO 80401

United Nations   1 United Nations Plaza, New York, NY 10017

United Nations Environment Programme   Regional North American Office, United Nations Room DC2-0803, New York, NY 10017, and 1889 F St. NW, Washington, DC 20006

U.S. Geological Survey   12201 Sunrise Valley Dr., Reston, VA 22092

World Bank   1818 H St. NW, Washington, DC 20433

# Units of Measurement

## LENGTH

### Metric

1 kilometer (km) = 1,000 meters (m)
1 meter (m) = 100 centimeters (cm)
1 meter (m) = 1,000 millimeters (mm)
1 centimeter (cm) = 0.01 meter (m)
1 millimeter (mm) = 0.001 meter (m)

### English

1 foot (ft) = 12 inches (in)
1 yard (yd) = 3 feet (ft)
1 mile (mi) = 5,280 feet (ft)
1 nautical mile = 1.15 miles

### Metric-English

1 kilometer (km) = 0.621 mile (mi)
1 meter (m) = 39.4 inches (in)
1 inch (in) = 2.54 centimeters (cm)
1 foot (ft) = 0.305 meter (m)
1 yard (yd) = 0.914 meter (m)
1 nautical mile = 1.85 kilometers (km)

## AREA

### Metric

1 square kilometer (km$^2$) = 1,000,000 square meters (m$^2$)
1 square meter (m$^2$) = 1,000,000 square millimeters (mm$^2$)
1 hectare (ha) = 10,000 square meters (m$^2$)
1 hectare (ha) = 0.01 square kilometer (km$^2$)

### English

1 square foot (ft$^2$) = 144 square inches (in$^2$)
1 square yard (yd$^2$) = 9 square feet (ft$^2$)
1 square mile (mi$^2$) = 27,880,000 square feet (ft$^2$)
1 acre (ac) = 43,560 square feet (ft$^2$)

### Metric-English

1 hectare (ha) = 2.471 acres (ac)
1 square kilometer (km$^2$) = 0.386 square mile (mi$^2$)
1 square meter (m$^2$) = 1.196 square yards (yd$^2$)
1 square meter (m$^2$) = 10.76 square feet (ft$^2$)
1 square centimeter (cm$^2$) = 0.155 square inch (in$^2$)

## VOLUME

### Metric

1 cubic kilometer (km$^3$) = 1,000,000,000 cubic meters (m$^3$)
1 cubic meter (m$^3$) = 1,000,000 cubic centimeters (cm$^3$)
1 liter (L) = 1,000 milliliters (mL) = 1,000 cubic centimeters (cm$^3$)
1 milliliter (mL) = 0.001 liter (L)
1 milliliter (mL) = 1 cubic centimeter (cm$^3$)

### English

1 gallon (gal) = 4 quarts (qt)
1 quart (qt) = 2 pints (pt)

### Metric-English

1 liter (L) = 0.265 gallon (gal)
1 liter (L) = 1.06 quarts (qt)
1 liter (L) = 0.0353 cubic foot (ft$^3$)
1 cubic meter (m$^3$) = 35.3 cubic feet (ft$^3$)
1 cubic meter (m$^3$) = 1.30 cubic yard (yd$^3$)
1 cubic kilometer (km$^3$) = 0.24 cubic mile (mi$^3$)
1 barrel (bbl) = 159 liters (L)
1 barrel (bbl) = 42 U.S. gallons (gal)

## MASS

### Metric

1 kilogram (kg) = 1,000 grams (g)
1 gram (g) = 1,000 milligrams (mg)
1 gram (g) = 1,000,000 micrograms (µg)
1 milligram (mg) = 0.001 gram (g)
1 microgram (µg) = 0.000001 gram (g)
1 metric ton (mt) = 1,000 kilograms (kg)

### English

1 ton (t) = 2,000 pounds (lb)
1 pound (lb) = 16 ounces (oz)

### Metric-English

1 metric ton (mt) = 2,200 pounds (lb) = 1.1 tons (t)
1 kilogram (kg) = 2.20 pounds (lb)
1 pound (lb) = 454 grams (g)
1 gram (g) = 0.035 ounce (oz)

## ENERGY AND POWER

### Metric

1 kilojoule (kJ) = 1,000 joules (J)
1 kilocalorie (kcal) = 1,000 calories (cal)
1 calorie (cal) = 4.184 joules (J)

### Metric-English

1 kilojoule (kJ) = 0.949 British thermal unit (Btu)
1 kilojoule (kJ) = 0.000278 kilowatt-hour (kW-h)
1 kilocalorie (kcal) = 3.97 British thermal units (Btu)
1 kilocalorie (kcal) = 0.00116 kilowatt-hour (kW-h)
1 kilowatt-hour (kW-h) = 860 kilocalories (kcal)
1 kilowatt-hour (kW-h) = 3,400 British thermal units (Btu)
1 quad (Q) = 1,050,000,000,000,000 kilojoules (kJ)
1 quad (Q) = 2,930,000,000,000 kilowatt-hours (kW-h)

## TEMPERATURE CONVERSIONS

Fahrenheit (°F) to Celsius (°C): $°C = \dfrac{(°F - 32.0)}{1.80}$

Celsius (°C) to Fahrenheit (°F): $°F = (°C \times 1.80) + 32.0$

# Major U.S. Resource Conservation and Environmental Legislation

## GENERAL

National Environmental Policy Act of 1969 (NEPA)
International Environmental Protection Act of 1983

## ENERGY

National Energy Act of 1978, 1980
National Appliance Energy Conservation Act of 1987
Energy Policy Act of 1992

## WATER QUALITY

Water Quality Act of 1965
Water Resources Planning Act of 1965
Federal Water Pollution Control Acts of 1965, 1972
Ocean Dumping Act of 1972
Ocean Dumping Ban Act of 1988
Safe Drinking Water Act of 1974, 1984
Water Resources Development Act of 1986
Clean Water Act of 1977, 1987

## AIR QUALITY

Clean Air Act of 1963, 1965, 1970, 1977, 1990
Pollution Prevention Act of 1990

## NOISE CONTROL

Noise Control Act of 1965
Quiet Communities Act of 1978

## RESOURCES AND SOLID WASTE MANAGEMENT

Solid Waste Disposal Act of 1965
Resource Recovery Act of 1970
Resource Conservation and Recovery Act of 1976
Marine Plastic Pollution Research and Control Act of 1987

## TOXIC SUBSTANCES

Hazardous Materials Transportation Act of 1975
Toxic Substances Control Act of 1976
Resource Conservation and Recovery Act of 1976
Comprehensive Environmental Response, Compensation, and Liability (Superfund) Act of 1980, 1986
Nuclear Waste Policy Act of 1982

## PESTICIDES

Federal Insecticide, Fungicide, and Rodenticide Control Act of 1972, 1988

## WILDLIFE CONSERVATION

Lacey Act of 1900
Migratory Bird Treaty Act of 1918
Migratory Bird Conservation Act of 1929
Migratory Bird Hunting Stamp Act of 1934
Pittman-Robertson Act of 1937
Anadromous Fish Conservation Act of 1965
Fur Seal Act of 1966
National Wildlife Refuge System Act of 1966, 1976, 1978
Species Conservation Act of 1966, 1969
Marine Mammal Protection Act of 1972
Marine Protection, Research, and Sanctuaries Act of 1972
Endangered Species Act of 1973, 1982, 1985, 1988
Fishery Conservation and Management Act of 1976, 1978, 1982
Whale Conservation and Protection Study Act of 1976
Fish and Wildlife Improvement Act of 1978
Fish and Wildlife Conservation Act of 1980 (Nongame Act)

## LAND USE AND CONSERVATION

Taylor Grazing Act of 1934
Wilderness Act of 1964
Multiple Use Sustained Yield Act of 1968
Wild and Scenic Rivers Act of 1968
National Trails System Act of 1968
National Coastal Zone Management Act of 1972, 1980
Forest Reserves Management Act of 1974, 1976
Forest and Rangeland Renewable Resources Act of 1974, 1978
Federal Land Policy and Management Act of 1976
National Forest Management Act of 1976
Soil and Water Conservation Act of 1977
Surface Mining Control and Reclamation Act of 1977
Antarctic Conservation Act of 1978
Endangered American Wilderness Act of 1978
Alaskan National Interests Lands Conservation Act of 1980
Coastal Barrier Resources Act of 1982
Food Security Act of 1985

# Further Readings

## GENERAL SOURCES OF ENVIRONMENTAL INFORMATION

**Ashworth, William. 1991.** *The Encyclopedia of Environmental Studies.* New York: Facts on File.

**British Petroleum. Annual.** *BP Statistical Review of World Energy.* New York: BP America, Inc.

**Brown, Lester R., et al. Annual.** *State of the World.* New York: W. W. Norton.

**Brown, Lester R., et al. 1992.** *Vital Signs 1992.* New York: W. W. Norton.

**Buzzworm Magazine Editors. Annual.** *Earth Journal: Environmental Almanac and Resource Directory.* Boulder, Colo.: Buzzworm Books.

**Council on Environmental Quality. Annual Report.** Washington, D.C.: Government Printing Office.

**Council on Environmental Quality and U.S. Department of State. 1980.** *The Global 2000 Report to the President.* Vols. I–3. Washington, D.C.: Government Printing Office.

**Environment Canada. Annual.** *The State of Canada's Environment.* Ottawa: Government of Canada.

**Frank, Irene, and David Brownstone. 1992.** *The Green Encyclopedia.* New York: Prentice-Hall General Reference.

**Grant, James P. Annual.** *The State of the World's Children.* New York: Oxford University Press.

**Kirdon, Michael, and Ronald Segal. 1991.** *The New State of the World Atlas.* 4th ed. New York: Simon & Schuster.

**Lean, Geoffrey, et al. 1990.** *Atlas of the Environment.* Englewood Cliffs, N.J.: Prentice-Hall.

**Population Reference Bureau. Annual.** *World Population Data Sheet.* Washington, D.C.: Population Reference Bureau.

**Renew America. Annual.** *Environmental Success Index.* Washington, D.C.: Renew America.

**Rittner, Don. 1992.** *Ecolinking: Everyone's Guide to Online Environmental Information.* Berkeley, Calif.: Peachpit Press.

**Seager, Joni, ed. 1990.** *The State of the Earth Atlas.* New York: Simon & Schuster.

**Stein, Edith C. 1992.** *The Environmental Sourcebook.* New York: Lyons & Burford.

**United Nations. Annual.** *Demographic Yearbook.* New York: United Nations.

**United Nations Development Programme (UNDP). Annual.** *Human Development Program.* New York: UNDP.

**United Nations Environment Programme (UNEP). Annual.** *State of the Environment.* New York: UNEP.

**United Nations Population Fund. Annual.** *The State of World Population.* New York: United Nations Population Fund.

**U.S. Bureau of the Census. Annual.** *Statistical Abstract of the United States.* Washington, D.C.: U.S. Bureau of the Census.

**World Bank. Annual.** *World Development Report.* New York: Oxford University Press.

**World Health Organization (WHO). Annual.** *World Health Statistics.* Geneva, Switzerland: WHO.

**World Resources Institute. Annual.** *The Information Please Environmental Almanac.* Boston: Houghton Mifflin.

**World Resources Institute and International Institute for Environment and Development. Biannual.** *World Resources.* New York: Basic Books.

## 1 ENVIRONMENTAL PROBLEMS AND THEIR CAUSES

**Asimov, Isaac, and Frederick Pohl. 1991.** *Our Angry Earth.* New York: St. Martin's Press.

**Bender, David L., and Bruno Leone, eds. 1990.** *Environment: Opposing Viewpoints.* Vol. I. San Diego: Greenhaven.

**Brown, Lester R., et al. 1992.** *Vital Signs: The Trends That Are Shaping Our Future.* New York: W. W. Norton.

**Brundtland, G. H., et al. 1987.** *Our Common Future: World Commission on Environment and Development.* New York: Oxford University Press.

**Catton, William R. 1980.** *Overshoot: The Ecological Basis of Revolutionary Change.* Urbana: University of Illinois Press.

**Commoner, Barry. 1990.** *Making Peace with the Planet.* New York: Pantheon Books.

**Dahlberg, Kenneth A., et al. 1985.** *Environment and the Global Arena.* Durham, N.C.: Duke University Press.

**Edberg, R., and A. Yablokov. 1991.** *Tomorrow Will Be Too Late: East Meets West on Global Ecology.* Tucson: University of Arizona Press.

**Ehrlich, Paul R., and Anne H. Ehrlich. 1990.** *The Population Explosion.* New York: Doubleday.

**Ehrlich, Paul R., and Anne H. Ehrlich. 1991.** *Healing the Planet.* Reading, Mass.: Addison-Wesley.

**Ehrlich, Paul R., and John P. Holdren, eds. 1988.** *The Cassandra Conference: Resources and the Human Predicament.* College Station: Texas A&M University Press.

**Ember, Lois R. 1990.** "Pollution Chokes East-bloc Nations." *Chemistry & Engineering News,* April 16, 7–16.

**Feshbach, Murray, and Alfred Friendly, Jr. 1992.** *Ecocide in the USSR: Health and Nature Under Siege.* New York: Basic Books.

**Global Tomorrow Coalition. 1990.** *The Global Ecology Handbook: What You Can Do About the Environmental Crisis.* Boston: Beacon Press.

**Goldfarb, Theodore D. 1989.** *Taking Sides: Clashing Views on Controversial Environmental Issues.* Guilford, Conn.: Dushkin.

**Goldsmith, Edward, et al. 1990.** *Imperiled Planet: Restoring Our Endangered Ecosystems.* Cambridge, Mass.: MIT Press.

**Gordon, Anita, and David Suzuki. 1991.** *It's a Matter of Survival.* Cambridge, Mass.: Harvard University Press.

**Gore, Al. 1992.** *Earth in the Balance: Ecology and the Human Spirit.* Boston: Houghton Mifflin.

**Hardin, Garrett. 1968.** "The Tragedy of the Commons," *Science,* vol. 162, 1243–1248.

**Hardin, Garrett. 1985.** *Filters Against Folly.* New York: Viking Press.

**Harrison, Paul. 1992.** *The Third Revolution: Environment, Population, and a Sustainable World.* New York: St. Martin's Press.

**Henning, Daniel H., and William R. Mangun. 1989.** *Managing the Environmental Crisis: Incorporating Competing Values in Natural Resource Management.* Durham, N.C.: Duke University Press.

**Lapp, Ralph. 1973.** *The Logarithmic Century.* Englewood Cliffs, N.J.: Prentice-Hall.

**Lehr, J., ed. 1992.** *Rational Readings on Environmental Concerns.* New York: Van Nostrand Reinhold.

**Meadows, Donella H. 1991.** *The Global Citizen.* Covelo, Calif.: Island Press.

**Meadows, Donella H., et al. 1992.** *Beyond the Limits: Confronting Global Collapse, Envisioning a Sustainable Future.* Post Mills, Vt.: Chelsea Green.

**Myers, Norman. 1990.** *The Gaia Atlas of Future Worlds.* New York: Anchor/Doubleday.

**Myers, Norman, ed. 1993.** *Gaia: An Atlas of Planet Management.* Garden City, N.Y.: Anchor/Doubleday.

**Peterson, D. J. 1993.** *Troubled Lands: The Legacy of Soviet Environmental Destruction.* Boulder, Colo.: Westview Press.

**Piel, Gerald. 1992.** *Only One World.* New York: W. H. Freeman.

**Porritt, Jonathan. 1991.** *Save the Earth.* Atlanta: Turner.

**Ray, Dixie Lee, and Lou Guzzo. 1993.** *Environmental Overkill: Whatever Happened to Common Sense?* Washington, D.C.: Regnery Gateway.

**Ruchlis, Hy, and Sandra Oddo. 1990.** *Clear Thinking.* New York: Prometheus Books.

**Silver, Cheryl S., and Ruth S. Defries. 1990.** *One Earth, One Future: Our Changing Global Environment.* Washington, D.C.: National Academy Press.

**Simmons, I. G. 1992.** *Earth, Air, Water Resources, and Environment in the Late 20th Century.* New York: Chapman & Hall.

**Simon, Julian L. 1981.** *The Ultimate Resource.* Princeton, N.J.: Princeton University Press.

**Simon, Julian L., and Herman Kahn, eds. 1984.** *The Resourceful Earth.* Cambridge, Mass.: Basil Blackwell.

**Thomson, Jon. 1991.** "East Europe's Dark Dawn: The Iron Curtain Rises to Reveal a Land Tarnished by Pollution." *National Geographic,* June, 36–69.

**Ward, Barbara, and René Dubos. 1972.** *Only One Earth: The Care and Maintenance of a Small Planet.* New York: W. W. Norton.

**Weiner, Jonathan. 1990.** *The Next One Hundred Years: Shaping the Fate of Our Living Earth.* New York: Bantam Books.

## 2 BRIEF HISTORY OF RESOURCE USE AND CONSERVATION

**Arrandale, Thomas. 1983.** *The Battle for Natural Resources.* Washington, D.C.: Congressional Quarterly Books.

**Axelrod, Robert. 1984.** *The Evolution of Cooperation.* New York: Basic Books.

**Borrelli, Peter, ed. 1988.** *Crossroads: Environmental Priorities for the Future.* Covelo, Calif.: Island Press.

**Bramwell, Anna. 1989.** *Ecology in the 20th Century.* New Haven, Conn.: Yale University Press.

**Bronowski, Jacob, Jr. 1974.** *The Ascent of Man.* Boston: Little, Brown.

**Burger, J. 1990.** *The Gaia Atlas of First Peoples: A Future for the Indigenous World.* New York: Doubleday.

**Callicott, J. Baird. 1989.** "American Indian Land Wisdom? Sorting Out the Issues." *Journal of Forest History,* vol. 33, no. 1, 35–42.

**Calvin, William H. 1990.** *The Ascent of Mind.* New York: Bantam Books.

**Carson, Rachel. 1962.** *Silent Spring.* Boston: Houghton Mifflin.

**Carter, V. G., and T. Dale. 1974.** *Topsoil and Civilization.* Norman: University of Oklahoma Press.

**Clawson, Marion. 1983.** *The Federal Lands Revisited.* Washington, D.C.: Resources for the Future.

**Coalition of Environmental Groups. 1989.** *Blueprint for the Environment.* Salt Lake City: Howe Brothers Press.

**Cohen, Mark N. 1989.** *Health and the Rise of Civilization.* New Haven, Conn.: Yale University Press.

**Cohen, Michael P. 1984.** *The Pathless Way: John Muir and American Wilderness.* Madison: University of Wisconsin Press.

**Crosby, Alfred W. 1986.** *Ecological Imperialism: The Biological Expansion of Europe, 900–1900.* New York: Cambridge University Press.

**Culhane, Paul J. 1981.** *Public Land Politics: Interest Group Influences on the Forest Service and the Bureau of Land Management.* Washington, D.C.: Resources for the Future.

**Debeir, Jean-Claude, et al. 1991.** *In the Servitude of Power: Energy and Civilization Through the Ages.* Highlands, N.J.: Humanities Press International.

Dunlap, Thomas. 1988. *Saving America's Wildlife.* Princeton, N.J.: Princeton University Press.

Dyson, Freeman. 1992. *From Eros to Gaia.* New York: Pantheon Books.

Eisler, Riabe. 1987. *The Chalice and the Blade: Our History, Our Future.* San Francisco: Harper & Row.

Fagan, Brian M. 1990. *The Journey from Eden: The Peopling of Our World.* London: Thames & Hudson.

Ferguson, Denzel, and Nancy Ferguson. 1983. *Sacred Cows at the Public Trough.* Bend, Ore.: Maverick.

Fox, Stephen. 1981. *John Muir and His Legacy: The American Conservation Movement.* Boston: Little, Brown.

Friends of the Earth et al. 1982. *Reagan and Environment.* San Francisco: Friends of the Earth.

Glover, James M. 1986. *A Wilderness Original: The Life of Bob Marshall.* Seattle: The Mountaineers.

Goudie, Andrew. 1990. *The Human Impact on the Natural Environment.* 3rd ed. Cambridge, Mass.: MIT Press.

Graham, Frank. 1971. *Man's Dominion: The Story of Conservation in America.* New York: M. Evans.

Hartzog, George B., Jr. 1988. *Battling for the National Parks.* Mt. Kisco, N.Y.: Moyer Bell.

Hays, Samuel. 1987. *Beauty, Health, and Permanence: Environmental Politics in the United States: 1955–1985.* New York: Cambridge University Press.

High Country News. 1989. *Reforming the Western Frontier.* Covelo, Calif.: Island Press.

Hughes, J. Donald. 1975. *The Ecology of Ancient Civilizations.* Albuquerque: University of New Mexico Press.

Hughes, J. Donald. 1983. *American Indian Ecology.* El Paso: Texas Western Press.

Hyams, Edward. 1976. *Soils and Civilization.* San Francisco: Harper & Row.

Jacks, G. W., and R. O. Whyte. 1939. *The Rape of the Earth.* New York: Faber & Faber.

Jacobsen, Judith, and John Firor, eds. 1992. *Human Impact on the Environment: Ancient Roots, Current Challenges.* Boulder, Colo.: Westview Press.

Jaimes, M., ed. 1992. *The State of Native America: Genocide, Colonization, and Resistance.* Boston: South End Press.

Krutch, Joseph Wood. 1956. *The Great Chain of Being.* Boston: Houghton Mifflin.

Lash, Jonathan, et al. 1984. *A Season of Spoils.* New York: Pantheon Books.

Leopold, Aldo. 1949. *A Sand County Almanac.* New York: Oxford University Press.

Livingston, John. 1973. *One Cosmic Instant: Man's Fleeting Supremacy.* Boston: Houghton Mifflin.

Mander, Jerry. 1991. *In the Absence of the Sacred: The Failure of Technology and the Rise of Indian Nations.* San Francisco: Sierra Club Books.

Marsh, George Perkins. 1864. *Man and Nature.* New York: Charles Scribner.

Marshall, Bruce, ed. 1991. *The Real World: Understanding the Modern World Through the New Geography.* Boston: Houghton Mifflin.

Martin, Calvin Luther. 1992. *In the Spirit of the Earth: Rethinking History and Time.* Baltimore: Johns Hopkins University Press.

Marx, Leo. 1964. *The Machine in the Garden: Technology and the Pastoral Ideal in America.* New York: Oxford University Press.

McCormick, John. 1989. *Reclaiming Paradise: The Global Environmental Movement.* Bloomington: Indiana University Press.

Meine, Curt. 1988. *Aldo Leopold: His Life and Work.* Madison: University of Wisconsin Press.

Mumford, Lewis. 1962. *The Transformations of Man.* New York: Collier.

Nabokov, Peter, ed. 1992. *Native American Testimony: A Chronicle of Indian-White Relations from Prophecy to the Present, 1492–1992.* New York: Viking Press.

Nash, Roderick. 1982. *Wilderness and the American Mind.* 3rd ed. New Haven, Conn.: Yale University Press.

Nash, Roderick. 1988. *The Rights of Nature: A History of Environmental Ethics.* Madison: University of Wisconsin Press.

Nicholson, Max. 1987. *The New Environmental Age.* New York: Cambridge University Press.

Odell, Rice. 1980. *Environmental Awakening: The New Revolution to Protect the Earth.* Cambridge, Mass.: Ballinger.

Oelschlager, Max. 1991. *The Idea of Wilderness from Prehistory to the Age of Ecology.* New Haven, Conn.: Yale University Press.

Osborn, Fairfield. 1948. *Our Plundered Planet.* Boston: Little, Brown.

Petulla, Joseph M. 1988. *American Environmental History.* 2nd ed. Columbus, Ohio: Charles E. Merrill.

Ponting, Clive. 1992. *A Green History of the World: The Environment and, the Collapse of Great Civilizations.* New York: St. Martin's Press.

Repetto, Robert, ed. 1986. *The Global Possible: Resources, Development, and the New Century.* New Haven, Conn.: Yale University Press.

Repetto, Robert. 1986. *World Enough and Time.* New Haven, Conn.: Yale University Press.

Roe, Frank G. 1970. *The North American Buffalo.* Toronto: University of Toronto Press.

Sabaloff, Jeremy A., and C. C. Lamberg-Karlovsky. 1975. *The Rise and Fall of Civilizations.* Menlo Park, Calif.: Benjamin/Cummings.

Scheffer, Vincent B. 1991. *The Shaping of Environmentalism in America.* Seattle: University of Washington Press.

Sears, Paul B. 1980. *Deserts on the March.* Norman: University of Oklahoma Press.

Shabecoff, Philip. 1993. *A Fierce Green Fire: The American Environmental Movement.* New York: Hill & Wang.

Shanks, Bernard. 1984. *This Land Is Your Land.* San Francisco: Sierra Club Books.

Shephard, Paul. 1982. *Nature and Madness.* San Francisco: Sierra Club Books.

Shephard, Paul. 1991. *Man in the Landscape: A Historic View of the Esthetics of Nature.* 2nd. ed. College Station: Texas A&M University Press.

Short, C. Brant. 1989. *Ronald Reagan and the Public Lands: America's Conservation Debate: 1979–1984.* College Station: Texas A&M University Press.

Simmons, I. G. 1989. *Changing the Face of the Earth: Culture, Environment, and History.* London: Basil Blackwell.

Stroup, Richard L., and John A. Baden. 1986. *Natural Resources: Bureaucratic Myths and Environmental Management.* San Francisco: Institute for Public Policy Research.

Tanner, Thomas, ed. 1987. *Aldo Leopold: The Man and His Legacy.* Ankony, Iowa: Soil Conservation Society of America.

Toynbee, Arnold. 1972. *A Study of History.* New York: Oxford University Press.

Turner, B. L., et al., eds. 1990. *The Earth as Transformed by Human Actions.* New York: Cambridge University Press.

Udall, Stewart L. 1963. *The Quiet Crisis.* New York: Holt, Rinehart & Winston. Reprint, with updating. Salt Lake City: Gibbs Smith.

U.S. Department of Agriculture, Forest Service. 1976. *Highlights in the History of Forest Conservation.* Washington, D.C.: Government Printing Office.

Vecsey, Christopher, and Robert W. Veneables, eds. 1980. *American Indian Environments: Ecological Issues in Native American History.* Syracuse, N.Y.: University of Syracuse Press.

Vig, Norman J., and Michael J. Craft. 1984. *Environmental Policy in the 1980s.* Washington, D.C.: Congressional Quarterly Press.

Vig, Norman J., and Michael J. Craft. 1990. *Environmental Policy in the 1990s.* Washington, D.C.: Congressional Quarterly Press.

Vogt, William. 1948. *The Road to Survival.* New York: Sloane.

Wallach, Bret. 1991. *At Odds with Progress: Americans and Conservation.* Tucson: University of Arizona Press.

Williams, Michael. 1989. *Americans and Their Forests: A Historical Account.* New York: Cambridge University Press.

World Resources Institute. 1989. *The Crucial Decade: The 1990s and the Global Environmental Challenge.* Washington, D.C.: World Resources Institute.

Worster, Donald, ed. 1988. *The Ends of the Earth: Perspectives on Modern Environmental History.* New York: Cambridge University Press.

Worster, Donald. 1992. *Under Western Skies: Nature and History in the American West.* New York: Oxford University Press.

Worster, Donald. 1993. *The Wealth of Nature: Environmental History and the Ecological Imagination.* New York: Oxford University Press.

Zaslowsky, Dyan, and Wilderness Society. 1986. *These American Lands.* New York: Henry Holt.

## 3 MATTER AND ENERGY RESOURCES: TYPES AND CONCEPTS

American Physical Society. 1975. *Efficient Use of Energy.* New York: American Institute of Physics.

Bauer, Henry H. 1992. *Scientific Literacy and the Myth of the Scientific Method.* Urbana: University of Illinois Press.

Berry, R. Stephen. 1991. *Understanding Energy: Energy, Entropy, and Thermodynamics for Everyman.* River Edge, N.J.: World Scientific.

Christensen, John W. 1990. *Global Science: Energy, Resources, and Environment.* 3rd ed. Dubuque, Iowa: Kendall/Hunt.

Colorado Energy Research Institute. 1976. *Net Energy Analysis: An Energy Balance Study of Fossil Fuel Resources.* Golden: Colorado Energy Research Institute.

Fowler, John M. 1984. *Energy and the Environment.* 2nd ed. New York: McGraw-Hill.

Gever, John, et al. 1991. *Beyond Oil: The Threat to Food and Fuel in Coming Decades.* Boulder: University of Colorado Press.

Glasby, G. P. 1988. "Entropy, Pollution, and Environmental Degradation." *Ambio,* vol. 17, no. 5, 330–335.

Kuhn, Thomas S. 1970. *The Structure of Scientific Revolutions.* 2nd ed. Chicago: University of Chicago Press.

Lovins, Amory B. 1977. *Soft Energy Paths.* Cambridge, Mass.: Ballinger.

Lovins, Amory B., and L. Hunter Lovins. 1986. *Energy Unbound: Your Invitation to Energy Abundance.* San Francisco: Sierra Club Books.

Miller, G. Tyler, Jr. 1971. *Energetics, Kinetics and Life: An Ecological Approach.* Belmont, Calif.: Wadsworth.

Miller, G. Tyler, Jr., and David G. Lygre. 1991. *Chemistry: A Contemporary Approach.* 3rd ed. Belmont, Calif.: Wadsworth.

Odum, Howard T., and Elisabeth C. Odum. 1981. *Energy Basis for Man and Nature.* New York: McGraw-Hill.

Rifkin, Jeremy. 1989. *Entropy: Into the Greenhouse World: A New World View.* New York: Bantam Books.

Rose, David. 1986. *Learning About Energy.* New York: Plenum.

Rothman, Milton A. 1992. *The Science Gap: Dispelling Myths and Understanding the Reality of Science.* New York: Prometheus Books.

Smil, Vaclav. 1991. *General Energetics: Energy in the Biosphere and Civilization.* New York: John Wiley.

## 4 ECOSYSTEMS AND HOW THEY WORK

Ahmadjian, V., and S. Paracer. 1986. *Symbiosis: An Introduction to Biological Associations.* New Haven, Conn.: University Press of New England.

Andrewartha, H. G., and L. C. Birch. 1986. *The Ecological Web: More on the Distribution and Abundance of Animals.* Chicago: University of Chicago Press.

Bolin, B., and R. B. Cook. 1983. *The Major Biogeochemical Cycles and Their Interactions.* New York: John Wiley.

Bradbury, Ian. 1991. *The Biosphere.* New York: Belhaven Press.

Brewer, R. 1993. *The Science of Ecology.* 2nd ed. Philadelphia: W.B. Saunders.

Burton, Robert, ed. 1991. *Animal Life.* New York: Oxford University Press.

Colinvaux, Paul A. 1986. *Ecology.* New York: John Wiley.

DiSilvestro, Roger L. 1990. *Fight for Survival.* New York: John Wiley.

Ehrlich, Anne H., and Paul R. Ehrlich. 1987. *Earth.* New York: Franklin Watts.

Ehrlich, Paul R. 1986. *The Machinery of Life: The Living World Around Us and How It Works.* New York: Simon & Schuster.

Ehrlich, Paul R., Anne H. Ehrlich, and John P. Holdren. 1977. *Ecoscience: Population, Resources and Environment.* New York: W. H. Freeman.

Elsom, Derek. 1992. *Earth: The Making, Shaping, and Working of a Planet.* New York: Macmillan.

Gates, David M. 1985. *Energy and Ecology.* Sunderland, Mass.: Sinauer.

Howe, Henry, and Lynn Westley. 1988. *Ecological Relationships of Plants and Animals.* New York: Oxford University Press.

Kormondy, Edward J. 1984. *Concepts of Ecology.* 3rd ed. Englewood Cliffs, N.J.: Prentice-Hall.

Krebs, Charles J. 1985. *Ecology.* 3rd ed. San Francisco: Harper & Row.

Macmillan Publishing. 1992. *The Way Nature Works.* New York: Macmillan.

Moore, D. M., ed. 1991. *Plant Life.* New York: Oxford University Press.

Odum, Eugene P. 1993. *Ecology and Our Endangered Life-Support Systems.* 2nd ed. Sunderland, Mass.: Sinauer.

Post, Wilfred M., et al. 1990. "The Global Carbon Cycle." *American Scientist,* vol. 78, 310–326.

Ramadé, François. 1984. *Ecology of Natural Resources.* New York: John Wiley.

Rickleffs, Robert E. 1990. *Ecology.* 3rd ed. New York: W. H. Freeman.

Smith, Robert L. 1990. *Elements of Ecology.* 4th ed. San Francisco: Harper & Row.

Springer, Victor G., and Joy P. Gold. 1989. *Sharks in Question: The Smithsonian Answer Book.* Washington, D.C.: Smithsonian Institution

Starr, Cecie, and Ralph Taggart. 1992. *Biology: The Unity and Diversity of Life.* 6th ed. Belmont, Calif.: Wadsworth.

Tudge, Colin. 1988. *The Environment of Life.* New York: Oxford University Press.

Tudge, Colin. 1991. *Global Ecology.* New York: Oxford University Press.

Watt, Kenneth E. F. 1982. *Understanding the Environment.* Boston: Allyn & Bacon.

Worster, Donald. 1985. *Nature's Economy: A History of Ecological Ideas.* New York: Cambridge University Press.

## 5 ATMOSPHERE, CLIMATE, WEATHER, AND LIFE

**See also the readings for Chapter 4.**

Aber, John, and Jerry Melito. 1991. *Terrestrial Ecosystems.* Philadelphia: Saunders.

Akin, Wallace E. 1991. *Global Patterns: Climate, Vegetation, and Soils.* Norman: University of Oklahoma Press.

Attenborough, David. 1984. *The Living Planet.* Boston: Little, Brown.

Attenborough, David, et al. 1989. *The Atlas of the Living World.* Boston: Houghton Mifflin.

Barry, R. C., and J. Chorley. 1987. *Atmosphere, Weather, and Climate.* 5th ed. London: Methuen.

Brown, J. H., and A. C. Gibson. 1983. *Biogeography.* St. Louis: C. V. Mosby.

Brown, Lauren. 1985. *Grasslands.* New York: Random House.

Burke, David G., et al. 1989. *Protecting Nontidal Wetlands.* Washington, D.C.: American Planning Association.

Carson, Rachel. 1955. *The Edge of the Sea.* Boston: Houghton Mifflin.

Clapham, W. B., Jr. 1984. *Natural Ecosystems.* 2nd ed. New York: Macmillan.

Couper, Alastair, ed. 1990. *The Times Atlas and Encyclopedia of the Sea.* Hagerstown, Md.: Lippincott.

Cousteau, Jacques-Yves. 1981. *The Cousteau Almanac: An Inventory of Life on Our Water Planet.* New York: Doubleday.

Culliny, John L. 1976. *The Forest of the Sea.* San Francisco: Sierra Club Books.

Daiber, Franklin C. 1986. *Conservation of Tidal Marshes.* New York: Van Nostrand Reinhold.

Elder, Danny, and John Pernetta, eds. 1991. *Oceans.* London: Michael Beazley.

Environmental Protection Agency. 1989. *Marine and Estuarine Protection: Programs and Activities.* Washington, D.C.: EPA.

Goldman, C., and A. Horne. 1983. *Limnology.* New York: McGraw-Hill.

Goldman-Carter, Jan. 1989. *A Citizen's Guide to Protecting Wetlands.* Washington, D.C.: National Wildlife Federation.

Goldsmith, Edward, et al. 1990. *Imperiled Planet: Restoring Our Endangered Ecosystems.* Cambridge, Mass.: MIT Press.

Golley, Frank B., ed. 1983. *Tropical Rain Forest Ecosystems: Structure and Function.* New York: Elsevier.

Graham, N. E., and W. B. White. 1988. "The *El Niño* Cycle: A Natural Oscillator of the Pacific Ocean-Atmosphere System." *Science,* vol. 240, 1293–1302.

Greenland, David. 1983. *Guidelines for Modern Resource Management: Soil, Land, Water, Air.* Columbus, Ohio: Charles E. Merrill.

Jeffress, J., et al. 1991. *Coasts in Crisis.* Washington, D.C.: U.S. Geological Survey, Circular 1075.

Kaufman, Wallace, and Orin Pilkey. 1979. *The Beaches Are Moving.* New York: Anchor/Doubleday.

Krutch, Joseph Wood. 1951. *The Desert Year.* New York: Viking Press.

Kusler, John. 1992. "Wetlands Delineation: An Issue of Science or Politics?" *Environment,* vol. 34, no. 2, 7–11, 29–36.

Lauw, G. N., and M. K. Seely. 1982. *Ecology of Desert Organisms.* New York: Longman.

Mabberly, D. J. 1983. *Tropical Rain Forest Ecology.* London: Blackie.

MacMahon, James A. 1985. *Deserts.* New York: Random House.

Maltby, Edward. 1986. *Waterlogged Wealth.* East Haven, Conn.: Earthscan.

McArthur, R. H. 1972. *Geographical Ecology.* San Francisco: Harper & Row.

Mitsch, William J., and James G. Gosselink. 1986. *Wetlands.* New York: Van Nostrand Reinhold.

Myers, Norman. 1984. *The Primary Source: Tropical Forests and Our Future.* New York: W. W. Norton.

National Academy of Sciences. 1990. *Managing Coastal Erosion.* Washington, D.C.: National Academy Press.

National Academy of Sciences. 1992. *Restoration of Aquatic Ecosystems: Science, Technology, and Public Policy.* Washington, D.C.: National Academy Press.

National Wildlife Federation. 1987. *Status Report of Our Nation's Wetlands.* Washington, D.C.: National Wildlife Federation.

Nicholas, Sara. 1992. "The War over Wetland." *Issues in Science and Technology,* Summer, 35–41.

Niering, William A. 1991. *Wetlands of North America.* Charlottesville, Va.: Thomasson-Grant.

Office of Technology Assessment. 1984. *Wetlands: Their Use and Regulation.* Washington, D.C.: Government Printing Office.

Pilkey, Orin H., Jr., et al. 1984. *Coastal Design: A Guide for Builders, Planners, and Homeowners.* New York: Van Nostrand Reinhold.

Pilkey, Orin H., Jr., and William J. Neal, eds. 1977–1991. *Living with the Shore.* 14 vols. Durham, N.C.: Duke University Press.

Simon, Anne W. 1978. *The Thin Edge: Coast and Man in Crisis.* New York: Harper & Row.

Teal, John, and Mildred Teal. 1969. *Life and Death of a Salt Marsh.* New York: Ballantine Books.

Thorne-Miller, Boyce, and John Catena. 1990. *The Living Ocean: Understanding and Protecting Marine Diversity.* Covelo, Calif.: Island Press.

Tudge, Colin. 1988. *The Environment of Life.* New York: Oxford University Press.

Urban Land Institute. 1990. *Wetlands: Mitigating and Regulating Development Impacts.* Washington, D.C.: Urban Land Institute.

Wallace, David. 1987. *Life in the Balance.* New York: Harcourt Brace Jovanovich.

Weber, Peter. 1993. "Reviving Coral Reefs." In Lester R. Brown et al., *State of the World 1993,* 42–60. New York: W. W. Norton.

Wells, Sue, and Nick Hanna. 1992. *The Greenpeace Book of Coral Reefs.* New York: Sterling.

Whittaker, R. H. 1975. *Communities and Ecosystems.* 2nd ed. New York: Macmillan.

Yates, Steve. 1988. *Adopting a Stream.* Seattle: University of Washington Press.

Yates, Steve. 1989. *Adopting a Wetland.* Everett, Wash.: Adopt-A-Stream Foundation.

## 6 CHANGES IN POPULATIONS, COMMUNITIES, AND ECOSYSTEMS

**See also the readings for Chapters 4 and 5.**

Anderson, Walter T. 1987. *To Govern Evolution.* New York: Harcourt Brace Jovanovich.

Berger, John J. 1986. *Restoring the Earth.* New York: Alfred A. Knopf.

Berger, John J., ed. 1990. *Environmental Restoration.* Covelo, Calif.: Island Press.

Boulding, Kenneth E. 1985. *The World as a Total System.* Beverly Hills, Calif.: Sage.

Busch, Lawrence, et al. 1990. *Plants, Power, and Profit: Social, Economic, and Ethical Consequences of the New Biotechnologies.* Cambridge, Mass.: Basil Blackwell.

Cairns, John, ed. 1988. *Rehabilitating Damaged Ecosystems.* Toledo, Ohio: CRC Press.

Constanza, Robert, et al., eds. 1991. *Ecosystem Health: New Goals for Environmental Management.* Covelo, Calif.: Island Press.

Cook, L. M. 1991. *Genetic and Ecological Diversity.* New York: Chapman & Hall.

Cowen, Richard. 1990. *History of Life.* New York: Basil Blackwell.

Davis, Bernard D., ed. 1991. *The Genetic Revolution: Scientific Prospects and Public Perceptions.* Baltimore: Johns Hopkins University Press.

Ehrlich, Paul R. 1980. "Variety Is the Key to Life." *Technology Review,* March/April, 599–608.

Ehrlich, Paul R., and Edward O. Wilson. 1991. "Biodiversity Studies: Science and Policy." *Science,* vol. 253, 758–762.

Eldridge, Niles. 1991. *The Miner's Canary: Unravelling the Mysteries of Extinction.* New York: Prentice-Hall.

Endler, John A. 1986. *Natural Selection in the Wild.* Princeton, N.J.: Princeton University Press.

Farvar, M. Tagi, and John Milton, eds. 1972. *The Careless Technology.* Garden City, N.Y.: Natural History Press.

Fincham, J. R. S., and J. R. Ravetz. 1991. *Genetically Engineered Organisms: Benefits and Risks.* New York: John Wiley.

Fox, Michael W. 1992. *Superpigs and Wondercorn: The Brave New World of Biotechnology and Where It All May Lead.* New York: Lyons & Burford.

Freedman, Bill. 1989. *Environmental Ecology: The Impacts of Pollution and Other Stresses on Ecosystem Structure and Function.* San Diego: Academic Press.

Gould, Stephen Jay. 1977. *Ever Since Darwin.* New York: W. W. Norton.

Gould, Stephen Jay. 1980. *The Panda's Thumb.* New York: W. W. Norton.

Hardin, Garrett. 1985. "Human Ecology: The Subversive, Conservative Science." *American Zoologist,* vol. 25, 469–476.

Harris, John. 1992. *Wonderwoman and Superman: The Ethics of Human Biotechnology.* New York: Oxford University Press.

Holland, Heinrich D. 1984. *The Chemical Evolution of the Atmosphere and Oceans.* Princeton, N.J.: Princeton University Press.

Joseph, Lawrence E. 1990. *Gaia: The Growth of an Idea.* New York: St. Martin's Press.

Krimsy, Sheldon. 1991. *Biotechnics and Society: The Rise of Industrial Genetics.* New York: Praeger.

Kusler, Jon A., and Mary E. Kentula, eds. 1990. *Wetland Creation and Restoration.* Covelo, Calif.: Island Press.

Lovelock, James E. 1988. *The Ages of Gaia: A Biography of Our Living Earth.* New York: W. W. Norton.

Lovelock, James E. 1991. *Healing Gaia: Practical Medicine for the Planet.* New York: Random House.

Margulis, Lynn, and Lorraine Olendzenski, eds. 1992. *Environmental Evolution: Effects of the Origin and Evolution of Life on Planet Earth.* Cambridge, Mass.: MIT Press.

Margulis, Lynn, and Dorion Sagan. 1986. *Microcosmos: Four Billion Years of Evolution from Our Microbiological Ancestors.* New York: Summit Books.

McArthur, Robert H., and E. O. Wilson. 1967. *The Theory of Island Biogeography.* Princeton, N.J.: Princeton University Press.

Meadows, Donella H., et al. 1992. *Beyond the Limits: Confronting Global Collapse, Envisioning a Sustainable Future.* Post Mills, Vt.: Chelsea Green.

Meyer, Christine, and Faith Moosang. 1992. *Living with the Land: Communities Restoring the Earth.* Philadelphia: New Society.

National Academy of Sciences. 1986. *Ecological Knowledge and Environmental Problem-Solving.* Washington, D.C.: National Academy Press.

National Academy of Sciences. 1992. *Restoration of Aquatic Ecosystems.* Washington, D.C.: National Academy Press.

Nilsen, Richard, ed. 1991. *Helping Nature Heal: An Introduction to Environmental Restoration.* Berkeley, Calif.: Ten Speed Press.

Nisbet, E. G. 1991. *Living Earth.* San Francisco: Harper-Collins.

Odum, Eugene P. 1969. "The Strategy of Ecosystem Development." *Science,* vol. 164, 262–270.

Olson, Steve. 1989. *Shaping the Future: Biology and Human Values.* Washington, D.C.: National Academy Press.

Pimentel, David, et al. 1989. "Benefits and Risks of Genetic Engineering in Agriculture." *BioScience,* vol. 39, no. 9, 606–614.

Pimm, Stuart L. 1992. *The Balance of Nature?* Chicago: University of Chicago Press.

Power, J. F., and R. F. Follett. 1987. "Monoculture." *Scientific American,* January, 30–36.

Rifkin, Jeremy. 1983. *Algeny.* New York: Viking/Penguin.

Rifkin, Jeremy. 1985. *Declaration of a Heretic.* Boston: Routledge & Kegan Paul.

Schneider, S. H., and R. S. Londer. 1984. *The Coevolution of Climate and Life.* San Francisco: Sierra Club Books.

Schneider, Stephen H., and Penelope J. Boston, eds. 1991. *Scientists on Gaia.* Cambridge, Mass.: MIT Press.

Slobodkin, Laurence B. 1980. *Growth and Regulation of Animal Populations.* New York: Dover.

Solbrig, Otto T. 1991. "The Origin of Biodiversity." *Environment,* vol. 33, no. 5, 17–20, 34–38.

Starr, Cecie, and Ralph Taggart. 1992. *Biology: The Unity and Diversity of Life.* 6th ed. Belmont, Calif.: Wadsworth.

Suzuki, David, and Peter Knudtson. 1989. *Genethics: The Clash Between the New Genetics and Human Values.* Cambridge, Mass.: Harvard University Press.

Thomson, William Irwin. 1991. *Gaia 2: Emergence.* Hudson, N.Y.: Lindisfarne Press.

Wilson, E. O. 1984. *Biophilia.* Cambridge, Mass.: Harvard University Press.

Wilson, E. O., ed. 1988. *Biodiversity.* Washington, D.C.: National Academy Press.

Wilson, E. O. 1992. *The Diversity of Life.* Cambridge, Mass.: Harvard University Press.

Woodwell, G. M. 1970. "Effects of Pollution on the Structure and Physiology of Ecosystems." *Science,* vol. 168, 429–433.

## 7 GEOLOGIC PROCESSES: THE DYNAMIC EARTH

Ballard, Robert D. 1988. *Exploring Our Living Planet.* Washington, D.C.: National Geographic Society.

Bolt, Bruce A. 1987. *Earthquakes.* Rev. ed. Berkeley and Los Angeles: University of California Press.

Brown, Bruce, and Lane Morgan. 1990. *The Miracle Planet.* Edison, N.J.: W. H. Smith.

Bullard, Fred. 1984. *Volcanoes of the Earth.* 2nd ed. Austin: University of Texas Press.

Craig, James R., et al. 1988. *Resources of the Earth.* Englewood Cliffs, N.J.: Prentice-Hall.

Dixon, Dougal, and Raymond L. Bendor. 1992. *The Practical Geologist.* New York: Simon & Schuster.

Erickson, Jon. 1989. *The Living Earth: The Coevolution of the Planet and Life.* Blue Ridge Summit, Pa.: TAB Books.

Ernst, W. G. 1990. *The Dynamic Planet.* New York: Columbia University Press.

Gregory, K. J., ed. 1990. *Earth's Natural Forces.* New York: Oxford University Press.

Hamblin, W. Kenneth. 1989. *The Earth's Dynamic Systems: A Textbook in Physical Geology.* 5th ed. New York: Macmillan.

Hansen, Gladys, and Emmet Condon. 1989. *Denial of Disaster.* San Francisco: Cameron.

Harris, Stephen L. 1990. *Agents of Chaos: Earthquakes, Volcanoes, and Other Natural Disasters.* Missoula, Mont.: Mountain Press.

Keller, Edward A. 1988. *Environmental Geology.* 5th ed. Columbus, Ohio: Charles E. Merrill.

Lambert, David, and the Diagram Group. 1988. *The Field Guide to Geology.* New York: Facts on File.

McAlester, R. A., et al. 1984. *The History of the Earth's Crust.* Englewood Cliffs, N.J.: Prentice-Hall.

Montgomery, Carla W. 1989. *Environmental Geology.* Dubuque, Iowa: Wm. C. Brown.

National Academy of Sciences. 1991. *A Safer Future: Reducing the Impacts of Natural Disasters.* Washington, D.C.: National Academy Press.

Plummer, C. C., and D. McGeary. 1985. *Physical Geography.* 3rd ed. Dubuque, Iowa: Wm. C. Brown.

Press, Frank, and Raymond Siever. 1986. *Earth.* New York: W. H. Freeman.

Redfern, Ron. 1983. *The Making of a Continent.* New York: Times Books.

Stanley, Steven M. 1986. *Earth and Life Through Time.* New York: W. H. Freeman.

Tilling, Robert I. 1982. *Eruptions of Mount St. Helens: Past, Present, and Future.* Washington, D.C.: U.S. Geological Survey, Government Printing Office.

Tilling, Robert I. 1989. *Volcanic Hazards: Short Course in Geology.* Vol. 1. Washington, D.C.: American Geophysical Union.

Van Andel, T. H. 1985. *New View of an Old Planet: Continental Drift and the History of the Earth.* New York: Cambridge University Press.

Westbrook, Peter. 1991. *Life as a Geological Force: Dynamics of the Earth.* New York: W. W. Norton.

Youngquist, Walter. 1990. *Mineral Resources and the Destinies of Nations.* Portland, Ore.: National Book Company.

## 8 POPULATION DYNAMICS AND POPULATION REGULATION

Barna, George. 1992. *The Invisible Generation: Baby Busters.* New York: Barna Research Group.

Bouvier, Leon F. 1992. *Peaceful Invasions: Immigration and Changing America.* Lantham, Md.: University Press of America.

Bouvier, Leon F., and Carol J. De Vita. 1991. "The Baby Boom—Entering Midlife." *Population Bulletin,* vol. 6, no. 3, 1–35.

Brown, Lester R., and Jodi Jacobson. 1986. *Our Demographically Divided World.* Washington, D.C.: Worldwatch Institute.

Brown, Lester R., and Edward C. Wolf. 1985. *Reversing Africa's Decline.* Washington, D.C.: Worldwatch Institute.

Callahan, Daniel. 1972. "Ethics and Population Limitation." *Science,* vol. 175, 487–494.

Crewdson, John. 1983. *The Tarnished Door.* New York: Times Books.

Croll, Elisabeth, et al. 1985. *China's One-Child Family Policy.* New York: St. Martin's Press.

Dankelman, Irene, and Joan Davidson. 1988. *Women and the Environment in the Third World.* East Haven, Conn.: Earthscan.

Davis, Kingsley, et al., eds. 1989. *Population and Resources in a Changing World.* Stanford, Calif.: Morrison Institute for Population and Resource Studies.

Day, Lincoln H. 1992. *The Future of Low-Birthrate Populations.* New York: Routledge.

Djerassi, Carl. 1989. "The Bitter Pill." *Science,* vol. 245, 356–361.

Donaldson, Peter J., and Amy Ong Tsui. 1990. "The International Family Planning Movement." *Population Bulletin,* vol. 43, no. 3, 1–42.

Dychtwald, Ken. 1989. *Age Wave: The Challenges and Opportunities of an Aging America.* New York: Jeremy Tarcher.

Ehrlich, Paul R., and Anne H. Ehrlich. 1990. *The Population Explosion.* New York: Doubleday.

Ehrlich, Paul, et al. 1981. *The Golden Door: International Migration, Mexico, and the United States.* New York: Wideview Books.

Formos, Werner. 1987. *Gaining People, Losing Ground: A Blueprint for Stabilizing World Population.* Washington, D.C.: Population Institute.

Goliber, Thomas J. 1985. "Sub-Saharan Africa: Population Pressures on Development." *Population Bulletin,* vol. 40, no. 1, 1–45.

Grant, Lindsey. 1992. *Elephants and Volkswagens: Facing the Tough Questions About Our Overcrowded Country.* New York: W. H. Freeman.

Gupte, Pranay. 1984. *The Crowded Earth: People and the Politics of Population.* New York: W. W. Norton.

Hardin, Garrett. 1993. *Living Within Limits: Ecology, Economics, and Population Taboos.* New York: Oxford University Press.

Harrison, Paul. 1992. *The Third Revolution: Environment, Population, and a Sustainable World.* New York: I. B. Tauris.

Hartmann, Betsy. 1987. *Reproductive Rights and Wrongs: The Global Politics of Population Control and Contraceptive Choice.* San Francisco: Harper & Row.

Haub, Carl. 1987. "Understanding Population Projections." *Population Bulletin,* vol. 42, no. 4, 1–41.

Haupt, Arthur, and Thomas T. Kane. 1985. *The Population Handbook: International.* 2nd ed. Washington, D.C.: Population Reference Bureau.

Hernandez, Donald J. 1985. *Success or Failure? Family Planning Programs in the Third World.* Westport, Conn.: Greenwood Press.

International Union for Conservation of Nature and Natural Resources and Planned Parenthood Federation. 1984. *Population and Natural Resources.* Gland, Switzerland: IUCN.

Jacobson, Jodi L. 1987. *Planning the Global Family.* Washington, D.C.: Worldwatch Institute.

Jacobson, Jodi. 1990. *The Global Politics of Abortion.* Washington, D.C.: Worldwatch Institute.

Jacobson, Jodi. 1991. *Women's Reproductive Health: The Silent Emergency.* Washington, D.C.: Worldwatch Institute.

Jones, Elsie F., et al. 1986. *Teenage Pregnancy in Industrialized Countries.* New Haven, Conn.: Yale University Press.

Keyfitz, Nathan. 1989. "The Growing Human Population." *Scientific American,* September, 119–126.

Keyfitz, Nathan, and Wilhelm Finger. 1991. *World Population Growth and Aging: Demographic Trends in the Late 20th Century.* Chicago: University of Chicago Press.

Lamm, Richard D., and Gary Imhoff. 1985. *The Immigration Time Bomb.* New York: E. P. Dutton.

Loup, Jacques. 1983. *Can the Third World Survive?* Baltimore: Johns Hopkins University Press.

McFalls, Joseph A., Jr. 1991. "Population: A Lively Introduction." *Population Bulletin,* vol. 46, no. 2, 1–43.

Menken, Jane, ed. 1986. *World Population and U.S. Policy: The Choices Ahead.* New York: W. W. Norton.

Merrick, Thomas W. 1986. "World Population in Transition." *Population Bulletin,* vol. 41, no. 2, 1–51.

Merrick, Thomas W., and Stephen J. Tordella. 1988. "Demographics: People and Markets." *Population Bulletin,* vol. 43, no. 1, 1–46.

Morgan, Robin. 1984. *Sisterhood Is Global.* New York: Doubleday.

Nafis, Sadik, ed. 1991. *Population Policies and Programmes: Lessons Learned from Two Decades of Experience.* New York: United Nations Population Fund.

National Academy of Sciences. 1990. *Developing New Contraceptives: Obstacles and Opportunities.* Washington, D.C.: National Academy Press.

Olshansky, S. Jay, et al. 1993. "The Aging of the Human Species." *Scientific American,* April, 46–52.

Peters, Gary L., and Robert P. Larkin. 1989. *Population Geography.* 3rd ed. Dubuque, Iowa: Kendall/Hunt.

Population Reference Bureau. Annual. *World Population Data Sheet.* Washington, D.C.: Population Reference Bureau.

Population Reference Bureau. 1986. *Women in the World: The Women's Decade and Beyond.* Washington, D.C.: Population Reference Bureau.

Population Reference Bureau. 1990. *World Population: Fundamentals of Growth.* Washington, D.C.: Population Reference Bureau.

Russell, Cheryl. 1987. *100 Predictions for the Baby Boom: The Next 50 Years.* New York: Plenum.

Saunders, John, 1988. *Basic Demographic Measures: A Practical Guide for Users.* Lanham, Md.: University Press of America.

Simon, Julian L. 1989. *Population Matters: People, Resources, Environment, and Immigration.* New Brunswick, N.J.: Transaction.

Simon, Julian L. 1990. *The Economic Consequences of Immigration.* Cambridge, Mass.: Basil Blackwell.

Soldo, Beth J., and Emily M. Agree. 1988. "America's Elderly." *Population Bulletin,* vol. 43, no. 3, 1–51.

Teitelbaum, Michael, and Jay M. Winter. 1985. *The Fear of Population Decline.* San Diego: Academic Press.

Tien, H. Yuan, et al. 1992. "China's Demographic Dilemmas." *Population Bulletin,* vol. 47, no. 1, 1–44.

United Nations. 1991. *Consequences of Rapid Population Growth in Developing Countries.* New York: United Nations.

United Nations. 1992. *Long-Range World Population Projections: Two Centuries of Population Growth, 1950–2150.* New York: United Nations.

Wattenberg, Ben J. 1987. *The Birth Dearth.* New York: Pharos Books.

Weber, Susan, ed. 1988. *USA by Numbers: A Statistical Portrait of the United States.* Washington, D.C.: Zero Population Growth.

Weeks, John R. 1992. *Population: An Introduction to Concepts and Issues.* 5th ed. Belmont, Calif.: Wadsworth.

Zero Population Growth. 1990. *Planning the Ideal Family: The Small Family Option.* Washington, D.C.: Zero Population Growth.

## 9 POPULATION DISTRIBUTION: URBAN LIVING

American Public Transit System. 1989. *Mass Transit—The Clean Air Alternative.* Washington, D.C.: American Public Transit Association.

Beewer, William E., and Charles P. Alter. 1988. *The Complete Manual of Land Planning and Development.* New York: Prentice-Hall.

Berg, Peter, et al. 1989. *A Green City Program for San Francisco Bay Area Cities and Towns.* San Francisco: Planet/Drum Foundation.

Bookchin, Murray. 1986. *The Limits of City.* New York: Black Rose.

Brenneman, Russell L., and Sarah M. Bates, eds. 1984. *Land-Saving Action.* Covelo, Calif.: Island Press.

Brown, Lester R., and Jodi Jacobson. 1987. *The Future of Urbanization: Facing the Ecological and Economic Restraints.* Washington, D.C.: Worldwatch Institute.

Cadman, D., and G. R. Payne, eds. 1990. *The Living City: Towards a Sustainable Future.* London: Routledge.

Canfield, Christopher, ed. 1990. *Ecocity Conference.* Berkeley, Calif.: Urban Ecology.

Cassidy, Robert. 1980. *Livable Cities: A Grass-Roots Guide to Rebuilding Urban America.* New York: Holt, Rinehart & Winston.

Choate, Pat, and Susan Walter. 1981. *America in Ruins: Beyond the Public Works Pork Barrel.* Washington, D.C.: Council on State Planning Agencies.

Coates, Gary. 1981. *Resettling America: Energy, Ecology, and Community.* Andover, Mass.: Brick House.

Corbett, Michael. 1990. *A Better Place to Live.* Davis, Calif.: agAccess.

Dantzig, George B., and Thomas L. Saaty. 1973. *Compact City: A Plan for a Livable Environment.* New York: W. H. Freeman.

Fabos, Julius Gy. 1985. *Land-Use Planning: From Global to Local Challenge.* New York: Chapman & Hall.

Farallones Institute. 1979. *The Integral Urban House: Self-Reliant Living in the City.* San Francisco: Sierra Club Books.

Frey, William H. 1990. "Metropolitan America: Beyond the Transition." *Population Bulletin,* vol. 45, no. 2, 1–49.

Garreau, Joel. 1992. *Edge City: Life on the New Frontier.* New York: Doubleday.

Gordon, Deborah. 1991. *Steering a New Course: Transportation, Energy, and the Environment.* Covelo, Calif.: Island Press.

Gottman, Jean, and Robert A. Harper, eds. 1990. *Since Megalopolis: The Urban Writings of Jean Gottman.* Baltimore: Johns Hopkins University Press.

Gratz, Roberta B. 1989. *The Living City.* New York: Simon & Schuster.

Hardoy, Jorge, and David Satterwaite. 1989. *Squatter Citizen: Life in the Third World.* East Haven, Conn.: Earthscan.

Hart, John. 1992. *Saving Cities, Saving Money: Environmental Strategies That Work.* Washington, D.C.: Resource Renewal Institute.

Heathcote, Willimas. 1991. *Autogeddon.* London: Jonathan Cape.

Herbes, J. 1986. *The New Heartlands: America's Flight Beyond the Suburbs.* New York: Time-Life Books.

Honachefsky, William B. 1992. *Land Planner's Environmental Handbook.* New York: Noyes.

Jacobs, Jane. 1984. *Cities and the Wealth of Nations.* New York: Random House.

Johnson, William C. 1989. *The Politics of Urban Planning.* New York: Paragon.

Kaplan, Marshall. 1989. *The Future of National Urban Policy.* Durham, N.C.: Duke University Press.

Kelbaugh, Doug, ed. 1989. *The Pedestrian Pocketbook: A New Suburban Design Strategy.* New York: Princeton Architectural Press.

Kemp, Roger L., ed. 1988. *America's Cities: Strategic Planning for the Future.* New York: Interstate Printers and Publishers.

Kozol, Jonathan. 1988. *Rachel and Her Children.* New York: Crown.

Kryter, Karl D. 1985. *The Effects of Noise.* 2nd ed. New York: Academic Press.

Leckie, Jim, et al. 1975. *Other Homes and Garbage: Designs for Self-Sufficient Living.* San Francisco: Sierra Club Books.

Lowe, Marcia D. 1989. *The Bicycle: Vehicle for a Small Planet.* Washington, D.C.: Worldwatch Institute.

Lowe, Marcia D. 1990. *Alternatives to the Automobile: Transport for Living Cities.* Washington, D.C.: Worldwatch Institute.

Lowe, Marcia D. 1991. *Shaping Cities: The Environmental and Human Dimensions.* Washington, D.C.: Worldwatch Institute.

Lowe, Marcia D. 1993. "Rediscovering Rail." In Lester R. Brown et al., *State of the World 1993,* 120–138. New York: W. W. Norton.

Luten, Daniel B. 1986. *Progress Against Growth.* New York: Guilford Press.

Mackenzie, Dorothy. 1991. *Design for Environment.* New York: Rizzoli International.

MacKenzie, James J., et al. 1992. *The Going Rate: What It Really Costs to Drive.* Washington, D.C.: World Resources Institute.

Makower, Joel. 1992. *The Green Commuter.* Washington, D.C.: National Press.

Mantrell, Michael L., et al. 1989. *Creating Successful Communities: A Guidebook to Growth Management Strategies.* Covelo, Calif.: Island Press.

Marcus, Clare C., and Wendy Sarkissian. 1986. *Housing As If People Mattered.* Berkeley and Los Angeles: University of California Press.

May, Richard, Jr., ed. 1989. *The Urbanization Revolution: Planning a New Agenda for Human Settlements.* New York: Plenum.

McHarg, Ian L. 1969. *Design with Nature.* Garden City, N.Y.: Natural History Press.

Morehouse, Ward, ed. 1989. *Building Sustainable Communities.* New York: Bootstrap Press.

Morris, David. 1982. *Energy and the Transformation of Urban America.* San Francisco: Sierra Club Books.

Mumford, Lewis. 1968. *The Urban Prospect.* New York: Harcourt Brace Jovanovich.

Nadis, Steve, and James J. MacKenzie. 1993. *Car Trouble.* Boston: Beacon Press.

Register, Richard. 1992. *Ecocities.* Berkeley, Calif.: North Atlantic Books.

Renner, Michael. 1988. *Rethinking the Role of the Automobile.* Washington, D.C.: Worldwatch Institute.

Replogle, Michael L. 1988. *Bicycles and Public Transportation: New Links to Suburban Transit.* 2nd ed. Washington, D.C.: The Bicycle Federation.

Ryn, Sin van der, and Peter Calthorpe. 1986. *Sustainable Communities: A New Design Synthesis for Cities, Suburbs, and Towns.* San Francisco: Sierra Club Books.

Sargent, Frederic O., et al. 1991. *Rural Environmental Planning for Sustainable Communities.* Covelo, Calif.: Island Press.

Spirn, Anne Whiston. 1984. *The Granite Garden: Urban Nature and Urban Design.* New York: Basic Books.

Stokes, Samuel N., et al. 1989. *Saving America's Countryside: A Guide to Rural Conservation.* Baltimore: Johns Hopkins University Press.

Stren, Richard, et al., eds. 1991. *Sustainable Cities: Urbanization and the Environment in International Perspective.* Boulder, Colo.: Westview Press.

Thornton, Richard D. 1991. "Why the U.S. Needs a MAGLEV System." *Technology Review,* April, 31–42.

Todd, John, and Nancy Jack Todd. 1993. *From Ecocities to Living Machines: Precepts for Sustainable Technology.* Berkeley, Calif.: North Atlantic Books.

Todd, John, and George Tukel. 1990. *Reinhabiting Cities and Towns: Designing for Sustainability.* San Francisco: Planet/Drum Foundation.

Todd, Nancy Jack, and John Todd. 1984. *Bioshelters, Ocean Arks, City Farming: Ecology as the Basis of Design.* San Francisco: Sierra Club Books.

Tolley, Rodney, ed. 1991. *The Greening of Urban Transport: Planning for Walking and Cycling in Western Cities.* New York: Pinter.

United Nations Population Division. 1991. *World Urbanization Prospects.* New York: United Nations.

Vranich, Joseph. 1991. *Supertrains: Solutions to America's Transportation Gridlock.* New York: St. Martin's Press.

Wachs, Martin. 1989. "U.S. Transit Subsidy Policy: In Need of Reform." *Science,* vol. 244, 1545–1549.

Walter, Bob, et al., eds. 1992. *Sustainable Cities: Concepts and Strategies for Eco-City Development.* Los Angeles: Eco-Home Media.

Westman, Walter E. 1985. *Ecology, Impact Assessment and Environmental Planning.* New York: John Wiley.

Whyte, William. 1988. *City: Discovering the Center.* New York: Doubleday.

Yang, Linda. 1990. *The City Gardener's Handbook.* New York: Random House.

Zuckerman, Wolfgang. 1991. *End of the Road: The World Car Crisis and How We Can Solve It.* Post Mills, Vt.: Chelsea Green.

## 10 DEFORESTATION AND LOSS OF BIODIVERSITY

Anderson, Anthony B., et al., eds. 1990. *Alternatives to Deforestation: Steps Toward Sustainable Use of the Amazon Rain Forest.* Irvington, N.Y.: Columbia University Press.

Anderson, Anthony B., et al. 1991. *The Subsidy from Nature: Palm Forests, Peasantry, and Development on the Amazon Frontier.* New York: Columbia University Press.

Anderson, Patrick. 1989. "The Myth of Sustainable Logging: The Case for a Ban on Tropical Timber Imports." *The Ecologist,* vol. 19, no. 5, 166–168.

Barber, Charles V., et al. 1993. *Breaking the Deadlock: Obstacles to Forest Reform in Indonesia and the United States.* Washington, D.C.: World Resources Institute.

Booth, Douglas E. 1992. "The Economics and Ethics of Old-Growth Forests." *Environmental Ethics,* Spring, 43–62.

Browder, John O. 1992. "The Limits of Extractivism." *BioScience,* vol. 42, no. 3, 174–182.

Burger, Julina. 1990. *The Gaia Atlas of First Peoples.* New York: Anchor Books.

Caufield, Catherine. 1985. *In the Rainforest.* New York: Alfred A. Knopf.

Chagnon, Napoleon A. 1992. *Yanomano: The Last Days of Eden.* New York: Harcourt Brace Jovanovich.

Clay, Jason W. 1988. *Indigenous Peoples and Tropical Forests.* Cambridge, Mass.: Cultural Survival.

Cockburn, Alexander, and Susanna Hecht. 1990. *The Fate of the Forest: Developers, Destroyers, and Defenders of the Amazon.* New York: HarperCollins.

Colchester, Marcus. 1990. "The International Tropical Timber Organization: Kill or Cure for the Rainforests." *The Ecologist,* vol. 20, no. 5, 166–181.

Collins, Mark, ed. 1990. *The Last Rainforests: A World Conservation Atlas.* Emmaus, Pa.: Rodale Press.

Connelly, Joel. 1991. "Big Cut: British Columbia's Lumber Lords Suffer Few Checks on Their Enterprise." *Sierra,* May/June, 42–53.

Cowell, Adrian. 1990. *The Decade of Destruction: The Crusade to Save the Amazon Rain Forest.* New York: Henry Holt.

Denslow, Julie S., and Christine Padoch, eds. 1988. *People of the Tropical Rain Forest.* Berkeley and Los Angeles: University of California Press.

Dietrich, William. 1992. *The Final Forest.* New York: Simon & Schuster.

Durning, Alan Thein. 1992. *Guardians of the Land: Indigenous Peoples and the Health of the Earth.* Washington, D.C.: Worldwatch Institute.

Eckholm, Erik, et al. 1984. *Fuelwood: The Energy Crisis That Won't Go Away.* East Haven, Conn.: Earthscan.

Ellis, Gerry, and Karen Kane. 1991. *America's Rainforest.* Minocqua, Wis.: North-World Press.

Ervin, Keith. 1989. *Fragile Majesty: The Battle for North America's Last Great Forest.* Seattle: The Mountaineers.

Friends of the Earth. 1992. *The Rainforest Harvest: Sustainable Strategies for Saving Tropical Forests.* Washington, D.C.: Friends of the Earth.

Friends of the Trees. 1988. *Green Front Report*. Chelan, Wash.: Friends of the Trees.

Gomez-Pumpa, A. 1990. *Rain Forest Regeneration and Management*. New York: Parthenon.

Goodland, Robert, ed. 1990. *Race to Save the Tropics: Ecology and Economics for a Sustainable Future*. Covelo, Calif.: Island Press.

Gradwohl, Judith, and Russell Greenberg. 1988. *Saving the Tropical Forests*. Covelo, Calif.: Island Press.

Head, Suzanne, and Robert Heinzman. 1990. *Lessons of the Rainforest*. San Francisco: Sierra Club Books.

Hecht, Susanna, and Alexander Cockburn. 1989. *The Fate of the Forest: Developers, Destroyers, and Defenders of the Amazon*. New York: Verso (Routledge, Chapman & Hall).

International Union for Conservation of Nature and Natural Resources (IUCN). 1992. *Tropical Deforestation and the Extinction of Species*. Gland, Switzerland: IUCN.

Jacobs, Marius. 1988. *The Tropical Rain Forest: A First Encounter*. New York: Springer-Verlag.

Johnson, Nels, and Brice Cabarle. 1993. *Looking Ahead: Sustainable Natural Forest Management in the Humid Tropics*. Washington, D.C.: World Resources Institute.

Jolly, Alison, and Frans Lanting. 1990. *Madagascar: A World Out of Time*. New York: Aperture.

Kelly, David, and Gary Braasch. 1988. *Secrets of the Old Growth Forest*. Salt Lake City: Peregrine Smith.

Living Earth Foundation. 1990. *The Rainforests: A Celebration*. San Francisco: Chronicle Books.

Mahony, Rhona. 1992. "Debt-for-Nature Swaps: Who Really Benefits?" *The Ecologist*, vol. 22, no. 3, 97–103.

Margolis, Marc. 1992. *The Last New World: The Conquest of the Amazon Frontier*. New York: W. W. Norton.

Maser, Chris. 1988. *The Redesigned Forest*. San Pedro, Calif.: R. & E. Miles.

Maser, Chris. 1989. *Forest Primeval*. San Francisco: Sierra Club Books.

Maybury-Lewis, David. 1992. *Millenium: Tribal Wisdom and the Modern World*. New York: Viking Press.

Miller, Kenton, and Laura Tangley. 1991. *Trees of Life: Protecting Tropical Forests and Their Biological Wealth*. Boston: Beacon Press.

Morgan, F., and J. R. Vincent. 1987. *Natural Management of Tropical Moist Forests: Silvicultural and Management Prospects of Sustained Utilization*. New Haven, Conn.: Yale School of Forestry.

Myers, Norman. 1984. *The Primary Source: Tropical Forests and Our Future*. New York: W. W. Norton.

Myers, Norman. 1989. *Deforestation Rates in Tropical Forests and Their Climatic Implications*. London: Friends of the Earth.

Newman, Arnold. 1990. *The Tropical Rainforest: A World Survey of Our Most Valuable Endangered Habitats*. New York: Facts on File.

Nichol, John. 1990. *The Mighty Rainforest*. London: David & Charles.

Norse, Elliot A. 1990. *Ancient Forests of the Pacific Northwest*. Covelo, Calif.: Island Press.

Office of Technology Assessment. 1992. *Combined Summaries: Technologies to Sustain Tropical Forest Resources and Biological Diversity*. Washington, D.C.: Office of Technology Assessment.

Onis, Juan de. 1992. *The Green Cathedral: Sustainable Development of Amazonia*. New York: Oxford University Press.

Orians, Gordon. 1990. "Ecological Concepts of Sustainability." *Environment*, vol. 32, no. 9, 10–15, 34–39.

Panayotou, Theodore, and Peter S. Ashton. 1992. *Not by Timber Alone: Economics and Ecology for Sustaining Tropical Forests*. Covelo, Calif.: Island Press.

Patterson, Alan. 1990. "Debt for Nature Swaps and the Need for Alternatives." *Environment*, vol. 32, no. 10, 5–13, 31–32.

Postel, Sandra, and Lori Heise. 1988. *Reforesting the Earth*. Washington, D.C.: Worldwatch Institute.

Reid, Walter V. C., and Kenton R. Miller. 1989. *Keeping Options Alive: The Scientific Basis for Conserving Biodiversity*. Washington, D.C.: World Resources Institute.

Reiss, Bob. 1992. *The Road to Extrema*. New York: Summit Books.

Repetto, Robert. 1990. "Deforestation in the Tropics." *Scientific American*, vol. 262, no. 4, 36–42.

Revkin, Andrew. 1990. *The Burning Season: The Murder of Chico Mendes and the Fight for the Amazon*. Boston: Houghton Mifflin.

Rice, R. E. 1990. "Old-Growth Logging Myths." *The Ecologist*, vol. 20, no. 4, 141–146.

Roselle, Mike, and Tracy Katelman. 1989. *Tropical Hardwoods: A Report*. San Francisco: Rainforest Action Network.

Rush, James. 1991. *The Last Tree: Reclaiming the Environment in Tropical Asia*. Boulder, Colo.: Westview Press.

Ryan, John C. 1991. "Goods from the Woods." *World Watch*, July/August, 19–26.

Ryan, John C. 1992. *Life Support: Conserving Biological Diversity*. Washington, D.C.: Worldwatch Institute.

Shoumatoff, Alex. 1990. *The World of Burning: The Tragedy of Chico Mendes*. Boston: Little, Brown.

Teitel, Martin. 1992. *Rain Forest in Your Kitchen: The Hidden Connection Between Extinction and Your Supermarket*. Covelo, Calif.: Island Press.

Terborgh, John. 1992. *Diversity and the Tropical Rain Forest*. New York: Scientific American Library.

Tree People. 1990. *The Simple Act of Planting a Tree*. Los Angeles: Jeremy Tarcher.

Trexler, Mark C., and Christine Rogers. 1993. *Keeping It Green: Using Tropical Forestry to Mitigate Global Warming*. Washington, D.C.: World Resources Institute.

Wellner, Pamela, and Eugene Dickey. 1991. *The Wood User's Guide*. San Francisco: Rainforest Action Network.

Wilderness Society. 1988. *Ancient Forests: A Threatened Heritage*. Washington, D.C.: Wilderness Society.

Wilderness Society. 1989. *Old Growth in the Pacific Northwest: A Status Report*. Washington, D.C.: Wilderness Society.

Wilson, E. O., ed. 1988. *Biodiversity*. Washington, D.C.: National Academy Press.

Wilson, E. O. 1992. *The Diversity of Life*. Cambridge, Mass.: Harvard University Press.

Winterbottom, Robert. 1990. *Taking Stock: The Tropical Forestry Action Plan Five Years Later*. Washington, D.C.: World Resources Institute.

World Bank. 1988. *Madagascar Environmental Action Plan*. Washington, D.C.: World Bank.

World Resources Institute (WRI), International Union for Conservation of Nature (IUCN), and United Nations Development Programme. 1992. *Global Biodiversity Strategy*. Washington, D.C.: World Resources Institute.

World Resources Institute, World Bank, and United Nations Development Programme. 1985. *Tropical Forests: A Call for Action*. Washington, D.C.: World Resources Institute.

Zuckerman, Seth. 1991. *Saving Our Ancient Forests*. Federalsburg, Md.: Living Planet Press.

## 11 GLOBAL WARMING AND OZONE LOSS: APOCALYPSE SOON?

American Forestry Association. 1993. *Forests and Global Warming*. Vol. 1. Washington, D.C.: American Forestry Association.

Ausubel, Jesse H. 1991. "A Second Look at the Impacts of Climate Change." *American Scientist*, Vol. 79, 210–221.

Balling, Robert C., Jr. 1992. *The Heated Debate: Greenhouse Predictions Versus Climate Reality*. San Francisco: Pacific Research Institute for Public Policy.

Bates, Albert K. 1990. *Climate in Crisis: The Greenhouse Effect and What We Can Do*. Summertown, Tenn.: Book.

Benedick, Richard Eliot. 1991. *Ozone Diplomacy: New Directions in Safeguarding the Planet*. Cambridge, Mass.: Harvard University Press.

Broome, John. 1992. *Counting the Cost of Global Warming*. Isle of Harris, United Kingdom: White Horse Press.

California Energy Commission. 1989. *The Impacts of Global Warming on California*. Sacramento: California Energy Commission.

Cogan, Douglas G. 1988. *Stones in a Glass House: CFCs and Ozone Depletion*. Washington, D.C.: Investor Responsibility Research Center.

Cogan, Douglas. 1992. *The Greenhouse Gambit: Business and Investment Responses to Climate Change*. Washington, D.C.: Investor Responsibility Research Center.

Council for Agricultural Science and Technology. 1992. *Preparing U.S. Agriculture for Global Climate Change*. Ames, Iowa: Council for Agricultural Science and Technology.

Department of Energy Multi-Laboratory Climate Change Committee. 1990. *Energy and Climate Change*. Boca Raton, Fla.: Lewis.

Dornbusch, Rudiger, and James M. Poterba. 1991. *Global Warming: Economic Policy Responses*. Cambridge, Mass.: MIT Press.

Dotto, Lydia. 1990. *Thinking the Unthinkable: Civilization and Rapid Climate Change*. Waterloo, Ontario: Wilfrid Lanier University Press.

Dudek, Daniel J. 1988. *Offsetting New CO₂ Emissions*. New York: Environmental Defense Fund.

Edgerton, Lynne T. 1990. *The Rising Tide: Global Warming and World Sea Levels*. Covelo, Calif.: Island Press.

Environmental Defense Fund. 1988. *Protecting the Ozone Layer: What You Can Do*. New York: Environmental Defense Fund.

Environmental Protection Agency. 1988. *The Potential Effects of Global Climate Change on the United States*. Washington, D.C.: EPA.

Environmental Protection Agency. 1989. *Policy Options for Stabilizing Global Climate*. Washington, D.C.: EPA.

Erikson, Jon. 1990. *Greenhouse Earth: Tomorrow's Disaster Today*. New York: TAB Books.

Fisher, David E. 1990. *Fire and Ice: The Greenhouse Effect, Ozone Depletion, and Nuclear Winter*. San Francisco: Harper & Row.

Fishman, Albert, and Robert Kalish. 1990. *Global Alert: The Ozone Pollution Crisis*. New York: Plenum.

Flavin, Christopher. 1989. *Slowing Global Warming: A Worldwide Strategy*. Washington, D.C.: Worldwatch Institute.

Gates, David M. 1993. *Climate Change and Its Biological Consequences*. Sunderland, Mass.: Sinauer.

Gordon, Anita, and David Suzuki. 1991. *It's a Matter of Survival*. Cambridge, Mass.: Harvard University Press.

Graedel, T. C., and Paul J. Cutzen. 1992. *Atmospheric Change*. New York: W. H. Freeman.

Graham, Robert L., et al. 1990. "How Increasing CO₂ and Climate Change Affect Forests." *BioScience*, vol. 40, no. 8, 575–586.

Greenhouse Crisis Foundation. 1990. *The Greenhouse Crisis: 101 Ways to Save the Earth*. Washington, D.C.: Greenhouse Crisis Foundation.

Gribbin, John. 1990. *Hothouse Earth: The Greenhouse Effect and Gaia*. London: Grove Weidenfeld.

Hammond, Allen L., et al. 1991. "Calculating National Accountability for Climate Change." *Environment*, vol. 33, no. 1, 11–15, 33–34.

Hileman, Bette. 1992. "Web of Interactions Makes It Difficult to Untangle Global Warming Data." *Chemistry & Engineering News*, April 27, 7–19.

Houghton, Richard A., and George M. Woodwell. 1989. "Global Climatic Change." *Scientific American*, vol. 260, no. 4, 36–44.

Idso, Sherwood B. 1989. *Carbon Dioxide and Global Change: Earth in Transition*. Tempe, Ariz.: Institute for Biospheric Research.

Ince, Martin. 1990. *The Rising Seas*. East Haven, Conn.: Earthscan.

Intergovernmental Panel on Climate Change (IPCC). 1990. *Climate Change: The IPCC Assessment*. New York: Cambridge University Press.

Intergovernmental Panel on Climate Change (IPCC). 1992. *The Supplementary Report to the IPCC Scientific Assessment*. New York: Cambridge University Press.

Jones, Philip D., and Tom M. L. Wiglet. 1990. "Global Warming Trends." *Scientific American*, August, 84–91.

Karplus, Walter J. 1992. *The Heavens Are Falling: The Scientific Prediction of Catastrophes in Our Time*. New York: Plenum.

Kimball, Norman J., et al. 1990. *Impact of Carbon Dioxide, Trace Gases, and Climate Change on Global Agriculture*. Madison, Wis.: Soil Science Society of America.

Krause, Florentin, et al. 1992. *Energy Policy in the Greenhouse*. New York: John Wiley.

Lamb, H. H. 1982. *Climate, History, and the Modern World*. New York: Methuen.

Leggett, Jeremy, ed. 1990. *Global Warming: The Greenpeace Report*. New York: Oxford University Press.

Levenson, Thomas. 1990. *Ice Time: Climate, Science, and Life on Earth*. San Francisco: Harper & Row.

Lovins, Amory B., et al. 1989. *Least-Cost Energy: Solving the CO₂ Problem*. 2nd ed. Andover, Mass.: Brick House.

Lyman, Francesca, et al. 1990. *The Greenhouse Trap: What We're Doing to the Atmosphere and How We Can Slow Global Warming*. Washington, D.C.: World Resources Institute.

Makhijani, Arjun, et al. 1992. *Saving Our Skins: The Causes and Consequences of Ozone Layer Depletion and Policies for Its Restoration and Protection*. Takoma Park, Md.: Institute for Energy and Environmental Research.

Manne, Alan S., and Richard G. Richels. 1992. *Buying Greenhouse Insurance: The Economic Costs of $CO_2$ Emission Limits*. Cambridge, Mass.: MIT Press.

Mathews, Jessica Tuchman, ed. 1991. *Greenhouse Warming: Negotiating a Global Regime*. Washington, D.C.: World Resources Institute.

McKibben, Bill. 1989. *The End of Nature*. New York: Random House.

Mintzer, Irving, and William R. Moomaw. 1991. *Escaping the Heat Trap: Probing the Prospects for a Stable Environment*. Washington, D.C.: World Resources Institute.

Mintzer, Irving, et al. 1990. *Protecting the Ozone Shield: Strategies for Phasing Out CFCs During the 1990s*. Washington, D.C.: World Resources Institute.

National Academy of Sciences. 1989. *Global Environmental Change*. Washington, D.C.: National Academy Press.

National Academy of Sciences. 1989. *Ozone Depletion, Greenhouse Gases, and Climate Change*. Washington, D.C.: National Academy Press.

National Academy of Sciences. 1990. *Confronting Climate Change*. Washington, D.C.: National Academy Press.

National Academy of Sciences. 1990. *Sea Level Change*. Washington, D.C.: National Academy Press.

National Academy of Sciences. 1991. *Policy Implications of Greenhouse Warming*. Washington, D.C.: National Academy Press.

National Academy of Sciences. 1992. *Global Environmental Change*. Washington, D.C.: National Academy Press.

National Audubon Society. 1990. *$CO_2$ Diet for a Greenhouse Planet: A Citizen's Guide to Slowing Global Warming*. New York: National Audubon Society.

Nilsson, Annika. 1992. *Greenhouse Earth*. New York: John Wiley.

Office of Technology Assessment. 1991. *Changing by Degrees: Steps to Reduce Greenhouse Gases*. Washington, D.C.: Government Printing Office.

Oppenheimer, Michael, and Robert H. Boyle. 1990. *Dead Heat: The Race Against the Greenhouse Effect*. New York: Basic Books.

Parry, Martin. 1990. *Climate Change and World Agriculture*. London: Earthscan.

Peters, Robert L., and Thomas E. Lovejoy. 1992. *Global Warming and Biological Diversity*. New Haven, Conn.: Yale University Press.

Public Citizen. 1989. *Turning Down the Heat: Solutions to Global Warming*. Washington, D.C.: Public Citizen.

Ray, Dixie Lee, and Lou Guzzo. 1990. *Trashing the Planet: How Science Can Help Us Deal with Acid Rain, Depletion of the Ozone, and Nuclear War (Among Other Things)*. Washington, D.C.: Regnery Gateway.

Reid, Walter V. C., and Mark C. Trexler. 1991. *Drowning the National Heritage: Climate Change and Coastal Biodiversity in the United States*. Washington, D.C.: World Resources Institute.

Revkin, Andrew. 1992. *Global Warming: Understanding the Forecast*. New York: Abbeville Press.

Roan, Sharon L. 1989. *Ozone Crisis: The 15-Year Evolution of a Sudden Global Emergency*. New York: John Wiley.

Rose, Chris, and Phil Hurst. 1992. *Can Nature Survive Global Warming?* Gland, Switzerland: World Wide Fund for Nature.

Rosenberg, Norman J., et al., eds. 1989. *Greenhouse Warming: Abatement and Adaptation*. Washington, D.C.: Resources for the Future.

Rowland, F. Sherwood. 1989. "Chlorofluorocarbons and the Depletion of Stratospheric Ozone." *American Scientist*, vol. 77, 36–45.

Rubin, et al. 1992. "Realistic Mitigation Options for Global Warming." *Science*, vol. 257, 148–149, 261–266.

Schneider, Stephen H. 1987. "Climate Modeling." *Scientific American*, vol. 256, no. 5, 72–80.

Schneider, Stephen H. 1989. *Global Warming: Are We Entering the Greenhouse Century?* New York: Random House.

Schneider, Stephen H., and R. S. Londer. 1984. *The Coevolution of Climate and Life*. San Francisco: Sierra Club Books.

Schotterer, Ulrich, and Peter Andermatt. 1992. *Climate— Our Future?* Duluth: University of Minnesota Press.

Shea, Cynthia Pollack. 1988. *Protecting Life on Earth: Steps to Save the Ozone Layer*. Washington, D.C.: Worldwatch Institute.

Trexler, Mark C. 1991. *Keeping It Green: Tropical Forestry and the Mitigation of Global Warming*. Washington, D.C.: World Resources Institute.

Trexler, Mark C. 1991. *Minding the Carbon Store: Weighing U.S. Forestry Strategies to Slow Global Warming*. Washington, D.C.: World Resources Institute.

U.S. Public Interest Group. 1989. *Du Pont Fiddles While the World Burns—Industry Inaction on Ozone Depletion*. Washington, D.C.: U.S. Public Interest Research Group.

Waggoner, Paul E., ed. 1990. *Climate Change and U.S. Water Resources*. New York: John Wiley.

Weiner, Jonathan. 1990. *The Next One Hundred Years: Shaping the Fate of Our Living Earth*. New York: Bantam Books.

White, Robert M. 1990. "The Great Climate Debate." *Scientific American*, July, 36–43.

Young, Louise B. 1990. *Sowing the Wind: Reflections on Earth's Atmosphere*. Englewood Cliffs, N.J.: Prentice-Hall.

## 12 SOIL RESOURCES

Ahmed, Y. J., and M. Kassas. 1987. *Desertification: Financial Support for the Biosphere*. London: Hodder & Stoughton.

Brady, Nyle C. 1989. *The Nature and Properties of Soils*. 10th ed. New York: Macmillan.

Brown, Lester R., and Edward C. Wolf. 1984. *Soil Erosion: Quiet Crisis in the World Economy*. Washington, D.C.: Worldwatch Institute.

Campbell, Stu. 1990. *Let It Rot: The Gardener's Guide to Composting*. Pownal, Vt.: Storey Communications.

Courtney, F. M., and S. T. Trudgill. 1984. *Soil: An Introduction to Soil Study*. 2nd ed. Baltimore: E. Arnold.

Donahue, Roy, et al. 1990. *Soils and Their Management*. 5th ed. Petaluma, Calif.: Inter Print.

Dregnue, Harold E. 1983. *Desertification of Arid Lands*. San Diego: Academic Press.

Dregnue, Harold E. 1985. "Aridity and Land Degradation." *Environment*, vol. 27, no. 8, 33–39.

Gorse, Jean E., and David R. Steeds. 1987. *Desertification in the Sahelian and Sudanian Zones of West Africa*. Washington, D.C.: World Bank.

Grainger, Alan. 1990. *The Threatening Desert: Controlling Desertification*. East Haven, Conn.: Earthscan.

Harpstead, Milo I., et al. 1988. *Soil Science Simplified*. 2nd ed. Ames: Iowa State University Press.

Hillel, Daniel. 1992. *Out of the Earth: Civilization and the Life of the Soil*. New York: Free Press.

Hudson, Norman. 1985. *Soil Conservation*. 2nd ed. Ithaca, N.Y.: Cornell University Press.

Lal, Rattan. 1990. *Soil Erosion in the Tropics: Principles and Management*. New York: McGraw-Hill.

Little, Charles E. 1987. *Green Fields Forever: The Conservation Tillage Revolution in America*. Covelo, Calif.: Island Press.

Mainguet, Monique. 1991. *Desertification: Natural Background and Human Mismanagement*. New York: Springer-Verlag.

Martin, Deb. 1991. *Rodale Guide to Composting*. Emmaus, Pa.: Rodale Press.

Mollison, Bill. 1990. *Permaculture*. Covelo, Calif.: Island Press.

Morgan, R. P. 1986. *Soil Erosion and Its Control*. New York: Van Nostrand Reinhold.

National Academy of Sciences. 1986. *Soil Conservation*. 2 vols. Washington, D.C.: National Academy Press.

Nelson, Ridley. 1988. *Dryland Management: The Desertification Problem*. Washington, D.C.: World Bank.

Paddock, Joe, et al. 1987. *Soil and Survival: Land Stewardship and the Future of American Agriculture*. San Francisco: Sierra Club Books.

Sheridan, David. 1981. *Desertification of the United States*. Washington, D.C.: Resources for the Future.

Sophen, C. D., and J. V. Baird. 1982. *Soils and Soil Management*. Reston, Va.: Reston.

Tompkins, Peter, and Christopher Bird. 1988. *Secrets of the Soil*. San Francisco: Harper & Row.

Wilson, G. F., et al. 1986. *The Soul of the Soil: A Guide to Ecological Soil Management*. 2nd ed. Montreal: Gaia Services.

World Bank. 1990. *Vetiver Grass: The Hedge Against Erosion*. Washington, D.C.: World Bank.

## 13 WATER RESOURCES

Allaby, Michael. 1992. *Water: Its Global Nature*. New York: Facts on File.

Anderson, T. L. 1986. *Water Rights: Scarce Resource Allocation, Bureaucracy, and the Environment*. San Francisco: Pacific Institute for Public Policy.

Ashworth, William. 1982. *Nor Any Drop to Drink*. New York: Summit Books.

Briscoe, John, and David de Ferrani. 1988. *Water for Rural Communities: Helping People Help Themselves*. Washington, D.C.: World Bank.

Clarke, Robin. 1993. *Water: The International Crisis*. Cambridge, Mass.: MIT Press.

Cousteau, Jacques-Yves, et al. 1981. *The Cousteau Almanac: An Inventory of Life on Our Water Planet*. New York: Doubleday.

Echeverria, John D., et al. 1990. *Rivers at Risk: The Concerned Citizen's Guide to Hydropower*. Covelo, Calif.: Island Press.

El-Ashry, Mohamed, and Diana C. Gibbons, eds. 1988. *Water and the Arid Lands of the Western United States*. New York: Cambridge University Press.

Ellefson, Connie, et al. 1992. *Xeriscape Gardening: Water Conservation for the American Landscape*. New York: Macmillan.

Falkenmark, Malin, and Carl Widstand. 1992. "Population and Water Resources: A Delicate Balance." *Population Bulletin*, vol. 47, no. 3, 1–36.

Feldman, David Lewis. 1991. *Water Resources Management: In Search of an Environmental Ethic*. Baltimore: Johns Hopkins University Press.

Franco, David A., and Robert G. Wetel. 1983. *To Quench Our Thirst: The Present and Future Status of Freshwater Resources of the United States*. Ann Arbor: University of Michigan Press.

Getches, David H., et al. 1991. *Controlling Water Use*. Washington, D.C.: Natural Resources Law Center.

Goldsmith, Edward, and Nicholas Hidyard, eds. 1986. *The Social and Environmental Effects of Large Dams*. 3 vols. New York: John Wiley.

Golfarb, William. 1988. *Water Law*. 2nd ed. Boca Raton, Fla.: Lewis.

Golubev, G. N., and A. K. Biswas. 1985. *Large Scale Water Transfers: Emerging Environmental and Social Experiences*. Oxford, England: Tycooly.

Gottlieb, Robert. 1989. *A Life of Its Own: The Politics and Power of Water*. New York: Harcourt Brace Jovanovich.

Hundley, Norris, Jr. 1992. *The Great Thirst: Californians and Water, 1770s–1990s*. Berkeley and Los Angeles: University of California Press.

Ingram, Helen. 1990. *Water Politics: Continuity and Change*. Albuquerque: University of New Mexico Press.

Ives, J. D., and B. Messeric. 1989. *The Himalayan Dilemma: Reconciling Development and Conservation*. London: Routledge.

Kotlyakov, V. M. 1991. "The Aral Sea Basin: A Critical Environmental Zone." *Environment*, vol. 33, no. 1, 4–9, 36–39.

Kourik, Robert. 1988. *Gray Water Use in the Landscape*. Santa Rosa, Calif.: Edible Publications.

Kourik, Robert. 1992. *Drip Irrigation*. Santa Rosa, Calif.: Edible Publications.

Leeden, Frits van der, et al., eds. 1990. *The Water Encyclopedia*. 2nd ed. Boca Raton, Fla.: Lewis.

Mather, J. R. 1984. *Water Resources Distribution, Use, and Management*. New York: John Wiley.

Matthiessen, Peter. 1992. *Baikal: Sacred Sea of Siberia*. San Francisco: Sierra Club Books.

McCutcheon, Sean. 1992. *Electric Rivers: The Story of the James River Project*. New York: Paul.

Meybeck, Michael, et al., eds. 1990. *Global Freshwater Quality*. Cambridge, Mass.: Basil Blackwell.

Mitchell, Bruce, ed. 1990. *Integrated Water Management*. New York: Belhaven Press.

Munasinghe, Mohan. 1992. *Water Supply and Environmental Management*. Boulder, Colo.: Westview Press.

Myers, Norman, ed. 1993. *Gaia: An Atlas of Planet Management*. New York: Anchor/Doubleday.

Naiman, Robert J., ed. 1992. *Watershed Management: Balancing Sustainability and Environmental Change.* New York: Springer-Verlag.

National Academy of Sciences. 1992. *Water Transfers in the West: Efficiency, Equity, and the Environment.* Washington, D.C.: National Academy Press.

Office of Technology Assessment. 1988. *Using Desalination Technologies for Water Treatment.* Washington, D.C.: Government Printing Office.

Okun, Daniel L. 1975. "Water Management in England: A Regional Model." *Environmental Science and Technology,* vol. 9, no. 10, 918–923.

Pearce, Fred. 1992. *The Dammed: Rivers, Dams, and the Coming World Water Crisis.* London: Bodley Head.

Pimentel, David, et al. 1982. "Water Resources in Food and Energy Production." *BioScience,* vol. 32, no. 11, 861–867.

Postel, Sandra. 1992. *The Last Oasis: Facing Water Scarcity.* New York: W. W. Norton.

Pringle, Laurence. 1982. *Water—The Next Great Resource Battle.* New York: Macmillan.

Reisner, Marc. 1986. *Cadillac Desert: The American West and Its Disappearing Water.* New York: Viking Press.

Reisner, Marc, and Sara Bates. 1990. *Overtapped Oasis: Reform or Revolution for Western Water.* Covelo, Calif.: Island Press.

Richardson, Boyce. 1991. *Strangers Devour the Land.* Post Mills, Vt.: Chelsea Green.

Rocky Mountain Institute. 1990. *Catalog of Water-Efficient Technologies for the Urban/Residential Sector.* Old Snowmass, Colo.: Rocky Mountain Institute.

Sloggett, Gordon, and Clifford Dickason. 1986. *Groundwater Mining in the United States.* Washington, D.C.: Government Printing Office.

Starr, Joyce R. 1991. "Water Wars." *Foreign Policy,* Spring, 12–45.

Waggoner, Paul E., ed. 1990. *Climate Change and U.S. Water Resources.* New York: John Wiley.

Waller, Roger M. 1988. *Ground Water and the Rural Homeowner.* Denver: U.S. Geological Survey.

Watson, Lyall. 1988. *The Water Planet.* New York: Crown.

Wijkman, Anders, and Lloyd Timberlake. 1984. *Natural Disasters: Acts of God or Acts of Man?* East Haven, Conn.: Earthscan.

Wilkinson, Charles F. 1992. *Crossing the Next Meridian: Land, Water, and the Future of the West.* Covelo, Calif.: Island Press.

Worster, Donald. 1985. *Rivers of Empire: Water, Aridity, and the Growth of the American West.* New York: Pantheon Books.

Zwingle, Erla. 1993. "Ogallala Aquifer: Wellspring of the High Plains." *National Geographic,* March, 80–107.

## 14 FOOD RESOURCES

Alexandratos, Nikos, ed. 1988. *World Agriculture: Toward 2000.* London: Belhaven Press.

Aliteri, Miguel A., and Susanna B. Hecht. 1990. *Agroecology and Small Farm Development.* New York: CRC Press.

Amato, Paul R., and Sonia A. Partridge. 1989. *The New Vegetarians: Promoting Health and Protecting Life.* New York: Plenum.

Bardach, John. 1988. "Aquaculture: Moving from Craft to Industry." *Environment,* vol. 30, no. 2, 7–40.

Bartholomew, Mel. 1987. *Square Foot Gardening.* Emmaus, Pa.: Rodale Press.

Bennett, Jon. 1987. *The Hunger Machine: The Politics of Food.* Cambridge, Mass.: Basil Blackwell.

Berry, Wendell. 1990. *Nature as Measure.* Berkeley, Calif.: North Point Press.

Berstein, Henry, et al., eds. 1990. *The Food Question: Profits Versus People.* East Haven, Conn.: Earthscan.

Bezdicek, D. F., ed. 1984. *Organic Farming: Current Technology and Its Role in a Sustainable Agriculture.* Washington, D.C.: American Society of Agronomy.

Brown, Larry. 1987. "Hunger in America." *Scientific American,* vol. 256, no. 2, 37–41.

Brown, Lester R. 1988. *The Changing World Food Prospect: The Nineties and Beyond.* Washington, D.C.: Worldwatch Institute.

Brown, Lester R., and John E. Young. 1990. "Feeding the World in the Nineties." In Lester Brown et al., *State of the World 1990,* 59–78. Washington, D.C.: Worldwatch Institute.

Carroll, C. Ronald, et al. 1990. *Agroecology.* New York: McGraw-Hill.

Clawson, David L. 1985. "Small-Scale Polyculture: An Alternative Development Model." *Philippines Geographical Journal,* vol. 29, nos. 3, 4, 1–12.

Cleveland, David A., and Daniela Soleri. 1991. *Food from Dryland Gardens: An Ecological, Nutritional, and Social Approach to Small-Scale Household Food Production.* San Francisco: Center for People, Food, and Environment.

Coleman, Elliot. 1992. *The New Organic Grower's Four-Season Harvest.* Post Mills, Vt.: Chelsea Green.

Crosson, Pierre R., and Norman J. Rosenberg. 1989. "Strategies for Agriculture." *Scientific American,* September, 128–135.

Curtis, Jennifer, et al. 1991. *Harvest of Hope: The Potential of Alternative Agriculture to Reduce Pesticide Use.* New York: Natural Resources Defense Council.

Dover, Michael J., and Lee M. Talbot. 1988. "Feeding the Earth: An Agroecological Solution." *Technology Review,* February/March, 27–35.

Doyle, Jack. 1985. *Altered Harvest: Agriculture, Genetics, and the Fate of the World's Food Supply.* New York: Viking Press.

Dunning, Alan B., and Holly W. Brough. 1991. *Taking Stock: Animal Farming and the Environment.* Washington, D.C.: Worldwatch Institute.

*The Ecologist.* 1991. Vol. 21, no. 2. Entire issue devoted to world hunger.

Editorial Research Reports. 1988. *How the U.S. Got into Agriculture and Why It Can't Get Out.* Washington, D.C.: Congressional Quarterly.

Editors of *Organic Gardening and Farming Magazine.* 1987. *The Encyclopedia of Organic Gardening.* Emmaus, Pa.: Rodale Press.

Edwards, Clive A., et al., eds. 1990. *Sustainable Agricultural Systems.* Ankeny, Iowa: Soil and Water Conservation Society.

Faeth, Paul, et al. 1993. *Agricultural Policy and Sustainability: Case Studies from India, Chile, the Philippines, and the United States.* Washington, D.C.: World Resources Institute.

Foster, Phillips. 1992. *The World Food Problem.* Boulder, Colo.: Lynne Rienner.

Fowler, Cary, and Pat Mooney. 1990. *Shattering: Food, Politics, and the Loss of Genetic Diversity.* Tucson: University of Arizona Press.

Francis, Charles A., and Richard Hardwood. 1985. *Enough Food: Achieving Food Security Through Regenerative Agriculture.* Emmaus, Pa.: Rodale Press.

Francis, Charles A., et al., eds. 1990. *Sustainable Agriculture in Temperate Zones.* New York: John Wiley.

Fukuoka, Masanobu. 1985. *The Natural Way of Farming: The Theory and Practice of Green Philosophy.* New York: Japan.

Gabel, Medard. 1986. *Empty Breadbasket: The Coming Challenge to America's Food Supply and What We Can Do About It.* Emmaus, Pa.: Rodale Press.

Gips, Terry. 1987. *Breaking the Pesticide Habit.* Minneapolis: IASA.

Goldsmith, Edward, and Nicholas Hildyard. 1991. "World Agriculture: Toward 2000: FAO's Plan to Feed the World." *The Ecologist,* vol. 21, no. 2, 8–92.

Gordon, R. Conway, and Edward R. Barbier. 1990. *After the Green Revolution: Sustainable Agriculture for Development.* East Haven, Conn.: Earthscan.

Granatstein, David. 1988. *Reshaping the Bottom Line: On-Farm Strategies for a Sustainable Agriculture.* Stillwater, Minn.: Land Stewardship Project.

Hamilton, Geoff. 1987. *The Complete Guide to Growing Flowers, Fruits, and Vegetables Naturally.* New York: Crown.

Harrison, Paul. 1987. *The Greening of Africa.* New York: Viking/Penguin.

Hellinger, Stephen, et al. 1988. *Aid for Just Development.* Boulder, Colo.: Lynne Rienner.

Hendry, Peter. 1988. "Food and Population: Beyond Five Billion." *Population Bulletin,* April, 1–55.

Huessy, Peter. 1978. *The Food First Debate.* San Francisco: Institute for Food and Development Policy.

Hunger Project. 1985. *Ending Hunger: An Idea Whose Time Has Come.* New York: Praeger.

International Rice Institute. 1988. *Science, Ethics, and Food.* Manila, Philippines: International Rice Institute.

Jackson, Wes. 1980. *New Roots for Agriculture.* San Francisco: Friends of the Earth.

Jackson, Wes. 1986. *The Unsettling of America.* San Francisco: Sierra Club Books.

Jackson, Wes. 1987. *Altars of Unhewn Stone: Science and the Earth.* Berkeley, Calif.: North Point Press.

Jackson, Wes, et al., eds. 1985. *Meeting the Expectations of Land: Essays in Sustainable Agriculture and Stewardship.* Berkeley, Calif.: North Point Press.

Jacobson, Michael, et al. 1991. *Safe Food: Eating Wisely in a Risky World.* Washington, D.C.: Planet Earth Press.

Jason, Dan. 1991. *Greening the Garden: Sustainable Growing.* Philadelphia: New Society.

Jeavons, John. 1982. *How to Grow More Vegetables.* Berkeley, Calif.: Ten Speed Press.

Jones, Byron. 1988. *The Farming Game.* Lincoln: University of Nebraska Press.

Juma, Calestous. 1989. *The Gene Hunters: Biotechnology and the Scramble for Seeds.* Princeton, N.J.: Princeton University Press.

Kidd, Charles V., and David Pimentel, eds. 1992. *Integrated Resource Management: Agroforestry for Development.* New York: Academic Press.

Klopenburg, Jack R., ed. 1988. *Seeds and Sovereignty.* Durham, N.C.: Duke University Press.

Kourik, Robert. 1986. *Designing and Maintaining Your Edible Landscape.* Santa Rosa, Calif.: Edible Landscape.

Lal, Rattan. 1987. "Managing the Soils of Sub-Saharan Africa." *Science,* vol. 236, 1069–1076.

Lambert, T. A. 1980. "Energy, Entropy, and Agriculture." *Cornell Journal of Social Relations,* vol. 15, no. 1, 84–97.

Landau, Matthew. 1992. *Introduction to Aquaculture.* New York: John Wiley.

Lappé, Francis M., and Joseph Collins. 1977. *Food First.* Boston: Houghton Mifflin.

Lappé, Francis M., et al. 1988. *Betraying the National Interest.* San Francisco: Food First.

League of Women Voters. 1991. *U.S. Farm Policy: Who Benefits? Who Pays? Who Decides?* Washington, D.C.: League of Women Voters.

LeMay, Brian, ed. 1988. *Science, Ethics, and Food.* Washington, D. C.: Smithsonian Institution Press.

Lockeretz, William G., ed. 1987. *Sustaining Agriculture Near Cities.* Ankeny, Iowa: Soil and Water Conservation Society.

Lowrance, Richard, ed. 1984. *Agricultural Ecosystems: Unifying Concepts.* New York: John Wiley.

McGoodwin, Russell. 1990. *Crisis in the World's Fisheries: People, Problems, and Politics.* Stanford, Calif.: Stanford University Press.

McKinney, Tom. 1987. *The Sustainable Farm of the Future.* Old Snowmass, Colo.: Rocky Mountain Institute.

Mollison, Bill. 1990. *Permaculture: A Practical Guide for a Sustainable Future.* Covelo, Calif.: Island Press.

Molnar, Joseph J., and Henry Kinnucan, ed. 1989. *Biotechnology and the New Agricultural Revolution.* Boulder, Colo.: Westview Press.

Morrimore, Michael. 1989. *Adapting to Drought: Farmers, Famines, and Desertification in West Africa.* New York: Cambridge University Press.

National Academy of Sciences. 1989. *Alternative Agriculture.* Washington, D.C.: National Academy Press.

National Academy of Sciences. 1989. *Triticale: A Promising Addition to the World's Cereal Grains.* Washington, D.C.: National Academy Press.

National Academy of Sciences. 1990. *Saline Agriculture: Salt-Tolerant Plants for Developing Countries.* Washington, D.C.: National Academy Press.

National Academy of Sciences. 1990. *Sustainable Agriculture Research and Education in the Field.* Washington, D.C.: National Academy Press.

National Academy of Sciences. 1992. *Marine Aquaculture: Opportunities for Growth.* Washington, D.C.: National Academy Press.

Norse, David. 1992. "Strategy for a Crowded Planet." *Environment,* vol. 34, no. 5, 7–11, 32–39.

Office of Technology Assessment. 1988. *Enhancing Agriculture in Africa.* Washington, D.C.: Office of Technology Assessment.

Phipps, Tim T., Pierre R. Crosson, and Kent A. Price, eds. 1986. *Agriculture and the Environment.* Washington, D.C.: Resources for the Future.

Pierce, John T. 1990. *Food Resources.* New York: John Wiley.

Pimentel, David, and Carl W. Hall. 1989. *Food and Natural Resources.* San Diego: Academic Press.

Pimentel, David, et al. 1989. "Benefits and Risks of Genetic Engineering and Agriculture." *BioScience,* vol. 39, no. 9, 606–614.

Poincelot, Raymond P. 1986. *Toward a Sustainable Agriculture*. Westport, Conn.: AVI.

Reaganold, John P., et al. 1990. "Sustainable Agriculture." *Scientific American*, June, 112–120.

Rifkin, Jeremy. 1992. *Beyond Beef: The Rise and Fall of the Cattle Culture*. New York: E. P. Dutton.

Ritchie, Mark. 1990. "GATT, Agriculture, and the Environment." *The Ecologist*, vol. 20, no. 6, 214–220.

Robbins, John. 1987. *Diet for a New America*. Walpole, N.H.: Stillpoint.

Robbins, John. 1992. *May All Be Fed: Diet for a New World*. New York: William Morrow.

Sanchez, Pedro A., and Jose R. Benites. 1987. "Low-Input Cropping for Acid Soils of the Humid Tropics." *Science*, vol. 238, 1521–1527.

Schell, Orville. 1984. *Modern Meat: Antibiotics, Hormones, and the Pharmaceutical Farm*. New York: Random House.

Schriefer, Donald L. 1984. *From the Soil Up*. Des Moines: Wallace-Homestead.

Shiva, Vandana. 1991. *The Violence of the Green Revolution*. Atlantic Highlands, N.J.: Zed Books.

Soil and Water Conservation Society. 1990. *Sustainable Agricultural Systems*. Ankeny, Iowa: Soil and Water Conservation Society.

Soule, Judith D., and Jon Piper. 1992. *Farming in Nature's Image: An Ecological Approach to Agriculture*. Covelo, Calif.: Island Press.

Steinman, David. 1990. *Diet for a Poisoned Planet: How to Choose Safe Foods for You and Your Family*. New York: Harmony Books.

Tarrant, John, ed. 1991. *Farming and Food*. New York: Oxford University Press.

Tivy, Joy. 1991. *Agricultural Ecology*. New York: John Wiley.

Todd, Nancy J., and John Todd. 1984. *Bioshelters, Ocean Arks, City Farming: Ecology as a Basis for Design*. San Francisco: Sierra Club Books.

Tudge, Colin. 1988. *Food Crops for the Future: Development of Plant Resources*. Oxford, England: Blackwell.

United Nations World Food Commission. 1989. *The Global State of Hunger and Malnutrition*. New York: United Nations.

U.S. Department of Agriculture. Annual. *Fact Book of Agriculture*. Washington, D.C.: Government Printing Office.

Vietmeyer, Noel D. 1986. "Lesser-Known Plants of Potential Use in Agriculture." *Science*, vol. 232, 1379–1384.

Whelan, Elizabeth M., and Frederick J. Stare. 1983. *The 100% Natural, Purely Organic, Cholesterol-Free, Megavitamin, Low-Carbohydrate Nutrition Hoax*. New York: Atheneum.

Widdowson, R. W. 1987. *Toward Holistic Agriculture*. New York: Pergamon Press.

Witter, Sylvan, et al. 1987. *Feeding a Billion: Frontiers of Chinese Agriculture*. East Lansing: Michigan State University Press.

Wojcik, Jan. 1989. *The Arguments of Agriculture: A Casebook in Contemporary Agricultural Controversy*. West Lafayette, Ind.: Purdue University Press.

Wolf, Edward C. 1986. *Beyond the Green Revolution: New Approaches for Third World Agriculture*. Washington, D.C.: Worldwatch Institute.

Yang, Linda. 1990. *The City Gardener's Handbook: From Balcony to Backyard*. New York: Random House.

## 15 BIODIVERSITY: FORESTS, RANGELANDS, PARKS, AND WILDERNESS

See also the readings for Chapter 2.

Allin, Craig W. 1982. *The Politics of Wilderness Preservation*. Westport, Conn.: Greenwood Press.

Ayres, Ed. 1992. "Whitewash: Pursuing the Truth About Paper." *World Watch*, September/October, 17–25.

Beattie, Mollie, et al. 1993. *Working with Your Woodland*. Hanover, N.H.: University Press of New England.

Cairns, John, Jr., and Todd V. Crawford. 1990. *Integrated Environmental Management*. Boca Raton, Fla.: Lewis.

Camp, Orville. 1984. *The Forest Farmer's Handbook: A Guide to Natural Selection Forest Management*. Berkeley, Calif.: Sky River Press.

Chase, Alston. 1986. *Playing God in Yellowstone: The Destruction of America's First National Park*. Boston: Atlantic Monthly Press.

Clary, David. 1986. *Timber and the Forest Service*. Lawrence: University of Kansas Press.

Collard, Andree, and Joyce Contrucci. 1989. *Rape of the Wild: Man's Violence Against Animals and the Earth*. Bloomington: Indiana University Press.

Conservation Foundation. 1989. *State Parks in a New Era*. 3 vols. Washington, D.C.: Conservation Foundation.

Deacon, Robert T., and M. Bruce Johnson, eds. 1986. *Forestlands: Public and Private*. San Francisco: Pacific Institute for Public Policy.

Defenders of Wildlife. 1982. *1080: The Case Against Poisoning Our Wildlife*. Washington, D.C.: Government Printing Office.

Dysart, Benjamin, III, and Marion Clawson. 1988. *Managing Public Lands in the Public Interest*. New York: Praeger.

Eckholm, Erik. 1982. *Down to Earth: Environment and Human Needs*. New York: Norton.

Fitzpatrick, Tony. 1993. *Signals From the Heartland*. New York: Walker.

Foreman, Dave, and Howie Wolke. 1989. *The Big Outside*. Tucson: Nedd Ludd Books.

Frederick, Kenneth D., and Roger A. Sedjo, eds. 1992. *America's Renewable Resources*. Washington, D.C.: Resources for the Future.

Friends of the Trees. 1989. *1988 International Green Front Report*. Whelan, Wash.: Friends of the Trees.

Fritz, Edward. 1983. *Sterile Forest: The Case Against Clearcutting*. Austin, Tex.: Eakin Press.

Frome, Michael. 1974. *The Battle for the Wilderness*. New York: Praeger.

Frome, Michael. 1983. *The Forest Service*. Boulder, Colo.: Westview Press.

Frome, Michael. 1992. *Regreening the National Parks*. Tucson: University of Arizona Press.

Gamlin, L. 1989. "Sweden's Factory Forests." *New Scientist*, January 26, 41–44.

Gillis, Anna Maria. 1991. "Should Cows Chew Cheatgrass on Commonlands?" *BioScience*, vol. 41, no. 10, 668–675.

Graf, William L. 1990. *Wilderness Preservation and the Sagebrush Rebellion*. Savage, Md.: Rowman & Littlefield.

Greenpeace. 1990. *The Greenpeace Guide to Paper*. Washington, D.C.: Greenpeace.

Harris, L. D. 1984. *The Fragmented Forest*. Chicago: University of Chicago Press.

Hartzog, George B., Jr. 1988. *Battling for the National Parks*. New York: Moyer Bell.

Hendee, John, et al. 1991. *Principles of Wilderness Management*. Golden, Colo.: Fulcrum.

Hess, Karl, Jr. 1992. *Visions upon the Land: Man and Nature on the Western Range*. Covelo, Calif.: Island Press.

Hunter, Malcolm L., Jr. 1990. *Wildlife, Forests, and Forestry: Managing Forests for Biological Diversity*. New York: Prentice-Hall.

Jacobs, Lynn. 1992. *Waste of the West: Public Lands Ranching*. Tucson, Ariz.: Lynn Jacobs.

Land Trust Alliance. 1990. *Starting a Land Trust: A Guide to Forming a Land Conservation Organization*. Washington, D.C.: Land Trust Alliance.

Lansky, Mitch. 1992. *Beyond the Beauty Strip: Saving What's Left of Our Forests*. Gardiner, Maine: Tilbury House.

Ledec, George, and Robert Goodland. 1988. *Wildlands: Their Protection and Management in Economic Development*. Washington, D.C.: World Bank.

Leopold, Aldo. 1949. *A Sand County Almanac*. New York: Oxford University Press.

Libecap, Gary D. 1986. *Locking Up the Range: Federal Land Control and Grazing*. San Francisco: Pacific Institute for Public Policy Research.

Lopez, Barry. 1989. *Crossing Open Ground*. New York: Vintage (Random House).

Mather, A. S. 1990. *Global Forest Resources*. London: Belhaven Press.

McNeely, Jeffery A., and Kenton R. Miller, eds. 1984. *National Parks, Conservation, and Development*. Washington, D.C.: Smithsonian Institution Press.

Mello, Robert A. 1987. *Last Stand of the Red Spruce*. Covelo, Calif.: Island Press.

Minckler, Leon S. 1980. *Woodland Ecology*. 2nd ed. Syracuse, N.Y.: Syracuse University Press.

Moll, Gary, and Sara Ebenreck. 1989. *Shading Our Cities: A Resource Guide for Urban and Community Forests*. Covelo, Calif.: Island Press.

Naar, Jon, and Alex J. Naar. 1993. *This Land Is Your Land: A Guide to North America's Endangered Ecosystems*. New York: Harper.

Nash, Roderick. 1982. *Wilderness and the American Mind*. 3rd ed. New Haven, Conn.: Yale University Press.

National Parks and Conservation Association. 1988. *Blueprint for National Parks*. 9 vols. Washington, D.C.: National Parks and Conservation Association.

National Park Service. 1992. *National Parks for the 21st Century*. Washington, D.C.: National Park Service.

National Wildlife Federation and Natural Resources Defense Council. 1989. *Our Ailing Public Rangelands: Condition Report—1989*. Washington, D.C.: Natural Resources Defense Council.

Oelschlager, Max. 1991. *The Idea of Wilderness from Prehistory to the Age of Ecology*. New Haven, Conn.: Yale University Press.

Office of Technology Assessment. 1992. *Forest Service Planning: Accommodating Uses, Producing Outputs, Protecting Ecosystems*. Washington, D.C.: Office of Technology Assessment.

O'Toole, Randal. 1987. *Reforming the Forest Service*. Covelo, Calif.: Island Press.

Perlin, John. 1989. *A Forest Journey: The Role of Wood in the Development of Civilization*. New York: W. W. Norton.

Postel, Sandra, and Lori Heise. 1988. *Reforesting the Earth*. Washington, D.C.: Worldwatch Institute.

Ramadé, François. 1984. *Ecology of Natural Resources*. New York: John Wiley.

Reed, P., ed. 1990. *Preparing to Manage Wilderness in the 21st Century*. Washington, D.C.: U.S. Forest Service.

Repetto, Robert, and Malcolm Gillis, eds. 1988. *Public Policy and the Misuse of Forest Resources*. New York: Cambridge University Press.

Rifkin, Jeremy. 1992. *Beyond Beef: The Rise and Fall of the Cattle Culture*. New York: E. P. Dutton.

Robinson, Gordon. 1987. *The Forest and the Trees: A Guide to Excellent Forestry*. Covelo, Calif.: Island Press.

Romme, William H., and Don G. Despain. 1989. "The Yellowstone Fires." *Scientific American*, vol. 261, no. 5, 37–46.

Runte, Alfred. 1987. *National Parks: The American Experience*. 2nd ed. Lincoln: University of Nebraska Press.

Runte, Alfred. 1990. *Yosemite: The Embattled Wilderness*. Lincoln: University of Nebraska Press.

Runte, Alfred. 1991. *Public Lands, Public Heritage: The National Forest Idea*. Niwot, Colo.: Roberts Rinehart.

Sampson, Neil, and Dwight Hair, eds. 1989. *Natural Resources for the 21st Century*. Covelo, Calif.: Island Press.

Savoy, Allan. 1988. *Holistic Resource Management*. Covelo, Calif.: Island Press.

Sierra Club. 1982. *Our Public Lands: An Introduction to the Agencies and Issues*. San Francisco: Sierra Club Books.

Simon, David J., ed. 1988. *Our Common Lands: Defending the National Parks*. Covelo, Calif.: Island Press.

Smith, D. M. 1982. *The Practice of Silviculture*. New York: John Wiley.

Society of American Foresters. 1981. *Choices in Silviculture for American Forests*. Washington, D.C.: Society of American Foresters.

Spurr, Stephen H., and Buron V. Barnes. 1980. *Forest Ecology*. 3rd ed. New York: Ronald Press.

Stoddard, Charles H., and Glenn M. Stoddard. 1987. *Essentials of Forestry Practice*. 4th ed. New York: John Wiley.

Thompson, Claudia. 1992. *Recycled Papers: The Essential Guide*. Cambridge, Mass.: MIT Press.

Valentine, John E., ed. 1990. *Grazing Management*. San Diego: Academic Press.

Wald, Joanna, et al. 1991. *How Not to Be Cowed—Livestock Grazing on Public Lands: An Owner's Manual*. Salt Lake City: Southern Utah Wilderness Alliance.

Waring, R. H., and W. R. Schlesinger. 1985. *Forest Ecosystems: Concepts and Management*. San Diego: Academic Press.

Weber, Thomas. 1990. *Hugging the Trees: The Story of the Chipko Movement*. New York: Penguin Books.

Westoby, Jack. 1989. *Introduction to World Forestry*. Cambridge, Mass.: Basil Blackwell.

Whelan, Tensie, ed. 1991. *Nature Tourism: Managing for the Environment*. Washington, D.C.: Island Press.

Wilcove, David S. 1988. *National Forests: Policies for the Future*. Vols. 1, 2. Alexandria, Va.: Global Printing.

Wilderness Society. 1991. *Keeping It Wild: A Citizen Guide to Wilderness Management*. Washington, D.C.: Wilderness Society.

Wright, Henry A., and Arthur W. Bailey. 1983. *Fire Ecology*. New York: John Wiley.

Wuerthner, George. 1989. *Yellowstone and the Fires of Change*. Salt Lake City: Dream Garden Press.

Wuerthner, George. 1991. "How the West Was Eaten." *Wilderness*, Spring, 28–37.

Zeveloff, Samuel I., and Lyrus M. McKell, eds. 1992. *Wilderness Issues in the Arid Lands of the Western United States*. Albuquerque: University of New Mexico Press.

## 16 WILDLIFE RESOURCES AND PRESERVING BIODIVERSITY

Abbey, Edward. 1988. *One Life at a Time Please*. New York: Henry Holt.

Ackerman, Diane. 1991. *The Moon by Whalelight*. New York: Random House.

Bailey, J. A. 1984. *Principles of Wildlife Management*. New York: John Wiley.

Baker, Ron. 1985. *The American Hunting Myth*. New York: Vantage Press.

Bonner, Nigel. 1989. *Whales of the World*. New York: Facts on File.

Boo, Elizabeth. 1990. *Ecotourism: The Potential and the Pitfalls*. Vols. 1, 2. Washington, D.C.: World Wildlife Fund.

Brooks, Paul. 1971. *Roadless Areas*. New York: Ballantine Books.

Burton, Robert, ed. 1991. *Nature's Last Strongholds*. New York: Oxford University Press.

Cadieux, Charles L. 1991. *Wildlife Extinction*. Washington, D.C.: Stone Wall Press.

Causey, Ann S. 1989. "On the Morality of Hunting." *Environmental Ethics*, Winter, 327–343.

Cohn, Jeffery P. 1990. "Elephants: Remarkable and Endangered." *BioScience*, vol. 40, no. 1, 10–14.

Constanza, Robert, et al., eds. 1992. *Ecosystem Health: New Goals for Environmental Management*. Covelo, Calif.: Island Press.

Cox, George W. 1993. *Conservation Ecology*. Dubuque, Iowa: Wm. C. Brown.

Credlund, Arthur G. 1983. *Whales and Whaling*. New York: Seven Hills Books.

Dasmann, Raymond F. 1981. *Wildlife Biology*. 2nd ed. New York: John Wiley.

DeBlieu, Jan. 1991. *Meant to Be Wild: The Struggle to Save Endangered Species Through Captive Breeding*. New York: Fulcrum.

Decker, Daniel J., and Gary R. Goff, eds. 1987. *Valuing Wildlife: Economic and Social Perspectives*. Boulder, Colo.: Westview Press.

DiSilvestro, Roger L. 1989. *The Endangered Kingdom: The Struggle to Save America's Wildlife*. New York: John Wiley.

DiSilvestro, Roger L. 1990. *Fight for Survival*. New York: John Wiley.

DiSilvestro, Roger L. 1992. *Rebirth of Nature*. New York: John Wiley.

DiSilvestro, Roger L., and Christopher N. Palmer, eds. 1991. *The African Elephant: Twilight in Eden*. New York: John Wiley.

Dixon, John A., and Paul B. Sherman. 1990. *Economics of Protected Areas*. Covelo, Calif.: Island Press.

Dunlap, Thomas R. 1988. *Saving America's Wildlife*. Princeton, N.J.: Princeton University Press.

Durrell, Lee. 1986. *State of the Ark: An Atlas of Conservation in Action*. New York: Doubleday.

Ehrlich, Paul, and Anne Ehrlich. 1981. *Extinction*. New York: Random House.

Ehrlich, Paul R., et al. 1992. *Birds in Jeopardy: The Imperiled and Extinct Birds of the United States and Canada, Including Hawaii and Puerto Rico*. Stanford, Calif.: Stanford University Press.

Eldredge, Niles. 1991. *The Miner's Canary*. New York: Prentice-Hall.

Elliot, David K. 1986. *Dynamics of Extinction*. New York: John Wiley.

Elton, Charles S. 1958. *The Ecology of Invasions by Plants and Animals*. London: Methuen.

Evernden, N. 1985. *The Natural Alien*. Toronto: University of Toronto Press.

Fiedler, Peggy L., and Subodh K. Jains, eds. 1992. *Conservation Biology: The Theory and Practice of Nature Conservation, Preservation, and Management*. New York: Routledge, Chapman & Hall.

Gaskin, D. E. 1982. *The Ecology of Whales and Dolphins*. London: Heinemann.

Gilbert, Frederick F., and Donald G. Dodds. 1987. *The Philosophy and Practice of Wildlife Management*. Malabar, Fla.: Robert E. Krieger.

Grumbine, R. Edward. 1992. *Ghost Bears: Exploring the Biodiversity Crisis*. Covelo, Calif.: Island Press.

Hargrove, Eugene C. 1992. *The Animal Rights/Environmental Ethics Debate*. Ithaca: State University of New York.

Harrison, R., and M. M. Bryden, eds. 1988. *Whales, Dolphins, and Porpoises*. New York: Facts on File.

Huxley, Anthony. 1984. *Green Inheritance*. New York: Anchor/Doubleday.

International Union for Conservation of Nature and Natural Resources. 1980. *World Conservation Strategy*. New York: Unipub.

International Union for Conservation of Nature and Natural Resources. 1985. *Implementing the World Conservation Strategy*. Gland, Switzerland: IUCN.

International Union for Conservation of Nature and Natural Resources. 1992. *Protected Areas of the World*. Vols. 1–4. Gland, Switzerland: IUCN.

Jasper, James M., and Dorothy Nelkin. 1992. *The Animal Rights Crusade: The Growth of a Moral Protest*. New York: Macmillan.

Klenig, John. 1992. *Valuing Life*. Princeton, N.J.: Princeton University Press.

Kohm, Kathryn A., ed. 1990. *Balancing on the Brink of Extinction: The Endangered Species Act and Lessons for the Future*. Covelo, Calif.: Island Press.

Koopowitz, Harold, and Hilary Kaye. 1983. *Plant Extinctions: A Global Crisis*. Washington, D.C.: Stone Wall Press.

Leopold, Aldo. 1933. *Game Management*. New York: Charles Scribner.

Lines, William J. 1992. *Taming the Great South: A History of the Conquest of Nature in Australia*. Berkeley and Los Angeles: University of California Press.

Livingston, John A. 1981. *The Fallacy of Wildlife Conservation*. Toronto: McClelland & Stewart.

Lopez, Barry. 1986. *Arctic Dreams: Imagination and Desire in a Northern Landscape*. New York: Charles Scribner.

Luoma, Jon. 1987. *A Crowded Ark: The Role of Zoos in Wildlife Conservation*. Boston: Houghton Mifflin.

Matthiessen, Peter. 1992. *Shadows of Africa*. New York: Frank Abrams.

McNeely, Jeffery A., et al. 1989. *Conserving the World's Biological Resources: A Primer on Principles and Practice for Development Action*. Washington, D.C.: World Resources Institute.

Miller, Debbie. 1989. *Midnight Wilderness: Journeys in Alaska's Arctic National Wildlife Refuge*. San Francisco: Sierra Club Books.

Miller, Kenton R. 1993. *Balancing the Scales: Managing Biodiversity at the Bioregional Level*. Washington, D.C.: World Resources Institute.

Morrison, Michael L., et al. 1992. *Wildlife-Habitat Relationships: Concepts and Applications*. Madison: University of Wisconsin Press.

Myers, Norman. 1983. *A Wealth of Wild Species: Storehouse for Human Welfare*. Boulder, Colo.: Westview Press.

Myers, Norman. 1987. "The Impending Extinction Spasm: Synergisms at Work." *Conservation Biology*, vol. 14, 15–22.

Nash, Roderick F. 1988. *The Rights of Nature: A History of Environmental Ethics*. Madison: University of Wisconsin Press.

National Academy of Sciences. 1988. *Use of Laboratory Animals in Biomedical Research*. Washington, D.C.: National Academy Press.

National Wildlife Federation. 1987. *The Arctic National Wildlife Refuge Coastal Plain: A Perspective for the Future*. Washington, D.C.: National Wildlife Federation.

Norton, B. G., ed. 1986. *Why Preserve Natural Variety?* Princeton, N.J.: Princeton University Press.

Office of Technology Assessment. 1986. *Alternatives to Animal Use in Research, Teaching, and Education*. Washington, D.C.: Government Printing Office.

Office of Technology Assessment. 1987. *Technologies to Maintain Biological Diversity*. Washington, D.C.: Government Printing Office.

Office of Technology Assessment. 1989. *Oil Production in the Arctic National Wildlife Refuge*. Washington, D.C.: Government Printing Office.

Oldfield. Margery L., and Janis B. Alcorn, eds. 1992. *Biodiversity: Culture, Conservation, and Ecodevelopment*. Boulder, Colo.: Westview Press.

Orians, Gordon H. 1990. "Ecological Concepts of Sustainability." *Environment*, November, 10–39.

Orenstein, Ronald, ed. 1991. *Elephants: The Deciding Decade*. San Francisco: Sierra Club Books.

Owens, Delia, and Mark Owens. 1992. *The Eye of the Elephant: An Epic Adventure in the African Wilderness*. Boston: Houghton Mifflin.

Passmore, John. 1974. *Man's Responsibility for Nature*. New York: Charles Scribner.

Peterson, Melvin N.A., ed. 1992. *Diversity of Oceanic Life*. Boulder, Colo.: Westview Press.

Pimentel, David, et al. 1992. "Conserving Biological Diversity in Agricultural/Forestry Systems." *BioScience*, vol. 42, no. 5, 354–362.

Prescott-Allen, Robert, and Christine Prescott-Allen. 1982. *What's Wildlife Worth?* East Haven, Conn.: Earthscan.

Preston-Mafbam, Ken. 1992. *Madagascar: A Natural History*. New York: Facts on File.

Primack, Richard B. 1993. *Essentials of Conservation Biology*. Sunderland, Mass.: Sinauer.

Pringle, Laurence. 1989. *The Animal Rights Controversy*. New York: Harcourt Brace Jovanovich.

Pringle, Laurence. 1991. *Exploring the World of Bats*. New York: Charles Scribner.

Reagan, Tom. 1983. *The Case for Animal Rights*. Berkeley and Los Angeles: University of California Press.

Reid, Walter V. C., and Kenton R. Miller. 1989. *Keeping Options Alive: The Scientific Basis for Conserving Biodiversity*. Washington, D.C.: World Resources Institute.

Reisner, Marc. 1991. *Game Wars: The Undercover Pursuit of Wildlife Poachers*. New York: Viking Press.

Reynolds, John E., III, and Daniel K. Odell. 1991. *Manatees and Dugongs*. New York: Facts on File.

Rolston, Holmes, III. 1988. *Environmental Ethics: Duties to and Values in the Natural World*. Philadelphia: Temple University Press.

Ryan, John C. 1992. *Life Support: Conserving Biological Diversity*. Washington, D.C.: Worldwatch Institute.

Schweitzer, Albert. 1949. *Out of My Life and Thought: An Autobiography*. New York: Holt, Rinehart & Winston.

Shafer, Craig L. 1990. *Nature Reserves: Island Theory and Conservation Practice*. Washington, D.C.: Smithsonian Institution.

Shaw, J. H. 1985. *Introduction to Wildlife Management*. New York: McGraw-Hill.

Shoshani, Jeheskel, ed. 1992. *Elephants: Majestic Creatures of the Wild*. Emmaus, Pa.: Rodale.

Singer, Peter. 1975. *Animal Liberation: A New Ethics for Our Treatment of Animals*. New York: New York Review of Books.

Soulé, Michael E. 1986. *Conservation Biology: Science of Scarcity and Diversity*. Sunderland, Mass.: Sinauer.

Soulé, Michael E., ed. 1987. *Viable Populations for Conservation*. New York: Cambridge University Press.

Soulé, Michael E. 1991. "Conservation: Tactics for a Constant Crisis." *Science*, vol. 253, 744–750.

Sperling, Susan. 1988. *Animal Liberators: Research and Morality*. Berkeley and Los Angeles: University of California Press.

Swanson, Timothy, and Edward B. Barber, eds. 1992. *Economics for the Wilds: Wildlife, Biodiversity, and Development*. Covelo, Calif.: Island Press.

Terborgh, John. 1992. "Why American Songbirds Are Vanishing." *Scientific American*, May, 98–104.

Tobin, Richard J. 1990. *The Expendable Future: U.S. Politics and the Protection of Biodiversity*. Durham, N.C.: Duke University Press.

Tudge, Colin. 1988. *The Environment of Life*. New York: Oxford University Press.

Tudge, Colin. 1992. *Last Animals at the Zoo: How Mass Extinction Can Be Stopped*. Covelo, Calif.: Island Press.

Tuttle, Merlin D. 1988. *America's Neighborhood Bats: Understanding and Learning to Live in Harmony With Them*. Austin: University of Texas Press.

Vitali, Theodore. 1990. "Sport Hunting: Moral or Immoral?" *Environmental Ethics*, Spring, 69–81.

Wallace, David Rains. 1987. *Life in the Balance*. New York: Harcourt Brace Jovanovich.

Watkins, T. H. 1988. *Vanishing Arctic: Alaska's National Wildlife Refuge*. New York: Aperture.

Wells, Michael, et al. 1991. *People and Parks: Linking Protected Area Management with Local Communities*. Washington, D.C.: World Bank.

Western, David, and Mary Pearl, eds. 1989. *Conservation for the Twenty-First Century*. New York: Oxford University Press.

Whelan, Tensie, ed. 1991. *Nature Tourism: Managing for the Environment*. Covelo, Calif.: Island Press.

Wilson, E. O., ed. 1988. *Biodiversity*. Washington, D.C.: National Academy Press.

Wilson, E. O. 1992. *The Diversity of Life*. Cambridge, Mass.: Harvard University Press.

Wolf, Edward C. 1987. *On the Brink of Extinction: Conserving the Diversity of Life*. Washington, D.C.: Worldwatch Institute.

Wolke, Howie. 1991. *Wilderness on the Rocks*. Tucson, Ariz.: Ned Ludd Books.

Woodwell, George, ed. 1990. *The Earth in Transition: Patterns and Processes of Biotic Impoverishment*. New York: Cambridge University Press.

World Resources Institute (WRI) et al. 1992. *Global Biodiversity Strategy*. Washington, D.C.: World Resources Institute.

World Wildlife Fund. 1992. *The Official World Wildlife Fund Guide to Endangered Species of North America*. Washington, D.C.: Beacham.

Yalden, D. W., and P. A. Morris. 1975. *The Lives of Bats*. New York: Quadrangle/New York Times.

## 17 PERPETUAL AND RENEWABLE ENERGY RESOURCES

See also the readings for Chapter 3.

American Council for an Energy Efficient Economy. Annual. *The Most Energy-Efficient Appliances*. Washington, D.C.: American Council for an Energy Efficient Economy.

American Council for an Energy Efficient Economy. 1988. *Energy Efficiency: A New Agenda*. Washington, D.C.: American Council for an Energy Efficient Economy.

American Council for an Energy Efficient Economy. 1991. *Energy Efficiency and Environment: Forging the Link*. Washington, D.C.: American Council for an Energy Efficient Economy.

American Institute of Physics. 1985. *Energy Efficiency and Renewable Resources*. New York: American Institute of Physics.

American Solar Energy Society. 1990. *Assessment of Solar Energy Technologies*. Boulder, Colo.: American Solar Energy Society.

Anderson, Bruce. 1990. *Solar Building Architecture*. Cambridge, Mass.: MIT Press.

Anderson, Bruce, and Michael Riordan. 1987. *The New Solar Home Book*. Andover, Mass.: Brick House.

Blackburn, John O. 1987. *The Renewable Energy Alternative: How the United States and the World Can Prosper Without Nuclear Energy or Coal*. Durham, N.C.: Duke University Press.

Bleviss, Deborah Lynn. 1988. *The New Oil Crisis and Fuel Economy Technologies*. Westport, Conn.: Quorum.

Bockris, J. O. 1980. *Energy Options: Real Economics and the Solar-Hydrogen System*. London: Taylor & Francis.

Brower, Michael. 1992. *Cool Energy: Renewable Solution to Environmental Problems*. 2nd ed. Cambridge, Mass.: MIT Press.

Butti, Ken, and John Perlin. 1980. *A Golden Thread—2500 Years of Solar Architecture*. Palo Alto, Calif.: Cheshire Press.

Davidson, Joel. 1987. *The New Solar Electric Home*. Ann Arbor, Mich.: Aatec.

Dinga, Gustav P. 1988. "Hydrogen: The Ultimate Fuel and Energy Carrier." *Journal of Chemical Education*, vol. 65, no. 8, 688–691.

Dostrovsky, I. 1989. *Energy and the Missing Resource*. New York: Cambridge University Press.

Echeverria, John, et al. 1989. *Rivers at Risk: The Concerned Citizen's Guide to Hydropower*. Covelo, Calif.: Island Press.

Energy Conservation Coalition. 1990. *Building a Brighter Future*. Washington, D.C.: Energy Conservation Coalition.

Flavin, Christopher, and Nicholas Lenssen. 1990. *Beyond the Petroleum Age: Designing a Solar Economy*. Washington, D.C.: Worldwatch Institute.

Flavin, Christopher, and Nicholas Lenssen. 1991. "Here Comes the Sun." *World Watch*, September/October, 10–18.

Flavin, Christopher, and Rock Piltz. 1990. *Sustainable Energy*. Washington, D.C.: Renew America.

Gever, John, et al. 1991. *Beyond Oil: The Threat to Food and Fuel in Coming Decades*. Boulder: University of Colorado Press.

Goldenberg, Jose, et al. 1988. *Energy for a Sustainable World*. New York: John Wiley.

Heede, H. Richard, et al. 1985. *The Hidden Costs of Energy*. Washington, D.C.: Center for Renewable Resources.

Helm, John L., ed. 1990. *Energy: Production, Consumption, and Consequences*. Washington, D.C.: National Academy Press.

Hinkel, Kenneth M. 1990. "Wood Burning for Residential Space Heating in the United States: An Energy Efficiency Analysis." *Applied Geography*, vol. 9, 259–272.

Hohmeyer, O. 1988. *Social Costs of Energy Consumption*. New York: Springer-Verlag.

Hollander, Jack M., ed. 1992. *The New Energy-Environment Connection*. Covelo, Calif.: Island Press.

Hubbard, Harold M. 1991. "The Real Cost of Energy." *Scientific American*, April, 36–42.

Johansson, Thomas B., et al., eds. 1992. *Renewable Energy: Sources for Fuels and Electricity*. Covelo, Calif.: Island Press.

Kozloff, Keith, and Roger C. Dower. 1993. *A New Power Base: Renewable Energy Policies for the Nineties and Beyond*. Washington, D.C.: World Resources Institute.

Krupnick, Alan. 1990. *The Environmental Costs of Energy: A Framework for Estimation*. Washington, D.C.: Resources for the Future.

Lenssen, Nicholas. 1992. *Empowering Development: The New Energy Equation*. Washington, D.C.: Worldwatch Institute.

Lovins, Amory B. 1989. *Energy, People, and Industrialization*. Old Snowmass, Colo.: Rocky Mountain Institute.

Lovins, Amory B. 1990. *The Negawatt Revolution*. Old Snowmass, Colo.: Rocky Mountain Institute.

Mackenzie, Dorothy. 1991. *Design for Environment*. New York: Rizolli.

Mackenzie, James L. 1993. *Electric and Hydrogen Vehicles: Transportation Technologies for the Twenty-First Century*. Washington, D.C.: World Resources Institute.

Mackenzie, James L., and Michael P. Walsh. 1990. *Driving Forces: Motor Vehicle Trends and Their Implications for Global Warming, Energy Strategies, and Transportation Planning*. Washington, D.C.: World Resources Institute.

McKeown, Walter. 1991. *Death of the Oil Age and the Birth of Hydrogen America*. San Francisco: Wild Bamboo Press.

National Academy of Sciences. 1988. *Geothermal Energy Technology*. Washington, D.C.: National Academy Press.

National Academy of Sciences. 1992. *Automotive Fuel Efficiency: How Far Can We Go?* Washington, D.C.: National Academy Press.

Nussbaum, Bruce. 1985. *The World After Oil: The Shifting Axis of Power and Wealth*. New York: Simon & Schuster.

Office of Technology Assessment. 1990. *Replacing Gasoline: Alternative Fuels for Light-Duty Vehicles*. Washington, D.C.: Government Printing Office.

Office of Technology Assessment. 1991. *Improving Automobile Fuel Economy: New Standards, New Approaches*. Washington, D.C.: Government Printing Office.

Office of Technology Assessment. 1992. *Building Energy Efficiency*. Washington, D.C.: Government Printing Office.

Office of Technology Assessment. 1992. *Fueling Development: Energy Technologies for Developing Countries*. Washington, D.C.: Government Printing Office.

Ogden, Joan M., and Robert H. Williams. 1989. *Solar Hydrogen: Moving Beyond Fossil Fuels*. Washington, D.C.: World Resources Institute.

Oppenheimer, Michael, and Robert H. Boyle. 1990. *Dead Heat: The Race Against the Greenhouse Effect*. New York: Basic Books.

Penny, Terry R., and Desikan Bharathan. 1987. "Power from the Sea." *Scientific American*, vol. 286, no. 1, 86–92.

Pimentel, David, et al. 1984. "Environmental and Social Costs of Biomass Energy." *BioScience*, February, 89–93.

Rader, Nancy, et al. 1989. *Power Surge: The Status and Near-Term Potential of Renewable Energy Technologies*. Washington, D.C.: Public Citizen.

Real Goods Trading Corporation. Annual. *Alternative Energy Sourcebook*. Ukiah, Calif.: Real Goods Trading Corporation.

Rocky Mountain Institute. 1991. *Practical Home Energy Savings*. Snowmass, Colo.: Rocky Mountain Institute.

*Scientific American*. 1990. *Energy for Planet Earth*. Entire September issue.

Shea, Cynthia Pollack. 1988. *Renewable Energy: Today's Contribution, Tomorrow's Promise*. Washington, D.C.: Worldwatch Institute.

Skelton, Luther W. 1984. *The Solar-Hydrogen Economy: Beyond the Age of Fire*. New York: Van Nostrand Reinhold.

Sklar, Scott, and Kenneth G. Sheinkopg. 1991. *Consumer Guide to Solar Energy*. Chicago: Bonus Books.

Smith, Ralph Lee. 1988. *Smart House: The Coming Revolution*. New York: CP.

Solar Energy Research Institute. 1981. *A New Prosperity: Building a Sustainable Energy Future*. Andover, Mass.: Brick House.

Sperling, Daniel. 1989. *New Transportation Fuels*. Berkeley and Los Angeles: University of California Press.

Starr, Chauncey, et al. 1992. "Energy Sources: A Realistic Outlook." *Science*, vol. 256, 981–986.

Starr, Gary. 1987. *The Solar Electric Book*. Lower Lake, Calif.: Integral.

Swan, Christopher C. 1986. *Suncell: Energy, Economy, Photovoltaics*. New York: Random House.

Tapp, B. A., and J. R. Watkins. 1989. *Energy and Mineral Resource Systems: An Introduction*. Cambridge, Mass.: Cambridge University Press.

Tester, Jefferson, ed. 1991. *Energy and the Environment in the 21st Century*. Cambridge, Mass.: MIT Press.

Underground Space Center, University of Minnesota. 1979. *Earth-Sheltered Housing Design*. New York: Van Nostrand Reinhold.

Union of Concerned Scientists. 1990. *Motor-Vehicle Efficiency and Global Warming*. Cambridge, Mass.: Union of Concerned Scientists.

Vale, Brenda, and Robert Vale. 1991. *Green Architecture*. Boston: Little, Brown.

Vine, Edward, and Drury Crawley, eds. 1991. *State of the Art of Energy Efficiency*. Washington, D.C.: American Council for an Energy Efficient Economy.

Wade, Herb. 1983. *Building Underground: The Design and Construction Handbook for Earth-Sheltered Houses*. Emmaus, Pa.: Rodale Press.

Wells, Malcolm. 1991. *How to Build an Underground House*. Brewster, Mass.: Malcolm Wells.

Wilson, Alex. 1991. *Consumer Guide to Home Energy Savings*. Washington, D.C.: American Council for an Energy Efficient Economy.

Woods, Charles G., and Malcolm Wells. 1992. *Designing Your Natural Home*. New York: Van Nostrand Reinhold.

Zweibel, Ken. 1990. *Harnessing Solar Power: The Challenge of Photovoltaics*. New York: Plenum.

## 18 NONRENEWABLE ENERGY RESOURCES

See also the readings for Chapter 3.

Ahearne, John F. 1993. "The Future of Nuclear Power." *American Scientist*, vol. 81, 24–35.

American Physical Society. 1985. *Radionuclide Release from Severe Accidents at Nuclear Power Plants*. New York: American Physical Society.

American Solar Energy Society. 1989. *Societal Costs of Energy: A Roundtable*. Boulder, Colo.: American Solar Energy Society.

Atomic Industrial Forum. 1985. *Nuclear Power Plant Response to Severe Accidents*. Bethesda, Md.: Atomic Industrial Forum.

Bartlett, Donald L., and James B. Steele. 1985. *Forevermore: Nuclear Waste in America*. New York: W. W. Norton.

Browning, William, and L. Hunter Lovins. 1989. *The Energy Casebook*. Old Snowmass, Colo.: Rocky Mountain Institute.

Burnett, W. M., and S. D. Ban. 1989. "Changing Prospects for Natural Gas in the United States." *Science*, vol. 244, 305–310.

Campbell, John L. 1988. *Collapse of an Industry: Nuclear Power and the Contradictions of U.S. Policy*. Ithaca, N.Y.: Cornell University Press.

Carter, Luther J. 1987. *Nuclear Imperatives and Public Trust: Dealing with Radioactive Waste*. Baltimore: Resources for the Future.

Chernousenko, Vladimir M. 1991. *Chernobyl: Insight from the Inside*. New York: Springer-Verlag.

Clark, Wilson, and Jake Page. 1983. *Energy, Vulnerability, and War*. New York: W. W. Norton.

Close, Frank. 1991. *Too Hot to Handle: The Race for Cold Fusion*. Princeton, N.J.: Princeton University Press.

Cohen, Bernard L. 1990. *The Nuclear Energy Option: An Alternative for the 90s*. New York: Plenum.

Energy Conservation Coalition. 1990. *Building a Brighter Future: State Experiences in Least-Cost Electrical Planning*. Washington, D.C.: Environmental Action Foundation.

Flavin, Christopher. 1985. *World Oil: Coping with the Dangers of Success*. Washington, D.C.: Worldwatch Institute.

Flavin, Christopher. 1987. *Reassessing Nuclear Power: The Fallout from Chernobyl*. Washington, D.C.: Worldwatch Institute.

Flavin, Christopher. 1988. "The Case Against Reviving Nuclear Power." *World Watch*, July/August, 27–35.

Flavin, Christopher. 1992. "Building a Bridge to Sustainable Energy." In Lester Brown et al., *State of the World 1992*, 27–55. New York: W. W. Norton.

Flavin, Christopher, and Alan B. Durning. 1988. *Building on Success: The Age of Energy Efficiency*. Washington, D.C.: Worldwatch Institute.

Flynn, James, et al. 1992. "Time to Rethink Nuclear Waste Storage." *Issues in Science and Technology*, Summer, 42–48.

Ford, Daniel F. 1986. *Meltdown*. New York: Simon & Schuster.

Fund for Renewable Energy and the Environment. 1987. *The Oil Rollercoaster*. Washington, D.C.: Fund for Renewable Energy and the Environment.

Golay, Michael W., and Neil E. Todreas. 1990. "Advanced Light-Water Reactors." *Scientific American*, April, 82–89.

Goldemberg, Jose, et al. 1987. *Energy for Development*. Washington, D.C.: World Resources Institute.

Gould, Jay M., and Benjamin A. Goldman. 1991. *Deadly Deceit: Low-Level Radiation, High-Level Cover-up*. New York: Four Walls Eight Windows.

Herman, Robin. 1990. *Fusion: The Search for Endless Energy*. New York: Cambridge University Press.

Holdren, John. 1982. "Energy Hazards: What to Measure, What to Compare." *Technology Review*, April, 32–38.

Hughes, Barry B., et al. 1985. *Energy in the Global Arena: Actors, Values, Policies, and Futures*. Durham, N.C.: Duke University Press.

Huizenga, John R. 1992. *Cold Fusion: The Scientific Fiasco of the Century*. Rochester, N.Y.: University of Rochester Press.

Humphrey, Craig R., and Frederick R. Buttel. 1982. *Environment, Energy, and Society*. Belmont, Calif.: Wadsworth.

Jacop, Gerald. 1990. *Sight Unseen: The Politics of Siting a Nuclear Waste Repository*. Pittsburgh: University of Pittsburgh Press.

Jagger, John. 1991. *The Nuclear Lion: What Every Citizen Should Know About Nuclear Power and Nuclear War*. New York: Plenum.

Jasper, James M. 1990. *Nuclear Politics: Energy and the State in the United States, Sweden, and France*. Princeton, N.J.: Princeton University Press.

Kaku, Michio, and Jennifer Trainer. 1982. *Nuclear Power: Both Sides*. New York: W. W. Norton.

League of Women Voters Education Fund. 1985. *The Nuclear Waste Primer*. Washington D.C.: League of Women Voters.

Lenssen, Nicholas. 1991. *Nuclear Waste: The Problem That Won't Go Away*. Washington, D.C.: Worldwatch Institute.

Lidsky, Lawrence M. 1983. "The Trouble with Fusion." *Technology Review*, October, 32–44.

Lidsky, Lawrence M. 1984. "The Reactor of the Future." *Technology Review*, February/March, 52–56.

Lovins, Amory B. 1986. "The Origins of the Nuclear Power Fiasco." *Energy Policy Studies*, vol. 3, 7–34.

Lovins, Amory B., and L. Hunter Lovins. 1982. *Brittle Power: Energy Strategy for National Security*. Andover, Mass.: Brick House.

Marples, David R. 1986. *Chernobyl and Nuclear Power in the USSR*. New York: St. Martin's Press.

Masters, C. D., et al. 1991. "Resource Constraints in Petroleum Production Potential." *Science*, vol. 253, 146–152.

May, John. 1990. *The Greenpeace Book of the Nuclear Age*. New York: Pantheon Books.

McCracken, Samuel. 1982. *The War Against the Atom*. New York: Basic Books.

Medvedev, Grigori. 1990. *The Truth About Chernobyl*. New York: Basic Books.

Medvedev, Zhores. 1990. *The Legacy of Chernobyl*. New York: W. W. Norton.

Morone, Joseph G., and Edward J. Woodhouse. 1989. *The Demise of Nuclear Energy?* New Haven, Conn.: Yale University Press.

Murray, Raymond L. 1989. *Understanding Radioactive Waste*. 3rd ed. Columbus, Ohio: Battelle Press.

National Academy of Sciences. 1990. *Energy: Production, Consumption, and Consequences*. Washington, D.C.: National Academy Press.

National Academy of Sciences. 1991. *Nuclear Power: Technical and Institutional Options for the Future*. Washington, D.C.: National Academy Press.

National Academy of Sciences. 1991. *Undiscovered Oil and Gas Resources*. Washington, D.C.: National Academy Press.

Office of Technology Assessment. 1984. *Managing the Nation's Commercial High-Level Radioactive Waste*. Washington, D.C.: Government Printing Office.

Office of Technology Assessment. 1991. *Complex Cleanup: The Environmental Legacy of Nuclear Weapons Production*. Washington, D.C.: Government Printing Office.

O'Hefferman, Patrick, Amory Lovins, and L. Hunter Lovins. 1984. *The First Nuclear World War*. New York: William Morrow.

Oppenheimer, Ernest J. 1990. *Natural Gas, the Best Energy Choice*. New York: Pen & Podium.

Park, Chris C. 1989. *Chernobyl: The Long Shadow*. New York: Routledge and Kegan Paul.

Pasqualetti, M. J. 1990. *Nuclear Decommissioning and Society: Public Links to a Technical Task*. New York: Routledge and Kegan Paul.

Patterson, Walter C. 1984. *The Plutonium Business and the Spread of the Bomb*. San Francisco: Sierra Club Books.

Pollock, Cynthia. 1986. *Decommissioning: Nuclear Power's Missing Link*. Washington, D.C.: Worldwatch Institute.

President's Commission on the Accident at Three Mile Island. 1979. *Report of the President's Commission on the Accident at Three Mile Island*. Washington, D.C.: Government Printing Office.

Public Citizen. 1987. *Nuclear Legacy: Too Costly to Continue*. Washington, D.C.: Public Citizen.

Public Citizen. 1987. *The Price-Anderson Act: Multi-Billion Dollar Nuclear Subsidy*. Washington, D.C.: Public Citizen.

Public Citizen. 1988. *Consequences of a Nuclear Accident*. Washington, D.C.: Public Citizen.

Public Citizen. 1989. *Forever Is the Debt*. Washington, D.C.: Public Citizen.

Public Citizen. 1989. *Nuclear Lemons: An Assessment of America's Worst Nuclear Reactors*. Washington, D.C.: Public Citizen.

Public Citizen. 1989. *On Again, Off Again: The Unreliability of U.S. Nuclear Power Plants*. Washington, D.C.: Public Citizen.

Public Citizen. 1989. *Runaway Costs: Rising Operating and Maintenance Expenses at U.S. Nuclear Plants*. Washington, D.C.: Public Citizen.

Read, Piers Paul. 1993. *Ablaze: The Story of Chernobyl*. New York: Random House.

Reddy, Amulya K. N., and Jose Goldenberg. 1990. "Energy for the Developing World." *Scientific American*, September, 111–118.

Resnikoff, Marvin. 1983. *The Next Nuclear Gamble: Transportation and Storage of Nuclear Waste*. Washington, D.C.: Council on Economic Priorities.

Resnikoff, Marvin. 1987. *Living Without Landfills*. New York: Radioactive Waste Campaign.

Resnikoff, Marvin. 1988. *Deadly Defense: Military Radioactive Landfills*. New York: Radioactive Waste Campaign.

Rocky Mountain Institute. 1988. *An Energy Security Reader*. 2nd ed. Old Snowmass, Colo.: Rocky Mountain Institute.

Rosenbaum, Walter A. 1987. *Energy, Politics, and Public Policy*. 2nd ed. Washington, D.C.: Congressional Quarterly.

Saleska, Scott. 1989. *Nuclear Legacy: An Overview of the Places, Problems, and Politics of Radioactive Waste in the United States*. Washington, D.C.: Public Citizen.

Schobert, Harold H. 1987. *Coal: The Energy Source of the Past and Future*. Washington, D.C.: American Chemical Society.

Shrader-Frechette, Kristin. 1991. "Ethical Dilemmas and Radioactive Waste: A Survey of the Issues." *Environmental Ethics*, vol. 13, Winter, 327–343.

Sierra Club. 1991. *Kick the Oil Habit: Choosing a Safe Energy Future for America*. San Francisco: Sierra Club Books.

Squillace, Mark. 1990. *Strip Mining Handbook*. Washington, D.C.: Friends of the Earth.

Taylor, John J. 1989. "Improved and Safer Nuclear Power." *Science*, vol. 244, 318–325.

Union of Concerned Scientists. 1990. *Safety Second: The NRC and America's Nuclear Power Plants*. Bloomington: Indiana University Press.

Union of Concerned Scientists et al. 1991. *America's Energy Choices: Investing in a Strong Economy and a Clean Environment*. Cambridge, Mass.: Union of Concerned Scientists.

U.S. Department of Energy. 1988. *An Analysis of Nuclear Power Operating Costs*. Washington, D.C.: Government Printing Office.

Watson, Robert K. 1988. *Fact Sheet on Oil and Conservation Resources*. New York: Natural Resources Defense Council.

Weinberg, Alvin M. 1985. *Continuing the Nuclear Dialogue*. La Grange Park, Ill.: American Nuclear Society.

Weinberg, Alvin M., et al. 1985. *The Second Nuclear Era: A New Start for Nuclear Power*. New York: Praeger.

Winteringham, F. P. W. 1991. *Energy Use and the Environment*. Boca Raton, Fla.: Lewis.

Yeargin, Daniel. 1988. "Energy Security in the 1990s." *Foreign Affairs*, Autumn, 93–116.

Yeargin, Daniel. 1990. *The Prize: The Epic Quest for Oil, Money, and Power*. New York: Simon & Schuster.

## 19 NONRENEWABLE MINERAL RESOURCES AND SOLID WASTE

Allen, Robert. 1992. *Waste Not, Want Not*. London: Earthscan.

Blumberg, Louis, and Robert Grottleib. 1988. *War on Waste—Can America Win Its Battle with Garbage?* Covelo, Calif.: Island Press.

Borgese, Elisabeth Mann. 1985. *The Mines of Neptune: Minerals and Metals from the Sea*. New York: Harry N. Abrams.

Boyd, Susan, et al., eds. 1988. *Waste: Choices for Communities*. Washington, D.C.: CONCERN.

Cameron, Eugene N. 1986. *At the Crossroads—The Mineral Problems of the United States*. New York: John Wiley.

Canby, Thomas Y., and Charles O'Rear. 1989. "Reshaping Our Lives: Advanced Materials." *National Geographic*, December, 746–781.

Carless, Jennifer. 1992. *Taking Out the Trash: A No-Nonsense Guide to Recycling*. Covelo, Calif.: Island Press.

Clark, Joel P., and Frank R. Field III. 1985. "How Critical Are Critical Materials?" *Technology Review*, August/September, 38–46.

Clarke, Marjorie J., et al. 1991. *Burning Garbage in the U.S.: Practice vs. State of the Art*. New York: INFORM.

Cohen, Levin, et al. 1988. *Coming Full Circle: Successful Recycling Today*. New York: Environmental Defense Fund.

Connett, Paul H. 1989. *Waste Management As If the Future Mattered*. Canton, N.Y.: Work on Waste.

Connett, Paul H. 1992. "The Disposable Society." In F. H. Bormann and Stephen R. Kellert, eds., *Ecology, Economics, Ethics*, 99–122. New Haven, Conn.: Yale University Press.

Debus, Keith H. 1990. "Mining with Microbes." *Technology Review*, August/September, 50–57.

Denison, Richard A., and John Ruston. 1990. *Recycling and Incineration: Evaluating the Choices*. Covelo, Calif.: Island Press.

Dorr, Ann. 1984. *Minerals—Foundations of Society*. Montgomery County: League of Women Voters of Montgomery County Maryland.

Durning, Alan Thein. 1992. *How Much Is Enough? The Consumer Society and the Future of the Earth*. New York: W. W. Norton.

Earth Works Group. 1990. *The Recycler's Handbook: Simple Things You Can Do*. Berkeley, Calif.: Earth Works Press.

Environment Canada. 1990. *Reduction and Reuse: The First 2Rs of Waste Management*. Ottawa: Environment Canada.

Environmental Protection Agency. 1989. *Solid Waste Disposal in the United States*. Washington, D.C.: Government Printing Office.

Environmental Protection Agency. 1990. *Methods to Manage and Control Plastic Wastes*. Washington, D.C.: Government Printing Office.

Environmental Protection Agency. 1992. *Characterization of Municipal Solid Waste in the United States*. Washington, D.C.: Government Printing Office.

Forrester, Tom. 1988. *The Materials Revolution: Superconductors, New Materials, and the Japanese Challenge*. Cambridge, Mass.: MIT Press.

Frosch, Robert A., and Nicholas E. Gallopoulos. 1989. "Strategies for Manufacturing." *Scientific American*, September, 144–152.

Gordon, Robert B., et al. 1988. *World Mineral Exploration: Trends and Issues*. Washington, D.C.: Resources for the Future.

Gourlay, K. A. 1992. *World of Waste: Dilemmas of Industrial Development*. Atlantic Highlands, N.J.: Zed Books.

Harben, Peter. 1992. "Strategic Minerals." *Earth*, July, 36–43.

Hershkowitz, Allen. 1987. "Burning Trash: How It Could Work." *Technology Review*, July, 26–34.

Hershkowitz, Allen, and Eugene Salermi. 1987. *Garbage Management in Japan: Leading the Way*. New York: INFORM.

Holdgate, Martin W. 1990. "Antarctica: Ice Under Pressure." *Environment*, vol. 32, no. 8, 4–9, 30–35.

Huls, Jon, and Neil Seldman. 1985. *Waste to Wealth*. Washington, D.C.: Institute for Local Self-Reliance.

Husingh, Donald, et al. 1986. *Proven Profits from Pollution Prevention*. Washington, D.C.: Institute for Local Self-Reliance.

Institute for Local Self-Reliance. 1988. *Recycling Goals and Strategies*. Washington, D.C.: Institute for Local Self-Reliance.

Kharbanda, O. P., and E. A. Stallworthy. 1990. *Waste Management: Toward a Sustainable Society*. New York: Auburn House.

Kimball, Lee A. 1990. *Southern Exposure: Deciding Antarctica's Future*. Washington, D.C.: World Resources Institute.

Kirshner, Dan, et al. 1988. *To Burn or Not to Burn*. New York: Environmental Defense Fund.

Leontief, Wassily, et al. 1983. *The Future of Nonfuel Minerals in the U.S. and World Economy: 1980–2030*. Lexington, Mass.: Lexington (Heath).

Lester, Stephen, and Brian Lipsett. 1988. *Incineration: The Burning Issue—A Manual on the Science and Politics of Hazardous Waste Incinerators*. Arlington, Va.: Citizens' Clearinghouse for Hazardous Waste.

Lester, Stephen, and Brian Lipsett. 1989. *Track Record of the Hazardous Waste Incineration Industry*. Arlington, Va.: Citizens' Clearinghouse for Hazardous Waste.

Lichiello, P., and L. Snyder. 1988. *Plastics: The Risks and Consequences of Its Production and Use*. Los Angeles: School of Architecture and Urban Planning, University of California.

Lipsett, B., and D. Farrell. 1990. *Solid Waste Incineration Status Report*. Arlington, Va.: Citizens' Clearinghouse for Hazardous Waste.

Maurice, Charles, and Charles W. Smithson. 1984. *The Doomsday Myth*. Stanford, Calif.: Hoover Institution Press.

May, John. 1989. *The Greenpeace Book of Antarctica*. New York: Doubleday.

McLaren, Digby J., and Brian J. Skinner, eds. 1987. *Resources and World Development*. New York: John Wiley.

McLenighan, Valjean. 1991. *Sustainable Manufacturing: Saving Jobs, Saving the Environment*. Chicago: Center for Neighborhood Technology.

National Academy of Sciences. 1990. *Our Seabed Frontier: Challenges and Choices*. Washington, D.C.: National Academy Press.

National Academy of Sciences. 1990. *Waste Reduction: Research Needs in Applied Social Sciences*. Washington, D.C.: National Academy Press.

Neal, Homer A., and J. R. Schubel. 1987. *Solid Waste Management and the Environment: The Mounting Garbage and Trash Crisis*. Englewood Cliffs, N.J.: Prentice-Hall.

Newsday. 1989. *Rush to Burn: Solving America's Garbage Crisis?* Covelo, Calif.: Island Press.

Office of Solid Waste. 1989. *Recycling Works! State and Local Solutions to Solid Waste Management*. Washington, D.C.: Environmental Protection Agency.

Office of Technology Assessment. 1985. *Strategic Materials: Technologies to Reduce U.S. Import Vulnerability*. Washington, D.C.: Government Printing Office.

Office of Technology Assessment. 1987. *Marine Minerals: Exploring Our New Ocean Frontier*. Washington, D.C.: Government Printing Office.

Office of Technology Assessment. 1988. *Advanced Materials by Design: New Structural Materials Technologies*. Washington, D.C.: Government Printing Office.

Office of Technology Assessment. 1989. *Facing America's Trash: What's Next for Municipal Solid Waste*. Washington, D.C.: Government Printing Office.

Office of Technology Assessment. 1989. *Polar Prospects: A Minerals Treaty for Antarctica*. Washington, D.C.: Government Printing Office.

Office of Technology Assessment. 1990. *Making Things Better*. Washington, D.C.: Government Printing Office.

Ortbal, John. 1991. *Buy Recycled! Your Practical Guide to the Environmentally Responsible Office*. Chicago: Services Marketing Group.

Platt, Brenda, et al. 1991. *Beyond 40 Percent: Record-Setting Recycling and Composting Programs*. Covelo, Calif.: Island Press.

Pollack, Cynthia. 1987. *Mining Urban Wastes: The Potential for Recycling*. Washington, D.C.: Worldwatch Institute.

Polprasert, Chongrak. 1989. *Organic Waste Recycling*. New York: John Wiley.

Rathje, William, and Cullen Murphy. 1992. *Rubbish! The Archaeology of Garbage: What Our Garbage Tells Us About Ourselves*. San Francisco: HarperCollins.

Reynolds, Michael. 1990–1991. *Earthship*. Vols. 1 and 2. Taos, N.M.: Solar Survival Architecture.

Seldman, Neil, and Bill Perkins. 1988. *Designing the Waste Stream*. Washington, D.C.: Institute for Local Self-Reliance.

Suter, Keith. 1991. *Antarctica: Private Property or Public Heritage?* Atlantic Highlands, N.J.: Zed Books.

Tapp, B. A., and J. R. Watkins. 1989. *Energy and Mineral Resource Systems: An Introduction*. New York: Cambridge University Press.

Tilton, John E., ed. 1990. *World Metal Demand*. Washington, D.C.: Resources for the Future.

Underwood, Joanna D., and Allen Hershkowitz. 1989. *Facts About U.S. Garbage Management: Problems and Practices*. New York: INFORM.

Westing, Arthur H. 1986. *Global Resources and International Conflict*. New York: Oxford University Press.

Williams, Susan, ed. 1991. *Trash to Cash: New Business Opportunities in the Post-Consumer Waste Stream*. Washington, D.C.: Investor Responsibility Research Center.

Wolf, Nancy, and Ellen Feldman. 1990. *Plastics: America's Packaging Dilemma*. Covelo, Calif.: Island Press.

Young, John E. 1991. *Discarding the Throwaway Society*. Washington, D.C.: Worldwatch Institute.

Young, John E. 1992. "Aluminum's Real Tab." *World Watch*, March/April, 26–34.

Young, John E. 1992. *Mining the Earth*. Washington, D.C.: Worldwatch Institute.

Youngquist, Walter. 1990. *Mineral Resources and the Destinies of Nations*. Portland, Ore.: National Book.

## 20 RISK AND HUMAN HEALTH

Amato, Paul R., and Sonia A. Partridge. 1989. *The New Vegetarians: Promoting Health and Protecting Life*. New York: Plenum.

Ames, Bruce N., et al. 1987. "Ranking Possible Carcinogenic Hazards." *Science*, vol. 236, 271–279.

Aral, Sevgi O., and King K. Holmes. 1991. "Sexually Transmitted Diseases in the AIDS Era." *Scientific American*, vol. 264, no. 2, 62–69.

Armstrong, David. 1984. *The Insider's Guide to Health Foods*. New York: Bantam Books.

Bernarde, Melvin A. 1989. *Our Precarious Habitat: Fifteen Years Later*. New York: John Wiley.

Bertell, Rosalie. 1986. *No Immediate Danger*. New York: Women's Press.

Bowen, Otis R., and Robert E. Windom. 1988. *Understanding AIDS*. Washington, D.C.: Government Printing Office.

Bower, John. 1989. *The Healthy House*. New York: Lyle Stuart.

Brill, Bertrand, ed. 1985. *Low-Level Radiation Effects: A Fact Book*. New York: New York Society for Nuclear Medicine.

Brodeur, Paul. 1989. *Currents of Death: Power Lines, Computer Terminals, and the Attempt to Cover Up Their Threat to Your Health*. New York: Simon & Schuster.

Calabrese, Edward J., and Michael W. Dorsey. 1984. *Healthy Living in an Unhealthy World*. New York: Simon & Schuster.

Caufield, Catherine. 1989. *Multiple Exposures: Chronicles of the Radiation Age*. San Francisco: Harper & Row.

Chandler, William U. 1986. *Banishing Tobacco*. Washington, D.C.: Worldwatch Institute.

Clarke, Lee. 1989. *Acceptable Risk? Making Decisions in a Toxic Environment*. Berkeley and Los Angeles: University of California Press.

Cohen, Mark N. 1989. *Health and the Rise of Civilization*. New Haven, Conn.: Yale University Press.

Cohrssen, John J., and Vincent T. Covello. 1989. *Risk Analysis: A Guide to Principles and Methods for Analyzing Health and Environmental Risks*. Springfield, Va.: National Technical Information Service.

Coogan, Patrica, and Terry Greene. 1992. *Environment and Health: How to Investigate Community Health Problems*. Boston: JSI Center for Environmental Health Studies.

Council on Environmental Quality. 1988. *Risk Analysis: Guide to Principles and Methods for Analyzing Health and Environmental Risks*. Springfield, Va.: National Technical Information Service.

Covello, V. T., et al., eds. 1989. *Effective Risk Communication*. New York: Plenum.

Crone, Hugh D. 1986. *Chemicals and Society*. Cambridge, Mass.: Cambridge University Press.

Desowitz, Robert S. 1991. *The Malaria Capers: More Tales of Parasites and People, Research, and Reality*. New York: W. W. Norton.

Douglas, Mary, and Aaron Wildavsky. 1982. *Risk and Culture*. Berkeley and Los Angeles: University of California Press.

Efron, Edith. 1984. *The Apocalyptics: Cancer and the Big Lie*. New York: Simon & Schuster.

Environmental Health Watch and Housing Resource Center. 1988. *The 1988 Healthy House Catalog*. Cleveland: Environmental Health Watch and Housing Resource Center.

Environmental Protection Agency. 1984. *Risk Assessment and Risk Management: Framework for Decision Making*. Washington, D.C.: Government Printing Office.

Environmental Protection Agency. 1987. *Unfinished Business: A Comparative Assessment of Environmental Problems*. Washington, D.C.: Environmental Protection Agency.

Environmental Protection Agency. 1988. *Future Risk: Research Strategies for the 1990s*. Washington, D.C.: EPA.

Environmental Protection Agency. 1990. *Reducing Risk: Setting Priorities and Strategies for Environmental Protection*. Washington, D.C.: EPA.

Environmental Protection Agency. 1991. March/April issue of the *EPA Journal*. Entire issue devoted to the debate about risk analysis.

Environmental Protection Agency. 1991. *The Environmental Challenge of the 1990s*. Washington, D.C.: EPA.

Environmental Protection Agency. 1992. *Respiratory Health Effects of Passive Smoking: Lung Cancer and Other Disorders*. Washington, D.C.: EPA.

Fischoff, Baruch, et al. 1984. *Acceptable Risk: Science and Determination of Safety*. New York: Cambridge University Press.

Freudenburg, William R. 1988. "Perceived Risk, Real Risk: Social Science and the Art of Probabilistic Risk Assessment." *Science*, vol. 242, 44–49.

Freudenthal, Ralph I., and Susan L. Freudenthal. 1989. *What You Need to Know to Live with Chemicals*. Greens Farms, Conn.: Hill & Garnett.

Gofman, John W. 1990. *Radiation-Induced Cancer from Low-Dose Exposure*. San Francisco: Committee for Nuclear Responsibility.

Gough, Michael. 1989. "Estimating Cancer Mortality." *Environmental Science and Technology*, vol. 23, no. 8, 925–930.

Gould, Jay, and Benjamin Goldman. 1990. *Deadly Deceit: Low-Level Radiation—High-Level Cover-Up*. New York: Four Walls Eight Windows.

Graham, J. D., et al., eds. 1988. *In Search of Safety: Chemicals and Cancer Risk*. Cambridge, Mass.: Harvard University Press.

Greenberg, M. R. 1987. *Public Health and Environment: The United States Experience*. New York: Guilford.

Hadden, Susan G. 1989. *A Citizen's Right to Know: Risk Communication and Public Policy*. Boulder, Colo.: Westview Press.

Hall, Bob, and Mary L. Kerr. 1991. *1991–92 Green Index: A State-by-State Guide to the Nation's Environmental Health*. Covelo, Calif.: Island Press.

Hall, Ross Hume. 1990. *Health and the Global Environment*. Cambridge, Mass.: Basil Blackwell.

Harte, John, et al. 1992. *Toxics A to Z: A Guide to Everyday Pollution Hazards*. Berkeley and Los Angeles: University of California Press.

Holleb, Arthur I., ed. 1990. *The American Cancer Society Cancer Book*. New York: Doubleday.

Hunter, Linda Mason. 1989. *The Healthy House: An Attic-to-Basement Guide to Toxin-Free Living*. Emmaus, Pa.: Rodale Press.

Imperato, P. J., and Greg Mitchell. 1985. *Acceptable Risks*. New York: Viking Press.

Jones, K., and G. Moon. 1987. *Health, Disease, and Society: An Introduction to Medical Geography*. San Diego: Academic Press.

Kamarin, M. A. 1988. *Toxicology: A Primer on Toxicology Principles and Applications*. Boca Raton, Fla.: Lewis.

Klaassen, C. D., et al. 1986. *Casarett and Doull's Toxicology: The Basic Science of Poisons*. 3rd ed. New York: Macmillan.

Krimsky, Sheldon, and Alonzo Plough. 1988. *Environmental Hazards: Communicating Risks as a Social Process*. Dover, Mass.: Auburn House.

Kupchella, Charles E. 1987. *Dimensions of Cancer*. Belmont, Calif.: Wadsworth.

Lave, Lester B. 1987. *Risk Assessment and Management*. New York: Plenum.

Lewis, H. W. 1990. *Technological Risk*. New York: W. W. Norton.

Mann, Jonathan, et al., eds. 1992. *AIDS in the World*. Cambridge, Mass.: Harvard University Press.

Manning, Willard G., et al. 1991. *The Costs of Poor Health Habits*. Cambridge, Mass.: Harvard University Press.

Mayo, Deborah G., and Rachelle D. Hollander, eds. 1992. *Acceptable Evidence: Science and Values in Risk Management*. New York: Oxford University Press.

Merrell, Paul, and Carol Van Strum. 1990. "Negligible Risk or Premeditated Murder?" *Journal of Pesticide Reform*, vol. 10, Spring, 20–22.

Moeller, Dade W. 1992. *Environmental Health*. Cambridge, Mass.: Harvard University Press.

Morone, Edward J., and Edward J. Woodhouse. 1986. *Averting Catastrophe: Strategies for Regulating Risky Technologies*. Berkeley and Los Angeles: University of California Press.

Mosley, W. Henry, and Peter Cowley. 1991. "The Challenge of World Health." *Population Bulletin*, vol. 46, no. 4, 1–39.

National Academy of Sciences. 1984. *Toxicity Testing: Strategies to Determine Needs and Priorities*. Washington, D.C.: National Academy Press.

National Academy of Sciences. 1986. *Environment Tobacco Smoke: Measuring Exposures and Assessing Health Effects*. Washington, D.C.: National Academy Press.

National Academy of Sciences. 1988. *Use of Laboratory Animals in Biomedical Research*. Washington, D.C.: National Academy Press.

National Academy of Sciences. 1989. *AIDS: The Second Decade*. Washington, D.C.: National Academy Press.

National Academy of Sciences. 1989. *Improving Risk Communication*. Washington, D.C.: National Academy Press.

National Academy of Sciences. 1990. *Health Effects of Exposure to Low Levels of Ionizing Radiation*. Washington, D.C.: National Academy Press.

National Academy of Sciences. 1991. *Malaria: Obstacles and Opportunities*. Washington, D.C.: National Academy Press.

National Academy of Sciences. 1992. *Eat for Life: The Food and Nutrition Board's Guide to Reducing Your Risk of Chronic Disease*. Washington, D.C.: National Academy Press.

National Academy of Sciences. 1992. *The Social Impact of AIDS*. Washington, D.C.: National Academy Press.

National Council on Radiation Protection and Measurements. 1987. *Ionizing Radiation Exposure of the Population of the United States*. Bethesda, Md.: NCRP.

Nelkin, M. M., and M. S. Brown. 1984. *Workers at Risk: Voices from the Workplace*. Chicago: University of Chicago Press.

Office of Technology Assessment. 1985. *Status of Biomedical Research and Related Technology for Tropical Diseases*. Washington, D.C.: Government Printing Office.

Office of Technology Assessment. 1986. *Alternatives to Animal Use in Research, Testing, and Education*. Washington, D.C.: Government Printing Office.

Office of Technology Assessment. 1989. *Biological Effects of Power Frequency Electric and Magnetic Fields*. Washington, D.C.: Government Printing Office.

Ottoboni, M. Alice. 1991. *The Dose Makes the Poison: A Plain-Language Guide to Toxicology*. 2nd ed. New York: Van Nostrand Reinhold.

Pearson, David. 1989. *The Natural House Book*. New York: Simon & Schuster.

Perrow, Charles. 1985. *Normal Accidents: Living with High-Risk Technologies*. New York: Basic Books.

Piller, Charles. 1991. *The Fail-Safe Society*. New York: Basic Books.

Pochin, Edward. 1985. *Nuclear Radiation: Risks and Benefits*. New York: Oxford University Press.

Robbins, Anthony, and Phyllis Freeman. 1988. "Obstacles to Developing Vaccines for the Third World." *Scientific American*, November, 126–133.

Rodricks, Joseph V. 1992. *Calculated Risks: The Toxicity and Human Health Risks of Chemicals in the Environment*. New York: Cambridge University Press.

Russell, Dick, et al. 1992. *Inconclusive by Design: Waste, Fraud, and Abuse in Federal Environmental Health Research*. Boston: Environmental Health Network.

Sandman, Peter M. 1986. *Explaining Environmental Risk*. Washington, D.C.: EPA, Office of Toxic Substances.

Schulman, Seth. 1992. *The Threat at Home: Confronting the Toxic Legacy of the US Military*. Boston: Beacon Press.

Shrader-Frechette, K. S. 1991. *Risk and Rationality*. Berkeley and Los Angeles: University of California Press.

Sternglass, Ernest J. 1981. *Secret Fallout: Low-Level Radiation from Hiroshima to Three Mile Island*. New York: McGraw-Hill.

Travis, Curtis C., and Sheri T. Hester. 1991. "Global Chemical Pollution." *Environmental Science & Technology*, vol. 25, no. 5, 814–819.

United Nations. 1990. *Radiation: Doses, Effects, and Risks*. New York: United Nations Publications.

U.S. Department of Health and Human Services. Annual. *The Health Consequences of Smoking*. Rockville, Md.: U.S. Department of Health and Human Services.

U.S. Department of Health and Human Services. 1986. *The Health Consequences of Involuntary Smoking: A Report of the Surgeon General*. Rockville, Md.: U.S. Department of Health and Human Services.

U.S. Department of Health and Human Services. 1988. *The Surgeon General's Report on Nutrition and Health*. Washington, D.C.: Government Printing Office.

Wilson, Albert R. 1991. *Environmental Risk: Identification and Management*. Boca Raton, Fla.: Lewis.

Wilson, Richard, and E. A. C. Crouch. 1987. "Risk Assessment and Comparisons: An Introduction." *Science*, vol. 236, 267–270.

## 21 HAZARDOUS WASTE

Agency for Toxic Substances and Disease Registry. 1988. *The Nature and Extent of Lead Poisoning in Children in the United States*. Atlanta: U.S. Department of Health and Human Services.

Block, Alan A., and Frank R. Scarpitti. 1984. *Poisoning for Profit: The Mafia and Toxic Waste in America*. New York: William Morrow.

Brown, Phil, and Edwin J. Mikkelsen. 1990. *No Safe Place: Toxic Waste, Leukemia, and Community Action*. Berkeley and Los Angeles: University of California Press.

Bryant, Bunyan, and Paul Mohai, eds. 1992. *Race and the Incidence of Environmental Hazards: A Time for Discourse*. Boulder, Colo.: Westview Press.

Bullard, Robert D. 1990. *Dumping in Dixie: Race, Class, and Environmental Quality*. Boulder, Colo.: Westview Press.

Centers for Disease Control and Prevention. 1991. *Preventing Lead Poisoning in Young Children*. Atlanta: Centers for Disease Control and Prevention.

Chepesiuk, Ron. 1991. "From Ash to Cash: The International Trade in Toxic Waste." *E Magazine*, July/August, 31–63.

Citizen's Clearinghouse for Toxic Waste. 1987. *Dealing with Military Toxics: What You Can Do*. Falls Church, Va.: Citizens' Clearinghouse for Toxic Waste.

Clean Sites. 1991. *What Works? Alternative Strategies for Superfund Cleanups*. Alexandria, Va.: Clean Sites.

Cohen, Gary, and John O'Connor. 1990. *Fighting Toxics: A Manual for Protecting Family, Community, and Workplace*. Covelo, Calif.: Island Press.

Commoner, Barry. 1990. *Making Peace with the Planet*. New York: Pantheon Books.

Costner, Pat, and Joe Thornton. 1989. *Sham Recyclers, Part 1: Hazardous Waste Incineration in Cement and Aggregate Kilns*. Washington, D.C.: Greenpeace.

Dadd, Debra Lynn. 1990. *Nontoxic, Natural and Earthwise*. Los Angeles: Jeremy Tarcher.

Davis, Charles E., and James P. Lester, eds. 1988. *Dimensions of Hazardous Waste Politics and Policies*. Westport, Conn.: Greenwood Press.

Dorfman, Mark H., et al. 1992. *Environmental Dividends: Cutting More Chemical Wastes*. New York: INFORM.

Enterprise for Education. 1989. *Hazardous Wastes from Homes*. Santa Monica, Calif.: Enterprise for Education.

Environmental Protection Agency. 1987. *The Hazardous Waste System*. Washington, D.C.: EPA.

Epstein, Samuel S., et al. 1982. *Hazardous Waste in America*. San Francisco: Sierra Club Books.

Gibbs, Lois. 1982. *The Love Canal: My Story*. Albany: State University of New York Press.

Gibbs, Lois, and Will Collette. 1987. *Solid Waste Action Project Guidebook*. Arlington, Va.: Citizens' Clearinghouse for Hazardous Waste.

Goldman, Benjamin A. 1991. *The Truth About Where You Live: An Atlas for Action on Toxins and Mortality*. New York: Random House.

Goldman, Benjamin A., et al. 1986. *Hazardous Waste Management: Reducing the Risk*. Covelo, Calif.: Island Press.

Gordon, Ben, and Peter Montague. 1989. *Zero Discharge: A Citizen's Toxic Waste Manual*. Washington, D.C.: Greenpeace.

Gordon, Wendy, and Jane Bloom. 1985. *Deeper Problems: Limits to Underground Injection as a Hazardous Waste Disposal Method*. New York: Natural Resources Defense Council.

Harte, John, et al. 1991. *Toxics A to Z: A Guide to Everyday Pollution Hazards*. Berkeley and Los Angeles: University of California Press.

Haun, J. William. 1991. *Guide to the Management of Hazardous Waste*. Golden, Colo.: Fulcrum.

Hirschorn, Joel S. 1988. "Cutting Production of Hazardous Waste." *Technology Review*, April, 52–61.

Hutchinson, T. C., ed. 1987. *Lead, Mercury, Cadmium, and Arsenic in the Environment*. New York: John Wiley.

Kenworthy, Lauren, and Eric Schaeffer. 1990. *A Citizen's Guide to Promoting Toxic Waste Reduction*. New York: INFORM.

Lappé, Marc. 1991. *Chemical Deception: The Toxic Threat to Health and Environment*. San Francisco: Sierra Club Books.

Lester, James P., and Ann O. M. Bowman, eds. 1983. *Politics of Hazardous Waste Management*. Durham, N.C.: Duke University Press.

Love Canal Homeowners Association. 1984. *Love Canal: A Chronology of Events That Shaped a Movement*. Arlington, Va.: Citizens' Clearinghouse for Hazardous Wastes.

Mazmanian, Daniel, and David Morrell. 1992. *Beyond Superfailure: America's Toxics Policy for the 1990s*. Boulder Colo.: Westview Press

Minnesota Mining and Manufacturing. 1988. *Low- or Non-Pollution Technology Through Pollution Prevention*. St. Paul, Minn.: 3M Company.

Montague, Peter. 1989. "What We Must Do—A Grass-Roots Offensive Against Toxics in the 90s." *The Workbook*, vol. 14, no. 3, 90–113.

Moyers, Bill. 1990. *Global Dumping Ground: The International Traffic in Hazardous Waste*. Cabin John, Md.: Seven Locks Press.

Muir, Warren, and Joanna Underwood. 1987. *Promoting Hazardous Waste Reduction*. New York: INFORM.

National Academy of Sciences. 1983. *Transportation of Hazardous Materials: Toward a National Strategy*. Washington, D.C.: National Academy Press.

National Academy of Sciences. 1991. *Environmental Epidemiology Vol. 1: Public Health and Hazardous Wastes*. Washington, D.C.: National Academy Press.

National Toxics Campaign Fund. 1991. *The U.S. Military's Toxic Legacy: America's Worst Environmental Enemy*. Boston: National Toxics Campaign Fund.

**North Carolina Pollution Prevention Pays Program. 1986.** *Accomplishments of North Carolina Industries.* Raleigh: North Carolina Department of Natural Resources and Community Development.

**Nriagu, Jerome O. 1990.** "Global Metal Pollution: Poisoning the Biosphere." *Environment,* vol. 32, no. 7, 7–32.

**Office of Technology Assessment. 1986.** *Serious Reduction of Hazardous Waste.* Washington, D.C.: Government Printing Office.

**Office of Technology Assessment. 1986.** *Transportation of Hazardous Materials.* Washington, D.C.: Government Printing Office.

**Office of Technology Assessment. 1987.** *From Pollution to Prevention: A Progress Report on Waste Reduction.* Washington, D.C.: Government Printing Office.

**Office of Technology Assessment. 1988.** *Are We Cleaning Up? 10 Superfund Case Studies.* Washington, D.C.: Government Printing Office.

**Office of Technology Assessment. 1989.** *Cleaning Up: Superfund's Problems Can Be Solved.* Washington, D.C.: Government Printing Office.

**Orum, Paul, et al. 1991.** *The "Recycling" Loophole in the Toxics Release Inventory: Out of Site, Out of Mind.* Washington, D.C.: Working Group on Community Right-to-Know.

**Padock, Todd. 1989.** *Dioxins and Furans: Questions and Answers.* Philadelphia: Academy of Natural Sciences.

**Piasecki, Bruce, and Gary Davis. 1987.** *America's Future in Toxic Waste Management: Lessons from Europe.* Westport, Conn.: Quorum.

**Pollack, Stephanie. 1989.** "Solving the Lead Dilemma." *Technology Review,* October, 22–31.

**Portney, Kent E. 1992.** *Siting Hazardous Waste Treatment Facilities: The NIMBY Syndrome.* New York: Auburn House.

**Postel, Sandra. 1987.** *Defusing the Toxics Threat: Controlling Pesticides and Industrial Waste.* Washington, D.C.: Worldwatch Institute.

**Scott, Ronald M. 1989.** *Chemical Hazards in the Workplace.* Boca Raton, Fla.: Lewis.

**Segel, Edward, et al. 1985.** *The Toxic Substances Dilemma: A Plan for Citizen Action.* Washington, D.C.: National Wildlife Federation.

**Shulman, Seth. 1992.** *The Threat at Home: Confronting the Toxic Legacy of the U.S. Military.* Boston: Beacon Press.

**Theodore, Louis, and Young C. McGuinn. 1992.** *Pollution Prevention.* New York: Van Nostrand Reinhold.

**Water Pollution Control Federation. 1989.** *Household Hazardous Waste: What You Should and Shouldn't Do.* Alexandria, Va.: Water Pollution Control Federation.

**Whelan, Elisabeth M. 1985.** *Toxic Terror.* Ottawa, Ill.: Jameson Books.


## 22 AIR POLLUTION

See also the readings for Chapter 20.

**Borman, F. H. 1985.** "Air Pollution and Forests: An Ecosystem Perspective." *BioScience,* vol. 35, no. 7, 434–441.

**Brenner, David J. 1989.** *Radon: Risk and Remedy.* New York: W. H. Freeman.

**Bridgman, Howard. 1991.** *Global Air Pollution: Problems for the 1990s.* New York: Belhaven Press.

**Brookins, Douglas G. 1990.** *The Indoor Radon Problem.* Irvington, N.Y.: Columbia University Press.

**Brouder, Paul. 1985.** *Outrageous Misconduct: The Asbestos Industry on Trial.* New York: Pantheon Books.

**Brown, Michael. 1987.** *The Toxic Cloud.* San Francisco: Harper & Row.

**Bryner, Gary. 1992.** *Blue Skies, Green Politics: The Clean Air Act of 1990.* Washington, D.C.: Congressional Quarterly Press.

**Coffel, Steve, and Karyn Feiden. 1991.** *Indoor Pollution.* New York: Random House.

**Cohen, Bernie. 1988.** *Radon: A Homeowner's Guide to Detection and Control.* Mt. Vernon, N.Y.: Consumer Report Books.

**Elson, Derek. 1987.** *Atmospheric Pollution: Causes, Effects, and Control Policies.* Cambridge, Mass.: Basil Blackwell.

**Environmental Protection Agency. 1988.** *The Inside Story: A Guide to Indoor Air Quality.* Washington, D.C.: EPA.

***EPA Journal,* 1991.** Vol. 17, no. 1. Entire issue devoted to 1990 Clean Air Act.

**French, Hilary F. 1990.** *Clearing the Air: A Global Agenda.* Washington, D.C.: Worldwatch Institute.

**Geller, H., et al. 1986.** *Acid Rain and Energy Conservation.* Washington, D.C.: American Council for an Energy-Efficient America.

**Havas, M., et al. 1984.** "Red Herrings in Acid Rain Research." *Environmental Science & Technology,* vol. 18, no. 6, 176A–186A.

**Lafavore, Michael. 1987.** *Radon: The Invisible Threat.* Emmaus, Pa.: Rodale Press.

**MacKenzie, James J., and Mohamed T. El-Ashry. 1990.** *Air Pollution's Toll on Forests and Crops.* New Haven, Conn.: Yale University Press.

**Malaspina, Mark, et al. 1991.** *Air Pollution Solutions: Report No. 1.* Washington, D.C.: Environmental Exchange.

**McKormick, John. 1985.** *Acid Earth: The Global Threat of Acid Pollution.* East Haven, Conn.: Earthscan.

**Mello, Robert A. 1987.** *Last Stand of the Red Spruce.* Covelo, Calif.: Island Press.

**Mohnen, Volker A. 1988.** "The Challenge of Acid Rain." *Scientific American,* vol. 259, no. 2, 30–38.

**Mossman, B. T., et al. 1990.** "Asbestos: Scientific Developments and Implications for Public Policy." *Science,* vol. 251, 247–300.

**National Academy of Sciences. 1988.** *Air Pollution, the Automobile, and Human Health.* Washington, D.C.: National Academy Press.

**Nero, Anthony V. 1988.** "Controlling Indoor Air Pollution." *Scientific American,* vol. 258, no. 5, 42–48.

**Nero, Anthony V. 1992.** "A National Strategy for Indoor Radon." *Issues in Science and Technology,* Fall, 33–40.

**Office of Technology Assessment. 1985.** *Acid Rain and Transported Air Pollutants: Implications for Public Policy.* New York: Unipub.

**Office of Technology Assessment. 1989.** *Catching Our Breath: Next Steps for Reducing Urban Ozone.* Washington, D.C.: Government Printing Office.

**Pawlick, Thomas. 1986.** *A Killing Rain: The Global Threat of Acid Precipitation.* San Francisco: Sierra Club Books.

**Public Citizen. 1989.** *Electricity Conservation: A Legislative Solution to Acid Rain.* Washington, D.C.: Public Citizen.

**Public Citizen. 1989.** *Radon: What You Don't Know Can Hurt You.* Washington, D.C.: Public Citizen.

**Regens, James L., and Robert W. Rycroft. 1988.** *The Acid Rain Controversy.* Pittsburgh: University of Pittsburgh Press.

**Schmandt, Jurgen, et al., eds. 1989.** *Acid Rain and Friendly Neighbors: The Policy Dispute Between Canada and the United States.* Durham, N.C.: Duke University Press.

**Smith, Kirk R. 1987.** *Biofuels, Air Pollution, and Health: A Global Review.* New York: Plenum.

**Smith, William H. 1991.** "Air Pollution and Forest Damage." *Chemistry and Engineering News,* November 11, 30–43.

**Wark, K., and C. F. Warner. 1986.** *Air Pollution: Its Origin and Control.* 3rd ed. San Francisco: Harper & Row.

**Wellburn, Alan. 1988.** *Air Pollution and Acid Rain: The Biological Impact.* New York: John Wiley.


## 23 WATER POLLUTION

See also the readings for Chapters 5 and 20.

**Ashworth, William. 1986.** *The Late, Great Lakes: An Environmental History.* New York: Alfred A. Knopf.

**Boon, P. J., et al., eds. 1992.** *River Conservation and Management.* New York: John Wiley.

**Borgese, Elisabeth Mann. 1986.** *The Future of the Oceans.* New York: Harvest House.

**Bullock, David K. 1989.** *The Wasted Ocean.* New York: Lyons & Burford.

**Center for Marine Conservation. 1989.** *The Exxon Valdez Oil Spill: A Management Analysis.* Washington, D.C.: Center for Marine Conservation.

**Colborn, Theodora E., et al. 1989.** *Great Lakes, Great Legacy?* Washington, D.C.: Conservation Foundation.

**Costner, Pat, and Glenna Booth. 1986.** *We All Live Downstream: A Guide to Waste Treatment That Stops Water Pollution.* Berkeley, Calif.: Bookpeople.

**Davidson, Art. 1990.** *In the Wake of the Exxon Valdez.* San Francisco: Sierra Club Books.

**Edmonson, W. T. 1991.** *The Uses of Ecology: Lake Washington and Beyond.* Seattle: University of Washington Press.

**Environmental Protection Agency. 1987.** *Lead and Your Drinking Water.* Washington, D.C.: EPA.

**Environmental Protection Agency. 1990.** *Citizen's Guide to Ground-Water Protection.* Washington, D.C.: EPA.

**Gabler, Raymond. 1988.** *Is Your Water Safe to Drink?* Mt. Vernon, N.Y.: Consumer Reports Books.

**Gray, N. F. 1992.** *Biology of Wastewater Treatment.* New York: Oxford University Press.

**Hansen, Nancy R., et al. 1988.** *Controlling Nonpoint-Source Water Pollution.* New York: National Audubon Society and Conservation Society.

**Harleman, Donald R. F. 1990.** "Cutting the Waste in Wastewater Cleanups." *Technology Review,* April, 60–68.

**Hitteman, Bette. 1988.** "The Great Lakes Cleanup Effort." *Chemistry & Engineering News,* February 8, 22–39.

**Holing, Dwight. 1990.** *Coastal Alert: Energy, Ecosystems, and Offshore Oil Drilling.* Covelo, Calif.: Island Press.

**Horton, Tom, and William Eichbaum. 1991.** *Turning the Tide: Saving the Chesapeake Bay.* Covelo, Calif.: Island Press.

**Ingram, Colin. 1991.** *The Drinking Water Book.* Berkeley, Calif.: Ten Speed Press.

**Irwin, Frances H. 1989.** "Integrated Pollution Control." *International Environmental Affairs,* vol. 1, no. 4, 255–274.

**Jefferies, Michael, and Derek Mills. 1991.** *Freshwater Ecology: Principles and Applications.* New York: Belhaven Press.

**Jorgensen, Eric P., ed. 1989.** *The Poisoned Well: New Strategies for Groundwater Protection.* Covelo, Calif.: Island Press.

**Keeble, John. 1991.** *Out of the Channel: The Exxon Valdez Oil Spill in Prince William Sound.* San Francisco: HarperCollins.

**King, Jonathan. 1985.** *Troubled Water: The Poisoning of America's Drinking Water.* Emmaus, Pa.: Rodale Press.

**Knopman, Debra S., and Richard A. Smith. 1993.** "20 Years of the Clean Water Act." *Environment,* vol. 35, no. 1, 17–20, 34–41.

**Lahey, William, and Michael Connor. 1983.** "The Case for Ocean Waste Disposal." *Technology Review,* August/September, 61–68.

**Loer, Raymond C. 1984.** *Pollution Control for Agriculture.* 2nd ed. San Diego: Academic Press.

**Loveland, David G., and Beth Reichfield. 1987.** *Safety on Tap: A Citizen's Drinking Water Handbook.* Washington, D.C.: League of Women Voters Education Fund.

**Lowe, Marcia D. 1989.** "Down the Tubes: Human Excrement Is Full of Valuable Nutrients." *World Watch,* March/April, 22–29.

**Marquardt, Sandra, et al. 1989.** *Bottled Water: Sparkling Hype at a Premium Price.* Washington, D.C.: Environmental Policy Institute.

**Marx, Wesley. 1991.** *The Frail Ocean: A Blueprint for Change in the 1990s and Beyond.* San Francisco: Sierra Club Books.

**Mason, C. F. 1991.** *Biology of Freshwater Pollution.* 2nd ed. New York: John Wiley.

**Matthiessen, Peter. 1992.** *Baikal: Sacred Sea of Siberia.* San Francisco: Sierra Club Books.

**Montgomery, Ted. 1990.** *On-Site Wastewater Treatment Systems.* East Falmouth, Mass.: New Alchemy Institute.

**National Academy of Sciences. 1984.** *Disposal of Industrial and Domestic Wastes: Land and Sea Alternatives.* Washington, D.C.: National Academy Press.

**National Academy of Sciences. 1984.** *Groundwater Contamination.* Washington, D.C.: National Academy Press.

**National Academy of Sciences. 1985.** *Ocean Disposal Systems for Sewage Sludge and Effluent.* Washington, D.C.: National Academy Press.

**National Academy of Sciences. 1985.** *Oil in the Sea.* Washington, D.C.: National Academy Press.

**National Academy of Sciences. 1986.** *Drinking Water and Health.* Washington, D.C.: National Academy Press.

**Natural Resources Defense Council. 1989.** *Ebb Tide for Pollution: Actions for Cleaning Up Coastal Waters.* New York: Natural Resources Defense Council.

**Office of Technology Assessment. 1984.** *Protecting the Nation's Groundwater from Contamination.* Washington, D.C.: Government Printing Office.

**Office of Technology Assessment. 1987.** *Wastes in Marine Environments.* Washington, D.C.: Government Printing Office.

**Office of Technology Assessment. 1989.** *Coping with Oiled Environments.* Washington, D.C.: Government Printing Office.

**Patrick, Ruth, E. Ford, and J. Quarles, eds. 1987.** *Groundwater Contamination in the United States.* Philadelphia: University of Pennsylvania Press.

Patrick, Ruth, et al. 1992. *Surface Water Quality: Have the Laws Been Successful?* Princeton N.J.: Princeton University Press.

Pryde, Philip R. 1991. *Environmental Management in the Soviet Union.* New York: Cambridge University Press.

Rail, Chester D. 1989. *Groundwater Contamination: Sources, Control, and Preventive Measures.* Lancaster, Pa.: Technomic.

Rice, Rip G. 1985. *Safe Drinking Water: The Impact of Chemicals on a Limited Resource.* Boca Raton, Fla.: Lewis.

Sierra Club Defense Fund. 1989. *The Poisoned Well: New Strategies for Groundwater Protection.* Covelo, Calif.: Island Press.

Simon, Anne W. 1985. *Neptune's Revenge: The Ocean of Tomorrow.* New York: Franklin Watts.

U.S. Geological Survey. 1988. *Groundwater and the Rural Homeowner.* Denver: U.S. Geological Survey.

## 24 PESTICIDES AND PEST CONTROL

See also the readings for Chapters 12, 14, and 20.

Bogard, William. 1989. *The Bhopal Tragedy: Language, Logic, and Politics in the Production of a Hazard.* Boulder, Colo.: Westview Press.

Bosso, Christopher. 1987. *Pesticides and Politics.* Pittsburgh: University of Pittsburgh Press.

Briggs, Shirley, and the Rachel Carson Council. 1992. *Basic Guide to Pesticides: Their Characteristics and Hazards.* Washington, D.C.: Taylor & Francis.

Brown, Joseph E. 1983. *The Return of the Brown Pelican.* Baton Rouge: Louisiana State University Press.

Bull, David. 1982. *A Growing Problem: Pesticides and the Third World Poor.* London: Oxfam.

Carr, Anna. 1985. *Good Neighbors: Companion Planting for Gardeners.* Emmaus, Pa.: Rodale Press.

Carson, Rachel. 1962. *Silent Spring.* Boston: Houghton Mifflin.

Dover, Michael J. 1985. *A Better Mousetrap: Improving Pest Management for Agriculture.* Washington, D.C.: World Resources Institute.

Dunlap, Thomas R. 1981. *DDT: Scientists, Citizens, and Public Policy.* Princeton, N.J.: Princeton University Press.

Environmental Protection Agency. 1989. *Pesticides Fact Book.* Washington, D.C.: EPA.

Flint, Mary Louise. 1990. *Pests of the Garden & a Small Farm: A Grower's Guide to Using Less Pesticide.* Oakland, Calif.: ANR Publications.

Foundation for Advancements in Science and Education. 1990. *Pesticide Export: Trafficking Biocides.* Los Angeles: Foundation for Advancements in Science and Education.

Friends of the Earth. 1990. *How to Get Your Lawn and Garden Off Drugs.* Ottawa, Ontario: Friends of the Earth.

Fukuoka, Masanobu. 1985. *The Natural Way of Farming: The Theory and Practice of Green Philosophy.* New York: Japan.

Garland, Ann W. 1989. *For Our Kids' Sake: How to Protect Your Child Against Pesticides.* San Francisco: Sierra Club Books.

Gips, Terry. 1987. *Breaking the Pesticide Habit.* Minneapolis: IASA.

Goldstein, Joan. 1990. *Demanding Clean Food and Water.* New York: Plenum.

Gough, Michael. 1986. *Dioxin, Agent Orange: The Facts.* New York: Plenum.

Heylin, Michael, ed. 1991. "Pesticides: Costs Versus Benefits." *Chemistry & Engineering News,* January 7, 27–56.

Horn, D. J. 1988. *Ecological Approach to Pest Management.* New York: Guilford.

Hussey, N. W., and N. Scopes. 1986. *Biological Pest Control.* Ithaca, N.Y.: Cornell University Press.

Hynes, Patricia. 1989. *The Recurring Silent Spring.* New York: Pergamon Press.

Jacobson, Michael F., et al. 1991. *Safe Food: Eating Wisely in a Risky World.* Los Angeles: Living Planet Press.

Kourik, Robert. 1990. "Combating Household Pests Without Chemical Warfare." *Garbage,* March/April, 22–29.

Kurzman, Dan. 1987. *A Killing Wind: Inside Union Carbide and the Bhopal Catastrophe.* New York: McGraw-Hill.

League of Women Voters. 1989. *America's Growing Dilemma: Pesticides in Food and Water.* Washington, D.C.: League of Women Voters.

Marco, G. J., et al. 1987. *Silent Spring Revisited.* Washington, D.C.: American Chemical Society.

Marquardt, Sandra. 1989. *Exporting Banned Pesticides: Fueling the Circle of Poison.* Washington, D.C.: Greenpeace.

Mollison, Bill. 1990. *Permaculture.* Covelo, Calif.: Island Press.

Mott, Lawrie, and Karen Snyder. 1988. *Pesticide Alert: A Guide to Pesticides in Fruits and Vegetables.* San Francisco: Sierra Club Books.

National Academy of Sciences. 1986. *Pesticide Resistance: Strategies and Tactics for Management.* Washington, D.C.: National Academy Press.

National Academy of Sciences. 1987. *Regulating Pesticides in Food: The Delaney Paradox.* Washington, D.C.: National Academy Press.

Natural Resources Defense Council. 1989. *Intolerable Risk: Pesticides in Our Children's Food.* New York: Natural Resources Defense Council.

Natural Veterans Legal Services Project. 1990. *Human Health Effects Associated with Exposure to Herbicides and/or Their Associated Contaminants–Chlorinated Dioxins.* Washington, D.C.: Natural Veterans Legal Services Project.

Olkowski, William, et al. 1991. *Common Sense Pest Control: Least Toxic Solutions for Your Home, Garden, Pets, and Community.* Newtown, Conn.: Taunton Press.

Pimentel, David, and Lois Levitan. 1986. "Pesticides: Amounts Applied and Amounts Reaching Pests." *BioScience,* vol. 36, no. 2, 86–91.

Pimentel, David, et al. 1991. "Environmental and Economic Effects of Reducing Pesticide Use." *BioScience,* vol. 41, no. 6, 402–409.

Pimentel, David, et al. 1992. "Environmental and Economic Cost of Pesticide Use." *BioScience,* vol. 42, no. 10, 750–760.

Postel, Sandra. 1987. *Defusing the Toxics Threat: Controlling Pesticides and Industrial Waste.* Washington, D.C.: Worldwatch Institute.

Preston-Mafham, Rod, and Ken Preston-Mafham. 1984. *Spiders of the World.* New York: Facts on File.

Schultz, Warren. 1989. *The Chemical-Free Lawn.* Emmaus, Pa.: Rodale Press.

Shrivastava, Paul. 1987. *Bhopal: Anatomy of a Crisis.* San Francisco: Harper & Row.

Van den Bosch, Robert. 1978. *The Pesticide Conspiracy.* New York: Doubleday.

Van den Bosch, Robert, and Mary L. Flint. 1981. *Introduction to Integrated Pest Management.* New York: Plenum.

Webb, Tony, et al. 1987. *Food Irradiation: Who Wants It?* Rochester, Vt.: Thorsons.

Weir, David. 1987. *The Bhopal Syndrome: Pesticides, Environment, and Health.* San Francisco: Sierra Club Books.

Yepsen, Roger B., Jr. 1987. *The Encyclopedia of Natural Insect and Pest Control.* Emmaus, Pa.: Rodale Press.

## 25 ECONOMICS AND ENVIRONMENT

Adams, P., and L. Solomon. 1985. *In the Name of Progress.* Toronto: Energy Probe.

Alperson, Myra, et al. 1991. *The Better World Investment Guide.* New York: Council on Economic Priorities.

Anderson, Bruce, ed. 1990. *Ecologue: The Environmental Catalogue and Consumer's Guide for a Safe Earth.* Englewood Cliffs, N.J.: Prentice-Hall.

Anderson, Terry, and Donald Leal. 1990. *Free Market Environmentalism.* San Francisco: Pacific Research Institute for Public Policy.

Anderson, Victor. 1991. *Alternative Economic Indicators.* New York: Routledge.

Banks, Ronald, ed. 1990. *Costing the Earth.* New York: Robert Schalkenbach Foundation.

Bennett, Steven J. 1991. *Ecopreneuring: The Green Guide to Small Business Opportunities from the Environmental Revolution.* New York: John Wiley.

Berle, Gustav. 1991. *The Green Entrepreneur.* New York: McGraw-Hill.

Berry, Wendell. 1987. *Home Economics.* Berkeley, Calif.: North Point Press.

Bhaskara, H., et al. 1989. *Against All Odds: Breaking the Poverty Trap.* London: Panos.

Binder, Alan. 1990. *Hard Heads, Soft Hearts: Tough Minded Economics for a Just Society.* Reading, Mass.: Addison-Wesley.

Borman, F. H., and Stephen R. Kellert, eds. 1992. *Ecology, Economics, Ethics.* New Haven, Conn.: Yale University Press.

Boulding, Kenneth E. 1985. *The World as a Total System.* Beverly Hills, Calif.: Sage.

Bowden, Elbert V. 1990. *Principles of Economics: Theory, Problems, Policies.* 5th ed. Cincinnati: South-Western.

Breton, Denise, and Christopher Largent. 1991. *The Soul of Economies.* Wilmington, Del.: Idea House.

Bromley, Daniel W. 1991. *Environment and Economy: Property Rights and Public Policy.* Cambridge, Mass.: Basil Blackwell.

Brown, Lester R., et al. 1991. *Saving the Planet: How to Shape an Environmentally Sustainable Global Economy.* New York: W. W. Norton.

Brundtland, G. H., et al. 1987. *Our Common Future: World Commission on Environment and Development.* New York: Oxford University Press.

Butlin, John A. 1981. *The Economics of Environmental and Natural Resources Policy.* Boulder, Colo.: Westview Press.

Cairncross, Frances. 1992. *Costing the Earth.* Boston: Harvard Business School.

Campbell, Monica E., and William M. Glenn. 1982. *Profit from Pollution Prevention.* Willowdale, Ontario: Firefly Books.

Cetron, Marvin. 1991. *Crystal Globe: The Haves and the Have-Nots of the New World Order.* New York: St. Martin's Press.

Clark, William C., and R. E. Munn, eds. 1986. *Sustainable Development of the Biosphere.* New York: Cambridge University Press.

Collard, David, et al., eds. 1988. *Economics, Growth, and Sustainable Environments.* New York: St. Martin's Press.

Conroy, Czech, et al. 1988. *The Greening of Aid: Sustainable Livelihood in Action.* East Haven, Conn.: Earthscan.

Co-op America. 1991. *Directory of Socially and Environmentally Responsible Businesses.* Washington, D.C.: Co-op America.

Corson, Ben, et al. Annual. *Shopping for a Better World.* New York: Council on Economic Priorities.

Costanza, Robert, ed. 1992. *Ecological Economics: The Science and Management of Sustainability.* New York: Columbia University Press.

Costanza, Robert, and Herman E. Daly. 1992. "Natural Capital and Sustainable Development." *Conservation Biology,* vol. 6, no. 1, 37–46.

Court, T. de la. 1990. *Beyond Bruntland: Green Development in the 1990s.* Atlantic Highlands, N.J.: Zed Books.

Daly, Herman E., ed. 1980. *Economics, Ecology, and Ethics.* New York: W. H. Freeman.

Daly, Herman E. 1991. *Steady-State Economics.* 2nd ed. Covelo, Calif.: Island Press.

Daly, Herman E. 1992. *Environmentally Sustainable Development: Building on Bruntland.* Covelo, Calif.: Island Press.

Daly, Herman E., and John B. Cobb, Jr. 1989. *For the Common Good: Redirecting the Economy Toward Community, the Environment, and a Sustainable Future.* Boston: Beacon Press.

Davis, John. 1991. *Greening Business: Managing for Sustainable Development.* New York: Basil Blackwell.

Dixon, John A., and Paul B. Sherman. 1990. *Economics of Protected Areas: A New Look at Benefits and Costs.* Covelo, Calif.: Island Press.

Dixon, John A., et al. 1988. *Economic Analysis of the Environmental Impacts of Development Projects.* East Haven, Conn.: Earthscan.

Douthwaite, Richard. 1992. *The Growth Illusion.* Devon, United Kingdom: Green Books.

Durning, Alan T. 1989. *Poverty and the Environment: Reversing the Downward Spiral.* Washington, D.C.: Worldwatch Institute.

Durning, Alan T. 1992. *How Much Is Enough? The Consumer Society and the Earth.* New York: W. W. Norton.

Elkington, John, et al. 1990. *The Green Consumer.* New York: Penguin Books.

Environmental Protection Agency. 1991. *Economic Incentives: Options for Environmental Protection.* Washington, D.C.: EPA.

Etizoni, A. 1988. *The Moral Dimension: Toward A New Economics.* New York: Free Press.

Finkelstein, J., ed. 1989. *Windows on a New World: The Third Industrial Revolution.* Westport, Conn.: Greenwood Press.

Fisher, Anthony C. 1981. *Resource and Environmental Economics.* New York: Cambridge University Press.

Flavin, Christopher, and John E. Young. 1993. "Shaping the Next Industrial Revolution." In Lester R. Brown et al., *State of the World 1993,* 180–199. New York: W. W. Norton.

Freeman, A. Myrick, III. 1982. *Air and Water Pollution Control: A Benefit-Cost Assessment.* New York: John Wiley.

French, Hilary F. 1993. "Reconciling Trade and Environment." In Lester R. Brown et al., *State of the World 1993,* 158–179. New York: W. W. Norton.

Galbraith, John Kenneth. 1988. *Economics in Perspective: A Critical History.* Boston: Houghton Mifflin.

Garbarino, James. 1992. *Toward a Sustainable Society: An Economic, Social and Environmental Agenda for Our Children's Future.* Chicago: Noble.

George, Susan. 1992. *The Debt Boomerang: How Third World Debt Harms Us All.* Boulder, Colo.: Westview Press.

Georgescu-Roegen, Nicholas. 1971. *The Entropy Law and the Economic Process.* Cambridge, Mass.: Harvard University Press.

Georgescu-Roegen, Nicholas. 1977. "The Steady State and Ecological Salvation: A Thermodynamic Analysis." *BioScience,* vol. 27, no. 4, 266–270.

Georgescu-Roegen, Nicholas. 1977. "Inequality, Limits, and Growth from a Bioeconomic Point of View." *Review of Social Economics,* vol. 35, 361–376.

Global Tomorrow Coalition. 1989. *Sustainable Development: A Guide to Our Common Future.* Washington, D.C.: Global Tomorrow Coalition.

Goldsmith, Edward, et al. 1992. *The Future of Development: Reflections on Environment and Development.* Berkeley, Calif.: International Society for Ecology and Culture.

Goodland, Robert, et al. 1992. *Environmentally Sustainable Economic Development: Building on Bruntland.* Paris: UNESCO Press.

Goodland, Robert, et al., eds. 1992. *Population, Technology, and Lifestyle: The Transition to Sustainability.* Covelo, Calif.: Island Press.

Gupta, Avijit. 1988. *Ecology and Development in the Third World.* New York: Routledge, Chapman & Hall.

Hamrin, Robert D. 1983. *A Renewable Resource Economy.* New York: Praeger.

Hamrin, Robert D. 1988. *America's New Economy: A Basic Guide.* New York: Franklin Watts.

Hare, W. L., ed. 1990. *Ecologically Sustainable Development.* Fitznoy, Victoria, Australia: Australian Conservation Foundation.

Harrison, Bennett, and Barry Bluestone. 1988. *The Great U-Turn: Corporate Restructuring and the Polarizing of America.* New York: Basic Books.

Hawken, Paul. 1983. *The Next Economy.* New York: Random House.

Heaton, George, et al. 1992. *Backs to the Future: U.S. Government Policy Toward Environmentally Critical Technology.* Washington, D.C.: World Resources Institute.

Henderson, Hazel. 1991. *Paradigms in Progress: Life Beyond Economics.* Chicago: Knowledge Systems.

Hirschorn, Joel S., and Kirsten U. Oldenberg. 1990. *Prosperity Without Pollution: The Prevention Strategy for Industry and Consumers.* New York: Van Nostrand Reinhold.

Holmberg, Johan, ed. 1992. *Making Development Sustainable: Redefining Institutions, Policy, and Economics.* Covelo, Calif.: Island Press.

Institute for Local Self-Reliance. 1990. *Proven Profits from Pollution Prevention.* Washington, D.C.: Institute for Local Self-Reliance.

Jacobs, Michael. 1991. *The Green Economy: Environment, Sustainable Development, and Politics.* New York: Pluto Press.

Jacobson, Jodi L. 1992. *Gender Bias: Roadblock to Sustainable Development.* Washington, D.C.: Worldwatch Institute.

Johnson, R. J. 1990. *Environmental Problems: Nature, Economy, and State.* New York: Belhaven Press.

Kane, Hal, and Linda Starke. 1992. *Time for Change: A New Approach to Environment and Development.* Washington, D.C.: Island Press.

Kassiola, Joel Jay. 1990. *The Death of Industrial Civilization.* Albany: State University of New York Press.

Kazis, Richard, and Richard L. Grossman. 1991. *Fear at Work: Job Blackmail, Labor, and the Environment.* Philadelphia: New Society.

Kennedy, Paul. 1993. *Preparing for the Twenty-First Century.* New York: Random House.

Kolko, Joyce. 1988. *Restructuring the World Economy.* New York: Pantheon Books.

Krutilla, John V., and Anthony C. Fisher. 1985. *The Economics of Natural Environments.* Washington, D.C.: Resources for the Future.

Kumar, Ranjit, and Barbara Murck. 1992. *On Common Ground: Managing Human-Planet Relationships.* New York: John Wiley.

Leonard, H. Jeffrey. 1988. *Pollution and the Struggle for the World Product: Multinational Corporations, Environment, and International Comparative Advantage.* New York: Cambridge University Press.

Lydenberg, Steven D., et al. 1989. *Rating America's Corporate Conscience.* Reading, Mass.: Addison-Wesley.

Makower, Joel, et al. 1991. *The Green Consumer Supermarket Guide.* New York: Penguin Books.

Maurice, Charles, and Charles W. Smithsonian. 1984. *The Doomsday Myth.* Stanford, Calif.: Hoover Institution Press.

McConnell, Campbell R. 1990. *Economics: Principles, Problems, and Policies.* 11th ed. New York: McGraw-Hill.

Meeker-Lowry, Susan. 1988. *Economics As If the Earth Mattered: A Catalyst Guide to Socially Conscious Investing.* Philadelphia: New Society.

Mikesell, Raymond F., and Lawrence F. Williams. 1992. *International Banks and the Environment.* San Francisco: Sierra Club Books.

Mishan, E. J. 1977. *The Economic Growth Debate: An Assessment.* London: Allen & Unwin.

Monks, Robert A. G., and Nell Minow. 1991. *Power and Accountability.* New York: HarperCollins.

Moran, Alan, et al., eds. 1992. *Markets, Resources, and the Environment.* London: UCL Press.

Morris, David. 1991. *The Trade Papers.* Washington, D.C.: Institute for Local Self-Reliance.

Neber, Philip A. 1990. *Natural Resource Economics: Conservation and Exploitation.* New York: Cambridge University Press.

Office of Technology Assessment. 1992. *Trade and Environment: Conflicts and Opportunities.* Washington, D.C.: Office of Technology Assessment.

Paepke, C. Owen. 1993. *The Evolution of Progress: The End of Economic Growth and the Beginning of Human Transformation.* New York: Random House.

Pearce, David, et al. 1991. *Blueprint 2: Greening the World Economy.* East Haven, Conn.: Earthscan.

Peet, John. 1992. *Energy and the Ecological Economics of Sustainability.* Covelo, Calif.: Island Press.

Peters, Tom J., and E. F. Waterman, Jr. 1982. *In Search of Excellence.* San Francisco: Harper & Row.

Plant, Christopher, and Judith Plant, eds. 1991. *Green Business: Hope or Hoax?* Philadelphia: New Society.

Pollution Probe Foundation. 1989. *The Canadian Green Consumer Guide.* Toronto: McClelland & Stewart.

Population Crisis Committee. 1987. *The International Human Suffering Index.* Washington, D.C.: Population Crisis Committee.

Portney, Paul, ed. 1990. *Public Policies for Environmental Protection.* Washington, D.C.: Resources for the Future.

Ramphal, Shridath. 1992. *Our Country, the Planet: Forging a Partnership for Survival.* Washington, D.C.: Island Press.

Redclift, Michael. 1987. *Sustainable Development: Exploring the Contradictions.* New York: Methuen.

Rees, B. 1990. "The Ecology of Sustainable Development." *The Ecologist,* vol. 20, no. 1, 18–23.

Renner, Michael. 1991. *Jobs in a Sustainable Economy.* Washington, D.C.: Worldwatch Institute.

Repetto, Robert. 1990. *Promoting Environmentally Sound Economic Progress: What the North Can Do.* Washington, D.C.: World Resources Institute.

Repetto, Robert. 1992. "Accounting for Environmental Assets." *Scientific American,* June, 94–100.

Repetto, Robert. 1992. "Balance Sheet: Incorporating Natural Resources in National Income Accounts." *Environment,* vol. 34, no. 7, 13–20, 43–44.

Repetto, Robert, et al. 1989. *Wasting Assets: Natural Resources in the National Income Accounts.* Washington, D.C.: World Resources Institute.

Repetto, Robert, et al. 1991. *Transforming Technology: An Agenda for Environmentally Sustainable Growth in the Twenty-First Century.* Washington, D.C.: World Resources Institute.

Repetto, Robert, et al. 1992. *Green Fees: How a Tax Shift Can Work for the Environment and the Economy.* Washington, D.C.: World Resources Institute.

Robertson, J. 1990. *Future Wealth: New Economics for the Twenty-First Century.* London: Cassell.

Roddick, Anita. 1991. *Body and Soul: Profits with Principles.* New York: Crown.

Sargoff, Mark. 1988. *The Economy of the Earth: Philosophy, Law, and the Environment.* New York: Cambridge University Press.

Schmidheiny, Stephan. 1992. *Changing Course: A Global Business Perspective on Development and the Environment.* Cambridge, Mass.: MIT Press.

Schramm, Gunther, and Jeremy J. Warford. 1989. *Environmental Management and Economic Development.* Baltimore: Johns Hopkins University Press.

Schumacher, E. F. 1973. *Small Is Beautiful: Economics As If the Earth Mattered.* San Francisco: Harper & Row.

Smart, Bruce, ed. 1992. *Beyond Compliance: A New Industry View of the Environment.* Washington, D.C.: World Resources Institute.

Smith, V. Kerry. 1979. *Scarcity and Growth Reconsidered.* Baltimore: Johns Hopkins University Press.

Sontheimer, Sally, ed. 1991. *Women and Environment: A Reader.* New York: Earthscan.

Stavins, Robert N., and Bradley W. Whitehead. 1992. "Market-Based Incentives for Environmental Protection." *Environment,* vol. 34, no. 7, 7–11, 29–42.

Stead, W. Edward, and John Garner Stead. 1992. *Management for a Small Planet.* New York: Sage.

Stone, Roger D. 1992. *Sustainable Economic Growth.* New York: Alfred A. Knopf.

Tasaday, Laurence. 1991. *Shopping for a Better Environment.* Deephaven, Minn.: Meadowbrook Press.

Theobald, Robert. 1987. *The Rapids of Change: Entrepreneurship in Turbulent Times.* Chicago: Knowledge Systems.

Theobald, Robert. 1987. *Turning the Century: Personal and Organizational Strategies for Your Changed World.* Chicago: Knowledge Systems.

Thurow, Lester. 1980. *The Zero Sum Society.* New York: Basic Books.

Tibbs, Hardin B. C. 1992. "Industrial Ecology: An Environmental Agenda for Industry." *Whole Earth Review,* Winter, 4–19.

Tietenberg, Tom. 1992. *Environmental and Resource Economics.* 3rd ed. Glenview, Ill.: Scott, Foresman.

Tisdell, Clement A. 1991. *Economics of Environmental Conservation.* New York: Elsevier Science.

Toffler, Alvin, and Heidi Toffler. 1990. *Powershift.* New York: Bantam Books.

Turner, Kerry, ed. 1988. *Sustainable Environmental Management: Principles and Practice.* Boulder, Colo.: Westview Press.

Wachtel, Paul. 1988. *The Poverty of Affluence.* Santa Cruz, Calif.: New Society.

Ward, Barbara. 1979. *Progress for a Small Planet.* New York: W. W. Norton.

Waring, Marilyn. 1988. *If Women Counted.* San Francisco: Harper & Row.

Wathen, Thomas A. 1992. *A Guide to Trade and the Environment.* New York: Environmental Grantmakers Association.

Watt, K. E. F. 1982. *Understanding the Environment.* Boston: Allyn & Bacon.

## 26 POLITICS AND ENVIRONMENT

Abbey, Edward. 1986. *The Monkey Wrench Gang.* New York: Avon Books.

Alinsky, Saul. 1972. *Rules for Radicals.* New York: Vintage Books.

Atkinson, Adrian. 1991. *Principles of Political Ecology.* London: Belhaven Press.

Bahro, Rudolf. 1986. *Building the Green Movement.* London: Heretic Books.

Barnaby, Frank, ed. 1988. *The Gaia Peace Atlas: Survival into the Third Millennium.* New York: Doubleday.

Basta, Nicholas. 1991. *The Environmental Career Guide: Job Opportunities with the Earth in Mind.* New York: John Wiley.

Benjamin, Medea, and Andrea Freeman. 1989. *Bridging the Global Gap: A Handbook to Linking Citizens of the First and Third Worlds.* Baltimore: Seven Locks Press.

Borrelli, Peter, ed. 1988. *Crossroads: Environmental Priorities for the Future.* Covelo, Calif.: Island Press.

Boulding, Kenneth E. 1989. *Three Faces of Power.* Beverly Hills, Calif.: Sage.

Branch, Melville C. 1990. *Planning: Universal Process.* New York: Praeger.

Brown, Janet W., ed. 1990. *In the U.S. Interest: Resources, Growth, and Security in the Developing World*. Washington, D.C.: World Resources Institute.

Buck, Susan J. 1991. *Understanding Environmental Administration and Law*. Covelo, Calif.: Island Press.

Caldecott, Leonie, and Stephanie Leland. 1983. *Reclaim the Earth: Women Speak Out for Life on Earth*. London: Women's Press.

Caldwell, Lynton K. 1990. *Between Two Worlds: Science, the Environmental Movement, and Policy Choice*. New York: Cambridge University Press.

Caldwell, Lynton K. 1990. *International Environmental Policy*. 2nd ed. Durham, N.C.: Duke University Press.

Capra, Fritjof, and Charlene Spretnak. 1984. *Green Politics*. New York: E. P. Dutton.

Carty, Winthrop P., and Elizabeth Lee. 1992. *The Rhino Man and Other Uncommon Environmentalists*. Washington, D.C.: Seven Locks Press.

Chiras, Daniel D. 1990. *Beyond the Fray: Reshaping America's Environmental Response*. Boulder, Colo.: Johnson Books.

Chomsky, Noam, and Edward Herman. 1988. *Manufacturing Consent: The Political Economy of the Mass Media*. New York: Pantheon Books.

Choucri, Nazli. 1991. "The Global Environment and Multinational Corporations." *Technology Review*, April, 52–59.

Chubb, John E., and Paul E. Peterson, eds. 1988. *Can the Government Govern?* Washington, D.C.: Brookings Institute.

Clark, John, ed. 1990. *Renewing the Earth: The Promise of Social Ecology: A Celebration of the Work of Murray Bookchin*. London: Green Print.

Cleveland, Harlan. 1990. *The Global Commons: Policy for the Planet*. Aspen, Colo.: Aspen Institute.

Cohn, Susan. 1992. *Green at Work: Finding a Business Career That Works for the Environment*. Covelo, Calif.: Island Press.

Cornish, Edward, ed. 1984. *Global Solutions: Innovative Approaches to World Problems*. Bethesda, Md.: World Future Society.

Costanza, Robert. 1987. "Social Traps and Environmental Policy." *BioScience*, vol. 37, no. 6, 407–412.

Cousins, Norman. 1987. *The Pathology of Power*. New York: W. W. Norton.

Dahlberg, Kenneth A., et al. 1985. *Environment and the Global Arena*. Durham, N.C.: Duke University Press.

Day, David. 1990. *The Environmental Wars: Reports from the First Line*. New York: St. Martin's Press.

Dobson, Andrew. 1990. *Green Political Thought: An Introduction*. New York: Routledge.

Durning, Alan B. 1989. *Action at the Grassroots: Fighting Poverty and Environmental Decline*. Washington D.C.: Worldwatch Institute.

Dye, Thomas R., and Harmon Zeigler. 1987. *The Irony of Democracy: An Uncommon Introduction to American Politics*. 7th ed. Pacific Grove, Calif.: Brooks/Cole.

Elkins, Paul, and Jakob von Uexhull. 1992. *Grassroots Movements for Global Change*. New York: Routledge.

Environmental Careers Organization. 1990. *The Complete Guide to Environmental Careers*. Covelo, Calif.: Island Press.

Erickson, Brad, ed. 1990. *Call to Action: Handbook for Ecology, Peace, and Justice*. San Francisco: Sierra Club Books.

Esckersley, Robyn. 1992. *Environmentalism and Political Theory: Toward an Ecocentric Approach*. Albany: State University of New York Press.

Firestone, David B., and Frank C. Reed. 1983. *Environmental Law for Non-Lawyers*. Salem, N.H.: Butterworths.

Florio, James, et al. 1990. *The Rebellion of the Planet: Environmental Policy in the 1990s*. New York: Pharos Books.

Foreman, Dave. 1990. *Confessions of an Eco-Warrior*. New York: Crown.

Foreman, Dave, and Bill Haywood, eds. 1988. *Ecodefense: A Field Guide to Monkeywrenching*. 2nd ed. Tucson, Ariz.: Ned Ludd Books.

Freedman, Leonard, and Roger A. Riske. 1987. *Power and Politics in America*. 5th ed. Pacific Grove, Calif.: Brooks/Cole.

French, Hilary E. 1992. *After the Earth Summit: The Future of Environmental Governance*. Washington, D.C.: Worldwatch Institute.

Gandhi, M. K. 1961. *Non-Violent Resistance*. New York: Schocken Books.

Gardner, Richard N. 1993. *Negotiating Survival: Four Priorities After Rio*. Washington, D.C.: Council on Foreign Relations.

Gorz, Andre. 1989. *Ecology as Politics*. Boston: South End Press.

Greenpeace. 1993. *The Greenpeace Guide to Anti-Environmental Organizations*. Berkeley, Calif.: Odonian Press.

Greider, William. 1992. *Who Will Tell the People?* New York: Simon & Schuster.

Halia, Yrjo, and Richard Levins. 1993. *Humanity and Nature: Ecology, Science, and Society*. Boulder, Colo.: Westview Press.

Hall, Bob. 1990. *Environmental Politics: Lessons from the Grassroots*. Durham, N.C.: Institute for Southern Studies.

Henderson, Hazel. 1981. *The Politics of the Solar Age*. New York: Anchor/Doubleday.

Henning, Daniel H., and William R. Manguin. 1989. *Managing the Environmental Crisis*. Durham, N.C.: Duke University Press.

Hirsch, F. 1978. *The Social Limits to Growth*. London: RKP.

Hurrell, Andrew, and Benedict Kingsbury, eds. 1992. *The International Politics of the Environment*. New York: Oxford University Press.

Irvine, Sandy, and A. Ponton. 1988. *A Green Manifesto*. London: Optima.

Kahn, S. 1982. *A Guidebook for Grassroots Leaders*. New York: McGraw-Hill.

Kazis, Richard, and Richard L. Grossman. 1991. *Fear at Work: Job Blackmail, Labor, and the Environment*. Philadelphia: New Society.

Killingsworth, M. J., and Jacqueline S. Palmer. 1992. *Ecospeak: Rhetoric and Environmental Politics in America*. Carbondale: Southern Illinois University Press.

Korten, David C. 1990. *Getting to the 21st Century: Voluntary Action and the Global Arena*. West Hartford, Conn.: Kumarian Press.

Kottler, Philip, et al. 1993. *Marketing Places: Building a Future for Cities, States, and Nations*. New York: Free Press (Macmillan).

Krannich, R. L. 1988. *Careering and Re-Careering for the 1990s: The Complete Guide to Planning the Future*. Manassas, Va.: Impact.

Lamay, Craig L., and Everette E. Dennis, eds. 1991. *Media and the Environment*. Covelo, Calif.: Island Press.

Landy, Marc K., et al. 1990. *The Environmental Protection Agency: Asking the Wrong Questions*. New York: Oxford University Press.

Learner, Steve. 1992. *Beyond the Earth Summit: Conversations with Advocates of Sustainable Development*. New York: Common Knowledge Press.

Lewis, Martin W. 1992. *Green Delusions: An Environmentalist Critique of Radical Environmentalism*. Durham, N.C.: Duke University Press.

Manes, Christopher. 1990. *Green Rage: Radical Environmentalism and the Unmaking of Civilization*. Boston: Little, Brown.

Marguglio, B. W. 1991. *Environmental Management Systems*. New York: Marcel Dekker.

Mathews, Christopher. 1988. *Hardball: How Politics Is Played—Told by One Who Knows the Game*. New York: Summit Books.

Mathews, Jessica Tuchman, ed. 1989. "Redefining Security." *Foreign Affairs*, Spring, 162–177.

Mathews, Jessica Tuchman, ed. 1990. *Preserving the Global Environment: The Challenge of Shared Leadership*. Washington, D.C.: World Resources Institute.

Meadows, Donella H. 1991. *Global Citizen*. Covelo, Calif.: Island Press.

Morine, David E. 1990. *Good Dirt: Confessions of a Conservationist*. New York: Ballantine.

Myers, Norman. 1988. "Environment and Security." *Foreign Policy*, vol. 74, 23–41.

Nadler, G., and S. Hibino. 1990. *Breakthrough Thinking*. New York: Prima (St. Martin's Press).

Nanus, B. 1989. *The Leader's Edge: The Seven Keys to Leadership in Turbulent Times*. Los Angeles: Contemporary Books.

National Academy of Sciences. 1992. *Global Environmental Change: Understanding the Human Dimensions*. Washington, D.C.: National Academy Press.

Ophuls, William, and A. Stephen Boyan, Jr. 1992. *Ecology and the Politics of Scarcity Revisited: The Unravelling of the American Dream*. New York: W. H. Freeman.

Ostrom, Elinor. 1990. *Governing the Commons*. New York: Cambridge University Press.

Paehilke, Robert C. 1989. *Environmentalism and the Future of Progressive Politics*. New Haven, Conn.: Yale University Press.

Parkin, S. 1989. *Green Parties*. London: Heretic Books/GMP.

Pearce, Fred. 1991. *Green Warriors: The People and Politics Behind the Environmental Revolution*. London: Bodley Head.

Peavey, Fran, Myra Levey, and Charles Varon. 1986. *Heart Politics*. Philadelphia: New Society.

Petulla, Joseph M. 1987. *Environmental Protection in the United States: Industry, Agencies, Environmentalists*. San Francisco: San Francisco Study Center.

Piasecki, Bruce, and Peter Asmus. 1990. *In Search of Environmental Excellence: Moving Beyond Blame*. New York: Simon & Schuster.

Plant, Judith, and Christopher Plant, eds. 1992. *Putting Power in Its Place: Create Community Control*. Philadelphia: New Society.

Porritt, Jonathan. 1984. *Seeing Green: The Politics of Ecology Explained*. Oxford, England: Blackwell.

Porter, Gareth, and Janet Welsh Brown. 1991. *Global Environmental Politics*. Boulder, Colo.: Westview Press.

Renew America. Annual. *Environmental Success Index*. Washington, D.C.: Renew America.

Renner, Michael. 1989. *National Security: The Economic and Environmental Dimensions*. Washington, D.C.: Worldwatch Institute.

Renner, Michael. 1990. *Swords into Plowshares: Converting to a Peace Economy*. Washington, D.C.: Worldwatch Institute.

Rifkin, Jeremy. 1991. *Biosphere Politics: A New Consciousness for a New Century*. New York: Crown.

Rifkin, Jeremy, and Carol G. Rifkin. 1992. *Voting Green: Your Complete Guide to Making Political Choices in the '90s*. New York: Doubleday.

Rosenbaum, Walter A. 1990. *Environment, Politics, and Policy*. 2nd ed. Washington, D.C.: Congressional Quarterly.

Sanjor, William. 1992. *Why the EPA Is Like It Is and What Can Be Done About It*. Washington, D.C.: Environmental Research Foundation.

Satin, Mark. 1991. *New Options for America*. Fresno: California State University Press.

Scarce, Rick. 1990. *Eco-Warriors*. Chicago: Noble Press.

Schlesinger, Arthur M., Jr. 1986. *The Cycles of American History*. Boston: Houghton Mifflin.

Schneider, Bertrand. 1988. *The Barefoot Revolution: A Report to the Club of Rome*. London: Intermediate Technologies Publications.

Shephard, Mark. 1987. *Gandhi Today: A Report on Mahatma Gandhi's Successors*. Arcata, Calif.: Simple Productions.

Sierra Club. 1987. *Conservation Action Handbook*. San Francisco: Sierra Club Books.

Sivard, Ruth. 1993. *World Military and Social Expenditures*. Cambridge, Mass.: World Priorities.

Smookler, Andrew Bard. 1984. *The Parable of the Tribes*. Berkeley and Los Angeles: University of California Press.

Snow, Donald. 1992. *Inside the Environmental Movement: Meeting the Leadership Challenge*. Covelo, Calif.: Island Press.

Snow, Donald, ed. 1992. *Voices from the Environmental Movement*. Covelo, Calif.: Island Press.

Spretnak, Charlene, and Fritjof Capra. 1986. *Green Politics: The Green Promise*. Santa Fe, N.M.: Bear.

Taylor, Ann. 1992. *A Practical Politics of the Environment*. New York: Routledge.

Telba, M. K. 1992. *Saving Our Planet: Challenges and Hopes*. New York: Chapman & Hall.

Timberlake, Lloyd. 1987. *Only One Earth: Living for the Future*. New York: Sterling.

Tokar, Michael. 1988. *The Green Alternative: Creating an Alternative Future*. San Pedro, Calif.: R. & E. Miles.

Vig, Norman, and Michael Kraft. 1990. *Environmental Policy in the 1990s*. Washington, D.C.: Congressional Quarterly.

Warner, David J. 1992. *Environmental Careers: A Practical Guide to Opportunities in the 1990s*. Boca Raton, Fla.: Lewis.

Washington, Haydn. 1993. *Ecosolutions*. Berkeley, Calif.: North Atlantic Books.

Watt, K. E. F. 1982. *Understanding the Environment*. Boston: Allyn & Bacon.

Weinstein, Mirriam. 1993. *1993 Making a Difference College Guide: Education for a Better World*. San Anselmo, Calif.: Sage Press.

Westman, Walter E. 1985. *Ecology, Impact Assessment and Environmental Planning*. New York: John Wiley.

Willhoite, Fred H. 1988. *Power and Governments: An Introduction to Politics*. Pacific Grove, Calif.: Brooks/Cole.

World Resources Institute. 1993. *A New Generation of Environmental Leadership: Action for the Environment and the Economy*. Washington, D.C.: World Resources Institute.

Yandle, Bruce. 1989. *The Political Limits of Environmental Regulation*. Westport, Conn.: Quorum.

Zimmerman, Richard. 1992. *What Can I Do to Make a Difference?* New York: Plume (Penguin).

## 27 WORLDVIEWS, ETHICS, AND SUSTAINABILITY

See also the readings for Chapters 2 and 16.

Anderson, Lorraine, ed. 1991. *Sisters of the Earth*. New York: Vintage Books (Random House).

Andruss, Van, et al. 1990. *Home! A Bioregional Reader*. Philadelphia: New Society.

Attfield, Robin. 1991. *The Ethics of Environmental Concern*. 2nd ed. Athens: University of Georgia Press.

Baldwin, J., ed. 1990. *Whole Earth Ecologue*. New York: Harmony Books.

Barbour, Ian G., ed. 1973. *Western Man and Environmental Ethics*. Reading, Mass.: Addison-Wesley.

Barbour, Ian G. 1980. *Technology, Environment, and Human Values*. New York: Praeger.

Barbour, Ian G. 1990. *Religion in an Age of Science*. San Francisco: Harper & Row.

Bateson, Gregory, and Mary Catherine Bateson. 1987. *Angels Fear: Toward an Epistemology of the Sacred*. New York: Macmillan.

Beckwith, B. P. 1986. *Beyond Tomorrow: A Rational Utopia*. Palo Alto, Calif.: B. P. Beckwith.

Berman, Morris. 1981. *The Reenchantment of the World*. Ithaca, N.Y.: Cornell University Press.

Berry, Thomas. 1988. *The Dream of the Earth*. San Francisco: Sierra Club Books.

Berry, Wendell. 1990. *What Are People For?* Berkeley, Calif.: North Point Press.

Bobo, Kim, et al. 1991. *Organizing for Social Change*. Cabin John, Md.: Seven Locks Press.

Bohm, David, and Mark Edwards. 1991. *Changing Consciousness: Exploring the Hidden Source of the Social, Political, and Environmental Crises Facing the World*. San Francisco: Harper & Row.

Bookchin, Murray. 1990. *Remaking Society: Pathways to a Green Future*. San Francisco: South End Press.

Botkin, Daniel. 1990. *Discordant Harmonies: A New Ecology for the Twenty-First Century*. New York: Oxford University Press.

Bowles, Samuel, et al. 1983. *Beyond the Wasteland*. New York: Anchor Press.

Boyer, William H. 1984. *America's Future: Transition to the 21st Century*. New York: Praeger.

Brennan, Andrew. 1988. *Thinking About Nature: An Investigation of Nature, Value, and Ecology*. Athens: University of Georgia Press.

Broder, Bill. 1992. *The Sacred Hoop: A Cycle of Earth Tales*. San Francisco: Sierra Club Books.

Brown, Lester R., et al. 1991. *Saving the Planet: How to Shape an Environmentally Sustainable Global Economy*. New York: W. W. Norton.

Cahn, Robert. 1978. *Footprints on the Planet: A Search for an Environmental Ethic*. New York: Universe Books.

Cahn, Robert, and Patricia Cahn. 1990. "Did Earth Day 1990 Change the World?" *Environment*, vol. 32, no. 7, 16–20, 36–42.

Caldicott, Helen. 1992. *If You Love This Planet: A Plan to Heal the Earth*. New York: W. W. Norton.

Callahan, Daniel. 1973. *The Tyranny of Survival*. New York: Macmillan.

Callenbach, Ernest. 1975. *Ecotopia*. New York: Bantam Books.

Callenbach, Ernest. 1981. *Ecotopia Emerging*. New York: Bantam Books.

Callicott, J. Baird. 1988. *In Defense of the Land Ethic: Essays in Environmental Philosophy*. Albany: State University of New York Press.

Campbell, Joseph. 1988. *The Power of Myth*. New York: Doubleday.

Capra, Fritjof. 1983. *The Turning Point: Science, Society, and the Rising Culture*. New York: Bantam Books.

Capra, Fritjof. 1988. *Uncommon Wisdom*. London: Century Hutchinson.

Capra, Fritjof, and Charlene Spretnak. 1986. *The Spiritual Dimensions of Green Politics*. Berkeley and Los Angeles: University of California Press.

Carson, Rachel. 1984. *The Sense of Wonder*. San Francisco: Harper & Row.

Catton, William R. 1989. *Overshoot: The Ecological Basis of Revolutionary Change*. Urbana: University of Illinois Press.

Chiras, Daniel D. 1992. *Lessons from Nature: Learning to Live Sustainably on the Earth*. Covelo, Calif.: Island Press.

Christensen, Karen. 1990. *Home Ecology: Simple and Practical Ways to Green Your Home*. Golden, Colo.: Fulcrum.

Clark, John, ed. 1990. *Renewing the Earth: The Promise of Social Ecology*. London: Green Print.

Clark, Mary E. 1989. *Adriadne's Thread: The Search for New Models of Thinking*. New York: St. Martin's Press.

Clark, Mary E., and Sandra A. Wawrytko, eds. 1990. *Toward an Integrated Interdisciplinary College Education*. Westport, Conn.: Greenwood Press.

Cohen, Michael J. 1988. *How Nature Works: Regenerating Kinship with Planet Earth*. Walpole, N.H.: Stillpoint.

Cohen, Michael J. 1989. *Connecting with Nature: Creating Moments That Let Earth Teach*. Eugene, Ore.: World Peace University.

Cook, Stephen, and Donella H. Meadows. 1990. *Coming of Age in the Global Village: The Science and Technology, Politics, Economics, and Ethics Literacy Book*. Russellville, Ark.: Parthenon.

Cornell, Joseph. 1989. *Sharing the Joy of Nature*. Nevada City, Calif.: Dawn.

Daly, Herman E., ed. 1980. *Economics, Ecology, and Ethics*. New York: W. H. Freeman.

de Haes, C. 1986. *The Assisi Declarations: Messages on Man and Nature from Buddhism, Christianity, Hinduism, Islam, and Judaism*. Gland, Switzerland: World Wildlife Fund.

Desjardins, Joseph R. 1993. *Environmental Ethics*. Belmont, Calif.: Wadsworth.

Devall, Bill. 1988. *Simple in Means, Rich in Ends: Practicing Deep Ecology*. Salt Lake City: Peregrine Smith.

Devall, Bill, and George Sessions. 1985. *Deep Ecology: Living As If Nature Mattered*. Salt Lake City: Gibbs M. Smith.

Diamond, Irene, and Gloria F. Orenstein, eds. 1990. *Reweaving the World: The Emergence of Ecofeminism*. San Francisco: Sierra Club Books.

Dillard, Anne. 1974. *Pilgrim at Tinker Creek*. San Francisco: Harper's Magazine Press.

Drengson, Alan. 1989. *Beyond the Environmental Crisis: From Technology to Planetary Person*. New York: Peter Lang.

Dubos, René. 1972. *A God Within*. New York: Charles Scribner.

Earth Works Group. 1990. *50 Simple Things You Can Do to Save the Earth*. Berkeley, Calif.: Earth Works Press.

Earth Works Group. 1991. *The Next Step: 50 More Things You Can Do to Save the Earth*. Kansas City: Andrews & McMeel.

Earth Works Group. 1991. *The Student Environmental Action Guide: 25 Things We Can Do*. Berkeley, Calif.: Earth Works Press.

Ehrenfeld, David. 1978. *The Arrogance of Humanism*. New York: Oxford University Press.

Ehrenfeld, David. 1993. *Beginning Again: People and Nature in the New Millennium*. New York: Oxford University Press.

Ehrlich, Paul R., and Anne H. Ehrlich. 1991. *Healing the Planet*. Reading, Mass.: Addison-Wesley.

Eisler, Riane. 1987. *The Chalice and the Blade*. San Francisco: Harper & Row.

Elder, Frederick. 1970. *Crisis in Eden: A Religious Study of Man and Environment*. Nashville, Tenn.: Abingdon Press.

Elgin, Duane. 1981. *Voluntary Simplicity: Toward a Way of Life That Is Outwardly Simple, Inwardly Rich*. New York: William Morrow.

Elkington, John, et al. 1990. *The Green Consumer*. New York: Penguin Books.

Engel, J. Ronald, and Joan G. Engel, eds. 1990. *Ethics of Environment and Development*. Tucson: University of Arizona Press.

Ereira, Allan. 1992. *The Elder Brothers*. New York: Alfred A. Knopf.

Evernden, Neil. 1985. *The Natural Alien: Humankind and Environment*. Toronto: University of Toronto Press.

Ferkiss, Victor. 1992. *Nature, Technology, and Society: Cultural Roots of the Current Environmental Crisis*. New York: New York University Press.

Fox, Stephen. 1981. *John Muir and His Legacy: The American Conservation Movement*. Boston: Little, Brown.

Fox, Warrick. 1990. *Toward a Transpersonal Ecology: Developing New Foundations for Environmentalism*. Boston: Shambhala.

Fritsch, Albert J. 1980. *Environmental Ethics: Choices for Concerned Citizens*. New York: Anchor Press.

Garbarino, James. 1988. *The Future As If It Really Mattered*. Longmont, Colo.: Bookmakers Guild.

Garbarino, James. 1992. *Toward a Sustainable Society*. New York: Noble Press.

Glacken, Clarence. 1967. *Traces on the Rhodian Shore: Nature and Culture in Western Thought*. Berkeley and Los Angeles: University of California Press.

Goldsmith, Edward. 1988. *The Great U-Turn: De-Industrializing Society*. London: Green Books.

Goldsmith, Edward. 1992. *The Way*. Cornwall, United Kingdom: WEC Books.

Golley, Frank B. 1989. "Deep Ecology: An Analysis from the Perspective of Ecological Science." *Trumpeter*, vol. 6, no. 1, 24–28.

Gore, Al. 1992. *Earth in the Balance: Ecology and the Human Spirit*. Boston: Houghton Mifflin.

Granberg-Michaelson, Wesley. 1984. *A Worldly Spirituality*. San Francisco: Harper & Row.

Gray, Elizabeth. 1982. *Green Paradise Lost*. Wellesley, Mass.: Roundtable Press.

Griffin, Susan. 1978. *Woman and Nature. The Roaring Inside Her*. San Francisco: Harper & Row.

Hardin, Garrett. 1977. *The Limits of Altruism: An Ecologist's View of Survival*. Bloomington: Indiana University Press.

Hardin, Garrett. 1978. *Exploring New Ethics for Survival*. 2nd ed. New York: Viking Press.

Hardin, Garrett. 1993. *Living Within Limits: Ecology, Economics, and Population Taboos*. New York: Oxford University Press.

Hargrove, Eugene C., ed. 1986. *Religion and Environmental Crisis*. Athens: University of Georgia Press.

Hargrove, Eugene C. 1989. *Foundations of Environmental Ethics*. Englewood Cliffs, N.J.: Prentice-Hall.

Harmon, Willis. 1988. *Global Mind Change: The Promise of the Last Years of the Twentieth Century*. Indianapolis: Knowledge Systems.

Heilbroner, Robert. 1974. *An Inquiry into the Human Prospect*. New York: W. W. Norton.

Henderson, Hazel. 1978. *Creating Alternative Futures*. New York: Berkeley.

Hiss, Tony. 1991. *The Experience of Place*. New York: Alfred A. Knopf.

Hollander, Jeffrey. 1990. *How to Make the World a Better Place*. New York: Quill.

Hynes, H. Patricia. 1990. *Earth Right: Every Citizen's Guide*. New York: Prima (St. Martin's Press).

Irvine, Sandy. 1989. *Beyond Green Consumerism*. London: Friends of the Earth.

IUCN, UNEP, WWF. 1991. *Caring for the Earth: A Strategy for Sustainable Living*. London: Earthscan.

Johnson, Lawrence E. 1991. *A Morally Deep World: An Essay on Moral Significance and Environmental Ethics*. New York: Cambridge University Press.

Johnson, Warren. 1978. *Muddling Toward Frugality*. San Francisco: Sierra Club Books.

Johnson, Warren. 1985. *The Future Is Not What It Used to Be: Returning to Traditional Values in an Age of Scarcity*. New York: Dodd, Mead.

Kidder, Rushworth M. 1989. *Reinventing the Future: Global Goals for the 21st Century*. Cambridge, Mass.: MIT Press.

Kleinig, John. 1991. *Valuing Life*. Princeton, N.J.: Princeton University Press.

LaChapelle, Dolores. 1989. *Sacred Land, Sacred Sex, Rapture of the Deep: Concerning Deep Ecology and Celebrating Life*. Silverton, Colo.: Finn Hill Arts.

Lamb, Marjorie. 1990. *2 Minutes a Day for a Greener Planet*. San Francisco: Harper & Row.

Lappé, Francis Moore. 1989. *Rediscovering America's Values*. New York: Ballantine Books.

Laszlo, E. 1989. *The Inner Limits of Mankind*. London: Oneworld.

Leopold, Aldo. 1949. *A Sand County Almanac*. New York: Oxford University Press.

Lewis, Martin W. 1992. *Green Delusions: An Environmentalist Critique of Radical Environmentalism*. Durham, N.C.: Duke University Press.

List, Peter C. 1993. *Radical Environmentalism: Philosophy and Tactics*. Belmont, Calif.: Wadsworth.

Little, Charles E. 1992. *Hope for the Land*. Newark, N.J.: Rutgers University Press.

Livingston, John A. 1981. *The Fallacy of Wildlife Conservation*. Toronto: McClelland & Stewart.

Livingston, John A. 1985. "Moral Concerns and the Biosphere." *Alternatives*, vol. 12, 3–9.

Lyon, Thomas J., and Peter Stine, eds. 1992. *On Nature's Terms*. College Station: Texas A&M University Press.

MacEachern, Diane. 1990. *Save Our Planet: 750 Everyday Ways You Can Help Clean Up the Earth*. New York: Dell.

Matre, Steve Van. 1990. *Earth Education*. Warrenville, Ill.: Institute for Earth Education.

McGaa, Ed. 1990. *Mother Earth Spirituality*. San Francisco: Harper & Row.

McLaughlin, Andrew. 1993. *Regarding Nature: Industrialism and Deep Ecology*. Ithaca: State University of New York Press.

Meeker, Joseph W. 1972. *The Comedy of Survival: Studies in Literary Ecology*. New York: Charles Scribner's.

Meeker, Joseph W. 1988. *Minding the Earth: Thinly Disguised Essays on Human Ecology*. Berkeley, Calif.: Latham Foundation.

Meine, Curt. 1988. *Aldo Leopold: His Life and Work*. Madison: University of Wisconsin Press.

Merchant, Carolyn. 1980. *The Death of Nature: Women, Ecology, and the Scientific Revolution*. San Francisco: Harper & Row.

Merchant, Carolyn. 1993. *Radical Ecology: The Search for a Liveable World*. New York: Routledge.

Milbrath, Lester W. 1989. *Envisioning a Sustainable Society*. Albany: State University of New York Press.

Molesworth, C. 1983. *Gary Snyder's Vision*. Columbia: University of Missouri Press.

Myers, Norman. 1990. *The Gaia Atlas of Future Worlds*. New York: Doubleday.

Naar, Jon. 1990. *Design for a Livable Planet*. San Francisco: Harper & Row.

Naess, Arne. 1989. *Ecology, Community, and Lifestyle*. New York: Cambridge University Press.

Nash, James A. 1991. *Loving Nature: Ecological Integrity and Christian Responsibility*. Nashville, Tenn.: Abingdon Press.

Nash, Roderick. 1988. *The Rights of Nature: A History of Environmental Ethics*. Madison: University of Wisconsin Press.

Nearing, Helen, and Scott Nearing. 1970. *Living the Good Life*. New York: Schocken Books.

Newman, Peter, et al. 1990. *Case Studies in Environmental Hope*. Perth, Australia: E.P.A. Support Services.

Norton, Bryan G. 1991. *Toward Unity Among Environmentalists*. New York: Oxford University Press.

Norwood, Vera. 1993. *Made from This Earth: American Women and Nature*. Chapel Hill: University of North Carolina Press.

Null, Gary. 1990. *Clearer, Cleaner, Safer, Greener: A Blueprint for Detoxifying Your Environment*. New York: Villard Books.

Oates, David. 1989. *Earth Rising: Ecological Belief in an Age of Science*. Corvallis: Oregon State University Press.

Oelschlaeger, Max. 1992. *After Earth Day: Continuing the Conservation Effort*. Denton: University of North Texas Press.

Olsen, Marvin E., et al. 1991. *Viewing the World Ecologically*. Boulder, Colo.: Westview Press.

Ornstein, Robert, and Paul Ehrlich. 1989. *New World, New Mind*. New York: Doubleday.

Orr, David. 1992. *Ecological Literacy*. Ithaca: State University of New York Press.

Passmore, John. 1980. *Man's Responsibility for Nature: Ecological Problems and Western Traditions*. New York: Charles Scribners'.

Peccei, Aurelio, and Daisaku Ikeda. 1984. *Before It Is Too Late*. Tokyo: Kodansha International.

Peterson's Guides. 1993. *Education for the Earth: A Guide to the Top Environmental Studies Programs*. Princeton, N.J.: Peterson's Guides.

Physicians for Social Responsibility. 1989. *Our Common Future: Healing the Planet: A Resource Guide for Individual Action*. Los Angeles: Physicians for Social Responsibility.

Piltz, Rick, and Shelia Machado. 1990. *Searching for Success*. Washington, D.C.: Renew America.

Plant, Judith, ed. 1989. *Healing the Wounds: The Promise of Ecofeminism*. Philadelphia: New Society.

Plant, Judith, and Christopher Plant, eds. 1990. *Turtle Talk: Fifteen Voices for a Sustainable Future*. Santa Cruz, Calif.: New Society.

Plumwood, Val. 1992. *Gender and Ecology: Feminism and the Mastery of Nature*. New York: Routledge.

Potter, Van Rensselaer. 1988. *Global Bioethics: Building on the Leopold Legacy*. Rensselaer: Michigan State University Press.

Quinn, Daniel. 1992. *Ishmael*. New York: Bantam Books.

Reed, Peter, and David Rothenberg, eds. 1992. *Wisdom in the Air: The Norwegian Roots of Deep Ecology*. Duluth: University of Minnesota Press.

Regan, Tom. 1984. *Earthbound: New Introductory Essays in Environmental Ethics*. New York: Random House.

Regenstein, Lewis. 1991. *Replenish the Earth*. London: SCM Press.

Rifkin, Jeremy. 1985. *Declaration of a Heretic*. Boston: Routledge & Kegan Paul.

Rifkin, Jeremy. 1989. *Entropy: Into the Greenhouse World: A New World View*. New York: Bantam Books.

Rifkin, Jeremy, ed. 1990. *The Green Lifestyle Handbook: 1001 Ways You Can Heal the Earth*. New York: Henry Holt.

Rodda, Annabel, ed. 1992. *Women and the Environment*. Atlantic Highlands, N.J.: Zed Books.

Rolston, Holmes, III. 1988. *Environmental Ethics: Duties to and Values in the Natural World*. Philadelphia: Temple University Press.

Romm, Joseph J. 1992. *The Once & Future Superpower: How to Restore America's Economic, Energy, and Environmental Security*. New York: William Morrow.

Roszak, Theodore. 1978. *Person/Planet*. New York: Doubleday.

Roszak, Theodore. 1988. *The Cult of Information*. London: Paladin.

Roszak, Theodore. 1992. *The Voice of the Earth*. New York: Simon & Schuster.

Rothburg, Paul, and Robert L. Olson, eds. 1990. *Mending the Earth: A World for Our Grandchildren*. Berkeley, Calif.: North Atlantic Books.

Rothenberg, D. 1987. "A Platform of Deep Ecology." *The Environmentalist*, vol. 7, no. 3, 185–190.

Rowe, Stan. 1990. *Home Places: Essays on Ecology*. Edmonton, Alberta: Newest.

Russell, Peter. 1992. *A White Hole in Time: Our Future Evolution and the Meaning of Now*. San Francisco: HarperCollins.

Sale, Kirkpatrick. 1985. *Dwellers in the Land: The Bioregional Vision*. San Francisco: Sierra Club Books.

Sale, Kirkpatrick. 1990. *Conquest of Paradise*. New York: Alfred A. Knopf.

Salleh, Ariel. 1992. "The Ecofeminism/Deep Ecology Debate: A Reply to Patriarchal Reason." *Environmental Ethics*, Fall, 195–216.

Santmire, H. Paul. 1985. *The Travail of Nature: The Ambiguous Ecological Promise of Christian Theology*. Philadelphia: Temple University Press.

Scharper, Stephen B., and Hilary Cunningham. 1993. *The Green Bible*. Maryknoll, NY: Orbit Books.

Scherer, Donald, ed. 1991. *Upstream/Downstream: Issues in Environmental Ethics*. Philadelphia: Temple University Press.

Schumacher, E. F. 1973. *Small Is Beautiful: Economics As If People Mattered*. New York: Harper & Row.

Seager, Joni. 1993. *Earth Follies: Coming to Feminist Terms with the Global Environmental Crisis*. New York: Routledge.

Seed, John, et al. 1988. *Thinking like a Mountain*. Madison, Wis.: Madison Rainforest Group.

Seymour, John, and Herbert Giradet. 1987. *Blueprint for a Green Planet: Your Practical Guide to Restoring the World's Environment*. Englewood Cliffs, N.J.: Prentice-Hall.

Shabecoff, Philip. 1993. *A Fierce Green Fire: The American Environmental Movement*. New York: Hill and Wang.

Sheldrake, Rupert. 1991. *The Rebirth of Nature: The Greening of Science and God*. New York: Bantam Books.

Shiva, Vandana. 1989. *Staying Alive: Women, Ecology, and Development*. London: Zed Books.

Shrader-Frechette, Kristin, ed. 1981. *Environmental Ethics*. Pacific Grove, Calif.: Boxwood Press.

Snyder, Gary. 1980. *The Real Work: Interviews and Talks, 1964–1977*. New York: New Directions.

Snyder, Gary. 1990. *The Practice of the Wild*. San Francisco: North Point Press.

Sombke, Laurence. 1990. *The Solution to Pollution: 101 Things You Can Do to Clean Up*. New York: MasterMedia.

Sowell, Thomas. 1987. *A Conflict of Visions*. New York: William Morrow.

Starke, Linda. 1990. *Signs of Hope: Working Towards Our Common Future*. New York: Oxford University Press.

Steger, Will, and Jon Bowermaster. 1990. *Saving the Earth*. New York: Alfred A. Knopf.

Stivers, Robert L. 1976. *The Sustainable Society*. Philadelphia: Westminster.

Stone, Christopher. 1987. *Earth, and Other Ethics: The Case for Moral Pluralism*. San Francisco: Harper & Row.

Stone, Christopher D. 1993. *The Gnat Is Older Than Man: Global Environmental Human Agenda*. Princeton, NJ: Princeton University Press.

Swan, James A. 1992. *Nature As Teacher and Healer: How to Reawaken Your Connection with Nature*. New York: Villard Books.

Swimme, Brian. 1984. *The Universe Is a Green Dragon*. Santa Fe, N.M.: Bear.

Swimme, Brian, and Thomas Berry. 1992. *The Universe Story: From the Primordial Flaring Forth to the Ecozoic Era*. San Francisco: HarperCollins.

Sylvan, Richard, and David Bennett. 1993. *The Greening of Ethics*. Western Isles, UK: White Horse Press.

Taylor, Paul W. 1986. *Respect for Nature: A Theory of Environmental Ethics*. Princeton, N.J.: Princeton University Press.

Theobald, Robert. 1987. *The Rapids of Change*. Indianapolis, Ind.: Knowledge Systems.

Theobald, Robert. 1992. *Turning the Century: Personal and Organizational Strategies for Your Changed World*. Indianapolis: Knowledge Systems.

Thomas, Lewis. 1992. *The Fragile Species*. New York: Charles Scribner (Macmillan).

Tobias, Michael, ed. 1985. *Deep Ecology*. San Diego: Avant Books.

Tobias, Michael. 1990. *Voice of the Planet*. New York: Bantam Books.

Todd, John, and George Tukel. 1990. *Reinhabiting Cities and Towns: Designing for Sustainability*. San Francisco: Planet/Drum Foundation.

Todd, Nancy Jack, and John Todd. 1984. *Bioshelters, Ocean Arks, City Farming: Ecology as the Basis of Design*. San Francisco: Sierra Club Books.

Tokar, Brian. 1987. *The Green Alternative: Creating an Ecological Future*. San Pedro, Calif.: R. & E. Miles.

Van Andruss, Christopher, et al. 1990. *Home! A Bioregional Reader*. Santa Cruz, Calif.: New Society.

Vonnegut, Kurt. 1990. *Hocus Pocus*. Berkeley, Calif.: Berkeley Books.

Wenz, Peter. 1988. *Environmental Justice*. Albany: State University of New York Press.

White, Lynn, Jr. 1967. "The Historical Roots of Our Ecologic Crisis." *Science*, vol. 155, 1203–1207.

Wilkinson, Loren, ed. 1980. *Earthkeeping: Christian Stewardship of Natural Resources*. Grand Rapids, Mich.: Eerdmans.

Willers, Bill, ed. 1991. *Learning to Listen to the Land*. Covelo, Calif.: Island Press.

Williams, Rosalind. 1990. *Notes on the Underground: An Essay on Technology, Society, and the Imagination*. Cambridge, Mass.: MIT Press.

World Resources Institute. 1989. *The Crucial Decade: The 1990s and the Global Environmental Challenge*. Washington, D.C.: World Resources Institute.

Zerzan, John, and Alice Carnes, eds. 1988. *Questioning Technology*. Seattle: Left Bank Distributors.

# Glossary

**abiotic**  Nonliving. Compare *biotic*.

**absolute humidity**  Amount of water vapor found in a certain mass of air (usually expressed as grams of water per kilogram of air). Compare *relative humidity*.

**absolute resource scarcity**  Situation in which there are not enough actual or affordable supplies of a resource left to meet present or future demand. Compare *relative resource scarcity*.

**acclimation**  Adjustment to slowly changing new conditions. Compare *threshold effect*.

**acid deposition**  The falling of acids and acid-forming compounds from the atmosphere to the earth's surface. Acid deposition is commonly known as *acid rain*, a term that refers only to wet deposition of droplets of acids and acid-forming compounds.

**acid solution**  Any water solution that has more hydrogen ions ($H^+$) than hydroxide ions ($OH^-$); any water solution with a pH less than 7. Compare *basic solution, neutral solution*.

**active solar heating system**  System that uses solar collectors to capture energy from the sun and store it for heating space and water. A liquid or air pumped through the collectors transfers the captured heat to a storage system such as an insulated water tank or rock bed. Pumps or fans then distribute the stored heat or hot water throughout a dwelling as needed. Compare *passive solar heating system*.

**adaptations**  Mutations that are beneficial and increase the survivability of offspring.

**adaptive radiation**  Period during which numerous new species evolve to fill vacant and new ecological niches in changed environments, usually after a mass extinction.

**advanced sewage treatment**  Specialized chemical and physical processes that reduce the amount of specific pollutants left in wastewater after primary and secondary sewage treatment. This type of treatment is usually expensive. See *primary sewage treatment, secondary sewage treatment*.

**aerobic organism**  Organism that needs oxygen to stay alive. Compare *anaerobic organism*.

**aerobic respiration**  Complex process that occurs in the cells of most living organisms in which nutrient organic molecules such as glucose ($C_6H_{12}O_6$) combine with oxygen ($O_2$) and produce carbon dioxide ($CO_2$), water ($H_2O$), and energy. Compare *photosynthesis*.

**age structure**  Percentage of the population, or the number of people of each sex, at each age level in a population.

**Agricultural Revolution**  Gradual shift from small, mobile hunting-and-gathering bands to settled agricultural communities, where people survived by learning how to breed and raise wild animals and to cultivate wild plants near where they lived. It began 10,000–12,000 years ago. Compare *Industrial Revolution*.

**agroforestry**  Planting trees and crops together.

**air pollution**  One or more chemicals in high enough concentrations in the air to harm humans, other animals, vegetation, or materials. Excess heat or noise can also be considered as forms of air pollution. Such chemicals or physical conditions are called air pollutants. See *primary pollutant, secondary pollutant*.

**albedo**  Ability of surfaces to reflect radiation.

**alien species**  See *immigrant species*.

**alley cropping**  Planting of crops in strips with rows of trees or shrubs on each side.

**alpha particle**  Positively charged matter, consisting of two neutrons and two protons, that is emitted as a form of radioactivity from the nuclei of some radioisotopes. See *beta particle, gamma rays*.

**altitude**  Height above sea level. Compare *latitude*.

**ambient**  Outdoor.

**anadromous fish**  Fish that, after birth, move from fresh water to the ocean and then back to fresh water to spawn. Examples include salmon, sturgeon, smelt, and shad.

**anaerobic organism**  Organism that does not need oxygen to stay alive. Compare *aerobic organism*.

**ancient forest**  See *old-growth forest*.

**animal manure**  Dung and urine of animals that can be used as a form of organic fertilizer. Compare *green manure*.

**animals (animalia)**  Eukaryotic, multicelled organisms such as sponges, jellyfishes, arthropods (insects, shrimp, lobsters), mollusks (snails, clams, oysters, octopuses), fish, amphibians (frogs, toads, salamanders), reptiles (turtles, lizards, alligators, crocodiles, snakes), birds, mammals (kangaroos, bats, cats, rabbits, elephants, whales, porpoises, monkeys, apes, humans). See *carnivore, herbivore, omnivore*.

**annual**  Plant that grows, sets seed, and dies in a single year. Compare *perennial*.

**annual rate of natural population change**  Annual rate at which the size of a population changes, usually expressed as a percentage.

**appropriate technology**  Form of technology that is typically fairly simple, locally adaptable, gentle, Earth-friendly, resource-efficient, and culturally suitable; that depends mostly on local resources and labor; that can be easily expanded, reduced, moved, and repaired; and whose failure temporarily jeopardizes or inconveniences a fairly small number of people.

**aquaculture**  Growing and harvesting of fish and shellfish for human use in freshwater ponds, irrigation ditches, and lakes, or in cages or fenced-in areas of coastal lagoons and estuaries. See *fish farming, fish ranching*.

**aquatic**  Pertaining to water. Compare *terrestrial*.

**aquifer**  Porous, water-saturated layers of sand, gravel, or bed rock that can yield an economically significant amount of water. See *confined aquifer, unconfined aquifer*.

**arable land**  Land that can be cultivated to grow crops.

**arid**  Dry. A desert or other area with an arid climate has little precipitation.

**asthenosphere**  Portion of the mantle that is capable of solid flow. See *crust, lithosphere, mantle*.

**atmosphere**  The whole mass of air surrounding the earth. See *mesosphere, stratosphere, thermosphere, troposphere*.

**atomic number**  Number of protons in the nucleus of an atom. Compare *mass number*.

**atoms**  Minute units made of subatomic particles that are the basic building blocks of all chemical elements and thus all matter; the smallest unit of an element that can exist and still have the unique characteristics of that element. Compare *ion, molecule*.

**autotroph**  See *producer*.

**bacteria**  Prokaryotic, one-celled organisms. Some transmit diseases. Most act as decomposers and get the nutrients they need by breaking down complex organic compounds in the tissues of living or dead organisms into simpler inorganic nutrient compounds.

**basic solution**  Water solution with more hydroxide ions ($OH^-$) than hydrogen ions ($H^+$); water solution with a pH greater than 7. Compare *acid solution, neutral solution*.

**beneficiation**  Separation of an ore mineral from the waste mineral material (gangue). See *tailings*.

**beta particle**  Swiftly moving electron emitted by the nucleus of a radioactive isotope. See *alpha particle, gamma rays*.

**bioaccumulation**  The retention or accumulation of nonbiodegradable or slowly biodegradable chemicals in the body, often in a particular part of the body. Compare *biological amplification*.

**biodegradable pollutant**  Material that can be broken down into simpler substances (elements and compounds) by bacteria or other decomposers. Paper and most organic wastes such as animal manure are biodegradable but can take decades to biodegrade in modern landfills. Compare *degradable pollutant, nondegradable pollutant, slowly degradable pollutant*.

**biodiversity**  See *biological diversity*.

**biofuel**  Gas or liquid fuel (such as ethyl alcohol) made from plant material (biomass).

**biogeochemical cycle**  Natural processes that recycle nutrients in various chemical forms from the nonliving environment, to living organisms, and then back to the nonliving environment. Examples include the carbon, oxygen, nitrogen, phosphorus, sulfur, and hydrologic cycles.

**biological amplification**  Increase in concentration of DDT, PCBs, and other slowly degradable, fat-soluble chemicals in organisms at successively higher trophic levels of a food chain or web. See *bioaccumulation*.

**biological community**  See *community*.

**biological diversity**  Variety of different species (*species diversity*), genetic variability among individuals within each species (*genetic diversity*), and variety of ecosystems (*ecological diversity*).

**biological evolution**  Changes in the genetic composition (gene pool) of a population exposed to new environmental conditions as a result of differential reproduction. Evolution can lead to the splitting of a single species into two or more different species. See *differential reproduction, natural selection, speciation.* Compare *chemical evolution.*

**biological oxygen demand (BOD)**   Amount of dissolved oxygen needed by aerobic decomposers to break down the organic materials in a given volume of water at a certain temperature over a specified time period.

**biological pest control**   Control of pest populations by natural predators, parasites, or disease-causing bacteria and viruses (pathogens).

**biomass**   Organic matter produced by plants and other photosynthetic producers; total dry weight of all living organisms that can be supported at each trophic level in a food chain; dry weight of all organic matter in plants and animals in an ecosystem; plant materials and animal wastes used as fuel.

**biome**   Terrestrial regions inhabited by certain types of life, especially vegetation. Examples include various types of deserts, grasslands, and forests.

**bioregion**   A unique life-place with its own soils, landforms, watersheds, climates, native plants and animals, and many other distinct natural characteristics.

**biosphere**   Zone of Earth where life is found. It consists of parts of the atmosphere (the troposphere), hydrosphere (mostly surface water and groundwater), and lithosphere (mostly soil and surface rocks and sediments on the bottoms of oceans and other bodies of water) where life is found. See *ecosphere.*

**biotic**   Living. Living organisms make up the biotic parts of ecosystems. Compare *abiotic.*

**biotic potential**   Maximum rate at which the population of a given species can increase when there are no limits of any sort on its rate of growth. See *environmental resistance.*

**birth rate**   See *crude birth rate.*

**bitumen**   Gooey, black, high-sulfur, heavy oil extracted from tar sand and then upgraded to synthetic fuel oil. See *tar sand.*

**breeder nuclear fission reactor**   Nuclear fission reactor that produces more nuclear fuel than it consumes, by converting nonfissionable uranium-238 into fissionable plutonium-239.

**calorie**   Unit of energy; amount of energy needed to raise the temperature of 1 gram of water 1°C. See *kilocalorie.*

**cancer**   Group of more than 120 different diseases—one for each type of cell in the human body. Each type of cancer produces a tumor in which cells multiply uncontrollably and invade surrounding tissue.

**capital goods**   See *manufactured capital.*

**capitalism**   See *pure market economic system.*

**carbon cycle**   Cyclic movement of carbon in different chemical forms from the environment, to organisms, and then back to the environment.

**carcinogen**   Chemicals, ionizing radiation, and viruses that cause or promote the growth of cancer. See *cancer, mutagen, teratogen.*

**carnivore**   Animal that feeds on other animals. Compare *herbivore, omnivore.*

**carrying capacity (K)**   Maximum population of a particular species that a given habitat can support over a given period of time. See *consumption overpopulation, people overpopulation.*

**cell**   Smallest living unit of an organism. Each cell is encased in an outer membrane or wall and contains genetic material (DNA) and other parts to perform its

life function. Organisms such as bacteria consist of only one cell, but most of the organisms we are familiar with contain many cells. See *eukaryotic cell, prokaryotic cell.*

**centrally planned economy**   See *pure command economic system.*

**CFCs**   See *chlorofluorocarbons.*

**chain reaction**   Multiple nuclear fissions taking place within a certain mass of a fissionable isotope that release an enormous amount of energy in a short time.

**chemical**   One of the millions of different elements and compounds found naturally and synthesized by humans. See *compound, element.*

**chemical change**   Interaction between chemicals in which there is a change in the chemical composition of the elements or compounds involved. Compare *physical change.*

**chemical evolution**   Period of about 1 billion years prior to biological evolution. It involves the formation of the earth and its early crust and atmosphere, evolution of the biological molecules necessary for life, and evolution of systems of chemical reactions needed to produce the first living cells. Compare *biological evolution.*

**chemical formula**   Shorthand way to show the number of atoms (or ions) in the basic structural unit of a compound. Examples are $H_2O$, NaCl, and $C_6H_{12}O_6$.

**chemical reaction**   See *chemical change.*

**chemosynthesis**   Process in which certain organisms (mostly specialized bacteria) extract inorganic compounds from their environment and convert them into organic nutrient compounds without the presence of sunlight. Compare *photosynthesis.*

**chlorinated hydrocarbon**   Organic compound made up of atoms of carbon, hydrogen, and chlorine. Examples include DDT and PCBs.

**chlorofluorocarbons (CFCs)**   Organic compounds made up of atoms of carbon, chlorine, and fluorine. An example is Freon-12 ($CCl_2F_2$), used as a refrigerant in refrigerators and air conditioners and in making plastics such as Styrofoam. Gaseous CFCs can deplete the ozone layer when they slowly rise into the stratosphere and their chlorine atoms react with ozone molecules.

**chromosome**   A grouping of various genes and associated proteins in plant and animal cells that carry certain types of genetic information. See *genes.*

**civil suit**   Lawsuit in which an individual plaintiff seeks to collect damages for injuries or for economic loss, to have the court issue a permanent injunction against any further wrongful action, or both. Compare *class action suit.*

**class action suit**   Civil lawsuit in which a group files a suit on behalf of a larger number of citizens who allege similar damages but who need not be listed and represented individually. Compare *civil suit.*

**clear-cutting**   Method of timber harvesting in which all trees in a forested area are removed in a single cutting. Compare *seed-tree cutting, selective cutting, shelterwood cutting, strip logging.*

**climate**   General pattern of atmospheric or weather conditions, seasonal variations, and weather extremes in a region over a long period—at least 30 years; average weather of an area. Compare *weather.*

**climax community**   See *mature community.*

**coal**   Solid, combustible mixture of organic compounds, 30–98% carbon by weight, mixed with varying amounts of water and small amounts of sulfur

and nitrogen. It is formed in several stages as the remains of plants are subjected to heat and pressure over millions of years.

**coal gasification**   Conversion of solid coal to synthetic natural gas (SNG).

**coal liquefaction**   Conversion of solid coal to a liquid hydrocarbon fuel such as synthetic gasoline or methanol.

**coastal wetland**   Land along a coastline, extending inland from an estuary, that is covered with salt water all or part of the year. Examples are marshes, bays, lagoons, tidal flats, and mangrove swamps. Compare *inland wetland.*

**coastal zone**   Relatively warm, nutrient-rich, shallow part of the ocean that extends from the high-tide mark on land to the edge of a shelflike extension of continental land masses known as the continental shelf. Compare *open sea.*

**coevolution**   Evolution when two or more species interact and exert selective pressures on each other that can cause each species to undergo various adaptations. See *evolution, natural selection.*

**cogeneration**   Production of two useful forms of energy such as high-temperature heat or steam and electricity from the same fuel source.

**commensalism**   An interaction between organisms of different species in which one type of organism benefits, while the other type is neither helped or harmed to any great degree. Compare *mutualism.*

**commercial extinction**   Depletion of the population of a wild species used as a resource to a level where it is no longer profitable to harvest the species.

**commercial fishing**   Finding and catching fish for sale. See *poaching.* Compare *sport fishing, subsistence fishing.*

**commercial hunting**   Killing of wild animals for profit from sale of their furs, meat, or other parts. See *poaching.* Compare *sport hunting, subsistence hunting.*

**commercial inorganic fertilizer**   Commercially prepared mixtures of plant nutrients such as nitrates, phosphates, and potassium applied to the soil to restore fertility and increase crop yields. Compare *organic fertilizer.*

**common law**   Large body of legal principles and rules based on past legal decisions; judge-made law. Compare *statutory law.*

**common-property resource**   Resource that people are normally free to use; each user depletes or degrades the available supply. Most are potentially renewable and are owned by no one. Examples include clean air, fish in parts of the ocean not under the control of a coastal country, migratory birds, gases of the lower atmosphere, and the ozone content of the upper atmosphere. See *tragedy of the commons.* Compare *private-property resource, public-property resource.*

**community**   Populations of all species living and interacting in an area at a particular time.

**community development**   See *ecological succession.*

**competition**   Two or more individual organisms of a single species (*intraspecific competition*) or two or more individuals of different species (*interspecific competition*) attempting to use the same scarce resources in the same ecosystem.

**competitive exclusion principle**   Inability of any two species to occupy exactly the same fundamental niche indefinitely in a habitat where there is not enough of a particular resource to meet the needs of both species. See *ecological niche, fundamental niche, realized niche.*

**compost** Partially decomposed organic plant and animal matter that can be used as a soil conditioner or fertilizer.

**compound** Combination of atoms, or oppositely charged ions, of two or more different elements held together by attractive forces called chemical bonds. Compare *element*. See *inorganic compound, organic compound*.

**concentration** Amount of a chemical in a particular volume or weight of air, water, soil, or other medium.

**condensation nuclei** Tiny particles on which droplets of water vapor can collect.

**confined aquifer** Aquifer between two layers of relatively impermeable Earth materials, such as clay or shale. Compare *unconfined aquifer*.

**coniferous trees** Cone-bearing trees, mostly evergreens, that have needle-shaped or scalelike leaves and that produce wood known commercially as softwood. Compare *deciduous plants*.

**conservation-tillage farming** Crop cultivation in which the soil is disturbed little (minimum-tillage farming) or not at all (no-till farming) to reduce soil erosion, lower labor costs, and save energy. Compare *conventional-tillage farming*.

**constancy** Ability of a living system, such as a population, to maintain a certain size. Compare *inertia, resilience*. See *homeostasis*.

**consumer** Organism that cannot synthesize the organic nutrients it needs and gets its organic nutrients by feeding on the tissues of producers or of other consumers; generally divided into *primary consumers* (herbivores), *secondary consumers* (carnivores), *tertiary and higher consumers, omnivores*, and *detritivores* (decomposers and detritus feeders). In economics, one who uses economic goods.

**consumption overpopulation** Situation in which people in the world or in a geographic region use resources at such a high rate and without sufficient pollution prevention and control that significant pollution, resource depletion, and environmental degradation occur. Compare *people overpopulation*.

**continental shelf** Submerged part of a continent.

**continuous grazing** Year-long or season-long grazing by livestock on a given area. Compare *deferred-rotation grazing*.

**contour farming** Plowing and planting across the changing slope of land, rather than in straight lines, to help retain water and reduce soil erosion.

**contraceptive** Physical, chemical, or biological method used to prevent pregnancy.

**conventional-tillage farming** Making a planting surface by plowing land, disking it several times to break up the soil, and then smoothing the surface. Compare *conservation-tillage farming*.

**convergent plate boundary** Area where Earth's lithospheric plates are pushed together. See *subduction zone*. Compare *divergent plate boundary, transform fault*.

**coral reef** Formation produced by massive colonies containing billions of tiny coral animals, called polyps, which secrete a stony substance (calcium carbonate) around themselves for protection. When the corals die, their empty outer skeletons form layers that cause the reef to grow. They are found in the coastal zones of warm tropical and subtropical oceans.

**core** Inner zone of the earth. It consists of a solid inner core and a liquid outer core. Compare *crust, mantle*.

**cost-benefit analysis** Estimates and comparison of short-term and long-term costs (losses) and benefits (gains) from an economic decision. If the estimated benefits exceed the estimated costs, the

decision to buy an economic good or provide a public good is considered worthwhile.

**critical mass** Amount of fissionable nuclei needed to sustain a branching nuclear fission chain reaction.

**critical mineral** A mineral necessary to the economy of a country. Compare *strategic mineral*.

**crop rotation** Planting a field, or an area of a field, with different crops from year to year to reduce depletion of soil nutrients. A plant such as corn, tobacco, or cotton, which removes large amounts of nitrogen from the soil, is planted one year. The next year a legume such as soybeans, which add nitrogen to the soil, is planted.

**crown fire** Extremely hot forest fire that burns ground vegetation and tree tops. Compare *ground fire, surface fire*.

**crude birth rate** Annual number of live births per 1,000 persons in the population of a geographical area at the midpoint of a given year. Compare *crude death rate*.

**crude death rate** Annual number of deaths per 1,000 persons in the population of a geographical area at the midpoint of a given year. Compare *crude birth rate*.

**crude oil** Gooey liquid consisting mostly of hydrocarbon compounds and small amounts of compounds containing oxygen, sulfur, and nitrogen. Extracted from underground accumulations, it is sent to oil refineries, where it is converted to heating oil, diesel fuel, gasoline, tar, and other materials.

**crust** Solid outer zone of the earth. It consists of oceanic crust and continental crust. Compare *core, mantle*.

**cultural eutrophication** Overnourishment of aquatic ecosystems with plant nutrients (mostly nitrates and phosphates) because of human activities such as agriculture, urbanization, and discharges from industrial plants and sewage treatment plants. See *eutrophication*.

**cyanobacteria** Single-celled, prokaryotic, microscopic organisms. Before being reclassified as monera, they were called blue-green algae.

**DDT** Dichlorodiphenyltrichloroethane, a chlorinated hydrocarbon that has been widely used as a pesticide.

**death rate** See *crude death rate*.

**debt-for-nature swap** Agreement in which a certain amount of foreign debt is canceled in exchange for local currency investments that will improve natural resource management or protect certain areas from harmful development in the debtor country.

**deciduous plants** Trees, such as oaks and maples, and other plants that survive during dry seasons or cold seasons by shedding their leaves. Compare *coniferous trees, succulent plants*.

**decomposer** Organism that digests parts of dead organisms and cast-off fragments and wastes of living organisms by breaking down the complex organic molecules in those materials into simpler inorganic compounds and absorbing the soluble nutrients. Most of these chemicals are returned to the soil and water for reuse by producers. Decomposers consist of various bacteria and fungi. Compare *consumer, detritivore, producer*.

**decreasers** Grass species that are easily depleted even when moderately grazed. Compare *increasers, invaders*.

**deep ecology** See *sustainable-Earth worldview*.

**defendant** The individual, group of individuals, corporation, or government agency being charged in a lawsuit. Compare *plaintiff*.

**deferred-rotation grazing** Moving livestock between two or more range areas. Compare *continuous grazing*.

**deforestation** Removal of trees from a forested area without adequate replanting.

**degradable pollutant** Potentially polluting chemical that is broken down completely or reduced to acceptable levels by natural physical, chemical, and biological processes. Compare *biodegradable pollutant, nondegradable pollutant, slowly degradable pollutant*.

**degree of urbanization** Percentage of the population in the world, or a country, living in areas with a population of more than 2,500 people (higher in some countries). Compare *urban growth*.

**democracy** Government "by the people" through their elected officials and appointed representatives. In a *constitutional democracy* a constitution provides the basis of governmental authority and puts restraints on governmental power through free elections and freely expressed public opinion.

**demographic transition** Hypothesis that countries, as they become industrialized, have declines in death rates followed by declines in birth rates.

**demography** Study of characteristics and changes in the size and structure of the human population in the world or other geographical area.

**depletion time** How long it takes to use a certain fraction—usually 80%—of the known or estimated supply of a nonrenewable resource at an assumed rate of use. Finding and extracting the remaining 20% usually costs more than it is worth.

**dermersal species** See *marine demersal species*.

**desalination** Purification of salt water or brackish (slightly salty) water by removing dissolved salts.

**desert** Biome where evaporation exceeds precipitation and the average amount of precipitation is less than 25 centimeters (10 inches) per year. Such areas have little vegetation or have widely spaced, mostly low vegetation. Compare *forest, grassland*.

**desertification** Conversion of rangeland, rain-fed cropland, or irrigated cropland to desertlike land, with a drop in agricultural productivity of 10% or more. Usually caused by a combination of overgrazing, soil erosion, prolonged drought, and climate change.

**desirability quotient** A number expressing the results of risk-benefit analysis by dividing the estimate of the benefits to society of using a particular product or technology by its estimated risks. See *risk-benefit analysis*. Compare *cost-benefit analysis*.

**detritivore** Consumer organism that feeds on detritus, parts of dead organisms, and cast-off fragments and wastes of living organisms. The two principal types are *detritus feeder* and *decomposer*.

**detritus** Parts of dead organisms and cast-off fragments and wastes of living organisms.

**detritus feeder** Organism that extracts nutrients from fragments of dead organisms and their cast-off parts and organic wastes. Examples include earthworms, termites, and crabs. Compare *decomposer*.

**deuterium (D: hydrogen-2)** Isotope of the element hydrogen, with a nucleus containing one proton and one neutron, and a mass number of 2. Compare *tritium*.

**dew point** Temperature at which condensation occurs for a given amount of water vapor.

**dieback** Sharp reduction in the population of a species when its numbers exceed the carrying capacity of its habitat. See *carrying capacity, consumption overpopulation, overshoot, people overpopulation*.

**differential reproduction** Ability of individuals with adaptive genetic traits to produce more living offspring than individuals without such traits. See *natural selection*.

**dioxins** Family of 75 different chlorinated hydrocarbon compounds formed as by-products in chemical reactions involving chlorine and hydrocarbons, usually at high temperatures.

**discount rate** How much economic value a resource will have in the future compared with its present value.

**dissolved oxygen (DO) content** Amount of oxygen gas ($O_2$) dissolved in a given volume of water at a particular temperature and pressure, often expressed as a concentration in parts of oxygen per million parts of water.

**divergent plate boundary** Area where Earth's lithospheric plates move apart in opposite directions. Compare *convergent plate boundary, transform fault.*

**DNA (deoxyribonucleic acid)** Large molecules in the cells of organisms; carries genetic information in living organisms.

**dose** The amount of a potentially harmful substance an individual ingests, inhales, or absorbs through the skin. Compare *response.* See *dose-response curve, lethal dose, median lethal dose.*

**dose-response curve** Plot of data showing effects of various doses of a toxic agent on a group of test organisms. See *dose, lethal dose, median lethal dose, response.*

**doubling time** The time it takes (usually in years) for the quantity of something growing exponentially to double. It can be calculated by dividing the annual percentage growth rate into 70. See *rule of 70.*

**drainage basin** See *watershed.*

**dredge spoils** Materials scraped from the bottoms of harbors and streams to maintain shipping channels. They are often contaminated with high levels of toxic substances that have settled out of the water. See *dredging.*

**dredging** Type of surface mining in which chain buckets and draglines scrape up sand, gravel, and other surface deposits covered with water. Also used to remove sediment from streams and harbors to maintain shipping channels. See *dredge spoils.*

**drift-net fishing** Catching fish in huge nets that drift in the water.

**drought** Condition in which an area does not get enough water because of lower than normal precipitation, higher than normal temperatures that increase evaporation, or both.

**dust dome** Dome of heated air that surrounds an urban area and traps and keeps pollutants, especially suspended particulate matter. See *urban heat island.*

**dust plume** Elongation of a dust dome by winds that can spread a city's pollutants for hundreds of kilometers downwind.

**Earth capital** Earth's natural resources and processes that sustain us and other species.

**Earth Wisdom Revolution** See *Sustainable-Earth Revolution.*

**Earth wisdom worldview** See *sustainable-Earth worldview.*

**earthquake** Shaking of the ground resulting from the fracturing and displacement of rock, producing a fault, or from subsequent movement along the fault.

**ecological diversity** The variety of forests, deserts, grasslands, oceans, streams, lakes, and other biological communities interacting with one another and with their nonliving environment. See *biological diversity.* Compare *genetic diversity, species diversity.*

**ecological land-use planning** Method for deciding how land should be used; development of an integrated model that considers geological, ecological, health, and social variables.

**ecological niche** Total way of life or role of a species in an ecosystem. Includes all physical, chemical, and biological conditions a species needs to live and reproduce in an ecosystem. See *fundamental niche, realized niche.*

**ecological population density** Number of individuals of a population per unit of habitat area. Compare *population density.*

**ecological succession** Process in which communities of plant and animal species in a particular area are replaced over time by a series of different and usually more complex communities. See *primary succession, secondary succession.*

**ecology** Study of the interactions of living organisms with one another and with their nonliving environment of matter and energy; study of the structure and functions of nature.

**economically depleted** See *economic depletion.*

**economic depletion** Exhaustion of 80% of the estimated supply of a nonrenewable resource. Finding, extracting, and processing the remaining 20% usually costs more than it is worth. May also apply to the depletion of a potentially renewable resource, such as a species of fish or trees.

**economic good** Any service or material item that gives people satisfaction.

**economic growth** Increase in the real value of all final goods and services produced by an economy; an increase in real GNP.

**economic needs** Types and amounts of certain economic goods—food, clothing, water, oxygen, shelter—that each of us must have to survive and to stay healthy. Compare *economic wants.* See *poverty.*

**economic resources** Natural resources, capital goods, and labor used in an economy to produce material goods and services. See *Earth capital, human capital, manufactured capital.*

**economics** Study of how individuals and groups make decisions about what to do with economic resources to meet their needs and wants.

**economic system** Method that a group of people uses to choose *what* goods and services to produce, *how* to produce them, *how much* to produce, and *how* to distribute them to people. See *mixed economic system, pure command economic system, pure market economic system, traditional economic system.*

**economic wants** Economic goods that go beyond our basic economic needs. These wants are influenced by the customs and conventions of the society we live in and by our level of affluence. Compare *economic needs.*

**economy** System of production, distribution, and consumption of economic goods.

**ecosphere** Earth's collection of living organisms (found in the biosphere) interacting with one another and their nonliving environment (energy and matter) throughout the world; all of Earth's ecosystems. See *biosphere.*

**ecosystem** Community of different species interacting with one another and with the chemical and physical factors making up the nonliving environment.

**efficiency** Measure of how much output of energy or how much of a product is produced by a certain input of energy, materials, or labor. See *energy efficiency.*

**electromagnetic radiation** Forms of kinetic energy traveling as electromagnetic waves. Examples include radio waves, TV waves, microwaves, infrared radiation, visible light, ultraviolet radiation, X rays, and gamma rays. Compare *ionizing radiation, nonionizing radiation.*

**electron (e)** Tiny particle moving around outside the nucleus of an atom. Each electron has one unit of negative charge (–) and almost no mass.

**element** Chemical, such as hydrogen (H), iron (Fe), sodium (Na), carbon (C), nitrogen (N), or oxygen (O), whose distinctly different atoms serve as the basic building blocks of all matter. There are 92 naturally occurring elements; another 15 have been created in laboratories. Two or more elements combine to form compounds that make up most of the world's matter. Compare *compound.*

**emigration** Migration of people out of one country or area to take up permanent residence in another country or area. Compare *immigration.*

**endangered species** Wild species with so few individual survivors that the species could soon become extinct in all or most of its natural range. Compare *threatened species.*

**energy** Capacity to do work by performing mechanical, physical, chemical, or electrical tasks or to cause a heat transfer between two objects at different temperatures.

**energy conservation** Reduction or elimination of unnecessary energy use and waste. See *energy efficiency.*

**energy efficiency** Percentage of the total energy input that does useful work and is not converted into low-quality, usually useless, heat in an energy conversion system or process. See *energy quality, net useful energy.*

**energy quality** Ability of a form of energy to do useful work. High-temperature heat and the chemical energy in fossil fuels and nuclear fuels is concentrated high-quality energy. Low-quality energy such as low-temperature heat is dispersed or diluted and cannot do much useful work. See *high-quality energy, low-quality energy.*

**enhanced oil recovery** Removal of some of the heavy oil left in an oil well after primary and secondary recovery. Compare *primary oil recovery, secondary oil recovery.*

**entropy** A measure of disorder or randomness. The higher the entropy, the greater its disorder. See *high-quality energy, high-quality matter, low-quality energy, low-quality matter.*

**environment** All external conditions and factors, living and nonliving (chemicals and energy), that affect an organism or other specified system during its lifetime.

**environmental degradation** Depletion or destruction of a potentially renewable resource such as soil, grassland, forest, or wildlife by using it at a faster rate than it is naturally replenished. If such use continues, the resource can become nonrenewable on a human time scale or nonexistent (extinct). See *sustainable yield.*

**environmental resistance** All the factors jointly acting to limit the growth of a population. See *biotic potential, limiting factor.*

**Environmental Revolution** See *Sustainable-Earth Revolution.*

**environmental science** Study of how we and other species interact with one another and with the nonliving environment of matter and energy. It is a holistic science that uses and integrates knowledge from physics, chemistry, biology (especially ecology), geology, geography, resource technology and engineering, resource conservation and management, demography (the study of population dynamics), economics, politics, and ethics.

**environmental unsustainability** See *overpopulation.*

**EPA** Environmental Protection Agency; responsible for managing federal efforts in the United States to control air and water pollution, reduce radiation and pesticide hazards, conduct environmental research, and regulate disposal of solid and hazardous waste.

**epidemiology** Study of the patterns of disease or other harmful effects from toxic exposure within defined groups of people to find out why some people get sick and some do not.

**epiphytes** Plants that use their roots to attach themselves to branches high in trees, especially in tropical forests.

**erosion** Process or group of processes by which earth materials, loose or consolidated, are dissolved, loosened, and worn away, and removed from one place and deposited in another. See *weathering*.

**estuary** Partially enclosed coastal area at the mouth of a river where its fresh water, carrying fertile silt and runoff from the land, mixes with salty seawater.

**ethics** What we believe to be right or wrong behavior.

**eukaryotic cell** Cell containing a *nucleus*, a region of genetic material surrounded by a membrane. Membranes also enclose several of the other internal parts found in a eukaryotic cell. Compare *prokaryotic cell*.

**eutrophication** Physical, chemical, and biological changes that take place after a lake, an estuary, or a slow-flowing stream receives inputs of plant nutrients—mostly nitrates and phosphates—from natural erosion and runoff from the surrounding land basin. See *cultural eutrophication*.

**eutrophic lake** Lake with a large or excessive supply of plant nutrients—mostly nitrates and phosphates. Compare *mesotrophic lake, oligotrophic lake*.

**evaporation** Physical change in which a liquid changes into a vapor or gas.

**even-aged management** Method of forest management in which trees, usually of a single species in a given stand, are maintained at about the same age and size, and are harvested all at once so a new stand may grow. Compare *uneven-aged management*.

**even-aged stand** Forest area where all trees are about the same age. Usually, such stands contain trees of only one or two species. See *even-aged management, tree farm*. Compare *uneven-aged management, uneven-aged stand*.

**evergreen plants** Plants that keep some of their leaves or needles throughout the year. Examples include ferns and cone-bearing trees (conifers) such as firs, spruces, pines, redwoods, and sequoias. Compare *deciduous plants, succulent plants*.

**evolution** Term normally refers to biological evolution. See *biological evolution, chemical evolution*.

**exclusive economic zone** Zone extending outward for 370 kilometers (200 nautical miles or 230 statute miles) from the shores of coastal countries. Under international law each coastal country has legal rights over all marine fishery resources and ocean mineral resources in this zone. Compare *high seas*.

**executive branch** Branch of government that in the United States consists of an elected president and vice president and the various agencies of government established by Congress to implement policy. Compare *judicial branch, legislative branch*.

**exhaustible resources** See *nonrenewable resource*.

**exploitation competition** Situation in which two competing species have equal access to a specific resource but differ in how quickly or efficiently they exploit it. See *interference competition, interspecific competition*. Compare *intraspecific competition*.

**exponential growth** Growth in which some quantity, such as population size or economic output, increases by a fixed percentage of the whole in a given time period; when the increase in quantity over time is plotted, this type of growth yields a J-shaped curve. Compare *linear growth*.

**external benefit** Beneficial social effect of producing and using an economic good that is not included in the market price of the good. Compare *external cost, internal cost, true cost*.

**external cost** Harmful social effect of producing and using an economic good that is not included in the market price of the good. Compare *external benefit, internal cost, true cost*.

**externalities** Social benefits ("goods") and social costs ("bads") not included in the market price of an economic good. See *external benefit, external cost*. Compare *internal cost, true cost*.

**extinction** Complete disappearance of a species from the earth. This happens when a species cannot adapt and successfully reproduce under new environmental conditions or evolves into one or more new species. Compare *speciation*. See *endangered species, threatened species*.

**family planning** Providing information, clinical services, and contraceptives to help individuals or couples choose the number and spacing of children.

**famine** Widespread malnutrition and starvation in a particular area because of a shortage of food, usually caused by a drought, war, flood, earthquake, or other catastrophic event that disrupts food production and distribution.

**feedback loop** Circuit of sensing, evaluating, and reacting to changes in environmental conditions as a result of information fed back into a system. See *information feedback, negative feedback, positive feedback*.

**feedlot** Confined outdoor or indoor space used to raise hundreds to thousands of domesticated livestock. Compare *rangeland*.

**fertilizer** Substance that adds inorganic or organic plant nutrients to soil and improves its ability to grow crops, trees, or other vegetation. See *commercial inorganic fertilizer, organic fertilizer*.

**first law of ecology** We can never do merely one thing. Any intrusion into nature has numerous effects, many of which are unpredictable.

**first law of energy** See *first law of thermodynamics*.

**first law of thermodynamics (energy)** In any physical or chemical change, no detectable amount of energy is created or destroyed, but in these processes energy can be changed from one form to another. You can't get more energy out of something than you put in; in terms of energy quantity, you can't get something for nothing (there is no free lunch). This law does not apply to nuclear changes, where energy can be produced from small amounts of matter. See *second law of thermodynamics*.

**fishery** Concentrations of particular aquatic species suitable for commercial harvesting in a given ocean area or inland body of water.

**fish farming** Form of aquaculture in which fish are cultivated in a controlled pond or other environment and harvested when they reach the desired size. See *fish ranching*.

**fishing** Hunting operation in which desirable species of fish and shellfish are found and captured. See *commercial fishing, sport fishing, subsistence fishing*. Compare *fish farming, fish ranching*.

**fish ranching** Form of aquaculture in which members of a fish species such as salmon are held in captivity for the first few years of their lives, released, and then harvested as adults when they return from the ocean to their freshwater birthplace to spawn. See *fish farming*.

**fissionable isotope** Isotope that can split apart when hit by a neutron at the right speed and thus undergo nuclear fission. Examples include uranium-235 and plutonium-239.

**floodplain** Flat valley floor next to a stream channel. For legal purposes, the term is often applied to any low area that has the potential for flooding, including certain coastal areas.

**flyway** Generally fixed route along which waterfowl migrate from one area to another at certain seasons of the year.

**food additive** A natural or synthetic chemical deliberately added to processed foods to retard spoilage, to provide missing amino acids and vitamins, or to enhance flavor, color, and texture.

**food chain** Series of organisms, each eating or decomposing the preceding one. Compare *food web*.

**food web** Complex network of many interconnected food chains and feeding relationships. Compare *food chain*.

**forage** Vegetation eaten by animals, especially grazing and browsing animals.

**forest** Biome with enough average annual precipitation (at least 76 centimeters, or 30 inches) to support growth of various species of trees and smaller forms of vegetation. Compare *desert, grassland*.

**fossil fuel** Products of partial or complete decomposition of plants and animals that occur as crude oil, coal, natural gas, or heavy oils as a result of exposure to heat and pressure in the earth's crust over millions of years. See *coal, crude oil, natural gas*.

**fossils** Skeletons, bones, shells, body parts, leaves, seeds, or impressions of such items that provide recognizable evidence of organisms that lived long ago.

**Freons** See *chlorofluorocarbons*.

**frontier worldview** Viewing undeveloped land as a hostile wilderness to be conquered, tamed, and cleared as quickly as possible so that its boundless resources can be developed. See *planetary-management worldview, spaceship-Earth worldview*. Compare *sustainable-Earth worldview*.

**full cost** Cost of a good when its internal costs and its short- and long-term external costs are included in its market price. Compare *external cost, internal cost*.

**fundamental niche** The full potential range of the physical, chemical, and biological factors a species can use, if there is no competition from other species. See *ecological niche*. Compare *realized niche*.

**fungi** Eukaryotic, mostly multicelled organisms such as mushrooms, molds, and yeasts. As decomposers, they get the nutrients they need by secreting enzymes that break down the organic matter in the tissue of other living or dead organisms. Then they absorb the resulting nutrients.

**fungicide** Chemical that kills fungi.

**Gaia hypothesis** Proposal that Earth is alive and can be considered a system that operates and changes by feedback of information between its living and nonliving components.

**game fish** Fish caught mostly for recreation. Compare *commercial fishing, subsistence fishing*.

**game species** Type of wild animal that people hunt or fish for, for sport and recreation and sometimes for food.

**gamma rays** A form of ionizing, electromagnetic radiation with a high energy content emitted by some radioisotopes. They readily penetrate body tissues.

**gangue** Waste or undesired material in an ore. See *ore*.

**gasohol**   Vehicle fuel consisting of a mixture of gasoline and ethyl or methyl alcohol—typically 10–23% ethanol or methanol by volume.

**gene mutation**   See *mutation*.

**gene pool**   All genetic (hereditary) information contained in a reproducing population of a particular species over time.

**generalist species**   Species with a broad ecological niche. They can live in many different places, eat a variety of foods, and tolerate a wide range of environmental conditions. Examples include flies, cockroaches, mice, rats, and human beings. Compare *specialist species*.

**genes**   Segments of various DNA molecules that control hereditary characteristics in organisms.

**genetic adaptation**   Changes in the genetic make-up of organisms of a species that allow the species to reproduce and gain a competitive advantage under changed environmental conditions. See *differential reproduction, evolution, natural selection*.

**genetic diversity**   Variability in the genetic makeup among individuals within a single species. See *biodiversity*. Compare *ecological diversity, species diversity*.

**geology**   Science devoted to the study of Earth's dynamic history. Geologists do this mostly by studying Earth's rocks and using this information to describe the processes and events that produce and change them.

**geothermal energy**   Heat transferred from the earth's underground concentrations of dry steam (steam with no water droplets), wet steam (a mixture of steam and water droplets), or hot water trapped in fractured or porous rock.

**glacier**   A flowing body of ice, formed in a region where snowfall exceeds melting.

**GNP**   See *gross national product*.

**GNP per capita**   Annual gross national product (GNP) of a country divided by its total population. See *gross national product, real GNP per capita*.

**grassland**   Biome found in regions where moderate annual average precipitation (25–76 centimeters, or 10–30 inches) is enough to support the growth of grass and small plants but not enough to support large stands of trees. Compare *desert, forest*.

**greenhouse effect**   A natural effect that traps heat in the atmosphere (troposphere) near the earth's surface. Some of the heat flowing back toward space from the earth's surface is absorbed by water vapor, carbon dioxide, ozone, and several other gases in the atmosphere, and then radiated back toward the earth's surface. If the atmospheric concentrations of these greenhouse gases rise, the average temperature of the lower atmosphere will gradually increase.

**greenhouse gases**   Gases in Earth's lower atmosphere (troposphere) that cause the greenhouse effect. Examples include carbon dioxide, chlorofluorocarbons, ozone, methane, water vapor, and nitrous oxide.

**green manure**   Freshly cut or still-growing green vegetation that is plowed into the soil to increase the organic matter and humus available to support crop growth. Compare *animal manure*.

**green revolution**   Popular term for the introduction of scientifically bred or selected varieties of grain (rice, wheat, maize) that, with high enough inputs of fertilizer and water, can greatly increase crop yields.

**gross national product (GNP)**   Total market value in current dollars of all goods and services produced by an economy for final use during a year. Compare *per capita GNP, per capita real NEW, real GNP, real GNP per capita*.

**gross primary productivity**   The rate at which an ecosystem's producers capture and store a given

amount of chemical energy as biomass in a given length of time. Compare *net primary productivity*.

**ground fire**   Fire that burns decayed leaves or peat deep below the ground surface. Compare *crown fire, surface fire*.

**groundwater**   Water that sinks into the soil and is stored in slowly flowing and slowly renewed underground reservoirs called aquifers; underground water in the zone of saturation, below the water table. See *confined aquifer, unconfined aquifer*. Compare *runoff, surface water*.

**growth rate (r)**   Increase in the size of a population per unit of time (such as a year).

**gully erosion**   Severe soil erosion caused when high-velocity water flow removes enough soil to form large ditches or gullies. Compare *rill erosion, sheet erosion*.

**gully reclamation**   Restoring land suffering from gully erosion by seeding gullies with quick-growing plants, building small dams to collect silt and gradually fill in the channels, and building channels to divert water away from the gully.

**habitat**   Place or type of place where an organism or a population of organisms lives. Compare *ecological niche*.

**half-life**   Time needed for one-half of the nuclei in a radioisotope to emit its radiation. Each radioisotope has a characteristic half-life, which may range from a few millionths of a second to several billion years.

**hazard**   Something that can cause injury, disease, economic loss, or environmental damage.

**hazardous chemical**   Chemical that can cause harm because it is flammable or explosive, or that can irritate or damage the skin or lungs (such as strong acidic or alkaline substances) or cause allergic reactions of the immune system (allergens). See *toxic chemical*.

**hazardous waste**   Any solid, liquid, or container-ized gas that can catch fire easily, is corrosive to skin tissue or metals, is unstable and can explode or release toxic fumes, or has harmful concentrations of one or more toxic materials that can leach out. See *toxic waste*.

**heat**   Total kinetic energy of all the randomly moving atoms, ions, or molecules within a given substance, excluding the overall motion of the whole object. This form of kinetic energy flows from one body to another when there is a temperature difference between the two bodies. Heat always flows spontaneously from a hot sample of matter to a colder sample of matter. This is one way to state the second law of thermodynamics. Compare *temperature*.

**heat island**   See *urban heat island*.

**herbicide**   Chemical that kills a plant or inhibits its growth.

**herbivore**   Plant-eating organism. Examples include deer, sheep, grasshoppers, and zooplankton. Compare *carnivore, omnivore*.

**heterotroph**   See *consumer*.

**high-quality energy**   Energy that is organized or concentrated (low entropy) and has great ability to perform useful work. Examples include high-temperature heat and the energy in electricity, coal, oil, gasoline, sunlight, and nuclei of uranium-235. Compare *low-quality energy*.

**high-quality matter**   Matter that is organized (low entropy) and contains a high concentration of a useful resource. Compare *low-quality matter*.

**high seas**   Ocean areas beyond the legal jurisdiction of any country—beyond the exclusive economic zone. Compare *exclusive economic zones*.

**homeostasis**   Maintenance of favorable internal conditions in a system despite changes in external conditions. See *constancy, inertia, resilience*.

**host**   Plant or animal upon which a parasite feeds.

**human capital**   Physical and mental talents of people used to produce, distribute, and sell an economic good. Labor includes entrepreneurs, who assume the risk and responsibility of combining the resources of land, capital goods, and workers who produce an economic good. Compare *Earth capital, manufactured capital*.

**humification**   Process in which organic matter in the upper soil layers is reduced to finely divided pieces of humus or partially decomposed organic matter.

**humus**   Slightly soluble residue of undigested or partially decomposed organic material in topsoil. This material helps retain water and water-soluble nutrients, which can be taken up by plant roots. See *humification*.

**hunter-gatherers**   People who get their food by gathering edible wild plants and other materials and by hunting wild animals and fish.

**hydrocarbon**   Organic compound of hydrogen and carbon atoms.

**hydroelectric power plant**   Structure in which the energy of falling or flowing water spins a turbine generator to produce electricity.

**hydrologic cycle**   Biogeochemical cycle that collects, purifies, and distributes the earth's fixed supply of water from the environment, to living organisms, and back to the environment.

**hydropower**   Electrical energy produced by falling or flowing water. See *hydroelectric power plant*.

**hydrosphere**   Earth's liquid water (oceans, lakes and other bodies of surface water, and underground water), Earth's frozen water (polar ice caps, floating ice cap, and ice in soil known as permafrost), and small amounts of water vapor in the atmosphere.

**identified resources**   Deposits of a particular mineral-bearing material of which the location, quantity, and quality are known or have been estimated from direct geological evidence and measurements. Compare *undiscovered resources*.

**igneous rock**   Rock formed when molten rock material (magma) wells up from Earth's interior, cools, and solidifies into rock masses. Compare *metamorphic rock, sedimentary rock*. See *rock cycle*.

**immature community**   Community at an early stage of ecological succession. It usually has a low number of species and ecological niches, and cannot capture and use energy or cycle critical nutrients as efficiently as more complex, mature ecosystems. Compare *mature community*.

**immigrant species**   Species that migrate into an ecosystem or that are deliberately or accidentally introduced into an ecosystem by humans. Some of these species are beneficial, while others can take over and eliminate many native species. Compare *indicator species, keystone species, native species*.

**immigration**   Migration of people into a country or area to take up permanent residence. Compare *emigration*.

**increasers**   Plant species present before grazing that increase in numbers after heavy grazing. Compare *decreasers, invaders*.

**indicator species**   Species that serve as early warnings that a community or an ecosystem is being degraded. Compare *immigrant species, keystone species, native species*.

**industrialized agriculture**   Using large inputs of energy from fossil fuels (especially oil and natural gas), water, fertilizer, and pesticides to produce large quantities of crops and livestock for domestic and foreign sale. Compare *subsistence farming*.

**Industrial Revolution**   Use of new sources of energy from fossil fuels and later from nuclear fuels, and use of new technologies, to grow food and manufacture products.

**industrial smog**   Type of air pollution consisting mostly of a mixture of sulfur dioxide, suspended droplets of sulfuric acid formed from some of the sulfur dioxide, and a variety of suspended solid particles. Compare *photochemical smog*.

**inertia**   Ability of a living system to resist being disturbed or altered. Compare *constancy, resilience*.

**infant mortality rate**   Number of babies per 1,000 born each year that die before their first birthday.

**infiltration**   Downward movement of water through soil.

**information feedback**   Process by which information is fed back into a system, causing it to change. See *negative feedback, positive feedback*.

**inland wetland**   Land away from the coast, such as a swamp, marsh, or bog, that is covered all or part of the year with fresh water. Compare *coastal wetland*.

**inorganic compound**   Any compound not classified as an organic compound. Compare *organic compound*.

**inorganic fertilizer**   See *commercial inorganic fertilizer*.

**input pollution control**   See *pollution prevention*.

**insecticide**   Chemical that kills insects.

**integrated pest management (IPM)**   Combined use of biological, chemical, and cultivation methods in proper sequence and timing to keep the size of a pest population below the size that causes economically unacceptable loss of a crop or livestock animal.

**intercropping**   Growing two or more different crops at the same time on a plot. For example, a carbohydrate-rich grain that depletes soil nitrogen and a protein-rich legume that adds nitrogen to the soil may be intercropped. Compare *monoculture, polyculture, polyvarietal cultivation*.

**interference competition**   Situation in which one species limits access of another species to a resource, regardless of whether the resource is abundant or scarce. See *exploitation competition, interspecific competition*. Compare *intraspecific competition*.

**intermediate goods**   See *manufactured capital*.

**internal cost**   Direct cost paid by the producer and the buyer of an economic good. Compare *external cost*.

**interplanting**   Simultaneously growing a variety of crops on the same plot. See *agroforestry, intercropping, polyculture, polyvarietal cultivation*.

**interspecific competition**   Members of two or more species trying to use the same limited resources in an ecosystem. See *competition, competitive exclusion principle, exploitation competition, interference competition, intraspecific competition*.

**intraspecific competition**   Two or more individual organisms of a single species trying to use the same limited resources in an ecosystem. See *competition, interspecific competition*.

**invaders**   Plants such as prickly cactus that infest severely overgrazed land. Compare *decreasers, increasers*.

**inversion**   See *thermal inversion*.

**invertebrates**   Animals that have no backbones. Compare *vertebrates*.

**ion**   Atom or group of atoms with one or more positive (+) or negative (–) electrical charges. Compare *atom, molecule*.

**ionizing radiation**   Fast-moving alpha or beta particles or high-energy radiation (gamma rays) emitted by radioisotopes. They have enough energy to dislodge one or more electrons from atoms they hit, forming charged ions in tissue that can react with and damage living tissue.

**isotopes**   Two or more forms of a chemical element that have the same number of protons but different mass numbers due to different numbers of neutrons in their nuclei.

**J-shaped curve**   Curve with a shape similar to that of the letter J; represents exponential growth.

**judicial branch**   Branch of government that in the United States consists of the Supreme Court and any lower federal courts established by Congress. Compare *executive branch, legislative branch*.

**kerogen**   Solid, waxy mixture of hydrocarbons found in oil shale rock. When the rock is heated to high temperatures, the kerogen is vaporized. The vapor is condensed and purified, and then sent to a refinery where gasoline, heating oil, and other products are produced. See *oil shale, shale oil*.

**keystone species**   Species that play roles affecting many other organisms in an ecosystem. Compare *immigrant species, indicator species, native species*.

**kilocalorie (kcal)**   Unit of energy equal to 1,000 calories. See *calorie*.

**kilowatt (kw)**   Unit of electrical power equal to 1,000 watts. See *watt*.

**kinetic energy**   Energy that matter has because of its motion and mass. Compare *potential energy*.

**K-strategists**   Species that produce a few, often fairly large offspring but invest a great deal of time and energy to ensure that most of those offspring will reach reproductive age. Compare *r-strategists*.

**kwashiorkor**   Type of malnutrition that occurs in infants and very young children when they are weaned from mother's milk to a starchy diet low in protein. See *marasmus*.

**labor**   See *human capital*.

**lake**   Large natural body of standing fresh water formed when water from precipitation, land runoff, or groundwater flow fills a depression in the earth created by glaciation, earth movement, volcanic activity, or a giant meteorite. See *eutrophic lake, mesotrophic lake, oligotrophic lake*.

**landfill**   See *sanitary landfill*.

**land-use planning**   Process for deciding the best present and future use of each parcel of land in an area.

**latitude**   Distance from the equator. Compare *altitude*.

**lava**   Magma that has been extruded onto the earth's surface; also a general name for the igneous rocks that form from it.

**law of conservation of energy**   See *first law of thermodynamics*.

**law of conservation of matter**   In any physical or chemical change, matter is neither created nor destroyed, but merely changed from one form to another; in physical and chemical changes, existing atoms are rearranged into either different spatial patterns (physical changes) or different combinations (chemical changes).

**law of conservation of matter and energy**   In any nuclear change, the total amount of matter and energy involved remains the same. Compare *first law of thermodynamics, law of conservation of matter*.

**law of pollution prevention**   If you don't put something into the environment, it isn't there.

**law of tolerance**   The existence, abundance, and distribution of a species in an ecosystem are determined by whether the levels of one or more physical or chemical factors fall within the range tolerated by the species. See *threshold effect*.

**LD$_{50}$**   See *median lethal dose*.

**LDC**   See *less developed country*.

**leaching**   Process in which various chemicals in upper layers of soil are dissolved and carried to lower layers and, in some cases, to groundwater.

**legislative branch**   Branch of government whose primary function is to develop, approve, and oversee policy—a planned course of action on a specific problem or topic. In the United States the elected members of Congress make up this branch of government. Compare *executive branch, judicial branch*.

**less developed country (LDC)**   Country that has low to moderate industrialization and low to moderate GNP per capita. Most are located in the Southern Hemisphere in Africa, Asia, and Latin America. Compare *more developed country*.

**lethal dose**   Amount of a toxic material per unit of body weight of the test animals that kills all of the test population in a certain time. See *median lethal dose*.

**life-cycle cost**   Initial cost plus lifetime operating costs of an economic good.

**life expectancy**   Average number of years a newborn infant can be expected to live.

**limiting factor**   Single factor that limits the growth, abundance, or distribution of the population of a species in an ecosystem. See *limiting factor principle*.

**limiting factor principle**   Too much or too little of any abiotic factor can limit or prevent growth of a population of a species in an ecosystem, even if all other factors are at or near the optimum range of tolerance for the species.

**linear growth**   Growth in which a quantity increases by some fixed amount during each unit of time. Compare *exponential growth*.

**liquefied natural gas (LNG)**   Natural gas converted to liquid form by cooling to a very low temperature.

**liquefied petroleum gas (LPG)**   Mixture of liquefied propane and butane gas removed from natural gas.

**lithosphere**   Outer shell of the earth composed of the crust and the rigid, outermost part of the mantle outside of the asthenosphere; material found in Earth's plates. See *crust, mantle, plates, plate tectonics*.

**loams**   Soils containing a mixture of clay, sand, silt, and humus. Good for growing most crops.

**low-quality energy**   Energy that is disorganized or dispersed (high entropy) and that has little ability to do useful work. An example is low-temperature heat. Compare *high-quality energy*.

**low-quality matter**   Matter that is disorganized (high entropy), is diluted or dispersed, or contains a low concentration of a useful resource. Compare *high-quality matter*.

**LPG**   See *liquefied petroleum gas*.

**macronutrient**   Element that a plant or an animal needs in large amounts to stay alive and healthy. Examples include carbon, oxygen, hydrogen, nitrogen, phosphorus, sulfur, calcium, magnesium, and potassium. Compare *micronutrient*.

**magma**   Molten rock below the earth's surface.

**magnitude**   Measure of the amount of energy released in an earthquake; usually reported in terms of the Richter scale.

**malnutrition**   Faulty nutrition. Caused by a diet that does not supply an individual with enough proteins, essential fats, vitamins, minerals, and other nutrients needed for good health. See *kwashiorkor, marasmus*. Compare *overnutrition, undernutrition*.

**mantle**   Zone of the earth's interior between its core and its crust. Compare *core, crust*. See *lithosphere*.

**manufactured capital**   Manufactured items made from Earth capital and used to produce and distribute economic goods and services bought by consumers.

These include tools, machinery, equipment, factory buildings, and transportation and distribution facilities. Compare *Earth capital, human capital.*

**manure**   See *animal manure, green manure.*

**marasmus**   Nutritional-deficiency disease caused by a diet that does not have enough calories and protein to maintain good health. See *kwashiorkor, malnutrition.*

**marine demersal species**   Fish and shellfish that feed mostly on or near ocean bottoms and usually don't range over a wide area. Examples include cod, flounder, haddock, sole, lobster, crawfish, and crab. Compare *anadromous fish, marine pelagic species.*

**marine pelagic species**   Ocean fish that usually feed near the surface and often migrate over a wide area. Examples include tuna, herring, pilchard (whose young are canned and sold as sardines), anchovy, mackerel, squid, and salmon. Compare *anadromous fish, marine demersal species.*

**market equilibrium**   State in which sellers and buyers of an economic good agree on the quantity to be produced and the price to be paid.

**mass**   The amount of material in an object.

**mass extinction**   A catastrophic, widespread— often global— event in which major groups of species are wiped out simultaneously over a relatively short time compared to normal (background) extinctions.

**mass number**   Sum of the number of neutrons and the number of protons in the nucleus of an atom. It gives the approximate mass of that atom. Compare *atomic number.*

**mass transit**   Buses, trains, trolleys, and other forms of transportation that carry large numbers of people.

**mass wasting**   Downslope movement of regolith or rock masses newly detached from underlying material under the influence of gravity, without being carried in, on, or under a glacier, stream, or other agent of erosion. Examples include rockfalls, rockslides, earthflows, and mudflows. Compare *erosion, weathering.*

**matter**   Anything that has mass (the amount of material in an object) and takes up space. On Earth, where gravity is present, we weigh an object to determine its mass.

**matter quality**   Measure of how useful a matter resource is based on its availability and concentration. See *high-quality matter, low-quality matter.*

**matter-recycling society**   Society that emphasizes recycling the maximum amount of all resources that can be recycled. The goal is to allow economic growth to continue without depleting matter resources and without producing excessive pollution and environmental degradation. Compare *sustainable-Earth society, throwaway society.*

**mature community**   Fairly stable, self-sustaining community in an advanced stage of ecological succession; usually has a diverse array of species and ecological niches; captures and uses energy and cycles critical chemicals more efficiently than simpler, immature communities. Compare *immature community.*

**maximum sustainable yield**   See *sustainable yield.*

**MDC**   See *more developed country.*

**median lethal dose (LD$_{50}$)**   Amount of a toxic material per unit of body weight of test animals that kills half the test population in a certain time. Compare *lethal dose.*

**meltdown**   The melting of the core of a nuclear reactor.

**mesosphere**   Third layer of the atmosphere, found above the stratosphere. Compare *stratosphere, thermosphere, troposphere.*

**mesotrophic lake**   Lake with a moderate supply of plant nutrients. Compare *eutrophic lake, oligotrophic lake.*

**metabolic reserve**   Lower half of rangeland grass plants; can grow back as long as it is not consumed by herbivores.

**metamorphic rock**   Rock produced when a preexisting rock is subjected to high temperatures (which may cause it to melt partially), high pressures, chemically active fluids, or a combination of these agents. Compare *igneous rock, sedimentary rock.* See *rock cycle.*

**metastasis**   Spread of malignant (cancerous cells) from a cancer to other parts of the body.

**micronutrient**   Element that a plant or an animal needs in small, or trace, amounts to stay alive and healthy. Examples include iron, copper, zinc, chlorine, and iodine. Compare *macronutrient.*

**migration**   Repeated departure and return of individuals or their offspring to and from an area. An example is migratory birds. Also used to describe emigration and immigration of individuals. See *emigration, immigration.*

**mineral**   Any naturally occurring inorganic substance found in the earth's crust as a crystalline solid. See *mineral resource.*

**mineralization**   Process taking place in soil in which decomposers turn organic materials into inorganic ones.

**mineral resource**   Concentration of naturally occurring solid, liquid, or gaseous material, in or on the earth's crust, in such form and amount that its extraction and conversion into useful materials or items is currently or potentially profitable. Mineral resources are classified as metallic (such as iron and tin ores) or nonmetallic (such as fossil fuels, sand, and salt).

**minimum-tillage farming**   See *conservation-tillage farming.*

**mixed economic system**   Economic system that falls somewhere between pure market and pure command economic systems. Virtually all of the world's economic systems are in this category, with some closer to a pure market system and some closer to a pure command economic system. Compare *pure command economic system, pure market economic system, traditional economic system.*

**mixture**   Combination of one or more elements and compounds.

**molecule**   Combination of two or more atoms of the same chemical element (such as $O_2$) or different chemical elements (such as $H_2O$) held together by chemical bonds.

**monera**   See *bacteria, cyanobacteria.*

**monoculture**   Cultivation of a single crop, usually on a large area of land. Compare *polyculture.*

**more developed country (MDC)**   Country that is highly industrialized and has a high GNP per capita. Compare *less developed country.*

**multiple use**   Principle of managing public land, such as a national forest, so it is used for a variety of purposes, such as timbering, mining, recreation, grazing, wildlife preservation, and soil and water conservation. See *sustainable yield.*

**municipal solid waste**   Solid materials discarded by homes and businesses in or near urban areas. See *solid waste.*

**mutagen**   Chemical, or form of ionizing radiation, that causes heritable changes in the DNA molecules in the genes found in chromosomes (mutations). See *carcinogen, mutation, teratogen.*

**mutation**   A heritable change in the kind, structure, sequence, or number of component parts of a cell's DNA. See *mutagen.*

**mutualism**   Type of species interaction in which both participating species generally benefit. Compare *commensalism.*

**national ambient air quality standards (NAAQS)**   Maximum allowable level, averaged over a specific time period, for a certain pollutant in outdoor (ambient) air.

**native species**   Species that normally live and thrive in a particular ecosystem. Compare *immigrant species, indicator species, keystone species.*

**natural gas**   Underground deposits of gases consisting of 50–90% by weight methane gas ($CH_4$) and small amounts of heavier gaseous hydrocarbon compounds such as propane ($C_3H_8$) and butane ($C_4H_{10}$).

**natural hazard**   Event that destroys or damages wildlife habitats, kills or harms humans, or damages property. Examples include earthquakes, volcanoes, floods, and mass wasting.

**natural ionizing radiation**   Ionizing radiation in the environment from natural sources.

**natural radioactive decay**   Nuclear change in which unstable nuclei of atoms spontaneously shoot out particles (usually alpha or beta particles), energy (gamma rays), or both at a fixed rate.

**natural recharge**   Natural replenishment of an aquifer by precipitation, which percolates downward through soil and rock. See *recharge area.*

**natural resource capital**   See *Earth capital.*

**natural resources**   Area of the earth's solid surface, nutrients and minerals in the soil and deeper layers of the earth's crust, water, wild and domesticated plants and animals, air, and other resources produced by the earth's natural processes. Compare *human capital, manufactured capital.* See *Earth capital.*

**natural selection**   Process by which some genes and gene combinations in a population of a species are reproduced more than others when the population is exposed to an environmental change or stress. When individual organisms in a population die off over time because they cannot tolerate a new stress, they are replaced by individuals whose genetic traits allow them to cope better with the stress. When these better-adapted individuals reproduce, they pass their adaptive traits on to their offspring. See *differential reproduction, evolution.*

**negative feedback**   Flow of information into a system that counteracts the effects of a change in external conditions on the system. Compare *positive feedback.*

**nematocide**   Chemical that kills nematodes (roundworms).

**net economic welfare (NEW)**   Measure of annual change in quality of life in a country, obtained by subtracting the value of all final products and services that decrease the quality of life from a country's GNP. See *NEW per capita.*

**net energy**   See *net useful energy.*

**net primary productivity**   Rate at which all the plants in an ecosystem produce net useful chemical energy; equal to the difference between the rate at which the plants in an ecosystem produce useful chemical energy (primary productivity) and the rate at which they use some of that energy through cellular respiration. Compare *primary productivity.*

**net useful energy**   Total amount of useful energy available from an energy resource or energy system over its lifetime minus the amount of energy used (the first energy law), automatically wasted (the second energy law), and unnecessarily wasted in finding, processing, concentrating, and transporting it to users.

**neutral solution**   Water solution containing an equal number of hydrogen ions ($H^+$) and hydroxide ions (OH⁻); water solution with a pH of 7. Compare *acid solution, basic solution*.

**neutron (n)** Elementary particle in the nuclei of all atoms (except hydrogen-1). It has a relative mass of 1 and no electric charge.

**NEW** See *net economic welfare*.

**NEW per capita** Annual net economic welfare (NEW) of a country divided by its total population. See *net economic welfare, real NEW per capita*.

**niche** See *ecological niche*.

**nitrogen cycle** Cyclic movement of nitrogen in different chemical forms from the environment, to organisms, and then back to the environment.

**nitrogen fixation** Conversion of atmospheric nitrogen gas into forms useful to plants, by lightning, bacteria, and cyanobacteria; part of the nitrogen cycle.

**noise pollution** Any unwanted, disturbing, or harmful sound that impairs or interferes with hearing, causes stress, hampers concentration and work efficiency, or causes accidents.

**nondegradable pollutant** Material that is not broken down by natural processes. Examples include the toxic elements lead and mercury. Compare *biodegradable pollutant, degradable pollutant, slowly degradable pollutant*.

**nonionizing radiation** Forms of radiant energy such as radio waves, microwaves, infrared light, and ordinary light that do not have enough energy to cause ionization of atoms in living tissue. Compare *ionizing radiation*.

**nonpersistent pollutant** See *degradable pollutant*.

**nonpoint source** Large or dispersed land areas such as cropfields, streets, and lawns that discharge pollutants into the environment over a large area. Compare *point source*.

**nonrenewable resource** Resource that exists in a fixed amount (stock) in various places in the earth's crust and has the potential for renewal only by geological, physical, and chemical processes taking place over hundreds of millions to billions of years. Examples include copper, aluminum, coal, and oil. We classify these resources as exhaustible because we are extracting and using them at a much faster rate than the geological time scale on which they were formed. Compare *perpetual resource, potentially renewable resource*.

**nonruminants** Animals such as pigs and chickens that cannot feed on rangeland vegetation and eat mostly cereal grains grown on cropland. Compare *ruminant*.

**nontransmissible disease** A disease that is not caused by living organisms and that does not spread from one person to another. Examples are most cancer, diabetes, cardiovascular disease, and malnutrition. Compare *transmissible disease*.

**no-till farming** See *conservation-tillage farming*.

**nuclear change** Process in which nuclei of certain isotopes spontaneously change, or are forced to change, into one or more different isotopes. The three principal types of nuclear change are natural radioactivity, nuclear fission, and nuclear fusion. Compare *chemical change*.

**nuclear energy** Energy released when atomic nuclei undergo a nuclear reaction such as the spontaneous emission of radioactivity, nuclear fission, or nuclear fusion.

**nuclear fission** Nuclear change in which the nuclei of certain isotopes with large mass numbers (such as uranium-235 and plutonium-239) are split apart into lighter nuclei when struck by a neutron. This process releases more neutrons and a large amount of energy. Compare *nuclear fusion*.

**nuclear fusion** Nuclear change in which two nuclei of isotopes of elements with a low mass number (such as hydrogen-2 and hydrogen-3) are forced together at extremely high temperatures until they fuse to form a heavier nucleus (such as helium-4). This process releases a large amount of energy. Compare *nuclear fission*.

**nucleus** Extremely tiny center of an atom, making up most of the atom's mass. It contains one or more positively charged protons and one or more neutrons with no electrical charge (except for a hydrogen-1 atom, which has one proton and no neutrons in its nucleus).

**nutrient** Any food or element an organism must take in to live, grow, or reproduce. See *macronutrient, micronutrient*.

**nutrient cycle** See *biogeochemical cycle*.

**oil** See *crude oil*.

**oil shale** Fine-grained rock containing varying amounts of kerogen, a solid, waxy mixture of hydrocarbon compounds. Heating the rock to high temperatures converts the kerogen into a vapor that can be condensed to form a slow-flowing heavy oil called shale oil. See *kerogen, shale oil*.

**old-growth forest** Virgin and old, second-growth forests containing trees that are often hundreds, sometimes thousands, of years old. Examples include forests of Douglas fir, western hemlock, giant sequoia, and coastal redwoods in the western United States. Compare *second-growth forest, tree farm*.

**oligotrophic lake** Lake with a low supply of plant nutrients. Compare *eutrophic lake, mesotrophic lake*.

**omnivore** Animal organism that can use both plants and other animals as food sources. Examples include pigs, rats, cockroaches, and people. Compare *carnivore, herbivore*.

**open-pit mining** Removal of ores of metals such as iron and copper by digging them out of the earth's surface and leaving a pit.

**open sea** The part of an ocean that is beyond the continental shelf. Compare *coastal zone*.

**optimum yield** Amount of fish (or other potentially renewable resource) that can be economically harvested on a sustainable basis; usually less than the sustainable yield. See *sustainable yield*.

**ore** Part of a metal-yielding material that can be economically and legally extracted at a given time. An ore typically contains two parts: the ore mineral, which contains the desired metal, and waste mineral material (gangue). See *beneficiation*.

**organic compound** Molecule that contains atoms of the element carbon, usually combined with each other and with atoms of one or more other elements such as hydrogen, oxygen, nitrogen, sulfur, phosphorus, chlorine, and fluorine. Compare *inorganic compound*.

**organic farming** Producing crops and livestock naturally by using organic fertilizer (manure, legumes, compost) and natural pest control (bugs that eat harmful bugs, plants that repel bugs, and environmental controls such as crop rotation) instead of using commercial inorganic fertilizers and synthetic pesticides and herbicides.

**organic fertilizer** Organic material such as animal manure, green manure, and compost, applied to cropland as a source of plant nutrients. Compare *commercial inorganic fertilizer*.

**organism** Any form of life.

**other resources** Identified and unidentified resources not classified as reserves.

**output pollution control** See *pollution cleanup*.

**overburden** Layer of soil and rock overlying a mineral deposit; removed during surface mining.

**overconsumption** Situation where some people consume much more than they need at the expense of those who cannot meet their basic needs and at the expense of Earth's present and future life support systems.

**overfishing** Harvesting so many fish of a species, especially immature ones, that there is not enough breeding stock left to replenish the species so it is not profitable to harvest them.

**overgrazing** Destruction of vegetation when too many grazing animals feed too long and exceed the carrying capacity of a rangeland area.

**overnutrition** Diet so high in calories, saturated (animal) fats, salt, sugar, and processed foods, and so low in vegetables and fruits, that the consumer runs high risks of diabetes, hypertension, heart disease, and other health hazards. Compare *malnutrition, undernutrition*.

**overpopulation** State in which there are more people than can live on Earth or in a geographic region in comfort, happiness, and health, and still leave the planet or region a fit place for future generations. It is a result of growing numbers of people, growing affluence (resource consumption), or both. See *carrying capacity, consumption overpopulation, dieback, overshoot, people overpopulation*.

**overshoot** Condition in which population size of a species temporarily exceeds the carrying capacity of its habitat. This leads to a sharp reduction in its population. See *carrying capacity, consumption overpopulation, dieback, people overpopulation*.

**oxygen cycle** Cyclic movement of oxygen in different chemical forms from the environment, to organisms, and then back to the environment.

**oxygen-demanding wastes** Organic materials that are usually biodegraded by aerobic (oxygen-consuming) bacteria, if there is enough dissolved oxygen in the water. See *biological oxygen demand*.

**ozone layer** Layer of gaseous ozone ($O_3$) in the stratosphere that protects life on Earth by filtering out harmful ultraviolet radiation from the sun.

**PANs** Peroxyacyl nitrates—a group of chemicals found in photochemical smog.

**parasite** Consumer organism that lives on or in and feeds on a living plant or animal, known as the host, over an extended period of time. The parasite draws nourishment from and gradually weakens its host, which may or may not kill the host.

**particulate matter** Solid particles or liquid droplets suspended or carried in the air.

**parts per billion (ppb)** Number of parts of a chemical found in one billion parts of a particular gas, liquid, or solid.

**parts per million (ppm)** Number of parts of a chemical found in one million parts of a particular gas, liquid, or solid.

**passive solar heating system** System that captures sunlight directly within a structure and converts it into low-temperature heat for heating space or for heating water for domestic use without the use of mechanical devices. Compare *active solar heating system*.

**pathogen** Organism that produces disease.

**PCBs** See *polychlorinated biphenyls*.

**pelagic species** See *marine pelagic species*.

**people overpopulation** Situation in which there are more people in the world or a geographic region than available supplies of food, water, and other vital resources can support. It can also occur where the rate of population growth so exceeds the rate of economic growth, or the distribution of wealth is so inequitable, that a number of people are too poor to grow or buy enough food, fuel, and other important resources. Compare *consumption overpopulation*.

**per capita GNP**   See *GNP per capita*.

**per capita NEW**   See *NEW per capita*.

**per capita real NEW**   See *real NEW per capita*.

**perennial**   Plant that grows from the root stock each year and that does not need to be replanted. Compare *annual*.

**permafrost**   Permanently frozen underground layers of soil in tundra.

**permeability**   The degree to which underground rock and soil pores are interconnected with each other and thus a measure of the degree to which water can flow freely from one pore to another. Compare *porosity*.

**perpetual resource**   Resource, such as solar energy, that is virtually inexhaustible on a human time scale. Compare *nonrenewable resource, potentially renewable resource*.

**persistence**   See *inertia*.

**persistent pollutant**   See *slowly degradable pollutant*.

**pest**   Unwanted organism that directly or indirectly interferes with human activities.

**pesticide**   Any chemical designed to kill or inhibit the growth of an organism that people consider to be undesirable. See *fungicide, herbicide, insecticide*.

**pesticide treadmill**   Situation in which the cost of using pesticides increases while their effectiveness decreases, mostly because the pest species develop genetic resistance to the pesticides.

**petrochemicals**   Chemicals obtained by refining (distilling) crude oil and used as raw materials in the manufacture of most industrial chemicals, fertilizers, pesticides, plastics, synthetic fibers, paints, medicines, and many other products.

**petroleum**   See *crude oil*.

**pH**   Numeric value that indicates the relative acidity or alkalinity of a substance on a scale of 0 to 14, with the neutral point at 7. Acid solutions have pH values lower than 7, and basic or alkaline solutions have pH values greater than 7.

**phosphorus cycle**   Cyclic movement of phosphorus in different chemical forms from the environment, to organisms, and then back to the environment.

**photochemical smog**   Complex mixture of air pollutants produced in the atmosphere by the reaction of hydrocarbons and nitrogen oxides under the influence of sunlight. Especially harmful components include ozone, peroxyacyl nitrates (PANs), and various aldehydes. Compare *industrial smog*.

**photosynthesis**   Complex process that takes place in cells of green plants. Radiant energy from the sun is used to combine carbon dioxide ($CO_2$) and water ($H_2O$) to produce oxygen ($O_2$) and carbohydrates (such as glucose, $C_6H_{12}O_6$) and other nutrient molecules. Compare *aerobic respiration, chemosynthesis*.

**photovoltaic cell (solar cell)**   Device in which radiant (solar) energy is converted directly into electrical energy.

**physical change**   Process that alters one or more physical properties of an element or a compound without altering its chemical composition. Examples include changing the size and shape of a sample of matter (crushing ice and cutting aluminum foil) and changing a sample of matter from one physical state to another (boiling and freezing water). Compare *chemical change*.

**phytoplankton**   Small, drifting plants, mostly algae and bacteria, found in aquatic ecosystems. Compare *plankton, zooplankton*.

**pioneer community**   First integrated set of plants, animals, and decomposers found in an area undergoing primary ecological succession. See *immature community, mature community*.

**pioneer species**   First hardy species, often microbes, mosses, and lichens, that begin colonizing a site as the first stage of ecological succession. See *ecological succession, pioneer community*.

**plaintiff**   The individual, group of individuals, corporation, or government agency bringing the charges in a lawsuit. Compare *defendant*.

**planetary-management worldview**   Belief that Earth is a place of unlimited resources. Any type of resource conservation that hampers short-term economic growth is unnecessary because if we pollute or deplete resources in one area, we will find substitutes; control the pollution through technology, and, if necessary, get resources from the moon and asteroids in the "new frontier" of space. See *frontier worldview, spaceship-Earth worldview*. Compare *sustainable-Earth worldview*.

**plankton**   Small plant organisms (phytoplankton) and animal organisms (zooplankton) that float in aquatic ecosystems.

**plantation agriculture**   Growing specialized crops such as bananas, coffee, and cacao in tropical LDCs, primarily for sale to MDCs.

**plants (plantae)**   Eukaryotic, mostly multicelled organisms such as algae (red, blue, and green), mosses, ferns, flowers, cacti, grasses, beans, wheat, rice, and trees. These organisms use photosynthesis to produce organic nutrients for themselves and for other organisms feeding on them. Water and other inorganic nutrients are obtained from the soil for terrestrial plants and from the water for aquatic plants.

**plates**   Various-sized areas of Earth's lithosphere that move slowly around with the mantle's flowing asthenosphere. Most earthquakes and volcanoes occur around the boundaries of these plates. See *asthenosphere, lithosphere, plate tectonics*.

**plate tectonics**   Theory of geophysical processes that explains the movements of lithospheric plates and the processes that occur at their boundaries. See *lithosphere, plates*.

**poaching**   Illegal commercial hunting or fishing.

**point source**   A single identifiable source that discharges pollutants into the environment. Examples are the smokestack of a power plant or an industrial plant, the drainpipe of a meat-packing plant, the chimney of a house, or the exhaust pipe of an automobile. Compare *nonpoint source*.

**policy**   A planned course of action on a specific problem or topic.

**politics**   Process through which individuals and groups try to influence or control the policies and actions of governments that affect the local, state, national, and international communities.

**pollution**   An undesirable change in the physical, chemical, or biological characteristics of air, water, soil, or food that can adversely affect the health, survival, or activities of humans or other living organisms.

**pollution cleanup**   Device or process that removes or reduces the level of a pollutant after it has been produced or has entered the environment. Examples include automobile emission control devices and sewage treatment plants. Compare *pollution prevention*.

**pollution prevention**   Device or process that prevents a potential pollutant from forming or from entering the environment or that sharply reduces the amounts entering the environment. Compare *pollution cleanup*.

**polychlorinated biphenyls (PCBs)**   Group of 209 different toxic, oily, synthetic chlorinated hydrocarbon compounds that can be biologically amplified in food chains and webs.

**polyculture**   Complex form of intercropping in which a large number of different plants maturing at different times are planted together. See *intercropping*. Compare *monoculture, polyvarietal cultivation*.

**polyvarietal cultivation**   Planting a plot of land with several varieties of the same crop. Compare *intercropping, monoculture, polyculture*.

**population**   Group of individual organisms of the same species living within a particular area.

**population crash**   Large number of deaths over a fairly short time, brought about when the number of individuals in a population is too large to be supported by available environmental resources.

**population density**   Number of organisms in a particular population found in a specified area. Compare *ecological population density*.

**population dispersion**   General pattern in which the members of a population are arranged through its habitat.

**population distribution**   Variation of population density over a particular geographical area. For example, a country has a high population density in its urban areas and a much lower population density in rural areas.

**population dynamics**   Major abiotic and biotic factors that tend to increase or decrease the population size and the age and sex composition of a species.

**population size**   Number of individuals making up a population's gene pool.

**porosity**   The pores (cracks and spaces) in rocks or soil, or the percentage of the rock's or soil's volume not occupied by the rock or soil itself. Compare *permeability*.

**positive feedback**   Situation in which a change in a system in one direction provides information that causes the system to change farther in the same direction. Compare *negative feedback*.

**potential energy**   Energy stored in an object because of its position or the position of its parts. Compare *kinetic energy*.

**potentially renewable resource**   Resource that theoretically can last indefinitely without reducing the available supply because it is replaced more rapidly through natural processes than are nonrenewable resources. Examples include trees in forests, grasses in grasslands, wild animals, fresh surface water in lakes and streams, most groundwater, fresh air, and fertile soil. If such a resource is used faster than it is replenished, it can be depleted and converted into a nonrenewable resource. Compare *nonrenewable resource, perpetual resource*. See *environmental degradation*.

**poverty**   Inability to meet basic needs for food, clothing, and shelter.

**ppb**   See *parts per billion*.

**ppm**   See *parts per million*.

**precipitation**   Water in the form of rain, sleet, hail, and snow that falls from the atmosphere onto the land and bodies of water.

**predation**   Situation in which an organism of one species (the predator) captures and feeds on parts or all of an organism of another species (the prey).

**predator**   Organism that captures and feeds on parts or all of an organism of another species (the prey).

**predator-prey relationship**   Interaction between two organisms of different species in which one organism (the predator) captures and feeds on parts or all of another organism (the prey).

**prey**   Organism that is captured and serves as a source of food for an organism of another species (the predator).

**primary consumer**   Organism that feeds directly on all or part of plants (*herbivore*) or other producers. Compare *detritivore, omnivore, secondary consumer*.

**primary oil recovery**   Pumping out the crude oil that flows by gravity or under gas pressure into the bottom of an oil well. Compare *enhanced oil recovery, secondary oil recovery*.

**primary pollutant**   Chemical that has been added directly to the air by natural events or human activities and occurs in a harmful concentration. Compare *secondary pollutant*.

**primary productivity**   See *gross primary productivity*. Compare *net primary productivity*.

**primary sewage treatment**   Mechanical treatment of sewage in which large solids are filtered out by screens and suspended solids settle out as sludge in a sedimentation tank. Compare *advanced sewage treatment, secondary sewage treatment*.

**primary succession**   Sequential development of communities in a bare area that has never been occupied by a community of organisms. Compare *secondary succession*.

**prime reproductive age**   Years between ages 20–29, during which most women have most of their children. Compare *reproductive age*.

**principle of multiple use**   See *multiple use*.

**prior appropriation**   Legal principle by which the first user of water from a stream establishes a legal right to continued use of the amount originally withdrawn. Compare *riparian rights*.

**private-property resource**   Resource owned by an individual or a group of individuals other than the government. Compare *common-property resource, public-property resource*.

**probability**   A mathematical statement about how likely it is that something will happen.

**producer**   Organism that uses solar energy (green plant) or chemical energy (some bacteria) to manufacture the organic compounds it needs as nutrients from simple inorganic compounds obtained from its environment. Compare *consumer, decomposer*.

**prokaryotic cell**   Cell that doesn't have a distinct nucleus. Other internal parts are also not enclosed by membranes. Compare *eukaryotic cell*.

**protists (protista)**   Eukaryotic, mostly single-cell organisms such as diatoms, amoebas, some algae (golden brown and yellow-green), protozoans, and slime molds. Some protists produce their own organic nutrients through photosynthesis; others are decomposers; and some feed on bacteria, other protists, or cells of multicellular organisms.

**proton (p)**   Positively charged particle in the nuclei of all atoms. Each proton has a relative mass of 1 and a single positive charge.

**public-property resource**   Land that is owned jointly by all citizens, but is managed for them by an agency of the local, state, or federal government. Examples include state and national parks, forests, wildlife refuges, and wilderness areas. Compare *common-property resource, private-property resource*.

**pure capitalism**   See *pure market economic system*.

**pure command economic system**   System in which all economic decisions are made by the government or some other central authority. Compare *mixed economic system, pure market economic system, traditional economic system*.

**pure competition**   State in which there are large numbers of independently acting buyers and sellers for each economic good in a pure market economic system. No buyer or seller is able to control the sup-

ply of, demand for, or price of a good. All buyers and sellers are free to enter or leave the market as they please but must accept the going market price.

**pure market economic system**   System in which all economic decisions are made in the market, where buyers and sellers of economic goods freely interact, with no government or other interference. Compare *mixed economic system, pure command economic system, traditional economic system*.

**purse-seine fishing**   Catching fish, such as tuna, that feed near the surface or in shallow water by surrounding them with a net whose bottom can be pulled closed. Compare *drift-net fishing, trawler fishing*.

**pyramid of biomass**   Diagram representing the biomass, or total dry weight, of all living organisms, that can be supported at each trophic level in a food chain or food web. See *pyramid of energy flow, pyramid of numbers*.

**pyramid of energy flow**   Diagram representing the flow of energy through each trophic level in a food chain or food web. With each energy transfer, only a small part (typically 10%) of the usable energy entering one trophic level is transferred to the organisms at the next trophic level. Compare *pyramid of biomass, pyramid of numbers*.

**pyramid of numbers**   Diagram representing the number of organisms of a particular type that can be supported at each trophic level from a given input of solar energy at the producer trophic level in a food chain or food web. Compare *pyramid of biomass, pyramid of energy flow*.

**radiation**   Fast-moving particles (particulate radiation) or waves of energy (electromagnetic radiation). See *ionizing radiation, nonionizing radiation*.

**radioactive decay**   Change of a radioisotope to a different isotope by the emission of radioactivity.

**radioactive isotope**   See *radioisotope*.

**radioactive waste**   Radioactive waste products of nuclear power plants, research, medicine, weapons production, or other processes involving nuclear reactions. See *radioactivity*.

**radioactivity**   Nuclear change in which unstable nuclei of atoms spontaneously shoot out "chunks" of mass, energy, or both, at a fixed rate. The three principal types of radioactivity are gamma rays and fast-moving alpha and beta particles.

**radioisotope**   Isotope of an atom that spontaneously emits one or more types of radioactivity (alpha particles, beta particles, gamma rays).

**rain shadow effect**   Low precipitation on the far side (leeward side) of a mountain when prevailing winds flow up and over a high mountain or range of high mountains. This creates semiarid and arid conditions on the leeward side of a high mountain range.

**range condition**   Estimate of how close a particular area of rangeland is to its potential for producing vegetation that can be consumed by grazing or browsing animals.

**rangeland**   Land that supplies forage or vegetation (grasses, grasslike plants, and shrubs) for grazing and browsing animals and that is not intensively managed. Compare *feedlot*.

**range of tolerance**   Range of chemical and physical conditions that must be maintained for populations of a particular species to stay alive and grow, develop, and function normally. See *law of tolerance*.

**real GNP**   Gross national product adjusted for inflation. Compare *GNP per capita, gross national product, real GNP per capita*.

**real GNP per capita**   Per capita GNP adjusted for inflation. See *GNP per capita*.

**realized niche**   Parts of the fundamental niche of a species that are actually used by a species. See *ecological niche, fundamental niche*.

**real NEW per capita**   Per capita NEW adjusted for inflation. See *net economic welfare, NEW per capita*.

**recharge area**   Any area of land allowing water to pass through it and into an aquifer. See *aquifer, natural recharge*.

**recycling**   Collecting and reprocessing a resource so it can be made into new products. An example is collecting aluminum cans, melting them down, and using the aluminum to make new cans or other aluminum products. Compare *reuse*.

**reforestation**   Renewal of trees and other types of vegetation on land where trees have been removed; can be done naturally by seeds from nearby trees or artificially by planting seeds or seedlings.

**regulations**   Rules for implementing laws passed by Congress.

**relative humidity**   Measure (as a percentage) of the amount of water vapor in a certain mass of air compared with the maximum amount it could hold at that temperature. Compare *absolute humidity*.

**relative resource scarcity**   Situation in which a resource has not been depleted but there is not enough available to meet the demand because of unbalanced distribution; can be caused by a war, a natural disaster, or other events that disrupt the production and distribution of a resource, or by deliberate attempts by its producers to lower production to drive prices up. Compare *absolute resource scarcity*.

**renewable resource**   See *potentially renewable resource*.

**replacement-level fertility**   Number of children a couple must have to replace themselves. The average for a country or the world is usually slightly higher than 2 children per couple (2.1 in the United States and 2.5 in some LDCs) because some children die before reaching their reproductive years. See *total fertility rate*.

**reproduction**   Production of offspring by one or more parents.

**reproductive age**   Ages 15–44, when most women have all their children. Compare *prime reproductive age*.

**reproductive isolation**   Long-term geographic separation of members of a particular sexually reproducing species.

**reserves**   Resources that have been identified and from which a usable mineral can be extracted profitably at present prices with current mining technology. See *identified resources, undiscovered resources*.

**resilience**   Ability of a living system to restore itself to original condition after being exposed to an outside disturbance that is not too drastic. See *constancy, inertia*.

**resource**   Anything obtained from the living and nonliving environment to meet human needs and wants.

**resource partitioning**   Process of dividing up resources in an ecosystem so species with similar requirements (overlapping ecological niches) use the same scarce resources at different times, in different ways, or in different places. See *ecological niche, fundamental niche, realized niche*.

**resource recovery**   Salvaging usable metals, paper, and glass from solid waste, and selling them to manufacturing industries for recycling or reuse.

**respiration**   See *aerobic respiration*.

**response**   The amount of health damage caused by exposure to a certain dose of a harmful substance or form of radiation. See *dose, dose-response curve, lethal dose, median lethal dose*.

**reuse**   To use a product over and over again in the same form. An example is collecting, washing, and refilling glass beverage bottles. Compare *recycling*.

**rill erosion**   Soil erosion caused when small streams (rivulets) of surface water flow at high velocities over the ground and cut small channels or ditches in the soil. Compare *gully erosion, sheet erosion.*

**riparian rights**   System of water law that gives anyone whose land adjoins a flowing stream the right to use water from the stream as long as some is left for downstream users. Compare *prior appropriation.*

**riparian zones**   Thin strips and patches of vegetation that surround streams.

**risk**   The probability that something undesirable will happen from deliberate or accidental exposure to a hazard. See *risk assessment, risk-benefit analysis, risk management.*

**risk analysis**   Identifying hazards, evaluating the nature and severity of risks (*risk assessment*), using this and other information to determine options and make decisions about reducing or eliminating risks (*risk management*), and communicating information about risks to decision makers and the public (*risk communication*).

**risk assessment**   Process of gathering data and making assumptions to estimate short- and long-term harmful effects on human health or the environment from exposure to hazards associated with the use of a particular product or technology. See *risk, risk-benefit analysis.*

**risk-benefit analysis**   Estimate of the short- and long-term risks and benefits of using a particular product or technology. See *desirability quotient, risk.* Compare *cost-benefit analysis.*

**risk communication**   Communicating information about risks to decision makers and the public. See *risk, risk analysis, risk-benefit analysis.*

**risk management**   Using risk assessment and other information to determine options and make decisions about reducing or eliminating risks. See *risk, risk analysis, risk-benefit analysis, risk communication.*

**rock**   Any material that makes up a large, natural, continuous part of Earth's crust. See *mineral.*

**rock cycle**   Largest and slowest of the earth's cycles, consisting of geologic, physical, and chemical processes that form and modify rocks and soil in the earth's crust over millions of years.

**rodenticide**   Chemical that kills rodents.

**r-strategists**   Species that reproduce early in their life span and that produce large numbers of usually small and short-lived offspring in a short period of time. Compare *K-strategists.*

**rule of 70**   Doubling time = 70/percentage growth rate. See *doubling time, exponential growth.*

**ruminant**   Grazing and browsing herbivores such as cattle, sheep, goats, and buffalo that have a three- or four-chambered stomach that digests the cellulose in grasses and vegetation they eat. Compare *nonruminants.*

**runoff**   Fresh water from precipitation and melting ice that flows on the earth's surface into nearby streams, lakes, wetlands, and reservoirs. See *surface runoff, surface water.* Compare *groundwater.*

**rural area**   Geographical area in the United States with a population of less than 2,500 people per unit of area. The number of people used in this definition may vary in different countries. Compare *urban area.*

**salinity**   Amount of various salts dissolved in a given volume of water.

**salinization**   Accumulation of salts in soil that can eventually make the soil unable to support plant growth.

**saltwater intrusion**   Movement of salt water into freshwater aquifers in coastal and inland areas as groundwater is withdrawn faster than it is recharged by precipitation.

**sanitary landfill**   Waste disposal site on land in which waste is spread in thin layers, compacted, and covered with a fresh layer of clay or plastic foam each day.

**scavenger**   Organism that feeds on dead organisms that either were killed by other organisms or died naturally. Examples include vultures, flies, and crows. Compare *detritivore.*

**science**   Attempts to discover order in nature and then use that knowledge to make predictions about what will happen in nature. See *scientific data, scientific hypothesis, scientific law, scientific methods, scientific theory.*

**scientific data**   Facts obtained by making observations and measurements. Compare *scientific hypothesis, scientific law, scientific theory.*

**scientific hypothesis**   An educated guess that attempts to explain a scientific law or certain scientific observations. Compare *scientific data, scientific law, scientific theory.*

**scientific law**   Summary of what scientists find happening in nature over and over in the same way. See *first law of thermodynamics, second law of thermodynamics, law of conservation of matter.* Compare *scientific data, scientific hypothesis, scientific theory.*

**scientific methods**   The ways scientists gather data and formulate and test scientific laws and theories. See *scientific data, scientific hypothesis, scientific law, scientific theory.*

**scientific theory**   A well-tested and widely accepted scientific hypothesis. Compare *scientific data, scientific hypothesis, scientific law.*

**secondary consumer**   Organism that feeds only on primary consumers. Most secondary consumers are animals, but some are plants. Compare *detritivore, omnivore, primary consumer.*

**secondary oil recovery**   Injection of water into an oil well after primary oil recovery to force out some of the remaining, usually thicker, crude oil. Compare *enhanced oil recovery, primary oil recovery.*

**secondary pollutant**   Harmful chemical formed in the atmosphere when a primary air pollutant reacts with normal air components or with other air pollutants. Compare *primary pollutant.*

**secondary sewage treatment**   Second step in most waste treatment systems, in which aerobic bacteria break down up to 90% of degradable, oxygen-demanding organic wastes in wastewater; usually done by bringing sewage and bacteria together in trickling filters or in the activated sludge process. Compare *advanced sewage treatment, primary sewage treatment.*

**secondary succession**   Sequential development of communities in an area in which natural vegetation has been removed or destroyed but the soil is not destroyed. Compare *primary succession.*

**second-growth forest**   Stands of trees resulting from secondary ecological succession. Compare *ancient forest, old-growth forest, tree farm.*

**second law of ecology**   Everything is connected to and intermingled with everything else.

**second law of energy**   See *second law of thermodynamics.*

**second law of thermodynamics**   In any conversion of heat energy to useful work, some of the initial energy input is always degraded to a lower-quality, more dispersed (higher entropy), less useful energy, usually low-temperature heat that flows into the environment; you can't break even in terms of energy quality. See *first law of thermodynamics.*

**sedimentary rock**   Rock that forms from the accumulated products of erosion and in some cases from the compacted shells, skeletons, and other remains of dead organisms. Compare *igneous rock, metamorphic rock.* See *rock cycle.*

**seed-tree cutting**   Removal of nearly all trees on a site in one cutting, with a few seed-producing trees left uniformly distributed to regenerate the forest. Compare *clear-cutting, selective cutting, shelterwood cutting, strip logging, whole-tree harvesting.*

**selective cutting**   Cutting of intermediate-aged, mature, or diseased trees in an uneven-aged forest stand, either singly or in small groups. This encourages the growth of younger trees and maintains an uneven-aged stand. Compare *clear-cutting, seed-tree cutting, shelterwood cutting, strip logging, whole-tree harvesting.*

**septic tank**   Underground tank for treatment of wastewater from a home in rural and suburban areas. Bacteria in the tank decompose organic wastes, and the sludge settles to the bottom of the tank. The effluent flows out of the tank into the ground through a field of drain pipes.

**sewage sludge**   Gooey mixture of toxic chemicals, infectious agents, and settled solids removed from wastewater at sewage treatment plants.

**shale oil**   Slow-flowing, dark brown, heavy oil obtained when kerogen in oil shale is vaporized at high temperatures and then condensed. Shale oil can be refined to yield gasoline, heating oil, and other petroleum products. See *kerogen, oil shale.*

**sheet erosion**   Soil erosion caused by surface water moving down a slope or across a field in a wide flow. Because it removes topsoil evenly, it may not be noticeable until much damage has been done. Compare *gully erosion, rill erosion.*

**shelterbelt**   See *windbreak.*

**shelterwood cutting**   Removal of mature, marketable trees in an area in a series of partial cuttings to allow regeneration of a new stand under the partial shade of older trees, which are later removed. Typically, this is done by making two or three cuts over a decade. Compare *clear-cutting, seed-tree cutting, selective cutting, strip logging, whole-tree harvesting.*

**shifting cultivation**   Clearing a plot of ground in a forest, especially in tropical areas, and planting crops on it for a few years (typically two to five years) until the soil is depleted of nutrients or until the plot has been invaded by a dense growth of vegetation from the surrounding forest. Then a new plot is cleared and the process is repeated. The abandoned plot cannot sustain crop growth for 10–30 years. See *slash-and-burn cultivation.*

**slash-and-burn cultivation**   Cutting down trees and other vegetation in a patch of forest, leaving the cut vegetation on the ground to dry, and then burning it. The ashes that are left add nutrients to the nutrient-poor soils found in most tropical forest areas. Crops are planted between tree stumps. Plots must be abandoned after a few years (typically two to five years) because of loss of soil fertility or invasion of vegetation from the surrounding forest. See *shifting cultivation.*

**slowly degradable pollutant**   Material that is slowly broken down into simpler chemicals or reduced to acceptable levels by natural physical, chemical, and biological processes. Compare *biodegradable pollutant, degradable pollutant, nondegradable pollutant.*

**sludge**   See *sewage sludge.*

**smelting**   Process in which a desired metal is separated from the other elements in an ore mineral.

**smog**   Originally a combination of smoke and fog, but now used to describe other mixtures of pollutants in the atmosphere. See *industrial smog, photochemical smog.*

**soil**   Complex mixture of inorganic minerals (clay, silt, pebbles, and sand), decaying organic matter, water, air, and living organisms.

**soil conservation** Methods used to reduce soil erosion, to prevent depletion of soil nutrients, and to restore nutrients already lost by erosion, leaching, and excessive crop harvesting.

**soil erosion** Movement of soil components, especially topsoil, from one place to another, usually by exposure to wind, flowing water, or both. This natural process can be greatly accelerated by human activities that remove vegetation from soil. See *gully erosion, rill erosion, sheet erosion.*

**soil horizons** Horizontal zones that make up a particular mature soil. Each horizon has a distinct texture and composition that varies with different types of soils.

**soil permeability** Rate at which water and air move from upper to lower soil layers.

**soil porosity** See *porosity.*

**soil profile** Cross-sectional view of the horizons in a soil.

**soil structure** How the particles that make up a soil are organized and clumped together. See *soil permeability, soil texture.*

**soil texture** Relative amounts of the different types and sizes of mineral particles in a sample of soil.

**soil water** Underground water that partially fills pores between soil particles and rocks within the upper soil and rock layers of the earth's crust, above the water table. Compare *groundwater.*

**solar capital** Solar energy from the sun reaching Earth. Compare *Earth capital.*

**solar cell** See *photovoltaic cell.*

**solar collector** Device for collecting radiant energy from the sun and converting it into heat. See *active solar heating system, passive solar heating system.*

**solar energy** Direct radiant energy from the sun and a number of indirect forms of energy produced by the direct input. Principal indirect forms of solar energy include wind, falling and flowing water (hydropower), and biomass (solar energy converted into chemical energy stored in the chemical bonds of organic compounds in trees and other plants).

**solar pond** Fairly small body of fresh water or salt water from which stored solar energy can be extracted, because of the temperature difference between the hot surface layer exposed to the sun during daylight and the cooler layer beneath it.

**solid waste** Any unwanted or discarded material that is not a liquid or a gas. See *municipal solid waste.*

**spaceship-Earth worldview** Earth as a spaceship—a machine that we can understand, control, and change at will by using advanced technology. See *frontier worldview, planetary-management worldview.* Compare *sustainable-Earth worldview.*

**specialist species** Species with a narrow ecological niche. They may be able to live in only one type of habitat, tolerate only a narrow range of climatic and other environmental conditions, or use only one or a few types of food. Compare *generalist species.*

**speciation** Formation of two species from one species as a result of divergent natural selection in response to changes in environmental conditions; usually takes thousands of years. Compare *extinction.*

**species** Group of organisms that resemble one another in appearance, behavior, chemical makeup and processes, and genetic structure. Organisms that reproduce sexually are classified as members of the same species only if they can actually or potentially interbreed with one another and produce fertile offspring.

**species diversity** Number of different species and their relative abundances in a given area. See *biolog-*

*ical diversity.* Compare *ecological diversity, genetic diversity.*

**spoils** Unwanted rock and other waste materials produced when a material is removed from the earth's surface or subsurface by mining, dredging, quarrying, and excavation.

**sport fishing** Finding and catching fish, mostly for recreation. Compare *commercial fishing, subsistence fishing.*

**sport hunting** Finding and killing animals, mostly for recreation. Compare *commercial hunting, poaching, subsistence hunting.*

**spreading center** See *divergent plate boundary.*

**S-shaped curve** Leveling off of an exponential, J-shaped curve when a rapidly growing population exceeds the carrying capacity of its environment and ceases to grow in numbers. See *overshoot, population crash.*

**stability** Ability of a living system to withstand or recover from externally imposed changes or stresses. See *constancy, inertia, resilience.*

**statutory law** Law passed by a state or national legislature or other governing body. Compare *common law.*

**stewardship** View that because of our superior intellect and power or because of our religious beliefs we have an ethical responsibility to manage and care for domesticated plants and animals as well as for the rest of nature. Compare *planetary-management worldview, sustainable-Earth worldview.*

**stocking rate** Number of a particular kind of animal grazing on a given area of grassland.

**strategic mineral** A fuel or a nonfuel mineral vital to the industry and defense of a country. Ideally, supplies are stockpiled to cushion against supply interruptions and sharp price rises.

**stratosphere** Second layer of the atmosphere, extending from about 17 to 48 kilometers (11 to 30 miles) above the earth's surface. It contains small amounts of gaseous ozone ($O_3$), which filters out about 99% of the incoming harmful ultraviolet (UV) radiation emitted by the sun. Compare *mesosphere, thermosphere, troposphere.*

**stream** Flowing body of surface water. Examples include creeks and rivers.

**strip cropping** Planting regular crops and close-growing plants, such as hay or nitrogen-fixing legumes, in alternating rows or bands to help reduce depletion of soil nutrients.

**strip logging** A variation of clear-cutting in which a strip of trees is clear cut along the contour of the land, with the corridor narrow enough to allow natural regeneration within a few years. After regeneration another strip is cut above the first, and so on. Compare *clear-cutting, seed-tree cutting, selective cutting, shelterwood cutting, whole-tree harvesting.*

**strip mining** Form of surface mining in which bulldozers, power shovels, or stripping wheels remove large chunks of the earth's surface in strips. See *surface mining.* Compare *subsurface mining.*

**subatomic particles** Extremely small particles—electrons, protons, and neutrons—that make up the internal structure of atoms.

**subduction zone** Area in which oceanic lithosphere is carried downward (subducted) under the island arc or continent at a convergent plate boundary. A trench ordinarily forms at the boundary between the two converging plates. See *convergent plate boundary.*

**subsidence** Slow or rapid sinking down of part of the earth's crust that is not slope related.

**subsistence economy** Economic system where the primary goal is to produce enough goods to meet

basic survival needs with little or no surplus for sale or trade; often a traditional economic system. See *traditional economic system.* Compare *mixed economic system, pure command economic system, pure market economic system.*

**subsistence farming** Supplementing solar energy with energy from human labor and draft animals to produce enough food to feed oneself and family members; in good years there may be enough food left over to sell or put aside for hard times. Compare *industrialized agriculture.*

**subsistence fishing** Finding and catching fish to get food for survival. Compare *commercial fishing, sport fishing.*

**subsistence hunting** Finding and killing wild animals to get enough food and other animal material for survival. Compare *commercial hunting, poaching, sport hunting.*

**subsurface mining** Extraction of a metal ore or fuel resource such as coal from a deep underground deposit. Compare *surface mining.*

**succession** See *ecological succession.*

**succulent plants** Plants, such as desert cacti, that survive in dry climates by having no leaves, thus reducing the loss of scarce water. They store water and use sunlight to produce the food they need in the thick fleshy tissue of their green stems and branches. Compare *deciduous plants, evergreen plants.*

**sulfur cycle** Cyclic movement of sulfur in different chemical forms from the environment, to organisms, and then back to the environment.

**superinsulated house** House that is heavily insulated and extremely airtight. Typically, active or passive solar collectors are used to heat water and an air-to-air heat exchanger is used to prevent buildup of excessive moisture and indoor air pollutants.

**surface fire** Forest fire that burns only undergrowth and leaf litter on the forest floor. Compare *crown fire, ground fire.*

**surface mining** Removal of soil, subsoil, and other strata, and then extracting a mineral deposit found fairly close to the earth's surface. See *open-pit mining.* Compare *subsurface mining.*

**surface runoff** Water flowing off the land into bodies of surface water.

**surface water** Precipitation that does not infiltrate the ground or return to the atmosphere by evaporation or transpiration. See *runoff.* Compare *groundwater.*

**survivorship curve** Graph showing number of survivors in different age groups for a particular species.

**sustainable agriculture** See *sustainable-Earth agricultural system.*

**sustainable development** See *sustainable economic development.*

**sustainable Earth** See *sustainable-Earth agricultural system, sustainable-Earth economy, Sustainable-Earth Revolution, sustainable-Earth society, sustainable-Earth worldview.*

**sustainable-Earth agricultural system** Method of growing crops and raising livestock based on organic fertilizers, soil conservation, water conservation, biological control of pests, and minimal use of nonrenewable fossil-fuel energy.

**sustainable-Earth economy** Economic system in which the number of people and the quantity of goods are maintained at some constant level. This level is ecologically sustainable over time and meets at least the basic needs of all members of the population.

**Sustainable-Earth Revolution** Cultural change involving halting population growth and altering lifestyles, political and economic systems, and the way we treat the environment so that we can preserve the earth for ourselves and other species, and can help heal some of the wounds we have inflicted on the earth. See *sustainable-Earth society*.

**sustainable-Earth society** Society based on working with nature by recycling and reusing discarded matter; by preventing pollution; by conserving matter and energy resources through reducing unnecessary waste and use; by not degrading renewable resources; by building things that are easy to recycle, reuse, and repair; by not allowing population size to exceed the carrying capacity of the environment; and by preserving biodiversity. See *sustainable-Earth worldview*. Compare *matter-recycling society, planetary management worldview, throwaway society*.

**sustainable-Earth worldview** Belief that Earth is a place with finite room and resources, so continuing population growth, production, and consumption inevitably put severe stress on natural processes that renew and maintain the resource base of air, water, and soil. To prevent environmental overload, environmental degradation, and resource depletion, people should work with nature by controlling population growth, reducing unnecessary use and waste of matter and energy resources, and not causing the premature extinction of any other species. Compare *frontier worldview, planetary-management worldview, spaceship-Earth worldview*.

**sustainable economic development** Forms of economic growth and activities that do not deplete or degrade natural resources upon which present and future economic growth depend.

**sustainable living** Taking no more potentially renewable resources from the natural world than can be replenished naturally, and not overloading the capacity of the environment to cleanse and renew itself by natural processes.

**sustainable society** A society that manages its economic development and population growth in ways that do no irreparable environmental harm. It satisfies the needs of its people without depleting Earth capital and thus jeopardizing the prospects of future generations of people or other species.

**sustainable yield (sustained yield)** Highest rate at which a potentially renewable resource can be used without reducing its available supply throughout the world or in a particular area. See *environmental degradation*.

**symbiotic relationship** Species interaction in which two kinds of organisms live together in an intimate association, with members of one or both species benefiting from the association. See *commensalism, mutualism*.

**synergistic interaction** Interaction of two or more factors so the net effect is greater than that expected from adding together the independent effects of each factor.

**synergy** See *synergistic interaction*.

**synfuels** Synthetic gaseous and liquid fuels produced from solid coal or sources other than natural gas or crude oil.

**synthetic natural gas (SNG)** Gaseous fuel containing mostly methane produced from solid coal.

**tailings** Rock and other waste materials removed as impurities when waste mineral material is separated from the metal in an ore. See *beneficiation*.

**tar sand** Deposit of a mixture of clay, sand, water, and varying amounts of a tarlike heavy oil known as bitumen. Bitumen can be extracted from tar sand by heating and is then purified and upgraded to synthetic crude oil. See *bitumen*.

**technological-economic growth worldview** See *planetary-management worldview*.

**technology** Creation of new products and processes that are supposed to improve our survival,

comfort, and quality of life. Compare *science*. See *appropriate technology*.

**temperature** Measure of the average speed of motion of the atoms, ions, or molecules in a substance or combination of substances at a given moment. Compare *heat*.

**temperature inversion** See *thermal inversion*.

**teratogen** Chemical, ionizing agent, or virus that causes birth defects. See *carcinogen, mutagen*.

**terracing** Planting crops on a long, steep slope that has been converted into a series of broad, nearly level terraces with short vertical drops that run along the contour of the land to retain water and reduce soil erosion.

**terrestrial** Pertaining to land. Compare *aquatic*.

**tertiary (higher-level) consumers** Animals that feed on animal-eating animals. They feed at high trophic levels in food chains and webs. Examples include hawks, lions, bass, and sharks. Compare *detritivore, primary consumer, secondary consumer*.

**tertiary oil recovery** See *enhanced oil recovery*.

**tertiary sewage treatment** See *advanced sewage treatment*.

**theory of evolution** See *biological evolution*.

**thermal enrichment** Beneficial effects in an aquatic ecosystem from a rise in water temperature. Compare *thermal pollution*.

**thermal inversion** Layer of dense, cool air trapped under a layer of less dense warm air. This prevents upward-flowing air currents from developing. In a prolonged inversion, air pollution in the trapped layer may build up to harmful levels.

**thermal pollution** Increase in water temperature that has harmful effects on aquatic life. See *thermal shock*. Compare *thermal enrichment*.

**thermal shock** A sharp change in water temperature that can kill or harm fish and other aquatic organisms. See *thermal pollution*. Compare *thermal enrichment*.

**thermocline** Zone of gradual temperature decrease between warm surface water and colder deep water in a lake, reservoir, or ocean.

**thermosphere** Fourth layer of the atmosphere; found above the mesosphere. Compare *mesosphere, stratosphere, troposphere*.

**third law of ecology** Any substance we produce should not interfere with any of Earth's natural biogeochemical cycles.

**threatened species** Wild species that is still abundant in its natural range but is likely to become endangered because of a decline in numbers. Compare *endangered species*.

**threshold effect** The harmful or fatal effect of a small change in environmental conditions that exceeds the limit of tolerance of an organism or population of a species. See *law of tolerance*.

**throwaway society** The situation in most advanced industrialized countries, in which ever-increasing economic growth is sustained by maximizing the rate at which matter and energy resources are used, with little emphasis on pollution prevention, recycling, reuse, reduction of unnecessary waste, and other forms of resource conservation. Compare *matter-recycling society, sustainable-Earth society*.

**throwaway worldview** See *planetary management worldview*.

**time delay** Lapse between the time when a system receives a stimulus and the time when the system takes a corrective action.

**total fertility rate (TFR)** Estimate of the average number of children that will be born alive to a woman during her lifetime if she passes through all her childbearing years (ages 15–44) conforming to age-spe-

cific fertility rates of a given year. In simpler terms, it is an estimate of the average number of children a woman will have during her childbearing years.

**totally planned economy** See *pure command economic system*.

**toxic chemical** Chemical that is fatal to humans in low doses, or fatal to over 50% of test animals at stated concentrations. Most are neurotoxins, which attack nerve cells. See *carcinogen, hazardous chemical, mutagen, teratogen*.

**toxic waste** Form of hazardous waste that causes death or serious injury (such as burns, respiratory diseases, cancers, or genetic mutations). See *hazardous waste*.

**traditional economic system** System in which past customs and traditions are used to make economic decisions. This system is found in most remaining tribal communities and is often a subsistence economic system. Compare *mixed economic system, pure command economic system, pure market economic system*.

**traditional intensive agriculture** Producing enough food for a farm family's survival and perhaps a surplus that can be sold. This type of agriculture requires higher inputs of labor, fertilizer, and water than traditional subsistence agriculture. See *traditional subsistence agriculture*.

**traditional subsistence agriculture** Production of enough crops or livestock for a farm family's survival and, in good years, a surplus to sell or put aside for hard times. Compare *traditional intensive agriculture*.

**tragedy of the commons** Depletion or degradation of a resource to which people have free and unmanaged access. An example is the depletion of commercially desirable species of fish in the open ocean beyond areas controlled by coastal countries. See *common-property resource*.

**transform fault** Area where Earth's lithospheric plates move in opposite but parallel directions along a fracture (fault) in the lithosphere. Compare *convergent plate boundary, divergent plate boundary*.

**transmissible disease** A disease that is caused by living organisms such as bacteria, viruses, and parasitic worms, and that is conveyed from one person to another through the air or water, in food or body fluids, or in some cases by insects or other organisms. Compare *nontransmissible disease*.

**transpiration** Process in which water is absorbed by the root systems of plants, moves up through the plant, passes through pores (stomata) in their leaves or other parts, and then evaporates into the atmosphere as water vapor.

**trawler fishing** Catching fish by dragging a funnel-shaped net along the ocean bottom. Compare *drift-net fishing, purse-seine fishing*.

**tree farm** Site planted with one or only a few tree species in an even-aged stand. When the stand matures, it is usually harvested by clear-cutting and then replanted. Normally used to grow rapidly growing tree species for fuelwood, timber, or pulpwood. See *even-aged management*. Compare *old-growth forest, second-growth forest, uneven-aged management, uneven-aged stand*.

**tritium (T: hydrogen-3)** Isotope of hydrogen with a nucleus containing one proton and two neutrons, thus having a mass number of 3. Compare *deuterium*.

**trophic level** All organisms that are the same number of energy transfers away from the original source of energy (e.g., sunlight) that enters an ecosystem. For example, all producers belong to the first trophic level and all herbivores belong to the second trophic level in a food chain or a food web.

**troposphere**   Innermost layer of the atmosphere. It contains about 95% of the mass of Earth's air and extends about 17 kilometers (11 miles) above sea level. Compare *stratosphere*.

**true cost**   See *full cost*.

**unconfined aquifer**   Collection of groundwater above a layer of Earth material (usually rock or clay) through which water flows very slowly (low permeability). Compare *confined aquifer*.

**undernutrition**   Consuming insufficient food to meet one's minimum daily energy requirement for a long enough time to cause harmful effects. Compare *malnutrition, overnutrition*.

**undiscovered resources**   Potential supplies of a particular mineral resource, believed to exist because of geologic knowledge and theory, though specific locations, quality, and amounts are unknown. Compare *identified resources, reserves*.

**uneven-aged management**   Method of forest management in which trees of different species in a given stand are maintained at many ages and sizes to permit continuous natural regeneration. Compare *even-aged management*.

**uneven-aged stand**   Stand of trees in which there are considerable differences in the ages of individual trees. Usually, such stands have a variety of tree species. See *uneven-aged management*. Compare *even-aged stand, tree farm*.

**upwelling**   Movement of nutrient-rich bottom water to the ocean's surface. This can occur far from shore but usually occurs along certain steep coastal areas where the surface layer of ocean water is pushed away from shore and replaced by cold, nutrient-rich bottom water.

**urban area**   Geographic area with a population of 2,500 or more people. The number of people used in this definition may vary, with some countries setting the minimum number of people anywhere from 10,000 to 50,000.

**urban growth**   Rate of growth of an urban population. Compare *degree of urbanization*.

**urban heat island**   Buildup of heat in the atmosphere above an urban area. This heat is produced by the large concentration of cars, buildings, factories, and other heat-producing activities. See *dust dome*.

**urbanization**   See *degree of urbanization*.

**vertebrates**   Animals with backbones. Compare *invertebrates*.

**volcano**   Emission of magma through a central vent or long fissure in the earth's surface, releasing ejecta, liquid lava, and gases into the environment.

**water consumption**   Water that is not returned to the surface water or groundwater from which it came, mostly because of evaporation and transpiration. As a result, this water is not available for use again in the area from which it came. See *water withdrawal*.

**water cycle**   See *hydrologic cycle*.

**waterlogging**   Saturation of soil with irrigation water or excessive precipitation, so that the water table rises close to the surface.

**water pollution**   Any physical or chemical change in surface water or groundwater that can harm living organisms or make water unfit for certain uses.

**watershed**   Land area that delivers the water, sediment, and dissolved substances via small streams to a major stream (river).

**water table**   Upper surface of the zone of saturation in which all available pores in the soil and rock in the earth's crust are filled with water.

**water withdrawal**   Removing water from a groundwater or surface water source and transporting it to a place of use. Compare *water consumption*.

**watt**   Unit of power, or rate at which electrical work is done. See *kilowatt*.

**weather**   Short-term changes in the temperature, barometric pressure, humidity, precipitation, sunshine (solar radiation), cloud cover, wind direction and speed, and other conditions in the troposphere at a given place and time. Compare *climate*.

**weathering**   Physical and chemical processes in which solid rock exposed on the earth's surface is changed to separate solid particles and dissolved material, which can then be moved to another place as sediment. See *erosion*.

**wetland**   Land that is covered all or part of the year with salt water or fresh water, excluding streams, lakes, and the open ocean. See *coastal wetland, inland wetland*.

**whole-tree harvesting**   Use of machines to cut trees off at ground level, or to pull entire trees from the ground, and then reduce the trunks and branches to small wood chips.

**wilderness**   Area where the earth and its community of life have not been seriously disturbed by humans and where humans are only temporary visitors.

**wildlife**   All free, undomesticated species. Sometimes the term is used to describe only free, undomesticated species of animals.

**wildlife management**   Manipulation of populations of wild species (especially game species) and their habitats for human benefit, the welfare of other species, and the preservation of threatened and endangered wildlife species.

**wildlife resources**   Species of wildlife that have actual or potential economic value to people. See *game species*.

**windbreak**   Row of trees or hedges planted to partially block wind flow and reduce soil erosion on cultivated land.

**wind farm**   Cluster of small to medium-sized wind turbines in a windy area to capture wind energy and convert it into electrical energy.

**work**   What happens when a force is used to move a sample of matter over some distance or to raise its temperature. Energy is defined as the capacity to do such work.

**worldview**   How individuals think the world works and what they think their role in the world should be. See *planetary-management worldview, spaceship-Earth worldview, sustainable-Earth worldview*.

**zero population growth (ZPG)**   State in which the birth rate (plus immigration) equals the death rate (plus emigration) so the population of a geographical area is no longer increasing.

**zone of saturation**   Area where all available pores in soil and rock in the earth's crust are filled by water. See *water table*.

**zoning**   Regulating how various parcels of land can be used.

**zooplankton**   Animal plankton. Small floating herbivores that feed on plant plankton (phytoplankton). Compare *phytoplankton*.

# Index

Note: Page numbers appearing in **boldface** indicate where definitions of key terms can be found in the text; these terms also appear in the glossary. Page numbers in *italics* indicate illustrations, tables, and figures.